Selected works of Jawaharlal Nehru

WITH MRS BANDARANAIKE IN COLOMBO, 15 OCTOBER 1962

Selected works of Jawaharlal Nehru

SECOND SERIES

Volume Seventy Nine (1 October – 30 November 1962)

Editor

MADHAVAN K. PALAT

Jawaharlal Nehru Memorial Fund

New Delhi

Enquiries regarding copyright
to be addressed to the publishers

PUBLISHED BY
Jawaharlal Nehru Memorial Fund
Teen Murti House, New Delhi 110 011

ISBN : 0-19-949665-X
ISBN : 978-0-19-949665-5

DISTRIBUTED BY
Oxford University Press
YMCA Library Building, Jai Singh Road, New Delhi 110 001
Mumbai Kolkata Chennai
Oxford New York Toronto
Melbourne Tokyo Hong Kong

PRINTED AT
Aditya Arts,
I-66, Jadunath Enclave,
Sector 29, Faridabad-121008

CONTENTS

x

(b) Africa

(c) Burma

(d) Ceylon

(e) Disarmament

(b) CHINESE INVASION: Explanation and Strategy

(c) CHINESE INVASION: Mobilising Popular Support

V. MISCELLANEOUS

VI. APPENDICES

FOREWORD

Jawaharlal Nehru is one of the key figures of the twentieth century. He symbolised some of the major forces which have transformed our age.

When Jawaharlal Nehru was young, history was still the privilege of the West; the rest of the world lay in deliberate darkness. The impression given was that the vast continents of Asia and Africa existed merely to sustain their masters in Europe and North America. Jawaharlal Nehru's own education in Britain could be interpreted, in a sense, as an attempt to secure for him a place within the pale. His letters of the time are evidence of his sensitivity, his interest in science and international affairs as well as of his pride in India and Asia. But his personality was veiled by his shyness and a facade of nonchalance, and perhaps outwardly there was not much to distinguish him from the ordinary run of men. Gradually there emerged the warm and universal being who became intensely involved with the problems of the poor and the oppressed in all lands. In doing so, Jawaharlal Nehru gave articulation and leadership to millions of people in his own country and in Asia and Africa.

That imperialism was a curse which should be lifted from the brows of men, that poverty was incompatible with civilisation, that nationalism should be poised on a sense of international community and that it was not sufficient to brood on these things when action was urgent and compelling—these were the principles which inspired and gave vitality to Jawaharlal Nehru's activities in the years of India's struggle for freedom and made him not only an intense nationalist but one of the leaders of humanism.

No particular ideological doctrine could claim Jawaharlal Nehru for its own. Long days in jail were spent in reading widely. He drew much from the thought of the East and West and from the philosophies of the past and the present. Never religious in the formal sense, yet he had a deep love for the culture and tradition of his own land. Never a rigid Marxist, yet he was deeply influenced by that theory and was particularly impressed by what he saw in the Soviet Union on his first visit in 1927. However, he realised that the world was too complex, and man had too many facets, to be encompassed by any single or total explanation. He himself was a socialist with an abhorrence of regimentation and a democrat who was anxious to reconcile his faith in civil liberty with the necessity of mitigating economic and social wretchedness. His struggles, both within himself and with the outside world, to adjust such seeming contradictions are what make his life and work significant and fascinating.

As a leader of free India, Jawaharlal Nehru recognised that his country could neither stay out of the world nor divest itself of its own interests in world affairs. But to the extent that it was possible, Jawaharlal Nehru sought to speak objectively and to be a voice of sanity in the shrill phases of the 'cold war'. Whether his influence helped on certain occasions to maintain peace is for the future historian to assess. What we do know is that for a long stretch of time he commanded an international audience reaching far beyond governments, that he spoke for ordinary, sensitive, thinking men and women around the globe and that his was a constituency which extended far beyond India.

So the story of Jawaharlal Nehru is that of a man who evolved, who grew in storm and stress till he became the representative of much that was noble in his time. It is the story of a generous and gracious human being who summed up in himself the resurgence of the 'third world' as well as the humanism which transcends dogmas and is adapted to the contemporary context. His achievement, by its very nature and setting, was much greater than that of a Prime Minister. And it is with the conviction that the life of this man is of importance not only to scholars but to all, in India and elsewhere, who are interested in the valour and compassion of the human spirit that the Jawaharlal Nehru Memorial Fund has decided to publish a series of volumes consisting of all that is significant in what Jawaharlal Nehru spoke and wrote. There is, as is to be expected in the speeches and writings of a man so engrossed in affairs and gifted with expression, much that is ephemeral; this will be omitted. The official letters and memoranda will also not find place here. But it is planned to include everything else and the whole corpus should help to remind us of the quality and endeavour of one who was not only a leader of men and a lover of mankind, but a completely integrated human being.

Indira Gandhi

New Delhi
18 January 1972

Chairman
Jawaharlal Nehru Memorial Fund

EDITORIAL NOTE

The Chinese invasion of 20 October to 21 November dominates this volume and other matters appear secondary, even such important ones as the proposal to amend the Constitution to deal with the DMK's secessionist utterances. The documents dealing with the invasion have been divided into thematic groups, but there is an inevitable overlap. An important set of documents are to be found in the appendices also. There is little available on the military aspects of the conflict. However, Nehru's numerous public statements and his letters to world leaders reveal quite clearly how he experienced this invasion. He was not remotely prepared for anything of this magnitude, it came as a surprise and shock, and the initial reactions expose disarray, politically, militarily, and administratively in the machinery of the state. Ever the good historian, he pointed out frequently that India was exceptional for not having experienced total war unlike China and Japan, the Soviet Union and Europe. Hence the image of India as peace-loving. But, in the crisis, he could invoke even Gandhi in the cause of war by reminding his audiences that Gandhi was one of the most courageous of men he had known and he would never have flinched from fighting. As he once said, it might have done India some good to have been shaken out of complacency.

Some of the speeches have been transcribed; hence the paragraphing, punctuation, and other such details have been inserted. Words and expressions which were inaudible or unintelligible have been shown by an ellipsis between square brackets thus: [...]. When no text or recording of a speech was available, a newspaper report has been used as a substitute. Such a newspaper report, once selected for publication, has been reproduced faithfully; other information has been added only by way of annotation. Most items here are from Nehru's office copies. In personal letters, and even in official letters composed in personal style to personal friends, the salutation and concluding portions were written by hand; such details are not recorded in the office copy. Therefore, these have either been inserted in Nehru's customary style for such persons or his full name has been used, but the editorial intervention is indicated by square brackets. Information on persons may always be traced through the index if it is not available in the footnote. References to the Selected Works appear as SWJN/FS/10/..., to be understood as Selected Works of Jawaharlal Nehru, First

Series, Volume 10. In the case of the Second Series, it would be SWJN/SS/....
The part and page numbers follow the volume number.

Documents, which have been referred to as items, are numbered
sequentially throughout the volume; footnote numbering however is continuous
only within a section, not between sections. Maps of the boundary between
India and China have been reproduce from official documents and are placed
at the end of the volume.

Nehru's speeches or texts in Hindi have been published in Hindi and a
translation into English has been appended in each case for those who might
need or want one.

A large part of Nehru's archives is housed in the Nehru Memorial Museum
and Library and is known as the JN Collection. This has been the chief source
for items here, and has been made available by Shrimati Sonia Gandhi, the
Chairperson of the Jawaharlal Nehru Memorial Fund. Unless otherwise stated,
all items are from this collection. The Nehru Memorial Museum and Library
has been immensely helpful in so many ways, and it is a pleasure to record
our thanks to it. The Cabinet Secretariat, the secretariats of the President
and Prime Minister, various ministries of the Government of India, All India
Radio, the Press Information Bureau, and the National Archives of India, all
have permitted us to use material in their possession. We are grateful to The
Hindu, the National Herald, Shankar's Weekly, and in particular to the late R.K.
Laxman for permission to reproduce reports and cartoons.

Finally, it gives me great pleasure to thank those who contributed to
preparing this volume for publication, most of all Bibhu Prasad Mohapatra. The
Hindi texts have been edited by Mohammed Khalid Ansari, and the translation
from the Hindi was done by Chandra Chari.

Madhavan K. Palat

LIST OF ILLUSTRATIONS

I. POLITICS

(a) General

1. To V.R. Radhakrishnan: Jayaprakash Narayan's Birthday Souvenir[1]

October 2, 1962

Dear Shri Radhakrishnan,

I have your letter of the 26th September. I am sorry I cannot send you any article for the Souvenir you are issuing on the occasion of the sixty-first birthday of Shri Jayaprakash Narayan. I send, however, my good wishes for him[2].

2. In New Delhi: Public Meeting[3]

English as Associate Language
Government not to Bow to Agitations, PM Warns Hindi Enthusiasts

New Delhi, October 3 – Prime Minister Nehru yesterday declared in firm tones that the pledge given in Parliament to give English an associate status in the Constitution would be fulfilled whatever happened.

Pandit Nehru, who was addressing a mammoth public meeting here, said that some people, who called themselves "lovers of Hindi", had started agitations against giving English an associate status.

Raising his voice, Pandit Nehru said: "Let them be under no illusion. The pledge we gave on the floor of Parliament to the people of South India that nothing would be done against their wishes in the matter of English will be fulfilled. This is crystal clear".

Pandit Nehru, who dwelt at some length on the agitations and demonstration being carried on against giving English an associate status, said that it was strange that no voice was raised when this pledge was taken in Parliament,

---

1. Letter to the General Secretary, Sri Jayaprakash Narayan's Sixty-First Birthday Celebrations Committee, 1, Thiruvalluvar Koil Street, Madras-4. PMO, File No. 9/2/61-PMP, Vol. 7, Sr. No. 9-A.
2. See item 11.
3. Speech, 2 October 1962. Reproduced from the *National Herald*, 4 October, 1962, p. 4, col. 4.

but a big noise was being made now. "Are we to break this pledge now? It is impossible".

Pandit Nehru, who was addressing a meeting called by the Delhi Citizens Committee on the auspicious occasion of Mahatma Gandhi's birthday to demand disarmament and a ban on nuclear arms and to foster national integration, cited the demonstrations against English as weakening the integration of country. It would only strengthen the hands of people demanding secession from India in the South.

Pandit Nehru said that there was a lot of noise being created by some people who opposed giving English an associate status by amending the Constitution, which had laid down that Hindi alone should be the official language after 1965. This proposal of an associate status English was made by him two years ago, as the people in the South had urged that English should be retained for some time more. "We agreed to it, because we did not want that we should impose Hindi on half or one fourth of the country against the wishes of the people there. Hindi of course, will grow and flourish in the whole country as is already happening. But it will be wrong and harmful to the cause of Hindi itself to spread it through the use of the lathi".

Resolution

The meeting, in a resolution, urged the nuclear powers to sign an agreement without delay for the complete prohibition of all nuclear tests. "This meeting feels that the proposals put forward by the eight non-aligned nations, at the disarmament committee at Geneva, offers a sound basis for the conclusion of such an agreement", the resolution added.

The meeting appealed to the current session of the United Nations General Assembly to review the progress made at the negotiations at the disarmament committee at Geneva, and to emphasise once again the necessity of an early agreement on a treaty for general and complete disarmament with adequate measures for inspection and control, ensuring the total ban on manufacture and stockpiling of all kinds of nuclear weapons.

Trend Abroad

Without naming any party, Pandit Nehru said: "There is a party in Madras which is propagating secession of that state from India.[4] How far they really want this in their hearts, I do not know. But to annoy and tease the people in

---

4.   Nehru is referring to the DMK in Madras State.

the South with these demonstrations against English will only strengthen the hands of those who are demanding secession".

Pandit Nehru said that even in European countries, like England, the trend was that people learn more foreign languages. In Britain, there was a big move for people to learn French, German, and Russian, because they felt they were remaining behind in science and other matters by not being able to read all the new books and scientific literature coming out in other languages. Even in Egypt, it had been made compulsory for every school going child to learn English and one additional foreign language. The Arabic language was a very fine and forceful language, but the Government of the UAR had made the knowledge of English and another foreign language compulsory for all school-going children. This was done to enable the people there to understand the fast-changing world.

Pandit Nehru warned that India would go down again if it did not keep the windows and doors of its mind open to learn from the world. The history of India gave ample evidence of the country falling time and again because it did not have knowledge of what was happening in the world in various spheres and keeping abreast of the times.

Pandit Nehru said that books in other languages could, of course, be translated into Hindi and other Indian languages. But it was not possible to translate thousands of new books coming out every day in various parts of the world.

"We cannot live in isolation. We must acquire knowledge of new inventions and achievements in various spheres. We can only do this by learning not only English but other foreign languages also. If we don't do it, then our freedom can also be endangered", he said.

In an obvious reference to the Socialist Party, Pandit Nehru said that there was one party which was indulging in childish nonsense by raising the slogan "Throw out English". In this age of the atom bomb and science, could big problems be solved by this kind of hooligan behaviour?

Pandit Nehru asked the people to clear their minds and hearts of fighting over a language. They should stop using the "weapon of the tongue" or the "lathi of tongue" against each other. This kind of thing was utterly wrong, especially when India faced danger on her borders. All linguistic, provincial and other disputes should cease and full nationalism should be created, he said. PTI.

3. Tribute to S. Radhakrishnan[5]

I join in paying my tribute to our President, Dr Radhakrishnan. He has served his country in many capacities. But, above all, he is a great teacher from whom all of us have learnt much and will continue to learn. It is India's peculiar privilege to have a great philosopher, a great educationist and a great humanist as her President. That in itself shows the kind of men we honour and respect.[6]

4. To Syed Qaim Mehdi: National Integration Committee[7]

October 5, 1962

Dear Maulana Saheb,
I have your letter of the 2nd October. I am glad to learn of the good work you have been doing for national integration.

So far as the Committee for National Integration is concerned, it was formed according to a resolution of the National Integration Council[8] held last year. According to this, the members are Chief Ministers of States, some leaders of political parties in Parliament and some prominent educationists. This committee was formed some time ago and I do not think it is feasible to add to it now.

Yours sincerely,
[Jawaharlal Nehru]

5. To P.N. Thapar: Military Secrets Leaked[9]

October 5, 1962

My dear Thapar,
I have just received a letter from the President which runs as follows:

"I am surprised and pained to see this morning a press report that a special task force was to be sent to NEFA, charged with pushing the Chinese out. Such secret military information is not given out. It will give previous warning to the other side and endanger the lives of our men. I do not know why our

5. Message, 3 October 1962. PMO, File No. 9/2/61-PMP, Vol. 7, Sr. No. 13-B.
6. See appendix 1.
7. Letter; address: Mujtahid, Moh. Pata Nala, Distt. Lucknow.
8. See SWJN/SS/72/item 78/p.228. Also, SWJN/SS/77/items 6, 7 & 8.
9. Letter to the Chief of the Army Staff.

press men do not exercise more restraint and responsibility. I thought I should convey to you my feelings in the matter. The Defence Minister who is with me feels as I do."

I was myself greatly surprised and distressed to see the report in the press this morning.[10] In a matter of this kind, special care has to be taken to keep any news secret. We are injuring ourselves by any leakage of information and endangering our own causes.

I am having an investigation made as to how this leakage in the press took place. I shall be glad to know if there was any talk, direct or indirect, by you or any members of your staff to any newspaper man or other person. I am much exercised over this as we cannot tolerate this looseness in our set-up.

Yours sincerely,
Jawaharlal Nehru

6. To S. Radhakrishnan: Military Secrets Leaked[11]

5th October, 1962
My dear Mr President,
I have just received your letter of October 5th about the press report regarding NEFA[12]. I was myself distressed to see this report and I consider it very improper for anyone to give this to the press. It is most unfortunate and regrettable that such leakages should occur.

We are having an inquiry made into this matter. Meanwhile, I have written to the Chief of Staff, General Thapar, about it. I have taken the liberty of sending him a copy of your letter. I hope you do not mind.

Yours affectionately,
[Jawaharlal Nehru]

7. P. Subbarayan[13]

I have just learnt with deep grief of the passing away of Dr Subbarayan. This came as a shock to me as I had recently learnt that he had recovered from his

10. In the *Times of India*, 5 October 1962, p.1.
11. Letter to the President.
12. See item 5.
13. Message, 6 October 1962, sent to the Chief Minister of Madras. Reproduced from the *National Herald*, 7th October, 1962, p.1, col. 1.

illness[14]. He was an old friend and colleague and a great patriot and we have suffered a great national loss.

Please convey my deep sorrow and sympathy to the members of his family.

8. To Moni Bagchee: Remembering Gandhi[15]

October 8, 1962

Dear Moni Bagchee,

Thank you for your letter of October 5th.[16] I remember meeting you long ago.

It is perfectly true that Gandhiji's living memory is going into the backwaters of our life. It is obvious that mere chanting of Ramdhun etc. is almost a dead thing without the living inspiration of Gandhiji.

To some extent, that is natural and almost inevitable. A new generation has grown up which only knows of Gandhiji rather vaguely as a historical person. The older generation that knew him more intimately, have either got lost in politics or in humdrum so-called constructive activities like spinning etc. Yet, I believe that Gandhiji has affected all our lives considerably and has influenced and will continue to influence people in India and abroad. Whenever I have gone abroad, just as recently I went to Nigeria, I have heard his name in all manner of odd places and the kind of influence he exercised on the struggles in Africa.

There is no one who can be called a true Gandhi-ite. Perhaps, the nearest approach to this is Vinoba Bhave.

I shall be glad to have from you any concrete scheme of what we should do in this matter.

Yours sincerely,
[Jawaharlal Nehru]

14. See also items 472 and 480.
15. Letter to Moni Bagchee, (1907-1983); writer and historian. PMO, File No. 2 (114)/56-66-PMS, Sr. No. 87-A.Also available in the JN Collection.
16. See appendix 5.

9. To T.T. Krishnamachari: Malaviya's Reform Proposals[17]

October 8, 1962

My dear T.T.,

Gulzarilal Nanda has written to me that the various matters you suggested in your papers, more especially those in regard to maintaining of prices of essential commodities, are being examined by a number of Committees, and he hopes to have papers ready on them in a few days' time.

I have received a letter from Keshava Deva Malaviya.[18] I have no doubt that the administrative system and its working are cumbersome and delaying, and should be improved. But I rather doubt if any Committee will be able to make any helpful suggestions.

The other point he raises is about speedy generation of greater power and the control of power schemes in a more efficient way. Obviously, we want as much power as we can possibly generate. But I do not quite understand his approach to this question. I enclose Keshava Deva's letter.

Yours affectionately,
[Jawaharlal Nehru]

10. To Suresh Asthana: No Quick Remedy[19]

October 8, 1962

Dear Suresh Asthana,

I have your letter of 1st October. It is perfectly true that there are all kinds of disruptive forces at play in India and that caste continues to play an undesirable part. Also that the Congress itself suffers from these evils. I cannot tell you of some sovereign remedy to meet these difficulties. We have to face evil and try to overcome it. I have no special revolutionary step in my mind at present to meet these difficulties.

Yours sincerely,
[Jawaharlal Nehru]

---

17. Letter to Minister without Portfolio.
18. See appendix 7.
19. Letter; address: 26 K, Kailash Colony, New Delhi-14.

11. To Jayaprakash Narayan: Birthday Greetings[20]

October 10, 1962

My dear Jayaprakash,

I had fully intended to come tomorrow to your sixtieth birthday celebrations at 30, Ferozeshah Road. But, rather suddenly, I have got an important engagement just at that time which I cannot forego. I am sorry, therefore, that I cannot come personally to congratulate you on your birthday. Please forgive me.

I send you all my good wishes.

Yours affectionately
Jawaharlal

12. To Shriman Narayan Agarwal: No Time for Wardha[21]

October 10, 1962

My dear Shriman,

Your letter of the 10th October with the article by Rajaji.[22] I am sorry, I cannot give you any firm date when I can go to Wardha. I doubt very much if I shall be able to go there this year. Perhaps it may be possible next year.

Yours sincerely,
J. Nehru

13. For Emotional Integration Seminar[23]

I send my good wishes to the Seminar on Emotional Integration organized by the Women's International League for Peace and Freedom. Emotional

---

20. Letter to the Sarvodaya leader. NMML, Jayaprakash Narayan Papers.
21. Reproduced from Shriman Narayan, *Letters from Gandhi, Nehru, Vinoba* (Bombay: Asia Publishing House, 1968) pp. 121-122.
22. The letter referred to C. Rajagopalachari's article on the language policy, published in the *Hindustan Times* of 15 August 1962. It also requested Nehru to inaugurate "the Golden Jubilee Celebrations of the Wardha Education Society, which was founded by the late Shri Jamnalal Bajaj more than 50 years ago."
23. Message, 10 October 1962, forwarded to Sushila Nayar, 1 Curzon Road, New Delhi. PMO, File No. 9/2/62-PMP, Vol. 7, Sr. No. 41-A.

integration is of vital importance to us in India, and I am sure that women can help in bringing this about even more than men.

14. To Jayaprakash Narayan: Hindi and English[24]

October 11, 1962

My dear Jayaprakash,

Some days ago, I saw a report in the press of your statement expressing your disapproval of "the manner in which the Prime Minister is carrying on the language controversy since his return from abroad". You compared this in some way to why people should misbehave in legislatures. I was much surprised to read this. But I did not think it worthwhile to say anything about it. This morning, I received, presumably from you, a copy of your full statement which I have read. I may be wrong, of course, in the views I hold or in the expression of them. But it does seem to me rather odd that you should immediately issue a statement without trying to verify what I said. I spoke in Hindi. Therefore, I did not call anything "stupid". No one was referred to. I do not think that I used the word "bewaqoof" either. I discussed certain policies only and probably said that the cry of "Angrezi hatao" etc. was rather childish. Perhaps, I might have used the word "jehalat" in this connection[25].

I referred to the statement made in Parliament both by Pant ji[26] and me two years ago that English should be an associate language at the Centre till such time as the non-Hindi-speaking States could say that it was not necessary. That is exactly what Vinobaji[27] has said.

I laid stress also on the medium of instruction being the regional language. I further pointed out that the Hindi-speaking States could certainly use as much Hindi as they liked. The question was of the language at the Centre and, in view of the opposition in some States, it was not desirable to do anything which would mean forcing it down their throats against their will. I was speaking at a National Integration meeting and I said that this would not help in integration, but would have the reverse effect. Further, I said that English and other foreign

---

24. Letter to the Sarvodaya leader. PMO, File No. 52(12)/57-63-PMS, Vol. I, Sr. No. 92-A. Also available in NMML, Jayaprakash Narayan Papers.
25. Here meaning "unbecoming behaviour". See items 2 and 122.
26. G. B. Pant, the then Home Minister headed a Parliamentary Committee on Official Languages, which submitted its report in 1959. The Committee recommended that Hindi should be made the primary official language with English continuing as a subsidiary language.
27. Vinoba Bhave.

languages should be taught not as a medium of instruction, but as necessary languages. I said further that we had been for long an inward-looking people and had cut ourselves off to a large extent from outside influences, while the world was changing rapidly. It would be a pity if we continued to do that[28].

The second time I referred to it was at the opening ceremony of a Girls' College where the question arose in some speech or other.[29] I have been unable to discover what was wrong with the manner in which I referred to these questions, and your statement has not helped me at all in doing so.

Yours affectionately,
[Jawaharlal Nehru]

15. To Maya Devi Chettry: A Ministerial Post[30]

October 11, 1962

My dear Maya Devi,
I have received your letter of the 8th October. Thank you for it.

You know that I have a high regard for you and I have no doubt you will discharge any responsibility that may be entrusted to you. I have not been thinking lately of any addition to our Government. I was not aware that any rumours had gone about in regard to it. If any occasion arises for my doing so, I shall certainly bear you in mind.

Yours sincerely,
[Jawaharlal Nehru]

16. To Chief Ministers[31]

12th October, 1962

My dear Chief Minister,
I have been wanting to write to you for some time, ever since my return from abroad, to tell you not only about my impressions of the countries I visited,

---

28. See item 2.
29. See speech at the opening ceremony of Janki Devi Memorial College, item 122.
30. Letter to Rajya Sabha MP, Congress, from West Bengal; address: Chettry Bhavan, Kurseong, Darjeeling.
31. Letter to all Chief Ministers and the Prime Minister of Jammu and Kashmir. PMS, File No. 25(30)/62-PM, Sr. No. 5-A.

but more so about our own problems. I suppose there is little I can say about my tour to foreign countries which has not appeared in the Press and of which you are not already informed.

[Five Year Plan]

2.   As for our problems in India, they are troublesome enough. What requires the greatest attention is the progress of our Five Year Plan and, more especially, the rise in prices. Just before I went abroad, our Cabinet appointed some committees and asked the Planning Commission especially to look into these matters and report to us. We expect to get their reports within a few days and then to consider them. As you will appreciate, these matters require the most careful consideration based on facts and not merely on theory. Hence, the delay in getting all these facts etc. together.

[International Situation]

3.   The international situation continues to be full of tension, though I believe there is also a desire not to push it to the ultimate crisis. Probably, the two most important questions today which might give rise to further trouble are Berlin and Cuba. In Yemen, there has been a revolution, and the old Imam, the autocratic ruler, has been replaced by a more or less military government. This government appears to be fairly firmly in the saddle, although Saudi Arabia and Jordan are opposed to it and would like to suppress it. The chances are that it will continue because it has already got the support not only of the UAR, but some other countries. In fact, there is some possibility of this revolutionary movement spreading to Saudi Arabia itself.

[Nepal]

4.   In Nepal, conditions have deteriorated fast. That is very unfortunate. We have tried our utmost to smooth difficulties that had arisen between Nepal and India. Just before going abroad, I received a letter from the King in which he accused us of arms-running into Nepal and otherwise encouraging the Nepalese rebels. I replied to him immediately that what he had stated was not true. We had issued explicit instructions, which I believe have been followed, to the effect that no arms should be allowed to go into Nepal from India. From our information very few arms have gone, probably some individuals taking them by some bypath. Most of the arms that the Nepalese rebels possess, have been acquired from police posts and army posts in Nepal which were overpowered by them. I wrote to the King a friendly letter assuring him of our policy of non-

interference in Nepal. In spite of this letter, a few days later, the Nepal King dismissed his Foreign Minister who was supposed to be perhaps slightly friendly to India, and issued a very provocative statement accusing India of various things. This statement was not based on any facts. We refrained, however, from replying to it, so as not to carry on this controversy. Our Ambassador in Kathmandu, however, pointed out to him the true facts.

5. Then occurred an incident at Raxaul on the border where some Nepalese people came and shot at and killed some persons in Indian territory and then escaped. The persons who did the shooting were recognised and their names were communicated to the Nepal Government. We asked for a joint enquiry into this incident. But the Nepal Government has sent us no answer to our request. Instead they have issued statements completely denying the facts and accusing India of various acts against them. In particular, they have accused us of stopping supplies from going to Nepal from India and thus blockading it. This was untrue. What happened was that people on our side of the border being greatly irritated at attacks on them from Nepal had for a while stopped some of the trucks etc. going across. This had nothing to do with any Government order and, in fact, Government took steps soon after to let these trucks pass. But much was made of this incident, and newspapers of Nepal, which are of course Government sponsored, have been writing the most vituperative articles about India. Meanwhile, the Chinese Foreign Minister stated that they were prepared to come to help Nepal if any other country attacked it. Obviously, the reference was to India.

6. This is a very disturbing situation. We have tried to remain calm about it because excitement does not do any good. The fact of the matter is that the economic and political situation in Nepal is progressively deteriorating and the King and his advisers, not knowing what to do, find a scapegoat in India and blame us. I hope that our restraint in the face of these provocations will help in easing the situation. But it is difficult to deal with persons who have developed a tremendous bias against us.[32]

[China and the Northeast]

7. What I particularly want to draw your attention to is the dangerous situation that has arisen on our NEFA border with Tibet-China. Till last month NEFA was intact and free from any Chinese aggression except a small village

32. See items 218, 220, 223, and 224; appendix 8.

on the border called Longju, which also had been vacated by the Chinese.[33] On the 8th of September, some Chinese forces came down through the Thagla Pass and occupied a mile or two of territory there. This was a new development, and we had immediately to take steps to meet the situation that had arisen. As elsewhere the Chinese have an advantage of lines of communication. They have roads almost right up to the international frontier in Tibet, while our people have to go through difficult mountain terrain for long distances. The normal altitudes of these places vary from 10,000 to 15,000 feet or more, we have taken steps to strengthen our position and to try to push the Chinese out. There have been a number of incidents involving firing at each other and resulting in some casualties on both sides. The latest one of these was two days ago when there were about eleven killed on our side and about ten or eleven wounded. On the Chinese side the casualties were much heavier, and probably about a hundred.

8.   This incident and other facts brought to light that the Chinese had been strengthening their forces very considerably in this area. That is the present position. It is a difficult one chiefly because we have to supply our forces by air in very difficult terrain. Meanwhile winter is coming on fast. Both sides, of course, will be affected by these wintry conditions. It is exceedingly cold there and snow has started falling.

9.   This situation in the North-East frontier is definitely a dangerous one, and it may lead to major conflicts. We shall, of course, try to do our best. But it seems likely that conflicts on a bigger scale might take place there. All this will involve a considerable additional burden on us. We cannot avoid it, and we have to face every danger to India and shoulder the burdens that this might involve. I would like you, therefore, to keep this in mind and be prepared for such burdens as we might have to carry.

10.   The Chinese Government has been, more especially during the last three or four weeks, carrying on an intensive campaign in China against India accusing us of committing aggression on their territory. It is a little difficult to understand this charge or this reasoning. Quite apart from any claims that China may make, and we are convinced that these claims have no foundation, the patent fact is that the Chinese were not there, that is, across the McMahon Line, up to early in September. Thus their coming across the pass then was a new move which can only be termed fresh aggression. While they commit

33.   See SWJN/SS/51/item 193 for Nehru's statement in Lok Sabha on the incident which took place on 26 August 1959. This incident also "placed all the border areas directly under the Military authority." Till then these border posts were patrolled by Assam Rifles, which was under the Governor, who represented the MEA in GOI. See also Nehru's communication of the incident to the US President and the Prime Minister of UK, 29 August 1959. Ibid, item 195.

aggression, they talk continuously of their wanting to have a peaceful settlement. We, for our part, have pointed out that while we are always willing to talk and to have a peaceful settlement, this cannot be done till a climate is created for such talks. Therefore, we had suggested that the representatives of the two countries might meet to discuss, to begin with, not the basic claims or positions of either party, but how to reduce this tension. Obviously, there can be no such reduction when the Chinese continue committing aggression daily. Now, of course, with these petty conflicts going on in the NEFA border and the ever present possibility of a large conflict, it has become still more difficult for us to sit down at the table to discuss our controversies.[34]

11. I cannot obviously go into details about this position in the North East border. All I wish to impress upon you is that it is a very serious situation and that in any event, whatever may happen in the near future, we shall have to face this situation for a considerable time. That must involve a great burden on us for which we have to be prepared. That is the price we pay for our independence and integrity.

12. While we have to keep all this in mind, we should avoid saying or doing anything which creates any alarm in the minds of some of our people.

13. I should like to say that even in the few conflicts we have had in the border, our Army has behaved with exemplary courage and our Air Force has carried out its task of dropping supplies from the air under very difficult circumstances with great ability in spite of the risks involved in it.

14. I am going today to Ceylon for four days. I shall return to Delhi on the 16th of October.

Yours sincerely,
Jawaharlal Nehru

17. To Swami Ananda: National Flag[35]

October 16, 1962

Dear Swamiji,

I have your letter of the 11th October.

You refer to the display of the National Flag. As a matter of fact, there are some rules covering it because it is thought that the National Flag should not

---

34. See items in section IV.
35. Letter to the Secretary of the Bharat Sadhu Samaj, Chanakyapuri, New Delhi – 21. PMO, File No. 52(8)/57-68-PMS, Sr. No. 21-A.

be misused in any way. Therefore, only certain persons are allowed to display it normally. On special days, however, like Republic Day, Independence Day, etc., any person can display it.

Particularly we do not want it to be used for election purposes. This is the rule in most other countries also.

There is a National Integration Council which is considering this question of integration. There is little point, therefore, in appointing a commission of enquiry.

Yours sincerely,
Jawaharlal Nehru

18. To L. Krishnaswami Bharati: Hindi and Jayaprakash Narayan's Protest[36]

16th October, 1962

Dear Shri Krishnaswami Bharati,

Thank you for your letter of the 13th October.[37] I have read it as well as your statement with interest. Shri Jayaprakash Narayan is needlessly agitated about what I had said. As a matter of fact, I was speaking in Hindi and therefore, I did not use the word stupid. Nor had I referred to any individual. All I had said was that a certain type of agitation was foolish.[38]

Yours sincerely,
Jawaharlal Nehru

19. For the All India Whips Conference[39]

I am interested to learn that an All India Whips Conference is going to be held in Bombay. I think it is a good idea to hold such a conference because Whips play an important part in our parliamentary institutions. Not only do they encourage Members to be present at voting time, but what is more important, they help in

---

36. Letter to an advocate, who had been Tamil interpreter at one of Nehru's public meetings in Madurai; address: 4 Avadi Road, Madras-10. PMO, File No. 52(12)/57-63-PMS, Vol. I, Sr. No. 94-A.
37. Letter not reproduced; available in the NMML.
38. See item 14 and appendix 9.
39. Message, 16 October 1962. NMML, JN Supplementary Papers, Box No. 143.

the establishment of practices which are in conformity with decorous behaviour and calm consideration of the problems that are discussed.

I wish the conference success.

[J. Nehru]

20. To K.B. Menon: Nothing Improper about Joining PSP[40]

October 18, 1962

My dear Menon,

Your letter of the 12th October.[41] I am glad to hear from you. But there is no reason at all for you to think that your behaviour towards me was not proper. It never struck me in this way. You were at perfect liberty to join the PSP without any impropriety. So please do not worry about this matter.

I hope you are keeping well.

Yours sincerely,
Jawaharlal Nehru

21. To S. Chellaswamy: Progress of Hindi[42]

October 19, 1962

Dear Shri Chellaswamy,

I have your letter of October 17.[43]

The Bill on the Official Language has not been finalised yet. But I do not understand why you should object to a provision in it to review the progress of Hindi from time to time. This is independent of English being an associate

---

40. Letter to a former PSP leader from Kerala; address: Thripuram, Empress Hotel Road, Calicut-1. NMML, K.B. Menon Papers.
41. See appendix 15.
42. Letter to Convener, Union Language Convention, South India, and President Madras Bar Association; address: Chandra Bagh Avenue, Off Edward Elliotts Road, Madras-4. PMO, File No. 52(12)/57-63-PMS, Vol. I, Sr. No. 98-A.
43. Not reproduced here; available at the NMML; PMO, File No. 52(12)/57-63-PMS, Vol. I, Sr. No. 97-A.

language. Any committee that is formed for this review will necessarily consist of representatives from all over the country.

Yours sincerely,
Jawaharlal Nehru

22. To J. B. Kripalani: Meeting[44]

October 25, 1962

My dear Jivat,
I shall be glad to see you at 12.30 mid-day on Saturday, the 27th October in my office in External Affairs Ministry, if this is convenient to you.

Yours affectionately,
[Jawaharlal Nehru]

23. To Lal Bahadur Shastri: Constitutional Amendment[45]

November 17, 1962

My dear Lal Bahadur,
I enclose two letters from Gopalan[46] about a Supreme Court decision.[47] I think that the result of this decision has been unfortunate. But I do not quite see what we can do in the matter now. We can hardly take up a constitutional amendment in this session of Parliament.

I am also enclosing a letter from Prakash Vir Shastri[48] about which I think I spoke to you. I do not agree with him in what he says. I do not know all the persons he mentions, but those I know are good servicemen and are doing good work.

Yours affectionately,
[Jawaharlal Nehru]

44. Letter to PSP leader; address: 30 Prithviraj Road, New Delhi.
45. Letter to the Home Minister.
46. A.K. Gopalan, Lok Sabha MP, CPI.
47. The case of A.K. Gopalan vs. State of Madras. See 1950 AIR 27, 1950 SCR 88.
48. Independent MP, Lok Sabha.

24. To M.N. Saravanam Pillay: Committee Membership[49]

November 17, 1962

Dear Shri Saravanam Pillay,

I have your letter of the 14th November.

Jagjivan Ram[50] is an old colleague of mine and I respect him. But membership of special committees does not depend on length of service, but on the Ministries that are specially concerned. This does not mean any disparagement to anyone.

Yours sincerely,
[Jawaharlal Nehru]

(b) Indian National Congress

25. To Damodar Swarup Seth: Finding Work[51]

October 8, 1962

My dear Damodar Swarup,

I have your letter of October 5th. I am very sorry to learn that you have not yet found any suitable work to do. I spoke to Shri C.B.Gupta[52] about it a day or two ago. He said that, in so far as governmental work is concerned, it is difficult to offer any to you, but it should be possible to find some Congress work. I am writing again to Shri Ajit Prasad Jain[53] on the subject. I hope he will be able to help you.

Yours affectionately,
[Jawaharlal Nehru]

---

49. Letter; address: 16 Thulasingam Mudaly Street, Perambur, Madras 11.
50. Minister of Transport and Communications.
51. Letter to a Congress Socialist leader from UP (1901-1965); address: Moti Mahal, Lucknow.
52. Chief Minister of Uttar Pradesh.
53. President of the Uttar Pradesh PCC.

26. To the CPP Executive[54]

Land Tax in States
Nehru Favours Gradual Levy
Step to Reduce Burden
(From Our Correspondent)

New Delhi, Oct. 17 – The Executive of the Congress Parliamentary Party which met here this evening devoted most of its time to a discussion of the formula to be applied for determining the additional payment due to sugarcane growers for the period 1958-62.

The two other subjects considered today were the European Common Market and land tax in States. On the ECM question, Nehru, it is learnt, gave an account of his meeting with President de Gaulle.

On the land tax, Mr Nehru is believed to have expressed himself in favour of the levy being made gradually to make it less burdensome. In this context, it is learnt that Mr Nehru pointed out that in asking the States to raise more funds for the Plans, the Planning Commission had not specified land tax as the only means.

The Prime Minister is stated to have told the Committee that the French President had promised every possible help to safeguard the interests of India, Pakistan and Ceylon when Britain entered the Common Market.

Sugar Formula

The discussion on the sugar formula took nearly 45 minutes and ended only when Mr Nehru allayed the fears of the critics of the Government decision by saying that the formula was intended only for determining the payment for the past four years and would not be applicable in the future.

PTI adds – During the discussion on the cane-sugar prices, Mr Nehru is understood to have explained that the formula devised by Government would only have retrospective effect and would not project itself to the future. He is also stated to have assured that the new formula would not involve any payment back by the cane-growers to the mills.

---

54. Report of CPP Executive meeting. Reproduced from *The Hindu*, 18 October 1962, p. 1.

27. To D. Sanjivayya: Choosing Rajya Sabha Candidates from Bihar[55]

November 22, 1962

My dear Sanjivayya,

Yesterday I received from the AICC Office a paper about nominations for the Rajya Sabha from Bihar. It appears that two names were considered or are being considered. One is that of, I think, L.P. Mishra. The other is of Shyam Nandan Mishra. L.P. Mishra was apparently suggested by the Bihar people although, I am told, no proper meeting of the Election Committee was held.

I have nothing against L.P. Mishra except that he has been defeated at the last election. We might even ignore that under special circumstances. But taking all in all, I do think that Shyam Nandan Mishra, who is senior Congressman and who has done good work and who did not stand for election last time, should be preferred. I have received quite a number of letters about this matter recommending Shyam Nandan Mishra and protesting against defeated candidates being chosen now.

Yours sincerely,
[Jawaharlal Nehru]

28. To Jainarain Vyas: Party Intrigues[56]

November 30, 1962

My dear Jainarainji,

Thank you for your letter of 26th November.

I am aware of the lobbying and intrigues that have been going on to some extent. I spoke about them in my own way at a recent meeting of the Executive Committee of the Party as well as meeting of the whole Party.

I do not know how speeches and statements can be limited except by a self-denying ordinance.

I think that whenever a change arises, we should make it clear that our basic ideals remain and will be pursued.

Yours sincerely,
[Jawaharlal Nehru]

---

55. Letter to the Congress President.
56. Letter to Rajya Sabha MP from Rajasthan; address: 83 South Avenue, New Delhi.

(c) Social Groups

29. To Mehr Chand Khanna: East Pakistan Refugees[57]

October 6, 1962

My dear Mehr Chand,

I enclose a copy of a letter I have received from Tridib Kumar Chaudhuri, MP.[58]

Is it possible to send these refugees or many of them to Dandakaranya? I think it would be desirable to do so. After all they are refugees from East Pakistan and something has to be done for them.

I am also enquiring from the Chief Minister of West Bengal.

Yours sincerely,
[Jawaharlal Nehru]

30. To S.K. Patil: YMCA Hostel[59]

October 16, 1962

My dear SK,

Your letter of October 16 about the proposal for the New Delhi YMCA to construct a tourist hostel. I had heard about this some time ago and had approved of it.

Personally, I have no objection to Government giving them a grant or loan for this purpose which, I think, is worthwhile. The YMCA has a Christian background as its name implies. But this is certainly not a denominational or narrow sectarian institution. It has done much good work. Therefore, I do not think that the fact of its being a Christian organisation should stand in the way of our helping it.

I did not know that we were keeping a list of so-called denominational organisations. There may be a general rule for Government not to help denominational institutions. That rule is good in so far as it goes, but each case has to be considered on its merits, and I think that the present case certainly deserves the help they ask for.

---

57. Letter to the Minister for Works, Housing and Supply.
58. Lok Sabha, Revolutionary Socialist Party, Behrampore, West Bengal.
59. Letter to the Minister of Food and Agriculture. PMO, File No. 27(50)59-65-PMS, Vol. I, Sr. No. 62-A.

In the booklet you have sent me, I see messages of goodwill from Dr Rajendra Prasad as well as our President and from many other eminent persons. Surely that should be enough to convince one of its bona fides.

I do not know what you wish me to do in this matter. You can send a copy of this letter of mine to the Ministry concerned.

Yours sincerely,
Jawaharlal Nehru

31. To C. P. Ranasinghe: Buddhism Good but no Religious Propaganda[60]

October 16, 1962

Dear Shri Ranasinghe,

Thank you for your letter of October 14.

Certainly, you should do whatever you can to spread knowledge of the Buddha's philosophy. I am glad that you are likely to be sent to the Ceylon Embassy in Washington.

My difficulty in helping you to present copies of your book[61] to large numbers of persons has nothing to do with the cost that might be incurred. It would not be appropriate for any Government agency to do this kind of propaganda on behalf of a religion, however good that might be. This should be done privately.

Yours sincerely,
[Jawaharlal Nehru]

32. To U. Dhammajoti: No Official Religious Position[62]

October 16, 1962

Dear Rev Dhammajoti,

Thank you for your letter of the 10th October. I have just come back from Ceylon and I hasten to reply to your letter.

60. Letter to Ceylonese author and philosopher; address: "Shanti", 53 Kandi Road, Mahara, Kadawata, Ceylon.
61. See also item 182.
62. Letter to the Principal of the Mangala College, 177 Deans Road, Maradana, Colombo, Ceylon.

Any attempt to lay stress on the common culture of Asian countries which have been affected by Hindu and Buddhist culture is to be welcomed. But such an attempt must be purely on a non-official level. I am afraid it will thus not be possible for me to associate myself formally with any such endeavour.[63]

Yours sincerely,
[Jawaharlal Nehru]

33. To Abdul Majid Khwaja: Illness[64]

November 11, 1962

My dear Khwaja,
I have just heard that you are ill and that you have been here in Delhi for some time. I am sorry to learn this. I hope proper arrangements have been made for your treatment. If I can help in any way, I shall gladly do so.

I am sending this note to you because I have heard that you might be returning to Aligarh tomorrow, the 12th November. I would suggest your staying here for your treatment and going back when you are better.[65]

Yours affectionately,
Jawaharlal Nehru

34. To Jamal Khawaja: Ill-health[66]

November 15, 1962

My dear Jamal,
Thank you for your letter of the 14th November. I am sorry that you have been unwell and have spent a month at the Balrampur Hospital, Lucknow. I hope you will recover your health soon.

We are having a difficult time. But there are many consolations. Above all, the tremendous emotional reaction all over the country has been most heartening. I am convinced that in the long run this will do good to our country and our people.

63. See item 31.
64. Letter to prominent lawyer and educationist; (1885-1962); address: Hameed Manzil, Daryaganj, Delhi. NMML, A.M. Khwaja Papers.
65. See also item 34.
66. Letter to Professor of Philosophy of Religion at Aligarh Muslim University and member of the second Lok Sabha; address: Samee Manzil, Aligarh.

I heard of your father's ill-health.[67] But I could not see him as he returned to Aligarh the very next day. I am glad he is better now.

Yours affectionately,
[Jawaharlal Nehru]

(d) States

(i) Andhra Pradesh

35. To N. Sanjiva Reddy: Flood Relief[68]

3rd October, 1962

My dear Sanjiva Reddy,
I returned to Delhi from abroad day before yesterday. Yesterday I read a copy of a letter from your Governor Shrinagesh[69] to the President. From this I found that you have had very heavy and continuous rains in Andhra Pradesh and that Hyderabad and Secunderabad have also suffered a great deal. I am sending a cheque for Rs 25,000/- from the Prime Minister's National Relief Fund to help in relief work.

Yours sincerely,
[Jawaharlal Nehru]

36. To Kumudini Devi: Flood Relief[70]

10th October, 1962

My dear Mayor,
I am very sorry to learn of the great damage caused by the floods in Hyderabad resulting in large numbers of people being displaced as their houses fell down. I am sending you a cheque for rupees twenty thousand from the Prime Minister's Relief Fund for your Mayor's Relief Fund[71].

As most of the damage done by the floods has been in the low lying areas containing many slums, I hope that you will not allow these slums to grow up there again. Now that part of the slums has been destroyed by the floods,

---

67. See item 33.
68. Letter to the Chief Minister of Andhra Pradesh.
69. S.M. Shrinagesh.
70. Letter to the Mayor of Hyderabad.
71. See item 35.

advantage should be taken of this and the slums should be removed completely and the area should be planned so as to have suitable buildings for houses as well as open spaces for children's playgrounds, etc. Usually if you put up multi-storeyed buildings for this purpose, they occupy less space on the ground and there is room for these playgrounds and open spaces. In making these changes the first priority should be of those who have been displaced. As far as possible, they should be rehabilitated in that area.[72]

I wish you all success in the work you are doing.

Yours sincerely,
[Jawaharlal Nehru]

37. To T. Anjaiah: Little Time to Meet[73]

October 16, 1962

Dear Shri Anjaiah,

I have your letter of the 13th October. I have just returned from Ceylon and am heavily occupied with many matters and the crises that face our country. I am afraid, therefore, that I cannot give much time to the industrial crisis that you tell me has arisen in Andhra. If you wish to see [me], I shall try to find a few minutes for you. I would suggest, however, if you come here, to see my Principal Private Secretary, Shri K. Ram, to begin with and explain the situation to him.

Yours sincerely,
[Jawaharlal Nehru]

38. For the Kosigi Panchayat Samithi[74]

My good wishes to the Kosigi Panchayat Samithi on the third anniversary of Panchayat Raj in Andhra Pradesh. Panchayat Raj is a great experiment and a great adventure. It means faith and reliance on the people of the country. I am sure that it will succeed and change our people in rural India, who are the backbone of the country. But this will need discipline and hard work and a spirit of cooperation.

72. See item 171.
73. Letter to Congress MLA, Barkatpura, Hyderabad.
74. Message, 20 October 1962, forwarded to P.O. Satyanarayana Raju, MLA, President Kosigi Panchayat Samithi, Kurnool. PMO, File No. 9/2/62-PMP, Vol. 7, Sr. No. 61-A.

25

39. To Atulya Ghosh: B.C. Roy Memorial at Hyderabad[75]

November 11, 1962

My dear Atulya Babu,

I enclose a letter which I have received form the Chief Minister of Andhra Pradesh.[76] He wants the consent of the Central Advisory Board of the Dr B.C. Roy Memorial Committee for a proposal to raise a suitable memorial to Dr Roy at Hyderabad. I think that we should agree to this, if you have no objection.

Yours sincerely,
[Jawaharlal Nehru]

(ii) Gujarat

40. To Balvantray Mehta: Charges Against the Chief Minister[77]

20th October, 1962

My dear Balvantray,

Your letter of the 18th October. I am sorry that you have got entangled in this business. I know that you did not ask for the inquiry but it seems to me that if serious charges are made in public against a Chief Minister and others, it is quite right for him to demand an inquiry.

I have not gone into this matter very carefully. The Chief Minister of Gujarat[78] certainly spoke to me about it and I have had a brief talk with Sadiq Ali.[79] From this it appeared to me that although you did not ask for the inquiry you were of opinion that there was much substance in the charges made. Such serious charges, if made, have either to be established or it has to be stated that they have not been proved. The matter cannot be left in the air. I gather that it is going to be considered by the Seven-man Committee who have Sadiq Ali's report before them. I have not read the report.

Regarding the resignation of a Congress MLA from Sihor in the Bhavnagar District and your standing for election from that seat, this is a matter which

---

75. Letter to Congress MP from Asansol; address: 19 Canning Lane, New Delhi.
76. N. Sanjiva Reddy.
77. Letter to President of the Lok Sevak Mandal.
78. Jivraj Mehta.
79. General Secretary, AICC.

should be considered separately, although Sadiq Ali's report may be one of the background matters which may be relevant to some extent.

Yours sincerely,
Jawaharlal Nehru

(iii) Kashmir

41. To Ghulam Mohammed Bakhshi: Visiting Kashmir[80]

October 4, 1962

My dear Bakhshi,

I have just received your letter of October, 4. Thank you for it. I have read also with interest the text of your inaugural speech at the meeting of the All India Editors Conference.

You renew your invitation to me to go to Kashmir. I am sorry to say that this is not feasible at all for me. I am heavily occupied during this month and November and December. Apart from my normal heavy occupations, our trouble in our border area in the East is a matter of great concern to us. And then there are many eminent visitors--Presidents and Prime Ministers--coming to India during these months. So, you must forgive me.

Yours sincerely,
[Jawaharlal Nehru]

42. On Bamzai's Book on Kashmir[81]

This book is a welcome addition to the long story of Kashmir. There are, I believe, some old histories of Kashmir written in the Persian language, and there is the famous *Raj-Tarangini* written in Sanskrit nine hundred years ago and brought up-to-date from time to time. The *Raj-Tarangini*, in fact, is supposed to be the only history as such in Sanskrit. This fairly comprehensive history of Shri P.N.K. Bamzai is, therefore, so far as I know, the only book of the kind and it is to be welcomed.

80. Letter to the Prime Minister of Jammu and Kashmir.
81. Foreword, 8 October 1962, to P.N.K. Bamzai's *A History of Kashmir: Political, Social, Cultural, from the Earliest Times to the Present Day* (Delhi: Metropolitan Book Co., 1962).

Apart from the story of kings and rulers, it gives some account of the social, economic and cultural elements in the history of Kashmir. It brings out a peculiar feature of the Kashmiris and how their mixed culture took shape. About two thousand years or more ago, Kashmir was a great Buddhist centre and some of the famous Buddhist councils were held there. From then onwards it continued to be one of the principal centres of Sanskrit learning. Nearly a thousand years ago, Arab and Persian influences first affected Kashmir and later, under Muslim rule, Persian became the recognised official language. Thus Kashmir experienced successively and sometimes together Buddhist, Hindu and Muslim influences, creating a mixed but harmonised culture which is so evident even today in Kashmir.

All over India something of this kind took place in varying degrees, more in the North than in the South. Thus we find this mixture of various cultures growing up in different parts of India in varying degrees. In Kashmir, however, this process went much further and resulted in blending these cultures effectively. The conflicts between the religions and cultures there, were less marked and the people of Kashmir broadly accepted all of them and thus created a blended cultural atmosphere which was peculiar to Kashmir. Shri Bamzai's history brings this out and shows the influence of Islam on Hinduism and of Hinduism on Islam. This blending resulted in a relative absence of communal feeling. In fact, the special characteristic of Kashmir was that of tolerance. Kashmir thus became, even more so than the rest of India, a laboratory for this process of the blending of cultures. Linguistically Kashmir was for long a home of Sanskrit learning and later became a centre of the Persian language also. Out of this mixture grew the present Kashmiri language.

Women in Kashmir have played a notable part in its history. Broadly speaking, women had greater rights there than in other parts of India.

Because of the beauty of nature in the valley and other parts of Kashmir perhaps, a special characteristic of the Kashmiris has always been a love of nature. Even now large numbers of the people go, whenever they have a chance, to the Moghul Gardens to sit there sipping their tea made from samovars that they carry with them and enjoy the beautiful flowers and trees there. Kashmiri poetry is full of nature's beauties and a certain pride in living in this delectable area.

The Moghul emperors were, as is well known, powerfully attracted to Kashmir and its beauty. Jehangir said that "Kashmir is a garden of eternal spring". The fame of Kashmir thus spread to Europe and other parts of the world both for its charm of nature and its lovely handicrafts.

But nature's beauties exist in many places and are often ignored. In Kashmir they were appreciated by the common people and not only by the rulers and the like, and the beautiful handicrafts were produced by the men and women of Kashmir. The influence of these two factors in addition to the blended and harmonised culture that grew up there led to the people being generally tolerant and free from communal conflict.

We must keep in mind these influences which have gone to mould the Kashmiri people and which explain, to some extent, its subsequent history and even more especially happenings [in] recent times. Kashmir was less affected by communal bigotry than most parts of India[82]. Even when, after the Partition of India, terrible occurrences took place in northern India, Kashmir was by and large free from any major conflict.

I am glad that Shri Bamzai has written in some detail about the events which took place in Kashmir's struggle for freedom and in the wake of the Partition of India. This makes us understand that the refusal of the people of Kashmir to accept the so-called two-nation theory was not a mere political development, but had its roots in their long past and the culture they had developed.

Kashmiris are known to be intelligent; they do very well in examinations. Their artisans are hardworking and have a sense of art and beauty. They love song and music. Perhaps because of these civilised traits they grew soft and other failings grew among them. They were not at all war-like and were thus very different from some of their neighbours. They liked a soft and quiet life. Perhaps it was this softness that attracted adventurous people from outside and ultimately led to the troubles that followed the Partition of India. That shock has had a powerful influence on them and has been an additional factor in moulding them.

Kashmir has been very much in the news in the last few years and many people talk of it as if it was just a piece of territory over which there is a conflict and lengthy arguments take place in the Security Council of the United Nations. But behind all these arguments lie the people of Kashmir, an attractive people in many ways who want to live their own lives and, now that they have tasted freedom, to progress according to their own ways and maintain the blended culture which has been their hallmark, whether they are Hindus or Muslims or Sikhs.

This book gives some idea of this background and I hope many people will read it and thus begin to understand something that lies behind the controversies relating to Kashmir.

[Jawaharlal Nehru]

82. See item 478.

43. To Sri Prakasa: Article on Kashmir[83]

9th October, 1962

My dear Prakasa,

I have just read your article on "Kashmir and Indo-Pakistan Relations: A Solution – II". I have not read the previous article.[84] This particular article was brought to me by Bakhshi Ghulam Mohammed[85] who is rather upset about it. It has thus far not been published in the press but it is stated on the type-script which was shown to me that it is not to be published before October 9, i.e. today.

I must confess to a feeling of surprise and great regret that you have written this article. I do not remember your mentioning to me your views as stated in this article. These views are, as you perhaps know, wholly opposed to the Government's views on the subject and your article will no doubt be used by the Pakistan authorities and press against us.

It is very far from true that Kashmir is de facto independent or nearly so, or not fully a part of the Indian Union. I need not go into any details about this. The fact that there is a Prime Minister there is a relic of the past and we have not thought it worthwhile to change it. The Supreme Court has authority there as elsewhere. Our Election Commission governs elections there. Our Parliament has authority to pass legislation governing it. There are some facts stated in the Constitution in which we do not choose to interfere. These are relatively minor things. The Governor is certainly appointed in a different way, but the appointment is by our President on the recommendations of the Kashmir Assembly.

I think it might have been wise for you to refer an article dealing with a very important issue of national and international significance to us before publication. I am afraid it is too late to do that now and your article is going to cause us any amount of difficulty and trouble with Pakistan as well as possibly with others. Whatever might have happened at the time of Partition or soon after, the position is entirely different now.

I am writing to you in some haste and, therefore, I do not wish to lengthen this letter. But I felt that I must let you know how I felt about your article as soon as possible.

Yours affectionately,
[Jawaharlal Nehru]

83. Letter to a Congressman, former Governor of Madras and Maharashtra.
84. Both reproduced, see appendix 2.
85. Prime Minister of Jammu and Kashmir.

44. To G.S. Pathak: Mridula Sarabhai's Note[86]

October 10, 1962

My dear Pathak,

I enclose a note I have received from Mridula Sarabhai. Forgive me for sending these notes on to you from time to time. I do not know what to do with them. Those which deal with the Conspiracy Case[87] or the under-trials there, I sometimes send on to you. It is for you to decide if anything is to be done or not.

Yours sincerely,
[Jawaharlal Nehru]

45. To Abdul Ghani Goni: Road and Rail in Jammu[88]

November 17, 1962

My dear Goni,
Your letter of November 12th.

I am afraid it will not be possible to take up the major road project to which you refer at this stage.[89] As you probably know, there is a proposal which we are trying to expedite, about the building of a railway to Jammu and beyond. There are also some roads likely to be constructed because of the minerals that have been found there.

Yours sincerely,
Jawaharlal Nehru

---

86. Letter to Rajya Sabha MP; address: 7/39 Kitchener Road, New Delhi.
87. The Kashmir Conspiracy Case involving Sheikh Abdullah.
88. Letter to Lok Sabha MP, National Conference; M842; address: 26 North Avenue, New Delhi. PMO, File No. 17(444)/61-70-PMS, Sr. No. 16-A.
89. Excerpt from Goni's letter: "Jammu & Kashmir is linked with the rest of the country only with one road, i.e. Pathankot to Jammu, which may be subjected to interference at any time."
    "I have been suggesting to build an alternate road connecting Chamba (Himachal) and Bhadarwah (J&K) to meet any emergency. This road not being the safest only but would serve as an alternate Defence line also as and when required. I would also request that the road from Kishtwar to Padar which is already under construction should be accelerated." PMO, File No. 17(444)/61-70-PMS, Sr. No. 15-A.

(iv) Kerala

46. To V.V. Giri: Grant for Kerala University[90]

October 17, 1962

My dear Giri,

Your letter of the 1st October was referred to the Education Ministry. I understand that letter is being examined by that Ministry. Usually such contributions are made through the University Grants Commission on the basis of certain approved projects. I hope it may be possible to give an ad-hoc grant to the Kerala University.

Yours sincerely,
[Jawaharlal Nehru]

(v) Madras

47. To Lal Bahadur Shastri: DMK and National Integration[91]

October 17, 1962

My dear Lal Bahadur,

Recently at Madras, T.T. Krishnamachari,[92] Subramaniam[93] and I met Kamaraj[94] and Bhaktavatsalam,[95] and discussed as to what we should do about the DMK agitation. The enclosed paper was considered. The first part of this paper is merely a repetition of Articles of the Constitution. It was suggested that Article 19(1) and (4) might be amended as stated at the bottom of the paper. It was further suggested that the Sub-Committee of the National Integration Council, of which C.P. Ramaswami Aiyar is Chairman, might be asked to make this

---

90. Letter to the Governor of Kerala.
91. Letter to the Home Minister. MHA, File No. 25/3/61-Poll (1), p.15, with enclosure.
92. Minister without Portfolio.
93. C.Subramaniam, Minister of Steel and Heavy Industries and former Minister of Law, Madras.
94. K. Kamaraj, Chief Minister of Madras.
95. M.Bhaktavatsalam, Minister for Finance and Education, Madras.

recommendation. Thereafter, we shall consider this question further. Kamaraj said he would speak to C.P. Ramaswami Aiyar about it.[96]

Yours affectionately,
Jawaharlal

[Enclosure]

Article 19(1):	All citizens shall have the right –
	(a) to freedom of speech and expression;
	(c) to form associations of unions;
Article 19(2):	Nothing in sub-clause (a) of clause (1) shall affect the operation of any existing law, or prevent the State from making any law, in so far as such law imposes reasonable restrictions on the exercise of the right conferred by the said sub-clause in the interest of the security of the State, friendly relations with foreign States, public order, decency or morality, or in relation to contempt of court, defamation or incitement to an offence.
Article 19(4):	Nothing in sub-clause (c) of the said clause shall affect the operation of any existing law in so far as it imposes, or prevent the law State from making any law imposing, in the interests of public order or morality, reasonable restrictions on the exercise of the right conferred by the said sub-clause.
Article 84:	A person shall not be qualified to be chosen to fill a seat in Parliament unless he –
	(a) is a citizen of India;
	(b) is, in the case of a seat in the Council of States, not less than thirty years of age and, in the case of a seat in the House of the People, not less than twenty-five years of age; and

96. Lal Bahadur Shastri replied on 18 October 1962 as follows: "My dear Panditji, I have received your letter No. 1686-PMH/62 dated 17th October, 1962. I had sent a note to you in the month of June last when you were in Srinagar regarding the amendment of the Constitution, i.e. amendment of Article 19(1) and (4). I shall look into that note further and when the C.P. Ramaswami Aiyar Sub-Committee recommendations are received, I shall finalise it and place it before you and the Cabinet. Yours affectionately, Lal." MHA, File No. 25/3/61-Poll (1), p.17.

(c) possesses such other qualifications as may be prescribed in that behalf by or under any law made by Parliament.

Article 19(1) & (4): Reasonable restrictions on the exercise of the rights under 1(a) and (c) in both these clauses should include "In the interests of the preservation of the integrity of the State".

Article 84(a): "… A citizen of a State and pledges himself to preserve the Constitution and the integrity of the State."

48. To S. Radhakrishnan: DMK and National Integration[97]

October 17, 1962

My dear President,
I enclose a paper which was considered by us at our meeting in Madras where Kamraj, T.T. Krishnamachari, Subramaniam and Bhaktavatsalam were present. The first part of this paper really quotes the present Articles. It was suggested that Article 19(1) and (4) might be amended as stated in the paper.[98]

Yours affectionately,
Jawaharlal Nehru

49. To Lal Bahadur Shastri: DMK and National Integration[99]

20th October, 1962

My dear Lal Bahadur,
I sent you the other day a note which had been discussed by me with Kamaraj and others in Madras. A suggestion was made in this about certain amendments of the Constitution. I sent a copy of that note to the President also. He has written to me on this subject and I enclose his letter. You may keep this for the present till we consider this matter more formally.[100]

97. Letter to the President. President's Secretariat, File No. 70/63, p.1.
98. See reply, appendix 19.
99. Letter to the Home Minister. MHA, File No. 25/3/61-Poll (1) p.18
100. See items 47 and 48, and appendix 19.

At present the idea is that some such suggestion should come from the Committee of the Integration Council. We can then consider it more precisely.

Yours affectionately,
Jawaharlal

50. To S. Radhakrishnan: Amending the Constitution[101]

20th October, 1962

My dear President,

Thank you for your letter of October 20 about the suggested amendments to the Constitution.[102] We shall consider what you have written with care when the time comes for actual drafting. For the present, as I think I wrote to you previously, we would like the Committee of the Integration Council to consider this matter and make recommendations to us.

The word "State" is used in the Constitution as referring to the entire Union, but it may perhaps be better to say the "Union".

Yours affectionately,
[Jawaharlal Nehru]

51. To Lal Bahadur Shastri: National Integration and Regionalism[103]

November 5, 1962

My dear Lal Bahadur,

I enclose a letter from C.P. Ramaswami Aiyar and a statement of the Committee on National Integration and Regionalism. I think that we should consider his proposal for the amendment of the Constitution in the Cabinet.

As for sending his statement to the Press, I think it would be desirable to do so. But it might be better to consult some of our colleagues before issuing it

101. Letter to the President.
102. See appendix 19.
103. Letter to the Home Minister.

to the Press. There is a Cabinet meeting on the 7th November. We can consider it then.[104]

Yours affectionately,
[Jawaharlal Nehru]

(vi) Maharashtra

52. To S. Radhakrishnan: Vijaya Lakshmi Pandit for Maharashtra Governor[105]

November 10, 1962

My dear Mr President,

I have spoken to Shri Yeshwantrao Chavan, Chief Minister of Maharashtra. He repeated to me his wish to have Shrimati Vijaya Lakshmi Pandit as Governor of Maharashtra.

He appeared to think that Mrs Pandit might take charge of her new office towards the end of this month or, at any rate, during the last week of the month. Apparently, the Acting Governor has fixed some engagements, and it would be desirable to give him some little time before he goes back to the High Court.

I would, therefore, recommend to you that Vijaya Lakshmi Pandit be appointed Governor of Maharashtra. The actual time of her taking charge of the Governorship might be fixed in consultation with the Chief Minister later.

If you are pleased to accept this recommendation, I would suggest an announcement to this effect being made in the course of the next two or three days.

Yours sincerely,
[Jawaharlal Nehru]

104. See item 47 and appendix 19.
105. Letter to the President. President's Secretariat, File No. 1/11/62, p. 1.

(vii) Mysore

53. Renaming Mysore as Karnataka[106]

Please reply to the attached letter as follows:

"Dear Shri Naidu,[107]
The Prime Minster has received your letter of the 27th September. He is surprised to learn that you propose to go on fast with the object of renaming the State of Mysore as Karnataka. To undertake a fast for this or any other purpose appears to the Prime Minister highly undesirable. Indeed, even a good object suffers because of a fast in its favour.

Yours sincerely,"
Jawaharlal Nehru

54. To S. Nijalingappa: No Time to Visit[108]

October 8, 1962

My dear Nijalingappa,
Your letter of October 5th. I am afraid there is very little chance of my being able to visit Bangalore or the Nandi Hills in the foreseeable future. I am very fully occupied in November and December, and January too is pretty full. Apart from my many engagements, the frontier situation is causing us a great deal of trouble, and I do not want to be away for long. Also, we are having any number of Prime Ministers and Presidents visiting us in November and December. You must, therefore, forgive me.

Yours sincerely,
[Jawaharlal Nehru]

106. Note, 3 October 1962, for a Private Secretary.
107. An activist of Karnataka Ekikaran Samithi.
108. Letter to the Chief Minister of Mysore.

(viii) Northeast

55. To Lal Bahadur Shastri: Mizo District[109]

October 20, 1962

My dear Lal Bahadur,

I enclose a letter from Chaliha, Chief Minister of Assam, about the Mizo district.[110] With this, he has sent reports of the Commissioner and the Deputy Commissioner.

Various suggestions have been made as to how to deal with the situation there. Some of these can only be given effect to by the Assam Government itself. Others require the initiative of the Government of India.

It has been especially suggested that the military forces there (apart from the Assam Rifles) should be removed. They are of no particular use there and only irritate the people. I have written to the Defense Minister on this subject. The armed police also, it is suggested, should be removed, only the Assam Rifles remaining there.

Yours affectionately,

[Jawaharlal Nehru]

56. For V. K. Krishna Menon: Mizo District[111]

The Chief Minister of Assam has sent me long reports about the Mizo district where there is a growing demand for independence.[112] Apparently this demand is not strong at present. Anyhow, various suggestions have been made. Among these is the withdrawal of some Army forces and Special Police there, apart from the Assam Rifles. These were put there apparently to stop Naga hostiles from escaping that way. I am told, however, there is no chance of Nagas going there. At the present moment, the presence of these armed forces is not really necessary there, and they have a bad effect on the people. It is suggested, therefore, they should be removed, and only the Assam Rifles should be left in the Mizo district.[113]

---

109. Letter to the Home Minister. NAI, MHA, File No. 15/1/62-SR(R)-A.
110. Appendices 13 and 48.
111. Note, 20 October 1962, for the Defence Minister.
112. See appendix 13.
113. See item 55.

2. The Governor of Assam had a talk with Lieutenant General Umrao Singh, who apparently agreed that there was no need for the military there. But he said orders must come from the Government of India. I suppose this means the Defense Ministry.

3. Could you kindly look into this matter and take the necessary steps?

57. To B.P. Chaliha: Mizo District and Chinese Invasion[114]

October 20, 1962

My dear Chaliha,

Thank you for your letter of the 12th October about the political situation in Mizo district.[115] I have read the reports of your Commissioner and Deputy Commissioner also. Among the recommendations made, some can be carried out by your Government. As for the Army and the Special Police (except the Assam Rifles) being withdrawn, this should certainly be done. I am writing to the authorities concerned about it.

I hope you will succeed in removing misunderstandings created by the Assam Official Language Act.

The Chinese aggression in NEFA has developed rapidly and, as you will no doubt know, there have been big conflicts today all over our border. The Chinese have come down in very large numbers and have pushed back our Army from several places. Both sides appear to have suffered heavy losses.[116] This is a matter which is causing us great concern and we are giving all our thought to it. There can, of course, be no surrender to this kind of thing. But we must be prepared for losses from time to time.

As for publicity being given, I think you will find that better publicity is given in future. We have, in fact, invited some representatives of news agencies to go there. They have taken some time in choosing suitable men as only hardy people who can survive the climate and the difficult conditions there, should go. We have a very difficult task, but we shall face it with a stout heart. We

---

114. Letter to the Chief Minister of Assam.
115. Appendix 13.
116. See Note by Ministry of Foreign Affairs, Peking, to Embassy of India in China, 20 October 1962, see A.S. Bhasin (ed.) *India-China Relations: 1947-2000 A Documentary Study*, published in cooperation with Policy Planning Division, Ministry of External Affairs, (New Delhi: Geetika Publishers, 2018)doc. no. 1876, pp.3921-3922.

must realise, however, that this is going to be a long drawn out affair. I see no near end of it.

Yours sincerely,
[Jawaharlal Nehru]

58. To K.D. Malaviya: Assam Oil[117]

November 4, 1962

My dear Keshava Deva,

Morarji Desai has sent me his report on the Oil question. I enclose a copy of this.[118] I accept this report and the recommendations made therein.

I have sent a copy of it to Chaliha also and suggested that this report might be given effect to from the 1st November, 1962.[119]

Yours affectionately,
Jawaharlal Nehru

59. To B.P. Chaliha: Oil Royalty Question Settled[120]

November 4, 1962

My dear Chaliha,

Shri Morarji Desai has sent me his report on the Oil Royalty question, of which I enclose a copy. As you know, he discussed this matter fully with your Government's representatives and also the representatives of our Ministry concerned. I accept this report, and I think this should form the basis of a decision on this issue. I would further suggest that his proposals might be considered to have come into effect on the 1st November, 1962.

Yours sincerely,
Jawaharlal Nehru

---

117. Letter to the Minister of Mines and Fuel. PMO, File No. 17(490)/62-70-PMS, Sr. No. 57-A.
118. See appendix 29.
119. See item 59.
120. Letter to the Chief Minister of Assam. PMO, File No. 17(490)/62-70-PMS, Sr. No. 56-A. See appendix 29; and SWJN/SS/78/appendices 11and 12.

60. In the Lok Sabha: Escape of Naga Leaders to London[121]

Question[122]: Will the Prime Minister be pleased to state:

(a) whether in September 1962, the Government of UK permitted the four Naga campaigners for "independence" to enter Britain; and

(b) if so, what are the reactions of the Government of India thereto?

The Minister of State in the Ministry of External Affairs (Lakshmi Menon):

(a) Yes.

(b) Before the four Indian Naga were allowed to enter the UK our High Commission in London informed the UK authorities that if the UK authorities decided to permit these Nagas to enter the UK, on the basis of identification papers issued to them by any other country, in full knowledge of the fact that they were Indian citizens, we would regard it as an unfriendly act on the part of the British Government. The UK authorities informed our High Commission that they accepted our High Commissioner's statement as to the place of birth of these persons and this statement established that under British laws, they were Commonwealth citizens. As such, they had a right to enter the UK under the Commonwealth Immigrants Act, 1962, since they had sufficient funds to support themselves as visitors in the U.K.

It was clarified in a press statement issued by our High Commission that the only commonwealth country of which these Nagas could be citizens was India and that they had been allowed entry into UK as Commonwealth citizens on the basis of their Indian citizenship.

Surendra Pal Singh[123]: Did these rebel Naga leaders seek an interview with our Prime Minister when he was in London in September last?

---

121. Oral answers to questions, *Lok Sabha Debates*, Third Series, Vol. IX, November 8-20, 1962, pp. 858-862.

122. By Surendra Pal Singh, P.C. Borooah, Savitri Nigam, F.H. Mohsin, S.B. Patil, Kapur Singh, N.S. Kajrolkar, T.H. Sonavane (Congress), Homi Daji, P.K. Vasudevan Nair, Indrajit Gupta, Sarjoo Pandey, Renu Chakravarty (CPI), Yashpal Singh, P.K. Ghosh, P.K. Deo (Swatantra Party), S.M. Banerjee (Independent).

123. Congress , from Bulandshahr.

The Prime Minister and Minister of External Affairs, Defence and Atomic Energy (Jawaharlal Nehru): No, Sir; there was no such proposal.

Surendra Pal Singh: May I know the significance of this term Commonwealth citizenship? When they were not recognised as Indian citizens, how is it that they were admitted into the United Kingdom as Commonwealth citizens? May we have a clarification about that?

Jawaharlal Nehru: The UK Government did recognise them as Indian citizens.

S.M. Banerjee[124]: I want to know whether it is a fact that these four Naga leaders went to meet Mr Phizo to enable him to raise the issue of Nagaland in the United Nations with the help of certain countries and, if so, whether these people have come back. Do you know anything about their activities?

Lakshmi Menon: They are still in London. They have not gone to the United Nations.

S.M. Banerjee: Sir, it came out in the newspapers that these four Naga leaders went to London to meet Mr Phizo and to enable him to raise this question of Nagaland, that is, his conception of Nagaland, in the United Nations with the help of certain countries. I want to know whether they are still there or whether they have come back. What is our source of information?

Shri Jawaharlal Nehru: All the four are in London. They did not go to the United States.

S.M. Banerjee: Mr Phizo was also in London at that time.

Speaker: If these four and Mr Phizo are there they might be meeting there. How can we know about that?

S.M. Banerjee: I never mentioned United Nations at all.

Indrajit Gupta[125]: I want to know whether it is a fact, as has been reported in the press, that after they had been allowed to enter Britain these Nagas

---

124. Independent, from Kanpur.
125. CPI, from Calcutta South.

issued a statement saying that they were not Indian citizens. In that case what is the position that the British Government took up? Although they may be Commonwealth citizens, I want to know whether they can enter Britain without any kind of a passport and then make a declaration denying that they are Indian citizens.

Jawaharlal Nehru: That is a question which can only be considered by the UK Government. The UK Government stated that they can only allow them to enter in their capacity as Commonwealth citizens which they derive from being citizens of India. They said that. It may be as the hon. Member says, that these people denied that. We pointed out even after that, that they can only be considered as Indian citizens.

Hem Barua[126]: May I know if the Government is aware of the fact that these Naga leaders in London are taking up their anti-Indian campaign anew and that the *Daily Express* is helping them by publishing their charges against India? If so, may I know whether the Government has brought this to the notice of the UK Government?

Jawaharlal Nehru: I have no particular knowledge of their propaganda activities there through the *Daily Express*. It is quite likely they are doing it. They have nothing else to do except to try to do propaganda as their course. But, I do not know whether the particular attention of the UK Government has been drawn to this or not.

Sonavane[127]: In view of these hostile Nagas working in Britain, has our High Commissioner been instructed to keep a watch on their activities so that we may be kept informed.

Jawaharlal Nehru: It is the business of the High Commissioner to find out and report to us what these people are doing.

Hem Barua: Has he?

Basumatari[128]: May I know what steps the Government will take against these Naga hostiles when they want to return?

126. PSP, from Gauhati, Assam.
127. T.H. Sonavane, Congress, from Pandharpur, Maharashtra.
128. D. Basumatari, Congress, from Goalpara, Assam.

Savitri Nigam[129]: It was widely publicised that these Naga hostiles have refused to say that they are Indian citizens and they did not have any travel papers or any passport. May I know whether the Indian Government has ever enquired from the UK Government on what basis they were recognised as Indian citizens?

बेरवा[130]: क्या मैं जान सकता हूं कि चीनी हमले के सम्बन्ध में नागा नेताओं की क्या प्रतिक्रिया देखी गई है?

अध्यक्षः जो चार वहां हैं, उन की, या सब नागरिकों की, जो यहां पर हैं?

बेरवाः मैं यह जानना चाहता हूं कि जो नागा नेता यहां पर हैं, चीनी हमले के सम्बन्ध में उनकी क्या प्रतिक्रिया देखी गई है। वे भारत के साथ हैं या विरूद्ध?

कछवाय[131]: श्रीमन् मैं यह जानना चाहता हूं कि इस समय कितने नागा विद्रोही इंगलैण्ड में हैं।

[Translation begins:

Onkarlal Berwa: May I know, what is the opinion of these Naga Leaders regarding the Chinese attack?

Speaker: Those four who are there, or all those who are here?

Berwa: I want to know about those Naga leaders who are here and what is there position regarding the Chinese attack. Are they with India or against?

H.C. Kachwai: Sir, I want to know how many Naga rebels are in England now.

Translation ends]

Speaker: That would be hypothetical.

---

129. Congress, from Banda.
130. Jana Sangh.
131. Jana Sangh.

61. To Moinul Haque Choudhury: Remain in Assam[132]

November 15, 1962

Dear Moinul Haque,

Thank you for your letter of November 11th offering your services in the present emergency. There is hardly any question of people being sent abroad now. We are in fact calling back such people as we can. We have to concentrate on our work in India. You are doing good work in Assam, and there are many other types of work in Assam which require to be done. I suggest that you should undertake such activities in Assam itself.

Yours sincerely,
[Jawaharlal Nehru]

62. To Liladhar Kotoki: Problems of Northeast in Perspective[133]

November 17, 1962

Dear Liladharji,

Thank you for your letter of the 17th November.

Of all parts of India, surely the north-east is today receiving the greatest attention. That is natural because the invasion of India by China has come through the north-east. So, we have to think of NEFA and Assam and consider their problems. Immediately we have to deal with a ruthless invasion. It is probable that the struggle will last a long time and will strain us to the utmost. But I am confident that it will end in our victory and that the aggressor will be pushed out of India.

This is the major issue. Everything else is secondary. It often happens that when a big issue arises, other matters lose importance. I think that, that is partly true of Assam today. So the problems which have troubled us, such as the demand of the tribal districts to form a separate state etc., have receded into the background.

132. Letter to Minister in Assam.
133. Letter to Lok Sabha MP, Congress, from Nowgong; address: 50 South Avenue, New Delhi.

45

I am afraid that any development scheme which is not directly connected with the war effort will have to be delayed. On the other hand, everything connected with it will receive special attention.[134]

Yours sincerely,
[Jawaharlal Nehru]

63. To R.S. Panjhazari: Defence of Northeast[135]

November 18, 1962

Dear Panjhazari,
Your letter of the 17th November with which you have sent a letter from Shri Liladhar Kotoki. I do not know what the Executive Committee of the Party can do in this matter. The main question he raises is that of Defence. Our Armies are chiefly in Assam and doing the utmost to defend it. A resolution of the Committee will not add to their strength.

As for the other matters referred to by Liladhar Kotoki, they are important no doubt, but they have to take second place because of the Chinese invasion.[136]

Yours sincerely,
[Jawaharlal Nehru]

64. In the Rajya Sabha: NEFA Official Financing Phizo's Relative[137]

A.D. Mani[138]: Will the Prime Minister be pleased to state:

(a) whether a senior official of the North Eastern Frontier Agency was involved in a case of violation of Foreign Exchange Rules in regard to financing the trip of Mr Phizo's relative to Europe; and

(b) if so what action has been taken against the said official?

---

134. See also item 63.
135. Letter to the Secretary of CPP.
136. See item 62.
137. Intervention in debate, *Rajya Sabha Debates*, Vol. XLI, Nos. 9-21, 20 November to 6 December 1962, Oral Answers, pp. 1740-1743.
138. Independent.

The Deputy Minister in the Ministry of External Affairs (Dinesh Singh):

(a) Yes.

(b) The adjudication proceedings against the officer were completed on the 30th December, 1961, and a penalty of Rs 1,750 was imposed on him.

A.D. Mani: Sir, I would like the hon. Minister to give more details about the case under (a).

The hon. Minister replied 'yes' to part (a) of the question which means that there was a case. What were the details of the case?

Shri Dinesh Singh: It will be difficult to give full details in this short time. One official in the NEFA Administration had given some foreign exchange to a lady student who was going to the United Kingdom and this was in contravention of the Foreign Exchange Regulations. He pleaded that there was some misunderstanding, that he had been away in NEFA and was not fully informed of the changes that had been made in the rules and as such he had given this money to her in good faith but in the adjudication proceedings it was felt that this penalty should be imposed on him and it was accordingly done.

A.D. Mani: I would like the hon. Minister to confirm or deny these facts. This gentleman was an official. He opened an account with his London Bank and gave a cheque to this lady who was in touch with Mr Phizo. This lady was searched on the aeroplane and the cheque was recovered from her. She was fined Rs 250 for violating the Foreign Exchange Regulations and this official was subjected to a nominal fine though he had not taken any authorisation from the Reserve Bank to issue a cheque on his London account to a lady whose antecedents in respect of Mr Phizo were doubtful. Would he confirm or deny these facts.

Dinesh Singh: There are too many questions to say yes or no outright.

Jawaharlal Nehru: May I point out that the fact that he issued a cheque, gave a cheque, to a young woman who was going for her studies there is established. His case was—he had given an explanation as far as I remember—that he had, what is called, a Zero Account, a Zero Account being an old account which is not subject normally to the new Exchange Regulations because it exists from pre-independence days. I do not know anything about the fact that this young woman was connected with Mr Phizo in any way.

47

A.D. Mani: Sir, this official was holding a responsible position as Adviser to the Governor and he should have known, whether it was a Zero Account or no. 1 Account, that no cheque can be issued on a London Bank without the authorisation of the Reserve Bank. And I am told that after he was involved in this case he has been sent for training in some special work with a view to eventual promotion to a higher job.

Jawaharlal Nehru: This matter was fully considered by the Enquiry Committee. They went into it and they gave a certain punishment, admonition or whatever it was, to him. I do not think they had been too lenient in what they said or did in this matter. They considered everything. The officer in question otherwise has an excellent record.

Bhupesh Gupta[139]: It seems that the whole matter was dealt with departmentally. May I know the reason why the matter was not referred to the Directorate of Enforcement under the Ministry of Finance where such cases are dealt with in view of the fact that under the Reserve Bank Rules nobody can issue such cheques whether in respect of Zero Account or Plus One Account without the sanction of the Reserve Bank authorities?

Jawaharlal Nehru: I am not sure that is the rule that one cannot issue cheques.

Lakshmi Menon: This was investigated by the Enforcement Directorate.

Jawaharlal Nehru: My colleague tells me here that this was investigated by the Enforcement Directorate. But cheques can always be issued. How is one to prevent cheques from being issued? Only information of that has to be sent to the proper authorities. I do not quite understand. A person has an account there and he sends by post a cheque to somebody. And if it is a Zero Account, then information of that has to be sent. No permission has to be sought.

A.D. Mani: I would like to ask a further question. After this lady went to London, remittances from Mr Phizo started flowing into the State Bank at Shillong to the family of Mr Phizo and the money was being sent by Mr Phizo. Have all these transactions been enquired into by the Enquiry Committee or did it confine itself only to the technical violation of the Foreign Exchange Regulations?

139 CPI.

48

Dinesh Singh: We are not aware of what the hon. Member has mentioned. If it is so desired, we shall find out about it.

Bhupesh Gupta: Did the Government find out from the person concerned the total amount in his credit with the Bank in England at the time of the issuance of this cheque, and may I know whether he was called upon to explain how that amount was accumulated there?

Jawaharlal Nehru: I do not understand all this. This is a matter which the Enquiry Committee and the Enforcement Directorate went into. I do not know all the details of it, nor am I supposed to know all of them.

Bhupesh Gupta: We would like to know the amount involved. That should be known to the Government, the total amount he had in this Account.

Lakshmi Menon: The official concerned had lived in England almost all his life and his father too and he had an account there even before 1947. As for the lady's relationship, I think that lady has only very distant relationship with Mr Phizo and families were not even on friendly terms. So, all those suggestions are not quite correct.

(ix) Pondicherry

65. In the Lok Sabha: Pondicherry Bill[140]

The Prime Minister and Minister of External Affairs and Minister of Atomic Energy (Jawaharlal Nehru): I shall move the motion. Then my colleague will carry on.

Sir, I beg to move:

"That the Bill to provide for the administration of Pondicherry and for matters connected therewith be taken into consideration."

I introduced this Bill the other day. It is a very simple measure. The House knows the past history of Pondicherry and how in November, 1954,

140. Moving the Administration of Pondicherry Bill, *Lok Sabha Debates*, Third Series, Vol. X, November 21 to December 4, 1962, pp. 2932-2934.

the French establishments of Pondicherry, Karaikal and Yanam were vested in the Government of India following an agreement between the Governments of India and France. The two Governments entered into a treaty in 1956 ceding full sovereignty over these territories to India. This treaty was to come into force on its ratification. The Instruments of ratification were exchanged on the 16th August, 1962. Accordingly, with effect from that date, these establishments have become a part of the Indian Union. In order to specify these former French establishments in the Union Territory called Pondicherry and to amend article 240 of the Constitution, to confer powers on the President to make regulations for their peace, progress and good government, the Constitution XIV Amendment Bill, 1962, was passed by both Houses during the last session. This bill has not yet secured the assent of the President as it has to be ratified by the State Legislature previously. Until this Bill becomes law, no Regulation can be promulgated in respect of Pondicherry under article 240 of the Constitution. It was, therefore, found necessary to provide for the continuance of the existing laws and officers, to take power to extend appropriate Indian enactments to the Union Territory and to provide for the extension of the jurisdiction of the High Court of Madras over Pondicherry as the power of the Courts of France over the Courts in Pondicherry ceased with effect from 18th August, 1962. As Parliament was not in session, the Pondicherry (Administration) Ordinance of 1962 was promulgated by the President on 6th November, 1962. As required under article 123(2) of the Constitution, the Pondicherry (Administration) bill is now being moved in order to replace the said Ordinance.

This is a relatively simple Bill. Section 3: the existing officers and institutions during the de facto period are to continue to exercise the same functions as before in the interests of smooth administration. Section 4: after the de facto agreement, effective from 1st November, 1954, the administration of Pondicherry was carried on by the Government of India on the basis of the then existing laws. However, Indian laws considered essential were extended to the territory under the Foreigners Jurisdiction Act. It is considered that all the laws as existed prior to the 16th August, 1962 should be validated. Sections 5 and 6: these sections are based on the Treaty of Cession which was signed by the Governments of India and France in 1956 and has already been ratified. Section 7: this section ensures the continuance of the existing taxes. Section 8: The Government of India has taken power to extend to Pondicherry such enactments as are in force in a State at the date of the notification. I need not say much about these specific matters. It is seen that they are very relevant and almost obvious such as extension of Jurisdiction of the High Court of Madras to Pondicherry. The complicated French judicial system now ceases to exist.

Ranga[141] (Swatantra Party): Ceases to exist?

Jawaharlal Nehru: Not entirely; I mean to say locally. It is cut off from France. Appeals will go to the High Court. That is all I have to say at this stage.

(x) Punjab

66. To Partap Singh Kairon: Flood Relief[142]

2nd October, 1962

My dear Partap Singh,
I returned yesterday from abroad. I am much grieved and distressed to learn of the terrible calamity that has descended upon Punjab. I feel sure, however, that you and your Government will face it with courage and determination.

I understand that my PPS[143] has already sent you Rs 50,000/- from the Prime Minister's National Relief Fund for relief work. I enclose another cheque for Rs 50,000/- for the same purpose.

Yours sincerely,
[Jawaharlal Nehru]

67. To Pattom A. Thanu Pillai: Governor of Punjab[144]

October 3, 1962

My dear Thanu Pillai,
Thank you for your note of the 2nd October. I was glad to learn almost immediately after my arrival here that you had been sworn in as Governor of the Punjab. I congratulate you upon it and I am sure you will make a success of it.

The Punjab is, in its own way a difficult province, but it is a vital province in the sense that its people are enterprising and hard-working.

With all good wishes to you,

Yours sincerely,
[Jawaharlal Nehru]

141. N.G. Ranga.
142. Letter to the Chief Minister of Punjab.
143. Kesho Ram.
144. Letter to the former Chief Minister of Kerala. See also items 68 and 71.

68. To A. N. Vidyalankar: Thanu Pillai as Governor of Punjab[145]

October 6, 1962

My dear Amar Nathji,

I have your letter of the 3rd October. I can understand your surprise and perhaps your initial disapproval of the appointment of Shri Thanu Pillai as Governor of the Punjab. But if you knew all the facts, I am sure you would change your opinion. I am quite clear in my mind that nothing should be done by us which is lacking in political integrity and decency.

The element of hurry certainly came in because of the last moment decision of Shri Reddy[146] not to go to the Punjab as Governor. We had to take some decision quickly and make arrangements within a certain time.

But Shri Thanu Pillai told me some months ago, without my asking him about it, that he was prepared to take a Governorship. Much later he told Lal Bahadurji[147] about it too. It was far from our minds to indulge in any political trickery in this matter. It is true that Shri Thanu Pillai had become a problem in Kerala. He has a long record of service, but he is a difficult person to get on with for colleagues in the Ministry. He is equally difficult, I am told, in the PSP and has seldom followed his Party's advice. His own Party in Kerala has split up. A number of people have resigned from it and asked to be taken into the Congress. We have specially refrained from doing so because we did not think it proper to do anything to break up the PSP there. As a matter of fact, if we had so wanted, we could have not only taken these persons but some other members of the PSP there. Our whole attempt has been not to break up the PSP in Kerala and to continue our cooperation with it. This was in spite of the acute tensions arising there both in the PSP and between the PSP and the Congress.

In view of all this and the fact that Shri Thanu Pillai himself wanted a Governorship and also because in spite of his temperamental difficulties he has a long record of service to his credit and is, I believe, an able man, we decided as we did.

---

145. Congress MP from Hoshiarpur, Punjab; address: 15 Ferozeshah Road, New Delhi.
146. According to press reports, K.C. Reddy, Union Minister for Commerce and Industry was supposed to succeed N.V. Gadgil as the Governor of Punjab. He was reported to have informed Nehru in the third week of September that in one of his weaker moments he had earlier agreed to accept the Governorship, but the people of his constituency were not happy over his decision to quit active politics. See *The Tribune*, 27 September 1962, p.4.
147. Lal Bahadur Shastri, Home Minister.

I am writing to you briefly on this subject.[148] I understand that Lal Bahadur Shastriji has explained the situation to Shri Asoka Mehta[149] also who had little to say after he had heard the facts.

Yours sincerely,
Jawaharlal Nehru

69. To Partap Singh Kairon: Flood Relief[150]

October 6, 1962

My dear Partap Singh,

I have already sent you Rs 1 lakh from the Prime Minister's Relief Fund directly for relief from the floods in the Punjab.[151] I have further sent you Rs 25,000/- from the American Ambassador and Rs 25,000/- from one of the Tata trusts.

I now enclose a cheque for Rs 100,000/- received from Shri Ghulam Mohammed Bakhshi, Prime Minister of J & K State for relief from the ravages caused by the recent floods in the Punjab. He specially mentions that this includes any relief to be given owing to the Spiti Valley tragedy.

Shrimati Rameshwari Nehru has specially asked me for some money for giving blankets etc. to Harijans in the Punjab who have suffered from these floods. I may give her some money for this specially. I would suggest, however, that you might give the Harijan Sevak Sangh of which she is in charge apparently, some money for this purpose.[152] You might give her Rs 20,000/- or Rs 25,000/-.

Yours sincerely,
[Jawaharlal Nehru]

148. See also item 71.
149. PSP leader.
150. Letter to the Chief Minister of Punjab.
151. See item 66.
152. See item 70.

70. To Rameshwari Nehru: Flood Relief[153]

October 6, 1962

My dear Bijju Bhabi,

I have sent Rs 1, 00,000 to the Chief Minister of the Punjab directly and I have also sent or am sending another Rs. 2, 00,000 for relief work.

I have informed the Chief Minister of the special needs of the Harijans and of your letter to me and requested him to give some money for this purpose. I hope you will get something from him.[154]

Meanwhile, I am sending you a cheque for Rs 20,000.

Yours affectionately,
[Jawaharlal Nehru]

71. To Harekrushna Mahtab: Thanu Pillai and Nepal[155]

October 11, 1962

My dear Mahtab,

Thank you for your letter of the 8th October.

I am sorry there has been so much misunderstanding about the appointment of the new Governor of the Punjab.[156] I do not think there is any impropriety in our doing so. It was certainly done in some haste because of circumstances. Reddy refused at the last moment, and it was not possible for us to force him to go there. I left immediately thereafter for England.

Thanu Pillai spoke to me about three months or more ago expressing a wish to be appointed Governor of some State. He said he was old and he wanted at the end of his career a relatively quiet office. He was having a lot of trouble in his Government. He is a man who is very temperamental and does not get on with anybody. He did not get on with his own Party, and did what he liked regardless of what the PSP advised him to do. As a result of this, four or five members of his Party resigned from it some time ago.[157] These persons who had resigned

---

153. Letter to Rameshwari Nehru, worked with the Harijan Sevak Sangh, Delhi-9.
154. See item 68.
155. Letter to Congress MP from Angul, Orissa and former Chief Minister of Orissa.
156. Pattom Thanu Pillai, PSP, former Chief Minister of Kerala. See item 68.
157. See appendix 15.

asked to be taken into the Congress. We refrained from encouraging them as we did not wish to do the thing that you accuse us of. The remaining members of the PSP were also not at all happy with the situation. The Government was not functioning properly.

So far as the Congress Party was concerned, it found it could not go on with the Government as it was. This was the position when Lal Bahadur[158] went to Trivandrum. I do not know exactly what the conversation there was, but as a result of it Thanu Pillai agreed to become Governor of the Punjab. It was not our intention to weaken the PSP or to end the Coalition Government. We said so clearly. Thanu Pillai was almost anxious to leave his post and become Governor, and we thought also that this was good solution of the tangle in Kerala. Therefore, Lal Bahadur decided as he did. He sent me a cable about it, and I replied that he could act as he thought fit.

We had dealt all along with Thanu Pillai. We had not directly dealt with the PSP central organisation at any stage, and as I have said above, Thanu Pillai was completely out of control in the PSP. It was perhaps for him to refer to the PSP people.

As regards the developments in Nepal, I agree with you that they are very disturbing. We have tried our best to smooth things there, and have gone rather out of our way to give assurances to the King. Just before my departure for England, I got a letter from him through his Foreign Minister. I replied to this immediately repeating my assurances.[159] The Foreign Minister was, I think, pleased with what I had written to the King. Some days afterwards, the King dismissed his Foreign Minister and issued a statement offensive to India. We swallowed that, and I did not issue any reply.[160]

The fact of the matter is that the King, I think, is off his head and he has got some very bad advisers. At least one of them is definitely pro-Chinese, if not worse. The Chinese are out to flatter the King and to injure our interests wherever they can.

We have issued definite instructions to the Bihar Government and to our people not to create any trouble in Nepal.[161] Unfortunately some PSP people in Bihar have been demonstrating against the present Nepal regime. Even so, nothing much has happened. From the other side, however, there has been the most offensive propaganda against us, and some of our people have been murdered in cold blood near the frontier.

158. Lal Bahadur Shastri, Home Minister.
159. See SS/78/ item 429.
160. See item 218.
161. See item 221.

The situation is bad on our North-East frontier also, and I fear this will give us a lot of trouble with the Chinese.

So far as the Third Plan is concerned, it is true that we are facing many difficulties. Before I went to England, we referred several matters of importance for immediate consideration of the Planning Commission and some committees. We propose to take them up soon.

Yours sincerely,
[Jawaharlal Nehru]

(xi) Rajasthan

72. To D. Sanjivayya: Jaisalmer Police Atrocities[162]

October 10, 1962

My dear Sanjivayya,
I am enclosing some papers sent to me by the Secretary of the Congress Party. These relate to certain alleged atrocities committed in the Jaisalmer area by the police. I have written to Shri Sukhadia, Chief Minister, about these and suggested that he should look into the matter.[163]

Perhaps you would be good enough to write to the President of the Pradesh Congress Committee on the subject.

Yours sincerely,
Jawaharlal Nehru

73. To Mohanlal Sukhadia: Jaisalmer Police Atrocities[164]

October 10, 1962

My dear Sukhadia,
I have been sent copy of the letter which Jai Narain Vyas[165] wrote to you on the 26th September and other papers, including some printed ones, about the alleged atrocities committed by the police in the Jaisalmer area. I know nothing about

162. Letter to the Congress President. NMML, AICC Papers, F. No. OD-30/A/1962, Box 10.
163. Item 73.
164. Letter to the Chief Minister of Rajasthan.
165. Rajya Sabha MP (1957-63) from Rajasthan.

this matter. But as so much publicity has been given to it, I think something should be done about it.[166]

Yours sincerely,
[Jawaharlal Nehru]

(xii) Uttar Pradesh

74. To C.B. Gupta: UP Land Holdings Tax Bill[167]

3rd October, 1962

My dear Chandra Bhanu,

Thank you for your letter of September 29th which I received on my return here from abroad. I have naturally not been in touch with various developments owing to my absence and so I am glad to have a full account from you.

I think the exemption limit that you have fixed is ample and there is no reason at this stage to make any further changes in your Bill. If any reference is made to me I shall say so.[168]

Yours sincerely,
Jawaharlal Nehru

75. To Mahavir Tyagi: UP Land Holdings Tax Bill[169]

8 October 1962

प्रिय महावीर,

मुझे तुम्हारा 7 तारीख़ का पत्र आज मिला।

मुझे यह ताज्जुब हुआ सुनकर कि यह कहा जाता है कि मैं ने ज़ोर दिया है कि लगान के बारे में नया क़ानून बने। मुझे तो इसका कुछ मालूम तक नहीं था सिवाए इसके कि कुछ अखबारों में मैंने पड़ा था। हां शुरू में प्लैनिंग कमीशन से उत्तर प्रदेश के मंत्रियों की

---

166. See also item 72.
167. Letter to the Chief Minister of Uttar Pradesh. PMO, File No. 31(124)/62-63-PMS, Sr. No. 10-A.
168. See SWJN/SS/78/items 184,191,192,193, and 194.
169. Letter to Congress MP from Dehradun; PMO, File No. 31(124)/62-63-PMS, Sr.No.14-A. Mahavir Tyagi's letter is available in the NMML, Mahavir Tyagi Papers, No. 1587, PMH-62.

बातें हुई थीं। पहली बार मेरी तवज्जो इस मामले में ख़ास तौर से कुछ हुई चन्द रोज़ पहले मेरे योरप जाने के। उस वक़्त भी और अभी तक मैं ने इस क़ानून की तफ़सील नहीं देखी मेरा ख़्याल था कि यह ग़ौर तलब मामला है। मैंने इस पर गुप्ता जी को लिखा कि इस पर फिर से ग़ौर होना चाहिए[170] और वह प्लैनिंग कमीशन से पूरा मशवरा करें। प्लैनिंग कमीशन से भी हम ने यही कहा।

यहां आ कर मैंने सुना कि यह मशवरे हुए थे और बहुत कुछ क़ानून में तबदीली की गई। प्लैनिंग कमीशन ने शायद उनसे कहा था कि वह पांच एकड़ तक लगान माफ़ कर दें। फिर मैंने सुना कि गुप्ता जी ने अपनी पार्टी में इसको पेश किया और वहां ज़्यादातर मेम्बर पांच एकड़ को सुनकर खुश हुए। कुछ लोगों ने कहा कि इसको ज़रा बढ़ा देना चाहिए, साढ़े छः एकड़ कर देना चाहिए। कुछ ने दस एकड़ तक कहा। आख़िर में उन्होंने फ़ैसला किया कि आठ एकड़ कर देना चाहिए, यह आठ एकड़ सबों को लागू होगा और यह नहीं है, जैसे कि तुम ने लिखा है कि चार से दस एकड़ तक छूट होगी।

यह मेरी समझ में नहीं आता, जो तुम ने लिखा है, कि बुलाने पर भी पार्टी की मीटिंग नहीं की गई। मैंने सुना है कि पार्टी की मीटिंग बार बार हुई और आख़री फ़ैसला भी पार्टी की रज़ामंदी से किया गया। फिर शायद कुछ सदस्यों ने मुमकिन है लिखा हो इसके बारे में। मैंने सुना है कि कुछ लोगों ने बाद में गुप्ता जी से कहा कि हमारा नाम ग़लत फ़हमी से शामिल हुआ था और हमें यह नहीं मालूम था कि आख़िरी तजवीज़ क्या है। चुनाव से उन्होंने अपने नाम वापस ले लिए।

यह भी कहा गया है कि जो रूपया आयेगा इस क़ानून से वह किसानों की पंचायत समितियों को दिया जायगा उनके कार्यक्रम के लिए।

मैंने इस मामले में कोई दखल नहीं दिया है, और मेरी समझ में नहीं आता कि अब मैं कोई ख़ास बयान दूं तो कहां तक मुनासिब होगा। जो बातें तुमने लिखी हैं क़रीब क़रीब वह सब बातें की जा चुकी हैं।

यह सही है कि लगान का मामला पेचीदा होता है और इसका असर किसानों पर काफ़ी पड़ सकता है। इस लिए मुझे फ़िक्र थी और मैंने बार बार गुप्ता जी से और औरों से इसका ज़िक्र किया। अब जो शकल निकली है उससे इस क़ानून का असर बहुत बदल गया है और यह ख़ाली उनपर लागू होगा जो आठ एकड़ या उससे ज़्यादा ज़मीन रखते हैं। बहुत कुछ ख़राबियां पुराने मसवदे की निकाल दी गई हैं। जैसे तुम ने लिखा है इसको बिल्कूल छोड़ देना अब मुनासिब नहीं मालूम होता।

तुम्हारा,
जवाहरलाल नेहरू

170. See items 74 and 76.

[Translation begins:

October 8, 1962

Dear Mahavir,[171]

I received your letter of the 7th today.

I was surprised to learn that it is being said that I had put pressure about levying the new tax. I knew nothing about this except what I had read in the newspapers. Yes, there were some discussions between the Planning Commission and the Ministers in Uttar Pradesh. My attention was drawn to this just a few days before I left for Europe. Neither then nor even till now, have I looked at the Bill in any detail. I had felt that this was a matter which should be carefully thought about. I had written about this to Guptaji[172] also saying that this must be re-examined and that he should consult the Planning Commission in detail. The Planning Commission also said the same thing to us.

I came here and learnt that discussions had taken place and many amendments had been made. The Planning Commission had perhaps told them that exemption should be given for up to five acres. Then I heard that Guptaji put it up to his Party and the majority of the members were very happy to hear about the five acres limit. Some others felt that it should be increased to six and a half acres. Some even said that it should be ten acres. Finally, they decided on not imposing the tax on eight acres. This will apply to everyone, eight acres, and not as you have written four to ten acres will be exempted.

I am not able to understand what you have written about a Party meeting not being called. I heard the final decision was taken with the concurrence of the Party. Then perhaps some members may have written about this. I heard that later on some members had told Guptaji that their names had been included by mistake and that they did not know fully well what the issue was. Hence, they took their names back.

It has also been said that the money collected by this tax will be handed over to the farmers' panchayat samitis for their development projects.

I have not interfered in this matter at all and I cannot understand how far it would be appropriate on my part to make a special statement. Whatever you have written has all been said already.

It is true that the matter of taxation is always complicated and it can have an adverse impact on the farmers. That is why I was worried and I had talked to Guptaji again and again and mentioned it to others too. Now the Bill has come out in a changed form, in which the tax will be levied only on those who own

171. See fn 169 in this section.
172. See fn 170 in this section.

eight acres or more land. Many of the shortcomings have now been removed from the old Bill. It does not seem possible to abandon it altogether now, as you have suggested.

Yours sincerely,
Jawaharlal Nehru

Translation ends]

76. To C.B. Gupta: Hydroelectric Potential of UP[173]

October 9, 1962

My dear Chandra Bhanu,

I have an impression that you have not perhaps explained to some of your Party members and even perhaps some of your colleagues in the Cabinet the present state of your proposals in regard to land revenue. You have no doubt done so at Party meetings and possibly at Cabinet meetings. But I think a personal approach would be helpful. This is always pleasing to the party approached.

I am told that some of your colleagues in the Party have been saying that the responsibility for this legislation is not yours or your Government's but entirely mine and that I have forced it upon you even against your will.[174] You know that is not correct. I have personally little to do with it. It is true that the Planning Commission laid stress on your raising funds for your development.

But there is one point I should particularly like to mention to you, quite apart from this question of additional taxation. The UP is unfortunately situated from the point of view of minerals etc. Thus Bihar, Orissa, and Madhya Pradesh have enormous potential because of their minerals. But the UP is fortunately situated in regard to hydroelectric works. You have the foothills of the Himalayas and other places too where it should be easy to get electric power. This electric power is the most important thing in the development of an area. Once you get it, industries grow. So far as I know, no proper survey has yet been made of hydroelectric possibilities in the UP. You have some schemes going, but that is not enough. You take them [up] if there is money for them.

---

173. Letter to the Chief Minister of Uttar Pradesh. PMO, File No. 31(124)/62-63-PMS, Sr. No. 15-A.
174. These complaints were made by Mahavir Tyagi in his letter of 7 October 1962. Available in the NMML, Mahavir Tyagi Papers. See item 75.

That is not the correct approach. What you should do, I think, is to appoint a small committee of competent engineers headed by somebody in the position of a Chief Engineer to investigate the possibilities of water power being used for producing electric power in the UP. Let them survey the whole province and report without going into details of the various places where this might be done.

The next stage would be to pick out the better ones and to have them examined a little more thoroughly and in details. This should be done regardless of whether you are including them in a plan or not. You should be ready with your schemes when the planning part comes in. Normally, the initial stages of enquiry etc. take some years. You could well utilise the present for that investigation and be ready with schemes when money is available. This will save you much time then.

This was suggested to me by A.N. Khosla, now Governor of Orissa, who is a top-ranking engineer specially connected with hydroelectric schemes. He was convinced that there were great potential power resources in the UP and that they should be investigated as soon as possible. The investigation will not cost you much, although it will cost some relatively small sum. But it will lay the basis of future advance.

Yours sincerely,
Jawaharlal Nehru

77. To C.B. Gupta: Land Holdings Tax Bill[175]

20th October, 1962

My dear Chandra Bhanu,

Thank you for your letter of October 17th. I am glad to find from it that you have repeatedly explained to your Cabinet and to Party members your proposals in regard to land revenue. Nobody exactly complained of this to me, but I did get the impression that probably you had dealt with this matter in party meetings and groups, which of course is desirable, and not on the personal basis with some people. In such matters a personal and friendly approach goes a long way.

There is one other matter which, I think, I mentioned to you. This was the desirability of your making it clear that the money that you will get from this taxation will be handed over to Panchayat Samitis for development purposes.

---

175. Letter to the Chief Minister of Uttar Pradesh. PMO, File No. 31(124)/62-63-PMS, Sr. No. 21-A.

You told me that this was so.[176] I think that if this was adequately publicised, it would go a long way to make people agree to it.

Yours sincerely,
Jawaharlal Nehru

78. To C.B. Gupta: Harassment of Farmers[177]

October 24, 1962

My dear Chandra Bhanu,

Here is a suggestion that has been made to me:

"Today kisans are very much harassed by the Lekhpals[178]and are unnecessarily implicated into litigation, only because they do not get the copy of their land records. The lekhpal charges Rs 5/- to Rs 25/- for this copy known as "Intekhab".[179] Let the Government make it a compulsory feature to give this Intekhab every year to each kisan and charge a fee of Rs 2/- to Rs 3/-. Every kisan would be paying this sum without any hitch and moreover it will save them from so many botherations. From it Government could collect three crores of rupees without any additional expenditure".

I do not know what virtue there is in this suggestion, but it seems to me it deserves consideration.

Lal Bahadur told me that he had telephoned to you to the effect that in view of the dangerous situation on our frontier, and the crisis that has arisen there, it might be worthwhile for States to avoid controversial legislation at this stage. I entirely agree with him.

Yours sincerely,
Jawaharlal Nehru

---

176. See item 75.
177. Letter to the Chief Minister of Uttar Pradesh. PMO, File No. 31(124)/62-63-PMS, Sr. No. 27-A.
178. A village level officer, who keeps land records.
179. The document given by a village level official detailing ownership of land, portion cultivated, and tax paid.

79. To Saiyi'd Raza Ali Khan Bahadur: Amroha Election[180]

October 25, 1962

My dear Nawab Sahib,

Thank you for your letter of October 24th. I am very sorry to learn that you have not been well. I hope you will recover soon.

As for the election in the Amroha constituency caused by the death of Maulana Hifzur Rahman, the matter has not come up before us from the UP Pradesh Congress Committee.[181] There is some talk, however, of elections being postponed because of the national crisis.

Yours sincerely,
[Jawaharlal Nehru]

(o) Law and Administration

80. To C.B. Gupta: A Price for Mohammad Mujeeb's House[182]

10th October, 1962

My dear Chandra Bhanu,

Professor Mohd. Mujeeb, the Vice-Chancellor of the Jamia Millia University, came to see me this morning. He referred to a certain private matter. He and his brother, Professor Habib[183] of Aligarh, own a house—Naseem Mansions, 2 Rana Pratap Marg, Lucknow. I enclose a paper containing some details of this house.

This was apparently requisitioned and occupied by certain offices. The rent paid was Rs 560/- per month. The house is a big one and about two or three months' rent was spent on repairs. Recently, a sum of rupees ten to fifteen thousand was spent on repairs.

It appears that it is proposed to buy it for the Motilal Nehru Education Trust for Rs 1,60,000/-. Professor Mujeeb and his brother have no objection to selling it, but they would beg of you to consider what the proper price should be. Habib has retired and Mujeeb is on the point of retiring. This is the sole

---

180. Letter to the Nawab of Rampur; address: KhasBagh Palace, Rampur.
181. See SWJN/SS/78/Items 189,190, and 195.
182. Letter to the Chief Minister of Uttar Pradesh.
183. Mohammad Habib, historian, Emeritus Professor at Aligarh Muslim University.

property they have and they were looking forward for help from its proceeds of rent or sale in their retirement. It would hit them badly if they did not get an adequate price.

The rent paid originally was Rs 560/-. Apparently it is being reduced to Rs. 450/- a month. As for the price of the house, it is supposed to be much more than the suggested Rs 1,60,000/-. Anyhow this could be valued.

The Posts & Telegraphs organisation have also been having talks to buy it. Probably they will pay much more.

I am not usually interested in such matters, but Mujeeb is a very fine man who has spent his whole life on a bare pittance in serving the Jamia, at first with Dr Zakir Hussain and then otherwise. His whole life is one of devotion and sacrifice. I should not like him to suffer in the days of his retirement. He is a fine scholar. I gather from Mujeeb that his brother Habib agreed to some proposal made by you or the UP Government. Apparently, he did not give much thought to the terms then.

The Vice-President, Dr Zakir Hussain, is naturally greatly interested in his own colleague and he mentioned this matter to me.

I hope you will be able to help in this matter so that the brothers, Habib and Mujeeb, may get proper rent or a proper price for the building.

Yours sincerely,
Jawaharlal Nehru

81. To Mehr Chand Khanna: Hyderabad House[184]

October 11, 1962

My dear Mehr Chand,

Your letter of October 10 about Hyderabad House.

I agree with you that, in the circumstances, we had better give up the idea of purchasing outright this house. The old condition, however, will remain, that there should be no alienation except with the consent of the Government of India.

I think we should continue the present arrangement by which we pay them some annual rent and use it for the guests of the External Affairs Ministry.

Yours sincerely,
[Jawaharlal Nehru]

184. Letter to the Minister of Works, Housing and Supply.

82. To Morarji Desai: Man Singh II's Visit to USA[185]

October 17, 1962

My dear Morarji,

I gather that the Maharaja of Jaipur[186] visited the United States recently when Rajaji was there. It is possible, of course, that his visit had nothing to do with Rajaji's presence there. Anyhow, the question does arise how he manages to get the foreign exchange for these visits abroad and if he takes any permission, as others, from the Reserve Bank.

Yours sincerely,
[Jawaharlal Nehru]

83. To V.K. Krishna Menon: Retiring Generals[187]

22nd October, 1962

My dear Krishna,

I enclose a letter I have received from General Rajendrasinghji.[188] He refers to the impending retirement of Lieutenant General Chaudhuri[189] and Lieutenant General Bahadur Singh.[190]

I think the point he makes deserves consideration. In the crisis we are passing through we should not retire anyone who is considered good. I do not know much about Bahadur Singh, but Chaudhuri is certainly very competent.

Yours affectionately,
[Jawaharlal Nehru]

---

185. Letter to the Finance Minister.
186. Man Singh II.
187. Letter to the Defence Minister.
188. Former Chief of Army Staff.
189. J.N. Chaudhuri (1908-1983) GOC-in-C Southern Command, 1959-1962. He officiated as the Chief of Army Staff when P.N. Thapar went on long leave from 20 November 1962.
190. K. Bahadur Singh (1910-2007) Kumaon Regiment.1961-1971.

84. M. S. Thacker for Planning Commission[191]

It was decided some time ago and I believe announced in public that Prof. M.S. Thacker was being made a member of the Planning Commission. Prof. Thacker has now returned to Delhi. I think, therefore, that the sooner we make formal announcement, the better. Please ask the Deputy Chairman of the Planning Commission, Shri Gulzarilal Nanda, about it and process this matter.

85. In New Delhi: To the Institute of Public Administration[192]

Friends and members of the Institute,

I am very grateful to you that you have gone through the business of this meeting with extreme speed and brevity. That is not only a recognition of the crisis and emergency that we are passing through, but also the adaptation of it to our work. We often recognise things but do not adapt ourselves so well to them. You have been good enough to elect me as your President and I thank you for it though I must confess that this honour is singularly ill-deserved—in the sense that apart from my attending the Annual Meetings, I don't perform any useful function for the Institute. Still if you think my attendance itself is of some use, I shall gladly, and I am glad to agree.

The question that is naturally filling my mind, and the minds of many amongst you, is how we can deal with various aspects, deal with the present crisis and emergency that we are facing. Because it is indeed a vital matter for us as to how we function. We have had many difficulties ever since we gained independence, economic difficulties and others. We have faced them and managed to carry on. The present crisis, however, is of a new kind, a novel kind and we have to adapt ourselves to it and prepare ourselves, whatever the demands may be on us, with extreme rapidity. I was just thinking how this Institute can help in this crisis. This Institute is largely a thinking body, perhaps a teaching body too. Not directly engaged in executive or other activities, still even the thinking part is important and it has always been important. And I should like your Executive Council to consider how you can help in our

191. Note, 25 October 1962, MHA, File No. 15/1/62-Pub.I. See item 95.
192. Speech, 29 October 1962, Presidential Address to the Eighth Annual General Body Meeting, held at Sapru House, New Delhi. Reproduced from P. L. Sanjeev Reddy and R. K. Tiwari, eds, *Jawaharlal Nehru and Public Administration* (New Delhi: Indian Institute of Public Administration, 2004), pp. 50-57; checked against NMML, AIR Tapes, TS No. 8716-17-18, NM No. 1700-01.

meeting this crisis. Obviously, most of you are not going to don a uniform and become soldiers and go to the front. But, as an Institute dealing with public administration, you can help by giving thought to the way public administration can function with speed, of course, and has to relax or change many of our rules which are time-consuming.

It is true that war is a bad thing. It is none of our choosing. But when one is attacked, one's country is attacked, there is no choice left about it. One has to defend, for to submit to it means the death of the soul of a nation. I am sure that India will never do that. We may look forward and we may work for peaceful solutions, but they must be in conformity with our honour and our integrity. Now, what I am suggesting to you and your Executive Council, is to think definitely and deliberately, of how our procedures can be expedited and tightened up. In such situations, where one has to meet very difficult and urgent problems and decide quickly, all kinds of new situations arise and so we have to not only think correctly but think how to lay down our procedures which are both rapid and effective and as good as we can make them. And I am sure that if you think of that, you will be able to offer suggestions which may be very helpful to Government. Naturally, Government itself is thinking of these things and from time to time, day-to-day almost, you will hear of some new action evolved by Government or new methods of procedure etc. Only recently, two or three days ago, the President issued an ordinance, the Defence of India Ordinance, which is a far reaching one, and normally only issued in war time.

We may not be technically at war. We have not declared war, although we have been attacked in a war-like manner and we have defended ourselves and are defending. Nevertheless, we are not at war, but the fact of the matter is that in effect we are. For various reasons, I think good ones, we have not made a declaration to that effect. And it is not necessary at the present moment, that we should do so. And it doesn't come in our way. So we don't propose to do so for the present, I don't know about the future.

And war brings all kinds of burdens and problems. It brings an enormous increase of expenditure in war-like activities, and war-like activities cover many branches of Government. It means a tremendous increase in production, not only in weapons of war, not only in our procuring those weapons of war in addition to our production of them as much as we can, but also many civil departments which are connected with the war. You can say food is an essential thing, of course, and it must be produced. That is our normal desire too—to increase the production of food and food articles. It becomes much stronger and more urgent in a crisis of this kind. Clothing, boots and I do not know how many things we require for war, it is a long list, because, it is no longer military operations at the front alone which matter. Each person at the front has to be supported by—I do not know by how many—dozens of people, hundreds of people behind the lines, and it is of the utmost importance that the apparatus of production should function rapidly and smoothly.

We have production in our public sectors and in the private sector --both have to be coordinated and directed to this one urgent and vital aim-- to produce generally, but especially to produce for anything required for these operations.

Then, the other very important aspect comes: of prices. That we should do our utmost to keep the prices low, not allow them to increase. That is no easy matter, when we may have to indulge in deficit financing, one can't help. Therefore, inevitably, some methods of control and distribution become necessary. Sometimes people argue, as to the desirability of control, some are for and some are against it. But we have passed that stage of argument in the emergency that we face. We have to have it - what kind of control I cannot say now. We have to face this problem of control of important commodities. Then, because we do think rapidly and in a big way, usually, war means great wastage, war means that because of this wastage many people slip into the wrong paths, taking advantage of the crisis of the nation and leaving the path of integrity. It is particularly necessary that, we must see to it that this has not happened in a small way or a big way. All these are matters, which might well be considered by your Executive and suggestions as to what should be done, made to the Government and as well as to the public. And I am sure that will help us all.

You know of the certain proposals made by Governments, certain steps taken, to some of you we are just giving some prizes and out of the prizes a part of them have been given to the national defence fund. Then there is talk about gold being given, which is very important and also there is some talk about some bonds being issued for gold and so on and so forth.

I should like to say in this connection, that in this moment of this great burden being carried by us, nothing has heartened me more and delighted me than the magnificent response of the nation and the people of the world. And I know that for you and for me to feel heartened by it, is natural. But I know that the representatives of foreign countries and people in foreign countries, not Indians, but others, have been agreeably surprised at the response in India. Now, that is the basic thing which we must have - the response of the people generally. It is not a question of few rich men, or moderately rich men giving part of their riches, but the poorest are taking part in it. Every morning in the course of the day, I have a stream of people coming to me. Little children of seven or eight, giving me their little money. They may have a few rupees which they may have collected in the course of a few weeks or months - workers and others come too. It is really a very moving sight, not only I, but the President every day sends me what he has collected and what has been given to him in the course of the day - not only money but gold and jewellery etc.[193] And that is happening all over India, I think that shows, if anybody had any doubts about it, that basically our country and our people are not only sound but full of that vital energy that a living nation should possess in facing a crisis. People seem to forget this and get wrapped up in their petty conflicts – whatever kind they may be-- whether they are based on religion or caste or language or provincialism; whatever they may be. Suddenly, we have risen above them, we are rising above them, and that is the test for all the people, whether they can rise when the demand is made of them.

We have risen and because of that, we can speak confidently of the future. I cannot say how long this crisis will last, what I have said and what I have felt was, it is not a short one and no one need to expect it to end quickly. So we have to be prepared for a long period, it will be a heavy time we shall all have and we shall have to work hard and with grim determination. But I am confident and certain in my mind, that however long this may last, we shall win in the end and triumph. Even if I had that confidence before, it has been strengthened a hundred fold and a thousand fold by what we have seen in the whole of the country and the magnificent and splendid response that has come from all people. Now the question is, as has often been said, how we can utilize this response and not allow it to fritter away. Also such a response coming suddenly is one thing and to keep spirit and the morale of the nation intact for a lengthy period, is a more difficult task. But I am convinced that will be done and that will happen.

It is often said, criticisms are made of the Government that why did we not prepare ourselves for the ordeals that we have faced. Why did we have to submit to some serious reverses on our frontiers. It is a legitimate question and I don't know that there is any adequate answer for it. But I will submit to you, that we have a fine army, good army, there is none braver. But the fact of the matter is that we have been conditioned for long past to think, not to think of war. We may theoretically think of it. We may think of some slight operation here and there, but not of a major war. And all our thoughts have been directed towards building up the economy of the country's development, Five Year Plans etc. We spent some money on our defence services, but in terms of war, that was very little. And always we had this in view, that any major diversion to possible war effort would have bad consequences for our plan. In fact if you think of war, we don't think merely of adding something to your defence forces. We will have to add everything that you have to it - in those terms. And

193. See items 362 and 443.

we talked of peace everywhere and we felt that way and we felt the importance of it too. But for us to decide, to devote all our strength and resources to a war effort, did not appeal to us. Because even from a point of view of war that is not carried on by weapons etc. which you buy or get from abroad, but it can only be carried on by the industrial strength of the nation -- the productive capacity in the industrial strength. So even from that point of view, our Five Year Plans were vital, apart from any other consequences that we aimed at. Therefore, we concentrated on that and hoped possibly, it was wishful thinking, that no war of this type would face us. We certainly have done a good deal in increasing our defence production, production of weapons etc. because you will remember that till we became independent, all our defence forces were practically controlled and guided by the White Hall, not only the officers and others, all our policy was laid down in White Hall and the officers merely carried out directions.

What is more important was that the British Government did not encourage the production of defence material here. Certain circumstances forced them to do something during the wars because they could not get them from England. Even then there was always a reluctance to produce them here, and we had to rely on Britain for those arms and material equipment. That is how we were when we became independent. Ever since then, we have tried to build up this industry of defence production, production of arms and defence equipment and what is very important is that we have built up a fairly strong defence science department. Because it is not merely a question of producing a rifle or something like that, weapons are much more sophisticated and unless we can produce or our scientists can keep abreast with modern developments, we cannot produce them ourselves and we have to buy them. And weapons are so terribly expensive, that it becomes exceedingly difficult for any country even the richest countries to keep pace with modern development. We do not go in for the highly sophisticated things like well, like atomic weapons, nor do we want to go into them. But even apart from atomic weapons, there are highly sophisticated things, which are little beyond our ken, far too expensive, and it will absorb all our resources. However, we built up the Science Department which is doing well. But, of course, we can't compare it to the highly militarised and scientifically developed nations which spend billions of pounds on this thing every year. So, we have made progress in our defence industries and the progress is a continuous one. And nevertheless, it is not enough to face a big crisis like this and that is why what we have to do today is not only to increase tremendously our production of defence requirements, but inevitably to obtain them from other countries, other friendly countries, which are prepared to give them to us, or to help us in this way, on such terms as we can afford - what I mean is, at longer terms of payments etc. And we shall do it of course, because the first need is defence, which has to be met, however much we may have to, however heavy the burden may be.

It is a fact, I can very well understand, the people feeling rather annoyed and asking, why this has happened, why we are not fully prepared? That is a justifiable thing, although it does not take all considerations into account. Such preparation would have meant not only a full preparation for war, but war against an apparatus of a government, which is in this respect - one of the strongest in the world.

China has not got all the sophisticated weapons, which the Soviet Union or the United States of America has. But it has an army which is bigger than any army in the world. And it has a system of Government, which is concentrated in the last 12 years of its existence on preparing for war and strengthening its country. We have a different system of Government. We do not like the idea of always living in a war atmosphere and preparing for it and it is very difficult to keep up this war apparatus, except at the cost of everything else. It is one thing when one is faced with the crisis, then the people realize it and everybody works for it. But apart from that, it is difficult and I would say almost undesirable to work only for war preparation for that means giving up the idea of economic progress in most other directions, Well, it is easy to be wise after the event, but I do not really know, how we could have done otherwise, in minor matters, yet but in major matters, because when you think of the major matters more, you have to think not only of crores or hundreds of crores, but of thousands of crores and that is a position we have to meet.

But it is true, that we in our thinking process have not been conditioned to war. Previously it was the British Government and the White Hall to give thought to it. We did not have any personal experience of war except perhaps a little bit in the North East Frontier. And it is not like countries of Europe which have had and partly some Asian countries too, where there is hardly a family, which hasn't lost some of loved one in the course of war and sometimes lost all - what has strengthened them, conditioned them. We talk of peace in India and we talked about it, we feel it not merely talking yet there is a little something superficial about our talking, because we do not know what war is. We like it in theory, in peace of course, and India is a peaceful country and we are more peaceful perhaps conditioned more peacefully than most others, but we have known war, the horrors of war and especially the horrors of a coming war, nuclear war. We easily sign protest against war and for peace and all against nuclear war-fare. Because it doesn't mean much to us and no harm in signing. And now we are suddenly thrown into this cauldron, I don't mean to say that we are going to have a nuclear war here. I think not anyhow. The country which has invaded us does not possess nuclear weapons and even if it did, have an

71

explosion and make little difference to frighten some people should make little difference. Because it takes many long years to develop a thing like that even after some experiment or test has been made. But whatever that may be in so called conventional arms we have to face the horrors of war? It is confined to our frontier and many people have suffered from it, many have died, many of our army people. I find that very exaggerated rumours are spread about the number of casualties. Now my difficulty is that we do not exactly know, we can put limits to it, but we do not exactly know, the reports have not come.

Well, I haven't talked to you very much about this Institute of Public Administration, except to suggest which I do again and that I like to think about these problems, they are affecting our country and make suggestions with both governmental and private affecting our economy, our procedures of Government or whatever else. You would hardly tell us about how to conduct a war. I do not ask you to do that. But you can need to tell us, how to deal with our economy and our procedures of Government especially in such a crisis.

Now to mention one or two other matters. There is our Five Year Plan which we consider very important. It would be a pity, if we had to put an end to that plan because putting an end to it means weakening ourselves for the future. So even from the limited point of view, limited but important point of view of the present crisis, we cannot put an end to it of course. It will have to be adapted may be some matters, which are not of the first importance may have to be given up. But by and large, in regard to all the important matters of the Five Year Plan, we should go ahead. After all, the expenditures involved on the burden, which will fall on us in defence and like matters is far greater than the whole Five Year Plan put together. So we should not as I said we may have to adapt it to change it here and there but basically I hope it will continue. Basically, I hope to take another aspect of it.

These are [that] the Panchayati Raj business must continue, these are strengthening things and not weakening things although we have to spend some money. And here may I make a suggestion or rather approval of suggestions already made in one of our pamphlets or books. This awful name that you have given to it, what is it decentralization, democratic decentralization? Horrible. One feels almost against a thing itself by the name you should never give a name which sticks in the throat or in the mouth. But I find much better than [this one] in one of your papers, decentralized democracy. It is just reversing the words, but it is much better, instead of what was the other thing? Democratic decentralization. It is far better, decentralized democracy. It sounds better and you lay stress on democracy, that is a basic thing to decentralize it, not in the decentralized at the end democracy is a kind of little off-shoot of it. So I hope you will encourage the use of that word which I think Dr Menon himself is responsible for it. Because, I do hope that in our other troubles the burden that we carry we will not forget the basic things, that about our Five year Plan and more especially things that go to make our nation strong.

There is always a danger in such crisis - for democracy itself being a victim and we should take care of that, because we attach value to that not only normally but even in crisis but democracy must be made to function in an effective and in a speedy way - not in the slow-moving methods, to which we are normally accustomed.

And I am very grateful to you for the speedy and efficient way, you have conducted the proceedings. I have taken more time than all of you put together and you will notice that. But I thought I might put before you what I had in my mind and ask your consideration of it.

Thank you. [Applause].

86. To Morarji Desai: Customs Insult to Nargis[194]

October 30, 1962

My dear Morarji,
I enclose a letter from Nargis (Mrs Sunil Dutt). This gives an account of the ill-treatment and insulting behaviour she had to put up with at the Bombay Customs. I wish our Customs people did not behave in this way and get a bad reputation for themselves and for our country.

Yours sincerely,
[Jawaharlal Nehru]

87. To Nargis: Apology for Customs Bad Behaviour[195]

October 30, 1962

Dear Nargis,
I have received your letter of October 26th. I have read it with some distress. I am exceedingly sorry that our Customs people should have treated you as they did. Customs people tend to behave badly. We have had so many cases of gold smuggling that it affects not only their temper, but their behaviour. Of course,

---

194. Letter to the Finance Minister.
195. Letter to the actor; address: Mrs Sunil Dutt, 58 Pali Hill, Bandra, Bombay-50. See item 86.

that is no reason why they should treat you and your little son in the way they did. I am exceedingly sorry, and I apologise to you.

I am drawing attention to this incident of the people in charge of Customs.

Yours sincerely,
[Jawaharlal Nehru]

88. To T.T. Krishnamachari: Phone Tapping[196]

November 1, 1962

My dear T.T.,

I was greatly distressed this morning to learn that somebody had been tapping your telephone. I asked Lal Bahadur[197] to inquire about it. I also had enquiry made from the DIB.[198] He was amazed and said it was unbelievable that anyone should have dared to do it. I have asked the DIB to inquire into this matter. I imagine it was someone in the telephone exchange who misbehaved in this way. We must find out.

Yours affectionately,
Jawaharlal Nehru

89. To Mahavir Tyagi: Phone Tapping[199]

November 2, 1962

My dear Mahavir,

Your letter of the 2nd November. I am indeed surprised to learn that your telephone was being tapped. I am surprised for a variety of reasons. The chief one is that our instructions are, and have been for a long time, that no such tapping should be done except in the case of two or three foreign embassies or some foreigners who were suspected. Apart from tapping, our instructions are that no report of the activities of the Congress Party or of Congress Members should be made. I receive numerous reports from Intelligence, but I do not remember having received a single report about the Congress Party or Congress Members.

---

196. Letter to Minister without Portfolio. NMML, T.T. Krishnamachari Papers, File 1962, Holo. See reply, appendix 38.
197. Lal Bahadur Shastri, Home Minister.
198. B.N. Mullik.
199. Letter to Congress MP. NMML, Mahavir Tyagi Papers.

I have no doubt whatever that our Intelligence Department has nothing to do with this matter. I have verified this from a talk I have had with the DIB who is I think—and I have known him for many years rather well and intimately—an able, conscientious and straightforward man. Pantji had a high regard for him. I got to know him through Pantji. I believe Lal Bahadur has the same opinion of him.[200]

You suggest that somebody in the Defence Ministry might be responsible for the tapping. I cannot say without enquiry that this was done. But it is not an easy matter for an outsider to do it. There are only two ways, as far as I know, of doing it. One is to put in a special line attached to a particular number and take it to another place where a recorder is used. This is a complicated process requiring the full assistance and work of the Engineering Department of P & T. The other is for a person to sit in the Exchange all the time in the hope that some number will turn up and then, with the assistance of the operator, to listen in. Nothing can be done without the cooperation of the operator. Also, in regard to an automatic exchange, this becomes exceedingly difficult, though not impossible.

It sometimes happens that wires get crossed. I have often, when beginning to telephone, suddenly found myself listening to some conversation that was taking place between two other persons. I was not interested in it.

Thus, it is no easy matter even to organise such telephone tapping without the assistance of the Telephone Exchange people.

However, I am enquiring into this matter.

Yours affectionately,
Jawaharlal Nehru

90. To K.L. Shrimali: A.C.N. Nambiar for UNESCO[201]

November 2, 1962

My dear Shrimali,

Rajkumari Amrit Kaur has sent me a copy of her letter to you dated 2nd November. In this she suggests that A.C.N. Nambiar[202] might be asked to join the UNESCO Delegation. I think it is a good idea, and he will make a good

---

200. B.N. Mullik.
201. Letter to the Minister of Education.
202. Former Ambassador to Germany.

representative. Our delegation is a small one now, and the addition of Nambiar should not be difficult.

Yours sincerely,
[Jawaharlal Nehru]

91. To T.T. Krishnamachari: Phone tapping[203]

November 2, 1962

My dear T.T.,

Your letter of today's date.[204] I am glad you met the DIB. I have known him for many years, ever since Pantji put him in touch with me. Pantji spoke in very high terms of his probity and competence. It was for this reason that he gave him a second term. My own experience of him has been, since then, very considerable, and I have found him to be able, conscientious and thoroughly straightforward.

About telephone tapping, it is perfectly clear, as you have said yourself that it had nothing to do with him or his Department. You suggest that it might have been done by military authorities. I am having that enquired into.

But, as far as I can find out, there are only two ways of tapping telephones properly. One is to sit in the Exchange and wait for a particular number to be called and then, with the help of the Exchange Operator, to listen in, or to have a special line laid to another place from a particular number and to have it connected with a recorder. No such line can be laid without the Engineering Department of the P & T coming into the picture. As for somebody sitting there all the time waiting for the possibility of a number being called, it is not a very feasible proposition, though it is a possible one. In any event, the full cooperation of the telephone operator is necessary. In regard to an automatic telephone, it is especially difficult to tap a particular number, although some complicated arrangements can be made for that purpose also.

Our general instructions to the Intelligence people have long been not to tap any person's telephone calls unless these be of two or three foreign embassies or usually some foreigner who is suspected.

However, I am further enquiring into this matter.

203. Letter to Minister without Portfolio.
204. See appendix 38.

It is wholly incorrect to say that there has been no real change in the Defence Ministry.[205] I am in full and direct charge of it and I have been spending a good deal of time there and trying to get a grip of its various departments as well as the situation in NEFA and Ladakh.

Yours affectionately,
[Jawaharlal Nehru]

92. To Mahavir Tyagi: Phone Tapping Again[206]

November 6, 1962

My dear Mahavir,

You wrote to me about your telephone being tapped, and I replied that I would have an immediate enquiry made into this matter.[207] I also pointed out that there were only two feasible methods of tapping. One was to have a wire laid on from the central exchange to some other house, and the other was for a person to sit all the time in the exchange office so that he might be there when a call to or from a particular number took place. This obviously could only be done with the approval of the operator.

As a result of the enquiry I have had, it seems clear that neither of these methods was adopted or practised by anyone.

There is always a possibility of somebody overhearing a conversation by wires being crossed. This is accidental. I do not know how else tapping can take place. If you can supply any further information, I could have the matter enquired into again.

As I pointed out, it is exceedingly difficult to tap an automatic telephone conversation. Also, the Defence have their separate lines.[208]

Yours affectionately,
Jawaharlal Nehru

---

205. He took over the Defence portfolio from 31 October 1962. See item 336.
206. Letter to Congress MP; address: 16 Dr Rajendra Prasad Road, New Delhi. NMML, Mahavir Tyagi Papers.
207. See item 89.
208. See also appendix 336; and items 88 and 91.

II. DEVELOPMENT

(a) Economy

93. To M.J. Jamal Moideen: Meeting Manubhai Shah[1]

October 4, 1962

My dear Shri Jamal Moideen.

I have your letter of the 1st October together with its enclosed papers.

It is often difficult for Ministers to find time for all the interviews they should give. Shri Manubhai Shah[2] is a heavily occupied person and sometimes it may be that he is unable to find time for an interview.

So far as the proposals for the European Common Market are concerned, these were dealt with fully at the Conference[3] and are being handled very competently by our Ambassador who is in charge of these matters, Shri K.B. Lall.

I am referring the papers you have sent to me to Shri Manubhai Shah.

Yours sincerely,
[Jawaharlal Nehru]

94. Visit to Rihand Dam[4]

I intend going to the Rihand Dam in Mirzapur District on November 6th to 7th. I suppose I had better go to Allahabad by the Viscount, and go if possible, by Helicopter or some small plane. There is, I am told, an airstrip near the Rihand Dam[5] which can accommodate even a Dakota.

Please find out from Air Headquarters what would be feasible.

[J. Nehru]

---

1. Letter to Rajya Sabha MP, Congress, from Madras; address: "Jamalia", 10 Perambur High Road, Madras-12.
2. Minister of State for Industry.
3. The Commonwealth Prime Ministers' Conference 10-19 September 1962. See SWJN/ SS/78/items 362 and 363.
4. Note, 7 October 1962; PMS (Public Section) File No. F.8 (231)62—PMP.
5. See also item103.

95. To G.L. Nanda: Planning Commission Appointments[6]

October 8, 1962

My dear Gulzarilal,

I think we should make an announcement about Thacker[7] joining the Planning Commission. He will be returning here in another week or so.

Before I went abroad, you told me something about Khera,[8] the Cabinet Secretary. So far as I can recollect, you said that he might also be made an ex-officio Member of the Planning Commission. I think that would be advisable. If you agree, we can go ahead with these matters.[9]

Yours sincerely,
Jawaharlal Nehru

96. To G.L. Nanda: Prices and Other Matters[10]

October 8, 1962

My dear Gulzarilal,

I have received your two letters, dated October 5th and 6th. Thank you for them. I am glad you are having various matters referred to [be] examined carefully and that soon you will be able to put your reports, or summaries of them, before the Cabinet. I feel that we must take some steps about the issue of prices of essential commodities.

Yours sincerely,
[Jawaharlal Nehru]

---

6. Letter to the Deputy Chairman of the Planning Commission. MO, File No. 17(189)/60-65-PMS, Sr. No. 43-A.
7. M. S. Thacker (1904-1979); Former Director General of Council of Scientific and Industrial Research and Secretary, Department of Science and Technology in the Ministry of Scientific Research and Cultural Affairs. He served as a member of the Planning Commission from 1962 to 1967.
8. S.S. Khera was given the additional responsibility of Secretary, Planning Commission.
9. See item 84.
10. Letter to the Deputy Chairman of the Planning Commission.

97. To T.T. Krishnamachari: Import Licences[11]

October 20, 1962

My dear T.T.,

Your letter of October 19.[12] I quite agree with what you say about extreme care being taken in regard to import licences. In view of the very serious situation that has developed on our frontiers, we have to revise our thinking completely.

Yours affectionately,
[Jawaharlal Nehru]

98. To K.C. Reddy: Imports[13]

October 20, 1962

My dear Reddy,

I enclose a letter and a cutting which T.T. Krishnamachari has sent me.[14] I agree with what he says in his letter. We have anyhow to be very careful about our imports but now that we have to face a serious and difficult situation on our frontiers, we have to be particularly careful and, in fact, we have to revise our thinking.[15]

Yours sincerely,
[Jawaharlal Nehru]

11. Letter to the Minister without Portfolio. NMML, T.T. Krishnamachari Papers, File 1962, Auto.
12. See appendix 18.
13. Letter to the Minister for Commerce and Industry.
14. See appendix 18.
15. See item 97.

99. To V.T. Krishnamachari: Acknowledging Gift of Book[16]

October 31, 1962

My dear V.T.,

Thank you for your letter of the 30th October and for the copy of your book *Fundamentals of Planning in India*.[17] I shall certainly endeavour to read this book. For the present, I confess I have no time to do so.

Yours sincerely,
Jawaharlal Nehru

100. To Morarji Desai: Gold[18]

November 20, 1962

My dear Morarji,

Your letter of November 20th about the steps you wish to take in regard to gold.[19] I entirely agree with the proposal you have made.

Yours sincerely,
Jawaharlal Nehru

---

16. Letter to former member of the Planning Commission. PMO, File No. 38(78)/61-71-PMS, Sr. No. 6-A.
17. V.T. Krishnamachari, *Fundamentals of Planning in India* (Bombay: Orient Longmans, 1962).
18. Letter to the Finance Minister. PMO, File No. 37/114/63-66-PM, Vol. I, Sr. No.1-C.
19. See appendix 61.

(b) Industry

101. To T.T. Krishnamachari: Naval Tata on Textile Policy[20]

October 9, 1962

My dear TT,

I enclose a letter from Naval Tata[21] with its enclosures.[22] I should like your advice in this matter before I reply to him.[23]

Yours sincerely,
Jawaharlal Nehru

102. To Keshava Deva Malaviya: Mulraj Kersondas on Gold Mining[24]

October 16, 1962

My dear Keshava Deva,

Mulraj Kersondas[25] of Bombay has written to me about various matters.[26] Among other things, he has referred to gold smuggling. About this, he goes on to say:

"I feel that the correct remedy for stopping this evil is to bring down the prices of gold. This will be done if exploration is made in this country for finding out gold mines in the country. I know of one such place, i.e., the Nilambur village, 30 miles from Ootacamund. This was the place where an Australian gold Mining Company had first discovered gold in India in the year 1875, but they had closed up because their working was uneconomical. The price of gold at that time was only about Rs 50/- per ounce which is equal to 1- 1/7 to 1- 1/8 of the present price and there are large quantities of gold ore at this place. I feel if your Ministry takes up mines in such places and sells the

---

20. Letter to Minister without Portfolio, PMO, File No. 17(438)/60-64-PMS, Vol. I, Sr. No. 11-A.
21. Naval H. Tata; Chairman, Ahmedabad Advance Mills, Tata Group; Chairman, Tata Electric Company; Deputy Chairman, Tata Sons Ltd
22. See appendix 6.
23. See reply, appendix 10.
24. Letter to the Minister of Mines and Fuel.
25. Gujarati entrepreneur and a long time acquaintance.
26. See appendix 14.

gold into the open market regularly, it will satisfy and bring the gold prices down and if the gold prices are brought down to about Rs 80 to 90 per tola, the temptation in smuggling will greatly be reduced, and this will save us a lot of foreign exchange which is disappearing in this racket."

Yours affectionately,
[Jawaharlal Nehru]

103. To Gulzarilal Nanda: G.D. Birla's Need for a Power Plant[27]

October 19, 1962

My dear Gulzarilal,

I shall be going to the Rihand Dam in the UP next month.[28] I shall also visit the aluminium plant[29] which has been put up there by the Birlas in collaboration with some American concerns.

Yesterday, G.D. Birla came to see me and spoke to me about the proposal to have what is called a captive power plant[30] for his aluminium factory. He said that everybody seemed to have agreed to this but somewhere this has got held up, and he cannot take any steps till he is given a final clearance.[31]

How do matters stand about this proposed power plant?

G.D. Birla also told me of the numerous administrative delays in coming to decisions by our Government. He said that this produced a bad effect in the USA. He has recently come from there.

Yours sincerely,
[Jawaharlal Nehru]

27. Letter to the Minister for Planning and Labour and Employment.
28. See item 94.
29. Hindustan Aluminium Corporation Ltd, Renukoot, became operational in 1962.
30. Renusagar captive thermal power plant near Renukoot, Sonbhadra District, UP.
31. See also item 104.

104. To Hafiz Mohammad Ibrahim: G. D. Birla's Aluminium Factory[32]

October 22, 1962

My dear Hafizji,

I shall be going to the Rihand Dam on the 6th and 7th November. I shall also visit the Aluminium Factory that has been put up there. G.D. Birla was asking me about the captive electric plant which it is proposed to put up there.

I wrote to Nandaji about it.[33] He has written to me that it has been decided that each such proposal should be considered individually. Therefore, it is for your ministry to put up a paper before the Cabinet about the proposal for a thermal plant in the Aluminium Factory.

Will you please expedite this so that before I go to Rihand, I can convey our decision.

Yours sincerely,
Jawaharlal Nehru

(c) Agriculture

105. To Ravi Garg: Good Wishes[34]

October 10, 1962

Dear Ravi Garg,

I have received the letter of the 29th September which you, S.K. Chaturvedi and Bharat Shah have sent me. I have read it with interest and appreciation.

The aims and objectives that you have set out are good and comprehensive. Perhaps they are too comprehensive for effective work. But you can keep all these objectives before you and concentrate on such as are feasible.

I wish you success.

Yours sincerely,
[Jawaharlal Nehru]

---

32. Letter to the Minister for Irrigation and Power. PMS (Public Section) File No. F.8 (231) 62, PMP.
33. See item 103.
34. Letter to Students; address: 65 New Hostel, Allahabad Agricultural Institute, Allahabad.

106. To Mulraj Kersondas: Food Production[35]

October 16, 1962

My dear Mulraj,

I have received your letter of October 12th today, on my return from Ceylon.[36] I am immediately referring it to the Planning Commission.

The part dealing with gold, I am sending to our Minister for Mines.[37]

I hope you are keeping well.

Yours sincerely,
Jawaharlal Nehru

107. To S. Husain Zaheer: K.N. Kaul[38]

November 8, 1962

My dear Munne,

I enclose a letter from Kailas Nath Kaul, Director of the National Botanical Gardens in Lucknow. He is here at present and gave me this letter.

I do not quite know in what way he can help as he has suggested. I should like you to discuss this matter with him and find out what he has in mind. Everything of course has to be judged now from the point of view of the emergency. I think he might be useful.

Yours sincerely,
[Jawaharlal Nehru]

---

35. Letter to an old acquaintance and entrepreneur; address: Kamani Chambers, 32 Nicol Road, Ballard Estate, Bombay-1. JNMF, D-23/M Series.
36. See appendix 14.
37. K.D. Malaviya. See item 102.
38. Letter to the Director-General of the CSIR.

108. To Panjabrao S. Deshmukh: Success of Bharat Krishak Samaj[39]

November 29, 1962

My dear Panjabrao,

Thank you for your letter of the 29th November. I am glad to learn of the success that the Bharat Krishak Samaj or the Farmers' Forum of India has achieved. I send you all my good wishes for it. ·

You ask me to become Chief Patron of it. I hesitate normally to become patron of [any] organisation. At the present moment with the crisis before us, I am even more reluctant. But you have all my good wishes.

Yours sincerely,
[Jawaharlal Nehru]

(d) Health

109. To Sushila Nayar: Chandiwala's Bequest to Cheshire Homes[40]

October 2, 1962

My dear Sushila,

I understand that you had a talk with my PPS[41] about the estate that Lala Banarsidas Chandiwala[42] gave to the Cheshire Home and which is now sought to be taken back from them for a private convalescent home. I think it would be unfortunate if this is done. The Cheshire Homes are doing extraordinarily good work and have an international status. To deprive them of what they have once been given would be odd and would be doing injury to a good cause. I do not understand why a private convalescent home should be preferred to some such home run by an organisation which is excellent and which is doing very good work.

---

39. Letter to Lok Sabha MP, Congress (1898-1965), farmer leader from Vidarbha; address: 3 Rafi Marg, New Delhi. PMO, File No. 31(126)/62-64-PMS, Sr. No.2-A.
40. Letter to the Minister of Health.
41. Kesho Ram.
42. Banarsidas Chandiwala (1860-1911), trader and philanthropist. The Estate was donated by Brij Krishan Chandiwala. NMML, B.K.Chandiwala Individual Collection.

So far as the name is concerned, Shri Banarsidas Chandiwala's name can be attached to it. The home is, in fact, used for poor people chiefly.[43]

Yours affectionately,
[Jawaharlal Nehru]

110. To J.A.K. Martyn: Kalkaji Estate and Cheshire Homes[44]

3rd October, 1962

Dear Mr Martyn,

I have received your letter of the 28th September, 1962, on my return from abroad.

Ever since January of last year I have been receiving letters and complaints from the original owners of the Kalkaji Estate. They complained that they had given it to Government of India for a particular purpose in accordance with the wishes of their late father. This had not been carried out by the Government and the Government's action in giving this estate to the Cheshire Homes was taken without the donors' consent and was not therefore valid. I referred the matter to my Principal Private Secretary and he has carried on extensive correspondence on the subject with the original donors and others. I lost sight of the matter.

Just before going to Europe early in September, I was again reminded of this and now on my return I have looked into all the previous papers and correspondence.

I need not tell you how much I admire the work of the Cheshire Homes. I have expressed my views about them previously and I hold to that opinion. I should like to help these Homes to the best of my ability. I am sure the work they do is of great value and should be assisted.

But I am in a difficulty when the donors of the Kalkaji Estate continually raise objections and demand that this estate should be put to the use they had laid down for it. I am not very much interested in the legal aspect of this matter, but there is a certain moral aspect which troubles me. This estate was originally given to the then Health Minister of the Delhi State Government, Dr Sushila Nayar, who is now the Health Minister of the Central Government. She tells me that it was on certain conditions specifically stated that it had been given to her. Therefore, there seems to be some substance in the objections raised by the donors.[45]

43. See item 110.
44. Letter to the Headmaster of Doon School, 1948-1966; address: Chand Bagh, Dehradun.
45. See item 109.

Apart from this, it seems to me undesirable for the Cheshire Homes to become the subject of an undesirable controversy which cannot do them good. I have tried to reason with the original donors, but without success. They have been particularly upset apparently by some communication addressed to them by someone on behalf of the Cheshire Home in Dehra Dun which they interpreted as a threat to them. This has made matters worse.

The question is what we should do now. We do not wish the Cheshire Homes to suffer or to be prevented from carrying on the good work they are doing in Delhi. At the same time I think it is no good carrying on a controversy which creates a bad atmosphere for any work. And, as I have said, there is some substance in the claim of the original donors. Of course, the Cheshire Homes are not responsible for this and the responsibility is that of the Government of India.

I would suggest, for the consideration of the trustees of the Cheshire Homes that they should agree to leave this particular estate after a convenient period. Meanwhile, they should be allotted suitable land elsewhere and Government may give them some grant also for building. Otherwise too the Government would help. Possibly, this would result in a more suitable building. I gather that you intended putting up another wing of the existing building.

If this course is followed, there should be no upsetting of the work that is being done by the Cheshire Homes or inconvenience caused to the inmates of it, and a new and more suitable home would be available.

The suggestion I have made above has been made to me by the present Health Minister of the Government of India, and it seems to me a good one. I hope you and your co-trustees will consider it. It is far better to settle this matter in a friendly way, without any harm done to the Cheshire Homes, than to carry on a controversy and create ill-will.

Yours sincerely,
Jawaharlal Nehru

111. To R.V. Wardekar: Leprosy Foundation[46]

October 8, 1962

Dear Dr Wardekar,
Shri R.R. Diwakar[47] wrote to me before he left India, inviting me to lay the corner stone of the Leprosy Foundation building sometime in November. I received his letter on my return to India.

46. Letter to R.V. Wardekar, Director of the Gandhi Memorial Leprosy Foundation, Wardha.
47. Chairman, Gandhi Peace Foundation, and Rajya Sabha MP, nominated.

I should have much liked to come for this purpose, but I am sorry that I cannot find even one free day in November. Every day is taken up by some important engagement or other. A number of eminent visitors from abroad are coming to Delhi and I have to be present then. Apart from this, there are the meetings of the Congress Working Committee and the AICC and Parliament session starts in the middle of November. This session is of great importance and I cannot afford to be away.

Please accept my apologies therefor. I hope you will kindly inform Shri R.R. Diwakar.

Yours sincerely,
[Jawaharlal Nehru]

112. To Bishanchander Seth: Equipment for Eye Care Centre[48]

अक्टूबर 10, 1962

प्रिय बिशन चन्द्रजी,

आपका 6 अक्टूबर का पत्र मिला। आपने जो नेत्र चिकित्सा का लिखा है वह एक आवश्यक बात है और उसकी सहायता करना ठीक है। लेकिन प्राईम मिनिस्टर का रिलीफ फण्ड विशेषकर उन लोगों की सहायता के लिए है जो कि बाढ़ या भूकम्प या आग से या किसी ऐसी ही मुसीबत से पीड़ित हों। इस लिए मेरे लिए कठिन है उनमें से कुछ हस्पताल के सामान के लिए देना।

आजकल आप जानते हैं कि भारत में बहुत बाढ़ से हानि हुई है और मेरे पास इसकी निस्बत बहुत मांगें आ रही हैं।

आपका,
जवाहरलाल नेहरु

[Translation begins:

My dear Bishanchanderji,

I got your letter of 6 October. What you have mentioned about helping the eye care centre is right and it should be done. But the Prime Minister's Relief Fund is especially meant for those who have suffered from earth quake or floods or some such similar calamity. Hence, it is difficult for me to give something from that fund for the hospital equipment.

48. Letter to Lok Sabha MP, Congress, from Shahjahanpur; address: Ornaments place, Shahjahanpur. PMH-62, No.1622.

You know these days India has suffered severe losses due to floods and I am getting a lot of requests for relief from various quarters.

Yours,
[Jawaharlal Nehru]

Translation ends]

113. For Amrit Kaur: Synthetic Rice[49]

Your note about synthetic rice. I am rather surprised to read the report. This matter has been before us for over a year and this is the first time I have received any criticism. We have been anxious to expedite it all this time. The Nutrition Advisory Committee apparently meets in a leisurely way. Of course, we should enquire into this matter fully before we take any steps. But for this purpose, urgent action must be taken.

114. In Ceylon: At the Ayurveda Research Institute[50]

Prime Minister,[51] Mr Health Minister,[52] Friends,
When you were good enough to invite me to attend this ceremony, I was put in a difficulty. Any ceremony in commemoration of the late Mr Bandaranaike[53] was something that appealed to me and I wanted to take advantage of it to pay my tribute to him, whom I respected and admired so much and who was an old friend of mine. Also, any request from you, Madam,[54] was difficult to refuse because even from the distance of Delhi I could see how you were carrying a great burden worthily and admirably and I wanted to show my appreciation of it by coming here personally. All that was on the credit side. On the other side, I wondered how far I was fitted for opening or inaugurating this institute of

---

49. Note, 11 October 1962, for Rajya Sabha MP, President of AIIMS, and a member of the Nutritional Advisory Group of Indian Council of Medical Research. MS, File No. 31(35)/48-PMS, Vol. I & II, Sr. No. 35-A.
50. Speech, 14 October 1962, at Nawinna. NMML, AIR Tapes, TS No. 19059, NM No. 2555.
51. Sirimavo Bandaranaike.
52. A.P.Jayasurya.
53. Solomon Bandaranaike, Prime Minister of Ceylon, 1956-1959.
54. Sirimavo Bandaranaike.

ayurveda because my knowledge was exceedingly limited and, shall I confess it, It was somewhat critical of ayurveda, not ayurveda, that is not quite correct, but in the way that ayurveda had come to be in the modern age, now-a-days, because I have always been convinced that ayurveda exhibited an amazing advance in medicine, in treatment, in fact in something much bigger than medical treatment of individuals.

Perhaps you know that ayurveda means the science of life, the science of living and it went into all manner of details about it, telling people what to do and what not to do, what to eat, how to dress, when to sleep, when to keep awake and so on and so forth. The ancients were remarkably thorough in their direction. And I have no doubt that ayurveda—and I am using ayurveda as a somewhat more comprehensive word than mere ayurveda, that is, including the unani system of medicine which then affected to some extent, I believe, or was affected by the Greek system and through the Greek system it affected the so-called modern science. But the unani system itself, it is said, I do not know on what authority, to have derived much of what it possesses from the older system of ayurveda in India. But there is no doubt that both ayurveda and unani systems made remarkable progress in those days and that progress to say that it was speculative progress is to do a grave injustice to it. It was, having regard to the conditions then prevailing, as scientific as anything could be then.

So I have always admired the great achievements of ayurveda as well as the unani systems. But my own impression and I speak completely as a layman without knowing much about the subject—which is a dangerous thing to do, but since I am put in the position like this I have to say what I have in mind—I found that the great advance that was made in ayurveda and unani systems, somehow, like many other things in India and Ceylon and many other countries, became static, unmoving, unprogressive, not looking forward but looking back, reciting some mantras or some recipe, using them, excellent recipes, wonderful remedies, curing people, but without a forward looking outlook. That prejudiced me against it. That is the present way of people who talk and work with ayurveda.

My own early training, my college training being somewhat scientific, I became a great believer in the scientific method. I realise that what I got, the kind of training I got in Cambridge more than half a century ago is completely out of date today. What I learnt in physics has been changed by subsequent discoveries. It was not quite so final as I thought it then. But anyhow, my belief, not in a particular axiom or dogma of science but in the method of science persists. And when I see the most excellent things being said or done without applying that method, I feel somewhat critical. So, that being my attitude generally, I was doubtful how far I was suited to be the inaugurator of this institute. But then I was assured that my disability would not be treated as such and that I was at perfect liberty to say what I liked. Of course, it was still nothing very bad, I might assure you anyhow. But nevertheless, it was not likely to be a paean of eulogy only, it was to be critical because I am critical, not of the ayurveda and its great achievements, but of the modern exemplars of ayurveda and the way they can only talk with the past. I do not like people who only talk with the past. I like more forward looking people, I like the spirit of science, by discovering things by trial and error and by experimentation, realising very well that science itself goes forward after numerous mistakes, it stumbles and falls and then gets up and goes again. And as I said, even the science that I learnt in my younger days is quite upset now by subsequent people like Einstein and others coming in and upsetting all, Newton and others. Well, that is so. Also, my own approach to medicine for long—I regret to say I have fallen from that high estate—was not to take it and I have avoided taking medicines for a long time, hardly any medicines, practically, drugs, and I advise everybody not to take it. Of course, that advice does not go far, I admit, when one is really ill. Fortunately, I was not ill and when I did take it off and on, in recent years, perhaps it cured me; I do not know, I might have been cured without it. But it certainly left after affects which I did not like. I do not like antibiotics. I think they are—I will not say worse than disease, but they are very near it, and the present habit of these miracle drugs and wonder drugs even, given by all and sundry, it may be by very competent persons knowing their patients fully, they might work, but the way they are given by every fledgling without knowing much about the patient or anything and who often succeed probably in killing the patients instead of curing them, and recently we heard of a drug which has led to the birth of deformed children and all this business of tranquillisers and the rest; it seems to me that modern medicine, as it is called, is going downhill with remarkable speed. It is a wonderful thing, modern medicine, modern medicine or scientific medicine, whatever you like to call it, and I think it has tremendous achievements to its credit in the last couple of hundred years or so, but I am beginning to think that it is not quite so sure of itself as it imagines it is. I am also beginning to think that the attitude of contempt to other forms of knowledge is neither a scientific way of looking at things, nor does it do much credit. Hippocrates is supposed to be the father of modern medicine, just as the father of the ayurveda is, I believe, supposed to be Dhanwantari and Bharadwaj, the two ancients, and in the unani medicine or Greek medicine, you will remember the name of Ibn Sina or Avicenna, the famous saint, and the great books in Sanskrit dealing with ayurveda, Susrut and Charaka. Later, other names come in, Nagarjuna and others. All these are famous names, and it would be foolish for any one attached to one branch of science to look down upon another branch, and even to not only look down, but refuse to look at it at all, imagining it as something superstitious and not worth consideration. That, I think, is a fundamentally wrong and unscientific attitude. It is true that the whole idea of medical treatment in the ancient days, very ancient days, was perhaps based on some wrong premises where it was thought that God is punishing a person for his sin, whatever it was, and all kinds of curious methods were evolved to appease the gods instead of looking at the patient. But that is very old. Then came gradually the approach of some, I would call it scientific certainly, whether it is ayurveda or unani system, because it was based on experiments and trial and error. They did not have the machines, the equipment to do so accurately as we have today but it was based on experimentation. And so it grew and it grew remarkably as any person who has studied the subject knows, grew remarkably in India and in Baghdad and in the Arab world and in the Greek world and in China—China was different, rather on a different basis it proceeded, and gradually seeped through to western countries through the Arab world. But in those days, anything about two thousand or sixteen hundred years ago, or less, when in India Taxila or Taksha Shila was a great school of medicine, and in Nalanda too, which was thought of greatly in other parts of Asia, Doctors from Taksha Shila were summoned to Harun al Rashid's bedside to treat him and there used to be hospitals in old Baghdad. And even the old Greeks speak highly of Indian medicine in those days. So it was fairly advanced and what is more, I am not referring to the practice of ayurveda now as I am rather critical of it, not knowing much about it, I might say, but the impression one gets is that ayurveda did not go about treating an odd disease by itself but wanted to treat the whole man or woman, whoever it was, the whole person, which is, I believe, gradually coming to be the approach of the modern physician. To my surprise, I found that there are some exhibits here which confirm my thoughts, even in surgery, which has made such wonderful advances nowadays in modern medicine; even in surgery the ancients in India did not do badly. Naturally, modern surgery has tremendously advanced, but they did not do badly. If that is so, then it is worth our while to study those for various purposes. It may be that some of the theories of the old medicine, whether here or in Greece or anywhere, were based on certain humours of the body. Now I do not pretend to understand that at all, what a humour of the body is, and so I can say nothing except that I am rather reluctant to accept anything which I do not understand; I cannot say no to it but I do not understand it and I am reluctant to accept it. These are the metaphysical or philosophical or other theories behind them. But there can be no doubt at all that in the realm of actual treatment it is a tremendous icon, ayurveda or unani, everybody knows it. I know it from personal experience and I have seen other people who have been despaired of by others being treated by the ayurveda and unani systems and getting well. There is something obviously in it, and if for nothing else, that very sphere is worthy of higher inquiry. So I am glad of this Institute. The only thing that I would lay stress on, and I consider it most important, is that every inquiry should be based on the method of science, and mere speculation, mere belief of what the ancients have said is not enough for me. What the ancients have said should be honoured, should be respected, should be studied and then should be proved by experimentation. It is, I think, likely, that what the ancients have said is correct. They were wise men, I do not say they should not, but it is a bad habit to accept things uncorroborated simply because somebody has said it. One thing, again I do not know much about it—modern health to some extent has been, curative and all that, but it is, the whole aspect has been more of public health, public hygiene, improving the environment, removing, let us say, putting an end to malaria, as has been done in Ceylon, largely in India too, putting an end to typhoid. In Europe and other countries all these diseases flourished but they have been put an end to in a mass scale. So far as I know I speak subject to correction, there was not that approach to public health in the old days, it was more of individual treatment. Particularly, of course, facilities were not available for that kind of thing in those days. Then again, what alarms me today is the growth of these drugs, the drug racket, and how ignorant people—and they appear to be quite a big number if not more so in western countries than in India or Ceylon—fall to any new drug that comes in and swallow it with very harmful consequences and to the great advantage of the makers of those drugs who make millions and billions of money over it. I think it is a horrible idea, this business of people trading en masse by producing some new drug every year and people falling on it and regardless of any, they take pride in scientific approach, they forget all science, and only discover that after suffering from it, how bad it is. Even great drugs which have done much good, like penicillin and antibiotic medicines, have been misused, as everyone knows. People think that it is a medical thing and it is given for everything. I wish something could be done to stop this business. Personally, I dislike the idea of a patent medicine. I dislike money being made out of the suffering of the people.[55] I think that there should be no such patent medicine. I think health is a thing which should be the concern of the State and there should be health services in the State. It is a big and expensive thing, perhaps every State cannot do it. But it should work along those lines, and when the motive of private profit somehow is taken away from this, there will be lesser exploitation than there is today.

55. See item 117.

Anyhow, believing as I do in the great advance of modern medicine, it has changed the world undoubtedly, modern surgery even more so, and believing as I do in the scientific approach to this whole subject, as to other subjects, I do think it is necessary and desirable for this scientific approach to be made to our old systems, which did wonders in their own times, to the ayurveda, to the unani systems, as well as to others, maybe. Well I am quite convinced that would lead to a substantial advance in human knowledge of the present day for the benefit of humanity. Therefore, I am happy that this Institute has been started by the Ceylon Government. I am sure it will do good not only to Ceylon but also to India.

115. To A. Hameed: Hamdard Institute[56]

October 16, 1962

Dear Dr Hameed,
I have your letter of October 16. I shall be glad to associate myself with the foundation stone ceremony of your institute. The only question before me was how to find the time for it. I am heavily occupied during the next two or three months. If you will suggest one or more dates, I shall try to find out which date suits me.[57]

Yours sincerely,
Jawaharlal Nehru

---

56. Letter to the President of the Institute of History of Medicine and Medical Research, Hamdard Buildings. Hamdard Archives and Research Centre, Hakim Abdul Hameed Papers, Correspondence with Jawaharlal Nehru.
57. See item 116.

116. To A. Hameed: Visit to Hamdard Institute[58]

October 18, 1962

Dear Dr Hameed

Your letter of October 18th. I can come to your function on the 15th November at 12.

Yours sincerely,
Jawaharlal Nehru

117. To Gulzarilal Nanda: Patenting Drugs[59]

22nd October, 1962

My dear Gulzarilal,

Sokhey[60] came to see me today and gave me the enclosed letter and a pamphlet[61] about drugs and the drug racket. He has in the past often seen me on the subject. His main suggestion is that the essential drugs should not be patented in India, or that their patents should not be registered in India. I entirely agree with him[62] in this as the drug racket in many countries is a scandalous thing. Recent secret enquiry committees in the US brought this out very forcibly. I think that we should expedite the Patents Act provision with this purpose, apart from other purposes. We lose large sums of money in this way and it is great burden on patients.

Yours sincerely,
Jawaharlal Nehru

58. Letter to the President of the Institute of History of Medicine and Medical Research, Hamdard Buildings, Delhi. Hamdard Archives and Research Centre, Hakim Abdul Hameed Papers, Correspondence with Jawaharlal Nehru. See also item 115.
59. Letter to the Minister of Planning and Employment and Labour. PMO, File No. 28(82)/61-68-PMS, Sr. No. 7-A.
60. S.S. Sokhey (1887-1971) Biochemist, member of First Rajya Sabha.
61. Extracts reproduced as was in enclosure. PMO File No.28 (82)61-68-PMS, Sr.No.6-A. For the complete argument see *Economic and Political Weekly*, 3 April 1965, pp.596-598.
62. See note in item 114, p. 94.

[Enclosure]

The Drug Racket: Patents make it Possible
S.S. Sokhey
Delhi

Both the Public sector and private industry are planning in a big way to put up plants to makethe country self-sufficient in all the essential drugs, such as anti-biotic, vitamins, synthetic drugs and drugs from medicinal plants, and make them available at the lowest possible prices by the end of the Third Five Year Plan.We are still almost entirely dependent for our supplies of modern life saving drugs on foreign countries and the high prices charged (an additional import duty has been imposed on them in the present budget) put them beyond the reach of most of our people. Even the public hospitals cannot use some of these drugs unless the patient can pay for them, which of course, most of them cannot.

The manufacture of drugs and their easy availability at reasonable prices are vital. The development of all industries and the prices of their products, particularly those of the drug industry, are, however, markedly affected by the patent laws in force in the country. The Government of India, therefore, appointed a one-man committee of Shri Rajagopala Ayyangar in 1958 to see if our Patents Act was conducive to national interests and to make necessary recommendations. He submitted his report in September 1959. But since then, to be precise, on June 27, 1961, Senator [Carey] Estes Kafauver Committee report on Administered Prices in Drug Industry has been published (Senate Report No.448, 87th Congress). The committee conducted a very exhaustive enquiry into all aspects of ethical drugs, that is, drugs not advertised to the layman but sold only on the prescription of a physician. The enquiry lasted two years during which numerous public hearings were held at which the leading drug manufacturers of the United States gave their evidence and had their full say. The committee's report throws a flood of light on the practices of the manufacturers and how they exploit drug patents to rigidly control the market to make excessive profits more than double made by the U.S. manufacturing industries as a whole, including oil, steel, automobiles, and chemicals.

India the victim of Drug Patents: - Senator Kefauver Committee cites India as an example of the disastrous effect of prices of patents on prices of drugs. It says: "India which does grant patents on drugs, provides an interesting case example. The prices in India for the broad-spectrum anti biotics, Auromycin and achromycin, are among the highest in the world. As a matter of fact, in drugs generally, India ranks among the highest priced nations of the world—a case of an inverse relationship between per capita income and the level of drug prices."

118. For the Foundation of the Red Cross[63]

I send my good wishes on the occasion of the Centenary of the Foundation of the Red Cross. During these hundred years, the Red Cross Organisation has done good work both during war and peace in many countries. I am glad, therefore, that the Indian Red Cross is organising a programme for the Centenary celebrations.

119. In New Delhi: To the World Medical Association[64]

Mr President,[65] distinguished delegates,
It is rather embarrassing to me, to follow our President. He has already welcomed you, on behalf of our country and I should like to add on behalf of the Government of India, our welcome to all the distinguished delegates that have come here at this General Assembly Meeting of the World Medical Council. You represent a great profession and a profession which has always meant to be one of service to mankind, whether you take the oath of Hippocrates or the ancient oaths to which reference has been made by our President and Dr Sen.[66] They all refer to the service and betterment of mankind. In India, this tradition is an old one and the principal treatises on it were written as long ago as the years before Christ. Later, if you have the time, you could visit some of the old seats of learning here which were famous here for their schools of medicine in the old days.

The medicine, Indian medicine, largely affected Arab medicine. In fact, in the old days in the Arabian Nights when the Caliph Haroun Al Rashid was ill, he sent for an Indian physician to Baghdad. From Arabia, this spread through various channels, Cordoba and Spain and elsewhere to the Western World. So in those days Indian medicine was for the time advanced and in its own way, it had a scientific basis. Unfortunately, in later centuries, it became rather static and it lost that scientific basis, just before the development of modern science as it is. And the torch of learning in medicine as in many other things went to countries where science was advancing at a rapid phase.

---

63. Message, 26 October 1962, forwarded to Major-General C.K. Lakshmanan, Secretary-General of the Indian Red Cross Society, Red Cross Road, New Delhi-1.
64. Speech at the World Medical Association General Assembly Council sessions 45-46 at New Delhi, Vigyan Bhavan, 11 November 1962. NMML, AIR Tapes TS No. 8618-19, NM No. 1696.
65. The reference here is to S. Radhakrishnan.
66. Dr S.C. Sen.

I do believe and I do think that any progress that can be made in this or other matters must be based on the scientific method and on the achievements of science. That is so, but I would submit to you that it is worthwhile even for modern people, modern medicine and modern science to find out what was achieved in olden times and perhaps to get some ideas from it, which examined by the scientific method might prove profitable. We read the history of medicine; unfortunately, so far as I know, the history of medicine [that is] taught rather ignores these earlier periods, which are full of information as to how in the old days, these matters were treated. They were treated always, I believe from the point of view of an integrated human being—mind and body. And I believe that is a fact which is fully recognised by the medical world today. That is a great objective. As our President said, health is important for the body, it is even more important for the mind. And in fact, if either of those do not come up to standard, the other suffers also. Then again, in seeking health, we may have enough hospitals, enough trained physicians and the like, but the basic thing for health is proper nutrition; and a country, which is not rich enough, wealthy enough, developed enough, to solve the food problem and like problems, naturally suffers in health. It is not a question of drugs and medicine, but good food.

Now in countries which are not developed in the modern sense of the word, the barest necessities of life are often lacking for large numbers of people and I should think that the first duty of the people who are responsible for the destiny of that country is to provide those basic necessities. In more industrially advanced countries, where the primary necessities have been supplied to all practically, there may be differences, but the primary necessities are fulfilled. And therefore, they seek other things, which may be worthwhile, which may not be. Then other problems confront them. But in countries, where these primary necessities are not fulfilled, that remains the primary and the chief problem. Naturally, you cannot confine yourself to only that aspect, other aspects have also to be viewed, because they are all interconnected in a system of development. But first of all, the primary necessities must be fulfilled. Apart from food and clothing, health and education are among the primary necessities. Health, particularly, is a matter with which you are intimately concerned. Now the problem for us in India is the same as in many other countries, how to give proper health services to the nation. In the last 15 years or so since we became independent, we have done something to that end. There are many more hospitals, many more medical colleges and the like, but still we have only touched the fringe of the problem of this country with a vast and growing population.

I read somewhere among your papers, that your Council does not approve very much of the State interfering in or taking direct part in organising health services. Now that may be good for some countries, but I do not know how we can face the problem in a country like India. There are enormous problems before us: unless the State interferes, not only interferes, but largely controls the health services of people, because her objectives as it must be for others too, to make the health services, the treatment of disease and all the matter connected with it, available to every human being and where human beings are poor, cannot afford much, how are we to deal with them? Only the State can do it on a big scale. Therefore, we feel here, that without infringing on private practitioners, State Medical Services become essential to meet this problem. No number of private practitioners can deal with it in a country like India, having regard to the conditions prevailing here. I merely mention this to you because of the difficulty I felt in this country that may apply to other countries also.

Then there is the question of modern drugs, which are many of them wonderful. Some almost miraculous, and yet it often happens that a drug which is called miraculous today falls into disuse very soon, something and some other miracle takes its place, and there we are: miracle after miracle comes, some good, some wrong miracles, and the whole of this drug business is associated with a kind of industry, which is good in its own way, but which has often done harm. I do not quite know how one can get over all these difficulties. I hope, your General Assembly or part of it and Committee, will consider this question of drugs.

Only recently, we have heard of great harm being done by some drug, which is not perhaps properly tested. But apart from that, my own reaction to drugs, perhaps fortunately, have been not to take them. And I have largely succeeded in doing that, not wholly. Because, when trouble comes one falls into the hands of a doctor, whether one wants to or not. And so sometimes, I have had to take them too, but rarely, I am glad to say, and it is better I think to err on that side than on the other, which seems to be a growing habit among the people. They seem to think that health lies in a pill. They will swallow any pill which is sufficiently advertised to bring this relief. This kind of thing, the drugs, do a lot of good, I have no doubt, but perhaps they also do a lot of harm and some methods should be found and adopted and encouraged by you who are experts in these matters, to check the overuse of drugs and somehow to separate the bad ones from the good. I am venturing to say something that is obvious and it must be in your minds. But because we ourselves have trouble in dealing with these problems here I thought I might mention them to you, so that you might give us the benefit of your knowledge and experience.

For the rest, we face apart from our very special problems, the general problems of the medical profession all over the world. Special problems are because we are changing over in India from a somewhat old pattern of society, to a modern pattern. We are modernising India in its industry, in its agriculture and that results in modernising it in many other ways. When I say modernising, that does not mean that we are uprooting ourselves from our past. We are the outcome of hundreds or thousands of years of the past of India and there is much in it that we value exceedingly. And if we uprooted ourselves from that past, we will be rootless. We do not wish to do that but keeping to that past, traditions of the past, we nevertheless, want to marry it to the present, to the modern age, the modern age of science and technology, keeping always some basis of the past too. A past is not always good, nor it is always bad, as one of the famous classical poets of India said long ago. So we try to bring about a synthesis and at the present moment we are endeavouring to bring the basic things of the modern age and that is a basic thing, leaving science and their applications and growth of science here and thereby trying to better the lot of our people to raise their standard of living. To give them first of all the basic necessities which, as I said, apart from material necessities include health and education specially, because from education come out all other things, and we want a long period of peace for this, so that we may work out our destiny accordingly. We may progress and we are convinced that we will make much greater progress. Unfortunately, in this world other things happen, come in the way. At the present moment, as some of the previous speakers have reminded you, we have trouble on our frontier.

It is extraordinary that we, who have loudly proclaimed, and I think truthfully that we stand for peace all over the world, who in our own struggle for freedom here adopted peaceful methods and achieved our freedom through peaceful methods against a powerful imperialist, that we who are so passionately fond of peace should suddenly have to face a war situation. It is a queer, an odd happening which apart from being undesirable, it shows what games destiny plays with the people in the country. Well, if it plays that game, we shall face it, we are facing it, we will face it. The only regret that comes from our minds is that possibly our march forward in developing the country and large number of projects for the benefit of our people may be delayed. But, however, that may be, nothing is more important than maintaining one's freedom and integrity. Therefore, we have to think a great deal and spend our resources on this primary matter. But even so, we realise that we cannot give up the basic objectives which we have set up before us to raise the level of our people and give them a better life. We shall endeavour to do so and I hope we shall succeed.

I should like to welcome you, ladies and gentlemen, again and I hope that your visit to this ancient city of Delhi which is not only old Delhi and New Delhi as you perhaps know, but old Delhi itself is the seventh city on or round about this site. Six cities have gone before the seventh which is old Delhi and New Delhi where you sit now is the eighth city. So, we are surrounded here by

101

a multitude of past happenings, old memories, racial memories and the like. We live in them, we have grown in them and yet we live in them in the present and work for the future and we hope it may be given to us to be able to bring about synthesis between our past and future which gradually unveils itself.

Thank you.

(e) Education

120. For the Inter-University Youth Festival[67]

I am glad that the Inter-University Youth Festival is again meeting in the Talkatora Gardens in Delhi. I am sure these Youth Festivals serve an important purpose in the development of our young men and women. Education does not consist merely of reading books and passing examinations, but also in developing the human being and stirring the enthusiasm of young people. I hope that this Festival helps in this process.

121. To Virendrakumar S. Shah: Use of English[68]

October 5, 1962

Dear Shri Shah,

I have received your letter of October 3.[69]

I have repeatedly expressed my views on the language question. Only this afternoon I did so again at a public function.

I think that the medium of instruction should be the mother tongue. I therefore think it is right for Gujarati to be medium of instruction. In the higher studies it may be necessary to use another medium, such as English also.

But I feel sure that it is essential for people to know foreign languages. For us in India English is the easiest foreign language to know and many people know it. Therefore, English should be taught in all schools at a fairly early stage.

Yours sincerely,
Jawaharlal Nehru

---

67. Message, 2 October 1962.
68. Letter; address: 8 Samarat Bhuvan, 3rd Floor, 174 Gujerat Society, Bombay 22. PMO, File No. 52(12)/57-63-PMS, Vol.I, Sr. No. 86-A.
69. Not reproduced here, but available in the NMML. PMO, File No. 52(12)/57-63-PMS, Vol-I, Sr. No. 85-A.

122. In Delhi: Languages and Indian Culture[70]

चेयरमैन साहब[71], बृजकृष्ण जी[72], और प्रिंसिपल साहिबा[73] और लड़कियों [हंसी], इसके माने ये नहीं हैं कि और जो लोग यहां मौजूद हैं उनको मैंने छोड़ दिया लेकिन ढाई बरस हुए मैं, मेरी दावत की गयी थी इसकी नींव डालने के लिए, बुनियादी पत्थर इस इमारत का। और आज मैंने आ के देखा कि वो एक पत्थर किता उसको औलाद कितनी हुई है [हंसी] और कितना लम्बा चौड़ा हो गया और एक सुन्दर इमारत बनी है। कोई बहुत ताज़्जुब की बात नहीं थी वो एक ढाई बरस में बन जाती, लेकिन मैंने सुना ढाई बरस में ज़्यादातर वक़्त तो गुज़रा नक्शे पे ग़ौर करने में, कार्पोरेशन में और कहां कहां और यह इमारत ख़ाली सात महीने में बनी है। तो सात महीने में इसको बनाना तो एक तारीफ़ के क़ाबिल बात है और मैं आपसे साफ़ कह दूं कि इसको दूर से भी देख के, अभी अन्दर तो गया नहीं हूं और बातें देख कर मेरे ऊपर असर हुआ है। [तालियां] दूसरे मैंने अभी सुना प्रिंसिपल की रिपोर्ट में किस तेज़ी से यह कालेज बढ़ा है हर तरफ़ से, खाते नम्बर में नहीं, लेकिन कामयाबी में, और मैंने ख़ुद देखा कि यह एन0 सी0 सी0 का जो आपकी एक फ़ौज तैयार हुई है [हंसी] यह बातें मुझे भली मालूम हुई। अब मैं जो यहां लड़कियां पढ़ती हैं उनकी निस्बत तो मैं बहुत कुछ कह नहीं सकता, मैंने कोई इस्तहान तो लिया नहीं है उनका [हंसी], लेकिन फिर भी कुछ अंदाज़ा हो जाता है चेहरे और शक्लों को देखकर, वो भी मुझे भली मालूम होते हैं। [हंसी]

यह सही है कि कुछ में हिन्दुस्तान की औरतों और लड़कियों की तरफ़ झुकता हूं, मेरी राय में तरफ़दारी की राय है ज़रूर, मेरी राय में वो किसी और मुल्क की लड़कियां औरतों का सामना कर सकती हैं और उनसे बेहतर भी हो सकती हैं और हैं। [तालियां] इसलिए मुझे ख़ास खुशी होती है लड़कियों कि शिक्षा में, तालीम में क्योंकि मेरा पक्का यक़ीन है कि एक मुल्क की तरक्की एक माने में लड़कियों के हाथो में ज़्यादा है बनिस्बत लड़कों के। यों तो दोनों को तरक्क़ी करनी चाहिए। लड़कियों को इसलिए मैं कहता हूं एक तो लड़के, लड़कों की तरफ़ अक्सर देखा जाता है उनकी पढ़ाई लिखाई का, लड़कियां ज़रा पिछड़ गईं हमारे मुल्क में, दूसरे यह कि लड़कियों का असर घरों पे ज़्यादा पड़ता है और तालीम ख़ाली स्कूलों कॉलेज में नहीं होती, शिक्षा शुरू होती है पैदा होने के वक़्त से, ख़ासकर माँएं देती हैं, घर पे पढ़ना लिखना नहीं है बातें होती है जिससे बच्चा सीखता है। और पहले बरसों में बच्चे, कहा जाता है पहले सात बरस में एक पक्की बुनियाद पड़ जाती है बच्चा कैसा होगा बढ़ के? लेकिन आमतौर से लोग नहीं समझते, वो समझते हैं स्कूल-कालेज में बहुत सीखेंगे लेकिन स्कूल जाने के पहले ही वो बहुत कुछ ढल जाता है। तो इसीलिए मैं लड़कियों की तालीम को बहुत ज़रूरी समझता हूं हिन्दुस्तान में।

70. Speech at the Janki Devi Memorial College, 5 October 1962. NMML, AIR Tapes, TS No. 8429, NM No. 1657.
71. Sri Krishan Chandiwala.
72. Brij Krishan Chandiwala, Secretary, Banarsidas Chandiwala Trust.
73. Ms P.N. Jungalwala.

फिर सवाल उठता है कैसे तालीम हो, किस ढंग की हो? इसका जवाब देना मुश्किल है, क्योंकि आजकल इतनी चीज़ें हैं सीखने को कोई एक शख़्स सब नहीं सीख सकता या कोई बहुत ऊंचे दर्जे के साहब हों वो सीख लें लेकिन कोई आमतौर से सीख नहीं सकता है इतनी बातें। बाज़ बातें जिसको हरेक को सीखना चाहिए एक बुनियादी बातें और फिर कुछ अलग अलग शाख़ाओं में जा सकते हैं। आजकल कुछ मैं नहीं जानता यहां कितना झुकाव है, लेकिन हमारी पढ़ाई में झुकाव विज्ञान की तरफ़, साइंस की तरफ़, टैक्नोलोजी की तरफ़ हो रहा है, यहां है, कुछ साइंस यहां नहीं है, कुछ कमी रह गयी है यहां। इसलिए नहीं कि आप बहुत बढ़ के साईंटिस्ट हो जाएंगे, हो सकता है, लेकिन इसलिए कि आजकल की दुनियां को समझने के लिए कुछ दिमाग़ की ट्रेनिंग विज्ञान की होनी चाहिए, आजकल हम दुनिया में रहते हैं वो उसकी बुनियाद विज्ञान है, और विज्ञान के बच्चे बहुत पैदा हुए हैं और रोज़ पैदा होते जाते हैं, इसलिए अच्छा है इसको सिखाना और उसके बग़ैर तो हम आजकल की बढ़ती हुई दुनिया में पिछड़ जाएंगे। इसके माने नहीं कि ख़ाली विज्ञान सिखाया जाये, और यह अक्सर होता है कि बाद हमारे लोग सीखते हैं, अच्छे वैज्ञानिक साईंटिस्ट हो जाते हैं, अच्छे इंजीनियर होते है वग़ैरह वग़ैरह, अच्छा काम करते हैं, लेकिन कुछ और दुनियां का हाल उन्हें न मालूम हो, यह भी होता है। यह भी बात ग़लत है। इंसान की पढ़ाई के माने हैं कि असल माने तो यह हैं कि वो अच्छा नागरिक हो, अच्छा नागरिक के माने हैं कुछ न कुछ काम करें, और उसको शख़्सी तौर से वो चारों तरफ़ बढ़ सकें, शरीर बढ़े, दिमाग़ हर तरफ़ बढ़े, जिसको अंग्रेज़ी में कहते हैं इंटीग्रेटिड परस्नैलिटी हो। उसमें ज़रूरी है आजकल कुछ विज्ञान जाने तो कुछ कलाएं जाने, साहित्य वग़ैरह भी जाने, यानी ह्यूमैनिटीज़ भी जाने और साइंस भी जाने, दोनों तरफ़ बढ़ना चाहिए, चाहे बहुत ऊँचा न हो लेकिन दोनों तरफ़ कुछ न कुछ होना चाहिए, नहीं तो [एक तरफ़ा] हो जाता है वहां। तो हल्के हल्के यह मैं चाहता हूं ऐसी जगह भी जहां साइंस वग़ैरह पढ़ाई जाती है वहां भी काफ़ी ह्यूमैनिटीज़, साहित्य कलाएं वग़ैरह सिखाई जाएं तब आदमी ज़रा बराबर का होता है। नहीं तो एक तरफ़ झुक जाता है।

आजकल एक बहस काफ़ी हमारे देश में हैं भाषाओं की, कुछ अंग्रेज़ी की, हिन्दी की और भाषाओं की [उनकी क्या] जगह है यहां, हालांकि सवाल मुश्किल है। मुश्किल बहस के माने में नहीं मुश्किल है, लेकिन इस सब को काबू में लाना और पढ़ाना कई भाषाएं, उसमें ज़रा कठिनाई होती है, लेकिन जो बहस होती है वो ग़लत ढंग की होती है। मैं अभी आ रहा हूं एक दस रोज़ हुए, मिश्र में था इजिप्ट में, वहां उनकी ज़बान अरबी है, एक मशहूर ज़बान है, बड़ी सुन्दर ज़बान है और इत्तेफ़ाक़ से वो उनकी पुरानी ज़बान भी है जैसे हमारी संस्कृत है, और जो नई हैं उसमें एक आसानी पड़ जाती हैं। तो अरबी में तो काम होता ही है वहां, लेकिन उन्होंने दो भाषाएं और ज़रूरी कर दीं हरेक को सीखने के लिए, हरेक बच्चे से ले के, एक तो अंग्रेज़ी और एक और योरोप की ज़बान या फ़्रैंच या जर्मन या रूसी, यह हरेक को सीखनी पड़ती है। यानी एक अंग्रेज़ी और एक इन तीन चार ज़बानों में से चुनते हैं, अलावा अरबी के। यह कोई वहां बहस नहीं करता कि अंग्रेज़ी न

सीखो, अंग्रेज़ी एक दूसरे देश की ज़बान है इसमें हमारी कुछ, हमारी शान के ख़िलाफ़ है, यह तो निकम्मी बातें है, जिस चीज़ से हमें फ़ायदा हो सके उसे हमें सीखना है।

मैं अभी वहां विलायत में था, इंग्लैंड में, वहां एक दूसरे क़िस्म की बहस मैंने सुनी, ख़ासकर उन लोगों के लिए जो साइंस और टैक्नोलोजी पढ़ते हैं। वहां यह बहस हो रही थी कि अंग्रेज़ी जानना काफ़ी नहीं है, आजकल विज्ञान इतना फैला हुआ है कि तो इस पर ज़ोर हो रहा कि जो विज्ञान पढ़ते हैं उनको दो भाषायें और सीखनी चाहिए। दो से ज़्यादा कह नहीं सकते वो चाहते हैं और भी सीखते, लेकिन दो उन्होंने कहा कम से कम और, अब जो कुछ हो रूसी हो, जर्मन हो, फ्रेंच हो वग़ैरह। तो हमारे यहां बहस एक अजीब होती है, यानी बजाए इसके कि हम कोशिश करें ज़्यादा सिखाने की, हम उसको बन्द करना चाहते हैं, गोया कि कोई बात सीखनी भी एक बुरी बात है, गुनाह है जैसे पुराने ज़माने में बड़ी बहस होती थी हिन्दी या उर्दू। अब बहस की कौन सी बात है, हिन्दी और उर्दू एक बिलकुल क़रीब का उनका रिश्ता है, बहनें हैं, दोनों में बहुत कुछ दौलत है और दोनों मिलाई जायें तो बहुत ज़बर्दस्त भाषा हो जाती है। ख़ैर वो अलग रहें या मिलाई जायें, यह हालत हो गयी थी और अब भी है, बहस होती है कि अगर कोई कोई उर्दू के शब्द का प्रयोग किया जाये तो हिन्दी वाले नाराज़ होते हैं उर्दू ले आये यहां, ज़्यादा हिन्दी कराई जाए तो उर्दू वाले नाराज़ होते हैं वो कहते हैं कि हमारी नहीं समझ में आता। ख़ैर न समझ में आए, लेकिन यह पहली दफ़ा मैंने देखा है कि लोग चिल्ला चिल्ला के कहें कि हम इत्ते अनपढ़ हैं कि समझते नहीं हैं, कोई बात को। आमतौर से लोग अपना अपना ऐब छुपाते हैं, न भी कुछ समझे तो कहता नहीं हैं कि मैं नहीं समझता, यहां ख़ासतौर से चिल्ला चिल्ला के कहते हैं हम नहीं समझते। जैसे फ्रांस में, जैसे इंग्लैंड में आप लीजिए, उनकी ज़बान है अक्सर उनकी ज़बान का सम्बंध फ्रेंच से है, तो कोई आदमी फ्रेंच में या कोई लेटिन में कुछ कहता है, वो न भी समझ में आये तो कोई कहेगा नहीं कि हमारी समझ में नहीं आया। वो समझेगा कि इसमें कोई हमारी इज्जत नहीं बढ़ेगी [अगर] हम कहें कि हम नहीं समझे फ्रेंच। यहां चिल्ला चिल्ला के कहेंगे हमें हिन्दी नहीं समझ में आयी, हमें उर्दू नहीं समझ में आयी, अजीब हालत है। तो यह तरीक़ा, यह तर्ज़ ग़लत है बिलकुल। मेरा [यह] मतलब नहीं कि आप झूठ बोलें, समझ में जो आपको न आये उसको कहें आता है। लेकिन यह दिमाग़ का तर्ज़, गोया कि बुरा है किसी बात को समझना, किसी बात को पढ़ना यह ग़लत बात है, और ख़ासकर हिन्दुस्तान में।

हिन्दुस्तान क्या चीज़ है, भारत क्या है? बहुत बड़ा देश है अनेकता इसमें बहुत है और उसी के साथ एकता भी है ज़बर्दस्त, जो कि उनको, भारत को रखा है मिलाकर। तो इसमें अगर हम अनेकता को पूरी तौर से पहचानें नहीं, और उसकी क़द्र न करें तो हमारी एकता कमज़ोर हो जाती है अजीब बात है। यह अनेकता को मानकर हम एकता मज़बूत कर सकते हैं अगर हम अनेकता को न माने तो एकता भी कमज़ोर हो जाती है और हिन्दुस्तान का सौन्दर्य ही अनेकता का है, अनेकता में एकता। तो भाषाओं के सिलसिले में इसलिए हमें यह तरीक़ा छोड़ देना चाहिए। अब आजकल हालत क्या है? ज़ाहिर है

हम यहां दिल्ली में हल्के हल्के या तेज़ी से हमारा काम हिन्दी में होगा, और प्रान्तों में भी हिन्दी में होगा, जो हिन्दी बोलने वाली प्रान्तें हैं उत्तर-प्रदेश, बिहार है, मध्य प्रदेश वग़ैरह होगा इसमें कुछ संदेह नहीं, लेकिन और जल्दी से जल्दी होना चाहिए, लेकिन अगर हम चाहें कि हिन्दी में काम, फ़र्ज़ कीजिए बंगाल हो, या मद्रास में हो तो यह ग़लत बात है। हम चाहते हैं हिन्दी सीखें वहां के लोग वो ठीक है लेकिन ज़रा भी हमने दबाव डाला, करो तो उनकी बड़ी भारी भाषा है बंगला, तामिल, बड़ी सुन्दर है बड़ी मशहूर है, बड़ी पुरानी है, तो लोग चिढ़ जाते हैं हम पर दबाव डालते हैं कि हम अपनी भाषा के बजाए दूसरी भाषा सीखें, यह तरीक़ा नहीं है। इस वक़्त भारत भर में हिन्दी काफ़ी सीखी जा रही है मद्रास में भी बहुत लोग सीख रहे हैं, बढ़ रही है और बढ़ेंगे, लेकिन अगर आप लाठी ले के कहें सीखो हिन्दी पढ़ो, तो हम उसके खिलाफ़ विचार हो जाते हैं, कोई तरीक़ा नहीं है। हम सारे अपने देश की भाषाओं को बढ़ाना चाहते हैं, हमारे विधान में लिखी हुई है और उसी के साथ हमारा विचार है कि हिन्दी बड़े हर हिस्से में बढ़े कि हिन्दी को, और भारत के हिस्सों में भी लोग जान लें ताकि कोई तो सम्बंध रखने की भाषा हो।

आजकल सच बात यह है कि हमारा संबंध अधिकतर अंग्रेज़ी का है, यहां मद्रास में मैं जाऊं तो मद्रास में मैं अंग्रेज़ी में बोल सकता हूं सब लोगों से, तामिल मैं जानता नहीं, हिन्दी में बोलूं तो कम समझते हैं। हम अंग्रेज़ी की जगह हिन्दुस्तानी को रखना चाहते हैं यानी हिन्दी को, कि वो हमें जोड़ने की भाषा हो, यानी अपनी अपनी भाषायें रखें, अपनी अपनी भाषा में काम करें लेकिन एक प्रान्त से दूसरे प्रान्त का सम्बंध और केन्द्र से, यह हल्के हल्के हिन्दी में हो यह बात ठीक है और यही हमारे विधान में भी लिखा है। लेकिन इसको अगर इस तरह से देखें कि अंग्रेज़ी को हम निकाल दें तो बार बार नारे उठते हैं कि जाने क्या, 'अंग्रेज़ी को निकालो', 'अंग्रेज़ी को भगाओ' तरह तरह के नारे होते हैं, वो जहालत[74] के नारे हैं, अंग्रेज़ी नहीं निकालनी चाहिए। मैंने आपसे कहा मिश्र को, मैं आपको और बहुत मुल्कों की, आपको रूस की मिसाल दूं, रूस में भी अंग्रेज़ी है सब स्कूलों में पढ़ाई जाती है, सब बच्चों को। रूसी ज़बान बड़ी ज़बर्दस्त है लेकिन एक उनको इस बात की फ़िक्र है कि उनका मुल्क बढ़े, अंग्रेजी से उनका सम्बंध होता है दुनियां से, बहुत बड़ी दुनियां से और भी भाषायें सिखाते हैं। और हम, हमने काफ़ी अंग्रेज़ी सीखी हिन्दुस्तान में हालांकि हमारे चालीस ब्यालीस करोड़ आदमियों को लेके एक थोड़े ही आदमियों ने सीखी कुछ लेकिन फिर भी काफ़ी सीखी उसको हम फैंक दें एक इल्म हासिल जो किया है। और नतीजा क्या है हम और दुनियां से मिलने के दरवाज़े बन्द कर देते हैं अपने और दुनियां को समझने के और ऐसे मौक़े पर जब कि और दुनियां में रोज़ नयी नयी बातें होती हैं, नयी-नयी तरक़्क़ी होती है। अब यह कोई हिन्दी का क़सूर तो नहीं है या बंगला का या गुजराती का। वाक़्या यह है कि हमारी भाषायें बहुत अच्छी हैं, सुन्दर हैं, साहित्य उनके अच्छे हैं लेकिन विज्ञान में और आज कल की दुनियां की बातें उसमें नहीं हैं, और आजकल की दुनियां की बातें इस तरह से नहीं हो सकती कि हम उसका अनुवाद कर के

---

74. See appendix 9 and item 14.

ले आयें, अनुवाद तो करते ही हैं और करना ही चाहिए लेकिन कहां तक हम हर साल करेंगे इन हज़ार किताबों का अनुवाद, हर साल दस-बीस हज़ार निकल रही है विज्ञान पर। तो इसलिए यह दरवाज़े बन्द कर देना और दुनियां को, यह हमें कमजोर करता है।

आप भारत का इतिहास पढ़ते होंगे, अच्छा है, बुरा है सब है लेकिन एक बात उसमें देखने की है कि पिछले ज़माने में, पिछले ज़माने से मेरा मतलब पिछले दो चार सौ बरस में भारत रोज़-ब-रोज़ कुछ अपने चारों तरफ़ दीवारें खड़ी करता गया, दिमाग़ की दीवारें। भारत में बहुत विविधा थी, बहुत इल्म था इसमें कोई शक नहीं, लेकिन और दुनियां की बातें वहां न आ सकें, वो करने लगा, शुरू शुरू में भारत का इतिहास पढ़िए तो भारतीय लोग दूर दूर आते थे बहुत दूर दूर समुन्दर पार करके बस गये, मिश्र गये, अरब देशों में गये, ईरान गये, इधर चीन गये, जापान गये, बौध धर्म को ले गये कहां कहां भारतीय लोग। आप उधर जाइए पूर्व एशिया में इंडोनेशिया है, भरी हुई है वो भारत की कलाओं से, भारत की कहानियों से। वहां इंडोनेशिया में आप जाइए, याद रखिए इंडोनेशिया एक मुस्लिम देश है वहां सब लोग क़रीब क़रीब सब लोग मुसलमान हैं, लेकिन उनके यहां सारे उनकी कलाएं हैं, उनके नृत्य हैं, नाच वग़ैरह सब हैं वो सब रामायण की कहानियों पे हैं या महाभारत की। इतने भरे हुए हैं इससे और बड़े सुन्दर नाच होते हैं। और तरह तरह की बातें होती हैं, उनके चित्र रामायण और महाभारत के हैं। यह कोई धर्म से ताल्लुक़ नहीं रखता यह तो एक देश के साहित्य से देश की सभ्यता से संस्कृति से संबंध रखती हैं यह बातें। तो गरज़ कि भारत से यह सब गई फिर बाद में कई सौ बरस गुज़र गये कि फिर हम कुछ ठंडे हो गये इस देश में और बजाए इसके कि बाहर देखें बाहर जायें हम सिकुड़ गये, हमारे पास काफ़ी दौलत थी उसी को देखते रहे लेकिन दायें-बायें नहीं देखा, नतीजा क्या हुआ, और दुनिया ने बढ़ती तरक्क़ी की ज़ोरों से। और तरक्क़ी करने के माने ये हैं कि उसकी शक्ति भी बढ़ती गयी और आख़िर में आके उन्होंने भारत पर हमला किया, भारत को गुलाम बना लिया।

छोटी छोटी बातें आप देखें कि किताबें छपना, हरेक के पास आजकल छपती हैं हर जगह छपती हैं सैकड़ों बरस से योरोप में किताबें छप रही थीं। कहा जाता है उसके पहले भी कुछ चीन में होती थी ब्लाक वग़ैरह बनते थे योरोप में छपना शुरू हुआ कई सौ बरस हुए। हिन्दुस्तान में किसी को नहीं ख़बर थी, न फ़िक्र थी, दरवाज़े बन्द कर लिये थे मालूम ही नहीं करते थे, क्या और जगह होता है? पहली दफ़े हिन्दुस्तान में छपी हुई किताब आयी थी अकबर या जहांगीर के ज़माने में, मुझे याद नहीं योरोप से कुछ मिशनरीज़ लाए थे। अकबर बड़ा आदमी था, बहुत लायक़ आदमी लेकिन मुझे ताज्जुब होता है कि उसको देख के भी उनको यह शौक़ नहीं पैदा हुआ कि हमारे यहां छापी जाये किताबें, फिर अटक गया मामला पड़ा रहा, आख़िर में जब अंग्रेज़ आये तो अंग्रेज़ों ने, कोई एक मालूम नहीं डेढ़-सौ, पौने दो-सौ बरस हुए पहला छापाखाना खोला सैरामपुर में, बंगाल में, वो भी कुछ मिशनरीज़ ने, तब छपना शुरू हुआ, हल्के हल्के फैला। मेरा मतलब यह कि जो बातें अब छपने से दुनिया को बदल दिया, छापने ने पढ़ाई को हरेक बात को आप सोचें आप के पास

किताबें छपी हुई न हों तो कैसे आप पढ़ें, पढ़ सकते हैं जैसे हमारे यहां पढ़ते थे एक गुरू के पास कुछ लोग रहते थे उनसे बातें करते थे, सीखते थे लेकिन इतने बड़े पैमाने में पढ़ाई या गवर्नमेंट का इंतज़ाम कुछ हो ही नहीं सकता, बग़ैर किताबों की छपाई के। यह बात इत्ती देर में आयी यहां क्यों हिन्दुस्तान में, इस लिए कि हमने दीवारें बना ली थी कि बाहर की दुनियां से हमारा संबंध बहुत कम था, हम जाते नहीं थे और हमारे यहां कभी कभी बाहर के लोग आयें वो देखें उन्होंने बड़ी-बड़ी लम्बी-लम्बी किताबें लिखीं, अपने सफरनामें, जो बाहर से आये थे हमारे लोगों ने सिवाए शुरू के, बाद में कुछ नहीं ऐसा लिखा बाहर जा के।

तो यह हमारे इतिहास में हिन्दुस्तान की कहानी में, यह एक बड़ी ग़ौरतलब बात है कि कैसे हमारे पूर्वज जो थे दूर-दूर जाते थे, हमारी संस्कृति को ले के, हमारी भाषा संस्कृत को लेकर। संस्कृत की पुस्तकें चीन में मिलती हैं, तिब्बत में मिलती हैं गोबी डेज़र्ट में मिलती हैं, वहां जाते थे और फिर एकदम से जाना बन्द कर दिया, और यहां बैठ गए किसी क़दर माफ़ कीजिएगा मेरा कहना कुंए के मेंढक हम बन गए। बाहर नहीं देखें हम बस अपने ही दायरे में देखें बस, यह कोई आदमी करता है खुद या कोई कौम करती है या कोई देश करता है वो सुकड़ने लगता है, उसका दिमाग नहीं फैलता और दुनियां से अलग हो जाता है और आख़िर में गिरता है, यही हमारा हशर हुआ।

खैर हम फिर बढ़े, हम अब बढ़ रहे हैं। तो अब कोई ऐसी बात भी करें जिससे हमारा दिमाग़ सुकुड़ जाये हम और दुनियां का हाल नहीं जाने, वो निहायत नुकसानदेह है। इसलिए भाषा के मामले में भी मुझे तकलीफ़ होती है आजकल की बहस पर, यह नहीं की यह सिखाया जाये वो यह तो पढ़ाने वाले पढ़ने वाले तय करें। लेकिन इस दिमाग के तर्ज पर इसको न करे, रोकने को इल्म हासिल करने से, और दुनियां से अलग हो जाने को, फिर दीवारें खड़ी करने को, यह तकलीफ़देह है। ज़ाहिर है हमें सब करना चाहिए हिन्दी को बढ़ाने के लिए, ज़ाहिर है रोज़-ब-रोज़ ज़्यादा हिन्दी में काम होगा, लेकिन उसके बढ़ाने की कोशिश में हम और भाषाओं को छोड़ दें। अपने देश की भाषाएं तो हैं ही उनको सीखना चाहिए और लेकिन अंग्रेज़ी को निकाल दें या फ्रेंच या रूसी यह ग़लत बात होगी और इससे हमारी तरक्की रूक जायेगी आजकल की दुनियां में।

मैंने आपसे ज़रा कुछ ज़रूरत से ज़्यादा भाषाओं के बारे में कहा, लेकिन मैं चाहता था आप लोग समझें, यह खाली भाषा का सवाल नहीं है यह भारत के भविष्य का सवाल है। भारत का दिमाग़ खुला रखना है, खिड़कियां अपने दिमाग़ की खुली रखनी हैं कि सारी दुनियां से हवायें आयें, जैसे महात्मा जी ने कहा था कि हमें अपनी दिमाग़ की खिड़कियां खुली रखनी चाहिए दरवाज़े और खिड़कियां सब तरफ़ से हवा आये। लेकिन उसी के साथ हमारे पैर अपनी ज़मीन पर जमें रहने चाहिएं यह नहीं कि हवा आ के हमें बहा दे यह भी गड़बड़ बात है। पैर ज़मीन पर रहें और हमारी ज़मीन मज़बूत है, ज़मीन से मतलब हमारे भारत की संस्कृति है पुरानी वग़ैरह, मज़बूत है उससे हम उखड़ जाते हैं तो बेजड़ के हो जाते हैं न इधर के न उधर के, फिर एक पत्ती की तरह से उड़ते हैं।

तो दोनों बातें होनी चाहिए कि हमारे पैर जमे रहें हमारी ज़मीन पर, हमारे साहित्य पर, हमारी बहुत पुरानी बातों पर, लेकिन उसी के साथ दुनियां का [साथ दे], दुनियां से हम सीखें क्या हो रहा है। उसको अपनायें, आजकल की दुनियां में ख़ासतौर से उसका विज्ञान सीखें, विज्ञान से क्या क्या निकला है? क्योंकि हर चीज़ आप दायें, बायें कहीं भी झुकिए विज्ञान आ जाता है सामने, रोज़मर्रा की हमारी ज़िंदगी में, हम क्या करते है? हम सफ़र करते हैं तो रेल पर करते हैं हवाई जहाज़ पर करते हैं, मोटर पर करते हैं। आपका यह मकान बना है, यह नए तरीकों से बना है जो विज्ञान ने बताए नहीं तो किसी और तरह का बनता पुराने तरीके का। और कोई काम आप नहीं कर सकते आजकल बगैर विज्ञान की दुनियां को समझे। तो दोनों तरफ़ बढ़ना है, और इस तरह से बढ़ना है कि बढ़ने में हमारी, हम अपनी जगह पे रहें कोई हम किसी के सामने शर्मिन्दा नहीं होते हैं भारत के लिए शर्मिन्दा होने की क्या बात, हमें उसका अभिमान है, ग़रूर है, सब बातों का नहीं वहां की, लेकिन जो हमारी बुनियादी बातें हैं वो अभिमान की ग़रूर करने की हैं, उस पर हम जमें रहें, अपनायें, उससे अलग होते हैं जैसे मैंने आपसे कहा फिर तो आप हवा की पत्ती हो जाते हैं। लेकिन उसी के साथ और चीज़ें भी सीखें, अपनाएं, तब हम आजकल की दुनियां में भी हैं और अपने देश की दुनियां में भी कायम रहते हैं।

तो आपका यह सुन्दर कालेज और सुन्दर सारी लड़कियां इसमें हैं तो मैं तो समझता हूं कि जो आजकल लड़के लड़कियां हमारे पढ़ रहे हैं, वो ज़रा कुछ नए ढंग के होंगे, मेरे ज़माने के लोगों से कुछ बेहतर होंगे। हम तो फिर भी एक पुराने बहुत लोग हो गये हैं इसलिए मुझे कुछ ज़रा दिक्कत भी होती है, मैं कुछ झिझकता भी हूं, कि मैं छोटे लड़के लड़कियों को बहुत सलाह दूं क्योंकि इतना फासला हो गया है मेरी उम्र में और उनकी उम्र में कि मुझे यकीन नहीं होता कि मैं उनके दिमाग में या दिल में जा सकता हूं कि नहीं। अकसर ऐसे फ़ासले हो जाते हैं अलग जैनरेशन्ज़ में। तो मुझे तो यकीन है कि आजकल जो लोग बढ़ रहे हैं लड़के-लड़कियां बावजूद इसके कि बहुत शिकायतें होती हैं उनकी कभी कभी, फिर भी वो एक नये ढंग के निकल रहें हैं जो भारत को मज़बूत करेंगे, जो शानदार करेंगे, जो भारत की संस्कृति में मज़बूती से क़ायम है और उसी के साथ दुनिया को संस्कृति भी जानते हैं और दुनिया में क्या क्या ख़ास बात हुई है दोनों बातें जोड़ना ज़रूरी है अलग करने से न हम इधर के रहेंगे न उधर के रहेंगे।

मैंने भारत की संस्कृति का कहा और भाषाओं का कहा। मेरी राय में हमारी संस्कृति की जड़ जो रही है वो संस्कृत है, और दुनिया की पुरानी भाषाओं में बड़ा ऊंचा दर्जा है संस्कृत का, और मैं चाहता हूं कि संस्कृत काफ़ी लोग पढ़ें, मैं नहीं कह सकता हरेक पढ़े तो बहुत बोझा हो जाए हरेक पे लेकिन संस्कृत की सेवा हमें काफ़ी करनी चाहिए क्योंकि उसी में, उसी के ज़रिए से भारत बड़ा है। मेरी राय है यह, तो अच्छा है उसको करें और उसके ज़रिए से हमारी भाषायें भी और दौलतमंद और धनी हो जाएंगे।

यह जो एन0 सी0 सी0 की आपकी लड़कियां थीं उनको देख के मुझे खुशी हुई, शायद यह सही है मुझे याद नहीं कि पहली बार एक लड़कियों की एन0 सी0 सी0 [कैडेट] कौर ने गार्ड आफ़ आनर मुझे दिया। लड़कियों को तो मैंने बहुत एन0 सी0 सी0 में देखा है,

109

इस वक़्त याद नहीं पड़ता गार्ड-आफ़-आनर उन्होंने दिया था कि नहीं दिया [हंसी और तालियां] । तो यह अच्छी बात है कि इसमें हैं और आप जितनी ज़्यादा इसमें हों उतना ही अच्छा है। इससे कुछ कई नए तरफ़ हम बढ़ते हैं यह बातें सीख के, मैं नहीं चाहता कि आप बड़े शूर-वीर सिपाही बन जायें सब, लेकिन सिपाहीपना भी कुछ अच्छा होता है मर्द में या औरत में अपने अपने ढंग का। तो बस फिर आपको जिन लोगों ने इस दो ढाई बरस से इस कालेज को चलाया है और तेज़ी से तरक्क़ी की है उनको मैं बधाई देता हूं और ख़ासकर लड़कियों को जो यहां पढ़ती है और जो पढ़ के मुझे उम्मीद है बड़े बड़े काम करेंगी। जयहिन्द!

[Translation begins:

Mr Chairman,[75] Brijkrishanji,[76] Madam Principal[77] and Girls [Laughter],
That does not mean that I have left out the others who are present here. Anyhow, I was invited to lay the foundation stone of this building two and a half years ago and I see today what one stone has yielded [Laughter]; a huge and beautiful building has come up. It is not surprising that it should have been completed in two and a half years. But I believe that most of that time was spent in drawing up the plans and getting them approved in the corporation and what not, and this building was actually built in seven months. Now that is really praiseworthy and I would like to tell you that even the glimpse that I have caught of it has impressed me profoundly. [Applause] Secondly, I have learnt from the Principal's report how rapidly this College has grown in every way, not only in numbers but in its achievements, and I have seen for myself the splendid NCC unit which has come up here. [Laughter] I liked what I saw. Now I cannot say very much about the girls who are studying here because I have not tested them. [Laughter] But I can form a fairly good impression just by looking at their faces which seem very nice to me. [Laughter]

It is true that I lean in favour of the girls and women of India. So my views are biased. In my opinion, they can compete with the women of any country and in fact outstrip them. [Applause] Therefore, I am particularly happy to see the spread of education among women because I am fully convinced that the progress of a nation depends more on girls than on boys. Of course, both sexes must progress. But I am stressing the education of girls because for one thing, attention has always been paid more to boys' education and the girls have been neglected. Secondly, women wield a greater influence in the home

75. See note 71 in this section.
76. See note 72 in this section.
77. See note 73 in this section.

110

and particularly on children, than the boys. In fact, a child's education does not start in schools or colleges but at home, at his mother's knees. A child learns many things at home. It is believed that it is in the first few years that a child's mind is moulded and the firm foundations of his personality are laid in the first seven years. But this is not generally understood by people who think that children learn everything in schools and colleges. As a matter of fact, a child's personality is moulded to a very large extent even before he joins school. Therefore, I consider the education of girls in India to be extremely important.

The question then arises as to the kind of education that should be imparted. It is a difficult question because there are innumerable areas of knowledge available. An individual cannot learn everything except perhaps a genius. But there are certain fundamental things which everyone must learn and then they can specialise in different branches. I do not know about this College, but generally speaking, we are laying greater stress on scientific and technological education in India. We do not have science here. Well, that is certainly a shortcoming. It is not that all of you can become great scientists except in a few cases. But in order to understand the world that we live in, we need to train our minds in science for it is the basis of the modern age. Innumerable offshoots of science are all around us and continue to increase day-by-day. Therefore, it is a good thing to learn science, for without it our education will remain incomplete. That does not mean that nothing but science should be taught. It often happens that some of our people grow up to be great scientists and engineers etc. and do good work. But they are completely divorced from the realities of the world. That is also wrong. The education of a human being really means that he should learn to become a good citizen and to do something useful. As an individual, there must be all-round development of his personality, mentally and physically, in order to become what is known as an integrated personality. For that it is necessary to know a little about modern science a little about arts and literature. Everyone must know the humanities and in scientific institutions, humanities, arts and literature must be taught.

Nowadays there is a great debate over the issues of languages. It is no doubt a difficult problem. It is difficult to teach several languages. But the argument is all wrong. I was recently in Egypt where they speak Arabic which is a beautiful language. It happens to be their ancient language too, like Sanskrit is for us. So it is somewhat easier for them. The official work is all done in Arabic. But they have made it compulsory for everyone to learn two more languages—English and another European language, like French, German, or Russian. So everyone has to learn three languages. There is no argument about it. They do not say English is a foreign language as we do. It is absurd. We must learn whatever is useful to us.

111

When I was in England recently, I heard a different kind of an argument particularly among those who are in the field of science and technology. The argument there was that though English is spoken in very large areas of the world, it is not enough for the purposes of studying science. Therefore, it is felt that those who are in the scientific field should learn at least two other languages, if not more, like Russian, German, French, etc. Here in India, instead of making an effort to learn as much as possible, we want to restrict our learning as though knowledge is a bad thing or learning, a crime. Some years ago, there used to be a debate over Hindi vs Urdu. What is there to argue about this? Hindi and Urdu are closely related and each is enriched by the other. Together they could make a very powerful language. But even now, the debate rears its head now and then. If Urdu words are used, the Hindi pundits get annoyed, and vice versa. This is the first time I have seen people shouting from the roof-tops parading their ignorance. Generally people would try to hide their ignorance. I cannot understand why anyone would want to parade their ignorance. For instance, in England, if some French or Latin word is used, nobody will admit to not understanding it because they feel it is beneath their dignity to say that they do not know these languages. Here on the other hand, we shout from the roof-tops that we do not understand Hindi or Urdu or something else. I feel that the whole attitude is wrong. I do not say that you should tell lies or say you know something when you don't. But the attitude of mind to think that any kind of knowledge is bad is wrong anywhere and particularly in India.

What is India? India is a very large country with great diversity and at the same time a tremendous unity which has bound the country together. If we fail to understand the diversity and respect it, our unity will be weakened. It is strange that we can strengthen our unity only by accepting the diversity. India's beauty lies in her diversity, the unity which exists in diversity. Therefore we must give up our old way of thinking in the issue of languages. What is the situation today? It is obvious that in Delhi, gradually we will switch over to Hindi for our official work and the states will also do so in due course, particularly in the Hindi-speaking provinces of Uttar Pradesh, Bihar, Madhya Pradesh, etc.. There is no doubt about that. But the process must be speeded up. However, it would be wrong to force it down the throats of the people in non-Hindi speaking states like Bengal or Madras. We want the people in these states to learn Hindi. But if we were to put the slightest pressure, the people whose languages are ancient, powerful and rich like Bengali and Tamil are annoyed. It is not right to force anything down the people's throats. At the moment, people in large numbers are learning Hindi in Madras and elsewhere and the number is bound to increase. But if you try to force them, the people will turn against the idea. We want to give a fillip to all our national languages as laid down in our constitution. At the same time, we want Hindi to spread in order to link the whole country together by a single language.

The fact is that nowadays our main link is only through English. When I go to Madras, I can speak to the people in English because I do not know Tamil and very few people understand Hindi. We want to substitute Hindi for English as a link language for the whole country. Every state will retain its own language and conduct its work in it. But Hindi will be a link between the various states and the centre. This is what our constitution lays down. But it is uncultivated behaviour[78] to go about shouting slogans saying English should be given up. I told you about Egypt. Let me give you another example. In the Soviet Union also, English is taught in all the schools. Russian is a very powerful language. But they are interested in progress and so they learn English to maintain contact with the outside world. They teach other languages too. We have learnt a lot of English in India though the number of English-speaking people may be very small when compared to the forty two crores of people in the country. Yet it is useful knowledge. If we do that, we will be shutting the doors on contact with the outside world at a time when new discoveries are being made every day in the world and new avenues of progress are opening up. Not that there is any defect in Hindi, Bengali or Gujarati. The fact is that our national languages are powerful and beautiful with rich literature. But they are not advanced enough for purposes of scientific education. We are translating the works from other languages. But it will take a long time to translate thousands of books. Every year thousands of books are published on scientific subjects. It would weaken us if we shut the doors on the outside world.

You must have read Indian history which is full of ups and downs. But one of the things that need to be borne in mind is that during the last few centuries, India had erected mental barriers all around her. There is no doubt about it that there was a great deal of knowledge and scholarship in India. But we cut ourselves off from the world. If you read the early history of India, you find that Indians used to travel far and wide, crossing the high seas, and went to Egypt, the Arab countries, Iran, China, Japan and elsewhere. People from India went carrying the message of Buddhism. If you go to East Asia, to Indonesia and other countries, you will find great evidence of the arts of India. You must remember that Indonesia is a Muslim country and most of the people are Muslims but their arts and dance and culture are all based on the Ramayana and the Mahabharata. They bear the unmistakable stamp of Indian culture. These things have nothing to do with religious beliefs. They are concerned with a country's literature, culture and civilisation. In short, Indian arts and culture

78. See note 74 in this section.

spread far and wide for centuries. Then came a time when we lost our vitality and instead of looking outward, we shrank within ourselves. We cling to our old ways of thinking and failed to notice what was going on in the rest of the world. The result was that the world continued to make progress while we remained backward. Finally, we lost our freedom and were enslaved by foreign powers.

Our stagnation was evident in very small things. Take printing for instance. Printing had been known in Europe for hundreds of years. It is believed that block printing was known in China even in ancient times. But printing began in Europe several hundred years ago. In India we were completely unaware because we had shut our minds to development in the outside world. Printed books were brought to the court of Emperor Akbar or Jehangir. I do not remember exactly—by the European missionaries. Akbar was a man of great catholicity but I am amazed that even after seeing printed books he did not have the curiosity to try printing in India. Finally it is only when the British came that the first printing press was set up in Serampore in Bengal about hundred and fifty years or so ago. Then it spread gradually. What I mean is that printing had revolutionised the spread of knowledge in the West. In ancient times children were educated by living in gurukuls. It was not possible to educate people on a large scale as we are doing now without printed books. But it took a long time for the knowledge of printing to reach India because we had erected barriers and cut ourselves off from the outside world. Foreigners have left long accounts of their visit to India for posterity. But there are no such memoirs written by Indians except in the ancient times.

One of the noteworthy things about Indian history is that in ancient times, our ancestors used to travel far and wide with our culture and literature. Sanskrit manuscripts have been found in China, Tibet, in the Gobi desert and elsewhere. Then suddenly we stopped our trips outside and became like frogs in a well. We refused to recognise what was going on in the world. When an individual or a nation does this, they begin shrinking within themselves. The mind shrinks if it is cut off from the outside world. Ultimately the country is weakened and falls. This is what happened to us.

Well, now we have been given another opportunity to grow again. It will be extremely harmful if we do anything which leads to the shrinking of the mind. Therefore, I find it extremely painful to quarrel over the issue of language. It is up to the teachers and the taught to decide what must be taught. But the attitude of mind which restricts the acquisition of knowledge or cuts us off from the rest of the world or creates barriers is harmful. It is obvious that we should do everything we can to encourage the spread of Hindi. But in that effort it will be wrong to give up our other national languages, including English and prevent people from learning French or Russian, because it will prevent our progress in the modern world.

I have spoken at unnecessary length because I want you to realise the implications. It is not merely a question of languages but of India's future. We must keep the doors and windows of our minds open and allow the fresh breeze of thought to blow in from all sides, as Mahatma Gandhi had said. But at the same time, our feet must be firmly planted on the ground instead of allowing ourselves to be uprooted. We must keep our feet firmly on the ground rooted in our own soil and culture. If we allow ourselves to be uprooted from our culture, we will lose our moorings and be cut adrift.

So we must maintain a balance and keep ourselves firmly rooted to our soil and ancient traditions and at the same time learn about what is happening in the outside world. We must imbibe the new scientific knowledge and learn about the new discoveries and inventions. Science and its off shoots are all around us in our day to day lives. We travel by motor car, trains and aeroplanes. The houses that we live in are constructed by modern methods. Today we cannot do anything without knowledge of science. So we must progress in both directions and make sure that we do not lose our moorings. We must not ever feel ashamed of India in any way. We must be proud of our heritage and cherish it. If we cut ourselves off from it, we will drift. But at the same time, we must imbibe and learn what the modern world has to offer.

This is a beautiful college for beautiful young girls and I think that the modern boys and girls will be different from and better than the people of my generation. Most of us are very old and there is a generation gap between us. I hesitate to give advice to boys and girls of the younger generation because the age difference between us creates a great gap and I am not sure that I can reach out to their hearts and minds. This generation gap is not unusual. I am convinced that in spite of innumerable complaints, the boys and girls of this generation are of very good material and will grow up to make India strong and proud by holding on to the ancient culture of India and at the same time keeping an open mind on what the world has to offer. A synthesis between the two is very essential for if we stuck to one or separate then, we will be neither here nor there.

I mentioned Indian culture and languages. In my opinion the roots of our culture lie in Sanskrit which is one of the oldest and most powerful languages in the world. I want people in large numbers to read Sanskrit. I cannot say that it should be made compulsory because it may impose too great a burden. But we must cherish the rich heritage of Sanskrit for we owe our past greatness to it in my opinion. We will be enriching the other Indian languages by doing so.

115

I was very happy to see the NCC cadets. I think it would be correct to say that for the first time a girls NCC group has given me a guard of honour. I have seen girls in the NCC before but I do not remember their giving me a guard of honour before this. So it is a good thing that you have NCC and the more of you who join the better it will be. This training contributes to the development of our personality in many ways. I do not want that you should become soldiers. But a certain soldierly discipline is good for men as well as women in its own way.

All right. I congratulate you on getting this building in two and a half years and for running it successfully. We have great hopes from the girls who are studying here and I am sure they will grow up to do great things. Jai Hind!

Translation ends]

123. For the NCC[79]

I send my good wishes to the National Cadet Corps on the occasion of NCC Day. The NCC, I am glad to find, has grown in strength. There are, I am told, over 4,20,000 Cadets in the Senior Division of the NCC and NCC Rifles. The Junior Division has 1, 84, 950, and the Auxiliary Cadet Corps 12, 64,380 Cadets. This is good progress. But we should not remain content. I think the training in the NCC is good for all our young men, and the more they participate in it, the better for them and for India.

I am particularly glad to know that the NCC is encouraging the love for adventure and mountaineering.

124. To Virendra Agarwala: Children's Education[80]

October 8, 1962

Dear Virendraji,

A letter of yours dated September 3rd has remained with me unreplied. As you perhaps know, I went away on a tour abroad.

I have read your article on "Basic Education" with interest. I agree with much that you say, but I do not agree that children might go to school from a later age if the period they can be kept in school is shorter than desired. I think it is essential that the process of education should start at an early age.

---

79. Message, 8 October 1962.
80. Letter to a researcher and educationist; address: 71 Pandara Road, New Delhi. A version of the article was published in *Yojana*, Vol. 22 (18), pp.41-42.

Of course it should be continued till fourteen or preferably fifteen, but not to begin at the early age would be wrong. Besides, we hope to increase the period at school before long.

Yours sincerely,
[Jawaharlal Nehru]

125. To P.E. Dustoor: Central Institute of English[81]

October 10, 1962

Dear Dr Dustoor,

I have received your two letters dated 29th September and 2nd October. I have delayed replying to you because I could not find a suitable date when I could visit you for the foundation-stone ceremony of the Central Institute of English. I am yet not sure when I can do so. But, as you must be waiting for my answer, I am writing these few lines.

In any event, I do not think I can go to Hyderabad in October or November. I shall consider further what possible date may be feasible.

Yours sincerely,
[Jawaharlal Nehru]

126. To M.C. Chagla: Foreign Exchange for Students[82]

October 11, 1962

My dear Chagla,

I received your letter of October 8 this morning, in which you discuss the question of foreign exchange for our students. As I told you, I think the matter deserves consideration. I have sent a copy of your letter to the Finance Minister.

I am going to Ceylon tomorrow morning for three or four days. I want to keep my engagement there although I am rather reluctant to leave Delhi at present. The situation in the North-East frontier is developing badly, and I fear there may be fighting on a fairly big scale there.

Yours sincerely,
[Jawaharlal Nehru]

81. Letter to the Chairman of the Board of Governors, Central Institute of English, "Bide-a-Wee", Kodaikanal.
82. Letter to the High Commissioner in London.

127. In New Delhi: To the Vice-Chancellors' Conference[83]

I am grateful to you for inviting me here to meet you. Dr Shrimali said that it is refreshing to hear my views. It may be that it is refreshing but not always profitable if it concerns some matter about which you ought to know much better because, as you know, politicians have to express their views about every subject. Education, which is so highly important, I think it would be far better that they were expressed by educationists than by politicians.

Yet, things being what they are, the politician has to play a part, and that part is not always as good as it might have been. I do think it is important in educational matters, especially higher education with which you as Vice-Chancellors are chiefly concerned, that your views should largely govern policy in this because, apart from other things, matters concerning education, I think, should be considered in a calm atmosphere and not exactly in the market-place of politics, and I take it that, however much you may feel strongly about some subjects, you would consider them calmly and objectively. We have great arguments today about the medium of instruction, about the place of the regional languages, of Hindi and of English. All these are eminent matters for calm and careful consideration, not only in regard to the ideal aimed at, but in regard to the process of changes which we have to go through.

One thing we have always to keep in mind, and that is the maintenance of quality, because without quality we fall back. We must have quality in our education, and that quality must be maintained throughout the process of education, not only the educational process, but by research. I am glad to find from the Chairman of the University Grants Commission[84] that he attaches a great deal of importance to post graduate courses and to research work. University education sinks to a lower level unless there are groups of persons in each university doing good research work, and I hope that it may be possible for these research centres to be organised in every university in some subject or other, and that the University Grants Commission will be of some help in this direction.

Now the medium of instruction has given rise to much argument. I have no doubt that the ideal to be aimed at is that of the medium being a regional language. That was one of the reasons why Rabindranath Tagore started Santiniketan. He insisted upon it and I think very rightly, if I may say so. That process is going on now, I think—the change over to the regional language as

83. Speech, 11 October 1962. PIB.
84, D.S. Kothari.

the medium of instruction. It may be that this change over might be staggered a little so as not to create a break in the process of education, not perhaps so much in literature and arts, but in technological and scientific subjects, and there is no reason why we should not use both the regional language and English at the same time, English for some subjects and the regional language for some other, so that education might not suffer and yet, the changeover may take place. People talk too much in terms of absolutes, either this or that. But there may be a middle course leading to the final change. So I have little doubt that the medium would ultimately be the regional language which is good for the student undoubtedly, but that creates a certain difficulty about the universities becoming quite isolated from each other. That is a grave danger. Now how should they keep contacts, for professors to be exchanged, and students also? That is a vital matter because it would be highly dangerous and harmful and will come in the way of progress if there are not these contacts. Now the contacts, so far as language is concerned, can apparently only be, as we are constituted today, either through Hindi or English. At the present moment they are in English; it is admitted, and even if the change takes place, it will probably be some time before those contacts are fully in Hindi, but any how Hindi and English are the two link languages you may call it, which should, I think, exist both on practical considerations and other.

I have just seen outside your exhibition of books, and it is gratifying to note what great progress has been made in the translation of books in our regional languages and the process, I think, will continue at a faster pace now. But one has to remember that however much you may translate textbooks or produce textbooks, knowledge is not confined to textbooks, and we have to read many other books, that is, in the higher stages of education, many books other than textbooks, and it is impossible for anyone to imagine that all the literatures of the world would be translated into Indian languages – it is physically impossible. Therefore, the necessity comes for people in the higher stages of education more especially for people in science and technology – which is the important modern fact of education--to know some foreign languages, because we cannot again be left behind in this race for knowledge, if you like, in scientific education, scientific thinking and scientific research work. I mentioned the importance of research. No research can take place isolated from what is being done in the rest of the world on a particular subject. When I was in England recently, I read a report of some commission or committee and I think it was about scientific education, and it laid stress on the fact that English was not enough for scientists. They pointed out three other languages, French, German, and Russian, as essential for science, and that they said over and above their language English, which is probably more prevalent than any other language today. Even that was not enough. Thus more so would it be insufficient for us, for any person, for such research work, not to know other foreign languages. Our regional languages, good as they are and they should be expanded—are not enough now or even at any time, any language for the matter of that. When English is not enough, when French is not enough, when German is not enough, how can we presume to say that regional languages can be enough to cover the world? Therefore, it becomes necessary to encourage the learning of foreign languages—most of the important ones. Now it is obvious, when they consider foreign languages, that the one with which we are most acquainted is English; we have a certain background; we need not start from scratch. So I do hope that efforts would be made to teach foreign languages, both for scientific purposes and cultural purposes, and in this way I say we have them in some universities where, as classical languages, we learn Arabic and Persian, which is good, because they are fine classical languages, but it is perhaps more important to learn modern Arabic and modern Persian than only classical Arabic and classical Persian. I hope that some efforts will be made to that end. There is a vast part of the world called the Arabic world, and purely for cultural contacts, political contacts and others, it is necessary to know Arabic, not for scientific purposes so much. Persian again is a language which used to be very widespread and still is. Now in scientific work probably Russian is more advanced than any other language; it probably comes next to English in the volume of work produced. So we have to produce people knowing these various languages but, as I said, inevitably it is both advantageous for us and the facts of the situation warrant it that we must use the English language we know already, and concentrate on English as a window to the outside world of knowledge. Therefore, I hope that the study of English will be widespread and will be good. I do not think it is good enough to say that English should be a language of understanding and no more. I do not know how you understand a language without understanding the language properly. You may understand a school book or some simple sentences, but in order to appreciate either a scientific book or literary book you have to know it rather well—the language—and we should aim at a thorough study of the languages we take up.

You know that there is some argument, especially in the political sphere, to continue having English as the associate language at the Centre. We stated, the then Home Minister, Pandit Govind Ballabh Pant, and I, stated in Parliament two years ago that it was the decision of Government that English should continue as an associate language.[85] We did not fix any period for it; vaguely

---

85. See *Report of the Committee of Parliament on Official Language, 1958*. (New Delhi: Government of India Press, 1959).

we stated that the period would be determined later and would be largely left to the wishes of the non-Hindi speaking States. There is some feeling, some strong feeling expressed now against it, against this continuation of English apart from the fact that a firm assurance was given on behalf of Government, and it would be highly improper to go back upon it. It is necessary and I think that Hindi or the other regional languages will profit by this association with foreign languages, especially English, English being the easiest foreign language for us, they will actually profit and grow more.

As a people, we in India have been in the past rather inward looking, rather ignoring the outside world. The outside world changed rapidly, especially in sciences and technology, and we remained immersed in our own learning which was very good, but still it was limited in so far as the world was concerned. Now the world grows into one and we cannot afford to have that limited outlook. We must remain in contact with the world. Languages play a most important part of maintaining those contacts with the world, with the young world, with the changes taking place in the world. So I feel that it is important that we should teach foreign languages and teach them well. And of the foreign languages, inevitably English is likely to suit us better than others though others should also be encouraged.

Now, even if you agree with the principles that I have suggested, yet a great deal remains to be done in the manner of doing it, that more than others these things should be decided by educationists, I think, and not by political decisions. Broad principles being laid down they should be worked out by educationists of universities themselves. But I hope that in doing so they will always keep in mind the necessity of not isolating themselves from other universities. Obviously that will impede their own growth. Take science. However eminent an individual scientist may be, scientific research is done more by a group than by an individual.

So also other forms of real research. Research should be common factors in universities. Universities may join together. For example, professors may go from some places to other places. If because of the linguistic barrier they cannot do so, our progress and research work will suffer.

So I have ventured to place before you some ideas of mine as a mere politician. But I do think that these matters are eminently fit to be determined by educationists, not that, I believe, educationists, are calm, they look at things calmly and philosophically always; they get excited too. But still they are relatively better situated than politicians even in other fields. Take a vital matter for the world's future—peace and war, nuclear testing, stopping of them and the like, disarmament. Now, there are committees and commissions meeting interminably without coming to an agreement. Yet we have found that when those particular matters are referred to a body of scientists coming from the very countries which are at loggerheads with each other, those scientists have usually found a way out of the difficulties and suggested a solution, because it may be that their training was somewhat different from that of the politicians. It would be a good thing, therefore, if these matters, which excite people so much, were considered in a more academic atmosphere, not divorced from the practical side of it but nevertheless not purely thinking in terms of day-to-day politics in our thinking, purely, in terms of some academic ivory tower.

After all we have our Five Year Plans and the like. The most important thing—I do not know what is most important. Everything is important—but education is, after all, the basis of all the progress that we are likely to make. And education, mass education, general education and specialised education, are all essential. And constantly we have to face a dilemma, quantity versus quality. Quantity is necessary. But it would be a pity if quality were sacrificed over it.

Now, today primary education has grown pretty fast. I do not know the number of students now. Two years ago I was told it was 45 million. Forty five million is a tidy number. It is impressive. When I repeat this figure in other countries they are impressed. It is more than the population of most of the countries. Yes, it is only a part of our problem. Probably it is now 47 million, I am told. But, then, if you look at the quality of the 47 million, it is not so satisfying. The schools and other places have little equipment. Perhaps not all of them have trained teachers. That is the difficulty that one has to face. But we should always try to improve the quality, at the same time the quantity. Ultimately the quality depends upon the teachers. In the higher branches of education the teachers usually have quality if they do research work. Because they go deeper in it they are honoured, more respected than merely people who read text books and repeat them to the students. I am sorry I am telling you some obvious things with which you are very well acquainted. But then if you ask a politician what can he do? He cannot enter deeper. I hope you will consider all these matters and give a proper lead to this great adventure of spreading education.

I have not said anything about one matter. My own education was – well, it might be called – scientific. I took my degree in science. That does not mean that I am a scientist. Now, there is this controversy now going on in the Western world between scientific education and the humanities. I have no doubt that both are necessary. I am quite sure that a scientist may be a very good scientist but he lacks something which is so essential for a human being. Also you cannot possibly leave science out and concentrate on Humanities. Then you get cut off from the world. And so far as it is possible, one should combine the two. I think —although I lack it—that where possible it is a very good thing for a

122

person to know classical languages. The difficulty is you cannot have all this together. I think Sanskrit, for instance, in India is of enormous importance. I should like to encourage it. But I feel I cannot simply make it a compulsory language for every one, but I should like to encourage it because so much has happened in India. In fact, the whole root and background of Indian culture is wrapped up in the Sanskrit language. Later many other elements came into it and created the mixed culture that we have. We welcome that, but Sanskrit has been the root of it. It is a magnificent language. I say so even though I do not know much of it. But how to cover all this wide field of knowledge in the course of one's educational career of school and college I do not know. That is for you to consider, how to produce an integrated individual with the depth that comes from the knowledge of the classics and the scientific training that is so essential in these days. Possibly we cannot have it. But anyhow, both should be encouraged and to some extent every scientist must know the Humanities, and to some extent even classical student must know science to some extent and not too much, must know at least the background of it, and it should not be said by somebody like Mr C.P. Snow[86] in England, I think that there are two cultures marching off in different directions and not meeting. The scientist does not understand a non-scientist and the non-scientist being at variance with the other. That is to some extent happening. There are many estimable people who are singularly ignorant of the other branch. I think something, especially in the high schools, should be done for the human being, for a student to have some basic knowledge of both these sciences. He can at least have some glimpse of an understanding of the modern world. After that he may develop it or not if he so chooses.

I do not know if I have said anything of any particular importance to you because I am rather hesitant to talk to experts in a field in which I am an amateur. Anyhow, I am grateful to you for inviting me and I wish you success in your labours.

---

86. Author of *The Two Cultures and Scientific Revolution* (Cambridge: Cambridge University Press, 1959).

128. To Prakash Vir Shastri: Official Language Issue[87]

October 16,1962

प्रिय प्रकाशवीरजी,[88]

आपका १६ अक्तूबर का पत्र मिला। भाषा के बारे में कुछ ग़लत फ़हमी मालूम होती है। अंग्रेजी का सहायक भाषा होना सिर्फ़ केन्द्र के लिए कहा जाता है। बाकी प्रान्त अपनी अपनी प्रान्तीय भाषा में अवश्य काम करें। ऐसी हालत में उत्तर प्रदेश, बिहार, मध्य प्रदेश आदि में हिन्दी में काम अधिक से अधिक हो सकता हैं।

जहां तक मैं आपको समझा हूं यही आपने स्वयं लिखा है उसमें कोई कठिनाई नहीं होनी चाहिए। केन्द्र में इस लिए अंग्रेज़ी भाषा सहायक रखी जाती है कि जिन प्रान्तों में हिन्दी नहीं बोली जाती उनको सुविधा हो।

आपका
जवाहरलाल नेहरु

[Translation begins:

Dear Prakash Vir ji,
I received your letter of 16 October.

There seems to be some misunderstanding regarding the language issue. English would be an associate language only for the Centre. The rest of the states can continue to work in their respective regional languages. Under these circumstances, states like Uttar Pradesh, Bihar, Madhya Pradesh etc. could do as much work in Hindi, as possible.

As far as I have understood, this is what you meant to convey in your letter. This should not pose any problem. English is being retained as an associate language at the Centre only to help the states where Hindi is not spoken.

Yours sincerely,
Jawaharlal Nehru

Translation ends]

87. Letter to Lok Sabha MP from Bijnor, Independent, 16 October 1962. PMH-62-No.1668.
88. (1923-1977), Independent MP and Arya Samaj leader.

129. For the Arya Samaj Education Conference[89]

I send my good wishes to the Conference of Educational Institutions formed under the auspices of the Arya Samaj. These institutions have done good work in spreading education through their colleges and gurukuls. In particular, it is good to know that the Depressed Classes are given free and equal admission and are encouraged in every way.

130. To Brij Mohan: Visiting Delhi University Students' Union[90]

October 17, 1962

My dear Brij Mohan,

Your letter of the 17th October. I would much like to visit the Delhi University Student's Union, but I must confess that it is not an easy matter nowadays as I am so heavily occupied with important work and engagements. Perhaps, I might be able to go on the 26th October at 6 p.m.

But it will be proper if the Students' Union approaches the Vice-Chancellor of the Delhi University[91] on the subject. It is appropriate for me to accept such an invitation only if the Vice-Chancellor supports it.

Yours sincerely,
[Jawaharlal Nehru]

131. For Indira Gandhi: Day Scholars at Visva-Bharati[92]

This question of Visva-Bharati accepting day scholars has come up repeatedly before me through the Vice-Chancellor. There is no doubt that the whole concept of Santiniketan was a residential one. To admit day scholars would change that concept, and possibly bring in local politics and troubles in its train.

2.   Anyhow the Act governing Visva-Bharati has laid it down clearly that it must be a residential university and we cannot accept any local day scholars unless we change the Act in Parliament. That is neither feasible nor desirable.

---

89. Message, 17 October 1962, forwarded to D. Vable, Principal, Dayanand College, Ajmer. PMO, File No. 9/2/62-PMP, Vol. 7, Sr. No. 52-A.
90. Letter to the President of the Delhi Pradesh Congress Committee, Ajmeri Gate, Delhi-6.
91. C.D. Deshmukh.
92. Note, 22 October 1962.

3. If the Bolpur people want to join Santiniketan, they can of course do so if they become residents of the university. Also there are a number of colleges roundabout Bolpur where they can easily go to.

4. The whole point is that Visva-Bharati is a special type of institution where, according to the directions of Gurudev,[93] much importance is attached to residents and personal contacts between teachers and students. We do not want it to be a replica of other universities where this personal contact hardly takes place.

5. I have discussed this matter with the Vice-Chancellor, Shri S.R. Das, and he is strongly of this opinion. I agree with him.

132. To the Delhi University Students Union[94]

छात्रसंघ के अध्यक्ष,[95] वाइस-चान्सेलर साहिब,[96] बहिनों और भाइयों, नौजवानों,

अजीब इत्तफ़ाक़ है कि आज मैं आपके सामने बोल रहा हूं, क्योंकि शायद अगर मुझे ज़रा भी यह ख़्याल होता कि एक नयी आज़माइश हमारी हो रही है और नये सवाल हमारे सामने पेश हैं, तो शायद मैं आसानी से अपने काम को छोड़ के न आता। जब आप का निमंत्रण मिला था मुझे,[97] उस वक़्त यों तो हज़ार सवाल रहते हैं पेचीदा लेकिन मैं खिंचा था आपके पास आने के लिए क्योंकि आख़िर में जो हमारे छात्र हैं, यूनिवर्सिटीज़ में कालेज में पढ़ते हैं उन्हीं को भारत का बोझा उठाना है आज नहीं तो कल, कल नहीं तो परसों [तालियां] और इसलिए यह बहुत ज़रूरी है और मुझे पसन्द है कि उनसे कुछ सम्बन्ध हो कुछ मैं उनसे कह सकूं और कुछ उनका मैं सुन सकूं।

मुझे अक्सर एक डर सा होता है कि मेरे ज़माने के लोग और मैं हमारा दिमाग कहां तक मिलता जुलता है आजकल के नौजवानों से, मुश्किल होता है हमेशा। बाप बेटा कभी पूरी तौर से नहीं मिलता है। ज्यों ज्यों जनरेशन आती है, बदलता है। नसीहत सब देने को तैयार होते हैं, मैं भी कभी कभी नसीहत देने को तैयार होता हूं। लेकिन नसीहत से कुछ फ़ायदा कभी हो, असल में समझना होता है और जब बहुत फ़र्क़ होता है उम्र में तो कुछ समझने में दिक़्क़त हो जाती है, कठिनाई हो जाती है और आप जानते हैं मेरी उम्र काफ़ी लम्बी-चौड़ी हो गयी [हंसी] आप एक ज़िन्दगी के अपने नये नये काम करने के दरवाज़े पर हैं।

---

93. Rabindranath Tagore.
94. Speech at the inauguration of the Union 26 October 1962. NMML, AIR Tapes, TS No. 8425, 8426, NM No. 1655, 1656.
95. Joginder Singh Sethi.
96. C.D. Deshmukh.
97. See item 130.

तो ख़ैर, जब आपके यहां से दावत आई, यहां के आपके छात्रसंघ के उद्घाटन के लिए, तो मैंने ख़ुशी से मंजूर किया। और मैंने सोचा कि आप लोगों को, आप लोगों से मिलकर, देख कर, मैं नहीं जानता कि मेरे कुछ कहने से आपको क्या फायदा हो, लेकिन आप सभी को देखकर आपके जोश को देखकर कुछ मुझे ज़रूर फ़ायदा हुआ [तालियां] और इसलिए ख़ुदगर्ज़ी से मैं यहां आया। [हंसी]

लेकिन फिर बाद में नयी नयी बातें हुईं, अजीब किस्मत का खेल है या शैतान का है, क्या है मैं नहीं जानता, के नये नये सवाल हमारे मुल्क के सामने पेश किये जो कि काफ़ी मुश्किल हैं, कठिन हैं। हम, अजीब बात यह है कि हम जो कि अपनी राय में और ख़ाली अपनी राय में नहीं औरों की राय में भी बहुतों की दुनियां में हम एक अमन और शान्ति का झण्डा ले के फिरते थे सब जगह। हमने जो कि मेरी जवानी के ज़माने में एक अपनी आज़ादी की लड़ाई भी हमने एक शान्ति के रास्ते पर चल के की। हमारे जो सिखाने वाले हमारे नेता जो बड़े थे, गांधी जी, उनका कुछ असर पड़ा। हालांकि हम नालायक़ थे, उनके असर को पूरा क़बूल हम नहीं कर सके, [हंसी] लेकिन फिर भी असर पड़ा, और कोई आदमी भी, कोई शख़्स भी, जिसको मौक़ा मिला हो उनके पास कुछ दिन रहने का, कुछ न कुछ असर हुआ है उस पर चाहे कित्ता ही नालायक़ हो वो। तो यह सब बातें एक तरफ़। फिर हम आज़ाद हुए और हमने लम्बी लम्बी बातें की शान्ति की दुनिया में फिर और बावजूद इन सब बातों के, अब हमें एक ऐसा इत्तफ़ाक़ हमारे सामने आ गया, कि जब हमें हथियारबंद होना पड़ता है और हथियारों को लेके लड़ाई लड़नी है। इसलिए मैं आपसे कहता था कि अजीब क़िस्मत का खेल है यह, कि हमें चिढ़ाने के लिए, हमें परेशान करने को, जो बाहर की परेशानी है वो तो जो कुछ है उसका सामना होता है, लेकिन एक दिल की परेशानी, ख़ैर वो हुई। फिर कुछ थोड़ा सा मेरा ख़्याल हुआ था कि मैं आपसे माफ़ी मांगू आज न आऊं। इसलिए नहीं कि यह वाक़्या हुआ, इसलिए कि बहुत काम में फंसा हूँ। लेकिन मुझे यह ग़लत मालूम हुआ, क्योंकि मैंने सोचा कि इससे ज़्यादा अच्छे एक सभा में आडियन्स मुझे कहां मिल सकती है। कि दिल्ली के यूनिवर्सिटी के छात्रसंघ के लोग हज़ारों लड़के लड़कियां मिलें, एक, एक तरह से भारत के नौजवानों का नमूना। तो अच्छा है कि मैं आऊँ और कुछ आपके उत्साह से आपके जोश से, आपके चेहरों से, कुछ मेरी भी कुछ ताक़त बढ़े।

क्या बात हुई? आप जानते हैं आपके सदर साहब ने भी कुछ ज़िक्र किया, चीनी आक्रमण का। वो तो हुआ, लेकिन एक बात हुई है जिसमें एक हमारा अध्याय ख़त्म कर दिया है, दूसरा अध्याय शुरू किया है हमारी क़ौमी ज़िंदगी में। एक सफ़ा उलट गया। नये सफ़े खुले हैं और उस पर हमको और आपको लिखना है क्योंकि हर ज़माने में क़ौम अपना इतिहास खुद लिखती है अपने काम से अपने कारनामों से अपनी हिम्मत से। वो इतिहास के लिखने वाले तो बाद में आते हैं, लेकिन असल इतिहास लोग अपने काम से, अपनी हरकतों से लिखते हैं। कभी कभी ज़ोरों का इतिहास लिखते हैं। हमने भी कुछ अपनी जवानी के ज़माने में हिन्दुस्तान की आज़ादी की जंग में कुछ न कुछ करा। हमने

127

मैंने नहीं लाखों आदमियों ने भारत के। आप तो नौजवान हैं शायद आपने कहानियां सुनी हों, आपको अपना तजुर्बा नहीं उसका। लेकिन जो लोग जिन लोगों ने उसमें हिस्सा लिया था उनके दिल पर छापा है उसका दिलो-दिमाग़ पर। कभी कभी मैं सोचता था कि कैसे आजकल के लोगों पर कुछ वो असर हो जो हम पर हुआ था, ज़बरदस्त असर हुआ था, जबकि हम भूल गये थे बहुत कुछ बातें जो आमतौर से जिसमें हम दिलचस्पी लेते थे और कुछ मजनूँ की तरह से एक तरफ़ चलते थे और फ़िक्र नहीं थी कि क्या उसका नतीजा हो जब तक कि हम ताक़त से चलते जायें। इस क़िस्म का अभ्यास, इस क़िस्म का तजुर्बा, क़ौम के लिए अच्छा होता है हालांकि तकलीफ़देह होता है और मैं देखता था कि हमारे हज़ारों सवाल हैं हिन्दुस्तान में, मुश्किल सवाल हैं, लेकिन कुछ एक कमी सी मुझे नज़र आती थी मुझे कभी कभी, कि लोग छोटी छोटी बातों में फंस जाते हैं, छोटे झगड़ों में फंस जाते हैं। बहसें होती हैं, कभी कभी वो फ़िरक़ापरस्ती में, साम्प्रदायिकता में, कभी भाषा के ऊपर झगड़े होते हैं कभी। और ऐसी बातें हैं हमारे देश में, बहुत ऐसी बातें हैं जो दीवारें खड़ी कर देती हैं एक के दूसरे के बीच।

प्रान्तीयता है, किस तरह से इसमें से निकल कर हम ज़रा एक अपने दिमाग़ को फैलायें, दिल को फैलायें और सारे हिन्दुस्तान को अपने सामने रखें? वाक़्या तो यह है कि ज़माना आने वाला है मेरी उम्र में तो न आये, ज़िंदगी में आपके आयेगा, जब कि जो यह एक एक देश की राष्ट्रीयता है वो भी फैल के शायद दुनियां भर को अपने साये में ले आये। वन-वर्ल्ड का आजकल सवाल होता है हालांकि वन-वर्ल्ड से हम बहुत दूर हैं लेकिन क्योंकि कोई चारा नहीं है कभी न कभी आयेगी, दुनियां तबाह हो जायेगी क्योंकि जो विज्ञान ने जो टैक्नोलोजी ने तरक्क़ी की है वो रोज़-ब-रोज़ दीवारें हटाती हैं। लेकिन हमारे दिल में और दिमाग़ में दीवारें बनी वो कैसे हटायें वो? तो वो आयेगा ज़माना, अभी नहीं है। लेकिन हम तो उस राष्ट्रीयपन पर भी हम उसका चर्चा बहुत करते थे लेकिन जब हमारा इतिहास होता है तो हम फ़ौरन छोटे से गिरोह में हो जाते हैं चाहे वह प्रान्त का हो चाहे एक भाषा बोलने वालों का हो या मज़हब के नाम से हो या जात-वात का हो। कित्ते हम पिछड़े हुए हैं राष्ट्रीयता से भी, दुनियां की बातें तो छोड़िए। यह ख़्याल आते थे मुझे, और सोचता था मैं कि ये बातें क़ौम अपने आप सीखले तो बहुत अच्छा। दिल्ली यूनिवर्सिटी में बहुत अच्छे, यक़ीनन आप पढ़ते लिखते हैं, सीखते हैं, और उससे आप ढलते हैं लेकिन वाक़्या यह है कि क़ौम आख़िर में ढलती है अपने तजुर्बे से, अपनी तकलीफ़ से, अपनी मुसीबत से, सामना कर के बड़े-बड़े सवालों का, बड़ी-बड़ी दिक़्क़तों का कठिनाईयों का इस तरह ढलते हैं लोग।

इसी तरह से गांधी जी का नाम आपने सुना, बहुत कम लोगों ने उनको देखा होगा। गांधी जी ने क्या किया? ख़ैर, उनका मुकाबला करना किसी से तो मुश्किल है अब या कभी भी इतिहास में। उन्होंने हिन्दुस्तान के करोड़ों आदमियों को और ऐसे लोगों को जो बेचारे अनपढ़ ग़रीब से ग़रीब किसान थे, मुरझाये हुए थे, जिनकी आंखें धसी हुई थी, नाउम्मीद थे, निराश थे। उनमें उन्होंने जान डाली उनको उन्होंने एक कुछ उम्मीद दी, आशाएं दी,

उनकी कमर सीधी की, उनकी आंखें कुछ चमकने लगी, बड़ी बात थी हालांकि उनके पास कुछ पैसा नहीं ज़्यादा आ गया जो असली चीज़ होती है, क़ौम में एक जान और एक हिम्मत, वो डाली। आपके बहुत पढ़े लिखे आदमियों को मैं नहीं कहता मामूली हिन्दुस्तान के ग़रीब आदमी क्योंकि वो उसी दर्जे पर उन्होंने अपने को रखा था। और हमने देखा इस जादू को, किस तरह से उन्होंने हिन्दुस्तान के करोड़ों आदमियों को बदल दिया और इसी वजह से हम कामयाब हुए, सफ़ल हुए, आज़ाद हुए। क्योंकि एक अजीब चीज़ थी वो, कि करोड़ों आदमी इस तरह से जानदार हो जायें और कुछ कुछ डिसिपलिण्ड हो जायें। ख़ैर वो ज़माना गया, बहुत नयी बातें हुई। इस तरह की बातें करने की हमें ख़ास ज़रूरत नहीं रही आजकल के ज़माने में लेकिन फिर भी यह सवाल अकसर मेरे सामने आता था कि कैसे कोई ऐसा तजुर्बा हो, लाखों करोड़ों को, जिससे वो फिर ज़रा ढलें, फिर से कुछ लोहापन आये उन को। और नहीं तो कुछ हम, हम कोई तो बड़े आरामतलब नहीं हैं हिन्दुस्तान में क़ौम हम ऐसे दौलतमन्द मुल्क नहीं है कि आरामतलब क़ौम हो। लेकिन आरामतलब न भी होते हुए एक कमज़ोरी आ जाती है इंसान में। कुछ आसमान की तरफ़ देखने की आदत नहीं होती, बहुत नीचे कदमों की तरफ़ देखते हैं। छोटी बातों में पड़ जाते हैं, छोटी बहसों की तरफ़ देखते हैं। छोटी बातों में पड़ जाते हैं, छोटी बहसों में और छोटी बहसों में लोग ज़्यादातर पड़ जाते हैं तो उनका मुल्क भी उस क़दर छोटा हो जाता है। यह ख़्याल थे।

आप देखें कि पिछले पचास बरसों में या कित्ते बरस हुए मुझे याद नहीं, दो बड़ी लड़ाइयां हुई दुनिया में। ज़बर्दस्त लड़ाइयां हुई अब हम इंतजार कर रहे हैं, कहिए, तीसरी का। वह दो लड़ाइयां हुई। उन दो लड़ाइयों में अच्छा बुरा मैं नहीं कहता कुछ, लेकिन एक ज़ाती तजुर्बा हासिल किया। योरोप के लोगों ने एशिया के कुछ लोगों ने, कुछ अमेरिका के भी। कोई घर नहीं है योरोप में, कोई परिवार नहीं है जिसमें से कोई न कोई रिश्तेदार लड़का वग़ैरह लड़ाई में मरा न हो। तो इससे वो लड़ाई एक दूर की चीज़ नहीं रही और हम अख़बारों में पढ़ें उसका अपना असर हुआ और क़ौम भर पर असर हुआ, बुरा या अच्छा जो कुछ है। इस क़िस्म का तजुर्बा हमें नहीं हासिल हुआ है ज़माने से। मैं लड़ाई के हक़ में नहीं हूँ। बहुत ग़लत समझता हूँ ख़ासकर आज कल जो लड़ाई हो उसको। लेकिन यह उसमें बात होती है, कुछ आदमी को मारती भी है और ज़िंदा भी करती है, जान भी देती है। तो यह तजुर्बा हुआ, योरोप में हम पहले तो अंग्रेज़ी हुकूमत के नीचे जो कुछ कहिए पैस ब्रिटेनिका कहलाती थी। हमें पसन्द नहीं थी, न होनी चाहिए थी। लेकिन नतीजा उसका यह हुआ कि हम समझने लगे कि क़ौम ख़ाली तक़रीर करने से आगे बढ़ती है।

गांधी जी आए, उन्होंने दिखाया कि क़ौम इस तरह से नहीं बढ़ती कुछ और करना होता है और बहुत लोगों ने किया वो और उससे वो बढ़े आगे मज़बूत हुए और हिन्दुस्तान का नाम अगर आजकल दुनियां में है तो गांधी की वजह से है, हम आजकल छुटभइये हैं, हम क्या उसका नाम करें? तो यह हुआ। लेकिन फिर भी कुछ हमारे दिमाग़ में यह बात रही, हमारे से मतलब है हिन्दुस्तान के लोगों के, कि तक़रीरें कर के जुलूस निकाल के,

129

नारे उठा के सब काम हो जाते हैं। अब मैं नारों के जलूस के ख़िलाफ़ नहीं हूं, वक़्त आये करना चाहिए अच्छा है जोश बढ़ता है लेकिन यह समझना कि उससे असली काम होते हैं यह अपने को धोखा देना है। तो कुछ समझ नहीं है हमें, हमारी क़ौम को। आजकल की दुनियां कैसी है, सख़्त है, बेरहम है और काफ़ी क़ीमत देनी पड़ती है तरक़्क़ी के लिए, मेहनत से मुसीबत से ले के, अपनी आज़ादी रखने के लिए भी काफ़ी क़ीमत देनी होती है। और यह न समझिए कि आज़ादी एक दफ़ा आ गयी तो आ गयी। आज़ादी को रोज़ आपको रखने के लिए रोज़ कुछ न कुछ करना होता है, हर वक़्त होशियार रहना होता है, और हिफ़ाज़त के लिए। हर वक़्त तैयार रहना होता है उसको जो कुछ हमें क़ीमत देनी है [आज़ादी] रखने के लिए, जहां ज़रा ग़फ़लत हुई ढील हुई वो फिसलने लगती है। हमारे इतिहास में काफ़ी हमने देखा है, कैसे हमारी आज़ादी बार बार फिसली। क्योंकि हमारी ग़फ़लत में, हमारी ना-इत्तफ़ाक़ी में, आपस की फूट में, बाहर का दुश्मन आया और उसने एक एक टुकड़े को दबा लिया और दूसरे लोग देखते रहे गये, फ़िक्र ही नहीं थी।

तो यह सब मैंने आपसे कहा इस सिलसिले में अब आप देखिए 15 वर्ष हुए हमें आज़ाद हुए हमारे देश को 16 बरस, 17 बरस कित्ते बरस हुए? और उसमें हमने मेरा ख़्याल है काफ़ी तरक़्क़ी भी की है बहुत बातों में, काफ़ी ग़लतियां भी कीं, अक्सर ठोकर खा के गिरे फिर उठे, फिर चले। ऐसे क़ौमें बढ़ती हैं, ठोकर खा कर गिरने से कोई नहीं डरना चाहिए। अगर जब एक, के आपके पास में दम हो फिर खड़े होके आगे बढ़ने का। तो वो सब हुआ। लेकिन वो बात मैं समझता हूं कुछ आप लोग, हिन्दुस्तान के लोग पूरे नहीं समझे, जो कि कुछ योरोप अमेरिका के लोग समझे हैं, क्योंकि उनको तजुर्बा है उन बड़ी लड़ाइयों का। हमारे लिए लड़ाई एक चीज़ है जिसको हम पढ़ते हैं क़िस्से कहानियों में। हां, हम लड़ाई के ख़िलाफ़ हैं आप कह दें। सभी कहेंगे कौन लड़ाई के हक़ में है? लेकिन वो एक तजुर्बा उसका एक इमोशनल इम्पैक्ट [emotional impact] उसका हमारे ऊपर नहीं हुआ है। ज़रा सी लड़ाई में कुछ आसाम के कोने में पिछली लड़ाई में हो गया था हम पर असर नहीं हुआ। तो इसलिए ग़फ़लत में हम थे।

यह सब भूमिका, मैंने आपको सुनाई, इसलिए कि अब जो वाक़्यात हुए हैं वो कुछ हमारी सारी क़ौम को हिलाने वाले हैं। क्या हुआ? एक कहानी आप जानते हैं, पिछले पांच बरस से चीनी लोगों ने हमारे देश पे कुछ न कुछ हमला किया, आक्रमण किया हल्के हल्के। लद्दाख़ के हिस्से को दबाया और हम उनसे डर नहीं गये, यह तो गलत बात है कहना। लेकिन हम चाहते थे कि हो सके तो यह मामला कुछ बा-अमन तरीक़ों से निश्चय किया जाये कुछ फ़ैसला हो क्योंकि हम जानते थे कि चीन जैसे महान देश से लड़ाई न हमारे लिए अच्छी, न उनके लिए, न दुनियां के लिए। हमने सारे तरीक़े किए, कोशिश की उसमें कामयाबी नहीं हुई। पांच बरस से यह सिलसिला चला आता था। और उसका हम भी चर्चा करते थे आप भी, कि हमारी सीमा के झगड़े। अब एक नयी बात हुई, यह सारी दिक्क़तें, ये सारी बातें झगड़े वग़ैरह हमले, आक्रमण लद्दाख़ की सीमा पर जो हुए।

अब सीमा प्रान्त जो हमारी है, जिसको हम नेफ़ा कहते हैं नार्थ ईस्ट्रन फरंटीयर ऐजन्सी उसकी भी जो सरहद थी, और है मैकमहान लाइन। कभी कभी कहते हैं जो कि हिमालय के सब में ऊंचा पहाड़ जो वाटर शैड है, जहां पानी इधर या उधर बहता है, जो एक ज़माने से बहुत ज़माने से वो समझा जाता है और मैकमहान का नाम उसमें लग गया। इसलिए कोई पचास बरस हुए एक समझौते के लिए बातचीत हुई थी, कुछ तिब्बती नुमाइन्दे आये थे हमारे थे, हमारे से मतलब गवर्नमेंट आफ़ इंडिया के थे और कुछ चीन के भी, तो मैकमहान इसमें था। तो बातचीत के बाद वो जो पुराने ज़माने से सरहद समझी जाती थी, यानी हिमालय के पहाड़ की चोटी उधर जो हिमालय की रिज है, कोई नयी लाइन इन्होंने नहीं खींची बल्कि पुरानी को मंज़ूर कर के उन्होंने कह दिया कि यह है और एक नक़शा बना दिया और लिख दिया कि हिमालय की वाटर शैड है।

ख़ैर, तो हालांकि चीन ने एक पुराने नक़्शे निकाले, पुराने से मतलब अभी बीस-पच्चीस बरस के जिसमें उन्होंने बड़े हिस्से लद्दाख़ के, बड़े हिस्से नेफ़ा के दिखाये थे, कि होने चाहिए? इस पर हमने उनके लोग हमारे लोग, मिले भी थे और मेरी राय में आप भी देख सकते हैं, छपी बातें हैं उन्होंने रिपोर्ट पेश की। और इसकी शहादत उन्होंने साफ़ कर दी जिससे कोई किसी को शक न रहे कि हमारा जो मुक़दमा था वो सही था उनका ग़लत था। ख़ैर यहां इस सीमा पर, पूर्वी सीमा पर, वो कभी इसके पार नहीं आये थे सिवाए एक छोटा सा गांव है। उसका शायद आपने नाम सुना हो लौंगजू ज़रा सा उस पर बहस थी कि वो मैकमहान लाइन के इधर है कि उधर है अलावा इसके वो नहीं आया इधर। बल्कि कई बातें हुई इस दौरान में जब कि उन्होंने अपने, अपनी कार्यवाही से एक्शन से एक माने में तसलीम किया कि वही हमारी हिमालय की रिज जो है वो वही हमारी सीमा, सरहद है। एक और बात हुई कि बर्मा से उनकी एक सन्धि हुई, वो मैकमहान लाइन वहां भी आगे जाती थी उसको वहां उन्होंने स्वीकार कर लिया, मंजूर कर लिया तो हमें और भी यक़ीन हुआ कि उसको मंजूर कर चुके। उसूल एक है तो यहां भी करेंगे और उन्होंने क़रीब क़रीब हमसे कहा भी, मैं नहीं कहना चाहता कि उन्होंने इक़रार किया कि नहीं है, लेकिन अपने बर्ताव से हमें ज़ाहिर किया कि उसको मंज़ूर करते हैं।

ख़ैर, बारह बरस से ये चीन में जो आजकल हुकूमत है वह क़ायम है वह, इस बारह बरस में और हम मैकमहान लाइन के इस पार वह कभी आए नहीं, ना कोई ख़ास कोशिश की। अब यकायक बावजूद इसके कि यह लद्दाख़ में बहुत बढ़े थे अब इस, कोई तारीख़ आठ सितम्बर को डेढ़ महीना पौने दो महीने हुए वो पहली दफे वहां जो पास है वहां से उतर के कुछ लोग आये। वहां हमारे पास के नीचे ही हमारे कुछ थोड़ी सी फ़ौज, थोड़े से पोस्ट थे, मिलिटरी पोस्ट, वह आये, उनके ज़रा दूर पर उतर के आ गये, और जो हमें एक पहली बात थी, पहले हम समझे कि कुछ यह थोड़े से आये हैं लोग कुछ मुलाहज़ा करने, देखने, हालांकि एक नई बात थी [हंसी] फिर भी हम उसको यह नहीं समझे कि यह कोई बड़ा हमला है। बहरसूरत मैं उस वक़्त, उसके एक रोज़ पहले चला गया था विलायत, कामन वैल्थ प्राइम मिनिस्टर्स कांफ्रेन्स में। लेकिन जैसे ही यह मालूम हुआ हमें, तो हमने यह कहा अपनी फ़ौज वालों से कि तुम वहां, हमारी थोड़ी बहुत ये पोस्ट थे सौ सौ आदमी

के डेढ़ सौ, बड़ी फौज तो थी नहीं कि ज़रा दूर थी तुम अपनी फौज भेजो वहां उनको हटाने के लिए जो आये हैं, यह वहां जम न जायें। अब उसमें एक बात थी उनको वहां आना आसान था हमें जाना ज़रा मुश्किल था। क्योंकि उनके इस पहाड़ के, हिमालय के उस तरफ़, तिब्बत का प्लाटो है, ऊंची चीज़ उसमें ज़रा ही सी थी और क़रीब मैदान तो नहीं लेकिन मैदान सा है, बड़े ऊंचे पहाड़ नहीं उसमें सड़के बन सकती हैं, बनायी चीनियों ने, तो सड़क-सड़क वह आ जाते थे उस रिज के पास तक, फिर ज़रा सा चढ़ाई चढ़ के वह रिज के ऊपर आ के, फिर इधर उतर आय। हमें, हमारी तरफ़ सारे हिमालय पहाड़ की बेहद चोटियां हैं और बहुत दूर तक, दूर से लाना पड़े और सड़के नहीं। कुछ नहीं, सड़कें हमने बहुत बनाई हैं, फिर भी बहुत जगह ख़ाली और यह जगह याद रखिये चौदह हज़ार, पन्द्रह हज़ार से अठारह हज़ार फ़ीट से ऊंची है जहां कि मामूली तौर से आप अगर जायें तो आपको सांस लेने में भी कुछ तकलीफ़ हो, कम से कम शुरू में। तो हमने कहा कि तैयारी करो फौज की तो उन्होंने कुछ फौज भेजनी शुरू की और भेजी भी कुछ, वहां पहुंच भी गयी और हम चाहते थे कि वहां से हटा दिये जायें। लेकिन जब हम फ़ौज भेज रहे थे वहां, उन्होंने भी फ़ौजें भेजी अपनी और उनको ज़्यादा आसान था क्योंकि, एक तिब्बत आप जानते हैं तिब्बत में उनकी बेशुमार फ़ौजें हैं शायद हमारी सब फ़ौजों को मिला के ज़्यादा फ़ौजें तिब्बत में जमा हैं क्योंकि तिब्बत में उनकी, तिब्बत को दबाने के लिए काफ़ी फ़ौजे ले गये थे वो। और वह सड़कों से हिमालय के उस पार तक आ जाती हैं। फिर ज़रा सी चढ़ाई चढ़ के उतर सकते हैं वह।

ख़ैर, यह सब कुछ हुआ। आठ सितम्बर से शुरू अक्टूबर आया। कुछ हमारी भी ताक़त वहां बन गई लेकिन फिर हमने देखा, मालूम हुआ कि उनकी ताक़त बहुत बढ़ गई है, बहुत फ़ौजें, बेशुमार फ़ौजें ले आये हैं। फिर बीस अक्टूबर को उन्होंने एक बड़ा हमला किया हमारी फ़ौजों पर। अब यह ग़ौरतलब बात है कि हम पर हमला किया, ख़ाली वहां नहीं क़रीब क़रीब सारे हमारी सीमा पर, लद्दाख़ से ले के वहां तक, उन्होंने हमला किया और जैसा वह हमला था वो ऐसा था कि जिसकी तैयारी में काफ़ी दिन लगते हैं, हफ़्तों लगे बहुत तैयारी से सामान लाये, बहुत तैयारी से और इंतज़ाम से वहां से यहां तक और बड़ी ज़बरदस्त फ़ौजें चारों तरफ़ ख़ैर वो आये। हमला किया और सारी दुनियां में मशहूर किया कि हम तो अपने घर में बैठे थे हिन्दुस्तान वाले हम पर हमला करते जाते हैं। और अजीब बात यह है कि उन्होंने पहले इस बात का एलान किया कि हिन्दुस्तान हमला कर रहा है, क़ब्ल इसके कि कोई भी वहां लड़ाई हुई हो एक आधे घण्टे पहले यह बात शुरू हुई। यानी पहले उन्होंने ऐलान कर दिया कि हिन्दुस्तान कर रहा है हमला। हिन्दुस्तान के हमले करने में कोई ग़लत बात नहीं थी अगर करता लेकिन वाक़्या मैं आपको बता रहा हूँ कि इत्ते बड़े पैमाने पर उन्होंने हमला किया और दुनियां में गुल मचाना शुरू किया कि हम बेगुनाह हैं, हम पर हमला कर रहा है।

ख़ैर, उसका नतीजा यह हुआ कि हमारे उन्होंने कई पोस्ट पर कब्ज़ा किया। धकेल दिया हमारी फ़ौज को क्योंकि उनकी बहुत फ़ौजें बहुत ज़्यादा थीं और कुछ हथियार भी ज़्यादा ज़बरदस्त थे जिनका असर दूर तक जाये। उससे हमें धक्का लगा। और कई बातें

उसके बाद हुई हैं। जिनकी ख़बर सुन के हमें तकलीफ़ हुई, परेशानी हुई और हमें कुछ परेशानी यहां दिल्ली में हो रही है। जो बेचारे हमारे सिपाही अफ़सर और सिपाही बहुत बहादुरी से लड़े उनकी परेशानी का हाल आप समझ सकते हैं क्या होगी।

अच्छा पहली बात मैं चाहता हूं कि आप समझ जायें। यह चीज़ इसका रंग बदल गया, यह कोई सरहद के किनारे कोई छोटी मोटी लड़ाई का रंग नहीं रहा, यह एक इत्ते बड़े पैमाने पर तैयारी से इन्होंने किया, और कर के करते जाते हैं अब भी यानी यह एक सारे हिन्दुस्तान पर एक हमला करना है, इन्वेजन-आफ इंडिया [invasion of India] है वह बात रह गई कि एक छोटे से सरहद पर कुछ बहस हो हम में उनमें, कोई झगड़ा हो ज़रा सा वह आगे आ जाये, यह हिन्दुस्तान भर पे हमला हो रहा है। उसी तरह से हमें समझना है। यह बात सही है कि न उन्होंने न हमने ज़ाप्ते से ये नहीं कहा है कि हिन्दुस्तान में और चीन में, घोषणा नहीं की है लड़ाई की, वार डिक्लेयर नहीं की। लेकिन वाक़्या यह है कि वही बातें हो रही हैं। हमने नहीं की, बाज़ लोग कहते हैं क्यों नहीं कर देते? यह मैं ज़्यादा नहीं जाना चाहता, लेकिन बात यह है कि जो कुछ हम कर सकते हैं वह करेंगे, कोई रूकावट नहीं है उसके करने से, कुछ और दिक्क़तें पेश आ जा सकती हैं, ख़ैर, वह समझने की बात है कोई बात नहीं है। लेकिन बात यह है कि हिन्दुस्तान के ऊपर एक बड़ा हमला ज़बरदस्त, बहुत दिनों बाद हुआ है और ख़तरनाक हमला बड़ी फ़ौजों से, बड़े हथियारों से और उसमें शुरू शुरू में हमें काफ़ी धक्का उससे पहुंचा, असर हुआ जहां जहां वह पहुंचा है। मैं नहीं कह सकता कि कित्ते और धक्के हमें लगे, लेकिन यह मैं ज़रूर कह सकता हूं कि चाहे एक धक्का लगे, दो लगे, आज लगे, कल लगे, हमें उसका सामना करके उसको हटाना है और आख़िरी धक्का हमारा ही होगा। [तालियां]

अब इसमें कोई शेख़ी की बात नहीं है, मैं शेख़ी करूं या आप करें? क्योंकि नारों और शेख़ी का ज़माना गुज़र गया। यह एक सख़्त मुकाबला है, इसमें कोई शक नहीं कि सख़्त मुक़ाबला है और सख़्त मुक़ाबले को हम अपनी आवाज़ी नारों से नहीं हटा सकते। काफ़ी हमें मुसीबत झेलनी पड़ेगी। हमारी सारी ज़िन्दगी का तर्ज़ कोई लड़ाई लड़ने का नहीं है। फ़ौज हमारी अच्छी है, एक फ़ौज है अलग है, ट्रेण्ड किया, अच्छी बहादुर है। लेकिन हमारा सारा ज़िन्दगी का हमारी आर्थिक हालत जो है वह लड़ाई लड़ने के लिए नहीं बनी है और भी योरोप के मुल्कों में आप देखिए अक्सर मुल्कों में कांस्क्रिपशन conscription है और तजुर्बा उनको लड़ाई का इत्ता है कि और भी उसके लिए एक माने में किसी क़दर तैयार रहते हैं। और इन मुल्कों में आप जाइए जैसे चीन है वह एक तो हर वक़्त उनकी बुनियाद है लड़ाई लड़ने की तैयारी, और उसी के लिए उसको अव्वल रख के उसके लिए तैयार रहना। वहां कोई बात उन्हें करनी होती है वह एकदम से कर सकते हैं, कानून बनाना होता है वह डिग्री निकाल देते हैं, हो गया। हम, ये जमहूरियत में, डेमोक्रेसी में क़दम पेचीदा होते हैं, देर लगती है उसमें और हज़ार नुक़्ताचीनी होती है। ख़ैर यह डेमोक्रेसी की कुछ कमज़ोरियां कहिए लेकिन मेरा ख़्याल है कि असल में डेमोक्रेसी का रास्ता सही है बिलकुल मुझे यक़ीन है। हालांकि शुरू में ऐसे मौक़ों पर उसमें कुछ कमज़ोरियां आ जाती हैं आख़िर

133

में वह ताक़त पकड़ती है और आख़िर में उसकी जीत होती है [तालियां] तो लेकिन शुरू में धक्के लगते हैं क्योंकि दूसरी दूसी मुख़ालिफ़ क़ौमें हैं, वह हथियार हर वक़्त रखती हैं तैयार। हमारे हथियार कहीं इतमीनान से आजायबघरों में रहते हैं या और जगहों पर रहते हैं ज्यादातर तो यह सवाल पेश हुआ। शायद बहुत इसमें काफ़ी इसके पहलु हैं, इस सवाल के नुक़सानदेह, लेकिन यह एक शायद अच्छा हो मुफ़ीद हो कि यह हमारे लोगों को ज़रा जगा दे और दिखा दे, कि कैसी दुनियां में हम रहते हैं।

एक बेरहम दुनियां है, सख़्त दुनियां है, कमज़ोरों की नहीं है, और ताक़त तभी आती है जब कि हम लोग एक दिल हो कर, मिलकर, एक क़ौम हो के कोई काम करें, बड़ा काम। और अगर हम हर वक़्त आपस में फूट हो, और बहसें करें छोटी-छोटी बातों पर, तो हम कमज़ोर होते हैं और मुल्क हमें दबा सकते हैं। तो शायद इससे फ़ायदा हो हमें। इत्ता मुल्क में अगर यह पूरी तौर से हो जाये, लेकिन मेरा कहना यह है और मैं एक इतमीनान से आपसे कहता हूं मुझे यक़ीन है कि यह जो चीनी हमला हुआ है इसको हम हटायेंगे लेकिन अब आप ज़ोरों की ताली बजाने लगिये तो यह भी बात है कि आप कुछ उसको नहीं समझे कि क्या क्या करना पड़ेगा आपको और हम सभी को, क़ब्ल इसके कि वह हटें। उसको समझ के ताली बजे तो ज्यादा माने हैं। नहीं तो इस तरह अगर हमारे दिलों की ख़्वाहिशें पूरी हो जाया करें तब तो बड़ा आसान है, दुनियां को हम अपने ढंग का बना लें। यह सब बातें लेकिन उसके लिए बड़ी मेहनत करनी पड़ती है।और यह समझना है हमें कि, इस वक़्त हमारा मुक़ाबला एक मुल्क से हो रहा है जिसकी शायद फ़ौज दुनियां में सब में बड़ी हो, कोई मुल्क से इसका नम्बर हो मैं नहीं कहता पर उनकी ताक़त इत्ती बड़ी है ज़ाहिर है रूस की ज्यादा है, ज़ाहिर है अमेरिका की ज्यादा है। लेकिन वो हथियारों की और बातों की है, लेकिन फ़ौज जित्ती बड़ी चीन की है इत्ती बड़ी किसी की नहीं है इस वक़्त। [हंसी] और यह मेरी समझ में नहीं आया यह हंसी की क्या बात हुई। [हंसी] आपने इसे कुछ मज़ाक समझा है?

तो इस तरह से कोई मुक़ाबला करना और ख़ाली फ़ौज की बात नहीं, एक पुराना मुल्क है ताकतवर मुल्क है और कट्टर मुल्क है, यह सब बातें ताक़त बढ़ाती हैं। हम नहीं चाहते थे, हम दो मुल्क एशिया के सब में पुराने जिनका इतिहास हज़ारों बरस से चला आता है और आज तक इन हज़ारों बरस में हमारा और चीन में कोई झगड़ा नहीं हुआ ग़ैर मामूली बात है। तो अब हम एक दूसरे के आमने सामने खड़े हो जाएं, मुक़ाबला करने। तो ज़ाहिर है वो नुक़सान हमें पहुंचा सकता है और मैं समझता हूं हम भी उनको पहुंचा सकते हैं और यह मुक़ाबला हो एक दूसरे को नुक़सान पहुंचाना, आजकल की दुनियां में यह कोई बहुत अक़्ल की बात नहीं है, सभ्यता की बात नहीं है। लेकिन क्या किया जाए हमारे ऊपर हमला हो तो हम उसको बर्दाश्त करें, हम उसको स्वीकार करें, सिर झुका लें, घुटने टेक लें, यह तो नामुमकिन बात है, और उसका मुक़ाबला करना ही पड़ता है। कित्ती ही उसमें परेशानी हो, तकलीफ़ हो, यह एक चुनौती है, चैलेंज है, जिसको हमें लेना ही है।

तो अब आप लोग मालूम नहीं आपके छात्र-संघ के अध्यक्ष ने कुछ कहा, पहली नवम्बर को आप करने वाले हैं, सुना नहीं मैंने क्या कहा? कोई प्रदर्शन करेंगे, कोई आप जोश दिखाने का, ख़ैर करें आप। [हंसी] लेकिन, लेकिन मैं आपसे कहूं कि अच्छी बात है ऐसे भी होना अच्छा होता है लेकिन बहुत ज़्यादा असर उसका नहीं होता। सो और भी गज़ हैं जिससे नापें जायेंगे आपका जोश कित्ता है, और जिसमें महज़ एक सभा में या एक जुलूस में जा के आप कुछ करें वो काफ़ी नहीं है और उसमें आप की ताक़त कुछ सर्फ़ हो जाए। मैं इस वक़्त नहीं कह सकता कि किस किस तरह से आप क्या कीजिए? लेकिन वक़्त आ रहा है कि आपको, आपको क्या हम सभी को की आज़माइश सख़्त हो, और कुछ न कुछ हिदायत वग़ैरह हम देंगे आपके लिए, सभी के लिए।

एक छोटी सी बात तो मैं कह दूं कि आपको नेशनल कैडिट कोर्प्स में तो होना ही चाहिए [तालियां] उससे आप महज़ सिपाही नहीं बल्कि कुछ अफ़सरी भी, इसमें सीखते हैं। और हमें अगर हमें, फ़ौज बढ़ाना पड़े जैसे पड़ रहा है काफ़ी लोग होंगे, काफ़ी अफ़सरों को सिखाना पड़ेगा। हमारी ज़िन्दगी एक पलटा खा रही है और इसको आपको समझ लेना है और उसके लिए तैयार होना है। यह तो मैंने छोटी बात कही आपसे कि एन0सी0सी0 में आप हो जाएं, यह तो होना ही चाहिए जित्ते ज़्यादा हो सकें लड़के लड़कियां। लेकिन और भी कई बातें हम करेंगे उसके अलावा सब लोगों के लिए कुछ फ़ौजी तालीम वोलेंटीयर कोर्प्स वग़ैरह, कई बनेंगे।

अलावा फ़ौज के बढ़ने के वो तो है ही और दूसरी बात जो है तैयारी की मुल्क की, असल में मुल्क की तैयारी होती है कि फ़ौज में बड़ा सिपाही खड़ा होता है लड़ने को, उसके पीछे मैं नहीं जानता कित्ते पचास आदमी काम करें, तो वो लड़ सकता है। पचास या सौ आदमी मेहनत करें, पैदा करें, उत्पादन हो, प्रोडक्शन हो, उसके सहारे के लिए। यानी प्रोडक्शन हमें बढ़ाना है, खेती से, कारख़ानों से हर तरफ़ से, तब हम कर सकते हैं। तो इसके माने क्या हैं? सब से पहली बात तो यही है कि हमारा इरादा बिल्कुल पक्का हो जाए, एक मज़बूत लोहे का सा कि हमें एक बात करनी है, हम नहीं चाहते, कुछ भी हो कुछ भी नतीजा हो, हमें यह मंज़ूर नहीं है इस मुल्क में कि हम ज़बर के सामने सिर झुकायें या हमें हमारी क़ौम घुटनों के बल रहे यह मंज़ूर नहीं है। चाहे जो भी कुछ नतीजा हो, हम आज़ाद रहेंगे, सिर ऊंचा रहेगा, कमर सीधी रहेगी। फिर यह तय किया आपने, फिर उसके लिए आपको तैयार होना है, उसकी कीमत देनी है। जो क़ीमत एक एक शख़्स को देनी है ख़ाली अख़बारों में आप पढ़ लें कि फ़ौज लड़ रही है वह काफ़ी नहीं है, मुमकिन है ज़रूरत हो आपकी भी जानें की लड़ाई के मैदान में, या लड़ाई या उसके पीछे लड़ाई का सामान कुछ और काम करने को। यह हो सकता है लेकिन अलावा उसके हमें इस प्रोडक्शन के सिलसिले में ज़ोरों से काम करने हैं चाहे ज़मीन से, चाहे कारख़ाने से।

आप पढ़ते हैं और पढ़ना एक ज़रूरी चीज़ है। हम नहीं चाहते कि हमारी सरहद पर लड़ाई हो, तो पढ़ना लिखना लोग छोड़ दें, यह तो एक आइन्दा के लिए अपने को कमज़ोर करना है। क्योंकि एक मुल्क की ताक़त होती है आख़िर में क्वालिटी की, ट्रेण्ड आदमियों

135

की, जित्ती ज़्यादा आपकी ट्रेनिंग होगी आपकी क्वालिटी अच्छी होगी उत्ता ज़्यादा मुल्क बढ़ेगा, नम्बर ख़ाली गिनती से तो नहीं बढ़ता, ट्रेन्ड आदमियों से। तो मैं नहीं चाहता कि आप लिखना पढ़ना, बल्कि और ज़ोरों से कीजिए, लेकिन ऐसा मौक़ा भी आता है जब पढ़ना लिखना भी छोड़ देना पड़ता है, ऐसा ख़तरा हो। [तालियां] उसमें भी पढ़ना लिखना छोड़ने के माने आप समझ लीजिए [हंसी] यह नहीं कि पढ़ना लिखना छोड़ने के माने यह हैं कि उसके बजाए मुझे और ख़तरे का सामना करना पड़ता है। यह नहीं कि आप घर बैठ के पढ़ना लिखना छोड़ दें। आप, मैं चाहता हूं आप पढ़ें-लिखें और ज़ोरों से पढ़ें खूब तैयार हों, जो भी आप काम करें इसको करें ताकि कुछ भी आप को काम करना हो, उसका ज़ोरों से आप कर सकें। लेकिन अगर ऐसी मुसीबत आये कि हमें अपने नौजवानों को लड़ाई के मैदान में भेजना है, भेज दीजिए, भेजना होगा चाहे साल दो साल के लिए उनकी पढ़ाई रूक जाए, जो कुछ भी हो। क्योंकि जब एक मुल्क ज़िन्दा रहने और मरने का सवाल हो जाता है तब हर चीज़ पल्ले में डालनी पड़ती है जित्ती हमारी ताक़त हो।

तो यह हमारे लिए एक ज़बरदस्त चुनौती है किस्मत ने भेजी है हमें। हम में से ढीलापन निकल जाए मज़बूत हों हम। पहले उसके माने तो यह हैं कि हम सीखें कि हम में जो नाइत्तेफ़ाक़ियां हैं, झगड़े होते हैं छोटे मोटे, उनको भूल जाएं। भूलें कि याद करके उनको ख़त्म कर दें और यह ख्याल रखें कि हिन्दुस्तान में झगड़े होते हैं, सूबे के सूबे में, कौन ज़िले बढ़ जाए, घट जाएं सूबे के टुकड़े हों, भाषा हो, तरह तरह के, सब कुछ अहमीयत रखते होंगे अपने वक़्त में। लेकिन बड़े सवालों के सामने उनकी कोई अहमीयत नहीं है और एक क़ौम का इम्तेहान होता है कि वो क़ौम या कोई आदमी बड़े सवालों को सोचता है कि छोटी बातों में पड़ा रहता है। अगर छोटी में पड़ा रहता है तो ज़ाहिर है छोटी क़ौम हो जाती है बड़ी को सोचता है तो बढ़ता है।

तो पहली बात यह, जो आपने सुना है हम एकता को इमोशनल इनटीग्रेशन कहते हैं हिन्दुस्तान में। तो उसको इस मौक़े से इस ख़तरे से फ़ायदा उठा के उसे हमें पूरा करना है और हो सकता है क्योंकि कोई हम कोई नक़ली बात हिन्दुस्तान के लिए नहीं कहते हैं, कोई नयी चीज़ नहीं कहते हैं। हिन्दुस्तान के इतिहास में हमेशा एकता रही है चाहे अलग अलग हुकूमतें भी हों, तब भी हिन्दुस्तान में एकता रही है हां, उसी के साथ अनेकता भी रही है, डाइवरसिटी रही है। फ़र्क़ रहा है और यह हिन्दुस्तान की खूबी रही है कि दोनों बातें साथ रहें और दोनों हम रखना चाहते हैं। इसलिए अनेकता के माने नहीं हैं कि लोग लड़ें, बल्कि हम नहीं चाहते कि एक सब एक नाप के हों, एक चौड़ान के हों, यह बात फ़िजूल है। अपने अपने रास्ते पर चलें, लेकिन बुनियादी एकता को रख के। और यह समझ के हर बात में, कि अव्वल बात हमारी अपनी मुल्क की ख़िदमत करनी, मुल्क की तरक्की करनी, मुल्क की एकता रखनी, नहीं तो हम सब कमज़ोर हो जाते हैं, मुल्क कमज़ोर हो जाता है। और हरेक को आप दिल्ली में रहते हैं यह एक पुरानी बहुत पुरानी जगह है। कुछ लोग मद्रास में हैं, कुछ लोग गुजरात में कहीं और हैं बंगाल में हैं। मैं नहीं चाहता, यानी आप महसूस करें कि आप मद्रास में रहते हैं तो सारा हिन्दुस्तान आप का है, ख़ाली

मद्रास आपका नहीं है। आप गुजरात में रहते हैं, हिन्दुस्तान में आप कश्मीर में रहते हैं तो कश्मीर का एक मद्रास में भी है, गुजरात में भी है बंगाल में भी है यानी यह हमारी विरासत है इनहैरीटेंस है यह सभी की है चाहे हम कहीं भी रहें। यह एक ज़बरदस्त बात समझ जायें, हमारा दिल समझ जाये तब हम, इसमें हमारी दिल की एकता हो, इमोशनल इनटीग्रेशन जिसे कहते हैं उसको करना है अगर हम यह करें तो बड़ी ताक़त हो जाती है फिर और बातें तो महज़ तैयारी की हैं, हथियार की हैं, फ़ौज की हैं। वो तो हम करेंगे ही, उसमें भी आपको शरीक होना है और मैं उम्मीद करता हूं और मुझे यक़ीन है कि जब जब कोई पुकार आयेगी हमारे नौजवान शरीक होंगे पूरीतौर से। [तालियां]

जो बात मैं चाहता हूं आप समझ जायें वो यह कि बग़ैर हमारे कुछ कोशिश किए, एक इम्तेहान का वक़्त आ गया, सारे मुल्क का, मेरा भी, आपका भी, मैं कौन चीज हूं, चन्द रोज़ का मेहमान हूं, लेकिन आपके ऊपर बोझे पड़ने वाले हैं, ज़्यादा इसके और इसके लिए आप आपने दिमाग़ को तैयार कीजिए और जो असली बुनियादी बातें हैं उनको सोचिए उनको मज़बूत कीजिए। क्योंकि एक बात तो क़ाबिले बरदाश्त नहीं है कि हम डर के, और घबरा के हम हार मान लें, झुक जायें, यह नहीं हो सकता। [तालियां] अगर यह नहीं हो सकता, तो यह भी याद रखिए कि आप कोई नारों से नहीं जीत जायेंगे, वो नहीं मैं देखता हूं एक वह बच्चे इधर उधर फिरते हैं, नारे उठाते हैं और उठायें वो, लेकिन वो बचपन का खेल है, बड़े आदमियों का नहीं है, उसके लिए तैयार होना है, मुसीबत झेलनी है और मुक़ाबला करना है, तब हम जीत सकते हैं। हमारी कोई अदावत नहीं है चीनी लोगों से। हमारी बदक़िस्मती है, कि आजकल की हुक़ूमत चीन की, हम पर हमला करती है, हमें हमले का जवाब देना है चाहे आज हम उसको, हमले को हटा दें। आज लगे, छः महीने बाद, साल भर बाद, दो साल बाद हम करेंगे। इस इरादे से कि वक़्त कित्ता ही लगे, हमें करना है और लम्बी बात है, छोटी बात भी नहीं है। इस ढंग से आप इसे देखें और इस ढंग से सामना करें। आख़िर हम और आप एक पुराने मुल्क के रहने वाले हैं जिसने बहुत ऊंच नीच देखी है और सब इस हजारों बरस ने हमको बनाया, हम को ढाला, हमारी कमज़ोरियां भी, हमारी अच्छाइयां भी। हम ज़रूर समझते हैं कि इस मुल्क में अच्छाइयां हैं बहुत, हमें मोहब्बत है उससे, यों भी होती, हम समझते हैं इसमें अच्छाइयां हैं, हम यह भी समझते हैं इसमें कुछ कुछ हमारे लिए तो है ही, कुछ और मुल्कों के लिए भी पैग़ाम हैं। जो कुछ समझें, लेकिन इस वक़्त हमारे और आपके सामने वो हज़ारों बरस जो पीछे हैं, वो खड़े हो जाते हैं देखने को, देखने को कि आजकल की क़ौम कैसे है, क्या करेगी? इसमें दम है कि ख़ाली कागज़ी है। तो हमें दिखाना है अपने पुराने ज़माने को कि हममें भी दम है और हम इस मुल्क को मोहब्बत हैं करते, इज़्ज़त करते हैं और उसके लिए हम सब कुछ करने को तैयार हैं एक हो कर और इस तरह से हम भविष्य को अपना बनायेंगे।

आप, आपके छात्र-संघ का आज उद्घाटन है? तो मैं बड़ी खुशी से उद्घाटन करता हूं [तालियां] लेकिन हां, लेकिन मैंने आपसे कहा था मैं यहां आया था कुछ आपके चेहरे देख कर कुछ अपने को भी ताज़ा करने के लिए, वो कुछ हुआ, कुछ असर हुआ, आपके

चेहरे देख के आपके उत्साह से और मैं यहां से जाऊंगा तो कुछ ताज़गी ले के जाऊंगा। मालूम नहीं मेरे, मैंने तो कोई आपने देखा कोई बहुत पुरजोश तक़रीर, व्याख्यान किया नहीं, क्योंकि पुरजोश व्याख्यान होते हैं, बाज़ लोग करते हैं, मुझे करना आता नहीं। क्योंकि जब कोई बड़ा सवाल सामने आता है तो उस वक़्त और भी ज़रूरी हो जाता है, मेरी राय में दिमाग़ को और ज़बान को ठण्डा रखना ताकि हम उस सवाल का जवाब ढूढ़ें, ताक़त से, ख़ाली गुलशोर मचा कर जवाब न हो, इसलिए मैंने आपसे ठंडी हालत में जो कुछ कहा, कहा। लेकिन शायद आपको झलक मिली हो मेरा दिलो दिमाग़ काफ़ी इस वक़्त गर्म है, गर्मी में है और गुस्सा भी है कि क्या बातें की गयी हमारे मुल्क के ख़िलाफ़ जो कि अलावा इसके कि हमारे मुल्क के ख़िलाफ़ है एक, एक जुर्म है इण्टरनेशनल ला [International Law] में इस तरह से करना मेरी राय में। कौन से हम क़ायदे क़ानून बनाते हैं, उनको इण्टरनेशनल ला कहते हैं, इण्टरनेशनल अफेयर्स, कि इस तरह से हमले करें, दूर मुल्क पर दूसरे और इसलिए भी कि हमारा फ़र्ज़ है कि हम इसका मुकाबला करें, अपने लिए तो करना ही है और बातों के लिए भी। और मुल्कों का फ़र्ज़ है कि वो इस बात को समझें कि इस क़िस्म की बातें अगर दुनियां में होती रहेंगी तो फिर कोई मुल्क अमन से नहीं रह सकता, यह तो एक जंगली क़ानून है। जंगल का। तो बस मैंने आपका बहुत वक़्त लिया आप माफ़ करेंगे।

जयहिन्द!

[Translation begins:

President of the Students Union,[98] Mr Vice Chancellor,[99] Sisters, Brothers, Young Men,

It is purely by chance that I am speaking before you today because if I had any idea that we would be facing a new kind of challenge and problems, perhaps I would not have left my work so easily and come here. When I received your invitation,[100] though I was beset as usual with innumerable problems I made some time to come here because after all, it is our students in colleges and universities who will have to shoulder the burdens of the country in the future. So it is very essential and I like to keep in touch with them.

I am often a little afraid that the generation gap between the people of my age and the youth of today is widening. Even a father and son often do not see eye to eye. Everybody is prepared to give advice including me. Though good advice may sometimes help, the thing that really counts is understanding. When there is a large gap in ages, there is difficulty in understanding. As you

98. See fn 95 in this section.
99. See fn 96 in this section.
100. See item 130.

know, I am pretty advanced in years [Laughter] while you are on the threshold of a new life.

Well, anyhow, when I received your invitation to inaugurate your student's union, I accepted gladly. I do not know if you are likely to derive any benefit from meeting me. But I have certainly benefited by seeing you and imbibing some of your enthusiasm. [Applause]. So I am here purely for selfish reasons. [Laughter].

But all kinds of new developments took place after that and by a strange quirk of fortune or whatever it is, India is facing extremely difficult and complex problems today. The strange thing is that we believe and so do other people in the world that we stand for peace. In my youth when we were struggling for freedom, we adopted peaceful methods. We were greatly influenced by our leader, Mahatma Gandhi, though it is our own shortcomings which prevented us from learning more from him. [Laughter]. Yet he exerted an influence on all those who had the opportunity of spending even a few days by his side, no matter how useless they were. Then we became free and took on the role of messenger of peace in the world. But in spite of all this, now we are faced with the necessity to arm ourselves and fight a war. That is why I said that it is a strange quirk of fate that we are in this situation today. It has to be faced but it is extremely perturbing. At first I thought of calling off this engagement not because of pressure of work. But it seemed wrong to me because where else could I get a better audience than in the student's union of the Delhi University where thousands of boys and girls—the epitome of India's youth—are assembled? So, I thought it would be a good thing to come here and derive some strength from your eager young faces, your enthusiasm and spirit.

All of you are aware of the Chinese aggression. What it has done is to close one chapter of our history and begin another in our national life. A page has been turned and new chapters are opening. You and I must write them because every age writes its own history by its deeds and courage and actions. Historians will record them later but actual history is made by the people. Sometimes it gathers great momentum. In our youth, we and millions of people in India played a role in our struggle for freedom. You must have heard about those days though you have not seen them first hand. But the people who actually took part in the struggle bear the imprint of those years on their minds and hearts. Sometimes I wonder how the people of this generation can experience the emotions that we did in those days, when we forgot about our normal daily cares and concerns and were propelled by a strange kind of madness towards one particular goal. We were not bothered about the consequences of our actions so long as we were marching together. An experience of this kind is good for a nation though it is painful. I have often found that though India is beset with innumerable

139

problems, the people are unconcerned about the larger issues and are immersed in their petty problems and quarrels. They fight in the name of provincialism, communalism, language or something else. There are many such things in India which erect barriers among the people.

How are we to get out of these influences and broaden our minds to think about the larger national issues? The fact is that soon a time is bound to come, if not in my life time, certainly in yours when nationalism will spread and embrace the entire world. We talk about one world and though we are still far from it, there is no alternative to it. It is bound to comesomeday. Otherwise the world will be destroyed. Science and technology are successfully breaking down the barriers of ignorance. But how are we to remove the barriers which are in our hearts and minds? Anyhow, a time will come when there will be one world. In India, we talk a great deal about nationalism too but throughout history, we have shown how backward we are in this respect by breaking ourselves up into small groups in the name of religion, languages, caste, province and what not. I often think about all this. I am sure you are learning a great deal in this university and are being moulded by the years you are spending in Delhi University. But the fact is that ultimately a nation is moulded by its experiences and hardships, the challenges it faces and the difficulties and problems that it has to undergo.

You have heard about Gandhiji though very few among you would have seen him. What did Gandhiji do? It is difficult to compare him with anyone in history. He breathed a new spark of life and vitality into India's poor, illiterate, down-trodden millions with their lacklustre eyes and hopeless demeanour, and gave them fresh hope. He taught them to stand erect once more and brought a new sparkle in their eyes. It was a great miracle though it did not suddenly make them wealthy. But it did something far more important and that was to infuse new life and vitality in the people. I am not referring to the intellectuals but to the poor, common man in India. Gandhiji put himself in their place and we saw how the strange magic of his personality transformed India's millions. So we were successful in winning freedom. It is a strange phenomenon when millions of people are suddenly filled with a new vitality, determination and discipline. Well, those days are gone and there has been no special need for us to gear ourselves to that pitch. But I have often wondered how the people could once again be made to experience what we did, so that they can be moulded by it and filled with a steely determination once again. We are not a wealthy or ease- loving nation. But even so, a weakness creeps into individuals when they are no longer in the habit of gazing at the stars and keep their eyes lowered to the ground. They get bogged down by petty arguments and quarrels and to that extent, a nation also shrinks in stature.

In the last fifty years or so there have been two great wars in the world. Now you might say we are waiting for the third. I will not go into the good or bad points about these wars. But the people of Europe, Asia and to some extent, the United States of America acquired a unique experience. There is no family in Europe which has not lost a life in the war. So war to them is not a distant thing which they read about in newspapers. It made a deep and everlasting impression upon these countries. This is something we have not experienced in ages. I am not in favour of war. I think it is very wrong, particularly modern wars. But while it kills, it also fills human beings with a new vitality. Europe has had this experience. We under Pax Britannica began to feel that nations can progress merely by shouting slogans or taking out processions.

Then Gandhiji came and showed us how wrong we were. Millions of people followed him and became strong and organized. If India is famous in the world today, it is because of Gandhiji. We are people of very short stature. But somehow, we still seem to think that it is enough to shout slogans, take out processions, etc. Now I am not against slogans or processions and they can whip up enthusiasm at the appropriate time. But we would be deceiving ourselves if we think that that is our real task, we are living in a ruthless world in which a great price has to be paid for progress in terms of hard labour and bearing hardships. We have to pay a great price for our freedom too. You must not think for a moment that once we have got freedom, it is our permanent possession. We have to make an effort every single day of our lives to hold on to that freedom, and remain constantly vigilant. We have to be prepared at all times to defend and protect that freedom. If we slacken even a little, freedom will slip away. We have seen this happening again and again in the course of our long history. We have allowed our freedom to slip away due to our foolishness, internal feuds and disunity which made us vulnerable to enemy attack. Invaders came from outside and swallowed the country piece by piece while the rest of us looked on.

More than fifteen years have gone by since India became independent and, I think, we have made great progress during this period. We have also made mistakes and often stumbled and fallen. But we have picked ourselves up and gone on. This is how nations progress, we must not be afraid of stumbling and falling occasionally so long as we have the spirit to pick ourselves up and go on. But I feel that one thing that the people of India have not understood fully is the reality of war. The people in the West have had experience of world wars. To us, war is something we read about in stories. It is true that we are opposed to war. But the emotional impact of that experience has not touched us. Even in the last war fighting was limited to a corner of Assam. It did not affect the rest of us.

I have given you this background because the incidents that have occurred recently shook up the entire nation. What exactly happened? As you know, for the last five years, the Chinese have been gradually occupying portions of our territory in Ladakh. It would be wrong to say that we were afraid of them. But we wanted as far as possible to solve the problem by peaceful methods because we knew that a war with a great country like China would bode no good for anyone. So we tried other methods but did not succeed. This had been going on for five years and we have been talking about the border dispute.

Now the Chinese invasion of the Eastern frontier is a new development. The area known as NEFA or the North Eastern Frontier Agency and the McMahon Line which is the watershed in the Himalayas constitute our borders. The name McMahon was given to that imaginary divide because fifty years ago, when the then government of India had reached an agreement with Tibet and China, it was a British representative of that name who presided. Since then the ridge in the highest Himalayan peak has been regarded as the border dividing India and China. It was not a new demarcation but merely confirmed an old agreement. It was agreed upon to regard that as the watershed.

Well, anyhow, the Chinese have been using some old maps in which large portions of Ladakh and NEFA were shown as part of their territory. We have several meetings with them about this. All our correspondence on the subject has been published. Our report presents evidence which leave no room for doubt that our case was right. Well, the Chinese have never set foot on our soil on the eastern border except for the dispute over the village of Longju and whether it was on this side of the McMahon Line or that. On the contrary many things happened in this period in which by their own action, they accepted, in a sense, the fact that the ridge in the Himalayas does constitute our border. Then they came to an agreement with Burma. The McMahon Line extends to that country and beyond. The Chinese accepted it as the boundary. When that happened, we were convinced that they would do so in India too for after all the principle was the same. I do not say that they made a promise but they did make it obvious by their behaviour that they accepted the boundary demarcation.

Anyhow, in the last twelve years since the present regime came to power in China, they have never tried to cross the McMahon Line. Now suddenly about seven weeks ago, on the eighth of September, they came down from the Pass and were very close to our military posts in that area. This was something new for us. At first we thought that they had come down to inspect something, though it was rather unusual. [Laughter]. But we did not think of it as a great attack on India. In fact, I had left for the Commonwealth Prime Ministers' Conference just the day before. But as soon as we came to know about this, we gave orders to our army to throw them out. The thing is that it was easy for the Chinese to reach that area for the Tibetan Plateau on the other side. Though that is also on a height, it was on level ground. The Chinese have built roads in that region and so they could easily go up and down the ridge to our side. We, on the other hand, had to scale the high mountain peaks in the Himalayas. There were no roads and though we have built some roads, there are large areas which are completely inaccessible. You must bear in mind that it lies at a height of fourteen-fifteen or even eighteen thousand feet where you will have difficulty in breathing, if you suddenly go there. Anyhow, we gave orders to our armed forces to make preparations. Then the Chinese started sending in their troops. We wanted to throw them out. But it was easy for them, to send in a large number of troops which had been stationed in Tibet ever since they occupied that country.

These were the events of those first few weeks. By the first week of October, our position had been strengthened. But we found that the Chinese had become even more strongly entrenched. Then, on the 20th of October, they launched a massive attack on our troops. What we must take into account is that they attacked on the entire Ladakh border. It was an operation which must have taken days and weeks of preparation. They attacked and then went about telling everyone in the world that it is India who was the aggressor. The strange thing is that they made an announcement half an hour before even a shot was fired-- that India had attacked China. India would not have been wrong even if she had attacked. But I am giving you the facts. They launched an attack on a massive scale and then made a noise in the world that they were innocent and that India was the aggressor.

Anyhow, the result was that they captured several of our posts and pushed our forces back by sheer superiority of numbers and weapons, it was a big shock to us. Various developments followed which perturbed us greatly. But whatever might have been our feelings in Delhi, you can imagine what our brave jawans and soldiers who fought so bravely must have felt.

Now I want you to understand one thing clearly. The incidents of October 20 changed the complexion of the situation completely. It was no longer a minor border skirmish. They had made preparations on a massive scale to launch an attack on India. So it became an invasion of India. The Chinese have gone beyond a border dispute and launched a full scale attack on India. This is how we must look at this. It is true that neither side has made a formal declaration of war. But the fact remains that that is what is happening. Some people feel that we should declare war. I do not want to go into the details. But the fact is that we will do whatever we can. We will not let anything stand in our way. But the fact is that after a long time, India has had to face a massive attack by enemy troops. In the beginning this led to a tremendous lowering of morale in the country for it was a great shock. I do not know what else is in store for us. But I can definitely say that no matter what happens, we will face the situation with courage and throw them out. The final blow will be struck by us. [Applause].

This is not an empty boast. The days of slogan-mongering and empty boasts are over. There is no doubt about it that this is a serious encounter which has to be faced squarely. We will have to undergo great hardships. We have never been a warmongering nation. Our armed forces are good, well-trained and courageous. But our entire economy is not geared towards fighting a war. You will find that there is conscription in most countries like China, for instance. Their efforts are always geared towards war. It is a very great priority with them. If they want to do something, all they have to do is to pass a decree. These processes are more complicated in a democracy and take time. There are innumerable criticisms. Well, these are some of the weaknesses of a democracy. But in my opinion, that is the only proper road to follow. Though it may create some initial difficulties once it takes roots, it is bound to win in the end. [Applause]. But in the beginning, a nation has to be prepared for shocks because the adversary is always well armed and prepared. Our weapons are stored in museums gathering dust. Anyhow, there are many aspects of the present crisis which are harmful to us. But I think perhaps the one good thing it may do is to wake us up a little and show us the kind of world we live in.

This is a ruthless world in which there is no place for the week. We can become a strong nation only if we are united and face the challenges that arise. If we are constantly turned apart by internal strife and arguments over petty things, we will become weak and other countries can subjugate us. So I think the present crisis may benefit us. I can say with complete confidence that we will throw out the Chinese. But you are cheering without understanding what you and I and all of us must do before that happens. It would make more sense if you were to realise fully what we have to do. If all our wishes can be fulfilled by merely cheering or clapping, it would be very easy to build a world of our dreams. But it requires very hard work and a full realisation that we are in conflict with a nation which has perhaps the largest army in the world. It is obvious that the United States and the Soviet Union are superior to China in military might. But that is because ofthe weapons that they possess. But the Chinese army is perhaps the largest in the world today. [Laughter]. I do not know what there is to laugh about. [Laughter].You seem to think this is a joke.

Anyhow, it is not merely a question of the armed forces, China is an ancient country, strong and determined and dogmatic in its attitude. All these things contribute to a nation's strength. India and China are the two most ancient countries in Asia with a history dating back to thousands of years. In this long period of time, not a single war has been fought between India and

China which is extraordinary. Now we are facing one another in armed conflict. So it is obvious that China can do us great harm and vice versa. This mutual destruction is not very wise or civilised. But what is to be done? We cannot sit quietly and allow the aggression to go unchallenged or bow down to their might. That is impossible. It has to be faced squarely, no matter how much we have to suffer in the process. We have to accept the challenge.

I think the student's union is planning to do something on the 1st of November, what is it? Oh, you are holding a demonstration. Well, you are welcome to do so. [Laughter]. But I would like to tell you that though such demonstrations may be a good thing, they do not have any impact. There are other yardsticks by which your spirit and determination will be measured. It is not enough to hold a meeting or take out a procession. It will only mean a waste of your energy. I cannot tell you off hand what you can do. But the time is coming when all of us will have to undergo a severe trial. We will be issuing general instructions to everyone soon.

I would like to mention one thing. It is a good thing for you to belong to the National Cadet Corps. [Applause]. It teaches you to be a soldier as well as an officer. If we have to expand our armed forces as we are having to do, we will need to train large numbers of officers. Our entire life is changing and you must realise it and prepare yourselves for it. So girls and boys must join the NCC in large numbers. But we will be doing other things too. Everyone will be given some military training and volunteer corps will be set up.

Apart from expanding the armed forces other things are involved in a nation's preparedness. The soldiers fight on the front. But innumerable people are needed to do various things to make it possible for them to fight. Production has to be stepped up in fields and factories. What does this imply? First of all, the most important thing is of course, to have a steely determination not to yield to brute force, no matter what the consequences are. We shall remain free and continue to hold our heads high. Once you are determined to do this, then you must be prepared to pay the price for that. Every single individual has to pay the price. It is not enough that you read in the newspapers about the war. You may have to give up, if necessary, even your lives. But apart from that, we must work hard to step up production in every direction.

You are students and education is extremely important. We do not want that you should give up your studies because of the border trouble for that will weaken the country in the future. A nation's strength lies ultimately in the number of people of quality and training who are available in the country. Therefore, the greater the number of such people, the more a nation can progress. A nation does not progress by mere numbers. What it needs is trained human beings. So I do not want you to give up your studies. On the contrary you must study harder than ever. But a time may come when you may have to give up your studies if greater danger threatens. However, you must understand that that does not mean that you can give up your studies and sit at home. It means that you will have to face greater dangers. I want you to concentrate on your studies and prepare yourselves for the future. If the necessity arises, we may have to send our youth into the battle field which may mean an interruption in their studies for a year or two. When it is a matter of life and death for a nation, then everything that makes for strength has to be given priority.

This is a tremendous challenge that fate has thrown in our way in order to shake us out of our slackness and make us strong. First of all, we must learn to forget our petty differences of caste, province, language and what not. They may have some significance. But when we are facing larger issues, they do not count at all. The best test of a nation lies in whether it thinks of larger issues or is bogged down by petty things. It is obvious that if it thinks big, it can rise to great heights.

You must have heard about emotional integration. We must take advantage of this crisis to complete that process. What we are trying to do is not something artificial or new. There has always been unity in the history of India though there were separate kingdoms. Amidst the great diversity which exists in India, there has always been a strand of unity and the beauty of India lies in the synthesis of the two. We want to keep both. But diversity does not mean that people must fight among themselves. On the other hand, we do not want complete uniformity throughout the country. That is absurd. Everyone must follow his own path while preserving a basic unity and understanding that our foremost duty is to our country. We must work for the progress of the country because otherwise we pave the way for weakness. You are citizens of Delhi which is a very ancient city. Then there are people in Madras and Bengal and Gujarat. I do not want you to think you belong only to Madras. The whole of India is our heritage whether we live in Gujarat, Kashmir, Madras, Bangalore or somewhere else. This is a very important thing which we must try to realise fully. Once there is emotional integration among the people of the country, it will automatically contribute to our strength which will be more invincible than mere arms or armed forces. We will of course pay attention to that aspect too and all of us must be prepared to answer the call of the nation. [Applause].

What I want you to understand is that willy-nilly, we have been thrust into a big crisis and the entire nation has to face the test. I am a bird of passage. The real burden of the nation will fall upon your shoulders and you must prepare yourselves mentally for that and understand the things that really matter. We will not tolerate any panic or acceptance of defeat. That is not possible. [Applause]. But at the same time you must also remember that you cannot win the war by shouting slogans. I often see children running here and there with placards. But that is child's play. Adults have to prepare themselves to bear hardships and to face any challenges that may arise if we wish to win the war. We do not have any bitterness against the chinese people but it is the Chinese government of the day which has chosen to commit aggression. We have to take up the challenge and throw them out even if it takes months or years. We must be firm in our determination no matter how long it takes. This is not a trivial matter. We must look at it in this light and face it. After all, you and I are the people of a very ancient country which has seen great ups and downs during the thousands of years of its history and been moulded by them, by our weaknesses as well as our good qualities. We think that there are great qualities in India and we love our country. We also feel that India has a special message not only for her people but to the other nations of the world too. In the present crisis, we have the history of thousands of years standing in judgment upon what we do. We must show that we too have courage and spirit that we love and respect our country and are prepared to do everything in our power in unity and cooperation.

This is the inauguration of your student's union. I inaugurate it with great happiness. [cheers] But as I was saying I came here to refresh myself by meeting you, I shall go away from here refreshed in spirit by your enthusiasm and spirit. I have not given you a fiery speech as some people do. But I do not know how to do that for whenever there is a crisis, I feel it is more than ever necessary to keep the mind and speech under calm control in order to find a solution to the problem. We cannot do that by making a noise. Therefore, I have said whatever I had to calmly. But you may have caught a glimpse of the fire and anger there is in my mind at the moment, particularly about some of the things that have been done against India. Apart from everything else, in my opinion, what has happened is a crime in international law. The nations of the world must realise that if such things are permitted to happen in international affairs, there can be no peace anywhere in the world. It is the law of the jungle. It is of course our duty to face the aggression squarely in order to defend our country.

I have taken up enough of your time for which you must forgive me.
Jai Hind!

Translation ends]

133. For African Studies Department of Delhi University[101]

I am glad that the Department of African Studies of the University of Delhi is bringing out a monograph on Tanganyika on the occasion of its independence on the 9th December 1961. This is an imaginative act on their part. We in India know very little about Africa even though Africa is in every one's heart and mind. Therefore, any measure taken to fill in this lacuna deserves encouragement. I hope the monograph will be worthy of the great occasion that it sets out to commemorate – the emergence of another independent country in the vast continent of Africa. We are looking forward to having the closest and the friendliest relations with Tanganyika, and I hope that this monograph will help towards this.

(f) Culture

134. To Swami Swahananda: Vivekananda Birth Centenary[102]

October 4, 1962

Dear Swamiji,

I have your letter of October 4th. I am glad to learn that you are celebrating in a fitting way the birth centenary of Swami Vivekananda. I shall be happy to be associated with it, but I fear I cannot give much time as I am heavily occupied in various ways.

If you wish to associate my name with it, you can certainly do so.[103]

Yours sincerely,
[Jawaharlal Nehru]

---

101. Message, 21 November 1962. PMO, File No. 9/2/61-PMP, Vol. 8, Sr. No. 95-A.
102. Letter to the Secretary of the Swami Vivekananda Birth Centenary Committee, Ramakrishna Ashram, New Delhi-1.
103. See also items136, 139,144.

135. To M.C. Chagla: Banning *Nine Hours to Rama*[104]

October 8, 1962

My dear Chagla,

I have your letter of October 2nd. You spoke to me about this subject of banning books when I was in London. I agree with you that it should only be in very special cases that a book is banned. I shall send a copy of your letter to the Finance Minister[105] who is likely to return to India in the course of the next few days.

I have not read *Nine Hours to Rama*.[106] I am told that it is a well written book and the only possible objection that people might take is that it puts the murderer in a good light. But the mere report of the book has created such a furore in India that it may be difficult now to undo what has been done. If it had not been banned to begin with, it would have been relatively easy.

Yours sincerely,
Jawaharlal Nehru

136. To K.L. Shrimali: Vivekananda Birth Centenary[107]

October 8, 1962

My dear Shrimali,

A representative of the Ramakrishna Mission in Delhi[108] came to see me today about the celebration of Swami Vivekananda's Birth Centenary. A Committee has been formed for this purpose. He discussed how we should celebrate this.

Among other things, he suggested that the youth of our country should be more closely acquainted with Vivekananda's teaching and inspiration which was "rooted in our past heritage but based on modern science and technology". He suggested that three of his small books which the Ramakrishna Mission has published, should be made widely available in various languages in India. These three books are:

---

104. Letter to the High Commissioner in the UK. PMO, File No. 43(183)/62-70-PMS, Sr. No. 24-A.
105. Morarji Desai.
106. A book by Stanley Wolpert, *Nine Hours to Rama* (New York: Random House, 1962). See also SWJN/SS/75/ item 211 and SWJN/SS/76/items 377,378,385 and 387.
107. Letter to the Minister of Education.
108. Swami Swahananda, Secretary, Swami Vivekananda Birth Centenary Celebration Committee, met Nehru at 9.30 in the morning the same day. Engagement Diary.

1. *To the Youth of India,* by Swami Vivekananda[109]
2. *Swami Vivekananda on India and Her Problems*[110]
3. *A Short Life of Swami Vivekananda*[111]

He suggested that these books may be prescribed for rapid reading in our Higher Secondary Schools and colleges. I do not know how far this is possible. Undoubtedly, Vivekananda's writings are worth reading by everybody and especially by every Indian. I should like them widely distributed.

Could you give some thought to this matter?[112]

Yours sincerely,
[Jawaharlal Nehru]

137. To D.S. Kothari: Vivekananda's Books[113]

October 8, 1962

My dear Kothari,

I enclose a letter I have written to Dr Shrimali about Swami Vivekananda's books.[114] I think we should do something to popularise these books among our young men in a big way. The Birth Centenary offers an occasion for doing this.

Yours sincerely,
[Jawaharlal Nehru]

138. For The Bharatiya Music and Arts Society[115]

I send my good wishes to the Annual Festival of Music and Dance which is being held under the auspices of The Bharatiya Music and Arts Society. I hope the Festival will be a success and will enable the Society to raise enough money for their Music School Building Fund.

109. (California: Vedanta Press, 1946).
110. Compiled by Swami Nirvedananda, edited and published by Swami Pavitrananda (Almora: Mayavati Press, 1946).
111. By Swami Tejasananda, edited and published by Swami Pavitrananda (Kolkata: Advaita Ashram Press, n.d.).
112. See also items 134 and 137.
113. Letter to the Chairman of the UGC.
114. See item 136.
115. Forwarded to P.R. Subramanyam, President, Bharatiya Music and Arts Society, 3/150 Kamalalayam, Wadala, Bombay 31.

139. For Swami Swahananda: Little Time for Meetings[116]

Please inform Swami Swahananda that although I would like to attend the two meetings he has mentioned,[117] I am not sure that I shall be able to do so. All I can say is that I shall try to do so. The situation in the country, and especially on our frontiers, is a very difficult one and much will depend on how it takes shape later.[118]

140. To Jagjivan Ram: Stamp on the Himalayan Panda[119]

October 20, 1962

My dear Jagjivan Ram,

Thank you for the special stamp commemorating wild life in India.

I would suggest that, among these wild life stamps, you might include the Himalayan Panda which is unique in India and is very attractive looking.

Yours sincerely,
Jawaharlal Nehru

---

116. Note, 20 October 1962. PMO, File No. 9/65/63-64-PMP, Vol. I, Sr. No. Minute-44.
117. From Swami Swahananda to Nehru's PS, 13 October 1962: "Dear Sir, During my interview with the Prime Minister a few days ago, [on 8 October 1962] he kindly agreed to participate in the following meetings to be held to celebrate the Swami Vivekananda Birth centenary:

  1.   Public meeting at Mission premises. The Prime Minister is to preside over this meeting.
  2.   Public meeting at the Ramlila Grounds. The Prime Minister is to speak at the meeting.

  We have now fixed up the dates and times for the meetings. The first meeting (at the Mission premises) has been fixed to take place on Sunday, the 3rd February, 1963 (from 5 p.m. to 6.30 or 6.45 p.m.). The second meeting (at the Ramlila grounds) has been fixed up to commence at 5 p.m. on Sunday, the 3rd March, 1963.

  We, therefore, request you to inform the Prime Minister about the dates and times of the two public meetings and to send us your confirmation at your earliest convenience.

  Yours in service,
  Swami Swahananda"

  PMO, File No. 9/65/63-64-PMP, Vol. I, Sr. No. 43-A.
118. See also item 134.
119. Letter to the Minister of Transport and Communications. PMO, File No. 27(19)57-62-PMS, Sr. No. 106-A.

141. To Swami Lokeswarananda: Schedules Uncertain[120]

October 20, 1962

Dear Swamiji,

I have your letter of October 18th. It is always a pleasure to me to be able to help the Ramakrishna Mission or its institutions in any way. I am afraid, however, that in view of the critical time we are passing through and our trouble on the border, I cannot give an assurance about any future engagement or fix even an approximate date for it. If I go to Calcutta in the future, perhaps this also might be fitted in. That is the most I can say at present. I do not know when I might be able to go to Calcutta.

Yours sincerely,
[Jawaharlal Nehru]

142. To Humayun Kabir: No Time for More at Rihand[121]

October 25, 1962

My dear Humayun,

Your letter of the 25th October. I have got entangled in a visit to Rihand. But I want to come back as early as possible. I cannot, therefore, accept any other engagement there.

Yours sincerely,
[Jawaharlal Nehru]

120. Letter to the founder of Narendrapur Ramkrishna Mission Centre; address: Ramakrishna Mission Ashrama, P.O. Narendrapur, 24 Parganas.
121. Letter to the Minister of Scientific Research and Cultural Affairs. See item 94.

143. To C.P. Ramaswami Aiyar: Foreword on Book on Art[122]

October 27, 1962

My dear C.P.,

Your letter of October 18th.[123] I am sorry for the delay in answering it. But you know how heavily occupied I am at the present moment of difficulty and crisis.

I have no doubt that your new book will be interesting and worthwhile. I would like to read it and also, if you so wish, to write a foreword to it. But I confess that I do not see at present when I shall have the time to do so. However, perhaps by the end of this year, conditions may be a little better.

Yours sincerely,
Jawaharlal Nehru

144. For Vivekananda Birth Centenary[124]

I send my good wishes on the occasion of Swami Vivekananda's Birth Centenary and the Sixth Shri Ramakrishna Mela which will be held to celebrate it. Swami Vivekananda's teachings are as vital and inspiring today as they ever were in the past. In the crisis we are passing through owing to the invasion of India by China, we can draw much inspiration from Swami Vivekananda.

145. To Ananda Mangala: Buddha Images[125]

November 9, 1962

My dear Ananda Mangala,

Thank you for your letter of the 6th November and your good wishes.

You refer in this to Buddha images being sent to you. You mentioned this before to me also. I am not sure what images you require, and I must confess

---

122. Letter to Chairman, Hindu Religious Endowment Commission; address: 5 Safdarjang Road, New Delhi. PMO, File No. 9/2/62-PMP, Vol. 7, Sr. No. 80-A.
123. See appendix 17.
124. Message, 29 October 1962, forwarded to Swami Lokeswarananda. PMO, File No. 9/65/63-PMP, Sr. No. 2-A.
125. To the Bhikkhu; address: Indian Buddhist Missionary, Buddhist Temple, Temple Road, Kuala Lumpur.

that I am terribly occupied to go out and search for a Buddha image. Old images of Buddha are normally not allowed to leave the country.

With all good wishes,

Yours sincerely,
[Jawaharlal Nehru]

146. To Nuruddin Ahmad: Ajmal Khan Commemoration[126]

November 15, 1962

My dear Nuruddin Ahmad,

Your letter of the 12th November. I would certainly like to pay my homage to the memory of Hakim Ajmal Khan. But you know how terribly occupied I am these days, and it is difficult for me to be certain when I might or might not be free. In any event, it would hardly be proper for me to preside over the function. I could at the most attend the function and say a few words.

You say that the "Ajmal Day" would be celebrated after the week which lasts from 3rd to 8th December. I can come perhaps on the 9th, if that suits you, or the 10th for a little while. About 5 p.m. would suit me.

Yours sincerely,
[Jawaharlal Nehru]

(e) Sport

147. Commonwealth Games[127]

I am glad to learn that there is a chance of the British Empire and Commonwealth Games being held in India in 1966. We shall be happy to have them here and to give a warm welcome to all the athletes who come here from various Commonwealth countries. One of the particular features of the Commonwealth is that it consists of people of all races and from every continent. We hope that this multi-racial society will come to India and take part in the friendly rivalry of sport in the spirit of the game.

126. Letter to the Mayor of Delhi.
127. Message, 8 October 1962, for the brochure of the Indian Olympic Association. PMO, File No. 40(204)/60-70-PMS, Sr. No. 6-B.

148. To Amrit Kaur: Commonwealth Games[128]

October 23, 1962

My dear Amrit,

Your letter of October 23rd.[129] On the whole, I think that we should not send a team of athletes and players to the Commonwealth Games which are being held in Australia.

Jawaharlal Nehru

(h) Women and Children

149. For the All India Women's Conference[130]

I send my good wishes to the next All India Women's Conference which is going to be held at Chandigarh. One of the big changes that are taking place in India, is in regard to women. As education spreads, more and more girls are going to primary and secondary schools and, later, to colleges and universities. Many of them are taking part in various professions and even in business. Social service has, of course been a domain for which they are especially suited. Because of all this growth and advance, it is all the more necessary that women's organisations should consider it and give a lead.[131]

150. For the Indian Council for Child Welfare[132]

I send my good wishes to the Indian Council for Child Welfare and to all children in India on the occasion of the next Children's Day. I entirely agree that the community should look after every child and assure him proper training

---

128. Letter to Rajya Sabha MP, Congress; address: 2 Willingdon Crescent, New Delhi. PMO, File No. 40(225)/61-72-PMS, Sr. No. 38-A.
129. See appendix 24.
130. Message, 2 October 1962, forwarded to Dr Phulrenu Guha, Honorary General Secretary, All India Women's Conference, 6 Bhagwan Das Road, New Delhi-1.
131. Another message apparently for the same Conference, was sent on 16 October 1962, to Ponnamma Thanu Pillai, the Chairman of the Reception Committee, All India Women's Conference, Raj Bhavan, Chandigarh. See item 152.
132. Message, 2 October 1962, forwarded to Radha Raman, Vice-President, Indian Council for Child Welfare, 14-15 Block A, Barracks B, Janpath, New Delhi-1. PMO, File No. 9/69/63/64 PMP, Sr. No. 4-A.

and affection. At present, often even the elementary amenities are lacking for our children. They should, of course, be provided. It is something that primary school education is growing fast. But that by itself is not enough. The community owes a special responsibility to the children of the country and this should be given priority

151. To Premlila V. Thackersey: Kasturba Trust Sammelan[133]

October 4, 1962

Dear Shrimati Premlila Thackersey,

I have recently returned from my trip abroad and I am overburdened with work. I am afraid that October, November and December are absolutely full up and I cannot accept any additional engagements. You have asked me to go to the Kasturba Trust Sammelan in Indore on any date from the 13th to the 15th November. These very dates have been fixed for the All India Congress Committee meetings in Delhi which I must attend. Immediately after, Parliament session begins and it will take up all my time. Apart from this, there are a number of other important engagements.

I am sorry to say, therefore, that I shall not be able to go to Indore as suggested. I hope you will forgive me. I wish all success to the Kasturba Sammelan.

Yours sincerely,
[Jawaharlal Nehru]

152. For the All India Women's Conference[134]

I send my good wishes to the next Annual Session of the All India Women's Conference to be held at Chandigarh. One of the most encouraging signs in India today is the growing part that Indian women are taking in many fields of public activity. This, taken together with the growth of education among girls and women, is, I feel, a revolutionary feature in the Indian situation. This

---

133. Letter to the Vice-Chancellor of the Shrimati Nathibai Damodar Thackersey Women's University, 1, Nathibai Thackersey Road, Queen's Road, Fort, Bombay-1. She was the Chairman of the Kasturba Gandhi National Memorial Trust from 1956 to 1972.
134. Message, 16 October 1962, sent to Ponnamma Thanu Pillai, the Chairman of the Reception Committee, All India Women's Conference, Raj Bhavan, Chandigarh.

revolution has to be guided right and I hope the All India Woman's Conference will help in doing so.[135]

153. On D.K. Karve's Death[136]

It is sad that Dr Karve[137] is no more. And yet Dr Karve's life and death at an advanced age is a story of triumph over great difficulties and of success. He has been a great man in every sense of the word and India is proud of him and his memory will endure. I pay my tribute and homage to this great son of India who has demonstrated what a man can do if he has perseverance and determination. Women's education especially owes him a very deep debt of gratitude.

(i) Welfare

154. To Brahm Perkash: National Cooperative Congress[138]

October 4, 1962

My dear Brahm Perkash[139],
Your letter of the 1st October.[140] I am glad that the cooperative movement in India is making good progress.

I enclose a brief message.[141]

As for my inaugurating the National Cooperative Congress, I shall gladly do so. But it is difficult for me to say anything definite about March next. Presumably Parliament will be meeting then and I shall be here. You can suggest some dates to me and I shall see how far they are convenient to me.

Yours sincerely,
[J.Nehru]

135. See item 149.
136. Message, 9 November 1962, to the Chief Minister of Maharashtra with the request to forward it to Karve's family members.
137. (1858-1962) Social reformer and educationist.
138. Letter to the General Secretary of the National Cooperative Union of India, 72 Jorbagh, New Delhi. PMO, File No. 17(439)/60-64-PMS, Sr. No. 15-A.
139. Lok Sabha MP, Congress, Outer Delhi.
140. Not reproduced but available in the NMML, PMO, File No. 17(439)/60-64-PMS, Sr. No. 14-A.
141. See item 155.

155. For the National Cooperative Union of India[142]

We have talked about Cooperation for a long time, but we have not caught up in action to what we have proclaimed. Now I believe good progress has been made by the cooperative movement in India. It is fortunate in having as its President Shri V.T. Krishnamachari[143] whom no one can excel in his knowledge of cooperation or his enthusiasm for it.

I am deeply convinced of the value of cooperation both in our rural life and in urban life. But sometimes under the broad cloak of cooperation many things occur which could hardly reflect the basic principles of it. I hope, therefore, that the foundations of cooperation will be well and truly laid. This can ultimately be done only by developing the cooperative outlook among our people. Cooperation is a way of life and not merely a skeleton structure.

I send all my good wishes on the occasion of the cooperative week.[144]

156. To Mehr Chand Khanna: Hindustan Housing Factory[145]

October 4, 1962

My dear Mehr Chand,

I have received your two letters dated October 2 and 4.

I am glad to know of the success of the Hindustan Housing Factory. It seems to me obvious that we can speed up our construction work through pre-fabricated material.[146] I think it is a good idea to have more of these factories in various parts of India.

Yours sincerely,
[Jawaharlal Nehru]

---

142. Message, 4 October 1962. PMO, File No. 17(439)/60-64-PMS, Sr. No. 15-B.
143. Rajya Sabha MP, nominated (1961-1964).
144. See item 154.
145. Letter to the Minister of Works, Housing and Supply.
146. See also item 171.

157. To Rajan Nehru: Inaugurating Seminar[147]

October 8, 1962

My dear Rajan,

Your letter of the 4th October. In your letter you ask me to inaugurate your seminar on the 23rd October, although you were aware of the fact that the Governors' Conference is opening that day and continuing the next day. I am afraid it is not at all possible for me to be away from the Governors' Conference even for a short time, especially at the opening session on the 23rd. I am sorry therefore that I cannot come to the seminar.

The 24th October, which is UN Day, will also be taken up by the Governors' Conference, but it is just possible that I might be able to get away from it at 5 p.m. that day. If that can be done, I shall try to come to your meeting at Sapru House[148].

Yours affectionately,
[Jawaharlal Nehru]

158. To Durgabai Deshmukh: Finding a Job for You[149]

October 8, 1962

My dear Durgabai,

Thank you for your letter of the 2nd October. I did not answer it immediately as I did not quite know what to answer. I have thought over it for some days.

I think that it would be a pity if your ability and energy are not utilised for some national work. But I cannot think of anything where I can be of help to

---

147. Letter to Rajan Nehru, address: 1 Thyagaraja Marg, New Delhi.
148. The Indian Council of World Affairs and All India UN Day Committee jointly held a two-day seminar to celebrate the 17th anniversary of the UN. Nehru attended the concluding reception on 24 October 1962 at Sapru House. See the *Times of India* 26 October 1962, pp.1 and 6.
149. Letter to the Chairman, National Council for Girls' and Women's Education; address: 40 Lodi Estate, New Delhi. [Citation from Bonnie G. Smith, ed., *Oxford Encyclopaedia of Women in World History*, Vol-1, p.42, Oxford University Press, online version 2008.]

you. I do not think that the Planning Commission would be suitable. For the rest, nothing at present comes to my mind. If I think of anything suitable, I shall certainly let you know.

Yours sincerely,
[Jawaharlal Nehru]

159. For the Conference on Moral and Social Hygiene[150]

I send my good wishes to the All India Conference of the Association for Moral and Social Hygiene. The object of this Conference is good and I have no doubt that its efforts have a beneficial result. Apart from these efforts, I think that an economic approach to this problem will be helpful.

I wish success to the Conference and to the Association.

160. For the All India Cooperative Week[151]

अध्यक्ष जी[152] और बहनों और भाइयों,

क़रीब एक महीना भर हुआ जब मेरी दावत हुई थी यहाँ, इस सप्ताह, का उद्घाटन करने की, शुरू करने की। तो मैंने ख़ुशी से मंज़ूर की थी और मुझे ये कहा गया था कि कोई संदेशा, मैसेज भेजूँ, वो भी मैंने भेजा, शायद छपा है इधर-उधर। लेकिन वो सब संदेश जो आये हैं, अपने वक़्त पर कुछ अहमियत रखें, लेकिन पुराने हैं वो। कुछ हिन्दुस्तान की दुनिया इस महीने में बदल गयी है और अभी दो-चार दिन हुए मैंने सोचा कि आजकल वक़्त की तंगी है, काम बहुत करने हैं। मैं ब्रह्म प्रकाश जी से माफ़ी-वाफ़ी माँगू और इजाज़त माँगू कि न आऊँ यहां आज, लेकिन फिर मैंने यह मुनासिब नहीं समझा। एक तो यह कि मैं सहकारिता, कोऑपरेशन वग़ैरा को बहुत अहमियत देता हूँ, दूसरे यह कि जो आजकल बड़े ज़बरदस्त मसले हमारे सामने पेश हैं उसमें मैंने सोचा कि आपकी कोऑपरेटिव्स बहुत मदद दे सकती है और इसलिए मैं आपके सामने हाज़िर हुआ आज।

तो आप लोग, ज़्यादातर यहाँ जो लोग हैं वो ख़ुद कोऑपरेटिव्स का काम करते हैं, जानते हैं, मैं तो दूर से इसकी चर्चा कर देता हूँ, लेकिन मुझे यह पक्का यक़ीन है कि आजकल के हिन्दुस्तान के सवाल या दुनिया के सवाल हल होंगे। हल होने का रास्ता है यही सहकारिता संघ का, कोऑपरेटिव्स का, बल्कि एक बात ज़्यादा कहूँगा मैं कि ख़ाली

---

150. Message, 8 October 1962, forwarded to Sushila Nayar, President, Association for Moral and Social Hygiene in India.

151. Speech, 3 November 1962, at Sapru House. NMML, AIR TS No. 8615, NM No. 1694.

152. V.T. Krishnamachari.

गाँव में या शहरों में कोऑपरेटिव्स बनाना अच्छा है, ज़रूरी है। हमारी निगाहों में तो एक ज़्यादा बड़ी चीज़ है यानी जैसे कि एक दफ़े हमने कांग्रेस के विधान में, आज़ादी के पहले, बहुत हमने लिखा था कि हिन्दुस्तान का विधान, हिन्दुस्तान का आईन बनना चाहिए ऐसा कि सारा भारत एक कोऑपरेटिव कॉमनवैल्थ हो, सारे हिन्दुस्तान को हमने एक सहकारी संघ माना था। क्या माने थे इसके? माने समझाने तो आसान नहीं हैं क्योंकि कोई क़ायदे क़ानून की बात नहीं है ख़ाली, बल्कि एक रहने का तरीक़ा, एक सोचने का तरीक़ा, एक आपस में रिश्ता क्या हो लोगों का, उसका तरीक़ा, और आख़िर में एक रिश्ता क्या हो एक मुल्क का दूसरे मुल्क के साथ उसका तरीक़ा। वो सब एक ही चीज़ से निकलती है। अभी आपने एक गीत सुना एक-दूसरे से, शायद था प्यार करो, क्या ठीक है वो एक अपना दृष्टिकोण, अपने नुक़्ते निगाह को बदलना जो आजकल है।

आजकल बहसें होती हैं समाजवाद, साम्यवाद, पूंजीवाद, वग़ैरा-वग़ैरा, कई वाद हैं और शायद आपको मालूम हो कि मेरा झुकाव उस समय समाजवाद की तरफ़, सोशलिज़्म की तरफ़, लेकिन मैं समझता हूँ एक तरफ़ से समाजवाद का एक ढंग है, बिल्कुल समाजवाद नहीं उसका एक ढंग है यह सहकारी संघ, सहकारी तरीक़ा। मैं समझता हूँ कि वो एक यही तरीक़ा है जो कि एक अलग-अलग बहसों को हल करने की एक कुंजी है। अगर हम सहकारी तरीक़े से काम मुल्क का चलायें, गाँव में, शहर में, कारख़ानों में और यहाँ तक मैं कहूँगा कि हुकूमत में सब जगह। और उस तरीक़े से हम रहें जो कि आसान नहीं है, क्योंकि हमें आजकल की दुनिया की आबोहवा से निकल के एक दूसरी हवा हमें ढूँढनी है, हल्के-हल्के होगी, एकदम से तो नहीं, जो-जो काम आप करते हैं गाँव में या शहर में, उसमें वो सब मदद करता है उसमें। लेकिन एकदम से कौन सारे मुल्क का रहन-सहन बदले, सोचने का तरीक़ा बदले, होता जायेगा, मुझे यक़ीन है।

इसलिए मेरे सामने जो तस्वीर रहे वो एक दूर तक देखने की है और मैं चाहता हूँ कि कोऑपरेशन का, सहकारी तरीक़ा जो कि एक ज़िंदगी को ढालता है, वो हमारे मुल्क की ज़िंदगी को ढाले और उधर ले जाये और यह न हो, आजकल का तरीक़ा क्या है किसी क़दर, मैं नहीं कहता कि लोग बुरे हैं, लेकिन तरीक़ा बहुत अच्छा नहीं है, एक-दूसरे का गला काटने का है, एक-दूसरे के नुक़सान से फ़ायदा उठाने का है। तो ये बातें अच्छी नहीं हैं और आजकल की दुनिया जो हो गयी है उसमें बहुत ज़्यादा चल भी नहीं सकती। हाँ, चल सकती है, मेरा मतलब यह नहीं है कि नहीं चल सकती, लेकिन हवा उसके ख़िलाफ़ होती जा रही है। इसलिए मैं चाहता हूँ, पहली बात आपसे अर्ज़ करूँ, मैं चाहता हूँ कि आप भी अपने सामने इस तस्वीर को रखें, चाहे जब कभी हम पहुँचे जिधर हम जा रहे हैं और अभी हम छोटे क़दम उठाते हैं, बाद में बड़े क़दम उठेंगे, लेकिन हम हिन्दुस्तान भर को एक सहकारी संघ बनाना चाहते हैं। एक माने में जैसा कि हमने तीस-चालीस बरस हुए कहा था और उस वक़्त से अब तक और भी ज़रूरी हो गया यह करना, कोई और चारा नहीं है। बड़ी बहसें होती हैं, और गाली गलौच भी होती है, एक-दूसरे को देते हैं एक साम्यवादी, समाजवादी, पूंजीवादी लड़ते हैं और जो उनके अच्छे-अच्छे ख़्याल हैं, वो भी ख़राब हो जाते हैं उनके तरीक़ों में, लड़ाई में, गाली गलौच में, क्योंकि वो बिल्कुल

बिल्कुल सहकारी तरीक़े के अलग हैं। सहकारी तरीक़ा है, सहयोग करना, मिलना, जिससे हमारे दिमाग़भी बदलें, जिससे हम दूसरे को दबा के फ़ायदा अपना न उठायें, सभी उठायें, सभों की मेहनत से, जिससे मिलजुल कर हम रहें। बाज़ लोग ऐसे हैं, वो समझते हैं कि आजकल की दुनिया को हम बिल्कुल तोड़ दें, ख़त्म कर दें, आजकल की जो आर्थिक स्थिति वग़ैरा है फिर उसपे नयी दुनिया बनायें। ये बातें तो एक स्वप्नों की हैं कि पहले दुनिया को ख़त्म कर दें आजकल की, फिर हम नयी बनायें, ज़्यादा अच्छी बनायेंगे, दुनिया के ख़त्म करने में जो तबाही आती है पहले वो लोग बरदाश्त करें और फिर उसके बाद, जाने क्या-क्या ख़राबियाँ आयें, उसका सामना करें, फिर नयी दुनिया कब बने, क्या बने। यह तरीक़ा ऐसा है कि बग़ैर दुनिया को तबाह किये, गिराये, हम उसको बदलते हैं, सभों की भलाई के लिए इसलिए मैं समझता हूँ कि यह कोऑपरेशन का तरीक़ा यह अच्छा है हर काम के लिए और हमारे हिन्दुस्तान के लिए ख़ासतौर से अच्छा है और हमें उसे हर तरह से बढ़ाना है।

हाँ, उसके साथ एक बात मैं आपसे कहूँ कि कोऑपरेशन के माने यह नहीं हैं कि नकली कोऑपरेटिव बना दिये, कहीं-कहीं होते हैं, मैं नहीं जानता कितने नकली हैं, कितने असली हैं। जो ब्रह्मप्रकाश जी ने बताया साढ़े तीन लाख कोऑपरेटिव हैं, भारत में हैं लेकिन वो असली होने चाहियें और यह मेरा पक्का ख़्याल है कि, कोऑपरेटिव्स कोई सरकारी चीज़ नहीं होनी चाहिए, आम लोग बनायें, सरकारी मदद मिले, सरकारी सलाह मिले, वो ठीक है क्योंकि हरेक का काम यह होना चाहिए इसको करने का, लेकिन जैसे कि पहले होता था, अब भी शायद कहीं होता हो एक क़रीब-क़रीब सरकारी महकमा वो हो जाता है और सरकारी अफ़सर उसके कोई अध्यक्ष हों, कोई सेक्रेटरी हों, इस तरह का। तो वो इसी तरीक़े से मुमकिन है कि कुछ थोड़ा बहुत काम अच्छा हो जाये। मुमकिन है सरकारी अफ़सर जो हों वो अच्छे हों, लेकिन वो ढंग ग़लत है और वो चीज़ वो नहीं पैदा करता जो कोऑपरेटिव्स की जड़ है, यानी एक ख़ुद अपने पैरों पर खड़ा होना, ख़ुद इंतज़ाम करना, ख़ुद मिलकर के रहना यह तो किसी दूसरे की हुकूमत से सब काम हो तो कोऑपरेटिव नहीं है, हो सकता है कि अच्छा काम हो लेकिन कोऑपरेटिव नहीं है। तो इस बात को आप याद रखें और जो काम आप करते हैं उनमें आप इस उसूल को लाइये, इस ढंग को समझ के, कि ख़ाली एक ऊपरी चीज़ नहीं है क़ानून की, लेकिन यह एक रहन-सहन का तरीक़ा है।

अब मैं अलग-अलग बातें तो कहता नहीं आपसे, कुछ आप इस पर बहस करेंगे, लेकिन दो-चार बातें मैं आपसे कहना चाहता हूँ। एक तो यह कि जैसे ब्रह्मप्रकाशजी ने कहा हमारा पंचायती राज है। पंचायती राज के कुछ ख़ास माने नहीं होंगे अगर वहाँ सहकारी संघ न हो, यह उसकी एक जड़ है, उसकी एक शाख़ है, जो कुछ कहिये, बहुत ज़रूरी, वो दोनों जुड़ के चलते हैं, अलग-अलग नहीं। और चुनांचे बहुत ज़रूरी है कि हम सारे मुल्क में इसको कर दें, सारे हमारे देहातों में। दूसरे यह ख़ासतौर से, ख़ासतौर से औरतों को इसमें शरीक होना चाहिए, हिस्सा लेना चाहिए, एक तो हम चाहते हैं हर बात में औरतों को लेना चाहिए, वो एक आख़िर हिन्दुस्तान की आधी आबादी उससे कुछ ज़्यादा हैं या कुछ कम

औरतें हैं, उनको छोड़ के हम कैसे काम करें। दूसरे यह कि जो काम है कोऑपरेशन का इसमें बहुत कुछ घरेलू बातें आती हैं, उसमें ख़ासतौर से उन्हें दिलचस्पी है, उनको समझना चाहिए, लेना चाहिए औरतों को, आपको सदस्य बनाना चाहिए इसका।

तीसरे यह मकान बनाने में, बहुत मकानों की ज़रूरत है, हर जगह, गाँव में, शहरों में, तरीक़े नये-नये निकल रहे हैं, हाउसिंग फैक्ट्रीज़, कारख़ाने बन रहे हैं, जहाँ हिस्से बने-बनाये मकान के मिल जाते हैं। वो सब ठीक हैं, सब चलाये जायेंगे, दिल्ली में एक है हाउसिंग फैक्ट्रीज़ [Housing factories] जो हमने पहले बनाई थी, लोगों ने बड़ा गुलशोर मचाया, क्योंकि शुरु में एकदम से वो कामयाब नहीं हुई, उसने जो बनाई, जो कुछ कहिये एक ईंट की तरह से चीज़ वो ठीक नहीं, चिटक जाती थी, लोगों ने गुल मचाया, बेईमानी हुई, यह हुआ, जितना अनजान आदमी होता है उतना ज़्यादा गुल मचाता है। यह एक निशानी है गुल मचाने वाले की, वो समझा नहीं है बात, कभी-कभी समझ जाये और बात है, लेकिन आमतौर से सबमें जाहिल लोग गुल मचाया करते हैं। [हँसी] वही गुल मचाया, पार्लियामेंट में गुल मचाया क्या-क्या, वह है यह है। एक बहुत अच्छा आदमी था उसके चार्ज में, बहुत लायक़ आदमी, वो घबरा के, परेशान होके गुल से छोड़ के चला गया और बड़े ऊँचे ओहदे पर वहाँ यूनेस्को का, किसका बड़ा अफ़सर है, बड़ा अच्छा काम कर रहा है, हमने एक बड़े अच्छे आदमी को छोड़ दिया। अब वही फैक्ट्री अब ज़रा आज़मा के, देख के, कुछ ग़लतियाँ थीं, संभाल के, शुरु में हो जाती हैं ग़लतियाँ, अब ज़ोरों से काम कर रही हैं और खूब मकान बन रहे हैं तेज़ी से, स्कूल बन रहे हैं तेज़ी से, दिल्ली में और जगह, सारे हिन्दुस्तान में तो काम कर नहीं सकती, दिल्ली में ख़ास काम कर रही है, हम चाहते हैं और ऐसी बनें।

ख़ैर, इससे कोऑपरेशन से कोई ख़ास मतलब नहीं लेकिन मकान बनाने के लिए बहुत ज़रूरी चीज़ है और यह कोऑपरेटिव तरीक़ा मकान बनाने का कोऑपरेटिव हाउसिंग सोसाइटीज़ यही एक तरीक़ा है तेज़ी से मुल्क में मकान बनाने का। अब कहाँ तक समझा जाये कि सरकार बनाती जायेगी, कहाँ तक अलग लोग बनायेंगे, एक कोऑपरेटिव तरीक़ा है जिसमें तेज़ी से बन सकते हैं और इसमें आप विचार करें, ग़ौर करें और बने वो जो साज़ो-सामान वहाँ मिलता है, कोई दूर से आप बहुत लायें वो नहीं होगा, उसका भी इंतज़ाम हो सकता है।

यह दो-तीन बातें मैंने आपसे कहीं और एक बात की हमेशा हमें ज़रूरत है, ख़ासकर आज, और वो यह कि हमारी पैदावार खेती से बढ़े, यह बुनियादी बात है। मैं बहुत चाहता हूँ कि हिन्दुस्तान में कारख़ाने बढ़ें, बग़ैर कारख़ानों के बड़े और छोटे, हम हिन्दुस्तान की दौलत को बढ़ा नहीं सकते, और दौलत नहीं हिन्दुस्तान की बढ़ती, तो लोगों के पास भी ज़्यादा नहीं बढ़ती आमदनी। इसलिए सबमें पहले, मैंने आपसे कहा कि मैं चाहता हूँ कारख़ाने बनें। लेकिन कारख़ाने जभी बनेंगे और कामयाबी से बनेंगे जब आपकी खेती की आमदनी काफ़ी हो, खेती की पैदावार बढ़े, जुड़े हुए हैं, अलग-अलग कहना यह ज़रूरी है उसके तो कोई माने नहीं हैं, ख़ासकर हमारे मुल्क में, एक खेतिहर मुल्क है, उसमें बिल्कुल ज़रूरी है कि हमारी तरक़्क़ी, कारख़ानों की और कोई भी और आम लोगों की तरक़्क़ी इस पर है

कि खेती से ज़्यादा बढ़े या ज़्यादा पैदा हो । और इसीलिए हमारा ख़्याल था कि पंचायती राज हमने इसीलिए किया और यह एक सहकारी संघ ।

हिन्दुस्तान में आप जानते हैं आमतौर से किसान, किसानों के पास बहुत कम ज़मीन है, औसत ली जाये तो शायद एक-दो एकड़ पड़े, कुछ लोगों के पास ज़्यादा है लेकिन वो भी बहुत ज़्यादा नहीं । अब हमारी खेती को बेहतर करने के लिए यह ज़रूरी है कि आजकल का जो खेती इल्म है और मुल्कों में जहाँ-जहाँ, उसको हम सीखें क्योंकि हमारी खेती पिछड़ गई इसलिए कि हम उसी तरीक़े से खेती करते गये जैसे कि हज़ार बरस पहले करते थे । वो बुरे तरीक़े नहीं हैं लेकिन हम पिछड़ गये, नई बातें नहीं सीखीं, नये हल नहीं चलाते, हम पुराने हल चलाते हैं, फ़र्टिलाइज़र वग़ैरा, खाद वग़ैरा नहीं काफ़ी देते, अब कुछ सीखने लगे हैं, कुछ देने लगे हैं जिससे यह लोग जो जानते हैं कहते हैं कि हम हिन्दुस्तान की पैदावार को चौगुना-पंचगुना कर सकते हैं, यानी पाँच सौ,चार सौ फ़ीसदी बढ़ा सकते हैं । अब ख़्याल कीजिये सारा नक़्शा हिन्दुस्तान का बदल जाये, अगर उसकी पाँच सौ न समझिये दुगना हम कर दें पैदावार को, दुगना बहुत है और वो हो सकती है, शर्तियन, हो सकती है, हम सब जानते हैं । और मुल्कों में क्यों हो गई दुगनी-तिगनी-चौगनी, इसके तरीक़े से हमारे मुल्क में आप देखिये जहां कोशिश हुई है वहाँ दुगनी-तिगनी हो गई है, तो हम क्यों न करें, सारे मुल्क में क्यों न करें । अच्छा अगर एक आदमी के पास थोड़ी सी ज़मीन है, एक एकड़, दो एकड़, उसकी हिम्मत नहीं है, उसके पास सामान नहीं है कि कुछ नये-नये तरीक़े करे, कर नहीं सकता, ताक़त नहीं है, पैसा नहीं है । लेकिन कोऑपरेटिव में हो वो तब कोऑपरेटिव उसका और, औरों को कर सकती है । या तो बड़ा ज़मींदार कर सकता है या कोऑपरेटिव कर सकती है । बड़े ज़मींदार हम नहीं चाहते हैं, ख़त्म हो गये इस मुल्क में, चुनांचे और कोई चारा नहीं है कि हम कोऑपरेटिव करें, नहीं तो हम पड़े रहें वैसे ही पिछड़े हुए, नये तरीक़े न लायें । इसलिए अज़हद ज़रूरी है कोऑपरेटिव्स हमारे देहात के काम में और और तरह से शहरों में भी बहुत ज़रूरी है, लेकिन देहात एक बुनियादी चीज़ है क्योंकि खाना पैदा करना जिससे अलावा इसके कि हमारी आबादी तीस करोड़ की है मुल्क की, देहाती, तीस करोड़ से कुछ ज़्यादा है, उनको फ़ायदा पहुँचे और दूसरे सारे मुल्क को फ़ायदा हो । तीसरे उसके पैदा करने से हमारे पास काफ़ी रुपया बचा रहेगा । खाने-पीने वग़ैरा का सब इंतज़ाम अच्छा करके इस रुपये से हम बाहर से जो कुछ हमें मशीन वग़ैरा मंगानी है कारख़ाने बनाने की, मंगा सकते हैं । इसलिए बड़ा हुआ है वो इंडस्ट्री की और कारख़ानों की तरक़्क़ी से । यह इतनी, इत्ती बात यह मिल सी गई है ।

हमारी पंचवर्षीय योजना है, उसमें एक अध्याय है, एक चैप्टर [Chapter] है कुछ कोऑपरेशन वग़ैरा का, ठीक है लेकिन असल में उस चैप्टर [Chapter] में ज़्यादा यह कोऑपरेशन, सहकारी काम यह सारे नक़्शा पे छाया हुआ है, उसके । अब आजकल यह सवाल उठता है कि हमारे ऊपर इतना बोझा पड़ा है चीनी हमले से, बेशुमार रुपया हमें ख़र्चना पड़ रहा है और पड़ेगा । क्या हम अपने पंचवर्षीय योजना को इसमें बन्द कर दें या बहुत कम कर लें । पेचीदा सवाल है, क्योंकि पहली बात हमारे सामने आ गई है जैसी कि आती है हर मुल्क के सामने, अपने मुल्क की इज़्ज़त, अपने मुल्क की आज़ादी

बचाना और हर बात दूसरी है, नम्बर दो है। ठीक है लेकिन अपने मुल्क की आज़ादी क़ायम रखने के लिए भी यह ज़रूरी है कि हम, जो हमारा पंचवर्षीय योजना का एक बड़ा विकास का काम है उसको ज़्यादातर जारी रखें। मैं नहीं कहता हर बात जारी रखें, उसको इधर-उधर बदलना है बदल दें, लेकिन ख़ालिस और बात को छोड़ दीजिये। ख़ास आजकल जो यह ख़तरनाक बातें हुई हैं हमारे मुल्क पर, हमारे मुल्क पर हमला किया है चीनियों ने, उसका सामना करने के लिए भी हमारे लिए ज़रूरी है कि मुल्क की ताक़त बढ़ायें। लोग समझते हैं कि ख़ाली फ़ौज करती है, फ़ौज तो करती है, लेकिन एक सिपाही के पीछे मैं नहीं जानता कितने लोग होते हैं। सौ-पचास आदमी पीछे होते हैं, पीछे से मतलब चाहे गाँव में काम करें, कारख़ाने में काम करें, उसका सामान उसको दें तब तो लड़े वो। यह कोई पुराने ज़माने की लड़ाई तो है नहीं तलवार रखके, एक नेज़ा लेके चले गये, बहादुरी दिखायी, उसको सामान देने के लिए सैकड़ों आदमी की बाहर ज़रूरत है काम करने की, चाहे खेत में, चाहे कारख़ाने में।

तो ज़रूरी है कि वो काम ठीकतौर से हो इसलिए ज़रूरी है कि हम उस काम को बढ़ाने की कोशिश करें, वही पंचवर्षीय योजना है। फ़र्ज़ कीजिये कि बिजली की शक्ति है, इलेक्ट्रिक पावर [Electric Power] है, इंतहादर्जे ज़रूरी चीज़ है, यानी इंतहादर्जे ज़रूरी चीज़ है वहाँ लड़ने के लिए, बिजली की पावर वहाँ नहीं होगी सरहद पर, लेकिन उसकी वजह से हम अपनी पैदावार को बढ़ायेंगे, हम गाँव-गाँव में पैदावार, हम छोटे कारख़ाने खोलेंगे, बड़े कारख़ाने खोलेंगे, किसान तक को इसमें कुछ मदद होगी बिजली आ जाने से। तो बिजली हमें बढ़ानी है और लड़ाई की वजह से और बढ़ानी है, कम नहीं करनी है। इसी तरह से हमें बहुत चीज़ें ज़रूरी हैं। तो जो बुनियादी बातें हमारी पंचवर्षीय योजना की हैं वो तो हमें करनी हैं, एक तो यों भी करनी थी, अब और भी ज़रूरी हो गई। यह लोगों का कहना कि इसको बन्द कर दो, पंचवर्षीय योजना को क्योंकि लड़ाई का मौक़ा है, यह बिल्कुल लड़ाई को समझना नहीं है, लड़ाई के लिए ज़रूरी क्या बात है और आइन्दा हम हिन्दुस्तान को क्या बनाना चाहते हैं, उसको भी भूल जाना है।

हम लड़ाई किस लिए लड़ते हैं? अपनी आज़ादी के लिए, अपने हिन्दुस्तान की एकता क़ायम करने के लिए, कोई हिन्दुस्तान के हिस्से पर कोई और कब्ज़ा न कर ले। यह ठीक है, बहुत माक़ूल बातें हैं लेकिन हिन्दुस्तान की तरक़्क़ी भी अब हमें करनी है। हम हिन्दुस्तान को बाद में एक ऐसा देश आख़िर में रह जाये, कि और भी ग़रीब हो जाये, दब जाये अपने बोझे के मारे। वो तो लड़ाई जीत लें लेकिन असली लड़ाई जो है हमारी ग़रीबी की वो हार गये। तो यह सब बातें सामने रखनी हैं, इसीलिए यह ज़रूरी है कि हम पंचवर्षीय योजना के बदले जो ग़ैर ज़रूरी काम है उसको निकाल दें, उसको मुलतवी कर दें लेकिन असली बात को, असली काम जो है बढ़ायें।

एक यह बात लीजिये, फ़र्ज़ कीजिये बाज़ लोग कहते हैं कि पढ़ाई है, शिक्षा है, बड़ा ख़र्चा हो रहा है उसमें हर तरफ़ बहुत तेज़ी से बढ़ रही है, इस वक़्त हमारे यहाँ कितने में भूल गया, पौने पाँच करोड़ लड़के-लड़कियाँ स्कूल-कॉलेज में पढ़ते हैं और ख़्याल है कि साढ़े

छः करोड़ हो जायेंगे इस साल में पाँच बरस के अन्दर और हर जगह माँग है। आप जानते हैं, पढ़ाई में बड़ा रुपया ख़र्चा होता है, इस वक़्त इसमें बेशुमार लोग, कोई एक पन्द्रह लाख, पन्द्रह लाख पढ़ाने वाले हैं, अध्यापक हैं, बड़ा ख़र्चा होता है, इमारतें हैं, यह, वो। कहते हैं कि पढ़ाई को ज़रा रोकथाम कर दो इसलिए कि लड़ें जाके। इससे ज़्यादा ग़लत बात कोई हो नहीं सकती। क्योंकि इन बातों से मुल्क की ताक़त बढ़ती है, पढ़े-लिखे आदमी से, वो आजकल लड़ाई भी लड़नी है वो अनपढ़ आदमी नहीं लड़ सकते, सीखना पड़ता है, अक़्लों से लड़ना होता है। तो यह ज़रूरी है कि हम अपनी शिक्षा की जो प्रबन्ध हम करना चाहते हैं उसको जारी रखें। हाँ, उसको कुछ मोड़ दें ऐसा कि ज़्यादा मदद हो उससे, यह और बात है लेकिन यह कि हम कम कर दें उसको यह इस वक़्त नहीं हो सकता, लड़ाई की वजह से, और बातें छोड़ दीजिये। इसलिए इस ढंग से हमें देखना है और इस ढंग से देखने से यह जो सहकारी संघ का ख़्याल है, कोऑपरेटिव्स का, यह बिल्कुल ज़रूरी है, लड़ाई के लिए भी, और बातें छोड़िये। चुनांचे, इसकी अहमियत आप समझ लीजिये आजकल की हालत में।

अब हमारे ऊपर यकायक यह ज़बरदस्त हमला हुआ, एक सदमा पहुँचा लोगों के दिल को, बहुत हमारे बहादुर जवानों की जानें गईं, और लड़ाई होगी और जायेंगी, लेकिन फिर भी एक और बात हुई उससे जिससे कम से कम मुझे बहुत ख़ुशी हुई है और यक़ीनन आपको भी होगी। इस सदमे का नतीजा जो हुआ, एक, एक कोई व्यक्ति हो, इंसान हो या कोई क़ौम हो उसकी आज़माइश होती है सदमों के सामने, ख़तरे के सामने, आरामतलबी से आज़माइश नहीं होती। और यह जो सदमा पहुँचा हमले का तो आपने देखा, हम सभों ने देखा कि हिन्दुस्तान भर में क्या हवा फैली, कोई डर की बात नहीं, घबराने की नहीं बल्कि हिम्मत की, बल्कि एक क़ुर्बानी की, बल्कि छोटे-छोटे सवाल जो आपस में बहस के थे, झगड़े के थे उसको हल कर देने की। और एक आवाज़ निकली हिन्दुस्तान के हर शख़्स से जो आपस में लड़ते भी थे वो भी भूल गये लड़ाई, कि मदद करें इस मौक़े पर, इस ख़तरनाक मौक़े पर अपने मुल्क की। और सब चाहे पैसा जमा किया जाये, चाहे वहाँ जाइये आप जहाँ रंगरूट भर्ती होते हैं हल्के-हल्के। वहाँ एक मजमा खड़ा था, हज़ारों आदमी खड़े थे भर्ती होने वाले, पाँच-छः हज़ार एक दफ़्तर में, बहुत सारे दफ़्तर हैं। इससे जोश, मालूम होता है कि मुल्क में जोश है, मुल्क में एक जोश नहीं बल्कि मुल्क की जान इससे मालूम होती है, जानदार मुल्क है और अगर वह चीज़ है, जान है, जोश है और एकता है तब कोई उस मुल्क को हरा नहीं सकता है, चाहे कुछ हो, तकलीफ़ें उठानी पड़ें, कुछ हो।

तो एक माने में एक कुछ यह कहना मुझे ख़ुशी हुई कि हम पे हमला हुआ यह तो ग़लत बात है लेकिन फिर भी एक ढंग उसका है, एक तरीक़ा है एक उसको देखने का यह जो मुल्क में यकायक एक नई जान हुई, नई लौ जली एक के दिल में, यह बहुत क़ीमती चीज़ है। और कोई बेजा नहीं है, कि हम ख़ुश हों कि मुसीबत भी आई, कि उसका नतीजा यह हुआ कि हमने इसको, इस लौ को फिर पाया, ज़रा धीमी कहीं-कहीं पड़ गई थी लेकिन यह हमें मालूम हो गया कि बुझी नहीं थी कहीं, हरेक दिल में मौजूद थी, फिर

तेज़ी से उठ खड़ी हुई। यह हाल है, लेकिन यह हाल तो है जोश है, लेकिन यह याद रखिए आप यह वक़्ती जोश काफ़ी नहीं होता है, इसको जारी रखना है क्योंकि सख़्त मुक़ाबला है, सख़्त मुश्किलेंहैं और सदमें पहुँचेंगे फिर भी हमें इस जोश को रखना है, और बढ़ाना है और ख़ासतौर से अपनी एकता को मज़बूत करना है। यह बड़ी बात हुई एक माने में, एक झलक हमें दिखी हिन्दुस्तान में उस चीज़ की जिस तस्वीर को हम दूर से रखके देख रहे हैं, यानी भारत, एक सारा भारत एक सहकारी संघ हो जाये वो झलक दिखी। क्योंकि जब सब लोग मिलके एकतरफ़ देखते हैं, एक काम करते हैं सहकारी तरीक़े पर तो वो मिलके एक मज़बूत, एक ताक़तवर चीज़ हो जाती है, अलग-अलग खींचने वाली नहीं। तो वो हमने देखा, इससे हम फ़ायदा उठायें और पूरीतौर से हम अपने-अपने जो काम करते हैं उसको अच्छा करें, मुल्क को मज़बूत करने के लिए और मुल्क को आज़ाद रखने के लिए।

एक बात और मैं आपसे कहूँ—मुझे रंज होता है एक तरफ़ तो यह है और दूसरे तरफ़ यहाँ दिल्ली शहर में, शायद कहीं और भी, पता नहीं, कुछ नादान लड़के स्कूल के, कॉलेज के जुलूस निकाल के हुड़-दंगा करते हैं, जाके कुछ दुकानें तोड़ दीं और इस क़िस्म की बातें कहीं, जला भी दीं, कोई कई जगह, इससे ज़्यादा कोई नुकसानदेह चीज़ नहीं है हमारे मुल्क के लिए, इस वक़्त यह सब मुल्क का सिपाही होना है, कोई लड़कों का खेल नहीं है कि जाके गुल मचाके यहाँ जला दिया और यहाँ किसी को मार दिया, यह तमाशा है। हम सभों को सिपाही होना है, सिपाही की तरह से रहना है, सिपाही की तरह से अपनी ताक़त को मिलाके लगाना है, इसमें बदनामी हासिल करना अपनी और मुल्कों में कि ऐसे मौक़े पर यह कुछ अनजान लोग मुमकिन है जोश में आके या कुछ बहकाए हुए यह बातें करते हैं। इससे ताक़त कम होती है मुल्क की, हमें एक एक ज़रा अपनी ताक़त को जमा करना है, मज़बूती से और जमा करके आगे बढ़ना है, छलांग मारनी है, मुल्क को आज़ाद करना है। यह दिल्ली के बाज़ारों में जुलूस निकाल के होंगी यह बातें, और हुल्लड़ मचाके मैं तो हैरान होता हूँ कि ऐसे मौक़ों पर भी लोग समझे नहीं हैं कि, क्या चीज़ है मुल्क की आज़ादी के लिए लड़ना। वो समझते हैं कि गुल मचाके या एक दल दूसरे दल के ख़िलाफ़ होके, इस वक़्त दल-वल नहीं है कोई हिन्दुस्तान में, इस वक़्त एक दल है वो हिन्दुस्तानी का दल है और हरेक को सामना करना है इसका और क़ायदे से, नियमित रूप से, डिसिप्लिन से, न कि हुल्लड़बाज़ी से।

तो यह हालत है इस वक़्त जब हम आपसे मिले हैं, मैंने कहा आपसे कि मैंने महीना भर हुआ एक सन्देश भेजा था वो पुराना हो गया। मुल्क का नक़्शा बदल गया, मुल्क की हवा बदल गई, हमारे सवालों की हवा बदली। अब मैं लिखता, शायद मैं कुछ और लिखता, लेकिन बावजूद इन सब बातों के यह सहकारी संघ का काम इतना बुनियादी है आइन्दा के लिए, हमारे भविष्य के लिए और इस वक़्त जो लड़ाई के मैदान में हमें जाना पड़ रहा है उसके लिए। इसलिए इस निगाह से आप देखें यह बड़ा काम है और हम जो उस काम में लगे हैं वो हम हिन्दुस्तान की ख़िदमत बड़े पैमाने पर कर रहे हैं। इस तरह से देखिये तो हम लोग जो अपने-अपने काम में फंसे हैं, छोटे-छोटे कामों में वो भी कुछ उनका क़द बढ़

167

जायेगा, क्योंकि जब आप कोई बड़े काम में लगते हैं चाहे आप छोटे से पुर्ज़े हों उसमें, बड़े काम का साया आप पे पड़ता है और आप भी बढ़ने लगते हैं। तो मौक़ा आया है फिर से हमें, हमारे मुल्क में, कि हम सब लोग इस ज़बरदस्त काम में लग के, हम सब बढ़ें, और हिन्दुस्तान बढ़े।

जयहिन्द!

[Translation begins:

Mr Chairman,[153] Sisters and Brothers,

When I was invited to come here a month ago, I accepted very gladly. I was also asked to give a message which I did.[154] I think it has been published somewhere. But the message, whatever significance it may have had at the time it was sent, has become somewhat outdated now. Our world has changed somewhat drastically in this one month and I was thinking of making my excuses to Brahma Perkashji[155] and not coming here today because nowadays there is great pressure on my time. But then I thought it would not be proper. For one thing, I attach great importance to cooperation. Secondly, I feel that the cooperatives can help a great deal in the tremendous problems that we are facing just now. So I have presented myself before you.

Most of you present here are involved in the working of cooperatives whereas I can talk about it only as an outsider. But I am fully convinced that the only way to solve India's problems is through cooperation. I think it is a very good thing to form cooperatives in the cities as well as the rural areas. We have something even bigger in mind. Before India became independent, we had laid down in the constitution of the Congress that the Constitution of India should be drawn up on the principle of a cooperative commonwealth. It is not easy to understand what we actually meant by that because it is not a question of merely passing laws. It is an entire way of life, of thinking and of relations between human beings and ultimately among nations. All that stems from the same thing. Just now you heard a song about loving one another. Cooperation involves changing one's entire thinking and viewpoint.

There are often debates about the various issues, socialism, communism and capitalism. You are perhaps aware that my own leaning is towards socialism. But in a sense, I feel that cooperation is a method of bringing about socialism. I think that is the only key to solve the argument about the various isms. We must use the method of cooperation to handle the tasks in villages and cities and

153. See note 152 in this section.
154. See items 154 and 155.
155. General Secretary of the National Cooperative Union of India.

factories, etc. In fact, I would go so far as to say that the entire administration should be based on the cooperative method though it is not easy. We have to create a new atmosphere in the country. It can be done only gradually and with the help of the people? You cannot change the entire way of life of a nation and its thinking very suddenly. I am convinced it will come about? So the picture that I have before me is a far-reaching one, I want that cooperation should mould the entire life of the nation instead of their cutting each other's throats as people do nowadays. I do not say that the people are bad, but the method of their dealing with one another certainly is. People take advantage of one another's misfortunes. But such things cannot last very long. Or, rather, they may. What I mean is that the atmosphere is changing.

So I want to request you to keep this broader picture in mind. Only then can we reach our goal some time. We are taking very small steps in that direction just now. But later we can go on faster. Ultimately, we want the whole of India to be one large cooperative in a sense, as we had said thirty or forty years ago. It has become more than ever necessary. There is no alternative. There are often very shrill debates between the followers of various isms, capitalism, communism and socialism. Even their good principles are vitiated by their methods of quarrelling, abusing one another, etc., which are far removed from the cooperative method. We must change our way of thinking and learn not to take advantage of others' misfortunes but to work in mutual cooperation. Some people seem to think that they must destroy the existing social organisation and economy and then build a new world of their dreams. They expect people to put up with the ruin that will descend upon the world and face all kinds of hardships before the new world is created. Cooperation is something by which we can change the existing system without destroying it. So I feel that it is the best way for everyone and particularly so for India and we must expand it in every way.

At the same time, I must tell you that cooperation does not mean putting up some artificial cooperatives here and there. I do not know how many of the existing cooperatives are real. Brahma Perkashji said that there are three and a half lakh cooperatives in India. But I hope they are the real thing. I am fully convinced that the cooperatives must not be run by government officials. They can help and advise but the task of the running the cooperatives must belong to the people. Very often, they become official institutions with government servants being ex-officio president and secretary. It is possible that wherever the government officials are good, the work may go on well. But the method is wrong for it did not create the spirit which is fundamental to cooperation, the self-confidence, ability to stand on one's feet, harmony, working together, etc. It is not a real cooperative if it functions by orders from above. It may do good work. But it is not a real cooperative. You must bear this mind and work upon this principle. You must understand that it is not a superficial thing imposed from above but an entire way of life.

I do not wish to go into all the details. There will be a debate on it anyhow. But I do wish to point out a few things. Brahma Perkashji said just now that there is panchayati raj here. But panchayati raj is meaningless until there is a cooperative society too. Both these things are linked together. Therefore it is essential that we have them all over the country, particularly in the rural areas. Secondly, women must participate in these activities, we want the women to play a more active role in national life. After all, they are a little more than half of India's population. How can we go ahead without them? Moreover cooperation is something which concerns a number of matters related to domestic life. Therefore women must take greater interest in it. You must enrol women as members.

Thirdly, housing is very important both in the rural and the urban areas. New methods of building houses are being devised and prefabricated houses are being produced in the housing factories. When we first set up a housing factory in Delhi, there was a great uproar because the bricks which were being used were cracking. There were accusations of dishonesty and what not. The more ignorant the people, the greater the noise there is generally? It is usually the uninformed people who make most noise. [Laughter] There was a very capable man in charge who left in a panic and is now occupying a very high position in the UNESCO. We have let a very able man go. Anyhow, after a period of trial and error, the factory is fully in operation now. Houses and school buildings are being produced on a large scale. We want more of these factories to come up elsewhere in the country?

Well, this has nothing to do with cooperation. Cooperative housing societies are the only answer to the problem of housing shortages. The government cannot provide houses for everyone? Arrangements must be made to ensure that locally available material is used.

There are two or three things, which are absolutely basic to our progress. One is the growth of agricultural production. Two, industries must come up because there is no other way to increase the national wealth. But the basic thing is increase in agricultural production which will provide the necessary surplus for industrialisation. The two things are closely linked. India is a predominantly agricultural country. Therefore the growth of industries and the betterment of economic condition of the masses are all dependent on the increase in agricultural production. It is with this in view that we started the panchayati raj system and cooperative societies.

As you know, the majority of the farmers in India has very small landholdings. On an average, an individual farmer may not have more than an acre or two. Therefore it is absolutely essential to adopt modern techniques of agriculture and to understand that we had become backward in this field. The old methods which farmers have been following for thousands of years are not bad. But we became backward because we failed to learn anything new. We have been using the old plough and do not use fertilisers, etc. Those who have adopted the improved techniques have increased production fourfold. The entire face of India would be transformed if everyone could even double the production from land. We know that it can be done. Even in India, wherever an effort has been made, production has doubled or even trebled. Why should we not try to do it all over the country? Those who have very small landholdings may not have the resources to adopt new techniques. But a cooperative society can help even the smallest farmer. We do not want big landlords any more in India. There is no alternative to cooperatives. Otherwise we will remain backward as before. Cooperation is absolutely essential for the rural areas. The population in the rural areas is a little more than thirty crores. Cooperatives will benefit all of them directly as well as the entire nation. Moreover, an increase in agricultural production will mean a surplus which can be used for importing machines and setting up industries, etc. So all these things are inextricably linked together.

There is a chapter on cooperation in our Five Year Plan. But it is something which underlies the entire Plan. We have had to spend an enormous amount of money due to Chinese aggression. The dilemma that we are facing is whether we should give up the Plan or curtail it. The most important consideration for any nation is its self-respect, honour and freedom. Everything else is secondary. That is no doubt true. But even to hold on to our freedom, it is essential that we should carry on the work of development that we have undertaken. We may have to make some changes. But even in view of the danger which threatens on our borders, it is essential that we make India strong. People think that it is only the armed forces which defend the borders. But behind every soldier there is the work of hundreds of people, in factories and villages, to keep them supplied with food and equipment, etc. Wars are no longer fought as in the olden days by soldiers marching off with their swords to prove their valour on the battlefield. Hundreds of men have to work hard behind the scenes, in the fields and factories to keep the armed forces supplied with all they need.

Therefore, it is extremely important to carry on as before with the Five Year Plans. For instance, take electricity, which is extremely important in the battlefield too. Therefore, we must increase generation of power, which in turn will help increase production, agricultural as well as industrial production. We have to increase power generation, not reduce it. Similarly, there are various

171

other things, which are essential. Therefore, we cannot give up the fundamental tasks that we have taken up under the Five Year Plans. They were important anyhow but have become more so now. Those who say that we should give up the Plan because of the border crisis do not understand what war is all about and forget the kind of India that we wish to build.

What are we fighting for? We are fighting to keep the unity and freedom of India intact which is a very good thing. But we cannot give up the path of progress that we have been following so far. If we continue to remain backward and poor, even if we win the military battle, we would have lost the war against poverty. So we should keep all this in mind. We can leave out the non-essential items from the Five Year Plan or postpone them. But we have to continue doing the things which are absolutely essential.

Take education, for instance. Some people feel that we are spending too much on education. I think nearly four crores and seventy-five lakh children are reading in schools and colleges and by the end of five years, the number may increase to six and a half crores. As you know, this means an enormous investment with fifteen lakh teachers to pay and buildings and so on. Some people say that we should stop this while we are at war. There can be nothing more harmful because a nation's strength lies in its qualified, educated men and women. A modem war cannot be fought by uneducated people. They have to learn to handle sophisticated machines and equipment. Therefore, it is essential that we continue the arrangements we have made for education. We can give it a slightly different slant. But we cannot bring our efforts to a halt because we are at war.

If you look at it from this point of view, the idea of cooperatives is absolutely essential, even for the war effort. You must understand its importance in today's situation. The unexpected Chinese attack has been a great shock to all of us. Many of our brave young soldiers have lost their lives in the battlefield. But there has been one outcome which has filled me at least with great happiness, as I am sure, it will do for you. It is only in a crisis that the character of an individual or a nation is truly tested. You must have felt the new atmosphere which has prevailed ever since the border crisis arose. There was no panic but only a spirit of sacrifice and courage. In fact, there has been a marked tendency to set aside petty disputes and India has risen as one man to face the situation. Donations have come pouring in and everywhere, you can see long lines of people waiting to be recruited into the army. All this shows the vitality and enthusiasm of the people and so long as we have that, no power on earth can defeat us.

It would be wrong to say that I am happy about the Chinese aggression. But the spirit of unity and camaraderie which it has engendered in the country is something very precious. There is nothing wrong in feeling happy that even in this hour of trouble, we have rediscovered our vitality which had dimmed at times. We have been reassured that it has by no means been snuffed out. It is present in every individual and is burning bright once again.

Anyhow, we must remember that momentary enthusiasm is not enough. We have to sustain it because there are goals ahead. We will have to face difficult times and must be prepared for shocks. We must keep up our spirit and present a united front. We have caught a glimpse of India as one large cooperative with the people united in their purpose leading to unity and strength. As I said, we have caught a glimpse of that and must try to take full advantage of the prevailing climate.

I was distressed to find that in Delhi and some other cities, ignorant young college boys take out processions and burn shops and what not. There can be nothing more harmful to India at present than such behaviour. Each one of you has to become a soldier in India's cause. This is not the time to be indulging in schoolboy pranks and irresponsible behaviour. We have to conduct ourselves with martial discipline. Hooliganism and disorderliness will earn a bad reputation for India and weaken us at a time when we should conserve our strength to defend India's freedom and honour. You cannot do that by taking out processions in the streets of Delhi. I am amazed that there should be people even in this crisis who refuse to understand what it means to be fighting for our survival. They seem to think of it as some party politics. There is but one party today in India, the party of Indians and every single citizen here must face the danger which threatens the country with discipline.

The message that I had sent over a month ago has become outdated today. The entire pattern has changed and we are suddenly facing a new set of problems. I would write a different kind of a message today. But in spite of that, cooperation is fundamental for us, at present as well as for our future and for our war effort too. I want you to look at it from this point of view, that we are engaged in the service of the nation on a very grand scale. If you look at it from this point of view, that we are engaged in the service of the nation on a very grand scale. If you look at it from this angle, even the small tasks in which most of us are engaged will assume a new importance and the people will grow in stature. When we are engaged in a great task, even if it is only as very small cogs, the greatness rubs off on us and we grow in stature. We have been given yet another opportunity to serve the nation in a big way.

Jai Hind!

Translation ends]

173

(j) Media

161. For *The Hindusthan Standard*[156]

I send my greetings and good wishes to *The Hindusthan Standard* on the occasion of its completing twenty-five years of existence as a daily newspaper. I remember its early days when it championed the cause of India's freedom bravely in spite of difficulties put in its way by the then British Government.

In these days the calls on a newspaper are more diverse. I hope that *The Hindusthan Standard* will continue to meet the challenge of the times and thus serve the cause of the people. In particular, unity and integration are the basis of all our freedom.

162. For *Kesari*[157]

I send my good wishes to the *Kesari* on the occasion of its being converted into a daily newspaper from Vijay Dasami day. That is a day of good omen for this project. But, apart from the day, the *Kesari* has had the great good fortune of being founded by Lokmanya Tilak and ever since then it has maintained a high tradition. I hope that the daily newspaper will carry this tradition on and serve the nation.

163. In New Delhi: To State Information Ministers' Conference[158]

Shri Gopala Reddi,[159] friends and comrades,
I must confess that my mind is not quite ready to deal with all your problems. I have accepted gladly your invitation to be present here at this conference, but since the various developments are taking place of which you are fully aware which fill my mind and I cannot adjust myself to other things. And yet these developments to which you, Mr Minister, have referred your remarks, the massive invasion on our frontier, and the amazing statements that have accompanied it are themselves a reason why, you, I mean, the Ministers of

---

156. Message, 1 October 1962.
157. Message, 3 October 1962.
158. Speech, 25 October 1962. NMML, AIR Tapes TS No. 8721-22, NM No. 1703.
159. Minister of Information and Broadcasting.

Information and Broadcasting, should not put such machinery as you have in gear to meet this kind of thing.

Our Plan is a basic thing. It is meant to strengthen the nation to increase the nation's welfare and the individual welfare in the nation. Ultimately, a country is only strong if its economy is strong and the people are progressing and their standard of living is being raised. That is why we have paid so much attention, to the plan. But sometimes a crisis occurs such as has occurred in India today, when all our energies have to be diverted to that end. That does not mean that we forget the plan, because a plan itself is one aspect of meeting the crisis in the long run, not in the immediate present. In the long run a nation which is economically strong and productive can meet any danger. Thus, for instance, even if we have to prepare for military conflicts on a large scale in the field for war, in fact, the only preparation is the real preparation; so you produce the stuff that you want, that means production, that means plan, you increase our productive capacity or electric power or agricultural capacity, all that becomes a part of the military effort, apart from everything else, so that the plan is by no means an alternative to a military effort, it is a part of it. It may, of course, be that the present plan has to be adjusted somewhat to the present day needs, those items in it which are not of high priority can be delayed. That is a different matter. But in the main, the plan has to go on. Apart from everything else, because of the situation created by the Chinese invasion. Now, apart from that I think this aspect should be understood and should be explained and publicised to our people. Because our people, all of us, not only we, you and I are not, if I may use the word, military minded. I am ashamed of not being military minded. Military minded does not mean that we have no knowledge of military affairs, we may have and we have studied them, but military-minded thinking and functioning in terms of the military mind. The far more military minded people are those who know nothing about military matters and who go up and down the streets shouting slogans; they are very military minded, very aggressive minded but very foolishly minded, very ignorantly minded, who do not help at all anybody.

So, we have been conditioned not only since independence but even long before that under British rule; Pax Britannica as it was called, who helped us then under British rule, and it was the job of the British to fight with the Indian army no doubt. But right, there were two great wars in our recollection and Indian armies took part in them. Nevertheless, it was not in India, may be a little corner of Assam, the Japanese came in last time and it did not affect India very much. We were not conscious of war—emotionally conscious—and just like countries in Europe, where they have suffered from war. They have seen the whole countryside and cities being wiped off. Every family in Europe has personally suffered from the war. In that sense we are not conscious and we talked big occasionally, but we did not get emotionally involved in it.

Since independence, naturally we have been anxious to protect our country and for the first time, our defence forces have been directed from the country, not from Whitehall. Till then they were directed from Whitehall and all the equipment etc. they required came from England, whether it was fully suited or not, it came from England. Since then the first thing that happened was that the direction was transferred from Whitehall to New Delhi of our defence forces, our army staff etc. who formed, and they became the expert advisors to the government on this subject. Before that remember, it is important, that we had no senior officers in the Indian army, Indians I mean, and the whole policy was laid down from Whitehall. That big change was made.

The second change was the manufacture of equipment in India. Now that is a part of the general process of industrialisation, which is not only equipment and [goods]. That is why the development of industry was considered important, the development of electric power etc. behind that again. Now take any war effort; it is not confined to guns and such like things, weapons of warfare. It covers any number of things it covers clothing, it covers food, it covers so many other things, that half the civil production is concerned with it. So that the whole industrial machinery of the state has to come up, has to grow up in order to feed and to sustain any war effort. Therefore, we had even from that point of view to build up our Plan. We did not forget the possible dangers to India, we had to build up the plan from that point of view. We have to build up our agriculture from that point of view apart from other points of view which are important. And we had built up especially our ordnance factories and the industries pertaining to defence directly. They started not from scratch, they did produce something, but almost from scratch. Because in British times they did not want and they did not encourage India producing her own armaments even, they wanted them to be obtained from England. It was only under the stress of the last war, last Great War, that something had to be done here because we could not get them from England. But still, it was very rudimentary and preliminary. Since then we have made very considerable progress in our manufacturing sectors, ordnance factories etc. and take even aircraft, we are doing very well. But that progress is not translated into immediate effect. We can make, we have made a supersonic aircraft. We are making another two or three, but we are not producing them by the dozens every day as these great countries do. They produce several a day in the assembly lines. We are producing many things, we are not producing all yet, but we are progressing fairly well, yet we have a long way to go to produce even the necessary things for our immediate requirements if danger threatens.

Now the first point that I would like you to bear in mind is this that while today inevitably circumstances have forced us to face this war effort in our country because none of you and no Indian I hope, will ever agree to surrender to invasion or aggression. Now if that is agreed to as it is, we should never agree, does not matter how many reverses we have to begin with, we will never agree and we will strengthen ourselves and prepare for the final victory. That is so. If that is so then it follows that we must prepare for it. We do not prepare for it by passing resolutions. Resolutions are good occasionally, but we have to prepare for it in every field, in the military field, in the scientific field, in the economic field, in the agricultural field, industrial field, every field, should be coordinated to help in adding to the strength of India to meet this crisis. It may take some time gradually but there is no other way. We cannot, we cannot, merely sit down and bemoan our lot. That is not a self-respecting nation's way to meet the crisis. It is not the right way, of course, to create conditions of alarm and panic in the public mind. That also is a sign of weakness, and we must and you must by your information and other services try to avoid that to give them.

Now, we have to in a democratic country more than elsewhere, you have to trust the public and our public is, by and large, a trustworthy thing, I think. I have great faith in them. And if you explain something fully to them, they understand it, most of them. Therefore, I would trust the public and give them as full information as one can. One cannot give them every information obviously in military matters, but keep them broadly informed of the position so that they may know and not be liable to being affected by rumours and gossip and all that, as sometimes they are. Therefore, it becomes very important, the publicity aspect of it is important; and you will see, if you watch the Chinese type of publicity which is quite astonishing that they get away with it in the shape of falsehood, there is no relation to fact; they just want pouring a stream of falsehoods hoping that some would stick—and some do stick—and what is more they even describe the event before it had happened, which is extraordinary. It is very interesting this, their big invasion, massive invasion of India took place five days ago on the 20th October. Before any fighting had started there, the Peking Radio let out that Indian forces had carried out a frenzied attack on them. Now this was a preparation for their attacking. The Indian forces at that time had not attacked them at all, but within half an hour or twenty minutes Chinese forces started attacking. Now before that they started the Chinese radio, i.e., the Peking Radio announced it that our forces are attacking and they are defending and they would defend. This went out. We heard first from the Chinese and from Australia. They had heard the Chinese radio reporting that we were attacking. While they were going to attack, they were preparing the public minds for that and then went on saying that they were acting in self-defence of fierce attacks from the

177

Indian forces. I think, the Indian forces were quite entitled to attack them since they are in our territory. That is not the point. But the way the Chinese put it, to appear as meek lambs who are being devoured by some tigers from India, and they have to defend themselves. It is quite extraordinary, the meek lamb goes on devouring our territory and that is not an example, I suggest that you should follow. That is the example of untruth and making statements of events which have not occurred and so on and so forth. Nevertheless, it is true that we are not quite wide awake enough in these matters and we should awaken both from the point of view of other countries and our own. There is no doubt that in other countries during these critical few days-- past few days-- they have got Chinese accounts far ahead of any Indian account reaching them by the radio or otherwise. We must be, therefore, more up to the mark. Now, I am saying, that is one thing and the other is with our own people.

Mr Gopala Reddi began by talking about national integration. That, of course, is always essential and now doubly so and I hope that out of the evil cometh out good. Out of this crisis, people forget their petty grievances and petty controversies and realise the essential nature of national integration, if we talk and go on arguing about small matters, relatively small matters, then it simply means that we have no larger outlook, we have no national outlook and we will suffer for it as we have suffered in the past, when in spite of great courage and bravery on the part of Indians they all thought of their area, their group and it was gradually swallowed up by the enemy in each area. So, national integration has become a very important thing in this context especially, and I am glad to say broadly speaking the whole atmosphere in India is in favour of that in view of this crisis and we should take advantage of it and we should avoid as far as possible controversies, except such as are essential. We cannot absolutely avoid them, but controversies about unessential matters can be postponed, should be postponed, so that we may create an atmosphere for hard work leading in this direction of preparing the country for war, for defence.

Now I want you to realise that shocked as we have been, the public and everyone, and I can quite understand the shock the public has suffered during the last week or so. It has brought us, made us realise that we were, shall I say, we are getting out of touch with reality in the modern world. We are living in an artificial atmosphere of our old creation and we have been shocked out of it, all of us, whether it is government, whether it is people, I am not referring to some, may be industrialists. People say, people talk, we are four hundred million, just as the Chinese talk, we are six hundred millions. It has some significance no doubt, but not very much. There can be six hundred million or four hundred millions sheep. There can be a few stronger animals. Numbers in a sense potentially count, but ultimately it is strength, cohesion, training of a nation that counts, all this Five Year Plan etc., is ultimately meant to give that strength and cohesion and training. But even from the point of view of warlike preparation, we have suffered a severe shock. It is no good, sitting down for us, now, and do a post-mortem on it, but the real thing that is out of joint, was our whole mentality, our whole government, the way government is run here. It has not run on that basis. Government takes time to do anything, slow moving processes of government. Now, you cannot move slowly in this matter, when you lose a battle by delay of a few days or you may lose a war if you do not change that. So, we have to get out of that rut and move swiftly, whatever we have to do, and war with all its evils is a tremendous energising process. May be, it will do us that good, may be it will stiffen us and make us function quickly and effectively and get out of this long bureaucratic method and machines that we are used to. I have no doubt, that in all these matters, information and broadcasting can help a lot. I cannot suggest you the details how you should do it, how you can do it but keep this in view and I am sure, you can help a lot by keeping the public informed and preventing them from developing any panicky attitude and even if there may be reverses, there have been serious reverses, there may be more. You will remember what happened in the last great war, when a very terrible thing happened to the British army, in France, Dunkirk— the whole British army was wiped off. They had to start from scratch. They were brave people, they did not give in and under a great leader Mr Winston Churchill, they started building anew and built and fortified themselves and ultimately defeated the enemy. So, to some extent, we have to function like that. We have to build up, not spend our time in criticising the past and bemoaning the past, but look to the future and build up for it, and I am quite sure in my mind and I say so completely honestly that the strength in India is considerable and directed to right ends and, it can be directed to right ends, and in the situation created by this conflict and other matters, there are other factors also in favour of us. Therefore, there is no reason for long-term alarm. There is reason for great concern and great effort to be laid down.

One thing more. Quite apart from our troubles on our frontier, the world is at present again on the brink of war over the Cuban affair, and if unfortunately that fuse is lit, it will be very disastrous for the whole world and we have and we shall not be in that war, but we will be affected and every country will be affected if it is nuclear, bound to be, if there is war, it is bound to be a nuclear war—a terrible affair. I remember when I was in England, a very responsible person quoting another responsible person said that in a nuclear war the estimate of scientists and other competent people was that within the first few days, there would be three hundred million deaths in Europe, in America and in Asia, partly in Africa. Now, imagine about 90 million people dying in America about 90 or

100 million in the Soviet Union and about another 100 million in Europe. We have come to this that we talk, people talk calmly, of 300 million deaths. It is a strange, well I will call it, deterioration of the human mind that we can take these things in our stride and call it practical view, and now we are again on the brink of it. We cannot do much about it. Some people will decide. We have enough trouble of our own anyhow. But all this means that we are entering a phase of our existence which is full of dangers and difficulties and we cannot afford to relax, we cannot afford to take things softly, we cannot afford to carry on petty controversies, and if we cannot live up to this period of danger and difficulty in the world and our own frontiers, then we imperil our own freedom. It is not a question of few miles here and there in the border, it is a much broader and much deeper question. So, I hope in this great effort that India is going to make, our Ministry for Information and Broadcasting will throw in their full weight.

164. To D. Tyerman: Press Institute Seminar[160]

October 25, 1962

Dear Mr Tyerman,

Thank you for your letter of October 22nd.

I would gladly attend the concluding session of the Seminar of the Indian Press Institute. But I cannot be quite sure as I am uncertain of my program in February next. Also, you will appreciate that, owing to the crisis that has arisen because of the Chinese invasion of India, it is difficult for me to accept firmly engagements nearly four months ahead. But if it is possible for me, I shall attend your meeting.

Yours sincerely,
[Jawaharlal Nehru]

---

160. Letter to the Editor of *The Economist*, 22 Ryder Street, St James's, London SW1.

165. To B. Gopala Reddi: Quality of Radio Programmes[161]

November 11, 1962

My dear Gopala Reddi,

Thank you for your letter of November 11, together with the statement attached to it.

I am afraid I have no time to listen in to the radio. Sometimes I hear the news at 9 p.m. But it is true that there is widespread complaint about the ineffectiveness of our radio programmes. I cannot judge how far this complaint is true. I think perhaps the manner of presenting news is not as good as it might be. It requires professional expertise, to do it in an attractive way.

The other day the radio said, and so also the press, that we were still retaining Chushul. I do not know what the word "still" meant. But it was understood to mean that we were hard pressed at Chushul and we were hanging on for the moment. This was not so, as a fact. We are strongly placed in Chushul and we expect to remain there. When I enquired from the Defence Ministry as to what news had been given out, they said they had not used the word "still".

I enclose a slip that I have received from Mridula Sarabhai. I do think that we should avoid the kind of language referred to in it.

It might be worthwhile for you to meet some Members of Parliament or the Consultative Committee for I & B and tell them what you are doing and ask for their suggestions.

Yours sincerely,
Jawaharlal Nehru

---

161. Letter to the Minister of Information and Broadcasting. PMO, File No. 43(192)/62-63-PMS, Sr. No. 25-A.

166. To Mahavir Tyagi: Ramnath Goenka's Mobilisation of the Press[162]

November 27, 1962

My dear Mahavir,

Thank you for your letter of the 27th.[163] I am returning Ramnath Goenka's letter to you.[164]

Yours affectionately,
[Jawaharlal Nehru]

167. To S.P. Jain: Support from *Times of India*[165]

November 30, 1962

Dear Shanti Prasadji,

Thank you for your letter of November 21st and for the offer of your personal service as well as that of the *Times of India* to interpret our policies. Newspapers have a great responsibility today and I am sure that they can do much good if they discharge it conscientiously and for the benefit of national policies.[166]

Yours sincerely,
[Jawaharlal Nehru]

(k) Urban Development

168. Hanging Gardens in Bombay[167]

I see from the note attached to Shri Dharma Vira's[168] letter that the State Government has formed a Sub-Committee to look into this matter. If that is so, we should await the report of the Sub-Committee.

---

162. Letter to Congress MP; address: 16 Dr Rajendra Prasad Road, New Delhi.
163. See appendix 69.
164. See appendix 68. See also item 167.
165. Letter to the owner of the *Times of India* Group of Publication.
166. See also item 166 and appendices 68 and 69.
167. Note, 2 October 1962, for Kesho Ram, the PPS. PMO, File No. 28/99/62-64-PMS, Minute No. 10.
168. Secretary, Ministry of Works, Housing and Supply.

2.   I would suggest that the W.H. & S. Ministry should enquire from the Chief Minister himself as to what is happening and what he recommends.

3.   I do not know what the "funnel" suggested was. But it was clear to me when I looked at the prospect from the hanging gardens that one of the very few beauty spots in Bombay city would be spoiled by fresh constructions and the cutting down of trees. Many trees had already been cut down. Personally, I am of opinion that there should be a law or a bye-law to the effect that nobody can cut down a tree without special permission being taken from the Municipality. There are such bye-laws in some of the cities I recently visited.[169]

169.   To Mehr Chand Khanna: Artists for Rajghat[170]

October 3, 1962

My dear Mehr Chand,

Your letter of the 29th September.[171] I think your new procedure about appointing artists for the Rajghat Samadhi is likely to yield good results.

Yours sincerely,
Jawaharlal Nehru

170.   For the Town and Country Planning Seminar[172]

Town and Country Planning is assuming increasing importance in India. That is right because our towns and cities are growing rapidly, often in an unplanned way. I am glad, therefore, that the Institute of Town Planners is again meeting and having and Annual Town and Country Planning Seminar at Bhopal. I hope they will deal not only with the broad principles, which should be kept in mind, but also give specific indications as to how they should be implemented.

---

169. See SWJN/SS/78/items 280, 281,282.
170. Letter to the Minister of Works, Housing, and Supply. PMO, File No. 2/129/56-71-PMS, Sr. No. 21-A.
171. See appendix 3 and SWJN/SS/78/item 5.
172. Message, 4 October 1962, forwarded to L.R. Vagale, Honorary Joint Secretary, Institute of Town Planners. PMO, File No. 9/2/62-PMP, Vol. 7, Sr. No. 19-A.

171. In New Delhi: Housing Ministers' Conference[173]

I have gladly come here for a while not to throw much light on the problem of housing but to express my own sense of its importance and urgency. Next to food and clothing, housing is the most important for any individual or any family. It is important from this point of view, of course; it is important also to increase his working capacity because the better the conditions in which he lives the more work and production he can do. So, there is no doubt about the importance of housing. But the problem is so huge; it exists in every country of the world today. In India it is naturally big as everything in India is big. Whatever you touch in India becomes hundredfold, thousand fold or a million fold because of our huge population and the extent of the country. Perhaps in the past—I am not saying of the immediate past, but in the long past—we have not thought much of this and therefore, we have to face the problems which have grown enormous.

Shri Mehr Chand Khanna[174] was just now referring to the amounts spent and the amounts necessary. That is perfectly correct, but I do not think it helps us at all to talk of percentage in this matter and say that the percentage in the First Plan was this much, in the Second Plan was this much and in the Third Plan is this much. Suppose we spend, as we must, a very large sum on agriculture, that is, irrigation and the like affecting agriculture. Naturally, housing should go ahead, but the percentage spent on agriculture to be taken to housing is no accurate method of judging. The more we can spend on housing the better. That is admitted, but one has also to remember the various demands on the public purse. They are very heavy. Some demands are, of course, whether it is agriculture or industry, to increase the wealth producing capacity of the country. To some extent we have to put up with this concept—it is difficult at present—so that in future we might be better off. That applies to all these social services important as they are.

Broad Approach

Take, for instance, education. If the Education Minister was here speaking to you, he would talk about the urgent necessity of a few hundred crores of rupees or of a few thousand crores of rupees more for education and he will be completely right. How are we to deal with this asking for money when there is no money or when there is not adequate money? We have to do the best we

173. Inaugural Address, 17 October 1962. PIB.
174. Minister for Works, Housing, and Supply.

can, not starving anything which comes in the way of future growth that is essential. Unless we grow in wealth, we cannot raise the standard of living of our people; we cannot ultimately give social amenities to our people. That is most important. At the same time in order to grow in wealth we have to give social amenities. We have to have education. I have said that schools are necessary, even if there are no buildings; let the schools be in the open. They are more necessary than the building. The teachers and the pupils are what constitute the school and not the building necessarily. Of course, if there are buildings, we can open schools; but we cannot wait for buildings for schools to be run. Schools have to be organised; if you like you may have a holiday period during the rainy season. I am merely suggesting to you the broad approach to these problems.

Slums Clearance

Now, take slums, in the removal of which I am deeply interested. It pains me to see them, because they reduce the human being living there to a slightly sub-human level. It is utterly bad for the children to live there. So, I think that we should concentrate on the removal of slums.

All this resolves itself into a question of money. That is so. Yet, I do not accept that explanation. Money, of course, is necessary, and we should try to find it out as much as we can. But there are many other factors.

Take slums in great cities. There are all manner of private interests which preserve these slums, are interested in them, and exploit the people dwelling in those slums. I think that it is very wrong, very anti-social and very objectionable for this kind of thing to be tolerated. There are all manner of obstructions. From what little experience I have had of Delhi city slums, it is quite extraordinary to get going, because there are so many obstructions put in the way that one loses heart almost. Quite apart from money, I am talking about obstructions put in the way by the owners of the land, the owners of the slums, by even the dwellers of the slums who are not prepared to leave them; they are so used to living there that they do not want to live elsewhere at a slightly higher cost.[175]

Then, talking about Delhi, there are so many authorities that it is impossible to get them all to agree, or it takes a mighty long time. All these are things which can be done without expenditure of any money, so as to expedite these processes and make them simpler and easier, which ultimately, even in terms of money, make for less cost, because delay is the most costly thing of all.

175. See item 36.

Multi-storeyed Buildings

Then, it seems to me that in a city, especially in a growing city, in a city like Delhi, you have no escape from putting up multi-storeyed buildings; where land becomes frightfully expensive, you cannot afford it simply to have little houses much as you may like them. You have not got the room; you have not got the wherewithal to put up little houses; you must put up multi storeyed buildings. They need not be sky-scrapers, but they have to be more than single-storeyed, I should imagine, three or four storeyed, with apartments inside them. I think that, that is more feasible proposition than little houses dotted all over the place. In Bombay, I believe that that is the only way they can grow, that is, grow high up; you cannot spread out much more. And I think that that has to be adopted in Delhi and in all places where there is concentration of buildings. Apart from the cost of land there, land values grow tremendously. There are other facilities about a big building, but there are some disadvantages also. Our way of life as practised may not suit these flats, but, unfortunately, as our population grows, there is no escape from it; we have to get used to it. We can make apartments as convenient as we can, and I think that ultimately it will be much cheaper too, that way.

Then, there is another aspect of ease of transport and communication. As the city spreads, people live some distance away. In every big city, they have to live far away. That means there should be the development of communication and transport so that people can get easily to their office or place of business. In Delhi, it is not adequate; the transport services are growing, no doubt; still, I hardly think that they are adequate. There, if you have built a colony or something some distance away, to go from there to the place of business, it takes time.

Civic Amenities

Of course, with regard to building of houses or apartments or anything the very first thing that should be done there is the provision of amenities, that is, proper water supply, proper lighting, proper drainage etc. It was a painful thing in Delhi for large number of houses to be put up without any proper drainage, latrines—there were some, of course—or lighting. It is scandalous, whoever may be guilty of that performance, because those houses are useless. You might not have built them; you might have left it an open space. It is, I think, much more important in India for the water supply, lighting, latrines, drainage etc. to be provided without a house. I would prefer that than a house without these amenities. It means nothing at all except some protection from the cold and the rain. All these things must go together. If there is any difficulty and if there is any delay, some new system should be evolved where there should be no delay. I am pointing out all these things because we cannot concentrate on money. Money is important, but money is less important in the way these things are done.

Prefabricated Houses[176]

In all the great cities there should be prefabricated houses. That is the only way to meet the situation and to build houses quickly. There is a housing factory here in Delhi which many of you may have seen or may see. I remember very well when this housing factory was started about ten to twelve years ago that there was an eminent expert in charge of it.[177] In the first few months of the housing factory the blocks that were made cracked or something happened; they were not good. Immediately a tremendous outcry was raised in Parliament. It was called the housing scandal, with the result, ultimately, that the very fine expert left it, went off somewhere else. He is doing good work in Africa or elsewhere, I do not know. This particular housing factory waited for a long time as to what to do and what not to do. It was rented out to private owners and all kinds of things were done. Ultimately, it has come back to its chief function, that is, housing, and it is succeeding; it is doing well. There is no doubt that in a thing of this kind you have to experiment; you have to make mistakes in the quality of material you make and then you arrive at the right mixture. Here some of our friends expect, by some magic, that the first attempt should be completely successful and they discard it if it is not. That is not being done anywhere in the world. This housing factory in Delhi is a peculiar example of our, call it what you like, impatience, if immediate success is not coming; therefore, our delaying its function and delaying still further what we wanted to do. Today you can be wise after the event and see how well it is functioning. It is producing, as you see in the corridors here, very good material for big houses even and for small houses. You can build houses rapidly by it. You can build schools and other buildings, which are so necessary, quickly. I understand the housing factory is going to be doubled and it is suggested that in other places too in India housing factories of this type should be built up.

176. See item 154.
177. Otto Koenigsberger (1908-1999); German Architect, Director, Hindustan Housing Factory, 1948-1951.

Change in Approach

There is no other way for quick work. Our whole attitude to housing has to change. It has to be with local materials. You cannot bring marble from Carrara or from far away to build houses. For rapid building, local materials must be available near the locality with which you can build. You can utilise other methods if you like, but principally I do think this pre-fabricated material will have to be used. There may be simple ways, not of these big factories, but simple ways, there are, I believe, of making blocks even in a village scale which can be used there. There are many ways. Attention should, therefore, be directed more and more to a scientific approach to this problem than merely carrying on as of old. I am afraid that our attitude in almost everything is hopelessly unscientific. We do not profit by the improvements suggested.

Take roads. In the last two years or three years, our Road Research Department has suggested a way of making roads, which is very much cheaper than the normal methods and is as good. When this was sent to our State Governments, the State Governments, the PWD and others would not accept it, saying, oh, no no; they put their noses, instead of experimenting with it, saying "Here is something which has come out of the Road Research Department after experimentation." But, no, they would not accept it. Even I wrote, and others wrote, and with great difficulty we have got them to move a little. We live in ruts of thought and action. It is a slowdown procedure. We do not profit by new discoveries and new methods, and, therefore, we are backward. We have to develop a more scientific methods of approach to housing, to roads, and to everything and take advantage of the new. After all, here is a suggestion about a road. A road is to be built. Now, what can be against it? The engineers say that it would not last. Well, if it does not last, we shall see and we shall experiment, but they refuse to experiment. I am astonished at the stick-in-the-mud attitude of the people who carry on old practices.

Our PWD standards—they are changing, I believe—are such nowhere in the wide world does anybody adopt them. They have outgrown them. Our PWD still functions in the 19th century; at least it was so; I do not know what is happening now. A certain width of the wall, a certain this and that all sorts of things come up. I am not criticising it. But, generally, the attitude is a very backward-looking attitude, not progressing, and not improving. You go to a place like New York, for instance. I do not put it forward as a comparison; there is no comparison, let us say, between New York and Delhi, between American conditions and Indian conditions, or French conditions, or British conditions, or the German conditions, especially. But, every year, if you go there, you see a new type of house, a completely new type. They experiment, all the time building. They do not mind knocking it down ten years later or five years later and building a new one, because they would always experiment. But we have got into the rut, and in housing, more particularly, we must get out of those ruts. We calculate according to old methods, old standards and old procedures, and we draw up plans and charts and multiply it by 400 million and say that so many crores are required. That does not help. It is true that there are 40 million people living here, and we get into colossal figures which stagger our minds. How can we do it? I think that it is all wrong, that is, this kind of approach, and more time should be spent on two things—forget the money part—firstly, on the best methods of building. Something is being done about it, but much more is to be done. And even when the methods are suggested, they are not accepted by our Departments and if one Department accepts it, the Finance Department comes in the way or some other Department, and they argue and argue, and nothing is done. It is this kind of approach that is harmful, not money, I shall again repeat. Money can come. It may not come in those colossal figures that were suggested. We have many other very important obligations today; we have another obligation, an essential one, namely the defence of our country. We cannot simply forget all these things. We have to face them. But much can be done without a rupee extra being spent—of that, I am convinced with a little more scientific approach, and a better organisational approach, not these hold-ups and obstructions all over, but adopting modern methods as far as possible. And this involves, as these things are connected, other things also.

It is no good sending people to live ten miles away from their place of business; it is very costly for them; they would not go unless you provide means of transport for them to go from there to their place of business. You go into any great city; even in Bombay and Calcutta, they come from far away by train or bus or some such thing. If you provide that, then they can live in more hygienic conditions and be able to get there, instead of living in those slums conditions.

You cannot remove slums without providing all these things. It is all a compact whole, not frittering away in the old way without thinking of the problem and the ways of solving it.

Though it is not relevant to our housing problem but take Chandigarh. It is a new city built on a new approach by one of the greatest architects in the world. I do not know if most people like it or do not like it. I approve of it hundred per cent not because I like everything in it but because it takes us out of the rut of the PWDs and the rest. It makes us think on different lines. It opens out windows to our mind to think. It is, I think, a remarkable achievement which is famous all over the world. I am not aware of that fame arising to our other housing developments; but Chandigarh is. I do not want Chandigarh to be repeated all over. It is expensive. That is not the point, but it is the new mind, that is the approach, that I want; get out of this rut and spend much more time and energy over research work, as to how to build houses cheaply.

Fortunately, you have a great deal of material for that in every country because every country is troubled with this housing problem. In England, housing is one of the major political issues. So, you get information as to what is being done all over the world. Learn from it and experiment yourself. You have got research institutions which are doing good work, I believe; but somehow they remain too long in the research stage and it is not applied because people think that it is quite good enough as their great grandfathers did and so why change it?

So, I should like this Conference and the Housing Ministers generally to think more and not merely to sit and write letters to the Central Government or to any Government saying, "Send us some money." You will not get it straight. We have too many burdens on us. The primary burden is defence, that is, protecting our territory and the country's integrity. That is a growing burden. Apart from that, there are many other things to be done in your States which perhaps you might consider of greater priority. Therefore, get what you can; ask, if you like, for more; but try to approach the problem in a different way as to how you can do these things expeditiously and relatively cheaper taking the same amount of money much further. Of course, if you build in a great city, different conditions prevail there. You go up and up; you cannot spread out. In a smaller town you have more room to spread out. In villages it is different again. You do not build skyscrapers or multi-storeyed buildings in villages. They should be built with local material with blocks of bricks that can be made locally of new materials. There are new materials today for building. Again, you need not copy New York to build in glass and all kinds of fancy things. But one should take advantage of what is being done elsewhere and of the knowledge that has been accumulated elsewhere in regard to building.

Aesthetics Side

I do not believe in always paying attention to the beauty of the building or of the city. We must not lose sight of the aesthetic side of life.

Now, some people imagine that beauty requires money. It may, sometimes, but normally it does not. It requires an eye for beauty and a hand for beauty. Your village craftsmen have a sense of beauty. They produce things which are very beautiful. That is one of the chief values of handicraftsmanship. So, there are many things which can be made beautiful without expense. The idea of some of our friends is that beauty means the use of marble. Personally, I am allergic to marble, generally speaking. There are buildings where marble can be useful, but not for public display too much. And I am surprised at the way marble is used. There are many more beautiful things than marble which are infinitely cheaper.

So, beauty is not a question of expense; it is a question of the person, the builder, having an eye for beauty. I think that that fact should not be forgotten.

Master Plans

You know that in Delhi we have got the Master Plan, a grandiose thing, and I hope that it will be given effect to as rapidly as possible; it will take some time, but we have to make a beginning. Everywhere I hope, in all cities, big cities, there will be planning done, and planning with a view not to meet the immediate difficulty, but looking ahead twenty years or thirty years what the city should be like and gradually working up to it.

There is another small matter about roads. I find that on the outskirts of the city, as the city grows, small roads are made, because wide roads are not necessary there. Gradually, houses grow up on each side of this narrow road, and traffic grows, and then it is very difficult to widen the road, because there are houses on both sides. You cannot acquire them or knock them down. All this is shortsightedness. Even in the outskirts of a city where there is no traffic, if a road is built it should be a wide road of a big city; or, at any rate, the road need not be wide, but there should be room for the road to expand, and no houses should be allowed there. Modern roads are 300 feet broad in some cities, I imagine, 300 feet broad, because traffic is so heavy. It is impossible in London or Paris or Rome to move; the fastest way to move there is on foot, not by cars because cars are jammed, and they block all the roads, and the roads are not wide enough. These are old cities, and just like in Old Delhi, you cannot knock down everything to broaden the road.

Therefore, care should be taken in a growing town, in the outskirts, to build broad roads or have broad expanses left open for roads to grow. All these things have to be thought out by the planners.

I remember a case in the great city of Bombay, of the road going to Trombay. There was not much traffic there, and a narrow road was built. Now, houses have sprung up, and the traffic is more, and there is difficulty. Either you have to spend large sums of money to acquire those houses and broaden the road or continue to face this difficulty. So, one must think ahead.

It is not a question of just putting up a house. You have to see that people can approach the house and people can get away from the house to their place of business easily, and that other facilities are provided. All these things have to be seen in an integrated way.

Therefore, planning is essential. Planning first of all, as I said, of the best way to build a house, that is to say, about the materials etc.; whether it is pre-fabricated or it should be multi-storeyed or not will depend upon circumstances. Then, there is the question of the approaches to the houses, the roads, and of course, of the amenities such as lighting, drainage etc. to these houses. If you build multi-storeyed apartments, it is obvious and it is necessary to give them electric light and electric fans; you need not even give them fans, but you must give a plug for a fan, because people, having regard to our climate, require a lot of air. Give them as much light and air as possible in all your houses. In the multi-storeyed houses people cannot easily go out and sleep in the open except on the roof. I should suggest that it is far better to have multi-storeyed buildings with roundabout garden etc. to be enjoyed by the dwellers in the houses and by the children etc. than have potty little houses without any room at all. You cannot afford to have room if you build a little high roof on all sides. You can have many services in the multi-storeyed houses which will add to the convenience of the dwellers.

There are many approaches to this. I have ventured to suggest to you one or two for you to think about. I am not an expert in this or in anything else; but I observe things. I see things in other countries and here. What worries me is not the implementation—implementation is always difficult—but even the mental approach is so slow here to change and that I want to shake up. I should like you, therefore, to think out all these things with the help of your experts etc. and approach the question in a somewhat novel way and not merely shout for money. Such money as you have you will get. If you have not got it, you will not get it. That is an obvious thing. There are certain limitations about that, but there are certain things about which there is no limitation. There is no limitation for a man's thinking capacity and energy to do things. We should try to exploit that and try to carry on our business in a more expeditious way without all these obstructions and blocks which occur in our method of administration and other business.

172. In the Lok Sabha: Land Acquisition for Delhi Master Plan[178]

D.N. Tiwary[179]: Will the Prime Minister be pleased to state:

(a) whether it is a fact that in the last week of August he met a large number of kisans from Meerut and Bulandshahr led by two Members of Lok Sabha and heard their grievances about the acquisitions of land for Delhi Master Plan; and

(b) whether he has sent any suggestions or directions, hopeful to the kisans to the proper authorities?

The Prime Minister and Minister of External Affairs, Defence and Atomic Energy (Jawaharlal Nehru): (a) and (b). Yes. The Prime Minister after listening to the grievances of the kisans, wrote to the Chief Minister, UP, that while it was inevitable that land near a great city would gradually have to be acquired for the extension of that city and industries, it might the better to vary the Master Plan somewhat and to acquire banjar [Fallow] land and leave the good land for agricultural purpose. The local authorities connected with the Delhi Master Plan were also apprised of the Prime Minister's views. Originally it was proposed to acquire about 34,000 acres of land but subsequently on further consideration it was reduced to about 6,000 acres. The Chief Minister, UP, has since sent a detailed reply and while explaining why it has become necessary to acquire 6,159 acres of agricultural land in 22 villages for planned and regulated development of the Ghaziabad region, has assured that the State Government are anxious to avoid any hardships to agriculturists and that they shall try to accommodate them as far as possible.[180]

---

178. Written answers to questions, *Lok Sabha Debates*, Third Series, Vol. IX, November 8-20, 1962, pp. 2203-2204.
179. Congress MP from Gopalgunj, Bihar.
180. See also item 173. SWJN/SS/78/items 116 and 188.

173. To C.B. Gupta: Ghaziabad Land and Delhi Master Plan[181]

My dear Chandra Bhanu,

You will remember my writing to you about a number of agriculturists from Ghaziabad who had come to see me and who were greatly distressed at the prospect of having their lands acquired for the purpose of some Master Plan. You were good enough to reply to me at some length.

Some of these persons again came to see me this morning and gave me the attached paper.

One thing that they said to me seemed to me to be worthy of consideration. They said that they were going to be deprived of their standing crops. This would cause great loss to them and would be of no good to anybody. If this is so, I think it has force. Whatever steps you may take about this land, the standing crops must be preserved. Preferably, therefore, they should be allowed to harvest these crops.[182]

Yours sincerely,
[Jawaharlal Nehru]

(i) Science

174. To Humayun Kabir: Steel Research Laboratory[183]

October 5, 1962

My dear Humayun,

I enclose a note I have received from Shri T.T. Krishnamachari[184]. I think it will be desirable for us to have a steel research laboratory as he has suggested.

---

181. Letter to Chief Minister of Uttar Pradesh.
182. See also item 172; SWJN/SS/78/items 116 and 188.
183. Letter to the Minister of Scientific Research and Cultural Affairs. MO, File No. 17(522)/62-66-PMS, Sr. No. 1-A.
184. Minister without Portfolio.

But it is not clear to me what exactly this means and what its financial effect on us will be. Could you please have this matter considered? You may consult the Director of the CSIR.[185]

Yours sincerely,
Jawaharlal Nehru

175. To D.C. Sharma: Visiting Trombay[186]

October 16, 1962

My dear Diwan Chandji,
Your letter of October 12th.

It would be a good thing for Members of the Informal Consultative Committee of Parliament on Atomic Energy to visit Trombay and see the Atomic Energy Establishment there. But I rather doubt about the advisability of holding a meeting of that committee at Trombay. It will be difficult for me to go there for this purpose and if we hold a meeting there, there will be hardly time to see the establishment. Generally, it is not desirable to hold meetings of Consultative Committees outside Delhi. There should be no difficulty, however, if Members of the Committee going there when Parliament is not meeting.

Yours sincerely,
[Jawaharlal Nehru]

176. For Seminar on Science and Spirituality[187]

I am much interested to learn that a seminar on Science and Spirituality is going to be held soon in Patna. I think that the subject of the seminar is of high importance. The future of the world is tied up with the growth of science and life becomes more and more dependent on science. At the same time, life with science only as its guide and without a spiritual basis is very likely to lead to disaster for humanity.

I send my good wishes to this seminar.

185. Syed Husain Zaheer.
186. Letter to Congress MP from Gurdaspur; address: 19 Windsor Place, New Delhi – 1.
187. Forwarded to Surendra Mohan Ghose, Rajya Sabha MP and a follower of Sri Aurobindo; address: 21 Janpath, New Delhi. PMO, File No. 9/2/62-PMP, Vol. VIII, Sr. No. 41-A.

177. To Husain Zaheer: CSIR Directors' Meeting[188]

October 26, 1962

My dear Munne,

Your letter of the 26th October.

I think you have done right in changing the character of your Directors' meeting. As for my being able to go there, I cannot promise to do so and cannot suggest any date. If it is possible for me to go, I shall do so. I shall be in Delhi for the first three weeks of December. Of course, Parliament will be sitting then and I will be very busy.

Yours affectionately,
Jawaharlal Nehru

178. In the Lok Sabha: Pugwash Conference of Scientists[189]

Narayan Das[190]: Will the Prime Minister be pleased to state:

(a) whether the Government have in any way interested themselves in the activities of scientists who recently met in Pugwash Conference in London and discussed problems of disarmament and world security;

(b) if so, the nature and manner of India's participation so far; and

(c) whether the next Conference will be held in India?

The Prime Minister and Minister of External Affairs, Defence and Atomic Energy (Jawaharlal Nehru): (a) and (b). The International Conferences on Science and World Affairs, known as Pugwash Conferences, are non-official conferences which are attended by eminent scientists of various countries in their personal capacity. They owe their origin to a suggestion made by the Prime Minister in 1954 regarding the setting up of a Committee of scientists to explain to the world the effect a war would have on humanity. This idea was pursued further by the Atomic Scientists' Association in Great Britain and the Federation of American Scientists' Association in Great Britain and

188. Letter to the Director-General of the CSIR. PMO, File No. 17(213)/56-64-PMS, Sr. No. 12-A.

189. Written answers, *Lok Sabha Debates*, Third Series, Vol. IX, November 8-20, 1962, pp. 891-892.

190. Congress MP from Darbhanga, Bihar.

the Federation of American Scientists in the USA and discussions were held subsequently with other scientists, including Soviet scientists.

The Tenth Conference in the series was held in London from the 3rd to the 7th of September, 1962 and was attended by Professor P.C. Mahalanobis in his personal capacity. The record of the discussions at the Conference has not yet been published.

Although the Government of India are not directly concerned in these non-official conferences, they support the Pugwash movement and believe that scientists can make significant contribution towards peace and disarmament as well as towards helping developing nations to modernise and secure the benefits of scientific progress. At the request of the organisers of the Tenth Conference the Prime Minister sent a message wishing success to the Conference.

Besides the Tenth Conference, the Third Conference held in Austria in September, 1958, was attended by Dr A.J. Bhalla, Dr K.S. Krishnan and Professor P.C. Mahalanobis, the Fifth Conference held in Pugwash, Canada, in August, 1959 by Dr M.L. Ahuja and the Ninth Conference held in Cambridge in August, 1962 by Dr Vikram Sarabhai.

(c) A suggestion has been made that the next conference be held in India. No final decision has, however, yet been reached.

179. To T.T. Krishnamachari: Scientific Mobilisation Council[191]

November 28, 1962.

My dear T.T.,

Your letter of November 28th about the formation of a Scientific Mobilisation Council.[192] I should like to avoid too many Committees with overlapping functions. But if you think this Scientific Mobilisation Council is necessary, I have no objection. You might discuss this matter with Homi Bhabha[193] and then we can consider this further.

Yours affectionately,
Jawaharlal Nehru

---

191. Letter to the Minister for Economic and Defence Coordination. NMML, T.T. Krishnamachari Papers, File 1962, Auto.

192. Excerpt: "I have been discussing with various friends in the scientific field about concentrated scientific thinking on problems connected with defence and production. There are various scientific bodies dealing with this subject. We have a Scientific Committee of the Cabinet. We have also the Council of Scientific and Industrial Research, which has a governing body. There is a small Defence Scientific Council functioning with the same end in view. All these bodies have specific functions to perform but for the purpose on hand a body differently constructed is needed.2. My intention, therefore, is to create a Council for this purpose. In order that the nomenclature may not overlap I could call it the Scientific Mobilisation Council. I shall be requesting Dr. H.J. Bhabha to be the Chairman." NMML, T.T. Krishnamachari Papers, File 1962, Copy.

193. Chairman of the Atomic Energy Commission.

III. EXTERNAL AFFAIRS

(a) General

180. In New Delhi: To the Press[1]

NEFA Incident No Bar to Talks with China
Nehru back in Delhi after Tour: Warm Welcome

New Delhi, Oct. 1 – Prime Minister Nehru today declared that he would always be prepared for talks with the Chinese, whatever happened, provided they were decent and self-respecting to India.

Pandit Nehru made this remark in reply to a correspondent's question whether in view of the recent development in NEFA, he would withdraw the proposal for talks between India and China.

The Prime Minister thumped his thigh and said: "I shall always be prepared for talks whatever happens, provided they are decent and self-respecting to us. I have never refused to talk to anybody".

Pandit Nehru was talking to pressmen at Palam soon after his arrival here after a three-week foreign tour.

Earlier, the Prime Minister was asked how he "took" the fresh Chinese intrusions in the NEFA area.

He said: "I do not like them. I do not know the latest developments there. I should like to find out what the latest development is".

A correspondent: "What are the prospects of talks proposed to begin on October 15 between India and China as suggested recently".

Pandit Nehru: "I cannot say. It depends on at least two parties".

Asked about the Panchen Lama's claim that Tawang in NEFA always formed part of China and was administered by it, Pandit Nehru said: "I can't bandy words with the Panchen Lama".

---

1. Report of interaction with the Press. Reproduced from *The National Herald*, 2 October 1962, p. 1.

Talks on ECM[2]

Answering a question about the "results" of his efforts to protect Indian economic interests at the Commonwealth Prime Ministers' Conference on the ECM issue, Pandit Nehru said: "I can't tell you now what the results of this would be".

A correspondent asked whether his subsequent consultations on the continent with French and Italian leaders had made a "difference" on this matter.

Pandit Nehru: "Nothing definite emerged out of these consultations, except that I found a friendly attitude there and understanding of the Indian position".

Pandit Nehru was asked whether the British Prime Minister's statement in the course of a TV interview soon after the Commonwealth Prime Ministers' Conference that Britain would join the ECM did not amount to "going back" on the joint communiqué.

Pandit Nehru: "That is not going back on that. As far as I can see, Mr Macmillan's attitude is clear".

Asked whether Britain would ultimately go into the ECM, Pandit Nehru said that it was "highly likely that Britain would go in".

Asked about the British Labour Party executive's stand that if the present British Government did not change its attitude on ECM, it would damage Commonwealth relations beyond repair, Pandit Nehru said: "Presumably, this is its (Labour Party's) view, I can't answer hypothetical questions".

The Prime Minister, however, went on to say that Mr Macmillan had always wanted to join the ECM. But he could not join if the British people were against it or if his own party was against it. There was a difference of opinion in England over this matter. There were many who wanted to join.

When asked about his experiences of his first visit to Africa, Pandit Nehru corrected the correspondent by saying, "first visit south of the Sahara", and added: "I find all people wherever I go very friendly. I liked my visit there".

Second Bandung

Replying to a question on the prospects of a second Bandung Conference, Pandit Nehru said that India had always stated that if a suitable or convenient opportunity arose, the so-called second Bandung Conference could be held.

2. See SWJN/SS/78/Item 325

About the possibility of India recognising the new regime in Yemen, Pandit Nehru said: "I cannot say. It depends on developments. We will have to consider this matter carefully".

He added that he told this to the Foreign Minister of the new government of Yemen, whom he met in Cairo for a few minutes.

The Foreign Minister himself told Pandit Nehru that he could not expect a sudden decision by India about recognition of his government.

Asked whether he had invited President de Gaulle to visit India, Pandit Nehru said: "I have invited him for the last two years. I have repeated the invitation. I don't know when he will come. He is busy at the present moment."

181. To Hubert Phillips: India, the Commonwealth and the Future[3]

October 5, 1962

Dear Mr Phillips,

I have your letter. I enclose a signed photograph.

I am afraid I cannot write much to you about the future of India or of the British Commonwealth of Nations. I am heavily occupied at present.

All my work is concerned with building up the future of India. I think that we shall succeed although it is a difficult journey. We are aiming, to begin with, at higher standards for all our people, leading to equality of opportunity for all. We want India to be a peaceful nation, friendly to all other countries and cooperating with them as far as possible.

As for the Commonwealth of Nations, I think that it has served a very good purpose in bringing people of different races and nations and from distant parts of the world together on a common platform. I hope it will continue as such. This kind of association seems to me far better than alliances and the like. I am not prophet enough to say what the future will bring.

Yours sincerely,
[Jawaharlal Nehru]

---

3. Letter to Hubert Phillips (1891-1964); British economist and journalist; address: The Oak House Annexe, Liphook, Hampshire, England.

182. To C.P. Ranasinghe: Buddha, Non-Violence and the Bomb[4]

October 9, 1962

Dear Shri Ranasinghe,

Thank you for your letter of October 5th which has just reached me.

It is true that the world is confronted today with a choice between what might be considered Buddha's way of peace and non-violence and the way of the atomic bomb. I believe that more and more people are inclined that way.

But this is not a question of approaching the modern world on the logical plane. If logic had much to do with it, the great nations would give up this armament race which can only bring disaster. It is, therefore, very doubtful if any book, however good it is, can convince people who are full of fear of each other and who react as a frightened person does. I do not think that any active propagation of Buddha's message to scientists, politicians, scholars and others will make much difference at this stage. The mind has to be prepared to receive before a gift is offered.

But, of course, it will be a good thing if your book[5] or other books reach these people in the outside world. One difficulty is that we cannot claim to reach others what we do not practise ourselves in our own countries. That, as you know, is not a mere repetition of some principles or dogmas, but a way of life. I am afraid neither we in India nor you in Ceylon have adequately imbibed the peaceful and non-violent way of life that the Buddha preached.

I shall gladly see you if it is possible during my visit to Ceylon. But as far as I can see, my programme there is fairly full.

Yours sincerely,
[Jawaharlal Nehru]

---

4.   Letter to C.P. Ranasinghe, Sri Lankan author and philosopher; address: "Shanti", 53 Kandy Road, Mahara, Kadawata, Ceylon.
5.   *The Buddha's Explanation of the Universe* (Colombo: Lanka Buddha Mandalaya Fund, 1957).

183. To Kusum Thakore: "Roses" not a Practical Global Mission[6]

October 10, 1962

Dear Kusum Thakore,

I have your letter of the 5th October. Your project about "The Roses of the World" is good in so far as intentions are concerned. But I am not sure about its practicability. Many of us who go abroad discuss matters with representatives of other countries and try to impress upon them the necessity for a newer and better outlook in world affairs. I am afraid, the effect we produce is very limited.

Therefore, I doubt very much if your visit abroad will produce any results. Also, we talk about telling other countries to behave in a better way. But in our own country we do not reach a high standard of behaviour in politics or in other activities. The best example would be our own behaviour.

Therefore, while I have no doubt about your motive, I have doubts about the success that you can achieve in realising your motive.

The kind of Missions that we send abroad are usually technical Missions or Parliamentary Missions consisting of Members of Parliament. It will be difficult to include you in either type of Mission. At the present moment with our difficulties in regard to foreign exchange, we are particularly reluctant to accept any expenditure involving foreign exchange.

Yours sincerely,
[Jawaharlal Nehru]

184. In Colombo: Press Conference[7]

[China]

Question: [Not clear].

Jawaharlal Nehru: I can hardly go into past history for years and years. According to us our frontiers are well known for a long time past, our maps have been given to them regularly. Those frontiers include high mountain ranges and unpopulated tracts; the terrain there is very difficult, very cold, nobody lives

---

6. Letter; address: Pestanji Villa, Fateh Gunj, Baroda-2.
7. Interaction with Press, 15 October 1962, at India House, Colombo. NMML, AIR Tapes, TS No. 19062, 19063, NM No. 2558, 2559.

203

there in winter, in summer some shepherds might come. When many years ago, at the beginning of the present regime in China, a little after, a year or two later, we discovered that some maps in China were giving different frontiers, that is, including large bits of India in the Chinese state, we drew the attention of the Chinese Government to this and said that obviously there must be some mistake because our frontiers were quite clear. Thereupon, the Chinese Government said that those maps were old maps of the previous regime, Chiang Kai shek's regime, and they have had no time to revise them. Every year we reminded them of this and they gave the same answer. I spoke about them when I went to Peking to Mr Chou En-lai. He said the same thing, we shall decide this in a friendly way when we have the time. Well, it is true he did not in as many words acknowledge our maps but the impression he created in our minds was that their maps were certainly wrong and would be revised. Then we dealt with Tibet. We had certain rights in Tibet, which we had inherited from the old British Government. In any event we did not wish to keep those rights, extra territorial rights and others in Tibet, we were not interested in keeping them. We were interested in our trade with Tibet and large numbers of people go to Tibet on pilgrimage from India. So we had a treaty with China about Tibet. When making that treaty it was said the following are outstanding problems between us and we dealt with those problems one by one, and came to an agreement. Nobody mentioned then the question of the frontier. It is surprising that when the problems are being dealt with we did not raise the question of the frontier except perhaps one or two small ones, we mentioned one or two small controversies about a mile or two here and there in some spots. So there is that treaty. Afterwards again, Mr Chou En-lai came to India, we discussed many matters and, as far as I remember, yes, we mentioned the frontier too, the maps, because we said there is no frontier question between us but your maps create misunderstanding. He said, we shall have to look into that carefully and settle it peacefully.

Then came in Tibet, the rebellion in Tibet. It began in the eastern side of Tibet adjoining China, in fact, in a part of Tibet which is included in China proper, and gradually spread. Ultimately it occurred in a big way and reached Lhasa. It was just about that time that the Dalai Lama came away from Lhasa and took refuge in India. Also about thirty, thirty-five thousand Tibetans came to India. For some odd reason which I cannot understand the Chinese Government thought that we were encouraging this rebellion from India, which was wholly untrue. Why should we encourage rebellion in Tibet and how could we? But because the refugees had come to India and because there were some Tibetans living on our side of the border, this led them to think that India was encouraging this rebellion. I am mentioning this because it might possibly explain, to some extent, their attitude. We had been friendly to China, we had recognised their special position in Tibet, we had been year after year, proposing China's recognition by the UN, and then this came. When the Tibet rebellion took place, the Chinese Government sent large forces to Tibet to suppress the rebellion and they came right up to our borders. The immediate border they came up to was the North-East border, that is, the North East Frontier Agency we have. They did not cross the border. We had a number of check posts there, not big military posts, but check posts there. They did not cross the border. But from the other side, more North-East of Kashmir, that is Ladakh, there their forces crossed the border and went right in. As I said, this is not inhabited territory and it is very wild, I mean very desolate, very high, varying from thirteen thousand to twenty thousand feet in altitude, treeless. At that height trees do not [grow] there, there are rock and snow and glaciers. They came in there without any obstruction from us. When we learnt of this we protested, and there had been numerous exchanges of notes and protests. Their answer always was, this is our territory and we are here as of right and you have occupied it because the British imperialism had done so. This thing went on till we were, naturally, worried. Mr Chou En lai came to Delhi about two and a half years ago and we could not come to an agreement about it. Of course, there is no doubt that the Chinese were not there before, leave out the original historical claims, they were not there and they had come in. I pointed out to him that all the trouble on the frontier is not due to any action that we have taken recently, it is due to movement on the Chinese side. Well, ultimately we said, let us refer this matter to a team of officials, Chinese and Indian, who would not decide it, officials cannot decide these major questions of policy, but who would go into all the evidence, documents, treaties, accounts, whatever they were, collect them and present reports about them, if possible a joint report, otherwise separate reports. These officials met first in Peking for about several weeks, then they came to Delhi and met there for several weeks, and then, lastly, they met in Rangoon, again for several weeks, altogether it lasted [for] about five or six months, these meetings, and they presented two separate reports, our officials gave one report, the Chinese officials a separate report. Anyhow, it served one good purpose. They collected such evidence as they had. As soon as we got their reports we published them, both our report and the Chinese report, with the evidence, fat volumes, because we had to place them before our Parliament. We placed them. They were published. Any of you, gentlemen, can see them. And then the Chinese did not publish them for a year or more, a year and a half. It was in the summer of this year, I think, that they placed extracts from those reports before their Congress. I do not yet know if they published most of it or part of it since then. Meanwhile, I might add, we were worried about this, about their continuous coming, creeping forward into Indian territory, which was relatively easy for them because on the other side there is the tableland of Tibet with roads, etc., and they could come right up to our border and even beyond it; they could make roads out there, while we had to cross several high mountain chains to reach the place, no roads, nothing. So we decided to build roads and had a programme called "roads in the mountains" on our border. And we have built many of them, still many remain, it is a long programme. Gradually we built up our check posts, military posts, further up till the position became—I am talking about Ladakh—till our military posts were facing their posts. Of course, it may be a difference of a mile or two, sometimes a little more or a little less. That is to say, it became difficult for the Chinese forces to advance more without coming into conflict with our forces. Broadly speaking, that is the position still in Ladakh area.

Meanwhile, a new development took place in the eastern side, that is, the North East Frontier Agency. Only last month, there was no doubt that the Chinese were not there previously except [in] a tiny village on the border about which there was some dispute, Longju,[8] they were not on this side. According to us, the border between China-India and Tibet-China is the watershed on Himalayas. The big mountain ranges water comes down this side and that side, that is a definite thing which you can recognise and which has been considered as the border for a long time past. About fifty years ago there was a conference between the representatives of the Government of India, that is, the British Government of India, of the Chinese Government and of the Tibetan Government. Among the many matters discussed was the question of the border. And at that time these people who met agreed to this watershed border; they did not define the borders, they said this is the border. It was not a new decision but recognition of a fact that they said was well-known and that is, the watershed was the border, and that extended, the watershed, even to Burma. It was called the McMahon Line because he was the English officer who was present then there. This was accepted by the Tibetan representatives there but subsequently the Chinese Government did not accept that, did not sign that treaty. But if you see the reports of those conversations, what they objected to was not this border but something else. Inner Tibet and outer Tibet—there is also a border—they objected to that, not to the border with India. However, they did not sign it. Therefore, the Chinese Government can well say, "we did not accept it then." But the fact remains that ever since then, that is, fifty years and according to the statements made then, for long before that was considered the border of India by us, by any government in India, all our maps said so. But, as I said,

8. In Subansiri district of NEFA. See note 33 in item 16.

these are not inhabited areas, a good part, except maybe some shepherds come and go. So there was no administration. Beyond that, in the east there are tribal people, and the British Government in its days did not have a proper system of administration over the tribal areas. They controlled them broadly but not the same system of administration. When we became independent, we introduced administration in all those areas, gradually of course, and went right up to the border in the North East and put up check posts, etc., more to check traffic, check posts are not strong enough to fight, but just to know what is happening. That has continued all this time.

Now, as I said, on the northern side, in Ladakh there is a stalemate, more or less, and their forces, they have come in about one hundred and fifty miles in our territory and are facing our posts in the mountains and sometimes there are small incidents of patrols and others. Much to our surprise, last month they started coming down in the eastern frontier, coming down the high passes—that was on the eighth of September where they had not come down yet. This naturally upset us very much and we took steps to send some of our forces to check them. They were checked a little on this side of the frontier. The frontier is the high mountain range. They had come down the high mountain range and come two or three miles on this side. There is a river there. The present position is that they are on the other side of the river and our forces are on this side of the river, and about five days ago there was a biggish engagement on the other side of the river when, I think, we lost eleven dead and about ten or eleven wounded. So far as we can make out the Chinese casualties were bigger. That is the position now. We had suggested, before this north east incursion took place last month, we had suggested that our officials should meet, not to consider the major problem—that would come later—but to consider means of reducing tensions and incidents. When this new aggression took place in the north-east, we pointed out to them, how could we meet to discuss the lessening of tension when every day you are advancing into our territory. So we must stop this on the east—they had come in a few miles—and go back to your original position on the other side of the pass and let us meet and discuss them. They go on saying, "this is our territory and you get out off our territory." It is very extraordinary, because if, I do not think they have the slightest claim on it, historically, politically or anything, I am not going back a thousand years but I am talking about the last hundred years, two or three hundred years. But even if they had any claim on any territory there, you do not enforce a claim by marching an army there but by talks. And we have necessarily to take some steps to defend our territory and we have done so. You can very well recognise, gentlemen that all our mentality is opposed to these conflicts, military conflicts; apart from the fact that they are a great burden on us when we are trying to build up our country we are not interested in fighting. But it becomes very difficult for us not to try to stop their advance in our country. Of course, there are statements which they send us every second day, a protest that we are encroaching on their territory. Nor it is really difficult to answer such peculiar charge when, I would again remind you, right from the earliest days of the present regime in China we have been pointing out to them our frontier by maps and things and they have been saying they will consider this and if necessary, revise their old maps. There has been no doubt in their minds about what we said was our frontier. And now they suddenly come in and say this is theirs. They send a note: if our aircraft flies on our land, they say you are intruding in our territory. It really is an extraordinarily difficult position. It is frightfully difficult to deal with this kind of statements which have no basis at all, which they are continuing to make. We should naturally gladly settle every question peacefully. But their idea apparently is to seize territory and then to talk about it. They have seized about twelve thousand square miles in Ladakh. In the north east it is not much yet, but if we did not defend ourselves there they would march on. What is there to prevent them from marching further and further? We have the outposts. That is the position.

I have given you a long reply. I do not know [if] it is an adequate reply in your opinion.

> Question: When Mr Chou En-lai visited New Delhi in 1960 he had agreed to the maintenance of status quo and that in the meanwhile...

Jawaharlal Nehru: I do not think it will be quite correct to say that he had formally agreed to it, but that was the impression which we got from the talks. And also in the recent treaty between China and Burma they have, in effect, agreed to the continuation of the McMahon line as border of Burma. So one might think that, that applies to India too, to the same border line.

> Question: [Not clear]. The latest Chinese note had given the impression that the latest that the problem India was concerned with, was only discussing the situation in the Western sector, whereas they considered the Eastern sectors the most pressing problem. Is that correct?[9]

Jawaharlal Nehru: Partly yes. We were, all the time. The Eastern sector till the 8th of September last month had not been infringed upon, they had not come

---

9. The question has been reproduced from a report in *The Hindu*, 16 October 1962, p.1. See also *White Paper*, Vol. VII, p.141.

there, and the question was our discussing the Western sector. It is only now that they have come in the Eastern sector, and we stated that they must get back on the Eastern sector. They have just come a little, as I said, about three or four miles in depth and about fifteen miles in length and we said, "what are we to discuss about it. You get back, we will discuss everything then." But we cannot permit their occupying a place and using it as a further bargaining matter. Possession is nine-tenths of the law.

[Nepal]

Question: [Not clear]

Jawaharlal Nehru: The present situation in Nepal, internal situation, is a matter for the Nepal Government to deal with. We are not concerned with it. If you are referring to the relations of the Nepal Government with the Government of India, the Government of India right from the beginning of this present order in Nepal, which began a little over two years ago when there was a coup d'état, parliament was dissolved and the ministers and the prime minister were put in prison, well, at that time when I was asked in my Parliament about it, I said that we regret this setback to democracy, but this is a matter entirely for Nepal, we are not interfering in any way. I have repeated that many times. Between Nepal and India there is a very long border, I forget, about fifteen hundred miles, I do not know how much. It is an open border, people can come and go on either side. When the king took that step there, a number of Nepalese came in to India, one or two ex-Ministers too, and they started an agitation in Nepal against the existing regime and calling for release of their ministers and others and some kind of a democratic regime. We did not interfere. But the King and his advisers constantly said that we were interfering. We told them that in so far as any peaceful, constitutional agitation is concerned, the Nepalese émigrés can function because it is our law. If we took any action, we get into trouble with our law courts. But we will not permit them to make India a base for operations in Nepal or to send any arms from India. That has been our policy. But in a thousand mile frontier it is very difficult for us -- and which is an open frontier -- to check anything which may be taken secretly. But our own information is that not much has been taken from India, and the trouble in Nepal is based, is in Nepal proper. It may be that some people in India send secret instructions to them; that I cannot help; but we prevent them from functioning openly against the Nepal Government in the sense of using India as a base and certainly in gun running. We have prevented that. But the Nepal Government goes on saying, accusing us of helping their opponents. I do not know what we can do about it. We have assured them that apart from helping, we have arrested some of the people who were on our side functioning against the Nepal Government. Lately the Foreign Minister of Nepal, Mr Rishikesh Shaha, he was dismissed and another foreign minister came in, who is not at all favourably inclined to India. He makes statements violently attacking us. Even the King has made some statements which have surprised me.[10] He is evidently misinformed. I have refrained even from giving any answers, having an argument or controversy about it because it only makes matters worse. Meanwhile, we have continued many schemes of economic aid to Nepal from India. They are continuing. We have not made any change, withdrawn or we have got a number of people there, experts and other, in charge of these schemes. They are carrying on.

Question: [Not clear]

Jawaharlal Nehru: I am not aware of any such application or request. I read some vague talk, I forget where, in newspapers or somewhere. There has been no such request.[11]

Question: [Not clear]

Jawaharlal Nehru: I said matters of mutual interest.

[Stateless People in Ceylon]

Question: [Not clear]

Jawaharlal Nehru: Well, I might tell you that we have not discussed the problem of the so-called stateless people here, partly because I have been rushed about from place to place and there is no problem which can be dealt with in five minutes or ten minutes. It requires careful consideration. I need not say that I am anxious, I would be very happy indeed to get some kind of satisfactory solution of this problem. I hope that efforts have been made, first, the official level, who can go into it in detail; then later of course, it can be considered at higher levels. Because our relations, between India and Ceylon, are very good, very friendly, very cooperative, and it is a pity that this problem of old standing should continue.

10. See item 218.
11. Apparently, a correspondent had referred to a report that Ceylon had asked India for aid to repatriate people of Indian origin. See report in *The Hindu*, 16 October 1962, p.1.

Question: [Not clear]

[The Language Question]

Jawaharlal Nehru: It is a handful of questions. Why should I forget my having been to Cambridge, I do not understand. But that has nothing to do with it. In the matter of the language problem in India, as you perhaps know, in our Constitution we recognise fourteen languages; officially recognise fourteen languages, regional languages. In addition to that, we said that we would like, we wanted to make Hindi as an all-India official language, all-India language for official purposes, they are all official languages, but for official purposes, that is to say, the purpose that was being served by English as being a link language of various parts of India, we said, should be served by Hindi. In the Constitution it was said that after fifteen years, given some time, [this will] change. Meanwhile, progressively, in each of our regional areas, their regional languages are being used and we are convinced, for instance, that for educational purposes, in fact it is our fundamental rule, the mother tongue should be used for primary schools. Thus, in a city like Bombay, which is a cosmopolitan city and people from all over India live there, the Corporation of Bombay runs, I forget now, schools in eighteen languages, eighteen or sixteen, I forget, in Hindi, Urdu, Bengali, Marathi, Gujarati, Tamil, whatever it is, if there are a sufficient number of people living in Bombay of that language stock, they get a school from the Corporation. Naturally, that cannot go right high up. It is only in the primary school. Otherwise the regional languages are used. And the problems in India today are, linguistically, the problem of higher education. In regard to that we have come to the conclusion, we have laid down a three-language formula; the language of the region, I am sorry, the mother tongue, which is normally the language of the region; secondly, Hindi as a language we wish to make to some extent all-India, and thirdly, a foreign language, usually English, because you know it better, but it may be Russian or German or French. That is the formula we have laid down, because we wanted a foreign language very much to keep in touch with modern developments of ideas, of science, technology and the rest; also as a link language. At the present moment the argument in India is about, I said, two years ago our Government said that even after the fifteen years laid down in our Constitution for the changeover to Hindi, that means Hindi of course is coming in, but we will continue to use English as an associate language for all-India purposes. That is to say, regionally each region has the complete freedom to work in its own language. We do not even compel people to learn Hindi, much as we would like to, and in many areas of India it is a compulsory second language, but in some areas it is not. It is learnt by large numbers but it is not a compulsory language because we do not believe in compulsion of this kind. So, in our various states, progressively, all the work is being done from top to bottom in their regional language. Partly it is still done in English through sheer habit and facility. The problem is at the Centre. We have said, let this develop in the regions, regional languages; at the centre too let Hindi develop as fast as it can, but owing to various factors we have agreed to English being the associate language of Hindi at the Centre. Now the various factors are, first of all, there are some states in India which do not want us to give up English at the present moment or in two or three years' time, and in deference to their wishes we do not wish to make a changeover, in fact, the real fear being that as Hindi comes in fully, it will be to some extent to the disadvantage of the non-Hindi speaking areas, in examinations, in jobs, etc. So we do not wish any such feeling of discrimination to arise anywhere in India. So we said, all right, we will not, we will leave English as an associate language till, I said, till the non-Hindi speaking areas agree to the full changeover. I left the choice to them. This was done, a statement was made by us two years ago in Parliament and it was generally welcomed everywhere. Now we are bringing in a piece of legislation to put that in black and white. And some people are objecting to it, some Hindi-area people, Hindi speaking people. Well, first of all, two years ago we gave a guarantee on behalf of the Government and I can hardly swallow my own guarantee, promise that I made. Secondly, for practical reasons it is not feasible to put a sudden stop to our central work. Remember, differentiate the all-India central work and the provincial work which can be carried on in the regional language. It is not easy and it will upset our work to change over too quickly. In the Government of India, we employ people from all over India, not Hindi speaking areas, others too, very much. It will put them at a disadvantage. English or a foreign language has to continue for many of our international obligations and things. So, we made it an associate language, the principal language being Hindi later on. I think it is a very reasonable approach. Apart from everything else we believe, we believe strongly in national integration. National integration is ultimately a thing not to be brought about by compulsion, a thing of the mind and heart, and we do not wish to compel people to do things. We want them to agree to it. And our language policy is also based on that.

Question: [Not clear] A correspondent drew attention to the difficulties faced by people in Ceylon and India regarding travel and whether these difficulties could be eased.[12]

12. Question reproduced from a report in *The Hindu*, 16 October 1962, p.1.

Jawaharlal Nehru: I entirely agree with you. I wish something was done to ease these travel conditions. I think if that was done it would be a good step forward in lessening these other difficulties between the two countries.

Question: [Not clear] May I know your views on the proposed second Bandung Conference?[13]

[Second Bandung Conference]

Jawaharlal Nehru: I have expressed them, I have said that at the present juncture it does not seem to me very opportune. The first Bandung Conference was a success, a marked success because there were many common points between all the countries that attended. Now there are many controversies and conflicts between those countries and therefore, meeting at the present moment would not be helpful. We have suggested it should be postponed for a more favourable period.

Question: [Not clear] What are your views on the formation of an Asian Common Market?[14]

[Asian Common Market]

Jawaharlal Nehru: Asian Common Market? Well, to begin with it is a phrase that at present has little meaning. It is natural for trade to develop between nearby countries. For instance, you might say the South-East Asian countries should develop contacts on trade. I entirely agree. Or similar regions. Asia is too big a region, it differs too much. But apart from that, while we may aim at greater facilities for trade and, if you like, a common market in Asian countries, that is a desirable thing to aim at but it can only grow gradually. You must remember that many of the Asian countries, all of them excepting Japan, are developing countries, not developed countries, as the western countries are. Therefore, Asian countries, by and large, do not fulfil each other's wants. If I want or Ceylon wants, let us say, machinery, you can only get it from a country which produces the machinery. Small things [we] can adjust between ourselves, raw materials, you may buy rice, you may sell rubber and all that. That is all right. These are raw materials and it will be a good thing if we, to some extent, came to agreement about those matters. But the real demand in developing countries is for capital goods and that is machinery, and the developed countries supply

13. Question reproduced from a report in *The Hindu*, 16 October 1962, p.1.
14. Question reproduced from a report in *The Hindu*, 16 October 1962, p.1.

that till you yourself become developed. The present trouble, the argument about the European Common Market, apart from its political implications, is that immediately it may affect the economies of India, Ceylon and Pakistan. Our market in the United Kingdom will be affected. Our exports will diminish just at the time when we badly want our exports to increase. It is for the British Government to enter the European Common Market or not, but we want our interests protected. What is really required now is a world market, world conditions of trade being defined. That is what has been suggested by the Economic and Social Council of the United Nations and the United Nations are going to consider this matter.

[Succession]

Question: [Not clear]

Jawaharlal Nehru: My successor? Those who speculate can vote about it and get done with it. I cannot understand this. How can you nominate a successor in a democratic structure or government? Gandhiji was pleased to mention my name but he did not mention it as Prime Minister. He mentioned it before I was Prime Minister or anybody was Prime Minister in India. That was a different matter. We were carrying on a struggle for independence. But in a democratic structure, the successor is presumably the head of the largest party in Parliament. If a certain person is named you put that person at a disadvantage because there will be jealousies and people, possibly, react against somebody being imposed upon them. I will give you an instance. Sir Anthony Eden was groomed by Sir Winston Churchill to become his successor. He did become his successor but within a few months of that he got into trouble over the Suez and things and ultimately he had to resign.

[China and Pakistan Border]

Question: Sir, how do you describe the present approach of Pakistan and China to demarcate the border between the two countries?[15]

Jawaharlal Nehru: They [Pakistan and China] are trying to demarcate that portion of the border [where] there is no common border between Pakistan and China; there is a border between Kashmir and China. In fact, a part of that has been overrun by the Chinese forces in Ladakh, north of that is that part

---

15. Question reproduced from a report in *The Hindu*, 16 October 1962, p.1.

of Kashmir which is occupied by Pakistan. So their border question comes only because they occupy a part of Kashmir. We have pointed out to them that it would be improper for them to come to any agreement with China about territory which does not belong to them.

Question: [Not clear]

Jawaharlal Nehru: How can I say when I shall come here [next]? It is difficult to make plans far ahead.
    Thank you, gentlemen.

185. To S. Radhakrishnan: Bertrand Russell Peace Foundation[16]

October 16, 1962

My dear Mr President,
I have today received a letter from Earl Russell, a copy of which I enclose.[17] From this, you will see that he wants me to be a sponsor of a Foundation which will spread knowledge of the dangers of nuclear war. The Foundation is to be called the Bertrand Russell Peace Foundation.
    I am reluctant to join any such Foundations outside India. But I feel that in the present case I should not refuse. What do you advise me to do?[18]

Yours affectionately,
[Jawaharlal Nehru]

16. Letter to the President.
17. See appendix 12.
18. Nehru wrote an identical letter the same day to R. R. Diwakar, President of the Gandhi Peace Foundation, Rajghat, New Delhi.

186. To Bertrand Russell: Bertrand Russell Peace Foundation[19]

October 19, 1962

Dear Lord Russell,

Thank you for your letter of 11th October which I received on my return from Ceylon.[20] I have been thinking about the suggestion you have made in this letter. Normally I do not join foundations outside India, but I feel the object of the foundation you mention is such that it deserves every support. To spread knowledge of the danger of nuclear war in a big way is certainly desirable, and if we can do anything to that end, we should do it.

I am, therefore, agreeable to becoming a sponsor of the foundation.

With all good wishes,

Yours sincerely
Jawaharlal Nehru

187. To Nuruddin Ahmad: Welcome Address to Cyprus President[21]

October 25, 1962

My dear Mayor,

I am returning your draft Address of Welcome to be presented to the President of Cyprus.[22] I have only made some minor verbal corrections.

Yours sincerely,
[Jawaharlal Nehru]

---

19. Letter, sent to Plas Penrhyn, Penrhyndeudraeth, Merioneth, UK. NMML, Jawaharlal Nehru Supplementary Papers.
20. See appendix 12.
21. Letter to the Mayor of Delhi.
22. Archbishop Makarios III (1913-1977).

188. To Jonkheer G. Beelaerts van Blokland: Beatrix's Visit[23]

October 31, 1962

My dear Ambassador,

Thank you for your letter of the 31st October. I am very glad that Princess Beatrix is coming to India. Unfortunately, we have the invasion by China giving us a lot of trouble. I am glad, however, that I shall have the pleasure of meeting Princess Beatrix at lunch in my house and possibly also at the President's lunch.

Thank you for understanding my difficulties about attending your Reception.

Yours sincerely,
[Jawaharlal Nehru

189. In the Rajya Sabha: Second Bandung Conference[24]

Dahyabhai V. Patel[25]: Will the Prime Minister be pleased to state:

(a) whether India is participating in the proposed preparatory committee meeting of the Second Bandung Conference; and
(b) if not, what are the reasons therefor?

The Prime Minister and Minister of External Affairs (Jawaharlal Nehru): (a) and (b). It is not yet clear to us whether the preparatory meeting called in connection with the second Bandung Conference is going to be held. We have, however stated that if the meeting is held and a majority of the countries invited participate in the meeting we shall also be prepared to join.

---

23. Letter to the Ambassador of The Netherlands.
24. Written answers, *Rajya Sabha Debates*, Vol. XLI, Nos. 1-8, 8 November to 19 November 1962, pp. 838-839.
25. Leader of Swatantra Party in Rajya Sabha.

190. In the Lok Sabha: Second Bandung Conference[26]

Question[27]: Will the Prime Minister be pleased to state:

(a) the stand taken by the Government of India on President Soekarno's proposal to hold second Bandung Conference of Afro-Asian Nations; and

(b) whether there is any proposal to invite Soviet Russia also?

The Minister of State in the Ministry of External Affairs (Lakshmi Menon):

(a) We are not aware of any firm decision as yet about the holding of the Second Bandung Conference. There was an idea of calling a preparatory meeting of interested countries to consider this matter but even on that differing views have been expressed. So far as we are concerned we have suggested that a meeting at the present moment would not be helpful and that it could be postponed for a more favourable time.

(b) We are not aware of any such proposal.

विभूति मिश्रः अभी प्रधान मंत्री जी यूरोप की यात्रा से वापिस आते हुए इजिप्ट में ठहरे थे और श्री नासिर से भेंट की थी तो क्या उनसे भी इस संबंध में कुछ चर्चा हुई थी?

प्रधानमंत्री तथा वैदेशिक कार्य, प्रतिरक्षा तथा अणुशक्ति मंत्री (जवाहरलाल नेहरू): जी हां, कुछ ज़िक्र हुआ था और उनकी भी राय नहीं थी कि इस वक़्त कान्फ्रेंस करना मुनासिब होगा।

विभूति मिश्रः बांडुंग कान्फ्रेंस किन कारणों से सरकार करना उचित नहीं समझती है?

जवाहरलाल नेहरूः मैं इस वक़्त सारी वजूहात में नहीं जाना चाहता। लेकिन हमारे और चीन के दरमियान जो लड़ाई चल रही है वही कारण ऐसी कान्फ्रेंस न करने के लिये काफ़ी है।

26. Oral answers to questions, *Lok Sabha Debates*, Third Series, Vol. IX, Nov. 8-20, 1962, pp. 2163-2166.

27. Bibhuti Mishra, P.C. Borooah, Surendra Pal Singh, Bhagwat Jha Azad, N.S. Kajrolkar, P. Venkatasubbaiah, Buta Singh (Congress), M.K. Kumaran, Vasudevan Nair, Ranen Sen (CPI), Tridib Kumar Chaudhuri, Yashpal Singh, Y.D. Singh, Dinen Bhattacharya, J.B. S. Bist, P.K. Ghosh (Swatantra Party), and L.M. Singhvi (Independent).

[Translation begins:

Bibhuti Mishra[28]: Recently during the Prime Minister's Europe visit, he stopped over in Egypt and met Nasser. Did he discuss with him this matter?

Jawaharlal Nehru: Yes, something like this came up and he too did not think that this is the appropriate time for the Conference.

Bibhuti Mishra: What are the reasons that the Government does not think that the Bandung Conference should not be held now?

Jawaharlal Nehru: I do not wish to go into the details of the reasons. But the war between China and us is reason enough for not holding the Conference.

Translation ends]

P.C. Borooah[29]: May I know whether the attention of the Government has been drawn to the suggestion made by the Chairman of the campaign against nuclear tests to Burma, Ceylon and Indonesia to call for another Bandung Conference on the Sino-Indian dispute and, if so, the reaction of the Government thereto?

Speaker: Sino-Indian dispute is altogether a different matter.

Hem Barua[30]: May I know if it is a fact that in the present political climate, not to speak of India, even other countries are not in favour of giving China an undue prominence, which it would undoubtedly seek, by holding a second Bandung Conference and, if so, whether other countries have conveyed their reactions or their opinions on this matter to our Government?

Jawaharlal Nehru: In the answer to the main question it has been stated that a number of countries were not in favour of holding this conference in the near future for various reasons; of course, the latest developments in regard to our war with China were not there then, these are later developments. But these developments make it all the more undesirable to hold such a conference now.

28. Congress MP from Puri, Orissa.
29. Congress.
30. PSP.

Indrajit Gupta[31]: How many of the countries which participated in the first Bandung Conference have supported India openly in this conflict with China and have any of them supported China?

Jawaharlal Nehru: I could not give the figure. A number of them have supported us and a number of them are more or less silent.

प्रकाशवीर शास्त्री: बांडुंग कान्फ्रेंस में जो राष्ट्र सम्मिलित हुए थे यह सही है जैसा कि प्रधानमंत्री जी ने कहा कि वर्तमान परिस्थितियों में ऐसा कोई सम्मेलन बुलाना सम्भव नहीं हो सकेगा लेकिन मैं जानना चाहूंगा कि क्या उनकी सहानुभूति प्राप्त करने के लिये हमारे ओर से कोई यत्न किया जा रहा है?

जवाहरलाल नेहरू: सहानुभूति प्राप्त करने का यत्न होता ही जाता है।

प्रकाशवीर शास्त्री: मेरा अभिप्राय है कि क्या विशेष यत्न किया जा रहा है?

[Translation begins:

Prakash Vir Shastri[32]: I understand and agree with the Prime Minister that in the present situation it is not possible to hold a Conference; but are we trying to get the support of the Bandung Group?

Jawaharlal Nehru: Yes, we are apprising them of the situation.

Prakash Vir Shastri: My question was whether any special effort is being made in that direction.

Translation ends]

---

31. CPI.
32. Independent MP from Bijnor.

(b) Africa

191. For the *East African Standard*[33]

The *East African Standard* has asked me for a message on the occasion of its Jubilee. I gladly do so, because of my interest in Africa.

Events are moving fast in East Africa and now Kenya is preparing for independence. I have no doubt that an independent united Kenya can be a most prosperous country and play an important part in the development of Africa and in world affairs.

In Kenya, as in the rest of East Africa, there are numbers of persons of Indian origin. We have consistently advised them to identify themselves with the lives and fortunes of the countries in which they live. I am glad to see that this is being done. I am equally glad to learn that in Kenya they will be treated in just the same way as other African citizens, with the same rights and duties. No country can go forward in the modern world without the loyalty and conscious efforts of all its citizens and this is possible only if every citizen is confident of receiving fair and equal treatment. Confidence breeds confidence. The urgent need all over the world today is for mutual sympathy, understanding and tolerance. These have long been accepted as the hallmark of a mature political society, no less than that of a civilised individual.

A prime need for newly independent countries is rapid economic development. Unless the common man is assured of certain minimum material benefits, a country cannot avoid internal convulsions or resist external pressures. Kenya, in her efforts at advancement will have the support of India. She will be happy to share her experiences of economic development with Kenya, and in other ways, help Kenya to the best of her ability and resources.

While congratulating the *East African Standard* on its anniversary, I wish it all success and hope that it will make every effort to propagate the ideals of tolerance, goodwill and mutual help.

---

33. Message, undated, but apparently 4 October 1962. See letter of 4 October 1962 from N. P. Alexander of MEA to K.R.F. Khilnani, Commissioner for India in Nairobi, enclosing the message. MEA, File No. A-IV/123/4/62, pp. 9-10/corr.

192. To B.P. Sinha: Inviting Chief Justice of Nigeria[34]

October 9, 1962

My dear Chief Justice,

When I was in Nigeria recently, the Chief Justice of the country expressed a wish to visit India. I told him that he would be very welcome. I suggest that, if you agree, you might send a letter to the Chief Justice inviting him and his wife to come to India. We shall make them our guests in India.

His name etc. are:

Sir Adetokunbo Ademola, Kt.,
Chief Justice of the Federal Supreme Court,
Racecourse Road,
Lagos (Nigeria).

His wife, Lady Ademola, is a cultured and distinguished person. She is a graduate from Oxford University and for many years was a teacher.

He has suggested that he might come here on or about the 22nd of January and stay for a period of three to four weeks. He is most anxious to make a detailed study of our entire judicial system.

I hope you will be good enough to invite him.

Yours sincerely,
[Jawaharlal Nehru]

193. To K.K. Shah: Attending Africa Seminars[35]

October 10, 1962

My dear Shah,

Your letter of October 9th.

I am afraid I cannot say at present whether it will be possible for me to attend your two seminars. I can understand that these are important occasions and I should like to be present at them. But it is not possible for me to accept any

---

34. Letter to the Chief Justice of India. MEA, File No. A-II/121/51/62, p.2/Corr.
35. Letter to Rajya Sabha MP, Congress (1960-1971), Indian Council for Africa, 5 Curzon Lane, New Delhi-1.

firm engagement then. Parliament will be sitting and apart from that, there are some very important things that I have to do here. Perhaps early in December I might be able to be more definite.

Yours sincerely,
[Jawaharlal Nehru]

194. To Pyarelal: Gandhi on Africa[36]

October 20, 1962

My dear Pyarelal,

Your letter of the 20th October with its enclosures.[37] I have read the papers you sent me. You can certainly use your article and the script for a broadcast.

I am very heavily occupied at present. After you come back from Calcutta, you might remind me, and I shall try to fix a date for our meeting.

I am returning the papers you sent me.

Yours sincerely,
Jawaharlal Nehru

195. Recalling Troops from Congo[38]

A number of suggestions have been made to me to call back our troops from the Congo because of the emergency here. I would not like to do so suddenly as this would upset the situation in the Congo. But it might be worthwhile to find out from the Secretary-General of the United Nations whether it will be possible in the fairly near future to call them back.

2. In a lesser degree, this applies to our troops in Gaza also.

36. Letter to Mahatma Gandhi's secretary and biographer. PMO, File No. 2(114)/56-66-PMS, Sr. No. 89-A.
37. See appendix 20.
38. Note, 27 October 1962, for the SG, MEA. MEA, File No. A-II/101/13/62, Vol. V, p. iii/n.

196. Interview to the Kenya Broadcasting Corporation[39]

Question: Prime Minister, now that military equipment has started to arrive from your allies, will the Indian armies soon be in a position to hold the Chinese back indefinitely.

Jawaharlal Nehru: That is a military question which I would not venture to answer. We are holding them back now and I hope that they would be held back, pushed back later. But there are many factors in this. Winter conditions are setting in and all that.

Question: Is any political solution yet insight?

Jawaharlal Nehru: Obviously not. If this has been in sight, this war-like conflict would not have arisen.

Question: This week-end India again supported Chinese admission to the United Nations. Why do you continue to support her in this matter when she is invading your frontiers?

Jawaharlal Nehru: This has been explained by our permanent representative in the United Nations. This is not a question of likes or dislikes. Obviously we are very much against China's policy specially at present. But there are two reasons. One is we have always proclaimed that the universality of the United Nations. Every country should be there and the other very important reason is that if China is not there, you can't hold her to account. If she had been there, we might have raised the question in the United Nations about what she has done in invading India. And thirdly the question of disarmament is so important and vital. It is pretty obvious, you can't have a world disarmed leaving China fully armed.

Question: In view of China's action will India have to revise her policy of peaceful co-existence.

Jawaharlal Nehru: Now, it is often said; I don't quite understand this. Peaceful co-existence is a firm policy, but obviously it depends on two parties or more. One person cannot peacefully exist and if the other person does not. We are not peacefully co-existing with China now. Obviously not. But the policy is the right policy or else the alternative is that, if you differ from a country you cannot have any peacefuldealings with her and one country tries to impose its policy on the other—at least war; and in the circumstances of today it leads

39. Interview, 2 November 1962.MEA, File No. AIV/103/27/62, pp. 21-25/Corr.

big countries to nuclear war, to destroy both and the rest of the world. There is no choice, whatever your views may be about that policy, there is no choice. The world has to live peacefully recognising that they differ, countries differ in their policies, ideologies etc. This means destruction.

Question: What effect will the defence effort have on India's Third Five Year Plan?

Jawaharlal Nehru: It will obviously have an effect and we do not want the Third Five Year Plan to be given up in the important aspects because that, the development envisaged in Third Five Year Plan, strengthens the industrial and the agricultural position of India which is very necessary even in war time. So that is, it may have to be changed here and there and more stress laid on the more important things today.

Question: In East-Africa the Indian community is raising large sums of money for the defence fund. Have you anything would you like to say to them?

Jawaharlal Nehru: I am glad to hear that they are raising money and even more so the sentiment behind their feeling about what is happening to India, and feeling warm-hearted about it in trying to help. That is more important than its being translated into money. My advice to Indians in East Africa or anywhere abroad has always been that they should work with the fullest cooperation with the people of the country. They should not seek any special position or special privileges. Naturally, they want good treatment but not at the expense, say of the Africans; and to treat themselves as they may be East Africans themselves and since they lived long enough and Kenyans. That is right. They owe their loyalty to Kenya or East Africa and they owe certain loyalty to India too. There is no conflict between them and they should serve the cause of freedom in East Africa and of the Africans. That should be their particular aim and now that we are in trouble in India, we welcome such help as they can give. That doesn't take away from their obligation to serve the people in Kenya.

Question: Prime Minister what have you to say about the response of the people in India itself?

Jawaharlal Nehru: I think, the response has been wonderful and a large number of our domestic problems have almost solved themselves—petty conflicts, petty arguments. We appointed a Committee. We have a Council of National Integration to tackle all these problems and that appointed a Committee specially, it was the name of it, but to deal specially with communalism and the like. This morning, yesterday, this morning's papers contained that report in which they say that our work has been done; and a new situation that has been created, the problems we are considering are no more there. So it has had one good effect—cohesive effect and it is really high, very pleasing indeed and heartening to see all kinds of people who are quarrelling through small matters pulling together.

Question: Sir, have you any comments to make on the reasons why you assumed the Defence portfolio?

Jawaharlal Nehru: Well, as a matter of fact even when I didn't have the Defence portfolio I was greatly interested in it and took part in all the important decisions, especially since this crisis arose. But I thought that it would be good for the country and many people who wanted me to do it in the country; and I also wanted to be more intimately connected with it. So I took it over. As a matter of fact, some little time ago, days ago, the Defence Minister Mr Krishna Menon asked me to take it over and so I decided that it would be best in the circumstances to take it over.

Correspondent: Thank you Prime Minister.

197. In the Lok Sabha: Situation in Congo[40]

Question[41]: Will the Prime Minister be pleased to state:

(a) to what extent situation in Congo has improved; and
(b) what steps have been taken to implement UN Secretary-General's new formula for integration?

The Minister of State in the Ministry of External Affairs (Lakshmi Menon):

(a) There has been no concrete improvement recently in the Congo situation. In fact, Mr Tshombe appears to be pursuing his old tactics of prolonging negotiations as far as possible, in order to avert decisive action being taken against him, and to gain time, which he utilises to strengthen himself politically and militarily.
(b) The implementation of the Plan of the 20th August, 1962, is in the hands of the Government of the Republic of Congo and the United

---

40. Intervention during question hour, *Lok Sabha Debates*, Third Series, Vol. IX, November 8 to 20, 1962, 8 November 1962, pp. 26-30.
41. By Harish Chandra Mathur (Congress), Indrajit Gupta, Homi Daji (CPI).

Nations. The Government of India do not know the details of the steps taken to implement the Plan. It is, however, understood that three Commissions, one on military and two on financial matters have been set up, and are working to settle the terms of the integration of Katanga into the rest of the Congo. Agreement in principle has been reached on certain matters, but it is only when these agreements are actually implemented that real progress can be said to have been made.

Harish Chandra Mathur[42]: In view of the answer given by the hon. Minister that the situation remains completely bogged down as it was and the trouble is likely to be a long drawn-out one and also in view of the emergency at home, may I know whether we have taken any steps to recall our troops from there?

Lakshmi Menon: May I submit that there is another question on the same subject? But I may say that we have apprised the Secretary-General about the emergency in our country and we have also asked when the Congo situation is likely to become normal.

Hari Vishnu Kamath[43]: I could not hear the answer.

Speaker: The answer is that we have informed the Secretary-General about the emergency and also enquired when the situation in Congo would improve when we can withdraw.

Harish Chandra Mathur: May I know which of the important countries, and whether particularly the USSR, the USA and the UK are all agreed to the Secretary-General's new formula, and if so, what the trouble is which stands in the way of its implementation?

Lakshmi Menon: I have stated in the main answer that the matter has to be settled between the Congo Government and the United Nations. The plan is the United Nations plan or what is called the U Thant Plan, and unless the Katanga Government agrees to the plan, nothing could happen.

Indrajit Gupta[44]: May I know whether it is a fact that the agreed communiqué of the Commonwealth Prime Ministers' Conference on this subject, in fact,

42. Congress, Jalore, Rajasthan.
43. PSP, Hoshangabad, Madhya Pradesh.
44. CPI, South West Calcutta, West Bengal.

approved of the British Government's position regarding this proposal made by Mr U Thant, and whether that did not, in fact, encourage Mr Tshombe's[45] adamant attitude towards it?

The Prime Minister and Minister of External Affairs, Defence and Atomic Energy (Jawaharlal Nehru): I have not quite understood to which communiqué of the British Government the hon. Member is referring.

Indrajit Gupta: I am referring to the communiqué issued after the Commonwealth Prime Ministers' Conference.

Jawaharlal Nehru: Of course, there is some reference in it, and as far as I remember, that said that the Conference approved of the proposals of Mr U Thant, and hoped that they would be given effect to by all parties concerned.

Narendra Singh Mahida[46]: What is the strength of our troops at present in the Congo?

Jawaharlal Nehru: I am afraid I cannot give the exact number; it may be five thousand or six thousand.

Hari Vishnu Kamath: Is it a fact that a contingent of our troops sailed from Bombay as late as last month, and if so, is it the Government's view that resolving the civil war in the Congo is more important than defending our own country?

Jawaharlal Nehru: The troops were sent from here were sent to Gaza to replace our forces there which will come back.

Hari Vishnu Kamath: My question has not been answered. Is it the Governments view that the task in Gaza or the Congo is more important than defending our own territory? Why should we deploy our troops abroad?

Speaker: He has said ...(interruption)

Hari Vishnu Kamath: He has not answered the question.

---

45. Moise Tshombe, leader of the local *Confédération des associations tribales du Katanga* (CONAKAT) political party. Served as President, 1960-1963.
46. Swatantra Party, Anand, Gujarat.

Speaker: Order, order. I was only repeating what he said.

Jawaharlal Nehru: The hon. Member puts a question to which he should very well knows the answer.

Hari Vishnu Kamath: How?

Jawaharlal Nehru: Obviously nothing is more important than protecting our own integrity. But there is such a thing as abiding by our word to the UN and elsewhere. We cannot suddenly upset the situation without the concurrence of the United Nations. As soon as possible, we can get them back, that is a different matter.

Hem Barua[47]: Is it not a fact that these 1,100 troops sent to Gaza are expected to do only police work in connection with a dispute on that border?

Jawaharlal Nehru: They are not supposed to fight. They are at the ceasefire line or whatever it is called. They were sent at the request of not only the United Nations but of the UAR Government. Obviously, we cannot suddenly take any action without the consent of the parties concerned.

N.G. Ranga[48]: Have Government taken steps to inform the UN Security Council or the Secretary-General that it would not be possible for India to retain her troops in these various places and, therefore, the UN should take necessary steps to release them as soon as possible?

Jawaharlal Nehru: We have informed the Secretary-General that we would like to have them back as soon as it is possible. It is for the Secretary-General to decide that.

Homi Daji[49]: Is the Prime Minister aware that the Commonwealth Premiers' communiqué has accepted U Thant's proposal as the basis which is exactly the word Tshombe used and the stand of the British Government, and this has been taken to mean not an endorsement totally of the proposal but rather an endorsement of the British-Tshombe stand, a stand commented upon by many newspapers including *The Statesman*? If so, what is the stand of the Government of India?

47. PSP.
48. Swatantra Party.
49. Homi F. Daji, CPI, from Indore.

Jawaharlal Nehru: I do not know what comments have been made in newspapers. But that statement, to the best of my recollection, was definitely in favour of U Thant's proposal. We do not go into all these details. I do not know how the hon. Member thinks that it was something else.

Homi Daji: I can read it out.

Jawaharlal Nehru: I do not accept *The Statesman*'s or any other newspaper's comments. I know better.

L.M. Singhvi[50]: When do we expect the return of our troops? Have we set a definite date for that? If not, why not?

Jawaharlal Nehru: We have not set a definite date because we observe our international agreements and arrangements. We cannot upset the United Nations because of this, but we have indicated to them that as soon as it is convenient we should like to get them back.

K. Hanumanthaiya[51]: Is it not the case that the placing of our troops at the disposal of the United Nations would be helpful to us in the same way when we are in difficulty?

Jawaharlal Nehru: It would be helpful to India in the wider world context.

Joachim Alva[52]: We have fulfilled a longer spell of duty in the Gaza strip and a lesser spell of duty in Congo. Is it not possible to regulate withdrawal in terms of the spell of duty so that in course of time we can call them back?

रामेश्वरानन्द[53]: कांगो आदि देशों में जो भारतीय सेनायें गई हैं, देश की ऐसी *स्थति* होने पर क्या उन्हें भारत वापिस बुलाने का कोई विचार है या नहीं? मैं यह भी जानना चाहता हूं कि देश की वर्तमान स्थिति कैसी है?

अध्यक्ष महोदयः आप बैठ जाइए अपने पड़ोसी से यह जान लीजिये।

---

50. Independent.
51. Congress, from Bangalore City, Mysore.
52. Congress, from Kanara, Mysore.
53. Jana Sangh, from Karnal, Punjab.

रामसेवक यादव[54]: देश के सामने जो वर्तमान संकट मौजूद है उस को देखते हुए क्या भारत सरकार ने यूनाइटेड नेशन्स को लिख दिया है कि भारतीय ट्रूप्स रिलीव कर दिये जायें?

अध्यक्ष महोदय: यह तो उन्होंने जवाब दे दिया है।

[Translation begins:

Rameshwaranand: I want to know about those troops who have been sent to Congo etc., are they being called back in view of the current situation here? I also want to know what the situation in the country is?

Speaker: Please sit down and get all these information from your neighbour.

Ram Sewak Yadav: Given the present state of the nation, has the Government of India written to the UN that the troops may be relieved?

Speaker: This has been already answered.

Translation ends]

198. To Abdul Haq G.H. Woolla: Loyalties of Indians in Africa[55]

November 24, 1962

Dear friend,

I have your letter of the 18 November.

There are two kinds of Indians in various parts of Africa. Some of them have become African citizens and some retain their Indian nationality. Those who are African citizens must give all their loyalty to the country of their choice. But those who remain Indian citizens still—and I was addressing such persons—should be loyal to Africa as well as to India and serve both. It was something of this kind that I said. It is not a question of dividing of our loyalty. Inevitably an Indian national owes a certain loyalty to India. In addition, he must be loyal to the country in Africa where he lives and does his business.[56]

---

54. Socialist Party, from Barabanki, UP.
55. Letter; address: PO Box 30245, Nairobi, Kenya.
56. See item 199.

We have encouraged Indians to become citizens of the country they live in Africa.

With all good wishes,

Yours sincerely,
[Jawaharlal Nehru]

199. Controversy over Statement on Indians in East Africa[57]

[Note, 28 November 1962, by Dinesh Singh, Deputy Minister, MEA, begins]

PM gave an interview to the Kenya Broadcasting Service on November 2, 1962.[58] During the course of the interview PM thanked the people of Indian origin in East Africa for their contributions to us in our hour of need especially for the sentiment behind their feeling about what was happening in India. He had mentioned that his advice to Indians abroad had always been that they should work in fullest cooperation with the people of the country they had made their home. They should not seek any special position or privileges and should treat themselves as citizens of the countries and owe their loyalty to those countries. He had also emphasized that they should serve the cause of freedom in East Africa and of the Africans. During this PM had mentioned of a kind of emotional feelings they have about India and their friendship towards us and kind of loyalty they owe to India also. (Transcript of the paragraph in question is at flag 'N').

This statement has been mischievously removed out of context and played up in Africa to give an impression that PM had suggested that Asians in Africa should have double loyalty. Photostat copy of a press cutting is at flag "R". Some telegrams have been received from Kenya about it and we have been asked by our acting High Commissioner in Uganda to clarify the position. The Acting High Commissioner has discussed the matter with the Secretary-General of the External Affairs Division of Uganda and apparently the Secretary-General conveyed to him that the Prime Minster of Uganda[59] was seriously worried about it. Since then, I believe, the Uganda People's Congress (the Government party of Uganda) has issued a strongly worded statement which is at flag "Z".

---

57. Note, 28 November 1962.
58. See items 191 and 196.
59. Milton Obote (1925-2005), held office from 1962 to 1966.

The Prime Minister of Uganda had also made a brief statement expressing his concern over the statement but terming it as alleged statement. It is, therefore, felt that some clarification should be issued to remove the misunderstanding. It has been suggested that we should issue a clarification or PM himself might make a brief statement.

I do not think it is necessary for PM to make a statement as it will give a new lease of life to the controversy. We could give full particulars to our High Commission in Uganda and ask the Acting High Commissioner to explain it suitably to Uganda Government and issue a Press statement. We could also inform our High Commission in Tanganyika and Commission in Kenya and ask them to meet any mischievous propaganda that might come to their notice there.

Dinesh Singh

PM

[Note, 28 November 1962, by Dinesh Singh,
Deputy Minister, MEA, ends]

[Note, 28 November 1962, by Nehru begins]

Yes. This may be cleared up by some statement. I have already written on this subject to someone in East Africa who drew my attention to this matter.[60]

2. I was distinguishing between Indians who are still Indian nationals and those who have adopted Kenya or East African nationality. I referred to the Indian nationals there and pointed out that although, as Indian nationals, they owe certain loyalty to India, nevertheless they should be loyal to the country they live in and work.

3. As a matter of fact, our general advice to Indians in East Africa has been to adopt the nationality of the country they live in. But those who do not adopt that nationality, even so, owe a certain loyalty to those countries.

J. Nehru
28.11.1962

Deputy Minister, EA

[Note, 28 November 1962, by Nehru ends]

60. See item 198.

200. To Hastings Kamuzu Banda: Indians should identify with Local People[61]

November 30, 1962

Dear Dr Banda,

Thank you for your letter of the 24th October 1962. I had the pleasure of meeting Mr R.B. Chidzanja, as well as Dr Kokri, Mr Gelu and Mr Cheriyan, and of hearing from them about recent developments in your country.

I am heartened to learn of the happy relationship that exists between the different Nyasa communities. I have no doubt that under your wise guidance and leadership Nyasaland[62] will more rapidly forward. As you are aware, we have consistently advised the people of Indian origin permanently domiciled abroad to adopt the citizenship of, and to identify themselves completely with, the people of the countries in which they live.

I am grateful to you for the expression of your sympathy in the wanton aggression launched by China against us. We are engaged not only in the defence of our sovereignty and integrity but of our very way of life and the values for which we and other like-minded nations stand. The support which we have received from our friends abroad has been a source of great encouragement to us.

Please accept our congratulations on the happy outcome of the recent London Conference. I have no doubt that the home rule which has been decided upon is only the first step towards the speedy attainment of complete independence by Nyasaland.

With kind regards,

Yours sincerely,
[Jawaharlal Nehru]

61. Letter to future Prime Minister (1964-1966) and subsequently President (1966-1994) of Malawi; address: P.O. Box 538, Blantyre, Nyasaland.
62. Until 1964 Malawi was known as Nyasaland.

(c) Burma

201. Inviting Ne Win[63]

[Note, 3 October 1962, by Y. D. Gundevia, the CS, MEA, begins]

I was speaking to the Prime Minister, this morning, about General Ne Win of Burma. I had only yesterday acknowledged two of our Ambassador's[64] letters, one of which deals with Ne Win[65] and the other with his lieutenant, Aung Gyi[66].

2. The Prime Minister said that he would not invite Ne Win to India yet. I shall press this on the Prime Minister, again, after some days, if I may. Democracy has not failed only in Burma. Some of our neighbours seem to want to learn a few things outside their own country, but they are not sure whether they are welcome in India. Our Ambassador in Rangoon has said on an earlier occasion, that Ne Win has almost been fishing for an invitation. I think the least that is necessary today, is for our Ambassador to let Ne Win know that he would be welcome if he wants to come to India.

Y.D. Gundevia
3.10.1962

PM

[Note, 3 October 1962, by Y. D. Gundevia,
the CS, MEA, ends]

[Note, 4 October 1962, by Nehru begins]

I still feel that in the circumstances we cannot invite General Ne Win to be our guest in Delhi. I cannot adjust myself to this idea. May be that sometime in the future we can consider this again. Apart from this, the next two or three months are very full with eminent persons from abroad and other engagements.

---

63. Noting, 4 October 1962, MEA, File No. SI/457/6/62, p.5/notes.
64. R.S. Mani.
65. Prime Minister of Burma, 1962-1974.
66. Member, Revolutionary Council of Burma.

The situation on our frontiers is a menacing one and may develop rapidly.

Apart from inviting General Ne Win, we should show them every courtesy and encourage our relations with Burma. If there is any occasion for it, we can send the Deputy Minister with some officials to discuss any pending matters in Rangoon.

J. Nehru
4.10.1962

CS

[Note, 4 October 1962, ends]

(d) Ceylon

202. In Colombo: Address to Parliament[67]

Mr Speaker[68] and Honourable Members of both Houses of Parliament,
I am deeply grateful to you for the honour you have done me in inviting me to address this august assembly. I have been many times to this beautiful Island and every time I have come here, I have been welcomed with great hospitality and friendship and I carry memories of those visits with me.

On this occasion, although I have spoken here previously, I believe it is the first time that I have addressed Members of Parliament as such. I do not quite know what you would desire me to speak about. But the first thing that strikes me is that Ceylon and India are among the very few countries in Asia which have a parliamentary form of government. And some other countries which have tried it, have reverted to other ways. Now the more experience I have gathered the less I feel inclined to say anything about the method of government of any country, because methods of government depend on so many factors, past history, traditions, environment and so many other things, that I think it is not right for anyone to think that the method of government one may prefer in one's own country is necessarily the ideal method for every country. Every country has to find out its own way, not only in political methods of government but in economic advancement, in the sense of the common goal

---

67. Speech, 13 October 1962. NMML, AIR Tapes TS No. 11633-11635, NM No. 2120-2121.
68. R.S. Pepola.

of most countries today that are developing. All I can say is what we like in our own country. We have adopted this parliamentary system of government in India after due deliberation, but at the same time without much doubt. I mean to say we accepted it wholeheartedly, and we have tried to work it during these years since we became independent. It was not an entirely novel form of government for us. We had some restricted form previously, and even if we go back to past history there has been a system in India, rather at the lower levels, of village republics and others, of representative government. So one cannot say that it has come as something entirely new to our people in the mass, but still it is a new form and we have carried it on with a large measure of success during these sixteen, seventeen years since we became independent. We have had, as you know, a number of general elections of the vast electorate that we have in India and it has been a tremendous job for us to organise that electorate. The electorate consists of a trifle over two hundred million, and over about sixty percent of them vote and in all kinds of conditions, in fact it is impossible for us to find a suitable time in the year when we can have elections everywhere at the same time, because some areas of ours are snowbound and it is not possible to approach them in winter, and yet winter is the right time for elections in the rest of the country. In spite of all these difficulties we have carried on with some success.

One very noted parliamentarian from England, Sir Winston Churchill, once said that the parliamentary form of government was pretty bad, it was full of difficulties and failings; but, he added, nevertheless it is the best form yet devised. I think that is the correct description. It is a difficult form and it has many failings, because, after all, the failings of the people are represented in parliament. But nevertheless, I think that it may be said, provided it fits in to the people generally in their habits, a good form of government, perhaps the best. I do not know. But it requires a great deal of some qualities in the people generally, qualities of tolerance, qualities of pulling together even though opinions may differ, because a parliamentary form of government means acceptance of certain basic things and a measure of cooperation even when we differ, a recognition of the rights of others, of even minorities and those who differ in opinion because if they do not agree at all they will put an end to the system of government. It is difficult to carry on. So there is a measure of tolerance, of working together and of coming to agreements as far as possible which are accepted by most people. All this is, of course, you may say it is a civilised approach to life carried up to the national stage. But it makes it difficult to be wholly civilised all the time. In the international sphere, as you know, we are not yet wholly civilised, we, meaning the world, not our countries, and we live in a period of what is called "cold war", which is not a good thing to have and which turns people's attention always to some kind of approaching conflict and turns it at a period when a conflict might really destroy civilisation. What is a cold war? It is always to think in terms of war. The very words are "cold war". Some countries are called neutral, some are not aligned to the great military blocs and when we talk about neutrality it is, really we are thinking in terms of war. There is no such thing as neutrality except in terms of war. In war some countries are belligerent, some are non-belligerent, [and] are [called] neutral. So we have brought in the terminology of war into times more or less of peace, and more and more one begins to think in military terms. I do not like the word neutral. We are called neutrals. India is called neutral. Perhaps Ceylon might also be called neutral. Neutral means, of balance between the two. I think non-aligned is a far better description. We are not tied up with any power bloc, we are friendly to all, we should try to be friendly to all, and we decide our course of action independently without being dragged into this or that course of action by alignment with any bloc. But it is a serious state of affairs in the world today when great and advanced nations face each other with armaments of tremendous quantity and tremendous force, and then there is always the possibility that even without a desire to have war some unfortunate accident may lead to it and then there is no withdrawal from it. It is an extraordinarily difficult situation. You will remember that in the Charter of the UNESCO the words occur that "wars begin in the minds of men". Now the cold war is something which begins in the minds of men and exists there. Therefore, it is a bad thing to have, lest it be translated into actual war. I do not presume to say this in criticism of any country, big or small, because the world is a difficult place to live in, and nobody should be presumptuous enough to criticise other countries, great powers or others, who have their own difficulties and who may find it a little difficult to solve them immediately. They are trying to solve them and it is our function, as much as we can, to help in creating an atmosphere which might perhaps lead to a solution. We cannot solve them. The big, the major quarrels of the world are between the Great Powers.

You know that there is a disarmament committee which has been functioning in Geneva for some time. It has not produced any remarkable results, although disarmament is probably the most important question today in the world. But I do think that the presence of eight countries, who are supposed to be neutral, in that committee has helped greatly in keeping the discussions on a nearly friendly level, without breaking the committee up, and various proposals have been made by those eight nations there which will help to bridge the gap a little. I must confess that the outlook is not very bright in regard to disarmament, but it is not quite hopeless either. There is a ray of light, because I think the Great Powers are earnestly trying for disarmament, and more immediately, for the cessation of nuclear tests. I hope that they will succeed. I said that I do not presume to criticise anybody, because who would want to criticise, who is one to accuse another person when one's own difficulties face one, which we cannot solve ourselves. As you perhaps know we are, all our conditioning in India has been, certainly in the last forty, fifty years, in favour of peaceful action and peace generally. I am not referring to the past period, I am referring to the period since when Mahatma Gandhi became our leader, and he conditioned us, the masses of India, very much in favour peaceful action, and we did indulge in it to an astonishing degree and succeeded by those means. Much more so have we been in favour of peace in the world and generally cooperation between nations. So, conditioned we have been in peace, and yet here we find ourselves by a strange succession of events, facing situations which are far from those of peaceful on our frontier area, having a great deal of trouble. It is an extraordinary thing that a country like India, so devoted to peace, with a passion for peace and so conditioned for peace, should have to face contingencies like we do today on our frontiers which do not lead to peaceful happenings and may trouble us still more in future.

I am merely mentioning this to point out the contradictions in the life we lead. We do not want to do a thing, we try to avoid it, and yet sometimes circumstances compel us to do something that we utterly and absolutely dislike. We will try to avoid that, because we have tried our best to be friendly with all countries, some naturally more than others, some [for] whom we [have admiration], but not to be unfriendly to any country. We shall continue to do so in spite of the difficulties that arise, because our business today, and ever since we became independent, is the primary business of bettering the lot of our people, of raising their economic level and higher standards for them. That is the essential task before us, and before you, and before any developing country. And so when we became independent almost the first thing we did was to apply ourselves to this problem of development and we did it in a more or less scientific way, appointing a high powered Planning Commission which went into these matters closely and made recommendations which the Government accepted, and thus started our First Five Year Plan. It was not a very ambitious plan but it was good beginning and we succeeded in that Five Year Plan. The next Five Year plan was much more ambitious and we did not do quite as well in it as we had done in the first. It was a much bigger thing. Yet, on the whole we succeeded. Now we are in the middle of the Third Five Year Plan and we have begun it well in some ways, not so well in others. Anyhow, we are carrying on with a stout heart and we hope to succeed. Therefore, the problems that really face us in our country, and I take it that face you in Ceylon, are problems of development. I do not want to get entangled in other problems, in international affairs, because all my time and energy I wish to spend on these problems of development in India. But you will see how we get entangled. We are entangled in the Congo in Africa, we have got considerable forces there, which we have placed at the disposal of the United Nations. They are there still. We are entangled in Southeast Asia, these international commissions in the states of Indo-China. We have got some forces on the boundary of the United Arab Republic and Israel. Somehow it becomes difficult to refuse to do something which an international organisation asks us, and which has to be done. So we get entangled, although such energy as we have we want to concentrate on our development, because the more we develop, the more we are in a position to help in the solution of international problems. It is no good jumping about from place to place when one's house is not very much in order. Then there is the United Nations, of course, which takes up a good deal of time normally. So that in spite of all our entanglements abroad, which are not exactly of our seeking, but which circumstances have compelled us to accept, the major problem before us in India is one of development.

Behind that development, of course, all kinds of other problems lie. We have, what we call movements in India, we call them national integration. What does that mean? India is of course a politically integrated country. There is no question of it being otherwise. But India is also a country of many religions, of huge states or provinces which in some ways differ from each other, in many ways. There is a great deal of difference between North India and South India, climatic differences and others. So India is a country which has a strong and abiding unity, and at the same time differences in different parts of India, whether the differences arise from different climatic conditions, different sense of statehoods, sense of differing religions and other aspects, which we call communal in India. And yet at the same time there is something very strong which holds India together; even when the distant parts of India were separated into many parts there was this holding together, at first culturally and later in more ways than that. Now we want naturally to make India not only politically one, which it is today, but something, a living unity in the minds of men. Politically it is one, and we work together, we have a Parliament, and we have so many other functions working together—but we want to make this something real in the minds of the people in the villages and other places. A country like India with this variety cannot carry on unless it recognises that variety and gives it opportunity to function. We do give it, in theory, in our Constitution we give privileges, we recognise these varieties, always keeping in view the fundamental unifying influences and the unity of India, but recognising the variety of India and giving it freedom to flourish, not merely because circumstances compel us to do it, because we think it is a good thing to have variety within that unity. All the variety enriches national life. It need not necessarily be a uniform pattern. And anyhow, if we adopt the democratic method, we have to do that. And I think we are making good progress towards that.

Every problem in relation to India becomes a vast problem by virtue of its population, 442 million in the last census, and everything has to be multiplied by 442 million. If we make progress and if we have to calculate the per capita income, we divide the total wealth by 442 million. So the figure we achieve in the end is a relatively small figure. So it is a vast undertaking to raise the level of all these four hundred and odd millions.

To come back to this development scheme, which is the most important for us, we have to develop on all fronts, agricultural front, industrial front, industrial front meaning big industry, heavy industry, light industry. Developing in that means the adoption of techniques provided by modern science and technology. That does not mean again that we should adopt everything that a great country like the United States does, or like the Soviet Union does, because conditions are different. It is no good copying it. I might tell you one thing. A little while ago the people, who taught us economics in India, whether they were Europeans, or whether they were Indians, taught that to us from the European and English textbooks. Now English textbooks on economics deal with the problems of England or Europe, deal with the problems of an industrially advanced community. Now patently we are not an industrially advanced community. Our problems are those of development. Therefore, those problems did not apply to India. Yet we were taught in the textbooks about those problems as applied to Europe. Gradually only, we came to realise that we have to develop our own economics. Basically, of course, the principle is the same, but we have to consider it in the context of our own problems. It is no good, not only we but foreigners began to recognise it too, it is no good applying the American view of economics to India, or the Russian view, but gaining from those views, we developed our own approach to these questions. So our Planning Commission has tried to look at it from many points of view and we have taken as our advisers from time to time people from all countries. You will be surprised to know the variety of people who have come to advise us from capitalist countries, from communist countries, from socialist countries. We have discussed the matter with them and come to our own conclusions. And the odd thing is, often we have had at the same time some people, say, from America, Canada, from England, from Russian and other places, from Poland, when made to consider the actual problem, the economic problem we had to face, without ideologies, frequently they came to more or less the same conclusion in their advice to us, because they were considering a specific problem, not ideological, not discussing wide ideologies on which they differed greatly. So we have to see

241

that in a pragmatic way keeping two or three broad things in view. One was that we should aim at raising [the] thinking of the common man in India, how to raise him, how to raise the masses of India, how to give an equal opportunity to all the people of India. It is a big thing, nevertheless, and I do not know when we will reach that stage. Anyhow we aim at it. That is why we said, we want a structure of society based on socialism. We did not take up doctrinaire attitude of some rigid form of socialism, but broadly socialism, meaning that we will try to give an equal opportunity to all, and remove the great differences which exist at present, unfortunately, between the very few rich and the many poor. We have adopted an economy which is called mixed economy, that is partly a public sector economy and partly a private sector economy, [in] the hope that the public sector will continue to grow and will occupy all the strategic points in our economy while the private sector also does its function, both sectors being more or less according to our plan. We cannot have them conflicting with each other. Difficulties arise at every stage. The more we thought of this, the more we came to the conclusion that without industrial development it was not really possible to raise the standards very much of our people. So we attach great value to industrial development. Industrial development, again, cannot take place adequately unless we have heavy industries, heavy industries like steel and others, and have a great deal of power resources. So our programme has been to develop heavy industry, as also light industry. But then another factor which we always thought of became more pressing. We found that basic to every kind of progress in India was the agricultural front. We attach the greatest value to industry, but if I may say so, it is difficult to compare the two, but we attach even more value to agricultural advance, because even industrial growth will only take place if agriculture is on a sound footing and gives us some surplus for industry. But really, in planning there is no such thing as first and second, you have to march along different paths together. But I, we, did wish to mention to you how much more importance we attach to agriculture. After all, seventy-five or eighty per cent of our people subsist on agriculture, [who live in] our villages.

In our villages, therefore, we first had a community development scheme to energise the villages, because we found that ultimately all these economic theories and others come up against the human being. More specially, agriculture comes very much up against the human being. If our peasants, agriculturists, still pursue methods of agriculture which they did, say five years ago or five hundred years ago, it is difficult to improve agriculture. We have to give them better tools, better implements, we have to get them used to [these tools]. We have, in fact, to change the human being, somewhat widen his outlook. So we have the community development schemes. They did some good. Lately, in the last year or two we made a radical change in our rural structure. It is quite a revolutionary change because we have given authority to the rural councils, very great authority. Each rural council, there are various stages of them consisting of, let us say, twenty or thirty villages, it has very considerable authority. In fact, it has authority in regard to all development schemes, and we give them the money for it too. The money we get from them in land taxes we return to the councils, practically, most of it. Now the purpose of doing this was not only to make them partners in development, to give them the feeling that they are also sharers in this, they have to work, but to take them out of the old rut, make them self-confident. They used to run up to me or to the officers and others, do this for us and do that. If they come up to me now, my answer is, "do it yourselves, you have got the power. Why come to me?" It develops a different approach in them, I do not say that this has succeeded everywhere in India, but they are going through that process of change and they are becoming more self-reliant. Even, oddly enough, even our programme for mass education is spreading more through the agency of those village councils than through the top officers, etc. The top officers are there but they advise them. For instance, in a village, attendance at school was not very good. No inspector coming from outside could help it. When he comes, they come up. But now that the village people themselves are responsible they see jolly well that every child attends the school. It is a matter of prestige for them. They are always there. And so in some ways a certain change is taking place in our rural masses which is of basic importance. We think in the ultimate analysis it is better than any change which is brought about superficially by some parliamentary legislation or something else. Parliamentary legislation of course is necessary to help this change, but ultimately we have to change our people's habits, minds, the approaches to life, and we are trying to do that in some of the ways I have mentioned to you, in many other ways, but making them do things for themselves rather than others do it for them. The old method, not only in British times—I do not know if you have it here—but even in pre-British times in India, where the district magistrate was the big boss who had very great authority for his district. He may be a good man but the whole outlook of the people was to look up to him. He was the initiator, the doer. If he was good he did good work, if he was not good he did not do good work. We, to some extent, had it also in the early years of our independence, we carried on the old administration in that way. Now the old boss system, whether British or Indian, is giving way to this system, which I have explained, because the village people are not ideal at all, they quarrel, they do all kinds of things. Nevertheless, they become self-reliant, they begin to do that, they begin to cooperate.

Now, another thing that we have laid the greatest stress on there is cooperation, the cooperative movement, because our peasant holdings are very small. The average holding is two acres, an acre, and nobody can expect them to do much modernising with an acre of land. We have put an end to the big landlords and we have put a ceiling on land and all that, and we do not want to revert to it. Therefore, the only way to adopt modern techniques is through the cooperative movement, so that peasants in a village or two or three villages come together and adopt the cooperative technique. We lay the greatest stress on that.

These are some of our approaches, because ultimately the problems of our country today are economic. Political problems are there, unfortunately, international and national, but the problems are economic. And in theory we should be able to solve all these problems, because modern scientific techniques are capable of production of wealth in a very large measure. There is no doubt that the whole world would be well fed today if by some scientific method we could use the resources of the world for that purpose and everybody would gradually have a high standard of living. I hope that will be so ultimately, just as some countries in Western Europe are called the affluent countries, the United States and the Western European countries and Russia, they are all among the affluent countries today, and the great part of the world lacks even ordinary necessities of life. It means that there is no doubt about it, it is only the political differences that keep us from utilising the world's resources to the world's advantage, and of course the vast, colossal sums spent on armaments, which might partly be diverted to the betterment of humanity. And so the problems really are economic, of want, and they can be solved, and I hope they will be solved, as they end the war which puts an end to others. And in economics, as I said, and I would like to repeat it, there is no sovereign remedy, there are certain lines of advance, but to say that we must follow the example of either a great capitalist country like America, or a communist country like Russia, is not very logical. We may accept some lines of advance here and there, the basic approach. But conditions are different. I give you an instance. India is a country, although very big, it has a very big population. The result is, and the population grows, per man there is not enough land in India. Both in America and in Russia the ratio of land to human beings is entirely different from that of India. Human beings are relatively few and land, there are enormous tracts of land in Russia, in both of them. Naturally, they have to think differently of agriculture than we have to. We cannot slaughter a large number of people to have less people in the land. We have to deal with them. We do try to control in some measure, the growth of population, but such as it is we have to deal with it. So our whole land problem becomes somewhat different from that in a country where there is more land than men relatively, like the Soviet Union, like America. And so therefore, every country has to look at its problem in its own light, learn from other communities but apply that knowledge to its own problems so as to fit in with the existing conditions there. Therefore, the more I have seen these difficulties in our own country, of people trying to apply it, you will find, for instance, sometimes we send people, let us say, to become, specialise in something in America. They are very good engineers, very good this, very good that, when they come back. But it takes quite a long time for them to adjust themselves to India. They are always shouting for the latest type of machinery which they saw in America. It is all right for America. It is totally out of place in India at the present stage of our development. I have no objection to machines, I like machines. But it must fit in with the conditions they have to work in. Sometimes it is cheaper for us and better, socially better for us to employ a large number of human beings to do a bit of work than a machine and to throw them out of employment, whatever it is. So that a person who comes from America may, not always, may become rather frustrated because he cannot find all the latest techniques and methods that he has been used to in America. So, through much experience we have come to the conclusion that learning everything from outside as far as we can, we have to think of applying it to the existing conditions in India in the way we think best. We have to draw up our own economics, again learning from others, keeping in view that the object is to serve the common man in India, the general poverty stricken people in India, rather than a select few. From that many things flow. That is, the public sector should grow and should dominate the economics of the country, the strategic points. We are not against the private sector. In fact all our land is private sector, much of our industry is still private sector, but we do hope that the public sector will grow and we are trying to do this without much conflict, as far as possible. Some conflict there is inevitably. And we hope to succeed. I cannot be a prophet about the future, because there are too many pitfalls in the way for us, and the world, and in India.

I have not ventured to say anything about Ceylon and Ceylon's problems, because it is for you to deal with them and I do not know enough to be able to suggest anything. But it may be that some of our experiences in India may possibly throw some light over similar problems here. You can only learn from other problems, from the experiences of others, if you are prepared to adapt them and you think best of your own. It is no good copying any country, whatever the country may be, because each country has a certain individuality. Ceylon certainly has very much an individuality. You may learn from America, England, Germany, France, Russia, Japan, but ultimately it will be your own version of what you have learnt that will do good, not the copying of something. And if you can learn something from our struggle during the last seventeen years of independence, well, I hope you will learn from them, adapting them to your own uses, not blindly learn from any country. That is all I can suggest to you, because this question of development is a common one for all countries, all the developing countries, which are sometimes called the under-developed countries. Developing countries is a better word than under-developed countries and we have similar problems to face but in different environments, in different circumstances, and therefore, we have to be wide awake to our own environment, to our ideals and then take every step which leads to that ideal.

One thing more I should like to mention, planning. I have said we talk of Five Year Plans but there is no such thing as planning for a year, or five years. Planning has to be perspective planning, looking far ahead. Now we are trying to plan at least for fifteen or twenty years ahead, not detailed plan but a broad plan, and then keeping that in view we plan for five years, we plan for one year. You have to keep a picture in view because many things cannot be done in five years. You cannot have a steel plant, if you want one, in five years, it overlaps periods. If we want a steel plant, we have to train engineers to run the steel plant and that takes ten or fifteen years. It is no good our planning in the air for the steel plant without training people who will run it and so a vital matter becomes the training of individuals, on the one hand, mass education which is essential, and on the other, specialised education for these specialised jobs, which takes a long time. Again, education, itself, becomes such a vast problem in India because of our numbers. At the present moment we have got forty-seven million boys and girls in schools and colleges, and they are growing. I think in about four or five years' time the number will be sixty-five million, huge numbers we have to deal with. That is general education, primary, secondary and college. But specialised education, especially scientific and technological, is also growing fast, but not faster than our requirement. We may have, as we do have, unemployment on a large scale in India, but there is no unemployment, practically none, among people who have specialised training, because they are being picked up by the growing economy of the country.

I can talk a great deal about our problems, economic, and Five Year Plans, and our difficulties. But I have tried to give you some glimpse of our major approaches to these things. Perhaps, in some aspects they may be similar to yours, the problems, and approaches may be similar to yours. But I would again repeat, do not try to copy the approach of any country, whether it is India, or America, or England, learn from it, from their mistakes as well as their successes and find your own approach.

I am deeply grateful to you, Mr Speaker, Sir, for this opportunity to address this assembly of parliamentarians and I thank you for it. [Applause].

203. In Colombo: Reception[69]

Prime Minister,[70] Excellencies, Friends

I am deeply grateful to you, Prime Minister, for your graceful words of welcome. I come back to Ceylon after several years and I am happy to be here because a visit to this beautiful and enchanting Island and to the enchanting people of this Island is always very welcome to me.

You have referred to our close relations, to our friendship. That friendship goes back well into the past, a past with historical, cultural association to which you referred. There is another bond and link between our two countries and that was the message of the Buddha which I believe is particularly required by the world today, the message of peace. And so it is a particular pleasure to me to come here today for a few days and to be able to meet you and all our friends here and discuss about our mutual problems. The last time I came here I was welcomed by a very distinguished Prime Minister[71] who is no more, and I feel a little sad that my visit on this occasion should be almost in a sense committed to the memorial of him.

I am grateful to you, Prime Minister, and I agree with you that we have to strengthen the bonds between our two countries and help and cooperate in many ways.

Thank you.

204. In Ceylon: To the Ramakrishna Mission[72]

Swamiji and Friends,

It always gives me great pleasure to visit what I would call the 'abodes of service', run by the Ramakrishna Mission. Wherever they have worked, and they have worked in many places not only in India but in neighbouring countries all round, they have created an ideal of service and a reputation for quiet unostentatious work and thus not only done good to numerous individuals but in their own way helped in soothing and bettering international relations. So I am happy to be here even for a short time during my brief stay of two and a half days in this Island.

---

69. Speech, 13 October 1962, NMML, AIR Tapes, TS No. 11353, NM No. 1979.
70. Sirimavo Bandaranaike.
71. Solomon Bandaranaike (1899-1959). Nehru Visited Sri Lanka in May 1957. See SWJN/ SS/38/pp.705-727.
72. Speech at the inauguration of the Ramakrishna Mission International Cultural Centre, 15 October 1962, Colombo. NMML, AIR Tapes, TS No. 19060, NM No. 2556.

I do not know what you would expect me to say on this occasion during a few minutes. But in the world today which is so full of conflict and so full of fears and suspicions, not only internationally but sometimes even nationally, within a country, how are we to approach these problems? I am not talking about the argumentative approach or the merits or the demerits of a particular problem but rather the mental, the psychological, emotional approach to the problems that affect us. It is obvious that where there is fear and suspicion it is all due to the wrong approach. It clouds the minds, it angers persons. Today in the world, we see this tremendous obsession, this fear complex among nations, with the result that we get, what is called the, cold war. What is the cold war? It is a war, not of weapons actually but of minds. It is a war of hatred and, if not violence, continuous preparation for violence, and thereby inducing the fear element to grow. It is, in fact, the very opposite and the very reverse of that feeling which, well, if I may say so, this Ramakrishna Mission tries to spread; a feeling of friendliness, of charity. It is the very opposite of what the Buddha stood for or the great sages anywhere.

So, while we discuss the problems, whether national or international, the real thing is in what frame of mind we discuss them. Are we out to grab, to injure the other party? Or even if we are not out for that, if we are so afraid of the other party grabbing and injuring us that we react in the same way; well, the result is that we become so tied up in complexes, in prejudices, in fears, that the real merits or demerits of the problems are hidden away. People do not think of them so much because their minds are clouded with anger and fear. That is the state of the world today. Everybody will say and does say that, "Oh! We must avoid the disaster, let us say, of war, world war." And yet logically, countries will do the exact opposite and do things which push the world towards that possible disaster. That is on the international scale. On the national scale that type of fear of war, etc., is not present, or at any rate should not be present, but, nevertheless, sometimes we see the same type of approach, not the human approach, not the cooperative approach but the approach of conflict, of imagining that we will benefit ourselves by injuring the other person, not realising that that can never happen. It may not be so obvious, but even now it is fairly clear in the context of the world that if one country tries to injure another country by war or something else, the ultimate effect of that is to cause injury to itself. If that is so in the world sphere then it is much more so in the national sphere. We are becoming [the same] too. We are all organic wholes; you cannot injure your arm without injuring the body, you cannot injure your little toe even, without having the sensation of pain, fever all over the body. It seems obvious enough and yet we function in that way all over the world, not realising that the way of hatred and violence does not yield results, practically speaking, quite apart

248

from ideals and noble sentiments. From the strictest, practical, opportunist point of view it is becoming clear that the way of trying to gain something by violence and hatred does not pay in the long run even though it might appear to yield some little result.

I am concerned, naturally, with the world's problems in so far as they affect my own country. It is none of my business to interfere in the world's problems. I have enough in my own country, more than enough. But I cannot help not only taking interest in it but sometimes participating in matters relating to international problems, whether in the United Nations or elsewhere, because they affect me. If there is war in the world it affects me and you and everybody. Or if there are tensions and fears it affects me and everybody. So, one has to take interest and participate in these matters. But my function, primarily, is to serve the sphere in which I work, my country. But I realise that I cannot isolate it from other major matters. Therefore, I mention them. We seem to have arrived at a stage in political development, in military development, when we have to take a turn, if I may say so, in terms of quality. What I mean is this. You have heard of atomic energy and atomic bombs. One of the great men of the age who was instrumental in bringing about atomic energy to the service or disservice of man was Einstein, a great scientist. He was very unhappy about what he had been instrumental in doing because he was not only a great scientist but a great man and a very humane man who disliked violence and hatred and all that, and just a little before his death he said, "Atom bombs cannot be conquered by other atom bombs, they can only be conquered by a change in the heart of man." That is what I meant, that it may be that we have to change our approach to some of our major problems qualitatively, approach them in a different way, not in the old way. I am quite certain that this question of atomic bombs and the rest can never be solved by a race in armaments. It is, on the face of it, a little absurd to imagine, by continuing evil you are going to put an end to evil. You go on setting fire all over the place and think that you are putting out the fire. It is illogical, it is completely unreasonable. That is obvious enough in the big things but it is equally obvious in the small day to day things of life, relations of groups, relations of individuals, relations of nations, of course. How to change our approach qualitatively, how to realise that we do not do any good to our country by perpetuating conflict and the feeling of hatred or dislike or aversion or fear and apprehensions?

Now that is a major problem of the age, almost, which takes us from the political and the economic planes, which are important no doubt, to something that might be called the moral or the ethical plane of approaching these subjects. That plane, of course, has always been there and the great men that the world has produced have always reminded us of that. But there is a difference today, between today and the times gone by. The difference is that it has ceased to be merely a moral principle, it has become an urgent and absolute practical necessity, than moral principle. Why? well, there are many reasons. But patently, the development of science and technology has altered and revolutionised the world. Neither you nor I, nor anybody anywhere can live an isolated life. Even countries that are distant to us become our neighbours. We can go there in three or four hours, we can listen to them in an infinitesimal fraction of a second, instantaneously, communications are tremendously fast; you take them for granted, whether it is the normal transport or news services or telephone or radio or radar, which is instantaneous as far as we can see. But that has changed the nature of the world. Every country is a neighbour of every other country in the world, and when you become neighbours like this, continuously rubbing each other up, if you rub each other the wrong way, well, it is bad for both. If on the other hand you realise that it is the benefit of all of us to develop the cooperative attitude in life then it is good for everyone. In ancient days, may be thousands of years ago, when the population of each country and the world was a relatively small one, and there were wide spaces unoccupied, I believe, in India it is very roughly calculated that long ago the population was very small and we talk of those days as days of a golden age. There may have been many virtues in those days but one forgets that in those days there were vast stretches of land unoccupied and people could easily occupy it, and lived, at any rate, so far as the necessities of life were concerned, fairly comfortably, not [in] luxury. Population grows, other things happen, nations come nearer, and within a nation people who live in separate village communities begin to rub each other up, each other's shoulders, rub against each other. Cities grow, more and more people live in a variety of occupations. Now, that can only be done satisfactorily by the growth of the civic sense, people cooperating with each other, not cooperating by the compulsion of an autocrat or of a dictator or somebody dominating over you, but cooperating by producing self-discipline. The cooperation comes from one's own decision, is not imposed upon one because an imposed cooperation is no cooperation. It is just as nothing imposed can ever be really worthwhile.

So, in the world today, these problems arise which have made it a practical and an absolute necessity for the way of cooperation, co-existence, sometimes between nations, just as within a nation, there has to be co-existence between various groups. The days of conflict are not over, obviously, but conflict becomes much more dangerous now, on any scale, than it used to be because of these developments. So that, the old moral idea becomes the urgently necessary practical idea today. Whether we take it or not is another matter. We live, as it is, on the brink, on the verge of a possible catastrophe, a world [of] catastrophe owing to war, atomic war, we live on the verge of that; and what I say is by no means just a play on words, it is a fact that we live on the verge of it and no man knows what the year or the years to come may bring about. And it just surprises me that people do not wake up to this prospect and still waste their time and energy over petty problems and petty conflicts when this major problem for the whole of mankind stares them in the face, when even the possibility of the extinction of humanity cannot be ruled out. That is the challenge of the time which you may put in any way you like; challenge, on the one side, if you like, of the atomic bomb and the hydrogen bomb, on the other the message, the old messages of the sages, the message of the Buddha which is the exact contrary, the opposite approach, the approach of compassion, of wisdom, of cooperation, of tolerance, of humanity.

Humanity, I said. Well, human relations ultimately are tremendously important. How would you divide the problems of the world, all the problems, almost, I suggest that you divide them, let us say, in three broad groups: the relationship of the individual with the individual, another individual; the relationship of the individual with the group; and the relationship of a group with another group. The latter includes national groups, one nation against another nation. Practically, this covers most problems that you have, apart from problems of the individuals in our development which is on a different level but which is helped, of course, by the way one functions in these other spheres. So we come back, we have to tackle these problems in the big scale, national, international, but the problem of human relationships, remains a vital one. And in this problem of human relationships an organisation like the Ramakrishna Mission plays, I think, a very vital part, because, by its quiet, unostentatious work and service it soothes these animosities, it brings people together, it calms them, it lowers the fever in their brains and thereby, creates an atmosphere where people can cooperate, can become normal, can get rid of their complexes; and so, perhaps this quiet, unostentatious work of service is far more important than what politicians and what the newspapers talk about so much.

Therefore, I am happy to be here and I hope that more and more people will think of these problems in this way and in the spirit of quiet service, of cooperative relations, of human relations, and realise that the old days of barriers, whether you call them religious barriers, political barriers, national barriers, class barriers or whatever barriers they might be, are no longer relevant in the context of the world today. They are there, of course, and I do not try to deny them. There is class conflict, I do not deny it; there is international conflict, national conflict, group conflict. But I say, all those conflicts are irrelevant today and one must realise that and, therefore, try to produce an atmosphere without that conflict, and to produce it not through conflict; it is not through conflict that you will remove conflict but by another approach, a peaceful approach, a non-violent approach, a friendly and cooperative approach.

Thank you. [Applause]

205. In Colombo: To the Ceylon Association for the Advancement of Science[73]

Survival of Humanity
Nehru's Appeal for Scientific Approach

Colombo, Oct. 15 – Mr Nehru today asked the scientists to cultivate "a scientific type of mind, an enquiring type of mind, a type of mind which does not accept anything without proving it and merely on authority."

Mr Nehru was addressing the Ceylon Association for the Advancement of Science here this evening on "The place of science in the development of nations."

"The modern world is a world based on science. There is little doubt about it. It is becoming more and more progressively based on science. By ignoring this fact, you get nowhere. By accepting it, not only accepting it in theory but in practice, you are likely to get somewhere," he said.

Mr Nehru said that he did believe quite stoutly that the whole approach of science was essential for the survival of humanity, because this kind of thing could not easily continue for long -- a small part of the world in affluent circumstancesand a large part of the world in depressing poverty. "It is producing crisis all the time," he said.

Science could and did produce the goods they wanted, provided they were always prepared to work hard for it.

Spiritual Influence

He said that science with all its manifold benefits and virtues, however, did not solve the moral or spiritual problems of a human being or society. There was something in addition to it.

In this connection, Mr Nehru referred to Acharya Vinoba Bhave who, he said, symbolised to him something which took him out of the common rut and made him think of something afresh just as Gandhiji did. Acharya Vinoba Bhave

---

73. Reproduced from *The Hindu*, 16 October 1962, p. 7.

had been saying lately that politics and religion were out of date and what was required now was science and spirituality. It was worth thinking about, he said, Vinoba Bhave talked of spirituality and did not lay stress on the ritual of it.

Mr Nehru said he thought that without science there was no future, for any society. But even here, unless science was controlled by some spiritual influence, there was no future.

It was said that the Industrial Revolution changed the face of the world, which it did. "How did the industrial revolution come about?" he asked, and added that it was preceded by a scientific revolution.

Those who had read an account of the difficulties of the Industrial Revolution, Mr Nehru said, would remember the painful condition of workers and others in those days, who were exploited to the utmost. But the fact remained that science led to the improvement of technology. Technology led to greater production and greater production led to a number of changes which revolutionised life.

Material Progress

On the kind of development that India wanted, Mr Nehru said that they obviously wanted to develop on the material plane. India wanted to build up a society where it was open to every person to lead what was called a good life. Science, he said, helped it. But science had also produced many bad things "to give an obvious example, nuclear weapons and atomic bombs, which threaten to exterminate humanity and put an end to civilisation as we know it."

206. In New Delhi: To the Press[74]

New Delhi, Oct. 16 – Prime Minster Nehru said here today that the Government and the people of Ceylon were very friendly and cordial to India.

Talking to newsmen on his return to the capital after a three day visit to Ceylon, Pandit Nehru said "I am very happy I went to Ceylon. I had a good time there. The Government and the people were very friendly and cordial to us."

Asked whether he discussed with the Ceylon leader the Sino-Indian border dispute, the Prime Minister said that he did not naturally discuss this question with them. "Obviously it came up. They (the Ceylonese) are very friendly to us," he added.

74. Report of interaction with press. Reproduced from the *National Herald*, 17 October 1962, p. 1.

Replying to another question whether he had seen the latest Chinese note, Pandit Nehru replied amidst laughter, "I do not know which is the latest. How can I say?"

The Prime Minster was received at the Palam airport by his cabinet colleagues and high officials. – PTI

207. In the Lok Sabha: Indians in Ceylon[75]

Question[76]: Will the Prime Minister be pleased to state:

(a) whether it is a fact that during his visit to Ceylon he had talks with the Prime Minister of Ceylon on problem of Indian settlers rendered Stateless by Ceylonese citizenship laws: and

(b) if so, the result of the talk?

The Deputy Minister in the Ministry of External Affairs (Shri Dinesh Singh):

(a) Yes, Sir.
(b) The talk was brief and of a general nature. Further discussions at official level are envisaged.

विभूति मिश्रः मैं जानना चाहता हूं कि जो हमारे भारतीय सीलोन में बसे हुए हैं और स्टेटलैस सिटीज़न की हालत में हैं उन्हें स्टेट का सिटीज़न बनाने के बारे में जो बातचीत हुई उसमें कितनी प्रगति हुई है?

दिनेश सिंहः उन्हीं के बारे में बातचीत हुई है और जैसा मैंनें अभी अर्ज़ किया कि इस सिलसिले मे जो हमारे अफसर हैं वे और बातें अभी कर रहे हैं।

विभूति मिश्रः मैं जानना चाहता हूं कि प्रधानमंत्री जी ने जो बातचीत की, उससे कहां तक यह मालूम पड़ता है कि यह जो हिन्दुस्तान के बाशिंदे वहां पर हैं उन्हें स्टेट सिटीज़न बनाया जायेगा और अन्य सम्बन्धित अधिकार मिलेंगें?

75. Oral answers, *Lok Sabha Debates*, Vol. IX, Third Series, November, 8-20, 1962, pp. 854-858.
76. Bibhuti Mishra, D.N Tiwary, K.N. Tiwary, P.C. Borooah, Maheswar Naik, Savitri Nigam (Congress), P.K. Deo, Yashpal Singh (Swatantra Party), Prakash Vir Shastri, Bishanchander Seth, L.M. Singhvi (Independent), Jagdev Singh Siddhanti (Haryana Lok Samiti), Yallamanda Reddy(CPI).

दिनेश सिंहः बातें अभी चल ही रही हैं अभी वे ख़त्म नहीं हुई हैं।

विभूति मिश्रः प्रधानमंत्री जी ने जो बातचीत की उस बातचीत से हमें क्या आभास मिलता है और आशा होती है?

प्रधानमंत्री तथा वैदेशिक कार्य प्रतिरक्षा तथा अणुशक्ति मंत्री श्री जवाहरलाल नेहरुः माननीय सदस्य यह याद रखें कि यह जो लोग हैं वहां हमारी राय में सीलोन के नागरिक हैं, वह हमारे नहीं हैं। वह वहीं पैदा हुए उनके बाप दादे सिर्फ़ यहां पैदा हुए थे इसलिये यह सीलोन गवर्नमेंट का काम है कि उनकी रक्षा करे और उनके जो नागरिकों के अधिकार होते हैं वह उन को दे। अब वह चाहते हैं उनको यहां भेज देना सबों को या बहुतों को, इस पर हमने कहा है कि जो लोग बग़ैर किसी दबाव के ख़ुशी से आना चाहतें हैं और हमारे विधान को पूरा करते हैं वे आ सकते हैं लेकिन हमें यह स्वीकार नहीं है कि वह यहां ज़बरदस्ती और बग़ैर उनकी मर्ज़ी के भेजे जायं इस पर बहस होती है कि क्या ढंग निकाला जाये, क्या नहीं। हमें यह मंजूर है कि किसी क़िस्म की कोई ज़बरदस्ती न हो। जो वहां से आना चाहें वे आ जाएं, हम उन को लेंगे और जो वहां रहना चाहें वे वहां रहें। लेकिन वे हमारे नागरिक नहीं हैं। उनके बाप दादे भारत से निकले थे, वह और बात है।

[Translation begins:

Bibhuti Mishra[77]: I want to know, what progress have been made in the talks regarding providing citizenship to those Indians who are settled in Ceylon and are in a status of stateless citizens.

Dinesh Singh: We are discussing this issue. As I said now, our officers there are continuing the discussion.

Bibhuti Mishra: I want to know about the discussion that the Prime Minister held there and how far is it going to help the Indians in Ceylon get their citizenship and other related rights?

Dinesh Singh: The discussions are not yet over, they are going on.

Bibhuti Mishra: The discussions that the Prime Minister has had, what can we understand from it, or how hopeful are we of success?

77. Congress.

Jawaharlal Nehru: The hon. Member should remember that those who are settled there, in our opinion are citizens of Ceylon, not ours. They were born there. Only their fathers or grand fathers were born in India. It is now up to the Ceylon Government to give them the citizenship rights and protect them. Now the Ceylon Government wants to send some of them or most of them to India. We said that those who are willing to come without any pressure and those who fulfil our legal necessities are welcome, but it is unacceptable to us that people should be sent without their consent by force. We are trying to find a way out. But we would not agree to any manner of force being applied to deport these people.Those who wish to come willingly, may come and those who wish to stay would stay there. But they are not our citizens at present. It is a different matter that their fathers and grandfathers were from India.

Translation ends]

L.M. Singhvi[78]: May I know whether the hon. Prime Minister realised that by a legislative fiat these Ceylonese of Indian origin have been rendered stateless and whether it has been proposed to set up any specific machinery for conciliation between these two States on this question on any agreed terms of reference?

Jawaharlal Nehru: These questions cannot be dealt with by any official machinery by itself unless first the principles are settled by the two Governments. The machinery is there; there are our High Commission, our agents and others who discuss with those people.

प्रकाशवीर शास्त्री: क्या मैं जान सकता हूं कि प्रधानमंत्री जी जब लंका गए थे, तो लंका के प्रमुख अधिकारियों से बातचीत करने के अतिरिक्त, जिन भारतीय नागरिकों की यह समस्या है, उनमें से भी कुछ कठिनाइयों का विवरण उनको दिया था?

जवाहरलाल नेहरू: मैं फिर अर्ज़ करूंगा कि भारतीय नागरिकों का सवाल नहीं है। थोड़ा सा है इधर उधर। वह तो दूसरा सवाल है। यह तो उन लोगों का सवाल है, जिनके बाप दादा वहां पर गए थे और जो क़ानून के मुताबिक़ हमारे नागरिक नहीं रहे। वे सीलोन वालों नें कुछ थोड़े से लोगों को शायद तीस चालीस हज़ार को, नागरिक बनाया है। लेकिन सात लाख के क़रीब अभी बाक़ी हैं। और कुछ हमने बनाए, जो स्टेटलैस लोग कहलाते हैं, जो कहीं के नागरिक नहीं हैं। हमारा कहना था कि मैं फ़िर दोहराता हूँ कि उनमे से जो लोग खुशी से और बग़ैर दबाव के यहां आना चाहें उनको हम ले लेंगे, अगर वे हमारे कांस्टीट्यूशन के हिसाब से हमारे नागरिक हो सकते हैं। हम कहते हैं कि बाकियों का वे प्रबन्ध करें।

78. Independent.

प्रकाशवीर शास्त्रीः अध्यक्ष महोदय मेरा प्रश्न यह था कि जो राज्य-विहीन लोग वहां पर हैं, क्या उनके प्रतिनिधी भी प्रधानमंत्री जी से मिले थे।

जवाहरलाल नेहरूः जो हमारे नागरिक हैं? वह तो मुझे याद नहीं है। लेकिन ज़्यादातर ये लोग वहां एस्टेट लेबर हैं और उनकी ट्रेड यूनियन्ज़ हैं उन ट्रेड यूनियन्ज़ के अधिकारी मिले थे।

[Translation begins:

Prakash Vir Shastri[79]: May I know, when the Prime Minister went to Ceylon and had discussions with their senior officials, did he also give some assurances to these Indian citizens, who are facing problems there?

Jawaharlal Nehru: I would urge again that this is not a question of Indian citizens. The matter of legal interpretations is there. That is a different question. This is a question of those whose fathers and grandfathers went from here, and no longer remained our citizens. The Ceylon people have made some— thirty or forty thousand people their citizen. But there are still more or less seven lakh people left. And we too have given citizenship to some, those who are called stateless people, who are citizens of no country. I am repeating that those who are willing to come without any pressure; we shall accept them, as long as they comply with our laws of citizenship. The rest are the problem of the Ceylon Government.

Prakash Vir Shastri: Mr Speaker, my question is, did any group representing these so called stateless people meet the Prime Minister during his visit?

Jawaharlal Nehru: Our Citizens? I do not remember. But most people there are estate labourers and they have trade unions. Some of the trade union leaders had met me.

Translation ends]

Hem Barua[80]: In view of Ceylon's decisions to reserve jobs for the Ceylonese, may I know whether the problem of security of employment for the so-called stateless persons of Indian Origin in Ceylon was specifically discussed between the two Prime Ministers and, if so, with what effect?

79. Independent.
80. PSP.

Jawaharlal Nehru: A great majority of the stateless persons are at present employed in the estates. The question was not discussed but it was casually referred to that if any of them is removed from their employment some other employment should be given to them.

K.K. Warior[81]: May I know whether the Ceylon Government is agreeable to retain these stateless persons until a final agreement with the Government of India is arrived at? Instead of repatriating them to India will they be allowed to remain there until a final settlement with the Government of India is arrived at?

Jawaharlal Nehru: They are there now and they cannot easily send them to India till we allow them to come back. Our position is that we will take back any person who fulfils the qualifications and chooses to come here without compulsion.

Savitri Nigam[82]: The hon. Prime Minister has just now stated that those people who are ready to come willingly could come here. I would like to know whether the Ceylonese Government is going to allow them to bring their assets and in what other way the Ceylonese Government is going to help them if they are willing to come.

Jawaharlal Nehru: I do not know what inducements the Ceylon Government may give them or in what other way they can help them. That is for the Ceylon Government to decide. As for us, we have stated that we will accept any person who fulfils our Constitutional requirements and decides without pressure to come here. That is the position. I suppose, the Ceylon Government would give them facilities for that purpose where it arises.

Savitri Nigam: I want to know whether the Ceylon Government would allow them to bring back their assets along with them or not.

81. CPI.
82. Congress.

(e) Disarmament

208. In the Rajya Sabha: Gandhi Peace Mission's Visit Abroad[83]

Sitaram Jaipuria[84]: Will the Prime Minister be pleased to state:

(a) whether the Gandhi Peace Mission went abroad during the month of September with the prior permission of the Central Government;

(b) who were the members of the Mission and which countries they visited;

(c) whether Government have given any financial assistance to the Mission and if so, to what extent; and

(d) what has been the outcome of the Mission?

The Minister of State in the Ministry of External Affairs (Lakshmi Menon):

(a) and (b)

In pursuance of a suggestion of the Anti-Nuclear Arms Convention which met in New Delhi from the 16th to the 18th June, 1962 under the auspices of the Gandhi Peace Foundation, two delegations went abroad during the September-October 1962 to persuade the nuclear powers to stop all nuclear weapon tests. One delegation, consisting of Shri C. Rajagopalachari, Shri R.R. Diwakar and Shri B. Shiva Rao, went to the United States of America and the United Kingdom. The other delegation consisting of Shri U.N. Dhebar and Shri C. Ramachandran, visited the Soviet Union. The Gandhi Peace Foundation is a non-official organisation and their delegations were non-official. Government were informed of these delegations and gave them the necessary facilities. The Government of India are in favour of immediate stopping of all nuclear weapon tests.

(c) No, Sir.

(d) It is understood that the delegations impressed upon the Heads of the Governments concerned the urgent need for banning of nuclear weapon tests.[85]

---

83. Oral Answers, *Rajya Sabha Debates*, Vol. XLI, Nos. 1-8, 8 November to 19 November 1962, , pp. 735-737.

84. Independent, from UP.

85. See SWJN/SS/78/ items 330-341.

Sitaram Jaipuria: May I know, Sir, whether, in view of the fact that the delegations which visited those places consisted of eminent personalities and they met the highest people in those countries through our Embassies, the Government has received any report through our diplomatic sources?

Lakshmi Menon: Sir, that has been given in the answer; they met the Heads of Governments and discussed the problem with them.

A.D. Mani[86]: Sir, the hon. Minister has stated that Government gave them facilities. I would like to know, in relation to part (c) of the question, what the foreign exchange component of this delegation was.

Lakshmi Menon: Sir, foreign exchange to the extent of Rs 10,000 was released—for the persons going to the United States five hundred dollars each and eighteen pounds each.

A.M. Tariq[87]: Sir, I would like to know from the hon. Minister one thing. When Rs 10,000 were sanctioned as foreign exchange, is it a fact that all the engagements and all the interviews were sanctioned as foreign exchange, is it a fact that all the engagements and all the interviews were fixed by our Embassies in the foreign countries? Is it also a fact that the delegation stayed with our Ambassadors there and they were given all sorts of facilities and if so, what kind of facilities were given to them?

Lakshmi Menon: Sir, I do not know whether they stayed with the Ambassadors everywhere. The usual facilities were extended to them. Whatever courtesies are usually extended to distinguished visitors by our Embassies, they were extended to them.

Satyacharan[88]: May I know, Sir, whether any nuclear test took place after this delegation had seen the Heads of those two countries, Russia and the United States of America?

Lakshmi Menon: I do not know whether any nuclear test took place after that.

---

86. Independent, from Madhya Pradesh
87. Congress, from Jammu and Kashmir.
88. Satyacharan Besra, Congress, from Bihar.

A.M. Tariq: I would like to know from the hon. Minister whether, before this delegation left for the countries they visited, they took the permission of the Government or they discussed that matter with the Prime Minister. And is it a fact Sir, that after their return from those countries they met the Prime Minister and, if so, what reports they gave to the Prime Minister?

Jawaharlal Nehru: Yes, Sir. There was no question of permission but I was told that this deputation had been decided upon by the Gandhi Peace Foundation. I agreed to it and welcomed it. After their return, I have also seen the members of the Mission, both those who went to the United States and those who went to Russia and they have told me of their talks with various people there.

209. To B. Shiva Rao: Not Rajaji at Geneva[89]

November 16, 1962

My dear Shiva Rao,

Your letter of November 15th.

Rajaji[90] is undoubtedly a person of high ability and we all have respect and affection for him. But I doubt very much if he will at all suit or fit in with the Disarmament Conference at Geneva which consists of senior officials. Also, unfortunately he disagrees with almost everything, in the domestic or international sphere, for which some of us stand.

We shall be utilising General Kulwant Singh in some way or other.

We shall give thought to some of your other suggestions. As for the Whitley Councils,[91] I did not think of them in my address to the employees of the Secretariat the other day.[92]

Yours sincerely
Jawaharlal Nehru

---

89. Letter to Journalist, politician, and a former member of Parliament; address: 85 Lodi Estate, New Delhi-3. NMML, B. Shiva Rao Papers.
90. C. Rajagopalachari, leader of the Swatantra Party.
91. Rao wrote, "I was hoping that you would announce the Government's decision to set up without further delay Whitley Councils, the formation of which I consider to be essential for ensuring fair treatment to all Government employees.... I regret that no progress has been made in that direction during the last two years." NMML, B. Shiva Rao Papers. See SWJN/SS/61/item 261 with appendix 80 in the same volume.
92. See item 300.

(f) Germany

210. To Vijaya Lakshmi Pandit: Recognising East Germany[93]

3rd October, 1962

[Nan dear,]

When you saw me in Bombay on the 1st morning you said something about your tour in Germany. I thought that you were giving me a programme, but I found that your letter dealt with other matters.

I have seen your programme which has been given in M.J. Desai's[94] letter to you dated September 27th. There is no objection to this programme if you can afford the time. I would not like you to go to Berlin as that is a very controversial issue. But, anyhow, Berlin is not included in the programme.

If you like, you can go to Munich.

The Chancellor[95], President and other Ministers may wish to discuss the Berlin issue or other controversial issues with you. I think it would be best if you avoided such discussions as far as possible. You may say that we are greatly interested in disarmament and if this is achieved, it would be easier to solve other issues.

I had said in the course of a press interview, probably in London or in Paris[96], that the question of East Germany should be considered realistically. I had not suggested that it should be formally recognized, but that it should be dealt with and not ignored. In fact, indirectly in the past there have been many contacts between West and East Germany. The fiction of not recognising it even for informal contacts does not help. This statement of mine created some minor sensation and they thought that this was a prelude to our formally recognising and having diplomatic relations with East Germany. We have no such intention, although we have trade relations with them.[97]

I gather that our Embassy in Bonn has been authorised to meet your travel and other expenses in Germany in case these are not met by your hosts there.

[Jawahar]

---

93. Letter to sister; address: 8-E Mafatlal Park, Bhulabhai Desai Road, Bombay-26.
94. The Foreign Secretary.
95. Konrad Adenauer (1876-1967).
96. See SWJN/SS/78/Item 378.
97. See also item 211.

211. To Vijaya Lakshmi Pandit: Visit to Germany[98]

October 4, 1962

[Nan dear,]

I have just received your letter of the 2nd October. I wrote to you a day or two ago about your visit to Germany.

I agree with you that the programme they have drawn up for you is unnecessarily long. It should be quite easy to shorten it by a day or so. Why should you spend three days at Bonn? And at Dusseldorf also you can shorten the visit. Otherwise there is no harm in your going to all these places.

There is certainly a slight difficulty in going about Western Germany and discussing any matter connected with Berlin in these days of cold war. But I am sure, you will be able to overcome this embarrassment. In your public speeches you can avoid the topic except in the most general terms. You can say that while we have full sympathy for the difficulties for and about Berlin, it seems to us that these can only be solved peacefully by agreement as war is ruled out. To have a peaceful settlement, the continuing cold war should give place to relatively more friendly approaches. Neither side should threaten the other. It should be possible to retain the individuality and freedom of West Berlin by agreement.

The whole question depends more on wider issues of the cold war. If the cold war could be lessened, the chances of settlement would be greater. If there could be some marked approach to disarmament, many of the fears expressed would disappear. Therefore, disarmament on a big scale appears to be both necessary and essential.

You can also explain to them in your personal talks that we did not wish to enter into this cold war conflict, whatever our sympathies may be. That will not help anyone. Recently, von Brentano[99] said something about my having a look at the wall put up between West and East Berlin. Without even seeing it, I can well realise the tragedy of it and the enormous suffering it has caused. How are we to get over this? Not by war; and not also by cold war. If once the atmosphere is much smoother and better, even the wall might, we hope, go.

We are expecting the President[100] of the Federal Republic in India and we are looking forward to his visit.

You might explain in your personal talks with people there that what I am reported to have said at a Press Conference in London or Paris had nothing

98. Letter to sister; address: 8-E Mafatlal Park, Bhulabhai Desai Road, Bombay-26.
99. Heinrich von Brentano (1904-1964), Leader of the CDU/CSU Group in the Bundestag.
100. Heinrich Lübke (1894-1972), President, Federal Republic of Germany, 1959-1964.

to do with recognition of East Germany.[101] What I had said was that certain existing facts should be recognised in dealing with day-to-day situations. In the main this flowed from a lessening of the cold war attitude. That would help in solving the problem. So far as we are concerned, we have no intention in the foreseeable future of giving formal recognition to East Germany, even though we have trade contacts, etc.[102]

Give my regards to the Chancellor[103] and the President.

If you have time, visit the Deutsche Museum in Munich which is one of the most attractive anywhere. But it is a tremendous affair and to see it adequately, one has to spend days, perhaps weeks.

Thank you for sending me Padmaja's letter. I have read it and am now returning it.

As for your expenditure incurred in travelling to Germany from London, if no other arrangements are made, our Ministry will meet it.

Indu is probably returning on the 8th morning. I do not quite know whether she passes through Bombay.

[Jawahar]

(g) Indonesia

212. To Sudhir Ghosh: Indonesian Politics[104]

11th October, 1962

My dear Sudhir,

Thank you for your letter of the 10th October. Your analysis of the situation in Indonesia is interesting and more or less according to our own appraisal.

Yours sincerely,
[Jawaharlal Nehru]

---

101. See SWJN/SS/78/ 325
102. See item 210.
103. Konrad Adenauer (1876-1967); Chancellor of the Federal Republic of Germany, 1949-1963.
104. Letter to Rajya Sabha MP, Congress. See appendix 11. NMML, Sudhir Ghosh Papers. See appendix 11.

(h) Japan

213. For Japan Government's Training Centre[105]

When I was in Japan in October 1957,[106] the Japanese Government offered to set up a Prototype Production and Training Centre in India. I welcomed this offer gratefully. This has now taken shape, and I understand that the inauguration ceremony will be performed next month. I send my greetings and good wishes on this occasion.

I attach importance to this Production and Training Centre because this type of training is particularly needed in India and will encourage the growth of small industries. I also welcome it because it is an additional symbol of Indo-Japanese cooperation. We are grateful to the Japanese Government for the help they have given in the setting up of this Training Centre. I am particularly happy at the growth of cooperation between the two countries in many ways.

(i) Malaya

214. In New Delhi: At Banquet for Tunku Abdul Rahman[107]

Prime Minister,[108] Excellencies, ladies and gentlemen,
We are very happy to have you here Prime Minister our guest and gracious lady.[109] I do not remember how many times and for how many years we have tried to get you here, invited you; but you were busy with your work and you could not come. First time we met is rather long ago, a trifle over a quarter of a century in Malaya,[110] when I went there when both of us were functioning in different capacities. We met subsequently in London at the Commonwealth Prime Ministers' Conferences and now that you have come here gives us much happiness.

---

105. Message, 27 October 1962, forwarded to K.C. Reddy, Minister of Commerce and Industry. PMO, File No. 9/2/62-PMP, Vol. 7, Sr. No. 76-A.
106. See SWJN/SS/39/pp.597-598.
107. Speech, 27 October 1962, in honour of the Prime Minister of Malaya. NMML, AIR Tapes, TS No. 8487, NM No. 1684.
108. (1903-1990); first Prime Minister of Malaya, 1957-1970.
109. Sharifah Rodziah (1939-1990).
110. In 1937.

Malaya and India have had many contacts in the past for hundreds of years, in fact almost from thousands of years, as we have all had contacts with countries of South-East Asia. We are not only geographically near each other but also historically, and in some ways culturally, we have many common things and at present other contacts are growing, because it seems natural that the countries of South-East Asia should pull together, should cooperate because most of these countries are engaged after achieving their independence in the task of bettering the condition of their people and development and generally in making the countries happier and stronger. We have been very much engrossed in this work ever since we became independent about seventeen years ago. I believe we have made some progress, we have big ideals, big objectives and step by step we are trying to realise them. But we also realise as I suppose you do Prime Minister, that it is easier to have ideals than to implement them and make them reality and the task of building up of a nation is not an easy one. However, it is an inevitable fate that has descended upon all these countries, which for various reasons were left behind in the race for progress and have now to make good. We have our difficulties and so have you, but we have the satisfaction and the joy of working for a worthy cause, just as many years ago, we had the great joy of working for another worthy cause—the independence of India. Now independence has come to us and to you and we face our problems. At the same time while we face these problems, we cannot, however much we may wish to ignore the major problems of the world because the world shrinks and becomes narrower and practically each country lives on the threshold of another country. Malaya is of course near to India and we are in each other's threshold but even distant countries have become very near because of technological improvements and the speed of travel and communications. So, the question of peace and war affects all countries. If unhappily a war starts, no country escapes its influence. So also freedom! It is difficult to keep the world half-free and half-unfree and therefore, ever since we became free and you became free, Prime Minister, we have thrown our weight in favour of the freedom in those countries in Asia or Africa which are not yet free.

Meanwhile, we face tremendous problems, world problems, I am not for the moment referring to our internal problems which are heavy enough. World problems and the question of peace and war. We have been devoted to peace even in our struggle for independence under our leader Mahatma Gandhi and we have tried to pursue the path of peace in India and in our policies outside. Yet such is the curious fate that has pursued us that at the present moment we are engaged in military operations, not of our choosing, but it has been thrust upon us; because much as we like peace and we shall labour for it and continue to work for it, something happened which endangered the very foundation of peace in another way; because there can be no peace, as I said, if there is domination of one country over another or there is aggression or there is an attack on the freedom of a country over its territory. So, we have to face today a major aggression on our country from a neighbour country with whom we tried to develop friendly relations, whom we considered as friends, whose cause we pleaded outside in the Council of the world, and yet by some unhappy fate today we have to suffer aggression and invasion from that very country. However much we may like peace and we are passionately devoted to it, a peace which is based on surrender of one's territory, of one's self-respect is not worth having. They are something worse even than conflict and that is a surrender to aggression, because that is neither peace not freedom. We have to face that and you have come, Prime Minister, at a time when we are very much occupied with these problems and when we have to fashion our lives somewhat differently to meet these rather novel problems for us because we have not been conditioned to ways of war and military conflict; yet, since fate has brought them before us we have to face them and face them with courage. Because one thing we learnt in our peaceful struggle against British imperialism, and that was, however much the pressure may be exercised over us, we did not submit to anything we considered wrong. For years our struggle went on till we attained victory in the sense of freedom for our country and it came to us in a good way, that is, by agreement ultimately, and therefore, it left no traces of bitterness behind and we are friends with those who are in conflict with us previously and so we are not trained to war, thinking of war or even preparing for war. Naturally as independent nations we have our defence forces to protect our country. But there is such a thing as a country being habituated to the idea of military conflict and preparing for it. We have not been so habituated in the past and perhaps we have deliberately tried not to think of it devoting ourselves to peaceful development. Now, it has been thrust down upon us and we have, we cannot refuse, to accept the challenge and so we are very much involved now, and I feel sure, that not only you, Prime Minister, in your country but in many other countries will give us their sympathy and where possible their support. Because it is not merely a matter of our own troubles but there are some principles involved in this, certain international standards which have been broken, and it will be an evil day if international standards are broken with impunity. Therefore, the matter has a larger interest, not only for us, and our neighbour countries but for every country in the world who wish to help in strengthening these international standards. This is the immediate issue before us and we have to devote all our strength to meet it and solve it in a proper way. Larger problems remained—problems of peace in the world. We have spoken for peace and worked for it and we feel now in this nuclear age

267

more specially. Without peace there is no hope for mankind and, therefore, we have aimed and struggled hard for disarmament, not that our voice means very much in regard to disarmament because we are not one of the heavily-armed countries or countries possessing modern engines of mass destruction but, nevertheless, however big or small we may be, we have a certain duty not only to ourselves but to mankind and we have sought to discharge it. Here comes the tragedy that we who spoke of peace so much and fashioned ourselves for the works of peace and development have to meet a condition, a situation which is far from peaceful, which is military, which is warlike. Well, I suppose, we shall get over it and, however long it takes we shall get over it, and there is no supposition over it, we shall get over it. But it is an anomaly and a bit of a tragedy that we should be drawn away from the problems that consumed our attention, the development of our country and to some extent giving our service to international causes of peace and disarmament, to something which is exactly contrary to that.

I hope you do not mind my mentioning these matters at this time, because my mind is so full of them that I could not very well suppress myself on such an occasion or on any other occasion. Nevertheless, I want to assure you that, however, much occupied we might be because of these developments on our borders and frontiers, we are very happy that you have come to us and we offer you our warmest welcome, not only I and my government, but our people. You have been to some places in India, some parts of India, and many other parts which should welcome you if you went there and wherever you have been our people have been happy to see you, and meet you and welcome you. I hope that the rest of your stay in India will be agreeable and pleasant that when you go back you will return with pleasant and abiding memories of your visit and that your visit here will strengthen the old ties and bind us together which have brought us near repeatedly in history and has brought us near again the present stage.

So may I ask you Excellencies, ladies and gentlemen to drink to the health of the Prime Minister of Malaya and the gracious lady.

215. In New Delhi: Welcome Address to Malayan Prime Minister[111]

प्रधानमंत्री जी, मेयर साहब, साहेबान,

आपने अभी सुना कि जो मलाया के प्रधानमंत्री आये हैं उनसे मेरी मुलाक़ात पहली बार पच्चीस बरस से ज़्यादा हुए हुई थी। मुझे याद पड़ता है कि उस वक़्त भी मैंने उनसे कहा था कि वो हिन्दुस्तान आयें। हालांकि मेरी हैसियत उस वक़्त कुछ और थी और उनकी भी कुछ और थी। तो पच्चीस बरस के बाद बहुत अरसे तक कोई मौक़ा नहीं मिला, मिलने का। फिर पिछले दस-बारह बरस हुए, कई दफ़े मिलना हुआ, कुछ लंदन में, कुछ एक आद दफ़े मलाया में। तो बार-बार मैंने फिर से दावत दी यहाँ आने की। अब जो यहां आये हैं तो मुझे इसकी बहुत ख़ुशी है। क्योंकि अलावा इसके जो एक शख़्सी हैसियत से मैं चाहता था उनका यहाँ आना, और एक अपने देश के बड़े नेता होने के। मेरे सामने पुराने ताल्लुक़ात, पुराने संबंध हमारे मुल्क के और उनके मुल्क के, तस्वीर की तरह सामने आते हैं। दो हज़ार बरस की पुरानी हमारी मुलाक़ात है, पुराने ताल्लुक़ात हैं, संबंध हैं। ऊँच-नीच हुई उसमें, लेकिन इस पुरानी ताल्लुक़ात की निशानी को आप वहां अच्छी तरह से देख सकते हैं।

तो फिर ख़ास मैं ये चाहता था कि हमारा आजकल के ज़माने में, सोलह बरस की आज़ादी के ज़माने में ताल्लुक़ बढ़े और हमारा रिश्ता बढ़े। इसलिए मैं चाहता था आप यहाँ आयें और अब जो यहां आये चंद रोज़ से और कुछ हिन्दुस्तान में घूमे, मद्रास में और हैदराबाद में और बम्बई में और अजमेर में, और अब यहाँ आये तो मुझे कोई पुरानी ख़्वाहिश की पूरे होने की ख़ुशी हुई। ज़ाहिर है कि इनका यहाँ एक स्वागत होता, कहीं भी हिन्दुस्तान में जायें। स्वागत महज़ इसलिए नहीं कि एक मुल्क के, बड़े मुल्क के प्राइम मिनिस्टर हैं, प्रधानमंत्री हैं और इसलिए उनकी इज़्ज़त करनी है। लेकिन स्वागत किसी क़दर इस तरह कि वे एक अपने थे, वो कोई बहुत ग़ैर नहीं। तो स्वागत इनका हुआ, इस मोहब्बत से हुआ, और अब जहाँ-जहाँ आप जायेंगे हिन्दुस्तान में ऐसे ही हर जगह पायेंगे।

आपने ग़ौर से सुना होगा इन्होंने जो कहा? कि जो हमारी इस वक़्त हमारे सरहद पर हमले हुए हैं इसके निस्बत उन्होंने क्या कहा? हमारे सामने वाक़्या जो है कि एक, ख़तरे काफ़ी बड़े ख़तरे हैं, और मुल्क ने समझ लिया और इस मौक़े का फ़ायदा उठाते हुए मैं आपसे कहना चाहता हूँ कि जो हवा मुल्क में पैदा हुई है, जो देश भक्ती की जो त्याग की, और जिस तरह से लोग इस बात को समझ के कि मुल्क पर ख़तरा है उसकी अच्छी तैयारी के लिए भाग के आये उसका मुक़ाबले करने, मुल्क की, उससे इतिहा दर्ज मुझे ख़ुशी हुई। [तालियाँ] हमारे जो कुछ आपस के छोटे-मोटे झगड़े थे, नाइत्तिफ़ाक़ी थी, ख़ामख़ाँ थी, वो सब इसके आने से अलग हो गयीं। क्योंकि जो लोग एक बड़े ख़तरे के सामने छोटी बातों में पड़े रहते हैं वो एक अपना छोटा सा दिल दिखाते हैं। हम एक बड़े मुल्क के रहने वाले

111. Welcome Address to Malayan Prime Minister at a civic reception, 28 October 1962. NMML. Speeches of Jawaharlal Nehru, AIR Tapes, T.S.No.10087. N.M.No.1812.

हैं, ज़रा दिमाग़ भी बड़ा होना चाहिए, दिलो-दिमाग़ भी। और बड़े मुल्क की हमें हिफ़ाज़त करनी है। और अगर हम इसमें ज़रा भी ग़फ़लत करें तो फिर और बातें भी निकल जाती हैं हाथ से, क्योंकि उसके बग़ैर और बातें होती हैं। चुनांचे इस वक़्त अव्वल काम हम सबों का चाहे हिन्दुस्तान के किसी हिस्से में रहें, कुछ भी हमारा पेशा हो, हमारा फ़र्ज़ है इसकी मदद करना, जिती हमारी ताक़त हो, मुल्क की, इस मुक़ाबले में। क्योंकि मुक़ाबला बड़ा ज़बरदस्त है एक बहुत बड़े ताक़तवर मुल्क के साथ। अफ़सोस तो मुझे ये है कि ऐसे मुल्क के साथ मुक़ाबला है जिससे हमने दोस्ती करने की कोशिश की, और जिसकी हमने सिफ़ारिश की दुनिया में सब जगह कि उनकी तरफ़ से पहल नहीं थी। उसका बदला हमें यह मिला कि हमारे ऊपर हमला हुआ।

ख़ैर, हमारे लिए तो एक ही रास्ता है चुनौतियों का कि हम अपने मुल्क की आज़ादी और इज़्ज़त को रखें, चाहे जो कुछ भी हो, उसमें क़ीमत देनी पड़े ऐसे मौक़े पर जब हमारे ऊपर इतना बड़ा बोझ है और वो रहेगा। प्रधानमंत्री जी ने जो कहा उसका सार हमें और आपको अच्छा लगा क्योंकि उन्होंने कहा, बहुत सफ़ाई से, कि उसमें लारजर अफ़ेयर्स नहीं, अपने मुल्क की और अपनी हमदर्दी पूरी तौर से हमको दी। और कहा कि हर तरह के जो भी कुछ हो सिलसिले में, वो हमारे साथी हैं और उस माने में ''हमसफ़र'' हैं।

तो इस तरह की बातें हमारे पुराना मुल्क, जिससे हमारी पुरानी दोस्ती है, वो अपनी दोस्ती को ऐसे मौक़े पर फिर से ताज़ा करें, दोहराएँ, जब कि हमारे ऊपर एक ख़तरा छाया है। और उसके लिए आप, प्रधानमंत्री जी, आपको मैं बहुत-बहुत शुक्रिया आपका अदा करता हूँ उसके लिए।

तो फिर से मैं आपको, राब्ते से यहां दिल्ली के कार्पोरिशन के तो मानपत्र मिला, स्वागत आपका हुआ, और दिल्ली के बहुत सारे शहरी यहाँ मौजूद हैं उन्होंने भी किया। मैं भी एक दिल्ली के शहरी की हैसियत से अपनी आवाज़ इस स्वागत में मिलाता हूँ। [तालियाँ] और मैं उम्मीद करता हूँ कि आप यहाँ से जायेंगे तो दो-चार रोज़ जो आप दिल्ली में रहें उसकी याद, ख़ुशगवार याद आपको रहेगी। और दिल्ली के लोगों को भी कुछ आप याद करेंगे और उनकी मोहब्बत को, जो उन्होंने आपके सामने पेश की।

[Translation begins:

Honourable Prime Minister,[112] Mr Mayor,[113] Gentlemen,
You have just heard that I first met the Prime Minister of Malaya, who is here with us today, more than twenty five years ago. I remember even then I had said that he should visit India, though my status then was somewhat different and so was his. Then after that first meeting twenty five years ago, we did not have occasion to meet for a long time. Then during the last ten to twelve years

112. See note 108.
113. Nuruddin Ahmed.

we have met several times, sometimes in London and once or twice in Malaya. And I invited him again and again to visit India, so I am very happy that he has come here because apart from wanting it in my individual capacity, his visit after becoming the great leader of his country brings back memories of the age old relationship between our two nations. Our relations go back to over two thousand years, very long period. There have been ups and downs but you can find symbols of those ancient ties clearly in Malaya.

So it has been my special wish our relations should grow and become strongest during this period when we have been free for sixteen years. That is why I wanted him to visit and in the last few days since he arrived, he has seen something of India, Madras, Hyderabad, Bombay and Ajmer and now he is here. So I am happy that an old wish of mine has been fulfilled. It is clear that he would be warmly welcomed wherever he went in India, not merely because he is the Prime Minister of a great country and so he has to be honoured, but also welcomed as though he is one of our own, not some stranger. So he was given a warm welcome with great affection and he will find that happening wherever he goes in India.

You would have listened carefully to what he said about the attack on our borders, about the danger that confronts us. It has made me extremely happy to see how the people of India have risen to the occasion and made sacrifices and stood up to defend the country. [Applause]. All the petty problems, tensions and internal tussles among us have been put aside because those who continue to indulge in petty squabbles even in the face of grave danger reveal a narrow psyche. The people of a great nation have to be large hearted in every way. And we have to rise to the defence of this great nation. If we slacken in any way, we will lose much more. Therefore, at the moment the foremost task before us is that no matter which part of India we live in whatever be our profession, we have to come forward to the best of our ability to help the nation. The challenge before us is a fierce one, our war is with a very strong and mighty nation. My regret is that this is the country with whom we have tried to build friendly relations, a country which we sponsored everywhere in the world without their asking us. In return they have mounted this attack.

Well we have the only course open to face the challenge and to uphold the independence and dignity of our country no matter what happens and whatever price has to be paid. The onus is upon us and it is a heavy burden. All of us liked what the Prime Minister has said because he has expressed the sympathy of his country and himself very clearly without larger affairs, and has stated that they are our comrades in every way, in whatever situation.

Therefore, I would like to express my heart-felt thanks Mr Prime Minister, that you have reiterated your friendship at a time when a grave danger threatens our country. Relations between our two countries go back a long way.

You have been formally welcomed by the Delhi Corporation with a Manpatra and the leading citizens of Delhi have also welcomed you. I would like to add my own voice to them in my capacity as a citizen of Delhi [applause]. I hope that when you leave after three to four days, you will carry pleasant memories of your visit and your stay in Delhi. The people of Delhi will also remember you with affection which they have demonstrated amply before you.

Translation ends]

216. In New Delhi: In Honour of Yang-di-Pertuan Agong[114]

Mr Prime Minister,[115] Your Excellencies, ladies and gentlemen, I have not risen to deliver a speech, I am going to propose a formal toast to the King of Malaya, but since you, Mr Prime Minister, have said a few words, I should also like to say how much we have enjoyed your visit, the visit of Madam and your colleagues.

We are near Malaya. I visited Malaya and enjoyed it, but your visit, I have no doubt, has brought Malaya very near to large numbers of people in this country. The memories of your visit and your friendship would linger long. So I hope and I must thank you for what you have said on more than one occasion of your sympathy and solidarity with us in our hour of crisis.

I wish you and Madam, your wife,[116] a happy return and pleasant memories of India to carry back and all our good wishes for the future of Malaya and the Malaya people.

I ask your Excellencies, ladies and gentlemen to drink [to] the health of His Majesty the Yang-di-Pertuan Agong, King of Malaya.

114. Speech at Banquet, 29 October 1962, toast to the King of Malaya. PIB.
115. Tunku Abdul Rahman Putra, Prime Minister of Malaya.
116. Sarifah Rodzia.

(j) Mexico

217. In Delhi: Civic Reception to the President of Mexico[117]

महामान्य राष्ट्रपतिजी,[118] मेयर साहब,[119]

कोई मेरा आपके समाने खड़ा होना ग़ैर ज़रूरी बिल्कुल है। शायद ग़ैर मुनासिब भी हो। लेकिन हुकुम मिला मुझे मेयर साहब का तो इतना मैं अर्ज़ कर दूं कि मुझे बहुत खुशी हुई आपके मैकसिको के राष्ट्रपति जी के यहां आने की। बड़े आदमी यहां बहुत सारे आए हैं हमने उनका स्वागत किया है लेकिन एक माने में मैकसिको कितनी ही दूर हो बहुत बातें हमारी ओर उनकी मिलती हैं, और पुरानी भी और नई भी। और बहुत कुछ हम उनसे सीख सकते हैं। आज़ाद होने के बाद, यानी सियासी आज़ादी के बाद उन्होंने जो तरीक़ा इक़्तियार किया, माने आम लोगों को उठाने का, उनको फ़ायदा पहुंचाने का और अपने समाज को उसी तरह से बनाने का, आर्थिक और उनसे हम सीख सकते हैं कुछ थोड़ा बहुत, ज़्यादा तो नहीं, अभी थोड़ा बहुत हम उस रास्ते पर चलें भी और उम्मीद है कि और भी उधर चलेंगे। उन्होंने कहा आपसे कि एक बात आपके ख़ासतौर से याद करने की है और उससे मालूम होता है कि उनकी निगाह किधर रहती हैं। उन्होंने कहा कि बड़े बड़े बादशाह आते हैं और जाते हैं बड़ी-बड़ी इमारतें गिर जाती हैं लेकिन वो आम जनता क़ायम रहती है। इसलिए उसको हमेशा सामने रखना है, उनका और उनके मुल्क का और किस ढंग से उन्होंने वहां हुकुमत की है और क्या क्या समाज के बदलने की कोशिशें की हैं। आपने सुना अभी कि मैं वहां पारसाल गया था। कुछ रोज़ रहा, कम रोज़ लेकिन फिर भी कुछ देखा, अफ़सोस है, कि ख़ाली उनके बड़े शहर राजधानी में गया और मुल्क में नहीं घूम सका। क्योंकि अगर और घूमता तो कई बातें जो मैं पसंद करता देखने का मौक़ा मिलता, क्योंकि मैकसिकों में एक अजीब मेलजोल हैं पुरानी क़ौमों का जिन्होंने वहां अपना साम्राज्य वग़ैरा बनाया था और नई क़ौमें जो योरोप से गई वहां, वो अब वहां बसीं। कई जगह नई दुनिया में ये हुआ है। अमरीका की, उत्तरी और दक्षिण अमेरिका में सभी लोग बाहर से आए हैं, लेकिन फ़र्क़ यह हैं कि मैकसिको में पुराने लोग और नए लोग जो गए वह मिल गए और कोई एक दूसरे के ख़िलाफ़ आदावत नहीं हैं। कोई रंजिश नहीं है, कोई दीवारें नहीं है चाहे ज़रा रंग का ज़रा फ़र्क़ क्यों न हो। यह ख़ास बात ग़ौरतलब है। और जगह आप जानते हैं, काफ़ी दिक़्क़तें पेश आई हैं और अब तक आती हैं।

तो दो बातों पर ख़ास तौर से मैं आपकी तव्वजोह दिलाउंगा। एक तो है कि किस तरह से वहां के लोग मिलजुल के रहे हैं पुराने लोग और नए लोग, और आजकल का जो

---

117. Speech, 9 October 1962, Red Fort. NMML, AIR Tapes, TS No. 8428, NM No. 1657.
118. Adolfo Lopez Mateos (1910-1969), President of Mexico, 1958 to 1964.
119. Nuruddin Ahmed.

मैकसिको है उनके मिलजुल के रहने की निशानी है। और दूसरी बात जो मैकसिको कि तरफ़ से सामाजिक बाते हुई हैं, समाज के बदलने की जिससे आम लोगों का फ़ायदा हो। दोनों बातों से हम सीख सकते हैं। और फ़ायदा उठा सकते हैं। इसलिए मुझे ख़ासतौर से खुशी हैं कि हमें मौक़ा मिला आपका स्वागत करने का और आपकी श्रीमती जी, जो की वहां मैंने खुद देखा, मैकसिको में, कि कितना काम करती हैं ख़ास कर बच्चों के सिलसले में[120]। बच्चों को स्कूलो में खाने का, जो कि इनके इंतजाम से मैकसिको भर में दिया जाता है।

तो यह सब बाते हैं जिससे हम सीख सकते हैं और ऐसे शक्सों का यहां आना हमारे लिए एक मुबारक बाद है, हमारे दिल्ली शहर के लिए मुनासिब है। आपने उन्हें एक Sifarishnama[121] दिया आज और आप लोगों को यह मौक़ा मिला कुछ उनसे मिलने को और कुछ मैकसिको के हाल सुनकर कुछ सीखने को। [तालियां]

[Translation begins:

Honourable President,[122] Mr Mayor,[123]

It is absolutely unnecessary for me to be standing here and perhaps slightly inappropriate too. But I have been ordered by the Mayor to do so. So I would like to say that I am extremely happy that the President of Mexico can be here today. Many great dignitaries have come to India and we have welcomed all of them. But in a sense in spite of the vast distance which separates Mexico and India, there are many things in common between the two countries. We can learn a great deal from them. Particularly the method of economic and social uplift that they have adopted since getting their political freedom, in order to raise the standard of living of the masses. In fact we have tried to adopt some of their techniques. The President said something just now which should be remembered because it shows which way they look. He said that great kings and emperors come and go, palatial mansions often crumble, but the masses are always there. Therefore we must always keep them in mind and work for their good. It is the minds and bodies of the masses which produce other things.

This gives you a glimpse of the way he and his country think. They have tried very hard to bring about changes in their society. You were told just now

---

120. Eva Samano, founded the National Institute for Infants and Children in 1961, Mexico's first social assistance organisation dedicated solely to children. It introduced the school breakfast system in primary schools. See obituary in *TheNewYork Times*, 9 January 1984.

121. The meaning of the word in this context is a letter of appreciation.

122. See note 118 in this section.

123. See note 119 in this section.

about my visit to Mexico last year. I was there for a very few days but managed to see something. My only regret is that I could not travel in the country. I visited only their capital city. If I had travelled elsewhere in the country, I would have had an opportunity to see many other things. Mexico is a strange amalgam of the old imperialist way of life and the new nations of Europe who have gone and settled there. This has happened in many places in the new world in North as well as South America, everyone has come from outside and settled down. The difference is that in Mexico, the foreigners have mingled with the native population and there was no friction or bitterness or barriers among them, in spite of the slight difference in colour. This is extraordinary because elsewhere, as you know, they have great problems which persist to this day.

I would like to draw your attention to two things particularly. One is the way the newcomers have mingled with the old inhabitants. The Mexico of today is a symbol of their intermingling. The second thing is the social changes which have been brought about in order to benefit masses. We can learn from both these things. Therefore, I am particularly happy that we have had the opportunity of welcoming the President and his wife. I have seen for myself the work that she is doing in Mexico, particularly for children's welfare.[124] Measures are being taken to provide mid-day meals in schools as we have done here in India. It is an excellent arrangement which is found throughout Mexico.

So these are the various things that we can learn from and we are to be congratulated for being in a position to welcome such dignitaries in the city of Delhi. You have presented him with a 'Letter of Appreciation'[125]and had the opportunity of meeting him and learning a little about Mexico [Applause].

Translation ends]

124. See note 120 in this section.
125. Nehru uses the word *Sifarishnama*, which is translated here as a 'Letter of Appreciation'.

(k) Nepal

218. For M. J. Desai: No Reaction to Mahendra's Behaviour[126]

I agree with both your suggestion in your note. I shall speak to the Home Minister[127] on this subject also. I have already spoken to the DIB.[128]

I have read the papers in this file and, more particularly, the note of your interview with Shri Rishikesh Shaha.[129] I am entirely opposed to his suggestion that a senior representative of the Government of India should go to Kathmandu to see the King.[130] I have had no desire to embarrass the King or even to do anything which might hurt his vanity. But, at the same time, I am certainly not going to pamper that vanity.

I am also not inclined to deal with the King's communiqué in a special public statement. Naturally if I am asked at a press conference or elsewhere about it, I shall say something. But on the whole I think it will be better to treat it with the contempt it deserves. I do not propose to write to the King on this subject either.[131]

219. Vinoba Bhave's Nepal Visit[132]

Certainly we can raise no objections to Vinoba Bhave going to Nepal and we would be prepared to give such facilities as are necessary. You may inform our Ambassador[133] accordingly. But I doubt very much if Vinobaji will upset his present programme in order to visit Nepal. He is touring West Bengal now and is likely to spend two-three months there. As you know, he only travels by foot and it will take a mighty long time for him to reach Nepal on foot.

---

126. Note, 2 October 1962, for the Foreign Secretary.
127. Lal Bahadur Shastri.
128. B.N. Mullik. Nehru met Mullik at 9.30 p.m. on 1October 1962, the day he arrived at New Delhi. NMML, Engagement Diary.
129. Nepalese Politician, (1925-2002); He was replaced as Foreign Minister on 22 September 1962.
130. Mahendra.
131. The Royal decree claimed that "…despite New Delhi's assurance, the rebels were launching raids into Nepal from across the border". The *Sunday Tribune*, 23 September 1962; p.1. See also SWJN/SS/76/items 472 and 473; and SWJN/SS/78/item 430.
132. Note, 9 October 1962, for M. J. Desai, the Foreign Secretary.
133. Harishwar Dayal.

If Vinobaji is to be invited to Nepal, it is not enough for Shri Tulsi Meher[134] only to do so. The Government should join in the invitation or at least express their agreement with it. When Vinoba Bhave went through East Pakistan recently, the Government there went all out to arrange for his tour and to help him in every way. In Nepal, in existing circumstances, the Government's attitude has to be fully known to the public as well as their help should be given. Otherwise, people will be afraid and there will be difficulties.

You may write to our Ambassador on the above lines. Make it clear that we shall have no objection whatever to Vinobaji, if he agrees, going to Nepal.

You may also mention or write to Shri Shriman Narayan that there is some talk of this in Nepal. We shall have no objection to Vinobaji deciding to go there and we shall give him every facility if it comes off, whenever that might be.[135]

220. Nepali Political Intrigues[136]

I give below an extract from the UP Governor's[137] letter to the President dated October 4th. The reference in this extract is to something that happened two months ago and it may be out of date.

Extract:

> "The Commissioner, Faizabad Division, has reported, for the second half of August, 1962, that the Nepali Congress workers are now busy making preparations to start some violent activities against the King's regime in Nepal. They are reported to be secretly securing illicit arms and ammunition, including hand-grenades, etc. The Nepal authorities are in their turn deadly against the Nepali Congress workers and are bent upon even shooting and killing them. The Nepali Congress workers recently tried to loot the Mail bag of Bardia district (Nepal) but failed. They, however, staged demonstrations in several villages against the King of Nepal across our border in Nepal. The Nepali Police remained busy in unearthing the 'bomb explosion' incident in the office of the Deputy Superintendent of Police, Nepalganj, recently".

134. Tulsi Meher Shreshtha, worked with Gandhi at Sabarmati, and ran the Gandhi Smarak Nidhi in Nepal.
135. See appendix 8.
136. Note, 10 October 1962, for M. J. Desai, the Foreign Secretary.
137. Biswanath Das, 1962-1967.

Another extract:

"On my return from the visit of the Nepal and Tibet borders in the month
of June, I had invited your attention to the serious propaganda carried
out by officials in Nepal against India and the Prime Minister, Pandit
Nehru. I had also stated that there was a move to claim all hill areas of
Uttarakhand and Kumaun Divisions as also areas extending up to Dehra
Dun. I had hinted that the Chinese were taking very good advantage of
these ill-feelings and were consolidating themselves in Nepal. There is little
reason to disbelieve that this position is further intensified due to events
that had taken place since then. It is also published that convenience of
communication arrangements between Lhasa and Kathmandu are agreed
between both the Governments of Nepal and China".[138]

221. Chinese Influence in Nepal[139]

I am sending you a copy of the daily *Tej* of October 11th, 1962. This was given
to me by P.N. Sharma, Photographer[140], today.

2. On the third page, there is a report to the effect that it is learnt from
a reliable source that Chinese forces are coming into Nepal in considerable
numbers; that they are coming in the guise of volunteers, also that considerable
numbers of so-called Chinese technicians are coming into Nepal, but probably
they are also soldiers. Further that they are being armed by the Nepal
Government with arms they have received from India.

3. It is also stated that the Nepal Government is thinking of introducing
a visa system for personnel going from India to Nepal.

4. The leading article of the *Tej* in the same issue is quite a good one.

5. If you like, you can send this issue of the *Tej* to our Ambassador in
Kathmandu.[141]

6. I do not think it would be advisable for the Ambassador to adopt any
minatory language to the King or his Government. Things have gone too far
for any such language to be used. It will have the opposite effect. At the same
time, to remain quiet is not right. I think the Ambassador should draw the
attention of the Nepal Government to these rumours and reports as well as the
other things that have happened and state that it is a matter of deep grief to the
Government of India that such steps should be encouraged.

138. See also item 16.
139. Note, 11 October 1962, for M. J. Desai, the Foreign Secretary.
140. A Rotarian and Delhi based reporter and photographer of repute.
141. Harishwar Dayal.

222. Chen Yi on Nepal[142]

Prime Minster Nehru today described as "rather showing off" the recent statement of the Chinese Foreign Minister, Marshal Chen Yi that if Nepal was attacked China would go to her help.

On his return to the capital today after his visit to Colombo, Pandit Nehru was asked to comment on Marshal Chen Yi's statement, particularly in view of India's close treaty relations with Nepal.

Pandit Nehru: "How am I to explain or justly justify his (Chen Yi's) saying? We are not going to attack Nepal. The whole idea is rather showing off." PTI.

223. To Rajendra Prasad: Nepal Politics[143]

October 19, 1962

My dear Rajendra Babu,

I received your letter of October 11th on my return from Ceylon.

The situation in Nepal is very disturbing and we are greatly concerned about it. How this has arisen is a long story, and I do not propose to trouble you with this. Briefly, ever since the coup d'état by the King,[144] we have made it clear to him that we do not wish to interfere with internal changes or developments in Nepal. It is true that I expressed my regret at the time in Parliament in answer to a question, and said that what had happened in Nepal was a setback to democracy. Apart from that, I have not criticised the regime there. I have told the King when he has pressed me to advise him, that the problem in Nepal cannot be solved by mere repression. Some conciliation should also take place. I further told him that we would not permit India to be made a base for any violent activities in Nepal or for any gun-running. We issued instructions accordingly, and I believe that by and large these instructions have been followed. I think that very few rifles have gone to the Nepali Congress people in Nepal from India. It is difficult on a long and free frontier to check every individual who goes. There may, perhaps about a year ago or more, have been some slackness by the Bihar Police in this matter. But for some time past we have issued very strict injunctions, and I believe they have been followed. Most of the arms that the Nepali Congress people within Nepal have managed to obtain, are from Police posts and Army posts in Nepal itself.

142. Report of statement. Reproduced from the *National Herald*, 17 October 1962, p. 1.
143. Letter to the former President.
144. Mahendra.

It might interest you to know that when the late King[145] was alive, he did not get on well at all with his eldest son who is the King now. I pleaded for the son with him. Indeed, the late King would not give his permission to Mahendra to marry the woman of his choice, who was the daughter of a Rana. Again, I pleaded with him to give this permission, and he agreed. Later, the question arose about Mahendra being acknowledged to be the heir. The late King was dead against it, but owing to pressures brought upon him by his advisers and others, he ultimately agreed. Even while doing so, he said before a number of persons that Mahendra would be the last King in Nepal as he would ruin the country.

Ever since Mahendra became King, we have treated him in a friendly way and with the utmost courtesy. Occasionally he wrote to me asking for my advice. At that time, I told him that the two strengthening features in Nepal were the King's position and the popular organisation that is the Nepali Congress. If the two pulled together, all would be well in Nepal. Neither could do without the other.

Right from the beginning, Mahendra had an acute dislike of B.P. Koirala. He wanted Subarna Shamshere to be Prime Minister. Subarna rightly said that the leader of the Party should be the Prime Minister, and the King ultimately agreed. I congratulated him upon it. After that, no particular occasion arose for me to have long talks with the King. I met him once or twice, and he complained of B.P. Koirala, just as B.P. Koirala complained to me of the King's attitude in various matters. Suddenly I heard of the coup d'état and B.P. Koirala and others being put in prison. Much later, the King wrote to me on the subject and sought my advice. I did not urge him to have a democratic structure, but I did suggest that a conciliatory attitude would help him. This was the advice given to him by others also. I have never pressed my advice upon him and I have not gone beyond this at any time. It was only when he has insisted on my advising him that I have said so. Unfortunately, Mahendra is a very foolish and conceited person. Further, he is in the hands not only of bad advisers, but a palace clique which is anti-India. Indeed, it is one of the stock in trade of Nepal politics to raise a cry against India. Even B.P. Koirala indulged in this kind of thing. After the coup d'état, Tanka Prasad and some others exercised much influence on the King. Tanka Prasad is very pro-Chinese. The King thought he could play a game between India and China.

During all this time, we have not interfered in any way and we have continued the help we have been giving in various projects. We have further not only stopped any kind of gun-running, but tried to use our influence to stop any incidents on the border. As a matter of fact, hardly any incident has

145. Tribhuvan.

happened in recent weeks on the border, except those which have taken place at the instigation of the King's men from across the border. Some two or three hundred hardened criminals have been released from Nepalese prisons and are utilised by the authorities there to create incidents on the border. We have received some information that the idea behind all this is to create incidents and then to condemn India. The Press in Nepal which is entirely under the direction of the King, goes on writing the most vituperative attacks on India and often praises China.

During the last six weeks or so, the King has issued two very objectionable statements attacking India. I was asked to reply to them, but I have remained quite silent and said nothing about them. The previous Foreign Minister of Nepal was suddenly dismissed because he took exception to the anti-India and pro-Chinese policy. Tulsi Giri was made Foreign Minister again.

In these circumstances, you will appreciate that it is no easy matter for us to deal with the situation. We have done everything to refrain from embittering it still further and have tried to avoid everything which might create an incident in Nepal or on the borders. The King has become a nervous wreck, afraid of everybody and trusting no one. He has got into such a mess that he cannot get out of it.

You have referred to our Ambassador.[146] It is probably true that the King's palace clique and his present advisers do not like our Ambassador. But according to my information, this unpopularity does not extend to the people either of the Terai or other parts of Nepal. Anyhow, the Ambassador can do little except occasionally to see the king and his advisers. He is one of our senior Ambassadors because we attach importance to that post, and I have no reason to think that he has acted wrongly. The mere fact of being an Indian Ambassador is, in prevailing circumstances, enough to make you unpopular with the king and his palace clique.

I can assure you that there is no gun-running from India to Nepal and that effective steps have been taken to that end. What the Nepal Congressmen may have done in the rest of India, I cannot say definitely because it is always possible to buy some arms in Calcutta or in Goa or elsewhere. Oddly enough, I have received some information of some gun-running being organised by the Foreign Minister, Tulsi Giri, on his own behalf so as to have an armed band to support him.

It is our belief that some of the incidents near the border have been directly organised by the King's men. There have been, as you might know, even murders of people on our side of the border. There is continuous propaganda against India. Perhaps, some of these stories have reached you also.

146. Harishwar Dayal.

We are closely watching the situation and trying our best so that it may not grow worse. But it is no easy matter to deal with a paranoiac who is at the same time exceedingly foolish and who surrounds himself with some of the worst persons in Nepal. I am afraid he will continue doing everything which will bring ruin to Nepal. I want to assure you that we are trying to prevent any incident happening on the border. We have made that perfectly clear and, what is more, we have largely succeeded.

My own information is that the King is not very popular in Nepal, although a certain sanctity attaches to the office.

I am sorry you have not been keeping well.

With regards,

Yours sincerely,
[Jawaharlal Nehru]

224. To M.P. Singh: Relations with Nepal[147]

November 26, 1962

Dear Mahesh Babu,

Your letter of the 24th November. I do not quite understand what all this is about. There is a reference to a Biography of King Mahendra. Some time back, I saw some parts of this Biography and it struck me to be rather absurd. The writing was florid.

Then there is some reference to "resolving the present tangle" and some kind of a peace formula is suggested. I do not know who makes this suggestion and under whose authority. We cannot deal with such matters in this way.

We are anxious, of course, to have good relations with Nepal, and I believe these relations are improving.

Yours sincerely,
[Jawaharlal Nehru]

147. Letter to Bihar Minister.

(l) Pakistan

225. On Nehru-Ayub Talk in London[148]

I do not think it will be quite correct to say in reply what you have suggested. I think the reply should be somewhat as follows:

"(a) There were no discussions between President Ayub Khan and Prime Minister about Indo-Pakistan issues at the time of the Commonwealth Prime Ministers' Conference in London. Casually and very briefly, the President referred, however, to the action taken by India in sending back illegal immigrants from Pakistan. Also he made some reference to the desirability of a Ministers' meeting to consider the problems of the use of river waters in East Pakistan and West Bengal.

(b) No conclusions were arrived at. The Prime Minister explained to him very briefly the position in regard to both these matters. The whole conversation on two occasions did not take more than five minutes."

226. For V. K. Krishna Menon: Pakistani Activity on Rajasthan Border[149]

I am told by the Chief Minister of Rajasthan that there is a great deal of activity across the border of Rajasthan on the Pakistan side. Telephone poles are being put up and some organisation of "blue shirts"[150] is particularly active there.

---

148. Note, 4 October 1962, for Y. D. Gundevia, the CS, being a draft reply for starred question No. 1570 (advance notice) for the Lok Sabha by Hem Barua, PSP, from Gauhati, Assam.
149. Note, 17 October 1962, for the Defence Minister. MHA, File No. 9/55/62-T, p. 12/c.
150. The Blue Shirts Society, founded in 1932, was a secret organisation within the Chinese Nationalist Party. See appendix 50.

227. To M.C. Davar: Visit to Pakistan[151]

November 6, 1962

My dear Shri Davar,

Your letter of the 6th November. I have no objection to your going to Pakistan, and there will be no difficulty in your way from our side. You will, of course, have to get a visa from the Pakistan High Commission.

Yours sincerely
Jawaharlal Nehru

228. Soviet Intelligence on Pakistani Machinations[152]

The Soviet Chargé d'Affaires came to see me tonight at my house[153]. He told me that he has been asked by his Government to convey a message to me confidentially.

For some little time past, Pakistan representatives had approached the Soviet authorities telling them that the Pakistan Government was thinking of making a radical change in their foreign policy. This would mean their quitting the various Blocs and Alliances and adopting a neutral policy. The military blocs like SEATO and CENTO had lost their meaning. Therefore, Pakistan wanted to adopt a neutral foreign policy and for this they wanted the support of the USSR. Pakistan's desire was to improve relations with the USSR.

In Moscow there was no belief in this approach on behalf of Pakistan. There was nothing to demonstrate that Pakistan wants to break these alliances with Western Powers. It was thought in Moscow that these attempts were made to exert more pressure on the US and other Western Powers to get more military and other aid from them. Also, to get their support for various things that Pakistan wanted.

It was even thought in Moscow that perhaps this approach on behalf of Pakistan to the USSR might have been taken on the direct advice of the United States in order to spoil the friendly relations existing between the USSR and India.

Perhaps also the internal difficulties of Pakistan induced them to make this approach.

151. Letter to freedom fighter and peace activist; NMML, M.C. Davar Papers.
152. Note, 27 November 1962, for M.J. Desai, the Foreign Secretary.
153. The meeting took place at 10 p.m. on 27 November 1962, Engagement Diary.

The Soviet Government was not inclined to put any faith in Pakistan's approaches and representations, but in order to clarify and find out what the real intentions of Pakistan are, the Soviet Government propose to carry on talks with the Pakistan Government in case the latter wishes to do so.

It was, the Soviet message said, quite out of the question that any possible improvement of the Soviet relations with Pakistan could affect the friendly relations existing between the Soviet and India.

I asked the Chargé as to who the persons were who had carried these messages to the Soviet Government. He said that he did not know and he had not been told who they were. Possibly these approaches had been made in several places by Pakistan representatives. It was indicated that these approaches were made by some persons in the Pakistan Government.

I told the Chargé that the Pakistan Government was trying its hardest to exploit the present situation and India's difficulties. They were completely opportunist and followed no principle. If they thought that something might benefit them in the near future, they took that course. It was also possible that this was done to exercise pressure on the United States to get more aid from them and their support in their various demands. There could be little doubt that the agitation in Pakistan going on now was at the encouragement of members of Government there. This agitation was not only against India but also partly against the United States to bring pressure to bear on the US.

I further told the Chargé that Pakistan's demands were going up from day to day. In Kashmir how it was said that Pakistan not only wanted some part of the State, but practically the whole State. Further, in north east India, it was bazar rumour that Pakistan would get Assam and North Bengal if the Chinese succeeded.

The Chargé asked me if there was any risk or danger of Pakistan taking any steps against India. I told him that they were quite irresponsible and I was unable to say what they would do or not do.

The Chargé particularly mentioned that the information he had given me should be kept secret.

Please show this note to CS.[154] I do not want several copies of it to go into the office.

---

154. Y.D. Gundevia, Commonwealth Secretary.

229. To Bhimsen Sachar: Jayaprakash Narayan and Pakistan[155]

November 27, 1962

My dear Sachar,

Your letter of November 24th.

It is true that some months ago I had told Jayaprakash Narayan that I had no objection to his going to Pakistan and forming some kind of a Conciliation Group. I rather think that this will not be fitting at the present stage. Pakistan has gone very far indeed with hostility to India and I doubt if any persons going there would make any difference.

Yours sincerely,
[Jawaharlal Nehru]

230. Duncan Sandys's Talk with MEA Officials[156]

Mr Duncan Sandys, Secretary of State for Commonwealth Relations Mr John Tilney, Under Secretary of State for Commonwealth Relations, and Sir Paul Gore-Booth, British High Commissioner, came over and had a brief talk with the Foreign Secretary[157] and myself, this morning.

2. Mr Duncan Sandys said that he had had very fruitful talks with the Prime Minister yesterday.[158] Mr Duncan Sandys talk with us this morning was mainly about Pakistan. He said that there is complete understanding between the British and the Indians on the questions of aid to India, but they were concerned about our relations with Pakistan. He kept on asking what was possible by way of a rapprochement.

3. We told Mr Sandys that the Prime Minster had written a second and very conciliatory letter on 12th November to President Ayub,[159] and we could not but expect some response from Pakistan before we could think of the next move from our side. Mr Sandys asked what the next move could be if there was a response from Pakistan and himself pressed there should be as quickly

---

155. Letter to the former Chief Minister of Punjab and Governor of Orissa and Andhra Pradesh; address: No. 12-G Sector 4, Chandigarh.
156. Note, 27 November 1962, by Y.D. Gundevia, the Commonwealth Secretary. MEA, No. P.V. 1043/7/62, p. 7-8/ notes.
157. M.J. Desai.
158. See item 408 and 228.
159. See item 399.

as possible a meeting between President Ayub and the Prime Minister. We said that there was standing invitation, and this had been renewed less than two months ago by our High Commissioner etc. Mr Sandys said that if there was a meeting the understanding should be that there would be no limitations on the discussions—he meant no pre-conditions. He said that the Prime Minster had told him that he was prepared to discuss Kashmir, but Mr Sandys felt that it would, perhaps, not be right to begin by saying that the settlement could be only on the cease fire Line. We did not comment on this. Mr Sandys asked where the meeting could take place.

The Foreign Secretary explained that President Ayub had never come to India, except for half an hour in transit, an airport halt only, and since the Prime Minster had visited Pakistan for four days, a return visit was due from the Pakistan President to India, and, therefore, the meeting should take place in Delhi. Mr Sandys seemed to think in terms of a meeting somewhere "half-way". The Foreign Secretary said that this would not be right; a meeting like this would not only not have the right popular appeal but may lead to the belief that Kashmir problem was being secretly negotiated and settled and cause a serious reaction in both countries as nothing of this sort can be achieved in one meeting at high level. The only correct thing would be for the President to come to Delhi, where he could be given all the honours due to Head of State on a ceremonial visit. This would have a welcome impact on public opinion in both countries. We said that there could be no difficulty about renewing the invitation, if this was still considered necessary. If President Ayub replied suitably to the Prime Minister's letter, we could send out to him yet another invitation to come to Delhi, to get over any possible difficulty. Mr Sandys pressed that no meeting at any lesser level than that between the Prime Minister and the President of Pakistan could be of any avail, today. He said that something dramatic had to be done to alter the present unfortunate situation, and time was the essence of the problem now.

We made it clear that one should not expect that in any such meeting the Kashmir problem could be resolved, but there could be better understanding and better mutual feeling between the two countries, if in such a meeting it was agreed that all problems can and must be solved peacefully and by negotiations between the two countries. I said that, if such an understanding could be brought about, we should, from then on, proceed on the basis that a settlement already had been reached between the two countries and function as though there were no insuperable disputes between the two countries. Mr Duncan Sandys said that, if this could be achieved, it would be very useful, indeed. Mr Sandys, however, admitted that he had no illusions on the difficulties that were likely to face him on his arrival in Pakistan. He was not sure of his reception in Pakistan, etc. etc.

The Prime Minster, speaking to Shri Rajeshwar Dayal and myself a little later, told us that he had spoken very frankly to Mr Duncan Sandys yesterday. He had told the Secretary of State that he was prepared to talk to Pakistan at any level, official, Ministerial, Prime Minster-level, etc. But one thing he wanted definitely understood and that was that on no account would he negotiate on the Kashmir Valley. The Kashmir Valley could not be given away. If anything like this was attempted or brought about, the Prime Minister said, this would have an immediate effect on our struggle against China. It would go against the morale of the country, in every sense, and would come in the way of our struggle against China.

231. In the Lok Sabha: Talks with Pakistan on Kashmir[160]

S.M. Banerjee[161] (Kanpur): Under Rule 197. I call the attention of the Prime Minister to the following matter of urgent public importance and request that he may make a statement thereon:

"The reported news about the proposed talk between India and Pakistan to resolve the Kashmir dispute peacefully."

The Prime Minister and Minister of External Affairs and Minister of Atomic Energy (Jawaharlal Nehru): Sir, as the House is aware, we have recently had visits from Mr Duncan Sandys, Minister of Commonwealth Relations in the United Kingdom, and Mr Averell Harriman, Assistant, Secretary of State in the United States. We had long discussions with them[162] about the Chinese invasion of India and our need for various kinds of equipment to meet this attack on our country. I am glad to say that these discussions were fruitful and we hope to get much of the equipment required from the United States and the United Kingdom as well as some other friendly countries. I am grateful to these countries for the help they are giving us in this crisis that we have to face.

In the course of my talks with Mr Duncan Sandys and Mr Harriman the question of our relations with Pakistan was raised. I told them that it had always been our policy to have friendly and cooperative relations with Pakistan because

---

160. Answer to Calling Attention Motion, *Lok Sabha Debates*, Third Series, Vol. X, November 21 to December 4, 1962, pp.3973-3978.
161. Independent.
162. See item 408.

this seemed to us essential not only because of geography, but because of our joint history, culture, language and the many bonds that had arisen between us during the long years. We had always aimed at that and we are sure that this is the only proper relationship that should subsist between two neighbouring countries and peoples which have had such close bonds in the past. The question of Kashmir was referred to and we explained to them our position in regard to it and pointed out that anything that involved an upset of the present arrangement would be very harmful to the people of Kashmir as well as to the future relations of India and Pakistan. We were, however, always ready to discuss this, as other matters, with representatives of the Pakistan Government at any level desired. In fact, we had suggested meetings at various levels in the course of the last few months, but no positive response had come from them

Mr Sandys and Mr Harriman appreciated our position, but still suggested that a friendly discussion about these matters between India and Pakistan might be helpful. I was agreeable to this, as indeed we have been ourselves suggesting some such meeting for some time past. I explained to them again, however, our basic principles and how it was not possible for us to bypass or ignore them.

Mr Sandys thereafter went to Pakistan and came back yesterday after consultation with President Ayub Khan suggesting that a joint statement should be issued on behalf of both the Governments stating that a renewed effort should be made to resolve the outstanding differences so as to enable India and Pakistan to live side by side in peace and friendship, further stating that discussions should be started at an early date initially at the ministerial level and later at an appropriate stage directly between the Heads of the Governments.[163] We suggested some variations in the draft joint statement. These were largely agreed to. Ultimately, the following joint statement was issued on behalf of the Governments of India and Pakistan.

"The President of Pakistan and the Prime Minister of India have agreed that a renewed effort should be made to resolve the outstanding difference between their two countries on Kashmir and other related matters, so as to enable India and Pakistan to live side by side in peace and friendship.

In consequence, they have decided to start discussions at an early date with the object of reaching an honourable and equitable settlement.

These will be conducted initially at the ministerial level. At the appropriate stage direct talks will be held between Mr Nehru and President Ayub."

Some Hon. Members rose –

Speaker: Is there anything still to be asked?

163. See note in appendix 71.

Shri S.M. Banerjee: It is not about the statement that the hon. Prime Minister has made. He has stated that the dates have not yet been fixed. I want to know when the meeting of the ministerial level will take place? Has any date been fixed for that?

Jawaharlal Nehru: No, Sir, no date has been fixed thus far.

P.K. Deo[164] (Kalahandi): Sir, anxious as we are for a settlement of this outstanding question, may I know if this meeting is to take place at Delhi or at Karachi?

Jawaharlal Nehru: All these matters have not been settled yet.

Hem Barua[165] (Gauhati): May I know whether Mr Sandys has suggested any broad basis for efforts to be made towards a solution of the outstanding problems between India and Pakistan as indicated by the BBC broadcast this morning to the effect that the broad basis is that the Jammu and Kashmir State be partitioned; if so, how far this is true? This is a BBC broadcast. That is why I want to know it from the Prime Minister.

Jawaharlal Nehru: I am glad the hon. Member has drawn my attention to this broadcast. I have not heard it. All I can say is, the broadcast has no basis or foundation.

बागड़ी[166] (हिसार): हिन्दुस्तान और पाकिस्तान के बीच बातचीत होकर दोनों गवर्नमेन्टस के हैडस ने एक ज्वाएंट स्टेटमेन्ट; निकाला है। मैं जानना चाहता हूं कि इस बातचीत के दौरान में कोई ऐसी बात तो तय नहीं हुई है जो कि अभी बिल्कुल फाइनेलाइज़ तो नहीं हुई लेकिन बुनियादी तौर पर यह मान लिया गया है कि हिन्दुस्तान के कब्ज़े में कश्मीर का जो इलाका है वह कुछ इलाका पाकिस्तान को देकर फैसला किया जायेगा? कोई ऐसी बात तो नहीं की गई है।

अध्यक्ष: यह तो जवाब आ गया कि पार्टीशन के बारे में कोई बातचीत नहीं हुई।

बागड़ी: दूसरी चीज़ मैं यह जानना चाहता हूं कि कश्मीर का जैसे एक मसला है उस के अलावा और भी छोटी छोटी बातों के लिए कहा गया है कि उनके बारे में

---

164. Swatantra Party, Orissa.
165. PSP.
166. Socialist.

भी समझौता करने की कोशिश की जायेगी तो जैसे कश्मीर का नाम लिया है कोई दूसरी चीजें भी है जैसे कि मुश्तरका महाज़ वगैरह का मामला है कोई और भी इशूज (issues) हैं जिन पर कि बातचीत होगी?

अध्यक्षः अब माननीय सदस्य बैठ जायं।

जवाहरलाल नेहरूः ख़ाली एक मसला था कि हम बातें करें आपस में और यह हमें मंज़ूर था हमेशा से, वह तो तय ही है लेकिन और कोई बात या किस ढंग से बातें हों, यह कोई निश्चित नहीं हुआ है।

बागड़ीः मेरे पूछने का मतलब था ...

अध्यक्षः आपने सवाल किया, जवाब आ गया कि ऐसी कोई बात अभी तक तय नहीं हुई है। अब और आप क्या चाहते हैं।

बागड़ीः कश्मीर का जैसे नाम आया है उसी तरीक़े से क्या किसी और चीज़..

[Translation begins:

Bagri (Hissar)[167]: After discussion between the heads of states of Hindustan and Pakistan, they have come up with a joint statement. I want to know whether during the discussion, any such understanding has been arrived at, though not finalised, that the parts in possession of India and Pakistan could be exchanged in order to resolve the issue?

Speaker: This has been already answered that there has been no talks regarding partition.

Bagri: My second question is that apart from Kashmir which has been mentioned, there are many minor issues which are pending and whether any understanding regarding resolving those issues have been arrived at?

Speaker: Now the Hon. Member can sit down.

Jawaharlal Nehru: The only issue was that we should talk, which we have been proposing throughout, but how and what would be the process and content of these talks has not yet been finalised.

167. Socialist Party.

Bagri: The point of my asking was…

Speaker: Whatever you asked the answer has been given; now what else do you want?

Bagri: The way Kashmir has been brought up, has there been any other issue…

Translation ends]

Speaker: Order, order. Shri Kamath.

Hari Vishnu Kamath[168] (Hoshangabad): Has the attention of the Prime Minister been drawn to certain tendentious reports in this morning's papers emanating from Rawalpindi regarding the basis of settlement in the course of which plebiscite and partition both have been mentioned; and, if so, can the House take it that as matters stand between the two governments at the moment there has been no talk or understanding about this matter prior to the talks that might ensue later?

Jawaharlal Nehru: I am sorry I have not read all that the newspapers may contain this morning; I did not have the time to do that. I only saw a little about it; so, I cannot specifically refer to that. But, as I said, when the hon. Member referred to the BBC broadcast which I have not heard, any such statement is completely without foundation. Our talks were concerned only based on our meeting and discussing it. It was not for Mr Sandys or anyone else to suggest what kind of talk we should have and what manner of talk we should have. I have told them what I have stated here, that for the last two months, certainly even earlier, we have suggested various meetings at official level, at ministerial level; but there was no positive response to that.

168. PSP.

(m) Rumania

232. In New Delhi: Civic Reception for Gheorghe Gheorghiu-Dej[169]

Not to Resist Aggression will be Going down to Unknown Depths

New Delhi, Oct. 18 – Prime Minister Nehru today declared that the honour, dignity and territorial integrity of India would be protected whatever the cost and consequences.

Pandit Nehru said that everyone in the world knew of India's desire and efforts for peace. "But it is an irony that we are being drawn into a situation where we are compelled to take to arms."

The Prime Minister stated that India was opposed to war as a means for settling disputes. "But we are not a people who would bow down before aggression," he declared.

He said that if India did not resist aggression and fight it back it would drag the nation down to unknown depths.

The Prime Minister was speaking at a civic reception given in the honour of the Rumanian President, Gheorghe Gheorghiu-Dej.[170]

Forced to Fight

Pandit Nehru referred to the speech made earlier by the Rumanian President in which he had stressed the need for peace, and said:

"I fully endorse the viewpoint of our honoured guest in the matter. It is known in the wide world that we have always stood for peace and have advocated peaceful solution of international problems. But it is an irony that today we are being drawn into a situation where we have to take to arms."

Pandit Nehru said: "This is not the occasion for me to refer to this matter in detail. But I wish to state that if we do not resist aggression and fight back it would drag us down to unknown depths. We wish to avoid it (fighting) but we cannot help it."

Thunderous cheers arose from the crowd when Pandit Nehru said that India was not a country which would bow its head down to an aggressor. The defence and honour of the nation should, and shall be protected at all costs, he added.

169. Report of speech, 18 October 1962. Reproduced from the *National Herald*, 19 October 1962.
170. (1901-1965); General Secretary, Rumanian Communist Party, 1947-1965.

Adherence to Peace

Pandit Nehru said that it should not be construed from his remarks that India would abandon her policy of seeking peaceful solutions to international problems. "It would be extremely painful and wrong for us to do so," he added.

He said: "I wish to assure our honoured guest this evening that India's voice has always been and shall continue to be, raised in favour of peace."

Pandit Nehru stated that India wished to be friendly to nations. If someone else did not respond India could not help it. "But we would not abandon our basic policies."

The Prime Minister said that India was one with Rumania in working for peace and disarmament, "We are opposed to military pacts. We want all nations to prosper side by side in a world free from wars and weapons" he added.

Gratitude to Rumania

Expressing his gratitude to Rumania for her help and assistance in the discovery of oil in India[171] Pandit Nehru said, "India and Rumania are friends. This friendship has been further strengthened by their help to us in our development, particularly in the sphere of oil."

The story of Rumania's progress after independence, he said, was a happy story, and India rejoiced in Rumania's rapid development.

He agreed with the Rumanian President that the Berlin problem was one of the most explosive problems in the world and that an early solution to it was necessary.

Pandit Nehru expressed the hope that the visit to India of the Rumanian President and the Rumanian Prime Minister[172] would help strengthen the ties between the two countries.

---

171. A public sector oil refinery was initiated in 1959 at Hugrijan and Moran with help from Rumania. It was commissioned in 1962.
172. Ion Gheorghe Maurer.

(n) Tibet

233. Freda Bedi is not a Communist[173]

I enclose a personal and confidential letter from Freda Bedi. Whatever varying views might have been in the past, I am sure she is not a communist. She is, in fact, a devout Buddhist and has, during the last year or two, devoted herself to the Tibetan refugees' welfare and especially to their children.

2. I do not know what I can do in the matter. I think the Dalai Lama will be here till tomorrow evening. It is possible to give him a message from me (perhaps Shri K.L. Mehta[174] could do it), this might be done. The message should be that Mrs Freda Bedi is not Communist and is devoted to the welfare of the Tibetan children. I would not have agreed to her looking after the children if I had doubted her in any way.

234. Talk with the Dalai Lama[175]

Education

In reply to PM's enquiry about the Dalai Lama's recent visit to Simla, Dalai Lama said that he had heard reports that the standard of living of the children at the Save the Children Fund Nursery was high. This would have created difficulties when the time came for the children to settle down in life in India. He was glad to say, however, that as a result of his personal inspection, he found that there was no truth in the reports.[176]

2. The Dalai Lama mentioned that the Tibetan Education Society School in Chhota Simla was greatly congested. I[t] had 498 pupils whereas available accommodation could not be stretched to take in more than a maximum of 300.

3. The Joint Secretary[177] explained that a decision had already been taken by the Society to rent one or more houses in Simla in order to remove the congestion. Unfortunately, enquiries so far made showed that no such accommodation was available. PM said that he was not prepared to accept

173. Note, 18 October 1962, for M. J. Desai, the Foreign Secretary.
174. Joint Secretary (East), MEA. See also SWJN/SS/68/pp.609-613.
175. Record of talk, 18 October 1962. Composed by K. L. Mehta JS (E). MEA, File No. E-IV/2 (167)/62, pp.2-2/Corr.
176. See notes in item 474.
177. K.L. Mehta, Joint Secretary (East) MEA.

this statement and expressed the desire that renewed efforts should be made at an appropriate level to find the necessary accommodation in Simla so that the children could be properly housed. If Education Ministry does not act promptly, EA[178] should intervene and take action by sending our officer to Simla.

4.   The Dalai Lama referred to certain squabbles which had developed amongst members of the staff and expressed the hope that as a result of the Headmaster's removal, things would now settle down. He added that he was looking for a suitable Tibetan for appointment as Principal of the School. The present incumbent was a good man but rather lenient. PM said that the matter of selection of the right type of Headmasters/Teachers was of the highest importance. The Education Ministry should do everything necessary to ensure that qualified teachers with appropriate background and capacity to work with the Tibetans are found for the schools being set up by the Tibetan Education Society. PM also enquired whether a new man had been appointed to fill the Headmaster's post in the School.

5.   PM then enquired whether some of the children from the Dharamshala Nursery had moved over to Simla etc. Dalai Lama replied in the affirmative and added that even so, the number of pupils in the Dharamshala Nursery still stood at slightly over 500. This was partly because the Nursery had to admit many children whose parents were in Nepal.

6.   PM then enquired about Mr Maurice Frydman's proposal to set up Children's Homes in Almora. Dalai Lama said that as no water was available at the site originally proposed, he had himself made a modest start of the scheme as originally envisaged by Frydman in Mussoorie. The Joint Secretary explained briefly the details of the scheme as worked out by Mr Frydman and which had been discussed recently with the Minister of Education. PM felt that the objective which Mr Frydman and the Dalai Lama had could be equally achieved by providing a goodly measure of home life in the existing hostels. It must be remembered, PM added, that in schools of this kind it was not just a question of giving a few lectures. It was equally important that a Tibetan-home atmosphere should be created in all the houses where children reside as boarders. Where the children were small, there should be matrons in adequate number to look after them. In addition, Tibetan couples selected by the Dalai Lama should be appointed to take charge of the children as "foster parents". One such couple could normally be expected to look after 40 pupils. It follows that Tibetan couples in appropriate numbers may be appointed in a boarding house where more than 50 pupils reside. Necessary number of houses should be taken on rent to remove congestion and to implement this idea of providing home atmosphere in hostels.

178. MEA.

7. The Dalai Lama mentioned that present arrangements such as they are, provide education facilities for 1600 Tibetan children against a total of some 4,000. He was glad that plans were afoot to open more residential schools and expressed the hope that such schools will be started soon. PM agreed.

8. The Dalai Lama expressed his happiness to find the Prime Minister sharing his views in the matter. He said that was the important thing and the details could be worked out to achieve the objective which PM and he had before them. The Prime Minister ordered that the Ministry of Education should be asked to progress these matters expeditiously.

Tibetan Refugee Boys between the Ages of 16 and 28

9. Dalai Lama said that some 10,000 of such boys and girls are at present living in India, and only a few have so far been provided with jobs in factories etc. There appears to be a need to widen the scope of the programme under which boys in this age group are given training in appropriate crafts with a view to provide jobs for them.

10. PM agreed and expressed the view that this problem would become even more important once the boys and girls, at present being taught in our schools, finished their primary education and are not considered fit to pursue higher studies. Alternative avenues for training and employment must, therefore, be found for them.

Mysore Scheme

11. Prime Minister enquired how the people were taking to the Mysore Scheme. The Dalai Lama replied that the Tibetans who had gone there were very willing to settle down as agriculturists. He added that the desire would be heightened once the Mysore State has been able to allocate land to individual families. PM agreed and said that this process should be expedited.

(o) UK

235. To John Graham: Election of Glasgow University Rector[179]

October 10, 1962

Dear Mr Graham,

I do not think it will be quite appropriate for me to intervene in any way in the election for Lord Rector in Glasgow University[180]. It has seemed to me in the past to be improper to express my preferences or my recommendation in internal matters in the United Kingdom. I hope you will appreciate my difficulty and excuse me.

Yours sincerely,
[Jawaharlal Nehru]

236. To Harold Macmillan: Cuban Crisis[181]

October 27, 1962

My dear friend,

Thank you for your message of October 23 on the situation in regard to Cuba. I am sorry for the delay in my sending you an answer as you will appreciate, we have been heavily occupied with our troubles nearer home.

I entirely agree with what you have said about the dangers of the situation. This crisis has come at a time when we ourselves in India are facing a grave danger. Naturally our concern is all the greater as a major conflict between the USA and the Soviet Union might easily spell disaster for the world.

Fortunately, since you wrote to me, some steps have been taken by the Secretary-General of the United Nation[182] to find ways of easing the crisis. We welcome his initiative and we hope that it will lead to satisfactory results. I need hardly say that any effort that you may make to avert the crisis and to strengthen peace and security will always have our fullest support.

179. Letter to member of the Edward Heath Rectorial Committee, Conservative Club, Glasgow University, Glasgow.
180. The Lord Rector was elected by students of the University. In 1962 Albert Luthuli (1898-1967), anti-apartheid leader of South Africa, Nobel Laureate, and an ardent admirer of Nehru was finally elected the Rector.
181. Letter to the British Prime Minister.
182. U Thant.

Although we are fully occupied with our own problems, I shall gladly keep in touch with you on further developments in regard to Cuba.

With warm good wishes,

Yours sincerely,
[Jawaharlal Nehru]

(p) UN

237. For Seminar on United Nations[183]

I send my good wishes to the Regional Seminar on Teaching About the United Nations. The United Nations started with a noble ideal and an inspiring charter. It is often criticised for not having lived up to all its ideals. Nevertheless, there is no doubt that it has not only helped repeatedly in preventing conflicts between nations, but has also spread the idea of international cooperation. We should, therefore, try to improve it and bring it more in line with existing conditions. It seems to me very desirable that people should be told what the United Nations stands for and the aims and objectives which it has in view.

238. In New Delhi: United Nations Day[184]

Madam Chairman,[185] Excellencies and Friends,
I have often come here usually to this hall on the United Nations Day and said something I hope appropriate, regarding the ideals and the charter of the United Nations and I hope that it would be implemented.

Today as the Chairman said, we meet under peculiar circumstances, circumstances of challenge, not only to the Charter but perhaps to the very existence of the United Nations. She referred to problems we are having on our border. It is a matter of very serious concern to us, but also apart from this as we all know a situation has arisen of the gravest moment in the Caribbean in regard to Cuba and the world is, again, possibly on the brink of disaster. I am not going to discuss these matters here. But I have merely mentioned them

183. Message, 20 October 1962. PMO, File No. 9/2/62-PMP, Vol. 7, Sr. No. 66-A.
184. Speech, 24 October 1962, on United Nations Day at Sapru House. NMML, AIR Tapes, TS No. 8726-8727, NM No. 1706.
185. Rajan Nehru. See item 157.

in the background of the time we are living and of today when we meet here to celebrate the United Nations Day. I think nobody present here and many outside will doubt the fact that the formation of the United Nations was a happy thing and an inevitable thing. Time had arrived. It would have arrived very much earlier, but after the great war everybody felt that something of this kind must be done. Previously, the League of Nations had laboured and done good work but ultimately expired in the flames of war. So, with that experience behind the nations, a new organisation called the United Nations was formed and we profited by that old experience and the Charter and the other rules and regulations governing it, as the result of that experience which reflected not a perfect organisation but an organisation which to some extent reflected conditions as they were in the world then. People criticise United Nations for not being a perfectly democratic body. That is a correct criticism. But the fact is that the world as it is constituted today, is not democratic in that sense. All manner of differences between great nations and small, powerful nations and weak, in their structures of government, the way they pursue, and some way has to be found to bring them all together to cooperate and in the process of cooperation to get to know each other better and to realise that the United Nations offered them an opportunity to realise the ideals of the Charter.

Well, we have had seventeen years of it and I have no doubt that during these years the United Nations had done much good work. I think it has prevented many crises from coming up to boiling point, has solved many problems and yet at the same time many grave problems remain, which it has not solved. That is not the fault of the United Nations. It is a fault of the conditions we live in, which to some extent, are sometimes reflected in the United Nations. Yet the fact remains that something like the United Nations is essential for the world, in fact something more is essential. The world technologically speaking and otherwise has grown rapidly and boundaries hardly count, and it is inevitably leading, that is, if it survives, to some kind of one world order. There is no escape from the conclusion. When that will happen or whether it will happen at all I cannot say, but logically that is the only conclusion we can aim at, and the United Nations was a powerful step in that direction. It has justified itself broadly, although it has failed in individual matters, although perhaps its Constitution today does not reflect the world as it is. When it was formed there were less than half the present number of members; now they are, I do not know 103, 104, I forget, the exact number goes on growing and that growth is not represented in some of its organs. But in spite of that we may try to improve it when occasion offers. But in spite of that we cannot condemn it, because it is not the perfect organisation which we should like to have.

Unfortunately, we are not perfect, either the countries there or the individuals there, and sometimes I wonder if this kind of organisational approach will bring the results we aim at unless the minds and the hearts of human beings change somewhat. Of course, the organisational approach helps; I suppose helps the minds and hearts to change a little, just as the minds of men who govern that organisation also. In the UNESCO Charter it is said that wars begin in the minds of men, which is perfectly true, but the minds of men are often conditioned by various factors. Today, for instance, I should imagine that the vast number of human beings in the world, in every country, abhor the idea of a war; they dislike it intensely; they want to avoid it, and in spite of that, some events seem to have forced them in that direction. It is something like a Greek tragedy which is being enacted before our eyes. Yet, we try to do our utmost to prevent the culmination of that tragedy. And if we can prevent it, and take another direction in human affairs, possibly then we shall not only avoid that tragedy in the present or in the near future, but altogether. This is a curious stage we have arrived at as the big choice before the world which we chose. There is not much room left for intermediate courses, for intermediate courses may be devised for the time being to lead to something, but the direction has to change. And I have no doubt that some such organisation as the United Nations is essential. If the United Nations is not there, we have to sit down to create it. So with all its drawbacks and shortcomings, which we have seen sometimes, the United Nations remains the real hope of mankind, and whether it will ultimately succeed in preventing these terrible disasters I do not know, I hope so. Anyhow, we have to work for it because if we did not, if we did not have that hope, there will be little urge left to us to work for anything worthwhile.

It is an odd thing, it is a tragedy, it is very painful for us that we, who have spoken so much of peace and of the United Nations' ideals and Charter, should be involved in military operations, practically a war on a major scale on our borders. Let me think how all of us are creatures of circumstances and circumstances push us in a particular direction against our will, against all our impulses and urges. Even so, I have the satisfaction even in this matter which has created so much trouble on our border and leading to so much unfortunate conflict and fighting. But we have not gone against the Charter of the United Nations, we have not transgressed on any person's territory and that whatever has happened, has happened on our territory. I regret it. But anyhow it shows, that we are not transgressors. We have to carry a heavy burden, but much heavier is the burden, which our people on the borders, on the frontiers, have to carry and shoulder and my heart goes out to them. And in so far as we can, we shall, of course, help them. Then as I said, there is a grave, a very grave situation being created in the Western seas, in the Caribbean Sea. I do not know what

301

will be the outcome of this, but the outcome will affect the world whichever way it is decided. Therefore, we must all be very much concerned about it. Again as I said, it is an odd thing that on this United Nations Day, when we should talk of peace and cooperation and one world, our minds should be filled with these conflicts and possible disasters. And yet, that is a state of the world we have to deal with and to contend against. It is a hard task before the United Nations and all those who cherish it. And the only way to do so is to hold on to that ideal and Charter and to try to spread, spread its knowledge, as widely as possible. I understand that efforts are made, are being made here too and elsewhere to teach in schools and elsewhere what the United Nations stand for. That is a good thing. Because that teaching at the early years of education will have greater affect perhaps then at a later stage.

We have seen two great wars. Perhaps the people of India did not experience those wars as many countries of Europe and Asia did. And we are accustomed, intellectually we know what it is; even emotionally to some extent we know, but nevertheless we have not had any real experience except on the borders a little. And most people perhaps in India have no realisation as to what it means. And nobody in the world, a very very few, have any realisation of what a modern war, a nuclear war might mean. We are told men who have studied the subject, scientists and others tell us of the terrible disaster, the disasters that may follow such a war. People, competent people, sit down as I read the other day, to the cold blooded calculation of what the first few days of the nuclear war might mean, and it is said that it should mean the death of three hundred million people chiefly in Europe, America and part of Asia. It seems to me extraordinary that we live in a world where one could think and calculate that three hundred million people may be exterminated within a few days of the war. And yet the people should continue, nations and people should continue preparing for that war which might result in this powerful catastrophe. Yet that is a world we live in. Yet some unseen urges push us in that direction and we are filled with fear and hatred. How we can face this contingency, I do not know. One can try one's best whether it is easier or better to change the minds and hearts of men and thereby, lead to a better result or change the environment and the rules and regulations and some organisations and nations, and thus lead to the changing of the minds of men. I suppose both the processes have to go together.

We find that while very great phenomenal and exciting advances have been made by science and technology, the minds of men have remained rather primitive, full of hatreds and fears, filled with the desire to injure the other, thinking that will bring profit to them. And nations as a whole do not represent, that is men in a mass, in a nation, do not represent the higher qualities of the individual. The higher qualities exist in individuals of course in the nation, but as a group when they function in excitement, the lower qualities come up and that is why we have wars and destruction and hatred and fear. I leave it to you to consider how you can face the situation. As I said perhaps, we have to, we have to deal with it in many ways, certainly one very important way, is the way of the United Nations and therefore, we gather here to pay homage to the United Nations and in a sense pledge ourselves to work for peace and the ideals laid down in the Charter of the United Nations. After all, the United Nations was principally formed as it says to put an end to war. If wars continue, the organisations like United Nations obviously cannot last. The war put an end to it and if anybody survives after the war they will try to make another United Nations. There is no hope for the world without some such organisation. It is a race, therefore, between the powers of destruction, almost inherent in human beings, fear, destruction, and hatred and the nobler impulses and urges that they have. We all hope that the latter will win, and the latter will win largely because of the lead given by the United Nations. So, it is right that we should gather here together today and remember United Nations Day and more particularly the Charter and its noble words which are very inspiring as you know. So, I have come here today to offer that homage.

(q) USA

239. To John F. Kennedy: Cuban Crisis[186]

October 27, 1962

Dear Mr President,

Thank you for your message of October 23 about the situation in regard to Cuba. This was delivered to me by Ambassador Galbraith a few days ago. I am sorry for the delay in answering it, as you will appreciate, we have been much occupied with troubles nearer home.

I share your deep concern at the dangerous crisis which has arisen in regard to Cuba. Unless some solution can be found, it might easily lead to disaster. Knowing your dedication to peace, I am confident that on your side no efforts will be spared to find such a solution. Fortunately, some steps have been taken by the Secretary-General of the United Nations to bring about an easing of the crisis. We have welcomed his initiative and we hope that this will lead to satisfactory results. As you know, Mr President, any effort that may be made

186. Letter to the President of USA.

to avert this dangerous crisis and to ensure peace and security will have our fullest support.

In your message you have also referred to Chinese aggression on our territory which is continually taking place at the present time. I have sent you a separate message on this matter yesterday.[187] I deeply appreciate your sympathy and support.

With renewed thanks and warm good wishes,

Yours sincerely,
[Jawaharlal Nehru]

240. Eleanor Roosevelt's Death[188]

We are deeply grieved and shocked to learn of Mrs Roosevelt's passing away. She was a great and outstanding lady and her devotion to peace and understanding will always be remembered. We admired her greatly for her unremitting efforts for the promotion of all good causes. She was a friend of India and the memory her gracious presence, the warmth of her personality and the largeness of her heart will always remain with us.

The Government and the people of India join with her countless friends and admirers all over the world, in expressing their profound sorrow at the passing away of a great figure of our times.

241. To John Sherman Cooper: You are Welcome[189]

November 16, 1962

My dear Mr Cooper,

Thank you for your letter of November 10th. I am glad to learn that there is a chance of your coming here soon. We shall be happy to meet you again.

We are living through difficult times now and I suppose we shall have many more difficulties to face. But I am confident that we shall win though.

With all good wishes to you and your wife,

Sincerely yours,
[Jawaharlal Nehru]

---

187. See item 388.
188. Message, 8 November 1962, to family members of Eleanor Roosevelt. PIB.
189. Letter to US Senator from Kentucky; former ambassador to India, 1954-55.

(r) USSR

242. To B.G. Gafurov: George Roerich Anniversary[190]

October 4, 1962

Dear Dr Gafurov,

I have learnt with pleasure that the Institute of Oriental Studies of the USSR Academy of Sciences will soon celebrate the sixtieth anniversary of Dr George Roerich[191]. On this occasion I should like to add my tribute to him. I met him during his stay in India and was much impressed by his learning and extraordinary linguistic ability, as also with the work he was doing. I am glad that this work is being adequately recognised by the USSR Academy of Sciences. It is right that we should honour such a man and, because he was so long connected with India, I wish to join on behalf of my people on this occasion.

Yours sincerely,
J. Nehru

243. For USSR National Day[192]

I send my greetings and good wishes on the occasion of the National Day of the Soviet Union which is being celebrated as the Forty-Fifth Anniversary of the Revolution. In particular, I hope that the cause of world peace for which the Soviet Union stands and has worked for, will meet with success and the great advance which the scientists of the Soviet Union have made in travels in outer space will be devoted to the furtherance of peace all over the world and the advancement of humanity.

---

190. Letter to the Director of the Oriental Institute of the USSR Academy of Sciences, Armiansky-2, Moscow. PMO, File No. 9/2/62-PMP, Vol. 7, Sr. No. 21-A.
191. See appendix 4.
192. Message, 10 October 1962, forwarded to V. N. Matyash, TASS, New Delhi. PMO, File No. 9/2/62-PMP, Vol. 7, Sr. No. 43-A.

IV. CHINESE INVASION

(a) China General

244. To Morarji Desai: NEFA Border Situation[1]

October 11, 1962

My dear Morarji,

I am sorry to say that the situation in the NEFA border is deteriorating fast. I am afraid that we are in for trouble there on a big scale. This will put a great strain on us, but there is no help for it. We shall have specially to organise additional production, especially of spare parts. We may also have to add to our forces somewhat.[2]

Yours sincerely,
[Jawaharlal Nehru]

245. Clearing NEFA of Chinese[3]

Army Told to Clear NEFA of Chinese
PM No Talks till this Aggression Ends

New Delhi, Oct 12 – Prime Minister Nehru said here today that instructions to the Indian armed forces were to free the Indian territory in NEFA of the Chinese Intruders.

"I cannot fix a date, that is entirely for the military," Pandit Nehru said.

Prime Minister was talking to newsmen at the Palam aerodrome before his departure for Madras on his way to Ceylon for a three-day visit.

Replying to a question whether the chances of talks with the Chinese had finished, the Prime Minister declared that so long as this particular aggression (in the eastern sector) continued, there appeared to be no chance for talks.

Asked when he expected the Chinese to be thrown out of NEFA Pandit Nehru replied "Wintry conditions have set in already. I cannot fix any date for it. They are strongly positioned, large numbers situated on a higher ground."

1. Letter to the Finance Minister.
2. See also item 126.
3. Report of a press conference, 12 October 1962. Reproduced from the *National Herald*, 13 October 1962, p. 1.

Replying to a question about the estimate of the number of the Chinese in the area, Pandit Nehru said that he did not know the exact number. "Apart from anything else their (the Chinese) base on the other side is quite near from where they came," he added

Fighting in spurts

Answering a series of questions on the latest situation in NEFA Pandit Nehru said: "There was as you know a rather major incident two days ago. We suffered some casualties. The other side suffered heavier casualties probably approaching a hundred. There is a little river there about two miles from the mountains. Mostly, we are on this side of the river and they are on the other side."[4]

Asked whether the fighting was still going on, the Prime Minister replied that it was not continuing but it occurred in spurts.

In answer to a question whether the Chinese aggressive attitude presented a menace to the free nations of Asia, Pandit Nehru replied, "I don't know about that. It is quite enough to me if they are a menace to us."[5]

Pandit Nehru who left by a special IAF Viscount was accompanied by Mrs Indira Gandhi, and the Commonwealth Secretary Mr Y.D. Gundevia. The Minister a for Steel and Heavy Industries Mr C. Subramaniam, and the Minister without Portfolio Mr T.T. Krishnamachari, travelled by the same plane to Madras.

The Prime Minister was seen off by ministers of the Cabinet, high officials and the Chargé d'Affaires of the Ceylon High Commission, Mr B.P. Tilakaratna.

After a night's stopover in Madras the Prime Minister and party will leave for Colombo tomorrow.

246. Admission of China to the UN[6]

[Note, 21 October 1962, from M. J. Desai, the FS, begins]

The Soviet Resolution on admission of China to the UN is likely to come up in New York tomorrow. We have, during the last year or two, been voting in favour of the admission of China without making any statement. Similar

---

4. The reference is to Kechilang River, in the Chihtung area. *White Paper*, Vol. VII, p.113.
5. See also item 16, section "China and the Northeast".
6. Noting, MEA, The Question of Admission of The People's Republic of China to the United Nations, p. 16, col. 2, and p. 50.

attitude this year is bound to be seriously misunderstood by all concerned. If Prime Minister agrees, the telegram placed below to Chakravarty[7] may issue.

M. J. Desai,
21-10-1962

PM

[Note, 21 October 1962, from M. J. Desai, the FS, ends]

[Note, 21 October 1962, by Nehru begins]
Yes, the draft may issue.

J. Nehru
21-10-1962

[Note, 21 October 1962, by Nehru ends]

[Telegram, No. 24507, 22 October 1962, from M. J. Desai to B.N. Chakravarty, New York, UN, begins]

When the Soviet Resolution on admission of People's Republic of China comes for debate in General Assembly, you should make a statement. You should point out how China has committed flagrant aggression on both the Eastern and Western sectors of our borders and condemn Chinese aggression. You should, at the same time point out that our Delegation is voting for the Resolution because, apart from principle of universality of membership of the UN, the only effective way to check Chinese military adventurism is to make her accept her responsibility as member of the world organisation and be subject to the views and discipline of this world organisation.

[Telegram, No. 24507, 22 October 1962, from M. J. Desai to B.N. Chakravarty, New York, UN, ends]

---

7.   B.N. Chakravarty, Permanent Representative at the UN, 1962-65.

247. To Chou En-lai[8]

Thank you for the copy of your message of 24th October[9] which was delivered to the Ministry of External Affairs by your Chargé d'Affaires in Delhi on the evening of 24th October along with a copy of the statement issued by the Government of the People's Republic of China on the morning of the 24th.

Nothing in my long political career has hurt and grieved me more than the fact that the hopes and aspirations for peaceful and friendly neighbourly relations which we entertained, and to promote which my colleagues in the Government of India and myself worked so hard, ever since the establishment of the People's Republic of China, should have been shattered by the hostile and unfriendly twist given in India-China relations during the past few years. The current clashes on the India-China border arising out of what is in effect a Chinese invasion of India, which you have described as "most distressing", are the final culmination of the deterioration in relations between India and China.

I would not, in this letter, go into the long history of this deterioration in India-China relations or argue as to where the fault lies because you are quite familiar with our views on this subject. All I would say is that the long preamble to the statement of the Government of the People's Republic of China of 24th October, enclosed with your letter, gives a distorted picture of the history of India-China relations. I agree with you, however, that we should look ahead and consider what can be done not merely to turn the tide as you suggest, but to reverse it and make a serious attempt to restore the relations between India and China to the warm and friendly pattern of earlier days and even to improve on that pattern.

As regards the three points mentioned in your letter which were put out in the statement of 24th October, the Government of India have already indicated their official reactions to the proposals on these three points. I enclose a copy of this official reaction for ready reference.

My colleagues and I have carefully considered the appeal made in your letter. We are not able to understand the niceties of the Chinese three-point proposals which talk about "lines of actual control", etc. I believe several other Governments interested in peaceful settlement of our differences have also not been able to understand or appreciate what these proposals actually mean.

---

8. Letter, 27 October 1962, to the Prime Minister of China. Reproduced from *Chinese Aggression in War and Peace. Letters of the Prime Minister of India* (New Delhi: Ministry of Information and Broadcasting, Publications Division, 8 December 1962), pp. 9-13.
9. See appendix 26.

We are of the considered view that a clear straightforward way of reversing the deteriorating trend in India-China relations would be for Your Excellency to accept the suggestion made in point (v) of the official reaction of the Government of India and to revert to the position as it prevailed all along the India-China boundary prior to 8th September 1962. If this is agreed to, it can be implemented by both sides. We will, thereafter, be glad to welcome you or a delegation from your country at any level that is mutually acceptable to discuss and arrive at further agreed measures which can facilitate a peaceful settlement of our differences on this border question, in one stage or in more than one stage as may be necessary.

There have been repeated declarations by the Government of the People's Republic of China that they want to settle the differences on the border question with India by peaceful means, though what is happening today is in violent contradiction with these declarations. I would, however, presume that your letter is a reaffirmation of the earlier declarations and indicates a desire to revert to the paths of peace and peaceful settlement. On this common basis of eschewing war and violence in the settlement of border differences, our proposal to revert to the status quo along the entire boundary as it prevailed before 8th September 1962 should be acceptable to you. We could, after this is implemented, discuss our differences and see whether we can arrive at agreed measures and settle the differences either in one stage or in several stages. If we fail, we can consider what other agreed peaceful method of settling our differences should be adopted.

Please accept, Your Excellency, the assurances of my highest consideration.

Enclosure

October 24, 1962

The Government of India have seen Press Agency reports of the three-point statement issued by the People's Republic of China which the New China News Agency has put out this morning. There has been no official communication from the Chinese Government on this matter so far.

The Government of India have in previous notes and in statements made by the Prime Minister clearly indicated their attitude in this matter. The Government of India's position is:

    (i) The Government of India wedded to peace and peaceful methods have always sought to resolve differences by talks and discussions in this case of border differences with the Government of China.

    (ii) On the 16th October 1962, in a note sent to the Government of China they proposed the restoration of status quo of the boundary as it prevailed before the Chinese aggression in the Eastern sector on 8th September 1962, prior to talks and discussions for easing of tension and for creating the appropriate climate for purposeful talks and discussions to resolve the differences between the Governments of India and China on the boundary question.[10]

(iii) Since then, it is the Government of China which on the morning of the 20th October 1962 hurled its vast armies at various points on all sectors of the India-China boundary and enlarged the conflict. These Chinese forces have advanced in all sectors into Indian territory and are still advancing. India cannot and will not accept a position under which Chinese forces continue to commit aggression into Indian territory, occupy substantial Indian territories and use these as a bargaining counter to force a settlement on their terms.

(iv) There is no sense or meaning in the Chinese offer to withdraw 20 kilometres from what they call "line of actual control". What is this "line of actual control"? Is this the line they have created by aggression since the beginning of September? Advancing 40 or 60 kilometres by blatant military aggression and offering to withdraw 20 kilometres provided both sides do this is a deceptive device which can fool nobody.

(v) If the Chinese professions of peace and peaceful settlement of differences are really genuine, let them go back at least to the position where they were all along the boundary prior to 8th September 1962. India will then be prepared to undertake talks and discussions, at any level mutually agreed to, to arrive at agreed measures which should be taken for the easing of tension and correction of the situation created by unilateral forcible alteration of the status quo along the India-China boundary.

(vi) India is always prepared to resolve differences by talks and discussions but only on the basis of decency, dignity and self-respect and not under threat of military might of any country however strong it may be.

(vii) India would be prepared to welcome the Chinese Prime Minister or any suitable representative of the Chinese Government on a mutually agreed date if China is sincere in its professions of peaceful settlement and accepts the constructive proposal made in point (v) above which is fully consistent with dignity and self-respect both of India and China.

10. See *White Paper*, Vol.VII, pp.117-120.

248. Chinese Treatment of Lhasa Consulate Staff[11]

[Note, 4 November 1962, by M. J. Desai, the Foreign Secretary, begins]

The Chinese have been putting all sorts of pressure on our Consulate General in Lhasa. Telegraphic communication between Lhasa and Delhi and Lhasa and Peking was cut off, so far as our Missions are concerned, from 12th October. Telephone connection of the Lhasa Consulate-General has been cut off since 14th October. All sorts of restrictions have been placed on the staff and they are denied essential commodities like milk, eggs, firewood, etc. The local Tibetan servants have been compelled to withdraw their services from 31st October and now demonstrations are being organised on a trumped-up demand that the local staff who have refused to work for the Consulate-General should be given gratuity at the rate of one month's salary per every year of service. The telegrams from the Lhasa Consulate General are always delayed by three or four days and none of our telegrams to Lhasa seem to have been delivered to the Consulate-General.

2. The Chinese are determined to eliminate our last contact in Tibet i.e., the Consulate-General in Lhasa. There has been no pressure of this kind so far against the Consulate General at Shanghai or against our Embassy at Peking.

3. We have taken up the matter with the Chinese Mission here several times but the Chinese Chargé d'Affaires here can hardly do anything to get the Chinese Government's policy regarding the Lhasa Consulate General modified.

4. I feel that we should not wait for further Chinese moves but take the initiative ourselves and close the Consulates-General at Lhasa and Shanghai and ask the Chinese to close their Consulate-General in Bombay and Calcutta. We will hold the staff of the Chinese Consulates here till the staff of our Consulate-General at Lhasa and Shanghai are allowed to leave China. This is necessary because the Chinese system of exit permits, etc. can impose a lot of hardship on our staff and the Chinese ought to know that reciprocal hardships will be imposed on their staff in India.

M.J. Desai
4.11.62

PM

[Note, 4 November 1962, by M. J. Desai, the Foreign Secretary, ends]

11. Noting, 4 November 1962. MEA, File No. C/551/25/62-TB, pp. 2-3/notes.

[Note, 4 November 1962, by Nehru, begins]

I agree with you that we shall have to take some such steps as you suggest. But I do not know if you have clearly told the Chinese Government about the treatment of our people in our Consulate-General at Lhasa. It might be worth while to send them a message stating clearly how our employees and others have been treated there and how it is becoming impossible for them to function or even to have proper foodstuffs etc. There should be reciprocal treatment and we have put no difficulties in the way of the Chinese Consulates here. It is obviously not possible for our Mission to function in Lhasa if they have to face all these difficulties and obstructions.

Some such message might be sent to them and then on receipt of their answer, we can take the initiative to close our Consulates at Lhasa and Shanghai and ask them to close theirs in Bombay and Calcutta.

J. Nehru
4.11.1962

FS

[Note, 4 November 1962, by Nehru, ends]

249. To Chou En-lai[12]

Thank you for your letter of 4th November.[13] Our Chargé d'Affaires in Peking to whom it was handed over sent us a copy by telegram.

My colleagues and I have carefully considered the elaboration of the three proposals of the Chinese Government of October 24,[14] given in your letter.

Apart from the Chinese claims regarding the territorial boundary in various sectors of the India-China boundary, one fact stands out quite clearly. This is the basic fact that till the 8th September, 1962, Chinese forces had crossed the frontier between India and China in the Eastern sector as defined by India, that is, along the highest watershed in the region, in accordance with the Agreement of 1914. It was on 8th September 1962, that your forces crossed this frontier and threatened the Dhola frontier post of India. We took limited defensive measures to reinforce this post and at the same time made repeated approaches

12. Letter to the Prime Minister of China 14 November 1962; *White Paper,* Vol. VIII, pp.10-17.
13. Appendix 39.
14. See appendix 26.

to the Chinese Government to withdraw their forces beyond the Thag La ridge which is the frontier in the region. Your forces not only did not withdraw to the position they occupied before 8th September, 1962, but, after some probing attacks, mounted a massive attack and are now in occupation of large areas of Indian territory in this region and also in various other frontier areas of NEFA. That the attack was pre-meditated and carefully planned is clear from the fact that this attack at the Thag La ridge frontier which commenced on the morning of the 20th October 1962, was not an isolated move; similar attacks against Indian defence posts started simultaneously along other parts not only of the eastern sector of the frontier, but also of the western sector of the frontier.

As I said in my letter of 27th October,[15] I do not want to go into the history of the last five years and the forcible, unilateral alteration of the status quo of the boundary by the Chinese forces in the western sector, on which a mass of notes and memoranda have been exchanged between our two Governments. The events since 8th September, 1962, however, have completely shattered any hope that anyone could have entertained about settling India-China differences peacefully in accordance with normal international principles observed by all civilised governments. This invasion, coming after 12 years of constant and consistent endeavour on our part to maintain and develop friendly relations with China, can only point to one and only one conclusion, namely, that the Government of China have taken a deliberate cold-blooded decision, in total disregard of all principles, which govern normal neighbourly relations between sovereign governments, to enforce their alleged boundary claims by military invasion of India. It is this crisis of confidence which has to be dealt with. I must state frankly that we find no attempt either in the three proposals as elaborated now or in the other parts of your letter, to deal with this main problem created by the massive Chinese aggression on India which began on 8th September, 1962, namely, the complete loss of confidence in the bona fides of the professions for a peaceful settlement repeatedly made in public statements of the Government of China. On the other hand, your letter proceeds on the unilateral assumption that the line of actual control created by the latest Chinese invasion of India should be accepted as a part of the cease fire arrangements and implemented on the ground, the boundary differences being negotiated thereafter between the two Prime Ministers. In brief, China will keep what it has secured by this further invasion and is prepared to negotiate on the rest. India can never agree to this position.

The three proposals of the Chinese Government of October 24, 1962, have been examined carefully and in detail. The result of the examination is

15. Item 247.

given in the memorandum that I am attaching to this letter. The memorandum speaks for itself.

You have mentioned in your letter that according to the Chinese proposals, the Chinese armed forces will have to withdraw by more than 20 kilometers from their present positions and that the fact that the Chinese Government have taken as its basis the 1959 "line of actual control" and not the present "line of actual control" between the armed forces of the two sides, is full proof that the Chinese side has not tried to force any unilateral demand on the Indian side on account of the advances gained in what you still choose to call "recent counter attacks in self-defence". What you call the 1959 "line of actual control" was no line but a series of positions of Chinese forces on Indian territory in Ladakh progressively established since 1957, which forcibly and unilaterally altered the status quo of the boundary. This was done even while assuring us since 1954 that China had no territorial claims against India. So far as the Central sector is concerned, the Chinese forces were always to the north of the Himalayan watershed ridge which is the traditional and customary boundary in this area.

The analysis given in the attached note will, however, show that even this 7th November, 1959 line of actual control is projected three years ahead to be identical with the line of actual control established by your forces since the massive attack on 20th October, 1962. Surely this must be clear to all concerned. To advance a few hundred kilometres and then offer to withdraw 20 kilometres is, as anybody can see, hardly a constructive proposal based on mutual accommodation. Your present proposal in brief amounts in broad terms to this because India had been pressing China to remedy the forcible alteration of the status quo since 1957 in the Western sector, China has undertaken since 8th September, deliberately and in cold blood, a further massive aggression and occupied larger areas of Indian territory and is now making the magnanimous offer of retaining the gains of the earlier aggression plus such other gains as it can secure by negotiations from the latest aggression on the basis of the Chinese three point proposals. If this is not the assumption of the attitude of a victor, I do not know what else it can be. This is a demand to which India will never submit whatever the consequences and however long and hard the struggle may be. We cannot do less than this if we are going to maintain the principles we cherish, namely, peace, good neighbourliness and peaceful coexistence with all our neighbours including China. To do otherwise would mean mere existence at the mercy of an aggressive, arrogant and expansionist neighbour.

Despite the crisis of confidence created by the earlier Chinese aggression, we are, as I said in my letter of 27th October, prepared to consider entering into talks and discussions to deal with our differences and to re-establish good neighbourly relations on the basis of peaceful coexistence between our two countries, each following its own way of life, provided it was agreed that the status quo along the entire boundary as it prevailed before 8th September, 1962, should be restored. This is the minimum corrective action necessary. The damage to the very principles of good neighbourliness and peaceful coexistence done by the further aggression since 8th September, 1962, must be corrected before any other constructive step can be taken.

You have referred to the peaceful friendly relations between our two countries till 1959 despite the differences on the boundary question and asked why we could not have these relations after 1959 despite the differences on the boundary question. The reason I feel should be clear to you. It was in January 1959 that you put forward a claim for 50,000 square miles of Indian territory under the guise of a boundary dispute. This was not a small adjustment of the boundary here or there involving a few hundred square miles but a demand for surrender of large areas of Indian territory. You did not stop at this preposterous demand. Though we agreed to talks and discussions at various levels to examine the relevant historical, cartographic and other data on the subject, your forces continued to forcibly occupy substantial areas of Indian territory even while these talks and discussions were going on. This process continued throughout the subsequent years and, on 8th September 1962, your forces started the further aggression in the Eastern sector which had been quiet and peaceful all these twelve years except for the minor differences over Longju.

In your letters as well as in the official note of your Government, there are references to the line of actual control as on 7th November 1959, as the basis of the three-point proposals. If the Chinese Government really mean what they say regarding the restoration of 7th November 1959 positions of their forces in all sectors of the boundary, their withdrawal to those positions and the restoration of the positions of the Indian forces as they were prior to 8th September 1962, would, by and large, meet the problem of disengagement as there will be enough distances between the position of the forces of the two sides to prevent any risk of a clash. To put it concretely, in the Eastern sector the Chinese forces will go back to the positions they held on 7th November 1959, that is, they will be on the other side of the boundary along the Himalayan watershed which they first crossed on 8th September 1962. In the Central sector the position will be the same, that is, they will be to the north of the highest watershed ridge. In the Western sector the Chinese forces will go back to the positions they held on 7th November 1959, as given in the attached note, that is, along the line connecting their Spanggur post, Khurnak Fort and Kongka La and then northwards to join the main Aksai Chin Road. The Indian forces will go back to the various defence posts they occupied in all the three sectors prior to 8th September 1962. This arrangement will secure not only adequate disengagement of forces of both sides but will not in any way prejudge either the alignment of the customary and traditional boundary in the Western and the Central sectors as claimed by the two sides or the alignment of the Mc Mahon line Boundary in the Eastern sector.

You have, Mr Prime Minister, referred in your letter to the appeal made by Asian-African countries. I agree that this appeal should evoke a constructive response. You must have seen in this connection the four-point suggestion made by the President of the UAR mentioned in the UAR Presidential communiqué of 31st October and my message to the President of the UAR dated 27th October.[16]

Please accept, Your Excellency, the assurances of my highest consideration.

Memorandum

The implications of the three-point proposal of the Chinese Government presented on the 24th of October and further elaborated upon in Prime Minister Chou En-Lai's letter dated 4th November, 1962, are given below:

Western Sector: The line of actual control in November 1959 was no line but a series of positions of Chinese forces on Indian territory. These positions had been progressively established since 1957 by forcibly and unilaterally altering the traditional status quo of the boundary, even while the Government of China were assuring the Government of India that they had no territorial claims against India. In November 1959, Chinese posts in the Western sector were at Spanggur, Khurnak Fort, Kongka La and along the main Aksai Chin Road. Within three years i.e. by September, 1962, the Chinese had constructed a large network of military roads and posts, beginning with posts opposite Daulat Beg Oldhi in the north, along the Chip Chap river valley and across the Galwan river to the Pangong and Spanggur lake areas. At certain points the network of military posts was more than one hundred miles to the west of Chinese positions in 1959.

The Chinese three-point proposal, taken with its clarifications, is that, in the Western sector, both parties agree to respect the "line of actual control" between the two sides. In his clarificatory letter Premier Chou En-lai states that "the line of actual control" is basically still the line of actual control as existed between the Chinese and the Indian sides in November 1959." The normal deduction would be that this line of control would, therefore, be a line connecting Spanggur, Khurnak Fort, Kongka La and proceeding northwards to

16. See item 389 and appendix 56.

join the main Aksai Chin Road. However, Premier Chou En-lai's letter states that "in the Western and Middle Sectors it (the line of actual control) coincides in the main with the traditional customary line". In short, while referring to the line of control as it existed in 1959, the Chinese actually project it to the line they claimed in the meeting between the officials of the two sides in 1960 and the line they physically hold now since their massive attack which commenced in this region on 20th October, 1962. This line not only includes all the Chinese posts established in the three years since 1959, but also includes all the Indian posts in the territory that existed till 30th October 1962, and extends even farther westwards, thus taking in an additional 5000 to 6000 square miles since their 7th November 1959 position.

According to the Chinese proposal, after this "line of actual control" is determined, India would have to further withdraw yet another 20 kilometers inside territory accepted by the Chinese as undoubtedly Indian, while the Chinese withdrawal of 20 kilometres would be only 20 kilometres inside Indian territory claimed by them leaving the Chinese forces well over a hundred kilometres deep into territory belonging to India. The total effect of this would be that the entire network of Chinese aggressive posts which existed on 20th October 1962, and some more would remain intact poised for a further attack, while all Indian defence posts in Indian territory claimed by China will be eliminated and even posts in territory accepted as Indian including much key posts as Daulat Beg Oldhi, Chushul and Hanle would be dismantled and eliminated.

Middle Sector: In the middle sector, the suggestion that the "line of actual control" whether on 7th November 1959 or now, coincides only "in the main" with the traditional and customary boundary is absolutely without foundation. The Chinese Government have never had any authority south of the main Himalayan watershed ridge, which is the traditional boundary in this sector. Some Tibetan officials along with some Chinese troops did intrude into Barahoti on various occasions since 1954; and, in 1958, the two Governments agreed to withdraw their armed personnel from the locality. But Indian civilian personnel have throughout been functioning in the area. A conference held in 1958 to discuss the question made clear that the Chinese Government had not even precise knowledge of the area they were claiming.

Eastern Sector: In the Eastern sector the Chinese Government are willing to withdraw their troops to the north of the "line of actual control". This "line of actual control" has been clarified in Premier Chou En-lai's letter as coinciding "in the main" with the McMahon Line. The Chinese Government by this ambiguous statement indicate that there are portions of the "line of actual control" as envisaged by them which do not coincide with the McMahon Line. These divergences have not, however, that Chinese positions have always remained to the north of the highest Himalayan ridge in the Eastern sector of the India-China border and the alignment of the McMahon Line has never been questioned by China. The Chinese were nowhere in the vicinity of this watershed boundary either in November, 1959 or later till 8th September, 1962, when they started their aggression into Indian territory in this region.

Premier Chou En-lai has in his letter referred to the 1914 original map of the McMahon Line and the coordinates given in this map. The Agreement of 1914 only formalised what was the traditional and customary boundary in the area which lies along the highest Himalayan watershed ridges. The maps attached to the Agreement were of small scale of 1 inch to 8 miles. They were sketch maps and intended to be only illustrative. All that they made clear was that the boundary ran along the main watershed ridges of the area. The parallels and meridians were shown only approximately in accordance with the progress achieved at that time in the sphere of scientific surveys. This is a common cartographic feature and the Chinese Government have themselves recognised this in Article 48 of their 1960 Treaty with Burma. If the maps and the co-ordinates given therein were taken literally it is impossible to explain the discrepancy between the existing distances and those given in the map between various villages in the area. Also Migyitun according to the maps is at latitude 28° 38' North while its actual position as ascertained by the latest surveys is much further north. Tulung La has been shown on the 1914 maps at 27° 47' N while its position on the ground is further north of this point. Strict adherence to the co-ordinates shown on the McMahon Line maps would result in advancing the Indian boundary in both the areas of Migyitun and Tulung La further north thereby including both these places inside Indian territory. In the area east of Tsari Sarpa, strict adherence to the coordinates of Lola in the McMahon Line maps would result in advancing the boundary of India into this area by at least 7 miles to the north. This would mean including at least 70 square miles of Tibetan territory within India. The Government of India recognising the principle underlying the McMahon Line agreement that the boundaries line along the highest watershed ridges actually confine their jurisdiction to the area south of this boundary and did not try to take over Tibetan territory beyond the highest watershed ridge on the basis of the inaccurate coordinates given in the 1914 maps. This must be known to the Chinese authorities and yet they ignore this and seek to use the inaccurate coordinates given in the maps when they are favourable to their fanciful claims made to support their latest aggression. The Chinese authorities cannot have it both ways. They cannot accept the highest watershed as the boundary in parts of the Eastern sector where it suits them though this is not consistent with the coordinates given in the 1914 maps and quote the coordinates in these very maps in their favour in other parts of the sector to make demands for territorial concessions from India.

The Chinese proposal envisages a further withdrawal of 20 kilometres on either side of the McMahon Line as understood by them. This would leave Chinese forces in command of the passes leading into India while Indian forces would be 20 kilometres to the south leaving the entire Indian frontier defenceless and at the mercy of any fresh invasion. The present Chinese invasion which commenced on 8th September, 1962, was known because there was a defence post near the border. If there are no border posts at or near the passes, Chinese aggression could recur without India knowing about it for quite some time.

The objective of the Chinese three-point proposal is to secure for the Chinese side guaranteed occupation of the Indian areas in the Western and Central sectors which they claim while they retain their right to negotiate, and negotiations failing, to enforce, whatever territorial adjustments they want in the Eastern sector.

Western Sector: India should not dispute on the ground, though it will be allowed to talk about its juridical claim, the Chinese occupation of 14,000 square miles of Indian territory including 2,000 square miles forcibly occupied since 20th October 1962. India has to agree not only to respect this so called line of actual control but must also dismantle and withdraw its defences in the region a further 20 kilometres into admittedly Indian territory involving withdrawal from points like Chushul etc.

Middle Sector: The Chinese claims must be fully satisfied so far as physical occupation is concerned.

Eastern Sector: The principles of the highest watershed, which is the boundary and which had been respected till 8th September, 1962, should be given up in favour of whatever interpretation the Government of China decide to put on the McMahon Line. There should be a further withdrawal of 20 kilometres. Thus, India must give up control of the passes in the highest watershed ridges in the areas, with no guarantee that the Chinese side will not cross the actual line of control whichever it may be.

In short, the Chinese three-point proposal, despite the manner in which it is put forth, is a demand for surrender on terms which have to be accepted while the Chinese forces in great strength are occupying large areas of Indian territory which they have acquired since their further aggression which commenced on 8th September, 1962, and the massive attack which they started on 20th October, 1962.

250. To N. Sri Rama Reddy: Possible Action[17]

November 15, 1962

My dear Sri Rama Reddy,

Your letter of the 15th November. I think you have somewhat misunderstood me. When I said that China could not defeat us ultimately nor could we defeat China, I meant this in the ultimate sense, that is to say, India surrendering to them and their dictating terms of peace or China surrendering to us and our practically dictating terms of peace to them. It is obvious that great countries do not surrender, even though they may suffer any number of defeats, until they are completely exhausted. We are not going to and cannot march into China proper and into Peking, nor do I think that China is capable of marching to Delhi.

This does not preclude our pushing them back from Indian soil completely. Indeed, I think we can do so and I hope this will be done, though it may take a little time. Nor do I mean that peace efforts are futile. What I said was that their peace offensives at present are traps for us; but peace always comes after the bloodiest war and it may well be that the pressures on China, partly due to our efforts and partly to world conditions may be such that they retire completely from our territory.

As for the nuclear bomb, it is a possibility that the Chinese may have a test in a year or two.[18] That does not mean that they can use it. They will require another several years to be in a position to use it. I do not think there is the slightest chance of such a bomb being used against India, apart from the time element. The use of such a bomb would involve all kinds of consequences which should be very serious for China.

---

17. Letter to Rajya Sabha MP, Congress; address: 122 South Avenue, New Delhi.
18. China's first test was on 16 October 1964.

What you suggest we should try to do in a year or two is neither feasible nor desirable except in so far as we try to drive out the Chinese from Indian soil completely. Of course, much can be done to weaken China's position in other ways. Much is happening indeed and is likely to happen to that end.

Yours sincerely,
[Jawaharlal Nehru]

251. To Lal Bahadur Shastri: Chinese Propaganda in Dehra Dun[19]

November 16, 1962

My dear Lal Bahadur,

G.S. Pathak[20] has sent me the enclosed paper. This has been issued apparently by the Chinese Embassy. Pathak says it was being distributed among the workers at Dehra Dun.

Yours affectionately,
Jawaharlal

252. In the Rajya Sabha: Chinese Cease Fire Announcement[21]

The Prime Minister (Jawaharlal Nehru): Mr Chairman, Sir, in view of certain developments that have taken place in the last few hours, I would like to make a brief statement to the House.

The Government of the People's Republic of China, it appears through radio broadcasts, has announced that they will have a ceasefire from midnight of the 21-22 November, and will start withdrawing their forces from the positions they occupy, from the 1st December. This is a unilateral announcement. We have thus far received no official confirmation of it. As soon as we receive any official message from the Chinese Government, we shall give it full consideration. Till then I would not like to express any opinion in regard to the Chinese proposals.

---

19. Letter to the Home Minister. MHA, File No. 4/34/62-Poll (I), p. 1/c.
20. (1896-1982); Rajya Sabha MP, Congress.
21. Statement on Chinese Cease fire Announcement, *Rajya Sabha Debates*, Vol. XLI, Nos. 9-21, 20 November to 6 December 1962, pp. 1969-1973. See also notes in Announcement of Chinese Cease fire in item 253.

Our position in regard to any negotiations continues to be what we have previously stated, that is, that the position as it existed prior to September 8, 1962, shall be restored.

We shall continue our efforts to obtain aid from friendly countries and strengthen our country's defences and its economic potential. We would like to express again our gratitude to the many friendly countries who have offered us aid and sympathy and support during the time of distress. We have made it clear previously and we repeat it, that we have no desire for any territorial expansion in any direction and our aim is to live in peace and amity with our neighbours.

A.B. Vajpayee[22] (Uttar Pradesh): Sir, in view of the Chinese offer, which could well be a deceptive offer, made to confuse world opinion, and lull India again into complacency, may I suggest that the decision to adjourn the present session of Parliament of the 23rd of this month be reversed, and that Parliament should be constantly in session till this new peace offensive is dealt with? Secondly, before arriving at a final decision with regard to the latest offer, may I submit that the Government should consult and should have exchange of views with all sections of public opinion so that the decision may be a national decision as such?

An Hon. Member: That will be a national decision.

Ganga Sharan Sinha[23] (Bihar): While associating myself with what my hon. Friend here has said just now, I would like to say that some steps should be taken to see that this offer of the Chinese, about a cease fire does not create any lull or any relaxation in our efforts, either in the Government's efforts or in the public mind. Special efforts should be made for that and the necessary steps should be taken, because everybody is not in Delhi. We in Parliament are sitting before the Prime Minister and know, but many people outside may have an entirely different impression. So, we should take special steps to let the country know what the Government is thinking and what the Prime Minister has said just now. This must be known to everybody in the land. Secondly, so far as our final decision is concerned, I would request the Prime Minister that before a final decision is taken, Parliament should be taken into confidence. At the same time, we would request him that in making a final decision, I would personally like—and I think all hon. Members also would like—that those who have come to

22. Jana Sangh.
23. Independent.

our aid in hour of need should also be taken into confidence and I do hope our Prime Minister will keep these things in view.

I would also request the Prime Minister to continue this session of the Parliament so that it may keep up the morale of the country and everything will be much more sober and it will be useful from the point of view of the safety and solidarity of the country. Therefore, I suggest that this session of the Parliament should continue.

Jawaharlal Nehru: I have already stated, Sir, that I do not propose at this stage to give any full reaction to the Chinese proposals. We have not received them officially, not even unofficially, but long statements issued by the Chinese Government have been heard on the radio. They require full consideration, of course, before we can have a full picture. I do not know how many hon. Members have had the opportunity to listen to those long, long statements. And in a matter of this kind, no government worth its name should without consideration come to a decision.

Now, that decision will have to be on the lines that we have always stated and they have been recently discussed in this House. The general principles are decided by Parliament and on them the Government functions. The hon. Member has said that we should, before we do what we do, have some kind of a public debate. This is a very remarkable suggestion which will be quite unique in diplomatic history. In a matter of this kind, principles are laid down, but we cannot consider the notes that we send or receive in this public or semi-public way. It would be very unusual and possibly not very profitable.

As for the hon. Members suggestion that we should continue our efforts, even in the statement I made just now, I said that we propose to do it that we shall continue our efforts to obtain aid from friendly countries and strengthen our country's defences and the economic potential of this country. All that we propose to do fully.

The hon. Member also said something about consulting other countries. We are in close touch with many of our friends in other countries and we shall continue to remain in close touch. We do not propose to consult them about every decision we arrive at, every letter or note that we may send to another foreign country. But we are in close touch and we shall continue to be in close touch with them.

Ganga Sharan Sinha: I did not mean that they should be consulted on every one of our letters and notes or on every matter. But in coming to a final conclusion they should be taken into confidence and we should consult them.

Jawaharlal Nehru: There is one thing more. As for the suggestion that this House, that Parliament should continue to sit, that is entirely for the House and for you, Sir, to determine. But I would point out that it is not a question of two or three days' extra sitting, because we may come to a provisional conclusion and it may be finalised later on, after seeing what they do. They themselves say that they will withdraw and begin withdrawing on the 1st December. I do not know whether they are going to give effect to that or in what manner they are going to give effect to it. So, it may be necessary for us to see that. Apart from any provisional conclusions that we may arrive at after considering their proposals fully, it may be necessary for us to watch what they do. What I mean to say is that this is going to be not a thing which could be decided in two or three days. It may take a much longer period and in considering whether this House should continue to sit or not, that should be kept in mind.

253. In the Lok Sabha: Chinese Cease Fire Announcement[24]

Jawaharlal Nehru: Sir, I should like to make a brief statement in regard to certain developments that have taken place.

The Government of the People's Republic of China, it appears from Radio broadcasts, has announced that they will have ceasefire from midnight of 21/22 November and will start withdrawing their forces from the positions they occupied from the 1st December. This is a unilateral announcement. We have thus far received no official confirmation of it. As soon as we receive any official message from the Chinese Government, we shall give it full consideration. Till then I would not like to express any opinion in regard to the Chinese proposals. Our position in regard to any negotiations continues to be what we have previously stated, that is, that the position as it existed prior to September 8, 1962 shall be restored. We shall continue our efforts to obtain aid from friendly countries and strengthen our county's defences and its economic potential.[25]

---

24. Statement on Chinese Cease fire, *Lok Sabha Debates*, Third Series, Vol. X, November 21 to December 4, 1962, pp. 2689-90, 2700-02.
25. "On 21 October 1962, 00:00 hours Peking time, Peking Radio announced that from 00:00 hours 22 November 1962, the Chinese frontier guards would cease fire all along the Sino-Indian border. From 1 December 1962, the Frontier guards would withdraw 20 kilometres behind the 1959 Line of Actual Control." *Peking Review*, vols. 47 and 48, 30 November 1962, p.5. See also appendix 62.

We should like to express again our gratitude to the many friendly countries who have offered us aid and sympathy and support during the time of our distress.

We have made it clear previous and we repeat that we have no desire for any territorial expansion in any direction and our aim is to leave in peace and amity with our neighbours.

[Omitted: exchanges on procedure]

Jawaharlal Nehru: In the little statement that I made a little while ago, I have stated that we shall consider any communication from the Chinese Government carefully and then express an opinion about it. I have not gone into it and there is much that can be said in regard to it. Other hon. Members have given their first reactions and I have listened to them. But in a matter of this kind or any serious kind, Government has to think carefully all aspects of it and then form an opinion and give effect to it. I do not wish to say more. There is only one matter the hon. Member Shri Kamath talked about my broadcast the other day as if there has been any change in my submission to this House here or broadcast anywhere. We said some time ago, after careful thought that the position prior to the 8th September should be restored; to that we have stuck all along; to that we stick even now...

Priya Gupta[26]: 8th September? People of India do not want that. In the main Resolution they hold Prime Minister never said so...

Speaker: Order, order.

Jawaharlal Nehru: I am merely stating what our position has been in regard to this matter and we do not shift it about every 24 hours. I think it is a good position and strong position and, as I have said before, we do not propose to consider negotiations till that position is restored. Negotiations themselves will be in various stages and when it comes the first thing will be how to create the conditions which will enable negotiations.... (Interruptions).

Priya Gupta: It has cost us. There cannot be negotiations at the cost of our country's prestige and honours.

[Omitted: Exchanges on procedure]

26. PSP, from Katihar, Bihar.

Jawaharlal Nehru: A suggestion has been made by one or two hon. Members that before we communicate and reply to the Chinese Government we should have it discussed here. I am afraid this is a very novel procedure. General principles are discussed here and we are guided by whatever the House may decide. But to discuss these communications between one Government and another would be a very extraordinary thing; and it is a very undesirable and harmful thing. We cannot carry on communications with Governments in that way.

Fourthly, an hon. Member has suggested that Parliament may be prolonged. That is entirely for you and the House to decide. It is not for me to say. But I would suggest this, we have not only to consider carefully any communication that comes to us from the Chinese Government, but also to find out and watch how they are giving effect to it before we can form an opinion. Even according to them—apart from the ceasefire which will be from tonight onwards—they will start withdrawing on the 1st December, and therefore, in order to watch what they do, it will involve some little time. It is not a question of extension by a few days, of Parliament. That is all I wish to submit.

Hari Vishnu Kamath[27]: I crave your pardon, Sir. The resolution that the House adopted the other day made no reference to the 8th September line. That is all that I want to say.

254. In the Lok Sabha: Cease fire[28]

Hari Vishnu Kamath[29] (Hoshangabad): Before you proceed, Sir, may I appeal to you to request the Prime Minister to make a brief statement on the war situation now, particularly with reference to that part of the Chinese Government's announcement that they would cease fire or would have ceased fire last midnight, midnight of 21st-22nd. We want to know whether there is any information available here in Delhi, in the External Affairs Ministry or not.

The Prime Minister and Minister of External Affairs and the Minister of Atomic Energy (Jawaharlal Nehru): Such information as we have got is to the effect that there has been no firing since last night.

---

27. PSP, from Hoshangabad.
28. Question Session, *Lok Sabha Debates*, Third Series, Vol. X, November 21 to December 4, 1962, pp. 2932-34.
29. PSP.

Hari Vishnu Kamath: Midnight?

Jawaharlal Nehru: There has been no firing—midnight or before that.[30]

Hem Barua[31] (Gauhati): May I know the exact position where the Chinese troops are now located so far as NEFA is concerned? Are they at the Foothills now or have they crossed Foothills? I want to know the exact location of Chinese at present.

Jawaharlal Nehru: I do not think they are at the Foothills; they are some way beyond that.

Hem Barua: There is a place called Foothills.

Jawaharlal Nehru: I know. They are not there.

255. For the National Broadcasting Company[32]

No Non-Alignment vis-à-vis China
Talks to be backed by Strength: PM

New York, Dec. 5 – Prime Minister Nehru has declared in a television interview: "There is no non-alignment vis-à-vis China." The filmed interview, recorded earlier in New Delhi was broadcast by NBC over its national network last night.

Questioned on the future of non-alignment, the Prime Minister said he still thought non-alignment a good policy for India, but it was true that Chinese aggression had weakened the idea in the minds of some countries. Moreover, non-alignment or Panch Sheel could not stand in the air. He added: "There is no non-alignment vis-à-vis China; there is no Panch Sheel vis-à-vis China. In spite of their loud talk, they broke it up." Pandit Nehru said whatever happened (even if the Chinese withdrew to the positions prior to September 8 and negotiations began) India's military preparations would continue.

"We have had rather bad shocks, and we do not propose to be careless or somnolent about matters. We shall continue our military preparations."

---

30. See appendix 64.
31. PSP.
32. Report of interview, reproduced from the *National Herald*, 6 December 1962, p.1. The interview was recorded on 27 November at 7 p.m. at the Prime Minister's House. NMML, Engagement Diary.

He expressed confidence that ultimately the Indian Army would drive them out from the NEFA area and very considerable portion of Ladakh—I cannot say the whole of Ladakh, because although we like to and try to ... long before that stage arises, we may have conditions favourable to us for talks with them."

Talks backed by Strength

Earlier, the Prime Minister said that even if India had to negotiate with China the "negotiations must be backed by strength and we have to build up our strength for that purpose; and we propose to do so." The Prime Minister said India had not yet thought of accepting American military advisory groups for training and other activities. "If the necessity arises, we shall take advisers", he added. He said he did not think any political considerations would come in, specially in respect of small advisory groups for training purposes, particularly of specialty weapons. It might be somewhat different if large numbers of people come.

Issue to UN

Asked about taking the Sino-Indian conflict to the United Nations, Pandit Nehru said: "We have not taken it. That does not mean we shall never take it."

China, Pandit Nehru said, was now making tremendous efforts by diplomatic contacts and publicity, which was not truthful, to influence Afro-Asian countries. However, India was getting tremendous sympathy and support from most of these countries. In the beginning, to some extent they hesitated to express their opinion because many of them wanted to mediate but later, realising what was happening, they have been clear in expressing sympathy to India, he added.

Soviet Attitude

On the attitude of the Soviet Union, the Prime Minister said that while the Russians had not done anything in a demonstrative way yet. It was a fact that the Russians were very friendly to India. Apart from the help they had given in building a steel plant, etc., there was something deeper he said.

He said that even in the present Sino-Indian crisis, during the last two or three years when the controversy grew, they refused to take the Chinese side, though pressed.

Answering further questions of the correspondent, Pandit Nehru said Pravda's first article had certainly disappointed India somewhat. But the later version was somewhat different. "Apparently they had pulled themselves for whatever reason they thought proper".

At present the Soviets were laying stress chiefly on "somehow or other there should begin negotiations", Pandit Nehru said.

Pandit Nehru said he did not expect "very much more" help from Russia, although the Soviet Union had been consistently friendly for the past several years. PTI and Reuter.

US Aid to Pak[33]

Asked about this earlier criticismof the United States military aid to Pakistan and the latter's current criticism of the US aid to India, Mr Nehru said he thought he was justified about past criticism, and "the present situation has partly proved my case."

He said American military aid was given to Pakistan for a particular purpose and not to be used against India. "Instead of that purpose their whole outlook appears to have changed."

Mr Nehru added: "Now it is a most extra ordinary situation that they are praising Communist China and blaming us and the United States for helping us with equipment. It is really quite extra ordinary. In a way they have fallen into the Chinese trap."

"I do not know what the Chinese have promised them. There are bizarre rumours, as you know, that they have been promised by the Chinese chunks of India in the east."

He Said, "Surely it is obvious any threat from outside to us is bound to be a threat to them."

(b) CHINESE INVASION: Explanation and Strategy

256. To Chief Ministers[34]

October 21, 1962

My dear Chief Minister,

The last two or three days have brought very disturbing news about the situation on our frontiers. As I write to you, we have not yet received any accurate information of this situation. But it is clear that the Chinese forces have attacked us all along the frontier in the NEFA and Ladakh in great numbers

---

33. This portion of the same interview has been reproduced from a report in *The Hindu*, 7 December 1962, p.1.
34. Letter to all Chief Ministers and the Prime Minister of Jammu and Kashmir.

and have dislodged positions that our forces had taken up at various places. They have been advancing. We do not yet know what our casualties or the Chinese casualties have been. But one of our helicopters used for removal of casualties has been shot down, and another is missing. In the Ladakh sector, one of our transport planes was shot at by the Chinese, but managed to return safely to its base.

The Chinese are issuing statement after statement trying to show that it was the Indian forces that organised a large scale attack on them in all the sectors and that they acted only in defense. It is amazing to what lengths the Chinese are going in disseminating utterly false accounts. In view of the overwhelming forces that the Chinese had with them, accompanied by artillery, mountain guns and automatics, we could not afford to carry out any large scale attack. Our instructions were to defend our line to the best of our ability.

As a matter of fact, the Chinese Government issued a statement at about 7 a.m. (Peking time) on the 20th October stating that the Indian forces had attacked them in large numbers.[35] It was only some time after this that the major attack of the Chinese started. It has become a habit for the Chinese to blame others for what they propose to do.

Anyhow, the fact remains that Chinese have attacked us with overwhelming strength and fire power, and this has led to a grave setback to our forces in NEFA where they have captured some of our posts and driven back our forces. In the Ladakh sector, some of our minor posts have also been captured by them. The position is a fluid one, rather to our disadvantage.

We are taking all possible steps to check this Chinese advance and have sent additional forces there. It is clear that the situation that has arisen is one of gravity and danger to India and its integrity.

It would be foolish for me to prophesy what further developments may take place in the near future. But about one thing we are certain: that we must throw all our strength and determination in resisting this blatant attack and aggression on India by the Chinese. We propose to do so. At the same time it must be realised that the situation before us is a difficult one and that it is likely to continue for a long time. Indeed, we must be prepared for a lengthy struggle which will affect India in various ways, even apart from the purely military aspect of it.

We have not declared war against China and we do not intend doing so at present or in the foreseeable future. Any such declaration of war is not beneficial to us in any way and would lead to far-reaching consequences. But the fact is

35. See "Note of the Chinese Government, 20 October 1962", *White Paper*, Vol.VII, pp. 123-124.

that we are in military conflict with the Chinese, and all the consequences of this conflict will be borne by us. We have thus to prepare ourselves in every way not only to carry on this conflict to its successful conclusion, but also to face the other consequences that may arise from it. Whatever happens, we cannot surrender to the Chinese aggression or bow down to it. However long a time it may take us, we shall fight with all our strength against this outrageous aggression on our territory.

The Chinese go on making statements which are so manifestly false that it is difficult to keep pace with this distortion of facts. They say that we have committed aggression on their territory, that our military aircraft are being used in the fighting, and that they had not crossed the McMahon Line which now, according to them, is not the high Himalayan watershed that we claim, but somewhat further south.[36] It is apparently their habit to consider every place that they have occupied by aggression as their territory. The fact is that neither our soldiers nor our planes have gone into Chinese territory or air space. Further, that no military aircraft has been used in these border encounters. We have used transport planes and helicopters to drop supplies or to remove casualties.

As for the so called McMahon Line, it is clearly stated in the old Treaty that the high ridge of the watershed of the Himalayas is the international frontier. The map attached to the Treaty is on a very small scale, and the line drawn covers a few miles in that scale. It is quite absurd to say that, in spite of the clear definition in the Treaty, the actual frontier is further south of it because the Line covers a few miles in a small scale map.

Apart from this, we have been long in possession of this area and the Treaty itself is nearly 50 years old.

But I need not go into these arguments because you know them and do not require to be convinced. The position now is that a full scale invasion by Chinese forces is taking place both in the eastern border and the northern, and we have to face it, whatever ups and downs there may be in the struggle.

It is a tragedy that we, who have stood for peace everywhere, should be attacked in this way and be compelled to resist attack by arms. But there is no help for it. No self respecting nation can tolerate this kind of aggression, and we will certainly not do so. I cannot say how long it may take us to clear our territory from the aggressors. However long that may be, we have to work to that and with resolution and the determination to achieve our objective.

It is not enough for us to say that and to shout slogans. We have to prepare for it and throw in all our strength and resources. We have been too long used

36. See Notes of Chinese Government of 11 and 17 October 1962; *White Paper*, Vol.VII, pp.141, 143.

to a relatively quiet and peaceful life and are not accustomed to meet such situations with speed. Even in the last two great wars, India did not come into the picture much, although our soldiers took part in them. We have now to face a dangerous crisis, such as we have not had since independence. Our procedures are slow moving. These have to be vitalised and speeded up. No military struggle can be carried on with slow civil procedures. We shall have to spend much money in procuring supplies and in adding to our forces.

We shall have to think of the economic aspect of all this and to introduce measures to control any untoward development. I am writing to you now in barest outline of the problem that faces us and asking you to make your colleagues and others realise the significance of it. We have to concentrate on this great struggle which threatens our integrity and freedom. Everything else will have to take second place. This is a matter which cannot be dealt with on party lines. It is a supreme national issue, and every person who is an Indian must realise his duty in this crisis. We must, therefore, concentrate on building up this unity to face this invasion of India and try to put aside, as far as we can, controversial matters. We have to create a sensation all over India that we stand together to oppose this invasion and shall continue to do so till we have freed India from the aggressor. This may be a long process. But, however long it may be and whatever temporary reverses we may suffer from, we must be determined to win.

We have felt no ill-will against the Chinese people. In international matters, we have often helped the Chinese Government. It has been a matter of great grief to me that, in spite of the friendly attitude to them, the Chinese Government should have paid us back by aggression and calumny. The Chinese newspapers are full of the utmost vituperation, against India and the Government of India.[37]

I do not want even now for us to indulge in calumny and vituperation, or to encourage hatred against a people. We must view the situation calmly and without panic or hysteria. But that calmness must be accompanied by a firm determination. China is a great and powerful country with enormous resources. But India is no weak country to be frightened by threats and military might. We shall build up our strength, both military and economic, to win this battle of Indian freedom. We shall always be willing to negotiate a peace, but that can only be on conditions that aggression is vacated. We can never submit or surrender to aggression. That has not been our way, and that will not be our way in the future.

37. Nehru is reacting in particular to an editorial in *Renmin Ribao*, 14 October 1962, entitled, "Mr Nehru, It is High Time for you to pull back from the Brink of the Precipice", reproduced in *Peking Review*, Vol.V, No.42, 19 October 1962, p.6.

We shall have to take measures in regard to prices going up etc. I would like you to think about these matters also and be wide awake so that no untoward happening takes place. There must, of course, be no panicky reaction to events. That is a sign of weakness.

Above all, I would beg of you to avoid controversial issues and to concentrate on the unity of the nation and our united resolve to meet this menace together and with full strength. I am sure that all parties will feel this way. It is always to be stressed that this is a national issue demanding the service of every Indian, to whatever group or party he might belong.

Yours sincerely,
[Jawaharlal Nehru]

257. Talk with PSP Leaders[38]

Chinese will be Repulsed
No Need for Panic, Says PM

New Delhi, Oct. 21 – Prime Minister Nehru today told two PSP members of Parliament, Mr H.V. Kamath and Mr Hem Barua, that recent "reverses", on the northern borders, should in no way cause alarm or panic because the army would take action to repulse the Chinese and regain the lost position.

Mr Kamath and Mr Barua met the Prime Minister here this morning.

Mr Kamath and Mr Barua told pressmen that while Pandit Nehru admitted that the armed forces had suffered certain reverses, he (Pandit Nehru) was of the view that the conflict with China "will probably be a long drawn affair."

The PSP leaders said that Pandit Nehru explained the present position in NEFA and Ladakh and said that the Chinese had penetrated three to four miles inside NEFA.

Summoning of Parliament

The PSP leaders had suggested to Pandit Nehru that as the country was "practically at war though undeclared", it was very necessary that Parliament should be summoned at the earliest, not later than November 5.

They said they got the impression that Pandit Nehru was seriously considering such a step. The Prime Minister had already given such an indication in his letter to Mr Kamath dated September 28.[39]

---

38. Report, reproduced from the *National Herald*, Oct 22, 1962, p. 1.
39. See SWJN/SS/78/ item 420.

Asked whether in the context of an undeclared war, severance of diplomatic relations with China was necessary or desirable, Pandit Nehru told the two leaders that the matter would have to be carefully considered in the light of the consequences that might possibly ensue from such a step.

The matter should therefore be left to the Government to judge and decide keeping in mind the various aspects of the questions, Pandit Nehru was said to have added.

On the situation on the border Pandit Nehru was reported to have said that China was at present in a position to bring up troops and supplies in lorries and trucks by road up to two to three miles of the fighting line while India had to depend on airdropping. India had however built and was building roads in that region and he was confident that they would soon overcome the present difficulties.

Danger to Bhutan

Asked whether there was any danger of attack on Bhutan, Pandit Nehru told the PSP leaders, that Chinese troops were only fifteen miles from Bhutan border but he could not say what their intentions were.

Replying to a question Pandit Nehru is reported to have remarked that perhaps the Chinese were concentrating on NEFA area with a view to strengthening their bargaining position in Ladakh.

Mr Kamath and Mr Barua also asked the Prime Minister whether without any shift in the policy pursued so far in acquiring military equipment the acceptance of any offer of aid without strings would be improper orundesirable.

Pandit Nehru told them that India was at present purchasing arms from different countries and there was no need to consider the matter from any other angle.

Mr Kamath and Mr Barua pointed out that China was often ahead of India in her news broadcasts over Peking Radio.

Pandit Nehru replied that the Chinese technique was to serve the news of an incident even before it took place and cited as an example the latest happenings in NEFA.[40]

Further, Pandit Nehru added, the Chinese had the habit of ascribing their sins to India in order to provide a cover for their own actions.

Pandit Nehru was said to have agreed with the view expressed by the PSP leaders that the Plan[41] might have to be pruned in order to raise more resources for defence purposes.

40. The reference is to the 20th October morning attack news by BBC before the attack actually took place. The *Times of India* 23 October 1962, p.1, col.6.
41. The Third Five Year Plan.

People's Committees

The PSP leaders suggested that people's committees should be set up at the state and if possible, at the district levels, to make the people aware of the danger and mobilise them both psychologically and physically, cooperation of all the parties should be sought in the task. The PSP offered its full cooperation in this.

They drew Pandit Nehru's attention to the latest resolution of the Communist Party on the border situation and suggested that it should be "watched". Pandit Nehru said that the party Chairman, Mr Dange,[42] had tried to explain the resolution, though it was only one side of it.[43]

258. In New Delhi: Interview to BBC[44]

Prime Minister Nehru said, in a BBC television interview broadcast here tonight, that India would not ask for Western military aid in her frontier conflict with Peoples, China. But, he added, India would buy military material from the West.

Mr Nehru said that the present conflict was most serious—it amounted to a war, even though there has been no declaration of war.

The Indian Defence Minister, Mr Krishna Menon, also interviewed, described the Chinese actions on the frontier as total aggression against India.

The interview with Mr Nehru and Mr Menon was recorded in New Delhi last night. Asked what the attitude of the Communist Powers towards the Sino-Indian conflict was likely to be, Mr Nehru replied, "So far they have been silent, but we hope that they will have an understanding of our position."

Mr Nehru said he thought the conflict would be a long-drawn out one. The fact that the Chinese had announced the fighting even before it started, he

---

42. S.A. Dange became Chairman of CPI after Ajay Ghose's death in January 1962.
43. While Dange said in a press conference that "the Chinese have violated the McMahon line," the General Secretary, E.M.S. Namboodripad said it was a border dispute which should have a negotiated settlement in his answer. Reported in the *Times of India*, 18 October 1962; p.1, col.6.
44. Report of interview of 21 October 1962. Reproduced from *The Hindu*, 24 October 1962.

stressed, showed that their action was premeditated and prepared.[45] He added that the present situation was the result of the peculiar Chinese habit of saying one thing and meaning something different. As long as that continued, one never knew where one stood with China.

Asked how he explained the outward calm in the Indian capital, Mr Nehru replied: "One gets angry and excited at times, but the situation has become so serious that we have got to be calm."

Mr Menon was asked whether India intended to refer the conflict to the United Nations. He replied that he would not say what would be done in the future, but one factor to consider was that the big powers had kept China out of the UN and referring the border conflict to the UN now would be deciding the question.[46]

Asked if India's position was properly understood in the Western countries, Mr Menon said that one got the impression from press reports there that it was India which had taken on something it could not cope with. What was not realised, he declared, was that it was China which had entered Indian territory by force and continued to occupy it, and India was trying to regain its territory.

259. Broadcast to the Nation[47]

भाइयों और बहिनों, साथियों और हमवतनों,

मैं बहुत दिन बाद आपसे रेडियो पर बोल रहा हूँ। लेकिन इस वक़्त मैंने बोलना ज़रूरी समझा, क्योंकि एक अहम हालत है और हमारे सीमा पर ज़बर्दस्त हमले चीनी फ़ौजों ने किए हैं और करते जाते हैं। ऐसी हालत उठी है जिसको हमें पूरी अपनी ताक़त से उसका मुक़ाबला करना है।

हमें इस देश में अमन पसन्द है, शान्ति पसन्द है और शान्ति के तरीक़ों के आदी हैं। हम नहीं आदी हैं लड़ाई की ज़रूरियात के। इसी वजह से और और भी वजूहात हैं।

45. A note to the Indian Embassy by the Ministry of Foreign Affairs, Peking, dated 20 October 1962, stated that "At 7 o'clock (Peking time) in the morning of 20th October the aggressive Indian forces …launched massive attacks against the Chinese frontier guards all along the Keichilang river and in the Khinzemane area." *White Paper*, Vol.VIII, p.123.This was 4.30 a.m. IST. The *Times of India* commented that "it was astonishing that at 4.30 a.m. IST, the BBC broadcast the alleged attack basing its message on a Peking Radio report which had obviously been issued before 4.30 a.m. IST." Which means that "the aggressor, aware of its planned offensive could only have announced the attack half an hour before it was actually made." 23 October 1962, p.1, col.6.
46. See item 246.
47. Speech, 22 October 1962, NMML, AIR Tapes T.S. No. 8805, NM No. 1707.

हमने एक शान्ति के रास्ते पर हम चले हैं और जब लददाख़ पर हमला भी पाचं बरस हुए हुआ था, उस वक़्त भी हमने कोशिश की कोई शान्ति का तस्पीया हो जाय और ऐसा कोई रास्ता हमें मिले। सारी दुनियां में हम शान्ति का कहते थे और ज़ाहिर है, अपने मुल्क में भी चाहते थे। हम जानते हैं कि आजकल के ज़माने में लड़ाई कितनी भयानक है और हमने पूरी अपनी तरफ से कोशिश की कि कोई ऐसी लड़ाई, जो दुनिया को डूबो दे, वह न हो। लेकिन हमारी कोशिशें हमारी ही सरहद पर कामयाब नहीं हुईं जहां एक बहुत ताक़तवर और बेशर्म-दुश्मन जिसको ज़रा फ़िक्र नहीं शान्ति के तरीक़ों की, उसने हमें धमकी दी और उसपर अमल भी किया। इसलिए वक़्त आ गया है कि हम इस ख़तरे को पूरी तौर से समझें जो कि हमारे मुल्क के लोगों की आज़ादी और हमारे मुल्क की स्वतंत्रता पर हमलावर हैं। मैं इसको कहता हूँ बावजूद इसके कि मुझे पूरा इतमीनान है कि कोई ताक़त ऐसी नहीं है जो हमारी आज़ादी को हम से छीन सके, आख़िर में। जिस आज़ादी को हमने इत्ती मुसीबत से, मेहनत से और त्याग से हासिल किया और बाद बहुत ज़माने के, जब कि हमारा मुल्क औरों की हूकूमत में था। लेकिन इस आज़ादी को और मुल्क के हर हिस्से को मुल्क में रखने के लिए हमें पूरी तैयारी करनी है, कमर कसनी है। और इस वक़्त सामना करना है। इस वक़्त, जो सब से बड़ा ख़तरा हमारे समाने आया है, जब से हम आज़ाद हुए हैं, मुझे कोई शक नहीं कि हम कामयाब होंगे और, हर और चीज़ का इसके बाद में नम्बर है, क्योंकि सब में अव्वल चीज़ हमारे लोगों की और मुल्क की आज़ादी है। और हमें तैयार होना चाहिए, कि हर चीज़ को हम इस पर न्योछावर कर दें।

मैं आपको कोई लम्बी कहानी नहीं सुनाउँगा इस वक़्त। जो पांच बरस से चीनियों ने हमला किया लददाख़ में और किसी तरह से उन्होंने उस हमले के हक़ में अजीब अजीब बयान और बहसें पेश कीं और कमाल की ग़लत बातें कहीं और उसी के साथ हमारे मुल्क को बदनाम किया। शायद ही आपको इतिहास में ऐसी मिसाल कोई मिले जैसे कि एक मुल्क यानी हिन्दुस्तान ख़ासतौर से कोशिश करके दोस्ती उसने की और सहयोग किया चीनी हुकूमत से और लोगों से वहां के और उसकी तरफ से वकालत की। दुनिया की अदालतों में और वही चीनी गवर्नमेंट ने इस भलाई का जवाब दिया बुराई से और यहां तक कि हमारे मुल्क पर हमलावर हुए और उसके बाज़ हिस्सों पर कब्ज़ा किया। कोई भी ख़ुददार मुल्क इसकी बर्दाश्त नहीं कर सकता, न इसको सहन करेगा। ज़ाहिर है कि हिन्दुस्तान, जिसके लोग आज़ादी से मुहब्बत करते हैं, कभी भी इसके नीचे सिर नहीं झुका सकता, चाहे जो कुछ भी नतीजा हो।

पांच बरस तक लददाख़ की सीमा पर हमले हुए। जो दूसरी हमारी सीमा है नेफ़ा में वह इनसे बरी रही। जब हम ख़ासतौर से बातें कर रहे थे कि कौन तरीक़ा निकले इस कशमकश को कम करने को ताकि हवा ऐसी हो, मुनासिब हवा हो, जिससे हम बातें कर सकें असली मामले पर और हमारे लोग यानी हिन्दुस्तान के और चीनी नुमाइन्दे मिलें इस बात पर ग़ौर करने को, कैसे वह हम करें, कैसे हवा को साफ करें और कशमकश को कम करें और उस वक़्त फिर एक नया हमला चीनियों ने हमारे ऊपर किया नेफ़ा की सीमा

पर। आठ सितम्बर को यह शुरू हुआ। यह एक अजीब तरीक़ा था हवा को साफ़ करना और कशमकश को कम करने का। यह एक नमूना है किस तरह से चीनी हुक़ूमत ने हमारे साथ बर्ताव किया है। हमारी सरहद चाईना के साथ तिब्बत के हल्क़े में और हमारी तरफ़ नेफ़ा के हल्क़े में, अच्छी तरह से लोग जानते हैं। और ज़मानों से वह एक मज़बूत सरहद रही है। कभी कभी उसको मैकमहाने लाइन कहते हैं, लेकिन यह लाईन कोई उस वक़्त नहीं बनी, मैकमहाने साहब ने नहीं बनायी। लेकिन हिन्दुस्तान और तिब्बत के बीच में जो सब में ऊंचे पहाड़ हैं, वह लाइन गिनी गयी है।

यह हमारे इतिहास में, हमारे साहित्य में, हमारे और सुलहनामों में हर जगह इसका ज़िक्र है, क़ब्ल इसके कि मैकमहाने लाइन कहलाई जाए। चीनियों तक ने इस को बाज़ तरीक़ों से माना, हालांकि वे कहते थे मैकमहाने लाइन ग़ैरक़ानूनी है। चीनियों ने कुछ नक़्शे अपने बनाये हैं। जो कि, जिसमें नेफ़ा का एक बड़ा हिस्सा उन्होंने अपनी तरफ़ खींच लिया है जो हिस्सा हमारी हुक़ूमत में एक ज़माने से है। चीन की नयी हुक़ूमत कोई 12 वर्ष हुए क़ायम हुई थी, उसके पहले तिब्बती लोग थे, उन्होंने कभी ऐतराज़ नहीं किया इस सरहद पर। और जो चीनी भी नक़्शे दिखाते थे, वो भी पुराने नक़्शे थे और वो ख़ुद कहते थे कि इनको फिर से हमें इन पर ग़ौर करना है और इसको सही करना है। बावजूद इसके यह सीमा, जहां कि कभी कोई झगड़ा नहीं हुआ था लड़ाई नहीं शान्ति की सीमा थी वहां चीनियों ने इस 8 सितम्बर को ख़ासतौर से हमला किया और बड़ी भारी फ़ौजें उधर भेजीं, बड़े इन्तेज़ाम के साथ एक बड़ी लड़ाई के लिए।

मुझे अफ़सोस है कि हमारी फ़ौज को जो कई जगह धक्के लगे और कई जगह से वह हटाई गयी। उनके ऊपर इत्ती ज़्यादा फ़ौजों के लोग उनके मुख़ालिफ़ हुए और हमारे लोगों के सामने बहुत मुश्किल हो गयी। मैं, अपने, हमारे अफसर और लोग, जिन्होंने इस बड़ी फ़ौज का सामना किया हिम्मत से, उनकी तारीफ़ करता हूं। अब भी फिर भी और हो सकता है कि हमें और धक्के लगें सरहद पर, हमारी फ़ौजें और हटायीं जाएं, लेकिन एक बात मेरी राय में तय है और वह यह कि आख़िरी नतीजा इस मुक़ाबले का हमारे हक़ में होगा और कोई हो नहीं सकता। एक ऐसे मुल्क जैसे हिन्दूस्तान है, भारत है जब वह अपनी आज़ादी के लिए लड़ता है। हमें एक ज़बर्दस्त मुल्क का सामना करना है, जो कि बहुत ज़ाब्तों में नहीं पड़ता है। हमें उसका सामना मज़बूती से करना है और अपने ऊपर भरोसा कर के।

यह झगड़ा मालूम नहीं कित्ते दिन चले, लम्बा हो सकता है हमें उसके लिए अपनी तैयार करनी है, दिमाग़ी और, और तरह से, अपने पर भरोसा हमें करना है क्योंकि मुझे इतमीनान है कि हमारे भरोसे से और अपनी तैयारियों से, हम आख़िर में जीतेंगे, और कोई नतीजा हो नहीं सकता।

तो हम पक्के इरादे से आगे बढ़ें, इस भरोसे से और इस इरादे से कि हम अपने मुल्क से, जो लोग हमला करके आए है, उनको हटा देंगे। हमें इस वक़्त करना क्या है? सब में पहले तो अपने दिल को और दिमाग़ को मज़बूत करना है और एक लोहे की तरह से

बनाना है और मुल्क की ताक़त को एक तरफ़ भेजना है, यानी इसका सामना करना ही करना है। और हम तरीक़े बदलें जो कि काम तेज़ी से हो सकें, और हल्के हल्के जैसे अब होते हैं, वो न रहें। हमें अपनी फ़ौजी ताक़त बढ़ानी है, लेकिन फ़ौजी ताक़त काफ़ी नहीं है, इसके पीछे मुल्क का सारा काम है, इन्डस्ट्री है, खेती है। तो मैं सभी से दरख़ास्त करूँगा जो हमारे काम करने वाले भाई-बहिन हैं कि इस मौक़े पर जबकि हमारा पहला काम है कि हम अपनी पैदावार बढ़ाए, कोई हड़ताल, स्ट्राइक न करें। गांवों में खेतों में और कारखानों में, दोनों जगह हमें अपनी पैदावार खूब बढ़ानी है। इस मौक़े पर, कोई क़ौम के ख़िलाफ़, मुल्क के ख़िलाफ़ या खुदगर्ज़ी की कार्यवाही तो बर्दाश्त नहीं हो सकती है जब कि मुल्क ख़तरे में है। हमें एक बड़ा बोझा उठाना है, हम सभी को, चाहे हमारा पेशा कुछ भी हो लेकिन आज़ादी की क़ीमत पूरीतौर से देनी होती है और कोई क़ीमत ज़रूरत से ज़्यादा नहीं है जब कि हमारे मुल्क की आज़ादी और हमारे मुल्क के दल जो हैं पार्टीज़ हैं और गिरोह हैं वो सब मिल जायेंगे और अपने आपस के झगड़ों को बन्द करेंगे। इस वक़्त मौक़ा आपस की बहस और झगड़ों का नहीं है, हमें सभी को मिल कर सामना करना है ख़तरे का, जो मुल्क के सामने आया है बोझा बहुत हमारे ऊपर होने वाला है।

हमें अपने पैसे बचाने हैं और उसको सेविंग में पोस्ट आफ़िस या बाण्डस में देने हैं ताकि हमारे पास रूपया आए अपनी रक्षा के लिए और जो हमें चीज़ें बनानी हैं, उनके कारखानों के लिए। अगर कोई क़ीमत बढ़ती हैं तो हमें उसको रोकना है। यह बहुत नामुनासिब बात है, ग़लत बात है, कोई आदमी मुल्क के ख़तरे के वक़्त अपने खुद फ़ायदा उठाने की कोशिश करें।

हम तीसरी पंचवर्षीय योजना के बीच में हैं। यह कोई सवाल नहीं उठता कि हम उसको छोड़ दें हां, उसको ज़रा सा हम संभालें, उसको ऐसा कहीं कहीं बदलें जिससे आजकल की ज़रूरत पूरी हो, लेकिन जो उसमें बड़ी बातें हैं। उसको हमें पूरा करना है। क्योंकि उसी से मुल्क की ताक़त बढ़ती है अब भी और बाद में भी। और बहुत सारी बातें हैं जो हमारे लोग कर सकते हैं। एक किसी और दिन बाद मैं आपका ध्यान उधर दिलाउँगा। लेकिन अव्वल चीज़ वही है कि हम सारे अपने दिमाग़ और दिल को मज़बूत करके ढालें आज़ादी के लिए, और आज़ादी की हमारी जो ताक़त है, वह मज़बूत हो और हम ज़ोरो से काम करें।

कोई हम नहीं कह सकते कितना वक़्त इसमें लगेगा। जब तक हम नहीं जीतें, हम इस लड़ाई को चलाएंगे, क्योंकि कुछ भी हो हम कभी सिर नहीं झुका सकते, दुश्मन के हमले से। हमें कोशिश करनी है कि कोई घबराना नहीं है। घबराये हुए लोग कुछ ठीक काम नही कर सकते हैं हमारे पीछे, और घबरायें हम क्यों? हमारे पीछे एक बड़े मुल्क की ताक़त है। इसमें हमें खुश होना है और इस ताक़त को हमें आज का जो सब में बड़ा काम है, उसमें लगाना है, यानी भारत की आज़ादी और उसकी ज़मीन कोई छीन न सके। और जो उसपे हमला करे उसको हटाना है। हमें इसका सामना करना है मज़बूती से। महज़ अफ़वाहों पर आप यक़ीन न कीजिए और जिनके दिल कमज़ोर हों, न उनका कीजिए। हमारा इम्तिहान है। यह मुमकिन है हम ज़रा ढीले से हो गये थे, हमें सख़्त हो जाना हैं।

एक बात और, हमने अब तक यह नीति पर अमल किया था कि किसी फ़ौजी गिरोह में हम नहीं जाएगें, दोस्ती सभी से करेंगे। अब भी वही हमारी पालिसी रहेगी, क्योंकि बुनयादी पालिसी छोड़ देना किसी दिक़्क़त से, ठीक नहीं है। बल्कि उसको रखने ही में कामयाब होगें मैं और आप। मैं चाहता हूँ कि आपका और हमारे देश का भला हो और हम लोग हमेशा अपना सिर ऊंचा रखें और पूरा इतमीनान रखें हमारे देश के भविष्य में।
जयहिन्द!

[Translation begins:

Comrades, friends and fellow countrymen,
I am speaking to you on the radio after a long interval. I feel, however, that I must speak to you about the grave situation that has arisen on our frontiers because of continuing and unabashed aggression by the Chinese forces. A situation has arisen which calls upon all of us to meet it effectively. We are men and women of peace in this country, conditioned to the ways of peace. We are unused to the necessities of war. Because of this we endeavoured to follow a policy of peace even when aggression took place on our territory in Ladakh five years ago. We explored avenues for an honourable settlement by peaceful methods. That was our policy all over the world and we tried to apply it even in our own country.

We know the horrors of war in this age today and we have done our utmost to prevent war from engulfing the world. But all our efforts have been in vain in so far as our own frontiers are concerned, where a powerful and unscrupulous opponent, not caring for peace or peaceful methods, has not only threatened us but even carried these threats into action. The time has, therefore, come for us to realise fully this menace that threatens the freedom of our people and the independence of our country. I say so even though I realise that no power can ultimately imperil the freedom we have won with so much sacrifice and cost to our people after long ages of foreign domination. But to conserve that freedom and integrity of our territory we must gird up our loins and face this great menace that has come to us since we became independent. I have no doubt in my mind that we shall succeed. Everything else is secondary to the freedom of our people, and of our motherland and if necessary, everything else has to be sacrificed in this great crisis.

I do not propose to give you the long history of continued aggression by the Chinese during the last five years, and how they have tried to justify it by speeches and arguments and the repeated assertion of untruths and a campaign of calumny and vituperation against our country. Perhaps there are not many instances in history, where one country, that is, India, has gone out of her way to be friendly and cooperative with the Chinese Government and people and to plead their cause in the comity of nations and then for the Chinese Government to return evil for good and even go to the extent of committing aggression and invade our sacred land. No self respecting country and certainly, not India, with her love for freedom can submit to this whatever the consequences may be. There have been five years of continuous aggression on the Ladakh frontier. Our other frontier at NEFA remained largely free from this aggression. Just when we were discussing ways and means of reducing tension and there was even some chance of the representatives of the two countries meeting to consider this matter, a new and fresh aggression took place on the NEFA border. This began on the 8th of September, last. This was a curious way of lessening tension. It is typical of the way the Chinese Government have treated us.

Our border with China in the NEFA region is well-known and well established from ages past. It is sometimes called the McMahon Line, but this line which separated India from Tibet was the high ridge which divides the watershed. This has been acknowledged as the border by history, tradition and treaties long before it was called the McMahon Line. The Chinese have in many ways acknowledged it as the border, even though they have called the McMahon Line illegal. The Chinese laid claim in their maps to a large part of the NEFA which has been under our administration for a long time. The present Chinese regime was established about twelve years ago. Before that the Tibetans did not challenge it. Even the maps the Chinese produced were acknowledged by them repeatedly to be old and out-of-date maps which had little relevance today. Yet, on this peaceful border where no trouble of fighting had occurred for a long time, they committed aggression and this also in large numbers and after vast preparations for a major attack. I am grieved at the set-back to our troops that have occurred on this frontier and the reverses we have had. They were overwhelmed by vast numbers and by bigger artillery, mountain guns and heavy mortars which the Chinese forces have brought with them. I should like to pay a tribute to our officers and men who face these overwhelming numbers with courage. There may be some more reverses in those areas. But one thing is certain that the final result of this conflict will be in our favour. It cannot be otherwise when a nation like India fights for her freedom and the integrity of the country. We have to meet a powerful and unscrupulous opponent. We have, therefore, to build up our strength and power to face this situation adequately and with confidence. The conflict may continue for long. We must prepare ourselves for it mentally and otherwise. We must have faith in ourselves and I am certain that faith and our preparations will triumph. No other result is conceivable. Let there be this faith, the focused determination to free our country from the aggressor.

What then are we to do about it? We must steel our wills and direct the nation's energy and resources to this one end. We must change our procedures from slow moving methods of peace time to those that produce results quickly. We must build up our military strength by all means at our disposal. But military strength is not by itself enough. It has to be supported fully by the industry and the farmers of the country and by increasing our production in every way that is necessary for us. I would appeal to all our workers not to indulge in strikes or in any other way which comes in the way of increasing production. That production has to be not only in the factory but in the field. No anti-national or anti-social activities can be tolerated when the nation is in peril. We shall have to carry a heavy burden together, whatever our vocations may be. The price of freedom will have to be paid in full measure and no price is too great for the freedom of our people and of our motherland. I earnestly trust and I believe that all parties and groups in the country will unite in this great enterprise and put aside their controversies and arguments which have no place today and put forth a solid, united front before all those who seek to endanger our freedom and integrity. The burden on us is going to be great. We must add greatly to our savings by the purchase of bonds, to help finance production and meet the increasing cost of national defence. We must prevent any rise in prices and we must realise that those who seek to profit at a time of national calamity are anti-national and injure the nation.

We are in the middle of our Third Five Year Plan. There can be no question of our giving up this Plan or reducing any important element of it. We may adapt it to the new requirements here and there. But essentially the major projects of the Plan must be pursued and implemented. Because it is in that way that we shall strengthen our country not only in the present crisis but in the years to come. There are many other things that our people can do and I hope to communicate some of them at a later stage. But the principal thing is for us to devote ourselves to forge the national will to freedom and to work hard to that end. There is no time limit to this. We shall carry the struggle as long as we do not win because we cannot submit to the aggression or the domination of others. We must avoid any panic because that is bad at any time and there is no reason for it.

We have behind us the strength of a united nation. Let us rejoice and apply it to the major tasks at hand today, that is, preserving our complete freedom and integrity and the removal of all these who commit aggression on India's sacred territory. Let us face this crisis not lightheartedly but with seriousness and with a stout heart and with firm faith in the rightness of our struggle and confidence in its outcome.

Do not believe in rumours, do not listen to those who have faint hearts. This is a time of trial and testing for all of us and we have to steel ourselves to the task. Perhaps we were growing too soft and taking things for granted. But freedom can never be taken for granted. It requires always awareness, strength and austerity.

I invite all of you to whatever religion or party or group you may belong to be comrades in this great struggle that has been forced upon us. I have full faith in our people and in the cause and in the future of our country. Perhaps that future requires some such test and determination on our part.

We have followed a policy of non-alignment and sought friendship of all nations. We believe in that policy fully and we shall continue to follow it. We are not going to give up our basic principles because of the present difficulty. Even this difficulty will be more effectively met by our continuing that policy.

I wish you well, and whatever may befall us in the future, I want you to hold your heads high and have faith and full confidence in the great future that we envisage for our country.

Jai Hind!

Translation ends]

260. To Biju Patnaik: Facing the Chinese Threat[48]

October 22, 1962

My dear Biju,

Your letter of the 20th October.

Since you wrote very grave and serious developments have taken place on the NEFA border. That occupies all our attention and our resources. We cannot add to our burdens. We have to watch carefully all developments and take such action as we can.

As it is, we face a prolonged conflict on our borders and we have a very hard task. We shall, of course, face it with all our strength and I have no doubt that in the end we shall succeed, even though we may have any number of reverses in the beginning.

We must not, because of momentary difficulties, forget our basic policy. That indeed would be most unfortunate; but our basic policy must be conditioned to circumstances. Goodness and mental charity are always good but they should not mean supineness and submission to evil. We have to meet violence

---

48. Letter to the Chief Minister of Orissa.

and invasion with all the strength we possess and the firm determination not to submit to them. The next two or three weeks will, probably, indicate what further developments are likely to take place. We shall keep our minds free to consider such developments and what we should do in regard to them. I do not think that we should, at this stage, involve ourselves in matters which would add to our difficulties. There is no question of our being soft to the Chinese after all they have done, but we have anyhow to be wise and farseeing and not to lose ourselves in taking wrong steps which may produce results that are not good for us.

Yours sincerely,
[Jawaharlal Nehru]

261. To N.S. Khrushchev: Chinese Aggression[49]

22nd October, 1962

My dear Prime Minister,

The Government of India appreciate the friendly interest shown by the Government of the USSR and their concern at the latest developments on the India-China border, expressed in their note which was handed over by the Soviet Ambassador to me on 20th October. The Government of India are grateful to the Government of the USSR for their anxiety, conveyed in the note, to remove as quickly as possible the difficulties in the relations between India and China.

The Government of India share the desire of the Government of the USSR to do whatever they can to resolve the differences between the Governments of India and China on the border question by peaceful talks and discussions in a spirit of understanding and cooperation.[50] They have throughout these last few years made serious attempts to resolve these differences by peaceful means.

The Government of India appreciated the position of the USSR and the cautious stand taken by them on the India-China border differences. That is why the Government of India did not so far place the merits of the case before the Government of the USSR. It was only a few days back on 18th September that our Foreign Secretary, on hearing about your Ambassador's interest in this matter, talked to him about the background of the case and the latest developments and gave the Ambassador copies of notes exchanged between India and China on the latest clashes in the Eastern Sector of the boundary.

49. Letter to the Chairman of the Council of Ministers of the USSR.
50. For the Soviet position on the Sino-Indian issue, see appendix 23.

As Your Excellency is aware, our policies ever since our attainment of independence have been conditioned by our own historical background and thinking. We have been strictly non-aligned, taking attitudes on the merits of each question. So far as the relations between India and the Soviet Union and even between India and China are concerned, the Government of India have never been, and will never be, influenced in any way by the views of attitudes of other Governments. The Government of India are, therefore, surprised at the references in the USSR Government's note to those "who are interested in intensifying world tension, who wish to line their coats by military clash between India and China", to "forces of reaction and war" and "imperialist circles" and how they "dream in their sleep of ways of disturbing the friendship of the Soviet Union with India and with China".

China-India relations have deteriorated because of certain things done by China in her relations with India in the last few years. The present crisis has not been of Government of India's making, but has been forced by deliberate aggressive moves made by the Government of China to alter the status quo of the boundary unilaterally by force instead of seeking a solution by talks, discussions and negotiations. It would be appropriate in this connection to state the following facts:

(i) Till 1954, i.e. about five years after the formation of the Government of the People's Republic of China and the establishment of their control in Tibet, there had been no trouble of any kind on the India-China frontier. On the contrary, the Governments of India and China negotiated an Agreement on Trade and Intercourse between India and the Tibet region of China, under which the Government of India, on their own initiative, gave up various extra-territorial privileges exercised by the Government of India in Tibet, which had come down from British times. This was done in a spirit of understanding to establish friendly and cooperative relations between two sovereign and independent countries, removing all traces of colonial traditions of the past.

(ii) The Government of India had no doubts about the customary and traditional boundary confirmed by treaties and agreements of the past; and this boundary was known to the Government of the People's Republic of China. There were inaccuracies in Chinese maps regarding this boundary and these were brought to the notice of the Government of China as early as 1954 and on several occasions afterwards. We were always given to understand that they were old maps which had not been revised.

(iii) The presence of Chinese forces in the area of Aksai Chin along the Sinkiang-Tibet caravan route came to the notice of the Government of India for the first time when the Government of China published a map of their projected road. An Indian patrol which went to the area in the course of its normal rounds was detained by the Chinese border forces and, on enquiry, the Government of China informed the Government of India "According to the report of the Chinese local authorities in Sinkiang, frontier guards of the Chinese Liberation Army stationed in the south-western part of Sinkiang discovered in succession on September 8 and 12, 1958, two groups of Indian armed personnel at Tahung-Liutan and Kezrekirekan on the Sinkiang-Tibet road on Chinese territory". This communication was dated 3rd November, 1958.

(iv) By the beginning of 1959, the Chinese forces had moved further west and as mentioned in the note of the Government of the USSR an armed clash took place at Kongko Pass when the Chinese border forces opened fire, killed 9 Indian personnel and captured the rest.

(v) Even after my meeting with Premier Chou En-lai in April 1960 and during the subsequent discussions of the officials of the two sides, the Chinese aggressive moves continued. By the middle of 1961, the Chinese border forces were nearly 70 miles south-west of the Sinkiang-Tibet road where they were in 1958.

(vi) Due to these aggressive intrusions by Chinese forces, the Government of India were compelled to take certain defence measures to halt the Chinese advance. While taking this action, the Government of India at the same time expressed their desire for talks and discussions to remove the border tension prevailing in these areas and made various proposals throughout last July, August and September. The Chinese responses to these approaches were negative and disappointing. The Chinese even refused to consider discussion of measures to correct the situation created by their unilateral alteration of the status quo of the boundary. Instead, they insisted on India accepting the precondition that the Chinese forces could not be asked to withdraw from the areas they had occupied over the last few years in the region of Ladakh.

(vii) It is pertinent to mention that according to the Chinese notes it was the Chinese frontier guards which detained the Indian patrol party in September 1958 at the north-western end of the Sinkiang-Tibet road. Chinese notes received during the last few months again refer to Chinese frontier guards who are now manning a series of posts nearly a hundred miles south-west of where they were in September 1958. Surely, the India-China frontier cannot be mobile and vary from year to year in accordance with the progress of Chinese forcible intrusions.

347

(viii) While notes regarding the scope of these talks and discussions were being exchanged and even dates and places were being specified, the Chinese forces crossed the Thagla Ridge, which constitutes the boundary between India and China in the Eastern Sector, and intruded into the north-west corner of North East Frontier Agency, of India., The Government of India had to take measures to meet this further attempt to alter forcibly the status quo of the boundary.

(ix) The Agreement concerning the McMahon Line, which is the same by which the boundary in this sector between India and the Tibet Region of China is often called, merely formalised what had been the traditional and customary boundary between the territories of India and Tibet. It was a well recognised and long-established boundary which was not "created", but only confirmed by treaty in 1914. The local authorities and inhabitants of the area as well as the Governments of the two sides had for centuries recognised the validity of this boundary alignment, and even the People's Government of China, after they established their control in Tibet, proceeded on the basis that this was the boundary. The same watershed boundary, represented by the McMahon Line of 1914, between Burma and China has recently been once more accepted in the treaty between the Governments of Burma and China.

(x) Any talks or discussions, whether they are regarding preliminary measures to relieve tension or substantive discussions are, of course, without prejudice to the position of either party regarding its claims in connection with the boundary. But there is no convention or precedent in international practice which justifies forcible occupation of territory without a declaration of war; and this is what the Government of China have done over the period of five years since 1957 in Ladakh and have been doing now since the beginning of September in the north-west corner of the Eastern Sector of the India-China boundary.

The Government of India agree that these border questions are difficult and complicated and have to be handled with patience to arrive at reasonable solutions. They have acted all along in this spirit even after the forcible occupation of about 12,000 square miles of Indian territory by the Chinese in the Ladakh region. They only took limited defensive measures to stop further Chinese intrusions and asked for talks and discussions to consider what measures should be taken, by agreement between the two Governments, for restoring the status quo of the boundary and easing tensions in the area, prior to discussion of the question on merits. The Government of India laid down no pre-conditions of any kind. It is the Chinese who, through their Foreign

Minister, stated that no one can make the Chinese withdraw from the Ladakh area that they had occupied during the last few years. It was this pre-condition about which notes were being exchanged when the Chinese thought it fit to cross the well known India-China boundary in the Eastern sector and commit further aggression into India. Consistent with her self respect and dignity, India had to take such action as it could to resist this new intrusion. On the very morning on which your Ambassador handed over the note of the Soviet Government to me, the Chinese mounted a well concerted and premeditated attack on our defense posts in the Western as well as Eastern sectors of the boundary and are advancing further into Indian territory. You will agree, Mr Prime Minister, that this blatant use of force by the Chinese to annex such territory as they can is at complete variance with the policy regarding exercise of patience and settling differences in a spirit of cooperation and understanding counselled in the Soviet Government's note. The Chinese chose to launch their carefully organised large-scale and vicious attack on Indian defense posts south of the McMahon Line, which is the international frontier and which had been quiet and peaceful for all these years, and also on our defense posts in the Western sector, on the very day on which you, Mr Prime Minister, were making sincere efforts to have the boundary differences between India and China resolved peacefully.

There is a reference in the note to the talks which our Defence Minister, Shri Krishna Menon, had with the Soviet Ambassador in Delhi on September 15 and October 8. You will appreciate, Mr Prime Minister, that these talks had taken place after the recent aggressive intrusion by China south of the international frontier into the north-west area of the eastern sector of the boundary. Even then the Defence Minister pointed out, in the context of the great patience and forbearance shown by the Government of India at Chinese aggression in Ladakh during the last few years, that India would certainly have to resist if the Chinese continued this new aggression in the eastern sector. Surely, neither you nor any of India's other friends would want her to submit to the arbitrary and blatant use of force by any Power, however strong.

It is not India who is attempting to settle the dispute by the use of force. China had already, by military action, forcibly occupied the greater part of the disputed area in the western sector, that is, in Ladakh, over the period of the last five years. Despite this unilateral and forcible occupation, India, because of its faith in peaceful talks and discussions, did not precipitate a clash but made proposals for a meeting between the representatives of the two countries. While the exchange of notes for the finalisation of these talks was going on, China in the beginning of September suddenly marched her forces in the eastern sector across the highest mountain ridge—the Thagla Ridge—which constitutes the boundary in that particular area, to spread the conflict and seize Indian territory by force. I agree with Your Excellency that this is a very dangerous path, but it is China which is following this path.

I can assure you, Mr Prime Minister, that so far as the Government of India are concerned, we are wedded to paths of peace and to the policy of settling outstanding differences by talks, discussions and negotiations.

All our past traditions and policy have clearly demonstrated our love of peace and our abhorrence of war. We have not set foot on an inch of Chinese territory, but have remained on our own territory which has been in our possession for a long time past and which has been clearly shown in all our maps as well as in our Constitution as being part of the Indian Union. It is true that this Indian area now occupied by China is mountainous and sparsely populated. But that does not lessen our undoubted claim to it. Politically, by treaty and tradition, it belongs to India and has all along been treated as such. Our literature for two thousand years or more is full of references to it as part of India and our people, nurtured in this literature and old tradition, are greatly attached to it. It has been and is a part of India's life and heritage. No country with any self-respect can accept any claim which is contrary to history, treaties and its own traditions, more especially when this is by aggression.

We know that China is a great and powerful country. We have sought, in the past, friendship and cooperation with it and pleaded its cause before the United Nations and elsewhere. It has been a matter of great surprise and regret for us that in spite of our friendly attitude, the People's Government of China has committed gross aggression on our territory and has carried on a propaganda against us which is vituperative in the extreme. You will appreciate, Mr Prime Minister, that India could not have acted otherwise than it did in challenging the Chinese claim which had no basis and in protesting strongly against their aggression. Even so, we have been prepared for discussions which might lead to a peaceful settlement, but how can we have any discussions when actual and new aggression is continuously taking place and vast Chinese armies are moving further into our territory? Any discussion can only be worthwhile if a suitable atmosphere is created for it. We, therefore, proposed that the first thing to do was to create that atmosphere by the Chinese Government restoring the status quo as it was prior to the 8th September. We could then consider what further agreed steps should be taken to correct the situation created by the earlier unilateral alteration of the status quo of the boundary and to ease the tensions, preparatory to the substantive discussions of the differences regarding the boundary.[51]

With kind regards,

Yours sincerely,
Jawaharlal Nehru

51. See also item 395.

262. To the Conference of Governors[52]

At the invitation of the President, the Prime Minister gave an account of the situation which had developed on the border with China. It was five years, the Prime Minister said, since the Chinese started their aggression in Ladakh. To meet this, we had built certain roads and set up border posts. Ultimately our posts and the Chinese posts were more or less facing each other. The Chinese were in a more favourable position because they could bring their supplies by roads across the Tibetan plateau almost up to their posts whereas our supplies had to be brought across high mountains or carried by air. A state of tension continued but no major clash had taken place. Recently there had been a proposal for talks between the Chinese and Indian representatives. We had made no conditions but had proposed that the initial talks should be not so much on the

[HIGH MORALE]

You Said It

By LAXMAN

(From *The Times of India*, 14 November 1962)

52. From the Proceedings of the conference on 23 and 24 October 1962 at Rashtrapati Bhavan. MHA, File No. 19/41/62-Public-I, pp. 21(A)/c. Only extracts are available at the NMML.

351

merits of the case but in order to find an agreed solution for lessening tension. While this correspondence was going on, a new development took place on the north-eastern frontier where the McMahon line is the international boundary.

The McMahon Line, the Prime Minister said, merely recognised the frontier which had existed for a long time past and is described in a treaty as the highest ridge of the watershed in the Himalayas there. The Chinese maps claim a great part in NEFA and in Ladakh. Soon after the new Chinese Government came into being, attention was drawn to this both in writing and subsequently orally to Prime Minister Chou En-lai. At that time, he said that these were old maps produced by the previous Chiang Kai-shek regime and that he had had no time to look into the matter and that anyhow this could be settled peacefully between the two Governments. When these maps were printed again the same way, we again drew the Chinese Premier's attention to them and received the same answer which gave the impression (though he did not himself) that the old maps could be changed and that while possibly there might be some minor differences there were no major differences. Meanwhile, five years ago, the Chinese started their aggression in Ladakh. No aggression took place in the NEFA area except for the incident at Longju which was not of much importance.

On the 8th September, the Chinese crossed the high ridge of the Thagla pass. Indian forces in the area were strengthened. The Chinese, however, were at a great advantage since their road system came right up to the foot of the ridge whereas our troops had to be supplied mainly by air. Reinforcements were sent but we were still greatly outnumbered. On the 20th October, the Chinese launched an attack all along the frontier in NEFA and simultaneously on the Ladakh frontiers. Half an hour earlier Peking radio announced that they were being attacked.[53] There had been severe fighting and heavy casualties on both sides. Many of our posts had been overwhelmed or had been compelled to withdraw and the Chinese were advancing towards Tawang.

The Prime Minister said this may well mean an interminable conflict between India and China and it was necessary to fashion our organisation accordingly from slow moving peace-time ways, both in civil and military matters, to a swift moving machine which can take decisions quickly and act on them effectively. This would mean a great additional burden on our country but it must be shouldered. There was no other way. The Chinese had crossed the McMahon Line which, in fact, they had never recognised. The position was serious. We had suffered a severe setback and must gear up the machinery to meet the situation. We had to increase our production and give a single-minded direction to all our efforts. People must give up minor controversies.

53. See note in item 258.

He was glad that there had been adequate response to the appeal to all parties. It would be necessary to raise more money by Government loans, savings and in other ways. We must keep down prices. The cooperation of the States would be necessary in all fields. It was proposed to call the National Development Council sooner than had been intended.

The Defence Minister then gave the Conference an account of the military situation on the frontier. On the 8th September, he said, the Chinese came over the Thagla ridge. Steps were taken to reinforce our positions. Our posts were small ones. There are no roads in the area and in places even animal transport cannot be used, the bridges in some places being rope bridges. The Chinese first surrounded our post at Dhola after destroying one of the bridges. Our troops resisted but were clearly outnumbered. Steps were being taken to contain the Chinese in the Thagla area when the Chinese launched their attack in great strength. Our forward positions had been taken by direct assault after severe fighting. The supply position was very difficult being dependent on air dropping. A threat was developing to Tawang. The Chinese had taken Khinzamane.

Lieutenant General B.M. Kaul, Chief of the General Staff, had been appointed Corps Commander to conduct operations on this front.[54]

In the West, the Defence Minister said, we had for the past eighteen months been building up posts between the international border and the 1960 line. The Chinese tactics had been to surround our posts. Until the present fierce fighting started, we took defensive action but had not gone in for waging war. Now there had been simultaneous attacks on our posts some of which had fallen in the face of heavy gun fire. In the Pangong lake area even tanks had been used and a threat was developing to Chushul.

The Defence Minister referred to Chinese propaganda according to which every time they attacked they accused India of doing so. They had recently announced that our air force was supported by our ground forces. They also announced that their forces would not respect the McMahon Line. As the Prime Minister had said, the situation required considerable reorganisation of the administrative machine. Augmentation of the army and supply of modern weapons had been under consideration and would be put into operation as soon as possible. He could not say how long the present struggle would continue but we would fight back; there was no other way. The morale of our troops was high though they were fighting under very difficult conditions. Our communication systems were limited and this was one of the main reasons why it would be some time before we would be in a position to recover lost ground.

54. On 4 October 1962. The *Times of India*, 5 October 1962, p.1, col.5. See also items 5 and 6, which concerned Kaul's appointment.

In answer to questions the Prime Minister said that the Chinese had not invaded Bhutan or Sikkim. They had made a declaration that they had nothing to do with Bhutan which is an independent country. It was difficult to say anything about the attitude of Russia. They appeared to be trying to maintain an attitude of not taking any sides. China was of course their ally.[55]

[Portions omitted]

International Situation

The Prime Minister informed the Conference that the Chief of the Army Staff would come with maps the next day and explain the situation on the borders.

He then told the Conference of the very tense situation that had developed in regard to Cuba. The day before, President Kennedy had broadcast an address to the American nation in which he said that Cuba was being used by the Soviets as a base for missiles carrying atomic warheads. They had established installations for ballistic missiles capable of carrying a nuclear warhead to Washington. This, President Kennedy had said, was a danger to the USA and all the American countries and he had, therefore, taken measures, including the placing of Cuba under close surveillance. No ship would be allowed there if carrying war material and therefore, every ship going there would be searched. The USA had also asked the Security Council that the United Nations should send observers to find out about the alleged missile bases and if there were any, to have them dismantled. President Kennedy had warned that any missile attack from Cuba on the United States would be answered by instant retaliation on the Soviet Union. Berlin also, the Prime Minister said, continued to be a cause of tension. The situation was very dangerous.

In regard to Pakistan there had been no particular development. Generally speaking the Pakistan Press had been giving prominence to Chinese reports and statements about the border conflict. He did not however think they were likely to create difficulty for India at this time because of the influence of America on whom they rely for support.[56]

Nepal, the Prime Minister said, was a very difficult problem. The King and the Ministers were aggressively anti-Indian. India did not wish to interfere in Nepalese affairs. Express instructions had been issued not to allow India to be used a base for anti-Government activity. There was however an open border with Nepal and it was very difficult to stop people coming from Nepal to India and carrying on activities from here. No incidents had occurred during the past two or three months. There have, however, been several incidents deliberately

55. See appendix 23.
56. See item 228.

engineered from Nepal. We had suggested joint enquires into these but the Nepalese had refused.[57]

The Governor of Uttar Pradesh mentioned a report he had heard of Chinese fishing operations in the vicinity of Indian islands and the possibility of their establishing submarine bases there.

[Portions omitted]

The Prime Minister said that questions had been asked about foreign exchange in the preceding discussions. The whole position was, however, very much governed by the new situation which was entirely outside our previous reckoning and would undoubtedly be a strain both on foreign exchange and domestic resources. The equipment of the army was not up to date. We had hitherto concentrated on manufacturing our own equipment and had made considerable progress but that was not enough. To have provided modern equipment for our army would have cost hundreds of crores and naturally we had to balance these demands with our other necessities. Originally, we had to consider only the situation vis-à-vis Pakistan but now a far greater menace had appeared and we would have to produce modern equipment as far as we could and also obtain it from outside and that was going to be a very heavy burden.

With regard to the European Common Market the Prime Minister said he had met the President of France and the Prime Minister of Italy who had shown themselves to be sympathetic and anxious to find a solution for India's difficulties.

The Prime Minister then read out the text of a statement issued by the Chinese Government which had not been received officially but of which a broadcast had been made. This statement proposed that both parties should affirm that the Sino-Indian boundary question must be settled peacefully through negotiations, pending which both should respect the line of actual control between the two sides along the entire border and that the armed forces of both sides should be withdrawn 20 kilometres from this line and disengage.[58] This, the Prime Minister said, was of course a typical Chinese gambit. If we accepted the line of actual control it would mean that if they penetrated deeper into our territory that would actually be the line of control. They had already occupied parts of NEFA and Ladakh and now they wanted to sit down for talks.

57. See items 220, 221 and 222.
58. Statement of the Chinese Government, 24 October 1962. See A.S. Bhasin (ed.) *India-China Relations: 1947-2000 A Documentary Study,* (New Delhi: Geetika, 2018), doc. no. 1881, pp. 3939-3942.

This would mean the acceptance of their aggression. It was impossible for us to accept this. India's position had been clearly stated in the President's speech the preceding evening which was that the Chinese should withdraw to the line held by them on the 8th September 1962 which meant that all fresh aggression in NEFA must be vacated and some changes in Ladakh also. We could not go beyond that whatever the consequences. The Chinese were massing troops in all sectors. The Chief of the Army Staff would explain the military position to the Conference.

263. To H.K. Mahtab: Offer to China[59]

October 27, 1962

My dear Mahtab,

Your telegram. You are wrong in thinking that we are asking for something now which China offered and we rejected previously. We asked earlier for a meeting to consider how to lessen tension, and if this was achieved then to meet to consider the merits.

What we ask now is for the position before 8th September to be restored and then for preliminary meeting to reduce tension to take place. This is in line with what we said before. As a matter of fact, if China agrees to this and goes back across the McMahon Line in the East and also back to some extent in the Western sector, that will be very advantageous to us, and China will lose all the advantages she has gained. There is practically no chance of her accepting this. I am sure that what we have proposed is both honourable and desirable for us. There is no question of confusion being caused anywhere.

Yours sincerely,
[Jawaharlal Nehru]

264. In New Delhi: To Congress MPs[60]

India to Get Arms from Outside: Nehru

New Delhi, Oct. 27 – Prime Minister Nehru told his party colleagues here today that India had made arrangements with some countries for securing armaments and equipment for the Indian forces now engaged in repelling the Chinese invaders.

59. Letter to Congress MP and former Chief Minister of Orissa.
60. Reproduced from the *National Herald*, 27 October 1962, p. 1.

He told about forty five Congress members of Parliament who called on him today, that efforts were also being made to step up production of the requisite armament indigenously despite the foreign exchange position.

Those present at the meeting included the Defence Minister, Mr Krishna Menon.

Pandit Nehru also told the members that the Government would utilise retired army officers and generals who had offered their services. The Government was considering certain measures by which best advantage could be taken of their experience without having dual arrangements with regard to actual operations.[61]

Pandit Nehru informed the members that India had already communicated her case to all countries barring Portugal and South Africa, with whom she did not have diplomatic relations.

India has told that the Chinese invasion of Indian territory, apart from raising other problems, constituted a crime under international law.

Explaining India's conditions to the recent Chinese proposal for resumption of talks, Pandit Nehru is understood to have said that the demand for withdrawal of the invading Chinese forces was made in order to relieve tension and create the proper climate for talks.

In reply to questions, Pandit Nehru told the members that India had no doubts with regard to her friendship with Bhutan.

The relations with Nepal were also friendly and he was sure both the countries would stand together. There were a large number of Nepali nationals in the Indian armed forces and a still larger number on the Indian reserve list inside Nepal.

He expressed surprise at the attitude of the Pakistani press in the present Sino-Indian conflict particularly the bitterness with which they wrote against India. Both in their bitterness and extent of writing, Pakistani papers seemed to have outdone the Chinese itself.

On the attitude of the Communist Party Pandit Nehru is understood to have said: "We have to do the right thing and not to do anything that would lead to unnecessary provocation of creation of enemies."

The members are understood to have told the Prime Minister that the people had responded well to the promulgation of the state of emergency by the President.[62]

Pandit Nehru assured them that the emergency powers sought under the Defence of India measure would be used to curb anti-social elements.

61. See items 291 and 383.
62. On 26 October 1962.

Why Arms Shortage

Carrying the background to the shortage of automatic weapons, Pandit Nehru is understood to have told the members that in the past, the British rulers had not created capacity in India for producing these. The requirements of the Indian army were supplied from Britain. Production of armaments was taken up in the country only after independence, but the pace of production was handicapped largely by the pressure on foreign exchange.

However, despite the foreign exchange, efforts were being made to step up their production.

Explaining the emergency decided on by the Cabinet, Pandit Nehru told the members that the proposed citizens' force should be a voluntary organisation.

He said that the Territorial Rifles and Home Guards would be expanded on a large scale for internal work.

He welcomed the formation of citizens' committees as had been done by the Mayors of Bombay and Delhi.

Pandit Nehru is understood to have stressed the need for utilising the services of all for the national cause, while replying to a question about the relative roles of the public and private sector in building up the nation's defence capacity.

He also emphasised the need for austerity both in the Government as well as private homes. There was also need to prevent rise in prices.

The members reported complete satisfaction after their meeting with the Prime Minister lasting over seventy minutes.

They said that their discussions with Pandit Nehru had cleared whatever little doubts or misgivings they had.[63]

265. In New Delhi: To the CPP Executive[64]

Arms Arrive: Supply Position. Improves
Country Better Prepared Now To Meet Aggression

New Delhi, Oct. 29 – Prime Minister Nehru and the Defence Minister, Mr Krishna Menon, are understood to have told the Congress Parliament Party executive here today that India was now in a better position to meet the Chinese threat in NEFA and elsewhere than a few days ago.

---

63. "Misgivings" about equipment. See NMML, Sudhir Ghosh Papers.
64. Report of conversation with CPP executive members; reproduced from the *National Herald*, 30 October 1962, p. 1.

They told the thirty-two-member executive that the supply position to the Indian forces had improved. Some arms had already arrived from abroad and more were on their way.

Pandit Nehru, however, laid great emphasis on indigenous production of arms and equipment needed by the defence forces, so that the nation could stand on its own feet.

Pandit Nehru is understood to have indicated to the members that he was not thinking of breaking diplomatic relations with China at the present moment.

Besides the Defence Minister, the Minister of State, for Defence, Mr K. Raghuramiah, was also specially invited to attend the meeting which lasted about an hour and forty-five minutes.

During the discussions, the members are reported to have strongly felt that every possible measure should be taken to improve the nation's military preparedness.

Aggressor's Advantage

Mr Menon is understood to have explained that in any military conflict, the aggressor had certain initial advantages of surprise moves. But the Chinese no longer had these advantages.

Pandit Nehru is stated to have told the members that the withdrawals by Indian forces from the forward positions were more in the nature of strategic moves.

The Minister for Agriculture, Dr Ram Subhag Singh, who returned to Delhi today after a four day study of supply position in Assam and other border areas, reported to the meeting that the morale of Indian forces was very high, they were cheerful and in good spirits.

Reviewing the measures that had been taken to maintain and improve the supply position to the border areas, the minister said quantities of food had already been allotted to the border areas on an emergency basis. Part of it had already reached their destination and more was on its way.

The minister told the committee that apart from having consultation with the officials in Assam, NEFA and bordering states, he had attended several meetings of the grain dealers, producers and others to discuss gearing up of the food production machinery.

No Second Grade Weapons

To a suggestion that in the absence of latest weapons, the country should acquire and produce second grade weapons, Pandit Nehru is reported to have remarked that there could be no question of securing or producing second grade weapons. Apart from securing latest weapons, the country must produce them. People should get out of the old habit of securing things from outside. There were still some who continued to think on the old lines, this mentality was no doubt changing, though slowly.

With regard to civil defence, Prime Minister told the committee that steps had already been taken to protect defence and other important installations.

Those who participated in the committee's discussions included Mr Mahavir Tyagi, Mr Bhakt Darshan, Mr K. K. Shaw, General Secretary of the All-India Congress Committee, Mr Ravindra Verma, Mr H. C. Mathur, Mrs Renuka Ray and Mr S. Shastri.

266. To T.T. Krishnamachari: Don't feel Despondent[65]

October 30, 1962

My dear TT,

Thank you for your letter of today's date.[66]

Much of what you said yesterday I agree with. Part of it I do not agree with. But that does not very much matter. Anyhow, whatever you said and repeat in your letter is very much in my mind. I think that we have set things moving and I hope they will bring quick results.

There is no need for you to feel despondent. I have no such feeling although I have received a number of shocks during the last few days.

You can see me when you like or write to me.

Yours affectionately,
[Jawaharlal Nehru]

267. To Surjit Singh Majithia: Strategy in NEFA[67]

November 3, 1962

My dear Surjit Singh,

Your letter of the 3rd November. I am writing a brief reply to you immediately. I wish I had time to write more fully.

---

65. Letter to Minister without Portfolio. NMML, T.T. Krishnamachari Papers, File 1962, Copy.
66. See appendix 33. See also documents in sub section (e) CHINESE INVASION: Krishna Menon, infra.
67. Letter to Deputy Minister of Defence; address: 9 Teen Murti Marg, New Delhi.

(a) Government knew that there were large forces of the Chinese in Tibet, but we did not think that several Divisions would be thrown across the Thagla Pass. As soon as the original incursion took place by the Chinese on the Thagla Pass, immediate steps were taken to send troops there. This was not an easy matter as many of them had to go by air. Every supply needed had also to be sent by air in difficult mountain terrain. Many of our air droppings were lost.

About the second week of October we found that the Chinese forces were increasing fast. Even then we could not imagine that two or three Divisions would come over rather suddenly.

(b) The Army appreciation of the situation was that we should try to push the Chinese a little wherever possible, but in effect we should hold a strong defensive line at the river Namchuko. This was, in fact, the direction given.

(c) I am not aware of this assessment. Opinions differed and it was thought that the longer we allowed the Chinese to entrench themselves fully, the more difficult it would be to push them back. In fact, hardly any aggressive action was taken by us except one or two minor incursions. The attack came from the Chinese side in a big and massive way.

(d) Tawang had certainly importance. But the main centre of attack was some distance away from it. If that was not held, Tawang would obviously have been weakened greatly. Anyhow, the final decisions were left to the military Commanders.

(e) There is no question of our sacrificing the lives of large numbers of our men deliberately. No one expected two Divisions of Chinese troops, highly trained and well armed, coming down on our forces then in a particular spot.

(f) It is easy to criticise the administrative arrangement, more especially after the event. Every effort was made to send supplies, but all these had to be sent by air, and our Air Force was strained to the utmost. And, as I have said above, many of the air droppings were lost.

(g) Such fire support as was available was given. But the Chinese had big artillery, heavy mortars, etc. Our Army does not possess these big mortars. Nor indeed do the UK and US armies possess them. They rely on air power much more.

(h) As I have said above, the final decision was left to the Commanders on the spot. No orders were given that they must do anything which they thought unwise. In fact, the final orders were to defend at the river as far as possible.

361

I am surprised that you should say that this was a fault of Defence Production, or of the person in charge of it.[68] Our Defence Production has been speeded up as much as possible, but it is true that it was not enough to meet the years of preparation and training of the Chinese. You will remember the difficulties of the American forces in Korea and the severe set-back they suffered there in spite of the latest equipment they had. Also, the wiping out of the British Army at Dunkirk by the Nazis in spite of good equipment and every effort made. It is easy to find scapegoats, but it does not show much wisdom to forget surrounding circumstances.

Yours sincerely,
[Jawaharlal Nehru]

268. To the National Development Council[69]

Friends, Comrades,

We are meeting today specially because a very special occasion has demanded it. You know all the facts and the recent occurrences. Nevertheless I should like to impress upon you what has happened. It is the Chinese invasion of India and it is something much more than aggression on a particular point and particular border area.

There has been a good deal of Chinese aggression in Ladakh for the last four or five years. Nevertheless, although it covered a great deal of area, it was one on a small scale in the sense that small forces went and occupied certain areas.

What has happened in NEFA in the months of September and October and more specially from the 20th October onwards, is qualitatively and quantitatively very different. It is not a frontier exchange. It is an invasion of India. What the Chinese may have in mind is anybody's guess work. We can all think about it. But anyhow it is a much bigger thing than what has happened yet, certainly since the Chinese came or since our Independence. It really marks, their coming and our reaction to it, if I may say so, a turning point in India's history.

We are at the crossroads of history and we are facing great historical problems on which depends our futures, our present of course, but our future. So whether we are big men or small, we have to undertake the work of big men because only big people can face big problems, not big in size but big in

---

68. At this time V.K. Krishna Menon was in charge of Defence Production. See sub section (e) CHINESE INVASION: Krishna Menon, infra.
69. Speech, 4 November 1962. Planning Commission, File No. F.8/6/62-Education, Education Division.

mind, big in vision, big in determination. This is the first point I should like to stress upon you to realise the extraordinary character of what has happened which has in effect changed or will change our whole national outlook and as well our history as it is going to be. So if we have to face this adequately, as we have every intention of doing, then we have to think in a big way. We have to forget many of our problems which normally pursue us and see this big problem which concerns us all.

It may be, I hope, it will and there are some indications that it will be, that in solving the big problem we shall almost automatically solve many of our smaller problems, conflicts, controversies, etc. At the same time it is clear that this big problem will require a tremendous effort on the Nation's part and those of us who have been placed by fate and circumstances in a position of Governmental authority, whether at the Centre or at the State, have a tremendous responsibility—a responsibility which a few persons by themselves can be big enough to shoulder but which, I am sure, all of us put together can and will shoulder. Therefore, it is necessary to view these problems in perspective and realise the full implications of what has happened and what might happen.

The Chinese invasion, I may use the word, came in its quantity and quality, as I said, it is something different from the previous thing. It came almost like a thunderbolt, and reactions today in India, good reactions, have also come like a thunderbolt. The response of the people all over the country has been truly magnificent and wonderful. Most of the problems that fill our newspapers, conflicts, this, that and other, are things of the past. Not for ever. They may raise their heads again but for the present they are not and we have to keep them there and there can be no doubt as you all know that the response of the people of all classes, of all areas in India, has been amazingly good and heartening. That itself shows the stuff that our people are made of. It is one thing to get entangled in small matters but when the big crisis comes, to rise above those matters and face it. While much had happened in the past to depress us, what has now happened has heartened me and I am sure heartened all of you.

We might say that this terrible shock has occasioned almost a new birth of the Indian spirit and the soul of India has awakened again after some stop. We who are privileged to serve the particular States, to serve India, it is a great privilege and a great responsibility. Well, all we can say is that we shall do our utmost to be worthy of this responsibility and not to allow any personal group or other matters to come in the way. We must put them aside. In this matter, constitutionally there might be Central Government and the State Governments, but actually we are all one and we have to face as on one people.

Now we normally meet, that is this National Development Council, to consider our Plan, and the Plan is not something apart from our national life.

It is of the warp and woof of it. How does it affect our Plan and our economic and social processes that are going on in the country. That is a matter which we will have to consider. You may not at this meeting go into great details about it but I do hope that we all have some discussion about it.

It is clear to begin with that the first priority and the first necessity is to do everything that helps us to meet this crisis and ultimately to push out the invader and the aggressor from our country. That is the first priority and everything else must give way to it. But even considering that we have to see what strength we have in us in doing it and prepare the ground not only for that purpose but for the time that comes afterwards. After all we have an immediate task, immediate I use the word, because the task has come to us now, though it may last a considerable time for us to give effect to it, is to free our country from the aggressor. But that itself is part of the task of strengthening and raising our country to higher levels.

It may be that some trick of destiny has put us to this test, to take our minds away from the petty things of life and to test us and to prepare us for bigger things in the future.

While we think of what might be called a war effort, we have always to think of the building up of the country as well.

War effort is not a question of enrolling soldiers and sending them to the front. That is a part of it, an important part. A soldier as everyone knows depends on the country, on the morale of the country, on the production of the country. Each soldier—I do not know how many he requires—requires hundreds of men behind to feed him and to send him supply. Even from the point of view of the war effort, we have to work all over the country in a variety of ways, in agriculture, in industry and so many other ways but also apart from the war effort that is necessary to produce the kind of India that we seek. The two are not contradictory. In fact they fit in. If we do not do that, the war effort will be lacking and the ultimate result would be very much lacking.

For people to say that the Plan must be largely scrapped because we have got trouble and invasion to face has no meaning to me. It shows an utter misunderstanding of the situation. It is a war effort that requires the Plan.

The basis of the Plan is to strengthen the nation, the basis of the plan is to increase production. Nothing is required more than production when you have such a problem to face. I am leaving out the military aspect; that is for our experts and soldiers to deal with. But the civil aspect is an essential part of any war effort of this kind. The civil aspect is important and production is important, training is important, technical personnel and all that.

It becomes essential to look at the Plan as apart, as an essential part of our effort. Therefore, all idea of giving up the plan which some people who in their shortsightedness suggest is very wrong. It is true that we shall have to examine the Plan, stick to essentials and those things that are not essential now or which might be essential tomorrow may be slowed down somewhat. That is a matter of examination. We cannot easily examine it in some details here in this Council. We can consider the main things.

It is obvious as I said that production must increase, agricultural production, industrial production. In industrial production things that are not essential may not increase; in fact may be even stopped. But those things that are essential must increase for our effort alone. Everything has to be judged from that point of view.

Then take training. We have to increase our technical training. Take normal education which may on the first view appear not so terribly important and yet it is essential and important that we may make variations in our system of training. We may not spend too much as I think we should not on big buildings and constructions and make some other use of other methods. We may have bigger classes. We may have in each school double shifts, three shifts if you like. But we cannot stop the educational process or slow down the pace because that itself is essential for the effort, not only for the effort today but for tomorrow. We cannot have a short vision and if I may use the word "win the war and lose the peace afterwards". It often happens when we have to face a crisis we have to keep both in view—win a war and win the peace.

Then again power. Now, every one of you realises the importance of power—electric power, thermal power whatever. Because on that depends the growth of industry, on that depends to some extent the growth of agriculture, on that depends so much. The modernising of agriculture and industry depends upon power. We cannot afford to lessen power and in fact we have to increase it, augment it. In this connection, we have at the present moment agreed to have an atomic power plant at Tarapore. Later on one in Rajasthan and we have in view one in South India. Now because of this crisis I do not think, for a variety of reasons, that we should interfere with that programme. Power is essential to increase our strength, to increase our industry, etc. and the growth of atomic energy is also essential from other points of view. Therefore, we cannot relax on that now. We cannot relax on most of the things that we have to do. After all our Plan is a selective plan. We wanted to do much more. How are we to do this? Inevitably it will involve tremendous burdens, not only the war effort, the plan effort, this is part of the war effort.

We have to cut down the non-essentials not only in the Plan but generally in our other activities. We have to economise and whatever we may do, we shall have to bear this burden and the consequences of it. Normally the increase in production in war time for war needs which are not only needs actually of war, that is armament, etc., but also other needs required by the armed forces, the increase in production is very considerable.

That means that a large amount of purchasing power will go to the people. What will be the effect on many things, on prices, etc., we have to consider it. It is important that in so far as possible, the price level should be maintained and I would like to say there have been tendencies for the price to rise which have worried us and we have considered this matter and the matter will come up before you. Considering everything, by and large, prices have not risen appreciably—in pockets they have. That is a very important matter because this affects not only the people but the whole economic structure. Several goods will have to be restricted to some extent, concentrate on other goods. There is a demand for them because of the increasing purchasing power. All these things have to be considered by us, organisation of civil supplies, etc., so that there may not be a lack of them amongst large groups of people and in abundance elsewhere.

One thing on which we have laid stress repeatedly has been the cooperative movement. I think it has advanced quite considerably in the last few years. I cannot at the moment say how far it has advanced in numbers, in quantity, in quality how much, I am not in a position to say. Perhaps you know better. I think even in quality it is advancing. Anyhow this movement, look at it from the point of view of the present emergency, is a very important thing apart from its general importance. So we have to push it. The maintenance of prices, cooperative stores and cooperative movement generally is important.[70]

There is one matter which I should like to draw your attention and consult my colleagues about it which just struck me. We might encourage in agriculture the short term crops immediately. Crops, anything, vegetable crops or other things like eggs. These are the necessities for troops and others.

We might utilise the next three months for this short-term. The Agriculture Ministry has to consider that more specially in Northern India.

It is a good thing in itself. To encourage these things, possibly sometimes we may have to give a little subsidy for them to do it. The return will be very considerable and would be good for the agriculturists and for the country.

Then you may have heard that we are forming some national committees. The National Defence Fund that we have formed and for which we are having your cooperation of course—we should like to have some of your representatives from the States on it. If you like we can have all the Chief Ministers. Or if you prefer not to make it too unwieldy you can choose your number to be on the National Defence Fund Committee.

---

70. See item 160.

In regard to the collections in States you know that the State Bank is accepting donations and contributions everywhere; the Reserve Bank too.

You will get to know a little more about it later. It has been suggested that some kind of State fund might be opened as a part of the big fund that will come to the big fund. This is the view to be considered. But it must be one major fund, National Defence Fund, which cannot be split up.

Then, you perhaps know that some days ago when the present emergency is supposed to have arisen on the 20th October i.e. just exactly two weeks ago, an Emergency Committee of the Cabinet was formed. Then there have been in the Central Government various other adjustments to speed up work. And on the whole this has resulted in speeding up the working of the Government. Gradually we will get into full stride.

Then it is proposed very soon to form a National Defence Council. The National Defence Council will broadly—we have not finalised the names etc, yet—will consist of the Emergency Committee of the Cabinet, the present Chiefs of Staff of course, certain retired Generals and retired senior people from the other Defence Services and some prominent public men. On the one hand we do not want it to be unwieldy. At the same time we wanted it to be representative. There again I want to consult you as to the representation of States. It may not be perhaps helpful to have every Chief Minister on it. We can have some of them or all of them and have their advice.

Further you know at various places, chiefly in cities like Bombay and other cities, Citizens Committees have been formed. It is a good thing but it is desirable to have some central coordination of them.

There will be some separate committees but if there is a Central Committee coordinating their activities, it will be better. But our idea of the Citizens Committees is it should be 100 per cent non-official, except for one thing that our President has kindly agreed to be the Patron but not in any executive capacity. We will advise them but it should be a non-official committee. In that also the question arises of how the State should be represented in it. Then you know that the Finance Minister has made appeals—we have all made appeals for contributions—and they are coming in and it is an exceedingly moving spectacle every day to see the kind of people who bring their life's savings, who bring them to us.

More moving is the response of the poor and children coming up. Daily in the morning I spend some time, an hour or so, at my house because large numbers of people come to my house, where a provisional branch of the State Bank has been opened. At the President's House the same thing occurs. I find, I am very greatly moved, the way people who come, the very little children and grown-ups and retired people, giving whatever they have saved. It is a very heartening sight. Now we have to organise this. Last night the Finance Minister[71] broadcast something about gold bonds which he proposes to issue very soon and he probably will give you some particulars about it.

The Citizens Committee can broadly, generally, help in keeping up the morale, in looking after even prices not shooting up, in not allowing wrong kind of rumours to spread. One grave danger in moments of crisis is this spreading of rumours. Particularly we in India—I do not know if we do it more than other people—but we are apt to listen to rumours and spread rumours. Everybody, in fact the whole world, does it specially in such times. How to deal with that situation.

Then again in Delhi some unfortunate things have happened, occurrences have taken place when people in their excitement going out and demonstrating against some Embassy or some office and sometimes doing a little damage. This is too serious a matter to be left in the hands of school boys, however well-intentioned it may be. It becomes a joke for them but it has bad consequences. We cannot afford to have these things now even though we might have had them before. We have to put up with that. It is the Citizens Committee's job to control the situation in a friendly way and generally to help in the maintenance of peace and order because all disciplined effort of the nation depends on peace and order in the country. Obviously, if our energies are absorbed in other matters we cannot deal with the major issues. But there are many other things that Citizens Committees can do, in the savings campaigns and others.

269. To the CPP Executive[72]

साथियों कल इसके, कि हम और कार्यवाही करें, कुछ Condolences के प्रस्ताव हैं। एक तो Dr. Subbarayan और दूसरे Vinayak Rao Vidyalankar Hyderabad तो अगर आप मंजूर करें तो खड़े हो जायें। बैठिए।

[Translation begins

Comrades, before we start the proceedings, we have some motions for condolences. One is for Dr Subbarayan and the other is for Vinayak Rao Vidyalankar of Hyderabad. So, if you agree, please stand up. Please sit down.

Translation ends]

71. Morarji Desai.
72. Speech at the meeting of the Congress Parliamentary Party Executive Committee, 7 November 1962. NMML, AICC Speeches, Tape No. M 64/C(i), M 64/C(ii) M 65/C(i).

Comrades and friends, we meet here today before the date previously fixed for the session to commence. You know the reasons for this. A new situation has arisen, a dangerous situation on account of the aggression and invasion of Chinese forces into India. You know also the reaction that this has caused all over India and naturally on Members of Parliament as well as so many others. It has been a wonderful and magnificent reaction and all of us in spite of what has happened on our frontiers have been greatly heartened by this reaction. It has shown, this reaction, the basic feeling of the Indian people which can rise on an emergency above all their petty quarrels and disputes and controversies. The realisation has come to them that this is one of the big things that happens to a nation and it has to be met in a big way. Perhaps almost, one might feel inclined to say, that the kind of shock we have had and the reaction it has produced may work out finally for the good of the nation.

That is good, but you will realise that the situation we have to face cannot be met by merely exhibitions of, rebel exhibitions of our deep feelings, to all we are, whether we declare it or not, in a state of war. In a state of war with a country which, for the purposes of war, is highly organised and is and possesses possibly the biggest army in the world, not only a big army but a highly trained army, trained during the last 20 or 30 years and trained in a particular way which need not be quite orthodox but which is very effective, because it is a mixture of army tactics and what might be called guerrilla tactics. In Tibet alone they have a very large army, all over Tibet, and Tibet has been connected by them by roads so that it is fairly easily possible for them to rush their forces to any particular part of the frontier of Tibet and India. So we have seen in the last, little more than a fortnight, massive forces of the Chinese army coming down into India over the mountain passes and overwhelming our forces.

It is, everybody knows, that our army is a well-trained and brave army. Everybody also knows that even in this contingency they fought with remarkable courage, but they were simply overwhelmed by these large masses of troops coming wave after wave. Now naturally the shock was great to all of us and many criticisms have been made of our stage of preparedness or unpreparedness, many charges have been made which sometimes are partly true, sometimes are completely untrue, but the basic fact is that we have to face a ruthless enemy and a very strong enemy and one can only meet that aggression by a total mobilisation of our resources and fortitude and determination. So it must be realised that we are in for a long time and that this is not some short time affair which can be concluded by a burst of energy. We are, as I said in my broadcast a fortnight ago, we are a peaceful nation, we may have a good army, but we are not mentally constituted, our thinking is not, does not go that way, to organise ourselves for war. We can, of course, we are doing it, but we have not been in the past.

Many people in Parliament, belonging to the opposition chiefly, have criticised us in the past for not driving the Chinese out of Ladakh. Some people have even said we should conquer Tibet. Now all that if I may say so with all respect, is so extraordinarily beyond the range of possible fact that it is surprising that intelligent people should make such remarks. When you come to war, it is not what your wishes are that count but what your strength, determination, discipline organisation is. We have seen mighty countries with mighty war apparatuses like Germany, like Japan, crushed completely, ultimately in a war. We have seen whole armies thrust into the sea like the British army, in France, Dunkirk. You have seen a great nation like France collapse before the Nazi onslaught, in spite of a huge army and the modern weapons. You have seen in another connection the Japanese in the last war driving out the whole strong British army in Malaya and so on. That is to say, in order to meet the crisis of this type fully, it is not enough to be excited about it, but cold-blooded, long sustained effort when almost everything is secondary but the primary job of freeing our motherland.

Now we have been known in the past as advocates of peace all over the world and of course in our country. We follow the policy of non-alignment. In our country we seek to establish the structure which we have described as a socialist structure. I think those objectives of ours who were and are today and I hope will be firmly pursued but the fact remains that today we have to meet a certain situation and nothing is more necessary than a firm adherence to the objectives and not to weaken national morale or national discipline in any way. Fortunately, we have got a good basis for it in the wonderful reaction we have seen in the country, the country wants and desires it, and it is up to us to give it proper direction, mobilise the millions of people in the country and do everything that is necessary. I may be saying something that of our attitude and now obvious to all of you but I am putting it to you so that we may give consideration to this problem of today in the light of this background.

For instance, again I refer to people saying we must conquer Tibet. Now, I won't go into any details but that is beyond the bounds of possibility however much we may want it. Our putting it means that we are justifying the argument that has been made by the Chinese and thereby other countries will think that all this has arisen by our aggressive activities. As it is, you will find many so-called unaligned countries in the world rather confused, rather afraid of being dragged into this conflict, and some have declared completely in our favour, some half and half, some, many have hesitated because, well, it is obvious the reason but even the facts underlining this are not so clear to them in spite of all efforts of ours, because Chinese propaganda is strong and they go on saying the most outrageous falsehoods about our having attacked them and they are defending themselves, our attacking them on Indian soil, this is absurd on the face of it. Now for us to talk of Tibet in this connection is to talk about the moon or some other distant object which is unattainable.

Some members have said drive them out from Ladakh. That was a desirable objective, we wanted to do it, I hope we will do it, but in the circumstances that then existed purely from the balance of military and like strength of us it was not a feasible proposition, we would have sent our soldiers to certain disaster not because soldiers were weak but all the conditions were such as to militate against them and against us. This has been happening now for four or five years and any attempt of ours to build ourselves up was a fairly lengthy process. When we had built up we might adopt other tactics but some people accused us, well, do it immediately. You will realise now how difficult this was when in a relatively more favourable position, relatively I say, in NEFA, the terrible difficulties we have had, Ladakh was much more difficult to deal with in that way.

So we have to take a view of the situation, a realistic view and not merely an enthusiastic view of what we want to do. Now it is my belief that looking at it realistically we can do it, that is, we can push out the invaders from our territory, but we can do it only with a mighty effort, with building up all the resources or our nation and everything up all the resources of our nation and everything that goes with it. It is going to be a tremendous burden to us, we may suffer setbacks but I have no doubt in my mind that the ultimate triumph will be ours if we remain true to our country. Thus we have to take this long view and not in our excitement to do something for the moment which may appeal to us but which may have consequences which are in the long run bad.

Now a good deal has been said about our state of unpreparedness. Partly it is true, partly things have been said are not true. It is true in the sense that our minds are not conditioned to this kind of major war, our country is not conditioned. There is always an advantage in favour of an aggressor which can concentrate its attack on a particular point and we had a choice all these years certainly of strengthening our defence apparatus, but also of strengthening our country economically and socially. In effect a great war against a powerful adversary can only be fought by a industrialised nation in modern conditions. For a moment you can fight, you can fight little actions and you can also perhaps get enough aid to fight some little war, but a long term effort cannot be made with all the help in the world, without your own people producing the goods you require, the weapons you require and all that, you will find no instance of that anywhere. So, we looked upon our Five Year Plan not only as good in itself but as something which strengthens the nation even for war. We had the choice of either proceeding with it or gradually strengthening the base of the nation for war or peace, for everything, or leaving it and immediately getting all the help we can in weapons and other things and concentrating our efforts then for an immediate crisis. When there is an immediate crisis, one has to do it, there is no choice left, as there is a crisis today we are getting weapons from wherever we can, we have asked all countries for it. We have asked of course the United States, UK, France, Italy we have asked the Soviet Union and other countries and we are getting them. I hope to get them, but that kind of thing can only be done in an acute crisis for the moment, and because there is no help for it, there is no escape from it and you try your utmost, it is question of survival. But otherwise one builds up one's strength, basic strength; that does not give basic strength, because basic strength must come from the people, from what they make, industry, science, etc. War is a question of science and industry today as well as agriculture, the food front is most important in this. You have to build that. Therefore the Five Year Plan, there is no question before us that the Five Year Plan was necessary, not only to build up the nation but even to build it up for defence in war, but it takes time as you know and we have succeeded to some extent but not nearly as much as we should like it to be, but we had always this choice, should we give up part of the Five Year Plan, a good part of it, and devote it only to arms etc. Remember when you talk of war and arms, you have to think in terms of thousands of crores, it is not a question of a few crores this way or that way, 10, 20, 50, 100, 200 thousands of crores. Normally no country except an authoritarian regime like in China or like Hitler can do it. No democratic country can. If you have vast resources like the United States you can do it, it has enormous resources. But a democratic country, specially a relatively poor democratic country, finds it exceedingly hard. You have always the choice of giving up all the building and concentrating on war effort. That war effort itself, if it is to be a long sustained one requires internal strength, you cannot always rely on others. Therefore, we chose, we tried to build up our army and our apparatus on those lines knowing that will take time and hoping that time will come to us, that is, no major attack will be made then and when we are strong enough. Meanwhile we did what we could, the construction of roads etc. in the construction of equipment in India and in buying such necessary articles as we could. I cannot go into these matters in detail because it would not be proper; I mean to say, it would not be proper because that would be giving out the information which may help the enemy, which may—I am talking about the past—which may be not quite fair to our services, for our colleagues and others, but always we had this in view.

Now we are being criticised for not giving proper weapons or clothing. That is not a correct thing. Take clothing, every soldier that was sent out—and they were sent out rather hurriedly to the North East—we had in NEFA a fairly well protected area in the normal sense and I said so in Parliament. I could not give any undertaking and I did not to Parliament that we hold NEFA against all odds. How can I say that but I did say it was a better protected area than Ladakh. It was a better protected area and it is. Then when they first started coming over the Thagla Pass in small numbers, well, we immediately decided to send more troops there, we had sent troops almost entirely by air, because the place is inaccessible otherwise not wholly inaccessible but not easy to access. We had to send all their supplies, arms, clothing, food, every little thing, which they wanted by air. Our Air Force has done a wonderful job carrying all these things under great strain, sometimes under fire too. We did that, and because of the hurry that we had to send them, we had to do something which normally should not have been done, that is sending people from the plains suddenly to a height of 14000 feet or more. Normally people have to get accustomed to it, acclimatised. Our soldiers are good, healthy persons, but one is weakened by this sudden transfer. When they went in September, in the second week of September, it was not so cold there. We gave every single soldier three stout blankets and two pairs of boots. They said, I do not know who said, the soldiers or their officers, that going by air they take up too much room, all these blankets, send them subsequently by air. They took a blanket each, sent others later. We did so, but owing to the hazards of air droppings many of them, many of the things we dropped, fell into the ravines, remember air dropping has to be done not only in highly mountainous country with huge ravines and khuds, but facing the enemy, so much of it was lost in the khuds, it was recovered by search party and others sometimes, sometimes not. Later, we went on supplying them with blankets, every one of them has four blankets. Then we discovered, we learnt something from the Chinese because they, after long years of war on mountainous territory and guerrilla war and others have rather perfected simple methods which do not burden the soldiers and costs them little. In the matter of food we have a complicated system of food, good food for the army. The Chinese soldier has his bag of rice and a little tea and nothing else, he boils the rice and eats it and has some tea. We have a complicated food, which is better food no doubt, but it takes time to cook; it is much more difficult to supply all that. Their clothing is principally thickly padded, cotton padded coat and cotton padded trousers, which is very warm, it does not look nice at all. One of our officers said the Chinese look like monkeys in this clothing, puffed up. Well, it may be, but very effective, they may not look very dainty and graceful in them. We adopted that, we have been supplying now for the last two to three weeks, we gave immediate orders, we have supplied at the rate of 500 to 1000 cotton padded coats to all our army in addition to the other too.

Then weapons, we supplied them, most of them had 303 rifles which are good rifles, and which have been used till now, till very recently in England in the British army and in other armies too. The British army and the American army rely much more on aircraft. They have not got even mortars which the Chinese have, big mortars, we have mortars too but not of that range, we could not get mortars. We have been making mortars, we make smaller ones and now we are making bigger ones, but the very big ones were not ready then in our factory. Gradually by experience we found that this was completely a different type of warfare. Well we might have been wise, perhaps some people are, this was matter of judgment of our general staff and others. You might have thought this might happen and will happen, but normally people in the army and elsewhere are thinking in routines, they are used to certain things and they carried on till by errors and mistakes and sufferings they learnt better. We should not. Some time ago we decided to have automatic weapons and we decided as we wanted to in everything to make them ourselves. A long argument was carried on whether we should get them from outside. If we get them from outside it meant a large sum of money and we do not build up our industrial strength. But it took considerable time and ultimately we did start it, time was wasted in argument apart from the fact that, which we always have to consider, our financial resources, our foreign exchange and all that. So we started making them, not enough to replace them, we are replacing them now. But I would like to tell you how even in the most efficient armies in the world 303 rifles are still being used and are being replaced now. I think in the British army they have actually been replaced just recently.

So all these things happened and some of them put us at a disadvantage there, but the major thing was the vast masses of Chinese troops that were brought down. It is difficult for us to estimate how many they will be, we saw them increasing and that is why our effort was to take action, to push them out in the early stages. Sometimes it has been said that the political direction we gave them interfered with their military activities. Well, I can tell you that from the first of October, the day I came back from abroad, daily I was going to the Defence Ministry, discussing with the generals and air chiefs and others the position, what they were doing, what they should do and certainly I pressed them, whenever, as soon as it was possible, to push these people back. We could not, nobody can tell, it is ultimately for the experts, the generals etc. to decide when to take and what action to take. We can tell them broadly that we like these people to be pushed back so we told them but not that they must stick there, whether it is militarily possible or not and get slaughtered, that was an absurd thing.

Then soon after we came back, on the 1st October, we decided to change our organisation, make it more effective there. The organisation then was the whole of the frontier of that side, not including Ladakh, apart from Ladakh the whole of this huge frontier UP, Punjab, Himachal Pradesh, NEFA, Naga Hills and all that were under one General. We thought that was too big a charge and he had to concentrate on this NEFA. So we divided up into two and appointed one of our very competent generals to be in charge of this, General Kaul.

He was on leave then, he was suddenly called back and within twenty-four hours of his coming back, he was sent to NEFA. He went there, with these directions as I have said, to take as early steps as he could to push them back. We did not exactly know what numbers they were because large numbers were hidden by the ridge on the other side, you can only see the numbers on this side. He went there, he functioned rather too actively in the sense that first of all he went from Delhi to 14000 feet height and walked and inspected every post there, perhaps walking 16 miles, 18 miles a day in high mountains, can you imagine at that height, sudden change, this affected somewhat his heart and other things. However he carried on. After five or six days, he came back to report and he gave us a report that the Chinese troops were far more than we had imagined and many more on the other side. Anyhow they are much more. Well after about a few days, after he reported, he went back. Even when he was here, he came back after his very strenuous time he spent there, he got high fever when he was here. In that fever he went back, he said I will get over it. But going back to the same height again instead of getting better, he got worse and ultimately the doctors in charge forced him, brought him forcibly almost back to Delhi, this was on the 18th and he was here for a number of days; when the action took place and the Chinese attacked on the 20th he was lying badly ill here and part of his illness was due to his feeling frustrated, to go back, he did go back, some days or about a week after or eight days or nine days I forget, now beginning of this month and he is there now. I want to say that that all kinds of totally false stories about him were circulated, and even some foreign correspondents sent stories to their papers abroad. Now General Kaul, I don't wish to, compare he is, to my thinking and my watching him for the last fifteen to sixteen years, one of the bravest and most active and energetic persons in our Army. Nobody can judge one's ability or high tactics till the thing occurs, but about his courage and his extreme perseverance and his capacity to do a job entrusted to him I doubt if there is anybody equal to him. Well unfortunately, he is there now, it is very unfair to our officers to cast doubts on their efficiency, ability or courage, specially on an officer who even in this episode showed extraordinary determination and when he became quite incapacitated for a few days by high temperature and palpitation of the heart,

375

etc, he was forced by the doctors to come away, so he came away here. After two, three days' rest he wanted to go back, he was forcibly restrained here by the doctors and others and even when he went back the doctors were not agreeable to his going back, but he went and we allowed him to go back because he was really feeling so frustrated being here when all this was happening there.

Well, this disaster took place there on the 20th and we do not yet know, it is really, how many our casualties were, because large numbers of our troops who were dispersed by that sudden onslaught, have been coming back from places round about, and that meant of course the more they came back the casualties were that much less. I do not exactly know but I think between 1000 to 1500 or 1600 persons came back, have been coming back, more may come back, but still there were heavy casualties which we have estimated at about 2000 or so. We do not know if the Chinese have taken any prisoners, I rather doubt it, may be a few, but I rather doubt it. The fighting was of such a character as it did not permit prisoners to be taken and as far as I know Chinese are not famous for taking prisoners. Apart from that initial upset and onslaught and the Chinese took advantage of that to move forward because our armies have been upset by this terrific onslaught and they were not reorganised rapidly. So they advanced somewhat in two or three directions, that is what happened, some places fell to them, but after a few days fresh advances were formed and they are there, fairly strong defences, as strong as we can make them, and I believe that they are giving a good account of themselves. But in a matter of this kind I cannot give a guarantee, nor can the bravest general give a guarantee, because it depends on factors; one can do one's best, depending on factors sometimes beyond one's control but I feel that both in Ladakh and in NEFA area we occupy strongly our defence position.

Now I have tried to give you some brief account of what has happened there. Ever since then we have been trying to strengthen them more but the difficulty about strengthening them is not just numbers of soldiers but all the logistics apparatus which goes with them, which has to be transported by air, sometimes by trucks to a certain distance, and as I said the strain on our Air Force has been tremendous and they have borne it well. Now naturally so far as pure military tactics are concerned, it is a matter for our army general staff etc. I can offer them no advice about tactics etc. I do not know anything about it, I can discuss it with them, I can put ideas that I may have, but it is for them to decide. We discussed these matters daily and we have been strengthening our posts there every day. I have no doubt Chinese have also been strengthening them. But whatever the future may bring I do not think the Chinese forces can bring about the same type of massive attack with large numbers which they did on the first day. That is the position.

Now suppose we hold on to where we are, and I think we will, suppose we even push them back a little here and there or suppose they push us back, all these are temporary things. It may be advantageous to us or slightly disadvantageous. But the basic thing is that this kind of thing does not defeat either party finally. So the struggle goes on and therefore, we have to be prepared for a long term effort. Now our general policy has been and continues to be to seek peace where it is honourable, not dishonourable to us, and which helps us to maintain the integrity of our country, and I hope we shall never give that up because it is, if I may say so respectfully, a little childish to talk bravely of defeating China and our going to march to Peking to defeat it or they going to march to Delhi, all these things. But what we have before us is a continuous struggle provided no extraordinary thing occurs, which is not, I do not expect their agreeing to our terms. Now some people have said, you should not offer terms, you should not talk to them till they have quitted the whole of our territory. It is a great thing to say but not a very wise thing to say in the circumstances. What we have said is this, that they should withdraw to the position on the 8th September, that means a big withdrawal in NEFA and partly in Ladakh. After that we are prepared to talk to them, not on the merits but to talk to them about reducing tensions so that in future we might be able to talk to them, that is our present position. We have to take up a position which is not by any means easy but which is at least possibly feasible and which gives us further opportunities, strengthens us. We have to talk to them, something which can be understood by other countries, all countries are interested. That is our present position. I think it is a very fair suggestion which they have rejected, that is a different matter. It is a fair suggestion which has been accepted by many other countries as a fair proposition. Some people like President Nasser when he understood this position, he himself proposed something very like this to the Chinese Government, because all these countries wanted to do something in the nature of mediation and did not want to jump into the fray on this side or that. He suggested and several other countries have done the same thing.

Now to come to the present, I have given you in some detail the development of this war and I want you fully to realise that it is going to be a long, long effort and in a long effort just like a runner runs, you must get your second breath, the nation must get its second breath and not start panting too much and may be unable to carry on and we have to prepare for that second breath in the long effort. That is why I do not very much like the mere exuberant enthusiasm of school boys and others, which is good in its own way, but which exhausts itself soon. If grown up people function like that they seem to think that they are helping the cause of their country, but they are only exhausting their energy and making themselves less capable of carrying on war for a long time.

One thing of course is definitely bad which has happened in Delhi, may be elsewhere, these organised attacks on the Chinese Embassy, the Communist Party headquarters and some shops, Chinese shops etc. It is not a sign of strength, it weakens one, and in other countries it creates a bad impression. Remember the Communists. I do not know what they have in their minds or hearts, but many of them are probably in their hearts pro-Chinese, many of them I think are not, not to that extent, they have passed a resolution which as resolutions go, is fully in support of all our policy and have condemned China, and have even criticised some articles in Russian newspapers which is a very unusual thing for them to do. You may say they were forced by some circumstances, whatever that may be, their resolution has helped us in other countries because when people see in other countries, in these unaligned countries, and even communist countries of Central Europe, Poland, etc., that the Communist Party has said this, then they are much more chary of criticising our national attitude, they realise this. However that is by the way. But this is not a good thing to encourage in any way this kind of loose behaviour, it is a fight which does not leave any strength behind.

Now we have got to build up the nation and build up the nation in a way to which we are not accustomed. We have carried on civil disobedience, non-cooperation and all that; we are by way of being experts, in that something which is a different approach which affects every human being in India, build up everything, total mobilisation of our resources, our industries, our agriculture, our human beings, take this part of our plan education, we dare not allow education to lapse. We dare not allow agriculture to go back because that affects our broad effort, we have to build up, we want to, increase our army. We want immediately 15000 officers, where will the officers come from, from our young men who have to be given special training, may be concentrated training, and there must be a background of people, even our soldiers must be educated because they are technically-minded today. So that all these processes have to be diverted to one end, mobilising the nation, preparing the nation and everything that comes in the way of that has to be sacrificed or put by. That is what we have to do. We have to build up the morale of the nation and the morale of the forces. Therefore, it is essential that we do not do anything which affects the morale of the nation or of our armed forces and everything, every word that you may say in Parliament is broadcast to India and to the world. Hence you be very careful not to say things which affects the morale of the nation and of our forces. As a matter of fact, people complain we do not tell them much about news from the front. We do not judge, it is entirely a matter for the military to judge, if they think some news may help the enemy, they did not want to give it out. Something that may help not only the enemy but any person, a saboteur or somebody committing sabotage. Now some aircraft have been bringing arms from America and from England and from other places. In no warring country is it ever advertised, what is coming when it is coming; it is an invitation, a person might commit sabotage on the airfield or wherever they can. Thus far we are not used to these restraints. Newspapers giving big headlines, this has arrived, that has arrived, it is all very well, but you take a risk and unless there are very stiff arrangements to prevent that happening, it is a bad risk, you would not take it. You know that even now we have got this Defence of India Act under which there are severe penalties for rumour-mongering, severe penalties for giving news about movement of troops, movements of equipment, and gradually we will have to get used to them, the sooner the better. Because it comes in the way of our war effort. We may have to get used to all kinds of things. In England, etc. in war time there was strict rationing, strict controls, we are not going to put them now, but if anything is necessary it has to be done, because everything has to be subordinated to one end. I have no doubt, I am sorry I am taking up your time by saying things which are well known, which are platitudes.

But now I come to one other matter. There has been a great deal of talk and criticism of our Defence Ministry of Mr Krishna Menon who was Defence Minister and partly of me too.[73] I do not mind criticism myself but the way it has been carried on has been most unfortunate and it hurts me very greatly. Because, shall I say, all these setbacks that we have suffered, have been cast on the Defence Minister, sometimes on others too, that would be cruel because all the major decisions and the minor decisions have been jointly undertaken by us. It is normal and I can tell you that I have been in touch with Defence rather closely all the time, but for the last five weeks or so I have been in daily, constant touch, going to the Defence Ministry, sitting down there, discussing it and so I am at least as much to blame as anybody else. It is easy, it is a cheap way of finding fault with people because something has occurred. And I can understand the public, the public irritation, frustration, anger and trying to find the scapegoat, that happens. But it is a dangerous way of thinking because if you do that our generals, suppose you started criticising our generals in that way, no general will be able to function, such ability he has he gives, why did this happen, why did you withdraw, why that, it simply cannot be done, you change your general, ultimately you may have to change the general, and I want to say I have been hurt very much by what has been said against my colleague Mr Krishna Menon. Sometimes his patriotism is doubted. Now none of us,

---

73. See infra sub section (e) CHINESE INVASION: Krishna Menon. See also items 28 and 446.

certainly including me, most of you too are free of failings, are merely a bundle of virtues. We have our failings, our faults, and so has Mr Krishna Menon. But I can say with complete confidence, I have had experience of five or six Defence Ministers here since Independence, and some of them very good, very able men, like Mr Gopalaswamy Ayyangar, a very fine man. But I can say with confidence that no Defence Minister has worked harder and more efficiently than Mr Krishna Menon. One might almost say he gave his, well I won't say gave his life to it, but all the energy he has, all the time he has, he does work, he is a very hard worker, all night he hardly sleeps, and he worked that way. He may have made mistakes here and there but he gave all the strength he had to it and it was a difficult matter because of the difficulty we are facing today

We have to think anew, we have to build a new type of nation, new type of public, used to these conditions. We are too used to a certain slackness, a certain, well, speechifying and pointing out the faults of others. In the army which is a good army I repeat, we are the successors of the British army, we follow their methods, our Indian Army, right up to Independence practically everything was decided in Whitehall, then we had the officers, he had to carry it out, they were English officers here till then, almost everything that we required for our ammunition and equipment was bought from England. Some change was made during the last war. Because of the difficulties of the war they could not get them from England so they had to produce them here. So some factories etc. were put up, ordnance factories, but still we were very, very backward in introducing everything. Our method of thinking was that the best way to get a thing is sign an order on some firms in Germany, America, England, etc. and we get them, we did get them but at a terrific price, nothing is more expensive than war material and not only is it expensive, the armaments racket is notorious. It makes you pay through your nose, private firms and others, it is not an easy thing which you can get. If you require something, you have to get it, whatever you pay, they make you pay. So the basic thing was this has to be changed and we have to produce ourselves. That was not an easy matter to shift from, because it is not copying a gun or something, sometimes they copy it, even in copying it we want their licence and their agreement and pay them royalties. It was having a Science Department which can produce these things, which can improve them, there was no such thing here previously. We have built up an effective science department, defence science department which not only thinks about these weapons but looks ahead and thinks about other weapons that are coming into the field like missiles and ballistics, things and all that. They have not very many, may not, but we have to think ahead, that was done. Ordnance factories, many of them were increased and advanced in many ways. Well that is all right. We made great progress subject always to our limitations of finance. Because when you think of war you have to think in terms of thousands of crores, it is not hundreds of crores, it means the whole, our annual revenue being thrown into it and we are chary of doing it, and I do not know if everybody justified it to anybody, people would have welcomed it, it is all very well now when they have the shock of this experience they are prepared to accept anything. If we say 10 thousand crores they will say yes, because they feel it is now a struggle for life and death but at that time, peace time, to get that, it was very difficult. And I can very well understand our Cabinet, our Finance Minister, myself, jibbing at vast expenditure.

So, it was to change the mentality behind defence, it is a difficult thing, which Mr Krishna Menon tried to do and which is essential, which now with the war of course we will do very rapidly and he succeeded to some extent, not to the extent of our making ourselves self-sufficient, of course not, it takes time. But we were moving in that direction and whatever has been done in the past few years, although it is wholly inadequate from the point of view of carrying on now, we can increase it rapidly on that strong foundation. That is why I said that Mr Krishna Menon has done according to my thinking and I have been in intimate touch with his work, very good work in the Defence Ministry, and from this point of view more effective work to build the foundation of the future strength than anyone else, although others, they were very able and very fine men and it has hurt me that a man who has devoted himself so utterly should be criticised in the way that he has been. I want you to distinguish two things: many people have said that he must go, resign, that is a different thing. I am sure one may be entitled to say in all the circumstances of the case he should resign, I can understand that. There are arguments for it and against it, but to condemn him for something which is the fault of many others including myself and which was inherent in the circumstances when you are facing a country with an army of I do not know 4 million people, the mere numbers are tremendous. We are a big country but our army is not one tenth of theirs. Their whole effort has been concentrated in building up a military apparatus and now we are engaged in building up a military apparatus to meet them, it is a different matter. So I should like to pay my tribute to Mr Krishna Menon's work. That does not mean that everything that he has done is perfect, he has made mistakes, I have made mistakes. First of all, most of us are jointly responsible for major decisions. Secondly, even in the other decisions with which I was largely connected I am largely responsible. He has made mistakes and sometimes he has got into trouble and all that and there is also to be said that however virtuous a minister might be, if for some reason or other, if the Department under him suffers a great deal, the minister is responsible. These are arguments which I can understand, but what has hurt me, well, it is not unexpected, it is a kind of propaganda which is carried on in the press, daily propaganda aligning him, that is carried on by some of our opposition parties, the Jan Sangh, Swatantra party and others. It is, it is morally bad, factually incorrect and does a lot of harm to the morale of the nation and our forces. I have expressed my opinion to you and behind it often I feel it is not so much what he has done or not done, but a desire—I am talking about the opposition parties—a desire to condemn us, condemn our party, the Congress and Congress Government and to take advantage of that situation in order to damn the Congress. Also I believe, some people, I do not say all, these opposition parties have opposed our policies, whether it is socialism, whether it is non-alignment, whether it is public sector, etc. etc. How they want to utilise this opportunity to go against all the basic policies that we have professed and tried to follow. That is a dangerous thing I think if that is done, not only will it weaken our war effort but otherwise do a lot of injury for us and we have to be very wide awake that that does not happen.

So, I was pained that many of our colleagues have, not entirely, partly, taken up that attitude. As I said it was, I can understand on a balance of considerations your coming to a decision or I, coming to a decision, that it is better for a minister to resign or the Prime Minister to resign. After all, I am here only by your goodwill, the moment you say no I go out, do some other job. That is a different matter, it is always in your hands and I said as I told the Executive Committee, if I feel at any time, that I do not have your confidence then I have no business to be here, I have not threatened resignation or anything like that, that would be a very bad thing for me in this crisis, in peace time one can do all such things, but in such a time nobody can run away from his job, unless of course it is your will, then of course everything stands.

Now I might tell you that during the last considerable time, well many weeks Mr Krishna Menon has several times offered his resignation to me and a letter he wrote to me about seven or eight days ago, I think it is dated 30 October, and I read to the Executive Committee, if you like I will read it. This was the letter he wrote to me then. It has come in the Radio? "In the situation that faces the country as a result of the unprovoked invasion of our territories by China I submit that it is appropriate and necessary that the portfolio of Defence should be taken over by you. I am conscious and concerned that this will impose a heavy burden on you. The determination of our people to eject the invader and to defend the honour and integrity of the motherland so overwhelmingly demonstrated by our people will I feel sure, add to your strength and capacity. No one other than you can guard or help to maintain that resoluteness to the fullness of this purpose and without deterioration. I conveyed these sentiments to you some days or weeks ago and much earlier in this crisis. I feel however that your assumption of charge should not he delayed. I had offered to serve and assist you in the task that faces us in any capacity you wished. I need hardly say that such ability or energies as I possess are unreservedly and entirely at your disposal now as always."[74] It was on the 31st that I made that change, I think on the 1st November perhaps that I took over Defence and asked Mr Krishna Menon to look after Defence Production in which he was greatly interested and which had been largely built up under his guidance and I should like to say, not work of Krishna Menon, but those of our army men, airmen and naval men, engineers. They are a fine lot of men and engineers, apart from courage, they are a fine lot of men who can do anything given the opportunities and the thing that Shri Krishna Menon did was to give our men opportunities. And until now the opportunities largely came in the way of purely fighting, I mean to say, the generals and colonels and others, but the engineers' job was rather in a lower grade. He was an adviser, he built, looked after an ordnance factory, but our scientific apparatus, we have got 2000 or 3000 scientists working on defence science and we have had this great advantage of having one of our ablest men till recently Dr Kothari, in charge of it. Now he is, as you know, of the University or what not, Grants Commission, head of it. So that these people are a very fine lot of men, and I am much impressed by their ability and what is more, having got the opportunity, they worked with tremendous enthusiasm, because they were making something new. They are not merely on parade, going up and down but they were making something, the best that was required, came out of them. So I am proud of those men. So that is what I decided on first. I thought defence was my complete charge including of course defence production but that particular department might be left to Mr Krishna Menon because he was good at it; he had devoted himself to it, and he worked hard for it. I thought that, well, meet the situation, but find after that a great deal of crisis still continuing and it has affected some of our members also. I have got letters of various kinds, some in his praise, some in his dispraise, some in his criticism and outside too as I ventured to say the other day somewhere, I am fairly in touch generally speaking with the pulse of the nation. Then because of all these factors and in spite of my opinions that he would do well, especially well in this restricted field of production, I thought that a person whose work has been criticised, even though wrongly criticised, cannot do good work. It upsets him, upsets others and I began to think then that repeatedly he has offered his resignation to me, should be considered by me previously, purely thinking there can be none of course, one may be affected personally by some factors. But I was trying to judge purely from the point of view of how we can conduct this war efficiently, how we can use our best men for particular jobs, which

74. See appendix 35.

they can do well and I have thought that then that he will do this job very well and we should ask him to do this defence production. But when later I began to feel that his work will be impeded by this constant controversy and criticism, it is immaterial whether most people criticise him or most people were for him, it is immaterial but there was this controversy, I thought of the resignation he sent me and which he kept on repeating and I have had his resignation letter in my pocket all the time. So finally, I decided to accept it.[75] I have at least, I have decided to accept it, I have not formally done so yet. That is a formal matter but I have decided to accept it and I have decided to accept it not without considerable hurt and pain because I did think and do think that a man of his extraordinary abilities, perseverance, determination at work should be utilised fully, and it will be harmful to us and to the nation I think if his abilities are wasted. After all there are not too many men in the country; there are of course many good men, many able men and in many fields of work but there are not too many of them about. So it is with regret that I acceded to his wish to resign. That is a decision now and I suppose formally speaking I shall write to him, may be tonight, may be tomorrow, finalising this matter.

Now we are meeting in Parliament tomorrow and I should like all our members, if I may say so with all respect, to function with determination and dignity and not descend as far as possible to personal levels. We do not want to treat this crisis for any party advantage, we have even I think the AICC has asked the Congress Committee to cooperate with other parties although I have been told this has not been very successful always and the other parties have rather not used the occasion to the advantage of the general cause. They have attacked Congress policy and made it rather embarrassing for Congressmen sitting on the same platform. I do not look at it from that point of view but remember that it is very difficult for us to sit down now without harm. Suppose we sat down and enquire into the working of our Army headquarters, Air headquarters some time this has to be done but this is no time. It is very harmful because all our senior officers are doing their best. Sometimes their best may not take them very far, that is a different matter because of circumstances and other things, sometimes an officer has to be changed or a minister has to be changed that is a different matter. I would remind you that in no war, no major war have the first set of senior officers continued long. Because they are peacetime officers when they have to face a crisis. Within six months of, the senior officers in England, in Russia, the last war, I am talking about and I am not sure what happened, in Germany because they were trained to it right from the beginning, were completely changed, war conditions brought out new men, new abilities

75. See appendices 45 and 46.

were recognised, younger men and all that. Well if that comes, that comes but normally a country facing a crisis does not indulge in mutual mud-slinging, it is bad form, it affects the morale of the people and therefore and as I said it is difficult for us even to say, give all the facts because all the facts may also be harmful from the morale point of view. So, I hope that tomorrow and after in Parliament, our party will function with discipline with dignity.

Thank you.

I do not wish in any sense to put a closure on speeches but, and it may be desirable, I do not know what the honourable member is going to speak, our colleague, he may be, I am saying is I have no idea whatever. He said he wanted some guidance about certain matters that may be necessary but perhaps it will be better for these points to be considered in subsequent meetings, points that are raised, we could consider them.

270. To Rajendra Prasad: Latest Position[76]

November 8, 1962

My dear Rajendra Babu,

Thank you for your letter of the 5th November. I have read the extract from the *Hindusthan Standard* which you have kindly sent me. We are taking such steps as are possible to protect the various routes of entry from Tibet to India. The Chinese have some advantages over us. They have an Army in Tibet alone which is far larger than the entire Indian Army; they have got roads all over Tibet so that they can rush troops at any point quickly and, being the aggressors, they can choose their point of attack.

We are protecting the Chungi Valley route, but some parts of Bhutan are easy of access to the Chinese. We cannot send any troops to Bhutan because the Maharaja thinks that will give an excuse to the Chinese to enter Bhutan. The Chinese have said that they will not enter Bhutan, but no one can really rely on their word.

Arrangements are being made about the collection of funds as well as about citizens' organisations in States.

76. Letter to the former President; address: Sadakat Ashram, Patna.

As you must have known, Krishna Menon has resigned. I do not think that the propaganda against him was at all justified. But I will not go into that question. I happen to have been connected with Defence very intimately for some time past. For the last five weeks I have been going there daily.

Yours sincerely,
[Jawaharlal Nehru]

271. In the Lok Sabha: Emergency and Appreciation of Defence Forces[77]

The Prime Minister and Minister of External Affairs, Defence and Atomic Energy (Jawaharlal Nehru): Mr Speaker, Sir, I beg to move:

"This House approves the Proclamation of Emergency issued by the President on the 26th of October, 1962, under clause (1) of article 352 of the Constitution."

Speaker: I shall place it before the House.
Resolution moved:

"This House approves the Proclamation of Emergency issued by the President on the 26th of October, 1962, under clause (1) of article 352 of Constitution."

The hon. Prime Minister may move the other resolution also.

Jawaharlal Nehru: I beg to move:

"This House notes with deep regret that in spite of the uniform gestures of goodwill and friendship by India towards the People's Government of China on the basis of recognition of each other's independence, non-aggression and non-interference, and peaceful coexistence, China has betrayed this goodwill and friendship and the principles of Panch Sheel which had been agreed to between the two countries and has committed aggression and initiated a massive invasion of India by her armed forces.

---

77. Moving Resolutions on National Emergency and Appreciation of Defence Forces, 8 November 1962. *Lok Sabha Debates*, Vol.9 November 8-20, 1962, pp. 106-133.

The House places on record its high appreciation of the valiant struggle of men and officers of our armed forces while defending our frontiers..."

Several Hon. Members: Hear, hear.

Jawaharlal Nehru: "... and pays its respectful homage to the martyrs who have laid down their lives in defending the honour and integrity of our Motherland.

This House also records its profound appreciation of the wonderful and spontaneous response of the people of India to the emergency and the crisis that has resulted from China's invasion of India. It notes with deep gratitude this mighty upsurge amongst all sections of our people for harnessing all our resources towards the organisation of an all out effort to meet this grave national emergency. The flame of liberty and sacrifice has been kindled anew and a fresh dedication has taken place to the cause of India's freedom and integrity.

This House gratefully acknowledges the sympathy and the moral and material support received from a large number of friendly countries in this grim hour of our struggle against aggression and invasion.

With hope and faith, this House affirms the firm resolve of the Indian people to drive out the aggressor from the sacred soil of India, however long and hard the struggle may be."

Speaker: I shall place this Resolution also before the House.
Resolution moved:

"This House notes with deep regret that, in spite of the uniform gestures of goodwill and friendship by India towards the People's Government of China on the basis of recognition of each other's independence, non-aggression and non-interference, and peaceful coexistence, China has betrayed this goodwill and friendship and the principles of Panchsheel which had been agreed to between the two countries and has committed aggression and initiated a massive invasion of India by her armed forces.

This House places on record its high appreciation of the valiant struggle of men and officers of our armed forces while defending our frontiers and pays its respectful homage to the martyrs who have laid down their lives in defending the honour and integrity of our Motherland.

This House also records its profound appreciation of wonderful and spontaneous response of the people of India to the emergency and the crisis that has resulted from China's invasion of India. It notes with deep gratitude this mighty upsurge amongst all sections of our people for harnessing all our resources towards the organisation of an all out effort to meet this grave national emergency. The flame of liberty and sacrifice has been kindled anew and a fresh dedication has taken place to cause of India's freedom and integrity.

This House gratefully acknowledges the sympathy and the moral and material support received from a large number of friendly countries in this grim hour of our struggle against aggression and invasion.

With hope and faith, this House affirms the firm resolve of the Indian people to drive out the aggressor from the sacred soil of India, however long and hard the struggle may be."

Jawaharlal Nehru: Mr Speaker, Sir, we meet in Parliament today earlier than was intended, because of a grave crisis that has arisen. This House, and everybody in India, and the greater part of the world know that the People's Republic of China has invaded India with massive forces, and there have been some bloody battles resulting in considerable casualties on both sides.

For five years, we have been the victims of Chinese aggression across our frontiers in the north. That aggression was, to begin with, rather furtive. Occasionally there were some incidents and conflicts. These conflicts might well be termed frontier incidents. Today, we are facing a regular and massive invasion of our territory by very large forces.

China, which has claimed and still claims to be anti-imperialist, is pursuing a course today for which comparisons can only be sought in the eighteenth and nineteenth centuries. In those past days, the European Powers in the full flood of imperialist aggression and with strength and weapons given to them by the Industrial Revolution took possession of large parts of Asia and Africa by force. That imperialism has abated now, and many of the colonies of European countries have been freed and are independent countries. But, curiously, the very champions of anti imperialism, that is, the People's Government of China, are now following the course of aggression and imperialist expansion.

[Omitted: Exchange on procedure]

Jawaharlal Nehru: It is sad to think that we in India, who have pleaded for peace all over the world, and who have sought the friendship of China and treated them with courtesy and consideration and pleaded their cause in the councils of the world should now ourselves be victims of new imperialism and expansionism by a country which says that it is against all imperialism. This strange twist of history has brought us face to face with something that we have not experienced in this way for over a hundred years or more. We had taken it almost for granted that despite some lapses in recent years, as in the

Suez affair, we had taken it for granted that this type of aggression was almost a thing of the past. Even the Chinese aggression on our borders during the last five years, bad as it was, and indicative of an expansionist tendency, though it troubled us greatly, hardly led us to the conclusion that China would indulge in a massive invasion of India. Now, we have seen and experienced this very invasion and it has shocked us, as it has shocked a large number of countries.

History has taken a new turn in Asia and perhaps the world, and we have to bear the brunt of it, to fight with all our might this menace to our freedom and integrity. Not only are we threatened by it, but all the standards of international behaviour have been upset and so all the world is affected by it, apart form the immediate consequences. No self-respecting country which lives its freedom and its integrity can possibly submit to this challenge. Certainly, India, this dear land of ours, will never submit to it whatever the consequences, we accept the challenge in all its consequences, whatever they may be …

It may be that this challenge is also an opportunity for us. Indeed, the people of India in their millions have demonstrated that they accept this challenge and have shown a unity and an enthusiasm such as has been very seldom in evidence. A crisis has come and we have stood up to face it and meet that crisis.

I have moved a Resolution seeking the approval of this House to the state of emergency that has been declared by the President. That was inevitable when foreign legions invaded India and our Constitution wisely provided for such a course to be followed by us in any serious crisis. I have no doubt that this House will approve of this declaration by the President and subsequently I hope also of the Defence of India Ordinance and the other steps that are being taken to face this crisis.

I should like this House for a moment to look at this matter in some perspective. We stand, I do believe, at a turning point not only in the history of India but of Asia and possibly even of the world, because what happens in this conflict will affect it obviously. It will affect Asia, of which two of the biggest countries are China and India. But it will affect the world also and, therefore, this conflict has very wide reaching consequences. We should try to look at it from this point of view. For the moment, we are shocked at this cruel and crude invasion of another country. The world has also witnessed the response of the people of the country invaded, that is, our country, and the world will yet witness the way the people of India act when their freedom is threatened and their dear liberty is imperilled.

So, we are shocked and in a state of high excitement. That is inevitable, and not surprising, but we have to remember that this turning point in history is not going to end soon. We may have to face this for a long period, for a number of years, I do not know how long, and we must train ourselves, and the nation to be prepared to face, however long the crisis may last. It is in the mood, in that mentality, that I seek this House to give a lead to the country.

Chinese aggression on our frontiers is five years old and during these years this House has discussed this matter repeatedly. On the last occasion this discussion took place on the 12th August, 1962. Many White Papers have been issued, giving the long drawn-out correspondence between the Government of India and the Government of China. Only today I have placed another bunch of these papers contained in White Paper No. 7. On the 22nd August, 1962 we sent a note to China. A reply was sent to this on the 13th September last. But before the reply was sent or received by us, even on the 8th September, China's forces crossed the international boundary in the northwest corner of NEFA across the Thagla ridge and began to threaten the Indian post at Dhola. We had a number of posts near the northern frontier of NEFA adequate enough to meet any minor or normal incursion. We hoped that we would be able to meet this new aggression and immediately we took steps to strengthen our forces in that area.

Five days after this new aggression, on the 13th September, the Chinese Government sent us a threatening reply, asking for discussions on the boundary question. We have previously demonstrated by a mass of evidence that our boundary is what has been called the McMahon Line, but the boundary was not laid down even by Mr McMahon, whoever is responsible for it. It was a recognition of the long standing frontier on the high ridge of the Himalayas which divided the two countries at the watershed. To some extent, though indirectly, the Chinese accepted this. Certainly, they accepted the continuation of this line in Burma. But, apart from the constitutional or legal aspects, it is undoubted and cannot be challenged that no Chinese has ever been in that part on this side of the line, excepting, as the House knows, in a little border village called Longju.

Even the McMahon Line which the Chinese have called illegal was laid down 48 years ago, in 1914, and that was a confirmation of what was believed in then. Legal or not, it has been a part of India for a long number of years and certainly let us say for 50 years or so, apart from its previous history which is also in our favour. Here then is a boundary which for nearly 50 years has been shown to be our northern frontier. I am limiting what I say to 50 years for the sake of argument; really it was even before that. Even if the Chinese did not accept it and I would like to say that the objection they raised in 1913 to this treaty was not based on their objection to the McMahon Line; it was based on their objection to another part of the treaty, which divided Inner Tibet and Outer Tibet, the McMahon Line did not come in that; however, it is a fact that they objected to the whole treaty because of that other objection. Even if the Chinese did not accept it then, this has been in existence now in our maps in our practice, in our Constitution, in our organization, administration etc., for nearly 50 years. Even the non-acceptance of it, can it entitle them to undertake an armed invasion to upset it? Even the Chinese know and say that independent India has been in possession of this territory right up to the Himalayan watershed. It is rather difficult for me to say what they say. Because, if any person takes the trouble to read through this vast correspondence, he will notice that their alleged frontier is a very mobile one; it changes. It is wherever they have laid the frontier and in this matter too they have stated many contradictory things. They have laid stress sometimes on the fact that we have occupied this area of NEFA or a large part of it since we became independent. That is a curious statement since, as I have said all along, it was fully recognised in 1913-14. Apart from that, when we became independent, we did one thing. We naturally wanted these tribal people in the frontier areas to share our independence. The British largely left them to their own resources and interfered only when there was some trouble. But there is no doubt that the British considered their frontier to be the McMahon Line. They did not have a full fledged administrative apparatus there. On gaining independence, we were naturally anxious to develop these area as we were trying to develop other areas of India. We tried, therefore not only to introduce our administration there but schools, hospitals, roads, etc. It is this which the Chinese say represents our occupying that. Any person who sees these papers and the history behind them would easily say that we have occupied it in every sense, legally, constitutionally, administratively, practically for a large number of years.

Now, the point is that whatever the legal and constitutional aspect of their claim might be—we think there is no force whatever—does that justify sudden invasion of this kind? The House will remember that we have discussed this matter many times previously; we discussed it largely in relation to their aggression in Ladakh because nothing had happened here except with the sole exception of the little frontier village Longju. Repeatedly, in the course of talks sometimes they are reflected in these papers too—we were given to understand something not absolutely, not clearly; as has now been discovered, always their phrases had a double meaning attached to them which could be interpreted any way, to assure us of something and later to deny that they had assured us. I remember the long talk I had with the Chinese Prime Minister, specially about the McMahon Line. I forget the exact date; it was five years ago or six years ago; I do not remember exactly. That was when he came to India. We had a long talk and immediately after the talk I put down in a note I prepared the contents of our talk so that I might not forget it. That note is here in our Office. Much later I sent an extract of my note of that talk to the Chinese Government and they denied the truth of it; I was very much surprised and hurt because I was quite certain. When we were talking it was not once I asked. I asked the same question two or three times and definitely the answer was given to me. He gave me to understand that although the Chinese Government considered the McMahon line an illegal line and a British imperialist line, nevertheless because of the large number of facts, because of their desire to be friendly with us, they would [be] prepared to do this. That was the clearest impression that I got. He denied it later on. So, it becomes a little difficult to say what they stood by at a particular time.

Anyhow, my point is that whether they acknowledge the McMahon Line or not undoubtedly it has been, till a few weeks ago, completely in our possession; the area on this side was completely in our possession; for generations past it has been in our possession; if you like it I can put a later date, 1913-14 and I may say that it was a recording of what had been happening previously. How does it justify the Chinese Government to carry on an invasion of it, by any law, international standards of behaviour or for any other reason?

The House may have noticed a very peculiar approach that the Chinese Government has made to what has happened recently in NEFA. They go on saying that India attacked them and their frontier guards as they are called, are merely defending themselves. I must confess that this complete perversion of facts and the attempt to make falsehood appear to be the truth, and the truth to be the falsehood has amazed me because nothing can be more utterly baseless than what they have been saying. Here is a single fact. We have been up to the McMahon line all these years; we have not gone one inch beyond nor have we covered another's territory. They have come, let us for the moment assume their case that there is some doubt about where the McMahon line is. But the point is that they have invaded an area which has not been in their possession ever, ever in the history of the last 10,000 years. After all the present Chinese Government came into existence 12 years ago or thereabout. Any claim that they may directly make to this territory can only be made either in these 12 years or possibly previously through Tibet. So, it becomes a question of what they can claim through Tibet or through their domination over Tibet. It is true that for a long time past there were some frontier questions between Tibet and India, even in British times. But all these questions were about little pockets or little frontier areas, small areas. Nobody has ever put forward, no Tibetan Government has ever put forward previously these large claims to what tantamount to two thirds of NEFA apart from the vast area in Ladakh.

So, we arrive at one firm conclusion which is not capable of argument or denial; that is, the Chinese have come to this territory with a massive force, territory which for a long time at least has been included in India, and administered in a vague way and a little fully administered by India. If they had any claim they could have discussed it and talked about it and adopted various means of peaceful settlement, appointed arbitrators, or gone to the Hague Court or whatever it was.

Here, I may say, it has been unfortunate, in this as in so many other cases, that the present Government of China is not represented in the United Nations. Hon. Members are surprised when we have supported the Chinese representation-the representation of the People's Government of China—in the United Nations, we have supported it in spite of this present invasion, because we have to look at it this way: it is not a question of likes or dislikes. It is a question, which will facilitate Chinese aggression; it will facilitate its misbehaviour in the future. It will make disarmament impossible in the world. You might disarm the whole world and leave China, a great, powerful country, fully armed to the teeth. It is inconceivable. Therefore, in spite of our great resentment at what they have done, the great irritation and anger, still, I am glad to say that we kept some perspective about things and supported that even now. The difficulty is one cannot call them up before any tribunal or world court or anywhere. They are just wholly an irresponsible country believing, I believe, in war as the only way of settling anything, having no love of peace and stating almost that, and with great power at their disposal. That is the dangerous state of affairs not only for India but for the rest of the world. I am not going into the question, as some people do, of communism or anti-communism. I do not believe that that is a major issue in this matter or any other. Communism may help; but the major issue is, an expansionist, imperialist-minded country deliberately invading into a new country...

[Interjection omitted]

Jawaharlal Nehru: I do not know what the hon. Member has said. I am not entering into that argument. I am laying stress on this fact, because as some countries do, they explain everything in terms of communism and anti-communism. I think the result is that they are unable to see many of the basic facts of the questions. Communism may help or communism may hinder. Communism may give them a certain strength of weakness, whatever it may be. But today we are facing a naked aggression, just the type of aggression which we saw in the eighteenth and nineteenth centuries there was then no communism anywhere.

[Interjection omitted]

Jawaharlal Nehru: So, we have to face this new type of imperialism on our border. Asia is facing this new type, and the whole world is concerned with that. For the moment, we are most concerned with it, and we have to face it and bear the burden ourselves, although some of our friendly countries are certainly helping us and we are grateful to them for that help.

To say that we are committing all this aggression on Chinese territory is a kind of double talk which is very difficult for a man of my simple mind to understand. "We commit aggression ourselves; we commit aggression on the soil of our own country and they defend it by coming over the mountains into our territory." It is really extraordinary to what length people can go to justify their misdeeds.

It is true that when we heard on the 8th September of their coming over the Thagla pass into our territory in some forces, we had quite adequate forces in our posts. We had no doubt some forces there to meet any incursion, but if large forces come over, an ordinary military post can hardly resist them. We took immediate steps to send further forces to reinforce our posts. We sent them immediately as we had to in the circumstances; yet there was one unfortunate factor which normally should be remembered. That was, if we send our forces, who are tough, young and strong, nevertheless, we send them from the plains of India suddenly to 14,000 ft. high. For any person; however strong he may be, it requires time to be acclimatised to these heights. But they went there. Then they went there, then began a process; we sent some further forces and thought that they would be adequate to meet the Chinese menace in so far as it was feasible. The Chinese also started increasing their forces there. Now, for them, it was a relatively easy matter, because they have vast forces in Tibet. I do not know how much they have. They used to have 11 divisions, and I told they now have 13 or 14 divisions in Tibet. Just imagine the very vast armies they are having in Tibet alone.

रामेश्वरानन्द [78]करनालः अब तो आपको चाइनीज की मनोवृत्ति का पता चल गया होगा ।

[Translation begins:

Rameswaranand: Now you must have understood the thinking process of the Chinese!

Translation ends]

Jawaharlal Nehru: I think, if the hon. Member feels keenly about it, we will send him to the frontier. Perhaps the speeches may convince the Chinese, so,

---

78. Jana Sangh.

first of all, the Chinese armies were fully acclimatised, living for long on the high plateau of Tibet. It was just not in the line with the ridge but only a little below the ridge.

Secondly, the whole of Tibet has been covered in the last few years by roads, and the roads there, in that extremely severe climate, mean simply levelling the ground, removing boulders, etc., because you do not require cement or anything at that height. The ground itself is so very hard. So, this is covered by roads, and they can travel perhaps at quick notice from one part to another in Tibet.

So, they could bring large forces to the other side of the Thagla ridge. They would not be immediately visible to us, because on the other side—and that is what we believe happened—although some forces were being added on by the Chinese crossing the Thagla ridge they could not be seen. They were adding large numbers of forces on the other side nearby and in the last few days of this battle that occurred there on the 20th, they poured in masses of the people. I do not know how much: six, seven and eight times the number of troops that we had. They have thus logistic advantage not only of bringing troops but supplying everything that could be brought immediately on the other side of the Thagla ridge and send them. We had a certain disadvantage. I am merely mentioning the facts—the logistic disadvantage of the people having been suddenly sent to those heights, everything that they require has to be sent by air, and our Air Force has done a very fine piece of work there in taking everything by air in spite, sometimes, of enemy fire and the difficulties that always occur in those high mountains. So, this went on.

May I add that there has been a great deal of attack about our unpreparedness. I think most of it is based on ignorance (Interruption).

Hari Vishnu Kamath[79]: We do not want to interrupt; you may go on replying in your own way.

Jawaharlal Nehru: I am glad of this generosity in not interrupting me. I say most of this talk is based on ignorance of facts. Some of them are true: first of all, it is perfectly true that we were not prepared to face two or three divisions of the Chinese army descending upon the forces there.

रामेश्वरानन्दः मैं जानना चाहता हूं कि अब तक आप क्या कर रहे थे ...

79. PSP.

अध्यक्षः आप सुन तो लीजिये आराम से? इस तरह इंटरप्शन करने से कैसे काम चलेगा?

रामेश्वरानन्दः यह दुराग्रह में आज तक फंसे रहे और अब हमारी बात सुनना भी नहीं पसन्द करते।

अध्यक्षः आप सुन तो लें आराम से।

रामेश्वरानन्दः मैं तो यह जानना चाहता हूं कि यह क्या कर रहे थे? वह लोग हमला कर रहे थे तब यह क्या कर रहे थे?

बागड़ी[80] (हिसार)ः जब स्वामी जी ने कुछ कहा तो हमारे प्राइम मिनिस्टर साहब ने कहा कि उनके फ्रंटियर को भेद दो। फ्रंटियर में जायेंगे हमारे बच्चे, वह बहादुर हैं। वह चीन तक जायेंगे और जीत कर आयेंगे।

[Translation begins:

Rameswaranand: I want to know what you were doing till now?

Speaker: Please listen to him first. If you interrupt like this how would we conduct the proceedings of the House?

Rameswaranand: He has been caught in this mistaken notion, and now he is not even prepared to listen to us.

Speaker: At least, listen to him with some patience.

Rameswaranand: I want to know what they were doing. Those people were attacking us and what were these people doing?

Bagri: When Swamiji was saying something, our Prime Minister said that penetrate their frontier. Our children will go to the frontier, because they are brave. They will go up to China and come back victorious.

Translation ends]

---

80. Socialist Party.

Shri Jawaharlal Nehru: Swamiji, I am afraid, has not acquired ...

रामसेवक यादव[81] (बाराबंकी): स्वामी जी की परेशानी यह है कि वह इस बोली को समझते नहीं हैं, आप उनको समझाइये।

जवाहरलाल नेहरुः यही मैं कह रहा था कि मुश्किल यह है कि स्वामी जी कुछ भी नहीं समझते।

रामसेवक यादवः स्वामी जी सब कुछ समझते हैं ...

जवाहरलाल नेहरुः यह बोली की बात नहीं है।

रामसेवक यादवः अध्यक्ष महोदय, किसी माननीय सदस्य के लिए यह कहना कि वह कुछ समझते नहीं हैं यह ठीक नहीं है।

अध्यक्षः आप मेरी तकलीफ़ को भी समझें। अगर स्वामी जी इस बोली को नहीं समझते और प्राइम मिनिस्टर साहब दूसरी बोली में बोलें तो कई और माननीय सदस्य नहीं समझेंगे। इसलिए यह तो सुन लीजिये। उसके बाद हम देखेंगे कि स्वामी जी को कैसे समझाया जाय।

रामसेवक यादवः प्रधान मंत्री जी ने एक बार यह भी किया था कि इस देश की बोली में यहां बोले थे। अब यह अंग्रेजी में बोल रहे हैं। यदि इस प्रश्न पर हिन्दी में बोलते तो अच्छा होता।

रामेश्वरानन्दः जब मैनें छः महीने पहले कहा था तो आपने कहा था कि वह सब भाषण छपे हुए हैं हिन्दी में।

अध्यक्षः यह तो कोई अजब बात नहीं स्वामी जी को इलहाम हो जाय पहले से लेकिन इस समय तो हमको सुनने दीजिये।

रामेश्वरानन्दः हमको हुआ है वही हम कहते हैं।

अध्यक्षः अब स्वामी जी आराम से बैठेंगे।

81. Socialist Party.

[Translation begins:

> Ram Sewak Yadav: Swamiji is agitated because he doesnot understand this language. You explain to him.

Jawaharlal Nehru: This is what I was saying. Swamiji does not understand anything.

> Ram Sewak Yadav: Swamiji understands everything.

Jawaharlal Nehru: This is not just a matter of language.

> Ram Sewak: Hon. Speaker, it is inappropriate to say that any hon. Member does not understand anything.
>
> Speaker: Please try to understand my problem. If Swamiji, does not understand this language, there are many other hon. Members who would not understand that language. Let us first listen to him and then decide how to make Swamiji understand.
>
> Ram Sewak: The Prime Minister had once spoken in this language in the house. If he could answer this question in this language, we would be grateful.
>
> Rameswaranand: When I had asked six months ago, you said all these speeches are printed in Hindi.
>
> Speaker: This is not a strange thing that Swamiji is unable to understand this, now. Let us listen to the Prime Minister first, and then decide.
>
> Rameswaranand: I have felt so, hence I have spoken so.
>
> Speaker: Now, Swamiji will sit quietly.

Translation ends]

Jawaharlal Nehru: I am sorry not to be able to oblige Swamiji. I would have been glad to oblige him, but my difficulty is, as you yourself have been pleased to remark, in a matter of this kind, there are many Members of this House who might not understand me otherwise.

I was talking about unpreparedness[82]. It is perfectly true, as I said that we were unprepared to meet a massive invasion of two or three divisions. But the other things that are said about roads, about blankets, etc. are very largely incorrect ... (Interruptions).

Mohan Swarup[83] (Pilibhit): what about arms?

Jawaharlal Nehru: It is really extraordinary that many persons here who know nothing about arms talk about arms. (Interruptions).

Speaker: Let us hear the hon. Prime Minister. All sections shall have their opportunity to express themselves, we are now listening to the Prime Minister.

Jawaharlal Nehru: I do not wish to go into details. I merely wanted to indicate that the criticisms that are made, partly justified, are largely not justified. About arms, it is not a thing which one normally talks about in Parliament openly. But I would be glad to explain what we have done, what we have not done and the difficulties that we had to face.

The hon. House will remember that till independence, our defence department was entirely under the War Office, and the War Office not only laid down the policy, but insisted that everything as far as possible should be acquired through Whitehall. During the last Great War, because of the difficulties of acquiring war material from abroad, from the United Kingdom, some of our ordnance factories grew up, but still they were rather elementary. The first problem we had to solve, therefore, was to get out of this Whitehall atmosphere and the practice of our acquiring everything from there, determining our own policy, and all that. I think we have done rather well to build up in these years this industry.

There is always a choice and there has been a choice in this and other matters for us to buy arms from abroad or to make them ourselves. Obviously it is infinitely better to make them ourselves, because that strengthens the country, industrially and otherwise; and secondly, you cannot altogether rely on outside supplies; any moment they may fail you and economically it is bad to get them from outside. So, our practice has been to try to build up our arms, the industry and the like in the country, and we have done fairly well. We might have done better; I do not know. All kinds of difficulties arise, because development of

82. See item 445.
83. PSP.

one industry depends on the whole industrial background of the country. We have laid stress on that. I would not go into that.

A great deal was said about arms, automatic rifles and the rest. For the last three or four years, we have been trying to make them and various difficulties arose about patents, this, that and the other, and sometimes about our own difficulties in finding enough foreign exchange. This has been a continuing difficulty, as to how much we should spend in the shape of foreign exchange. Ultimately, we got over these difficulties and we started their manufacture, I forget the date, but sometime this year, and we are now making them.

The only alternative was previously for us to get a large number of those weapons from abroad. We hesitated; we wanted to make them ourselves. Undoubtedly, we could have got them, but remember this. If we had tried to get all those weapons from abroad in what might be called relatively peace time, we would have had to spend enormous sums of money. Our whole planning, etc. will have gone, because when you talk of weapons in terms of war, you talk in terms of thousands of crores. It is not a question of a few crores, but thousands of crores and it would have smashed our economy. It is a different matter when we have to face this tremendous crisis, which both our people feel so much and the world sees; we can get better terms to get the things and our people are prepared to spend much more.

I am merely pointing out some things; they may not be an adequate explanation, but 1 want you to appreciate that every attempt has been made and continually being made to build up industry—an aircraft industry, an arms industry, etc., an up-to-date one. Obviously, we cannot be up-to-date in the sense of competing, let us say, with America or the Soviet Union or England. It is just not possible for us to advance our basic industries and science so much. But we have made good advance scientifically. One of the most important features is that the defence science department that we have built up is a high class affair, employing about 2,000 scientists.

Anyhow, if there were mistakes committed or delays committed, it is not for me to go into that now. It is not a good thing for us to apportion blame and say that such and such officer or such and such Minister, etc. is to blame. We are all to blame, in a sense. (Interruptions).

It is a fact that ever since 1st October, when I returned from abroad, every day I have been connected—previously I was connected through the Defence Ministry, but from the 1st October, I have been there every day. We, the Chiefs of Staff and others sat together and discussed the matters. And, naturally, it is for the experts, the Chiefs of Staff and their advisers to determine the tactics, the strategy etc., of fighting, and not for me; I do not know enough about it.

I canonly put questions to them, make suggestions to them, leaving the final carrying out of it to their hands.

We took several steps. On the very next day, on 2nd October, we called back the Chief of the General Staff, General Kaul, who was on leave then. I want to mention his name specially because, quite extraordinarily unjust things have been said about him. We sent for him and we changed the method of command, separating Naga Hills etc., from NEFA. He went there practically within 24 hours. Some people say he had not had any experience of fighting. That is not correct. He had the experience of fighting in Burma. He was our Military Attaché in Washington when the trouble occurred in Kashmir, but he begged us to send him there. We sent him there and he was there. I doubt, knowing a good many of our officers and others, many of them are good in sheer courage and initiative and hard work, if we can find anybody to beat him. Anyhow, it is very unfair for our officers who are bearing a heavy burden, whether it be Kaul or anybody else, to be criticised in this way, criticised by foreign correspondents sending messages abroad. That is a highly improper, highly irresponsible thing to be done when they are bearing such heavy burden.

Then General Kaul, as soon as he went over there—he went there suddenly from here to 14,000 feet—daily walked 16 to 20 miles from post to post over highly precipitous mountain area. He fell ill and he came here to report after four or five days.

रामेश्वरानन्दः जो मारे गये उनका क्या बना जी? क्या उनका वहां इलाज नहीं हुआ?

जवाहरलाल नेहरूः मैं स्वामी जी से एक प्रार्थना करूंगा। हम इस वक़्त हंसी मज़ाक नहीं कर रहे हैं जिनसे भारत का भविष्य बंधा हुआ है। वह समझते हैं कि हम हंसी मज़ाक कर रहे हैं। हम बहुत अहम बातों पर गोर कर रहे है जिनसे भारत काका भवष्यि बन्धा हुआ है।

रामेश्वरानन्दः हम आपके साथ हैं ... हम आपके साथ हैं। देश के लिए मरने के लिए तैयार हैं। हमारी सुनो तो सही।

[Translation begins:

Rameswaranand: Those who died, what happened to them? Didn't they get treatment there?

Jawaharlal Nehru: I would like to beg Swamiji that what we are discussing here is not a matter of joke. It is tied to India's future. He thinks that we are having fun. We are discussing here a very grave issue.

Rameswaranand: We are with you...we are with you. We are ready to die for the country. Please listen to us at least.

Translation ends]

Speaker: Order, order. I would first ask the hon. Members on these benches, on the Congress side, not to interfere or take into their own hands the right to silence any other hon. Member. I think I am competent enough. I will deal with any hon. member who interrupts or who says things like that. Whenever I need the help of all those hon. Members I will request them. But I think I would not need that. I hope hon. Members on this side would not compel me to go to that extent. They will have ample opportunity to have their say. I will allow them as much as they want. Now they should listen patiently. When their turn comes and when they speak, if they are interrupted in this manner, they would not like that. Therefore, we should listen to the Prime Minister in order to be able to criticise what he has said. If they do not listen to him, how shall the hon. Members on this side criticise those facts that he is giving. Let him have his say. When their opportunity comes they can criticise him.

रामेश्वरानन्दः आप हमें समझाने लगे हैं तो दो शब्द हिंदी में बोल दें।

अध्यक्षः मैंने यही कहा कि आप अभी ख़ामोश रहें, आपकी भी बारी आएगी और उस वक़्त आप ख़ूब कहें जितना आपका जी चाहे।

[Translation begins:

Rameswaranand: Since you have started explaining to us, please say a couple of words in Hindi also.

Speaker: I said that you keep quiet for now. When your turn comes you can speak as much as you wish.

Translation ends]

Jawaharlal Nehru: I would like to point out to the house a fact, which is no doubt known, that this invasion by the Chinese did not merely take place in NEFA on the 20th October. On that very day it was a coordinated attack all along the line from Ladakh to NEFA. Therefore, to say that because we had attacked them, we are perfectly justified in pushing them and attacking them in NEFA. To make that an excuse and say that we had attacked them in NEFA and therefore, they are attacking us on that day all among the line of Ladakh is a thing which is manifestly a false statement, a made-up thing.

Now, a few days after the 20th October—I think it was 24th—a message was sent to the heads of Governments or heads of States in cases where it may be so, almost all of them, pointing out the background of Chinese invasion and stating our firm resolve to resist it—a copy of it I have placed on the Table of the House [26/27 October 1962 was the date of the message]. We have received many replies, not from all yet, but from many of them, extending their sympathy and support at the present crisis.

Just soon after, four or five days after this massive attack, the Chinese Prime Minister came out with what is called, a "three-point proposal", on which a ceasefire might be arrived.[84] This was very vague. It was not quite clear what he meant. But what appeared to us and what appeared later on to us on further elucidation was that it meant our not only acknowledging or partly acknowledging their right to be where they were on our territory, but our force retiring still further, some 20 kilometres or so; that is to say, although the Chinese armies would retire a little on our territory we would retire further and they would have an opportunity to build up their strength on our territory to attack us further later. It is an impossible thing for us to agree to. There has been more confusion about this in the country, not only here but in other countries too, but as we have explained it. Most people have understood it—I am talking about other countries.[85]

We, in reply or independently rather, proposed that they should retire to the line prior to the 8th September, that is, behind the McMahon Line there and they should also retire the advances they had made since the 8th September in Ladakh. Some of our friends have said that this was a weak proposal, we should have asked them to go out completely. Well, it is for the House to judge our weakness and strength, and the proposals must have some realities because we have not only to abide by it but we have to convince all our friends elsewhere that we are making something, a proposal which is reasonable and which can be given effect to. The proposal was that they should retire to that line as it stood on 8th September both in NEFA and Ladakh. Then we were prepared to meet their representatives to consider what further steps should be taken to lessen tension etc. Once that was agreed to, then would come as a third step our meeting together to consider the merits of the question, we have

---

84. See appendix 26.
85. See Chou En-lai's rejection of this proposal, appendix 39, and Nehru's rejection of Chou En-lai's position, item 395.

made that proposal and we stand by it. I think it is a reasonable proposal and certainly not in any sense a dishonourable or a weak one.

Then, meanwhile, many of our friends abroad, well intentioned countries, made various efforts to bring about ceasefire, stoppage of fighting and a consideration of the matter on the merits. Their efforts, or rather their desire, to help in stopping this fighting is very laudable, and we welcome their desire. But, not knowing all the detailed facts, sometimes they made some proposals which had no great relevance to the situation.

I shall refer only to one of them and that was the reference made by President Nasser of the UAR. I must pay my tribute to President Nasser in this matter because he did not make a vague proposal in the air. People advise us to be good and peaceful, as if we are inclined to war. In fact, if we are anything, as the House well knows, we do not possess the warlike mentality and that is why for the purpose of war there is weakness. We may have developed it, but that is a different matter, I am talking of the past. So, people talking to us to be good boys and make it up has no particular meaning, unless they come to grips with the particular issues involved. Now, President Nasser took the trouble to understand the facts and, thereafter, issued a presidential decree or communiqué issued by the President—in the Council of the UAR,[86] in which he made certain proposals. These proposals were not exactly on the lines we had suggested but were largely in conformity with our proposals. They laid special stress on troops withdrawing to their lines where they stood prior to the 8th of September. That was a major thing. That fitted in with our proposal. China has rejected this proposal, made by President Nasser.[87]

Now, this crisis is none of our making or seeking. It is China which has sought to enforce its so-called territorial claims by military might. Indeed, she has advanced beyond the line of her territorial claims. As I said, their frontier is a mobile one; anything they could grasp becomes their frontier.

---

86. On 31 October 1962.
87. See item 389. Nasser proposed on 26 October that both India and China should revert to the situation prior to 20 October 1962 and cease fighting forthwith; a no-man's zone be established between the two sides and then enter into peace talks. China declined, as it felt that "neither the restoration of the state of boundaries as before September 8, nor restoration of the state boundaries as before October 20 when the clashes began, constitute a reasonable basis for a peaceful settlement". [In fact, the 4-point proposals were an improvement on the earlier proposals from the Indian perspective since they clarified the withdrawal line of 20 October 1962 as the one that existed on 8 September 1962.] *South China Morning Post*, no.2865, 23 November 1962, pp.28-29.

In this task, in defending our frontiers and our motherland, we have sought help from all friendly countries. I wish to express my gratitude for the prompt response to our appeal for sympathy and support which have been given to us by various countries. This help that is given is unconditional and without any strings. It does not therefore, affect directly our policy of non-alignment which we value. Those countries, which have helped us have themselves recognised this aid, made it clear that they do not expect us to leave that policy. Help has been given to us swiftly by the United States, by the United Kingdom and by some other friendly countries. We are in touch with many others. We have also made approaches to other friendly countries like the Soviet Union and France for supply of equipment.

We have often declared that we do not covet any territory of anyone else; we are quite satisfied with our own territory such as it is. But there is another aspect of that. We do not submit to anyone else coveting our territory and although the aggressor in this instance has gained some initial successes—I do not know what they have in mind, whether they want to use it as a bargaining counter or they have some other evil designs—as I have said we cannot submit to it, whatever the consequences.

There is one other aspect which I should like to mention, which is not indirectly connected with this matter but directly connected, and that is our development plans and the Five Year Plan. Some people have said "let us give up these Plans so that we may concentrate on the war effort." What is the war effort? People think of the soldiers in the front, which is perfectly right. They are bearing the brunt of the heat and danger. But in this matter, in the kind of struggle that we are involved in, every peasant in the field is a soldier, every worker in a factory is a soldier. Our work, our war effort essentially, apart from the actual fighting done, is in ever greater production in the field and factory. We must remember that. It is an effort which depends greatly on our development. Today we are much more in a position to make that kind of effort in field and factory than, let us say, ten or twelve years ago; there is no doubt about that. We are not still adequately developed. I hope this very crisis will make us always remember that an army today, a modern army, fights with modern weapons, which it has to manufacture itself in that country. It is based on the development of industry, and that industry must have an agricultural base if it is to succeed. Therefore, we have to develop all round, apart from agriculture and industry, which are the basic things in our Five Year Plan. Then there is power, which is essential from the point of view of war effort, from the point of view of industry, from the point of view of even agriculture, so that to talk of scrapping the Five Year Plan is not to understand the real springs of our strength. We have to carry the Five Year Plan and go beyond it in many respects. It may be, in some matters which are considered non-essential, we may tone down or leave them but in the major things of the Five Year Plan we have to make the fullest effort. Among the major things agriculture is highly important. How can a country fight when it is lacking in food? But do not think we will be. We have to grow more and more, which is a difficult thing. We have laid down the targets for our agricultural produce in our Five Year Plan, but in the last year or two, this year especially, we have fallen behind because of floods and all kinds of things.

Now, although we have fallen behind, I take it that we have to aim at higher targets than we have laid down even in the Third Plan, and I am sure we shall get that. I am not talking vaguely. I think we can get that, we cannot get it so easily if we laid down certain targets in the office here in the Food Ministry. We must go down to the agriculturist, and transform his present enthusiasms, his present energy into greater production. Nothing is more cheering and heartening than the reaction amongst the people, amongst the peasants, who have given their little mite. Let them transform them into greater production. I am sure they can if we approach them rightly. So also with industry; so also with many other things like education etc. We must look upon all of them as part of the war effort that we have to make. In this process I hope we shall not only build up our nation more swiftly but will make it stronger, make it more social-minded, and lay the base of the socialist structure that we aim at.

This peril we have to face is a grave menace. This challenge may be converted into opportunity for us to grow and to change the dark cloud that envelops our frontiers into the bright sun not only of freedom but of welfare in this country.

In effect we have to look at this matter as an effort of the whole nation. We may say—some people say—we want an armed people. That is true in a sense. But what we really want is the whole people mobilised for this effort doing their separate jobs whether it is in the field, the factory, or the battlefield, thus combining together and strengthening the nation and bringing successto us. We have to be armed, therefore, not only by weapons of warfare but by weapons of agriculture, industry and all those as well.

We do not minimise our task. Let no man minimise it or have any illusions about it. It is not a thing which we can deal with by momentary enthusiasm, enthusiasm of the moment or lasting a month or two. It is a long effort that we require, a difficult effort, and we shall have to go out to do our utmost. It is not merely enough to pay something to the Defence Fund or to do something else. That is good in its own way. It is very welcome how people are paying them by straining every nerve to the utmost. We have to keep up our strength and our determination to the end. And that end may not be near. Therefore we have to prepare in every way to strengthen the nation not only for today and tomorrow but for the day after also to meet this menace. If we do that, I have no doubt that we shall be able to show the determination and fortitude that is required of our people. We have had a glimpse of it in their present enthusiasm which has been a most moving sight. To see our people come, not only the young but the old—old men and old women—and the young, little children and their enthusiasm has been a sight to gladden any heart.

Now before I end I should like to say a word about our soldiers and airmen who are working under extraordinarily difficult circumstances. I want to send on your behalf our greetings and assurance of our full assistance. To those who have fallen in defence of the country we pay our homage. They will not be forgotten by us or by those who follow us. I am confident that all sides of this House will stand united in this great venture and will demonstrate to the world that free India which has stood for peace and will always stand for peace and friendship with other countries can never tolerate aggression and invasion. If we have worked for peace as we have done and we shall continue to do so, we can also work for war effectively if we are attacked as we have been.

Sir, I commend these Resolutions to the House.

272. In the Rajya Sabha: Emergency and Chinese Attack[88]

The Prime Minister (Jawaharlal Nehru): Chairman, Sir, I speak on the Resolution moved by my friend and colleague, the Home Minister.[89] As a matter of fact, I do not think it is necessary for anyone to speak in commending that Resolution because every party and group and every individual in this House, I gather, approves of it and gives it full support. And what is much more important, that support has come in a tremendous and magnificent measure from the people of this country.

I shall, therefore, say something about some points, some outstanding features of this situation more particularly about the way we have to condition our mentality to face it. Some people have criticised our unpreparedness and may I add that I hope, not now but somewhat later at a more suitable time, there will be an enquiry into this matter, because there is a great deal of misunderstanding and misapprehension and people have been shocked—all of us have been shocked—by the events that occurred from the 20th October

88. Statement on Resolution on Emergency, *Rajya Sabha Debates*, Vol. XLI, Nos. 1-8, 8 November to 19 November 1962, pp. 402-426.
89. Lal Bahadur Shastri.

onwards for a few days and the reverses that we suffered. So I hope there will be an enquiry so as to find out what mistakes or errors were committed and who was responsible for them. But for the present that cannot be done and I do not wish to state before the House anything in regard to those matters though I do think that many of the charges made have little substance. The real thing, the basic thing, is that we as a nation, in spite of brave speeches now and then, have been conditioned in a relatively peaceful manner, in a democratically peaceful manner, which is somewhat opposed to the type of conditioning that a country like China at present has had, especially in the last dozen years or so. They have been conditioned, even previously they have been in a sense at war, I should say for thirty years, in a condition of war, not war with foreign countries but war in their own country, and the House will remember how constantly this idea of war was being put forward by them. America has been their chief *bête noire*, their chief enemy and constantly they were rousing up their people against America, against imperialists and the like so as to keep up that mentality of war, that constant preparation for war, for building up for war and all that. We, on the other hand, have constantly spoken about peace and we are, in spite of sometimes using excited language, a peaceful people, and we have pleaded for peace all over the world and in our own country and naturally that conditioning is of a different type than the type of conditioning that China, for instance, has had during the last dozen years. Having conditioned their people, they can turn the direction, they can turn the people's thinking in any way they choose. It was against America; suddenly India becomes enemy no. 1. Not that America ceases to be in their minds the enemy, but they turn it round saying that we are the stooges of America. Therefore, all the previous conditioning against America is turned round to us. For them it is really as if we are doing a job for America, as if it did not directly concern us. Now, in normal times, even apart from this conditioning and the rest, democratic countries do not normally behave like, well, countries—if I may give you an instance—like Hitler behaved in Germany. Now, great countries—not countries which are pacifists—like England, like France and the rest had powerful armies; yet they were not conditioned in the way that Germany was under Hitler, and when war came the result was that in spite of their vast armies, the French army and the British army with the fullest equipment they had with them could not stand up against Hitler and they were swept off. France was humiliated and humbled and then the British army, almost the whole of it, was swept into the English Channel. Not that it was not a good army, but the aggressor has an advantage and the conditioning of the aggressor makes it a more fit instrument for the initial attack. First of all, the aggressor chooses the point of attack, the day and the time of attack, which is an advantage. So this has to be borne in mind. Now, we in the last many years have thought certainly of keeping our army, air force, etc., but we have thought that the essential way of gaining strength is industrialising the country and improving our agriculture because struggles are fought today even more than at the battle front in the field and factory and we thought—and we still think—that even from the point of view of strengthening our defence forces the background behind them in the field and factory was essential. Without a proper industry no modern war can be fought. We may get as we are getting—and we are thankful for getting them— arms from abroad because the emergency compels us to do so, to get them. Yet we cannot fight for any length of time with merely aid from abroad. We have to produce the weapons of war here and behind those weapons of war and behind that industry which is so essential is the agricultural background. No industry can be built up unless agriculture is functioning. So we come back to the growth of agriculture and industry and we have been trying to do that in the last so many years by Five Year Plans and the rest. Naturally, the Five Year Plans were meant to raise the level of living of our people, to give them certain amenities, to raise the national income and all that; but essentially, if I may venture to state to this House, they were meant to strengthen the country, to strengthen even the defence forces of the country. Now, many people thought, being used in the past to getting everything from abroad, that this was the easiest way—getting arms and everything from abroad. Originally, our Indian Army before Independence consisted of very brave men, but it was essentially an outgrowth of the British Army. Most of the officers, all the senior officers were foreign, were British. Gradually, some of our officers rose in rank and a very, very few became Brigadiers. For the rest, I think, Colonel was the topmost rank. All the policy was laid down in Whitehall. They did not bother. They had to carry out that policy. Almost all the fighting material—not human beings but arms, etc.—came from England chiefly. There was only a slight advance in our arms production during the Second World War because it became very difficult to supply India from England. Their own demands were terrific and there was distance. Therefore, the British Government encouraged the production of certain arms and ammunition in our ordnance factories. Even so, nothing except the most ordinary arms were allowed to be made here. The rest had to come from there. That was the state of affairs when we took charge. First of all, all the policy, direction, etc. changed, from Whitehall direction to Indian direction. We had good people. Yet all the training and thinking was originally derived from Whitehall or from Sandhurst, etc., which is good training. I do not say that it is bad. And they are very fine men. Nevertheless, it was somewhat out of touch with Indian conditions. Gradually, we had to bring that round, to fit in more with Indian conditions, but more particularly the whole question of production was before us. We could not rely on foreign sources for arms, etc. After all, when one is forced to do, one gets it from anywhere, as we are doing it today. But that is not a safe thing and that does not produce a sense of self-reliance and self-dependence. Now, to build up a modern arms industry requires not only some prototype being obtained and copying it. That is difficult enough. But it requires an industrial background in the country. It is out of a background of industry that these things arise, not a specific thing. You make something which may be good for war without any background. We have to have a vast number of scientists, technicians, etc. and long experience of doing it. All these years we have been trying to do that and I think we have made very considerable progress. We have today in our Defence Science Department—I do not exactly know it—I think more than two thousand scientists working. Because you cannot get the real thing here, to get some idea of it, you have to build up your own prototypes and then after building them up you have to experiment with them, try them, and then finally decide in favour and then produce them in large quantities. All this takes time. We have always had this idea that the way to strengthen our army is to go through these processes. It is true that in defence one has to fix some period with some idea in one's mind as to when one may be confronted with a war crisis. Suppose, we are confronted with a war crisis in a year's time. In our thinking everything else has to be conditioned to that year. We can not produce big things within that year. We have to do something. If a war is suddenly thrust upon you, immediately you have to do as best as you can. But in doing the best we can, for the time being, we really lessen our capacity for the future, even to carry on with war for the future, unless we build it up from below as I have said. That was the problem always before us. Every country when it thinks of arms, etc.—apart from this point of building up the arms industry—has to consider when the time for trial will come. I remember the first time I came into the Government, before I became Prime Minister, I was Vice-President of the Council and one day a problem came up before us about the Army. What Army should we keep? That was just after the World War. This was before Pakistan came into existence and before there was any particular danger. And we were put this question; "When do you expect, what time do you expect to have before a war will take place?" Any war. We had nobody in view. That is to say, we can concentrate more on preparations for it in the sense of long-term preparations. If we think the war is next year, then the approach is different. And it was said; "Let us think, for the moment, ten years." At that time there was no question of building up the arms industry here. It was only a question of acquiring weapons. Ten years has no particular meaning. It was just a period, so that whatever we required should be spread out over ten years. That was the idea and that should be obtained from abroad. Later when we became independent we laid much greater stress on production here in this country. There were difficulties. Many people used to old methods, not only for our Army but for everything, for our railways, etc., preferred just giving a big order—a team going abroad and coming back here—for tanks, for this, that, and the other. It was simpler and they knew that tank. And they rather suspected or were afraid that if we made it ourselves it may not be quite as good. It may fail us. But that was not good enough for a long-term effort, we had to do it ourselves and gradually it was built up. And then we had also, you will remember, always certain financial or foreign exchange difficulties, how much we should turn over to defence. Defence expenditure has gone up somewhat by normal peace time standards considerably. It affected our whole planning, our First Plan and Second Plan. So, we had to strike a balance somewhere, with all these difficulties and delays, nevertheless, we built up our defence industry, not by any means as we wanted it. The process continued and continues, but still I think with considerable success. If I could show you the rate at which our production in defence industry has gone up, you will notice that it is very considerable. I will not go into those figures. I am merely mentioning these things. Some people criticised that our ordnance factories have been making civilian goods. It was to the tune of about five per cent because when labour was unemployed it had to be turned to do something. And always the normal test is that ordnance factories or any arms manufacturing concerns cannot manufacture in peace time as fast as they are supposed to make in war time. Otherwise, you get stocked up with things tremendously. You cannot do anything with them. They get spoiled no doubt. The normal rate is—I forget the exact figure—that in war time you have to advance your rate of production between 15 and 20 per cent of peace time. Because you are spending so much, your ammunition is being fired at a tremendous pace, it must be replaced. In peace time you do it only when there are exercises. So, all these problems came to us. I was saying that our production has gone up very considerably—not civil production. It is a mere bagatelle, nothing—arms production for the Army, Navy and Air Force and especially for the Army and the Air Force. And now for the last month or two, of course, we have done extraordinarily well. I should like to say a word in commendation of those in charge of our arms production, the Director-General of it, who is a very able and very enthusiastic man, and all his workers and others. Their scientists and chiefly technicians are working today twenty-four hours a day. There is not a minute's interval when they stop. So, this process went on. It did not go on, I admit, completely, as fast as a country bent on war would do it, because we had always to check it, because the more we spent on it, the less we had for other basic things, even for defence. As I said, I think agriculture is as important as guns in defence. I think the growth of industries is as important as guns. I think that power is as important as guns. All these things help in producing guns, all these things help in producing a well fed army and well fed country, all these things help us conserving our foreign exchange. All these things are inter-connected. One must not think of defence as something by itself, training people, parading them about and handing them guns for defence. So this process has been going on naturally limited by our resources, limited by many other factors, limited by the growth of our industrial development, and it has made a fairly good progress. It might have made more.

And now I should like to carry this argument to its conclusion. I would like to say that we have today, as everyone realises, a terrific problem which cannot be solved obviously by brave gestures and processions or anything like that, which are good in their own way, but obviously it is something when we are up against one of the biggest powers in the world. We have seen in the past, in the Great War and others, how great powers mauled at each other till ultimately, after three or four years or more they were all exhausted, utterly bled, and the greatest powers were defeated, defeated absolutely France, Germany, Japan for instance. They did not lack enthusiasm, they did not lack good armies or good navies or air force, they did not lack the industrial background. Yet they were defeated because it was a trial ultimately of something basic, not a question of a few guns or something but of the nerve and basic strength of a nation, the morale of a nation. That is what we have to face. I think we can face it with confidence, but I want you to think of the ordeals before us. We may have, as every army has, as every defence force has, reverses and all that, we have to survive them, we will survive them and not get terribly dispirited because we had a reverse. That is not a right outlook at any time but more specially when we are up against a highly organised and trained military machine like that of China which has, I believe, the biggest army in the world. Even in Tibet I understand, they have got a vast army, leave out the huge legions in China. That is the problem before us. Now, in facing it, we face it today, as we try to do, with all the material we have and all the material we can get from abroad, and we have asked a large number of countries to supply it. The main countries which have supplied us thus far have been the United States and the United Kingdom, and we are grateful to them for it, but we have, if I may use the word, impartially asked many countries including the Soviet Union. I may add about the Soviet Union that all the previous commitments they made, I believe they stand by them, what further commitments they will make I cannot say. We have asked them, we have not got an answer yet. But on previous commitments they have said that they stand by them in spite of these developments.

So, we have to meet the situation, but if we realise, as we should realise, that this is a long-term effort, this may take, I cannot say how long, but mentally we must be prepared for a long, long time, for years, two years, three years or four years, the people and the country straining themselves to the uttermost—it is not a question of giving some money to a fund, it is not a question of some people being recruited, but every man and woman in the country being strained to the uttermost. If that is so, that can only be carried on if together with it we are thinking constantly of increasing our industrial potential and behind that our agricultural potential, and the industrial potential and the agricultural potential give us the war potential. War potential is not something apart from industrial potential and agricultural potential. That is why I have said that we dare not even for the sake of this war and the defence of our country slacken our efforts at increasing our industrial and agricultural potential or in other words give up our Five Year Plan. We may give up some bits of it—that is a different matter—which we consider non-essential, but the basic things of that have to continue, if for nothing else, just for the sake of this war situation. That is how I would like the House to consider this problem because it requires, apart from what we do, a certain mental adjustment to it. If we have not got that mental adjustment, we will be constantly having shocks, not being able to do what we can. It is not a hundred yards race or a hundred metres race where we make a violent effort and go as fast as we can for a hundred yards in nine or ten seconds. You do it if you are fast runner and get exhausted at the end of it. If it is a very long race, and if you have to run a long race, let us say, of three miles or more, you run differently from how you run a hundred yards race. You have to keep your breath and get your second breath and carry on whatever happens, so that in that sense we have to look at this and not exhaust our energy, our capacity in initial spurts, and not have the energy left for something else because there is a limit to a nation's energy. To courage you may say there is no limit. Many men show courage unto death. Fewer men show courage living on the verge of death and yet working hard. That is true, but there is a limit to the totality of a nation's, I will not say courage but, strength, if you like, and you see that in these great wars that have taken place that limit was reached in the case of some countries like Germany and Japan. They collapsed six months before the other party might have collapsed. Mr Winston Churchill, I believe, talking about the First World War said—I forget his words—it was just a pure chance, he said, ultimately which side collapsed. It is a very well worded thing but I do not remember it. However, one has to think ahead and preserve that courage so that we could outlast the other party, our opponent, our enemy. That is the problem before us, and this requires not only tremendous mobilisation of the nation's resources but a mental adaptation to it. Some of us are not

413

accustomed to facing these questions of a nation's life and death in war time—and we are not accustomed, let us be clear about it—we have heard of wars, read about wars, the first World War, the second World War and all that, but we were not emotionally concerned with them in the sense of that type of terrible suffering which people in Europe, people in the warring countries had, whether it was this side or that side, Germany, England, France and Russia. All these countries suffered terribly and to the last ounce of their blood they went on doing it, and then those people survived who had just the last ounce more than the others, they survived. That is the kind of struggle we are in. It is not a joke. And now of course in a war one has to think of nuclear weapons; not we, we are not producing them and we do not intend producing them. China says it will produce them. It has not done so. It might—in a year's time—and even if it does, it will be an experimental thing, and it will not be a thing which they can use for several years. However, war now has become a different thing and that is why apart from our natural desire for peace in the world and in our country, it is too terrible to contemplate, even by people who like war but fear the annihilation of mankind. So, we have pleaded for peace, and the world generally has been responding to the call of peace, not our call but the general call of peace all over. Even the great leaders of nations are powerfully affected by it because they faced—as we faced only two or three weeks ago—suddenly a turn of events in Cuba, and the Cuba affair might have led to war, war in 24 hours or 48 hours. Well, they shrank back and wisely decided to avoid it. Now, that has been the past, and we, apart from—I imagine—every thinking person wanting to avoid wars—are particularly trained to some extent, even more, inclined that way because of Gandhiji, not that I say Gandhiji made any of us terribly peaceful or made us what he thought he would like to have made us, but we did not reach his ideal. With all that behind us we pursued a certain policy which at no time—I may tell the House—was a pacifist policy, which at no time meant weakening our defence forces but strengthening them to the utmost of our capacity having regard to the resources and finances at our disposal. Our defence forces, our army at the present moment is much larger than the limit placed on it by ourselves. It has simply grown by circumstances bigger. Even so it is a very small army compared to China's millions; there you go into many millions, we do not go into them; we only go into hundreds of thousands and, as I said, we thought of defence chiefly from the point of view, first of all, of defence science—which is the basis of defence production, of technicians and others. To get all that takes time. For a soldier to be trained, it does not take very much time. And in the same way we take weapons because it is often said that we did not give our people adequate weapons. That is both true and not true; that is to say, we have not an army shifted over completely to automatic weapons; we are in the process of doing it. It is a lengthy process, manufacturing it ourselves, and we did not want, previous to this crisis, to spend large sums of money in getting those weapons from outside. We decided to make them ourselves, and we are making them now. But when the crisis came we had to give them—that is a different matter. We are trying to give them now, and in this connection, I might say that even an army like the British Army has only recently got automatic weapons. They are changing over now, in the course of some months, because their thinking is along different lines now, and we largely have followed their thinking; our officers and others who are responsible for this kind of thing have been trained there, have been in contact with them and think that way. The whole concept of war has changed. First of all, the air arm has become very important. Secondly, the nuclear weapons have become so important that conventional arms get relatively less important, and there is an argument whether the conventional army should be built up, or nuclear. All that is going on there. For us there is no choice. We do not have nuclear weapons and we are not likely to have them. But in the confusion of arguments this element of automatic weapons, even in an up-to-date and modern army like the British, was neglected in their military thinking; they did not think it was necessary or essential; they preferred some other weapons, 303 rifles, something which we have. Anyhow for the last two or three years we have been thinking of making the automatic weapons, not only thinking but also moving in that direction. But then all manner of difficulties are involved in it, because we have to get the prototypes, we have got to get the blueprints of them, and we have to make them ourselves making some adjustments for conditions here. Then we have tests and trials of them. It takes a long time. Last year we had been carrying this out, and now they are being produced or will be produced next month. Meanwhile we have got many of them from abroad. What I was venturing to point out to the House, were the problems that we had to face all the time, and at no time did we think that we can be complacent about this matter, about China or about their doings. But we did think that we should build up the basic thing which will enable us to convert it into a proper war machine when the necessity arose, because, if we did not have the base, then the war machine would be without foundations, would be superficial and would depend only on some outside help that we can get. We get it no doubt as we are getting it now, but it will not be able to carry us through for very long, and also it was, shall I say, a question of judgment as to when this final challenge would come. Of course, previously hon. Members here and elsewhere asked us—I remember a speech delivered here too--"why did we not push them out two or three years ago in Ladakh?" Well, it is rather difficult to go into that because that kind of thing, if one goes to details, may help our enemy, but broadly speaking we wanted to be fully prepared for that. We did not want to go into it half prepared or quarter prepared, and again, the preparation involved roads, a tremendous deal of roads, and big arms factories being built, the old ones being modernised and enlarged and all that, which takes time. So we wanted that. It was no good our hitting out at the Chinese and being pushed back with force and being helpless after that. So, we prepared for that and tried to build up the roads and build up the posts, which posts were, obviously, not strong enough to hold them back if a big army came. A post of 100 or 200 men is more a signal post, that thus far you advance and no more, but if they decide to bring in a big army, they can sweep it away. That was the position in Ladakh and, therefore, we tried to hold them there and prepared to make ourselves stronger for a future tussle. In the NEFA region, as the House knows, they had not come at all except, originally, to a small village Longju which again—according to them—they claimed to be on the side of the McMahon Line. It is actually on the border, and even that, according to them, was not coming over the McMahon Line. Apart from that they had not come over at all during all this period. What they had stated all this time, and their actions, say, in regard to the Burma-China Treaty and others, led one to believe that they would not encroach any further. That does not mean that they were satisfied with that. They might proceed further if they liked, but nevertheless there was this idea which was spread abroad by themselves, by their statements and activities. Although they said that this was an illegal McMahon Line, that they did not recognise it, nevertheless they always said that they would not cross it, and all these years we were in a sense better prepared here than in Ladakh, and especially lately we have built some more roads. But again, however prepared we were, it is a comparative question. No man can say that he is thoroughly prepared to meet anything. A hundred men may be prepared to meet five hundred men, but a hundred or five hundred or five thousand men are not prepared for a hundred thousand men to swoop down upon them or something. It is always a comparative thing. And we suddenly had to face a thing which certainly was not in our minds and we are, if you like, to blame for it, that an army of forty thousand or fifty thousand men will swoop down a small corner of NEFA and face our force which was about, I do not know—I do not wish to mention figures—but very much smaller.

Then, again, they have the facility of bringing large forces at short notice from Tibet. Tibet having a huge reservoir of Chinese army, they can bring it by road right up to the edge of the ridges because that is the end of the Himalayas there. They can bring it in, go over a little ridge there and down they are in our territory, the ridge being the watershed, while we have to go hundreds of miles of difficult territory. Now, although we have some roads, we have built them, yet almost everything that we had to send to the army had been by air. It is a terrific strain on our Air Force which have done remarkably well.

So, I want to keep this background before you that we were all the time thinking of producing conditions, both in our arms factories, in our defence science and the roads, etc. we built, which would enable us to meet them as strongly as possible. It was a question of whether we will be forced to face a big challenge, what time we might be forced and we could hurry these things up, but there is a limit to your hurrying an arms factory being built. Now we are thinking, and I hope the House will also think, in terms of a long-term effort, we cannot say how long it will be, but as things are, we dare not allow ourselves to think of a short-term effort, because if we think so, we will be disappointed, and that is disheartening thing if you do not make up your mind for a long-term effort and prepare for a short-term one, because then all your calculations are upset. Also, if we think in a short-term way, we will prepare for a short-term thing; we would not be able, perhaps, to carry on for a long term. We must think in terms of years.

Also there is a good deal of talk on the Chinese side, a good deal of, what I may say, peace offensives. Now, whatever happens we shall always favour peace provided that peace is an honourable one, a peace that leaves our territory in our hands. That is a different matter. I hope that we shall never become war-mad and forget the objectives that we have, as in the Great War and other wars, a certain madness seizes a nation for which they may even win the war but they lose the peace. That is so. We are all for peace always. Why should we spend vast sums of money? And money required for these things, for this kind of operations, is such that all the money we spend in our Five Year Plans is a bagatelle before its enormous sums. We thought we are brave to put a certain sum for our Five Year Plans. But here there is no choice left. We have to spend much more for the initial stages of the war and for subsequent stages. So while we are for peace, we must not allow ourselves to be taken in by these so-called peace offensives which are not peace, which are merely meant to some extent to humiliate us, to some extent to strengthen their position where they are for a future advance maybe, because, I am sorry to say it, it has become impossible to put trust in the word of the Chinese Government.

Now, even now their descriptions all the time are that we have attacked them and the brave Chinese frontier guards are defending themselves, the brave Chinese frontier guards having come on our territory, we are apparently attacking them and they are defending themselves. Apparently, the idea is that they should have a free run on our country and we should do nothing.

Some of the hon. Members have criticised our publicity arrangements and, if I may say so, there is a great deal of truth in that criticism. We are trying to

417

improve them. I think, they have improved somewhat, and I hope, they will improve, because it is not an easy matter to build up these things in a few days, war publicity and all that, and also because we do not quite function, we are not used to functioning, quite in the way the Chinese Government are used to functioning, that, is, stating complete untruth, one after the other, a set of lies. We are somewhat more careful about what we say. Take the 20th of October. Before even their own attack had commenced, they started broadcasting that we were attacking them. Before that, that is, a little before that, about half an hour before, I think, they started that. People said "Oh, we hurt them first and they afterwards." Now, what is one to do? Even before they attacked they started broadcasting that we were attacking them. Nothing was happening there. Then they attacked. When we learnt of that a couple of hours later, they got an advance of two or three hours. So you have to face a machine of propaganda publicity which originally was often called Goebbels machine in Nazi Germany. There is extraordinary similarity in many things between the Chinese publicity, etc., and the old Nazi publicity. And, of course, that can only be carried on with a certain rigid authoritarian pattern behind it—nobody dare say anything.

Here I do not wish to criticise our newspapers, but very often they say and do things which do not help the war effort, although they are very keen in helping it but they do not think in that way. Everybody can say anything in a public meeting, and many people say amazing things in public meetings here which certainly do not help the war effort. They shake their fists. "We will drive out the Chinese" and all that, and say all manner of things which prevent the Chinese being driven out.

You have to face the background of a democratic country, democratic freedoms. To some extent they have to be limited. There is the Defence of India Act which is not wholly functioning now but it is meant for that. But even in working that Defence of India Ordinance or Act we do not do it wholeheartedly, we do not like to do it unless we are forced to. I do not know, in the course of war it may gradually become stiffer in its operations. That is possible. But at the moment we have got inhibitions in acting, in stopping a man from writing or publishing something. But there it is, a completely regimented apparatus in private life and public life. That is helpful in a war effort, but I do not think it is ultimately helpful. I do think that a democratic background ultimately is the stronger of the two, and I think, you can see something of it; some glimpse of it you can have here even in the last fortnight, two or three weeks in India, by the wonderful response that we have had from our people. Now, that is not a regimented response. It is a spontaneous response which has come out of the people's minds and hearts and it does show that our fifteen year old democracy has taken roots in the people, that it is all very well for us to quarrel with each other and to make all kinds of demands, but when they see, when they feel, that there is danger to their democratic set-up they have come up like this. That is a very healthy sign, a very hopeful sign and something that has heartened all of us. So, I do think that the democratic apparatus is ultimately good even from the point of view of war, provided of course that the apparatus and everything else is not swept away at the first rush. But we can be sure that it will not be swept away. Therefore, it becomes a question of utilising that enthusiasm in a democratic manner with such limitations as war imposes upon us and directing it to defend the country and repel the invader. There again we have to think from a long-term view, and it should not be a question of our panting too soon, losing our breath too soon. We may have to run long, long distances and for a long, long time we have to carry on with determination and with fortitude. Well, our demonstrations and processions will not help in that. They may be good for rousing enthusiasm here and there, but we require something much deeper, much stronger, much more enduring for that.

Now, one further matter, which I should like to mention is that it is really painful and shocking to me the way the Chinese Government has, shall I say, adhered repeatedly to untruths. I am putting it in as mild a way as I can. What are they doing today? In the other House, I said it is aggression and invasion which reminds me of the activities of the Western powers in the nineteenth or the eighteenth century. Perhaps I was wrong. It is more comparable to the activities of Hitler in the modern age, because one thought that this kind of thing cannot happen nowadays. Of course, some aggression may take place here and there but this well thought out, premeditated and well organised invasion is what one thought was rather out-of-date and not feasible. We know the whole Chinese mentality, of the Government at least. It seems to think that war is a natural state of affairs, and here we are disliking it, excessively disliking the idea of war, emotionally disliking it, apart from not liking its consequences. We have, therefore, to realise that we are up against an enemy which is well conditioned, well prepared for the type of action it has taken and which is prepared also to cover it up with any number of falsehoods. And whatever we may do, to some extent this kind of propaganda of the Chinese, naturally, has some effect on other people in their own countries. I do not say that the Chinese persons are all against India but listening to their own propaganda they are influenced by it and other countries, the so-called non-aligned countries, getting that propaganda in full measure are affected by it, or at any rate, are confused by it. Therefore, it is no good our getting angry with them that they do not stand forthright in our defence, in support of our position, because they are confused. Not only are they confused, but sometimes they are a little afraid too. So, whatever the reason, we have to meet this and meet it with truth. Now, in war, Sir, unhappily—it has been said—the first casualty is truth, that is perfectly true, and the sad part of a war is not that people die in large numbers—that is sad of course—but the sad part of it is that war brutalises a nation and individuals. Well, death comes to all of us at its proper time but the brutalising of a country and of people is a more harmful thing. Now we have undergone a process under Gandhiji which is the reverse of this. I do not mean to say that we in India, our people, are any better than other people. I do not agree to that. We have numerous failings, weaknesses and we are even violent in small matters when other countries may not be. But the fact is that basically we are a gentle people, basically we have been conditioned by Gandhiji, especially, in peaceful methods, and however violent we may become occasionally, at the back of our minds there is that training. And it alarms me that we should become, because of the exigencies of war, brutalised, a brutal nation. I think that would mean the whole soul and spirit of India being demoralised, and that is a terribly harmful thing. Certainly, I hope that all of us will remember this.

Now, only the other day—two days ago—I saw a statement made by Acharya Vinoba Bhave for whom I have the greatest respect. I do not agree with everything that he says. Of course, I have the greatest respect for him because I do think in the whole of India he represents Gandhiji's thinking more than anybody else. And it heartened me—what he said about this Chinese invasion. He condemned it in his own gentle language, but he condemned it and he said himself he was not a man of war, he could not take a gun and meet it, but inferentially, he said India had to do it. But then he added that he hoped very much that even in doing so we would not be full of hatred, our minds full of hatred and ill-will and brutalised and all that. Well, I hope so earnestly. Now, what will happen. I cannot say, because war itself is a powerful agent for metamorphosis—varied experiences and brutalities. We may have to undergo all that, not the men. The men in the battlefield who face death all the time still sometimes survive this hatred. It is the people sitting behind who indulge in all this hatred. The energy and courage of the men in the battlefield is exercised in action but the men sitting at the counters in their money-houses and who encourage them too indulge in all this hatred business and create this brutalised mentality. Well, I do hope that somehow, we shall escape it; we shall try our best to escape it.

Now, some people criticise us for having suggested that we are prepared to talk to the Chinese representatives if they withdraw to the position before the 8th of September. And some people say "No, you must not talk to them, you must not do any such thing until they withdraw completely from Ladakh and everywhere." Now, the 8th of September was the day when they came in NEFA across the Thagla Ridge and also attacked Ladakh and went and captured some more territory in Ladakh. Now, let us be brave but let us also be sensible. Our saying to them "We will meet you only when you surrender and confess defeat" is not a thing which is likely to happen. Whatever happens, they are not defeated nor are we defeated. In fact, it is very difficult for China to defeat us and it is still more difficult for us to defeat China. We are not going to march to Peking. Even if we have success here, as we hope to, it does not defeat China even and even if they have success in the mountains, it does not mean that they defeat India. You must remember that this type of war is a war which may go on indefinitely, simply sucking the blood of either country and brutalising us. Therefore, to talk of conditions which are manifestly not going to be fulfilled in the foreseeable future is not a wise thing. What do we seek after that? We seek after that, if these conditions that we have set are fulfilled, to talk to them about what? It is to talk to them—our representatives and theirs—as to how we can produce conditions to relax tensions, etc. may be other withdrawals which will lead to the third stage which is talking to them on the merits of the question, we do not agree to anything in between and I think, it is a perfectly fair and legitimate proposal, honourable to us. As a matter of fact, as the House knows, the Chinese have rejected it completely out of hand. So, the various friends in other countries are putting forward numerous mediatory proposals, more or less all of them based on some kind of a ceasefire immediately and about the Chinese proposals. I need not go into them because they are so manifestly meant to favour their aggression and to give them a chance to establish themselves and push us out and then, may be at a later stage, to commit aggression again. But these people are confused. They put forward proposals which are very much to our disadvantage. Fortunately, after we had explained these various matters, President Nasser of the UAR put forward certain proposals which are very, very near our proposals.[90] They are not exactly the same but are very near; basically, our proposals that they should retire behind the Thagla Ridge, that conditions before the 8th of September should be produced. That is the basic part of his proposals. That too the Chinese have rejected. I think that the proposals we have put forward are honourable, legitimate and not coming through weakness but strength and they are having a good impression on the rest of the world. The rest of the world also counts in such matters.

Many people have said that we should close up our Mission in Peking and they should close the Chinese Mission here. Now, that is a legitimate thing for us to say or to do but we have to balance certain advantages and certain disadvantages, and for the moment, I need not and I cannot go into all the details. For the moment, we do not think it will be advantageous to us to

90. See note 87.

do that, when the time comes, if it is necessary, we shall do that. Again other Members, I believe, have talked about our withdrawing our forces from the Congo and the Gaza Strip. It is true that we would like to withdraw them, we have suggested that we should withdraw them but we have felt that we should not do something suddenly without adequate preparation for it on the other side, something which will upset all the two years' effort in the Congo and cast a heavy burden on the UN. Therefore, we have told them that we would like to withdraw them and we would like them to make other arrangements but for the present we will not withdraw them till they agree to it. We have certain international obligations. It is true that where the safety of our country is concerned, that is the first consideration. Nevertheless, in the balance we thought that we owed something to the international community, to Africa, and withdrawing them in a panicky condition would not be good and the amount of help that we derive from it, would be less than the harm we cause by our acting in that manner, out of course, we want to withdraw them as soon as we conveniently can.[91]

Finally, I should like to say that this is a tremendous challenge to our manhood and our nationhood, something which is far above our party bickering and party conflicts. Of course, parties have their views and they are entitled to them, but for the moment, this is something bigger than those things and the challenge has also another aspect of it and that is, it is an opportunity to build up our nation, an opportunity to build up on right lines—that is my trouble—lest we in our excitement or in our folly should go into wrong lines because that would be a tragedy, a deeper tragedy than war. That is not to be corrupted by war, to use war to the utmost of our strength, not to be corrupted, and to use that war situation to change our pattern or economic and social structure on the right lines. If we do that, then out of this great trouble that we face, good will come for the nation and I would like this House and our Parliament and our Members to give this lead to the nation that we are not interested in the so-called victory by itself, because victory is a hollow thing if you miss the fruits of victory. The fruit of victory is not a little territory. We have seen great wars in Europe and elsewhere, mighty countries fighting each other and countries have won, won decidedly and yet somehow the fruits of victory have escaped them. That is the lesson of the last two wars. It has slipped out of their fingers and new problems have been created which they cannot solve today and they think of the third war. Therefore, we have to think of the basic things we aim at because something has come in the way, a very bad thing—aggression—which is bad from our national point of view, from every point of view, therefore,

91. See item 197.

we have to get rid of it and we will try our utmost to get rid of it but that by itself is not enough. In doing so, because the process of doing so shakes up the nation completely, we have to see that that shaking up of the nation is of the right kind and they yield right results.

Thank you.

273. Defending Sikkim[92]

India Will Defend Sikkim: PM

Gangtok, Nov. 10 – Prime Minister Nehru has assured the Sikkim Congress President that "Sikkim will be defended by us with all our strength, just as any part of India."

He has conveyed this in a letter to the President of the Sikkim Congress, Mr Kashiraj Pradhan

Earlier in a letter to the Prime Minister, Mr Pradhan had expressed concern over the speech of Pandit Nehru in Parliament as reported by a Delhi newspaper which read: "The Prime Minister said that he could not give the assurance that Sikkim would not be lost to the Chinese."

Replying to Mr Pradhan, Nehru said: "The extracts from the newspapers you have given is not correctly reported."

274. To Sheikh Abdullah: Chinese Invasion[93]

November 13, 1962

My dear Sheikh Sahib,

I received your letter of the 5th November, 1962, some days ago.[94] Immediately, I wrote a brief acknowledgement which I hope has reached you. As you will appreciate, I have been terribly busy, and hence the delay in writing to you more fully.

I quite agree with you that the trouble on our borders is no mere border incident. We have had such border incidents now for five years, while China was encroaching on our territory. This time, however, in the North-East Frontier Agency, there has been what can only be described as a full scale invasion. The Chinese, in accordance with their way, twist everything, and call it aggression on our part. As a matter of fact, no Chinese have come into NEFA at any

92. Reproduced from a report in the *National Herald*, 1 December 1962, p.1.
93. Letter to the former Prime Minister of Jammu and Kashmir; address: Special Jail, Jammu.
94. See appendix 41.

time previously. Before the present regime came into existence in China, the Tibetans never laid claim to it. But I need not go into history. It is patent that the Chinese have deliberately and after much preparation, carried out this invasion. They have huge armies in Tibet, which they can turn easily to any particular point of attack. The aggressor has always this advantage. Also, they have another advantage—that they can come right up to our border easily by road, while we have to go across high mountains, without adequate roads, to reach the place. We have to send supplies etc. all by air-dropping. But, in spite of our initial reverses, I am quite confident that we shall not only check them, but, ultimately drive them back.

This is going to be a long process, as I have said, and it will take all our strength and resources to do so. I am quite convinced of the gravity of this situation, which you point out, and I think that gradually many other people are realising this. It is because of this that we are seeing an amazing upsurge of enthusiasm and emotion all over the country. The causes of the clash are, as you say, much deeper.

I appreciate what you say—that this invasion of India by China is dangerous for both India and Pakistan. Unfortunately, Pakistan has not realised this or, having realised it, wishes not to say or act in that way. The Pakistan newspapers are playing up China, and some leading personalities in Pakistan have even said that they must take advantage of this situation. I think that is a very short sighted and unwise policy for them. We have tried, and are trying our best, to be friendly to them and to make them realise the dangers inherent in the situation both for India and Pakistan. It is patent to me that the present danger to India will lead to a serious danger to the freedom of Pakistan. In fact, in a sense, Pakistan, by being in military pacts with Western countries, is really essentially more hostile to China. It is inconceivable to me that China can ever be friendly or cooperative with Pakistan. I hope that the realisation of this will come to the leaders of Pakistan.[95]

It has always been our basic policy to become friendly with Pakistan. It will continue to be harmful to both countries to be hostile to each other. We have tried our best to pursue this basic policy. But, unfortunately, it has not so far produced the results we aimed at. We shall continue our efforts. Perhaps, in the crisis that has overtaken us, some way out may be found.

I hope you are well.

Yours sincerely,
Jawaharlal Nehru.

95. See item 228.

275. In the Lok Sabha: Emergency and Chinese Invasion[96]

The Prime Minister and Minister of External Affairs, Defence and Atomic Energy (Jawaharlal Nehru): Mr Speaker, Sir, since I had the honour of moving this resolution, we have had a long debate in this House, almost perhaps a record debate in this House and perhaps in other parliaments also, I do not quite know how many Members have spoken.

Speaker: 165.

Jawaharlal Nehru: 165 Members have spoken. While it may have been said that perhaps a very large number of speeches rather take away from the pointedness of the question before the House and our minds wander into details, yet I am glad that so many Members have spoken because the point that stands out is this, not they have not made various suggestions, various criticisms, but that fundamentally and basically every person who has spoken in this House has spoken in the same refrain more or less, and that our Members have reflected the mood of the country.

I have put forward a longish resolution before this House, and it is clear from the speeches made that the resolution as it is welcome to this House and will be accepted as it is. But I have almost felt that it would have been, shall I say, suitable to add a small paragraph to the resolution thanking the Chinese Government for taking some action against us—which of course, we have resented—which has suddenly lifted a veil from the face of India. During the last three weeks or a little more we have had a glimpse of the strength of the serene face of India, strong and yet calm and determined, that face, and ancient face which is ever young and vibrant. We have not seen her face but rather this House, say a million faces representing that face of India or Bharat Mata.

That has been an experience worth having for all of us and it has been our high privilege to share in that emotion and experience. Whatever the future may bring, I do not think we shall ever forget this powerful emotional upheaval that India has had in which we have all shared. I repeat, all of us whatever party or group we may belong to. Any person who gives thought to these matters will realise, and I hope, other countries also realise—I hope that even the Chinese Government realises that—what this signifies because it seems to me obvious that no country which evokes that feeling in a moment of crisis can ever be suppressed or defeated. In fact many countries of the West and, I hope, many

96. Reply to debate on Resolution on Emergency, *Lok Sabha Debates*, Third Series, Vol. IX, November 8-20, 1962, pp. 1644-1671.

countries of the East also realise that today. They are surprised that such an amazing upheaval should have taken place among our feelings that all our petty controversies which seemed so big to us suddenly become of no moment and are a swept aside before the one thing before us, that is how to meet this crisis and emergency, how to face this invasion and to repel it. That is the major issue.

We may—I am going into that a little more later—have failed here and there. We might not have been quite prepared to meet this invasion. Our mentality may be built towards peace. Although we prepared for any such emergency, nevertheless it is true that the mind of the people and of the Government while preparing sought peace all the time. I am not sorry for that. I think, it was a right urge and it is that right urge that has led to this enormous upheaval in the Indian mind.

Much has been said about our unpreparedness. In some degrees many hon. Members have referred to it. I shall deal with that matter presently. I do not seek to justify any error that we might have committed, but I do think that many hon. Members have done an injustice, not to any Minister of others, but to our Armed Forces as a whole in making serious charges. I hope to disabuse their minds by stating some facts. The one real fact, as I said, is that our whole mentality has been governed by an approach to peace. That does not mean that we did not think of war or of defending our country. That, of course, we had always in mind. But there is such a thing as being conditioned in a certain way and, I am afraid, even now we are conditioned somewhat in that way.

Shri Anthony said—I am not quite sure of his words but he said something to the effect that now we must …

An Hon. Member: Brutalise.

Jawaharlal Nehru: I had an idea that he used the word "bloodthirsty"—I am not sure. Anyway, he said that our nation must be brutalised, that Jawaharlal Nehru must be brutalised. I hope that our nation, much less my humble self, will never be brutalised, because that is a strange idea that one can only be strong by being brutal. I reject that idea completely. Our strength lies in other factors. Brutality is a thing which we have associated with certain movements which we have objected to or rejected. By becoming brutal and thinking in those brutal ways we lose our souls and that is a tremendous loss. I hope that India which is essentially a gentle and peace loving country will retain that mind even though it may have to carry on war with all its consequences to the utmost.

There is a definite distinction between being strong and being brutalised. I need not mention an instance which has lent prestige to our history—the instance of the long period when Gandhiji was controlling the destinies of our movement for freedom. No man can say that Gandhiji was brutal, he was the essence of humility and of peace. No men can say that Gandhiji was weak. He was the strongest man that India or any country has produced. It was that peculiar fixture of strength with sacrifice to the uttermost, yet a certain humility in utterance and a certain friendly approach even to our opponents and enemies, that made him what he was. Those of us who were privileged to serve with him and under him do not claim, of course, to be much better than we are. We are humble folk who cannot be compared with the truly great, but something of the lesson that he taught came down upon us and we learnt it in a small measure. In the measure we learnt it, we also became strong though, I hope, not brutal. So, I would like to stress that I do not want to become brutal; I do not want that aspect of the cold war and the hot war which leads to hatred and dislike of a whole people and looking upon them is something below normal.

Some of us who are old, remember the First World War and the tremendous propaganda in it against the Germans. I do not hold any brief for the Germans. I think they were wrong in the First World War and, I think they were wrong in the Second World War. But the type of propaganda against the Huns and all that, against the whole people, not against an individual, was shocking. I have no doubt that the same type of propaganda was being carried on in Germany against the Western allies.

War is terrible and millions of people die; much destruction is caused. Yet, after all, death comes to all of us and if it comes a little earlier than otherwise in the great cause, it is not to be sorrowed for. We have to face it as men. Death in a good cause is not a thing to regret, even though we may regret the parting with our colleagues and comrades. But brutality is something which degrades a person. Death does not degrade a person. Brutality and hatred and the offspring of these things do degrade a nation and the people. So, I should like to say right at the beginning that, I hope, no such emotion will rise in our country and, if it does rise, it will be discouraged. We have nothing against the Chinese people. We regret many things that their Government has done. We think that their Government has acted infamously towards us. We regret many things that their Government has done in their country. We cannot help them. Anyhow, we must always distinguish between the people of my country—much more so of a great country, great in size, great in history—and its government, and not transfer somehow our anger and bitterness at what has been done by the Government, to the people.

Perhaps, if I understand, many Members, sometimes, listen to broadcasts from Peking. I have not done so at any time. They have told me of the constant appeals that Peking broadcast makes to the Indian people. It distinguishes the Indian people from the Indian Government or the Indian Parliament. It carries on propaganda that the present Government are just some reactionary people who are sitting and crushing the Indian people and making them do things against their will. I am sorry if they are so utterly mistaken, because even the blind can see that all the Indian people are one today. It does not require much perspicacity. But, I want the House to note the reason for their propaganda, that is trying always to distinguish between the Indian people and the various governmental agencies and parties. There is something in that. We must not lump together the Chinese people and the Chinese Government and everything that is in China together.

I cannot say how the Chinese people feel now, because they have no chance to express their feelings. Even if they had a chance, their minds are so conditioned by constant propaganda, by one-sided news that they are likely to feel one way even though otherwise they might not have done so. We should always distinguish between governmental action and the people as a whole. Therefore, I have not liked some poor Chinese shopkeepers, some restaurant-keepers being attacked in Delhi or elsewhere, as if they were the symbols of the attack on us. Perhaps some people thought so. But it was wrong for them to think so. It brutalises us and gives us a bad name. I should particularly like to lay stress on this aspect because it does not add to our strength in the least; but it weakens the nervous energy that we posses by using it in wrong directions.

War in these days is something infinitely more than it was in the old days. When I say old days, I am talking about India. I am not talking about the Great Wars and other things. War involves not only courage. It tends to became total war in which every human being, man, woman, and perhaps child, somehow helps or hinders, may hinder; and the total energy, nervous and otherwise of the nation, is involved in it, organised and mobilised.

We have seen in these great wars that have happened in the past, in the First World War and the Second, very powerful nations, very brave nations, armed to the teeth with the latest weapons, contending against each other, killing millions on either side, yet carrying on, but ultimately the whole nervous energy of the nation collapsing. Perhaps if the one which collapsed could have carried on a little while longer, the other would have collapsed, as Mr Winston Churchill said at the end of the First World War. It was the sheerest fluke that we won, the sheerest chance, sheerest fluke. Because both sides were determined to carry on. They were trained people in war and they had strength and determination. Ultimately, it becomes a thing of the whole basic energy of a nation collapsing, however it might be. It so happened that the Germans collapsed a little sooner. This is what Mr Churchill said. Perhaps, if they could have carried on, the decision might have been otherwise. So also in the Second World War. Throughout the War, it almost appeared, except towards the end, that Germany might win. Yet, ultimately, the other people won. So, we must realise that it is a question not only of a few weapons here and there, but of this entire energy of the nation, the mind of the nation being concentrated to achieve a certain objective and holding to it whatever happens and not wasting our energy or frittering it on any minor things, minor expressions and minor disputes.

I hope, of course, that we will mobilise the nation. We will, profit by many of these suggestions made in this House and other suggestions that are continually coming before us. But, even if we make mistakes, as any person is bound to do, the real thing that counts is not an odd mistake leading to an odd reverse, but ultimately keeping up this united front and united nervous energy of the nation to face this crisis.

The fact of the matter is that before these three and a half weeks, before the 20th of October, it was not realised by the people at large what danger possibly might confront us. They thought of frontier incidents. Hon. Members in this House criticised us for not taking steps in Ladakh to drive them out, not realising that it is not such an easy matter. Perhaps they realise it a little more now that these things are not such easy matters, that they require not only the strength of a nation, but properly utilised properly directed, enormous field of preparation and consideration of military factors. Where these factors are against us, naturally we suffer a reverse, it does not matter what your strength is. Our jawans were very strong.

I might mention just for the information of the House that it was not today, but some years back—by some years, I mean a couple of years back—that is, after the Chinese started nibbling at our territory in Ladakh, that we had before us the question of NEFA. We considered it, what we should do if they attacked. We hoped that they would not attack there. Certainly, we hoped, we expected that they would not attack in such large numbers as to bring about a regular invasion with several divisions, which they did. Nevertheless, we had to consider if they did, what should be done. The advice that we received then was that it will be disadvantageous for us to try to hold to the exact frontier line, the McMahon Line, but that we should delay them, we should harass them, we should fight them a little but the real defence line should be lower down wherever a strong defence line could be made. Partly because to the last moment we did not expect this invasion in overwhelming numbers, partly from the fact that we disliked it—I frankly tell you that we disliked the idea of our walking back in our own territory, whatever it was—we faced the Chinese there under very disadvantageous circumstances from a military point of view. In addition to that, enormous numbers came over. It is no criticism at all of our officers

429

or men that they were somewhat overwhelmed by this deluge and they had to retire to more defensive positions.

Frank Anthony[97], I think, said that we have been enabled to put up some kind of line of defence, because we have received arms from abroad. Now, we are very grateful for the arms and material and equipment that has come from abroad, but that was not correct then; no arms which were brought had reached our troops by then; they are gradually dribbling in and going there, but by that time when we achieved the present position, these arms which were brought had not been given and had not reached them. It was with the existing equipment that they brought the Chinese advance to a standstill.

So, the real reason, the basic reason for our reverses in the early days of this campaign was the very large forces the Chinese threw in; in a restricted sphere or field, they outnumbered our forces, by many, many times. Even the question of better arms did not arise. They had slightly better arms, but that question did not arise so much. They had better mortars to hit at some distance. They still have them, but they had stopped. That was the main reason, and there was nothing that we could do about it because the geography of the place, the military appraisal of the place was against us in that particular area. The only fault we made, it may be, if it is a fault, was even to stick out where the military situation was not very favourable. It was not that we told them to stick out; it is folly for any politician to say so. But our soldiers themselves have a reluctance to go back, and they stuck on at considerable cost to them.

I referred to the great unity in the country, which is a wonderful factor. It is not unity of parties so much as the unity of hearts and minds. We can see that in the thousands of faces. When I talked about the face of India, I really should have talked about the million faces of India, because they all bear the same impress today, whatever community or party he or she may belong to.

And I should like to say something even about the Communists. Now, the Communist Party's manifesto as a manifesto was, I think, as good as if it has been drafted by any non-communist. People may think or say that it does not represent their real views, but because of pressure from outside they did it. Let us suppose that it did not represent some of their views, some no doubt, some there are in the Communist Party who even objected to this manifesto, and were overruled. Even so, the fact that conditions in the country were such that they decided to issue that manifesto is a factor of some importance. It shows how these conditions mould people's minds in India, all of us, whatever party we may belong to, even to a party which for reasons known to Members was inclined in the past to favour somewhat the Chinese, because they are also

97. Nominated Member from the Anglo-Indian Community.

communists. Even then, they stood out, and stood up four square against this attack as any hundred per cent nationalist would do. That is a good thing. Why should we not take full advantage of it instead of deriding it and seeking causes why they did it? After all, there are some leaders among the Communists, and they sometimes quarrel amongst each other about ideologies, theses and what not, but the large number of ordinary workers or others who may belong to the Communist Party are simple folk. They are attracted by something in it, and those simple folk are affected just as they are affected by the situation which affects every Indian; they have also been affected by this manifesto of the Communist Party, that is, the ordinary communist members, that is a great gain. They should be affected in this way. Why should we lessen the effect of that by telling them that it is a wrong manifesto? So, I welcome that manifesto, and we should take full advantage of it in forging the unity against aggression that we have in fact forged.

Then, I do not wish to go into the hundred and more minor criticisms and suggestions made in this House. All suggestions made by hon. Members will be carefully examined. Some, as I said, were made because of not knowing that the thing had been done; some perhaps we cannot adopt; others we may adopt.

I should like rather to lay stress now on the general question of our preparedness, because hon. Members seem to think, some Members, that we sent our soldiers barefoot and without proper clothing, to fight in the NEFA mountains. It is really extraordinary to say that they were almost unarmed, and barefooted.

Some soldiers were stationed there. Others were sent rather in a hurry in September. Our time for issuing winter clothes is September, about the middle of September, when they were sent. They went there, of course, at that time in full uniform, full warm uniform, woollen uniform, and every man had two boots, good boots. As they were going, they were given three blankets apiece. Later on, it was made into four blankets; now, they have been issuing four thick army blankets. But these blankets took up so much room, and as they were going by air, the people decided, that is, the officer in charge, and the men themselves said, "They take so much room, and therefore send them later on to us." It was not so very cold then. So, they took, each one of them, one blanket, and left the others to be sent later on. That was a little unfortunate, because sending them later, as we did, meant air-dropping them. And air-dropping was a hazardous business in those days. Apart from the fact that the Chinese then could fire at them, airdropping in those very precipitous areas in the mountains could not be accurately carried out. Often, they went into the khud, into the deep ravine below, and it was difficult to recover them. So, we lost a good deal of our supplies, many of these blankets and other things.

431

Then, we even went further. We provide for high mountain altitudes snow-boots; they had good boots, they had two boots apiece; they had snow boots; these boots had been provided to these soldiers of ours who were permanently located there. The others that were sent were all in Assam; they were not here; but they were in Gauhati and other places. But, again, the difficulty arose of sending them by air.

Broadly speaking, I would say that all our Army in NEFA as well-clad, and well-booted, but towards the end, that is, towards the end of September, realising that the Chinese forces were increasing very rapidly, we decided to send more troops quickly. These troops were sent in a hurry. And sometimes, it so happened that troops that were being sent somewhere else were diverted to NEFA, and these troops certainly had not the full complement of winter clothing then. Of course, it was decided to send them later. Except for these troops that went later and which did not have the full complement and subsequently it was supplied to them, all others had the full Army complement, and many of them had snow-boots also. In any event, everyone had good stout Army boots.

Some people have heard stories of frostbite. All the cases of frostbite occur naturally due to the cold and due also to the high altitude. I do not quite remember the number, but I have an idea that out of a large number of people, I do not quite know, about two or three thousand, the total number of frostbite cases was only a handful. Even the cases of bronchitis, pneumonia etc., were only about forty, which is a very small percentage considering the conditions there. Of these too, we may say that more than half was due just to the altitude and not to lack of foot covering. This occurred not to our regular army serving on the front, but most of this occurred to people when on the 20th October, when this fierce onslaught of the Chinese came, our forces in that particular place—one or two places there—were dispersed. They could not return to the base of their army. They dispersed and for some days, they wandered about the mountains and ultimately returned. That was also the reason perhaps for people saying that the casualties were very heavy. Of course, a large number of our forces had not returned in order, they were wandering about the mountains, returning a few days later. I think these persons who returned a few days later were over 1,600. During these few days, these persons, naturally, were not well-protected. When they were wandering they did not have the facilities of the army blankets and other things they would at the base camp. They were not carrying them. They were wandering in high altitudes and they suffered a great deal. That was where the frostbite cases chiefly occurred, along with lack of other comforts. When they came back, they were put in hospital, and they are doing fairly well.

So I would submit to the House that it is not correct to say that our people were not sufficiently clad or sufficiently booted. It was an unfortunate thing that this was the time for changeover from summer clothing to winter clothing. Suddenly a small number of our army which was in summer clothing at that time was diverted to the east without coming back to their base, and the winter clothes took a little time to reach them. As regards boots, they had very good boots. Even snow boots were supplied. Some people do not have them. We do not supply snow boots to large numbers, to everybody. We do supply them to people in these high altitudes.

Apart from clothes and boots which were, I do think, excellent, normally our army is not clad for the winter. They were clad, for instance, in the special clothes, but normally our army is not clad for the severe winter. They have got all kinds of winter things, but not for these very high altitudes and the cold winter there.

It might interest hon. Members to know that in Ladakh, round about the Chushul area, the temperature at present is 30 degrees below zero. Such is the ferocity of that climate. Ordinarily, it does not matter how many clothes you may have in a temperature 30 degrees below zero at an altitude of over 14,000 ft. unless you are used to it. Now, learning from experience, we have provided, in addition to all the winter materials that our soldiers have, thick cotton padded coats and trousers. They are very warm. They may not look so smart as with the other clothes, but they are there. We started providing them these within a few days of the 20th, as soon as we felt that they ought to have these and it became colder there. We have been sending these cotton padded coats and trousers at the rate first of 500 a day and later at the rate of nearly 1000 a day.

The other charge made is about weapons, that they did not have proper weapons. Now the soldiers, jawans, who went there were supplied with all the normal equipment, that is, 303 rifles and the normal complement of automatic weapons such as light machine guns and medium machine guns. They did not have semi-automatic rifles because our army does not possess them. I might point out that many up-to-date armies in the West do not possess them yet. Even in England, the changeover to semi-automatic rifles has just fully taken place. It has just been completed; it took about four or five years; it has just been completed, this year, a few months ago. It is a lengthy process. And the British Army is relatively smaller than ours.

For about four years now, we have been considering and discussing this matter. Various difficulties arose. Points of views were different. The easiest way is always to order some ready-made article. But the easy way is not always a good way. Apart from the continuing difficulty we have to face, that is, lack

433

of foreign exchange etc., it is not the way to build up the strength of a nation. If we get something today, we have to get ammunition for that all the time and we are completely in the hands of some other country. And specially if we have to deal with private suppliers in other countries, the House knows that the arms racket is the worst racket of all; because you need something, they make you pay through the nose.

So we were very much against getting it from private suppliers outside and we thought that we should build up our arms industry to manufacture semiautomatic rifles. These arguments, especially in peace time, take a long period to determine. Of course, if we had this crisis before, we would have functioned better. But it took about two to three years to determine what type to have. Ultimately, we started the first processes of manufacture and we have just arrived at a stage when within about three weeks or four weeks—infact, some prototypes have been prepared—they will begin to come in larger numbers and will increase in numbers in another month, two months and three months to a substantial quantity.

It is not, a question merely of semi-automatic rifles. As I have said, we had automatic machine guns, LMGs and MMGs light machine guns and medium machine guns. Every regiment had its complement of these. Certainly, they did not have semi-automatic rifles for the reasons I have given, namely, we wanted to manufacture them ourselves and this changeover to automatic rifles has been relatively a modern development. As I said, even in England, it is a recent thing. But this outlook of ours, about manufacturing things ourselves rather than buying them, covered our whole approach to this question. We are manufacturing a great many things in arms today which we did not previously. I shall give you some figures. The first pressure upon us is always that of finance, that is, foreign exchange. We could not really afford it. Do not compare that situation two or three years ago with the situation today when we have to meet a crisis. When we meet a crisis like this, it just does not matter what happens. We have to face it. We have to buy it here and there; we have to get it from wherever we can. That is a different matter. But normally, the whole approach was to make them ourselves.

How did we make them? The usual thing was that we brought some with the proviso attached that the persons we bought it from would give us the license and the blueprints to manufacture it here. So we bought some to begin with, and then started with the blueprints and the license we had got to manufacture it, and supply it with everything, whether it is tanks or other things.

Also, it is all very well to build a factory here and there, but really you want to have a strong industrial background. You cannot, out of a relatively agricultural background, suddenly put up a highly sophisticated factory. All this time the work we have done, not in the Defence Ministry, but all over the country, in our First Five Year Plan, the Second and the Third, has been meant to strengthen the nation by making it more modernised, more industrialised and build up this base out of which you can produce the things you require. Perhaps some hon. Members will no doubt realise this, some may not. You have to have a strong base, industrial base. You have to have indeed not only a strong base, you have to have a literate people. People may think for the time being that education can be stopped. Education is essential for a real war effort. It is essential because you want every soldier today to be a better mechanic; he has to be educated as much as possible. So it all goes together. The whole basis of our Five Year Plan was to better our people, to raise their level and all that, but it was essential to make India stronger to face any trouble that arose, whether it was invasion or anything. And we are in a much better position today to face this trouble than we were ten or twelve years ago, there is no doubt, because of the growth of our industrial base in the public sector and the private sector, both. If we had to face this business ten or twelve years ago, our army was the same as today, a very brave army, but it had no industrial background and it would have been very difficult for it. We had to develop that industrial background as fast as we could. Now we have at least a base to develop, and I hope, therefore, that no conflict will arise in any person's mind whether we should go ahead with the Third Five Year Plan or devote ourselves to the war effort. That is part of the war effort—I do not say everything in the Third Plan—some things may be avoided, slowed down, even dropped, if you like. But take agriculture. It is the base of all industry. It is only on a strong agricultural base you can build up industry. The industrial base is the foundation of any war effort. So, the two are connected, intimately connected.

Education again. We want today, we shall want, not only a widely educated mass of people, but vast numbers of technically trained people. That comes in. Power is essential for industry, and so on. So, really, all the major things that we want were in the Five Year Plans, and are required today.

But the point I wish to lay stress on is this, that all our thinking in the past even from the point of view of the army has been concentrated on industrialisation, on making things ourselves.

Today we are getting large numbers of arms and equipment from other countries, and we are very grateful to the United States, to the United Kingdom especially, and other countries. But please remember that this kind of thing, and this kind of response, could not have occurred in peace time. Obviously, it is when danger threatens us, just as we feel in a particular way, and others feel too, and they think, as they rightly think, that this is not a mere matter of India being invaded by China, but it raises issues of vast importance to the world, to

435

Asia, and realising that they do it, they help us; that is, they feel this involves many issues in which they themselves are intensely interested. This could not have happened in peace time.

Someone asked us we could have brought some of the things at a very heavy price. Today I hope we get them on very special terms whatever the terns are, they are being worked out, but it is understood special terms, not to put any heavy burden on us today. That kind of thing could not have taken place then. We would have brought these things, or even one-tenth of what we are buying, at a heavy cost, which would have made our Finance Minister shiver. But apart from that, in any long-term view, it was a wrong thing. The thing is to make them ourselves.

What has China done? The main difference—there are many differences between China and India—but one difference is that first of all they started about twenty years before, the success of the revolution there, they were fighting all the time. They had a heavily trained army fighting in the mountains. They are especially good at mountain warfare; lightly clad with a bag of rice and a bag of tea in their pockets, they march on, with no questions of supplies or anything for days, with cotton-padded coats and trousers. They were highly trained in that warfare. But what I am saying is this, that they concentrated right from the beginning, apart from other developments in the country, on the development of armaments manufacture. They got a good deal of help from the Soviet Union; vast numbers, thousands of people set up their armament industries, did not concentrate on that, certainly not. We thought: better build up the whole industrial complex of India, and out of that other things would also be built up. Nevertheless, we did build up, I think fairly adequately, our armament industry, not as much as we would have liked, it was being progressed.

I shall just read out to you some figures of our ordnance factories production. In 1956-57, the issues to the army from the ordnance factories amounted to—I cannot tell you the details, it is not right for me to tell you the details, it is not right for me to tell you, I am only telling you how much they cost.

Some Hon. Members: No, no.

N.G. Ranga[98] (Chittoor): We know the results anyhow. We do not want all that, it will only help the enemy.

Jawaharlal Nehru: It has grown about 500 per cent. I do not mind telling you. I am not going to give you what they are making, but the issues to the army in

98. Swatantra Party.

1956-57 were Rs 8.64 crores; civil orders Rs 3.52 crores; Air Force and Navy Rs 1.93 crores. In 1957-58, issues to the Army Rs 12.78 crores; civil orders 3.27 crores; Air Force and Navy Rs 2 crores. Then the figure for the army goes up to Rs 12, Rs 14, Rs 19, Rs 24 and in 1961-62 to Rs 33¼ crores, and at the present moment it is estimated at Rs 60 crores.

Much has been said about civil orders, that we make thermos flasks and the like in ordnance factories. It is very unkind, that kind of criticism. Without knowing anything. Most of the civil orders are for Railways and the Government. A few things are made, some things like thermos flasks, simply because in the process of manufacturing other things, some things are manufactured which can easily be converted into thermos flasks etc., and there was surplus labour about. You will see that, civil orders have not progressed much. They have become, from Rs 3½, to Rs 6 crores in these eight years, while the issues to the Army rose from Rs 8 to Rs 60 crores. It has advanced much more, again with the difficulty of trying not to import machinery as much is possible. We did import some. Again foreign exchange, that awful thing stares us in the face. And the result was that much of the machinery used was revamped, reconditioned machinery, which we got from old stocks; and our engineers are good men, they made it to suit their purposes. Of course, it is far better to get new machinery. We are trying to get new machinery. But it is remarkable what they did with the material they had before them and I should like to pay a tribute to the men in charge of our ordnance factories, not only because they are thoroughly competent but, what is more, they are filled with a certain enthusiasm. They are patriotic and they want to show results. They work night and day and at the present moment they are working 24 hours a day in the factories.

I should like to mention how pressure of circumstances makes one a hard realist. The food we supply to our army, though good, is complicated and not easy to throw about or be supplied from above. In the last two or three weeks both our Armed Forces Food Department and Defence Science Organisation as also the Food and Agriculture Ministry have been experimenting with foods which could be concentrated foods and which could be carried about easily in your pocket also and which should be enough for several days. Only this morning I was looking at an exhibition, demonstration rather, in the Defence Ministry of these foods, quite a large number, very attractive and very palatable. They looked palatable. I did not eat them. There are all kinds of preparations of gur and nuts. They are excellent preparations, I may also tell the House that gur is a good thing for high altitudes. We are making very good progress. We have in fact sent these things to the front to find out the reaction of the soldiers to that.

437

Some hon. Member asked a question about the newspaper items about our soldiers getting notices from courts or some such thing. I do not know that. Anyhow we have immediately taken action to stop any such thing happening. And every such thing will have to be postponed for the duration of this emergency.

Some people criticised our diplomatic missions abroad for not doing as good a job of work as they ought to in putting our case and countering the Chinese propaganda. My information is that our diplomatic missions abroad, by and large, are doing very good work. But another country's outlook is not determined solely by what we tell there. There may be many factors, may be sometimes fear, sometimes other things. I think our missions abroad are doing well and, what is more, their work is being rewarded. The first reaction of many countries, many of these Asian and African countries, was regret and surprise at what had happened here and they hoped that it would be quickly ended by some ceasefire and compromise and all that, because they found themselves in a difficult position. Gradually this surprise is giving way; it has given way in the case of the UAR and even Ghana, which took up an attitude to our regret originally and later, supported the UAR making some suggestions to the Chinese Government. It was very near to the suggestions we made about the cease fire business. So, I do not think it will be right to criticise our diplomatic missions abroad. You must remember that these countries have their own diplomats too here who report to them, and most of them have got their newspaper correspondents. There are many ways of getting news about what is happening.

This question comes up in various ways about Pakistan and Nepal. It is difficult for me to say anything definite. But about Nepal I should like to say that latterly the attitude of Nepal has been relatively much more friendly. Naturally, we have always made it clear it is unfortunate that they thought that we were creating troubles. We have made it clear right from the beginning that we do not want trouble in Nepal. Apart from the Chinese invasion and the trouble there, they are largely internal. Anyhow, now, I think they believe our word and are very friendly and I hope that our relations will continue to be friendly and cordial.

As for Pakistan, there also, I will not be quite definite, but their newspapers have been peculiarly virulent about this matter against us. But I do not think their newspapers reflect very much the opinion of the people of Pakistan or even of those in authority in Pakistan. Gradually they are realising it; at first, apparently they thought this was a small frontier matter and nothing much. Now, they are realising how far reaching are the consequence of this and they are making a reappraisal.

I should like to say a few words about the Soviet Union. The Soviet Union has been, as the House knows, consistently friendly to us all along. It has been put in a very difficult position in this matter, because they have been, and are, allies of China, and hence the embarrassment to them as between a country with which they are friendly and a country which is their ally.[99] We have realised that and we do not expect them to do anything which would definitely mean a breach over there. It is not for us to suggest to any country. But we have had their goodwill and good wishes all along, even very recently, and that is a consolation to us and we certainly hope to have that in future.

The Chinese Government has been making a lot of propaganda about our Defence of India Act as if that was specially passed to deal with some Chinese here. It has obviously been passed because of the situation we have to deal with. Everybody who is mischief-maker, if it be a Chinese who makes a mischief, he comes under its purview; otherwise not. The difficulty with the Chinese is that they have a singularly perverted opinion and perverted view of what happens in the rest of the world. It is an odd characteristic of the Chinese. Being a great nation with a vast territory, it begins to think all outside the limits of its frontiers are subhuman types and not so advanced as they are.

One thing more. There has been some criticism about our offer for a cease fire. We have said that before we discuss anything, the Chinese forces must go back and restore the position as it existed before the 8th September, that is, a little over two months ago, when they first came over the Thagla pass. They have suggested something different, and something that is apt to delude the people. They say, let us go back, to the position of November 1959. Now, the people who do not know this might well wonder, they are going back three years, not now. But November, 1959 was roughly the date or period when the first claim was made by the Chinese Government, by Mr Chou En-lai, to these territories according to their maps. Previously, they were included in their maps, but nobody had made any official claim. In fact, officially they have said that their maps are old and not up-to-date, and they will revise them. But in 1959 for the first time, they claimed them, meanwhile, of course, they having gone into a good bit of Ladakh.

In 1959, our counter-measures started taking effect. In 1959-60 and 1961, we went into Ladakh much more and more and established many posts there. Now, we realised, as I think I told this House then, that the object of these posts is to prevent their further advance unless they fight it out. It was difficult for us to have a major armed conflict with them there, because they had great advantages. Their roads came right up there. They could bring all kinds of

99. See appendix 23.

weapons, tanks, etc., there from Tibet which is near, which is relatively a flat country, while for us, although we made some progress and the road is recently made--at that time even that was not made--it is very difficult; it meant months of effort to get there. Nevertheless, we put up those posts to check their advance and they did check their advance. In fact, we pulled them back a little. In the NEFA area, we had previously put up our posts at the border or just under it, because one cannot have a high-ridge post. Even in Thagla pass, our post was two or three miles on this side, but not on the pass itself.

Now, if we accept their proposals, which seems so innocuous, they would retire, they said, up to the McMahon Line, but then they add that their idea of McMahon Line was different from ours and it is on this side of the ridge, and we should have to retire from where we are today—another 20 kilometres, that is, leaving about 40 kilometres of territory which was not occupied either by their armies or ours. That is to say, they would have a fixed base on this side of the Thagla pass, an open territory which they can walk across any moment they like. It was impossible for us to agree to. And in Ladakh, it meant our withdrawing still further from where we are, and their [they are] not exactly marching immediately, but our facilitating their advance in the future if they want to come, so, we rejected those proposals.

We said, there should be a reversion to the 8th September line both in NEFA and in Ladakh. That meant in NEFA not only their going back but our going forward to those posts that we held, with no vacant space left, and in Ladakh our going back a good way.

Some people say, "How can you say that? You must not negotiate. You must not have any talk with them till you completely push them out from the Indian territory." That is a very good thing. But one does not talk with anybody whom one has defeated completely and pushed out. The question of talks does not arise. If we have gained our objective without talks, the question of talks does not arise. I would suggest to the House to remember that in these matters, one has to take a strong view, but a realistic view. The suggestion that we have made, they have rejected, because it strengthens us and weakens them. What is more the suggestion we have made about the 8th September line is one which has been appreciated in a great part of the world—non-aligned countries and others because merely saying that we shall not talk to you till you have confessed defeat is not the kind of suggestion that any country makes to another. So I hope that the House will realise that what we have suggested is a right suggestion and will support it fully. Some Members talked about our stating that we are going to liberate Tibet. Some other even mentioned I think the hon. Member who just intervened said something about Mansarovar.

Shri Raghunath Singh[100] (Varanasi): Mansar village. (Interruptions).

Jawaharlal Nehru: Unfortunately, history is not made by men like the hon. Member opposite. It is really amazing to see that some other Members and others outside talk that we should lay down that we would liberate Tibet. It is a very happy idea if it is liberated. But our undertaking that job at the present moment or at any moment seems to me extraordinary and fantastic and having no relation to reality.

I have said that in a war between India and China, it is patent that if you think in terms of victory and defeat there might be battles and we might push them back, as we hope to—but if either country thinks in terms of bringing the other to its knees, it manifestly cannot and will not happen. Let us be realistic. Are we going to march to Peking? (Interruptions.)

Priya Gupta[101] (Katihar): Are we going to allow them to march to Delhi?

Jawaharlal Nehru: I am sorry I cannot enter into an argument. But I appreciate that a war like this cannot be ended as far as I can foresee by surrender by either party. They are two great countries and neither will surrender. Therefore, some way out has to be found to finish the war in terms honourable to us. We have said that we will finish the war when we liberate our own territory which is in their possession. Our saying that we are going to liberate Tibet is a thing which we cannot do; even if we had the atom bomb, we could not do it. It is manifestly absurd to talk about it, and it justifies everything that China has said about it, in the sense ... (Interruptions.).

They have always been saying that their chief grouse against us is that we have been encouraging a revolt and rebellion in Tibet. That is the thing which ultimately turned them against us. If we say that, it will justify their argument, which had no foundation, and give them in international circles and everywhere considerable strength. It will mean our saying something which we cannot possibly, feasibly do. It is impossible. We have got a big enough task, a tremendous task, which we should realise, to push them back to their own territory from our own country. We are going to do it. It is going to be mighty difficult; it might take us a long time. So, I hope that while we should be strong and determined, as we must be, we must not just for the sake of appearing braver than others say things which are, I regret to use the word, manifestly nonsense.

100. Congress.
101. PSP.

Now, the resolution I have placed before the House is a fairly comprehensive one. It is a resolution of resolve, of determination and of dedication. I hope, therefore, that in accepting the resolution, as I hope this House will, the House thinks in terms of dedication, not in bombast, not in tall talk, but realising that we have a very difficult task before us, we are determined to fulfill it however long it may take, and whatever the consequences might be. And, in doing so, we will be heartened by the biggest thing that a country can do and which India has done thus far, and that is, produce this enormous emotional upheaval that we see all over India among men, among women and, perhaps more than all among children. So, I put forward this resolution before the House in the hope, faith and with the strong determination that all those who are present here and the country will abide by it and will act up to it.

Hari Vishnu Kamath[102]: Mr Speaker, may I by your leave, ask just one question? The Maharajkumar of Sikkim is reported to have said in Darjeeling two days ago that there has been a tremendous Chinese military build-up on Sikkim's borders during the last few days or weeks. Is the Prime Minister in a position to assure the House and the nation, in view of the agreement which India has with Sikkim for the responsibility of its defence, that our Army is better prepared to resist the Chinese aggressor in Sikkim than it was, unfortunately, in NEFA a few weeks ago?[103]

Jawaharlal Nehru: I regret, Sir, that such questions are put to me. I will give no assurance of any kind. How can I give assurances? I can give no assurance except that we are taking all measures that we can if such a thing occurs there. How can I give assurance about the future in matters which are determined not by my assurances but by other factors?[104] But I do not think that the Chinese, if they venture to invade and come from Chumbi valley, will be allowed to come or will find it an easy job.

One thing I have to mention it is unconnected with this question. I have received today a letter signed by 35 Members of Parliament offering their services to serve anywhere. I am very grateful to those 35 Members and I welcome their offer. I do not quite know how we can immediately profit by it. But I am sure as our organisation progresses work would be found for more and more people in all grades and departments of life.

---

102. PSP.
103. See item 273.
104. See item 276.

276. To Bishan Chandra Seth: Resolve to Fight back[105]

प्रिय बिशनचन्द्र जी,

आपका 17 नवम्बर का पत्र मिला।

आपने ठीक लिखा है कि जो मुझ से सिक्किम के बारे में प्रश्न हुआ, उससे मैं कुछ चिड़ गया और जो जवाब मैंने दिया उससे मुमकिन है किसी को धोखा भी हो जाए।[106] मुझसे कहा जाए कि मैं आश्वासन दूं कि एक बात होगी कि नहीं होगी लड़ाई के बारे में, यह मुझे ठीक नहीं लगा। मैं सिर्फ़ इतनी कह सकता था कि हमारा कर्तव्य है कि हम पूरी शक्ति से उसको हमले से बचायें, और इसका पूरा इरादा हमने किया है।

एक बात मैं निश्चय से कह सकता हूं और मुझे इसका विश्वास है, वह यह, कि चीन का आक्रमण हम अन्त में हटा देंगे सारे भारत से और सिक्किम से। लेकिन बीच में क्या क्या हो वह लड़ाई की बात है, और उसकी निसबत इक़रार करना कठिन होगा। आपको याद होगा कि बार बार पिछले बरसों में मुझ से कहा गया था कि हमें चाहिए चीनियों को लद्दाख़ से निकाल दें। मैं भी यह चाहता था। लेकिन उस समय मैं जानता था कि हम अपनी शक्ति से इस बात को नहीं कर सकते क्योंकि वहां चीनियों को बहुत सहूलियत है, और हमें बड़ी कठिनाई थी।

तिब्बत के बारे में हमसे कोई शख़्स कहे कि हम उसको भी चीनी फ़ौजों से साफ़ कर दें, यह बात समझ की नहीं है और हमारी शक्ति के बिल्कुल बाहर है। चीन में खुद कोई क्रान्ति हो तो और बात है, या कोई महायुद्ध दुनिया भर में हो तो उसका नतीजा कुछ भी हो सकता है।

तीसरी बात आपने लिखी है कि मुझे अपनी स्पीच को लिखकर पढ़ना चाहिए था। यह प्रायः सही हो। लेकिन मेरी यह आदत नहीं है और न ही मुझे समय मिलता है स्पीच लिखने का।

आपने जो लिखा है कि राष्ट्रपति जी को डिफेन्स कौन्सिल का अध्यक्ष होना चाहिए, यह बात मुझे उचित मालूम नहीं होती। किसी जगह भी जहां पार्लमेंटरी सरकार हो वहां यह उचित नहीं समझा गया, न किया जाता है। राष्ट्रपति जी की सलाह ली जाती है अक्सर, और उनकी सलाह का असर होता है, हमारे विधान के विरुद्ध।

पाकिस्तान पूरी सहायता अमरीका से ले रहा है और वह दे रहा है। हमारा सिर्फ़ फ़ौजी समझौता करना मैं गलत समझता हूं। हमको इससे कोई अधिक लाभ नहीं होगा, और दुनिया भर से हानि भी हो सकती है। रूस हमारे साथ हो या नहीं, मैं नहीं कह सकता, लेकिन अगर हमारे साथ न भी हो और चीन की मदद न करे, इससे भी हमें बहुत फ़ायदा होगा। आजकल रूस और चीन का सम्बन्ध अच्छा नहीं है। एक दूसरे को गाली देते हैं।

---

105. Letter to Bishan Chandra Seth, Congress MP from Saharanpur; 17 November 1962; address: 28 South Avenue, New Delhi; PMH-No.1999-62.
106. See note 104 in this section.

हमें कोई ऐसी बात नहीं करनी चाहिए जिससे हम रूस को चीन की तरफ़ और धकेल दें। अगर रूस पैट्रोल चीन को न दे इससे बड़ी सहायता हमें होगी।

यह मुमकिन है कि चीन की लड़ाई हवा से भी हो। इसके लिए हमें तैय्यार होना चाहिए। लेकिन इस वक़्त चीन की हवाई शक्ति बहुत बड़ी है और काफ़ी हानि हमें पहुंचा सकता है।

आसाम, बंगाल और कश्मीर के शासन तोड़ देना यह भारत के लिए अच्छा नहीं होगा, और बजाय जनता की पूरी सहायमा मिलने के, जोकि इस समय मिल रही है, वहां झगड़े पैदा हो जायेंगे।

आपका
जवाहरलाल नेहरु

[Translation begins:

Dear Bishan Chandra Ji,
Your letter of the 17th.

You are right in pointing out that when I was asked about Sikkim, I got a little irritated. And the answer I gave might be misconstrued by some.[107] If I am asked to give assurance whether something will happen or not during a war, I feel it is not right. I could only have said that we would defend Sikkim and we have all the intention of doing so.

One thing I can say with confidence, that we will repel the aggression of China from all of India and Sikkim. But in between what will happen is difficult to predict. You would remember that for years I have been asked to expel the Chinese from Ladakh. I too wanted that. But I knew that with our forces we cannot do so, since the Chinese were in an advantageous position and we were on difficult terrain.

If someone asks me to throw out the Chinese from Tibet, it is completely beyond reason and our capability. Well, if there is a revolution in China or a World War, anything can happen.

The third thing that you have pointed out is that I should write my speeches before delivering them. Neither is it my habit, nor do I get time to write speeches.

You have written that the President should be the head of the Defence Council, does not go down well with my understanding. Wherever there is parliamentary government, this is neither practised nor preferred. The president's views are taken and if they are impactful, it would go against our constitution.

107. See note 106.

444

Pakistan is taking all the help from the US and they are providing it also. Our entering into a military pact sounds wrong to me. We will not gain much from such a pact, and on top of that the whole world will suffer. Whether Soviet Russia is with us or not, I cannot say; but if they are not with us and yet, do not help China, then also we would stand to gain a lot. These days the Sino-Soviet relationship is not very good. They abuse each other in public. We should not do anything that would push the Soviets towards China. If Russia stops supplying petrol to China, that would be of great advantage to us.

It is possible that the war with China could be fought in the air. We should be prepared for it. But now China has much greater strength in air power and can harm us immensely.

Dissolving the governments of Assam, Bengal and Kashmir will not augur well for India; instead of getting full popular support, which we are getting now, it would start terrible in fighting.

Yours,
Jawaharlal Nehru

Translation ends]

277. To Vishnu Sahay: Defence Strategy[108]

November 17, 1962

My dear Vishnu Sahay,
I have your letter of the 14th November. I am passing on copies of it to the Home Minister and the Cabinet Secretary.

I agree with you that Tezpur is being over-visited. I have been thinking of going there myself, but for the present, I have postponed the visit. This is chiefly because of the fighting going on in the Walong area. I did not wish to come in the way of what is being done there.

What you say about the possibility of Chinese coming in via Tirap is true. There is that possibility though for the moment I do not think it is at all likely. But obviously we cannot station our forces in small numbers in various places. I think what might be done soon is, first of all, to have a good Intelligence service in this area and, secondly, to build up Volunteer Corps or Home Guards. I think also the time has come for us to train Guerrilla Units. We are taking this in hand elsewhere in NEFA using Khampas and tribal people.

108. Letter to the Governor of Assam.

As for Bhutan, we are in some difficulty. Any attempt of our Army to go there in numbers would probably be an invitation to the Chinese also to go there. For the present we have sent some people to train the Bhutanese and taking some other steps also.

Yours sincerely,
[Jawaharlal Nehru]

278. In the Rajya Sabha: NEFA and Ladakh[109]

The Prime Minister (Jawaharlal Nehru); Mr Chairman, Sir, I have to give grievous news to the House. Both Walong and the Sela Ridge in NEFA have fallen to the enemy. In the Chushul area fighting is proceeding.

In Walong the enemy attacked on the night of the 15-16 November. This was a two-pronged attack. The battle continued till the morning of the 17th. The enemy succeeded in shelling the airfield which was the only source of supply to our forces. On the 17th afternoon, our troops started withdrawing to defensive positions in the rear. In the Jung area, the enemy attacked our positions on the 17th November. Their attack was repulsed four times. Ultimately, there was an attack in greater strength and the Jung position had to be given up. Our troops fell back to the main position on Sela. In the meantime, the enemy by-passed our main post by a wide flanking movement between Sela and Bomdila. They attacked in the early hours of the 18th November and cut the road between Sela and Bomdila. The infiltrators were forced to withdraw. They formed up again, however, and renewed the attack. The situation is somewhat confused and fighting is going on, but our commander had to withdraw from Sela.

In Chushul sector in Ladakh heavy artillery—attacks were made on the Chushul airfield and outposts. Our post at Rezang La was attacked on the 18th November morning. After fierce fighting, this post was overwhelmed. A part of another post, six miles east of Chushul, was also attacked. Other attacks on the Chushul area were repulsed, fighting is still going on.

This is bad news. I cannot go into any further details at this stage. I should like to add that in spite of the reverses suffered by us, we are determined not to give in any way and we shall fight the enemy, however long it may take, to repel him and drive him out of our territory.

109. Statement in the House, *Rajya Sabha Debates*, Vol. XLI, Nos. 1-8, 8 November to 19 November 1962, pp. 1652-1659.

Ganga Sharan Sinha[110] (Bihar): I would like to have some clarification. It has appeared in today's papers that we had to withdraw from Walong because we were outnumbered. Secondly, it has also appeared in the Press today that Chinese trucks and buses were seen in Tawang. I do not know whether both these news items are correct. The first is that it has appeared in today's Press that one of the main reasons why we withdrew from Walong was that we were outnumbered there by the Chinese. Is that correct? The second thing is that it has also appeared in the Press today that Chinese buses and trucks were seen at Tawang. Is that news correct?

Jawaharlal Nehru: I can hardly discuss the details of the fighting, Sir, in Walong. It is difficult. We have not got all the details yet but the major fact is that the enemy managed to attain a high position, a position of height, there and shelled our airfield which was the sole source of supply to the Walong base and they also attacked the Walong post. The Commander there decided to withdraw and he was withdrawn from it. This has always to be decided by the Commander on the spot subject to such instructions as the superior officers give. The civil authority hardly comes into the picture.

As far as the other matter that the hon. Member has mentioned is concerned trucks and buses being seen there at Tawang, they may well be there because in the small area there between Tawang and Bumla pass, some kind of road appears to have been constructed by the Chinese.

K. Santhanam (Madras): May I know whether the airstrip at Walong has been made unusable by the Chinese?

Jawaharlal Nehru: I am sorry I cannot answer that question. I have no information on that.

Rajendra Pratap Sinha[111] (Bihar): I want to ask one question. The Prime Minister just now told us that there was an outflanking movement to capture Sela. Am I to believe that the Chinese forces came to this area from our adjoining State of Bhutan to attack?

Jawaharlal Nehru: No, Sir. It is on the other side. Bhutan is on the left side and nobody has entered Bhutan to our knowledge.

---

110. Independent.
111. Congress.

Chairman: He is talking of the outflanking movement at Sela.

Jawaharlal Nehru: Sela movement has nothing to do with Bhutan territory. It came from another side.

Chandra Shekhar[112] (Uttar Pradesh): The situation has turned out to be very serious. A National Defence Council was formed in the country and emergency was declared. I fail to understand why no meeting of the National Defence Council has been held so far. I should like to have one more assurance from the Prime Minister. I would like to know whether he is going to give up the old policy of vacillation and hesitation and declare that we are going to fight firmly, whether he will talk like a war leader who is going to put before the nation an example of his vitality, strength and determination. I want that clear and categorical assurance from the Prime Minister because at this juncture if we are in a hesitant mood, I think we cannot fight the enemy. The way civil defence arrangements are going on in the country, I think it is not intended to meet the situation in the country and the emergency that has arisen.

Jawaharlal Nehru: I can hardly answer the hon. Member's question. Not today but for some time past there has been no question of hesitation or vacillation. We realised certainly from the 20th October, if not before, that we are meeting a very well-prepared determined enemy who could throw in vast forces and overwhelm us at any point and we decided then to take every possible measure, including, of course, getting every kind of aid that we could from friendly countries. We have asked for every kind of aid. Some has come, some others will come in. We have not hesitated to do that. There is no inhibition about that and we propose to go on doing that and it is not only a full-fledged war but a very difficult war for us because of various situations. The hon. Member referred to civil defence. Civil defence is helpful but it has nothing to do with the immediate conflict. Civil defence comes in, may come in and we should certainly look after it but the immediate problem is somewhat different.

Chandra Shekhar: The whole trouble is that we become wiser after the event. Civil defence will come in later on but we must prepare for it. I should like to mention one more point. It was reported from Jorhat that there was an attempt to sabotage the railway line. It was reported from Warangal that some members of the public who went round to make collections for the

112. Congress.

Defence Fund were attacked by the Communists. It was reported from Burdwan that demonstrators against the Chinese were stoned from the Communist Party office. All these things are happening in the country and the national emergency is there, but our Government is keeping mum over all these issues, when people resisted all these attempts our Prime Minister told the public that all these attempts are not going to serve the country. I want to know from the Prime Minister whether this national upsurge is not going to serve the country but that only such attempts of sabotage are going to serve this country. (Interruptions) We are not going to burn the houses of the Communist Party but if stones come from the office of the Communist Party, those Communist Party offices cannot be protected by any Government and by any person whatsoever. (Interruptions)

Jawaharlal Nehru: The hon. Member referred to some incidents in today's papers about somebody being stoned apparently in front of the Communist Party office. I am told that those people who stoned them, especially the leader of the Party there, were arrested immediately and the Bengal Government has also taken other steps. There is no doubt that any such activity must be dealt with severely but I had ventured to say on a previous occasion that certain, fortunately very few incidents had occurred where some shops had been destroyed or burnt or looted out that does not add to our strength. It is undignified and harmful but any person coming in the way of our war effort must be dealt with firmly.

Dahyabhai V. Patel[113] (Gujarat): I do not wish to embarrass the Prime Minister or the Government in any way but we are opposing a massive onslaught of the Chinese who have been well prepared. They have been preparing themselves for a long time. The country feels, a very great section of the country, a large section of the country feels that our request for aid from friendly countries has been rather hesitant, we have not demanded the full measure of the aid that is available and we are hesitant to ask that. Are we going to ask for unstinted and full measure of aid to come to enable us to drive the Chinese out? I would like the Prime Minister to make that categorical declaration.

Jawaharlal Nehru: I think I had made that clear that we are asking, for all the aid that we require. There has been no delay on our part but aid naturally had to be phased. We wanted some things immediately, some things in the next two months or so and some things in the next six months but we have given

113. Leader of Swatantra Party in the House.

long lists of what we require to several friendly countries and we are anxious to get them as soon as possible.

M. Ruthnaswamy[114] (Madras): May I know by whom, the Cabinet or the Army Council, is the strategy of defence in the NEFA area laid? I also want to know whether the Commander who was sent there is allowed to modify that strategy whether he has anything to do with the course of the tactics followed day after day?

Some Hon. Members: How can that question be answered? No, no.

G. Murahari (Uttar Pradesh): I want to know why the Prime Minister is not ordering the air arm to go into action to destroy the supply bases of the enemy which are situated in our own territory.

Anand Chand (Himachal Pradesh): The hon. Prime Minister has just now said that it is a full-scale war. May I respectfully ask him, now that the position is changed—previously it was infiltration of the Chinese in very large numbers—whether the Government would now revise their stand—because up till now we have been saying that this is Chinese aggression—and we would now say that it is war and take all steps that are necessary because this emergency, Sir, as I put it before the House, was based on certain of our territories having been occupied by the Chinese? Now, it is full-scale war and if it is full-scale war, I think something should be done about the closure of our Embassy in China as well as the closure of the Chinese Embassy here and all other steps that follow, because I want to know whether we are going to declare war now that the Chinese have come into our soil or whether we are going to wait for the Chinese to declare war against us?

Chairman: You think the declaration is immensely important?

Jawaharlal Nehru: This is obviously a war, a kind of a brutal and callous war. We are treating it as such and taking all steps about it. As for the hon. Member's question about declaration of war and closing our Embassy and their Embassy here, there is no question of, shall I say, any inhibition in doing that. One has to consider it from various aspects as to whether it will be helpful in our carrying on this effort or not at the present moment. We shall certainly consider it very carefully.

114. Swatantra Party.

A.B. Vajpayee[115] (Uttar Pradesh): May I know whether the attention of the hon. Prime Minister has been drawn to a statement made by the Prime Minister of Australia that they have not received any request for military aid from India? May I seek a clarification whether Australia has been approached for military aid?

Jawaharlal Nehru: I think Australia has been approached, not in a big way because big aid was obviously likely to come from some big countries like the United States, like the United Kingdom and to some extent from France but I think we have approached them for some things.

M.H. Samuel (Andhra Pradesh): May I know if the Prime Minister has any information about the casualties we have inflicted on the enemy at Walong?

Ganga Sharan Sinha: Last Friday it was announced that our house will adjourn on the 23rd. In view of the serious situation that is developing, will the Prime Minister reconsider this and call the leaders of all the groups and find out some method so that Parliament can remain in session or some other via media, by which Members can be kept in touch because that is very necessary? And I think before we adjourn this decision should be taken.

Jawaharlal Nehru: I am in the hands of the house, this House and the other House. The sole test should be what will further our war effort. Many hon. Members have been eager to go back to their constituencies or elsewhere to do work. It was really under pressure from them that we decided to shorten this session. If it requires to be extended a little longer, we shall certainly agree.

279. In the Lok Sabha: NEFA and Ladakh[116]

The Prime Minister, Minister of External Affairs, Defence and Atomic Energy (Jawaharlal Nehru): Mr Speaker, Sir, I have to give grievous news to this House. Both Walong and the Sela ridge in NEFA have fallen to the enemy. In the Chushul area fighting is proceeding.

---

115. Jana Sangh.
116. Statement, *Lok Sabha Debates*, Third Series, Vol. IX, November 8-20, 1962, pp. 2230-2234.

In Walong, the enemy attacked on the 15th/16th night. This was a two-pronged attack. The battle continued till the morning of the 17th. The enemy succeeded in shelling this air field, which was the only source of supply to our forces. In the 17th afternoon, our troops started withdrawing to defensive positions in the rear.

In the Jung area, the enemy attacked our positions on the 17th November. Their attack was repulsed four times. Ultimately there was an attack in greater strength, and this Jung position had to be given up. Our troops fell back to the main position at Sela. In the meantime, the enemy bypassed our main post by a wide flanking movement between Sela and Bomdila. They attacked in the early hours of the 18th November, and cut the road between Sela and Bomdila. The infiltrators were forced to withdraw. They formed up again and renewed the attack. The situation is somewhat confused, and fighting is going on, but our Commander had to withdraw from Sela.

In the Chushul sector in Ladakh, heavy artillery attacks were made on the Chushul air field and the outposts. Our post at Rezang La was attacked on the 18th morning. After fierce fighting, this post was overwhelmed. A part of another post six miles east of Chushul was also attacked.

Other attacks in the Chushul area were repulsed but fighting is still going on.

This is bad news, I cannot go into further details at this stage. I should like to add that in spite of the reverses suffered by us, we are determined not to give in, in any way, and we shall fight the enemy, however long it may take to repel him and drive him out of our country.

Hari Vishnu Kamath[117]: On a point of clarification.

Speaker: I have received, and probably the Prime Minister may have received, a call attention notice from several hon. Members. That was specific about the fall of Jung to the enemy, and the reportedly precarious position of Chushul. Would the Prime Minister like to say anything more?

Jawaharlal Nehru: I would not like to say anything beyond what I have said. I have referred to both Jung and Chushul.

Hari Vishnu Kamath (Hoshangabad): I am sure the House is distressed and shocked beyond measure to hear of this most calamitous reverse since October 20. Our gallant jawans are being killed and taken prisoner in thousands.

117. PSP.

The former Defence Minister, on the eve of his resignation, stated in Bombay or elsewhere, that the position was that we are not only outnumbered, but out-weaponed.[118] May I ask the Prime Minister whether steps, and vigorous steps, are being taken now to obtain arms and equipment from all friendly nations on a massive scale and thus allay the widespread public apprehensions that our armed forces are not yet fully equipped to meet the enemy?

Jawaharlal Nehru: As the House knows, every effort is being made to get arms and other equipment from foreign countries, and we have received some, and they have been immediately sent on to our forward posts.

Priya Gupta[119] (Katihar): May I know the extent to which foreign military aid is taken, and whether Government have a blueprint for further military aid to meet this crisis arising out of the fact that there is a reported mutual understanding between China and the Pakistan Government to the effect that China would help Pakistan to get Kashmir and West Bengal and Assasm according to Group C proposal of the British Cabinet Mission?

Speaker: All this question is not relevant here.

[Omitted: Exchanges on procedure]

Speaker: Order, order. He (Bagri[120], Hissar) has put a question and the Prime Minister has said that he has not this information with him; and that whenever it is got it would be supplied to the House ... (Interruptions).

Hem Barua[121] (Gauhati): In view of the fact that a very grave situation has emerged with the fall of Walong and Jung and Sela pass has also fallen according to my latest information ... (Interruptions) and the Chinese are making a headlong thrust into the heart of Assam, in this context may I know whether the Government proposes to go in for a total war with military aid in men and materials from our friendly countries or the Government proposes to go in for immediate negotiations for peace on the basis of cease fire at whatever cost? These are the things that I want to know from the Prime Minister; the situation has become very serious.

118. See item 453.
119. PSP.
120. Mani Ram Bagri, Socialist Party.
121. PSP.

Jawaharlal Nehru: I have myself stated that it is a grave news and it creates a serious situation. Naturally our Armed Forces will do their utmost to meet it. It is all that I can say. I cannot go into details.

280. Broadcast to the Nation[122]

भाइयों और बहिनों,

क़रीब एक महीना हुआ मैंने रेडियो पे आपसे कुछ कहा था और आपको बताया था किस तरह से चीनी फ़ौजों ने हमारे ऊपर हमला किया और हमारे मुल्क में घुस आये[123]। उधर पूर्वी सीमा प्रान्त जो है, नेफ़ा से, हमारी सरहद से आये इधर और उन्होंने हमारे फ़ौजी जो वहाँ दस्ते थे उनपे हमला किया था। उसके बाद काफ़ी एक बड़ी जंग हुई वहाँ और चीनियों ने इत्ती बड़ी फ़ौज वहाँ डाली कि उन्होंने हमारी छोटी सी फ़ौजों को हटा दिया और दबा दिया। उस वक़्त मैंने आपसे कुछ कहा था रेडियो पर और उस वक़्त भी मैंने आपसे जहाँ तक मेरा ख़्याल है इस बात को साफ़ किया था कि यह जो हमारे ऊपर हमला है इसको हमें पूरी ताक़त से इसका मुक़ाबला करना है, सामना करना है और हमलावर लोगों को हटा देना है। यह पक्का इरादा था और यह भी मैंने आपसे कहा था कि हमें तैयार होना चाहिए अगर बीच में कुछ सदमें हों, कुछ नुकसान हों, कुछ छोटी-मोटी हार हो, उसके लिए तैयार होना चाहिए क्योंकि हमारा मुक़ाबला एक बड़े मुल्क, बड़े ताक़तवर मुल्क से है जो कि कोई क़ायदे-क़ानून को बज़ाहिर नहीं मानता है।

आज फिर से मैं आपको इसी बारे में कुछ कहना चाहता हूँ क्योंकि पिछले दो-तीन रोज़ में और ख़ासकर कल और आज बुरी ख़बरें हमारे पास आई हैं, तकलीफ़देह ख़बरें आई हैं, कुछ हमारी फ़ौजों को हटा देने की और कहीं-कहीं कुछ हार जाने की। मैं नहीं चाहता कि इस ख़बर को सुन के आप यह समझें कि ज़रा भी हमने अपने दिल को नरम किया है, ज़रा भी अपने पुराने इरादे को, पक्के इरादे को छोड़ा है। जैसे पहले मैंने कहा था वैसे ही अब और भी बल्कि उससे ज़्यादा हमारा इरादा पक्का है कि इस लड़ाई को जो कि हमारी दावत से नहीं आई, हमारे ऊपर डाली गयी है, इस लड़ाई को हम जारी रखेंगे जब तक कि हिन्दुस्तान पूरीतौर से फिर से आज़ाद न हो जाये और कोई हिस्सा हिन्दुस्तान का दुश्मन के क़ब्ज़े में न रहे, इस बात का मैं पहले आपको इतमीनान दिलाना चाहता हूँ। चीनी लोग हमारे साथ एक अजीब खेल सा खेलते हैं, एक तरफ़ हमलावर हैं हमला करते हैं और बेशुमार फ़ौजों को भेजा है, दूसरी तरफ़ कहते हैं हम तो सुलह चाहते हैं और सुलह की शरायत पेश करते हैं वो ऐसी ग़लत हैं कि जिसके माने हैं हम तसलीम कर लें बहुत दर्जे कि जो वो कर रहे हैं वो सही है। हम नहीं इसको कर सकते चाहे जो कुछ हो। यह बात साफ़ आप समझ लीजिये कि हम किसी सूरत से भी कोई ऐसी शर्त को नहीं मंज़ूर

---

122. Speech, 19 November 1962. NMML, AIR Tapes NM No. 8596, NM. No. 1689.
123. On 22 October 1962.

करेंगे जिससे ज़रा भी हिन्दुस्तान की शान गिरती हो या हिन्दुस्तान का कोई हिस्सा किसी को देना होता है, यह पक्का इरादा है।

तो फिर इसके माने यह हैं कि जो लड़ाई हमारी हमारे सामने है उसको हमें जारी रखना है, थोड़े दिन नहीं बहुत दिन, महीनों नहीं सालों रखना है जारी, हम लड़ते जायेंगे और अगर बीच में कहीं-कहीं हारे तो उससे हम और ताक़त पायेंगे, और आगे-आगे बढ़ेंगे क्योंकि हम इस बात को बरदाश्त नहीं कर सकते कि हम डर के मारे या किसी वजह से हम दब जायें चीनी हमलों से। आज और कल की ख़बरें आयी थीं वहाँ पूर्वी सीमा प्रान्त में वालोंग एक जगह है, उसको हमारी फ़ौज को छोड़ना पड़ा, सेला एक "पास" (Pass) है, पहाड़ है बोमडिला के ऊपर, तवांग और बोमडिला के बीच में और बोमडिला भी हमारे हाथ से निकल गया। रंज हुआ इसको सुनकर, रंज हुआ कि हमारी फ़ौज को हटना पड़ा वहाँ से, लेकिन रंज होने से और भी हमारा इरादा पक्का हुआ, इससे हम डर जायें और घबरा जायें यह तो ठीक नहीं है। इस वक़्त कुछ आसाम के ऊपर, आसाम के दरवाज़े पर दुश्मन है और आसाम ख़तरे में है। इसलिए ख़ासतौर से हमारा दिल जाता है हमारे भाई और बहिनों पर जो आसाम में रहते हैं, उनकी हमदर्दी में, क्योंकि उनको तकलीफ़ उठानी पड़ रही है और शायद और भी तकलीफ़ उठानी पड़े। हम उनकी पूरी मदद करने की कोशिश करेंगे और करेंगे, लेकिन कित्ते ही हम मदद करें, हम उनको तकलीफ़ से नहीं बचा लेंगे इस वक़्त। हाँ, एक बात का हम पक्का इरादा रखते हैं और दोहराते हैं हमारी प्रतिज्ञा को और वो यह है कि हम इस बात को आख़िरी दम तक चलायेंगे जब तक कि आसाम और सारा हिन्दुस्तान बिल्कुल दुश्मन से ख़ाली न हो जाये। हम कोई ग़लत तसफ़िया नहीं करते, ग़लत फैसला नहीं, ग़लत समझौता नहीं।

अब इसके माने हैं कि हमें और मुल्क को काफ़ी बोझे उठाने होंगे। मुल्क ने दिखाया है कित्ता उसे जोश है, कित्ता इस पिछले दो-चार हफ़्तों में जो भारत का रूप हमने देखा है उसको देख के दिल ख़ुश हुआ है, दिल मज़बूत हुआ है। अब और भी ज़बरदस्त हमारे सामने इम्तहान आने वाले हैं और उनका भी हम सामना करेंगे। मुझे पूरा यक़ीन है कि उनका भी हम सामना करेंगे दिलेरी से, हिम्मत से और बग़ैर ज़रा भी ढील दिये। पहली लड़ाई है यह जिसको आज़ाद हिन्दुस्तान अपनी आज़ादी क़ायम रखने के लिए लड़ रहा है। इससे ज़्यादा पवित्र लड़ाई क्या हो सकती है। अगर हम अपनी आज़ादी का ज़रा भी हिस्सा छोड़ दें या हमसे छूट जाये तो हम फिर किस मुँह से रहेंगे और किसका मुँह देखेंगे। हमें अपने मुल्क को, पूरे मुल्क को आज़ाद रखना है और उसके लिए जो भी कुछ देना हमें है हम देंगे, जो भी कुछ क़ुर्बानी करनी है करेंगे, इस इरादे से कि हम हिन्दुस्तान की आज़ादी को पूरीतौर से क़ाबू में रखें और जो कोई उस पर हमला करे उसका पूरा मुक़ाबला करें और उसको हरायें। इसी तरह से मुल्क बनते हैं और शायद यह भी क़िस्मत ने तय किया हो कि हमारा मुल्क भी ज़रा ढीला हो गया था, उसको फिर से चुस्त और चालाक होना है, तगड़ा होना है।

इस मामले में हम सभों को मिलके काम करना है, इस वक़्त पार्टी और दल की बातें नहीं होनी चाहियें, इस वक़्त हरेक हिन्दुस्तानी है और हरेक दुश्मन का मुक़ाबला करता है, चाहे वो सिपाही है वो करता ही है, चाहे वो हवाई जहाज़ को चलाने वाले बहादुर हमारे नौजवान हैं, चाहे वो खेत में काम करता है, चाहे कारख़ाने में या दुकान में, कहीं भी, हरेक हिन्दुस्तान का सिपाही है। और आने वाले दिनों में और महीनों में और बरसों में सिपाही रहना है हरेक को और हर चीज़, हर काम में अव्वल काम यही है, उसके बाद और काम आते हैं, चाहे हमारे घर के या किसी और बात के, अव्वल काम यह है कि हम वो बातें करें जिससे हिन्दुस्तान मज़बूत हो, हिन्दुस्तान की हिफ़ाज़त हो, जिससे हमारी फ़ौजें मज़बूत हों और बहादुरी से लड़ सकें। यह बात मुझे आपसे इस वक़्त कहनी थी, बाद में मौक़े आयेंगे फिर मैं आपसे कहूँगा, लेकिन इस बात को आप याद कर लीजिये कि इस मामले में चाहे जो कुछ कहीं न कहीं हमारी छोटी हार हो या हमारी फ़ौजें हटा दी जायें या दबा दी जायें कसरत के नम्बर से, हम इस बात को कभी नहीं भूलेंगे कि हमें हिन्दुस्तान की आज़ादी की रक्षा करनी है, हम कोई ऐसी बात मंज़ूर नहीं करेंगे जिससे ज़रा भी हिन्दुस्तान की शान किरकिरी हो। आप और हम सब इस बात की प्रतिज्ञा लें और साथ मिलकर, पैर मिलाकर, हाथ पकड़ के आगे चलें। यक़ीनन, मुझे पक्का यक़ीन है कि हमारी जीत होगी और हिन्दुस्तान आज़ाद रहेगा और पहले से ज़्यादा मज़बूती से रहेगा और किसी की हिम्मत नहीं होगी फिर कि आँख उठा के हिन्दुस्तान की तरफ़ देखे।

जयहिन्द!

[Translation begins:

Comrades and friends,

Nearly a month ago I spoke to you on the radio and told you of the Chinese invasion of India.[124] They had come across our frontier in the North East Frontier Agency. At first in small numbers and then in ever increasing numbers, and suddenly on the 20th October they had made a massive attack with overwhelming numbers on our military posts and our forces stationed there. That was a severe set-back for us and it naturally grieved us.

Now today I have to tell you of further set-back which have occurred in the last two or three days and even today. Huge Chinese armies have been marching in the northern part of the North East Frontier Agency and we have suffered reverses at Walong, on the Sela Ridge and today Bomdila—a small town in NEFA has also fallen. In the North also in Ladakh, in the Chushul area, the Chinese have been attacking fiercely, though they have been held. Now what has happened is very serious and very saddening to us and I can well understand what our friends in Assam must be feeling because all this is happening on their

124. See item 259.

doorstep, one might say. I want to tell them that we feel very much for them and that we shall help them to the utmost of our ability. We may not be able always to succeed in what we are trying now because of various factors and of the overwhelming numbers of the Chinese forces, but I want to take a pledge to them, here and now, that we shall see this matter to the end and the end will have to be victory for India. We are not going to tolerate this kind of invasion of India by any foreign country. This is the first war of independent India to maintain her independence. And India is not going to lose this war, however long it lasts and whatever harm it may do us meanwhile. Therefore, on this day which has been a sad day for us bringing news of reverses and set-backs, I want to send my greetings to the people of Assam specially, to the people of NEFA, and to the rest of India, and to tell them that we must not get worried about this. Sad we must be necessarily, but we must train ourselves and steel ourselves to meet all these reverses and to even make our determination still firmer to do all that we can to repel and throw out the invader from India. We shall not be content till that invader goes out of India or is pushed out. We shall not accept any terms that he may offer because he may think that we are a little frightened by some set-backs. I want to make that clear to all of you and more specially to our countrymen in Assam, to whom our heart goes out at this moment.

There has been a great deal of expression of determination in India, great enthusiasm, which has heartened us. People even the very poor have contributed to our funds, defence funds and in many ways, people have shown their determination. I hope that this will continue in ever increasing measure and any set-backs that may come, in this is war which has been thrust upon us, will not permit us to waver in our determination, because we will not waver. We shall carry out this fight which has been thrust upon us to the end, and that end is going to be victory for us, whatever in between there might be. So, with that pledge to you, I want to end; I do not wish any person to doubt what the end will be, and I do not want any Indian—man or woman or child, to get dismayed because the Chinese forces have won some successes at this beginning. This is war, and in war successes come and failures come also. What counts is the end, not the intermediary stages of that war.

So, at present, I shall only say this to you, I shall not say much. I hope in future to keep in touch with you, a little more frequently to tell you what is happening and to mobilise the nation to meet this grave menace. For this menace is not of Assam or Ladakh or of India only; it is a menace for Asia and a menace for the entire world. We see the most, the grossest form of imperialism functioning here across our borders in India. China has said often enough that it is anti-imperialist. Now we see this so-called anti-imperialist country becoming itself an imperialist of the worst kind and committing aggression and invading a friendly country without rhyme or reason or excuse and justifying it by saying that they are being attacked. I must confess, that I have seldom come across such a travesty of truth and of decency in international behaviour. We must stand up for it, not only we but all decent-minded persons and decent-minded countries who value their freedom, anywhere in Asia or Africa or in Europe or America.

I should like to say that we are grateful for the speedy help that came to us from our friendly countries abroad, more especially from the United States and the United Kingdom. We shall require more help and we have asked them for it and we shall certainly use all the help they can give us, because this is a matter of survival for us. It is not a game that we are playing or if you like, it is a game of life and death. The life and death of a nation and the life and death of millions in this country, and we are going ahead whatever happens, with the firm conviction of the rightness of our cause and that success and victory will be ours. I want you to join in this conviction and not to be downhearted at any time. And so, let us all say today with real meaning repeat our old cry: Jai Hind!

Translation ends]

281. In the Rajya Sabha: Situation in Ladakh and NEFA[125]

The Prime Minister and the Minister of External Affairs and Minister of Defence (Jawaharlal Nehru): Mr Chairman, I should like to keep the House informed of the developments on the various battle fronts. In the Ladakh area I said yesterday that Chushul had been fiercely attacked repeatedly, but the attacks had been repulsed. One of the distant outposts in Ladakh, Rezang La, had been attacked and it has changed hands twice. That outpost is in the possession of the enemy, but Chushul remains very much in our possession.

Then, in the other side the Chinese forces have advanced. They were near Bomdila yesterday. They have taken possession of Bomdila and they are at the present moment a few miles beyond Bomdila.

These are the chief facts which have happened. I need not add that all the steps possible for us are being taken by our Army authorities.

---

125. Statement in the House, *Rajya Sabha Debates,* Vol.XLI, Nos.9-21, 20 November to 6 December 1962, pp.1763-1767.

M.S. Gurupada Swamy[126] (Mysore): May I know, Sir, whether it is a fact that the intention of the Chinese troops is to march further and reach our Assam frontier, so that they may have a strategic hold over certain area? (Interruptions)

Chairman: How can anybody say what they want to do, how can the Prime Minister know what they want to do?

M.S. Gurupada Swamy: I want to know this. He said that the Chinese troops in Bomdila were advancing further. May I know whether the advance has been checked according to the information available or whether they are still advancing?

Jawaharlal Nehru: Obviously their advance is being obstructed and checked. I cannot answer what the intentions are of the Chinese troops, but we should expect the worst from them and prepare for it.

Faridul Haq Ansari[127] (Uttar Pradesh): Yesterday the hon. Prime Minister assured the House that very strict measures would be taken against those people who contravened the Defence of India Rules and Ordinance. May I know whether the hon. Prime Minister is aware that a map of the NEFA area by the Chinese showing Assam, Bihar and West Bengal as part of China is even now being sold in Calcutta? Secondly, there is a book, collections of Urdu poems by one Taban[128], which indicates welcome to the Chinese forces in India. Not only that. There is couplet which warns the Prime Minister of India that the Chinese invasion is death to him, Truman and other men. Why is action not taken against this?

Jawaharlal Nehru: I cannot answer these questions about which I do not know much, but action is being taken. We have specially asked the Bengal Government, as other Governments to take action wherever they consider necessary. It is for them to pick and choose and determine what action they have to take.

---

126. Congress.
127. PSP.
128. Mehtab Rai Taban. See also MEA memorandum to Chinese Embassy in India, 2 November 1962 regarding spreading propaganda material through post. *White paper*, Vol.VIII, p.126.

A.D. Mani[129] (Madhya Pradesh): May I ask the Prime Minister where was the need for our Chargé d'Affaires in Peking to meet the Chinese Foreign Office officials yesterday, when the situation is so grave as it is today and it is having a very weakening effect on our morale to find that when the crisis has developed, our Chargé d'Affaires is meeting the Chinese Foreign Office officials on his own initiative to discuss the matter? The news is published in today's paper.

Chairman: Was it on his initiative? Does the news say that it was on his initiative?

A.D. Mani: The news says that he called on the Foreign Office. If he had been invited by the Foreign Office, it would have been mentioned. I infer that he went and saw on his own initiative.

Jawaharlal Nehru: I do not know exactly how he went. Very likely he conveyed a message from us to the Foreign Office and he went to convey that message.

Bairagi Dwibedy (Orissa): May I know, Sir, what is the total number of evacuees from the towns that have fallen to the Chinese and how they have been rehabilitated?

Jawaharlal Nehru: I could not give the exact number. Tawang is a very small town and a considerable number of people came away from Tawang when the Chinese went there and they have been placed in various camps, etc. They have been looked after.

There is one other matter Sir, I should like to mention. General P.N. Thapar, Chief of our Army Staff, has this morning applied for long leave on grounds of health. He has been granted leave and on his recommendation the senior Army Commander Lieutenant General J.N. Chaudhuri, is being appointed to officiate as Chief of Army staff.

ए0एम0 तारिक़ (जम्मू और कश्मीर): अभी एक आनरेबिल मैम्बर ने डिफेंस आफ इंडिया रूल्स के बारे में सवाल पूछा। तो मैं प्राइम मिनिस्टर साहब से साफ़ लफ़्ज़ों में यह जानना चाहता हूं कि इस सिलसिले में हमारी क्या पालिसी है, और मैं उनकी तवज्जोह उस कार्टून की तरफ़ दिलाना चाहता हूं जो आज के "हिन्दुस्तान टाइम्स" में छपा है, जिसमें यह दिखाया गया है कि वज़ीरे आज़म के हाथ में एक मशाल है और हिन्दुस्तान के मकान में आग लगी है और श्री जयप्रकाश नारायण श्री अयूब

129. Independent.

को बचाने के लिये बुलाने जा रहे हैं। अगर हुकूमत ने यह कार्टून देखा है तो इस सिलसिले में क्या कार्यवाही की गई है।

जवाहरलाल नेहरू: मैंने कम से कम नहीं देखा और हुकूमत के किसी हिस्से ने नहीं देखा। अगर बेजा है तो उस पर ज़रूर कार्यवाही होनी चाहिये।

[Translation begins:

A.M. Tariq (Jammu and Kashmir): Just now an Hon. Member asked about the Defence of India Rules. I wish to ask the Prime Minister in clear terms, what is our policy regarding this. I would also like to draw his attention to a cartoon published in today's *Hindustan Times*, where it has been shown that the Prime Minister is holding a Mashaal and the house of Hindustan is on fire. And Jayaprakash Narayan is going to ask Ayub to save the house. If the Government has seen this cartoon, what action has been taken against it?

Jawaharlal Nehru: At least I have not seen it and if any government official has, then we would certainly take action.

Translation ends]

R.S. Khandekar [130](Madhya Pradesh): The hon. Prime Minister gave the position regarding Ladakh and Bomdila. May I know what is the position on the Walong front?

Jawaharlal Nehru: As you know on the Walong front, some miles on this side of Walong, conflicts are going on between our Army detachments and certain forward Chinese forces.

Bhupesh Gupta (West Bengal): May I know, Sir, if the Prime Minister is aware that the *Ananda Bazar Patrika* of Calcutta published a cartoon on the appointment of Mr Chavan as the Defence Minister, ridiculing his appointment in that paper and in other papers, calling the Prime Minister a gorilla and carrying on a scurrilous campaign against him? May I know whether the Home Minister has placed these materials before him, since what we need is national unity at this hour?

Jawaharlal Nehru: I am not aware of that cartoon or the articles.

130. PSP.

282. To Sudhir Ghosh: Military Tactics[131]

November 21, 1962

My dear Sudhir Ghosh,

Your letter of the 21st November.[132] I do not know to what documents you refer that have been shown to the President, and who showed them. At a very early stage, that is, late in September or the beginning of October, we did say that it was desirable to push the Chinese across the frontier. Later, when we got further information about the strength of the Chinese, definite instructions were given to defend at the most feasible line. We were not told that they had to move troops from Tawang, and we made it clear that the final decision must rest with the Commanders on the spot.

Yours sincerely,
[Jawaharlal Nehru]

283. To Gopal Singh: Future Strategy[133]

November 22, 1962

My dear Dr Gopal Singh,

Your letter of November 22. I quite agree with your analysis. What we require most now is a little breathing time to reorganise our forces and our equipment. At the same time, we cannot accept the Chinese proposal which is a very tricky one, and which we have refused previously. Any decision which might result in war on a bigger scale soon would be to our great disadvantage. We are trying our best to get the equipment necessary.

As for Pakistan, we have done a great deal recently to cultivate friendly relations, but they are getting more and more aggressive. Some people say that they have made some arrangement with China. Pakistan is thinking of greater ambitions—something even more than Kashmir. I do not see how we can possibly give in to this kind of bullying. India will go to pieces.

Yours sincerely,
[Jawaharlal Nehru]

---

131. Letter to Rajya Sabha MP, Congress; address: 95 South Avenue, New Delhi.
132. See appendix 64.
133. Letter to Rajya Sabha MP, nominated; address: 62 South Avenue, New Delhi.

284. To Chief Ministers: War and Five Year Plan[134]

November 23, 1962

My dear Chief Minister,

Our minds are full of the Chinese war in the North-East of India. This has been obviously a much bigger thing than a frontier affray. It is a regular invasion of India with far-reaching consequences and we cannot possibly submit to it.

2. The cease-fire and withdrawal proposals made by the Chinese are very tricky. Of course, we cannot object to their withdrawal. But we cannot admit even indirectly to their withdrawal. But we cannot admit even indirectly their claim to parts of our territory. We are considering what reply to send them.

3. But I am now writing to you not so much about the direct war effort, which is important and to which a great deal of attention has been paid, but certain other matters which ultimately are equally important even from the war point of view.

4. There is a tremendous response from our people, and it has been most heartening and moving to observe it. The problem is how to take advantage of this great response. To a small extent, the answer is recruiting for the Army or the volunteers; the NCC or Home Guards; or the National Defence Fund; or the Citizens' Committees that are being formed. All this does not cover a very large number of people. We can have large scale teaching of nursing and first aid and civil defence.

5. But it has to be realised that the war effort essentially means greater production in agriculture and industry. This means a concentration on certain basic aspects of our Third Five Year Plan. Industry, I take it, will gather momentum because of more needs and the like.

6. What of agriculture? I have had very pleasing news of the response of the peasantry. I think every effort should be made to direct this enthusiasm into right channels. For instance, they should be asked to undertake special works to increase agriculture. Even the digging of water channels, tanks, bunding and other important things which people can do without any expenditure of foreign exchange. We might fix a time table for this, say six months, during which they should build their water channels as well as do many other things.

7. If this is undertaken under proper direction and a strong push is given to it, the results may be very gratifying indeed.

8. I am merely mentioning one or two matters which come to my mind. You can consider other matters. The point is to tie all this up with the war effort and make people realise that they are serving this effort by these measures and,

134. Letter to all Chief Ministers and the Prime Minister of Jammu and Kashmir.

above all, to fix time limits. I hope you will give full and urgent consideration to this matter.

9. It is of the utmost importance that we should not allow defeatist rumours to spread. Unfortunately, there are many people engaged in this nefarious task which tends to demoralise our people. But fortunately, the majority of our people are not inclined that way, and they respond very well indeed to the right approach.

Yours sincerely,
Jawaharlal Nehru

285. To Mahendra Mohan Choudhury: Assam is India[135]

November 25, 1962

My dear Mahendra Mohan,

Your letter of the 22nd November reached me two or three days ago. The letter is signed not only by you, but by a number of others also.

I have read your letter with care and thank you for it. I have also been told of conditions in Assam at present by Shri Lal Bahadur Shastri, Indiraji and others who visited it.

I need not tell you how deeply pained we have been at recent events in NEFA and Assam. Our hearts have gone out to all of your people there. I can assure you that there will be no peace till we have rid India and, of course, Assam also, of this Chinese menace. Assam is a living part of India, and what happens to Assam happens to the whole of India. I cannot, of course, guarantee what ups and downs we may have in the near future. But of the end, I am quite certain, and I hope that the people of Assam will bear with determination and fortitude whatever burdens they may have to shoulder, remembering always that they have the entire people of India behind them. We have to deal with a strong, capable and ruthless enemy. We have to look ahead and prepare ourselves for this conflict. We cannot possibly surrender to them even indirectly.

We are carefully considering their recent offer. We are unable to accept it as such. At the same time, we do not want a quick resumption of operations. We want a little time to prepare ourselves.

Please do not be despondent. We must hold together stoutly and work and prepare for a better Assam and a better India.

---

135. Letter to the Speaker of the Assam Legislative Assembly.

If possible, I shall try to come myself for a day or two to Assam. At present, I am terribly occupied here with our war effort and other preparations.

You can share this letter of mine with your co-signatories. But please do not give publicity to it.

Yours sincerely,
[Jawaharlal Nehru]

286. In the Lok Sabha: After Cease Fire[136]

Jawaharlal Nehru: There have been so many questions of different types that I am a bit confused and may forget answering some of them.

Speaker: My intention was only to bring to the notice of the hon. Prime Minister all these questions. The hon. Prime Minister might choose which are to be answered at this moment.

Jawaharlal Nehru: I shall answer as many as I can remember here and now.

The first thing is about the hon. Law Minister[137] and the Secretary-General[138] going to Cairo and Accra. That is true. Very probably the Deputy Foreign Minister, Shrimati Lakshmi Menon, will go to some countries, that is, Burma, Indonesia and possibly Cambodia. These countries are those that have been invited by the Ceylonese Government to go very soon, early in December, to Colombo to discuss these matters connected with our conflict with China. We were not, naturally, invited and we were not even informed of it. Afterwards we heard about it. The countries invited are the UAR, Ghana, Indonesia, Burma and Cambodia. I think, that is the whole number; I cannot think of any others. So, we decided to send my colleague the law Minister and the Secretary-General to Africa, to these two countries invited from Africa and the Deputy Foreign Minister and probably some senior official of the External Affairs Ministry to the countries in Asia. That is apart from any others whom we may send to other places. Their object is to explain our position more thoroughly in regard to these so-called proposals of the Chinese Government so that there may be no confusion in their mind as to what we think about them.

---

136. Question hour, *Lok Sabha Debates*, Third Series, Vol. X, November 21 to December 4, 1962, pp. 3328-3336.
137. Asoke Sen.
138. Secretary-General, MEA, R.K. Nehru.

About the other questions, I really forget, …

S. M. Banerjee[139]: About clarification.

N.G. Ranga[140]: What about informing all other Governments? Press campaign?

Jawaharlal Nehru: We, of course, inform all Governments through our Ambassadors and in other ways. But, these we specially decided to approach because they were going to meet in Colombo soon at the invitation of the Prime Minister of Ceylon.[141]

The hon. Member asked for clarification. It is natural to ask for clarifications of various points which are not clear and in so far as they can be cleared it will be desirable so that our reply should be based not merely on any doubt about these matters. We have not received a full reply yet. Possibly in a day or two we will get it.

N.G. Ranga: Does the Prime Minister expect to receive their reply so soon in the light of the way in which the Chinese have been taking so long a time in all their replies?

Jawaharlal Nehru: Sometimes their replies come soon. Sometimes they take a long time. I cannot say precisely.

Hem Barua[142]: Position of civil defence in Tezpur.

Jawaharlal Nehru: I think the position in Tezpur is almost normal now. The hon. Member mentioned something about evacuation.

Hem Barua: There is an order by the Commissioner of Civil Supplies and Movements and Liaison Officer with the Government of India. It says:

"Employees whose homes are outside Assam may, however, be anxious to send away their families; this the State Government desires should be done in as orderly a manner as possible. Arrangements are accordingly being made to give all facilities for such employees to send their families home." I say, any order after the cease fire was announced, would it not create panic among the rest of the population in the State?

139. Independent Member.
140. Swatantra Party.
141. Sirimavo Bandaranaike.
142. PSP.

Jawaharlal Nehru: May I know the date of that?

Hem Barua: It was issued on 21st November, 1962. It was circulated to the different offices on the 22nd November this month.

Jawaharlal Nehru: I am afraid this notice was issued by some official in the Assam Government.

Hem Barua: No. He is an officer with the Government of India stationed at Shillong. Here it clearly says: Commissioner of Civil Supplies and Movements and Liaison Officer with the Government of India.

The Minister of Railways (Swaran Singh): That means Assam Officer for liaison work with us.

Jawaharlal Nehru: Assam Government's officer in liaison with our Government. I cannot say in what conditions he sent it. But it does not represent our view point. I agree with the hon. Member that there should be broadly speaking no question of anybody withdrawing from where he is. This refers, I think, to women and children chiefly.

Speaker: Women and children.

Hem Barua: Central Government employees....

Hari Vishnu Kamath[143] (Hoshangabad): This should be rescinded by the Government here.

Hem Barua: Withdrawn.

Speaker: Order, order. Now that it has been brought to the notice of the Government, the Government has a definite opinion about that and the Government would act accordingly. There was one other proposal whether it would be possible to place a map of those lines in the Central Hall so that Members may have an idea and might be able to appreciate what the difference is.

143. PSP.

N.G. Ranga[144]: How is that such an important order came to be passed without the knowledge at all of the Government of India? (Interruption).

Speaker: Order, order. Under the shadow of a previous event, some officer issued it. (Interruption). Order, order.

Jawaharlal Nehru: Certain orders were issued, I believe, some little time ago that in the event of any contingency arising, what should be done so that they may be prepared for it.

Hem Barua; It is not like that. The language is different.

Jawaharlal Nehru: I quite agree with the hon. Member that it was undesirable to issue this order. And those orders were perhaps misinterpreted or exaggerated by the local people.

Speaker: In regard to the maps, can anything be said for the present?

Jawaharlal Nehru: I shall endeavour to have some kind of map placed in the Central Hall.

Speaker: Is there any information about those jawans of ours who were taken in between Sela and Bomdila?

Jawaharlal Nehru: Some of them have returned. I believe—I am not quite sure—about a thousand of them have returned.

Hem Barua: There are conflicting press reports that the number is between 1000 and 3000.

Indrajit Gupta[145] (Calcutta South West): What is the estimate of the number of those persons?

Jawaharlal Nehru: They have not returned actually to headquarters. A few of them have been brought back when they were traced by our helicopters. The exact number is not known. It is an estimate. I hope that those people will be soon back. But that does not comprise of all those; it is possible that some of them, quite a fair number, may be in a different column round about.

144. Swatantra Party.
145. CPI.

287. At the CPP[146]

Jawaharlal Nehru: I have to announce that Shri Jagannath Rao Chandrike and Shri Amarnath Vidyalankar have been elected unopposed as Members of the AICC representing the Congress Party in Parliament.

A Member: Friends, with the permission of the leader I would like to announce 3 points: one is Shri Bakhshi Ghulam Mohamed will address the members of the party tomorrow the 30 November 1962 at 5.5 p.m. in the Central Hall; the second announcement is there will be a film show, a documentary on war efforts, in the Central Hall on Monday, the 3 December 1962 at 5.5 p.m.; third announcement is; 120 members of the Congress Party in Parliament have offered their services for the defence services in the following categories. Their names should be sent to the Ministries concerned and defence department so that their services may be utilised. Advocates 25, Agriculturists 8, Atomic Energy 3, Cooperation 3, Defence 5, Defence publicity 10, Doctors 8, Education 13, Engineering 2, Nursing 6, Publicity General 18, Miscellaneous 19, 120 altogether. Thank you.

Jawaharlal Nehru: I think that apart from individuals who may be chosen for some particular work which is possible, most of them will have to serve in their own states. They may serve in many ways, but almost every member can become a member of the territorial army or some voluntary organisations, official, I am not talking about the non-official, official voluntary organisations. I do not know,

Atomic energy is a full time job, if they are good enough they are chosen then they will work there and if they do not, they remain here. But there are many points, for instance publicity, in which members can be useful in their States and some of them here. But I would suggest that somebody the secretary or a small committee should keep this list in view, consult people, the defence and others, how to follow this up.

Well, friends and comrades there is nothing else on the Agenda, but as we are meeting after some time, I shall say a few words about the general situation etc. in the country. It is totally unnecessary for me to point out to you that the crisis that we have to face is extraordinary and dangerous, well vitally and in facing that crisis we have to do many things. We have passed a fine resolution in both Houses of Parliament. We have to act up to them. But something much more obviously. By passing that resolution and by the general upsurge which

146. Speech, 29 November 1962. NMML, J.N.'s Speeches from Tapes, Tape No. M 65 (II).

we have seen in the country which has been remarkable and most heartening. I think each one of us will agree with me that we have not seen anything like it previously; in another sense we have not seen, there was the independence movement, many things that moved us tremendously, and affected us. So this has moved us and it is, if you analyse it, why did this happen? Well, fundamentally because they felt they had something which they stood to lose, something of value which they stood to lose, by this Chinese invasion. That is to say I do not make a great point of it, but I do think it is a point worthy of mention. That since we became independent all our work, the work that has been done in the country has brought something to them which they value and consider precious and the fear of losing it brought about this tremendous reaction in the people. Of course, normally people, many people, react to any such invasion as they have, done but there is something more about it. Suppose we had been a complete failure in the last fifteen years since we became independent, government, development, whatever. I am sure the reaction would not have been as it has been. There has been a great deal of criticism of us during these years by, often by opposition parties, sometimes by our own colleagues, and sometimes it has been justified. But nevertheless, the fact remains that what has been done in these fifteen years or so has, when it came to the test, we find that it left a tremendous impression on the people and they did not want to lose it. That is very heartening.

Now the question arises about how we are to utilise this enthusiasm. This is a difficult question to answer immediately. There are various ways. One is of course for young people to join the army itself. I doubt if many Members of Parliament will be considered suitable for that, apart from their desire to do so. I mean to say even they, unfortunately, even the normal recruits that count and that is not so in India only, in other countries too, it is applied, about 75 percent are rejected for being physically unfit, even young people even those just and beyond that age of course little more. Our physical condition as a whole is not good, because even normally a soldier has to be tough and fit and specially in the kind of war we are waging in the mountains of high altitudes. It requires a man of extreme fitness and capacity to be able to fit too. One of the factors somewhat against us, I am not mentioning this as an excuse, was that our armies were sent rather at quick notice, suddenly transported from these low altitudes to 14000 feet high, not all 14000, 12000, and I doubt how many of you sitting here if you are suddenly put 14000 feet high, how you would function. You will find it difficult even to breathe. You will be panting all the time and if you live long there it may affect your heart seriously. I know of several very good officers of ours who were posted in Ladakh, army officers, not now, I am talking about a year and two ago, but merely living there about

6 or 8 months at Leh which is not so high, which is 11500, they died quickly after coming back, it affected their heart and what not. Now if I may say so, having to work hard at 14000 feethigh and then the cold coming and all that, the result was that not that our people are not fit enough, but they did not have the time to acclimatise themselves to that altitude and to that climate and therefore they were physically not as fit as they might have been. They went from here and went straight to the front, within a week or two they had to fight. That was perhaps one reason which lessened their capacity, there were others too. So I was saying about what we can do but there is the army, then there is the territorial army which I do think many of us should join, may I mention. Now I have spent a good deal of time in earlier years mountaineering and I was very fond of the mountains. Now I find if I go beyond 10,000 or so I get into difficulties, breathing difficulties, it does not matter if I go for a few hours, I recover doctors have told me, you must not go above 8000, 7000. I remember they told me some years ago, I was at Manali, and I had decided to go up to that Pass, what is it called? Rohtang Pass, which is 13500 feet and my doctor here who had examined me did not like it, he said he will report to the doctor, a person, who often sees me in London whenever I go, a very eminent man. They took my cardiogram and all that. We were going from morning to Rohtang, early in the morning and stopped for the night. At night, all arrangements were made, at night I got a telegram from this British doctor through the High Commissioner that I should not go above 7000 feet. Now Rohtang is 13500, I suppressed that telegram, I did not show it to anybody, and next morning we went up to the Rohtang and well fortunately I came back without being affected by anything. I spent only two or three hours. But I have felt unhappy since then because of my lesser capacity to go up to heights. It is natural I suppose after all I cannot forget that I am 73 now. So I had to come back. People should go. Then I went the very next year to Bhutan and I had to pass 3 passes to reach Pari, 3 passes of 14500 feet. We went, of course, we did not stay there, but we passed them and came down and went up.

Now I do think that it will be a good thing for many members to join the territorial army units. Those who are very old, from very old I mean relative to the ages required, perhaps may not, but I think they should try to get in and get some training and it will do them good, perhaps it will be a very good example to others, because the territorial army was meant for people of all classes in England I mean. Here normally the territorial army has workers in factories and some agriculturists, chiefly technical people and all that. We have not had broadly speaking middle-class elements there, they should go there as they did in England and that will include others to join too. Then there are other volunteer organisations which are being formed and there are many other types of direct work that people can do and indirect work of course there are any number, they are gradually growing. I cannot go into that, but the thing has been worked out, but essentially people have to work in their states, we cannot gather them all here, give them work except special individuals who may fit into some scheme of things that is much less our concern. I get a large number of letters offering their services. Now what am I to do? I cannot appoint them, I am not a public service commission taking them for a war effort, but I can thank them and refer them to their states.

Now I want to say something about the present position that we are facing. All of you know that a few days back the Chinese made some proposals. Unilaterally they announced a cease fire and a withdrawal will probably, I imagine, take effect from day after tomorrow. It may take a few days, but I suppose it will begin, they will do it. Now, people have expressed their opinion about this, many people, that what do we think about it, why didn't the Government reject it outright, why have we asked for clarification and elucidation of their offer and so on and so forth. Well, to begin with it is always good to understand an offer clearly before you deal with it. It is a good thing that we asked for this clarification, some has come, some has not yet come. And I suppose within a few days we shall send an answer. Now we were anxious to find out exactly what they did apart from what they have said. For instance we wanted to find out how they withdraw, have they withdrawn or not, that we shall know in two or three days time. There was no hurry to answer. Some of our friends and critics who stay with other parties had expressed their strong feelings that, why are we waiting for this, why do not we reject it, why do not we get up, gird our loins and drive the Chinese out. Well, that is a matter which is not a purely political matter for us to decide in our chambers but which concerns the army and our strength and what tactics we should pursue. All that has to be taken into consideration. It is not an expression of a public meeting, what we should do. Now clearly it would be rather absurd for us to say and they say we will withdraw, we say do not withdraw, we object to your withdrawing, it is ridiculous, they are withdrawing from our territory. We may find that they do not withdraw enough, that's a different matter. But so long as they withdraw it is a good thing.

But a basic factor before us I am reluctant to say, although it is fairly well known and I do earnestly hope that no member present will give publicity to this in the newspapers or elsewhere. The basic factor is time. Time for us to get prepared, to get ready. We have, we have had very serious set backs. In the larger scheme of things they are not very big in that sense, but they have been very severe, they have not been very big in the sense of numbers involved on our side. You may say it would be perhaps a legitimate criticism, why did not we have enough numbers. Well, much can be said in answer, but nevertheless the criticism is partly justified.

In other words, why were we not adequately prepared to meet this onslaught. Among the things that might be said is that we certainly did not expect a massive invasion of India; we expected a relatively small conflict on the frontier, we did not expect several divisions suddenly to pour in. But it is easy for them to do so because they can bring them in Tibet. Our estimate is that they have got 14 divisions in Tibet alone, the whole of the Indian Army consists of 10 divisions, all over India. I do not mean to say that they brought 14 divisions in one spot but they are easily accessible to them by roads and by large number of roads and those roads bring them up right up to the Indian frontier whether in Ladakh or here, and then all they have to do is to go up a little and then come down into India. On the other side we have to go sometimes hundreds of miles, no roads, sometimes a road comes up partly which we have built recently, but we have to do still nearly 100 miles, 80 miles, 70 miles by trek, which takes a long time. In other words, we have to, the only way we can reach there, send armies their food or clothing or arms is by air and not by air even. There is no airstrip there to land, by air droppings, which is very difficult process, laborious process and the more men we put there the harder it becomes to feed them and to give them arms etc. That is one of the reasons why we sent large quantity of winter clothing, they had gone there before winter had set in, it got rather cold suddenly and unfortunately many of these things we sent by air, dropped from the air, went into the khuds, into the ravines. It is highly deceptive country and the enemy sitting in the front, sometimes having pot shots at them, they could not come down very low and we lost much of the stuff. So, the difficulty in sending larger armies there was because we could not maintain them, because we had to maintain them through air droppings, and frankly to begin with we did not think they would throw in such a vast number of people and they could throw them in at two days' notice, a day's notice. At the last moment two or three days, we threw all these troops in across the pass and they were, after a few hours march.

Some people are of the opinion, our military people, that we should not have fought them at all on the border. That is we should have come to a proper defensive line, that is to say defensive line, first, which is capable of defence and secondly, which is connected by roads into our bases. We should not leave the bases and rely on air supply. It is a military problem, it is up to them to decide. Against that there was always a feeling one does not like to withdraw in one's own territory while the enemy marches on, one wanted to resist them and one did not know, how many people they have been, we thought that their numbers would also be limited.

So all these things happened and we suffered serious reverses, the serious reverses I would repeat are not so much from the point of view of numbers involved in big wars, large numbers, hundred or thousands are involved. We have not such a big army, or the fact that we lost, whatever we lost, two or three thousand persons as prisoners and casualties altogether. Actually, it was serious, and the psychological reaction to it was serious both for the public of India and the Army. It is easy to be wise after the event and to criticise them and it should be enquired into, who failed in this, whose fault it was. We cannot sit down, have a court of enquiry at the present moment, but it is being in a sense enquired into, what happened exactly. But the point is having got that experience we have to adapt ourselves to meet that. It is no good our saying that we shall fight everywhere, here, there and everywhere, under the same disadvantageous conditions that we have here (interruptions). That is so, that is, we gave to them at Chushul a very good fight.

Now I do not know, now what they do it is said there, somebody objected to our saying they come in waves after waves. There is nothing to object about that, because that involves two things, having very large numbers of troops and being willing to sacrifice very large numbers. We are not conditioned that way to throw away lives easily although our jawans are brave enough, very brave. But we do not send them in human masses.

Now I do think that in spite of our defeats the casualties suffered by the Chinese are probably much greater than ours. It is said, I do not know how, the Chinese put into front rows Tibetans whom they have got into their army, and somebody else in the second row and the third row they come up themselves. So that they sacrificed the poor Tibetans in large numbers, they fall down, then second row comes and third row, their troops come later. Now this was exactly what happened, apart from Tibetans, I mean in the Korean war, where you will remember the American army which had the latest type of weapons which no army possesses, suffered very serious defeats to begin with, and the Chinese had no modern arms then and yet by their method of warfare, which is a mixture of regular warfare and guerrilla warfare and there was a large number of people and they are very specially trained in mountain warfare. They did not go up to a pass; we go and defend the pass, they do not go to the pass; they climb the hill on the either side of the pass and having got at the hill and they take their small mountain guns at the top of the pass, they carry them themselves in bits, four or five persons carrying them, parts of the mountain guns, fix it there, sitting on the top of the mountain, they hold the pass, and they climb all round and usually they attack, not frontal attacks but all round attacks. It is normally rather disconcerting to the party holding a position. They expect a frontal attack, they have developed this kind of tactics and strategy after thirty years of fighting. We may read about, it we have read about it, but the real experience of it is different from reading about it in Korea or somewhere else. They took a mighty long time, the Americans, to get used to this warfare and with the help chiefly of their air power and others they could gradually control them. Now my point is, having got this experience we have to adapt our fighting methods to it so that we might be able to defeat them.

Now another thing, they proclaim their cease fire and withdrawal, when they were approaching the plains. They were still about 30, 40 miles away of the plain area, why they did it, maybe some political reasons, and some practical reasons. The advantages they have, being specially trained in mountain warfare largely vanishes on the plains, and they did not want therefore to meet our forces on the plains. Though political reasons too, I have no doubt. One thing is pretty obvious, that the Chinese did not look forward to a long campaign. Apparently, they wanted to hit us hard blows, to frighten us, and then even to appear to be generous having regard to the position they had gained by those hard blows and to come to some understanding or arrangement with us, which was less than they had gained by their hard blows, but nevertheless gave them an advantageous position for the future when they could have another or whatever it was. That has been their practice and that is I believe, now we are told, Chairman Mao Tse-tung's tactics, which is Chinese tactics, it is interesting to know, are largely derived, they have been worked up in the last hundred years in China. Of course, modern things are applied to it too, but in a sense all this trouble that has happened internally in China about 60 years ago, all that some tactics was applied. It is a curious tactic, avoiding fight, chiefly guerrilla work, if the enemy can be overwhelmed with numbers overwhelm them, or else avoid the fight. Now of course they have improved upon that with modern weapons. But the basic idea is still the same. So for whatever reasons it is partly political and partly lack of their desire not to get entangled in the plains, because then, and partly also their lines of communication, become lengthened. Now you must remember that all the Chinese armies in Tibet, as big as they are, are supported from China. It is a terrible job. You cannot get anything in Tibet, very little in the shape of food, even for the population, and large armies have to be fed from China, their arms are to be supplied, everything. The result is they have to face a very difficult logistic problem. They can send things by train, even so there is one thousand miles of road to cover. I suppose they use trucks and lorries for that. Now I have no doubt that in the last may be year, may be two years, they have been stocking supplies in Tibet for their army and they could rely on these stock of supplies for their attacks. But if there is a long continued war, you cannot carry it on because of past supplies, you have to get them. Therefore, it is not very easy for them to get this continuous flow of supplies for a large army and long campaign; therefore, it is disadvantageous to them. They want short, swift campaigns, yielding some results, which can be capitalised and then prepare for the next, whenever the time may come. All these reasons may perhaps have induced them to seek an arrangement after this initial success.

Also, you will see on the 20th October, they came down for the first time in massive strength from the Thagla pass and that was the first serious defeat we suffered. On the 24 October that is 4 days afterwards came Mr Chou En lai's offer, three-point offer. The mere fact of it following closely on the first, shows that it was carefully thought out beforehand, not suddenly in a day's time, that is, in their mind because it was this very policy of a hard hit and stunning a party and then offering some terms which might appear to them relatively good.[147] We did not accept those terms. So, for the next three weeks they prepared again and gave us a hard blow at Sela Pass and other places. Soon after that they come out again with their offer. The offer was the same as they had done on the 24 October this difference that they added to it unilaterally cease fire and withdrawal which is of course important, but essentially the offer was much the same as on 24 October which we had rejected.

So now we have before us a position when we must profit by the experiences and the reverses we had, and build ourselves up to meet the situation with strength, and that is the process we are going through now. Fortunately for us, some countries, notably the US and the UK came rapidly to our help, and although that help could not be used by us in the early days, because however much help they gave, which came rapidly, was not enough, and sending and distributing this material to our armies there took, takes time ,and so far as automatic rifles and others are concerned, does not merely take time but requires a little practice, not much, but some practice. So, it was not, it did not help us very much in these critical days. Anyhow we are grateful to them for having sent it and we are using it now and gradually they are spreading.

Also, we realised that any large scale help must be, there is, a limit to the help you can get from outside, and we must produce our own things, both for practical reasons and economic reasons. So, we took steps immediately in October to triple, quadruple our production from our ordnance factories. They are working night and day and producing a great deal. That is not enough, we are getting some equipment, machinery etc. so as to produce new types of things

147. In fact, the Chinese peace offer was known to the Soviets even before the attack of 20 October was launched. See "Central Committee of the Communist Party of the Soviet Union, Presidium Protocol 58," October 11, 1962, http://digitalarchive.wilsoncenter. org/document/115070 Accessed on 6 September 2018.

which we require, our ordnance factories are new ordnance factories. That is, we are aiming at producing most things that we may require ourselves, it may take a few months to have new factories, new things still there are some things which probably we cannot produce soon. Ultimately, we will produce almost everything, because of our industrial base today can almost produce everything we require, and in the last, that is for example because of the last 12, 13, 14 years of our First Plan, Second Plan, etc. we have got an industrial base which can be used. If this had happened ten years ago, we had not an adequate base for it, as some say of course from the last war, it is not enough. Now we can make many of these things and with a little further equipment we can do so. Now all this requires a little time. Quite apart from the other questions of producing them or getting them from abroad, getting them to be effectively used by people, by our Army or just as we are recruiting fresh armies, that requires a little time. Therefore, time is an important matter for us to consider. We cannot rush in unprepared and face possibly the same type of reverse that would be foolish from any point of view, and yet some of our friends in parties of the opposition and others go about delivering speeches that we must jump in and push them out. The gentlemen who say so, probably has never touched a rifle in life, being out of the other equipment. It is really extraordinary I suppose I can only say which has no reason or logic for perhaps some political reasons. Now that is the position we face. We want time to prepare and to give an effective reply to China's invasion. I have often said in public that we must be prepared for years, I have mentioned five years or even more, and I do not know how long we will have to do this, carry on with this. But in any event, we have to prepare as if we are carrying on for five years, may be a little less, may be a little, we have to prepare for that because I look upon this not merely as a present effort to drive them out but to create conditions, strength, to prevent any future onslaught.

Remember this that we are up against, in some ways, from an army point of view, the most powerful country in the world, army I repeat. The Chinese army is the biggest in the world, bigger than America or Russia: they have got good weapons for an army and they are better trained than, any American or Russian or anybody, because they have been continuously at it for the last 30 years in some form or other, whether civil war or anything, highly trained, fairly well armed. Of course they cannot be compared with Americans or Russians in regard to superior sophisticated weapons, they cannot compare with them, apart from nuclear weapons, even in their aircraft. They have got a very big air arm. I do not know how much bigger, but about ten times or eight times bigger than ours. But still in that, they are very much third rate, I mean to say compared to America and Russia. So far as pure army is concerned they are as good as any, and better.

So, it is a difficult matter, you must realise that we are fighting with one of the great powers of the world. It is not a local fight with a country more or less like us or little better or little worse. Therefore, we have to prepare and we have to take steps which are conditioned by our strategy, tactics and our preparation. We cannot just take steps without thinking of the military aspects. In all this in the last two months since October 20th and before, beginning of October or September even, we have naturally, in these matters one has inevitably to rely on the military advice one gets. We cannot, Ministers or Prime Ministers, we cannot tell them to do this or that, if it is against military advice. We may stress certain political aspects, that, for instance, we did not like the idea of their retiring a good deal from our frontier without challenging their coming in. Purely from a military point of view perhaps it was better to retire and allow them to come in and meet them on a more advantageous ground for us. We did not overrule military persons. If they had said no, we cannot do, perhaps submit, but we did say that something else should be done and they accepted it, therefore we agreed to it. However, I am talking about the future. One has to accept the advice of the military. There are defence experts as to what preparations we have to make and where we should meet the Chinese and try to push them back, defeat them. This is not a matter for political decision, sometimes it is, but this is not, and for us to do anything at present which involves a major military conflict unless we are prepared for it, it would not be very wise. The choice is not ours, the choice is Chinese, if they want to fight we have to fight. But if we have to fight according to our choice we fight on suitable ground with suitable arrangements and preparations, and, as I said, we should like some time for that. In a sense there is. The winter has come there and fighting may tone down, but nevertheless even winter does not stop it. It is in this context that we have to view the Chinese offer. As I have said, it would be absurd for us to say, do not withdraw, it is ridiculous. When they said they will have a cease fire, we could have said, you may have cease fire, we will go on shooting at you. But it is not practical politics, before arrangements of anything. We merely shoot at them, they are an army which has won a victory, preparing to depart, and we come in their way and invite them to advance further on us without proper preparations. It is not practical. So inevitably we accepted, we have not said anything about it, but we have accepted the cease fire to prepare ourselves for the next offer, and we certainly are going to accept their walking out, withdrawing.

The question is they have made, if you read their proposals carefully, they have laid down certain conditions. The first conditions were that if we fire at them as they are withdrawing, then they will hit back and something else like that. Some other conditions are about how far they will withdraw and how far they expect us to remain and there is some vacant land about 25 miles in between, where they are, according to them where we should be, what kind of arrangements should be made there, whether armies can go there or civil authority should go, these are other matters which we have to consider and reply to. But my point is that let us presume that we do not agree to all the conditions they said, we probably will not, but we cannot merely say we reject your offer, fight, because we have to be ready for it, we are preparing for it. So, we have to consider this with some wisdom and so as to produce conditions which are favourable for us to meet their challenge effectively.

Now I do hope, I have said nothing very secret, but I do hope what I am saying was not going to he repeated outside or published, I would beg of you to avoid that.

Now one thing else I should like to put to you. We have just been meeting in Executive Committee and there was a good deal of discussion there about some Congress members saying and doing things which produce an impression that the Congress party is not solid and disciplined.[148] Now about this I shall partly repeat what I said there. I am not going into any particular cases of individuals, that is important, but the fact of the matter is that in existing conditions you will realise that it is very easy for rumours to spread. We are only at the beginning of our trouble. Suppose bombs started falling on Delhi, then many of our people who are very brave on the platform, may function differently and then you will find all kinds of wild rumours going about. It is no disrespect to our courage, but we are a gossiping people, all people are really to some extent, and we spread, almost extraordinary stories spread out. I have known them, you must have known them, that there is a petty riot, or communal riot or something, the way the stories are made up, it is amazing and each story excites the other party. So such a contingency occurs. Well we might have to train our people.

My first experience of bomb dropping took place in 1938 in Spain where civil war was going on. I went to Barcelona on a visit to the Republican Government which was the legal Govt. Franco was attacking them. I was staying at a hotel in Barcelona on the 6th or 7th floor, I was there for two or three days. Every night aircraft came to bomb Barcelona. It is absurd to try to run away, I could not have run away from the 7th floor of the building, so I went on to the balcony to have a good look and I saw these bombs dropping all over and they went away after some practice. The next morning, I went to see the houses, a group of houses burning or ruined, shattered but I saw them. It was remarkable, they had got used to it, the people there. At first they were very frightened. Within ten minutes of the all clear signal which was given by the city authorities, the city was functioning again, city was functioning except

148. See item 28.

for the areas of the bomb which were bombed, which were ruined, others functioning, shops opened, large number of, on the road side, people selling things, it is extraordinary how rapidly they came back, because human beings adapted themselves with amazing facility to anything. In England or other places, these took place on a much bigger scale, subsequently in China in 1939 when I want to pay a visit to Mr Chiang Kai shek's Govt. I was in China when the great world war was declared. It started with invasion on Poland by Hitler. And I had gone to China to spend a month, or more there but I had been there only for five or six days and I came back immediately. But during those five or six days there, there were air raids, overnight Japanese air raids, and we had to retire to air shelter. I spent at least two nights in air shelters with Marshal Chiang Kai-shek and Madam Chiang Kai-shek and suddenly at dinner time and after dinner and the air raid alarm and they took us to their own shelter. But the view I had from the sixth or seventh floor from the Barcelona Hotel I did not have here, because I was on the ground, I could see when they come, and in Barcelona they had no anti-aircraft guns or anything, they had no aircraft or hardly any and it is very discouraging not to be able to do anything. It is the aircraft bombing either by anti-aircraft guns or in the air; they can come down fairly low and take pot shots at you. But in London of course in the last war infinitely more than this and other things. Gradually even though people got used to it first they are of course relatively speaking more disciplined people.

Now we have got to develop that discipline because it may be that we have to face these air raids and other things, not immediately. We did not in this present conflict with China to begin with the first month or so, we did not use our air, for the simple reason that we thought that if we use our air power they would use theirs and they had much more valuable targets than we had. We could attack Tibet; there is nothing which we can do, anything we could use in aiding the ground forces; certainly, we could a little, but with the risk of their also not only adding to their ground forces but destroying our ground forces and their air power is about eight or ten times of ours. The real thing was it was easy for them if they so chose, very easy for them to go and destroy Bhakra Nangal... [Tape inaudible]

मैं कुछ ख़ास बोलने नहीं खड़ा हुआ हूं आपका शुक्रिया अदा करने, धन्यवाद। कुछ इस वक़्त मौजूं नहीं है मेरा बोलना, लेकिन मेरे निस्बत जो बातें की गयीं वो, उससे मेरे ऊपर असर होता है और ज़िम्मेदारी बढ़ती जाती है। आप जानते हैं जो कोई आदमी हो चाहे मैं आपका लीडर हूं इस पार्टी का या नहीं, वो बहुत कम काम कर सकता है बग़ैर एक संगठित पार्टी के जो साथ-साथ चले उसके। तो असल में ये तो आप लोगों के हाथ में है कि इस तरह से, कि हम सब लोग मिलके जो काम करना है उसको करें। फिर से धन्यवाद आपको।

[Translation begins:

I have not stood up to say anything special. I have stood up to show my gratitude to you, Thank you. It is not the right time to say this, but whatever has been spoken about me or to me that has some impact and that also increases my responsibility. You all know that whoever is a leader, of this party or any other, can do very little without an organised and disciplined cadre, which walks alongwith him. So, it is actually upto you people to do what we all want to do. Thank you all again.

Translation ends]

(c) CHINISE INVATION: Mobilising Popular Support

288. National Defence Front[149]

I do not understand what this National Defence Front is likely to be. I think the initiative should either be taken by the Congress Working Committee or the Central Government.

1. I am told that today in Bombay the Chief Minister is making some appeal for a national front. I do not know the details.
2. I understand that it has already been decided to hold a meeting of such members of the Working Committee as are in Delhi on the 26th October at 3.30 p.m.
3. The whole question of economic policy will have to be considered from the point of view of the new development that has arisen because of the invasion on the frontier. First a priority will have to be given to production, especially Defence production. The other matters suggested should also be considered.
4. I am inclined to think that it would be better to postpone our Congress elections because of the present situation. But I am not sure about this as I do not know what the position is. This may perhaps be considered at the meeting on the 26th or, if the Congress President thinks it should be postponed, he can take steps by himself to that end.

149. Note, 23 October 1962, apparently for K. K. Shah, General Secretary, AICC, quoted in a letter of 24 October 1962, to K. K. Shah by S. P. Khanna, Nehru's PS. NMML. AICC Papers, Box No. 381, F. No. G-2(N), 1963.

289. Deepavali[150]

Soon we shall celebrate Deepavali, the Festival of Lights. This is an occasion for joy. But we shall have little joy or light in our hearts because a part of our Mother land has been invaded and the officers and men of our army on the borders have passed through an ordeal of great suffering. To all the men of our Army and Air force on our frontier areas, I send my heartfelt sympathy and good wishes. Indeed, not only I, but the whole nation does so, and the whole nation pledges itself to do its utmost to help those who are battling for our freedom and the integrity of our country. I can assure them on behalf of our nation that we shall not relax our efforts and shall continue them till we free our Mother land from the intruder. Then we shall celebrate Deepavali properly with joy and thanksgiving.

290. To Bhabani Prashad Bannarji: Volunteer Corps[151]

October 25, 1962

Dear Bhabani Prashadji,
I have your letter of 22nd October. Thank you for the message and for offering to raise a volunteer corps. A volunteer corps can only be of service in its own locality. For the Army something more than a volunteer corps is necessary and people have to be recruited to that. You may, if you like, raise a volunteer corps for local service for the present.

Yours sincerely,
[Jawaharlal Nehru]

291. To V.K. Krishna Menon: Veterans' Offers[152]

October 25, 1962

My dear Krishna,
I enclose two telegrams and a letter. The telegrams are from General Rajendrasinghji and Lt. Gen. Kalwant Singh; the letter from Lt. Gen. Thorat.

---

150. Message, 24 October 1962, NMML, JN Supplementary Papers, File No. 25, Box No. 134.
151. Letter to the Convenor of the Madhya Pradesh Congress Committee.
152. Letter to the Defence Minister.

I have received many other messages too.

I should like to know how you are utilising some of these people. I am repeatedly asked about them.

I am also enclosing another letter from Captain Rattan Singh.[153]

Yours affectionately,
[Jawaharlal Nehru]

292. To Vijaya Raje Scindia: Gwalior People's Response[154]

October 29, 1962

My dear Vijaya Raje,

Thank you for your letter of the 29th October. I am sure that you and the people of Gwalior will help in the present crisis to the utmost of your ability. We have to face a grave emergency, but perhaps it may do us good in toning all of us up.

Yours sincerely,
[Jawaharlal Nehru]

293. To Rajendra Prasad: People's Response[155]

October 30, 1962

My dear Rajendra Babu,

Thank you for your letter of October 25th which for some odd reason has only reached me today. I entirely agree with you about the magnificent response of our people to the crisis that we are facing. We are now doing our utmost to canalise this in effective activities.

I agree also that this is not some temporary interlude. We have to think not only in the short term but in the long term.

With regards,

Yours sincerely,
[Jawaharlal Nehru]

---

153. On 27 October 1962, Nehru informed the Congress MPs that the Government has decided to "utilise retired army officers and Generals, who had offered their services." *The Hindu*, 28 October 1962, p.1. See item 264.
154. Letter to the Maharani of Gwalior; address: Jaivilas, Gwalior.
155. Letter to the former President; address: Sadakat Ashram, Patna.

294. To V.R. Krishna Iyer: CPI on China[156]

October 30, 1962

My dear Krishna Iyer,

I have your letter of the 27th October. Indeed, I remember you well.

You have described in strong and effective language the action of China in invading India. You have been deeply pained by this. It is not surprising, therefore, that the vast majority of the people of our country should also feel that way without the restraining influences which enable you to see things in better perspective.

Many members of the Communist Party have openly condemned China's aggression. But there are still some important members who continue to equivocate and find excuses for China in spite of all that has happened. Surely you can imagine what effect this has on the country which is feeling so deeply about this aggression.[157] We should certainly try to prevent excess and to build up national unity. But what am I to do when some people take up an attitude which angers others?

Yours sincerely,
[Jawaharlal Nehru]

295. To Sant Fateh Singh: Views on Chinese Invasion[158]

November 4, 1962

My dear Sant Fateh Singh,

Thank you for your letter of November 2nd which was handed to me personally by your messenger. I appreciate what you have written, and I am glad to learn that your views in regard to the Chinese invasion of India are similar to ours.

---

156. Letter to an MLA; address: Advocate, M.G. Road, Ernakulum.
157. In a private conversation with Ivan Benedictov, Namboodripad was reported to have said: "In this connection we very much would like to find out if Soviet leaders could help the CPI give an understanding to the Chinese comrades that it is extremely desirable to give the possibility to Nehru to move toward peace negotiations and cease military actions without damage to the prestige of India and of Nehru himself...." "Entry from journal of Ivan Benedictov, Soviet ambassador to India (1959-1967) regarding conversation with E.M.S. Namboodripad, General Secretary, CPI; 26 October 1962";Wilson Centre Archives, http://digitalarchive.wilsoncentre.org/document/113000. Accessed on 6 September 2018.
158. Letter to Akali Dal leader; address: Shiromani Akali Dal, Teja Singh Samundari Hall, Amritsar.

There can be no doubt that this invasion must be resisted by all of us and the aggressors pushed back to their own territory. As you must have noticed, the response in India among all classes and groups of people has been wonderful. The Sikhs, of course, are a brave community and we are confident that they will play their full part in the defence of our Mother land.

The National Development Council has just met here in Delhi[159] and it will be issuing a declaration to the country. This will give some guidance to all of us. All I can suggest to you is to lend your support to this declaration and to all the other measures that are being taken to further the war effort in India.

Yours sincerely,
[Jawaharlal Nehru]

296. For Workers[160]

The grave crisis that has arisen in the country on account of the Chinese invasion has led to a very fine response from all parts of India and all sections of our people. Among these are the industrial workers who have pledged themselves to help in every way in higher production. I am happy to see this patriotic response of our industrial workers. The struggle for freedom and to repel the aggressors on our frontier has to be conducted not only by our soldiers but also by our workers in field and factory who have to increase production to their utmost capacity to help in every way the military effort of our Defence Services and to keep up the economy of the country.

I, therefore, welcome the assurance that has been given by the trade union organisations of the industrial workers and congratulate them on their wise and patriotic decision. We have to explore every avenue of giving help in this crisis. I am sure that our workers friends will be in the fore front of this great struggle.

159. See item 268.
160. Message, 5 November 1962. PMO, File No. 9/2/62-PMP, Vol. 7, Sr. No. 88-B.

297. To Ram Subhag Singh: Schemes of Populating NEFA[161]

November 6, 1962

My dear Ram Subhag,

I enclose a telegram which I have received today from the Governor of Assam.[162] This is, I think, about the statement you made a few days ago. You might keep in mind what he says about the effect of your scheme in Nagaland and other hill areas.[163]

Yours sincerely,
Jawaharlal Nehru

298. To Ram Subhag Singh: Settlements in NEFA[164]

November 8, 1962

My dear Ram Subhag,

Your letter of the 8th November.[165] I have sent a copy of it to Vishnu Sahay and written to him myself. I suggest your writing to him directly as full particulars as you can of what you have in mind. In any event, I would suggest starting the scheme in a small way. Any large numbers of people introduced in NEFA create problems.[166]

Yours sincerely,
[Jawaharlal Nehru]

---

161. Letter to Minister for Agriculture. MHA, File No. 16(7)-NI/62, p. 11/c.
162. The telegram is probably the following, No. 150, 6 November 1962, Vishnu Sahay, Governor of Assam, to M. J. Desai, FS: "Have you seen the item called 'scheme to populate NEFA under way' on page six of the *Statesman* of 3rd November. This may be grist to the mill of those opposed to us in Nagaland and other hill areas." MHA, File No. 16(7)-NI/62, p. 12.
163. See also item 298 and, appendices 47 and 49.
164. Letter to the Minister for Agriculture. MHA, File No. 16(7)-NI/62, p. 14.
165. Appendix 47.
166. See item 299 and appendix 49.

299. To Vishnu Sahay: Settlements in NEFA[167]

November 8, 1962

My dear Vishnu Sahay,

I saw your telegram in which you have expressed your apprehension about cultivators being sent to NEFA.[168] I spoke to the Minister for Agriculture who has sent me a letter, copy enclosed.[169]

I think I realise the difficulties you have in view. On the other hand, if we want to introduce better agriculture in NEFA, some model farms of the type intended are desirable. Provided this is done on a small scale as a beginning, it should not do any harm.

It might even be arranged that the persons who go there, should not permanently settle down, but should train up local people.

This would apply only to NEFA and not to Nagaland.

Yours sincerely,
Jawaharlal Nehru

300. In New Delhi: To Government Employees[170]

सभा मंत्री जी,[171] बहिनों, भाइयों और साथियों,

इस मैदान में अक्सर मुझे बोलने का मौक़ा मिला है और जब-जब बोला हूँ मैंने ज़ोर दिया है कि दुनिया में और हमारे मुल्क में हमें अमन और शान्ति की कोशिश करनी चाहिए। ज़माना ऐसा आया कि जब लड़ाइयाँ न्यूक्लीयर-बॉम्ब (Nuclear Bomb) वग़ैरा के ज़रिये से हो सकती हैं जो कि दुनिया को तबाह करें। हमारी नीति, पालिसी जो रही है दुनिया में, हर जगह वो कुछ ऐसी रही कि शान्ति हो और हथियारबन्दी बन्द हो। हमने कोशिश की सब मुल्कों से दोस्ती करने की, और कामयाब भी बहुत दर्जे हुए। अजीब इत्तिफ़ाक़ है कि हमें, हम जो समझे जाते थे कि हम बहुत अमन और शान्ति चाहते हैं दुनिया में हर जगह, क़िस्मत का खेल ऐसा हुआ कि हम इस वक़्त एक लड़ाई में फंसे हैं और एक हमारे भारत के इतिहास में एक नया अध्याय शुरू हो रहा है, उसका शुरू अब है, कैसे वो ख़त्म होगा यह बाद में देखा जायेगा। अजीब बात है कि चीन जिसके साथ हमने दोस्ती की

---

167. Letter to the Governor of Assam. MHA, File No. 16(7)-NI/62.p/c
168. See item 297.
169. See appendix 47.
170. Speech at the Ramlila Maidan, 9 November 1962. NMML, AIR Tapes, TS No. No. 8576, 8577, 8578, NM No. 1687, 1688.
171. S. Madhusudan, the Convener of the meeting.

कोशिश की पूरी, जिसके साथ, जिसको हमने उनके क्रान्तिकारी जो उनकी हुकूमत बनी, बारह बरस हुए, उसको हम क़रीब-क़रीब अव्वल लोगों में था हमारा देश जिसने उसको स्वीकार किया। हमने उनकी पैरवी की संयुक्त राष्ट्र में, यूनाइटेड नेशन्स में, उनके वहाँ लाने की और आमतौर से उनका साथ दिया और अब हम पे हमला कर रहे हैं और आज नहीं इस समय बल्कि पाँच बरस हुए वो शुरु हुआ था लद्दाख़ में, बहुत कुछ ख़त लिखे हमने उनको, उन्होंने लिखे हमें और मुलाक़ात भी एक दफ़े बीच में हुई, कुछ वारदात भी हो गयी जिसमें दस-बीस आदमी मर गये, कुछ फिर भी कुछ रोक-थाम रही कि लड़ाई बड़े पैमाने पर न छिड़े। बातचीत हो रही थी कि हम किस तरह से इस अहम मसले को शान्ति से तय करें। हमने तजवीज़ की थी कि पहले हमें मिलना चाहिए, हमारे नुमाइन्दों को, और उनके नुमाइन्दों को मिलना चाहिए और पहली बात यह हो कि कैसे हम ऐसी हवा पैदा करें जिससे बातचीत कामयाब हो सके, यानी क़ब्ल इसके कि हम जो असली सवाल है उनसे उसपे बहस करें, हवा होनी चाहिए हमारी राय थी, हमने पहले भी कहा था कि वो हवा जभी ऐसे हो जब जो हमारी ज़मीन पर वो आये हैं वो वहाँ से बहुत दर्जे हटें।

[WE WANT HONOURABLE EXIT]

(From *The Times of India,* 23 November 1962)

ख़ैर, यह बातचीत हो रही थी पिछले अगस्त में ख़त हमने भेजा, उनका जवाब आया, फिर हमने भेजा कि यकायक आठ सितम्बर को वो पहली बार नेफ़ा में यानी जो हमारा

प्रान्त है, सरहदी प्रान्त है पूरब में, उसपे वो उतर आये हैं, एक बड़े पास से, अब तक उसपे नहीं उतरे थे वो बिल्कुल। और एक वहाँ हमारी सरहद गिनी जाती है, बहुत पुरानी सरहद हिमालय के ऊँचे ऊँचे पहाड़ जो वहाँ हैं उसमें कोई निशान लगाने की ज़रूरत नहीं है। हिमालय के ऊँचे पहाड़ जिसके इधर-उधर पानी बहता है यानी जो पानी इधर को गिरता है वो हिन्दुस्तान की तरफ़ आता है, उधर तिब्बत की तरफ़। यह ज़माने से, सैकड़ों बरस से समझी जाती है, हिन्दुस्तान में बहुत ऊँच-नीच हुई, सल्तनतें बदलीं लेकिन तिब्बत में हिन्दुस्तान के हिस्से में सह-सरहद गिनी जाती थी। फिर क़रीब पचास बरस हुए इस पर बहस हुई, इसी सरहद पर यानी अंग्रेज़ी ज़माने में हिन्दुस्तान के, उसमें हिन्दुस्तान के नुमाइन्दे थे, अंग्रेज़ों के नुमाइन्दे थे और तिब्बत के थे और चीन के थे, तीनों। तिब्बत का हाल उस वक़्त यह था कि वो एक क़रीब-क़रीब आज़ाद मुल्क था लेकिन चीन का एक ऊपर से कुछ हुकूमत तो नहीं थी कहा जाये, लेकिन ऊपर से कुछ उनके इख़्तियारात थे, इसको अंग्रेज़ी में कहते हैं सॉवरेनटी, यानी चीन से मिला था लेकिन उनको अन्दरूनी इख़्तियारात थे। यही बात कि उस कॉन्फ्रेंस में तिब्बत के लोग भी आये और चीन के भी और हिन्दुस्तान के भी, इससे ज़ाहिर होता है कि तिब्बत के अलग-अलग अख़्तियार थे काफ़ी। उस कॉन्फ्रेंस में जो कि पचास बरस हुए हुई थी कुछ समझौते हुए उस पर, वो समझौते हुए इसी बारे में कि, हिन्दुस्तान की तिब्बत की सरहद क्या है। जिसका नाम बाद में पड़ गया मैकमहाने लाइन, क्योंकि मैकमहान साहब थे अंग्रेज़, जो कि इस कॉन्फ्रेंस में मुक़र्रर हुए थे अंग्रेज़ों की तरफ़ से। अब मैकमहाने लाइन जो थी वो उन्होंने कुछ नहीं बनाई थी, उन्होंने तो यह निश्चय किया कि पुराने ज़माने से क्या सरहद है, पहाड़ी सरहद है, पहाड़ की चोटियाँ, तो उन्होंने नयी बात नहीं लिखी, लेकिन एक पुरानी तसलीमशुदा बात को साफ़ लिखा। उसपे कुछ दस्तख़त भी हो गये तीनों के, लेकिन बाद में चीन की हुकूमत ने, उस वक़्त की हुकूमत ने इंकार किया उस समझौते पे दस्तख़त करने से उनको इंकार करना इसलिए नहीं था कि हिन्दुस्तान और तिब्बत की सरहद क्या है बल्कि एक और हिस्सा था समझौते का। कहती है शक्ल नहीं दिख रही, चलो हटो, मेरी शक्ल काफ़ी आप लोग देख चुके हैं, काफ़ी पुरानी हो गयी है शक्ल, अब क्या किया जाये, (हँसी) अरे हटो भाई मुझे बातें करनी हैं। तो उन्होंने जो एतराज़ किया था वो एक और हिस्सा था सुलहनामे का, तिब्बत के अन्दर दो हिस्से हैं, समझे, एक आउटर तिब्बत, एक इनर तिब्बत, उसपे उन्होंने एतराज़ किया था, इस ख़ास बात पर एतराज़ किया। लेकिन यह बात सही है कि चीनी हुकूमत ने ऐसे वक़्त भी, उस पर, उस सुलहनामे पर दस्तख़त नहीं किया, मंज़ूर नहीं किया। ख़ैर, बावजूद इसके हिन्दुस्तान के और तिब्बत वालों के, जो कुछ समझा गया वो ठीक है, उस पर अमल हुआ है यानी अलावा पहले के अमल के, पचास से तो हुआ ही है अमल। जब हिन्दुस्तान आज़ाद हुआ तो हमें फ़िक्र हुई कि सारे हिन्दुस्तान में तरक़्क़ी होनी चाहिए, इंतज़ाम होना चाहिए। इस हिस्से में नेफ़ा के उस वक़्त तक कोई माक़ूल इंतज़ाम नहीं था क्योंकि अंग्रेज़ी हुकूमत के ज़माने में उनको बहुत फ़िक्र नहीं थी, कभी-कभी लोग अपने अफ़सरों को भेज देते थे सरहद पर, कभी कुछ झगड़ा होता था तो

कुछ फ़ौज थोड़ी सी भेज देते थे, लेकिन और कुछ इंतज़ाम नहीं था। तो हमें फ़िक्र हुई कि इंतज़ाम वहाँ तक पहुँचना चाहिए और सड़कें हैं, अस्पताल हैं, स्कूल हैं ये सब होना चाहिए। चुनांचे यह होने लगा, हुआ, बढ़ रहा है, बहुत कुछ हुआ, और बढ़ता जाता है। यह इसका इतिहास है इस बात का।

अब चीनी हुकूमत की तरफ़ से कोई हमसे कोई बात ख़ास नहीं कही गयी है इसकी निस्बत जो नयी हुकूमत आयी है। लेकिन हमने देखा कि उनके नक़्शे जो हैं उसमें एक बड़ा हिस्सा हिन्दुस्तान का लद्दाख़ में और नेफ़ा में उन्होंने अपना दिखाया है, कि गोया कि चीन का है, तिब्बत के साथ है। हमें बहुत ताज्जुब हुआ और हमने उनसे कहा कि आपने यह क्या किया, यह तो बिल्कुल ग़लत नक़्शे हैं, बार-बार हमने कहा और बार-बार उन्होंने जवाब दिया कि नक़्शे हमारे पुराने हैं, पुराने हैं, वो पुरानी हुकूमत के जब चांग-काई-शेक थे और हमने इस पर ग़ौर नहीं किया, न फ़ुरसत हमें मिली है, हम ग़ौर करेंगे और आपसे बातचीत करेंगे और फिर अमन से, शान्ति से यह मसला हल हो जायेगा, यह उन्होंने कहा। ख़ैर, हमने पहली दफ़े कहा मान लिया, दूसरी दफ़े कहा कि हमारी समझ ही में नहीं आया कि उनको फ़ुरसत ही नहीं मिली है इस बात के सोचने की, तीसरे दफ़े कहा यहाँ तक कि मैंने ख़ुद जो वहाँ के प्रधानमंत्री हैं चाउ-एन-लाइ साहब से मैं मिला था, उनसे कहा, हमेशा जवाब उनका यही मिला था कि पुराने नक़्शे हैं उन पर ग़ौर करके हम, हम तुम बातचीत करके इसको अमन से तय कर लेंगे।

हमने इसको मंज़ूर किया और मंज़ूर करते न करते यह वाक़िया था करना पड़ा। और फिर तिब्बत में आप जानते हैं बलवे हुए हैं बड़े-बड़े, आप जानते हैं चीनी हुकूमत के ख़िलाफ़। अब किसी वजह से हमारी हमदर्दी कुछ तिब्बत की तरफ़ थी लेकिन हमने, उसमें हमारा कोई दखल नहीं था, लेकिन चीन की हुकूमत समझी ग़लत या सही, अपनी उनकी राय यह हुई, कि हमने वहाँ उनके ख़िलाफ़ बलवा करवाया। यह बिल्कुल निकम्मी बात थी, हम वहाँ तिब्बत में जायें बलवा करवाने। हम उनसे दोस्ती करते थे और हमारी ताक़त क्या कि हम तिब्बत में जाके करायें, लेकिन उन्होंने कहा नहीं कि हिन्दुस्तान में बैठके वहाँ कालिम्पाँग से और दार्जिलिंग से बलवा कर रहे हैं। मेरे समझ में नहीं आता कि अक़्लमन्द आदमी हैं वह, ऐसी हिमाक़त की बात कैसे उन्होंने मंज़ूर की और ख़ैर समझे वो। मैंने इसलिए आपसे यह बात कही और इससे शुरू बात की जिससे उनका कुछ दिमाग़ का तर्ज़ बदलने सा लगा हमारी तरफ़ से। और तिब्बत के बलवे की बात आप जानते हैं कि, दलाई लामा साहब, पैंतीस-चालीस हज़ार आदमी वहाँ से शरणार्थी होके हिन्दुस्तान आये, हमने उनको आने दिया यहाँ और उनसे कहा कि हम तुम्हारी देखभाल करेंगे और यह भी उनसे कहा कि हम यह नहीं चाहते तुम हमारे मुल्क में रहकर यहाँ कुछ हमारे मुल्क को अपना अड्डा बनाके तिब्बत में बलवे करवाने की कोशिश करो। उन्होंने मंज़ूर किया और जबसे वो यहाँ हैं हमने उनकी बहुत मदद की है और कई जगह बसे हुए हैं, कई छोटी-छोटी आबादियाँ हैं उनकी और उनके बच्चों का पढ़ाई-लिखाई का सब प्रबंध हो रहा है। यह सब बातें।

बावजूद इन सब बातों के, अब बावजूद इसके उन्होंने साफ़-साफ़ तो नहीं कहा, चीनी हुकूमत ने, बल्कि इशारे किये कि हालांकि कहा कि यह मैकमहान की लाइन ग़लत है, ये क़ानून के ख़िलाफ़ है लेकिन फिर भी हम उसको मंज़ूर कर लेंगे, हमारी तुम्हारी दोस्ती है, झगड़े की क्या बात है, यह बार-बार कहा। तो हमें कुछ इत्मीनान हुआ कि वहाँ नहीं आयेंगे, पक्का इत्मीनान तो नहीं हुआ सच बात यह है, लेकिन कुछ इत्मीनान हुआ, चाहे वो लद्दाख़ में जो भी कुछ करें, इधर नहीं आयेंगे। फिर भी हमने अपनी सरहद पर वहाँ अपने फ़ौजी दस्तों को रखा, पच्चीस-तीस दस्ते थे। अब ज़ाहिर है फ़ौजी दस्ते जो रहे वहाँ वो लम्बे-चौड़े तो नहीं थे, सरहद पर, कहीं बीस आदमी हों, कहीं पचास हों, कहीं सौ हों, वो कोई बड़ी लड़ाई लड़ने के लिए तो नहीं थे, उनको वहाँ रखा और कम से कम उनसे कोई आ नहीं सकता था छिपके, और कोई आ नहीं सकता था बग़ैर लड़ाई लड़े, यह उसके माने थे। और चुनांचे वहाँ कोई आया नहीं, न आने पाया इन सब बरसों में, हालांकि लद्दाख़ में काफ़ी बढ़े आगे। यह अब तक की बात मैं आपसे कहता हूँ।

अब आठ तारीख़ को, आठ सितम्बर को पहली बार उनके फ़ौजी लोग एक वहाँ पास है उसपे से उतरने लगे और उतर के आये, हमारे जो वहाँ फ़ौजी दस्ते आस-पास थे, ज़रा एक मील भर इधर थे, पास के नीचे उनको घेर लिया, घेर के पहले तो वो कुछ हट गये पीछे और छोटे, छोटे-मोटे वाक़ियात हुए, गोली-वोली चली लेकिन ज़्यादा नहीं। हमने सोचा कि यह मुनासिब नहीं है, इनको यहाँ से हटा देना चाहिए। तो हमने इंतज़ाम किया और फ़ौजें वहाँ चली जायें और उनको वहाँ से हटा दें। चुनांचे हमारी फ़ौजें जाने लगीं लेकिन यह याद रखिये आप कि यह जगह जो है यह बहुत ऊँचे पहाड़ों पर है, चौदह हज़ार फ़ीट ऊँची है और उससे भी ज़्यादा और आप एकदम से दिल्ली से वहाँ जायें तो आपको काफ़ी दिक़्क़त होगी सांस लेने में, ऊँचे पहाड़ों पे होती है अलावा और दिक़्क़तों के, सर्दी-वर्दी होती है लेकिन सांस लेने की दिक़्क़त होती है। और हमने वहाँ भेजी फ़ौजें कुछ और, वो वहाँ अपने पुराने अड्डों को मज़बूत किया, और नये बनाये, यह होता रहा कुछ दिन तक। मैं उस ज़माने में यूरोप में था, इंग्लैंड में, मैं जैसे वापिस आया शुरू अक्टूबर, पहली अक्टूबर को, हम उम्मीद करते थे कि उस वक़्त तक सब हमारी तैयारी हो गयी है। अब हम उनको हटाने की कोशिश करें, लेकिन हमने देखा कि जहाँ हम तैयारी कर रहे थे और वह भी हमसे ज़्यादा कर रहे थे और उनके लिए आसान था करना बामुक़ाबले हमारे, क्योंकि वो जो पहाड़ की चोटी है, उसके पार जो हमारी सरहद हम गिनते थे, उसके बाद तिब्बत का मैदान है, मैदान नहीं क़रीब-क़रीब मैदान है, वो भी बड़ा ऊँचा मैदान है, क़रीब ग्यारह हज़ार, बारह हज़ार फ़ीट ऊँचा।

तो उधर तो चीनियों ने सड़कें बहुत सारी बनायी थीं और सड़क भी वहाँ आसान है बनाना, क्योंकि इत्ती सर्दी होती है वहाँ कि सीमेंट वग़ैरा कुछ नहीं लगाते, वहाँ ज़मीन को हमवार करते हैं और कंकर पत्थर हटा देते हैं, ज़रा निशान की वो सड़क हो जाती है, कोई सीमेंट वग़ैरा की जरूरत नहीं होती है। और अलावा इसके यह भी कहूँगा कि वो सड़क वग़ैरा बनाने में मालूम होता है काफ़ी माहिर हैं, वो काफ़ी तेज़ी से बनाते हैं क्योंकि वहाँ

तिब्बती लोगों को लगा देते हैं हज़ारों और साफ़ की ज़मीन । यह विद्या तो वो लोग तिब्बत भर की अपनी फ़ौज को जो कि बड़ी थी बड़ी आसानी से ला सकते थे कहीं भी हो, हमारी सरहद के पास, फिर उनको सिर्फ़ ज़रा सा चढ़ना और फिर हमारे हिन्दुस्तान में उतर आना और उनके खाना-पीना, सामान, फ़ौजी सामान सब आ सकता था वहाँ लारी से, बस से । हमें दिक्क़त यह थी कि हालांकि हमने सड़कें बनायी थीं, पूरीतौर से बन नहीं सकीं, बाज़ बनीं वो सारी बड़े ऊँचे पहाड़ों पर, सैकड़ों मील तक थी । चुनांचे उनको बनाने में बरसों लगे, कुछ बन गयी हैं, नहीं तो वहाँ पहुँचना बड़ा मुश्किल था पगडंडियों वग़ैरा से फ़ौजों को और या हवाई जहाज़ से जायें । हवाई जहाज़ से उनको ख़ाली भेजना नहीं, एक-एक चीज़ जो उनको ज़रूरत है, उनका खाना, पीना, लड़ाई का सामान, एक-एक तिनका उनको चाहिए वो हवाई जहाज़ से भेजना पड़ेगा । तो हमारे हवाई जहाज़ों से किया यह, काफ़ी उनको मुसीबत पड़ी, काफ़ी दिक्क़त हुई लेकिन किया । इस वजह से जित्ती फ़ौज हम वहाँ भेजें वो भी कुछ रुकावटें थीं क्योंकि हरेक को हवाई जहाज़ से खिलाना पड़ता था, सामान भेजना पड़ता था । तो यह दिक्क़त थी । ख़ैर, हमने भी यह किया, उन्होंने भी किया । मैं पहली अक्टूबर को आया तो यह मालूम हुआ कि उनकी फ़ौजें बढ़ गयी हैं, हमारी भी बढ़ी हैं, उनकी भी ज़्यादा बढ़ी हैं, ठीक तो मालूम नहीं था क्योंकि पहाड़ के उस पार थे, जल्दी से आ सकते हैं । तो हमने फिर भी सोचा कि हमें कोशिश करनी चाहिए उनको धकेल देने की और यही हमने हिदायत दी । ख़ैर, जो कुछ भी उसका हम सोच रहे थे क्या करें, कुछ फ़ौजें बढ़ायें ।

यकायक बीस अक्टूबर को बड़े पैमाने पर बड़ी फ़ौजों से उन्होंने हमपे हमला किया । उनकी फ़ौजें जो हमला करने वाली थीं हमारी फ़ौजों पर मुश्किल है कहना, पंचगुनी, छः गुनी, सातगुनी, कहीं दसगुनी थीं, बहुत ज़्यादा उतर आये । उनका लड़ाई का तरीक़ा यह है कि छापा मारते हैं बहुत बड़ी फ़ौजों से और इस बात की फ़िक्र नहीं करते हैं कि, कित्ते लोग मरते हैं, एक के बाद एक लहर आती है फ़ौजी सिपाहियों की और हमारी बहुत कम फ़ौजें थीं, उनको उन्होंने दबा दिया और तितर-बितर हो गयीं वो । यह बीस तारीख़ को यह बड़ा हादसा हुआ, इससे हमें बड़ा सदमा पहुँचा, उस वक़्त से उसमें कुछ न कुछ होता जाता है, कुछ और बढ़ आये हैं लोग, कुछ नेफ़ा में आस-पास एकाध छोटे शहर को क़ाबू में ले आये हैं और अब इस अर्से में कुछ हमारी फ़ौजें फिर से उन्होंने अपनी जगह चुनी और उन जगहों पर मज़बूती से रहीं, और हैं वहां, जो कुछ भी हो कुछ रोकथाम किया है, वो भी बढ़ाते जाते हैं अपनी फ़ौजें और, और जैसे मैंने आपसे कहा उनका लाना आसान है । दूसरी बात यह है कि उनकी फ़ौज जो है वो आदी हो गयी है ऊँचे पहाड़ों पे रहने की, तिब्बत की ऊँचाई ग्यारह-बारह हज़ार फ़ुट है, बरस दो बरस से हैं, हमारी फ़ौजें एकदम से यहाँ मैदानों से गयीं ऊँचे पहाड़ों पर । फ़ौजें हमारी बहुत अच्छी हैं, तगड़ी हैं लेकिन एकदम से वहाँ से जाने में ऊँचे पहाड़ों पर कुछ सांस वग़ैरा फूल जाती है, कुछ काम करने की शक्ति कम हो जाती है जब तक कि आदी न हो जायें, पन्द्रह-बीस रोज़, महीना भर लगता है आदी होने में । यह सब बातें थीं ।

तो हमपे कई सदमें पहुँचे वहाँ और हमने महसूस किया जो हम पहले नहीं समझते थे, यह असल में एक हमला है सारे हिन्दुस्तान पर। यह कोई सरहदी छोटी लड़ाई नहीं है जैसे लद्दाख़ में हुई थी, यह एक पक्कीतौर से हमला है और तो उनकी एक शक्ल बदल गयी और हमारे सामने यह बात आयी कि इसके माने यह हैं कि चीन और हिन्दुस्तान में लड़ाई है, हालांकि एलान न की जाये लड़ाई, लेकिन है। और उसके लिए पूरा हमें तैयार होना है और जब से हम सवाल हमारा तैयारी का है, फ़ौज का और फ़ौज के पीछे।

अब मैं आपसे कहूँ, सुभद्रा जी ने कहा कि यह बहुत अफ़वाहें हैं, अजीब-अजीब अफ़वाहें हैं कि हमने फ़ौज को कपड़े ठीक नहीं दिये और गरम कमीज़ नहीं दिया और जूते नहीं दिये और हथियार नहीं दिये। यह तो बहुत ही ग़लत बातें हैं। वाक़िया यह है कि फ़ौजें जो भेजी गयीं नीचे से उसको पूरी वर्दी उसकी है, अच्छी गर्म कमीज़ नहीं और गर्म कोट वग़ैरा वो सब थे और उनको कम्बल भी दिये गये, उस वक़्त भी तीन-तीन मोटे कम्बल, फ़ौजी कम्बल बड़े मोटे होते हैं दिये गये। उन्होंने, हवाई जहाज़ से सब जा रहे थे, उन्होंने कहा कि कम्बल तो बड़ी जगह लेते हैं हवाई जहाज़ में उसको पीछे भेज देना है। एक, एक कम्बल ले गये थे अपने साथ, बाक़ी कम्बल पीछे भेज देना कहा गया, पीछे भेजे गये। पीछे भेजे गये तो उसमें एक दिक़्क़त वाक़िया हुई, पीछे भी हवाई जहाज़ से भेजे गये और हवाई जहाज़ वहाँ उतर नहीं सकता है, हवाई जहाज़ से फेंके जाते हैं, उनका खाना फेंका जाता है, एयर-ड्रोपिंग (air-dropping) होती है, उनके कम्बल वग़ैरा सब फेंका गया। तो फेंकने में ख़ासकर दुश्मन के सामने ज़रा ऊँचे से फेंके जाते हैं। अब वो ऊँच-नीच वहाँ पहाड़ों में बहुत है। तो जो पारसल भेजे जायें, बंडल, वो बजाय ऐसी जगह फेंके कि जहाँ मिल सकें, वो खड्ड में चले जायें, बड़ी तपअमते में चले जायें तो उनका तलाश करना मुश्किल हो जाये, कुछ तलाश करके आ जायें कुछ नहीं है। इससे कुछ दिक़्क़तें हुईं उनको पूरा मिलने में, उस वक़्त सितम्बर में सर्दी भी इत्ती नहीं थी लेकिन दिक़्क़त हुई, बार-बार हमें भेजना पड़ा, हमारा नुकसान भी हुआ। तो यह कोई सवाल नहीं है कि कपड़े उनको दिये नहीं गये थे, पूरी वर्दी दी थी लेकिन कम्बल कुछ वो ले नहीं गये थे ख़ुद समझ के कि भर जायेगा हवाई जहाज, और बाद में भेजे थे, कुछ ज़ाया हो गये। अब तो उनके पास, सभों के पास चार-चार मोटे कम्बल हैं।

अलावा इसके हमने एक सबक़ सीखा चीनियों से कि, चीनी फ़ौज कोई बहुत शानदार वर्दी वग़ैरा नहीं पहनती है, न उनका बहुत तूल, का खाना-वाना होता है, हमारी फ़ौज को अच्छा खाना देते हैं, तरह-तरह का, उस सबको भेजना पड़े हमें हवाई जहाज़ से, फेंकना पड़े चीनी फ़ौज कुछ चावल एक, एक छोटे थैले में रखते हैं चावल और कुछ चाय की पत्तियाँ, क़रीब-क़रीब यही है, जहाँ पहुँचे चावल को उबाल के खा लिया, चाय बना ली। अब यह सादगी है, आसान है, हमारे पेचीदा खाने के भेजने में मुश्किल थी। ख़ैर, खाने में हम कुछ तरमीम कर रहे हैं, कुछ जो मामूली खाना तो हम देते हैं ही, कुछ नये खाने हमने बनाये हैं जो कि थोड़े से खाने में काफ़ी असर हो, कई क़िस्म की चीज़ें हैं, मामूली चीज़ें हैं, पेचीदा नहीं हैं। मसलन, मसलन गुड़ की कई चीज़ें बनती हैं, गुड़ बहुत अच्छी

चीज़ है ख़ासकर पहाड़ों पर उसके सत्तू के कई तरीके हैं बनाने के जो मामूली लोग हमारे खाते हैं, उसका बना दिये हैं यानी अलावा मामूली खाने के उनके पास रहें, वक़्त ज़रूरत कभी न हो और आसान है उनको जेब में रख सकते हैं। तो यह हुआ। (हाँ, मैं कह रहा था) हाँ, यह इंतज़ाम किया है। अब जब वो, अब तो मैंने आपसे कहा सबके पास तो हो, हमने कपड़े के लिए, उनके लिए जो नक़ल की चीनियों की, नक़ल कहिये, कुछ वो एक रूई से भरे हुए ग़देले, कोट लम्बे, चीनी लोग रूई के कोट पहनते हैं और रूई के पायजामें यानी क़रीब-क़रीब लिहाफ़ के कोट, लिहाफ़ के पायजामें। (हँसी) अब यह चीज़ कोई बहुत ख़ूबसूरत नहीं लगती है और शुरु-शुरु में हमारे फ़ौजी अफ़सरों ने देखा, उन्होंने, वो भी तो, उन्होंने कहा यह कौन है, यह तो बन्दर की सी शक्ल हो जाती है इसको पहनके। (हँसी) यह क्या पहनावा है लेकिन शक्ल कैसी हो, वो आराम की चीज़ थी सर्दी में और उसी को पहनके वो सोते थे बर्फ़ पर, उठते थे, सब करते थे। तो हमने भी बहुत तेज़ी से रूई के कोट बनवाये उनके लिए, लम्बे कोट, ख़ूब रूई भर के, उनको फ़ौरन दो-चार रोज़ में बन गये, और भेजे उन्हें और भेज रहे हैं, क़रीब-क़रीब रोज़ एक हज़ार आदमियों को मिल जायें, भेजे, और जा रहे हैं। तो इस तरह से इंतज़ाम पहले से कुछ कर रहे हैं।

यह सही है कि यह इंतज़ाम उस वक़्त नहीं हुआ था जब पहला हादसा हुआ बीस अक्टूबर को, बीस-इक्कीस को और हमेशा जब कोई हमलावर होता है तब उसको फ़ायदा होता है क्योंकि वो चुन सकता है कहाँ हमला करेंगे, वहाँ अपनी फ़ौजों को जमा करता है और जो डिफ़ेंस में रहता है उसको हर जगह तैयार रहना पड़ता है जाने कहाँ हमला करे। तो चीनियों ने जिस जगह हमारी थोड़ी सी फ़ौज थी, वहाँ बीस-तीस हज़ार आदमी एकदम से उस पार से ले आये और अच्छे बाहथियार आदमी और पहाड़ों के रहने वाले, जो वहाँ के ऊँचे पहाड़ों की हवा के आदी हैं वो आये, मुश्किल हो गया, कोई फ़ौज उनके मुल्क का मुक़ाबला नहीं कर सकती।

हथियारों का कहा जाता है, हथियार हमारी फ़ौज के पास मामूली, जो हिन्दुस्तान की फ़ौजों के हथियार हैं वो सभों के पास थे ज़ाहिर है। हम कुछ दिनों से बदल रहे हैं, उन हथियारों को ऑटोमैटिक हथियार कर रहे हैं। यह एक नई चीज़ है जो कि अंग्रेज़ी फ़ौज में भी विलायत में अभी हो रही है चन्द महीने से। हमने यह सोचा लेकिन हम नहीं चाहते थे कि बाहर से मंगवायें, उसका बहुत पैसा देना पड़ता है और और ख़ुदमुख़्तारी नहीं, अपने ऊपर भरोसा नहीं हो सकता, बाहर से मंगाना पड़ता है, उसमें बहुत पैसा देना पड़ता है। हमने उसका इंतज़ाम किया, यहीं बनाने का किया, उसके बनाने में, कुछ यह बात कुछ दो-तीन बरस से चल रही थी कि, कैसे, कौन सी बने, उसका ब्ल्यूप्रिंट क्या हो, उसका नक़्शा क्या हो। और बाज़ लोग कहें कि नहीं तुम बाहर से मंगा लो, बाज़ लोग कहें नहीं तुम यहाँ बनाओ इस बहस में। फिर आख़िर में उसका बनाने का तय हो गया और वो बनने का इंतज़ाम हो गया और वो बन रही है आजकल और अब नई निकल रही है और मेरा ख़्याल है एक महीने भर के अंदर एक बहुत काफ़ी तादाद में निकलेगी। उस वक़्त तक नहीं बदली गई यह, हमारी जो बंदूक़ थी बहुत अच्छी है, लेकिन ऑटोमैटिक नहीं है और

जैसी अंग्रेज़ी फ़ौज में थी वैसी है। तो यह बातें कहना कि हमने उन्हें ठीक हथियार नहीं दिये, यह बात सही नहीं है। सही बात यह है कि बाज़ बातों में उनके पास ज़्यादा अच्छे हथियार थे जैसे मोर्टर हैं। मोर्टर हमारे पास भी हैं, वो थोड़ी दूर जाते हैं, उनका फेंका हुआ बम, वो फेंकते हैं काफ़ी उसकी दुगनी दूर। अब मोर्टर लीजिये आप, यह एक चीज़ है, हम बनाते हैं उसे छोटा और बड़ा भी बना रहे हैं जो कि अंग्रेज़ी फ़ौज में नहीं है, जो कि अमेरिकन फ़ौज में नहीं है, उनका लड़ने का तरीक़ा दूसरा था, वो हवाई जहाज़ पर ज़्यादा भरोसा करते हैं और कुछ हमारा नक़शा अंग्रेज़ी फ़ौज का पुराना बना है और वो चलता जाता था। तो ख़ैर, हमारे जो कुछ कहिये पुराने नक़्शे पे चलने से या कुछ नातजुर्बेकारी उससे ज़रूर चीनियों को फ़ायदा हुआ, उनके पास बड़े-बड़े मोर्टर थे और कुछ ऑटोमैटिक हथियार थे और, और बातों में कुछ था फ़ायदा।

लेकिन यह सब बातें कमोबेश ज़्यादा नहीं हैं, असल बात जो उनकी है वो यह कि इस क़दर फ़ौज को भेजते हैं, नम्बर में फ़ौजों को भेजते हैं बग़ैर इस बात का लिहाज़ किये कि, कितने मरते हैं। मेरा ख़्याल है उनकी फ़ौज में मरे और घायल हुए कहीं ज़्यादा हैं हमारे से। अब यह भी कितने हुए हमारे, हम कह नहीं सकते, यकायक इसलिए मैंने कहा नहीं और ख़बरें अफ़वाहें फैलीं बहुत, किसी ने कहा आठ हज़ार, दस हज़ार मर गये। तो यह तो हमारी पूरी फ़ौज भी नहीं थी उस जगह, लेकिन जहाँ तक हमें मालूम हुआ है अब तक, अभी तक हम ठीक नहीं कह सकते, ग़ालिबन दो हज़ार से ढाई हज़ार तक हमारी फ़ौजों को नुक़सान हुआ, बहुत सारे लोग जो कि ग़ायब हो गये थे, समझे जाते थे शायद मर गये हों वो वापिस आ गये हैं, तितर-बितर हो गये थे वापिस आये हैं। तो यह हुआ।

अब यह जो चीनियों ने किया वहां, यह, यानी हर नुक़्ते से जो बातें उन्होंने हमसे कहीं थीं, जो इशारे किये थे, वायदे किये थे उसके ख़िलाफ़ हैं और फ़र्ज़ कर लीजिए कि उनका मुक़दमा है कि ज़मीन उनकी थी, हमारी राय में बिल्कुल फ़िज़ूल है, बेमाने है लेकिन फ़र्ज़ कर लीजिये है मुक़दमा, तो यह कौन सा तरीक़ा है कि मुक़दमे को मज़बूत करने के लिए वो बड़ी फ़ौज लेके हमला करें। और तय होते हैं और तय करने के तरीक़े होते हैं इससे बातचीत करें मिलके। कहीं न तय हो तो किसी सालिस को मुक़र्रर करें, कुछ कोई अदालत हो, वर्ल्ड कोर्ट हो, कुछ हो। तो यह बिल्कुल बुनियादी तौर से ग़लत बात है, ख़राब बात है और अजीब हालत है कि वो अपने सब, सब अपने रेडियो में कहते हैं कि हिन्दुस्तान की फ़ौजों ने हमपे हमला किया, हम तो अपने को बचा रहे हैं। बचा कहाँ रहे हैं, हमारी छाती पे बैठके अपने को बचा रहे हैं, हमारे मुल्क में आकर बचा रहे हैं, हमारी ज़मीन पर, अजीब तमाशा है। मैं तो हैरान हो गया किस क़दर ग़लत बातें, झूठी बातें कहते हैं। और यानी अब तक बहुत लड़ाई झगड़े के सवाल रहे, और जगह झगड़ा हुआ लेकिन जिस क़िस्म की बात उन्होंने की इसका अगर आप सोचें कि इस क़िस्म की बात कभी नहीं हुई पहले। थोड़ी सी कोशिश हुई थी होने की तो कामयाब नहीं हुई दो-चार रोज़ में ख़त्म हो गयी वो, यानी पाँच-छः-सात बरस हुए स्विज़ (suez) में फ्रांस ने और इंग्लैंड ने यकायक हमला किया था मिस्र पर। ग़लत बात थी बिल्कुल, और चार-पाँच रोज़ में, हफ़्ते

495

भर में उसको ठंडा करना पड़ा उन्हें, क्योंकि दुनिया उसके ख़िलाफ़ हुई। लेकिन असल में मुक़ाबला कीजिये तो इस क़िस्म की चीज़ें हैं जो इन्होंने बात की है, जो हिटलर ने की थी पिछली लड़ाई के पहले, फ़ौज़ें दौड़ा के उसने कब्ज़ा कर लिया था और फिर लड़ाई हुई थी। फिर भी आपको याद होगा उस लड़ाई का शुरू क्या था, जो कि हमेशा हमलावर को फ़ायदा होता है। उसके सामने शुरू में फ्रांस की बड़ी भारी फौज थी, अंग्रेज़ों की फ़ौज थी जो फ्रांस गयी थी, उसने उनको ढकेल दिया, अंग्रेज़ी फ़ौज को तो बिल्कुल समुद्र तक फेंक दिया, ख़त्म हो गयी, उसने फ़ौज फिर से, दोबारा अंग्रेज़ों ने फ़ौज बनायी और फिर हल्के-हल्के तैयार होके, हमला करके और अमेरिका भी आ गया और बातें भी हुई, रूस भी आ गया, तब हटाया उन्हें। तो यह बात हिटलरशाही की चीन ने की। अपने को कहते हैं हम साम्यवादी मुल्क हैं, समाजवादी, साम्यवादी और अपने को कहते हैं हम साम्राज्यवाद, इम्पीरियलिज्म के ख़िलाफ़ हैं, बिल्कुल वही बातें कीं जो कि इम्पीरियलिस्ट मुल्क करते हैं, हमलावर मुल्क करते हैं। अफ़सोस की बात है और रंज की बात है कि साम्यवाद और समाजवाद की एक, एक चादर ओढ़ के उसके अन्दर ये बातें करते हैं।

ख़ैर, यह बात हुई और यकायक नहीं हुई, जो उन्होंने हमला किया वो इतने बड़े पैमाने पे था कि उसकी तैयारी में महीनों लगे होंगे, हर तरह से और हमसे बात कर रहे थे इस सुलह की और हमला किया। यह बात न क़ानून के मुनासिब है, ना दुनिया के, न शराफ़त के, न किसी बात के और फिर अब कहते जाते हैं कि हिन्दुस्तान ने हमला हम पर किया, हमने ख़ाली अपनी रक्षा की। और अब उसके बाद उन्होंने एक तजवीज़ की और कहा, हम नहीं चाहते कि लड़ाई हो, हम तो अमनपसन्द लोग हैं।

तो तीन बातें हम कहते हैं कि एक तो लड़ाई रुक जाये, दूसरे हम बीस किलोमीटर या क्या, बीस किलोमीटर कोई एक बारह मील हुए, हम बारह मील पीछे हट जायें और तुम भी बारह मील हट जाओ। यानी वो बारह मील पीछे हटें हमारी ज़मीन जिस पर उन्होंने हमला करके कब्ज़ा किया है और हम हटें और भी हट जायें पीछे पर अपनी ज़मीन पर और चुनांचे नतीजा क्या हो कि वो जो असली जगह है, पास, वगैरा के, उस पर क़ाबिज़ रहें और बीच की ज़मीन ख़ाली हो जाये अगर हम भी हटें, मंज़ूर कर लें उनका और उनके लिए आसान है, जब वो चाहें उस पर कब्ज़ा कर लें और आगे आ जायें और उनको मौक़ा मिल जाये और तैयार होने का। यह तो एक अजीब बात है देखने में, यकायक कुछ लोगों ने और मुल्कों में देखा, उन्होंने कहा, वही तो कहते हैं, अच्छी बात कहते हैं—तुम भी हट जाओ वो भी हट जायें, दोनों बराबर के हैं लेकिन बराबर के कहाँ हैं। हमारे मुल्क में आके और इसका नतीजा यह हो लद्दाख़ में और यहाँ हिन्दुस्तान में कि जो-जो जगह हमारी हमने अपने फ़ौजी अड्डे बनाये थे वो सब हट जायें, उन सभों में पीछे हटायें और उनके लिए छोड़ दें चाहे बिलफ़ेल वो ख़ाली रहें लेकिन जब चाहे वो आ सकते हैं और उनका वहाँ रहना एक तरह से हम क़बूल कर लें, मंज़ूर कर लें कि उन्हीं का है। ज़ाहिर है उसको हम मंज़ूर कर नहीं सकते, क्योंकि कोई मुल्क नहीं कर सकता है जिसको ज़रा भी अपनी इज़्ज़त का ख़्याल हो, तो हमने इससे इंकार किया। हमने जो उनसे कहा वो यह कि हम

496

आपसे बात उसी वक़्त करेंगे जब आप पहली बात यह कीजिये कि जो आठ सितम्बर के पहले हालत थी वो पहले हो जानी चाहिए यानी नेफ़ा में भी और लद्दाख़ में भी, यानी जब से यह नया हमला उन्होंने किया, दो महीने हुए वो हटें और हम वहाँ चले जायें, जो पहले हालत थी, हम चले जायें वहां, तुम हट जाओ। यह काफ़ी हमने भी नर्मी की बात कही उनसे। आज हमारे साथी कहते हैं तुम्हें उनसे कहना चाहिए कि बिल्कुल पूरीतौर से लद्दाख़ से हट जायें, हट जायें अच्छा है लेकिन जान के हमने ऐसी बात कही जो कि हमारी राय में मुमकिन हो सकती है, न हो और बात है। क्योंकि इस तरह से हम उन्हें कहें गोया कि बड़ी लड़ाई हम जीत के उनसे हुक्म दे रहे हैं उन्हें, यह बात चलती नहीं है, अक़्ल से काम लेना है। इसलिए हमने एक बात कही जो कि सभी की समझ में आ सकती है और जिसका होना नामुमकिन नहीं है, हालांकि उन्होंने नामंज़ूर कर दिया। वो आठ सितम्बर की लाइन पे यानी नेफ़ा में बिल्कुल उस पार हो जायें हमारी सरहद के और हम पुरानी जगह अपनी आ जायें, और लद्दाख़ में भी जो आगे बढ़े हैं वो आठ सितम्बर के बाद वो हट जायें। यह कोई ऐसी बात कहनी कि जो जिसके माने हों कि उनकी बड़ी ज़िल्लत हो रही है और वो ज़ाहिर है आसान नहीं है उनका मानना। याद रखना है हमें यह कोई शेख़ी की बात नहीं है कि हम शेख़ी से हट जायें हम, जुलूस आप निकालें यहाँ से हटा दें, यह बड़ी सख़्त बात है। इत्ते बड़े मुल्क से लड़ाई लड़ना आख़िर, दुनिया में सबमें बड़ी ज़मीन की फ़ौज चीन की है, अमेरिका और रूस की ताक़त ज़्यादा है क्योंकि उनके पास एटम-बम्ब वग़ैरा हैं लेकिन ज़मीन की फ़ौज चीन की सबमें बड़ी इन सभों से, बड़ा मुल्क है, बड़ी ताक़त है और हम यह समझें कि एक वो हम, हमने उसे हरा लिया यह तो एक फ़िज़ूल बात है। हम उनको रोक सकते हैं, हम उनको पीछे कर सकते हैं और मुझे इत्मीनान है लेकिन वक़्त लगेगा।

तो यह हालत इस वक़्त है और उन्होंने हमें हमारे साथ बहुत बुरा बर्ताव किया है, हमें धोखा दिया। हम उनसे दोस्ती करते गये इसका उन्होंने ग़लत फ़ायदा उठाया और इस तरह से हमपे हमला करके और करते जाते हैं, एक तरफ़ सुलह की बातें करते जाते हैं। हाँ, अब वो रुका हुआ है, हमारी फ़ौजों ने रोक दिया है। लेकिन मालूम नहीं वहाँ फिर ज़ोरों से, लड़ाई थोड़ी बहुत तो होती जा रही है, ज़ोरों से कब छिड़ जाये और यह कोई समझते हैं हम कोई ज़ोरों से रोकेंगे, कहीं रोकें, कहीं न रोकें, अब हमें और सदमें हों, बड़ी लड़ाई है, मैंने आपसे कहा कि यह सारी अंग्रेज़ी फ़ौज की फ़ौज समुद्र में फेंक दी थी हिटलर की फ़ौज ने, सारे फ़्रांस पर क़ब्ज़ा कर लिया था चन्द महीनों के अन्दर शुरू में। बड़े-बड़े मुल्क हैं, आख़िर में हिटलर की फ़ौज और जापान की फ़ौज दोनों बड़े ज़बरदस्त मुल्क हैं, बहादुर मुल्क हैं, फ़ौजें ज़बरदस्त वो हार गयी थीं, बिल्कुल उनको हार माननी पड़ी थी सोलह आने। तो ये बातें कोई शेख़ी की तो हैं नहीं, यह तो काफ़ी जब बड़े मुल्क, बड़ी क़ौमों की मुठभेड़ होती है तो ज़बरदस्त होती है। उस क़ौम को फ़ायदा पहुँचता है जिसने लड़ाई के लिए सारे अपने को तैयार किया है जैसे कि चीन ने किया, शुरू से लड़ाई लड़ी है। चीन एक मुल्क दुनिया में है जो कि कहता है, खुल्लमखुल्ला कहता है कि लड़ाई ज़रूर

होगी, हमसे नहीं दुनिया में लड़ाई ज़रूर होगी, और आप ग़ौर करें कहता है, हाँ एटम-बम्ब वग़ैरा आ गये, बहुत लोग मरेंगे। फ़र्ज़ कर लो हमारे मुल्क में, उनके मुल्क में, चीन में बीस करोड़ आदमी मर गये, बीस करोड़ फिर भी हमारे चालीस करोड़ बाक़ी रहेंगे। यानी एक दिमाग़ अजीब है कि वो इस तरह से कहें कि बीस करोड़ आदमी और मर जाना, बीस-तीस करोड़ एटम-बम्ब से, फिर और जगह भी मरेंगे, हमारे ज़्यादा बाक़ी रहेंगे, यानी इंसान की कोई क़ीमत नहीं है। (हँसी)

तो यह तो हमारे आपके सामने आपका जोश मुबारिक हो आपको और हमें, और जो हिन्दुस्तान में इस ज़माने में हमने तस्वीर भारत की देखी है उससे इंतहा दर्जे हमारे दिल बड़े हैं, दिल ख़ुश हुआ है। क्योंकि जैसा कि कहा आपसे कि अभी एक बयान में कहा गया कि यकायक हमारे सब आपसी बहसें, आपसी झगड़े, माँगें वग़ैरा सब दबा दी गयीं और एक शक्ल भारत की निकली कि सब लोग अलग-अलग दलों के, अलग पार्टीज़ के, अलग-अलग रुतबों के सब लोग तैयार हो गये या हो रहे हैं इसका मुक़ाबला करने, अपने मुल्क की हिफ़ाज़त करने। यह एक अजीब तस्वीर है, हमारे लिए तो है ही, बेहद हमारे ऊपर असर हुआ, दिल मज़बूत हुआ, लेकिन दुनिया भर में इसकी शोहरत हुई, तो हमारी इज़्ज़त बढ़ी, क्योंकि लोग कहा करते हैं दुनिया में हिन्दुस्तान में तो आपस में लड़ा करते हैं, आपस में बड़ी दलबन्दी है, यह है और वो है। और बड़े सवाल हैं, कहीं भाषा पर लड़ते हैं, कहीं कभी फ़िरक़ेवाराना बहस होती है, कम्युनल बातें होती हैं, कभी कुछ, कभी प्रान्तीयता होती है और एकदम से तस्वीर निकली कि सब बातें ग़ायब हो गयीं या दबा दी गयीं या मुलतवी कर दी गयीं और हिन्दुस्तान के सब लोग मिल के एक उन्होंने ये शक्ल दिखाई कि हम अपने हिन्दुस्तान को बचायेंगे। इसी से बहुत बातें ज़ाहिर होती हैं लेकिन ज़ाहिर होता है कि बुनियाद में जो हमारे ऊपरी झगड़े रहते थे एक ऊपरी चीज़ थी, ऊपर की थी और असली चीज़ हममें जो राष्ट्रीयता है, हमारा नेशनलिज़्म है वो मज़बूत है, दिल का है और आज़ादी हमें प्यारी है। हम आज़ादी के लिए, आज़ादी के एवज़ में कुछ नहीं लेने को तैयार हैं और आज़ादी पर जब कोई हमला हो तो हर बात को उसके लिए उसपे न्यौछावर करने को तैयार हैं, बड़ी बातें हैं। (तालियाँ)

आप जानते हैं यहाँ की कम्यूनिस्ट पार्टी ने अभी चन्द रोज़ हुए, आठ-दस रोज़ हुए, कितने दिन हुए एक बयान निकाला। अब कम्यूनिस्ट पार्टी बड़े पेंच में आ पड़ी, क्योंकि उनका रिश्ता रूस से और चीन से ख़ास है, क्योंकि कम्यूनिस्ट वो भी अपने को कहते हैं और यह भी कहते हैं, और इस वजह से कुछ अक्सर हमारी उनकी राय में बहुत फ़र्क़ हो जाता है। वो समाजवाद नीति, हम भी समाजवाद चाहते हैं, हमारे तरीके हैं शान्ति से लाने के उसे, कोई लड़ाई झगड़ा करके नहीं और हम समझते हैं हम ले भी आयेंगे। तो उसमें फिर भी बहुत बातों में नाइत्तिफ़ाक़ी थी, लेकिन बावजूद इन सब बातों के एक उनका ख़ास रिश्ता है। और आप जानते हैं कम्यूनिस्ट जैसे बाज़ बड़े कट्टर मज़हबी होते हैं, वो भी बड़े कट्टर हैं लेकिन बावजूद इसके उनमें भी इस मौक़े पर एक जज़्बात पैदा हुआ, कम से कम ज़्यादातर उन्होंने कि जो बयान उन्होंने लिखा, बयान निकला, वो सोलह

आने एक क़ौमी बयान था, जो बातें हम कहते थे उनको उन्होंने बयान में लिखीं। अब बाज़ लोग कहते हैं कि उनका दिल काला है, वो ज़बानी उन्हों ने कहा है, हो सकता है बाज़ का हो, बाज़ का न हो, लेकिन उनका वो बयान ही निकालना एक अच्छी बात है। (तालियाँ) क्योंकि बहुत सारे उनके, उनके वो नेता हैं उनके जो कुछ दिल काला है, सफ़ेद है, बाद में मालूम होगा, लेकिन आम लोग जो हैं सीधे-साधे बेचारे कम्युनिस्ट पार्टी में हैं जो जिनमें क़ौमियत, राष्ट्रीयता है, नेशनलिज़्म है, एक तरफ़ खींचते हैं उनके लिए, यह बयान निकालने से उनको आसानी हो गयी। उन्होंने देखा किधर जा रहे हैं कि इस वक़्त कम्युनलिज़्म का सवाल नहीं है, हमारे मुल्क में, उनकी निगाह में इस वक़्त हिन्दुस्तान को बचाने का सवाल है। और एक और फ़ायदा हुआ उससे कि उनका बयान निकालने से और जो दुनिया में कम्युनिस्ट पार्टीज़ हैं वो देखेंगे कि जो चीन की तरफ़ से पब्लिसिटी वग़ैरा होती है वो ग़लत है। जब यहाँ कम्युनिस्ट तक चीन के ख़िलाफ़ आवाज़ उठा रहे हैं तो कोई बात चीन ने बहुत ग़लत की है, और मुल्कों के कम्युनिस्ट, यहाँ तक कि चीन के कम्युनिस्ट भी इस पर ग़ौर करेंगे कि हिन्दुस्तान कि कम्युनिस्ट पार्टी जो है उसने ज़ोरों की आवाज़ निकाली तो कुछ न कुछ हमसे ग़लती हुई। तो अच्छा हुआ, मैं नहीं कहता कि वो और क्या करें, क्या न करें, कित्ते लोग इसको मानते हैं या हमारे हिन्दुस्तान में जो ज़ोरों की हवा पड़ी क़ौमियत की उसके दबाव से उन्होंने कर दिया, डर में आके। कुछ लोग उनमें हैं जिन्होंने इसको मंज़ूर नहीं किया था लेकिन ज़्यादातर लोगों ने किया जो उनकी तरफ़ से बयानात हुए हैं पार्लियामेंट में, लोकसभा में, राज्यसभा में वो काफ़ी साफ़ हुए हैं, काफ़ी ज़ोरों के हुए हैं चीन के ख़िलाफ़। यहाँ तक, ऐसी बात तक, उन्होंने स्वीकार की बयानों में जो कि आमतौर से उनके गले नहीं उतरती कि हम अमेरिका से, इंग्लैंड से हथियार लें, ले रहे हैं हम, तेज़ी से लड़ने को चीन से। यह तक उन्होंने मंज़ूर किया।

इससे ज़ाहिर होता है कि हिन्दुस्तान की हवा क्या है, कोई उसके ख़िलाफ़ इस वक़्त उठ नहीं सकता और हिन्दुस्तान का दिल कित्ता मज़बूत है इस मामले में, अच्छी बातें हैं और मैं चाहता हूँ, मुझे रंज हुआ कि दिल्ली में कुछ मुज़ाहिरे हुए, कुछ डिमांस्ट्रेशन हुए, यहाँ के कम्युनिस्ट पार्टी के दफ़्तर के ख़िलाफ़, और क्या कुछ दुकानें दो-चार चीनियों की थीं उनके ख़िलाफ़ और ऐसे ही हुए कुछ। यह अच्छी बात नहीं होगी, यों भी अच्छी नहीं है क्योंकि शान के ख़िलाफ़ बात है हमारे, हाँ शान के ख़िलाफ़ है और उससे कुछ नुकसान होता है हमारा भी। हमें, काफ़ी बड़ा मुक़ाबला है, उसको पूरी ताक़त से करना है और बच्चों की तरह से हम यह बातें करें, समझें कि हमने बहादुरी दिखायी तो हमारी ताक़त कम होती है, बहादुरी की निशानी नहीं है, बहादुरी अंदाज़ ज़रा ज़बरदस्त होने वाले हैं हमारे और आपके और सभों के और यह हम समझें कि इससे काम चल जायेगा तो यह ग़लतफ़हमी है।

बात यह है हमें कोई तजुर्बा है नहीं असल लड़ाई का, जैसे यूरोप के मुल्कों को है। वो दो बड़ी-बड़ी लड़ाइयों में गये और, और कोई घराना नहीं है फ्रांस में या इंग्लैंड में, या जर्मनी में या जापान में या रूस में कोई ख़ानदान, परिवार नहीं है जहाँ के लोग मरे नहीं

हैं, जिसने मुसीबत नहीं झेली है, कोई दूर की लड़ाई नहीं है कि जवान लोग लड़ रहे हैं, हम यहाँ से ताली पीट रहे हैं। आजकल की लड़ाईयाँ ऐसी होती हैं जब बढ़ती हैं कि वो हरेक इंसान पे, पड़ती हैं, वो तजुर्बा हमें नहीं है, शायद हो मालूम नहीं, लेकिन इसलिए हमें पूरी समझ नहीं क्या चीज़ है लड़ाई। जवानों को भेजना ठीक है, भेजने ही पड़ते हैं हमारे सिपाहियों को, लेकिन यह हमारा समझना यह कुछ ताली पीट-पीट के और जुलूस निकाल के काम चल जायेगा यह ठीक नहीं है। आजकल की लड़ाई फ़ौजी लोग लड़ते हैं, हवाई जहाज़ वाले लड़ते हैं, समुद्री जहाज़ वाले लड़ते हैं, लेकिन आजकल हरेक किसान, हरेक काम करने वाला दफ़्तर में, कारख़ाने में, वो समझिये लड़ाई के मैदान में काम कर रहा है क्योंकि जो लड़ाई के मैदान में है सिपाही, वो मौत का सामना करते हैं लेकिन वो जभी कर सकते हैं जब किसान ठीक काम करे, कारख़ाने वाला काम करे, दफ़्तर में काम करे। क्योंकि यहाँ से जो काम करके तैयार करते हैं, उनको भेजते हैं तब तो वो लड़ सकते हैं। खाना पूरा पहुँचे, कारख़ाने में हथियार बनें, और सामान बने, उनके लिए दफ़्तर में काम हो, इन सब बातों को ठीकतौर से चलाने का यानी आजकल की लड़ाई में हरेक आदमी सिपाही है, आदमी और औरत, चाहे जो काम करता हो अपना-अपना। आप लोग जो कि गवर्नमेंट के कर्मचारी हैं ज़ाहिर है एक बड़ा ज़िम्मेदारी का काम करना पड़ता है, ये सब बातें जो होती हैं चाहे आप गवर्नमेंट के कर्मचारी हों, चाहे आप गवर्नमेंट के कारख़ानों में काम करें या दफ़्तरों में, ज़रूरी काम है लड़ाई का इंतज़ाम करना, लड़ाई का सामान पैदा करना।

यानी, इस वक़्त यह सवाल उठा, कि हमारा पंचवर्षीय योजना है उसको हम चलायें कि न चलायें, लड़ाई की वजह से, ज़ोरों से लड़ें और और बातों में इत्ता रुपया या ताक़त क्यों ख़र्च करें, इस सवाल को उठाना भी एक ग़लतफ़हमी की बात है। हम क्यों पंचवर्षीय योजना वग़ैरा रखते थे। इसलिए कि मुल्क ताक़तवर हो, मुल्क की हालत बेहतर हो, ख़ुशहाली हो, लोगों की ग़रीबी दूर हो वग़ैरा-वग़ैरा। हमने हिसाब लगाया कि यह सब तरीक़ा एक ही तरह से हो सकता है कि हम अपने मुल्क को नयी दुनिया में लायें, नयी दुनिया कारख़ानों की, और जगहों की, नयी दुनिया विज्ञान की, साइंस की, जिसमें आकर इंग्लेंड, जर्मनी, रूस वग़ैरा आगे बढ़े, और कोई ज़रिया नहीं है, कोई हम कोई रेज़ोल्यूशन पास करके अपनी ग़रीबी को दूर तो नहीं करते, हम दौलत पैदा करते हैं। तो पंचवर्षीय योजना वग़ैरा इसीलिए थी। दौलत कैसे पैदा हो? हमें उसमें बहुत बातें करनी हैं, महज़ कारख़ाना चला देना नहीं है, हमें लोगों को पढ़ाना है, लोगों को सिखाना है विज्ञान, टेक्नीकल बातें सिखानी हैं, तो पढ़ाई हो, सभों की पढ़ाई, आम पढ़ाई हो। कुछ तो आम पढ़ाई हो प्राइमरी, सैकेन्डरी हरेक आदमी, लड़के और लड़की की और ख़ास पढ़ाई हो कारख़ाने चलाने की, विज्ञान के काम करने की, यह तो बुनियाद है और फिर कारख़ाने बढ़ें, इंडस्ट्रियलाइज़ करें। इस तरह से मुल्क की ताक़त बनती है, वक़्त लगता है। इसी काम में हम लगे थे और लड़ाई के लिए भी यही चीज़ ज़रूरी है। लड़ाई लड़ने में हमें ज़रूरी है कि हमारे खेती अच्छी हो, हमारे कारख़ाने ठीक चलें, हमारी पढ़ाई अच्छी हो। इसके बग़ैर लड़ाई लड़ना, आजकल तो

सिपाही को भी पढ़ा-लिखा होना है, पुरानी लड़ाइयाँ लड़ी गयीं, जो हथियार आजकल हैं उसमें सीखना-पढ़ना-लिखना है। इसलिए बहुत ज़रूरी इसलिए कहते हैं सारे क़ौम को, मुल्क को मोबिलाइज़ करना, मैन पावर को। और ख़ासकर आप लोग जैसे के आपके बयान में कहा गया आप लोग यह बड़ी कल जो है यह गवर्नमेंट, एक ज़बरदस्त उसके पुर्ज़े हैं, हम सब पुर्ज़े हैं, मैं और आप हैं। अगर पुर्ज़े ठीक नहीं हों तो कल कैसे चले और कल ठीक न चले तो फिर लड़ाई कैसे हो, ये सब बातें मिलीजुली हैं। हमारे सामने मैंने शुरू में कहा था एक नया वर्क़ हिन्दुस्तान के इतिहास का खुल रहा है, कहाँ ले जाये यह हम नहीं कह सकते, लेकिन हमें पूरी कोशिश करनी है और मेरा ख़्याल है कि हमारी कोशिशें कामयाब होंगी। कि वो हिन्दुस्तान को बड़ी तकलीफ़ें उठानी पड़ेंगी लेकिन हम कामयाब होंगे और ख़ाली कामयाब नहीं एक बेहतर हिन्दुस्तान उसके बाद निकलेगा। (तालियाँ)

तो आपने एक प्रतिज्ञा ली है, उसको मैंने सुना और मुनासिब प्रतिज्ञा है जो आपने ली है क्योंकि हमारी ख़ुद्दारी को तलब करती है, ऐसे ही हमारे मुल्क की आज़ादी तलब करती है दुश्मन को हटाना वग़ैरा और उसके लिए हमें पूरी ताक़त से काम करना है जहाँ-जहाँ हम ताक़त का काम करते हैं। सवाल हमारे सामने यह है कि कोई हमारी ताक़त ज़ाया न हो किसी बात से, हमारा कारख़ाना हिन्दुस्तान का चले चाहे खेती का, चाहे कारख़ानों का, चाहे दफ़्तरों का, फ़ौज का, उसका इंतज़ाम पूरा हो, हल्के-हल्के यह हो रहा है। और हिन्दुस्तान एक अमनपसन्द मुल्क, उसमें फ़ौज अच्छी है हमारी, लेकिन हमारा दिमाग़ हम कित्ता ही गुल मचायें, लड़ाई का दिमाग़ नहीं रहा है, न था और आजकल की लड़ाई का नहीं है, होगा वो हल्के-हल्के। मुझे एक बात की फ़िक्र है और वो हो जायेगा, हम ज़ोरों से लड़ेंगे। मुझे एक बात की फ़िक्र है कि लड़ाई का बड़ा बुरा असर होता है क़ौम पर, इंसानों पर, वो इंसानों को बेरहम कर देती है, इंसानों में मोहब्बत का जज़्बा कम होता है, अदावत का, दुश्मनी का बहुत हो जाता है और चुनांचे इंसान गिर जाता है। और मुझे इस बात का रंज है वो गिर गया हो तो, मुश्किल बात है। रंज हो कि हमारे सबक़ जो गांधीजी ने सिखाये अगर वो हम भूल जायें, उन्होंने हमें ट्रेंड किया, वो सब पानी की तरह से निकल जायें और हममें जो लड़ाई से वहशियाना बातें आती हैं वो आ जायें। मैं नहीं चाहता हूँ कि क्योंकि मुझे ग़रूर है हिन्दुस्तान में, हिन्दुस्तान की संस्कृति में, इसके माने नहीं हैं हिन्दुस्तान कमज़ोर हो, लड़ाई के लिए लड़ें हम ज़ोरों से, लेकिन इसके माने नहीं हैं हम वहशी हो जायें। हम कुछ याद रखें गांधीजी को जो आजकल जैसे गांधीजी के एक असली नुमाइन्दा है हिन्दुस्तान में वो आचार्य विनोबा भावे हैं। उनकी हर बात मैं नहीं स्वीकार करता, लेकिन, लेकिन उनकी मैं बहुत क़दर करता हूँ, बहुत बातें उनकी बहुत दर्जे की हैं। तो इस तरह से हमें अपने को तैयार करना है, अपनी ज़मीन नहीं छोड़ देनी है, अपनी संस्कृति नहीं छोड़ देनी है, मज़बूत रहना है, और त्याग करना है, हिम्मत से करना है सब बातें, लेकिन फिर भी अपनी-अपनी जगह पर रहके। यह हमें करना है और आप लोग जो काम करते हैं उसको भी अच्छी तरह से करें। आपने ख़ुद इक़रार किया है, उसके अच्छे करने ही से आप लड़ाई की मदद करते हैं।

अब हमारी कुछ बुनियादी बातें हैं जो आप भी जानते होंगे, एक तो वही थी दुनिया में अमन रहे हमारे मुल्क में, हमने कहा समाजवाद हो, हमने कहा कि हम दुनिया में सब मुल्कों से दोस्ती करेंगे, किसी फ़ौजी गिरोह में नहीं शरीक होंगे, नॉन-एलाइन्मेंट (Non Alignment) जिसको अंग्रेज़ी में कहते हैं। फ़ौजी गिरोह हैं, दो बड़े गिरोह, एक अमेरिका अंग्रेज़ों वग़ैरा का, एक रूस वग़ैरा का। हमने कहा हम फ़ौजी समझौता, एलाइन्स नहीं करेंगे किसी से, हम नॉन-एलाइन्स, हम दोस्ती सभों से करेंगे। हमने कोशिश की है यह करने की और कामयाबी भी हुई बहुत दर्जे। हमारी दोस्ती अमेरिका से है, इंग्लैंड से है, और मुल्कों से है और उधर के पश्चिमी मुल्कों से, हमारी दोस्ती सोवियत रूस से है और हम पूरी कोशिश करेंगे रखने की, हम इस नीति को, नॉन-एलाइन्मेंट को नहीं छोड़ेंगे। हम अपने मुसीबत के वक़्त मदद लेंगे हरेक जो दें, कोई मुल्क दें, हम लेंगे मदद, लाचार हैं, हमारे ऊपर जो हमला हुआ, हम हथियार वग़ैरा लेंगे, और सामान लेंगे जहाँ से भी मिलेगा, हम ले रहे हैं और हम मशकूर हैं उन-उन मुल्कों के जो दे रहे हैं।

इसके माने नहीं हैं कि हम एक गिरोह में हो गये, इसके माने नहीं हैं कि फ़र्ज़ कीजिये कि हम रूस से हमारी दोस्ती कुछ हम कम करना चाहते हैं। हम जानते हैं कि रूस इसमें, पेंच में पड़ा है क्योंकि रूस का पुराना समझौता है चीन से, वो उनका ऐलाइ (ally) है। हालांकि उसके बाद बहुत नाइत्तिफ़ाक़ी हुई है उन दोनों में और वो आपस में एक-दूसरे को बुरा-भला भी कहते हैं, ये सब बातें हैं, बहुत पसंद नहीं करते, बहुत मोहब्बत नहीं है लेकिन फिर भी ऐलाइ हैं एक-दूसरे के, बावजूद इसके उन्होंने हमारे साथ दोस्ती की, रूस ने, हमने पसन्द किया, उन्होंने हमारी मदद भी पिछले ज़माने में की है बनाने में कई बड़े-बड़े कारख़ाने। कुछ दिन हुए आपको याद होगा हमने कुछ हवाई जहाज़ उनसे लेने का तय किया था, निश्चय हुआ और वो लेने का वक़्त अभी आया नहीं, दिसम्बर में और मुझे पूरा यक़ीन है, वो कहते हैं हम देंगे आपको पूरा करेंगे, शायद और भी चीज़ें दें। तो यह माने नहीं हैं, मैं इसमें नहीं पड़ना चाहता कि कोई धोखे में हो, कि हम कोई अपनी पुरानी नीति नॉन-एलाइन्मेंट को छोड़ रहे हैं और हम किसी फ़ौजी समझौते में और गिरोह में पड़ जाते हैं। हाँ, कुछ वाक़ियात का दवाब है इसलिए हम हथियार वग़ैरा लेते हैं और लेंगे जहाँ हमें मिलेंगे, क्योंकि लड़ना है हमें, अपने मुल्क को बचाना है, अव्वल बात वो है।

लेकिन हम कोशिश करेंगे पूरीतौर से जो हमारी बुनियादी नीति है उसको क़ायम रखें और जो मदद दे सकता है दे और एक तरफ़ से जितनी हमारी ताक़त है हम उसको इस्तेमाल करें, करना ही है, और कोई चारा नहीं। और उसी के साथ हम अपने बुनियादी उसूलों को भूल न जायें, गांधीजी को भूल न जायें, हालांकि गांधीजी कोई लड़ाई के मामले में बहुत सलाह देने वाले नहीं थे कि कैसे लड़ें। लेकिन यह भी याद रखिये आप काश्मीर पे हमला पाकिस्तान से हुआ था, उनको बहुत रंज हुआ, दुख हुआ, लेकिन हमने तय किया कि हम फ़ौजें भेजें काश्मीर में। मुझे याद है मैं परेशान था तो उनके पास गया दो-तीन महीने के बाद उन बेचारे की हत्या हो गयी और मैंने उनसे कहा तो उन्होंने कहा कि मैं इन बातों में तुम्हें क्या सलाह दूँ, मैं तो जानता नहीं ऐसा लड़ाई का तरीक़ा, मेरे और तरीक़े हैं, लेकिन

काश्मीर पर हमला हुआ है, उसका मुक़ाबला करना है। (तालियाँ) गांधीजी ने कहा था और क़रीब यही बात इन्हीं अल्फ़ाज़ में विनोबा भावे जी ने कही। (तालियाँ) उन्होंने कहा कि मैं, मैं न लड़ना जानता हूँ, न किसी को बता सकता हूँ कि, कैसे हथियारबन्द लड़ाई लड़ें, मैं शान्ति का आदमी हूँ लेकिन इसमें कोई शक नहीं कि चीन ने हमला किया, चीन सेना ने एग्रेशन किया, इनवेड किया है हिन्दुस्तान को और उसका मुक़ाबला करना चाहिए। तो यह बात है, बात बिल्कुल साफ़ है, इसमें कोई धोखे की गुंजाइश नहीं और इसीलिए मुझे ख़ुशी है कि इस बात को कम्यूनिस्ट पार्टी के लोग भी समझ गये बावजूद इत्ते पुराने रिश्ते के। आख़िर वो भी हिन्दुस्तानी हैं और हिन्दुस्तानियत ज़्यादा सामने आयी। तो यह कि हम इसकी लड़ाई को समझें। यह एक कम्युनिज़्म के ख़िलाफ़ लड़ाई वग़ैरा है, यह बात अव्वल तो है नहीं और ग़लत होगी और नुकसानदेह होगी। हम जो चाहते हैं अपने मुल्क में करें, हमारा उसूल है, हम अपने मुल्क में जैसा चाहते हैं करेंगे, जैसा समाज बनाना चाहते हैं वैसे हम रखेंगे, हम दूसरे मुल्क के दबाव से नहीं कुछ करेंगे और दूसरे मुल्क जैसा चाहें वो रखें, हमें अदावत नहीं कोई उससे।

तो यह लड़ाई है हमारी और चीन की हुकूमत से, जिसने हमारे मुल्क पर हमला किया और जो कि एक बिल्कुल एक साम्राज्यवादी हमला है, साम्राज्य अपना बढ़ाना चाहते हैं इसलिए हमारी लड़ाई है और कोई दख़ल दे हमारी नीति वग़ैरा में तो हम उसके दबाव डालने में, उसमें नहीं आयेंगे। इस तरह से हमें देखना है और अपनी क़ौम को मिलाके चलना है। अच्छा है, ख़ुशी है मुझे कि इसमें फ़िरक़ेवाराना बातें, हिन्दू-मुसलमान-सिक्ख यह हट गयीं, भाषा की, प्रान्तीयता सब दब गयीं। लेकिन एक, एक इस माने में हमारा फ़ायदा, जो एकता पैदा हो हमारे में, उसी एकता से हम इस मुल्क को बनायेंगे और ज़बरदस्त और मज़बूत और जो हमला करता है उसका मुक़ाबला करेंगे। आज नहीं, कल नहीं, अगर सालों लगे तो सालों तक करेंगे। (तालियाँ)

तो आपको शुक्रिया जो आपने अपने बयान में कहा और जो आप कर रहे हैं, जो आपने प्रतिज्ञा ली, उसके लिए आपको मुबारकबाद।

जयहिन्द!

[Translation begins:

Mr Chairman[172], Sisters, Brothers, and Comrades,
I have often had the opportunity of speaking here and whenever I have done so, I have laid stress on peace in the world and India. We are in an age when a nuclear war can destroy the whole world. Our policy has been aimed at establishing peace in the world and disarmament. We have tried to maintain friendship with all the nations and succeeded to a very large extent. It is a strange quirk of fate that we who have always worked for peace in the world are now

172. See note 171 in this section.

engaged in war. A new chapter is beginning in the history of India. How it ends remains to be seen. It is strange that China with whom we have always made an effort to maintain friendship ever since their revolutionary government came to power twelve years ago, should now be attacking us. We were among the first nations to recognise them and sponsor their entry into the United Nations and to generally cooperate with them. Their hostility started five years ago in Ladakh. We have had a great deal of correspondence and some talks with them. There have been some incidents in which about 20 soldiers were killed. But our effort has been to see to it that the situation did not escalate to war. Talks were going on to find a peaceful solution to the problem. Our proposal was that our ambassadors should first meet and talk in order to create the climate in which our talks could succeed. It was our view that before we discussed the real issues, a climate should be created and that was possible only when they left the territory which they had occupied illegally.

Well, all these talks were going on. Last August we had sent them a note to which they replied. We wrote again and suddenly on the 8th of September, they marched into our frontier province of NEFA. They had never come so close before. That area has been regarded as our borders in the Himalayas for a long, long time and it had not been considered necessary to put up any signs. The river waters which flow down from the heights of the Himalayas and on the Indian side are considered to belong to us. For hundreds of years, in spite of great ups and downs and change of dynasties, this had been regarded as our border on the Tibetan side. Then, about fifty years ago, there was a dispute over this demarcation during British rule in India. India, China and Tibet were represented in these talks. Tibet's status then was that of an autonomous country under the suzerainty of China. It enjoyed internal independence. Therefore representatives from Tibet were present at that conference. This in itself shows that Tibet enjoyed independent rights. Certain agreements were reached in that conference more than fifty years ago and what came to be known as the McMahon Line was accepted as the boundary demarcated between the two countries, after the British representative, McMahon. The boundary itself was not a new one. It merely demarked the boundary which had been traditionally accepted. So, the British did not suggest anything new but merely clarified something which had always been accepted. The three countries signed the agreement but later on the then Chinese Government repudiated it, their refusal was not because of the boundary demarcation between India and Tibet but something else. Their objection was to the other half of the agreement which talked about an outer Tibet and an inner Tibet. But it is true that the Chinese government at that time did not accept the agreement.

However, in spite of that, the agreement between India and Tibet was accepted and implemented for the last fifty years. When India became independent, we were concerned that there should be uniform development all over the country. The NEFA area had been completely neglected during the British rule. They were not concerned with the remote border regions and made no other administrative arrangements except to occasionally send some troops to maintain law and order whenever there was a dispute. Anyhow we wanted to build schools and hospitals and roads in that area. So the process of development began and it goes on. This is the history of that area.

When the Communists came to power in China, they did not bring up this subject. But we found that in their maps, a very large area of Indian territory in Ladakh and NEFA was shown as being part of Chinese territory. We were surprised and so we pointed out over and over again that their maps were wrong. They replied that their maps were very old, belonging to the Chiang Kai-shek regime and that they had not had the opportunity of revising them. They said they would discuss the matter at a more opportune moment and find a peaceful solution. Well, we accepted it the first time. When we pressed the issue a second time, we could not understand why they had not found the time to think about it. On the third occasion, I mentioned the matter myself to Prime Minister Chou En-lai when we met. His reply was once again that they were old maps and that they would examine them and then settle the matter amicably with us.

We accepted it or rather, we were forced by circumstances to do so. As you know, there was a revolt against the Chinese Government in Tibet. Our sympathies lay with Tibet. But we did not interfere in any way. However, the Chinese Government seemed to mistakenly believe that we had incited the people of Tibet to revolt against them. That was absolutely absurd. We were friendly towards the Chinese and in any case, we lacked the resources to be able to incite a revolt in Tibet. But the Chinese insisted that the Indians sitting in Kalimpong and Darjeeling were aiding and abetting the people of Tibet. I cannot understand how any thinking individual can accept such a foolish thing. I am merely trying to point out how their attitude changed. As you know, after the revolt in Tibet, the Dalai Lama with 35-40,000 of his followers sought asylum in India. We allowed them to come and promised to look after them. But at the same time, we warned them that we did not want them to make India a base for their political activities in Tibet. Dalai Lama accepted our condition. We have helped the Tibetans to settle down in India. Many small Tibetan settlements have come up and we are making arrangements for the education of their children.

In spite of all this, the Chinese government had repeatedly hinted in the past that though they considered the McMahon Line to be illegal, they will accept it because there was friendship between India and China. So, we were somewhat reassured that they would not launch an attack, though we were not fully convinced. We felt that whatever they may do in Ladakh, they will not come down into the plains. Even so, we had posted 25 or 30 of our units in the border areas. It is obvious that they were not very large units. Most of them consisted of fifty or hundred jawans. They were not equipped to fight a major war but were there more for patrolling. In any case, no one could get past them without fighting. It is for this reason that no intrusion had taken place in all these years though the Chinese had advanced a great deal in Ladakh. I am telling you what has happened so far.

On the 8th of September, the Chinese troops began to come down from the Pass into the plains and surrounded our military posts. Then they retreated a little. There was an exchange of artillery but it was nothing much. We thought that it would not be proper to let them remain and that they should be thrown out. So we sent in more troops. But you must bear in mind the fact that this area lies high in the mountains, 14,000 feet above sea level. If you go there directly from Delhi, you will find it difficult even to breathe, apart from the extreme cold. Anyhow, we sent in our troops, strengthened our existing check posts and established new ones. All these things took some time. I was in Europe, in England, then. I came back at the beginning of October—on the first. We had hoped that our preparations would be complete by then and that we could make an attempt to throw them out. But when we found that their preparations were even more advanced than ours and their task was easier because beyond the mountains on their side of the border lay the plateau of Tibet at a height of 12,000 feet. The Chinese had built roads there which was easy for them because in the intense cold, it was not necessary for them to use much cement, etc. All they had to do was to level the ground. Moreover, it seems that the Chinese are experts at building roads. They employed thousands of Tibetans to clear the ground. So, it was very [easy] for the Chinese to move their huge army to our borders. After that all that they had to do was to climb a little and get down into India. It was very easy for them to transport food and equipment by lorries. Our difficulty was that though we had been building roads, they did not reach right up into the mountains. It had taken us years to build hundreds of miles of road. The troops had to be transported by planes and helicopters. Every single thing had to be transported by aeroplane which was an extremely difficult task. So, it was not easy to send a large number of troops. Anyhow, we did our best. Then when I came back on the 1st of October, I came to know that the troops on both sides had advanced. They had an edge over our forces though we did not know exactly how much. But we thought that we must make an effort to push them back and we gave the orders accordingly.

Suddenly on the 20th of October, the Chinese launched a massive attack. Their troops outnumbered ours six, seven or ten times. They came down in large numbers and mounted surprise attacks, uncaring about how many were killed. Their troops kept on coming, wave after wave, and Indian troops were hopelessly outnumbered. So, they were routed and retreated in great disarray. This happened on the 20th of October which was a great shock to us. Since then the Chinese troops have been advancing steadily and captured some small towns in NEFA. In the meanwhile, our forces have regrouped themselves and are holding on to their positions. They have been able to check the advance of the Chinese troops though more and more of them are pouring into the plains. As I said it is easy for them to do. Moreover, their troops have got acclimatised to the difficult conditions and height. Tibet lies at a height of 12,000 feet. Our troops have gone up from the plains and though they are strong and well-trained, the sudden change makes them breathless. Their vitality is lowered until they get acclimatised. It takes a few weeks to get acclimatised.

So, we have suffered shocks and we realised that this was a full-scale attack on India and not a small border skirmish as it had been in Ladakh. This was a proper attack and then the entire complexion changed. We were faced with the reality that India and China were at war, though they had been no declaration to that effect. Anyhow we have to be fully prepared in every way to meet this aggression.

Subhadraji[173] said just now that all kinds of strange rumours are floating around that our troops were not properly clad and that they had to fight without shoes or equipment. This is absolutely wrong. The fact is that the troops which were sent up had been issued warm coats and blankets, etc. Each jawan had been given three thick, warm blankets. But they could carry only one each as there was a problem of weight when the troops were transported by aeroplanes. The other blankets were sent later. Unfortunately, the problem that arose was that the transport planes could not land in that difficult terrain, with the result that the food-stuff and blankets, etc., were air-dropped. In many cases, the bundles fell into the rivers and it was difficult to search for them. So, there was a problem. In any case the weather had not turned cold in September. But we had to keep sending things and had to suffer losses. So it is not true to say that the troops were not properly clad. Initially some of the shipments which were air-dropped got lost. By now, each one of them has four thick blankets apiece.

Apart from that, we have learnt one thing from the Chinese. Their troops do not wear grand uniforms, nor are their rations very elaborate. We send

173. Subhadra Joshi (1919-2003). Chairman, Sampradayikta Virodhi Committee, an anti-communal political platform.

food for our troops. The Chinese troops carry their ration of rice and tea in their knapsacks. They boil the rice and make tea. We have been facing great difficulties in supplying complicated dishes. We are making some changes in their rations and trying to supply a new diet which is satisfying though limited in quantity. There are many simple substitutes like sweets made with jaggery which gives energy. Then there is sattu made out of flour which the common man in India eats. The troops can carry these things easily in their pockets.

So, we have been making all these arrangements. We are copying the Chinese style of clothing too, thick quilted coats and trousers like pyjamas which may not look very elegant but keep them extremely warm. In the beginning, our officers used to make fun of the Chinese saying that they looked like monkeys. But these garments are extremely practical. So we too had these quilted coats made. It took just a few days and we are supplying them to our jawans. All these arrangements are under way.

It is true that at the time of the attack on the 20th-21st of October, we were not fully prepared. The advantage always lies with the side which attacks because it can choose the time and the place. Those who are on the defensive are at a disadvantage. The Chinese attacked at a spot where our troops were not in a large number, with a force of twenty or thirty thousand men, well-armed and used to living at high altitudes and braving cold winters. No force could have withstood such an onslaught.

Then take the question of weapons. It is obvious that our men had all the weapons and equipment of the ordinary armed forces. We have been trying to switch over to automatic weapons which are fairly new even in the West. We did not want to import them at high cost. So we decided to become self-reliant and produce them here. The process was started two or three years ago and the blue-print is being drawn up for it. There has been a great argument about it with some people saying that we should import the weapons and others saying we should produce them here. Ultimately it was decided to set up a factory and the arrangements were completed. We have gone into production and I think within a month or so, we will be producing these weapons in large numbers. Our guns are very good but they are not automatic. But it is not correct to say that our soldiers were not given weapons to fight with. The fact is that in some things, their weaponry is superior and the trajectory of their guns is longer. We also have motors but theirs are superior. We are producing them in the country. The British and Americans rely more on their air force and our armed forces have been modelled on the British system which has continued until now. Anyhow, you can say that our somewhat outmoded system of defence and inexperience did benefit the Chinese who possess huge motors and automatic guns, etc.

However, these are not of great importance. The fact is that the Chinese troops outnumber ours many times over. They keep sending them in wave after wave, without bothering as to how many are killed. I think the dead and the wounded on their side are far more than on our side. We do not have the exact figures of our casualties though rumours abound. One rumour has it that eight or ten thousand people were killed when our total number of troops stationed there did not number that many. But as far as we know, I think our casualties have been between two thousand and two thousand five hundred. Many soldiers who were reported missing have come back.

The Chinese action has been against all the assurances, promises and hints that they had given us in the past. For instance, even if they had a case about the disputed territory, though we think that is meaningless, it does not warrant a full-scale attack on our territory. This is no way of settling a dispute. We should have talked this over and tried to find a solution by going to the World Court or whatever it is. It is fundamentally wrong and extremely dangerous to resort to such methods. It is strange that in their radio broadcasts, they are saying that it is India who attacked China and that they are fighting in defence. It is really strange that they should be fighting in defence. It is really strange that they should be fighting a war of defence on our territory. I am amazed at the lies that the Chinese are telling. Many wars have been fought in the past between various countries. But it is very rarely that the kind of action that the Chinese have resorted to has been known before. An attempt was made during the Suez crisis but it did not succeed. England and France launched a sudden attack on Egypt. It was absolutely wrong and they had to declare ceasefire within a week because world opinion was against them. But in fact, the Chinese action can only be compared to what Hitler had done before the beginning of the Second World War. His forces had overrun a large part of Europe. It was once again the same the same old story of the side which attacks having the advantage. Hitler's forces faced the French and the British army and soon pushed them back. The British forces were completely destroyed. They had to rebuild their forces once again. But they gradually prepared and rearmed themselves and the United States also joined the war. Then the Soviet Union joined in too and ultimately Hitler was defeated. China has behaved as Hitler did. They claim to be a communist country and anti-imperialistic and yet they are doing exactly the same thing as an imperialist nation would. It is indeed strange that China sh ould do things like this under the cloak of communism.

The Chinese attack was not sudden. They must have spent months preparing for it. They kept talking to us about a peaceful agreement and suddenly launched this attack. It was neither a legally permissible action nor civilised behaviour.

Now they are accusing us of attacking them. They have even made a proposal that they are a peace-loving people and do not wish to continue fighting.

They have three conditions. One, there should be a cease fire. Two, both sides should withdraw to a distance of twenty kilometers, that is twelve miles, that would mean that they would vacate the territory they had occupied and by withdrawing twelve miles into our own territory we would in effect leave the Chinese in occupation of the Pass. The territory in between will be no man's land which they can occupy at will. It would give them an opportunity to prepare themselves. Strangely enough, many countries are supporting the Chinese proposal and suggesting that both sides should withdraw an equal distance. But it is not equal. The result will be that we will be vacating all our military outposts in Ladakh so that they can claim that area as their own. In a sense, we would be acquiescing in the Chinese occupation of our territory. It is obvious that we cannot accept this just as no country with the slightest self-respect would. So we refused.

We told the Chinese that we will agree to talks with them only after they vacate the territory occupied by them since the 8th of September in NEFA and in Ladakh. We said this in extremely moderate tones. Now our colleagues say that we should have told them to get out of Ladakh altogether. It would be a good thing if they did. But we deliberately said this because we felt it was possible. After all, we cannot talk to them as if we have won a great battle and are ordering them to move out. We must be sensible about it. So we made a proposal which anybody could see was entirely feasible, though the Chinese have refused to withdraw to the position before the 8th of September in NEFA and Ladakh. It is obvious that they are not going to agree to anything easily. We must remember that we cannot achieve anything by bravado. You cannot throw them out by taking out a procession. This is a very serious matter. We are at war with a very great power. China has the largest infantry in the world. The superpowers may have nuclear weapons. But China has the largest forces on land. It is a very great power and it is absurd to think that we have defeated them. I am convinced that we can stop them and throw them back. But it will take time.

So, this is the situation at the moment. The Chinese have behaved very badly and betrayed our trust. We were friendly and they took undue advantage of it. They have committed aggression while all the time talking about a peaceful solution. Our forces have been able to stop them. But there are minor skirmishes in that area and nobody knows when it may escalate to a large-scale battle. We may have to suffer greater reverses. As I told you, Hitler's forces had backed the entire British army into the sea and overrun the whole of France in a matter of a few months. Ultimately Germany and Japan, both great powers with large armies were completely defeated.

Anyhow, this is no mere boast. Wars often taken place between large nations. The country which is fully prepared as China was, has the advantage. China is one country in the world which says quite openly that there will be another world war. They are fully aware that a nuclear war can kill millions. But their argument is that even if twenty crores of people were killed in China, they will still have another forty crores living. What I mean is that their entire thinking is very strange that they can accept 20-30 crores of people being killed. They feel that large numbers of people will die elsewhere too and they will still come out on top. They do not value human life. [Laughter].

Anyhow, I want to congratulate you on your enthusiasm. The picture of India that has emerged in the last few days is extremely heart-warming. As someone pointed out in his statement just now, suddenly we have put all our personal quarrels and demands behind us, and people belonging to different parties and communities have come together in defence of their country. This is a strangely moving picture of India which has made a profound impact upon me. It has enhanced our stature in the world. The general belief outside is that Indians are always at loggerheads with one another and that groupism, communalism and provincialism separate the people. But suddenly, all these things have disappeared or have been suppressed or postponed and the people of India have shown a united front to the world with a determination to protect India. This makes many things clear. But the most important point that it demonstrates is that our internal feuds and quarrels are superficial and the spirit of nationalism and love of freedom are deeply rooted in us. We are not prepared to trade our freedom for anything and if there is an attempt to take away that freedom, we are prepared to sacrifice everything to defend it. [Applause].

As you know, the Communist Party has issued a statement recently. It is in a great dilemma because of its special relationship with the Soviet Union and particularly China. Very often there are differences of opinion between the communists and us. We want socialism just as they do. But we want to bring about socialism by peaceful methods and I am convinced that we will succeed. The differences between the Communists and the Congress arise over other issues too. But in spite of their special relationship with the Chinese communists and their rigid bigotry, the Indian communists were moved by a strange emotion on this occasion. Their statement reflected a spirit of nationalism hundred per cent. Some people feel that they do not really mean what they say. Anyhow, their statement itself was a good thing [Applause]. I do not know about their leaders and time will show whether they are sincere or not. But by and large, the members of the Communist Party are simple, straightforward individuals, filled with a spirit of nationalism. The official statement has made things easier for them. They have realised that at the moment, it is not a question of communism but of defending the country against external aggression. Another advantage that has accrued from their statement is that the other communist parties in the world can see that the publicity on the Chinese side is wrong. When even the communists of India are raising their voice against China, it is obvious that the Chinese have done something very wrong. This will make even the communists in China pause and think whether they are in the wrong. So it is a good thing. I am not prepared to say what they will ultimately do and whether their present attitude has been born out of the intense atmosphere of nationalism which prevails in the country just now. There are some communists in India who have not accepted the official statement. But the majority of them have done so and there have been statements in Parliament, in the Lok Sabha and the Rajya Sabha, denouncing the Chinese aggression. They have even gone so far as to agree to our getting arms from the West to fight against the Chinese, which they would not be able to swallow otherwise.

It is pretty evident from all this what the atmosphere in India is like. Nobody can run counter to that spirit just now. It shows that India is extremely stout-hearted in a crisis. I was a little upset about the demonstrations in Delhi in front of the Communist Party office and some of the Chinese shops and restaurants. It is not befitting our dignity and such activities do harm to our reputation. We must do our best to contribute to the national effort. But to indulge in such childish activities weakens our strength. It is not a sign of bravery. Our courage will have to stand a great test and if we think that we can discharge our duties by demonstrations, we would be entirely mistaken.

The fact is that we have no real experience of fighting as the western countries do. They have gone through two great world wars and there is not a single household in France, England, Germany, Japan or the Soviet Union which has not lost some lives. For them, war has not been a distant affair. Modern warfare involves every single citizen in the country. We have not had that experience yet and so we are unable to understand fully what we are in for. Our jawans will no doubt fight the actual battle. But the rest of us cannot stand in the wings and cheer or demonstrate and take out processions. Today a war is fought not only by the army, navy and air force but by every single farmer, office and factory worker. It is true that the soldiers in the battlefield fight at the cost of their own lives. But they can do so only when the others, the farmer, the office or the factory worker, discharge their duties well. The people behind the lines have to work hard to keep the soldiers supplied with food, weapons and equipment. So, in a sense, every single man, woman and child in the country is a soldier. It is obvious that the Government employees have to shoulder a very great responsibility, whether you work in Government factories or offices. You are responsible for the administrative arrangements to ensure proper supplies to our forces.

The question that has arisen is whether we should continue with our Five Year Plans and whether we should be spending so much money on it when we are at war. It is a misconception to even raise this question. We are implementing the Five Year Plans to make the country strong and prosperous to get rid of our poverty, etc. We have calculated that all this is possible only in one way and that is by modernising the country through industrialisation and a knowledge of science and technology. This is how the West has advanced. There is no other alternative. We cannot get rid of our poverty by passing resolutions. So we started the Five Year Plans. How can we produce wealth in the country? Many things need to be done. It is not enough to set up industries. The people must be educated and scientific and technological training must be given to selected students. Primary and secondary school education must be available to every single individual in the country. Then specialised training can be given to the bright boys and girls. It is only on a firm foundation like this that we can build industries. We have been engaged in these tasks. Even in war, these are essential. In order to fight well, we must ensure that our food production is good and the factories work efficiently. Education must spread and even soldiers must be educated. Gone are the days when soldiers had to learn only how to use their weapons. Today it is extremely important that they should be educated. This is what is known as mobilising the manpower in the country. As you were told just now, the government in particular are great cogs in a giant machine. That includes all of us. If the cogs do not work well, the machine will come to a halt and then it is not possible to fight a battle. All these things are linked to one another. As I said in the beginning, a new chapter is beginning in the history of India. I cannot say where it will lead us. But we must continue to work hard and I am convinced that our efforts will succeed. Even if we have to bear great hardships now, we will succeed in the end and a better India will emerge out of our trials and tribulations. [Applause].

You have taken a pledge today. It is a good pledge by which you undertake to defend and protect our freedom and to throw out the enemy. We must work hard at whatever jobs we are doing. The important thing is not to waste our strength in any way. We must keep up our food and industrial production, work efficiently in the offices and ensure that our armed forces are kept supplied with everything that they need. Our armed forces are very good. But India is a peace-loving country and though we make a lot of noise, our attitude has never been belligerent or warlike. We will have to change our thinking somewhat. I have no doubt about it that we will fight with all our might. What bothers me is that one of the side-effects of war on a nation or human beings is that it makes them ruthless. It destroys emotions of love and creates bitterness and enmity and as a consequence, human beings are degraded. I am afraid that if we forget the lessons taught by Gandhlji, we will let our more bestial instincts take over. I do not want that to happen because I am proud of India and Indian culture. That does not mean that we should be weak. We should fight with all our might but at the same time not allow ourselves to behave in an uncivilised manner. We must bear in mind the lessons taught by Mahatma Gandhi and one of his real disciples in India today, Acharya Vinoba Bhave. I do not accept everything he says. But I have great respect for him and many of the things that he advocates are definitely superior. We must prepare ourselves well and remain true to our cultural heritage and traditions of strength, bravery and sacrifice. We must do all this in whichever field we happen to be in. Every one of you must work hard at whatever job you have, as you have pledged to do, for it is only by doing so that you can best help the war effort.

As all of you are aware, some of our basic principles have been to work for world peace, socialism in India and non-alignment in our foreign policy. We have refused to join either of the power groups into which the world is divided headed by the two superpowers, the Soviet Union and the United States. Our efforts to remain non-aligned have been crowned with success by and large. We have friendly relations with the western countries as well as with the Soviet Union. We will continue to abide by our policy of non-alignment. We will take the help of both sides in a crisis. We are helpless in the present situation and have to seek arms aid from whichever country that is willing to give. We are grateful to those who are helping us.

That does not mean that we are aligning ourselves with any one side. It does not mean that we wish to distance ourselves from the Soviet Union. We are aware that the Soviet Union is in a bit of a dilemma because it has a long-standing agreement with China which is their ally, in spite of the fact that there have been great differences of opinion between them. They abuse each other and there is not much love lost between them. But they are still allies. However, we have had friendly ties with the Soviet Union in spite of this and they have helped us a great deal in setting up our big industrial plants in the past. You may remember that a few days ago, it was decided that we would purchase some aircraft from them. They are to supply them by December and I am convinced that they will keep their word. Anyhow, I want to clarify for those who are under some misapprehension that we are not giving up our policy of non-alignment or getting into any military alliance. Due to the pressure of circumstances, we have to ask for some arms and equipment. We will take them wherever they are available because the most urgent priority is to fight for the defence of the country.

However, we will make every effort to stick to our fundamental policy. We will utilise whatever resources we have at our disposal and take any help that is forthcoming. But at the same time, we must not forget Gandhiji's principles though he was not one to advise about wars. You may remember how grieved he was when Pakistan had attacked Kashmir and we decided to send in our troops. I remember I was extremely perturbed. This was just three months before he was assassinated. When I asked him what to do, he said he could not advise me on this because his method of fighting was quite different. However, he was of the opinion that Kashmir must be defended. [Applause]. This is what Gandhiji said and Vinoba Bhave has used almost the same words now. [Applause]. He has said that he does not know how to fight nor that can he advise anyone how to fight an armed battle. "I am a man of peace. But there is no doubt about it that China has committed aggression and invaded India and we must combat that." So this is quite clear. There is no scope for confusion. I am happy that in spite of their long-standing relationship with China, even the Communist Party has understood this. After all, they are also Indians and nationalism has won. I want everyone to understand that it would be wrong and extremely harmful to think that this is an ideological war against communism. We believe that we should build a society according to our own principles but not under external pressure. At the same time, we have no quarrel with what other countries do in their internal affairs.

This is our war with the Chinese Government which has launched an imperialist aggression on our country. It is a protest against interference in our internal affairs. We will not yield to pressure of any kind. This is how we must regard the present war and march in step. I am happy to see that communalism, provincialism and linguistic differences have been suppressed. So in a sense, this war has done us some good. We must learn the valuable lesson of unity from this for that is crucial in order to build a strong and powerful country. We will fight the aggressor for years if need be. [Applause].

I thank you for the pledge that you have taken. My congratulations to you. Jai Hind!

Translation ends]

301. To Tashi Namgyal: Sikkim Support[174]

November 10, 1962

Your Highness,

Thank you for your letter of the 1st November, 1962, which was forwarded to me by our Political Officer[175] in Sikkim.

I was not able to see your son, the Maharajkumar,[176] during his brief visit to Delhi, but the Maharajkumar met our Foreign Secretary and other officials in the Ministry who briefed the Maharajkumar fully about the background of the unprovoked Chinese aggression and the various measures being taken to resist this aggression and to get it vacated.

I am grateful for Your Highness' pledge of your fullest cooperation and support in organising our national defence and getting the Chinese aggression along the Indian borders vacated.

With kind regard,

Yours sincerely,
Jawaharlal Nehru

302. In New Delhi: Public Meeting[177]

भाइयों और बहिनों,

परसों मैं यहाँ इसी मैदान में हाज़िर हुआ था और क़रीब-क़रीब इसी मज़मून पर जो आज मेरा होगा मैंने कुछ कहा था। मालूम नहीं आप लोग जो यहाँ मौजूद हैं इस तादाद में कितने लोग परसों भी थे, वो ख़ास थी गवर्नमेंट के कर्मचारियों की एक सभा, बहुत बड़ी सभा थी। ख़ैर, अगर मैं कुछ फिर से वही बातें दोहराऊँ तो आप माफ़ कीजियेगा। कहने को तो बहुत बातें हैं लेकिन मैं चाहता हूँ ज़रा आप सोचें कि तीन हफ़्तों में, ठीक तीन हफ़्ते आज हुए हैं, तीन हफ़्तों में हिन्दुस्तान का और आपका और हमारा रूप कैसे बदला?

तीन हफ़्ते हुए, चीन ने, चीन की फ़ौजों ने बड़े ज़ोरों का हमला किया। यों तो हमले उनके पाँच बरस से लद्दाख़ में थे, और नेफ़ा में भी, हमारी सीमा प्रान्त में भी शुरु सितम्बर में कुछ उतरे थे वो, पहाड़ों से, लेकिन थोड़े पैमाने पर हल्के-हल्के बढ़ते गये, लेकिन बीस अक्टूबर को, इसको ठीक तीन हफ़्ते हुए या शायद बाईस दिन हुए उन्होंने एक कार्यवाही

---

174. Letter to the Maharaja of Sikkim, Gangtok.
175. I.J. Bahadursingh.
176. Palden Thondup Namgyal.
177. Speech, 11 November 1962, at Ramlila Grounds. NMML, AIR Tapes TS No. 8462, 8463, 8464, NM No. 1671, 1681, 1682, 1683.

की जिसका धक्का पहुँचा हम सभों को। धक्के के अलावा एक, एक क्या कहूँ आपसे एक नया ज़माना हमारे सामने आ गया, एक नया अध्याय हुआ दुनिया के तमाशे में। यह अजीब तमाशा है जिसमें कभी अच्छा होता है ज़्यादातर तकलीफ़देह होता है, दुनिया के थियेटर में नया सीन उठा जिससे हम वाक़िफ़ नहीं थे, हमसे मतलब लोग हिन्दुस्तान के, और एकदम से हमारी तवज्जोह नयी-नयी तरफ़ जाने लगी। मैंने उसके दो रोज़ बाद एक रेडियो में ब्रॉडकास्ट किया था और मैंने कहा था कि हम लोग कुछ आजकल की दुनिया से पूरीतौर से वाक़िफ़ नहीं हैं, नहीं थे। इसके माने क्या थे? लोग समझें, लोगों ने अजीब-अजीब माने पहनाये। मेरा मतलब यह था, यह नहीं कि हम कोई ग़लत रास्ते पर चल रहे थे पहले, बल्कि कुछ मैं क्या कहूँ—हम लोग कुछ जो असली बात है दुनिया उस की है जिसके पास ताक़त होती है। एक दुनिया एक बेरहम चीज़ है, कमज़ोर के लिए, कमज़ोर मुल्क के लिए और एक माने में इसको हमें समझना चाहिए था, हम ग़फ़लत में रहे और ग़फ़लत में इस माने में नहीं कि हम बड़े शान्तिप्रिय हो गये थे, थे, कुछ न कुछ हो ही गये थे, बरसों से हमारी संस्कृति यह है और गांधीजी ने सिखाया और उसके बाद भी हम दुनिया में मशहूर हुए, शान्ति और अमन का पैग़ाम लेके गये और सब ठीक किया मेरी राय में। लेकिन बावजूद इसके यह भी आप जानते हैं कि ऐसे हादसे हुए हिन्दुस्तान में हमारे देखते-देखते जिससे शान्ति से कोई मतलब नहीं था। मैं फ़ौजी लड़ाई का नहीं कहता, आपस की लड़ाई का कहता हूँ जब पाकिस्तान बना, दिल्ली शहर में, पंजाब में कहाँ-कहाँ हादसे हुए, एक वहशियाना हादसे हुए। तो वो कोई शान्ति के नमूने तो नहीं थे।

तो हम शान्ति के असली माने समझते। गांधी की मानें तो हमारी ताक़त बढ़ती और बढ़ी जहाँ तक हम उसको समझें, हमारी ताक़त बढ़ी, हम आज़ाद हुए, लेकिन शान्ति के माने हैं एक दिल की मज़बूती ऊपर से, हाथ-पैर न चलाना ख़ाली माने नहीं हैं। अब गांधीजी से ज़्यादा मेरी बहत्तर बरस की उम्र में मैं नहीं जानता कौन ज़्यादा बहादुर आदमी है, उनसे ज़्यादा, लेकिन एक बहादुर थे, एक लोहा थे जो कि ग़लत बात की तरफ़ नहीं झुकते थे चाहे जो कुछ हो जाये, एक बड़े साम्राज्य के सामने नहीं झुके और अपने लोगों को तैयार किया, उसका मुक़ाबला करने को शान्ति के तरीकों से। तो ये शान्ति के माने होते हैं ताक़त बढ़ाना, मज़बूत होना, अपने उसूल के लिए खड़ा होना चाहे जो कुछ हो। हमने ऊपरी तौर से सबक़ को सीखा और उससे भी हमें फ़ायदा हुआ और बाद में जब हमारा इम्तहान हुआ हम कभी आपस में लड़ें, कभी फ़िरक़ेवाराना लड़ाइयाँ हों, कभी बड़े पैमाने पे आज़ादी के ज़माने में जो हुई थी, हिन्दुस्तान के दो टुकड़े हो गये, वो शान्ति की निशानी नहीं थी, वो कमज़ोरी की, अदावत की, ताक़त की नहीं थी। तो इसलिए मेरा मतलब था कि हम समझने लगें कि गुलशोर मचाने से, जुलूस निकालें, नारे उठायें, गुल मचायें यह एक ताक़त की निशानी है, हम भूल गये कि दुनिया में ताक़त और चीज़ है, चाहे आप ताक़त कैसी ही देखें, चाहे वो फ़ौजी ताक़त हो। फ़ौजी ताक़त क्या है? फ़ौजी ताक़त है हमारे फ़ौज के लोग, हवाई जहाज़ के लोग, बहुत सिखाये जाते हैं, डिसिप्लिंड

517

होते हैं, हुल्लड़बाज़ी नहीं करते हैं, उनकी ख़ामोश ताक़त है, वक़्त पर, वक़्त पर दुश्मन का मुक़ाबला करते हैं, एक ताक़त है, ज़बरदस्त ताक़त है, बड़ी-बड़ी लड़ाइयों में ऐसी ताक़त चली है, दो बड़े-बड़े, दो-तीन-चार मुल्कों में बड़ी लड़ाई हुई, सेकन्ड वर्ल्ड वॉर हुई, उसमें मुनज्ज़म मुल्क ने मुक़ाबला किया, बड़ा ज़बरदस्त मुक़ाबला हुआ, करोड़ों आदमी मरे, तबाह हुए, शहर, मुल्क तबाह हुए। उस वक़्त आप सोचें यह ताक़त जो समझी जाती है, ताक़त गुलशोर मचाने की वो किसी गिनती में नहीं है, वो तो अपने एक-दूसरे को धमकाने की हो जाये, वो असली मुक़ाबले की नहीं है, वो कमज़ोर करती है। आप जाके, बहुत लोग कहते हैं मेरे पास आके हमें सरहद पर भेज दो, हम भी लड़ेंगे, क्या वो करेंगे मेरी समझ में नहीं आता जब तक उनको ट्रेन्ड न किया जाये, सिखाया न जाये, मज़बूत न हों और बरदाश्त करने की ताक़त हो तब कुछ ख़्याल यह है, कि महज़ जोश और गुल मचाने से हमारी ताक़त दिखायी जाती है।

तो मेरा मतलब यह है कि बीस तारीख़ को जो हुआ एकदम से लोगों के दिमाग़ में एक नयी तस्वीर आयी, जिसमें उन्होंने देखा कि हमारे सामने एक, एक बड़ा हादसा हुआ और हमारे सामने बहुत ज़बरदस्त मुक़ाबले हैं जो कि महज़ वक़्ती जोश से नहीं हटते, और हमारे लिए नहीं ख़ाली एशिया के इतिहास में, दुनिया के इतिहास में एक नया-नया अध्याय शुरू हुआ, नया वर्क़ खुला। यों तो लड़ाई जो कुछ हमारी या चीन की फ़ौजों से हुई है वो छोटी है, सरहद पर ज़रा है लेकिन फिर भी छोटी होने पर भी उसके पीछे बहुत इमकानात हैं। चीन और हिन्दुस्तान का लड़ना ही है, एक दो एशिया के बड़े मुल्क, यह एक, यह एक ऐतिहासिक बात है और दो बड़े मुल्क जो इस तरह से लड़ते हैं तो एक-दूसरे की धमकी से नहीं वो हट जाते हैं, बहुत बातें उसमें होती हैं, एक मुल्क की शान है, होनी ही है, एक मुल्क की इज़्ज़त है, एक मुल्क की ज़मीन है जो उस पर कब्ज़ा करे, सब बातें हैं। चुनांचे ऐसी लड़ाई कोई फुटकर नहीं है, कोई साहब समझें कि ज़रा सा कुछ दो-तीन रोज़ का तमाशा हुआ था, कब, चौदह बरस हुए या कित्ते बरस हुए हैदराबाद में, या एक खेल हुआ था गोवा में, कोई इन बातों का मुक़ाबला नहीं है, यह असली और सख़्त चीज़ है और इसलिए हल्के-हल्के लोगों में, लोग समझने लगे, पूरीतौर से नहीं समझे, शायद आप भी पूरीतौर से न समझें हों कि, इसके माने क्या हैं, लेकिन फिर भी एक झलक हो गयी कि दुनिया कैसी चीज़ है और क्या करना होता है आज़ाद मुल्कों को अपनी आज़ादी रखने के लिए।

तो इस माने में मैंने कहा कि तीन हफ़्ते हुए नया चैप्टर, अध्याय हिन्दुस्तान के इतिहास में शुरू हुआ, मालूम नहीं कब तक यह चले, लेकिन कित्ता ही चले यह हिन्दुस्तान को बदल के छोड़ेगा और यह एक ग़ौरतलब बात है, जो बदलेगा हिन्दुस्तान को, वो किस तरफ़ ले जाके बदलेगा। मेरा मतलब नहीं चीन की फ़ौजों को हटाने का, मैं समझता हूँ हम उन्हें हटायेंगे, कामयाब होंगे, लेकिन उसके अलावा इस दौरान में हमें कित्ता हम बदलेंगे, बदलना ज़रूरी है क्योंकि बदल ही के हम मुक़ाबला कर सकते हैं। यों तो फ़ौजें बनेंगी, नयी फ़ौजें बनेंगी, पुरानी फ़ौज तैयार होंगी उनकी, तरह-तरह के हथियार मिलेंगे, यह सब बातें हैं।

518

लेकिन यह चीज़ ऐसी है जिससे सिपाही का काम ख़ाली वर्दी पहन के सरहद पर जो है वो सिपाही या जवान नहीं है, इसमें हरेक आदमी को, आदमी और एक माने में औरत को भी एक तरह की सिपाहीगिरी करनी है, चाहे वो किसान है, खेती करता है, चाहे वो कारख़ाने में काम करता है, चाहे वो दफ़्तर में काम करता है, चाहे दुकान में करता है, चाहे हाथ-पैर से। हमारे विद्यार्थी हैं जो स्कूल-कॉलेज में हैं, स्कूल को छोड़ दीजिए अभी बच्चे हैं, ये बढ़ें, हरेक को अपना काम नियमित रूप से करना है, डिसिप्लिंड तरीक़े से, तब ताक़त आती है। आप जानते होंगे कि सिपाही वहाँ लड़ता है, या हवाई जहाज़ पे जाते हैं, उसके पीछे कित्ते लोग काम करते हैं तब वो लड़ सकता है यानी यों तो फ़ौज को खिलाने का पिलाने का सवाल है, किसान पैदा करता है, कारख़ानों में सब सामान पैदा होता है, ख़ाली लड़ाई का नहीं बल्कि हर चीज़ जिसकी उसको ज़रूरत है चाहे वर्दी हो, चाहे वो हथियार हो, चाहे और पचासों चीज़ों की ज़रूरत होती है। तो अगर फ़र्ज़ कीजिये एक लाख आदमी लड़ रहे हैं वो एक लाख आदमी के पीछे बीस-तीस-चालीस लाख आदमी काम करते हैं तब वो लड़ सकते हैं और ज़्यादा फ़ौजों से, बीस-तीस लाख मैंने कहा इससे बहुत ज़्यादा, क्योंकि सारा मुल्क उनकी मदद करता है काम करके नियमित रूप से, डिसिप्लिंड तरीके से तब उनकी ताक़त बनती है और आपकी हमारी ताक़त बनती है।

यह बात मैं चाहता हूँ आप अच्छी तरह से समझ लें, क्योंकि मैं अब भी सुनता हूँ कि बाज़ लोगों का यह ख़्याल है कि गुलशोर मचा के जाके कहीं हमला कर दें, यहाँ चीनी सफ़ीर का मकान है, उस पर वो बड़ी बहादुरी दिखाते हैं। हम बदनाम होते हैं दुनिया में, ये नहीं जानते कि दुनिया इससे ज़्यादा समझदार है, होशियार है हम लोगों से, दुनिया से मेरा मतलब सारी दुनिया नहीं, दुनिया समझ लीजिए यही यूरोप की, यूरोप की, रूस की वग़ैरा। क्योंकि उस दुनिया ने मेरे देखते-देखते और आपके, बहुत लोगों के देखते-देखते दो बड़ी जंग लड़ी हैं जिसमें एक कोई घराना नहीं था मुल्क भर में जिसके लड़के ख़त्म न हो गये हों, कोई घराना नहीं था जिसमें तबाह न हों, शहर के शहर बिल्कुल मिट्टी के ढेर कर दिये गये। तो एक ज़बरदस्त लड़ाई आपके घर आयी, यह नहीं कि बैठे आप यहाँ अख़बारों में पढ़ें और ताली बजायें कि हमारे जवान बहुत बहादुर हैं। ठीक है, बहादुर तो हैं वो, और उनकी हमें पूरी मदद करनी चाहिए लेकिन यह बात जो कि यूरोप में, मैं कोई यूरोप के लोगों को, उनके ख़्यालात को हर बात में पसन्द नहीं करता और बहुत बातों में हम ज़्यादा अच्छे हैं उनसे, लेकिन इस बात में यूरोप के लोगों को तजुबा है ज़बरदस्त, कि लड़ाई क्या चीज़ है और फिर मज़ाक नहीं समझते कि हम ज़रा एक हुल्लड़ मचा दें या हम ताली पीट दें कि, इससे हम जीत जायेंगे या हम ज़ोरों से कहें कि हम निकाल देंगे चीनियों को, कहें आप अच्छा है लेकिन उसके बाद कुछ और करना है।

यह तस्वीर हल्के-हल्के हमारे सामने तीन हफ़्ते हुए आयी थी, पूरीतौर से नहीं आयी है, आती जायेगी और अच्छा है उसके पीछे जो हमने देखा हिन्दुस्तान में जो एक क़रीब-क़रीब हर आदमी में, हर औरत में, हर बच्चे में जोश चढ़ा, वो एक अजीब नज़ारा था और है। जिससे एकदम से एक और तस्वीर हमारे सामने आयी, एक बड़ा मुल्क जिसमें हज़ार

बहसें, हज़ार झगड़े थे सारे एकदम से ख़त्म कर दिये गये और और सब एक तरफ़ देखने लगे और कम से कम उनकी ख़्वाहिश हुई एक तरह का काम करने की जिससें इस जंग में मदद हो। यह बात अच्छी थी हमारे मुल्क के लिए, हालांकि जिस वजह से यह हुई वो एक हादसा हुआ, हमारे वहाँ सिपाही बहुत मरे, बहुत बहादुर जवान बड़ी हिम्मत से लड़े लेकिन जब उनके आठ गुने, दस गुने चीनी फ़ौजें आके उनपे छा गयीं तो मुश्किल होता है उनका मुक़ाबला करना उस वक़्त। ख़ैर, तो हिन्दुस्तान जाग गया, एक नया जीवन हिन्दुस्तान का हुआ और यह बात अच्छी हुई और बुनियादी बात हुई, और जो बातें हों, वो इसके बाद होती हैं।

हम क्या-क्या तैयारी करें? हो रही हैं तैयारियाँ और आप सुनेंगे, कुछ आपने सुनी भी हैं क्या-क्या हुआ है, क़ानून बदले हैं, नयी-नयी जमातें तैयार हुई हैं, नये सिपाही भर्ती हो रहे हैं, फ़ौजें, और तरह-तरह की बातें हैं, सामान आ रहा है, हमारे कारख़ानों से जो सामान बनता था वो अब पहले के मुक़ाबले में इस तीन हफ़्ते में तिगुना-चौगुना बनने लगा, फ़ौजी सामान (तालियाँ) और क्यों उन्हीं कारख़ानों में जहाँ बहस होती थी कि झगड़े होते थे कि हमारी तनख़्वाह बढ़ायी जाये, हमारी रोज़ाना की मज़दूरी बढ़ायी जाये और हम इत्ता कम काम करेंगे, ज्यादा नहीं करेंगे, यकायक क्या हुआ।

अब आप देखिये हमारे जो आर्डिनेन्स फ़ैक्ट्रीज़ हैं उसमें आजकल चौबीस घंटे काम होता है, रुकता नहीं है। यह मेरा मतलब नहीं एक आदमी चौबीस घंटे करता है, वो तो नामुमकिन है, लेकिन तीन शिफ्ट्स में एक आदमी आठ घंटे काम करे, दूसरे हों, तीसरे, हाँ दिन-रात काम होता है और इससे और हूँ-हाँ नहीं ख़ुशी से काम होता है और ख़ुशी के काम का नतीजा ज़्यादा अच्छा होता है, ज़्यादा होता है क्योंकि वो समझ रहे हैं, महज़ यह नहीं कि वो दो-चार रुपये के लिए काम कर रहे हैं बल्कि समझ रहे हैं, हम एक काम मुल्क के लिए कर रहे हैं, एक नये जोश के साथ। तो उसका असर ज़्यादा होता है और वो चीज़ भी ज्यादा क़ीमती हो जाती है जिसको वो पैदा करते हैं। तो यह सब हुआ और आप जानते हैं दिल्ली शहर या बम्बई, कलकत्ता कहीं भी जाइये, या गाँव में कैसे एकदम से एक नयी-नयी लौ जल गयी लोगों के दिलों में, हालांकि मैं फिर आपको याद दिलाऊँगा, अभी तक शायद आप लोग समझे न हों कि क्या-क्या होने वाला है, कोई भी नहीं जानता है और तैयार हमें हरेक बात के लिए होना है।

बहुत लोग, बाज़ लोगों ने बहुत नुक़्ताचीनी की कि हम तैयार नहीं, ख़बरें मशहूर कि ठीक-ठीक बन्दूकें नहीं दीं, ठीक कपड़े नहीं दिये और क्या-क्या, ज्यादातर वो ख़बरें सही नहीं हैं, कुछ सही हैं लेकिन ज़्यादातर सही नहीं हैं। यह फ़िज़ूल बात है कपड़े नहीं दिये, पूरे कपड़े दिये, पूरे कम्बल दिये, सब कुछ दिये, वो जगह ऐसी है कि आप महसूस नहीं कर सकते। अब एक जगह है लद्दाख़ में जहाँ लड़ाई हो रही है। अब मैं कैसे आपको समझाऊँ, वहाँ का टेम्परेचर पानी जमने के टेम्परेचर से बीस और तीस डिग्री नीचा है यानी जब बर्फ़ जम जाती है तो सर्दी होती है। अब उसका आप ख़्याल कीजिये कि तीस डिग्री उसके नीचा हो जाता है शाम को, रात को टेम्परेचर, तो आप महसूस करें कित्ता क्या अजीब हाल है पहाड़ों पर।

तो ख़ैर, वो तो है लेकिन फिर लोगों ने एक तरफ़ से, बहुत सभों ने, बहुत लोगों ने कहना शुरू किया ठीक कहा कि हम एक हैं, हम यह नहीं करेंगे, वो नहीं करेंगे, सब मिलके जायेंगे। दूसरी तरफ़ बाज़ लोग हैं, बाज़ संस्थायें हैं मैंने सुना दिल्ली में, दिल्ली के बाहर भी हों, वो कहती फिरती हैं, बस बदनाम करती फिरती हैं, हर काम को, कि यह तैयारी नहीं वो नहीं, और ये निकम्मे लोग हैं, निकम्मे हम लोग हैं। तो ख़ुशी आपकी, कोई, कोई ज़बरदस्ती तो आप पे कोई है नहीं, आप लोग हैं, हिन्दुस्तान के लोग हैं, पार्लियामेंट के लोग हैं, हमें हटा दूसरे को कर सकते हैं। मुझे कोई एतराज़ नहीं लेकिन जब तक हम हैं तो फिर हमें मिलके चलना है, (तालियाँ) यह एक, यह एक बिल्कुल पहला सबक़ है जिसको हमने पूरीतौर से नहीं सीखा। पहला सबक़ हमें इसका ज़ोरों का मिला था गांधीजी का।

मुझे याद है एक आपको पुरानी याद बताऊँ उनके असहयोग आन्दोलन और उत्तर के सवालात और क्या-क्या थे उसके पहले, एक कांग्रेस ने उस वक़्त तक इसको मंज़ूर नहीं किया था, उसके सामने नहीं आया था यह, गांधीजी ने नहीं रखा था। आपको शायद याद हो उस वक़्त गांधीजी ने पहले इसको कहा जो उस ज़माने में थी, क्या, ख़िलाफ़त कमेटी। ख़िलाफ़त कमेटी को गांधीजी ने उस वक़्त अपनाया था और और बातें भी थीं, पंजाब का मार्शल-लॉ था और फिर दोनों मिलके स्वराज्य आया, चन्द महीनों की बात है। ख़िलाफ़त कमेटी में बैठे थे वो और बहुत सारे बुज़ुर्ग वहाँ बैठे थे, बड़े ज़ोरों की तक़रीरें हो रही थीं—यह अंग्रेज़ों ने हमारे साथ ग़द्दारी की और यह किया और वो किया, और लोग कर रहे थे। गांधीजी दुबले-पतले आदमी उठे, उन्होंने कहा कि जो बातें आपने कहीं हो सकता है बहुत कुछ सही हों लेकिन सवाल आपके मेरे कहने का नहीं, सवाल यह आप करेंगे क्या और हमकरेंगे क्या? हमें मुक़ाबला करना है, ज़बरदस्त मुक़ाबला करना है, मेरे तरीक़े से मुक़ाबला एक ढंग से होता है, शान्ति से, लेकिन वो शान्ति हो, कुछ हो, वो, वो एक तरह की लड़ाई है,शान्ति की लड़ाई है और उसमें लड़ाई की जितनी अच्छी बातें हैं वो होनी चाहियें। लड़ाई में एक फ़ौजी सिपाही की तरह सिखाया जाता है, सिपाही बनता है, सिखाया जाता है, ट्रेन्ड होता है और एक डिसिप्लिंड होता है, नियमित रूप से काम करते हैं। और आपको हक़ है उन्होंने कहा कि, आप मुझे चाहे अपना नेता इस लड़ाई में चुनिये या न चुनिये मुझे कोई फ़िक्र नहीं, लेकिन अगर आप चुनते हैं तो मैं कमान्डर-इन-चीफ़ हूँ और मैं बताऊँगा कैसे चलना है, सभों को चलना पड़ेगा, (तालियाँ) यह उन्होंने कहा था। यह, उसके साथ यह भी कहा कि जिस वक़्त आप मुझसे नाराज़ हों उस वक़्त मेरा सिर काट के मुझे अलग कर दीजिये, यह आपको हक़ है। लेकिन जब तक मैं हूँ वहाँ उस वक़्त यह फ़ौज है, फ़ौज की तरह से हम लड़ेंगे, यह नहीं हरेक आदमी अपना गाना गाये, गीत गाये, इधर-उधर टहल आये। अब यह एक नयी आवाज़ पहली दफ़ा गांधीजी की उस वक़्त सुनने में आयी थी और मुझे याद है बड़े-बड़े बुज़ुर्ग वहाँ बैठे थे जो बड़ी लम्बी-चौड़ी बातें कह रहे थे, वो ज़रा घबरा से गये इसको सुनकर, हालांकि इसमें उन्होंने बहुत नर्मी से कहा था, लेकिन कहा था आप, अगर यह हमें लड़ाई लड़नी है तो मार्शल-लॉ होगा यहाँ हिन्दुस्तान में। मार्शल-लॉ अंग्रेज़ों का किया हुआ नहीं, उनका मतलब था हमें मार्शल-लॉ की

तरह रहना है और और जो कोई अफ़सर आप चुनिये उसका कहना मानना जैसे सिपाही मानता है अपने अफ़सर का। उस वक़्त एक तो चाहे कोई भी जमात हो, कांग्रेस हो, कुछ हो, हमारा तरीक़ा यह था कि लम्बे-लम्बे प्रस्ताव, रेज़ोल्यूशन पास करते थे या घर बैठे रहते थे। अब एक नया ढंग उन्होंने निकाला कि जो कहें वो कम कहें, कोई और गाली-गलौच कुछ न हो, कम कहें, इतना कहें कि हमें यह करना है और उसको करें चाहे जो कुछ हो और एक फ़ौज की तरह से, मुनज़्ज़म फ़ौज की तरह से करें। यह शुरू था। ख़ैर, मैं उस वक़्त मेरी उम्र कम थी और जोश चढ़ता था गांधीजी की बातें सुनके, मुझे पसन्द आयीं लेकिन मुझे बहुत कुछ दिल में हँसी आयी, मैं ज़ाहिर तो कर नहीं सकता था और लोग जो वहाँ मौजूद बुज़ुर्ग, बुज़ुर्गानि क़ौम बहुत सारे उनके चेहरे देखकर, जो कि बड़े ज़ोरों की तक़रीरें कर रहे थे थोड़ी देर पहले, लेकिन यहाँ तक़रीर से नहीं ठंडे दिल से गांधीजी ने कहा कि अब यह-यह करना है और एक फ़ौज की तरह से करना है और हटना नहीं है अपनी जगह से। ख़ैर, फिर कई बरस तक गांधीजी ने सारे हिन्दुस्तान में हमें हल्के-हल्के सिखाया, कुछ हम सीखे, कुछ हम नालायक़ थे नहीं पूरा सीख सके। लेकिन जो कुछ थोड़ा बहुत सीखा भी, उससे भी मुल्क की ताक़त बहुत बढ़ी और बढ़ते-बढ़ते आख़िर में उसी रास्ते पर चलके गांधीजी ने आज़ाद किया।

शायद आप लोग बहुत बैठे हैं, आप गांधीजी का नाम जानते हों, कुछ लोगों ने देखा हो दूर से, कुछ लोगों ने देखा भी न हो और कम से कम कुछ भूल गये हों उस ज़माने को, हमारे लिए भूलना मुश्किल है क्योंकि बीस-पच्चीस बरस तक उसी हवा में रहे, उसी काम में रहे, धक्के पहुँचे, ख़ुशी हुई और हमारे दिलों पर, दिमाग़ों पर वो जम गया, चुनांचे हम भूलें कैसे। लेकिन मुझे ज़माना याद आता है कि मैं आजकल देखता हूँ किस तरह से लोग बहके-बहके फिरते हैं और ताक़त की निशानी समझते हैं हुल्लड़बाज़ी, और हमले करने, इस तरह से जिसमें कुछ दुनिया में हमारी वक़अत कुछ कम हो जाती है। क्योंकि जब इंग्लैंड और फ़्रांस और जर्मनी और रूस लड़ाई में थे तो ये बातें आप कहीं नहीं देखते थे, वहाँ तो एक-एक मुल्क का एक-एक आदमी और औरत और लड़का एक सिपाही हो गया, वर्दी पहने चाहे न, और यह फ़ुर्सत नहीं किसी को वैसी गुल मचाने की बातें करें और जाके एक डिमॉन्स्ट्रेशन करें वग़ैरा। तो वो इससे समझते हैं कि हम अभी असली तौर से हमारी आँखें नहीं खुलीं इन बातों से, जो कुछ लड़के या बड़े, उम्र में बड़े लेकिन दिमाग़ से लड़के जो आजकल किया करते हैं कहीं-कहीं। और मुझे रंज हुआ यह सुनकर कि उनको हक़ है नुक़्ताचीनी करने का वग़ैरा, लेकिन कोई ऐसी बात करने का नहीं हक़ है जिससे हमारी क़ौमी ताक़त कम हो इस वक़्त। यह हरेक कहने को तैयार है कि हमारे जवान बड़े बहादुर हैं लेकिन फ़र्ज़ कीजिये यह भी उसी के साथ कहेंगे कि जवान बहादुर हैं लेकिन उनके अफ़सर ठीक नहीं या और लोग जो इंतज़ाम करते हैं ठीक नहीं, उन्हें कपड़े नहीं दिये, ये नहीं दिये, बिल्कुल फ़िज़ूल और लाहौल बातें हैं, न जानते हैं न कुछ, कहने की तरह कहते जाते हैं। वाक़िया है, वाक़िया यह है हमारा दिमाग़, मुल्क का दिमाग़ लड़ाई की तरफ़ नहीं झुका था, हम अमन-अमन कहते थे और दिमाग़ का झुकना आसान नहीं

होता, हल्के-हल्के हो जाता है, हो रहा है तेज़ी से और उसमें नयी-नयी बातें, नये-नये हुनर, नयी-नयी ताक़तें चाहियें।

तो इस बात को आपको समझना है। तीन हफ़्ते हुए आज से एक नया ज़माना हिन्दुतान के लिए खुला है, नया युग खुला है। इसमें क्या-क्या होने वाला है, यह तो ख़ैर बाद में इतिहास के लिखने वाले लिखेंगे लेकिन हम और आप उसको देखने वाले हैं, हमें और आपको उसकी बरदाश्त करनी है, हमें और आपको उसका सामना करना है, कैसे हम करते हैं यह हम पर और आप पर मुनहस्सर है और यह उसका सामना करना, ख़ाली ऊपरी जोश दिखाना नहीं है, रोज़मर्रा का काम हमारा बदल जाना चाहिए और इस ढंग से हो, हम अपना काम करते जायें, हरेक आदमी तो फ़ौजी सिपाही नहीं है। अगर हम किसान हैं तो उसे यह सोच के ज़ोरों से अपनी खेती करनी है कि, खेती की जो पैदावार है उसको दुगुना कर दें, तिगुना कर दें, कारख़ाने हैं तो वहाँ ज़्यादा पैदा करें, क्योंकि आख़िर में फ़ौज महज़ हिम्मत से नहीं लड़ती, हथियारों से भी लड़ती है, एक हथियार के पीछे मुल्क की आर्थिक ताक़त होती है, मुल्क की पैदावार होती है और जो उनको रखती है और उसी से आप सामान ले सकते हैं उनके लिए, फ़ौजी सामान, हवाई जहाज़ वग़ैरा, इस तरफ़ ध्यान देना है।

लड़के हैं, मैं अभी दिल्ली यूनिवर्सिटी गया था, जवान हैं वो, मैंने उनसे कहा कि आपको काम इस वक़्त बहुत काम करने होंगे, आप अपने पढ़ते जायें ज़ोरों से, अपने को तैयार कीजिये, वक़्त ज़ाया न कीजिये क्योंकि शायद मौक़ा न मिले फिर आपको करने का, पूरीतौर से उस काम को कीजिये जो आप करते हैं। और और बातें भी मैंने उनको सलाह दीं—आप एन.सी.सी. है, नेशनल कैडेट कोर, उसमें आप भर्ती होइये, ए.सी.सी. है, स्कूल के लड़के उसमें भर्ती हों और वक़्त आने पर शायद सोलह आने फ़ौज में भर्ती होना पड़े, लेकिन उसके लिए तैयार होना है। हम अब चाहते हैं और होगा कि हरेक कॉलेज में लड़का जो पढ़ता है उसको एन.सी.सी. में भर्ती होना पड़ेगा। इस वक़्त भी हैं, मुझे याद नहीं कित्ते हैं, तीन-चार लाख हैं लेकिन तीन-चार लाख नहीं हरेक लड़के को भर्ती होना पड़ेगा और उसमें से फिर हम चुन सकते हैं, जो अच्छे हुए उनको अफ़सर बनना पड़ेगा, ज़रा ट्रेनिंग देके। और बच्चे भी ए.सी.सी. में हों स्कूल वाले, वो भी अच्छा है, बुनियादी तालीम उनकी हो जाये, उसके अलावा टेरीटोरियल (territorial army) आर्मी है, यह सब असली फ़ौज से अलग हैं। इन सभों को हम बढ़ायेंगे और असली फ़ौज भी बढ़ रही है, तेज़ी से बढ़ेगी और सबमें मुश्किल बात है अफ़सरों का तैयार होना। अफ़सर कोई एकदम से तो हो नहीं जाते तैयार, अगर माक़ूल अफ़सर हों तो उनको सीखना पड़ता है, फ़न लड़ाई का करते हैं, कैसे करते हैं, क्या करते हैं, ख़ाली जोश नहीं। उनको सिखाने में वक़्त लगता है तेज़ी से हम उन्हें सिखाने का भी ज़रा ऐसा कर देंगे कि, जो साल भर में सीखते थे वो छः महीने में सीखें, ज़्यादा मेहनत करें। यह सब करना है।

लेकिन इन सब बातों के पीछे दो बातें हैं, कई बातें हैं—एक तो हमारी खेती तरक़्क़ी करे और एक हमारे कारख़ाने, माक़ूल तरह से वहाँ काम हो, दिल लगा के उसमें। अब

कोई सवाल नहीं रहा हड़ताल का या लॉकआउट का और उसके साथ यह भी है कि हम जो उनके साथ बर्ताव करें, हम से मतलब जो उनके कारख़ानों के मालिक हैं वो मुनासिब होना चाहिए। अब झगड़े की हमें बरदाश्त नहीं है वहाँ, यह सब करना है और आम लोगों को चाहे आप दुकानदार हों या जो भी आपका काम हो यह सोच लेना है आपको कि आप भी एक, एक पुर्ज़े हैं हिन्दुस्तान की फ़ौज के, हम सब पुर्ज़े हैं, हमारी अलग ताक़त कुछ न हो लेकिन मिलके ताक़त होती है, लेकिन मिलके ताक़त जभी होती है जब, जब मिलके काम करें। एक, एक बड़ी मशीन होती है, आप जानते हैं एक पुर्ज़ा निकाल लीजिये मशीन गड़बड़ हो सकती है, उसके अलग-अलग टुकड़े हैं, यह करना है। यह बात आप समझ लें, समझें। हो सकता है कि हम जिसके हाथ में इतनी बड़ी ज़िम्मेदारी है हम उसके पूरे लायक़ न हों, क्योंकि वाक़िया यह है इतनी बड़ी ज़िम्मेदारियों के बहुत कम लोग लायक़ होते हैं, लियाक़त हो, सब्र हो, घबरा न जायें आदमी, सांस न फूल जाये, यह सब बातें हैं। कम होते हैं मुल्कों में ऐसे मौक़े, पर, लेकिन हम उम्मीद करते हैं कि हल्के-हल्के बनते जायें, नये आदमी इस तरहसे नहीं बनेंगे चिल्ला-चिल्ला के। तो यह सब तस्वीर आप सामने रखिये। हो सकता है यह भी कि हमें काफ़ी धक्के लगें, हमारी फ़ौज को कभी-कभी हटना भी पड़े, यह सब खेल है लड़ाई का, कोई पहली दफ़ा हट जाने से कोई लड़ाई थोड़ी हार जाती है या जैसे उन्हें हटना पड़ा।

मैं आपको बताऊँ कि आज नहीं बरस-दो बरस हुआ हमने नक़्शे बनाये, हमने, मैंने नहीं, हमारे फ़ौजी अफ़सरों ने नक़्शे बनाये थे कि अगर चीनी हमला करें तो हम इस जगह उस जगह पर क्या करें और उन्होंने नक़्शे बना के राय दी थी यहाँ करें। उसमें यह भी लिखा था कि बिल्कुल सरहद के पास हमें बहुत ज़ोरों से उनको रोकना नहीं चाहिए, कहीं रोक सकें। इसलिए वो जगह ज़्यादा मौज़ू होगी चीनियों कि लिए और वो हम, हमें हटा तो देंगे लेकिन हमें बहुत नुक़सान से हटायेंगे। इसलिए उनकी कुछ रोकथाम करें लेकिन असल हमें मुक़ाबला ज़रा पीछे हट के करना पड़ेगा। ये बातें आज की नहीं हैं, अब लोग बड़े ज़ोरों से कहेंगे क्यों हटें, क्यों हटे, किसका क़सूर है, क़सूर क्या है यानी फ़ौजी मामले हैं, बड़े मुल्कों के साथ हैं, कोई छोटी बात नहीं है, उसमें हमें हमेशा इस बात पर ग़ौर करना होता है कि, कि हम आख़िर में ताक़तवर हों काफ़ी, उनको हराने को उनको हटाने को बीच में कोई एक तमाशा नहीं दिखाना है कि हम शुरु में एक छोटी सी लड़ाई जीत गये, बाद में हार गये। ये सब बातें सीखनी होती हैं।

बड़ी-बड़ी लड़ाइयाँ हुई हैं आपने सुना होगा, पढ़ा होगा क्या असर हुआ, जर्मनी इत्ता ज़बरदस्त मुल्क, ताक़तवर बड़ी फ़ौजों का, उसने हमला करके फ्रांस पर फ़तह कर लिया, इंग्लैंड की फ़ौज को समुद्र में फेंक दिया, पूरी फ़ौज को, और कित्ते मुल्कों को दबा लिया लेकिन आख़िर में जर्मनी हारा, ज़ोरों से हारा। मैं नहीं कहता, मैंने मिसाल दी, इस मिसाल की यहां मौज़ू न समझिए, क्योंकि मैं नहीं समझता कि चीन वाले इत्ते ताक़तवर हैं, ज़बरदस्त हैं, हिन्दुस्तान से इस तरह से खेल करें।

लेकिन मैं बताता हूँ कि हमें तैयार रहना चाहिए, ऐसे वाक़िये होंगे जिससे हमें धक्का लगे, बरदाश्त करें उससे और हम अपनी हिम्मत बढ़ायें और कोशिश करें, क्योंकि

इससे कोई हार नहीं जाता है या घबरा नहीं जाता है जैसे कुछ लोगों को यह मालूम हुआ था और इसमें आपका क़सूर नहीं कुछ हमारे अख़बारों का कुछ थोड़ा सा क़सूर है, इस ढंग से उन्होंने रखा जिससे परेशानी हुई लोगों को। यह मामला क्या है? हमारी फ़ौज को हटाना पड़ा, हमारी फ़ौज एक छोटे से मुक़ाबले में हार गयी, किसका क़सूर है? हो सकता है किसी का क़सूर हो कहीं पर यह मैं नहीं कहता, लेकिन यह दिमाग़ ग़लत है इस तरह से करना। यह तो वही है दिमाग़ जैसे कोई आदमी बीमार हो, ज़रा सा उसका एक पारा बढ़ जाये तो डाक्टरों को दिखाओ, दूसरे डाक्टर को लायें, हकीम को लायें, वैद्य को लायें, रोज़-रोज़ बदलते जायें घबराए हुए कि, क्या होने वाला है। इस तरह से न इंसान अच्छा होता है न मुल्क अच्छा होता है।

तो अब आप देखिये कि हुआ क्या है? पाँच बरस हुए यों तो पहले-पहले की कहानी आपसे कहूँ कि जब से चीन में क्रान्ति हुई, बारह बरस हुए चीन ने क्रान्ति की, बारह-तेरह बरस, उस वक़्त से हमारे सामने, ख़ैर चीन में कोई हमारी मदद से या रुकावट से तो नहीं हुई, और बड़ी क्रान्ति हुई दुनिया की बड़ी क्रान्तियों में। तो हमने उस पर ग़ौर किया, हमने निश्चय किया कि हमें पसन्द हो या ना-पसन्द हो चीन, हमें उसको मान लेना चाहिए जो हुकूमत है, क्योंकि एक हुकूमत है शरीअन, हम न मानें तो उनका तो कोई नुक़सान नहीं होता, हमारा होगा। हमने माना हल्के-हल्के, और बहुत मुल्कों ने माना, हम दूसरे मुल्क थे जिसने माना था अलावा कुछ साम्यवादी मुल्कों के, पहले बर्मा ने फिर हमने, शायद जहाँ तक मुझे याद है 31 दिसम्बर 49 को हमने माना था या 1 जनवरी 50 को समझ लीजिये। ख़ैर, माना और हमारा इरादा था कि उनसे दोस्ती करके रहें और इसके हमने बहुत काफ़ी सबूत दिये बाद में भी, हालांकि शुरु-शुरु में ख़ासतौर से उनकी तरफ़ से बहुत बदतमीज़ी की बातें हुई, उनके अख़बारों में। एक, मुझे हैरत होती थी कि एक ऐसे सभ्य देश जैसे चीनी हैं, बहुत पुरानी संस्कृति सभ्यता है कैसे वो बहक जाते हैं? अब यह किसका क़सूर? उनकी सभ्यता ख़त्म हो गयी एक नये क्रान्ति के आने से या क्या। बहरसूरत, यह एक बदतमीज़ी की बात है, हमको कुत्ता कहें, यह कहें, फ़िज़ूल बातें, हम साम्राज्यवाद के कुते हैं और यह कुछ वाक़िया हो न हो कोई शरीफ़ाना बातें नहीं मुल्क की निस्बत कहना। ख़ैर, हल्के-हल्के उनके दिमाग़ में बैठा कि वो ग़लत रास्ते पर थे और शराफ़त से हमारे साथ बर्ताव करने लगे और चन्द बरस ऐसे गुज़रे कि कमोबेश अच्छे गुज़रे हमारे उनके बर्ताव में।

एक बात हमें चुभती थी—हमने देखा कि उन्होंने जो नक़्शे बनाये हैं, उनके नक़्शे हैं उसमें उन्होंने दिखाया है कि हिन्दुस्तान का एक काफ़ी हिस्सा लद्दाख़ में, सरहदी प्रान्त में, वो चीन में है या कहिये तिब्बत में है लेकिन तिब्बत को चूंकि उन्होंने हज़म कर लिया, उन्होंने कहा कि हमारा है तो हमने उनकी तवज्जोह दिलाई यह क्या माने हैं, हमने अपने नक़्शे भेजे। उन्होंने कहा हमारे नक़्शे तो पुराने ज़माने के हैं, क्रान्ति के पहले के, हमें वक़्त नहीं मिला उनको बदलने का, हम उस पर सोचेंगे और फिर आपस में हम तय कर लेंगे, जब वक़्त आयेगा सोच लेंगे। हमने एक दफ़ा, दो-तीन-चार दफ़ा उनसे कहा कि देखिये

अभी आपके नक़्शे नहीं बदले, उन्होंने हर दफ़ा यही जवाब दिया कि फ़ुर्सत से इसको देखेंगे, ज़बानी मैंने कहा, उनसे मिला, पीकिंग गया, ये यहाँ आये, तब भी उनका यही जबाब था। अब इस जवाब के माने यह नहीं थे कि उन्होंने हमारा नक़्शा बिल्कुल तसलीम कर लिया, लेकिन कम से कम ये माने थे कि पुराना नक़्शा वो बदलने वाले हैं और पुराना नक़्शा सही नहीं है।

ख़ैर हमने, जब उन्होंने तिब्बत पर फ़ौजें भेजी बाज़ लोग कहते हैं तुमने ग़लत बात की, तुमने तसलीम कर लिया तिब्बत में उनकी, हुकूमत। यह भी मेरी समझ में नहीं आता कि कोई आदमी समझ के देखे तो क्या कहे। अव्वल तो यह वाक़िया है कि तिब्बत के सैकड़ों बरस के इतिहास में अक्सर वो चीन के मातहत रहा, कभी नहीं रहा और कभी ऐसा रिश्ता रहा कि समझ में नहीं आता मातहत था कि नहीं, क्योंकि पेंच यह था तिब्बत में जो दलाईलामा वहाँ के दोनों सियासी और मज़हबी पेशवा थे उनकी चीन में भी, क्योंकि वो भी ठनककीपेज मुल्क था, उनकी बहुत क़दर थी मज़हबी तौर पर, सियासी तौर पर न हो। तो कुछ धोखा हो जाता था उनकी इज़्ज़त करें कि उनकी एक मज़हबी पेशवा की हैसियत से इज़्ज़त करते हैं या वो, लेकिन यह हुआ, उसका उलटफेर होता रहा, कभी चीनी वहाँ गवर्नर रहे, कभी तिब्बत अपने मुल्क में आज़ाद रहे। लेकिन फिर भी चीन को कुछ माने, कभी बिल्कुल आज़ाद हों, इस तरह का रहा। किसी और मुल्क ने तिब्बत की पूरी आज़ादी कभी तसलीम नहीं की थी और यही निशानी होती है, हिन्दुस्तान ने नहीं की थी यानी हिन्दुस्तान से मेरा मतलब अंग्रेज़ी हिन्दुस्तान ने, जब अंग्रेज़ यहाँ थे उन्होंने नहीं की थी। हाँ, उनकी राय यह थी कि तिब्बत चीनी निगरानी में है यानी सॉवरेनटी, में है लेकिन अपने घर में वो आज़ाद है, ऑटोनमी है उसकी, यह था। यह तो इतिहास कहता था, हम उसको कैसे पलट देते जो कि एक बात थी जो अंग्रेज़ों ने मानी थी, हमने, लेकिन अलावा इसके उसूल के हम करते क्या? हम क्या अपने पहाड़ हैं, हिमालय पहाड़ के पार फ़ौजें भेजते चीन से लड़ने के लिए कि तिब्बत को आज़ाद रखो। ज़ाहिर है नामुमकिन बात थी, हमारी क़ाबिलियत नहीं, हम कर नहीं सकते थे, हम यह कर सकते थे कि हम समझते, हम कुछ न करते ख़ाली इन्कार करते चीन की हुकूमत का वहाँ जाना। इन्कार करने से क्या फ़ायदा होता, तिब्बत वालों को हम ज़रा नहीं बचा सकते थे, ज़रा नहीं मदद कर सकते उनकी, और चीन वालों को उससे और भी उकसायें जिससे तिब्बत वालों को बहुत सतायें वो, जैसे उन्होंने बाद में बहुत सताया दो-चार बरस छोड़ के। हम कुछ कर नहीं सकते थे, कोई बात नहीं है कि हम अपने-अपने दिल में जो हमारी ख़्वाहिशें हों, पूरा हरेक आदमी नहीं कर सकता, ख़ासकर मुल्क नहीं कर सकते। फिर यहाँ, थोड़े दिन बाद वहाँ बड़ा बलवा हुआ आप जानते हैं और दलाईलामा उनके साथ हज़ारों, पैंतीस हज़ार आदमी क़रीब यहाँ आ गये, उनको हमने आने दिया और रहते हैं हमारे यहाँ, उनकी हम मदद कर रहे हैं, उनके बच्चों को हम पढ़ा रहे हैं, सब बातें। इस बात से चीनी लोग बहुत नाराज़ हुए। अब लाचारी है उनकी नाराज़गी, इस बात से तो हम बाज़ नहीं आये थे, हमें करना ही था। लेकिन मैं कहता हूँ कि वो आजकल बाज़ साहिबान को कुछ ज़रूर सोचना

चाहिए जो बहुत कहते हैं कि यह तुम से बारह बरस हुए गुनाह हुआ था उसका नतीजा है। गुनाह क्या कि तिब्बत वालों की तुमने मदद नहीं की यानी ग़ौर करने की बात है कि हम हिमालय पहाड़ के उस पार किसकी मदद कर सकते हैं फ़ौज से, हम नहीं कर सकते थे।

ख़ैर, लेकिन जिस वक़्त से तिब्बत में चीनी आये, इसको दस बरस हुए, क़रीब बारह बरस हुए हमारे सामने एक बात आ गयी कि सब जो हमारा और तिब्बत की सरहद है, सीमा है, जो कि एक सोयी हुई सीमा थी क्योंकि तिब्बत की कोई ताक़त नहीं थी, हमारी तरफ़ कोई इरादा नहीं था उधर जाने का। तो कोई उसमें जान नहीं थी सीमा में। अब चीनियों के आने के बाद वो एक जानदार सीमा हो गयी है, ख़तरनाक सीमा हो गयी है, हमने सोचा हमारी तरफ़ चीनी कोई हमला नहीं कर रहे थे उस वक़्त और उस वक़्त हमने सोचा कि हम इसकी हिफ़ाज़त कैसे करें, मामूली हिफ़ाज़त, कोई बड़ी लड़ाई की हिफ़ाज़त नहीं है। अब हमारी सीमा चाहे लद्दाख़ में, चाहे सीमा प्रान्त में ऐसी थी जो कि कोई सड़क वहाँ नहीं थी, सैकड़ों मील तक सड़कें नहीं थी और बेहद मुश्किल ज़मीन थी, पहाड़ी इलाक़े, बहुत ज़बरदस्त खायी-ख़ुन्दक और ऊँचे पहाड़, ख़ासकर लद्दाख़ में तो इत्ते ऊँचे कि वहाँ जाइये आप एकदम से, मैं गया हूँ वहाँ, यकायक सांस लेना मुश्किल हो जाता है, इतने ऊँचे। तो हमने कोशिश की, हमने सड़कें बनानी शुरू कीं और बनायीं और सैकड़ों मील सड़कें बन गयीं लेकिन इत्ते बड़े इलाक़े हैं, सब नहीं बन सकीं। सड़कें बनाने में, हर काम करने में हर चीज़ हमें वहाँ हवाई जहाज़ से ले जानी पड़ी हर चीज़, सड़क बनाने वाले ले जाना पड़े, उनके हथियार, उनका खाना, पीने का पानी, हर चीज़ ले जाना पडा, दिक़्क़तें थीं जो कि दिक़्क़तें चीनियों को नहीं थीं क्योंकि तिब्बत उस पार था सरहद के हमारे, वो हमवार ज़मीन है कमोबेश, वहाँ आसानी से आ सकते थे और सड़कें बना सकते थे वहाँ, मोटर ला सकते थे, हमें ऊँचे पहाड़ों को हिमालय को, पार करना। ख़ैर, यह तो वाक़िया था।

तो हमें उसी वक़्त से अन्देशा था कि हमारी सरहद पर कहीं कोई चीनी लोग गड़बड़ न करें, हमने उस वक़्त से कोशिश की हल्के-हल्के, क्योंकि हम यह नहीं समझते थे कि बहुत जल्दी होने वाली है और उसमें वक़्त भी लगता था। हमने सीमा प्रान्त पर, नेफ़ा पर अपने फ़ौजी अड्डे बनाये सरहद के पास। फ़ौजी अड्डे बहुत बड़े नहीं थे, यह पचास आदमी रख दिये, तीस-चालीस, इतने आदमी के अड्डे थे वो तो एक निशानी थी कि ज़मीन हमारी है, वो कोई बड़ी फ़ौज से तीस आदमी पचास आदमी तो नहीं लड़ सकते थे।

इसी तरह से हमने लद्दाख़ में बनाना शुरू किया, लद्दाख़ में ज़रा पीछे क्योंकि वहाँ ज़्यादा मुश्किल था आगे बढ़ना। और आप याद रखिये लद्दाख़ वग़ैरा हमारे उस वक़्त तक जब हम आज़ाद हुए वो कश्मीर की रियासत थी। कश्मीर की रियासत में कुछ भी नहीं किया था वहाँ, कुछ भी इंतज़ाम वहाँ नहीं था क्योंकि तिब्बत से कोई लड़ाई झगड़ा नहीं था। उसके बाद ही, आज़ाद होने के बाद ही हमारी, हमारी लड़ाई हुई कश्मीर के बारे में, पाकिस्तान से कश्मीर में। पाकिस्तान की फ़ौजों ने इधर-उधर भी कुछ और काश्मीर का

एक हिस्सा कब्ज़े में किया, अब तक है, लद्दाख़ का एक हिस्सा कब्ज़े में किया, फिर बाद में हमारी फ़ौजों ने उनको लद्दाख़ के बाज़ हिस्सों से अलग कर दिया, निकाल दिया। तो इसमें हम फंसे रहे और गुंजाइश ही नहीं थी कि हम जाके लद्दाख़ के दूसरे सिरे पर कुछ इंतज़ाम करें, सड़कें बनायें, उसके बाद जब कुछ ख़त्म सा हुआ तब हमने शुरू किया। यह सब पुराना है। और चीनियों के लिए आसान था क्योंकि वहाँ आदमी तो बहुत ही कम रहते हैं, उस हिस्से में लद्दाख़ के पहाड़ हैं, कुछ मैदान हैं, मैदानों में आये, पहाड़ों पर सड़कें बना के आगे आ गये, फिर हमने बनाये अपने फ़ौजी दस्ते रखने को, वो रखे। वो कोई इसलिए नहीं थे कि बड़ी लड़ाई लड़ें, उसके लिए बड़ी फ़ौजों की ज़रूरत है लेकिन इसलिए थे कि उनको रोकने के लिए, कि उसके बाद, कि बग़ैर लड़े न आयें वो, उसमें हम कामयाब हुए और एक कोई दो बरस से वो नहीं आगे बढ़े वहाँ। यों बढ़ सकते थे, बड़ी फ़ौज लाते तो हमारे छोटे दस्तों को हटा सकते वो लेकिन लड़ के हटाना है।

यह मैंने आपको पुराना क़िस्सा सुनाया। फिर इस सारे ज़माने में कुछ न कुछ हमारी बहस होती रही उनसे कि तुम ग़लत आये हो, यह हमारी ज़मीन है तुम क्यों आये और इधर तो हम तैयारी कर रहे थे सड़क बना के, दस्ते रखके, और उधर उनसे ख़तो-किताबत हो रही थी, काफ़ी बयान हमारी गवर्नमेंट और उनकी गवर्नमेंट के।

फिर यहाँ चाऊ-एन-लाई साहब आये थे दो-ढाई बरस हुए, उनसे बातें हुईं, इत्तिफ़ाक़ नहीं हुआ उनमें। तो फिर मैंने तजवीज़ किया अच्छा जो-जो हम कुछ अफ़सर मुक़र्रर करें आप भी कुछ कीजिये और वो लोग मिलकर देखें कि शहादत क्या है, आपकी क्या शहादत है हमारी क्या है, उस पर ग़ौर करें और रिपोर्ट करें दोनों हुकूमतों को। ख़ैर, यह वो हुआ, वो मिले, पीकिंग में मिले, दिल्ली में आके मिले, फिर रंगून में मिले, कोई पाँच-छः-सात महीने तक इस तरह से मिलते रहे और बहुत शहादत उन्होंने जमा की हमारी उनकी और फिर रिपोर्ट दी। रिपोर्ट दो थीं एक हमारे आदमियों की और एक उनकी, एक नहीं थी। हमारी राय में उस शहादत से हमारे लोगों ने पूरीतौर से साबित कर दिया कि जो चीनी नक़्शे हैं वे बिल्कुल ग़लत हैं, हमारे सही हैं। ख़ैर, उस पर मामला अटका, फिर उसके बाद से हमने उसको छाप दिया, अपने यहाँ छिपाने की बात नहीं थी, पार्लियामेंट में रखा, लोग पढ़ सकते थे। चीन में नहीं छपा, वो साल भर तक नहीं छपा, फिर भी पूरा नहीं छपा, कुछ थोड़ा सा बाद में उन्होंने कहा था। यह सिलसिला चलता गया, अभी पार साल, फिर इस साल में आपने सुना होगा कुछ लद्दाख़ में कुछ वाक़ियात हुए, बहुत बड़े नहीं लेकिन हमारा पैट्रोल है उनके पैट्रोल से मुठभेड़ हो गयी, गोली चल गयी, दो-एक आदमी मर गये इधर, दो-चार उधर मरे, यह हुआ, बहुत बड़ा नहीं।

अब इस सारे दौरान में, नेफ़ा में यानी सरहदी प्रान्त, पूर्वी सरहदी प्रान्त में कोई हिस्सा नेफ़ा का, किसी हिस्से में चीनी नहीं आये थे और उन्होंने कहा था, कोई इक़रार नहीं किया था लेकिन कहा था कि जिसे हम यही समझे कि इधर ये नहीं आयेंगे। इसके माने नहीं थे कि हमने तैयारी नहीं की, हमने की, कुछ, लेकिन उनकी तरह नहीं। इस चार-पाँच बरस से बहस हो रही है वो नहीं आये वहाँ। तो पहले दफ़े वो इधर उतरे थागला एक पास है,

आठ सितम्बर को थोड़े से आदमी उतरे, थोड़े से मतलब सौ, दो सौ, तीन सौ उतरे होंगे, फिर ज़्यादा होते गये। उस वक़्त से हम होशियार हो गये हैं इधर। और हमारे दस्ते जो थे फ़ौज के वो काफ़ी थे नहीं बड़ी फ़ौज से लड़ने को, हम अपनी फ़ौज वहाँ भेजने लगे, उसमें वही दिक़्क़तें जो मैंने आपसे कहा कि वहाँ हवाई जहाज़ से जाना पड़ा, हवाई जहाज़ से खिलाना पड़ा, पिलाना पड़ा, सामान देना पड़ा, सड़कें आसपास से, हालांकि हमने बहुत सड़कें बनायीं लेकिन वहाँ तक नहीं पहुँची थीं और हज़ार दिक़्क़तों से हमने भेजे, पहुँच गयीं फ़ौजें, उनको मैंने आपसे कहा कि खिलाने-पिलाने में काफ़ी दिक़्क़त हुई, वो सब हवाई जहाज़ से भेजा गया। उनको तो हमने भेजा, ज़रा जल्दी भेजा था, नहीं तो आमतौर से जब ऊँचे पहाड़ पर लोगों को भेजते हैं, बहुत ऊँचे पहाड़ों पर, ऊँचे पहाड़ इसको मैं नहीं कहता हूँ शिमला मसूरी, वो तो मामूली हैं लेकिन इसके दुगने ऊँचे पहाड़ हों क़रीब। तब जहाँ सांस लेना दुश्वार होता है, वहाँ कुछ आदी हो जाना पड़ता है आदमी को यानी कुछ ज़रा नीचे पहले रखके फिर ऊँचे, ज़रा ऊँचे, फिर आदी हो जाता है। आप चढ़ें जाके हिमालय की चोटियों पर तो लोग महीनों लगाते हैं, आदी हो जाते हैं हल्के-हल्के, नहीं तो दिल में बुरा असर पड़ता है, धड़कने लगता है और सांस भी कठिन होती है। हमें तेज़ी से भेजना था, हमने भेज दिया। ख़ैर, हमारे जवान तगड़े हैं उसको बरदाश्त कर गये, हालांकि कुछ न कुछ काम करने की क़ुव्वत कम हो जाती है इस तरह से ऊँचे पहाड़ों पर एकदम से जाने में, यह समझ लें, लेकिन कुछ बीमारी भी ज़्यादा हुई, नमूनिया वग़ैरा ज़्यादा हुई इस तरह से। जब गये थे वो उस वक़्त इतनी सर्दी नहीं थी, सितम्बर के बीच में हल्के-हल्के बढ़ती गयी सर्दी, अक्टूबर में काफ़ी हो गयी सर्दी, कहा जाता है कपड़े-कम्बल का। कपड़े, उन्हें माक़ूल कपड़े जो फ़ौजी हैं पूरे दिये गये थे। गर्म कम्बल, उनको पहले तीन कम्बल दिये गये थे फ़ी-सिपाही। जाने में तीन कम्बल फ़ी-सिपाही बड़ा बंडल हो गया, उन्होंने कहा हवाई जहाज़ से जा रहे थे कि हवाई जहाज़ में बहुत जगह लेते हैं इसको आप बाद में भेजिये, एक-एक कम्बल ले गये। उनके अफ़सरों ने कहा अच्छा बाद में भेज देंगे, बाद में भेजे गये तो हवाई जहाज़ से फेंक-फेंक के भेजे गये। अब फेंकने में पहाड़ी इलाक़े में पूरीतौर से वो मुहय्या नहीं हुए, बाज़ खड्ड में चले गये, क्योंकि दुश्मन सामने था याद रखिये। तो उसमें कुछ ज़ाया हो गये, कुछ कहीं-कहीं कमी हो गयी, बाद में हमने भेजा लेकिन कुछ कमी हो गयी, सर्दी बढ़ती जाती थी। यह बातें हुईं। और हथियार जो उनके पास, कहते हैं हथियार नहीं थे उनके पास काफ़ी, यह बिल्कुल ग़लत बातें हैं, हथियार जो थे वो हमारी हिन्दुस्तान की फ़ौज के जो अच्छे से अच्छे हथियार हैं वो थे। हाँ, कुछ नये तरीक़े के हथियार निकले हैं जिनको ऑटोमैटिक कहते हैं, वो उनके पास नहीं थे और वो अभी तक थोड़े दिन हुए अंग्रेज़ी फ़ौज के पास भी नहीं थे, अक्सर फ़ौजों के पास नहीं हैं बड़े मुल्कों के, क्योंकि वो दूसरी तरह से लड़ते हैं, वो हवाई जहाज़ से ज़्यादा भरोसा करते हैं, हमारी फ़ौज में भी नहीं थे लेकिन फिर भी हम पिछले दो बरस से सोच रहे थे बदलने के लिए और उसमें कुछ वक़्त लगा, अरसा लगा उसकी ब्ल्यू प्रिंट्स, नक़्शे लाने में और एक क़रीब साल भर से बनाने की पूरी कोशिश हो रही है। चुनांचे, अब, अब निकल रहे

हैं बनके, उस वक़्त नहीं थे वहाँ। तो यह जिस तरह इसकी नुक़्ताचीनी होती है हर जगह, गोया कि उनको नंगा भेज दिया, कपड़े नहीं, जूते नहीं, फ़िज़ूल बात है इसकी। अब यह सही बात है कि हमें इन सब बातों को बहुत तेज़ी से करना पड़ा, ख़ासकर वहाँ की अज़हद सर्दी के मारे और चूँकि हर चीज़ हवाई जहाज़ से फेंकनी पड़ती थी, वो कुछ मिलती थी कुछ ज़ाया हो जाती थी, नुक़सान होता था।

असल बात यह है मैंने आपसे पहले कहा कि हमने साल-दो साल हुए इस पर ग़ौर किया था, हमारे फ़ौजी अफ़सरों ने, उन्होंने कहा था कि चीनी अगर इधर से आये तो उनसे लड़ने की जगह हमें चुननी है। यह बेवक़ूफ़ी है, कि हम ऐसी जगह पर उनसे लड़ें जहाँ कि उनको फ़ायदा हो और आसानी से शायद वो जीत जायें। इसलिए हमें अपनी ज़मीन चुननी है उनसे लड़ने के लिए चाहे उसमें कुछ हट जाना पड़े शुरु में। यहाँ अख़बार वाले या और लोग समझे नहीं, समझे हट गये, भाग गये वग़ैरा, यह गुल मचाया। तो यह पहले से तय था और चुनांचे कुछ ऐसा ही इंतज़ाम था, कुछ होता गया और बीस तारीख़ को उन्होंने बड़े पैमाने पर हमला किया यानी हमारी फ़ौजों की पंचगुनी, छ: गुनी फ़ौज, अच्छे हथियार लेके, तोप-बन्दूक लेके किया। उनकी चुनी हुई फ़ौजें हैं, ये जिनको ख़ास सिखाते हैं पहाड़ी लड़ाई, यह उनकी ख़ास बात है और वो एक बीच में होते हैं फ़ौजी लोग और गुरीला लोग, दोनों काम सीखते हैं और अपने-अपने पीठ पर लाद कर लाते हैं, यह छोटी-छोटी तोपें आदमी लाते हैं जो आमतौर से नहीं ले जाते, उसके टुकड़े करके दो-दो, चार-चार आदमी उठा के ले जाते हैं, पहाड़ की चोटी पर बैठ जाते हैं जाके, वहाँ से तोप चलाते हैं। और खाना-पीना सब में ज़रा सादगी है उनमें, खाना वो चावल थैले में रखके जेब में रख लेते हैं, कुछ न कुछ चाय रख लेते हैं, जहाँ पानी गर्म कर सकें, उन्होंने चावल बनाया, चाय बनायी और खा लिया। कपड़े उनके हैं आप देखिये तो उनमें कोई शान नहीं है, हमारे फ़ौजी अफ़सर उन्होंने पहले दफ़े देखे तो उनको बहुत नागवार गुज़रे। यह क्या हैं फ़ौजें? वो एक रूई का गदेला पहने हुए थे, रूई का, मोटी रूई का कोट, गर्म तो रखता था उन्हें, अब वो देखने में शान का नहीं था, सही बात है। यह हमारी कुछ आदतें हैं कुछ ज़रा अंग्रेज़ीयत रखने की, यानी अंग्रेज़ीयत से मेरा मतलब अंग्रेज़ी फ़ौजी बातें करने की अच्छी फ़ौज, हमारे पास अच्छी वर्दी है, मज़बूत है, शानदार है, ये सब बातें थीं। अब हल्के-हल्के तजुर्बे से हम सीख रहे हैं, हमने जहाँ, यह वहाँ सर्दी अज़हद आयी, हमें मालूम हुआ यह, हमने फ़ौरन अपने कारख़ानों से कहा कि जल्दी से जल्दी रूई के कोट बनाओ और चुनांचे दो-चार रोज़ बाद ही हम भेजने लगे, पाँच सौ कोट रोज़ जाते थे उनके यहाँ, अब शायद एक हज़ार रोज़ कोट जा रहे हैं।

तो ये नये तजुर्बे थे, नयी-नयी बातें सीख रहे हैं, उससे फ़ायदा उठा रहे हैं, अपनी ग़लतियों से और औरों की और चीनी लोग बीस बरस से लड़ रहे हैं और वहाँ तिब्बत में जमा हैं, बड़ी फ़ौजें जमा हैं, इतनी फ़ौजें हैं कि आपसे क्या कहूँ, सारे हिन्दुस्तान की फ़ौजों से ज़्यादा तिब्बत में मौजूद हैं उनके यहाँ, चीन में तो बहुत ज़्यादा हैं और वहाँ सड़के उन्होंने बना लीं, जब चाहें फ़ौज को एक जगह पर ले जायें और हिन्दुस्तान में उतर आयें। ख़ैर,

यह सब है। मैं वाक़ियात बताता हूँ कि इसमें कोई परेशान होने की बात नहीं है, परेशान तो होने की, एक माने में लड़ाई अच्छी चीज़ नहीं है और लड़ाई में परेशानी होती है लेकिन यह समझना कि चीनी फ़ौज ज़्यादा अच्छी है या चीनियों ने ज़रा हमें हटा दिया, इससे कोई हम हमारे हाथ-पैर फूल जायें, यह तो बिल्कुल ग़लत बात है। मेरा पक्का यक़ीन है कि हमारी फ़ौज, हमारे जवान चीन के लोगों से या कहीं से भी अच्छे हैं। (तालियाँ) अब कुछ हो जाता है, कुछ एक आदमी जो हमला करता है वो चुन लेता है कहाँ हमला करे, जो उसका मुक़ाबला करता है उसको मालूम नहीं कहाँ हमला करे, वो फैला हुआ होता है। ये सब बातें हैं, हुई और हमारी कुछ नातजुर्बेकारी वग़ैरा, यह तो हो गया।

मैंने कहानी आपको इसलिए बतायी कि अजीब-अजीब ग़लत बातें कही जाती हैं और उनको आप न मानिये और ख़ामख़ाह ग़लत बातें कही जायें मुझे ऐतराज़ नहीं है, मेरे ख़िलाफ़ कही जायें या हमारे गवर्नमेंट के ख़िलाफ़, उनको हक़ है। लेकिन ऐसी ग़लत बात कहें जिससे हमारी फ़ौजों पे असर पड़े, उनको रंज हो फ़ौजों के अफ़सरों को, यह ग़लत बात है, इससे मुल्क की ताक़त कम होती है। इसलिए ऐसी बातें नहीं कहनी चाहियें और आप कम से कम समझ लीजिये। ख़ैर, यह बात हो गयी।

अच्छा चीनी आये मैंने आपसे कहा, वो थागला पास से सीमा प्रान्त के ऊपर। आज तक चीनी वहाँ नहीं आये थे, उस प्रान्त भर में सिवाय एक छोटा सा गाँव है जिसका नाम लोंगजू है, बिल्कुल सरहद के ऊपर है, वहाँ दो बरस हुए आये थे, ढाई बरस हुए, आज तक नहीं आये थे और उनकी तर्ज़ से, बातों से, लिखा भी था, उससे मालूम होता था कि इस बात से यहाँ नहीं आयेंगे कई इशारे उन्होंने किये थे और उन्होंने मान ली थी जो सरहद है, पहाड़ की चोटी वो बर्मा में भी जाती है, वहाँ उन्होंने बर्मा को मान लिया था। अगर उसी मिसाल को लगायें तो यहाँ भी मानना ही था। ख़ैर, हम समझते ही नहीं थे आयेंगे लद्दाख़ में, जो कुछ करें, आयें और आयें कैसे? यह कह के बीस तारीख़ को उन्होंने हमला किया, बीस-तीस हज़ार आदमियों से। और कहा क्या, कि, हम पर हमला कर रहे हैं, हम अपने को बचा रहे हैं। अजीब हालत, हम अपनी, हमारी ज़मीन पर आयें और हम उनको रोकने की कोशिश करें तो उनपे हमला हो गया। अब रोज़ उनकी ख़बरें आती हैं कि हिन्दुस्तानी फ़ौज ने, हिन्दुस्तान की इन्वेडिंग आर्मी, हमलावर फ़ौज ने हमारे ऊपर गोली चलायी, हम अपने ही मुल्क पर हमला करते हैं। ख़ैर, कमाल हासिल है उन्हें, सच्चाई को उलट-पलट के उसको बिल्कुल ही झूठ को सच बनाने की कोशिश करें, यह है। और यह होता जायेगा और हल्के-हल्के सच बात यह है, आपसे मैं कहूँ, हमें इन बातों का तजुर्बा नहीं है, इन बातों से मतलब लड़ाई लड़ने का नहीं, लेकिन हमारी रेडियो है, रोज़ होता है सुबह-शाम, उसको आप देखिये, उसको सुनिये और चीनी का सुनिये, वो लम्बे-लम्बे झूठ और क्या-क्या कहते हैं बार-बार कि लोग सुनते जायें उस पर असर हो। हमारे जो लोग कहते हैं वो नापतौल के बातें कहते हैं, ठीक है नापतौल के कहें, लेकिन कुछ जानदार हों तो ज़्यादा अच्छा है वो बातें उनकी। अब, हल्के-हल्के अब हम उसको भी कुछ कोशिश कर रहे हैं कि ज़रा वो भी बेहतर हो जायें, और बातें भी हों और हमारे सामने सारा, सारा

हमारे कारख़ानों का कैसा इंतज़ाम हो, फ़ौज में भर्ती हो रहे हैं, ग़रज़ कि गाड़ी चल रही है, हल्के-हल्के ज़्यादा तेज़ होगी, हिन्दुस्तान भी तो एक हाथी है, ज़रा उसके उठने में ज़रा देर लगती है लेकिन उठ जाता है, तो हाथी है। (तालियाँ)

तो अब आप फिर से मैं दोहराता हूँ कि इस बात को समझ जायें कि एक नया युग हमारे लिए शुरू हुआ है और मेरा ख़्याल है ख़ाली हमारे लिए नहीं एशिया भर के और शायद दुनिया भर के लिए और, और हमें, हमें ज़बरदस्ती ढकेल रहा है वो आजकल की दुनिया में, क्योंकि हम आमतौर से लोग रहते आजकल हैं लेकिन हमारे ख़्यालात सैकड़ों बरस पुराने हैं । पुरानी बातें बाज़ अच्छी हैं, उनको तो रखना है लेकिन फिर भी नयी बातों को पूरा समझना होता है और लड़ाई में बहुत ख़राबियाँ हैं, लेकिन एक उसमें ख़ूबी है, वो धकेल के लोगों को बढ़ाती है आगे। वो बातें हो रही हैं, होंगी और हमें और आपको तैयार होना है और हर वक़्त यह सोचना है कि लड़ाई महज़ होश से नहीं जीती जाती, वो ट्रेन्ड लोगों की, जोश तो ज़रूरी है। ट्रेन्ड लोगों के लिए, सिखाए हुए लोग, हर बात में, चाहे वो कारख़ाने में काम करता है, चाहे वो कहीं और, चाहे सिपाही है, सभों को अपना-अपना काम करना है और जो लोग हमारे नौजवान हैं, उनके ऊपर ख़ास इसका बोझा पड़ने वाला है। इस बात की फ़िक्र न करें वो कि वो छूट जायेंगे इससे, वो नहीं छूटेंगे, उनको बोझा उठाना है और जित्ते ज़्यादा वो तैयार हो जायें उत्ती ज़्यादा अच्छी तरह से उठायेंगे। एक जगह मुझे याद नहीं कहाँ का था, कुछ याद नहीं, शायद दिल्ली का था, कहाँ था, कुछ लड़कों ने कहा कि अब यह वहाँ सरहद पर क्राइसिस आ गयी है, मुश्किलें हैं, हमें छुट्टी मिल जानी चाहिए। यह तो एक अजीब बात है, यह दिमाग़ जिस दिमाग़ से निकलता है, समझे ही नहीं क्या बात है, छुट्टी का सवाल न कारख़ाने वाले का है, न किसान का है, न लड़कों का है, न आपका है, न मेरा है। कोई छुट्टी लेनी होती है रात को सोना पड़ता है वग़ैरा वो और बात है लेकिन अपने दिमाग़ को, अपने जिस्म को तैयार करना है इसके लिए। अगर लोग पढ़ते हैं तो उनको पढ़ने जाना है, वक़्त आयेगा उनका, वो आयें, उनको भर्ती करना हो तो भर्ती करेंगे और वो सब बड़े अफ़सर नहीं हो जायेंगे, मामूली सिपाही की हैसियत से भर्ती करेंगे जैसे इंग्लैंड, फ़्रांस वग़ैरा में हुआ, वहाँ कोई फ़र्क़ नहीं हुआ जब भर्ती का हुक्म हुआ, कांस्क्रिप्शन (conscription) जिसे कहते हैं। तो उसमें अमीर आदमी, ग़रीब आदमी कोई हो सब मामूली सिपाही की हैसियत से हो गये, सब मामूली सिपाही की हैसियत से जाना पड़ा। तो ज़रा एक बराबरी भी हो गयी। तो यह सब तो हो सकता है, आयेगा आपके सामने सभों के, उसके लिए अपने जिस्मों दिमाग़ को तैयार कीजिये और जो कुछ ट्रेनिंग आपको मिल रही है चाहे यूनिवर्सिटी में, चाहे किसी जगह काम करने में उसको अच्छी तरह से कीजिये ताकि आप ज़्यादा तैयार हों।

अभी इसी ज़माने में आपने देखा होगा दो हफ़्ते की बात है जब क़रीब-क़रीब उसी वक़्त जब हमारे ऊपर हमला हुआ, चीन ने किया, उसी वक़्त एक क्यूबा का मामला बहुत बढ़ गया था अमेरिका में और रूस में। और यकायक मालूम हुआ कि शायद चौबीस घण्टे के अन्दर और अढ़तालीस घण्टे में बड़ी लड़ाई छिड़ जाये और लड़ाई कैसी जिसमें एटम

बम्ब चलें, दो रोज़ तक या तीन रोज़ तक दुनिया एक तलवार की धार पर रही, पता नहीं क्या होने वाला है। अगर वो चल जाते एटम बम्ब वग़ैरा तब करोड़ों आदमी तबाह हो गये होते, दो-चार रोज़ के अन्दर ख़त्म हो गये होते। यह अन्दाज़ा है एक अमेरिकन साहब का, अन्दाज़ा है कि ऐसी लड़ाई में मैं भूल गया उनके अलफ़ाज़, कोई एक पचास-चालीस करोड़ आदमी मर जायेंगे पहले दो-चार रोज़ में। ज़रा ग़ौर कीजिये, दिमाग़ में आती नहीं यह बातें। अमेरिका में, रूस में, यूरोप में, इन्हीं तीन-चार जगह कोई चालीस-पचास करोड़ आदमी मर जायेंगे चन्द दिनों में एटम बम्ब से। यह भयानक चीज़, इसीलिए हम कहते हैं लड़ाई वग़ैरा ग़लत है। ख़ैर, वो बात ठंडी हुई, किसी क़दर कुछ समझौता सा हो गया, ठंडी हो गयी लेकिन हर वक़्त हम इस पर रहते हैं कगार पर, ख़तरे की। तो इसका भी कुछ असर पड़ा यहाँ चीन के मामले में। मैं नहीं जानता, चीन वाले जानते थे यह होने वाला है कि नहीं। ऐसा वक़्त उन्होंने चुना आने का जबकि एक दूसरा मामला दुनिया के सामने था।

अब हमारा क्या तर्ज़ रहे? चीन का हम मुक़ाबला कर रहे हैं, करेंगे पूरी ताक़त से और यक़ीनन आज नहीं साल भर बाद, दो बरस बाद जब कभी हो हम कामयाब होंगे। (तालियाँ) यह आप, पहली बात तो मेरी यह है कि आप अपने दिल को घबराइये नहीं, छोटी-छोटी बातों से हाथ-पैर ठंडे न हो जायें, जो लोग मैंने देखा है, सबमें ज़्यादा गुल मचाते हैं, ज़ोर दिखाते हैं, उनके हाथ-पैर ठंडे सबमें जल्द हो जाते हैं। तो इस तरह से, आप यक़ीन रखिये कि हम इस किसी सूरत से चाहे जो कुछ भी हो, हम अपने मुल्क की बेइज़्ज़ती नहीं होने देंगे, (तालियाँ) हम अपने मुल्क की आज़ादी क़ायम रखेंगे, रखी है, और कुछ उसमें जो कुछ हमें क़ुर्बानी करनी है वो हम करेंगे। और बीच में धक्के लगे, कोई ख़बर बुरी आई, जो हमें सदमा हो उसको बरदाश्त हम करेंगे, उससे हम और सीखेंगे, और ताक़त लेंगे। यह आप यह अपने सामने हर वक़्त रखिये और यह भी याद रखिये कि यह कोई चन्द हफ़्तों की, चन्द महीनों की बात नहीं है, मुमकिन है सालों लगें इसमें, मुश्किलें काफ़ी आयें, तो इसका हमें सामना करना है। मैं नहीं चाहता कि आप इस वक़्त जोश दिखाके महीना-दो महीना बाद ज़रा थक जायें, कहें हम तो थक गये क्योंकि यह थक जाना, थक जाने की गुंजांइश नहीं है ऐसे मुल्क में। आख़िर में अब जर्मनी जैसा बड़ा ज़बरदस्त मुल्क हारा, आख़िर नहीं उसको बरदाश्त हुई, जापान हारा क्योंकि उसमें पूरी मुल्क की ताक़त लग जाती है और सिर्फ़ फ़ौजें नहीं हारती हैं इसमें, मुल्क की कमर टूट जाती है आख़िर में। मैं नहीं समझता हमारी कमर कोई तोड़ सकता है, (तालियाँ) बावजूद इसके कि बीच में कोई आगे-पीछे कोई हार भी हो। अगर हम अपना फ़र्ज़ अदा करते हैं और मुल्क में मज़बूती से सब काम करते हैं उसी से ताक़त बढ़ती है।

तो हाँ, तो हमारी आप जानते हैं हमारी नीति रही है, पोलिसी रही है शुरू से, हमने कोशिश की सब मुल्कों से दोस्ती करने की, हमने चीन से कोशिश की। अब अगर वो हमसे हमारे ख़िलाफ़ जायें, हमसे दोस्ती के बजाय अदावत करें, अब इसका मैं क्या कहूँ, हमारा क़सूर तो नहीं है और यह कहें दोस्ती करना बुरा है, इसलिए यह भी ग़लत बात है।

हमने पंचशील एक चीज़ निकाली और लोग हंसी मज़ाक़ करते हैं। पंचशील क्या चीज़ है? मैं अब कहता हूँ कि पंचशील एक ही तरीक़ा है, दो मुल्कों के अन्दर। पंचशील क्या है? पंचशील है एक-दूसरे की आज़ादी मंज़ूर करना, एक-दूसरे पर हमला नहीं करना, एक-दूसरे के अन्दर मुल्क में कोई दख़ल न देना यानी हमले के अलावा लोग भेज दें जासूस वग़ैरा जो झगड़ा फ़साद करें। और एकाध चीज़ और है और आप इसी तरह के और एक-दूसरे का चाहे वो अलग-अलग क्यों न हों उनके तरीक़े, उनके समाज के तरीक़े जैसे कोई समाजवाद हो, साम्यवाद हो, पूँजीवाद हो, कुछ हो, हर मुल्क जैसा चाहे करे, हमें हक़ न हो दख़ल दें उसके मुल्क में, उसके मुल्क में जाके न उनको हक़ न हमारे को। अब यह बात मुनासिब बात है, ठीक है होना ही चाहिए, और कोई तरीक़ा नहीं है, अगर आप यह नहीं मंज़ूर करते तो इसके माने यह हैं कि हर वक़्त एक मुल्क दूसरे मुल्क को उखाड़ने की कोशिश करे जो लड़ाई की जड़ है, हो नहीं सकता। अब इस वक़्त दुनिया में सबमें बड़े मुल्क दो हैं, अमेरिका और रूस है। ज़ाहिर है कोई अमेरिका रूस को नहीं दबा सकता, न रूस अमेरिका को दबा सकता है, लड़ाई हो अगर तो दोनों तबाह हो जाते हैं, तो भी अक़्ल की बात यही है कि दोनों मंज़ूर कर लें कि भई तुम अपने रास्ते पर चलो हम अपने रास्ते पर, दख़ल न होवे, एक-दूसरे को दख़ल न दें, जिसको पीसफुल कोइग्ज़िस्टेंस (Peaceful co-existance) कहते हैं, क्योंकि जहाँ दख़ल देने का हुआ दूसरा लड़ेगा और लड़ाई होगी, तबाही आयेगी सभी को। तो पंचशील में जो कुछ हमने कहा था वो बिल्कुल सोलह आने सही है और करना पड़ेगा। अब हमारी बदक़िस्मती से इसमें, चीन ने पंचशील-पंचशील बहुत कहा और चीनी-हिन्दी भाई-भाई कहा, लेकिन उनके दिल में और दिमाग़ में उनकी नीयत ख़राब थी, नहीं उसपे रहे। तो इसके माने यह तो नहीं हैं मैं कहूँ आपसे कि सच बोलना अच्छा है और कोई झूठा आके कह दे, कि सच बोलना बुरा। झूठा, उसमें झूठ हो, मैं क्या करूँ दूसरे की ग़द्दारी का।

तो इसलिए अच्छा, तो हमारी पालिसी यह रही जिसको अंग्रेज़ी में नॉन-एलाइन्मेंट कहते हैं यानी जो बड़े-बड़े फ़ौजी गिरोह हैं, जिसके सरदार एक तरफ़ से रूस है, दूसरे तरफ़ से अमेरिका है और बाहथियार, रोज़ हथियार बढ़ते जाते हैं। हमने कहा हम किसी गिरोह में नहीं जायेंगे, हम दोनों से दोस्ती रखाना चाहते हैं, हम फ़ौजी समझौता किसी से नहीं करेंगे, यह हमने कहा और हल्के-हल्के इसको दुनिया भी समझने लगी और पहले शिकायत थी कि रूसी कहें कि इसके माने ये हैं कि छिपते हैं, यह हमारे, हमारे ख़िलाफ़ हैं, अमेरिका वाले कहें हमारे ख़िलाफ़ हैं, हल्के-हल्के समझने लगे वो कि हम किसी के ख़िलाफ़ नहीं हैं। इसकी आवाज़ अक्सर उठती है, अब फिर उठने लगी कि यह ग़लत है, उसूल नॉन-एलाइन्मेंट का हमें छोड़ देना चाहिए इसे। मैं समझता हूँ बिल्कुल यह आवाज़ ग़लत उठ रही है और जो हमारा उसूल नॉन-एलाइन्मेंट का वो सही है और सही रहेगा चाहे दूसरा कोई ग़लती करे, ख़राबी करे या बेईमानी करे उससे क़सूर नहीं ग़लत हो जाता।

अब हमें इस वक़्त बहुत ज़रूरत थी हथियारों की, तरह-तरह के सामान की और हमने एक मुल्क को नहीं, दुनिया के सब मुल्कों, सिवाय दो-चार के, सब मुल्कों को यहाँ का

534

अपना हाल लिखा कि, क्या हो रहा है इस चीनी हमले के बाद। अभी कोई दो हफ़्ते हुए और उनसे कहा हमें आपकी हमदर्दी चाहिए और जहाँ तक आप मदद कर सकें कीजिये। हमने अमेरिका को भी लिखा, रूस को भी लिखा, और मुल्कों को लिखा, हमने उसमें फ़र्क़ नहीं किया, अब जो दें हमें। अमेरिका ने, अंग्रेज़ों के मुल्क ने, एकाध और ने हमें बहुत जल्दी मदद दी, कुछ पहुँचायी, और पहुँचा रहे हैं, और पहुँचायेंगे, हम उनके बहुत मशकूर हैं (तालियाँ) और हम, लेकिन उन्होंने भी कहा, आख़िर वो भी तो समझदार हैं, उससे ज़्यादा समझदार हैं जो उनके पैरोकार हैं, यहाँ हैं बाज़ लोग। उन्होंने कहा कि हम नहीं चाहते हमारी मदद से तुम अपनी नीति जो है, नॉन-एलाइन्मेंट की, वो छोड़ दो, हम इस तरह से मदद हम तुम्हें देंगे, दे रहे हैं, लेकिन इसलिए नहीं कि हम तुम्हें ख़रीद लें, अपने-अपने पीछे बाँध लें अपनी नीति से। क्योंकि वो ग़लत बात थी और एक हमारी, हमें अपनी सारी पालिसी बदल देना जो कि सही है डर के मारे, हमारी हैसियत क्या रहती है, हमारी इज़्ज़त क्या रहती है और हम और हमारी ताक़त भी कम हो जाती है। हाँ, एक उनके, उनके ताक़त पर हम कुछ थोड़ा बहुत रहते भी, यह ठीक नहीं था तो और उन्होंने तसलीम किया इस बात को। लेकिन फिर बाज़ लोग यहाँ हैं हिन्दुस्तान में जो कि सलाह देते हैं कि तुम नॉन-एलाइन्मेंट छोड़ दो।

मैंने आपसे कहा रूस है। रूस ने हमसे, हमें कुछ हवाई जहाज़ देने को कहा था कुछ महीने हुए, और कुछ कारख़ाना हवाई जहाज़ बनाने का शुरू करने के लिए। वो उससे नहीं हटे, वो उन्होंने कहा कि हम जो वक़्त मुक़र्रर है उसको कुछ महीने शायद दिसम्बर कहा है, उस वक़्त तक हम दे देंगे हवाई जहाज़, और बनायेंगे कारख़ाना। तो हमें हर तरफ़ से, या बहुत तरफ़ से मदद मिल रही है हम ख़ामख़ाँ के लिए कूद के हम कहें कि इस फ़ौज में उसमें नहीं, दूसरे को दुश्मन बनायें, यह कौन सी अक़्ल की बात है उसूलन मेरी राय में ग़लती है और अलावा इसके, आजकल की हालत में और भी ग़लती है यह करना, हम जहाँ-जहाँ, हमें मदद मिलती है हम उससे लेते हैं, हम कोई, कोई रुकावट नहीं है हमारी नॉन-एलाइन्मेंट (non-alignment) की नीति में, कि हम किसी की मदद न लें जो देता है। हम हरेक की मदद लेते हैं और जो देगा लेंगे लेकिन पालिसी मेरी राय में हमें मज़बूती से उसको रखना चाहिए। अब हालत यह है कि इस लड़ाई की हवा हो जाने से, लड़ाई छिड़ जाने से बाज़ लोग समझते हैं कि मौक़ा अच्छा है लोगों के जज़्बात उठें, लोग गुस्से में हैं तो उनसे उनकी यह बुनियादी बातों को हमें बदल देना चाहिए या दबाव डालना चाहिए, सब बातों में।

मैंने आपसे नॉन-एलाइन्मेंट (non-alignment) का कहा लेकिन हमारे, हम चाहते हैं समाजवाद हो, सोशलिज़्म हो, जो लोग इसको नहीं चाहते आमतौर से नहीं कह सकते थे, अब दूसरे ढंग से कहें कि हाँ नहीं होना चाहिए और लोगों को धोखा देंगे। मैं समझता हूँ और भी ज़रूरी है इस लड़ाई की वजह से कि हम उन बातों को पक्का करें, क्योंकि एक हमारी लड़ाई फ़ौजी लड़ाई नहीं है, फ़ौजी है लेकिन फ़ौजी लड़ाई तो उसका एक छोटा हिस्सा है, हमारी लड़ाई होती जाती है जैसे आजकल की लड़ाइयाँ होती हैं, जिसको कहते

हैं एक मुल्क के सब रहने वाले उसमें सिपाही हैं 'ए. नेशन इन आर्म्स' यह हो जाता है।
मेरा मतलब नहीं है कि हरेक आदमी बन्दूक लेके फिरे लेकिन हरेक सिपाही अपना-अपना
फ़र्ज़ अदा करे, सारा मुल्क लड़ता है और अगर कहीं इत्तिफ़ाक़ से, बदक़िस्मती से लड़ाई
ने यह ढंग इख़्तियार किया कि आपके दिल्ली में बम्ब के गोले पड़ें तब आप क्या करेंगे?
तब तो आपके घर, आपके घर में आ गयी लड़ाई, उस वक़्त आपको हिम्मत दिखानी है,
घबरा के भागना नहीं है, चारों तरफ भाग रहे हैं लोग परेशान होके, बल्कि सामना करना
है उसका, जो इंतज़ाम करना है करना है, मदद करनी है, हज़ार बातों के लिए तैयार हमें
होना चाहिए।

मैं बार-बार आपसे इसलिए कहता हूँ कि हमें ख़्याल, अब तक हम समझे नहीं हैं क्या
लड़ाई चीज़ है, किती ख़तरनाक चीज़ है, ख़तरनाक या कुछ हम अपनी आज़ादी तो नहीं
छोड़ेंगे उसके लिए, और मेरा ख़्याल है कि हमारी काफ़ी ताक़त है। हाँ, शुरु में चीनियों
की ताक़त जमा थी तिब्बत में, बहुत दिन से तैयारी थी, बड़ा फ़ायदा उन्हें हुआ, और भी
फ़ायदा हो जाये, लेकिन हमारी ताक़त है अगर हम उसको मुनज़्ज़म करें, ठीकतौर से बढ़ें
और जाने क्या-क्या बातें बढ़ें।

मैंने आपसे हवाई जहाज़ का कहा, कोई हवाई जहाज़ इस वक़्त दिल्ली नहीं आता
लेकिन मैं तो नहीं कह सकता नहीं आयेगा, लड़ाई नहीं बढ़ेगी, दिल्ली क्या और जगह
हैं, बड़ी-बड़ी हमारी जगह हैं। फ़र्ज़ कीजिये हमारे बड़े-बड़े कारख़ाने हैं उस पर हमला हो,
कारख़ाना ख़त्म हो जा सकता है। इस सभों को हमें ख़्याल करना है, हिफ़ाजत करनी है
और ख़ासतौर से लोगों के दिमाग़ों को तैयार रखना है कि जो भी कुछ हो हम उसको
बरदाश्त करेंगे, तैयार होंगे, और उसका सामना करेंगे और मुक़ाबला करेंगे। यह बात थी,
मैं चाहता हूँ, यह बात है, आजकल के हिन्दुस्तान ने दिखा दिया हमें यह बात है लेकिन
फिर भी मैं आपसे दोहराता हूँ कि इस बात को समझ लेना चाहिए, यह न समझें कि हम
गुलशोर मचा के काफ़ी हैं हम जीत जायेंगे और इस बात से मैं आपको चाहता हूँ, आपके
दिमाग़ को ख़ासतौर से होशियार कर दूँ कि इस लड़ाई के नाम पर लोग हमारी बुनियादी
जो नीति है, बुनियादी पालिसी है जो कि मुल्क के लिए अच्छी समझ के हमने रखी थी
उसको न हटा दें, उसको न पलट दें। क्योंकि अगर लड़ाई हम लड़ते हैं तो ज़ाहिर है सारा
मुल्क लड़ाई नहीं लड़ रहा है, इसलिए कि एक छोटा सा गिरोह उससे फ़ायदा उठाये, छोटा
सा गिरोह रुपया पैदा करे, रुपया बन जाये, लखपति-करोड़पति हो जाये, कुछ लोगों को
फ़ायदा हो, बाक़ी लोगों को बोझा उठाना पड़े, बोझा तो उठाना है मुल्क को, सभों को।
ऐसा मुल्क लड़ाई के बाद हुआ, तो हमारी लड़ाई से फ़ायदा क्या, बहुत कम फ़ायदा हुआ
इसलिए हमें उस बात को सामने रखना है जो हमने कही थी कि हम एक उधर जा रहे हैं
चाहे हल्के-हल्के जायें लेकिन जा रहे हैं समाजवाद की तरफ, सोशलिज़्म की तरफ, जिसमें
सब लोगों को बराबर का मौक़ा तरक़्क़ी का मिले, जिसमें ऊँच-नीच कम हो और बल्कि
कोशिश करनी चाहिए कि लड़ाई के दौरान में भी ऐसे काम करें जिससे उधर हम जायें।

इसलिए इन बातों से आप होशियार रहिये यह जो बहकाने वाली बातें होती हैं अब लड़ाई के पर्दे में ग़लत बातें लोग तय करवाते हैं, ग़लत लोगों को आज शायद सामने कर दें और आप असली बात नहीं समझ के उन बातों को मंज़ूर कर लें ।

फिर मैं आपसे बहुत वक़्त आपका लिया और कुछ समझाने की मैंने कोशिश की कि क्या हाल है, क्या-क्या हमें करना है, दिमाग़ को तैयार करना है, हमारी कई कमेटियाँ बनी हैं, एक दिल्ली के मेयर साहब ने दिल्ली की कमेटी बनायी है और एक हर सूबे में बन रही है, हिन्दुस्तान भर की एक सिटीज़न सेंट्रल कमेटी है, एक ख़ास डिफ़ेंस की कमेटी है, एक रुपया जमा करने की, सब तरफ़ हल्के-हल्के नक़्शा बनता जाता है और रास्ता आपको दिखता जाता है कि क्या-क्या करना है, उसके लिए आप तैयार हों । अगर आपके दिलो-दिमाग़ तैयार हैं तो बातें हल्के-हल्के होती जायेंगी और इस दौरान में हम भी एक मुल्क में, तकलीफ़ें बहुत होंगी लेकिन एक मज़बूत, ताक़तवर और एक ट्रेन्ड मुल्क हो जायेंगे जो कि हर मुसीबत का सामना कर सकें। (तालियाँ) इस तरह से हमें इसको देखना है और आगे बढ़ना है ।

अब आप जो मैंने आपसे कहा कुछ सोचिये उसको और क्योंकि मैंने इसी नीयत से कहा कि नक़्शा आपके सामने रखूँ ताकि आप उसको सोच सकें, समझ सकें और हल्के-हल्के दिमाग़ आपका आये और इस तस्वीर को समझें जो हमारे सामने है और जो आने वाली है और उसके लिए हम तैयार हों ।
जयहिन्द !

[Translation begins:

Brothers and Sisters,
I spoke here day before yesterday more or less on the same subject that is on the agenda today. I do not know how many of you were present here then. That was a special meeting of government servants and was attended in very large numbers.[178] Anyhow, please forgive me if I repeat some of the things that I said earlier. There are many things to talk about. But I want you to think how our lives in India have changed during the last three weeks.

Three weeks ago, the Chinese forces attacked us. They had occupied some of our territory in Ladakh more than five years ago. Their troops have been seen trickling down from the mountains into the NEFA area since September. But exactly three weeks ago, on the 20th October, they launched a massive attack which was a great shock to all of us. Apart from that, I would say that the Chinese aggression has ushered in a new era in the crazy game of international politics which is sound at times but mostly painful. A new science which we in India have been unfamiliar with so far, has begun in the world theatre. Our

178. See item 300.

attention is now being drawn in a completely new direction. Two days later I had made a radio broadcast[179] in which I said that we in India were not completely familiar with the realities of the modern world. What did that imply? People have chosen to interpret it in strange ways. I did not mean that the path we had been following so far was wrong. What I meant was that we should have been more in touch with reality. The world is a ruthless place especially for the weak. We should have realised that and also what constitutes power in international politics. We were labouring under a delusion. It is not because we were peace loving. Thousands of years of culture and Gandhiji's precepts conditioned us towards peace and India became well known in the world as a messenger of peace. What we did was right. But in spite of that as you know, terrible events which have had nothing to do with peace, have shattered the country from time to time. I am not talking about military warfare but internal dissensions. The communal riots which rocked the city of Delhi and the Punjab were no examples of peace.

If we had understood the real meaning of peace in the sense that Gandhiji meant it, we would have become strong. To the extent that we were able to grasp the true meaning of peace and non-violence, we did become strong enough to overthrow the foreign yoke. But peace implies real moral courage. In all my seventy two years, I have not come across anyone who was braver than Gandhiji. He had courage and an iron will which did not bend towards wrong means, no matter what the consequences were. He did not bow down to the might of a great imperial power and trained his people to challenge that might by peaceful means.

So that is what peace really means, to make oneself strong and courageous, to stand up for one's principles, unmindful of the consequences. We learnt his lesson only superficially but even to that extent, we benefited. However, when our knowledge was put to the test, we failed miserably. The country was divided into two and in the aftermath of Partition, barbaric communal riots rocked North India which showed our weakness and not our peace loving nature or strength. It was a sign of anger, weakness and bitterness. We began to think that shouting slogans and taking out processions are symbols of strength. We forgot that power means something else in the world, no matter how you look at it. What is military power, for instance? It is the armed forces, army, navy and air force. They are extremely disciplined and a source of silent strength in a crisis. Military power has played a great role in the two world wars in which millions of people were killed and entire cities lay in ruin. Compared to that, what we consider strength by shouting slogans, is nothing. It may be used to

179. See item 259.

threaten one another. But it cannot stand a real challenge. People come to me asking to be sent to the frontier to fight. I do not know what they can do there without rigorous training. They seem to think that they can show their strength by making a noise.

Anyhow, what I mean is that the events of 20th October have jolted us into the realisation that we need more than mere enthusiasm to face the challenges of the modern world. A new era has been ushered in the history not only of India, but of Asia and the world. The conflict on our borders has been on a small scale. But in spite of the limited nature of the conflict it has grave import. For one thing, a war between India and China, the two giants in Asia, is in itself a historic event. When two great countries engage in a conflict, many considerations like national dignity and honour, territorial sovereignty, etc., assume significance. Therefore, it cannot be ruled out as a minor conflict lasting a few days, something like the events which occurred years ago in Hyderabad or in Goa recently. There is no comparison. This is harsh reality which people have not been able to grasp fully yet. But we have been given a glimpse of what the world is really like and what independent nations must do to hold on to their freedom.

So, it is in this sense that I said a new chapter in the history of India has begun. I do not know how long this state of affairs will last. But however longer it lasts, it is bound to change India. What we must consider is where that is likely to take us. I do not mean throwing out the Chinese troops. I am sure that we will succeed in doing that. But what we have to be clear in our minds is how much we will change in the process. It is essential that we should change because only by changing can we combat this challenge. We will increase our military strength and modernise and train the existing forces, equip them with new weapons, etc. But this is a task which cannot be accomplished by the uniformed soldier on the border alone. Every man and woman must become a soldier in the national cause. The farmer, the factory worker, the shopkeeper and the white collared worker must all do their duty by working hard in their chosen profession. Everyone must acquire discipline for that is a great source of strength. Do you know how many people there are, working behind the scenes to keep the soldiers at the front? Firstly, there is the problem of keeping them fed and properly equipped. The farmer and the factory worker are responsible for supplying everything, including uniforms and weapons and equipment, that a soldier needs. So, if we have a lakh of soldiers engaged in battle, there are twenty, thirty, forty lakhs human beings working behind the lines to keep them there. In fact, their number would be even larger. The whole nation assists the soldiers in their task. A disciplined people working together contribute greatly to a nation's strength.

I want you to understand this clearly. I hear that some people think they are showing great bravery by agitating in front of the Chinese ambassador's house, or throwing stones at it. Such behaviour condemns us in the eyes of the world. The world, particularly the western world, is more experienced than us in the matter of warfare. The countries of Europe and the Soviet Union, etc., have fought two great world wars within my own living memory. There was not a single family which did not lose a son in the war and entire cities were reduced to rubble. So the war was forcibly brought to their door steps. In India, we sit at home, reading about the brave acts of our soldiers in the newspapers. We must help in the war effort. The fact is that I am not always in agreement with western ideas and thought. I think we are better than them in many ways. But the West has much more experience of war. So they do not take us seriously when we make a noise and say that we will throw out the Chinese. We must no doubt have faith in ourselves. But it has to be backed up in other ways.

This is the picture that emerged, though hazily, three weeks ago and it will become clearer as time goes by. We also saw the tremendous wave of emotion which the Chinese aggression aroused in almost every man, woman and child in India. It was indeed a strange spectacle. We were suddenly confronted with the phenomenon of a vast country, burying its innumerable internal quarrels, rallying forth in a spirit of patriotism and expressing a desire to help in the war effort. This was a good thing for our country though the circumstances in which it happened were painful and shocking. A number of our brave young soldiers died, fighting gallantly. But they were outnumbered almost one to eight by the Chinese troops. It was difficult to face them successfully. Anyhow, a great reawakening has taken place in India which is of great significance.

Now we are engaged in preparations—you must have heard a little about what we are doing. Laws have been altered, new regiments have been formed and we have stepped up the production of armaments and military equipment [Applause]. The ordnance factories where earlier there were daily labour disputes and demands for increase in wages and fixed working hours, etc., we suddenly find that work is being done twenty-four hours a day. I am told that the work is done in three shifts of eight hours each. The important thing is that people are working willingly. They are working not only for the sake of the overtime wages but because they feel that they are helping the war effort. This has a greater impact and the goods they produce become more valuable as a consequence. Wherever you go in India, in Bombay, Delhi, Calcutta or in the rural areas, you find a new spirit of patriotism burning bright in the hearts of the people. At the same time, I would like to remind you that even now most people have not understood the full implications of what the future hold for us. We must be prepared for every eventuality.

540

People have been levelling all kinds of criticism against the government saying that we were not prepared and that the soldiers did not have proper uniforms and guns, etc. There is only a small grain of truth in that. It is not completely true. It is absurd that they were not given proper clothes. Everyone had uniforms and blankets. The fact is that Ladakh where the fighting is taking place at a great height and the temperatures are usually 20 or 30 degrees below freezing. You can imagine how inhospitable the conditions would be.

Anyhow, on the one hand, people have rallied around and made declarations of unity and cooperation. On the other hand, I have heard that there are various parties, in Delhi and elsewhere which keep criticising the government, that we were not prepared and what not. Well, if we are useless, the people of India have the power to throw us out and elect someone else. I have no objection. But so long as we are in power, we must march in step (cheers). This is a lesson which we have not yet learnt fully. This was one of the first things that Gandhiji taught us.

Let me remind you of a very old incident at the time of the non cooperation movement. The Congress had not accepted it then, or rather, Gandhiji had not put it before the Congress. You may remember that Gandhiji had become a member of the Khilafat committee. At one of the meetings a number of our leaders were sitting together and a heated debate was taking place over the imposition of martial law in the Punjab. Somebody said that the British government had behaved treacherously. Gandhiji, a frail little man, got up and said that while it was possible that what they were saying was true, the question was what we were going to do. He said we must take strong and positive action. The method he advocated was of peace and non-violence and yet it would be a war with all the good characteristics of battle. There would be martial discipline and training. He said that he was not bothered whether he was elected leader in this war or not. But if he was chosen as the commander-in-charge, all would have to follow the path chalked out by him [Applause]. He also said that the moment the people became dissatisfied with him, they had the right to remove him. But so long as he was in charge, he would expect the people to behave like soldiers. Everyone cannot be allowed to sing his own tune or pull in a different direction.

Now this was a new thing which was being heard in India for the first time. I remember that the other elderly leaders sitting there were somewhat taken aback by this, though Gandhiji had said everything in a very mild manner. But what Gandhiji said in effect was that if we engaged in the battle for freedom, there will be martial law in India. Not the kind of martial law imposed by the British. What Gandhiji meant was that the people would have to behave in an extremely disciplined way and live as if under a martial law obeying the leader's orders like a soldier obeys his officer. Until then, the Congress had been content to pass resolutions or do nothing. Gandhiji was showing a new path in which there was to be very little talk and more of practical work. He said that we must determine on a course of action and then do it with military orderliness and precision.

That was the beginning. Well, I was young then and liked what Gandhiji said. But I also filled with silent laughter when I saw the other older leaders' faces who had been making impressive speeches a little while earlier. Here was Gandhiji saying something entirely new in his calm way and issuing a call to the nation to fight intrepidly. Well, for years after that, Gandhiji trained and moulded us. We were small people and ignorant. So we were not able to learn everything that he taught us. But even the little that we managed to learn contributed greatly to the country's strength and ultimately by following the path shown to us by Gandhiji, we got freedom.

Many of you present here may have heard Gandhiji's name or seen him from afar. Others may not have even seen him or at least have forgotten those years. It is difficult for us to forget because we lived under his shadow for twenty-five years and worked with a single-minded dedication towards one goal. We stumbled occasionally but were more often uplifted by the spirit of nationalism. Those years have left a deep imprint on our hearts and minds. I am reminded of that bygone age when I see people being led astray and thinking that hooliganism is a symbol of strength. If we behave in this manner, our stature in the world suffers. When England, France, Germany and the Soviet Union were engaged in war, you could not see such behaviour anywhere. Every man, woman and child became a soldier whether they were in uniform or not. Nobody had the time to make a noise or stage demonstrations and what not. So the western countries think that we are not fully aware of realities and we behave childishly. I was very sorry to hear these criticisms levelled against us. Everyone in India has the right to speak out against a wrong. But we do not have the right to do anything which weakens us as a nation. Everyone says that our jawans are extremely brave. But at the same time they criticise their officers and others who are responsible for arrangements. It is absurd. They do not know what they are talking about. The fact is that India's thoughts had never leaned towards war. We have always talked about peace. So, it is not easy to change one's thinking suddenly. We need to acquire all kinds of new skills and power. We are doing our best.

A new era has been ushered in the history of India. Later on historians will record how it will affect the country. But at the moment, you and I and all of us have to live through it and face the challenge with courage. How we do it depends on all of us. We must realise that it is not enough to show a superficial enthusiasm. We must change our attitude towards our day-to-day working in such a way that we can contribute effectively to the national effort. The farmer must increase his production and the factory worker must work hard to produce more goods. Ultimately, the armed forces cannot fight with courage alone. They need weapons too. But the real thing is a nation's economic strength. The more a nation produces the more surplus it has to buy military equipment and aeroplanes, etc.

I had recently visited the Delhi University. I told the students that they should work hard at their studies and not waste time. The opportunity for studying may not come again. Therefore, they must utilise the time at their disposal to the full. I also advised them to join the NCC. School boys can join the ACC.[180] If necessary they may all have to join the regular army. Anyhow, we must be well prepared. NCC will be made compulsory for everyone in college. Even now there are about three or four lakh students in the NCC. Soon every single boy will have to join. The good cadets can then be selected for further training. The children will be given basic training in the ACC. Then we have the territorial army. All these things are apart from the territorial army. We are concentrating on improving them and of course, increasing the strength of the armed forces. The most difficult thing is to train officers for it takes time. We are making arrangements to accelerate the process of training.

However, there are some essential requirements behind all this. One is to improve agriculture. Then the industries must function effectively. There is no question of a strike or a lock out. At the same time, the factory owners must treat the workers well. There should be complete unity in the country. Each one of us must think of ourselves as a cog in India's armed forces. Our strength lies in unity and cooperation. As you know, a huge machine can go out of order. All of us are cogs in a large machine. You must bear this in mind. It is possible that we who hold the reins of power are not fully qualified for the responsibility that we have been entrusted with. The fact is very few people are ever fully qualified to handle such great responsibilities with ability and patience without giving in to panic. There are very few people in any country who can rise to the occasion in a crisis. But we hope that gradually, more and more people will develop a quiet strength and determination. I want you to bear all this in mind. It is possible that we may suffer reverses in battle. But that is part of the game, losing a battle or an initial retreat does not imply losing the war.

Let me tell you that more than two years ago, some of our top military generals had drawn up an operational plan in case of an attack by China. The opinion of top military experts was that we should not make an attempt to stop the Chinese at the border since conditions there would be more favourable to

180. Auxiliary Cadet Corps

them. Even if we are able to throw them out, it would be at an enormous cost. Therefore we should retreat a little and then make a stand. Now people are asking why we have retreated and who is to blame, etc. No one is at fault. This is a military matter in which two great powers are involved. The important consideration is to choose a position most advantageous to us. It is not a game in which minor victories are more important than winning the war.

There have been great battles in the history of the world. Germany had become extraordinarily powerful. It conquered France and inflicted a crushing defeat on British forces to begin with. But ultimately Germany lost. Please do not think that I am making comparisons. I do not think China is so powerful as to play such games with India. But we must be prepared for shocks. We must face them with equanimity and not give into panic. We are not going to lose. I am aware that it is the fault of the newspapers that the situation appears alarming. Questions are being asked about who is to blame for our retreat after minor engagement and what not. I cannot say anything about that. But the entire attitude is wrong. It is like panicking in a minor illness and changing doctors every day. This no way for an individual or a nation to get well.

Now let us look at what has happened. To go back a little, a great revolution occurred in China, about twelve to thirteen years ago. We came to the conclusion that whether we agreed with their ideology or not, we must recognise the new government because it was the legitimate government. If we did not do so, we would be the ones to suffer. So, we were the second nation to recognise the new Chinese government and gradually other countries followed suit. Burma was first. As far as, I remember we recognised the People's Republic on the 31st of December, 1949 or rather the 1st January, 1950. It was our intention to maintain friendly relations with China and we gave ample proof of this, though in the beginning, their newspapers behaved very badly. It used to amaze me that an ancient country like China with its old culture and civilisation could be so carried away. But nobody was to blame. The old culture and civilisation came to an end with the new revolution. They called us imperialist dogs and what not. Whether it is true or not, it is not becoming of any nation to say such things about another. Well, it began to penetrate very gradually into their heads that they were on the wrong track. So they changed their tune and began to behave in a civilised way. A few years passed in mutual good relations.

One thing that irritated us was the maps that they had drawn up showing a very large part of Ladakh on the borders to be Chinese or rather Tibetan territory. Since China had swallowed up Tibet, they laid claim to Ladakh too. We drew their attention to this discrepancy and sent our own maps. Their reply was that their maps belonged to the pre-Revolutionary days and that they had not had time to change them. They said that we could meet at a mutually convenient time to settle the matter. We drew their attention again and again to the fact that they had not changed their maps and they continued to stall. On my visit to Peking and again when the Chinese came to India. I mentioned the matter orally and the reply was that they would do it at leisure. Now that did not mean that they accepted our version of the border demarcation. But at least, they said that the old map was not correct and that they would change it.

Well, when China sent its troops into Tibet and occupied it, some people criticised us for having accepted their occupation. I cannot understand how anyone who knows the facts can say such a thing. First of all, the fact is that during the hundreds of years of its history, Tibet has been off and on under Chinese suzerainty and at other times, the relationship between the two countries has been pretty ambiguous. The problem was that the Dalai Lama was both the political and religious head of the state in Tibet, China being a Buddhist country had always treated Dalai Lama with great respect, at least as the religious head even if not politically. So it was misleading. Anyhow, the situation was thoroughly confusing because at times, there have been Chinese governors in Tibet and at other times, it was independent but recognised Chinese suzerainty. No country had even accepted Tibet's complete freedom which is what really counts. The British government in India had not done so because their view was that Tibet was autonomous but under Chinese suzerainty. This is the historical record. Could we have sent in our troops across the Himalayas to fight the Chinese for Tibet's independence? It was obviously an impossible task for us. We simply did not have the resources or ability to do that. We could have protested against the Chinese invasion of Tibet. But it would have been no use for we could not have saved the Tibetans and on the contrary, our protest might have led to greater atrocities by the Chinese. In fact, that is what happened a few years later.

Anyhow, we could have done nothing, no matter what our wishes in the matter were. No individual or nation can fulfill all their desires. As you know there was a great revolt in Tibet and the Dalai Lama along with 35 thousand of his followers sought asylum in India. We are doing everything we can to help him and are educating the Tibetan children. All this angered the Chinese. But we were not daunted. We had to do what was right. Those who are saying today that we have come by our just deserts because we did not help the Tibetans twelve years ago must bear all this in mind. We could not have helped anyone militarily across the Himalayas.

However, ever since the Chinese occupied Tibet about ten or twelve years ago, we realised that the border which had been quiescent until then, since Tibet was a small power, had suddenly become alive and fraught with danger. Even then we began to think of ways of defending that border from a purely security point of view. There were no regular roads for hundreds of miles in the NEFA and Ladakh area. It is extremely difficult mountain terrain with dangerous gorges and steep climbs, particularly in Ladakh. It is at such a great height that it becomes difficult to breathe.

So, we started building roads and have managed to cover hundreds of miles. But the border is so long that it has not been possible to cover the entire area. We have had to use aeroplanes even to transport material for building roads and food and equipment for the workers. These are difficulties which the Chinese did not have to face because Tibet is a plateau. They could come over easily, bringing road building material by lorries and trucks whereas we have to cross the high Himalayan range.

We have had a suspicion since then that the Chinese may stir up trouble on the border though we did not think anything was likely to happen in a hurry. We started establishing border posts with small army units of thirty, forty troops each. It was merely a symbol to show that, that was our territory. We could not hope to fight a great war with a handful of troops.

Similarly, we started establishing military posts in Ladakh too though it was more difficult in that area. Until independence Ladakh was a part of the Kashmir state. No arrangements had ever been made for its defence because there was no quarrel with Tibet. After independence, we had to go to war with Pakistan over the Kashmir issue. A part of Kashmir was occupied by Pakistani troops and it continues to be so till today. Indian forces managed to throw Pakistani troops out of part of Ladakh. So, we were absorbed in all these problems and there was no chance for us to begin building roads at the other end of Ladakh for a long time. We could start only when the war with Pakistan was over. All this is old history. It was easy for the Chinese because for one thing, most of the border area is no man's land. They could come down easily into the plains and build roads. Then we established our own check posts, not with any aggressive intentions but purely as a defensive measure. We succeeded in this for a while and the Chinese did not advance any further for a year or two. They could have easily removed our small check posts with superior numerical strength. But they would have had to fight. I am giving you the background. In the meanwhile, the debate continued with India pointing out that the Chinese occupation was illegal. The correspondence between the governments grew in volume. At the same time we continued our preparations for defence by building roads and establishing check posts, etc.

Then Mr Chou En-lai came to India two and a half years ago. We had talks but could not reach an agreement. Then I suggested that we should appoint officers from both sides to try to find a solution acceptable to both. This was decided upon and they met in Peking, Delhi and then in Rangoon. The meetings continued over a period of six or seven months and having collected a great deal of information, a report was submitted. In our view, on the basis of those facts, we had clearly established that the Chinese maps were absolutely wrong and we were right. Well, the matter stopped there. We published a report and placed it on the table of the House.[181] In China, the report was not published for a year and even then, only excerpts were made known. This went on. Then as you heard, there were some incidents on the Ladakh border last year and again this year. There were some exchange between our patrols and theirs and firing took place in which a few soldiers were killed on both sides. It was not a major incident.

During this entire period, the Chinese had not set foot inside the NEFA border. No definite promises were made but it was tacitly accepted that they would not encroach in that area. Yet we made preparations. In all these four or five years, the Chinese had not advanced in that sector. Then for the first time, on the 8th of September, about 200 or 300 Chinese troops crossed over into the NEFA area. The number kept increasing. We became vigilant immediately. Our forces stationed there were not enough to fight against a vast army. So we started sending in reinforcements. But as I mentioned there were several difficulties in the way. The only means of transport was aeroplanes. Though we had been building roads in that area, they did not go right up to the border. So everything, food, equipment, arms and ammunition had to be transported by planes. Moreover, the troops had been sent in a hurry and so they did not have the time to get acclimatised to the heights. Breathing is difficult at great heights until one gets used to it. It takes months for an individual to get acclimatised. In the beginning there is a severe strain on the heart and breathing becomes difficult. But we were in a hurry. So they had to be sent anyhow, our jawans were strong and braved all these difficulties. But the vital capacity is usually lowered in the initial few months. Many of them fell ill with pneumonia.

In September when we had sent the troops, it was not very cold. But by mid-October, it had become bitterly cold. It is not true that they were not given enough warm clothes. Each jawan had been given three blankets but could carry only one with them when they went by air. The rest were sent later. But unfortunately many of them were lost when they were air dropped. So there may have been some shortfalls.

It is also wrong to say that they did not have enough weapons to fight with. Our troops had excellent weapons though they did not have automatic weapons. But they are not to be found in many countries even today. Greater reliance is placed on air power. We had been planning to modernise our weapons but it took

181. SWJN/SS/66/Supplement.

nearly a year to complete the blueprints. Now they have gone into production. From the criticisms that are levelled, it would seem that we had sent in the troops naked with no weapons to fight with. It is true that some losses occurred in air lifting the arms and ammunition and blankets, etc.

As I told you earlier, we had held a military review of the situation a couple of years ago. The army generals said that if the Chinese came from the NEFA area, we must choose the place to fight. It would have been foolish to engage in combat at a place which was to their advantage. Therefore, it was considered wiser tactics to choose our ground even if it meant retreating a little initially. The newspapermen and others failed to understand this and made a great noise that our troops had run away. It was something which had been decided in advance.

Anyhow, on the 20th, they launched a massive attack, with troops outnumbering ones by five or six times equipped with guns and cannons. The Chinese troops were specially trained in mountain warfare and are a cross between regular troops and guerrillas. They could carry small cannons on their backs which is not possible normally. They would sit on the mountain-tops and fire their cannon. Their food requirements are also simple. They carry rice and tea in their backpacks and cook it on a stove wherever they camped. Similarly, their uniforms are also extremely simple. Our officers were rather disgusted when they first saw them. Cotton filled coats would keep them warm though they may not look very good. We have been spoilt by English training with our insistence on good uniforms, etc. We are now learning from experience. We have ordered quilted cotton coats to be made in our factories and within a few days were sending five hundred coats a day. Now, I think, a thousand are being sent daily.

We are learning from our new experience and our mistakes. The Chinese have been fighting for the last twenty years. Their forces have been stationed in Tibet in large numbers. In fact, their forces far outnumber the entire Indian army. They have built roads which facilitate their troops movements.

I am merely giving you the facts. There is nothing to be perturbed about. War is not a good thing. It always leads to problems. But it is wrong to think that the Chinese troops are superior to us or that they have defeated us. There is no cause for panic. I am convinced that our jawans are far superior to the Chinese troops [Applause]. Reverses in battle are nothing to be ashamed of. We must attribute them to our inexperience.

I am telling you all this because all kinds of rumours are floating around. I have no objection to people spreading falsehoods about me or the government. But to do so against our armed forces is wrong because it lowers their morale and weakens the nation. I want you to understand that it is wrong.

All right, as I was saying, the Chinese came down the Thagla Pass in the NEFA area where the Chinese had never set foot before except in the village of Longju near the border where they had come a couple of years ago. From their activities, it seemed that they had no intention of crossing the border in the NEFA. From the many hints that they let drop, it seemed that they had accepted the border demarcation on the mountain which spread into Burma as final. At least, they had done so on the Burmese side. By the same token, they had to accept it on the Indian side too.

Well, anyhow, we simply did not expect them to march into that area. But on the 20th they launched a massive attack, all the time making protestations that it was in self defence. It is strange that they should march into our territory and then call us the aggressor. Every day there are broadcasts and news reports from their side saying that the invading army of India had opened fire upon them. It is indeed a strange feat to have turned the truth upside down. The fact of the matter is that we have no previous experience of such matters like wartime propaganda, and telling blatant lies on the radio, etc. We weigh our words carefully. We are trying to present our own version more forcefully now, and have stepped up the preparations in the factories, and recruitment to the armed forces, etc. India is like a huge elephant which takes a while to get going but it is bound to come up on top [Applause].

Let me repeat that a new era is beginning for us not only in India but the whole of Asia and perhaps to some extent the world too. We are being pushed willy-nilly into the modern age. The masses had until now been steeped in the old mental ruts of thousands of years. We must no doubt retain all that is best in our old traditions. But we have to grasp the realities of the new age too. There are many evils in war but one good thing that it does is to jolt the people out of their lethargy. This is what is happening in India now. We have to prepare ourselves in every way for a war cannot be won by enthusiasm alone. Everyone must work doubly hard in his own chosen profession, whether he is a soldier or a factory worker or something else. The greatest burden will fall on the youth. They need not worry that they will be left out. It is they who will have to shoulder the burden and the more they prepare themselves, the better equipped they will be to discharge their responsibilities. I remember that some students, perhaps in Delhi, have demanded that in view of the border crisis, they should be given a holiday. It is strange that anyone should talk like this. There is no question of a holiday for any of us, in factories, farms or in schools and colleges. The only rest that we can afford is the sleep at night. Otherwise we have to keep ourselves physically and mentally alert. Those who are in schools and colleges will have their chance. If necessary, we may have to introduce compulsory military training as it is done in England, France and other countries.

The boys from rich as well as poor families serve in the capacity of ordinary soldiers. This ensures a sense of equality. You must prepare yourselves mentally and physically for the responsibilities that the future may hold.

Just two weeks ago, at about the same time that the Chinese launched their attack on India, matters came to a head between the United States and the Soviet Union over the Cuban Missile crisis. Suddenly the world was on the brink of a nuclear war and for two or three days, the situation was suspended at razor's edge. If there had been a nuclear war millions of people would have been killed in days. An American scientist has estimated that in the first three or four days of a nuclear war, between forty and fifty crores of people would be killed. It is something which is extremely difficult for an ordinary mind to comprehend. People will die like flies in Europe, in the Soviet Union and the United States. It is a terrible thing to contemplate. Anyhow the matter was finally resolved. But the world is constantly on the brink of disaster. Perhaps this crisis influenced the Chinese decision to launch an attack on India. They chose a moment when the world was busy elsewhere.

What should be our attitude now? We shall face the Chinese challenge squarely and succeed, if not today, sometime in the next year or two [Applause]. My request to you is that you should not allow panic to grip you. I have often found that those who talk big and make a great deal of noise break up most easily in a crisis. Please believe me, we will not let dishonour come to India, no matter what happens [Applause]. We shall maintain our freedom, no matter what it costs us. We will make sacrifices and brace ourselves against unexpected shocks and news. In fact, we must learn to gain strength from our reverses. I want you to remember this at all times as also the fact that this is not a matter which is likely to end in a few weeks or months. It may take years and we may have to face enormous difficulties. I do not want you to fritter away all your energy and enthusiasm in the initial effort. We cannot afford to let up our efforts. Great powers like Germany and Japan were ultimately defeated by the concerted efforts of the Allied nations. I do not think that anyone can break our spirit [Applause]. There may be reverses initially. We must continue to do our duty by the nation and go from strength to strength.

As you know, it has been our policy right from the beginning to have friendly relations with all nations. We tried with China too. It is not our fault if they repay friendship with enmity. We cannot give up our efforts to maintain friendly relations with everyone.

Panch Sheel is one of the cornerstones of our foreign policy. People often laugh about it. I maintain that Panch Sheel is the only sensible way for two nations to deal with one another. Panch Sheel means accepting the sovereignty of the other nation, non-interference in one another's internal affairs and one or two other similar principles. There should be no interference in one another's internal affairs, no matter how conflicting the ideologies may be. Unless everyone accepts and follows this principle, there will be constant efforts to destabilise one another which is the root cause of war.

The two great superpowers in the world today are the United States and the Soviet Union. It is obvious that neither can get the better of the other. If there is a war between them, both will be ruined. Therefore, the sensible thing is to live and let live without interference in one another's affairs. There should be peaceful coexistence among nations. Our policy of Panch Sheel is absolutely right. It is unfortunate that though the Chinese paid lip service to Panch Sheel and Sino-Indian friendship, their intentions turned out to be traitorous. But we cannot accept it if a liar comes and tells you that speaking the truth is bad.

Anyhow, we have been following the policy of non alignment and kept ourselves aloof from the two armed camps into which the world has got divided under the leadership of the superpowers. We have tried to maintain friendly relations with both sides and refused to enter into any military alliance. In the beginning, there was deep mistrust on both sides of India. But gradually they have begun to realise that we are against no one. There has been great opposition to our policy of non-alignment in our own country. Voices are once again being raised that we should give it up which I think is absolutely wrong. It is the right policy and somebody else's wrong doing and dishonesty do not make it wrong.

We are in need of weapons and equipment. So we wrote to all the great powers except a few telling them what had happened and asking for their sympathy and help. We wrote to the United States as well as the Soviet Union. Some of the western powers have come very quickly to our aid for which we are grateful to them [Applause]. But even they have assured us that their aid was without any strings attached and that they did not want us to abandon our policy of non- alignment. They have shown themselves to have greater insight than some of the people here in India who are critical of our policy. It would be wrong to give up our policy out of fear. We would have no stature or respect left in the eyes of the world. It would weaken us too. The other countries have accepted it and yet there are people in India who advise us to give up non-alignment.

I told you about the Soviet Union. We had asked for some planes from them and cooperation to set up an aeroplane factory. They have not withdrawn their offer of supplying the planes by December as promised.[182] So we are getting help from all directions. Why should we alienate one or the other of them. In any case, I think it is fundamentally wrong on principle. There is no obstacle

182. See item 447.

to asking for aid from any country. But I feel that we should remain firm on our stand. Some people seem to think that this is a good time to bring about basic change when the people's emotions are churned up.

Then there is socialism. The critics could not openly oppose socialism. But I think the war with China has made it more than ever necessary to bring about socialism. Military warfare is only a small part of it. In modern warfare, it is a question of an entire nation in arms. I do not mean that everyone should sport a rifle but that everyone should do his duty by the nation. Suppose, by some misfortune, a bomb falls on Delhi. It would bring the war straight into your home and you would have to face the situation with courage. You cannot turn tail and run away in panic. You will have to help in every way that you can.

I am stressing this repeatedly because I think we have still not understood what a war is all about and how dangerous it is. We cannot give up our freedom. I feel that we have the stamina to face the crisis for as long as it lasts. The Chinese had amassed troops in Tibet and had an initial advantage. But we must gear ourselves to throw them out.

There has been no aerial warfare so far. But I cannot promise that it will not escalate. There could be aerial bombardment of our great industrial establishments. Therefore, we have to make arrangements to protect these sensitive areas. But more particularly, we must prepare the people mentally to put up with hardships and problems. India has already demonstrated what her people can do. But I would like to repeat that we cannot win a war by shouting slogans. I would like to warn you we cannot make this war an excuse to give up our fundamental policies which have been evolved as best suited to the national interest. We are not fighting this war in order to enable a small minority to amass fortunes while the rest bear the burden. The entire nation has to share the burden. Therefore we must keep going in the direction of socialism, equality and equal opportunity for all even when we are at war. I want you to be vigilant against people who try to incite others by spreading false rumours and not be led astray in a momentary fit of anger or passion.

I have taken up a great deal of your time, trying to explain what we have to do. Committees are being formed all over the country. The Mayor of Delhi has formed one. There is an all India Central Citizens Committee for defence fund. The path is gradually becoming clearer. You must prepare yourselves mentally for all eventualities. We will have to face hardships but it would have been worthwhile if we emerge a stronger and better trained nation [Applause]. I want you to think about all these things and understand what the future may have in store for us in order to be prepared for it.

Jai Hind!

Translation ends]

303. To the Youth[183]

To Students and Young Men and Women

Every generation has to fight anew the battle for freedom. Otherwise we grow soft and forget the basic values of life and freedom and tend to lose their essence. My generation had the inestimable privilege of serving under Gandhiji in the struggle for our freedom.

Now a chance comes to all of us and, more especially, to the young to test their mettle and their patriotism. Already the wonderful response of the people of the country has shown our basic strength. Let this not be frittered away in petty things. Let this challenge be considered an opportunity and be met with strength, dignity, discipline and fortitude, so that out of this trial a new and better India might be fashioned by the efforts and sacrifices of her children.

There are many ways of serving this cause, and many more will be pointed out to us from time to time. Meanwhile, I should like all our University students to join the National Cadet Corps or the NCC Rifles to get some elementary training. It may be necessary to have higher training later on. Let us live a life of some austerity and save as much as we can, so that our savings might help in increasing the nation's effort.

Let us continue our education and training and prepare for the time when more is required of us.

Let us not waste our energies in futilities and in anything which is beneath the dignity of a nation determined to carry out the great tasks before us, and let us avoid every kind of abuse and vulgarity in our language and deeds. That is unbecoming and degrading to a mature nation out to perform great deeds.

Let us remember that we are passing through a time of grave national emergency and that we are determined to profit by this opportunity in building up a great nation in which all of our people have equal opportunities of progress.

304. In the Lok Sabha: Compulsory Military Training[184]

The Prime Minister and Minister of External Affairs, Defence and Atomic Energy (Jawaharlal Nehru): Mr Deputy-Speaker, Sir, I am intervening at this early stage of the debate to indicate what Government's views are in this matter. Obviously, I take it that no one in this House can be opposed to this Resolution

---

183. Message, 11 November 1962.
184. Intervention in Debate, *Lok Sabha Debates*, Third Series, Vol. IX, November 8-20, 1962, pp. 1842-1846.

as such. Even apart from the crisis, it is a thing for every young man to have some training. It will make him a better citizen and will make him better fitted for any other duty that he might perform. But at this stage for us to say what we cannot do effectively would not be desirable.

I imagine that the persons who would be affected by this, if this Resolution is passed, would be about 30 million in India. To pass a Resolution or to decide on a measure without fully being able to implement it would not be proper. We are, as a matter of fact, increasing the numbers that are going to be trained very considerably in various ways. The hon. Member who has just spoken referred to the NCC. At the present moment it consists of about 4.2 lakhs, that is, over 400,000. We are increasing it, the NCC and the NCC rifles to cover practically every university student in India.

Then there is the Territorial Army which we are increasing fairly rapidly. Then there is a Lok Sahayak Sena. In addition, there are the Home Guards. If all these are totalled up, the figure comes to a formidable figure. That is as much as we can take in hand considering the need of officers and trainers and others. As the hon. Member says, "Give them wooden rifles." That, I accept, may be necessary here and there. But we should like to give a majority of these people some rifle training so that they may know the weapons fully and later on, if necessary, they can utilise them. At this moment we are expanding and extending our training programme very greatly, as much as we can possibly deal with. With all my sympathy for this resolution therefore, we are unable to accept it at this stage because we just will not be able to do it in view of the number of officers and trainers required. This would probably rather come in the way of the more intensive and better training that we are giving to those lots of people who come under the various categories that I have mentioned.

I did not mention, of course, the additional recruitment prograame for the Regular Army which is very considerable. It will mean our dispersing our efforts and possibly will rather impair the kind of training we are giving.

I entirely agree with the hon. Member who has just now spoken about our recruiting people from Nagaland and from all the border areas specially, we hope to touch all these people and to increase our capacity in regard to trained people very, very considerably. In fact, even now our capacity for training is stretched to the utmost.

We should remember that fortunately for us in India there is no lack of volunteers. The question of compulsory training I have no objection to it—comes in when volunteers are lacking. If and when that need arises we can certainly go in for conscription. But at the present moment we have millions of people at our disposal as much as we can train.

I suggest therefore, that it is better to concentrate on the steps that we are taking and gradually expand our programme ultimately, if need arises even accept a resolution of this kind. But at the present moment it would not be wise to accept a resolution which we cannot give effect to.

Hem Barua[185] (Gauhati): May I seek a clarification from the hon. Prime Minister? In view of the fact that this war is going to be a long-drawn out war, as the hon. Prime Minister has said so very often, why is it that we cannot spread out the programme to impart military training over a number of years, take them from now on and adopt this Resolution?

Jawaharlal Nehru: But we are spreading it out very fast, as much as we can deal with. I have no objection to spreading it out more and more, but merely saying that we will include almost everybody in India does not mean that we will be able to do more than we can. We cannot.

I had forgotten to mention another scheme of voluntary rifles. There are four or five major schemes where we could give effective training, not with wooden rifles and things of that kind, but with regular rifles and all these comprise millions and millions of people.

Narendra Singh Mahida[186] (Anand): May I seek some information? Will the hon. Prime Minister allow voluntary organisations to function under Government supervision for this military training? I had experience in 1947 when we had raised about a lakh of volunteers without Government assistance, completely voluntary work and without Government finances. So, I will again say that without Government assistance of a penny but under Government supervision we shall do our best. With the enthusiasm that has been aroused in our country people should be given the fullest opportunity in the rural areas. I think, they should not be hindered in their enthusiasm. In their self defence and even in civil defence they should be completely trained with voluntary efforts. So, I propose that the hon. Prime Minister invite voluntary organisations and if they want to give civil defence training, they should be allowed to do this.

Jawaharlal Nehru: There is plenty of opportunity for them in the volunteer rifles that we are raising and the Home Guards which is something even more than civil defence. The hon. Member can utilise all the enthusiasm he can find

185. PSP.
186. Swatantra Party.

for this. If he wants to raise some other volunteers, it is difficult for me to say unless I see the scheme how it fits in because one of the difficulties will be, when millions and millions of people are being trained to provide them with arms. We may not immediately be able to do so. But I will suggest to him that there are very large opportunities of training in the various categories that I have mentioned.

305. In New Delhi: To the TA, NCC, AAF[187]

टेरीटोरियल आर्मी जवान, नेशनल केडेट कोर और ऑग्ज़िल्यरी एयरफ़ोर्स के लड़के और जवान, क़रीब-क़रीब हर साल मैं आया हूँ इस मैदान में टेरीटोरियल आर्मी के दिन और आप लोगों से मिला हूँ, कुछ देखा है, कुछ कहा है, कुछ चाय पानी में भी शिरकत हुई है। (हँसी) आज कम से कम यहाँ जो लोग जो बुलाये गये हैं यहाँ मेहमान वो महरूम रहेंगे चाय से। ठीक है क्योंकि हमने सोचा कि यह मौक़ा नहीं है कि हम एक ख़ुशी से मनायें आजकल के ज़माने में किसी बात को, क्योंकि हमारे दिल में दुख है, रंज है, क्योंकि हमारे मुल्क के एक हिस्से पर दुश्मन का क़ब्ज़ा है और हमारे बहुत सारे भाई, नौजवान इस लड़ाई में जो सरहद के पास हो रही है उसमें उनका अन्त हो गया, देहान्त हो गया, कुछ लोग, बहुत लोग पकड़े भी गये, गिरफ़्तार हुए। जब हमारे देश भारत के जिस्म, शरीर के एक हिस्से को कोई दबाता है, कोई गिरफ़्तार करता है तो सारे जिस्म को बुख़ार चढ़ आता है। आप जानते हैं अगर आपके शरीर के एक छोटी सी उंगली में या अंगूठे में कुछ तकलीफ़ हो तो ख़ाली अंगूठे की नहीं रहती, वो सारे जिस्म की हो जाती है, बुख़ार चढ़ जाता है। तो यह आजकल हाल है।

हम सब लोग तकलीफ़ में हैं क्योंकि जिस्म के, एक हमारे भारत के शरीर का एक हिस्सा दुश्मन के क़ब्ज़े में है और हम सब लोगों का पहला काम यह हो गया है कि उसको छुड़ायें उससे, जो लोग ज़बरदस्ती अपने-अपने ताक़त के ज़ोर में या अपने हथियारों के ज़ोर में या जो कुछ हो वो हमारे मुल्क पर हमलावर हुए उनको हटायें।

आप जानते हैं कि जबसे हम आज़ाद हुए और उसके पहले भी हमारा पैगाम दुनिया को, शान्ति और अमन का था और कुछ हमने शोहरत भी हासिल की दुनिया में कि हिन्दुस्तान के लोग, हिन्दुस्तान की गवर्नमेंट बहुत शान्ति पसन्द है। अजीब क़िस्मत का खेल है कि हम जो शान्ति पसन्द अपने को समझते थे और कहलाये जाते थे वही आज एक लड़ाई में फंस जायें। लेकिन यह लड़ाई साबित कर रही है और करेगी कि शान्ति पसन्द होने के माने ये नहीं हैं कि कमज़ोर हों और कोई भी बेइज़्ज़ती या हमला अपने मुल्क पर उसको बरदाश्त करें। (तालियाँ)

187. Speech at the Red Fort, 18 November 1962. NMML, AIR Tapes, TS No. 8617, NM No. 1695.

तो यह अजीब बात हुई कि दुनिया में बड़े-बड़े देश हैं, बड़े और छोटे जो कि बाहथियार हैं, बहुत ज़ोरों की फ़ौजें हैं, सब कुछ हैं और बड़ी तैयारी लड़ाई-झगड़े की रहती है लेकिन इन सभों में हमारा देश जो कि सबमें कम चाहता था, कि दुनिया में लड़ाई हो, हमें ही इसका सामना करना पड़ा। ख़ैर, इसको बाद में जो तारीख़ लिखते हैं लोग इस पर सोचेंगे, समझेंगे और इसकी कहानी बनायेंगे, लेकिन इस वक़्त हमारे लिए तो आज अपनी तारीख़ लिखनी है, किताब में बाद में लिखी जायेगी, अपनी तारीख़ अपने क़लम दवात से, काग़ज़ से नहीं, लेकिन अपनी हिम्मत से, अपनी बहादुरी से, अपनी त्याग से और क़ुर्बानी से, क्योंकि आख़िर में कोई क़ौम जो कि आज़ाद हो और आज़ादी पसन्द करती हो वो उसी वक़्त उसके लायक़ होती है जबकि उस आज़ादी कि हिफ़ाज़त करने कि लिए वो सब कुछ देने को तैयार हो जाये। जो लोग झिझकते हैं, जो क़ौम झिझकती है उसके करने में, उसके हाथ से आज़ादियाँ ही निकल जाती हैं।

पन्द्रह बरस हुए हमें आज़ाद हुए और इस पन्द्रह बरस में बहुत कोशिशें हुई मुल्क को आगे ले जाने की, मुल्क से ग़रीबी निकालने की, बहुत कुछ बाक़ी है। तो सारी हमने ताक़त इसमें लगायी इस उम्मीद में कि हमें मौक़ा मिलेगा कि हम ग़रीबी को निकाल दें, मुल्क भर ताक़तवर हो, मुल्क में हमारी खेती अच्छी हो, ज़मीन का काम अच्छा हो, मुल्क में कारख़ाने बनें, हरेक को काम मिले और पैदावार हमारी बढ़े हर जगह हर क़िस्म की, उसकी हमने बुनियाद डाली, काफ़ी मज़बूत बुनियाद डाली और हम उम्मीद करते थे कि उसके फ़ायदे जो होंगे वो मुल्क की जनता को मिलें। और एक फ़ायदा उसका यह भी था कि मुल्क की ताक़त बढ़ने से मज़बूत होगा मुल्क अपनी हिफ़ाज़त करने के लिए, क्योंकि आप यह जानते हैं कि आजकल की लड़ाई भी ख़ाली इंसान की हिम्मत की नहीं है, हालांकि हिम्मत तो हमेशा ज़रूरी होती है बल्कि नये-नये हथियार, नये-नये औज़ार, उनकी है और वो जभी हो सकते हैं किसी मुल्क में जब वो ख़ुद पैदा करें उसे। बाहर से ख़रीद लेना आसान है, एक ख़रीदा, दो ख़रीदे, सौ, हज़ार, लाख ख़रीदे लेकिन वो सिलसिला चलता नहीं है जब औरों के ऊपर हमें भरोसा करना होता है, वो दें या न दें, जब चाहे दें।

तो इस बात की कोशिश की कि हम अपने यहाँ नये हथियार भी बनायें, नये हवाई जहाज़ बनायें, उसमें कुछ वक़्त लगता है, उसमें भी कुछ कामयाबी हुई, और बढ़ती जाती है। यह सब हमने किया और आइन्दा करने का इरादा था। हम देखते थे कि शायद एक और पाँच-सात बरस के बाद जो हमने बीज बोया है मुल्क में नयी-नयी बातें होने का, वो उगेगा, निकलेगा और एक ज़बरदस्त दरख़्त बन जायेगा, जिसके साये के नीचे सारे हिन्दुस्तान के मर्द और औरत और बच्चे ख़ुशहाल होके रहें। (तालियाँ) ऐसे, ऐसे मौक़े पर हमारे ऊपर चीन देश ने हमला किया। यों तो आप जानते हैं कि पाँच बरस से कुछ न कुछ हमलावर था वो, और लद्दाख़ के पहाड़ों में बढ़ता जाता था और हमको दबाता जाता था अपने नीचे। हमने उस पर एतराज़ किया, हमने शिकायत की, हमने आख़िर में कुछ रुकावट भी की, उनको रोकने की कोशिश भी की, रोका भी, लेकिन फिर भी हमारी कोशिश यह रही कि बाअमन तरीक़ों से इस मामले को हल किया जाये, क्योंकि हम दुनिया

में भी कहते थे कि वो ज़माना गुज़रा कि जब ऐसे दो मुल्कों के जो मसले हों वो लड़ाई झगड़े करके तय किये जायें, और ज़रिये होने चाहियें तय करने के। मुमकिन है कोई लोग कहें कि हमने इस ज़माने में, इस पाँच बरस में ढील ज़्यादा दी, मुमकिन है वो यह कहें तो सही भी हो क्योंकि हमारी कोशिश रही कि कोई लड़ाई आसानी से नहीं होनी चाहिए, ख़ासकर इन दो बड़े मुल्कों में, हिन्दुस्तान में और चीन में।

आख़िरी दम तक, अभी ढाई महीने हुए उस वक़्त तक हम इसी की कोशिश कर रहे थे लेकिन फिर यकायक बिल्कुल एक नयी जगह, नयी तरफ़ हिन्दुस्तान की सरहद पर एक नया हमला चीन ने किया। पहले तो लद्दाख़ में आये थे, अब हमारे पूर्वी सीमा प्रान्त, नॉर्थ ईस्ट्रन फ़्रन्टियर एजेंसी जहाँ कि हमारी सीमा में कोई शक नहीं था और लद्दाख़ की हिमालय का सब में ऊँचा पहाड़ जो उधर का है वो सीमा है। एक तरफ़ नदी का पानी इधर बहता है, एक उधर बहता है, उसके पार आये चीनी फ़ौजें और जब से वो और ज़्यादा आती गयीं। फिर भी हमने उनकी तवज्जोह दिलायी कि बिल्कुल ग़लत है और हमने कोशिश की कि हम भी फ़ौजें भेजें वहाँ उनका मुक़ाबला करने और उनको हटाने। यह सब पिछले दो महीने की कहानी है। अजीब बात यह है कि चीन के जो हुकमराँ हैं उन्होंने, वो यही कहते जाते हैं कि गोया कि हमने उनके मुक़ाबले पर हमला किया और वो तो हिफ़ाज़त कर रहे हैं अपने मुल्क की, उनका मुल्क बढ़ता जाता है और जो उसकी हिफ़ाज़त करे वो उनपे हमला करता है। आप लोगों में से मैं नहीं जानता, किसने सुना, मैं तो नहीं सुनता, पीकिंग के चीनी जो रेडियो हैं उसमें जो बातें कही जाती हैं उसको सुनने से ताल्लुक़ है, यक़ीन करना तो ख़ैर और बात है, इस क़दर झूठ, इस क़दर सच को झूठ बनाना और ग़लत बातें कहना, तबियत नाराज़ हो जाती है।

कुछ बरस हुए, बीस बरस हुए जब बड़ी लड़ाई हो रही थी, जर्मन लड़ाई, उसमें एक साहब थे उस वक़्त की जर्मन हुकूमत में, उन्होंने शोहरत हासिल की थी हमारे पर झूठ बोलने में, वो थे डॉ. गोबलज़। अब जो उन्होंने शोहरत हासिल की थी वो कुछ ढीली पड़ जायेगी चीनी झूठ के साथ। (हँसी) ख़ैर, झूठ और सच बात तो पीछे होगी, मोटी बात यह है कि हमारे मुल्क पर उन्होंने हमला किया, और एक निहायत बदतमीज़ी का, ग़लत और बेहूदा हमला किया और कुछ फ़ायदा उठा के। उसके लिए ज़ाहिर है जिस तरह से उन्होंने हमला किया बहुत ज़बरदस्त तैयारियाँ की थीं सालों से, तिब्बत में बड़ी फ़ौजें जमा थीं और सड़कें बनायीं जो बिल्कुल हमारी सरहद तक आ गयी थीं। तो उन सड़कों से और फ़ौजों से फ़ायदा उठाके वो आसानी से हमारे यहाँ आ सके, हमें दिक्क़तें थीं, बड़े-बड़े पहाड़ थे, उन पर जाना था, सामान भेजना था उन पर।

तो ख़ैर, उनको कुछ आसानी हो गयी और फिर उन्होंने आके हमारी जो हमने फ़ौजें भेजी थीं उन पर ज़ोरों का हमला किया। यों तो वो आये थे शुरु सितम्बर में, लेकिन बीस अक्टूबर को एक ज़बरदस्त हमला उन्होंने किया, बहुत तैयारी के साथ और जो हमारी बहुत तादाद में जो हमारी फ़ौजें थीं उससे बहुत ज़्यादा, और उन्होंने हटा दिया हमारी फ़ौजों को वहाँ से और अपने लोगों को बढ़ाते गये वो। और पहली बार बीस अक्टूबर के बाद हमारे

लोगों ने कुछ समझा कि कोई अहम वाक़िया हुआ है, कुछ दुनिया की भी आँखें खुलने लगीं, लोग समझते थे कि सरहदी बातें हैं, छोटी-मोटी बहस हो जाती है, छोटी-मोटी लड़ाई होती है, मुश्किल लड़ाई नहीं है। बीस अक्टूबर को मालूम हुआ, हमें तो फ़ौरन मालूम हो गया, हल्के-हल्के और मुल्कों को भी मालूम हो रहा है कि यह, कि यह मामूली सरहद का कोई छोटा-मोटा झगड़ा नहीं है बल्कि यह पक्का हमला है हिन्दुस्तान के ऊपर चीन का, सरहद के छोटे झगड़ों पर लाखों फ़ौजें नहीं आतीं बीच में। और चुनांचे आपने देखा कि यहाँ भी, हिन्दुस्तान में भी कई बातें हुईं अपने मुल्क को तैयार करने के लिए, क्योंकि ऐसी लड़ाई जो हो रही है वो ज़ाहिर है फ़ौज है, हवाई जहाज़ के नौजवान हमारे हैं, हो सकता है समुद्री जहाज़ भी, उनका काम तो है ही मुल्क की हिफ़ाज़त करना, लेकिन ऐसी लड़ाई में बोझा हरेक आदमी को उठाना पड़ता है, मर्द और औरत को मुल्क भर के। आजकल की लड़ाई ख़ाली वो नहीं लड़ते हैं जो वर्दी पहन के, फ़ौज में होके आगे जायें, वो तो लड़ते हैं लेकिन उनके पीछे बहुत बातें हैं, उनके पीछे हमारे कारख़ानों, ऑर्डिनेन्स फ़ैक्ट्री में, और जगह हज़ारों चीज़ें बनती हैं उनके लिए, हथियार बनते हैं, ऐम्यूनिशन बनती हैं तब तो लड़ें। तो ग़रज़ के आजकल की लड़ाई ऐसी हो गयी है कि मुल्क भर, एक तरह से मुल्क के सब लोग, मर्द और औरत किसी न किसी काम में सिपाहीगीरी दिखायें। यानी सब लोग एक तरह से बाहथियार हो जायें और हिस्सा लें मुल्क की हिफ़ाज़त में। आपने एक क़ानून बनाया चन्द रोज़ बाद, पिछले महीने अक्टूबर में क़ानून यहाँ मंजूर किया गया, डिफ़ेंस ऑफ़ इंडिया एक्ट जो कि काफ़ी दूर तक जाता है। इसलिए कि उसकी ताक़त लोगों को मुल्क के तैयार करने के लिए है । फिर उसमें छोटी रुकावटें नहीं होने देता है कि तेज़ी से काम हो, जो कुछ होना है ज़ोरों से हो, कोई नाजायज़ फ़ायदा उससे न उठायें, और सारी ताक़त मुल्क की एक तरफ़ झुके कि उसको बचाने के लिए, उसकी हिफ़ाज़त करने के लिए। अभी दो-चार दिन हुए हमारी लोकसभा में, पार्लियामेंट में भी यह मसला पेश हुआ और उन्होंने इसको मंजूर किया और एक प्रस्ताव, रेज़ोल्यूशन हमने वहाँ मंजूर किया, जिसमें उन्होंने इसका इक़रार किया। उन्होंने, पार्लियामेंट के माने हैं कि हिन्दुस्तान के जितने नुमाइन्दे वहाँ थे, उन्होंने इसको स्वीकार किया, प्रतिज्ञा ली हम इसका सामना करेंगे पक्कीतौर से, चाहे कितने ही दिन लगें, चाहे कित्ता ही हमारा नुकसान हो लेकिन सामना करेंगे जब तक हम अपने मुल्क को आज़ाद नहीं कर लेते हमलावर लोगों से। (तालियाँ) अक्सर रेज़ोल्यूशन होते हैं आम जलसों में जो कि पेश होते हैं, लोग मंजूर कर लेते हैं, अपने-अपने घर जाते हैं लेकिन यह जो रेज़ोल्यूशन था पार्लियामेंट का यह ऐसा नहीं, क्योंकि हमें एक काम करना है, हमें उसका सामना करना है, उसके लिए तैयार करना है मुल्क को, सब लोगों को।

तो वो तो हर वक़्त सामने हमारे रहेगा, हरेक शख़्स के और मालूम नहीं, मैं नहीं कह सकता कि कब हम उसको पूरा करें, लेकिन मुझे इसमें कोई शक नहीं है कि हमें उसको पूरा करना है और करेंगे हम, और चाहे यह जो लड़ाई हमारे ऊपर आयी, हमने उसको दावत नहीं दी। यह तो हमलावर लोगों ने हमला किया हमारे ऊपर एक मुल्क ने जिसका

हमने कोई बुरा नहीं किया था, हमने उससे दोस्ती रखी थी, यह जवाब हमें मिला दोस्ती का। तो अब हमारे सामने देश में, अव्वल काम यह है और सब काम चाहे जाति के हों, चाहे ख़ानदानी हों, चाहे कुछ हों वो दूसरे हो गये, अव्वल काम यह है कि मुल्क को तैयार करें, मुल्क को मज़बूत करें ताकि वो पूरी ताक़त से सामना कर सकें दुश्मन का। क्योंकि ज़ाहिर है अगर हम यह नहीं कर सकते तब और काम हम क्या करेंगे, हमलावर बन के करेंगे किसी और पर, हम क्या, मुल्क को, अपने को आज़ाद किया बहुत दिक़्क़तों से, परेशानियों से, त्याग से, क़ुर्बानी से, इसलिए अंग्रेज़ों से आज़ाद किया इसलिए कि चीनी धमकी में हम आ जायें और दब जायें, यह तो नामुमकिन बात है। (तालियाँ) लेकिन कहना तो काफ़ी नहीं है, इस बात को करना है और करने के माने हैं सामना करना, तकलीफ़ का, मुसीबत का। हमारे देश भारत के लिए यह ज़रूरी है कि हम ज़रा ढीले पड़ते जाते हैं, फिर से हम चुस्त और चालाक हों, आरामतलबी ज़रा कम हो जाये हमारी, और जो बुनियादी बातें हैं आज़ाद मुल्कों के सीखने की वो हम सीखें। फिर से हमारा इम्तहान हो रहा है और हमें रंज होता है कि हमारे नौजवान सिपाही और और लोग वहाँ मरे पहाड़ों पर, वहाँ बर्फ़ीले पहाड़ों पर, गिरफ़्तार हों, तकलीफ़ हो, रंज होता है। हमें रंज होता है कि चीनी फ़ौजें बड़ी कसरत से हैं, बहुत ज़्यादा हैं हमारी फ़ौजों से, वो आगे बढ़ें हमारे मुल्क में, हमें हटना पड़े उनके सामने, दिल दुखता है लेकिन उसी के साथ दिल कड़ा होता है और यह एक यह प्रतिज्ञा, यह क़सम या जो कुछ कहिए इक़रार हमने लिया है उनको हटाने का, उसको हमें फिर दोहराना होता है कि हम जब तक मुल्क को पूरीतौर से ख़ाली न कर दें चीनी हमलावर लोगों से उस वक़्त तक हम नहीं अपना कर्त्तव्य पूरा करेंगे, हमारा धर्म पूरा नहीं होगा । यह बरदाश्त की बात नहीं है इस तरह से आजकल के ज़माने में, जैसे पुराने ज़माने में इतिहास में पढ़ते थे मुल्क पर क़ब्जा कर लिया और मुल्क को दबा लिया, इस बात को हम बरदाश्त करें।

याद रखिये कि यह चीज़ कोई एक सरहदी बहस की नहीं रही, सरहद तो एक छोटी सी बात है, यह एक हमला है हिन्दुस्तान पर, हिन्दुस्तान की आज़ादी पर, हिन्दुस्तान की जान पर और कोई मैं समझता हूँ ऐसा हिन्दुस्तानी नहीं होगा मर्द या औरत, ख़ासकर बच्चे जो इसकी मुख़ालफ़त करने को तैयार न हों। यह हमारे सामने है और मैं आपसे कहूँ हमें इस पिछले महीने में अक्सर ख़बरें मिली हैं जिससे हमारा दिल दुखा है, तकलीफ़ हुई है, बार-बार मिली हैं और शायद और भी मिलें, क्योंकि हमारा दुश्मन बहुत तैयारी करके आया है, बहुत-बहुत बड़ी फ़ौजें लेके यकायक आ गया, शायद कहा जाये हम ग़फ़लत में पड़े थे, जो भी कुछ हो। तो ज्यों-ज्यों ऐसी ख़बरें आती हैं हमारे पास, उसमें रंज होता है ज़रूर, लेकिन उससे हमारा इरादा और भी लोहे का हो जाता है कि इसका मुक़ाबला करके इसको हटाना है। हमारा मुल्क ऐसा नहीं है कि ज़रा धक्का खाके घबरा जाये या डर जाये, कितने ही धक्के लगे, कितनी ही मुश्किलों का सामना करना पड़े हम अपने रास्ते पर चलेंगे, हिन्दुस्तान की ख़िदमत करेंगे और हिन्दुस्तान की आज़ादी को पक्का करके छोड़ेंगे। आप लोग जो टेरीटोरियल आर्मी के हैं, आप में से अक्सर लोग फ़ौज में शामिल

होंगे, असली फ़ौज में इम्बोडीड हो गये और भी हो जायेंगे और आपको सामना करना पड़ेगा इन बातों का। लेकिन हम चाहते हैं कि टेरीटोरियल आर्मी और जो ऐसी जमातें हैं वो बढ़ें, जो एन.सी.सी. है नौजवान लड़कों की, होनहार लड़कों को उनको भी इन दिक्क़तों का, मुसीबतों का, ख़तरों का सामना करना पड़ेगा। (तालियाँ) बहुत सारे माँ-बाप होंगे जिनको रंज होगा अपने प्यारे बच्चों को जाते हुए देखकर लेकिन, लेकिन रंज हो, कुछ हो इस बात की बरदाश्त करनी है, क्योंकि यह बात जल्दी ख़तम नहीं होती। और मुमकिन है ख़ाली जो, हम तो चाहते हैं कि हरेक शख़्स जो कॉलेज, यूनिवर्सिटी में पढ़े, पढ़ता है वो एन.सी.सी. में हो, हम चाहते हैं टेरीटोरियल आर्मी बहुत बढ़े और मुमकिन है कि बाद में, और हम फ़ौरन एन.सी.सी. राइफ़ल्स को हम बढ़ाना चाहते हैं, हम होमगार्ड किया चाहते हैं, हल्के-हल्के इसका दायरा बढ़ता जायेगा और मुमकिन है कि शायद ही कोई नौजवान मुल्क में रह जाये जिसको कुछ न कुछ सीखने का मौक़ा, ट्रेनिंग का मौक़ा न मिले ताकि ज़रूरत आने पर वो मुल्क की ख़िदमत करे इस तरह से, क्योंकि बोझा हम सभों को उठाना है। वो दिन गया कि फ़ौज को छोड़ दिया और हम बैठे हैं, अपने मामूली काम करते रहे। ज़माना ख़तरे का है हमारे मुल्क के लिए और ख़तरे के ज़मानों में मुल्क बनता है, ढलता है, आरामतलबी में नहीं बनता है, उसको आप समझ लें।

तो आप लोग जो यहाँ आज हैं टेरीटोरियल आर्मी के और एन.सी.सी. के और ऑग्ज़िल्यरी एयरफ़ोर्स के और लोग जो हैं उन लोगों को मुबारिक हो कि आपने इस ज़िम्मेदारी को ओढ़ा और जो और भी आपके सामने काम आये उसको यक़ीनन आप ज़ोरों से अपने मुल्क की शान हमेशा रखकर करेंगे, हमारे मुल्क की शान का तक़ाज़ा है, शान से ज़्यादा उसकी जान का तक़ाज़ा है। लेकिन सब लोग समझे नहीं हैं, लेकिन सख़्त मुक़ाबला है और मालूम नहीं कब तक चले और मालूम नहीं इस ज़माने में कित्ता भारत में फ़र्क़ हो, क्योंकि लड़ाई में मुल्क भर का ढंग बदलता जाता है, क्या-क्या हो मालूम नहीं और दुनिया में क्या हो, लड़ाई फैले, न फैले। एक अजीब ज़माना हमारे सामने आ रहा है, सख़्त ज़माना, आज़माइश का ज़माना और हिम्मत दिखाने का।

तो आप लोगों को मुबारक हो कि आपको मौक़ा मिल रहा है, ऐसे मौक़े पर मुल्क की ख़िदमत करनी है और मैं आपसे फिर याद दिला देता हूँ कि हमें अपने दिल कड़े करने हैं और कोई भी हमें धक्का लगे, कोई भी हमें नुकसान हो, कोई भी छोटी-बड़ी हार हो इस सबको ले के, अपने को मज़बूत करना है और आगे बढ़ना है। हम किसी एक बुरी ख़बर से डर नहीं जायेंगे क्योंकि ऐसी लड़ाईयों में पचासों ऊँच-नीच होती हैं। सवाल यह है कि आख़िर में किसका दम उखड़ता है, कौन आख़िर तक रहके अपनी मंज़िल पर पहुँचता है और हमारा पूरा पक्का इरादा है और मुल्क का इरादा है, हम कौन चीज़ हैं कि दिल नहीं उखड़ेगा, चाहे जो कुछ हो हम आख़िरी मंज़िल पर पहुँचेंगे। (तालियाँ)

बस यही मैं आपसे कहना चाहता था और हमें इत्ता साहस है कि अब हमारे आपस के जो भी कुछ बहसें हों, आपस की नाइत्तफ़ाक़ी हो, झगड़े हों वो ख़त्म हो गये। बड़े झगड़े का सामना है, इसमें मुल्क, सारा देश, हमारा भारत भर उसका मुक़ाबला है एक बड़े देश,

दूसरे देश से जो उस पर हमला कर रहा है। तो यह तो बहुत जहालत और बेवक़ूफ़ी की बात हो कि हम छोटी बातों में पड़ के अपनी ताक़त ज़ाया करें उसमें। अक्सर हम जयहिन्द कहते हैं और फिर भी करेंगे, लेकिन असल में उसके माने और हो गये हैं। हम चाहते हैं कि हिन्दुस्तान की जीत हो।

जयहिन्द!

[Translation begins:

Jawans of the Territorial Army, National Cadet Corps & Auxiliary Air Force, Nearly every year, I have come to the Red Fort on Territorial Army Day, met you, seen your work, made a speech, and had tea with you. [Laughter]. Today the invited guests will not be staying to tea which is proper. We felt that this was not an occasion for festivities when our hearts are filled with grief and a part of our country is in the enemy's possession. Many of our young men have lost their lives in the battlefield, and others have been captured by the enemy. When something like this happens, the entire nation suffers just as a wound in any part affects the whole body.

This is the situation today. All of us suffer because a part of India is under enemy occupation. It has become an urgent task for all of us to throw out the enemy who has committed aggression upon us on the strength of brute force of arms.

As you know, ever since we became free, and even before that, we had always carried the message of peace to the world and were famous in the world as a peace-loving people and government. It is a strange quirk of fate that we who were known as peace-lovers should be involved in a war today. But this war is proving and will continue to do so that to love peace does not mean we have to be weak or tolerate humiliation or aggression upon our country. [Applause].

It is a strange thing that there are constant preparations for war and most of the big powers in the world are armed to the teeth. Yet of all these countries India which was least interested in war is facing one today. The historians will later on ponder about it and try to find an explanation. But at the moment, it is we who have to make history, not with paper and pen, but by our courage and sacrifice. Ultimately a nation which is free and cherishes its freedom can become worthy of it only when it is prepared to sacrifice everything for its sake. Those who hesitate to do so will allow freedom to slip away.

Fifteen years have gone by since India became independent and great efforts have been made during this time towards progress, to remove poverty from the country. There has been considerable progress but a great deal remains to be done. We have pitted our entire strength into this task, in the hope that we can get rid of our poverty, make India strong to improve agriculture, industrialise the country in order to provide employment to everyone and increase production in every sphere of our national life. We have laid the firm foundations for this and had hoped that the people would now reap the benefit. It is only by being strong that we can defend our freedom. As you know, in modern warfare, courage alone is not enough though it is always essential. We need new kinds of weapons and tools which a nation must be able to produce. It may be easy to buy from outside but it cannot go on forever. If we depend on others, we will be at their mercy.

So, we have tried to produce weapons and aeroplanes, etc., in India and succeeded to a large extent. But it takes time. We had hoped that if we had another five years or so, the seeds that we had sown would grow into huge trees and in their shadow, the men, women and children of India would become prosperous. [Applause]. It is at such a time as this that China attacked us. As you know, for the last five years, they had been slowly spreading their tentacles into Ladakh. We had protested and complained and finally even tried to stop them from grabbing any more territory. But our effort has always been to try to find a solution by peaceful methods. We had been saying to the world that gone are the days when disputes between two nations are settled by means of war. Other means must be found. It is possible that people may accuse us of having been too lenient during the last five years and perhaps they would be justified. Our effort has always been not to resort to war easily, particularly as the dispute is between two great countries like India and China.

Till the last moment, until two and a half months ago, we were trying to find a peaceful solution. But suddenly, China attacked in a completely new sector. Until then, their activities were confined to Ladakh. Now suddenly, they crossed the watershed in the Himalayas and poured into the North Eastern Frontier Agency where our borders were demarcated clearly. We continued to point out to them that what they were doing was wrong and sent in our troops to stop the Chinese forces and push them back. This is the development during the last two months. The strange thing is that the Chinese propaganda claims that it is we who attacked and they are fighting purely in self-defence. They continue to advance into our territory and accuse us of being the aggressor. I do not know how many of you listen to Radio Peking—I do not because they tell blatant untruths which have no bearing upon reality and one feels enraged.

Nearly twenty years ago, when the Second World War was on there was a gentleman in the German administration named Goebbels who had earned great fame for telling lies. But even that would pale in comparison to what the Chinese can do. [Laughter]. Anyhow, truth and falsehoods can be sorted out later. The broad fact is that the Chinese have committed aggression upon India and behaved in a completely uncivilised, wrongful manner. It is obvious that they had been making preparations for years. Their troops were amassed in Tibet and they had built roads right up to our borders which gave them easy access to our territory. We on the other hand had to battle against great odds to transport our troops and equipment to the battle zone.

Well, they had some advantages over us and so they launched a massive attack on our borders on the 20th of October. They pushed them back and kept advancing. For the first time, we in India and the world woke up to the fact that something significant had occurred. Until then everyone had thought of the problem merely as a border dispute, not as a major conflict. On the 20th of October the truth suddenly dawned on everyone. The world has now realised that this is no minor border dispute but a full-scale aggression by China on India. Thousands of troops are not used for a minor border skirmish.

You must have noticed the preparations that we have been making in India. It is, of course, the duty of the armed forces to fight in the country's defence. But in modern warfare, every single man and woman in the country has to bear the burden. It is no longer the armed forces in uniform who fight a war. They have to be backed by the country's resources industrial and agricultural output, production of ammunition and weapons by the ordinance factories, etc. In short, modern wars are such that every single individual in the country has to behave like a soldier and arm themselves in same way or the other and participate in the country's defence. We passed an Act called the Defence of India which is very wide in scope. It leaves no room for obstacles in the way of rapid preparation for defence and prevents people from taking undue advantage of the crisis. We want the entire strength of the nation to be pitted into the task of defence.

Recently a resolution was passed in Parliament in which the representatives of the whole country took a pledge to face the Chinese aggression with calm determination and to throw them out, no matter how long it takes or what sacrifices we have to make. We are determined to go on fighting until we have freed India from the aggressors. [Applause]. Resolutions are often passed in public meetings, accepted by the people and forgotten once they go home. But this resolution passed in Parliament is different because we have a job to do, we prepare the nation to face external aggression. Every one of us will have to prepare ourselves for the job. I cannot say how long it may take. But I have no doubt about it that we will succeed in the end. We did not choose to go to war. This is an aggression committed upon us by a country whom we had always befriended and never done any harm to. This is the repayment we have got for our friendship.

Now the most urgent priority before us is to prepare ourselves to face the enemy. Everything else is secondary. It is obvious that if we cannot defend our national honour, we cannot do anything else either. We have been able to free India of British rule after tremendous problems and hardships and sacrifices. Have we done that only to give up our freedom to the Chinese? That is impossible. [Applause]. But it is not enough to say so. We have to prove that we mean what we say, which involves facing the problems that arise and learning great hardships. In a way, it is a good thing for our people because we had become somewhat slack. This crisis has jolted us out of our apathy. We must became smart and vigilant once again, and give up some of our ease-loving ways. We have to concentrate our bearing on some of the fundamental lessons necessary to hold on to our freedom.

We are being tested once again. We are grieved at the loss of our valiant young soldiers who have died fighting on the icy mountain peaks or been arrested. It is painful that we have had to withdraw in the face of the massive onslaught of the Chinese troops. At the same time, it hardens our determination to throw them out. We must remember our pledge not to rest until we have rid India completely of the Chinese aggression. Our duty will not be over until then. It is not something which can be tolerated. We cannot sit by and watch another nation overrun our territory as in the olden days.

I want you to bear in mind that this is no ordinary border dispute. It is an aggression committed upon India, her freedom and her very life and I think there would be no man, woman or child in India who would not be prepared to oppose it. In the last month or so, we have often received reports which have pained and grieved us and perhaps there will be more. Our enemy is well prepared and has launched a sudden attack upon us with an enormous force. It is being said that we were labouring under a false sense of confidence. Whatever it is, we are undoubtedly filled with grief about each report of reverses that we get. But at the same time, we are becoming more then ever determined to face the Chinese and throw them out. India is not a nation which panics easily. We will stick to our path no matter how many hardships and difficulties we have to face in order to strengthen India's freedom. Many of you who belong to the Territorial Army may be embodied in the armed forces and will have to face all these things. But we want the Territorial Army and other such organisations like the NCC to expand. All the bright young lads in these organisations will have to face dangers and difficulties. [Applause]. The parents will be filled with sorrow to see their children go. But whatever happens, we will have to put up with it because the present trouble will not be over so quickly. We want every single individual who is in college or university to join the NCC. We also want the Territorial Army to expand, if possible. At the moment, we want to expand the NCC Rifles. We want to gradually increase the scope of the Home Guards and soon there will be no youth in the country who has not tied the opportunity of getting some military training in order to serve the nation in its hour of need. All of us in the country have to share these burdens. Gone are the days when armies fought and the rest of the population went about their daily tasks. This is a time of danger for India and it is only by facing crises and dangers that a nation is moulded, not by slackness or life of ease.

I congratulate all of you who are in the Territorial Army, NCC and the Auxiliary Forces who have chosen to take on this responsibility. I am sure you will discharge your duty well and uphold the honour of India. At the moment the very life and honour of our country are at stake. But many people have not yet understood this. It is a fierce challenge and nobody knows how long it will continue or how it will change the course of our history. We cannot say whether the war is likely to spread to the rest of the world. This is a testing time for us and we must prove our mettle.

I congratulate all of you for you are getting an opportunity to serve the nation. I would like to remind you once again that we must harden our hearts and show a brave front, no matter what dangers threaten and losses we have to put up. We must go ahead with firm bold steps, taking the good as well as the bad in our stride. We shall not panic at slight reverses. There are bound to be great ups and downs in such wars. The question is who is strong enough to last out the entire course of the war and reach the final goal. We are fully determined not to allow ourselves to lose heart, no matter what happens, and to reach the goal we have set before ourselves.

That is all that I wished to say to you. [Applause]. The people have come together in a remarkable way, forgetting their petty differences and quarrels. We have to present a united front to the aggressor and it would be foolish to fritter away our energies in petty disputes. We often shout Jai Hind. But it has acquired a new significance for us. We want India to be victorious.

Jai Hind!

Translation ends]

306. To Students: Join the NCC[188]

Every generation has to fight a new the battle for freedom. Otherwise we grow soft and forget the basic values of life and freedom and tend to lose their essence. My generation had the inestimable privilege of serving under Gandhiji in the struggle for our freedom.

188. Message, 18 November 1962. PIB.

Now a chance comes to all of us and more especially, to the young to test their mettle and their patriotism. Already the wonderful response of the people of the country has shown our basic strength. Let this challenge be considered an opportunity and be met with strength, dignity, discipline and fortitude, so that out of this trial a new and better India might be fashioned by the efforts and sacrifices of her children.

There are many ways of serving this cause, and many more will be pointed out to us from time to time. Meanwhile, I should like all our University students to join the National Cadet Corps or the NCC Rifles to get some elementary training. It may be necessary to have higher training later on. Let us live a life of some austerity and save as much as we can, so that our savings might help in increasing the nation's effort.

Let us continue our education and training and prepare for the time when more is required us.

Let us not waste our energies in futilities and in anything which is beneath the dignity of a nation determined to carry out the great tasks before us, and let us avoid every kind of abuse and vulgarity in our language and deeds. That is unbecoming and degrading to a mature nation out to perform great deeds.

Let us remember that we are passing through a time of grave national emergency and that we are determined to profit by this opportunity in building up a great nation in which all of our people have equal opportunities of progress.

307. To Youth Rally[189]

The whole of India has been deeply moved by the crisis that has arisen on account of the Chinese invasion of India. The response all over the country has been magnificent. It is natural that young men and women should feel the call of India at this moment even more than others.

It is good to have a rally, but I hope this enthusiasm will be channelled on right lines and will lead to effective work which will strengthen our motherland. We have to face a long struggle and a difficult one. We shall with this, as we must, discipline, hard work and sacrifice. We must not imagine that the struggle will be over soon because of various diplomatic moves.

I send my greetings to the mass Youth Rally.

189. Message, 21 November 1962. PMO, File No. 9/2/62-PMP, Vol. 8, Sr. No. 3-A. The Rally, organised by the Indian Youth Congress, was to be held on 23 November 1962 at 5.30 p.m. on the LIC Grounds opposite the Theatre Communication Building, Connaught Place, New Delhi. Indira Gandhi was to inaugurate it, and various chief ministers were to address it. See circular letter, undated, by Puran Chand Azad, Secretary, Indian Youth Congress. PMO, File No. 9/2/62-PMP, Vol. 8, Sr. No. 2-A.

308. To Raja Hutheesingh: Citizens' Committees[190]

November 21, 1962

My dear Raja,

I have just received your letter of November 19. It is certainly desirable to canalise the great response of the people. There are many ways of doing it. Almost all of them have to be on a State basis. The Citizens Committees that have been formed have really to function also on a State basis. It is difficult to do that through a central organisation. The Citizens Central Committee has been set up to coordinate the State and like organisations.

I am afraid it is physically not possible for me to give any time to these matters now.

The chief areas which might be affected are in the north. But it would be a good thing, as you suggest, to give training in civil defence etc. in all parts of India. You might, with others, take the initiative in Bombay. But I would suggest your consulting the local Citizens Committee. I do not know who runs it.

The army officer who will be appointed to organise civil defence is a good man and retired long ago. He is specially acquainted with northern India, and his duties are rather special, including, if necessity arises, destruction. But I agree with you that this should be essentially a popular movement for civil defence.

Yours affectionately,
[Jawaharlal Nehru]

309. In New Delhi: To Red Cross Rally[191]

प्यारे नौजवानों, लड़कों और लड़कियों,

मुझे ऐसे मौक़े पर आने में हमेशा ख़ुशी होती है लेकिन आज ख़ासतौर से मुझे ख़ुशी है तुम सभों को देखकर और तुम्हारा जोश, उत्साह भी देखकर। एक मुल्क अपने लम्बान और चौड़ान से मज़बूत नहीं होता है, न उसकी आबादी से ख़ाली, वो उत्ता ही मज़बूत होता है जित्ते मज़बूत उसके नागरिक हों, उसके सिटिज़न्स हों, और उनकी मज़बूती है जोश और उत्साह हो ज़रूर, लेकिन सीखने का, एक सिपाही ज़्यादा मज़बूत है बनिस्बत एक आदमी के जिसने सिपाहीपन नहीं सीखा है। तो जो भी कुछ तुम सीखो, तुम रेड क्रॉस में सीखते

---

190. To Raja Hutheesing, youngest brother-in-law of Nehru; a philanthropist and politician based in Bombay.
191. Speech, 22 November 1962, at the Football Stadium. NMML, AIR Tapes, TS No. 9700, NM No. 1805.

हो या और बातें, तुम उसमें, नेशनल केडेट कोर में, वो सब बातें तुम्हारे लिए फ़ायदेमन्द हैं और मुल्क के लिए, क्योंकि उससे हमारी आबादी तगड़ी होती है, मज़बूत होती है और सीखी हुई होती है। आजकल ख़ासतौर से एक अजीब हमारे सामने संकट है, उसका चर्चा अभी हो चुका है और इसलिए ख़ास ज़रूरी है कि हम इन बुनियादी बातों की तरफ़ ध्यान दें जिसको मुल्क में होना चाहिए, नहीं तो वो कमज़ोर हो जाता है। गुलशोर से ताक़त नहीं आती, एक महज़ जुलूस निकालने से ताक़त नहीं आती लेकिन अपने निज़ाम को दुरुस्त करने से, डिसिप्लिन्ड करने से, काम सीखने से एक मुल्क तैयार होता है। तुम लोग अभी कम उम्र के हो, बच्चे हो, बढ़ोगे और, ज़िम्मेदारियों को तुम तभी अदा कर सकोगे पूरीतौर से जबकि आजकल तो तुमने फ़ायदा उठाया है कुछ सीखकर। इसलिए तुम्हारा देखना, आज थोड़े से आये हुये यहाँ, मैंने सुना कि दिल्ली में क़रीब-क़रीब तीन लाख ऐसे लड़के-लड़कियाँ हैं लेकिन सब आ नहीं सके, लेकिन तुम को भी देखकर मुझे ख़ुशी हुई, क्योंकि तगड़े लड़के-लड़कियाँ हो तुम, और बढ़कर इस क़ाबिल होगे कि मुल्क की सेवा, ख़िदमत कर सको अच्छी तरह से और जो भी कुछ संकट का सामना करना पड़े उसका करो हिम्मत से। अभी तुमने एक प्रतिज्ञा ली है, प्रतिज्ञा अच्छी है लेकिन प्रतिज्ञा लेने के माने बड़े होते हैं, ख़ाली एक दोहरा देना नहीं बल्कि उसको हर समय अपनी आँखों के सामने रखना है, दिल में याद रखना है क्योंकि जित्ता याद रखोगे उत्ता ही तुम उस पर अमल करोगे, उत्ता ही ज़्यादा तुम्हारी ताक़त बढ़ेगी।

एक मैंने कहा कि हमारे देश के सामने एक संकट का समय है, दुश्मन हमारी ज़मीन पर आया हुआ है, तरह-तरह की धमकियाँ देता है, किसी भी मुल्क को यह गवारा नहीं होना चाहिए, ख़ासकर, विशेषकर हमारा देश इसको गवारा नहीं कर सकता। हमें कुछ नुकसान हुआ, हानि हुई, हमारी फ़ौजें हटीं, हटाई गईं, धकेली गईं, यह बातें तो होती हैं ऊँच-नीच की। लेकिन हम सभों को इस बात का पक्का इरादा कर लेना चाहिए कि हम इस संकट का सामना करेंगे, चाहे जब तक भी हो, जब तक कि हम अपने देश की आज़ादी को पूरीतौर से सुरक्षित न कर सकें और करेंगे हम उसे। तुम्हारे लिए एक अजीब ज़माना है बजाय इसके कि ख़ाली खेलकूद में तुम पड़ो, पढ़ने में, खेलकूद में, कुछ सीखने में, यह सामने आ गया है। तो हम तो नहीं चाहते तुम अपना सीखने का समय कम करो, क्योंकि उससे तुम्हारी ताक़त बढ़ती है और मुल्क की ताक़त, लेकिन उसी के साथ नये संकट के आने की वजह से तुम ज़रा ढलोगे अच्छी तरह से। मुल्क बनते हैं आरामतलबी से नहीं बल्कि कठिनाई का, दिक़्क़त का सामना करने से मज़बूत होते हैं। एक आदमी जो हर वक़्त पड़ा रहे पलंग पर उसका शरीर भी अच्छा नहीं होता, शरीर के लिए भी तरह-तरह की कसरतें, वर्ज़िश करने की ज़रूरत होती है। तो ऐसे देशें को भी ज़रूरत होती है कि संकट का, मुसीबत का सामना करने से देश मज़बूत होता है, क़ौम मज़बूत होती है, तगड़ी होती है।

तो जो कुछ हमारे सामने है उससे हमें तकलीफ़ हुई, दुख हुआ, लेकिन उससे हमें फ़ायदा उठाना है, अपने को मज़बूत करना है, तगड़ा करना है और देश को ऐसा करना है

जैसे कि हम चाहते हैं और देश की आज़ादी का हमें संरक्षक बनना है। क्योंकि आज़ादी तो भली चीज़ है लेकिन आज़ादी ऐसी चीज़ नहीं है कि जो एक दफ़ा ले ली जाती है, आज़ादी उसी वक़्त तक रहती है जब तक कि लोग उसकी रक्षा करने को तैयार हों, उसके लिए बलिदान करने को तैयार हों। तो हर समय उसके लिए तैयार होना चाहिए, जहाँ ढील होती है हममें वो कुछ फ़िसल सी जाती है आज़ादी। तो इस वक़्त एक हमारे सभों की आज़माइश का, इम्तहान का मौक़ा आया है, सारे देश, बड़ों का, छोटों का और वो आज़माइश और इम्तहान हमारा हो रहा है और होयेगा आज, कल, परसों नहीं, लेकिन बहुत दिन तक होगा। यह मामला छोटा नहीं है कि थोड़े दिन में ख़त्म कर दें हम गुल मचा के, या किसी वजह से, यह मुमकिन है बरसों तक चले। तुम ज़रा उम्र में बढ़ो, तब भी चलता जाये यह, तुम्हें मौक़ा मिले, सभों को मौक़े मिले। तो एक तरह से यह तुम्हारे लिए और देश के लिए मुबारिक मौक़ा भी है, हालांकि कठिन मौक़ा है, मुबारिक भी है। इस तरह से हम हिन्दुस्तान को, भारत को मज़बूत बनायेंगे और दुनिया को दिखायेंगे कि हम कैसे अपनी स्वतंत्रता को, आज़ादी को प्यार करते हैं, कैसे उसके लिए हम बलिदान करते हैं, कैसे उसकी सेवा करते हैं।

तो बस, इत्ता ही मैं तुमसे कहता हूँ कि, और याद रखो कि ताक़त आती है देश की एकता से, इत्तेहाद से। हमारे देश में अनेक प्रकार के लोग रहते हैं अलग-अलग, उत्तर में, दक्षिण में, पूरब, पश्चिम, अलग-अलग धर्म हैं, सब हमारे देश के हैं लेकिन एक हमारा धर्म सभों का है, वो देश का धर्म है, चाहे कहीं भी हम रहें, चाहे कोई भी हमारा मज़हब या धर्म हो, कोई भी हमारा पेशा हो अव्वल धर्म है देश का धर्म, उसमें सब शामिल हैं। इसलिए हमें एकता मज़बूत करनी चाहिए और ऊँच-नीच भी हमें बहुत नहीं समझना चाहिए क्योंकि सभों को भारत के बच्चों को बराबर के अधिकार हम चाहते हैं हो जायें, अभी तो सभों के नहीं हैं लेकिन हम चाहते हैं हो जायें, ऊँचता-नीचता कम हो।

तो इस एकता को हमेशा मज़बूत करने की कोशिश करनी चाहिए। तुम सभों को मैं अपना प्यार और आर्शीवाद देता हूँ।
जयहिन्द!

[Translation begins:

Dear Boys and Girls,
I am always happy to participate in such functions. But I am particularly happy to be here among you today and to see your enthusiasm and spirit. A nation does not become great because of its size or population. It can only be as strong as its citizens and their strength depends on their enthusiasm and spirit, of course, but more important, their training and skill. A trained soldier is stronger than an untrained individual. So whatever you learn in the Red Cross and the NCC, ACC. etc., would benefit you and the nation because it makes our population stronger and better trained.

The crisis that we are facing at the moment has already been mentioned. It makes it more than ever necessary for us to pay attention to these fundamental things without which a nation becomes weak. Strength does not come from shouting slogans or taking out processions. It can come only by discipline and training. You are young, mere children but you will grow up to great responsibilities. You can discharge these responsibilities fully well only if you take advantage of the opportunity for learning and training your minds and bodies.

There are only a few of you present here today. I have heard that there are nearly three lakh such boys and girls in Delhi but everyone could not come. I am happy to see you because you are strong boys and girls who will grow up to serve the nation well and face any crisis that may arise with courage, you have just taken a pledge. It is a good pledge. But it is not enough merely to repeat a pledge. You must always keep it in mind because the more you remember the better you will practice what you have pledged, and become stronger as individuals and add to the nation's strength in the process.

As I said, this is a time of crisis for us. There is an enemy on our soil which threatens all kinds of things. No nation can tolerate that and particularly not India. We have suffered some reverses and loss of life. Our forces were pushed back. These ups and downs are quite normal. But we must be determined to face this crisis, no matter how long it takes and to defend India's freedom. It is a strange time for you that instead of merely studying and playing you have to face this experience. We do not want you to give up your studies. But at the same time, by facing this crisis, you will be better moulded. Nations are moulded not by a life of ease but by going through difficult experiences. A man who lies in bed all the time cannot be strong in body or mind. You need to do exercises to keep your body fit. Similarly, a nation needs to face difficulties and crisis to become strong.

The present crisis has been a painful experience. But we must take advantage of it to make the nation strong. We have to be the defenders of India's freedom. Freedom is not something which can be won once and for all. Freedom can be maintained only so long as the people are willing to defend it and make sacrifices for its sake. It demands constant vigilance and if there is the least complacency, freedom slips away.

So, this is a period of test for all of us, adults and children and it may last for a long time. This is not a small matter that can be ended within a few days, by making a noise. It may go on for a long time, perhaps till you are grown up. All of you will have the opportunity of serving the country. In a sense, it is a difficult but a welcome challenge for we shall come out of this experience a stronger nation and demonstrate to the world how deeply we value our freedom we are willing to make sacrifices and serve its cause.

All right, the only thing I want to tell you is that strength lies in unity. People in the different parts of the country have different life styles. There are various religions in India and all of them belong here. But the one religion common to all of us irrespective of the province we live in or religion or occupation we follow, is duty to our country. Therefore, it is very important for us to foster unity in the country and not allow any disparities. Every single son and daughter of India has equal rights and we want to ensure equality among the people which does not obtain at present. We want to reduce the disparities which exist today. We must try to foster unity among the people. My love and blessings to all of you.

Jai Hind!

Translation Ends]

310. To Antonio Colaco: Mobilisation for Peace[192]

22nd November, 1962

Dear Dr Colaco,

Thank you for your letter of the 21st November which I appreciate greatly.

What you say about mobilisation for peace is important. I think that it is essential that in our thinking and preparing for the war we must not forget the ultimate objective of the war which is peace, and we should take particular care that no harm is done to our ideals as well as our cultural and other monuments in the prosecution of the war. It is not clear to me, however, how a committee of the kind you have suggested will be helpful in this matter. It will be difficult even to get the members of the committee together and apart from issuing some statements there is little they can do at this stage. Such statements could be issued by them separately.

I agree that the case of India must be stated with clarity and force.

Yours sincerely,
[Jawaharlal Nehru]

---

192. Letter to Lok Sabha MP from Goa; address: Room No. 58, Western Court, New Delhi.

311. To Prabodh Chandra: Mobilisation into the Armed Forces[193]

22nd November, 1962

My dear Prabodh Chandra,

Thank you for your letter of the 21st November. I am glad to notice the great response we are having in the Punjab, as in the rest of India, from all classes of people for the help of the war effect.

As for enrolling members of assemblies and Parliament in the Army, the idea is a good one, but at the present moment we have to enrol people who fully qualify from the point of view of physical standards for this purpose. We may have to enrol others of a higher age later. I suggest that those who are of the proper age may offer themselves for enrolment in their respective localities. If they are considered fit, they will be enrolled.

In any event, it would be a good thing if they enrolled themselves in the Territorial Army and the Home Guards.

Yours sincerely,
[Jawaharlal Nehru]

312. To Lal Bahadur Shastri: Arresting Communists Counterproductive[194]

November 22, 1962

My dear Lal Bahadur,

I hope your visit to Tezpur and your night travel has not tired you out too much. You must take proper rest.

Indira has given me a depressing account of what she found at Tezpur. I am glad, however, that this is improving now. I think some of the Assam Ministers should stay there and tour about.

Some Communist MPs came to see me today. They were much depressed and exercised about the large scale arrests of Communists all over India. They said that while we were doing everything to fight the Chinese our people were being arrested. They would not mind if any individual mischief maker is arrested, but large numbers of arrests of this kind mean something different. As a matter of fact, this morning while they were sitting down writing a strong

193. Letter to the Speaker of the Punjab Vidhan Sabha.
194. Letter to the Home Minister.

article for the *New Age* condemning the Chinese, the police came and arrested Namboodripad[195] who was with them. This upset them greatly. Dange,[196] who was to have gone in a day or two to Moscow, specially to speak about the Chinese invasion of India, and to plead for the support of Communist Parties there, has written to me that he has cancelled his visit and will not be going now. He does not want to run away from India when his colleagues are in trouble.

I think that the States have rather overdone this matter, and your Ministry's instructions were rather vague. We decided that only those who were known to be mischief makers were to be arrested or detained. I do not think it was at all right to arrest Namboodripad. I still think that it would be better to release him. Also, I think the States might be asked to consider the lists of those persons who have been arrested again carefully and release those who have not been misbehaving or are expected to misbehave. By these large scale arrests, we shall lose some quite efficient propagandists against China.[197]

While arrests of Communists have taken place, those on the other side who are constantly criticising everything that Government does and demoralising the people are not touched. I think something should be done against some individuals to teach them that this kind of thing will not be permitted.

I enclose a letter from an MP together with a cyclostyled letter. I do not know if the signatures to the cyclostyled letter are real or forged. The DIB might find out.

Apart from this letter, Delhi is full of much more poisonous stuff. So many people have come to me and told me about it. So also Bombay. Vijaya Lakshmi came here today and gave me a lurid account of how the Swatantra Party people were behaving.

Yours affectionately,
[Jawaharlal Nehru]

---

195. E. M. S. Namboodripad, General Secretary of the CPI. On 21 November 1962, in a countrywide operation 350 CPI leaders were arrested. Namboodripad was arrested from Delhi on 22 November 1962. See reports in *The Times of India*, 22 and 23 November 1962, pp. 1 and 1 respectively.
196. S.A. Dange, Chairman of the CPI.
197. See "Entry from journal of Ivan Benedictov, Soviet ambassador to India (1959-1967) regarding conversation with E.M.S. Namboodripad, General Secretary, CPI; 26 October 1962"; Wilson Centre Archives, http://digitalarchive.wilsoncentre.org/document/113000. Accessed on 6 September 2018.

313. To G.L. Nanda: Spending on INTUC Uniforms[198]

November 25, 1962

My dear Gulzarilal,

I enclose a letter from S.R. Vasavada[199]. In this, he suggests that we might give a lakh of rupees to the Assam INTUC organisation for their volunteers. On looking at the details of the proposed expenditure, I find that two lakhs out of Rs 2,20,675/- is to be spent on some kind of a special dress or uniform for ten thousand volunteers.

I do not quite know what to do with this demand. We are forming volunteers and Home Guards and other formations on behalf of Government. For us to pay for the uniforms of INTUC volunteers would be unusual and odd.

Anyhow, I should like to have your advice in the matter.

Yours sincerely,
[Jawaharlal Nehru]

314. To Y.B. Chavan: Tribals for Guerrilla Warfare[200]

November 25, 1962

My dear Chavan,

We have various schemes of training people in arms etc. I think we should pay special attention to our tribal people in the Northeast. These border people are tough and fit and especially good at some kind of guerrilla warfare.

Even recruiting people for the Army, we might pay attention to them, or for Home Guards or the Assam Rifles.

I have been approached repeatedly about the Second Battalion of the Assam Regiment which was disbanded in J & K last year, I think, for some kind of minor mutiny. The fault lay partly at least with their officers who treated them badly and did not listen to their demands about food etc. Anyhow, it was bad to mutiny. Many of them were punished and convicted, and the whole battalion was disbanded. It has been suggested to me that we might get these people, who have been disbanded, re-instated in the Army and use them for active service. I should like you to consult the Chief of Army Staff on this subject. I think it

---

198. Letter to Minister of Labour and Employment.
199. Working Committee member of the INTUC.
200. Letter to the Minister of Defence.

will be worth while doing so as thereby you will get good trained soldiers and also create a good impression in Nagaland etc.

Yours sincerely,
[Jawaharlal Nehru]

315. To C.B. Gupta: Mobilising Popular Enthusiasm[201]

November 26, 1962

My dear Chandra Bhanu,

I do not know if you intend forming some kind of a State Committee to further war efforts. I think it would be desirable to do so. This would not be connected directly with the Defence Services, but it could help in considering the questions of Home Guards, volunteers, etc. It would especially keep in view the border areas. It would keep in touch with the Central Defence Council.

If you form such a Committee, it would be desirable to have some Muslim representatives in it. Indeed, I would suggest that some effort should be made to welcome Muslims in the Home Guards and volunteer organisations.

Mahavir Tyagi is very keen on starting some kind of volunteer corps in every district to utilise the present enthusiasm. The idea is a good one, but I am not quite sure what form it should take. Duplicating many organisations is not good. Perhaps Home Guards could be spread out in every district and some arrangements made to train them.

Yours sincerely,
[Jawaharlal Nehru]

316. To N.G. Ranga: Negative Role of Opposition Members[202]

November 27, 1962

My dear Ranga,

Your letter of the 24th November.

I was not aware of any circular issued by the AICC of the kind you have mentioned. I quite agree with you that it was very improper to describe

---

201. Letter to the Chief Minister of Uttar Pradesh.
202. Letter to Lok Sabha MP, Swatantra Party. NMML, N.G. Ranga Papers, Acc No. 301.

members of the Jan Sangh and Swatantra Party as traitors, or indeed anyone who criticises me.

I must say, however, that some members of the Swatantra Party and Jan Sangh have made very irresponsible statements.

Yours sincerely,
Jawaharlal Nehru

317. To C.B. Gupta: Abuse of Power[203]

November 27, 1962

My dear Chandra Bhanu,

I understand that your State Publicity Department is not doing anything at all to give publicity to the Chinese invasion and our war effort. I hope you will utilise this Department effectively for these purposes.

There are some complaints that pressure has been exercised by some officials for collection for the Defence Fund. This must be avoided.[204] Also that you have authorised Lekhpals to collect money for this purpose. Lekhpals are not usually popular or trusted. I suggest that some other machinery should be used.

Is it possible to use Thanas as rifle training centres?

Yours sincerely,
Jawaharlal Nehru

318. To Y.S. Parmar: Creating Volunteer Corps[205]

November 27, 1962

My dear Parmar,

Your letter of the 24th November.

I think it is desirable for all States to build up Volunteer Corps or Home Guards. Even if they cannot be given rifles at the present moment, some

---

203. Letter to the Chief Minister of Uttar Pradesh. PMO, File No. 43(192)/62-63-PMS, Sr. No. 48-A.
204. See also item 377.
205. Letter to the former Congress Chief Minister of Himachal Pradesh; address: 7-A Sujan Singh Park, New Delhi-3.

measures of discipline would be introduced and this would create a good effect in the surrounding area. You might discuss this with the Lieut. Governor.

As for the passes, we shall bear this in mind.

Yours sincerely,
[Jawaharlal Nehru]

319. To S. Chellaswamy: Thanking Well-wisher[206]

November 28, 1962

Dear Shri Chellaswamy,

Thank you for your letter of the 23rd November, with which you have sent some "Prasad". I am grateful to you for this.

Yours sincerely,
Jawaharlal Nehru

320. To S.K. Dey: Involving Panchayats[207]

November 30, 1962

My dear Dey,

Your letter of November 30th. I have read your "blue print of action." I like your broad approach to this problem, making the village panchayat and the other rural bodies the basis of this scheme.

You can certainly go ahead, but I think this will have to be worked out a little more carefully. More particularly, the State Governments should be brought into the picture so that they may give their support.

It seems to me on a first reading that the Panchayat might be burdened with too many responsibilities. Also, recruitment to the armed forces can only be done by the special recruiting staff who have to apply their standards. The

---

206. Letter to Convener, Union Language Convention, South India, and President Madras Bar Association; address: Chandra Bagh Avenue, Off Edward Elliots Road, Madras-4. Reproduced from *Letters from Late Prime Minister Mr Jawaharlal Nehru & Other Statesmen on National Issues. Selection of Letters To and From Mr S. Chellaswamy*, Printed in Madras, 1965, p. 7.

207. Letter to Minister for Community Development, Panchayati Raj and Cooperation.

NCC and the ACC are connected with our Universities, colleges and schools. I do not think isis possible to bring in the Panchayat into their training. The Block can create an atmosphere in favour of such recruitment.

So many other ministries are concerned that they should be consulted so that they may not create difficulties later.

I am writing in some haste after a first reading of your scheme. I shall of course gladly meet you in the course of the next two or three days. Perhaps you could come and see me on Sunday, 2nd December, at 11.30 a.m. in my office.

Yours sincerely,
[Jawaharlal Nehru]

321. To Tarkeshwari Sinha: Village Work for Defence[208]

November 30, 1962

My dear Tarkeshwari,
Your letter of the 30th November.

Many things that you have said are being organised. Thus, community development movement and panchayati raj are, it is proposed, to be utilised for a great deal of village work, including civil defence.

As for the military potential of industrial plants, this is being particularly looked into by the Ministry of Economic & Defence Coordination. So also necessarily the question of Supplies.

The question of doctors and engineers is also being considered.

As for the road building, certainly this must have priority.

Members of Parliament can go to their respective constituencies, but they must clearly understand that they must not put a burden on the people there. Thus, we do not want MPs to go to Assam and ask the administration or others to make arrangements for them to tour about. The Assam people are tired of VIPs visiting them.[209] The only way to go is to go on one's own steam and make one's own programme and stay in some village areas for a while. It is no good going just for a day or so and coming back.

Yours sincerely,
[Jawaharlal Nehru]

208. Letter to the Deputy Minister for Finance.
209. See also item 469.

322. To Sushila Nayar: Training Medical Personnel[210]

November 30, 1962

My dear Sushila,

I gather that you offered the services of the Health Ministry to the Defence Ministry for the training of doctors and nurses. The reply you got was, so I am told, not very encouraging. It is manifest that we want a large number of doctors and nurses and all our resources, both of the military and civil medical services, must be yoked to this end. It is a matter for consideration whether we could give shorter and condensed courses for this purpose to begin with.

If I can help you in this matter, please let me know.

Yours affectionately,
[Jawaharlal Nehru]

(d) CHINESE INVASION: Administrative Changes

323. To Raghunath Singh: Committee on External Affairs[211]

October 22, 1962

My dear Raghunath Singh,

Your letter of October 22nd. Yesterday, I received a letter from Vidya Charan Shukla suggesting that members of the Congress Standing Committee for External Affairs, many of whom are here, might meet me to discuss the border situation. I am afraid it is very difficult for me to find the time. But, nevertheless, I have suggested 9.15 a.m. on the 25th October, at my office in External Affairs for them to meet me. I can give them about 20 minutes then.

As for holding an Executive Committee meeting, the only time I can give you is the 27th October at 9.30 a.m.[212]

Thank you for the cheque for Rs 25/- to be used for the benefit of the armed forces. Please convey my thanks to the donors.

Yours sincerely,
[Jawaharlal Nehru]

210. Letter to the Minister of Health.
211. Letter to the Secretary of the CPP.
212. See also items 345 and 346.

324. To Humayun Kabir: Husain Zaheer and Defence Council[213]

November 8, 1962

My dear Humayun,

Your letter of November 8th. Dr Bhabha's[214] name was included in the National Defence Council. But, unfortunately, it was left out by inadvertence. I am having this rectified.

As for Hussain Zaheer,[215] he is doing good work and I agree with you that it might be useful to have him in the Defence Council. But I hesitate to add further names. The Defence Council is largely a policy-making body, and the list of its members is already too long a one. But of course, Husain Zaheer, can always be invited to it. He should really keep in close contact with the Defence Ministry. To add him now to the Defence Council would require consultation with many others.

Yours sincerely,
[Jawaharlal Nehru]

325. To K. Raghuramaiah: Defence Production Ministry[216]

November 8, 1962

My dear Raghuramaiah,

Krishna Menon's resignation will be formally announced tomorrow afternoon from Rashtrapati Bhavan.[217]

I am afraid I can give little time to the Defence Ministry's work. I hope to make some further arrangements in regard to it. Meanwhile I would specially

---

213. Letter to the Minister of Scientific Research and Cultural Affairs.
214. Secretary of the Atomic Energy Commission and Secretary, Department of Atomic Energy.
215. Director-General of the CSIR.
216. Letter to the Minister in the Ministry of Defence.
217. Menon, resigned on 7 November 1962. See appendices 45 and 46. See sub section (e) CHINESE INVASION: Krishna Menon; infra.

request you to look after Defence Production. It is important that there is no slackness there. It has been doing well lately and this tempo has to be kept up.

I shall see Admiral Shankar[218], the Controller-General of Defence Production, soon.

Yours sincerely,
[Jawaharlal Nehru]

326. To S. Radhakrishnan: Ministerial Appointments[219]

November 13, 1962

My dear President,

I have invited Shri Yashwantrao Balwantrao Chavan, at present Chief Minister of Maharashtra, to become our Minister of Defence. He has agreed, I recommend, therefore, that Shri Chavan be appointed Minister of Defence.

Shri Kotha Raghuramaiah who is a Minister of State in the Defence Ministry and is at present chiefly concerned with Defence Production, should I think be in independent charge of Defence Production as Minister of State.

I recommend also that Shri Tiruvallur Thattai Krishnamachari, at present Minister without Portfolio and in charge of Economic Coordination, should be appointed Minister of Defence and Economic Coordination. He will be assigned the Department of Technical Development and will be in charge of coordination of Defence and Civil production and supplies and such other subjects as may be assigned to him from time to time by the Prime Minister.

It is my intention to have a small committee to supervise Defence production and help in coordinating it with other productive and technical activities. This committee will consist of Prime Minister, Shri T.T. Krishnamachari, Shri Y.B. Chavan and the Minister of State for Defence Production, Shri K. Raghuramiah. I do not think it is necessary for you to mention this committee in any order that you may be pleased to issue, as that can be done without a Presidential Order. I am mentioning it to you to inform you of how my thinking is about coordination etc.

It is also my intention in the near future to appoint a Minister of State in charge of the Ministry of Supply which will be separated from the present Ministry of Works, Housing and Supply. About this I shall write to you a little later.

218. D. Shankar.
219. Letter to the President. President's Secretariat's File No. 8/62, p. 112.

It is also my intention to have a Department of Technical Development. This need not be mentioned at this stage in the order that you may be pleased to issue.

I shall be grateful to you if you will be good enough to accept my recommendations as stated above.[220]

Yours sincerely,
Jawaharlal Nehru

327. To S. Radhakrishnan: Department of Supply[221]

November 15, 1962

My dear President,

The question of supplies is becoming increasingly important in view of the large quantities that we are getting for war and other purposes from different countries. At present supplies is a part of the Ministry of Works, Housing & Supply. For some months past, I have been thinking of separating Supply from that Ministry and making it a charge of a Minister of State.

At present this question has become highly important some effective steps have to be taken. I would, therefore, recommend that the Department of Supply should be separated from the Ministry of Works, Housing & Supply and placed in-charge of a Minister of State, who will function in the Ministry of Economic & Defence Coordination.

I recommend that Shri Jaisukhlal Hathi, at present the Minister of State for Labour, should become Minister of State for Supply and his Department of Supply should be placed within the Ministry of Economic & Defence Coordination which is under the overall charge of the Minister Shri T.T. Krishnamachari.

I would also recommend the creation of a Department of Technical Development, replacing the present Development Wing in the Ministry of Commerce & Industry. This Department of Technical Development should also be located in the Ministry of Economic & Defence Coordination.

I trust you agree to these recommendations and will have Presidential Order issued to give effect to them.

The removal of Shri Jaisukhlal Hathi from Labour will create a vacancy in Labour. For the present, I do not suggest any new appointment for that Office.

---

220. See also item 327.
221. Letter to the President. President's Secretariat's File No. 8/62, p. 120.

Shri Gulzarilal Nanda is already the Minister for Planning and Labour and is thus in overall charge of Labour. A little later, we might have to appoint a new Minister of Labour under Shri Gulzarilal Nanda. I shall write to you about this sometime later.

I am communicating this to the Cabinet Secretary and he will take your orders in this matter and help in processing them in the proper form.[222]

Yours affectionately,
Jawaharlal Nehru

328. Appointments of Officials[223]

Shri T.T. Krishnamachari[224] has written to me about the proposed Ministry of Supply. He suggests that it should have a very senior Secretary who would, apart from looking after supply and resources and the Department of Technical Development, also coordinate civil production, besides being the senior secretary in the Ministry of Defence & Economic Coordination. He suggests the name of Bhoothalingam[225] for this post. He has had experience of Supply and Industry for a period of 22 years and knew the working of the Supply Department during the last war. He is, at present, I believe, Secretary Expenditure, in the Finance Ministry.

2. Shri T.T. Krishnamachari also would like to appoint his present Secretary, P.V.R. Rao, as Second Secretary for his Ministry for Coordination of Defence, Railways, Transport & Communications, Civil Aviation etc.

I have no objection to these appointments. Will you please mention these to the Finance Minister[226] and if he agrees take steps accordingly.

---

222. See also item 326 and appendix 55.
223. Note, 15 November 1962, for S.S. Khera, the Cabinet Secretary.
224. Minister of Defence & Economic Coordination. See appendix 55.
225. S. Bhoothalingam.
226. Morarji Desai.

329. To T.T. Krishnamachari: New Departments[227]

November 15, 1962

My Dear TT,

Your letter of November 15.[228] You are right in pointing out slight discrepancy between my letter to the President and his Presidential Order about the Minister of Defence Production. I am afraid, I am responsible for this. I was asked what exactly I meant whether the Minister of Defence Production should continue formally in the Ministry of Defence. Without thinking much at the time, I said that he might do so but he will be intimately connected with the Ministry of Economic and Defence Coordination. If you think this will not affect your work and you will be able to function adequately, we can leave it as it is, and at any time, if you so wish, I can make a change as was originally intended. Perhaps it might be worthwhile to continue things as they are. We have of course emphasised and everyone knows that the Minister of Defence Production will be in effect working largely under your directions.

I enclose a copy of a letter I have written to the Cabinet Secretary. I am also writing to the President directly.[229] This is about the creation of a Department of Supply and locating it in the Ministry of Economic & Defence Coordination. Also the creation of a Department of Technical Development, replacing the present Development Wing and locating it in the Ministry of Economic & Defence Coordination.

I am appointing Jaisukhlal Hathi as Minister of State for Supply and he and his Department will function under your Ministry.

I have had a talk with Gulzarilal Nanda and Mehr Chand Khanna. Gulzarilal was rather sorry to leave Jaisukhlal Hathi but he agreed that Supply was an urgent and vital matter now and if Hathi was required for it, he should go there. I have also spoken to Hathi.

Mehr Chand Khanna has two Deputy Ministers, P.S. Naskar and Jagannath Rao. Now that the Department of Supply has been removed from his charge, he obviously does not require these two Deputies. Perhaps you could take over one of them either of the two that you prefer. I think both are fairly good.

Yours affectionately,
[Jawaharlal Nehru]

---

227. Letter to the Minister of Economic and Defence Coordination.
228. See appendix 55.
229. See item 327.

330. To Rameshwar Tantia: National Defence Council[230]

November 16, 1962

Dear Tantiaji,

Your letter of the 15th November. The Chief Ministers appointed to the National Defence Council[231] were more or less chosen at the National Development Council meeting. It is a little difficult to add to them at the present moment. But I have no doubt that the Chief Minister of Rajasthan[232] will be consulted whenever any occasion concerning his border region arises.

Yours sincerely,
[Jawaharlal Nehru]

331. In the Lok Sabha: Economies during Emergency[233]

The Prime Minister and Minister of External Affairs and Minister of Atomic Energy (Jawaharlal Nehru): Mr Deputy Speaker, Sir, the main object and the reason behind this Resolution is one with which the whole House will be in agreement. The object is economy, no waste and efficiency. But how to bring it about is another matter. As a matter of fact, in war time what has normally happened in other countries is a vast increase in the apparatus of Government because vast new obligations arise and new duties are to be performed. I should very much like that to be avoided as far as possible here. To some extent it will have to be done because the normal peace time apparatus of Government cannot adequately discharge all the new functions that come to government.

It is obvious that no one would say that we should have economy at the expense of efficiency.

An hon. Member: Certainly not.

Jawaharlal Nehru: Nothing is more important in war time than speed and efficiency. What we mean by speed and efficiency is a matter for consideration and judgment. The hon. Member says that the number of Ministers or the

---

230. Letter to Lok Sabha MP, Congress, from Sikar; address: 12-D Ferozeshah Road, New Delhi-1.
231. See item 268.
232. Mohanlal Sukhadia.
233. Moving resolution on economy during Emergency, *Lok Sabha Debates*, Third Series, Vol. X, November 21 to December 4, 1962, pp. 3252-3264.

size of the Ministry should be reduced. That is a question which can only be considered from the point of view of efficiency. It is not a thing which can be reduced or expanded. If it is expedient to lessen it in the interest of efficiency, well and good; if it is expedient to expand it in the interest of efficiency, well and good. There is no other test except the work to be done and the efficient way of doing it. The amount spent on the increase of Ministers, if the Ministers are not necessary, is wasteful. In the circumstances that we face, for instance, all kinds of new work and new types of work have to be done. Even the staff has to be increased, with more Secretaries and more others. Therefore, the test of it is purely how we can effect and prosecute the war and matters connected with it. There is no other test. It is, if I may say so, a little unreasonable to have some adhoc test and say: Have so many Ministers regardless of the effect of that.

Then, again, the hon. Member said that Upper Houses are useless. That may be his opinion. There are some people who think that Lower Houses are also useless. I do not think so. I am saying that some people are of opinion that Parliament is useless. Some people think that we should have a dictatorship or that we should have an authoritarian government. We do not agree with them, I hope nobody agrees.

प्रकाशवीरशास्त्री[234] (बिजनौर): कुछ प्रान्त ऐसे भी तो हैं जहां अपर हाउससिस नहीं हैं।

जवाहरलाल नेहरु: जी हां।

[Translation begins:

Prakash Vir Shastri (Bijnor): There are some countries, where there are no Upper Houses.

Jawaharlal Nehru: Yes, sir.

Translation ends]

What I was venturing to say was that this line of argument is a dangerous line of argument which takes us ultimately really to say—some people say, not we—that the whole apparatus of Parliament wastes time and energy when we are prosecuting a war and that it is expensive.

---

234. Independent.

Surendra Nath Dwivedy[235]: That was never my suggestion.

Jawaharlal Nehru: I know, it is not the hon. Member's view point. I am saying that, that argument is extended by some people. I think, it is highly important at this crisis in our destiny that we should maintain the parliamentary form of government fully.

Surendra Nath Dwivedy: Certainly.

Jawaharlal Nehru: ...and show to the world that even parliamentary form of government can deal with grave problems that confront a country in war. That is an important consideration. Parliamentary form of government is a relatively expensive form of government compared to a dictatorship or an authoritarian government. Nevertheless, it is not only better from every point of view but possibly in the long run it is even less expensive than the other ways.

Hari Vishnu Kamath[236]: It is not necessarily bicameral. That is all.

Jawaharlal Nehru: That is true. It is not necessarily bicameral. As the hon. Member there pointed out in some states there is only one House. But at the present moment, I would submit, demolishing or trying to demolish the second chambers would encourage a very wrong tendency in the country as if second chambers are useless; let them go. There are some people and some groups in the country which think so, I think wrongly. I wish to discourage that. Ultimately, second chambers were adopted and it was left to the choice of the States, I believe. Some States chose a second chamber and some did not. If at some future time the States want to get rid of the second chamber, it is up to them. We should not take any steps to compel them to do so.

I submit, therefore, that so far as the question of Ministers is concerned, the sole consideration is the kind of work that we have to do and the persons required to do it efficiently. It is very difficult to judge about the efficiency of every Ministry. The hon. Member may not agree that such and—such a Ministry is efficient. We are not discussing the efficiency of the Ministry. I am merely pointing out the test to be applied.

Even now in our Cabinet which consists of 18 people ...

Hari Vishnu Kamath: 19.

---

235. PSP, from Kendrapara, Orissa.
236. PSP.

Jawaharlal Nehru: No. 18.

Hari Vishnu Kamath: Cabinet Ministers are 19. Anyway, it does not matter.

बागड़ी[237] (हिसार): कैबिनेट इतनी बड़ी कि प्रधानमंत्री जी को भी पता नहीं है कि उस में कितने मिनिस्टर्ज हैं।

[Translation begins:

Bagri (Hissar): The cabinet is so big that even the Prime Minister does not know how many ministers are there.

Translation ends]

L.M. Singhvi[238]: Now there are 58 Ministers.

Jawaharlal Nehru: Even now in our Cabinet there is an Emergency Committee of the Cabinet which consists of six or seven members. It is found that the full Cabinet could not deal efficiently and quickly with all the matters that come up from day to day and where decisions are required to be given almost from day to day. Therefore, an Emergency Committee of Cabinet Ministers specially concerned with the war effort was formed. The fact that a Cabinet Minister was not taken in it was not because he was considered less important but that his department was not directly concerned. Indirectly every Ministry and every department is concerned. It is called the Emergency Committee of the Cabinet consisting now, I believe, of seven members. It meets very frequently and confers, where necessary, with our defence officers and officials, receives reports daily and comes to conclusions. The full Cabinet could not deal with it adequately. It could not meet every day. Therefore, this device was adopted. It is often adopted in war-time and even in peace-time sometimes.

Now, whether the rest of the Cabinet can or should be reduced is a matter to be judged, as I said, from the point of view of what work has to be done by Government. At present the work of the Government, I might venture to submit to the House, is very heavy. It may be that in some departments it is not very heavy and in some it is excessively heavy both for the officials and the Ministers. War-time does not reduce the work. Quite apart from the actual war operations the preparation for it is a very heavy task and, I think, hardly any Minister

237. Socialist.
238. Independent.

today is, shall I say, working on the same level as he was working before. It is at a much higher level. But it has to be kept in mind that we should not have unnecessary work being done by Ministers who may not be very necessary in the context of the present situation. That has to be borne in mind. But merely to say that the Ministry should be reduced has no meaning to me. If the work is greater, it has to be done efficiently. I am very much afraid, I might inform the House, that owing to very heavy work that we have to face some of our officials who are working very heavily might not have a break down very soon. It will be unfortunate if they do. They are working in the Secretariat, some of them, from morning till very late at night. It is not a five, six or seven hour day but it is a twelve hour day or more for them. But, I entirely agree with the hon. Member about reducing unnecessary work, unnecessary expenditure, etc. I may just mention some instances. We have issued directions that the holding of meetings and conference other than those necessary in the interests of war work should be avoided. Parties, functions and State entertainments should be cut out. Proposals regarding deputation abroad of government servants should be rigorously screened. I might say, deputations will continue; but they are chiefly concerned directly with the war work or indirectly with it. Then, tours except those essential, should be avoided. Ministries and departments should cut down the consumption of electricity as much as possible. Minimum use should be made of the transport services. Ministries should locate surplus staff so that they can be utilised elsewhere for activities in furtherance of the defence effort. Every effort should be made to cut down the consumption of paper of various types, and so on. A number of other instructions have been issued. The main object is what the hon. Member has said that we must avoid waste and enforce strict economy.

One thing else. There has also been instruction sent to all Central Ministries for a cut of 10 per cent of expenditure of staff, so that the budget proposals for staff for 1963-64 are restricted to a ceiling of 90 per cent of the budget provision made for such expenditure for last year. Various other reductions have been made.

बागड़ी: अगर 10 परसेंट स्टाफ घटाया जाय तो 10 परसेंट मिनिस्टर्स भी घटाये जायें।

[Translation begins:

Bagri: If there is a reduction of 10 per cent of staff, then let there be 10 per cent reduction in the number of ministers.

Translation ends]

Jawaharlal Nehru: Ten percent on the expenditure on staff; not on the staff. Staff is being reduced also just as the hon. Speaker has agreed to reduce the staff in the Lok Sabha by 20 persons or so. They have not been dismissed overnight. These persons have been placed at the disposal of the Central pool to be utilised otherwise. So, in other Ministries, people are being placed at the disposal of the Central pool to be utilised for various kinds of new war work, etc.

One more thing is important. One hon. Member has moved an amendment which says, suspension of organisations like the Bharat Sevak Samaj, Sadhu Samaj, Lalit Kala Akademi. There is no question of suspension.

Some Hon. Members: Not moved.

Tyagi: Khadi Commission also.

Ram Sewak Yadav[239]: Not suspension, but stopping the aid being given to them.

Jawaharlal Nehru: The hon. Member's amendment is different. The other amendment talked about suspension. There is no question of suspension of private organisations. The point I wish to lay stress on is this. As a matter of fact, today, in the context of the war effort, the effects and after effects of war, we want as many voluntary organisations as possible to work. Organisations like the Bharat Sevak Samaj do far more important work now than they ever did before. It depends on the quality of work and the kind of work. For instance, I shall mention the work that has been allotted to them. Assistance to families of military personnel; maintenance of morale and solidarity of the community; service as construction agency for the needs of Defence; assistance in the preventing rise of prices; rendering emergency service; mobilisation of savings, and so on. It is war effort.

As the hon. House will remember, State committees have been formed. Citizens committees they are usually called, or by some other name. A Central citizens committee has also been formed with many branches, Women's committees and others. All these have been formed specially to help in the prosecution of the war and in meeting the after effects—highly important. A minor thing, if I may say so, a small thing, but which is considered important is that people should keep in direct touch by letters with our soldiers at the front—even unknown soldiers, not only friends, but others—just to tell them that people are interested in them. Personal touch comes in. It heartens them.

239. Socialist.

They do not get news every day from here. Personal letters like that is a very small matter. But, it requires some organisation. A large number of people should get letters from other people. I merely wanted to mention this.

Economy if it comes in the way of keeping up the morale or doing essential work in the war effort is bad economy. We are likely to spend vast sums of money, because war is an expensive thing. We should economise for that. But, economising so as to diminish the effect of our effort is bad obviously. We spend one crore of rupees on war. If perhaps a saving of 50,000 or 1 lakh would impair that one crore effort, it is bad economy.

Another thing that I should like again to stress before the House is this. Take the question of these Five Year Plans, etc. Some people seem to imagine that there is a conflict between carrying on a war and carrying on the Plan. Obviously there are some portions of the Plan which might, in these circumstances, be postponed, if you like, put off for the moment. But, what is the essential part of the Plan? The essential part is agricultural production part, industries part, power part, and so on. Agriculture is of the highest importance from every point of view. When we are spending so much, if the agricultural base weakens, that injures us more than anything. Therefore, we have to go ahead with greater production in agriculture at all costs. Industry, not industry dealing with luxuries and other things, but basic industries, have the highest importance. If we have a steel plant, we have to go on with the steel plant. If we have a big industry, the machine building industry, we have to go on with it. That always happens in war time. We have to go on with them for the purposes of war apart from industrial development. Power is the essence of the thing. We have to increase our power. Because we have to increase our power, we have to use every opportunity to increase it, not only hydro-electric and thermal power, even atomic energy, civil stations for power. I can go on mentioning the core of the Plan. The core of the Plan becomes highly important for war. Superficial things or relatively secondary things may be dropped. But, that does not help us very much in economising. It is the core of the Plan that swallows large sums of money.

There is another aspect not directly connected with this which I should like to mention. As the House knows, there is tremendous response all over the country, wonderful response. A most heartening thing. The surprising thing is this. Response in a city which we see is easy to understand. But, you go to the remotest village. You find that response whether in the north or south of India, everywhere. In order to give a certain direction to that response, we have to find ways and means. It is very important. Of course, we are recruiting for the Army. NCC we are enlarging, NCC Rifles we are constituting and enlarging; Home Guards and all that. But, even so, that affects at present a relatively small proportion of the entire population. It might affect more and more as we enlarge our recruiting for the various services. There are other services which might well be used in this work like civil defence, nursing. All these are good things. I do not mean to say that in a city like Bombay there is much likelihood of bombing. Nevertheless, it is a good thing to have the practice of civil defence, to get a large number of people trained, and teach them many good things such as fire-fighting, this, that and the other, which are good in themselves and which may be useful; and when they are required, trained people can come up. But the important point is that they are doing something in the national effort and it gives them a sense of satisfaction; apart from doing useful things and apart from improving themselves, it gives them a sense of satisfaction as being part of the national effort and not being frustrated saying "I want to do something, but I have nothing to do." Therefore, these things can be explored, this kind of finding suitable opportunities for work; and essentially, they must be non-official. There may be official, cooperation, and official guidance, but essentially they should be non-official efforts, and we have formed the Citizens' Committees for that purpose. They, no doubt, will expand their activities.

There is another thing that I would like to put before the House. This is specially meant for the rural areas. As I said, agriculture is of the highest importance. We all know how to increase the output from agriculture. There are various ways, such as having proper channels, proper irrigation, fertilisers, building, and so on and so forth, tanks etc. There are many ways which do not involve any foreign exchange or anything or that sort, but which do involve, of course, some local expenditure.

I would suggest that the State Governments and where possible the Central Government also should lay down some rules, some objectives to be attained, say, within six months, for, instance with regard to water channels etc. We have got major canals, but the water channels are missing. In the old days, the big zamidars and landlords were responsible for the water channels. Somehow, there was a break in the tradition. Now, Government is expected to do everything. We calculated the other day, and it means, I do not know how many, thousands of miles of water channels and at vast expense Government have to undertake it. If, however, the local village community does it, they do it quickly, and it is done all over the country in limited time. That is clear. But that requires organisation. And there is no reason why at present the enthusiasm of the people should not be directed to something which is directly good for them, and good for the country. Let them during the next six months dig these water channels in their own villages. Let them repair or dig new tanks or wells. Let them do bunding there, and other operations. These are simple things. Let them be connected with the war effort; let them think, Yes, we are doing something for the war. In this sense, a great deal of work can be done which

593

is of paramount and basic importance in improving agriculture. There may be other ways even in industries organised somewhat differently. But there are many ways in small industry etc. which can be pursued in that way, so as to increase production and thus ultimately increase the war effort.

So, I submit that this is the way of approach to this problem. The resolution that the hon. Member has moved, I regret, I cannot accept, because it is bad in principle, it is just laying down an ad hoc thing, say, that Ministers should be cut by half, or you might say that all members of Parliament should be five feet in height, and their heads should be raised or should be cut off.

Hari Vishnu Kamath: It is not so bad; the suggestions are not so bad.

Jawaharlal Nehru: It is an ad hoc approach; I do not quite understand. Some people will lose their heads and some people will lose their feet!

But I accept the general principle that there should be economy in every possible way. The test should always be efficacy and efficiency of the war effort. And there should be no wastage.

I trust that the hon. Mover will, after this debate is over, withdraw his resolution, because basically we agree with him.

Mahavir Tyagi[240]: May I get a clarification from the hon. Prime Minister? He has been good enough to take the House into confidence as to the items on which Government are trying to effect economies. I would like to know how much is expected to be saved by these small items which he has narrated. My fears are that Government lack that idea or the imagination of the colossal nature of the expenditure which they will have to incur inside the country; it is not only foreign exchange but expenditure inside the country also. The exchequer of Government will have to be stretched to an extent where they cannot go on unless they effect economy to the tune of about Rs 100 crores per year. That will be the incidence of war on them. I wonder if these small items which he has narrated would go anywhere near that. So, drastic changes have to be effected.

240. Congress.

Jawaharlal Nehru: It is obvious that these items would not bring about very major economies, but the small economies they bring about will help to that extent. Apart from that, the object is one of introducing a climate of economy and saving. As a matter of fact, in regard to some of these things like paper, it may well be that paper is in short supply; we just cannot give it. So, we have to save. We have to save the use of paper and other things. So, we are compelled to do that, apart from economy, apart from saving money, saving the stuff itself which is in short supply.

Mahavir Tyagi: Can the hon. Prime Minister re-examine the position once again to find out in what way drastic economy could be effected and savings could be effected?

Jawaharlal Nehru: The hon. Member is quite right in laying stress on drastic economies, and one should examine it from time to time, and again and again. But the fact is that war is terribly expensive business.

Mahavir Tyagi: Therefore, economy should be there.

Jawaharlal Nehru: The hon. Member mentioned a sum of about Rs 100 crores. I think that it is very small. The sum involved will be much greater.

Hari Vishnu Kamath (Hoshangabad): By your leave, may I ask the hon. Prime Minister to throw light on one small point? The other day, when you, Sir, were in the Chair, the Supplementary Demands for Grants were being discussed, and the Deputy Finance Minister in the course of his reply to the debate said that the suggestion with regard to the scrapping of prohibition was under the consideration or will be under the consideration of the Finance Minister and the Prime Minister. Is it being considered at all? That is what I would like to know. I do not want any decision or any answer now whether it will be scrapped. I just want to know whether it is being considered.

Jawaharlal Nehru: There is no question which cannot be considered. But this question has not come up before me in any shape or form yet.

332. To S.K. Patil: Adapting to New Demands[241]

23rd November, 1962

My dear SK,

Your letter of November 23.[242] I quite understand your feeling in this matter. The crisis came to us very suddenly and we are trying gradually to adapt ourselves to it. Most of the work that we have had to do has been:

1) of obtaining supplies, chiefly from the USA and UK,
2) some internal defence arrangements, and
3) addressing various countries to explain to them our position.

The burden of the work has specially fallen on External Affairs Ministry and the Defence Ministry, though others have had to join occasionally. No policy decisions have been taken, so far as I can remember, without reference to the Cabinet as a whole. The Emergency Committee deals with Defence supplies in some detail.

I shall try to keep the Cabinet informed more fully whenever possible.

Yours sincerely,
Jawaharlal Nehru

333. To Jagannath Rao: Reorganising WH & S Ministry[243]

November 25, 1962

My dear Jagannath Rao,

You know that a considerable part of the old Ministry of Works, Housing & Supply has been transferred to the Ministry of Economic & Defence Coordination. The part transferred deals with all supplies which have become very important in view of the large purchases we are making because of the emergency.

Mehr Chand Khanna[244] told me the other day that he would not require two Deputy Ministers now. T.T. Krishnamachari[245] has asked for you in his Ministry.

241. Letter to the Minister of Food and Agriculture. NMML, S.K. Patil Papers.
242. See appendix 65.
243. Letter to the Deputy Minister, Works, Housing and Rehabilitation.
244. Minister of Works, Housing and Supply.
245. Minister of Economic & Defence Coordination.

I am therefore instructing the Cabinet Secretary[246] to take the necessary steps in this matter.[247]

Yours sincerely,
[Jawaharlal Nehru]

334. To Sushila Nayar: From North Block to Patiala House[248]

November 30, 1962

My dear Sushila,

I have your two letters of November 28 and 29, about the question of your Ministry shifting from the North Block to another place. I have also heard from the Minister of Labour and Employment. For a variety of reasons, he cannot move to Patiala House. I sympathise with your difficulties, but, in the circumstances, I think that it will be desirable for your Ministry to move to Patiala House. You will have more space there.

The Ministry of Economic & Defence Coordination will occupy the accommodation vacated by you in the North Block. This has to be done as speedily as possible as the work of that Ministry is of considerable importance in view of our war effort and they are suffering from lack of a fixed abode.

I am sure you will understand the need that has arisen and will appreciate my decision.

Yours affectionately,
Jawaharlal Nehru

---

246. S.S. Khera.
247. See transfer of Jagannath Rao as DeputyMinister in the Ministry of Economic & Defence Coordination, on 26 November 1962. President's Secretariat, File No. 8/62, pp. 139, 140. See items 327, 328, and 329.
248. Letter to the Minister of Health.

335. To S. Radhakrishnan: R.K. Malaviya for Labour Ministry[249]

November 30, 1962

Dear Mr President,
As you know, Shri Jaisukhlal Hathi who was Minister of Labour, has now been made Minister of Supply in the Ministry of Economic & Defence Coordination. Shri Gulzarilal Nanda, Minister of Planning and Labour & Employment, finds that the work he has to deal with, especially in regard to labour, requires some assistance, now that Shri Jaisukhlal Hathi has left his Labour portfolio. Shri Nanda has suggested to me that his Parliamentary Secretary, Shri R.K. Malaviya, should be appointed Deputy Minister in his Ministry in charge of Labour and Employment.

I think that Shri Gulzarilal Nanda's suggestion should be accepted. I recommend to you for your approval that Shri R.K. Malaviya, now Parliamentary Secretary, should be appointed Deputy Minister for Labour and Employment. I trust you will be good enough to agree.

Yours sincerely,
Jawaharlal Nehru

(e) CHINESE INVASION: Krishna Menon

336. To S. Radhakrishnan: Krishna Menon removed from Defence[250]

31st October, 1962

My dear Mr President,
At the request of Shri Krishna Menon[251] I am taking charge of Defence. Shri Krishna Menon will be Minister of Defence Production. He will continue to be a Member of the Cabinet. As Minister of Defence Production, Shri Krishna Menon will be in charge of the ordnance factories and other manufacturing and industrial establishments in the Ministry of Defence, including also the establishments such as Hindustan Aircraft, Bharat Electronics and Mazagaon and Garden Reach Docks. He will also be responsible for Defence Research

249. Letter to the President. President's Secretariat, File No. 8/62, p. 147.
250. Letter to the President. President's Secretariat, File No. 8/62, p.100.
251. See appendix 35.

598

and Development, the Border Roads Organisation and any other matter that may be allotted to him from time to time.

These arrangements will take effect from tomorrow, 1st November, 1962. I hope you approve of these arrangements.

Yours affectionately,
Jawaharlal Nehru

337. To V.K. Krishna Menon: Change of Portfolio[252]

November 2, 1962

My dear Krishna,

It was good of you to send me your letter of the 30th October.[253] I am sorry for the delay in answering it in writing. But I have already given you my answer orally, and as you know, I have taken certain steps.

We have a very difficult task before us, and the difficulties have increased by all kinds of wild accusations. The shock that the country has received by the Chinese invasion has naturally upset most people. All of us have to show forbearance and charity and, at the same time, carry on our work with a fixed determination to succeed.

Yours affectionately,
Jawaharlal

338. To S. Radhakrishnan: Appointments[254]

November 2, 1962

My dear President,

Thank you for your letter of November 2nd with cash donations of Rs 1,570.85 np and cheques, drafts, etc. for Rs 1,369.75 np and $ 75.00. Also, a gold chain and a gold bangle.

As for Dilip Roy's[255] letter, it is difficult for us to help him, as you yourself have said. If he chooses to give a concert, he can do so but we can hardly make ourselves responsible for arrangements, etc.

---

252. Letter to the former Defence Minister, now Minister of Defence Production. NMML, V.K. Krishna Menon Papers.
253. Appendix 35.
254. Letter to the President.
255. Dilipkumar Roy (1897-1980); musicologist, musician, poet, novelist and essayist; friend of Romain Rolland.

The *Statesman* cutting is not quite correct. Probably Krishna Menon said something casually which does not give the right impression. I am in charge of Defence and am dealing with it myself directly and am going to the Defence Ministry daily. Krishna Menon has got a limited responsibility in regard to production matters which are under the Defence Ministry.

Krishna Menon sent me a letter which I have given to the Cabinet Secretary to show to you. You will remember that when I went to you I said that the Defence Minister had asked me to take charge of Defence at this particular crisis, or something to that effect.

I hope to see you this evening at about 5.45 p.m.

I am returning Dilip Roy's letter and a copy of your reply.

As for Shrinagesh's[256] letter, I think that he had better stay on as Governor. Apart from other matters, he is not too well for any strenuous and active work.

Yours affectionately,
[Jawaharlal Nehru]

339. To J. Rameshwar Rao: Krishna Menon and Defence Ministry[257]

November 3, 1962

My dear Rameshwar Rao,

Your letter of November 3. The press cutting you have sent is not correct. It was some casual remark presumably by Shri Krishna Menon even before he had seen the announcement, although he knew broadly what was coming. Anyhow, the change in the Defence Ministry is not one in name only. I am in complete charge and am responsible for it fully.

This is not a question of any individual being demoted or promoted. If I am to be in charge, I have to decide what I think best as to the most effective means of pursuing our aims and achieving results.

Yours sincerely,
[Jawaharlal Nehru]

---

256. S. M. Shrinagesh, Governor of Andhra Pradesh, and a retired general.
257. Letter to Congress MP from Mehboobnagar; address: 9 Electric Lane, New Delhi.

340. To Iftikhar Ali Khan: Krishna Menon not a Communist[258]

November 3, 1962

My dear Nawab Sahib,

Thank you for your letter of the 2nd November. I think you are wrong in your judgment of V.K. Krishna Menon. Like all of us, he has his failings, but unlike most of us, he has some remarkable virtues also. It is wholly wrong to say that he is a "violent Communist".

Yours sincerely,
[Jawaharlal Nehru]

341. To B.K.P. Sinha: Krishna Menon and Defence Ministry[259]

November 3, 1962

Dear Shri Sinha,

Your letter of November 2nd.

Shri Krishna Menon had decided to go to Tezpur before any change in the set-up here was made. Indeed, he must have heard about it for the first time in Tezpur, although he knew broadly what was going to happen. Apart from this, he or any other Minister can certainly go to Tezpur where we think it is necessary for important people to visit from time to time.

The remarks you quote from him were made casually apparently to someone who asked him. As a matter of fact, there is a complete change in the Defence set-up. We certainly wish to utilise Shri Menon's abilities and his driving power in Defence production, also to consult him occasionally about other matters. But I am in definite and full charge of the Defence Ministry.

Yours sincerely,
[Jawaharlal Nehru]

258. Letter to the Nawab of Malerkotla.
259. Letter to Lok Sabha MP, Congress; address: 74 South Avenue, New Delhi.

342. To V.K. Krishna Menon: Resignation[260]

November 7, 1962

My dear Krishna,

Thank you for your two letters dated the 7th November offering your resignation from the Government.[261] You have already spoken to me about this matter more than once. I appreciate the reasons which have influenced you in coming to this decision.

I should like to express my warm appreciation of the fine work you have done in the Defence Ministry during all the years you have been connected with it. As you know, I have spoken about this at the Party meeting today.[262] In the grave crisis we are facing today, I am sure your help in many ways will be of great assistance. I hope that it will be possible in the future to utilise your high abilities in the cause of the nation.

I deeply regret to part with you in the work we have been doing together for so long in Government. This is, of course, not a parting as both you and I are dedicated to serving our country in whatever position either of us may be placed.

I am forwarding your two letters to the President recommending to him to accept your resignation.[263] The formal acceptance can only take place after the President has indicated his wishes in the matter. I have already informed him of your letters and he has orally agreed to my recommendation. But I think we should wait for his reply in writing. This may be delayed by a day or two as I understand he is going to Tezpur very early tomorrow morning for the day.

With all good wishes to you,

Yours affectionately,
Jawaharlal

260. Letter to the Minister of Defence Production. NMML, V.K. Krishna Menon Papers.
261. See appendices 45 and 46.
262. See item 269.
263. See item 343.

343. To S. Radhakrishnan: Krishna Menon's Resignation[264]

November 7, 1962

My dear President,

I enclose copies of two letters I have received from Shri Krishna Menon offering his resignation from Government. I have already shown you these letters.

I propose to write to him accepting his resignation after I learn your wishes in the matter. These wishes have been conveyed to me orally by you already. But I would be grateful if you would kindly repeat them in writing.

Yours affectionately,
[Jawaharlal Nehru]

344. To V.K. Krishna Menon: Resignation Accepted[265]

November 8, 1962

My dear Krishna,

Thank you for your two letters dated the 7th November offering your resignation from the Government.[266] You have already spoken to me about this matter more than once. I appreciate the reasons which have influenced you in coming to this decision.

I should like to express my warm appreciation of the fine work you have done in the Defence Ministry during all the years you have been connected with it. In particular, Ordnance production has gone up very greatly during these years.

I deeply regret to part with you in the work we have been doing together for so long in Government. This is, of course, not a parting as both you and I are dedicated to serve our country in whatever position either of us may be placed. In the grave crisis we are facing today, I am sure your help in many ways will be of great assistance. I hope that it will be possible in the future to utilise your high abilities in the cause of the nation.

---

264. Letter to the President. See appendices 45 and 46.
265. Letter to the Minister of Defence Production. NMML, V.K. Krishna Menon Papers.
266. See appendices 45 and 46.

I forwarded your two letters to the President recommending to him to accept your resignation. I have just received from him a letter in which he says that, in the circumstances, we have to accept your resignation with regret. I am now requesting him to issue a formal announcement to this effect tomorrow.

With all good wishes to you,

Yours affectionately,
Jawaharlal Nehru

(f) CHINESE INVASION: Special Meetings

345. To A.M. Tariq: Parliament Session[267]

October 22, 1962

My dear Tariq,

Your two letter of October 22.

I am not at present inclined to call a session of the Parliament before the due date. We shall, however, keep this matter in view.[268]

Vidya Charan Shukla asked me to have a meeting of such members of the External Affairs Standing Committee as are here. I have suggested a brief meeting at 9.15 a.m. on 25th October.

If the Executive of the Congress Party wants to donate some money for sweets for the Armed Forces, this may be agreed to. I think, however, that it will be better to give this money to the families of those who have died on the frontier.[269]

Yours sincerely,
[Jawaharlal Nehru]

267. Letter to Congress MP; address: 19 Rakabganj Road, New Delhi.
268. See item 347, 348, 350.
269. See also items 323 and 346.

346. To R.S. Panjhazari: CPP Members Meeting[270]

October 23, 1962

Dear Panjhazari,

Your letter of the 23rd October.

As you say, I have asked certain Members to come to my office on the 25th October at 9.15 a.m. I am afraid I cannot stay for very long as I have to go to Vigyan Bhavan a little before 10. I think that it would be desirable to have a meeting of the Executive Committee on the 27th at 9.30 a.m.[271]

You might put up the question of a donation for the use of families of the army personnel etc. at the Executive Committee meeting.

I am sorry to know that you have had to go to the hospital.

Yours sincerely,
[Jawaharlal Nehru]

347. To Satya Narayan Sinha: Recalling Parliament Early[272]

October 25, 1962

My dear Satya Narayan,

At the Cabinet meeting today, it was decided to convene the next session of the Lok Sabha for the 8th November, that is eleven days before the date previously fixed. I suppose the Rajya Sabha will come two or three days later.

I find that the Speaker[273] is away from India and is expected to come back on the 9th November. I have asked his office people to send him a telegram informing him that we would like to have the Lok Sabha session beginning on the 8th November, and hoping that he will be back by then.

The Deputy Speaker[274] is also away. I think he should be informed and asked to come back before that date.

Yours sincerely,
[Jawaharlal Nehru]

270. Letter to the Secretary of the CPP.
271. See also items 345 and 323.
272. Letter to the Minister of Parliamentary Affairs.
273. Hukam Singh.
274. S.V. Krishnamoorthy Rao

348. To H.V. Kamath: Recalling Parliament[275]

October 28, 1962

My dear Kamath,

Your letter of October 26th has only just reached me.

The meeting of the Congress Standing Committee on External Affairs plus some others was held the other day because I was requested to hold such a meeting. There is no question of being partial to it.

You must have learnt that the next session of Parliament will now be held on November 8th. It has thus been advanced by eleven days. Both the Speaker and the Deputy Speaker are at present far away, and it was partly to accommodate their convenience that we have fixed the date for November 8th. Otherwise it might have been a little earlier still.[276]

Yours sincerely,
[Jawaharlal Nehru]

349. To Yashpal Singh: Secret Session of Parliament[277]

October 31, 1962

Dear Yashpal Singhji,

I have received your telegram of the 30th October suggesting that a secret sitting of the Lok Sabha should be called to discuss the situation on Indian borders and Chinese aggression.

We propose to move a resolution on behalf of the Government on the first day of the Lok Sabha Session approving of the President's Order in regard to Emergency. This is necessary constitutionally. There will, probably, be a debate on it for a day or two. On the whole, we think that this debate should not be a secret one. In any event, it can hardly be treated as secret, except for the press purposes, when five hundred Members are present. Purely military information will naturally have to be kept secret and cannot be given out as it will be of advantage to our enemy. Naturally, it will be desirable for Members to speak with some restraint and not say anything which might be injurious to our military operations.

---

275. Letter to PSP MP.
276. See also items 345, 347, 350, and 264.
277. Letter to Lok Sabha MP, Independent, from Kairana; address: 40 South Avenue, New Delhi.

If at any later time it is desirable to hold a secret session, we shall consider that. At present with the great public interest, a secret session will, probably not [be] advisable.

Yours sincerely,
[Jawaharlal Nehru]

350. To L.M. Singhvi: Secret Session of Lok Sabha[278]

November 6, 1962

Dear Dr Singhvi,
I have your letter of the 6th of November.

The suggestion about having a secret session of the Lok Sabha has previously been made to me. I feel that at this stage this is not desirable. If necessary and occasion arises for it, we can have it later on.[279]

Even a secret session of Parliament can hardly be called secret when about 500 persons are present. All that is done is that it is not properly reported and instead unauthorised rumours spread.[280]

Yours sincerely,
[Jawaharlal Nehru]

351. In the Lok Sabha: Secret Session[281]

L.M. Singhvi [282] (Jodhpur): Mr Speaker, I had suggested that this House go into a secret sitting to consider the National Emergency. I understand that a large number of Opposition leaders also concurred in the view. Although the Prime Minister earlier said that this was not the opportune time for this purpose, I understand the Minister for Parliamentary Affairs had undertaken or indicated that he would convey this to the Government and convey to us the decision of the Government finally on this matter.

---

278. Letter to Lok Sabha MP, Independent; address: 38 South Avenue, New Delhi.
279. See item 351.
280. See items 345, 347, and 348.
281. Re: Secret Session, *Lok Sabha Debates*, Third Series, Vol. IX, November 8-20, 1962, p. 105.
282. Independent.

The Prime Minister and Minister of External Affairs, Defence and Atomic Energy (Jawaharlal Nehru): Sir, I received a request to that effect from some Members.[283] I gave careful consideration to it. I think that, at the present moment, it would not be desirable to have a secret session. If it is desirable in future, I shall make my submission to you. The issues before the House are of high interest to the whole country. Right at the beginning to ask for a secret session would have a bad effect on the country. I am sure hon. Members would agree.

352. To Hafiz Mohammed Ibrahim: No Muslim Conference on Kashmir Now[284]

November 11, 1962

My dear Hafizji,
Your letter of November 10.

I do not think it is necessary or desirable to hold a special Muslim conference now on the subject of Kashmir. It is better for all of us to concentrate on the situation created by the Chinese invasion and not to talk much about Kashmir or Pakistan. Even for that purpose, I rather doubt if a special Muslim conference is necessary at present.[285]

Yours sincerely,
[Jawaharlal Nehru]

(g) CHINESE INVASION: Contributions to War Effort

353. To Zakir Husain: War Contribution[286]

October 25, 1962

My dear V.P.,
Thank you for your letter of the 25th October and the cheque for Rs 501/-. I am grateful to members of the Rajya Sabha Secretariat for this contribution for our soldiers at the front.

Yours sincerely,
[Jawaharlal Nehru]

283. See item 350.
284. Letter to the Minister of Irrigation and Power.
285. See also item 379.
286. Letter to the Vice-President.

354. To D. Sanjivayya: Contributions to Defence Fund[287]

October 26, 1962

My dear Sanjivayya,

Thank you for your letter of October 26th and a sum of Rs 501/-. This will be sent to the Defence Fund. Thank you also for the two packets of ornaments.

Yours sincerely,
[Jawaharlal Nehru]

355. To Mohanlal Sukhadia: National Defence Fund[288]

October 26, 1962

My dear Sukhadia,

Your letter of the 24th October.

Any money donations can be sent on to the Prime Minister's National Defence Fund.

As for the directions, you will get full information of the decisions of our Cabinet and the steps we are taking and want the States to take.

Yours sincerely,
[Jawaharlal Nehru]

356. To Patricia Gore-Booth: Mrs P. P. Roy's Gift[289]

October 26, 1962

Dear Lady Gore-Booth,

Thank you for your letter of the 5th October with the two sovereigns which Mrs P. Roy has sent. I am grateful to Mrs Roy for her gift.

I appreciate the decision of the Delhi Commonwealth Women's Association to knit comforts for the troops.

Yours sincerely,
[Jawaharlal Nehru]

287. Letter to the Congress President.
288. Letter to the Chief Minister of Rajasthan.
289. Letter to the wife of the British High Commissioner and patron of Delhi Commonwealth Women's Association.

357. To M.P. Birla: Blankets for Troops[290]

October 26, 1962

Dear Madhav Prasadji,

Thank you for your letter of the 25th October and for presenting 1500 blankets to the Defence Ministry for our soldiers.

Yours sincerely
[Jawaharlal Nehru]

358. To Humayun Kabir: CSIR Contribution to Defence Fund[291]

October 26, 1962

My dear Humayun,

Your letter of the 26th October, I appreciate and am grateful to the employees of your Ministry and the CSIR for their decision to contribute one day's salary to the Defence Fund. Please convey my thanks to them.

Yours sincerely,
[Jawaharlal Nehru]

359. To Lal Bahadur Shastri: Contribution to Defence Fund[292]

October 26, 1962

My dear Lal Bahadur,

Thank you for your letter enclosing a cheque for Rs. 261/- for the Defence Fund. I am grateful to those who have contributed this amount.

Yours affectionately,
[Jawaharlal Nehru]

---

290. Letter to Calcutta-based entrepreneur and philanthropist, (1918-1990); address: 15 India Exchange Place, Calcutta-1.
291. Letter to the Minister of Scientific Research and Cultural Affairs.
292. Letter to the Home Minister.

360. To M.G. Ramachandran: Contribution for Troops[293]

27th October, 1962

Dear Shri Ramachandran,

I have received your letter of the 22nd October. I am grateful to you for your generous donation of rupees seventy five thousand for the benefit of our soldiers on the front. I note that you have given rupees twenty five thousand of this to Shri Kamaraj, Chief Minister of Madras, and the balance will be paid in due course.

Yours sincerely,
[Jawaharlal Nehru]

361. Appeal for Contributions[294]

Appeal for Generous Contributions

New Delhi, Oct. 27 – Prime Minister Nehru today appealed for generous contributions to the Prime Minister's National Defence Fund as he declared: "It is a time of trial and testing for all of us."

Stating that he rejoiced at the spontaneous response from the public to the call of duty, Pandit Nehru said: "I am convinced that no power can ultimately imperil the freedom we have won."

The fund, started recently, would be utilised for providing amenities to the jawans fighting the Chinese on the northern frontiers and helping their families.

Freedom at Stake

Pandit Nehru said: "As I have already said in my recent broadcast,[295] the continuing and unabashed Chinese aggression on our frontiers has created a situation in the country which calls all of us to meet it effectively.

Being essentially a peace loving nation, we endeavoured to follow a policy of peace even when aggression took place on our territory in Ladakh five years ago. But as is well-known, all our efforts have been in vain—the Chinese have invaded our sacred land.

We have now to prove to the world that we are a self-respecting nation and will not submit to aggression, whatever the consequences may be. The time has, therefore, come for us to realise fully this menace that threatens the freedom of our people and the independence of our country.

---

293. Letter to Madras MLC; address: 160 Lloyds Road, Madras 14.
294. Reproduced from the *National Herald*, 28 October 1962, p.1.
295. On 22 October 1962. See item 259.

"I have rejoiced at the spontaneous response from the public to the call of duty. I am convinced that no power can ultimately imperil the freedom that we have won at so much sacrifice and cost to our people after a long period of foreign domination. I, therefore, call upon my countrymen, to realise that the hour has come when all of us should sink our differences, if any, and present a united front to the invader."

No Reason for Panic

Pandit Nehru said: "The hardships which our soldiers are facing are not unknown to you. The Government are no doubt doing their very best to look after our fighting forces, but the cooperation of the public is also essential to supplement the Government's effort. I, therefore, invite all of you to be comrades in this great struggle that has been forced upon us, and appeal to you in all earnestness to rise to the occasion and to contribute generously to the Prime Minister's National Defence Fund which has recently been started for the purpose. This Fund will be used for all purposes connected with defence. In particular, it will be utilised for providing amenities to our soldiers at the front and helping their families whenever necessary.

"There is no reason to be panicky. We have behind us the strength of a united nation. It is a time of trial and test for all of us, and we have to bend all our energies to the task of defending our sacred land and throwing out the aggressor. With a firm faith in the righteousness of our struggle, I once again appeal to my countrymen to extend their full co-operation and to strengthen the hands of the Government by contributing for this noble cause.

"All contributions should be sent to the secretary, Prime Minister's National Defence Fund, Prime Minister's Secretariat, New Delhi."

362. To S. Radhakrishnan: Contributions[296]

October 29, 1962

My dear President,

Thank you for your letter of today's date, enclosing cash, cheques, postal orders and gold ornaments for the National Defence Fund. I have received cash and cheques etc. for Rs. 16,088.50 np, and gold ornaments as follows: four bangles, two rings and one nose-ring. The response of our people to the crisis that has suddenly faced us, has been magnificent.

---

296. Letter to the President.

I am grateful that you have handed over to the Army authorities seven armoured cars and for placing the services of Army officers and the Bodyguards at the disposal of the Defence Ministry.

Yours affectionately,
[Jawaharlal Nehru]

363. To V.K. Krishna Menon: Clubs for Troops[297]

October 30, 1962

My dear Krishna,

G.D. Birla[298] has written to me saying that he understands that there is great need for some organisation to cater for the Jawans in Tezpur—a kind of club with canteen and some entertainments. Lal Bahadur Shastri[299] suggests that this is not only needed at Tezpur, but also at Gauhati. So, G.D. Birla offers to make, at his own expense and through a non-official organisation composed of local people, these clubs at Tezpur and Gauhati immediately.

I am replying to him thanking him for his offer and saying that Tezpur is certainly indicated for this. Perhaps, Gauhati also, but I would let him know later.

Do you think that Gauhati would be a suitable place?[300]

Yours affectionately,
[Jawaharlal Nehru]

364. To G.D. Birla: Clubs for Troops[301]

October 30, 1962

My dear Ghansyamdasji,

Thank you for your two letters of the 30th October and the cheque for Rs 74,151/-. This cheque, you say, is meant for the Prime Minister's National Relief Fund. I just want to make sure that this is meant for the National Relief Fund and not for the National Defence Fund.

297. Letter to the Defence Minister.
298. Industrialist.
299. Home Minister.
300. See items 364 and 365.
301. Letter to industrialist and founder President of Harijan Sevak Sangh; address: Birla House, New Delhi.

As for your proposal to build up some kind of clubs with canteens for our Jawans at Tezpur and Gauhati, I think it is an excellent proposal. But please do not call it "Nehru Club". There can be many other more appropriate names.

Tezpur will obviously be an appropriate place for it. About Gauhati I do not at present quite know. I shall let you know about it later.[302]

Yours sincerely,
[Jawaharlal Nehru]

365. To G.D. Birla: Canteens for Troops[303]

October 30, 1962

My dear Ghanshyamdasji,

I have consulted the Defence Ministry. They would be glad if you construct club houses and canteens at Tezpur and Gauhati for our troops.[304] They have pointed out, however, that all such canteens and club houses are managed and run by the Canteen Department of the Defence Ministry, which is a very large organisation. It would produce some measure of confusion and difficulty if any of these is privately run. Often there is a parameter surrounding the places which are occupied by troops, where entry is not unrestricted. Therefore, they suggest that after you have constructed these, they should be handed over to this Department of the Defence Ministry for the purpose of running them.

Yours sincerely,
[Jawaharlal Nehru]

366. To Sri Prakasa: Contribution to the National Defence Fund[305]

October 30, 1962

My dear Prakasa,

I have just received your letter of October 26th and your cheque for Rs 550/-. Thank you for both.

302. See also item 365.
303. Letter to industrialist; address: Birla House, New Delhi.
304. See items 363 and 364.
305. Letter to the former Governor of Madras and Maharashtra; address: House Veerana, 9 Ballupur, Chakrata Road, Dehra Dun.

We have all had great shocks during the last few weeks. To balance that has been the magnificent response of our country to this crisis. After all an emergency and a crisis have to be faced and we cannot live merely in shocked conditions. We shall have a heavy time but I have no doubt whatever that we shall win through.

You can send any contributions that you may receive for the National Defence Fund to Shri K. Ram, my Principal Private Secretary, who will send you a receipt for them.

Yours affectionately,
[Jawaharlal Nehru]

367. For V. K. Krishna Menon: Award for Valour[306]

The President has written to me as follows: -

"Sepoy Kewal Singh, 4th Battalion, the Sikh Regiment, who came out of his trench, charged the attacking Chinese and killed with his bayonet seven Chinese was shot dead as he was returning. I think an immediate announcement of some decoration will give great encouragement to our Jawans."

I agree with the President. It would be a good thing if we give a posthumous decoration to him and announce it soon.

368. To S. Radhakrishnan: Contributions and Bravery Award[307]

October 30, 1962

My dear President,

Thank you for your letter of October 30 with its enclosures, which was handed over to me by your ADC.

I have received the gold coins from the Raja of Faridkot, six bangles and a ring; also a cheque for Rs 101/- and a blanket.

I entirely agree with you that Sepoy Kewal Singh of the 4th Battalion of the Sikh Regiment deserves some special recognition.[308]

306. Note, 30 October 1962, for the Defence Minister.
307. Letter to the President.
308. See item 367.

I think that brief visits by you outside Delhi will be good and there is no apparent reason why you should cancel them.

I am returning the cheque which was sent by you. I shall be grateful if you will kindly endorse it and make it payable to the National Defence Fund.

Yours affectionately,
[Jawaharlal Nehru]

369. To Chou Hsiang-Kuang[309]: Offer of Services

November 1, 1962

Dear Dr Chou,

Thank you for your letter of October 26th, and for the offer of your services.

There is no intention at present of our severing diplomatic ties with the People's Government of China.

Yours sincerely,
[Jawaharlal Nehru]

370. To Hukam Singh: Lok Sabha Secretariat Contributions[310]

November 6, 1962

My dear Speaker,

Thank you for your letter of November 5th and the cheque for Rs 2500/- for the National Defence Fund. I shall be grateful to you if you will kindly convey my thanks to the Lok Sabha Secretariat for this contribution.

I am very glad you have taken various measures to effect economy in expenditure as also to simplify procedures to lessen the parliamentary work of the Ministries.

I am asking the Cabinet Secretary to consider your kind suggestion to spare some manpower from the Lok Sabha Secretariat.

Yours sincerely,
Jawaharlal Nehru

---

309. Letter to Chinese scholar of Budhism, 1 November 1962.
310. Letter to the Speaker.

371. To the Dalai Lama: Contribution of Gold[311]

November 6, 1962

Your Holiness,

Thank you for your letter of October 31, which was handed to me today. I am grateful for the 150 tolas of gold that you have sent for the National Defence Fund.

The aggression and invasion by the Chinese has shocked all of us. But, as you will have noticed, the reaction in the country has been one of rousing everybody to meet this menace and has produced a feeling of unity among all our people.

With warm regards,

Yours sincerely,
[Jawaharlal Nehru]

372. To C.D. Deshmukh: University Contributions[312]

November 6, 1962

My dear Vice-Chancellor,

I have your letter of November 5. We do not encourage too much ear-marking of donations for the National Defence Fund, but there is no objection whatever if college and university collections are earmarked for the education at various levels of dependents of those members of our Armed Forces who die or are wounded.

As a matter of fact, the National Development Council decided yesterday that the dependent children of members of our Armed Forces who die or are wounded should be educated free. Both the Central Government and the State Governments gladly assumed this responsibility. Nevertheless, I think it will be a good thing for University collections to be earmarked for this purpose.

Yours sincerely,
[Jawaharlal Nehru]

311. Letter to the Dalai Lama, Upper Dharamshala, Kangra District.
312. Letter to the Vice-Chancellor of Delhi University.

617

373. To V.B. Singh Deo: Defence Fund Contribution[313]

November 10, 1962

Dear friend,

Thank you for your letter of the 9th November which I have read with interest. I note that you propose to contribute 13 per cent of your privy purse to the Defence Fund until such time as we free our country from the aggressors.

I think you are quite right in going back to your constituency to explain the emergency to your constituents and raise their morale in every way.

Yours sincerely,
[Jawaharlal Nehru]

374. To Asoke K. Sen: Deduction from Salaries[314]

November 10, 1962

My dear Asoke,

Thank you for your letter of November 10[315] and the cheque for Rs 1001/- for the National Defence Fund from Shri Murari Mohan Dutta.

I am sending your letter to the Finance Ministry drawing his attention to your proposal about making some arrangements for the collection of one day's earnings every month from Government employees etc.

As for the Territorial Army, it would certainly be a good thing for our employees to join it. But owing to the stress of work, it may not always be possible for many of them to be relieved for this purpose.

Yours sincerely,
[Jawaharlal Nehru]

---

313. Letter to Lok Sabha MP, Congress; address: 340 Vinay Marg. He was Raja of Sarguja.
314. Letter to the Law Minister.
315. Letter not reproduced, but available in the NMML.

375. To Padmaja Naidu: Contribution[316]

November 12, 1962

Bebee dear,

This evening Nan[317] told me about your telephoning to her, and now, rather late at night, I have received your note of the 12th November with your cheque for Rs 5000/- for the National Defence Fund. This is indeed the best birthday gift[318] that you could send in the circumstances, although of course whatever birthday gifts you have sent me previously have always been very welcome.

We are passing through not only a national crisis, but a personal one also for many of us. Fortunately, I do not have much time to think of it as work of some kind or other keeps me fully occupied.

I am glad to know that your stay in Darjeeling has done you good and you have returned full of health and vigour.

I send you all my love and good wishes for your birthday on the 17th.

Love,
Jawahar

376. To Husain Kamil Kidwai: Use Rafi Anniversary Funds for Troops[319]

November 12, 1962

My dear Husain Kamil,

Your letter of the 12th November. Certainly, you can use the funds earmarked for the Birth and Death Anniversaries of Rafi Saheb for providing amenities for our soldiers and refugees.

I am glad to know that you are organising the resources of Masauli for this purpose.

Thank you for your good wishes for my birthday.

Yours sincerely,
[Jawaharlal Nehru]

---

316. Letter to the Governor of West Bengal. NMML, Padmaja Naidu Papers.
317. Vijaya Lakshmi Pandit.
318. Nehru's birthday was on 14 November.
319. Letter to the youngest brother of the late Rafi Ahmed Kidwai; address CII-73 Wellesley Road, New Delhi.

377. To Partap Singh Kairon: Coerced Collections for Defence Fund[320]

November 15, 1962

My dear Partap Singh,

Money is pouring in for the National Defence Fund, and the Punjab is doing especially well. This is very gratifying. I should like, however, to draw your attention to some complaints that we have received. One such complain is that in a village of 5,000 inhabitants, the Tehsildar was expected to produce a sum of Rs 20,000/- for the National Defence Fund. Another is that a District Officer in the Punjab went to the proprietor of a Bus Company and asked him to give Rs 25,000/- for the Fund. On his being told by the proprietor of this company that he did not have all that money, the officer produced a letter signed by the District Magistrate cancelling his bus permit. The proprietor of the Company had, therefore, no option but to promise to make this payment as soon as he was able to arrange the money.

I think these methods adopted to collect money are undesirable and do not leave a good taste. They might well create ill-feeling and resentment among the rural people. The grace of the collection goes. As a matter of fact, it is most heartening how the poorest have given and how even children have contributed.

I do hope you will instruct your officers not to use any coercive methods like the ones I have mentioned.

Yours sincerely
[Jawaharlal Nehru]

378. To Madanjeet Singh: Contributions[321]

November 19, 1962.

My dear Madanjeet,

Thank you for your letter of the 14th November and your good wishes. Also, for your cheque for 2,100 dollars which I appreciate very much. More particularly, I am grateful to Dhyanwati for the amount she realised from the sale of her jewellery. I am sure she will never regret this.

---

320. To Chief Minister of Punjab.
321. Letter to a sculptor, painter, author and philanthropist (1924-2013); address: Embassy of India, Stockholm.

We are living through difficult times but I am confident that we will triumph in the end.

Yours sincerely,
[Jawaharlal Nehru]

379. To Hafiz Mohammad Ibrahim: No Muslim Bodies for Fund Collection[322]

November 20, 1962

My dear Hafizji,

Your letter of November 20th. I do not think it is necessary for the Muslim MPs to form a separate body. The funds they collect might be sent either directly to me for the National Defence Fund or preferably to the Mayor of Delhi who has been asked by the Central Citizens' Committee to appoint authorised agencies for collecting funds in Delhi.[323]

Yours sincerely,
[Jawaharlal Nehru]

380. To Krishna Hutheesing: Something to do[324]

November 20, 1962

[My dear Betty]

Thank you for your letter of the 15th November and the snapshot of Nikhil.

I received Raja's and your letter offering your services. I could not do anything to it and so I passed it on, together with the very large number of similar letters that I receive, to the appropriate people who might perhaps suggest something.

I am surprised to learn that Ghanshyamdas Birla imagines that you are not in my favour. I cannot imagine how he gets these astonishing and utterly wrong notions. He has never spoken to me about you.

---

322. Letter to the Minister of Irrigation and Power.
323. See also item 352.
324. Letter to youngest sister; address: Anand Bhavan, 20 Carmichael road, Bombay 26.

I am terribly occupied. I wish I could suggest something for Raja to do, but I cannot find time to deal with such matters. The position is changing daily, much to our disadvantage. The Tezpur rest transit camp you refer to is now not possible.

[Jawaharlal Nehru]

381. To Hukam Singh: Acknowledging Contributions[325]

22nd November, 1962

My dear Mr Speaker,

Thank you for your letter of November 22nd and the cheque for Rs 2,100/- that you have sent on behalf of the Central Sikh Council for the Defence Fund. I have noted the other amounts that you have already forwarded to the Defence Fund.

I am grateful to you for all the steps you have taken to spare experienced persons from the Lok Sabha Secretariat for other work, as also the economies effected in stationery, printing, etc.[326]

Yours sincerely,
[Jawaharlal Nehru]

382. To Hanna Reitsch: Diamond Brooch[327]

November 25, 1962

My dear Hanna,

I am delighted to receive your letter of the 12th November through our Embassy in Bonn. Also, your diamond brooch. It is very good of you to send this for our Defence Fund, and I thank you for it.

We are having a difficult time. But we are confident that, however long our trouble may last, we shall succeed in the end. It is very heartening during these critical days to know that we have the goodwill of so many friends.

Yours sincerely,
[Jawaharlal Nehru]

---

325. Letter to the Speaker of the Lok Sabha.
326. See item 331.
327. Letter to German Test Pilot (1912-1979); visited India at Nehru's invitation in 1959 and, in 1962 was working with Kwame Nkrumah, building the African National Gliding School.; address: Kettenhofweg 55, Frankfurt/M, Germany.

383. To Y.B. Chavan: Roy Bucher and Nathu Singh Offer of Help[328]

November 25, 1962

My dear Chavan,

I enclose a telegram from Roy Bucher who was our first Commander-in-Chief of the Army after independence. Also, a letter from Lieutenant General Nathu Singh.[329]

As for Roy Bucher, I think a letter might be sent to him by you thanking him for his offer. I do not think he can be of any use to us here.

As for Nathu Singh, he can be of no use to us in any important capacity. He might perhaps help in recruiting. You might write to him saying that we have taken steps to have some of our old senior Army officers to help us, and mention to him that he could be of much use in recruiting etc. You could ask the Chief of Army Staff[330] what else to write to him. But I am sure we should not bring him in any way to Army Headquarters.

Yours sincerely,
[Jawaharlal Nehru]

384. To Partap Singh Kairon: Orderly Fund Collection[331]

November 29, 1962

My dear Partap Singh,

Your letter of the 21st November to my PPS about Government servants associating themselves with fund collections. I still think that Government servants, big or small, should keep apart from fund collections. Only those persons, who are authorised, should be allowed to collect. Senior Government servants might see to it that funds are collected properly and no parts of them are in danger of being embezzled or improperly used.

Yours sincerely,
[Jawaharlal Nehru]

328. Letter to the Minister of Defence.
329. Former Commander of the Eastern Command.
330. J.N. Chaudhury.
331. Letter to the Chief Minister of Punjab.

385. To Sushila Nayar: Fund Collection in Jhansi[332]

November 29, 1962

My dear Sushila,

Your letter of the 29th November. I am happy to learn that the Village Societies and Cooperative Banks in Jhansi area are collecting money in a systematic manner for the Defence Fund. Please convey my appreciation and gratitude to them.

Yours affectionately,
[Jawaharlal Nehru]

(h) CHINESE INVASION: International Action

386. To William Tubman: Chinese Aggression[333]

I am grateful for your telegram of 17th and your friendly concern regarding the recent serious incidents in the Eastern sector of the Sino-Indian boundary.[334]

You are probably aware that the Chinese have, over the last few years, forcibly occupied by unilateral action about twelve thousand square miles of Indian territory in the Ladakh region of India in the Western sector of the India-China boundary. Despite this, we did not, because of our firm belief in settling differences by discussions, resort to any precipitate action and force a clash. We continued exchange of notes and communications on the issues involved and I also met and discussed this matter with Chou En-lai in Delhi in 1960.[335] As a result of the decision taken at this meeting, officials of both sides met at Peking, Delhi and Rangoon over a period of some months and produced a Report giving the claims regarding the entire boundary made by both sides and the material in support of these claims. We published this Report of Officials early in 1961[336] but the Chinese Government did not publish it till a year later.

This Report of officials has been studied and reviewed by independent authorities in various countries who have supported our view that the Chinese

---

332. Letter to the Minister of Health. She represented Jhansi constituency.
333. Letter to the President of Liberia, telegraphed 20 October 1962. MEA, File No. A/103/23/62, pp.2-4/Corr.
334. See appendix 16.
335. See SWJN/SS/60.
336. SWJN/SS/66/Supplement.

case is flimsy and the Indian claim regarding the boundary is substantially established.

The Chinese did not stop their aggressive activities in the Western sector which had continued unabated even during the talks between the officials. We had, therefore, to take limited defensive action to contain further Chinese advance into Indian territory. At the same time, we made proposals to the Chinese to start talks and discussions at the appropriate level between the representatives of the two countries to devise measures for easing the tension in the Western sector, particularly measures to correct the situation created by the forcible alteration of the status quo of the boundary in the Western sector so that the implementation of these measures can create the appropriate climate in which differences between the two Governments on the entire border question can be discussed calmly and dispassionately with a view to resolving them.

While exchanges of these proposals were going on between the two Governments throughout July and August this year, the Chinese, for reasons best known to them, decided to commit further aggression into Indian territory in the Eastern sector, which had all along been quiet and peaceful, by crossing the international boundary in this region. They crossed over the Thagla ridge which is the international boundary in this area in the beginning of September. We had to resist this new aggression as there was no other way that we could adopt consistent with dignity and self-respect.

You will appreciate that it is hardly possible to tackle a situation of this sort by a group conference or by appeals for a cease fire. We are always prepared to talk and discuss with a view to settling differences by peaceful means. But you will agree that it is neither decent nor consistent with self-respect to negotiate with an aggressor under duress.

In the various notes on this new aggression exchanged in the last six weeks, we have been urging the Chinese to go back to their own territory on the northern side of the ridge. We have informed the Chinese in the latest note sent on 6th October that we are prepared to initiate talks and discussions of measures to be taken to relax tension and create the appropriate climate for further detailed talks on the boundary differences as soon as the Chinese terminate their latest aggression in the Eastern sector started by them in the beginning of September by returning to their side of the boundary, i.e., the north of the Thagla Ridge.[337] We hope the Chinese will, even at this late stage, see the error of their ways and take measures to correct situations.

With kind regards,

Jawaharlal Nehru

---

337. Available at NMML, *White Paper*, Vol.VII, pp. 123-124.

387. To Ibrahim Abboud: India-China Conflict[338]

I am grateful to Your Excellency for your kind message on the armed conflict between India and China and your appeal for peaceful settlement by negotiations addressed to our President.

As you are generally aware, China had by military action, forcibly occupied about 12,000 square miles of Indian territory in Ladakh in the Western sector of the boundary over the period of the last five years. Despite this unilateral and forcible occupation of Indian territory, we, because of our dedication to peace and peaceful methods, did not precipitate a clash but made proposals for a meeting between representatives of the two Governments.

While exchange of notes for the finalisation of those talks was going on, China on 8th of September suddenly marched its forces into India in the Eastern Sector across the highest mountain ridge, which constitutes the boundary in this particular area, to spread the conflict further and seize more Indian territory by force. We had to make arrangements to resist this further aggression by China. Even then, we maintained a defensive attitude and continued to send notes to China asking it to correct the situation created by this latest aggression and withdraw its forces to its side of the international frontier in the Eastern Sector to create an atmosphere for talks and discussions. We made it clear, at the same time, that if this further aggression continues, we will have to resist it.

The Chinese, however, for reasons best known to them, mounted a concerted well-planned attack in the early hours of the morning of 20th of October at several places in the Eastern sector as well as the Western sector with massive forces, with heavy offensive equipment—though they still continued to allege that these were border guards—and have advanced into Indian territory along the entire India-China border and are still advancing despite stiff resistance from our limited armed forces in these border areas.

These are the facts of Chinese blatant aggression and attempt to enforce alleged territorial claims by military might. We know that China is a great and powerful country. We have sought in the past friendship and cooperation with it and pleaded its cause before the United Nations and elsewhere, but you will appreciate, Mr President, that we cannot submit to brute force, India could not have acted otherwise than it did in challenging the Chinese aggression. Even so, we have been prepared for discussions which might lead to a peaceful settlement; but how can we have any discussions when actual and new aggression is continuously taking place and vast Chinese armies are moving

---

338. Telegram, 25 October, 1962, to President of the Sudan. MEA, File No. 1 (China)/62, Vol. III, p. nil.

further into our territory? Any discussion can only be worthwhile if a suitable atmosphere is created for it. We, therefore, proposed that the first thing to do was to create that atmosphere by the Chinese Government restoring the status quo as it was prior to the 8th September.

We are by our background and tradition against war and violence and wedded to peaceful methods and policies. In the context of conditions that have been created by the latest Chinese aggression, however, it is our clear duty to continue our resistance unless the Chinese heed to the advice of disinterested friends like you and others and correct the situation created by them by accepting the suggestion made in the above paragraph. If the Chinese aggression continues, we will continue to resist and we hope we will have your sympathy and support and the sympathy and support of all right-minded countries in this sacred task of maintaining the honour and integrity of our motherland.

With kind regards

[Jawaharlal Nehru]

388. To Heads of Government 26/27 October[339]

I am taking the liberty of addressing you in regard to a very serious situation that has arisen on our frontiers because of the armed aggression of Chinese forces on our territory. The consequences of this large scale aggression are not only serious for India but also for the rest of the world.

Conditioned as we are by our historical background and traditions of tolerance, understanding and peace, we have, ever since India became independent, consistently followed a policy of peace and friendly relations with all countries. Abhorrence of war and violence is part of our national tradition.

We understand the horrors of war, and all our efforts have been directed to the prevention of war and the preservation of peace. We have endeavoured to follow the same policy of peace in our differences with our neighbours. That is why when the Chinese aggression first started in Ladakh five years ago, we showed patience and restraint. Even though 12,000 square miles of Indian territory was occupied by the Chinese forces, we did not force a crisis but continued to explore avenues of a peaceful and honourable settlement. In 1960, the Chinese Prime Minister expressed a desire to meet me, and I met

339. Letter to Heads of Nations, 26/27 October 1962, reproduced from *Chinese Aggression in India. Letters of the Prime Minister of India* (Ministry of Information and Broadcasting, Publications Division, 8 December 1962), pp. 31-34.

him readily in order to find some way of resolving the differences between us peacefully.[340] The differences were not resolved, and we agreed that officials of both the Governments should examine all the facts. The report produced by our officials fully supported our position in regard to the traditional and customary boundary between India and Tibet, which had been repeatedly confirmed by agreements and treaties.[341] It was my hope that these facts would be considered by the Chinese Government and a further effort would be made to resolve the differences peacefully. However, the Chinese aggression continued and was even intensified. We were obliged, therefore, to take limited defensive measures to halt this aggressive advance. While taking these measures, however, we continued to make peaceful approaches with a view to easing tensions so that a proper climate might be created for further talks to resolve the differences.

While these approaches were being made, and we were hoping that they would lead to results, the Chinese forces suddenly, on the 8th September, 1962, made a fresh incursion into our territory. They crossed the international boundary in the Eastern sector which they had respected for twelve years since they came into Tibet. Our frontier in that sector traditionally and by treaty is the high ridge of the Himalaya mountains which forms the watershed. We could have taken immediate action to resist this further aggression. However, being wedded to the ways of peace, we continued our effort to persuade the Chinese to end this aggression by withdrawing from our territory, more particularly in the Eastern sector, which had been invaded for the first time for ages past on the 8th September. We pointed out the correct facts to them about the location of the border which was the high ridge of the Himalaya mountains. We also took some steps for the defence of the border.

While an exchange of notes of this subject was going on, the Chinese, after a number of probing attacks, made a massive attack on our Defence forces on the morning of the 20th October all along the India-China border in the Eastern sector as well as the Western sector. An attack on this scale could only have been made after careful preparation. Our Defence forces have put up a stiff resistance, but they have been pushed back by greatly superior numbers and massive weapons. In spite of these set-backs, our resistance will continue, for we are determined to defend our country and to put an end to aggression.

It is a matter of deep regret that the Chinese in their relations with India have paid back evil for good. Friendly and peaceful relations with China have been our basic policy ever since India became independent. We have consistently followed this policy and gone out of our way to support China's case in the

340. Record of meeting, SWJN/SS/60.
341. Report reproduced as SWJN/SS/66/Supplement.

councils of the world. We regret that in their relations with India, China has not merely shown a hostile attitude, but has also resorted to dissimulation. Even the pre-meditated and massive attack on our Defence forces on the 20th October has been represented by China as an attack by Indian forces on China's border guards. That this assertion is completely false is clear from the weight and intensity of the Chinese attack which is not confined to the Eastern sector but includes other sectors of the India-China border. No self-respecting country, and certainly not India with her love of freedom, can submit to such aggression, whatever may be the consequences. Nor can India allow China's occupation of Indian territory to be used as a bargaining counter for dictating to India a settlement of the differences regarding the boundary on China's terms.

This is not a mere boundary dispute or a question of small territorial frontier adjustments. Apart from the vast and fantastic claims that China has made, China had already occupied 12,000 square miles of Indian territory during the last five years. While notes were being exchanged for arranging talks and discussions to ease tensions and even dates and places were being suggested, further aggression by China started on 8th September and further areas of Indian territory were occupied in a new sector. The issue involved is not one of small territorial gains, one way or the other, but of standards of international behaviour between neighbouring countries and whether the world will allow the principle of "Might is Right" to prevail in international relations. Bearing this in mind, India will continue to resist aggression, both to preserve her honour and integrity and to prevent international standards from deteriorating into the jungle law of "Might is Right". When aggression is continuously taking place and vast Chinese armies are moving further into our territory, how can we discuss or talk about a peaceful settlement? The first essential is that the Chinese forces along the India-China border should go back at least to where they were prior to the 8th September, 1962.

I have ventured to give you this short account of the crisis that has arisen on the Indian frontier with China. The story of aggression is a long one going back several years. The most recent aggression in our Eastern sector which began on September 8, and has since the Chinese massive attack along the entire India-China frontier which started on 20th October, resulted in serious conflicts, has brought matters to a crisis. This crisis is not only of India but of the world and will have far reaching consequences on the standards of international behaviour and on the peace of the world. We cannot submit to this law of the jungle which affects our integrity and the honour of our motherland.

In this hour of crisis, when we are engaged in resisting this aggression, we are confident that we shall have your sympathy and support as well as the sympathy and support of all countries, not only because of their friendly

629

relations with us, but also because our struggle is in the interest of world peace and is directed to the elimination of deceit, dissimulation and force in international relations.

389. To Gamal Abdel Nasser[342]

Dear Friend,
Your Ambassador in Delhi has communicated to us the suggestions you have made to the Chinese Ambassador in Cairo. I am grateful for the suggestions you have made to the Chinese Government.

Prime Minister Chou En-lai sent me a message dated 24th October. I understand a copy of this message has also been given to you. I have replied to Prime Minister Chou En-lai this morning. I enclose a copy of this reply along with a copy of the official reaction referred to in my reply.

You see from this communication that the suggestions you have made for the consideration of the Chinese Government are broadly the same as those made in my reply to Prime Minister Chou En-lai. The essential preliminary to any talks and discussions to settle the matter peacefully is the restoration of the status quo along the entire India-China boundary as it existed before the further Chinese aggression started on 8th September. It is only after the Chinese Government accept this essential preliminary that we can go into the question of cease fire, the arrangements for withdrawal by both parties to the positions that they occupied prior to the Chinese aggression on 8th September and the detailed arrangements for talks and discussions for peaceful settlement of the differences on the border question in one stage or several stages as may be necessary.

With kind regards,

Yours sincerely,
Jawaharlal Nehru

390. To Ali Yavar Jung: French Government Statement[343]

Your telegram 253 October 27th. We would certainly welcome a clear expression of sympathy and support made on behalf of the French Government.

342. Letter, 27 October 1962, to the President of Egypt. PIB.
343. Telegram PRIMIN 21154, 28 October 1962, for Ambassador in Paris.

There need be no reference in this to the Soviet attitude. It might refer only to the invasion of India by Chinese forces and also to international aspects of it.

2. We are anxious to get such military material or equipment as we require with utmost speed.

391. To Kwame Nkrumah: Chinese Invasion[344]

October 29, 1962

Dear Mr President,

Thank you for your message of 27th October on our present crisis forced on us by Chinese massive invasion of our territory. I sent you a message on this subject on 27th October[345] which must have been presented to you by our High Commissioner in Accra. I have taken the liberty in that message of giving in brief the background of the China-India border differences, the various attempts made by us to have these resolved peacefully, the further aggression started by China on 8th September 1962 and of the massive attack by Chinese forces all along the frontier since 20th October. You will appreciate, Mr President, that no self-respecting country can submit to the dictates of blatant aggression and to military force. The first essential, therefore, as mentioned in my message of 27th, is to undo this latest aggression and for the Chinese forces at least to go back to where they were prior to the 8th September 1962 all along the India-China boundary.

In the last few days I have received two messages from President Nasser, one on 21st October and the other on 27th October. I have replied to both these messages.[346] I also received a message from Prime Minister Chou En-lai on 24th October to which I replied on the 26th.[347] I am asking our High Commissioner to give you copies of these messages which clearly state our position.

With kind regards,

Yours sincerely,
Jawaharlal Nehru

---

344. Letter to the President of Ghana. MEA, File No. A-II/103/26/62, p. 2/corr.
345. See item 388.
346. See item 389.
347. See appendix 26 and item 247.

392. To M.R. Pistone: No Time to write Article[348]

October 29, 1962

Dear Mr Pistone,

Thank you for your letter of the 23rd October.

I am sorry I cannot find time to send you an article. But surely the reasons for our resisting Chinese aggression are obvious and do not require any elucidation. Every self-respecting country must resist aggression or invasion of this kind, and we certainly have no intention of submitting to it.

Yours sincerely,
[Jawaharlal Nehru]

393. To Karan Singh: UNESCO Meeting[349]

29 October 1962

My dear Tiger,

Thank you for your letter of 27th and your personal cheque for Rs 1 lakh for the National Defence Fund. This is a generous donation which I appreciate.

I also received your letter of the 29th October.[350] I think you are right in not going to the UNESCO meeting in Paris.

Yours as ever,
Jawaharlal Nehru

394. To John Grigg: More than a Frontier Dispute[351]

November 3, 1962

My dear Lord Altrincham,

Thank you for your letter of the 1st November. I am grateful for what you have written. The Chinese invasion has come as a great shock to all of us. But it has certainly done one good. It has roused the entire country as nothing else has

---

348. Letter to the Editor of *Incontri Mediterranei*, 28 Via Sardegna, Roma, Italy.
349. Letter to the Sadar-i-Riyasat of Jammu and Kashmir. Reproduced from J. Alam, ed., *Jammu and Kashmir (1949-64): Select Correspondence between Jawaharlal Nehru and Karan Singh*; (New Delhi: Penguin India ltd.2006); pp. 290-291.
350. See appendix 30.
351. Letter to British journalist and politician; address: 32 Dartmouth Row, London SE 10.

done for a long time. It is extraordinary how our petty internal disputes have been forgotten before this crisis. I have no doubt that we shall pull through though this may take long.

I do not know what to suggest to you as to what you can do. You are the best judge. Of course, a great deal can be done in explaining not only the present situation, but the background of it. I have no doubt that this is not merely a frontier dispute, but something much deeper. I cannot definitely say what the Chinese Government might have in mind.

Yours very sincerely,
[Jawaharlal Nehru]

395. To N.S. Khrushchev: Terms of Settlement[352]

4th November, 1962

Dear Mr Prime Minister,

Thank you for your message of 31st October, which was given to me by your Ambassador in Delhi on the afternoon on 2nd November. Minister Malaviya,[353] whom you were good enough to see and who had the benefit of exchanging views with you on the current border clashes between India and China, has given me a full report of his talks with you.

As you know, Mr Prime Minister, we value greatly your friendship and the friendship of the Soviet Union. Frank and informal exchange of views on all matters of mutual interest to our two countries has been the basic feature of this friendship. We, therefore understand your concern at the conflict between China and India and fully appreciate the reasons underlying your message.

I attempted in my last message of 22nd October[354] to put before you frankly our position in regard to this current conflict between India and China. Minister Malaviya used the opportunity of his visit to the Soviet Union to discuss this question in further detail with you.

I appreciate your desire to avoid going into details and into the reasons for the emergence of the current conflict. I hope, however, that my previous message of 22nd October and the talk that Minister Malaviya had with you would have convinced you of our deep dedication to the paths of peace and our horror of conflict, war and bloodshed.

---

352. Letter to the Soviet Prime Minister. MEA, File No. 1(China)/62, Vol. I, p. nil.
353. K. D. Malaviya, Minister of Mines and Fuel met Khrushchev on 26 October 1962.
354. See item 261.

What we are facing today is a massive invasion of India by China. Large Chinese armies are on our soil. Prime Minister Chou En-lai's three-point proposals,[355] which you say contain the main basis for the settlement of the dispute, are only a reiteration of an earlier proposal of 7th November, 1959, which the Government of India did not accept at that time.[356] Shorn of its wrappings, therefore, this is in effect a demand for surrender. You will appreciate, Mr Prime Minister, that no country, much less India, can submit to the military dictates of the aggressor.

As you say "one need not glance back at yesterday one has to look into the future". This is exactly what causes us such concern. If it were merely a question of differences regarding territorial boundaries, these could, given the will on both sides, be settled by talks and discussions. One does not go to war on these matters. What is at stake, however, is the question of peaceful co-existence of states with different social systems. The Chinese Government seem to have decided against peaceful co-existence between the Chinese social system and the Indian way of life. All the restraint and tolerance that we had shown against Chinese aggressive activities during the last few years and our repeated proposals for talks and discussions have been answered by haughty, abusive and scurrilous notes by the Chinese Government and they have simultaneously carried on a vast propaganda offensive against the Indian way of life and all that India stands for. The further aggression since 8th September, 1962, was the final act in the Chinese attempt to disrupt by force any possibility of peaceful coexistence between the Chinese and the Indian ways of life. This challenge to the very principle of peaceful co-existence is a matter that affects not only India's security but the peace of the world.

I agree with you, Mr Prime Minister, "that attempts to solve outstanding questions by means of war do not lead to good." I also agree that "to carry on shooting, while being governed by considerations of acquiring an advantageous position, means that the military conflict can continue indefinitely." What has happened, however, is not of our seeking. We have sought no advantageous position. It is the Chinese armies that crossed over into India on 8th September and, as can be seen from developments since then, solely with a view to establishing an advantageous position from which they can force a settlement on their terms. All that we are now asking for is that at least the status quo prior to 8th September should be restored before both countries arrange for talks and discussions at appropriate levels to settle their differences regarding the boundary.

355. See appendix 26.
356. See appendix 39.

We appreciate your friendly feelings and the spirit in which you have expressed your views on the crisis that has arisen. We fully understand that you are not assuming the functions of a mediator in this matter. I would, in this connection, like to mention that President Nasser had, after contacting me as well as Prime Minister Chou En-lai and getting our views, made some suggestions.[357] I understand that these have, however, been rejected by the Government of China. Your Excellency must be aware of the details of President Nasser's suggestions and the Chinese Government's reply.

I would like to assure you, Mr Prime Minister, that we have not the slightest desire to continue the military conflict indefinitely nor do we want an inch of anyone's territory. But we have no alternative but to resist when a concerted and a premeditated invasion on our soil is mounted by the Chinese. You will appreciate that there can be no compromise with aggression and that there can be no peaceful talks while the aggressor's armies are on Indian soil.

With kind regards,

Yours sincerely,
Jawaharlal Nehru

396. To Mahendra: Chinese Attack[358]

November 6, 1962

My dear friend,

I write to thank you for your letter of the 30th October, which was sent to me through our Ambassador in Kathmandu.

I can quite understand your great concern in regard to the aggression and invasion of China on our northeast frontier. You will further, I am sure, appreciate our distress, constituted as we are, at the occurrence of large scale military operations and conflict on that border and beyond. We have pleaded for peace all over the world and are passionately attached to it. To us, therefore, it is a special misfortune and a tragedy that we should be involved in some kind of a war. But what is any self respecting country to do when it has to meet a massive invasion? For the last five years, we have tried our utmost to solve this question peacefully, but have not succeeded. In September last, for the first time, there was a regular invasion of our territory in the northeast, and on the 20th October this took the shape of a massive attack on a big scale by the

357. See item 389.
358. Letter to the King of Nepal.

Chinese forces. The conflict is not of our choosing. But there was no escape from it for us, and we had to face this contingency. We shall continue to do so with all the strength at our command till we repulse the invaders.

But we are always anxious for peace and we shall continue to explore all honourable methods of securing it. We have made a proposal to the Chinese that they should withdraw to the position they occupied on our borders before the 8th September, when this new invasion took place. This seems to me a very fair and honourable way to release the present tension and avoid a worsening of it. Then we can consider further measures to lessen tension and, later, to discuss what steps we should take to solve this problem.

The Chinese Government has also made some proposals which they call three-point proposals. These, in effect, leave the aggressors in possession of the fruits of aggression while we have to withdraw still further on our own territory. This will leave them in a position to launch further attacks on us at a time of their own choosing, and at the same time offer a still graver threat to our neighbours, including Nepal. We could not possibly accept this position.

Your Majesty will have observed the tremendous upsurge all over India in the face of this brutal invasion. All our internal problems have been hushed, and every part of India and all communities and groups here are united behind this national effort to repel this invasion. I have no doubt in my mind that success will come to us, however long this struggle may last.

Many brave sons of Nepal are with us in this fight and have already performed feats of valour which have aroused the admiration of their comrades. I have no doubt that Your Majesty must be maintaining vigilance against any suspicious military movement on your northern border as well as against the infiltration of enemy agents into Nepal.

During this emergency, when all our resources have to be thrown into the fight against our common danger, the strain on supplies and on our transport facilities may occasionally cause temporary shortages of certain essential commodities. We shall do our best to maintain normal supplies to Nepal so that the way of life of the people there and the execution of development plans are not unduly hindered. These matters can be discussed between our Governments as occasion arises.

Our Ambassador, Harishwar Dayal, will tell Your Majesty of the measures we have taken and continue to take to see that the tranquility of our common border is not disturbed. I believe these measures have already met with considerable success, and I have no doubt that these steps will be fully affective. I trust your Majesty will issue appropriate instructions for reciprocal action on your side.

I can assure Your Majesty that it is my earnest desire to have not only a peaceful border between Nepal and India, but also friendly and cooperative relations between the two countries.

With kind personal regards,

Yours sincerely,
Jawaharlal Nehru

397. Meeting with Czech Ambassador[359]

The Czech Ambassador has just seen me and given me the attached letter from his Prime Minister.[360] After reading it I told him what the facts were, more especially since the 8th of September, 1962, and of the Chinese invasion which had completely altered the situation. It was bad enough during the last five years, but this large scale invasion was of a different type, and the Chinese amazingly said that we had invaded their territory, and so on. I told him that the only possible way was for the position prior to the 8th September being restored. The Chinese talked of peace etc. and yet they went on advancing even beyond their claimed lines.

I further told him that the old imperialist countries had certainly often in the past adopted an objectionable line, but in the present case they did not come in at all. It is the Chinese Government that had attacked us and invaded us and there was no other way for us except to defend ourselves.

I then asked him if it was true that the Czech Government was sending large quantities of arms to the People's Republic of China. He said that this was completely untrue and they were not sending any arms to China.

398. To Bernard Montgomery: No Mediation[361]

November 11, 1962

My dear Field Marshal,

Thank you for your letter of the 5th November 1962. It is very good of you to offer to help in some way to solve the conflict that has arisen between China and India. This is a matter of great concern to us, and has shocked us.

---

359. Note, 10 November 1962, for R. K. Nehru, the SG at the MEA, and M.J. Desai, the FS.
360. Viliam Široký, Prime Minister of Czechoslovakia (1953–1963).
361. Letter to British Field Marshal; address: Islington Mill, Alton, Hants, England.

For five years there has been continued aggression by China on Indian territory, chiefly Ladakh. There have been petty incidents. We have tried our best to find some way of settling this question honourably. We have not succeeded.

On the 8th September 1962, Chinese forces suddenly appeared on our North-East Frontier Agency border and came down the Thagla Pass. We had some military posts in that region, small in numbers. This was an entirely new development which was wholly unexpected by us, as it had been repeatedly, though not formally, stated that there would be no aggression in this area. No Chinese had been there ever since our Independence. We have been building schools, colleges and roads there and establishing an effective administration. You may know that in 1913-14, there was a tripartite conference between the then Government of India, the Government of China and Tibet. This conference confirmed that the border between India and Tibet was the high ridge and watershed of the Himalayas, a well known geographical feature. It was not a new decision, but a recognition of a very old boundary. Subsequently the Chinese Government refused to sign that treaty. As a matter of fact, their refusal was not due to this line, called the McMahon Line, but to the line dividing inner Tibet with outer Tibet. Anyhow, from that date nearly fifty years ago, the Government of India has been in possession and there has been no interference of any kind. Even before that, of course, the Government was in constructive possession, although it did not build up the normal administrative services there and left it to the tribal people inhabiting it.

Thus, the appearance of the Chinese Forces on the 8th of September was something that had not happened for ages past. If the Chinese had any claim to it, they could discuss that peacefully and not suddenly invade our country. We took some steps to defend ourselves and sent some additional forces there. The place is difficult of access and we had to send our troops by air and all supplies were by air. Meanwhile the Chinese increased their forces very considerably. On the 20th of October, they began a well coordinated attack on our forces both in NEFA and in Ladakh, and they used apparently about three Divisions. Our forces were hopelessly outnumbered. It was easy for them to bring in large numbers of men quickly across the ridge as their roads came across the table land of Tibet right up to the edge of the ridge. There was a minor battle there and our people were greatly outnumbered and driven back. The Chinese advanced somewhat and are now being held a little further south.

I do not propose to tell you the long story of these five years of aggression or of what has happened since the 8th of September. It was patent to us that this was no frontier incident but a well thought out and well prepared invasion of India with large forces. The Chinese go about saying that we attacked them and they are defending themselves. This is an extraordinary and patently false statement.

This has led to a tremendous reaction in India and there is a great deal of irritation and even anger. It has, however, done one good. All our petty disputes and controversies have ended, and I have never experienced the sense of unity in India to the extent I have done now. You know how we have always talked of peace and how we utterly dislike the thought of war. It is an irony of fate that this invasion and warfare should have come down upon us. Yet, it is impossible for us to submit and surrender to aggression and invasion, whatever the consequences. We have proposed that we are prepared to talk to the Chinese if they go back to the position as it existed prior to 8th September 1962. They have rejected this, and meanwhile continue pouring in their troops across our frontier and are trying to advance. They have, on their side, made a three-point proposal which would enable them to strengthen their positions in India while we are supposed to retire further still. We cannot possibly accept this, and we have said so.

That is the position now, and there appears to be no way out. Meanwhile the winter is coming fast. The winter on these high altitudes is very severe indeed. In Ladakh the temperature now is between 20 and 30 degrees below zero. Perhaps the fighting may tone down because of this winter for some time.

It is very good of you to offer your services, but I do not quite know what you or anyone else can do. We can hardly accept some kind of mediation of this type, and I doubt if the Chinese Government will do it either. A time may arise when some such effort might be helpful provided the Chinese accept what we say and retire to the position before September 8. We are wholly unable to talk to them under threats and continuing invasion. We realise the far-reaching consequence of this, but there is no other choice open to us.

With my kind regards,

Yours sincerely,
Jawaharlal Nehru

399. To Ayub Khan[362]

November 12, 1962

My dear President,

Thank you for your letter of 6th November,[363] 1962 which I received from your High Commissioner in New Delhi.

I had, in my letter of 27th October,[364] given a brief account of the aggression by the forces of the People's Republic of China on Indian territory along the Eastern and Western sections of the India-China border. I agree with you that the military clashes that have taken place between Chinese and Indian forces are a matter of common concern to all of us who are interested in the maintenance of peace and stability in this sub-continent.

With your experience as a distinguished soldier, you will no doubt realise that the Chinese aggression is not merely in the nature of a border incident but is an invasion of India on a massive scale and has a significance wider than that of a mere border conflict between China and India. Whatever our differences may be, the disturbance to stability and peace in this sub-continent is a matter of common concern to both of us and you would not, I am sure, want any weakening or submission to Chinese aggression on our part as that will affect not only the future of India but of all independent countries in this region.

In spite of our love of peace, we could not submit to this further aggression by China and we have, therefore, much against our wishes, had to take all possible steps to meet the Chinese invasion. Just as I appealed to you in my letter of 27th October for your sympathy and support in our efforts to meet the crisis created by Chinese aggression, we also requested all friendly countries for their sympathy and help. Some of these countries have been good enough to agree to help us with urgently required defence stores and equipment.

This struggle against Chinese aggression is none of our seeking. It is painful for us to be involved in warlike measures and to turn our limited resources to warlike activities when there are so many demands for developments to be met by us. We are, however, facing a powerful and unscrupulous invader who has mounted a well-planned and massive invasion. All our energies and resources have to be devoted to resistance against this Chinese aggression. The help given to us by way of defence equipment and stores by friendly countries will be utilised solely in this resistance to Chinese aggression. We have to build up adequate war potential to meet the Chinese aggression, to which you refer

362. Letter to the President of Pakistan. PIB
363. See appendix 42.
364. See item 388.

in your letter, [and it] cannot and will not be used for any purpose other than effective resistance against this further Chinese aggression.

I entirely agree with you that we should strive for a world of peace and friendly relations with all countries and that the only methods which we should adopt are the methods of peace. Both our countries are engaged in tremendous task of development and of modernisation so as to raise the standards of living of our people. To this we are firmly dedicated. You can rest assured, Mr President, that this policy will be applied even more specially in our relations with Pakistan. The idea of any conflict with Pakistan is one which is repugnant to us and we on our part will never initiate it. I am convinced that the future of India and Pakistan lies in their friendship and cooperation for the benefit of both.

As for our conflict with China, we would welcome an end of that conflict so that we can direct our energy to peaceful development. But so long as China continues to invade and commit aggression against our country, we have to defend it, as you would no doubt do if any country committed aggression against Pakistan. While we shall always seek an end of this conflict, it has to be in a manner which preserves the honour and integrity of India. It may be that this conflict will last a long time, draining our resources and diverting our energies from the programmes of development.

In any event, we cannot submit to the aggressor. I am sure you would not want us to do so. Resisting the aggressor will cost us dearly but, I am sure, you would agree with me that this high cost must be said to maintain our independence and territorial integrity. Any weakening by India or submission to the aggressor will endanger the independence and territorial integrity not only of India but of all sovereign States in this region.

With kind regards,

Yours sincerely
Jawaharlal Nehru

400. To Louis Johnson: Chinese Menace[365]

November 16, 1962

My dear Louis,

Thank you for your letter of November 13th. It was a very welcome one and I appreciate what you have written. We are certainly having a difficult time

365. Letter to US politician and former Secretary of Defence; (1891-1966); address: c/o Messrs Steptoe and Johnson, Shoreham Building, Washington DC.

and we want all the help that we can get to meet this Chinese menace to our country's freedom and integrity.

Whatever the near future might bring us, I am quite certain in my mind that we shall drive the invader from our territory.

With warm regards,

Sincerely yours,
[Jawaharlal Nehru]

401. To Y.B. Chavan: Rebuke[366]

November 16, 1962

My dear Chavan,

I was rather surprised and distressed to read a report of your speech delivered at Poona on November 14. In this you are reported to have said that You were not "among those who believed that Russia would side with India in this crisis". You were "firmly of the opinion that Russia would ultimately be on the side of China because the Russians had recently described the Chinese as their brothers while the Indians were their friends only".

"There were people in India who believed Russia would help us in the present crisis, but Russia could not do it because of its policy of spreading Communism by force."

Whether your opinion or belief is wholly justified or not, it is certainly unfortunate that you should have made these statements. There is a tremendous inner struggle going on at present between Russia and China. This may even result in the break between the two, though perhaps that is unlikely. Even otherwise, it is likely to result in very strained relations between the two countries. Whether Russia helps us or not—and I agree with you that it is very unlikely that Russia will help us—the important point is about Russia helping the Chinese. It would make a tremendous difference if Russia helps them not only in regard to arms and aircraft, but even more especially about petrol. To say anything now which pushes Russia more into the Chinese hands, is unfortunate.

As you are coming here as Defence Minister soon,[367] your views on this matter will naturally attract a great deal of attention not only in India, but outside

---

366. Letter to the Chief Minister of Maharashtra.
367. Chavan was sworn in on 21 November 1962.

India. I hope, therefore, that you will be a little careful in your references to this topic.

Yours sincerely,
[Jawaharlal Nehru]

402. To P.C. Borooah: Soviet Position and Indian Statements[368]

November 18, 1962

Dear Borooah,

Your letter of November 17. I shall try to get news about your nephew, B.K. Borooah. As you say, there has been heavy fighting round about Walong and we have suffered a setback there. As soon as I have news of your nephew, I shall let you knew.

We realise the importance of the corridor connecting Assam with the rest of India, as well as the oil fields etc.

There is a great deal of propaganda going on on behalf of the Chinese stating that while they are quite prepared to put an end to the fighting, it is India that is coming in the way. It is necessary, therefore, for us to state the initial conditions which might make us agreeable to proceed further in this matter. We cannot appear before the world as if we are totally opposed to any peaceful approach. The suggestions we had made would have greatly strengthened us both psychologically and practically. The Chinese have rejected them.

I do not think it was wise for Shri Chavan[369] to say what he did about the USSR.[370] What he said might happen or it might not, but the world situation today contains a big enigma—the relations of Russia with China. Nobody quite knows what these are likely to be. There is no love lost between them. We do not expect much help from the Soviet Union, but the question is how far they will help the Chinese. This is a vital matter from the Chinese and our point of view. If the Russians, for instance, stop petrol supplies, this will hit the

---

368. Letter to Lok Sabha MP, Congress; address: 1 Gurdwara Road, New Delhi.
369. Y. B. Chavan, Chief Minister of Maharashtra, took over as the Defence Minister on 21 November 1962.
370. See item 401.

Chinese very hard. It is not wise, therefore, to say things which might induce the Russians to incline more towards the Chinese.

Yours sincerely,
[Jawaharlal Nehru]

403. To Nicolas Nabokov: Invasion not Skirmish[371]

November 18, 1962

Dear Mr Nabokov,

Thank you for your letter of the 14th November and for your good wishes on the occasion of my birthday.

It is true that we are passing through very difficult times because of the Chinese invasion of India. I am afraid our difficulties are likely to continue. But I am confident that ultimately, we shall push the Chinese back.

I do not know what I can suggest for you to do. You are the best judge. It seems to me rather surprising that some people still think that this is just a minor frontier affray while it is in effect a major invasion of India made after the most careful preparation and with very large forces.

Yours sincerely,
[Jawaharlal Nehru]

404. Mischievous Map in The *Times* of London[372]

The President has drawn my attention to a small map in the London *Times* of November 21. I am sending this to you. This little map is very mischievous as it shows the pre-McMahon Line frontier as something very different from the McMahon Line.

---

371. Letter to Russian born composer and author; (1903-1978); address: 6 Rue Jean-Goujon, Paris 8.
372. Note, 22 November 1962, for M.J. Desai, the FS. MEA, File No. XPP/307(4)/14/62, Part III, p.1.

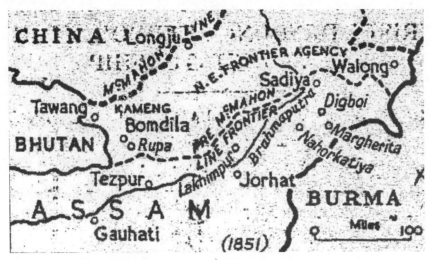

The Frontier between India and Tibat before
The McMahon Line was established at The
Simla Convention in 1914

405. To Asoke K. Sen: Correspondence Leaked[373]

November 23, 1962

My dear Asoke,

Your letter of the 22nd.

I do not think we sent any of the letters addressed to President Kennedy or to Macmillan to the press. If they have appeared in the press, this must have come from London or Washington.

We are daily sending any number of messages to various Heads of States or Governments. These are not normally circulated to members of the Cabinet, although there is nothing secret in them. Sometimes the recipient does not like any publicity being given.

We have suddenly entered into this crisis without adequate preparation. Gradually, I suppose we shall improve all this. At present our work is rather unbalanced. Most of the work done has been in connection with obtaining supplies from the USA, UK and some other countries. We do not wish to give any publicity to this, especially when we do not know what we will get. The

373. Letter to the Law Minister.

burden of the work has necessarily fallen especially on the Defence Ministry and the External Affairs Ministry.

Yours sincerely,
[Jawaharlal Nehru]

406. To Sudhir Ghosh: Kingsley Martin's Excess[374]

November 27, 1962

Dear Sudhir,

Thank you for your letter of the 27th November and the cutting from the *New Statesman*. I am afraid Kingsley Martin[375] has lost his balance. He accuses Indians of being jingoistic.

Yours sincerely,
Jawaharlal Nehru

407. In New Delhi: At Civic Reception for Heinrich Luebke[376]

No more traps for India: Nehru

New Delhi, Nov. 27 – Prime Minister Nehru said here today that the Chinese invasion had opened the eyes of India and she would never be caught in any trap hereafter.

Pandit Nehru, who was speaking at a civic reception given in honour of Dr Heinrich Luebke, President of the Federal Republic of Germany, warned the nation that the struggle against China would be a long drawn affair.

He said: "It is not going to be a matter of days or weeks or even months. May be, it will take years and we must prepare ourselves for it both mentally and militarily."

---

374. Letter to Rajya Sabha MP; address: 95 South Avenue, New Delhi. NMML, Sudhir Ghosh Papers.
375. Editor of the *New Statesman* of London.
376. Report of speech in honour of the President of the Federal Republic of Germany. Reproduced from the *National Herald*, 28 November 1962, p.1.

The Prime Minister said that it must be understood everywhere that India would not bow her head to the aggressor and would meet the Chinese invasion whatever the cost and consequences.

He said: "Perhaps we will have to learn new techniques of fighting. We will learn them. But there can be no question of our tolerating this aggression or being cowed down by China."

Thanking the friendly countries for their help, Pandit Nehru said: "We are grateful to them. It is but natural that they are taking interest in this matter. What China is doing is violation not only of international law but of all canons of international behaviour."

He, however, warned the people that it was they who would have to bear the brunt of the Chinese invasion. "Help from friends in the time of need is always welcome. But we must guard ourselves against leaning too much on friends. A people who forget their own duty in times of crisis and sit idly thinking that their friends will help them, lose their independence," Pandit Nehru said.

Pandit Nehru said that India did believe for some time that naked invasions had become things of the past and that disputes between nations could be resolved without wars. But the Chinese seemed to believe otherwise.

He told the people that the battle against China had to be fought on both fronts—civil and military. "While our jawans defend frontiers on the battle field, each civilian has to do his duty in the rear".

The Prime Minister said: "Military weapons, aeroplanes, etcetera, are symbols of a nation's strength. But behind them stand the fields and factories which produce the raw materials and manufactured things."

Earlier, Pandit Nehru welcomed Dr Luebke as "representative of a great country and personally a brave man."

Turning to Dr Luebke, Pandit Nehru said, "You have come to our country at a time when we are facing a mighty invasion. But it is a pleasure for us to welcome you, not only as the distinguished representative of a great and friendly country, but also as a man of courage and one wedded to noble ideals." – PTI.

408. Talks with W. Averell Harriman[377]

Harriman met Prime Minister Nehru four times; courtesy call shortly after arrival November 22; November 23 with Ambassador [Galbraith], [Paul] Nitze,[378] [Carl] Kaysen and M.J. Desai present; November 25 alone and November 28 with Ambassador.

At November 23 meeting in response Harriman question Nehru said ChiCom primary purpose to humiliate India. Nehru then reviewed history of border dispute, recalling Chou En-lai December 1956 statement to Nehru he would accept McMahon Line de facto and Chou's later denial of statement; Chou's 1956 offer trade NEFA status quo for ChiCom Ladakh claims which Nehru rejected; unproductive talks by officials following Nehru's rejection Chou's offer. Nehru observed that Aksai Chin and road valuable to ChiComs but rest Ladakh had no value. Harriman asked whether India had ever made offer to ChiComs on that corner Ladakh. Nehru said no, explained his offer of mutual withdrawal to line claimed by other side after which India prepared let ChiComs use road for civil purposes; said this offer repeated May 1962. Nehru emphasized India in undisputed possession NEFA for 50 years whatever ChiComs said about legal basis McMahon Line. ChiCom attack in NEFA obviously required long preparation. Nehru several times said ChiCom intention was to deliver hard blow and make it [an] agreement, then use time prepare for next blow and repeat pattern. Thus, October 20 attack followed by October 24 offer, November 15 attack followed by November 21 cease fire. Nehru said India sure ChiComs would look forward to prolongation of truce for a while. Harriman asked whether ChiComs would carry discussions through if initiated now or break off. Nehru replied ChiComs would carry through if they could get agreement favourable them. Harriman asked what Nehru intended do in immediate future. Nehru replied cease fire now in effect and he assumed ChiComs will withdraw December 1. It Nehru's understanding India could not go into territory vacated by ChiComs. M.J. Desai intervened say India could keep troops up to 20 kilometers south McMahon Line and send administrative and police personnel up to line. Ambassador asked whether there had been any actual withdrawals yet. Nehru said there had; Desai said only in Ladakh but in NEFA ChiComs only had said they prepared withdraw. Harriman asked what would happen December 1. Nehru said ChiComs would withdraw and

---

377. Galbraith's telegram to Department of State, 30 November 1962; Kennedy Papers. https://www.jfklibrary.org/Asset-Viewer/Archives/JFKNSF-111-016.aspx Accessed on 21 August 2018.

378. Paul Nitze, Deputy Secretary of Defense, USA.

wait for India act. Harriman asked what would happen if India did nothing to which Nehru replied ChiComs would still withdraw. Nehru added it would be foolish for India march forward. Harriman asked whether Nehru inclined change his position on ChiCom offer expressed in his letter of November 14. Nehru said he would not accept ChiCom offer; he must say something but offer had previously been rejected. Ambassador asked about other possibilities, noting that ChiComs had best of propaganda in Afro-Asian countries[379] and suggesting India might call for neutral observers with or without involving UN. Further discussion ChiCom proposal followed and Harriman asked whether cease-fire would last indefinitely if India made no response ChiCom offer. Nehru replied that ChiComs would probably advance further after some interval. Nehru mentioned difficult situation created by Brahmaputra river strike in East Pakistan and its effects on tea exports. Harriman asked whether Nehru had decided give answer to ChiComs and if so what would he say. Nehru said he obviously had to answer. In three or four days he would say something and raise various objections. Harriman and Ambassador referred to public presentation Indian case and importance of making reasonable counter offer to put onus on ChiComs. At moment ChiComs look reasonable and this advantage had to be taken away from them. Desai reviewed ChiCom offer in Ladakh and indicated why he thought it unacceptable. Nitze gave his preliminary view that it would take at least until end of next year for Indians to get into good military position.

Second Harriman meeting with Nehru alone November 25 was for primary purpose discussing India-Pak relations and possibility of Kashmir settlement. Harriman explained there two aspects: 1) immediate problem of calming Ayub and Paks from their emotional binge against India and US and pro-China; 2) long-run problem of defense of subcontinent; said unless tensions relieved US position untenable if it was asked give aid both Pakistan and India with part of aid being used for defense against the other. In response first point Nehru said he could not make further gesture towards Ayub. He had written letter he considered cordial and had had no reply.[380] In addition, India had been humiliated by ChiCom attack and public opinion would not stand for further humiliation in making concessions to Pakistan. When pressed on this point Nehru went into considerable detail on history negotiations with Pakistan over Kashmir and constant failure reach agreement on any basis acceptable to India. If GOI were now to make concessions public would not stand for it. In fact it might touch off violent communal rioting endangering lives of 40 million Indian Muslims. Harriman said number of Nehru's colleagues indicated

379. See appendix 56.
380. See item 399.

they thought time right for settlement. Discussion at some length followed on possible basis for settlement. Nehru rejected giving half to Pakistan or independent status for Kashmir but agreed some arrangements such as those proposed by M.J. Desai and Ambassador Galbraith might be acceptable. Harriman pressed Nehru on immediate importance relieving tensions and suggested discussions might begin between two governments. At first Nehru rejected this on grounds that if discussions failed it would make situation even worse. He finally agreed that if Ayub were willing he would join in starting negotiations preferably on Ministerial level. Nehru indicated that present not best time for settlement from standpoint Indian opinion but agreed that more favorable climate might develop. This climate might be encouraged if Ayub and his colleagues would make some friendly gesture towards India to offset torrent of abuse which had poured forth since ChiCom aggression. Harriman asked Nehru think over situation and expressed hope Nehru could arm him with some proposal before his departure for Pakistan on November 28. Harriman raised subject Nehru's request to President for air assistance. Nehru said he not pressing matter now as he did not believe ChiComs would attack at least for some months. He thought ChiComs wanted make deal and cited in support this view that ChiComs pressing Afro-Asian bloc to bring pressure on India.[381] Harriman said our military were discussing air assistance request with British and Indian Air Force. If anything to be provided Commonwealth countries should come in first. Harriman explained subject being discussed without commitment. Harriman told Nehru that Duncan Sandys had been informed by Morarji Desai that Soviets had definitely declined supply MIGs. Nehru replied that Desai could not have had latest information and what he had told Sandys must have been based on earlier talk by Indian Ambassador Moscow with a Soviet Deputy Commissar of Foreign Affairs. Recently Khrushchev assured Indian Ambassador that MIG factory would be delivered in couple of years and in meantime the few MIGs under discussion would be delivered in ample time for training purposes. Nehru gave impression he trying minimize importance of matter. Meeting lasted little less than hour. At parting Nehru thanked Harriman again for US aid and promptness of US response to India's request.

At final meeting with Nehru November 28 Harriman and Ambassador stressed to Nehru Ayub's domestic difficulties and urged it in India's interest work out settlement with Paks. Also pointed out to Nehru necessity of devising formula that would help Ayub domestically and strengthen him against his critics

---

381. There were talks among African and Asian countries regarding convening a six-nation peace conference to resolve the Sino-Indian crisis (Burma, Cambodia, Egypt, Ghana, Indonesia and Ceylon). See item 286.

there. Nehru said he amenable talks but indicated he had very limited concept in mind such as adjustment cease fire line. Ambassador said this not enough. By end of talks Nehru agreed he willing enter talks with open mind and without preconditions. Harriman impression of last meeting was that Nehru had become clearer minded and more down to earth than he had been at earlier meetings.

409. To U Thant: Withdrawing Indian Contingents[382]

November 30, 1962

My dear Secretary-General,
I acknowledge, with thanks, the receipt of your letter of 23rd November 1962.[383]

Being dedicated to the cause of peace and the promotion of understanding among nations, we have always tried staunchly to support the United Nations in its peace-keeping functions. We have, whenever requested, assisted the United Nations to the best of our ability, with troops and personnel and in other ways, in the discharge of the responsibilities entrusted to it. Fairly considerable Indian forces are therefore committed to the United Nations in the Congo and Gaza at the present time.

But now, as we are ourselves the victims of a massive and premeditated aggression, we must marshal all our strength and resources in defence of our own security and territorial integrity. It was in these circumstances that I was compelled to ask our Permanent Representative to see you in connection with the return of our troops in the Congo and Gaza.[384]

We do not wish to take any action which would undermine that United Nations operations in the Congo by any sudden withdrawal of our troops. We hope that speedy and effective action will be taken for the implementation of your plan for the Congo and that the measures which you have in mind will enable the release of the Indian troops as soon as possible, and not later than February 1963. We appreciate the understanding that you have shown of our situation arising out of the invasion of our territory.

---

382. Letter to the Secretary-General of the United Nations.
383. Not reproduced, but available in NMML. He wrote, "the measure of our gratitude is in the fact that at this stage without the contingent from India, it would be extremely difficult to implement the United Nations' resolution in respect to peace keeping operations in Congo…. Your decision, therefore, not to withdraw the Indian Contingent…is a decisive contribution to the continued success of the United Nations operations in Congo and Gaza."
384. See items 195 and 197.

I realise that some time will be required to arrange for the transport of the large Indian contingent with its equipment etc. But I hope that this can be reduced to the minimum in view of our dire needs.

With the assurances of my highest consideration,

Yours sincerely,
Jawaharlal Nehru

410. To N. Raghavan: Tibet Policy[385]

November 30, 1962

My dear Raghavan,

Thank you for your letter of November 22nd with a note attached. I have read this note with interest. With much that you say, I agree, but I do not agree about making the liberation of Tibet one of our war aims. That will be talking about things which are very difficult to attain. If we can drive the Chinese out of India and hold our frontier firmly, that itself will produce a new situation both in Tibet and elsewhere.

Yours sincerely,
[Jawaharlal Nehru]

(i) CHINESE INVASION: International Support

411. To John F. Kennedy: Thanking for Support[386]

Dear Mr President,

Your Ambassador Mr Galbraith has just handed to me your letter of October 27th.[387] I am deeply grateful to you for what you have written and for your sympathy and the sympathy of the great nation whose head you are at a moment of difficulty and crisis for us.

---

385 Letter to former Ambassador Extraordinaire and Plenipotentiary for Government of India to China; address: Hermitage, Ormes Road, Kilpauk, Madras.

386. Telegram from Galbraith, PRIMIN 21156, 29 October 1962, to the US President. Kennedy Papers, https://www.jfklibrary.org/Asset-Viewer/Archives/JFKNSF-111-016. aspx Accessed on 21 August 2018.

387. See appendix 28.

I have told your Ambassador that he can always come and discuss matters with me frankly. Such requests as we are making for your Government's assistance in this crisis have my full backing and support and we are very grateful to you for your assurance in regard to them.

With warm personal good wishes to you Mr President,

Sincerely,
Jawaharlal Nehru

412. International Reactions[388]

Sino-Indian Dispute,
Soviet Attitude
Nehru Sees No Basic Shift

New York, Oct. 30 – Mr Nehru today expressed the view that the change in Russia's attitude in the India-China dispute was probably caused by international developments including Cuba.

The Prime Minister of India expressed this view in an interview to the New Delhi correspondent of the Columbia Broadcasting Station. The interview was recorded earlier but broadcast tonight over the national network here.

Mr Nehru said: "I should imagine that developments of the world situation in regard to Cuba, etc., probably made it necessary for them (Russia) not to fall out with China." He had been asked to comment about the shift in Soviet policy.

Asked whether Russia's endorsement of Peking's proposals did not amount to a change, Mr Nehru said: "It has been different all this time. Even now, I do not think there has been any basic difference in their attitude."

Replying to further questions, Mr Nehru "The shift, I think, is because of developments of international situation. But I do not think it is a basic shift (in Soviet Union's attitude) between us and China." Mr Nehru added: "Now that I hope Cuba is out of the way, possibly it is easier for them (Russia) to revert to their neutral attitude."

388. Interview to Columbia Broadcasting Station; reproduced from *The Hindu*, 1 November 1962, p. 5.

Nigeria Condemns China Stand

The Nigerian Prime Minister has assured Mr Nehru of Nigeria's sympathy for India in the conflict.

In a letter to Mr Nehru in reply to a message from him, Sir Abubakar Tafawa Balewa said:

"The Chinese theory of 'might is right' cannot be tenable and any country that embraces it should stand condemned."

Stating that India has shown no aggressive intentions towards any of her neighbours since she became independent in 1947, the Nigerian Prime Minister said: "We cannot view the border dispute in isolation and we consider that its peaceful solution is very important for the preservation of world peace."

Sir Abubakar's letter said: "Since the first Chinese aggression in Ladakh five years ago I have watched with great admiration and respect the role which you have played entirely on your own to use persuasion in place of retaliation to contain the aggressive tendencies of China. I also knew that having regard to the implications for world peace and order of an open clash between India and China, you would have preferred to deal with the matter in your own way of peace and tolerance. But the intransigence which China has constantly displayed leads me to think that all friends of India should now speak out in defence of what is right and in the cause of world peace and concord."

413. To Arvind Jamidar: Support from Kenya[389]

November 5, 1962

Dear Mr Jamidar,

I was glad to receive the message brought by Mr John Bierman, and I would like to offer my sincere thanks to the organisations representing the Kenyan people of all races for their expression of sympathy and solidarity with us in our struggle against a blatant aggression. The whole country is united in its determination and resolve to resist the unscrupulous Chinese attack on our territory and it is heartening to have the sympathy and support of freedom loving people the world over.

Thanking you again for the spontaneous expression of your friendly sentiments and support.

Yours sincerely,
Jawaharlal Nehru

389. Letter to the Minister of Tourism, Nation House, Victoria Street, Nairobi.

414. To John XXIII: Acknowledging Good Wishes[390]

November 7, 1962

Your Holiness,

I am grateful to Your Holiness for your gracious letter of 30th October which was handed over to me by His Eminence Cardinal Gracias.

I am deeply touched by your invocation upon me and the people of India, of the heavenly gifts of peace, happiness and prosperity which we so earnestly desire. As you are aware, we have always endeavoured to work in the interest of peaceful settlement of disputes and differences between nations and people but, in the face of this evil of unabashed military aggression we have no other option but to defend our territorial integrity and the honour of our motherland.

With warm regards,

Yours sincerely,
[Jawaharlal Nehru]

415. For Kwame Nkrumah: On Message to Chou En-lai[391]

November 9, 1962

Dear Mr President,

Thank you for your letter of 27th October, and a copy of your message to Prime Minister Chou En-lai which you enclosed with your letter.[392]

I am grateful for the suggestion that you have made to Prime Minister Chou En-lai in your message of 27th October.

With kind regards,

Yours sincerely,
Jawaharlal Nehru

---

390. Letter to the Pope.
391. Telegram, No. 24584, 9 November 1962, from MEA to High Commission, Accra. MEA, File No. A-II/103/26, p. 3/Corr.
392. Nkrumah had written to Chou En-lai requesting China to retreat to the position held on 8 September 1959 or positions held before 20 October 1962. See report in *The Times of India* 20 November 1962, p.11.

416. Italian Sympathy[393]

New Delhi, Nov. 9 – The Prime Minister of Italy[394] has, in a message to Prime Minister Nehru, expressed his country's sincere sympathy towards India in fighting the Chinese aggression.

The Message says: "The Italian Government is fully aware of the gravity of the events which are at present causing concern to your country; their developments are followed here with a spirit of sincere sympathy towards the Indian people and with deep concern for the cause of peace.

"Whereas I fully agree with your opinion that the practice of international relations should not be altered by the predominance of force over the law, I am also confident that a fair settlement of the dispute which will take into account the rightful position of India may be reached through peaceful means."

417. To Sirimavo Bandaranaike[395]

Thank you for your message of the 30th of October,[396] which was received through your High Commissioner. I am grateful for your concern and your appreciation of the gravity of the situation and its consequences not only for India but also for the rest of the world.

2. I am fully conscious of the common ideals which we both share. We believe in peace, tolerance and observance of civilised norms of international behaviour. We also believe that either as individuals or nations, we cannot compromise with evil. History, tradition and heritage have strengthened the faith of our peoples in these precepts of our great teachers throughout the centuries.

3. I am deeply thankful to you for your understanding and your appreciation that we could not adopt any course which prejudices our territorial integrity or self-respect by submitting to negotiating under the pressure of armed force. Large Chinese armies are at present in occupation of our land as a result of treacherous, massive and pre-planned aggression. All canons of international behaviour and our common crusade to ensure international peace and justice demand that the Government of the People's Republic of China should agree at least to the restoration of the status quo prior to 8th September, 1962 when they started this further aggression against India.

---

393. Message, 9 November 1962, reproduced from *The Hindu*, 11 November 1962.
394. Amintori Fanfani (1908-1999) held office from February 1962 to June 1963.
395. Letter to the Prime Minister of Ceylon. MEA File No. 1 (China)/62, Vol I, p. nil.
396. See appendix 36.

4. I would in this connection, mention that President Nasser, after approaching me and Premier Chou En-lai and getting our views, had made some suggestions for a peaceful solution of the conflict. I understand there has been no response to President Nasser from the Chinese.

With kind regards,

[Jawaharlal Nehru]

418. For Pham Van Dong[397]

I thank your Excellency for your communication expressing concern at the serious situation that we face today in our border regions.[398] While joining in the hope that China and India, given the goodwill and mutual effort in the superior interest of peace and friendship, may find out a mutual agreement in the present dangerous situation by peaceful negotiations, I am sure that you will appreciate the fact that India has never claimed an inch of territory belonging to another country. Although she is traditionally and fundamentally wedded to ideals of peace and friendly settlement of disputes, she cannot but resist aggression on here own soil. As far as a satisfactory solution through negotiation of the Sino-Indian border question is concerned, it can only be achieved if the Government of China agrees to withdraw its troops at least to positions which they occupied before the 8th September, 1962.

2. I take this opportunity to renew to your Excellency the assurances of my highest consideration.[399]

---

397. Message to the Prime Minister of the Democratic Republic of North Vietnam. Telegram, No. 9424, 19 November 1962, from MEA to Consul-General in Hanoi. MEA, File No. SI/101/6/62, Vol. III, p. 138/Corr.

398. See appendix 53.

399. On 24 November 1962, Ho Chi Minh observed to the Chinese Chargé d'Affaires that "Nehru is of the capitalist class, and is also himself an aristocrat. Before Indian independence, he was fairly progressive, but the present Nehru is no longer the same. However, among India's ruling circles, he can still be considered a leftist. Right now, the titans of the ruling class are pressuring him, and have forced him to eliminate [Krishna] Menon's post. Since Menon's removal from office, Nehru has been even more isolated." Cable from the Chinese Embassy in Vietnam, November 24, 1962. Wilson Centre Archives http://digitalarchive.wilsoncenter.org/document/121295 Accessed on 6 September 2018.

419. To John F. Kennedy: Appeal for Support-I[400]

19 November 1962

Dear Mr President,

It is now a month since the Chinese massive attack on India started on 20th October. I think I must write to you again to acquaint you with further developments that have occurred since my letter of 29 October.[401] Before I deal with these further developments, however, I would like to say that we are extremely grateful to you and the Government and the people of the USA for the practical support given to us. We particularly appreciate the speed with which the urgently needed small arms and ammunition were rushed to India.

There was a deceptive lull after the first Chinese offensive during which the Chinese mounted a serious propaganda offensive in the name of three point proposals which, shorn of their wrappings, actually constituted a demand for surrender on their terms.[402] The Chinese tried, despite our rejection of these proposals,[403] to get various Afro-Asian countries to intercede with varying offers of mediation.

After my clear and categorical statement in Parliament on 14 November[404] rejecting the three-point proposals of Chou En-lai, the Chinese, who had made full preparations to put further military pressure on us, restarted their military offensive. I am asking our Ambassador[405] to give you a copy of a statement on the developments in the military situation during the last few days which I made in the Parliament this morning.[406] Bomdila, which was the headquarters of our North East Frontier Agency, has been surrounded and the equivalent of two divisions engaged in the operations in the NEFA area are fighting difficult rear-guard actions. It is not quite certain how many of them will be able to extricate themselves and join the Corps Headquarters at Tezpur, further south.

The Chinese are, by and large, in possession of the greater portion of the North East Frontier Agency and are poised to overrun Chushul in Ladakh. There is nothing to stop them after Chushul till they reach Leh, the headquarters of the Ladakh province of Kashmir.

---

400. Letter to US President. Kennedy Papers, https://www.jfklibrary.org/Asset-Viewer/ Archives/JFKNSF-111-016.aspx Accessed on 21 August 2018.Earlier reproduced in *The Indian Express*, 17 November 2010, p. 13.
401. See item 411.
402. See appendix 26.
403. See item 247.
404. See items 275 and 249.
405. B.K. Nehru.
406. See items 278 and 279.

Events have moved very fast and we are facing a grim situation in our struggle for survival and in defending all that India stands for against an unscrupulous and powerful aggressor.

Our defence experts have been discussing our detailed requirements with the technical experts in your Embassy here and have given them a full picture of the magnitude of the operations and the need for air transport and jet fighters. These are absolutely necessary to stem the Chinese tide of aggression. A lot more effort, both from us and from our friends, will be required to roll back this aggressive tide. I hope we will continue to have the support and assistance of your great country in the gigantic efforts that have to be made and sustained to deal with the unscrupulous and powerful enemy we are facing.

I am also writing to Prime Minister Macmillan to keep him informed of these developments.

With kind regards,

Yours sincerely,
Jawaharlal Nehru

420. To John F. Kennedy: Appeal for Support-II[407]

19th November, 1962

Dear Mr President,

Within a few hours of dispatching my earlier message of today,[408] the situation in the NEFA Command has deteriorated still further. Bomdila has fallen and retreating forces from Sela have been trapped between the Sela Ridge and Bomdila. A serious threat has developed to our Digboi oil fields in Assam. With the advance of the Chinese in massive strength, the entire Brahmaputra Valley is seriously threatened and unless something is done immediately to stem the tide, the whole of Assam, Tripura, Manipur and Nagaland would also pass into Chinese hands.

---

407. Letter to US President. Kennedy Papers, https://www.jfklibrary.org/Asset-Viewer/ Archives/JFKNSF-111-016.aspx Accessed on 21 August 2018. Earlier reproduced in *The Indian Express*, 17 November 2010, p. 13. Inder Malhotra, the journalist, records as follows about B. K. Nehru's (Ambassador to the US) reaction on receiving this letter: "He never made a secret of the fact that on receiving and reading the second letter, his impulse was not to deliver it. But realising that he was a civil servant and it was his bounden duty to obey his prime minister, he immediately headed for the White House." Inder Malhotra, "Letters from the darkest hour," *The Indian Express*, 17 November 2010, p. 13. See also appendix 59.

408. See item 419.

2.   The Chinese have poised massive forces in the Chumbi Valley between Sikkim and Bhutan and another invasion from the direction appears imminent. Our areas further North West on the border with Tibet in the States of UP, Punjab and Himachal Pradesh are also threatened. In Ladakh, as I have said in my earlier communication, Chushul is under heavy attack and shelling of the airfield at Chushul has already commenced. We have also noticed increasing air activity by the Chinese air force in Tibet.

3.   Hitherto we have restricted our requests for assistance to essential equipment and we are most grateful for the assistance which has been so readily given to us. We did not ask for more comprehensive assistance particularly air assistance because of the wider implications of such assistance in the global context and we did not want to embarrass our friends.

4.   The situation that has developed is, however, really desperate. We have to have more comprehensive assistance if the Chinese are to be prevented from taking over the whole of Eastern India. Any delay in this assistance reaching us will result in nothing short of a catastrophe for our country.

5.   We have repeatedly felt the need of using air arm in support of our land forces, but have been unable to do so as in the present state of our air and radar equipment we have no defence against retaliatory action by the Chinese.

6.   I, therefore, request that immediately support be given to strengthen our air arm sufficiently to stem the tide of Chinese advance.

7.   I am advised that for providing adequate air defence minimum of 12 squadrons of supersonic all weather fighters are essential. We have no modern radar cover in the country. For this also we seek your assistance. Our needs are most immediate. The United States Air Force personnel will have to man these fighters and radar installations while our personnel are being trained. US fighters and transport planes manned by US personnel will be used for the present to protect our cities and installations from Chinese air attacks and to maintain our communications. We should if this is possible also like US planes manned by US personnel to assist the Indian Air Force in air battles with the Chinese air force over Indian areas where air action by the IAF against Chinese communication lines supplies and troop concentration may lead to counter air action by the Chinese.

8.   Any air action to be taken against the Chinese beyond the limits of our country, e.g. in Tibet, will be taken by IAF planes manned by Indian personnel.

9.   Determined as we are to liberate all parts of our territory which may pass into the hands of the Chinese aggressors it is clear that sooner or later we would have to neutralise their bases and air fields by striking from the air. For this purpose, I request you to consider assisting us with two Squadrons of

Bombers of B-47 type. To man this indispensable arm, we would like to send immediately our Pilots and Technicians for training in the United States.

10. The Chinese threat as it has developed involves not merely the survival of India, but the survival of free and independent Governments in the whole of this sub-continent or in Asia. The domestic quarrels regarding small areas or territorial borders between the countries in this sub-continent or in Asia have no relevance whatever in the context of the developing Chinese invasion. I would emphasise particularly that all the assistance or equipment given to us to meet our dire need will be used entirely for resistance against the Chinese. I have made this clear in a letter I sent to President Ayub Khan of Pakistan.[409] I am asking our Ambassador to give you a copy of this letter.

11. We are confident that your great country will in this hour of our trial help us in our fight for survival and for the survival of freedom and independence in this sub-continent as well as the rest of Asia. We on our part are determined to spare no effort until the threat posed by Chinese expansionist and aggressive militarism to freedom and independence is completely eliminated.

With kind regards,

Yours sincerely
Jawaharlal Nehru

421. To Bertrand Russell: Terms for Cease Fire[410]

Thank you for your telegram dated November 8.[411] Chou En-lai's offer of a ceasefire on the basis of the Chinese three-point proposal is, in effect, a demand for surrender on terms to be accepted and implemented where large Chinese armies are on Indian soil. No country, much less India, can submit to the military dictates of an aggressor.

We have no desire to continue military conflict, nor do we desire any part of Chinese territory, but there can be no compromise with aggression. The first

---

409. See item 399.
410. Reproduced from report "Russell calls for effort for cease fire," in the *National Herald*, 21 November 1962.p. 1.
411. Russell had issued a statement on 20 November 1962: "It is clear to me that the failure to stop this war soon will exorably involve the nuclear powers, the consequence of which can only be total disaster for India and China and for the mankind." He urged that every effort should be made to bring India and china to cease fire "pending arbitration of the entire area in dispute." He also released the text of replies from Chou En-lai and Nehru to an appeal he made to them on 8 November 1962. Ibid.

essential, if we are to revert to peaceful processes, is to undo the aggression by restoring the status quo ante September 8, 1962.

422. To M.H. Mohammed: Support in Ceylon[412]

November 21, 1962

Dear Mr Mayor,

I am grateful to you for your letter of the 10th November conveying to me a resolution passed at a public meeting held in Colombo on the 8th November. I shall be obliged to you if you will kindly convey my thanks to the sponsors of that meeting for their full sympathy and support of India in the crisis that has arisen here owing to the invasion of India by China.

Yours sincerely,
[Jawaharlal Nehru]

423. To J.E. de Quay: Dutch Support[413]

November 21, 1962

Dear Mr Prime Minister,

I thank you for your message of the 2nd of November, which was passed on to me by our Ambassador at The Hague. I am grateful to you for your Government's sympathy and support in our determination to resist the massive aggression mounted by China against our country.[414]

With kind regards,

Yours sincerely,
[Jawaharlal Nehru]

412. Letter to the Mayor of Colombo.
413. Letter to the Prime Minister of the Netherlands.
414. The Dutch played a crucial role in getting Indonesia to support India's position and refrain from allying with the Communist bloc. See Telegram from Dutch Ambassador to Home, 1 November 1962. Wilson Centre Archives, http://digitalarchive.wilsoncenter.org/document/114791 Accessed on 6 September 2018.

424. To A. Sékou-Touré: Response to Cease Fire[415]

Thank you for your telegram of 21st on the subject of the Chinese Government's decision to apply the ceasefire unilaterally.

I had given detailed factual background of India-China reactions during the last 12 years, of the further Chinese aggression on India which commenced on 8th September, 1962, and of the massive attack which started on 20th October, 1962, in the letter I sent to you on 27th October, 1962.

We received a copy of the Chinese statement from the Chinese Chargé d'Affaires in Delhi on the evening of 21st November. Though this statement gives a perverse and distorted account of the factual history of the past and of the latest Chinese aggression which led to serious clashes between Chinese and Indian forces, it is being studied by our Foreign Office. There are several points in the statement which are vague and not precise. Our Foreign Office will try to get necessary clarification on these points from the Chinese Embassy in Delhi.

We are still of the view that peaceful talks and discussions are only possible provided there is the appropriate atmosphere of confidence. This atmosphere can only be created by the restoration of the status quo prior to 8th September, where the further Chinese aggression on India began.

We are wedded to peace and peaceful ways and to the policies of non-alignment and peaceful co-existence which we have followed ever since our independence. We will continue to adhere to these policies which we hold so dear. When, however, our independence and our territorial integrity are threatened by an aggressor, who is also out to destroy the principles of peaceful co-existence and non-alignment, we have to take all such measures as are necessary to resist aggressor. Submission or surrender to the dictates of the aggressor would mean not only the loss of some territory here or some territory there, but also deal a shattering blow to the policies of non-alignment and peaceful co-existence which we, along with our other friends in Africa and Asia, hold so dear.

---

415. Telegram, 21 November 1962, to the President of Guinea. MEA, File No. 1 (China)/62, Vol. II, p. nil. See appendix 63.

425. To Ne Win: Nasser's Suggestions[416]

November 21, 1962

Your Excellency,

Thank you for your message of the 29th October which I received through your Ambassador in New Delhi. I am grateful to you for your concern and for your appreciation of the seriousness of the situation which we are facing.

It is a matter of deep regret to us that China has started this wanton aggression of India. After a lull, there has been another massive and pre-planned attack with deeper penetration of our territory. As you are aware, President Nasser made certain suggestions for a peaceful solution of the conflict, but these, I understand, did not get a constructive response from China[417].

Please accept, Your Excellency, the assurances of my highest consideration.

Jawaharlal Nehru

426. To Habib Bourguiba: Chinese Betrayal[418]

22nd November, 1962

My dear President,

I am very grateful to Your Excellency for your message brought by your personal envoy, Ambassador Taieb Slim, with whom I have had a useful exchange of views. I deeply appreciate the sentiments of friendship and sympathy which you have expressed in regard to the premeditated and wanton aggression committed against us by China.

As Your Excellency has observed, we have throughout tried to establish our relations with the People's Republic of China on a basis of good neighbourliness and mutual respect and have lent our support to China's legitimate interests in the counsels of the world. China, however, has responded with deceit and treachery and has launched a massive invasion of our territory, seizing by force large areas in Assam and Ladakh.

China's actions have been cynical betrayal of the principles accepted by her at Bandung and a flagrant violation of all canons of international behaviour. The Chinese leaders alternate their brutal aggression with spurious cease fire

416. Letter to the Chairman of the Revolutionary Council of the Union of Burma, MEA, File No. 1 (China)/62, Vol. I, p. nil.
417. Nasser had made these suggestions for immediate cease fire on 26 October 1962 to Heads of African and Asian nations, which China rejected.
418. Letter to the President of Tunisia. MEA, File No. 1(China)/62, Vol. III, p.nil.

proposals whose only aim is to deceive the world and to enable the aggressor to consolidate his position for further aggressive actions. While we ardently believe in peace, we will never accept an ignominious peace or submit to impossible terms sought to be imposed on us by force.

For the massive Chinese invasion of India is not merely an attack over a piece of territory; it is aimed at destroying our entire way of life and all the values that we hold dear. It is equally a threat to the countries of Asia and Africa and indeed is a menace to the peace of the whole world.

We have firmly resolved to repel the aggression with all our might and strength and with the help of all friendly countries. Though the struggle which has been forced upon us will be long and hard one, we are determined to wage it till the end, confident that truth and justice will triumph over treachery and deceit. It is indeed gratifying to have Your Excellency's renewed assurance that in this struggle your sympathy and support is so abundantly with us.

With renewed thanks and with the assurances of my highest esteem and consideration,

Yours sincerely,
Jawaharlal Nehru

427. To Mrs Frank E. Evans: Acknowledging US Support[419]

November 22, 1962

Dear Mrs Evans,
I am grateful for your letter of the 21st November and for the good wishes it contains. We are having a difficult time, but I am confident that we shall overcome all these difficulties. Meanwhile, may I express my gratitude for the help we are receiving from the United States?

Yours sincerely,
[Jawaharlal Nehru]

419. Letter to widow of Brigadier General Frank Evans; address: 238 Spring Road, Lake Charles, La.

428. To Josip Broz Tito: Thanking for Support[420]

November 23, 1962

Dear Friend,

Thank you for your letter of the 12th of November which I received through your Ambassador in New Delhi.[421] I am grateful to you for your support and your understanding of the gravity of the Chinese recourse to arms and its consequences for the world.

I am conscious of the common ideals we held regarding peace and peaceful negotiation of disputes, non-involvement and co-existence.[422] The Chinese invasion of our country is an assault both on our territory as well as on these principles. We are, therefore, determined to resist the Chinese aggression. At the same time, we cannot accept, to use your expression, a fait accompli achieved through aggression and have suggested that China should at least restore the status quo prior to the 8th September when her armed forces mounted their latest invasion of our territory. We are gratified to know that we have your support in this matter.

With kind regards,

Yours sincerely,
[Jawaharlal Nehru]

429. To John G. Diefenbaker: Thanking for Support[423]

November 23, 1962

My dear Prime Minister,

I thank you for your message of the 29th of October which was forwarded to me by our High Commissioner in Ottawa. I am grateful to you for your sympathy and support in our determination to resist the Chinese aggression. I have appreciated the friendly and warm sentiments that you and many distinguished countrymen of yours have expressed on various occasions towards our country and our people.

420. Letter to the President of Yugoslavia.
421. See appendix From Josip Broz Tito 12/11 APP
422. See Tito's statement regarding India-China Conflict to delegation of Rumanian National High Assembly during their visit to Yugoslavia, 12-22 November 1962. Report by Stefan S. Nicalau, 22 December 1962. Wilson Centre Archives, http://digitalarchive. wilsoncenter.org/document/115794, Accessed on 21 August 2018.
423. Letter to the Prime Minister of Canada. MEA, File No. 1 (China)/62, Vol. I, p. nil.

I also take this opportunity of thanking your Government, and you personally, for the prompt supply of our urgent defence requirements and for your readiness to give us further assistance that we may require for defence against Chinese aggression.

With kind regards,

Jawaharlal Nehru

430. To Assadullah Alam: Thanking for Support[424]

November 23, 1962

Your Excellency,

I thank you for your message of the 30th October, which was forwarded to me by our Ambassador in Tehran. I am grateful to Your Excellency and the Imperial Government of Iran for your support and sympathy in our determination to resist the massive, pre-planned and treacherous aggression committed on our soil by the Government of China.

With kind regards,

Yours sincerely,
[Jawaharlal Nehru]

431. To Konard Adenauer: Acknowledging Concern[425]

November 24, 1962

Your Excellency,

Thank you for your letter of the 1st of November which I received through your Ambassador in New Delhi. I am grateful to you for your friendly concern and for your appreciation of the gravity of the situation arising out of the blatant aggression committed by China against our country.

We value greatly the friendship and the support given to us by your great country in our present crisis.

With warm greetings and best wishes,

Yours sincerely,
[Jawaharlal Nehru]

424. Letter to Prime Minister of Iran (1962-1964).
425. Letter to the Chancellor of the Federal Republic of Germany. MEA, File No. 1 (China)/62, Vol.III, p. nil.

432. To Ismet Inönü: Acknowledging Support[426]

November 24, 1962

Your Excellency,

Thank you for your letter of the 6th of November which your Ambassador in New Delhi handed over to me. I am grateful for your understanding and support in our determination to resist the pre-planned and massive invasion mounted by China on our country.

I agree with Your Excellency that all differences among nations should be settled by peaceful negotiations between them without recourse to arms or threat of arms. Friendship, peaceful coexistence and mutual cooperation are, to us, abiding principles of international living. I, therefore, share Your Excellency's hope that in the context of the threat posed by the Chinese aggression on India, which is equally a threat to international peace and security and to the ideals of civilised international behaviour, we in this sub-continent should direct our efforts towards avenues of cooperation with a view to solving our differences or at least postponing them. The Chinese aggression on India has far-reaching consequences for India, for this sub-continent, for Asia and the world.

Our faith in peace and friendship among nations remains unshaken. All our efforts over the years to negotiate peacefully our border differences with China have, however, been rudely thwarted by the latest invasion committed by China on the 8th of September. We are determined to resist this aggression and are heartened in our efforts by Your Excellency's sympathy and support.

With kind regards,

Yours sincerely
Jawaharlal Nehru

433. To Charles de Gaulle: Thanking for Support[427]

November 25, 1962

Dear Mr President,

Thank you for your message of the 3rd of November which was handed over to me by your Ambassador in New Delhi.[428] I am grateful to you, Mr President, for

---

426. Letter to the Prime Minister of Turkey.
427. Letter to the President of France, MEA, File No. 1 (China)/62, Vol. II, p. nil.
428. Jean-Paul Garnier,

your sympathy and support in the situation facing us as a result of the massive and pre-planned aggression committed by China on our territory.

We value greatly the friendship shown to us by your great country under your distinguished leadership and are heartened by your support in our efforts to resist the wanton Chinese aggression on our land.

I take this opportunity to convey to you, Mr President, the assurance of my highest consideration.

Yours sincerely,
Jawaharlal Nehru

434. To Kwame Nkrumah: Visit by Asoke Sen and R.K. Nehru[429]

November 26, 1962

My dear President Nkrumah,

At my request, my colleague in our Cabinet, Shri A.K. Sen, our Law Minister, and Shri R.K. Nehru, our Secretary-General, are visiting Accra to convey our greetings and thanks to you for your sympathy in the grave crisis that has confronted us. They will also be available to you to explain any facts in regard to the Chinese invasion of India.[430]

This invasion has been on a massive scale and has deeply pained us. It is in fact changing our way of life. We cannot possibly submit to aggression and dictation from any country, however powerful it might be. It is a strange twist of destiny that we who have stood for peace everywhere should be subjected to this blatant aggression and invasion. We have reacted as any country would and tried to resist this invasion and we shall go on resisting it, however long the process might be.

The recent proposals of the Chinese to have a cease fire and withdrawal itself indicates that they have committed aggression on our territory. We want peace but not on terms which are dishonourable to us. I regret that we can put little faith in Chinese words and promises after our experience of them.

With all good wishes,

Yours very sincerely,
Jawaharlal Nehru.

429. Letter to the President of Ghana.
430. Burma, Cambodia, UAR, Ghana, Indonesia and Ceylon had proposed a conference of the Bandung Group to ease India-China tensions.

435. To Norodom Sihanouk: Thanking for Support[431]

November 27, 1962

Your Royal Highness,

I thank your Royal Highness for your message of the 5th of November which I received through our Ambassador in Phnom Penh and for your anxiety and apprehension at the situation explained in my letter of the 27th October to you.

India and Cambodia share common ideals of peace, tolerance and observance of civilised norms of international behaviour. The treacherous, pre-planned and massive invasion committed by China is as much an assault on our territory as on these principles. We are therefore determined to resist the Chinese aggression.[432]

Our faith in the principles of peace and peaceful negotiation of disputes remains unshaken. At the same time, as individuals or nations, we cannot compromise with evil. We have, therefore, suggested that in order to create an atmosphere conducive to peaceful negotiations, China should at least restore the status quo prior to the 8th of September when her armed forces mounted their latest invasion of our territory.

Please accept, Your Royal Highness, the assurances of my highest consideration.

Yours sincerely,
[Jawaharlal Nehru]

436. To V.K. Joshi: Helping India's Cause from Aden[433]

27th November, 1962

Dear Mr Joshi,

Thank you for your letter of November 20th and for your generous offer to assist in repelling the Chinese aggression against India. You have correctly understood the dimensions of the struggle in which we are engaged, for the wanton attack against us is not merely over a piece of territory but an attempt to destroy our way of life and the values for which India and other like-minded

---

431. Letter to the Head of State of Cambodia.
432. For Sihanouk's position, see: "Minutes of Conversation between Chinese Vice Foreign Minister Huang Zhen and Cambodian King Norodom Sihanouk," November 30, 1962, Wilson Centre Archives, http://digitalarchive.wilsoncenter.org/document/121900, Accessed on 21 August 2018.
433. Letter to the Minister for Works and Aviation, Government of Aden.

nations stand. This menace we are determined to resist with all our might and with the help of all our friends.

In your work in Aden you are serving the larger cause of democracy and understanding among peoples. I am sure you are using your influence to rally sympathy and support for our cause, a cause which is common to the entire Afro-Asian family of nations, and indeed to all peace loving countries the world over.

Thanking you again and with best wishes.

Yours sincerely,
Jawaharlal Nehru

437. To Haile Sallassie[434]

November 28, 1962

Your Imperial Majesty,

I have sent a telegram on the 9th of November, acknowledging with thanks the sympathy and support which Ethiopia has given us in our present crisis. In view of the special friendly relations which exist between our two countries, however, I felt I would again write personally to Your Imperial Majesty.

India and Ethiopia share common ideals in international affairs. We continue to subscribe to these ideas and our faith in principles of peaceful co-existence and settlement of disputes by negotiation remains unshaken. The Chinese invasion of our land is an aggression both on Indian territory and on these principles of civilised international living. As I said in our Parliament a few days ago, the Chinese behaviour is reminiscent of the imperialists and fascist dictators of the past and irrespective of consequences, we are determined to defend our territory and not to compromise with aggression. At the same time, in consonance with our principles, we have suggested that in order to create an atmosphere conducive to peaceful negotiations, China should at least restore the status quo prior to the 8th of September when her armies mounted their latest invasion of India. In this context, we are heartened by Your Imperial Majesty's support to us.

With kind regards,

Yours sincerely,
[Jawaharlal Nehru.]

434. Letter to the Emperor of Ethiopia, MEA, File No. 1 (China)/62, Vol. II, p. nil.

438. To Robert Frost: Thanking for Support[435]

Thank you for your message which we have appreciated greatly.[436] The Chinese invasion apart from the evil it has done, has produced good results also. There has been a wonderful demonstration of unity in India and our friends all over the world have sent us their good wishes. I am deeply grateful to all of them. Their messages have strengthened us.

439. To M.C. Chagla: Labour Party Support[437]

November 29, 1962

My dear Chagla,
I have received the following message from the General Secretary of the British Labour Party[438]:

"National Executive Committee of the Labour Party send to you and the Indian people a message of support in your struggle and of sympathy for those who have suffered in the recent fighting. The Labour Party fully supports maximum British assistance to India in her struggle."

Will you please convey my thanks for their sympathy and support in our struggle against China?

Yours sincerely,
[Jawaharlal Nehru]

440. To Abdulla Al Salim Al Sabah: Thanking for Support[439]

November 30, 1962

Your Highness,
I thank you for your friendly message of 12th November, 1962, in which you have conveyed your anxiety and concern about the situation created by the wanton aggression by China against our territory and for the sentiments expressed by you in support of our stand. You have correctly gauged the issues

435. Telegram, 29 November 1962, to Robert Frost, the poet.
436. See appendix 40.
437. Letter to the High Commissioner in London.
438. Leonard Williams.
439. Letter to the Ruler of Kuwait, from 1950 to1965.

at stake for the struggle we are engaged in is not merely in defence of the integrity of our country but of our very way of life and the values for which India and other like-minded nations stand.

Your message of 18th November has just been received. In regard to your proposed official visit to India, please rest assured that we shall be glad to welcome you here at any time convenient to Your Highness. I, however, appreciate the reasons which prompt you to suggest a postponement of your official tour for the time being. I note that you are planning a private visit to Bombay during the month of Ramadan and I shall look forward to the pleasure of meeting you if I happen to go to Bombay at that time.

Please accept my best wishes for your continued good health and well being and for the continued progress and prosperity of your people.

Yours sincerely,
Jawaharlal Nehru

(j) CHINESE INVASION: Foreign Supplies

441. To N. Sri Rama Reddy: UN not a Source of Equipment[440]

October 24, 1962

Dear Sri Rama Reddy,

Thank you for your letter of the 23rd October. The crisis before us is such a big one that it will require all our effort to meet it, and it will probably last a long time. We shall try to get such equipment as we require from any friendly country. The United Nations is not an organisation which supplies equipment.

Yours sincerely,
[Jawaharlal Nehru]

442. To M.C. Chagla: British Government Supplies[441]

Your telegram 3682 October 26th.

British Government is not putting any difficulties or obstructions in the way now about our purchasing supplies. Previously this used to be the case. It is

---

440. Letter to Rajya Sabha MP, Congress; address: 122 South Avenue, New Delhi.
441. Telegram, PRIMIN 21152, 27 October 1962, to the High Commissioner in London.

not true that we prefer dealing with commercial firms. We would always prefer deals on Government basis.

2. All such demands will be through your High Commission. Please keep in touch with your military attaché. Sometimes there are informal talks here with foreign Ambassadors.

443. To S. Radhakrishnan: Military Supplies from Abroad[442]

October 27, 1962

My dear President,

Thank you for your letter of the 27th October and the various cheques, postal orders and cash amounting in all to Rs 6759/- which you have been good enough to send me. These monies will be sent to the National Defence Fund.

I agree with you that the response of the country has been very heartening.

You have referred to what the US Ambassador told you.[443] This is partly true but not wholly so. We have been trying to get aeroplane parts etc. from the USA. We are getting very soon mortars, automatic weapons from France and Belgium. We are getting something else from the United Kingdom. We have made thus far no fresh demand from the United States as we are busy preparing a full list of what we want which, I hope, will be ready by day after tomorrow. We can then make additional efforts to obtain them from the USA and other countries.[444]

Yours affectionately,
[Jawaharlal Nehru]

---

442. Letter to the President.
443. See telegram No. 1340 from Galbraith to Dean Rusk and J.F. Kennedy regarding his meetings with Radhakrishnan, 26 October 1962. Kennedy Papers, https://www.jfklibrary.org/Asset-Viewer/Archives/JFKNSF-111-016.aspx Accessed on 21 August 2018. See also Telegram 1384 from Embassy in India to the Department of State, 25 October 1962; *Foreign Relations of the United States, 1961-1963, Vol.XIX, South Asia*. Doc. No.180.
444. See item 444 and 445.

444. To V.K. Krishna Menon: Military Supplies from Abroad[445]

October 27, 1962

My dear Krishna,

In the course of a letter from the President to me he says:

"USA Ambassador, Galbraith,[446] was here last evening and said the USA were willing to supply us with any equipment we need but that they had not been asked.[447] We should not lose time in getting equipment from any source."

I entirely agree with the President.

We have received complaints from our Ambassadors abroad, more especially from London and Paris, I think, that they are not being kept informed of what we are trying to get from the respective countries and that we apparently deal directly with the Governments concerned. I think that the Ambassador or High Commissioner should be kept in full touch with the steps we are taking.[448]

Yours affectionately,
[Jawaharlal Nehru]

445. To V.K. Krishna Menon: Equipment Shortage[449]

October 28, 1962

My dear Krishna,

As you told me the other day, we have to consider the present situation in a short term aspect and a long term one. Even the long term aspect requires steps to be taken immediately; but the short term is evidently a matter of great urgency.

I am specially thinking of equipment. As you told me you are getting some things from France, Belgium, UK, etc. From the telegrams that are coming to

---

445. Letter to the Defence Minister. See notes in item 443.

446. J. K. Galbraith.

447. In his telegram to Dean Rusk of 26 October 1962, Galbraith had said "He wants aid desperately, but agrees we cannot offer it [without a formal request]. I have made guarded reference to the problem of providing aid while the DEFMIN is in office—American inclination is to help India, not Krishna Menon. The discharge of Menon will take Thapar who shares responsibility. He says that Kaul must also go."Kennedy Papers, https://www.jfklibrary.org/Asset-Viewer/Archives/JFKNSF-111-016.aspx Accessed on 21 August 2018.

448. See item 442.

449. Letter to the Defence Minister.

us you will notice that there is every desire to help in various countries. I have just seen the telegram from Canada, USA and UK.

It is not clear to me how far we are taking advantage of this general attitude and offers. We must rather overdo things than underdo them. The immediate need is great. I do not know how I shall explain to Parliament why we have been found lacking in equipment. It is not much good shifting about blame. The fact remains that we have been found lacking and there is an impression that we have approached these things in a somewhat amateurish way.

I should like to know exactly what we have done or are going to do about equipment. We shall have to inform the Emergency Committee of the Cabinet[450] that has been formed.

I suggest that if you are free you might come to see me at 9.30 p.m. tonight at my house.[451]

Yours affectionately,
[Jawaharlal Nehru]

446. To J. K. Galbraith: Publicity about Arms Supplies[452]

November 7, 1962

Dear Mr Ambassador,

Thank you for your letter of November 7.

As you know, we welcome and are very grateful to the United States for the help that is being given to us. There has been no question before us that news of the arms lift should be played down out of deference to any country's susceptibilities. The only question that was placed before us by our military authorities was the necessity of security. This seems to us to be a reasonable way of looking at the matter. It is quite possible that there might be attempts at sabotage if it is known that planes carrying arms are landing at a particular place and a particular time. This need not come in the way of subsequent publicity. It is difficult for us to guarantee safety in landing. I regret to say there are quite a considerable number of people about who might take advantage of any news that might reach them and try to commit sabotage. You may perhaps remember how an Air India Constellation was sabotaged by some one, I think, from Formosa when it was going from Canton to Djakarta. That tragedy is very much present still in our minds and that of the Indian public.[453]

---

450. On Emergency Committee, see https://ids.nic.in/history.htm Accessed on 26 August 2018.
451. Menon did meet Nehru at 9.30 p.m. that night. Engagement Diary 1962.
452. Letter to the US Ambassador.
453. See also item 449.

If any sabotage occurs now, it will have a very bad effect on our public and on our Government.

It should not be difficult to find ways of giving publicity without running this risk of possible sabotage.

As for press correspondents going to Tezpur, we have already relaxed conditions for them and opened a press camp at Tezpur. They will be allowed to go, accompanied by an officer, to the front or near it. It is difficult, however, to allow large numbers of them to wander about the front. Pictures can be taken also, but not of the arrangements made for defence. This, I believe, is the normal practice, and our military insist upon it. There is no question of our being anxious to avoid any publicity of any possible lack of efficiency.

Yours sincerely,
[Jawaharlal Nehru]

447. Soviet MIG Deliveries[454]

MiG Planes by Mid-December:
Soviet to Keep Commitment

New Delhi, Nov. 10 – The Soviet Union has told India that she would stick to her commitments to supply MIG aircraft to India by the contracted delivery dated – middle of December.

[MIGS & SELF RELIANCE]

By R.K. Laxman, (From *The Times of India*, 18 November 1962)

454. Report of a Consultative Committee of Parliamentarians, 10 November 1962; reproduced from the *National Herald*, 11 November 1962, p. 1.

Prime Minister Nehru is understood to have disclosed this at a meeting of the informal consultative committee of Parliament on external affairs, this evening in reply to questions by some members.

The meeting, which lasted an hour, covered questions like India's relations with Nepal, publicity of India's case abroad and the present situation in the border.

Pandit Nehru informed the committee that the President of Czechoslovakia had replied to his communication of October 26, to heads of government, expressing his country's distress at the conflict and favouring a peaceful settlement.[455]

A member drew Pandit Nehru's attention to the reported decision of the Nepali leaders to call off the agitation for restoration of democratic set-up in Nepal and sought Pandit Nehru's view on the impact it would have on Indo-Nepal relations.

Relations with Nepal

Pandit Nehru is understood to have replied that the country's relations with Nepal were improving.

Pandit Nehru is understood to have told the committee that President Ayub Khan's latest letter to him was not very encouraging.[456]

Pandit Nehru regretted that Pakistan press continued to be unfriendly to India in her present situation.

Replying to criticism about external publicity, especially the role of All India Radio, which occupied most of the discussions, Pandit Nehru is understood to have said that there was already a committee consisting of representatives of AIR, the Information and Broadcasting Ministry and the External Publicity Division to coordinate the activities.

455. See item 397.
456. See appendices 42 and 50.

448. To Foreign Journalists: Military Supplies[457]

Manufacture of Arms
US Approached for Equipment

New Delhi, Nov, 12 – Prime Minister Nehru told a group of visiting foreign journalists here today that India had asked the United States for equipment for manufacturing arms.

Pandit Nehru said requests were being put forth continually for US arms.

Pandit Nehru repeated that the Soviet Union had promised to send MIG-21 jet fighters to India and to provide a factory for manufacturing them.

Asked by a correspondent whether Russia would also supply spare parts to the MIG planes, Pandit Nehru said that, if a factory was established in India for the manufacture of MIGs, naturally the factory would produce the spares also.

The group of journalists had been flown to India on the American Arms aircraft.

Replying to a question, Pandit Nehru said he did not think the Chinese would withdraw voluntarily from the territory they now held.

He said the Soviet Union was obviously in an embarrassing position because she was an ally of China and a friend of India. The Soviet Union was seeking a cease fire on the border.

Asked if he thought the Russians had influence in Peking, Pandit Nehru said they must have some, but he did not know how much.

Asked whether the former Defence Minister, Mr Krishna Menon, would return to the leadership of India's UN delegation, Pandit Nehru said he doubted whether he could, but he could not say for certain.

449. To S.C. Bose: Publicity about Arms Supplies[458]

November 15, 1962

Dear Shri Bose,
Thank you for your letter of the 12th November.

Shri T.T. Krishnamachari is already in charge of a highly important portfolio. As such, of course, he will be consulted in many other matters including that of international trade. Some other changes are being made, which you will no doubt notice.

457. Reproduced from the *National Herald*, 13 November 1962, p. 1.
458. Letter to a concerned citizen.

It is true that newspapers have not been very careful in giving news. The difficulty has been, in regard to the arms arriving by air that publicity has often been given by the American representatives.[459]

Yours sincerely,
[Jawaharlal Nehru]

(k) CHINESE INVASION: Sundry Matters

450. To Sri Prakasa: No Time for Full Reply[460]

20th October, 1962

My dear Prakasa,

Thank you for your letter of October 17th.

I shall not refer to the various matters you have touched upon as that would mean writing to you at considerable length. I think, however, that if you had been in touch with subsequent developments you might change your opinion.[461]

For the present we have got something more dangerous and difficult to deal with i.e. the Chinese invasion, especially across the North East Frontier.

Yours affectionately,
[Jawaharlal Nehru]

451. In New Delhi: In Honour of Cyprus President[462]

राष्ट्रपति जी[463], मेयर साहब[464] और भाइयों और बहनों,

आज कार्पोरेशन के मानपत्र में कुछ थोड़ा सा ज़िक्र है साइप्रस के इतिहास का। एक सुन्दर टापू है, छोटा सा लेकिन बहुत पुरानी उसकी कहानी है। एक माने में कहा जाये कि जैसे हिन्दुस्तान का पुराना इतिहास है उसी ज़माने तक इसका भी जाता है। और एक सुन्दर है

---

459. See item 446.
460. Letter to former Governor of Madras and Maharashtra; address: "House Verana", 9 Bellupur, Chakrata Road, Dehra Dun, UP.
461. See appendix 2 and item 43.
462. Speech, 1 November 1962, at a civic reception in the Red Fort. NMML, AIR Tapes, TS No. 11272, NM No. 1959.
463. Archbishop Makarios.
464. Nuruddin Ahmed.

और इसकी संस्कृति मशहूर रही है, ज़्यादातर उस पर और बड़े देशों की हुकूमत रही है। रोम की हुकूमत रही, सिकन्दर की हुई हुकूमत, पुराने मिस्र की हुई, ईरान की हुई, सैकड़ों बरस तक ये रहा क्योंकि छोटा है टापू, लेकिन फिर भी अपनी ज़िंदगी को संभाले रखा उसने, अपनी संस्कृति को संभाला। वहाँ के लोग रहने वाले ज़्यादातर यूनानी हैं, ग्रीक बोलने वाले हैं, कुछ तुर्की भी हैं। हाँ, मैं भूल गया कई सौ वर्ष तक तुर्की हुकूमत वहाँ रही थी, आख़ीर में अंग्रेज़ी हुकूमत हुई और पिछले चन्द बरस में हमने देखा कैसे हिम्मत से वहाँ के रहने वालों ने अपनी आज़ादी के लिए एक जंग चलाई अंग्रेज़ी हुकूमत के ख़िलाफ़, काफ़ी उसका असर दुनिया में हुआ। छोटा सा टापू, बहादुर आदमी और एक बड़े मुल्क, बड़े ताक़तवर मुल्क के ख़िलाफ़ उन्होंने चलाया। आख़ीर में अभी दो-तीन वर्ष की बात है, समझौता हुआ, और एक पेचीदा विधान वहाँ बना है और हमारे आज के मेहमान वहाँ के राष्ट्रपति चुने गये। यह भी ज़रा ग़ैर-मामूली बात है कि एक बड़े धार्मिक पेशवा, मज़हबी पेशवा सियासत में, लड़ाई में उन्होंने बड़ा हिस्सा लिया, उसके आगे हुए और आख़ीर में वो उस अपने छोटे मुल्क के राष्ट्रपति चुने गये, प्रेज़ीडेंट चुने गये। शायद पहली बार हमने यहाँ इस लाल क़िले में कोई ऐसे आदमी का स्वागत किया है जो कि हमने राष्ट्रपति की हैसियत से किया, लेकिन उनकी एक बड़ी जगह है धार्मिक बातों में भी। आर्कबिशप हैं, आप जानते हैं।

तो एक अच्छा है, मुझे बहुत अच्छा लगा कि हमें मौक़ा मिला उनके स्वागत करने को। एक तो, एक बहुत छोटा मुल्क है लेकिन बहुत पुराना है, सभ्य है, संस्कृति उसकी है। दूसरे, उसका इतिहास ऐसा है जो हमें खेंचता है। तीसरे, ख़ासतौर से इस ज़माने में जो उन्होंने हिम्मत और बहादुरी से अपनी आज़ादी हासिल की, जिनकी लड़ाई में हमारी पूरी हमदर्दी और सहानुभूति उनके साथ थी। मुझे याद है कि छः-सात वर्ष हुए जब बांडुंग की कॉन्फ्रेंस हुई थी उस वक़्त साइप्रस आज़ाद नहीं था, वो अपनी जंगे आज़ादी में पड़ा था तो आर्कबिशप साहब जो आज राष्ट्रपति हैं साइप्रस के, वो आये थे बांडुंग में, और लोगों से मिलने को

और अपना, अपने मुल्क का कहा जाये मुक़दमा पेश करने को आज़ादी के लिए। उसी वक़्त से, मैं भी मिला था उनसे वहाँ, और मेरे ऊपर असर हुआ था उनकी शख़्सियत का। आप देखेंगे कि दूर से देखने से भी असर होगा आप पर उनका, बग़ैर जाने भी। उसके बाद, ख़ैर पिछले दो-तीन वर्ष से मिलने का इत्तिफ़ाक़ हुआ लन्दन में जो वहाँ प्राइम मिनिस्टरों की कॉन्फ्रेंस होती है, प्राइम मिनिस्टरों की या राष्ट्रपति की, आप भी साइप्रस के नुमाइन्दे होकर वहाँ आते थे, वहाँ मुलाक़ात हुई। तो अच्छा है कि हम आपकी एक बहादुर और बड़े आदमी की क़द्र करें, अच्छा है कि हम मुल्क की क़दर करें जिसकी नुमाइन्दगी और जिसके नेता हैं ये। और ऐसे मौक़े पर जो बातें उन्होंने कहीं यहां पर, या दो-एक रोज़ और जगह भी कहीं, जो उन्होंने हमदर्दी का इज़हार अपनी सहानुभूति का किया, जो हमारे ऊपर एक हमला हुआ है, ज़बरदस्त चीनी हमला, और जिसका हम कोशिश कर रहे हैं पूरीतौर से मुक़ाबला करने की। तो उन्होंने, आपने सुना पूरी हमदर्दी का इज़हार किया।

ज़ाहिर है साइप्रस जैसा छोटा टापू कोई ऐसी मदद तो हमारी कर नहीं सकता, कहा जाये हथियारी मदद, फ़ौजी मदद, लेकिन इसकी मदद फिर भी निहायत क़ीमती है हमारे लिए क्योंकि एक सभ्य सांस्कृतिक देश है और अभी ख़ुद अपनी आज़ादी की लड़ाई से निकला है। तो उनकी सहानुभूति एक बड़ी मदद है। मदद ख़ाली हथियार की नहीं होती है, और उससे भी ज़्यादा क़ीमती होती है। इसलिए मैं उनका बहुत मशकूर हूँ और बहुत-बहुत शुक्रिया उनको अदा करता हूँ जो बातें उन्होंने इस ख़ास मौक़े पर जब हम दिक़्क़त में पड़े हैं, कशमकश है, कठिनाई है, उन्होंने अपनी सहानुभूति का पूरीतौर से ख़ुद आश्वासन दिया और अपने लोगों की तरफ़ से भी।

यों तो ज़ाहिर है कि जो कुछ हमारे ऊपर मुश्किलें आयी हैं उसका सामना हम करेंगे, कर रहे हैं। और मैं आपसे कहूँ और आप जानते हैं इसको कि इस मौक़े पर जिस तरह से हिन्दुस्तान भर में एक उत्साह के साथ, जोश के साथ, उत्साह और जोश का इज़हार हुआ है और बहुत सारे आपस के छोटे झगड़े अलग रख दिये गये हैं, इस बड़ी बात के सामने उससे आप सभी को और मेरे ऊपर बड़ा असर हुआ। जो हमारे बहादुर सिपाही सरहद पर लड़ रहे हैं, हिम्मत दिखायी, बहादुरी दिखायी उन्होंने, उसमें कोई कमी नहीं है। ये कहिये कि कमी तो रही वो जो हमारे मुख़ालिफ़ीन हैं, जो हमारे दुश्मन हो गये, उनकी सभ्यता में, कि उन्होंने यकायक बहुत बड़ी फ़ौज से हमारे देश पर हमला किया। यह कोई सरहदी मामला नहीं रहा कि सरहद पर बैठकर फुटकर हो गयी इधर झड़प, उधर झड़प। जब कोई इत्ती बड़ी, लम्बी, चौड़ी फ़ौज से उतर आये हमारे मुल्क में, पहाड़ों से और बड़े-बड़े तोप और बन्दूक़ लेके, तो वो एक सरहद की बात नहीं है, वो तो एक हमला है, वो तो एक आक्रमण है देशके ऊपर। इसका हमें सामना करना है, हम करेंगे, हम कर रहे हैं और करेंगे और जित्ते दिन ज़रूरत हुई उत्ते दिन करेंगे, क्योंकि ऐसे मामले में कोई आधे रास्ते पर तसफ़िया नहीं हो सकता है, कोई अपनी इज़्ज़त और आज़ादी की निस्बत तसफ़िया नहीं करता है। यों तो हम तसफ़ियाकुन, हैं, हम अमन चाहते हैं, हम अमन का रास्ता ढूँढते हैं और ढूँढते रहेंगे, लेकिन अमन जिसकी क़ीमत हो अपनी इज़्ज़त को गँवा देना, वो अमन नहीं है।

तो मुझे खुशी है—खुशी तो कमज़ोर लफ़्ज़ है—हिन्दुस्तान में जो आबोहवा पैदा हुई है, आप लोगों में, दिल्ली शहर में, और सारे हिन्दुस्तान में, एकदम से एक जोश चढ़ा है जिसमें हिन्दुस्तान की एकता और मज़बूत हुई है और जिससे ज़ाहिर होता है कित्ती ताक़त छिपी हुई है हिन्दुस्तान में हैं। ज़ाहिर भी है और छिपी हुई भी है। उसको देखकर एक माने में खुशी होती है कि ऐसी मुसीबत हमारे ऊपर आयी जिसने ग़फ़लत से लोगों को निकालकर जगा दिया। कोशिश हम करें कि यह बात क़ायम रहे और जो एकता क़ायम हुई है, मज़बूती, वो रहे और हम छोटे-छोटे झगड़ों में न पड़ें।

एक बात मैं आपसे अर्ज़ करूँ—कल शायद एक यहां साम्यवादी दल के दफ़्तर में हमला हुआ, जला भी दिया गया कुछ। अब साम्यवादी दल से कोई लोग नाखुश हों, ठीक है, उनकी अजीब नीति है, पता नहीं चलता साफ़-साफ़, कभी कुछ कहते हैं, कभी कुछ

कहें, नाराज़गी हो। सब ठीक है, लेकिन ये नाराज़गी के माने नहीं हैं कि इस तरह से बदतमीज़ी की जाये और हम बदनाम हों और मुल्कों में, और जगह, ये ताक़त की निशानी नहीं है। एक बहुत बड़े और ताक़तवर मुल्क का मुक़ाबला हमें करना है और आप ये एक हुड़दंगापन—जाकर मकान जला दें, बदतमीज़ी करें, ये कोई ताक़त की निशानी है। आप समझें, ये तो कमज़ोरी की निशानी, बुढ़िया औरतों की बातें हैं ये, इंसानों की नहीं हैं कि बैठकर कोने में कोसें और जाकर एक चिंगारी लगा दें, आग लगा दें एक भीड़ जाकर। कहाँ की हिम्मत की निशानी है, बहादुरी की निशानी है, शान की निशानी है, सभ्यता की निशानी है, किस चीज़ की निशानी है? बदतमीज़ी की निशानी है, नालायक़ी की निशानी है। तो ये बातें नहीं होनी चाहियें, दिल्ली शहर को बदनाम करना हिन्दुस्तान को बदनाम करना है, हमारी ताक़त इस तरह से निकल जाये, ताक़त असल मुक़ाबला करने की फिर कहां रहे। ये कोई मौज़ू नहीं था मेरा इस वक्त इस चीज़ का ज़िक्र करना, लेकिन मैंने सोचा आपके सामने खड़ा हूँ तो मैं इसको कह दूँ क्योंकि हमें शान से इस काम को करना है, शान से हमें लड़ाई लड़नी है, शान से जीतना है और ये शान नहीं है, ये बिल्कुल नामुनासिब बातें हैं। ख़ैर, तो मैं नहीं चाहता, मैं उम्मीद करता हूँ आपकी मदद मिलेगी इसमें, कि हम अपने इस मौक़े पर जबकि हमारा इम्तिहान है दुनिया के सामने कि हिन्दुस्तान में कित्ती हिम्मत है, कित्ती शराफ़त है, कित्ता डिसिप्लिन है और हरेक की, दुनिया की आँखें हमारी तरफ़ हैं। तो हम एक अच्छी तस्वीर हिन्दुस्तान की और अपनी खेंचे दुनिया के सामने। कुछ बहुत बातें हो चुकी हैं, इंतज़ामात कुछ और भी हो रहे हैं जिसकी इत्तला आपको चन्द रोज़ में मिल जायेगी। इस माने में कि जो कुछ गवर्नमेंट करती है, जो कुछ फ़ौज करती है वो तो करती ही है, लेकिन इत्ते लोग हैं जो कि कुछ न कुछ चाहते हैं मदद करना, ये करना, उनको मौक़ा मिले। तो आप जानते हैं बहुत लोग पैसे दे रहे हैं, सोना दे रहे हैं, और भी तरीक़े हैं बहुत कुछ। तो इनके लिए कुछ शहरी लोगों की, सिटीज़ंस की कमेटियाँ बनेंगी। इरादा यह है कि एक केन्द्रीय कमेटी हो सारे हिन्दुस्तान की और अलग-अलग शहरों में बनें, जिसमें लोग तरह-तरह से मदद करें। ख़ाली पैसे और सोने वग़ैरा की नहीं, वो तो है ही, लेकिन इस बात में भी कि कोई ग़लत बात न हो। फ़र्ज़ कीजिये कि क़ीमतें न बढ़ जायें ज़रूरत से ज़्यादा। कोई वजह नहीं है बढ़ने की, लेकिन ऐसा मौक़ा देखकर अक्सर लोग मुल्क का नहीं समझते, जनता का नहीं सोचते, अपने फ़ायदे के लिए बढ़ा देते हैं, यह ग़लत बात है। तो इसका सरकारी इंतज़ाम जो है वो तो होगा और आपको मालूम होगा कि एक क़ानून है और अभी चार रोज़ हुए, पाँच रोज़ हुए बनाया गया है, डिफ़ेंस ऑफ़ इंडिया एक्ट, (Defence of India Act) हिन्दुस्तान की रक्षा के लिए क़ानून बना है जो कि सख़्त इख़्तियार देता है हुकूमत को ऐसी बातों के ख़िलाफ़ जो कि मुल्क के साथ कोई ग़द्दारी करे। मुल्क से ग़द्दारी होती है तरह-तरह की—एक तो मोटी तौर से होती है, दूसरे यह भी ग़द्दारी है कि पैसा बनायें, औरों की मुसीबत बढ़ायें, मुल्क की, यह भी ग़द्दारी है। तो इस सबकी रोकथाम करने को गवर्नमेंट जो कुछ करे वो तो करेगी, लेकिन वो चीज़ ऐसी है जिसमें ज़रूरत है आम लोगों की मदद की। आम लोगों की मदद इस माने में नहीं कि हरेक अपने रास्ते पर चल रहा है, जो चाहे करता है, इस माने में

नहीं कि हुल्लड़बाज़ी करते हैं, जैसे कल हुई, वो मदद नहीं है, वोतो और नुकसानदेह है करना। यह भी मैं आपसे कहूँगा, मुझे पसंद नहीं है, पैसे की ज़रूरत है, इसके माने नहीं हैं हरेक आदमी पैसे जमा कर रहा है, मालूम नहीं कहाँ जाये वो, वो भी क़ायदे से होना चाहिये जिनके पास, जिनको अख़्तियार हो जमा करने का, उनके पास देना चाहिये, उसके बहुत जगह हैं, बैंक में आप दे सकते हैं सीधे जाकर। ख़ैर, जो कुछ हो, नहीं तो ख़ामख़ाँ के लिए ग़लत आदमी उससे फ़ायदा उठायेंगे, लोगों के जोश से। लेकिन ख़ासतौर से जो कमेटियाँ होंगी उनका काम होगा कि ये ग़लत अफ़वाहें फैलती हैं उनको रोकें, और लोगों में कोई परेशानी न बढ़े। क्योंकि ज़रूरत भी होती है आम मौक़े पर कि दिल और दिमाग़ ठंडे हों, बहुत मज़बूत हों, बाहें मज़बूत हों। तो इसमें हम चाहते हैं आप लोगों की, सभी की मदद हो। और सरकारी काम के अलावा, ख़ासकर नागरिक काम होगा जो कि एक केन्द्रीय कमेटी होगी और सब सूबों में होगी। शायद, मुझे ठीक मालूम नहीं, आपके दिल्ली शहर में भी मेयर साहब कुछ ऐसा शुरु करें। हम नहीं चाहते कि उसमें कोई गवर्नमेंट का हाथ हो ज़्यादा, गवर्नमेंट की मदद है वो एक ख़ासतौर से ग़ैर सरकारी चीज़ होगी। तो उसकी ख़बर भी आपको चन्द रोज़ में मिल जायेगी। अभी दो रोज़ के अन्दर या तीन रोज़ में नेशनल डेवलपमेंट काउंसिल (National Development Council) होने वाली है हमारी, उसमें सूबों के सब मुख्यमंत्री आयेंगे, चीफ़ मिनिस्टर्स वग़ैरा, इन बातों पर ग़ौर करेंगे, क्या करना है, क्या नहीं करना है। ग़ौर तो रोज़ ही होता है, लेकिन उनके साथ करेंगे, और उसकी ख़बरें आपको पहुँचेंगी और, और भी आपको इत्तला करने का ठीक इंतज़ाम होगा। और मुझे उम्मीद है कि आपका उसमें पूरा सहयोग, मदद मिलेगी। सहयोग मिल रहा है, आपके दिल हैं इस तरफ़, लेकिन मैं क़ायदे से चाहता हूँ और कि उसका पूरा फ़ायदा उठा सके मुल्क।

मैंने बहुत सारी बातें कह दीं, राष्ट्रपति जी मुझे माफ़ करेंगे, कुछ अपने दिल में बातें थीं, आप इत्ते लोग यहाँ जमा हैं मैंने सोचा आपसे कह दूँ। असल में तो हम जमा हुए इनका स्वागत करने, इस्तक़बाल करने, आपने किया, आपकी कार्पोरेशन ने किया, मेयर साहब के ज़रिये से, और मैं भी उसमें कुछ अपनी आवाज़ जोड़ देना चाहता था, वो मैंने किया।

शुक्रिया!

[Translation begins:

Mr President,[465] Mr Mayor,[466] Brothers and Sisters,
There is a brief mention of the history of Cyprus in the Manpatra [Welcome Address] that the Corporation has presented to the President. It is a beautiful little island with a history almost as old as that of India. It has a very rich culture.

465. See note 463 in this section.
466. See note 464 in this section.

It has been under foreign domination most of the time, first under Rome, then Alexander, Egypt, Iran and so on, for centuries because of its size. And yet it has retained its cultural identity. The majority of the people of Cyprus speak Greek, Turkish is also spoken. Oh, yes, I had forgotten. The Turks ruled Cyprus for centuries. Ultimately, the British took over and we have seen how in the last few years, the people of Cyprus have been fighting for freedom with great valour. It has made a deep impression upon the world. A small little island of brave people have taken on the might of a vast empire. Finally, just a few years ago, a compromise was reached and a complex constitution drawn up. Our guest today was elected as the President. This in itself is rather unique that a great religious head like him should have played a key role in the political struggle for freedom. He led the movement and was ultimately elected President of that small nation. I think it is for the first time that we are welcoming a man of the Archbishop's stature who is not only a great political leader but a religious head as well.

So, I am happy to have this opportunity of welcoming the Archbishop. For one thing, Cyprus is a small but ancient country, civilised and cultured. Secondly, its history draws us closer together. Thirdly, all our sympathies are with them for the manner in which they have fought for and won freedom. I remember that even six or seven years ago, at the time of the Bandung Conference, Cyprus was not independent. It was in the throes of its freedom struggle. The Archbishop who is the President of Cyprus today had come to attend the Bandung Conference and to present his country's case for freedom. I had met him then and was deeply impressed by his personality. You will find that you are impressed by him even if you catch a glimpse of him from afar, even if you are not acquainted with him. Anyhow, in the last two or three years I have had the opportunity of meeting him in London at the Prime Ministers' Conference and Heads of State conferences. So it is fitting that we should honour a brave and great man like him. It is fitting too that we should honour the country which he represents. He has expressed here and elsewhere his sympathy for us in our troubles, with the Chinese and our efforts to throw out the aggressor. It is obvious that a small little island cannot help militarily. And yet its help is invaluable to us because it is a civilised, cultured nation and has just emerged as an independent country after a long struggle. Its sympathies also help because mere arms and ammution alone cannot help. I am very grateful to him and give my thanks for the sympathy that he has expressed in our time of trouble and tension.

It is obvious that we shall face the problems that we are facing resolutely. The wave of enthusiasm and patriotism which is sweeping the country, setting the petty squabbles and wrangling to face a grave challenge, have made a deep

685

impression upon all of us. Our brave soldiers fighting at the front have shown great valour and courage. There has been no dearth of bravery on our part. The shortcoming lies in the culture or our enemy that they should have suddenly launched an attack on our borders. This is no mere border skirmish because vast armies have rolled down the mountainside armed with powerful guns and cannons. It is a full-fledged attack on our country. We have to face it and we shall continue to do so for as long as it takes. There is no stopping midway or compromises. No nation can compromise its honour and freedom. Normally we are a peace loving nation and we shall continue to look for peaceful solution. But peace maintained at the cost of our honour is no peace at all.

I am happy to see the electric change in the atmosphere in India, in Delhi and all over the country, and the wave of enthusiasm that has been sweeping the people binding together. It is obvious that there is a great latent strength in India. In a sense, it makes one happy that such a crisis has descended upon us for it has shaken the people out of their complacency. We should make an effort to hold on to this unity and strength and not to slide back into petty quarrels.

I would like to mention one thing. Yesterday there was an attack on the Communist Party office and parts of it were burnt. Some people may be unhappy with the policies of the Communists. It is indeed strange. They say different things at different times. But anger should not lead us to behave in an uncivilised manner which brings us disrepute in the eyes of other nations. This is not a sign of strength. We have to face the might of a powerful nation and indulging in such activities as burning buildings does not add to our strength. It is on the contrary a sign of weakness, something that old women might do, to sit in a corner and heap curses or to go out in a mob setting fire. Is this a sign of culture, civilised behavior or bravery? It is a sign of helplessness, of uncivilised behavior. Such things ought not to happen. It brings Delhi and the whole of India into disrepute. We cannot afford to fritter away our strength in such futile activities at a time when we have to show a united front. It is perhaps not quite appropriate that I should mention this at this gathering. But I thought that since I was here, I should say this because we must conduct ourselves with dignity. We must fight our battles and win them with dignity. What we are doing is most improper and detracts from our dignity. Well, I hope that we shall have your full cooperation and help at a time when India is being tested in the eyes of the world. All eyes are upon us to see how much courage and discipline and civility there is in us. We must render a good account of ourselves in the eyes of the world.

We have taken a number of steps about which you will be informed shortly. The government and the armed forces will of course do what they have to do. But we want to give full opportunities to the large numbers of people who want to help. People are contributing cash and gold and helping in various ways. We shall be forming citizen's committees for this purpose. The intention is to have a central committee with branches all over the country to which people can send in their contributions. The committees will ensure that there is no misuse of funds and anti-national activities. For instance, prices should not rise needlessly. Very often people try to take advantage of a national crisis to line their own pockets. That is wrong. We shall be issuing an ordinance against such activities. You may be aware that the Defence of India Act has been passed a few days ago which arms the government with vast powers to deal stringently with people who indulge in anti-national activities. Anti-national activities can be of many kinds. One is the general way in which it is understood. Raising prices and hoarding, etc. are also anti-national activities. The government will take strong measures to control such activities. But we need the full cooperation of the people also to deal with them. That does not mean that everybody does what they like or indulging in hooliganism as it happened yesterday. Such things only hinder, not help, the nation.

Secondly, though we need money, I do not like the idea of every individual taking up collections because nobody know where the money goes. Collection of funds must be done methodically. Contributions should be given only to authorised individuals and institutions like banks. Otherwise some individuals may take advantage of the people's enthusiasm.

But the most important duty of the committees that will be formed would be to scotch rumours which unnecessarily create worry and panic among the people. In times of crisis, the people must be calm and strong. We need your help in this. The citizens must participate fully in such activities. I think the Mayor of Delhi will form a committee. We do not wish for too much governmental pressure in such committees. They should be wholly non-governmental. Very soon the National Development Council is to meet which all the Chief Ministers will attend. We will deliberate on the various steps that need to be taken. Such deliberations are going all the time. But these meetings with the Chief Ministers will be important. You will be kept informed of all the decisions that are taken and I hope that we will get your full cooperation and help. I know that you are wholeheartedly with us but I want that your cooperation should be put to good use so that the nation can benefit fully.

I hope the President will forgive me for straying away and sharing my thoughts. I felt that it would be a good idea to do so when you are gathered here in such large numbers. As a matter of fact, we are gathered here to welcome our honoured guest which the Corporation and the Mayor have done on your behalf and I have added my voice to theirs.

Thank you.

Translation ends]

452. To D. Shankar: Defence Production[467]

November 8, 1962

My dear Shankar,

As you know, some changes have been made in the Defence Ministry. Possibly some further changes or additions might be made there. I am now in charge of the Ministry, but it is not possible for me to devote enough time for this important work.

I am particularly interested in Defence Production of which you are in charge. This has done well, and I gather that the tempo of work has increased greatly in recent weeks. I want this to be kept up and for us to keep production at the highest possible level. I am sure you will be able to do it. You will have all the help that I can give you.

I gather that there are some shortages in regard to some machinery. These must be made good as soon as possible. I suggest that you might see Shri S.S. Khera, Cabinet Secretary, about them.

As soon as I am a little more free, I should like you to come and see me and tell me about the work of the factories engaged in Defence Production. Meanwhile, I am especially writing to you to convey to you and others engaged in Defence Production work my great interest in this work and my appreciation of the great progress made in it.

Yours sincerely
Jawaharlal Nehru

453. To S.S. Khera: Shortages in Military Supplies[468]

November 8, 1962

My dear Khera,

I am anxious that owing to the changes in the Defence Ministry, Defence Production should not suffer in any way. I am, therefore, asking Shri Raghuramaiah particularly to look after Defence Production till such time as further changes are made.[469]

Shri Krishna Menon gave me a paper today about the production in Ordnance Factories. I enclose this. This shows a considerable increase in

---

467. Letter to the Controller-General of Defence Production, Ministry of Defence.
468. Letter to the Cabinet Secretary.
469. See item 325.

production last year. I gather that the cost of production has gone down because of better work being done by the workers and there being no surplus labour. Hence the actual production is somewhat greater than the figures indicate.

The important thing to consider immediately is the filling up of shortages which are mentioned in this paper. Some of these shortages, if not quickly remedied, will affect production. Thus, the Filling Factories are quite essential for ammunition. I think this matter should be looked into immediately.

Shri Krishna Menon has given me another paper about winter clothing and equipment.

The President has written to me accepting Shri Krishna Menon's resignation. I am, therefore, asking him to have a formal announcement made to this effect tomorrow. After this announcement has been made I should like Shri Krishna Menon's two letters to me offering his resignation to be sent to the press. Also, my letter in reply to him. Copies of these papers are enclosed. Please have these sent to the press after the Presidential announcement.

You might keep in touch with Shri Krishna Menon during the next few days. This will help you to tie up loose ends.

Yours sincerely,
[Jawaharlal Nehru]

454. To S. Bhagwantham: Food for the Army[470]

November 8, 1962

My dear Bhagwantham,
The Food and Agriculture Minister has sent me a letter which I enclose. This relates to certain concentrated foodstuffs, ready to eat, which might be useful for our defence forces under conditions of emergency. I am sending this note to you together with the samples he has sent. They look to me to be palatable and good.

I do not quite know who is dealing with this matter in Defence. Will you kindly get in touch with him?

Yours sincerely,
Jawaharlal Nehru

---

470. Letter to the Scientific Adviser to the Ministry of Defence. PMO, File No. 31/125/62-71-PMS, Sr. No. 2-A.

455. To H.K. Mahtab: Soldiers' Frostbite[471]

November 12, 1962

My dear Mahtab,

Your letter of November 12.

I agree with you that photographs of the kind you sent me should not be published. The cases of frost-bite are of the soldiers who were dispersed by the Chinese on the 20th October and who wandered about the mountains for several days without adequate covering or food before they managed to get back to our headquarters. This has nothing to do with proper footwear not being supplied to the soldiers. Two pairs of Army boots were supplied to each.

Yours sincerely,
[Jawaharlal Nehru]

456. To Cardinal Valerian Gracias: Padres for the Army[472]

November 12, 1962

My dear Cardinal,

Your letter of the 9th November. I have enquired into the matter from the Defence Ministry. I understand that Padres are authorised for each unit, station or formation where the strength of Roman Catholic or Protestant soldiers is not less than 120. There are at present ten Roman Catholic Padres in the Army. They are all working in a civilian capacity. None of them accepted combatisation in the first instance, but one has now agreed to get combatised although the time limit for the same has expired. The question of extending the time limit up to March 1963 in order to accommodate him and any others who may now reconsider and accept combatisation, is under consideration.

---

471. Letter to Congress MP; address: 36 Canning Lane, New Delhi.
472. Letter to the Archbishop of Bombay, 12 November 1962; address: Casa Generalizia della Congregazione di Gesu-Maria, Via Nomentana 325, Roma.

A proposal, for permitting the employment of civilian religious teachers in NEFA area is at present under consideration in Army Headquarters. It is also being considered that one Roman Catholic Padre and one Protestant Padre should be attached to each Divisional Headquarters.

With all good wishes,

Yours sincerely,
[Jawaharlal Nehru]

457. To Morarji Desai: Gold Bonds Purchase Offer[473]

November 16, 1962

My dear Morarji,

I enclose a letter which was handed to me this morning. This is from the Tilkayat of Nathdwara Temple who is engaged in litigation with the Rajasthan Government.[474] He is not a very desirable person. However, he is making an offer, which you might consider, about purchasing Gold Bonds.

Yours sincerely,
[Jawaharlal Nehru]

458. On Refugees from Chinese Occupied Territory[475]

Short Notice Question No. 22 – Lok Sabha by Shri Raghunath Singh[476]

I regret I am unable to accept this Short Notice Question. Information about the areas of Indian territory under the illegal occupation of the Chinese and the number of Indians residing at present in these occupied territories is not readily available. Nor has there been any proper census of refugees who have come over from the Chinese occupied territory.

2. The situation is a fluid one and attacks and counter-attacks are taking place. It would be against our security interests to make an attempt to give detailed information on these points.

---

473. Letter to the Finance Minister.
474. Tilkayat Govindlal Ji.
475. Note, 16 November 1962, for the Lok Sabha Secretariat.
476. Congress Member from Varanasi.

459. To V.K.R.V. Rao: Maintaining Decency in Conflict[477]

November 16, 1962

My dear Rao,

Thank you for your letter of the 14th November and your good wishes which I value.

We are in for a hard time, but I have no doubt that we will win through. I hope that in doing so we shall not descend to hatred and vulgarity but try to maintain our standards.

Yours sincerely,
[Jawaharlal Nehru]

460. To B.P. Sinha: Appreciation[478]

November 17, 1962

My dear Chief Justice,

Thank you for your letter of November 16th, with which you have sent a copy of your letter to the President. I am sure the President will appreciate, as I do, the step you and your colleagues have taken.

Thank you also for the letter from Shri S. Pandey of the University of Hawaii. A receipt will be sent to him directly.

Yours sincerely,
[Jawaharlal Nehru]

461. To M. Muhammad Ismail: Appreciating Son[479]

November 17, 1962

Dear Mr Muhammad Ismail,

Thank you for your letter of the 16th November. I have read the copy of your son's letter with pleasure. It does him credit and I congratulate you on having such a gallant son.[480]

---

477. Letter to the Director of the Institute of Economic Growth, University Enclave, Delhi-6.
478. Letter to the Chief Justice of India.
479. Letter to Lok Sabha MP from Kerala, IUML; address: 5D Western Court, New Delhi.
480. He offered to enlist in the army.

I think that it will be far better if he finds some work connected with the war effort in Madras. The crisis we are facing is likely to last for a considerable time and every one of us will have to give our best to it.

I am returning your son's letter.

Yours sincerely,
[Jawaharlal Nehru]

462. To K.M. Cariappa: Balm to Wound[481]

November 19, 1962

My dear Cariappa,

I have just received your letter of the 18th November. Thank you for it.

I am sorry you have a feeling that I have been belittling you in the public. It is true that some things you did or said irritated me and I thought them quite wrong. Also, at once I used a phrase about you which I regretted afterwards. Apart from this, I do not remember having belittled you in the public or elsewhere. Anyhow I should like to assure you that this has not been so. In some matters we have not agreed, but I have always respected you and felt some affection for you.

Yours sincerely,
[Jawaharlal Nehru]

463. To Partap Singh Kairon: Protecting Bhakra Nangal[482]

November 20, 1962

My dear Partap Singh,

Your letter of November 15th about the protection of Bhakra Nangal. I quite agree with you about the importance of this vital installation. As a matter of fact, at present with our resources we are wholly unable to undertake such protection

---

481. Letter to a former Chief of the Army Staff; address: 10 Janpath, New Delhi.
482. Letter to the Chief Minister of Punjab.

of important installations. But we are trying to make some arrangements with other countries for this purpose and I hope they will be successful.

Yours sincerely,
[Jawaharlal Nehru]

464. To J.D. Weerasekera: Socialism Hurt[483]

November 21, 1962

Dear Shri Weerasekera,
Thank you for your letter of the 14th November and your good wishes on the occasion of my birthday.

The invasion of India by China has not only injured us in many ways, but it has also been a great blow to many things we believe in. I quite agree with you that it has hurt the cause of socialism. We have decided not to submit to this, however long the struggle may last.

Yours sincerely,
[Jawaharlal Nehru]

465. For the Armed Forces Flag Day[484]

The Armed Forces Flag Day occurs this year at a time of big crisis when our dear motherland has been invaded and our armed forces are fighting the invader. Thus this day has a special significance and all of us must show our high appreciation of the courage and devotion to duty of our armed forces.

Indeed all of us in the country must function as soldiers of India and work for India's freedom and integrity in whatever capacity our work may lie. Nevertheless, the major effort has to be borne by our armed forces and we must send our greetings and good wishes to them on this day. The donations we give will only be a minor way of showing our appreciation.

---

483. Letter to the Chief Government Whip, House of Representatives, Colombo.
484. Message, 22 November 1962. PMO, File No. 9/2/62-PMP, Vol. 8, Sr. No. 7-A. Published in the newspapers 7 December 1962.

466. To Lal Bahadur Shastri: Messy Evacuation from Tezpur[485]

November 23, 1962

My dear Lal Bahadur,

I understand that some instructions sent from the Home Ministry about evacuation of people in enemy threatened areas created a lot of trouble in Tezpur. From what I have heard of these instructions, they seem to me very unhappy. It is said that they were passed by the Cabinet. I do not remember. Anyhow we did not consider them in any detail.[486]

I think you might bring these matters up at the Cabinet meeting tomorrow so that they might be amended where necessary.

Yours affectionately,
[Jawaharlal Nehru]

467. To Swaran Singh: Siliguri Traffic Jam[487]

November 23, 1962

My dear Swaran Singh,

Lal Bahadur and others who went with him to Assam have told me of the terrible jam at Siliguri and elsewhere of railway carriages, trucks, etc. Vast numbers are held up. This probably is not the fault of the Railway people at all but of the civil authorities who could not take charge of the stuff sent in these trucks. I hope that Lal Bahadur's visit and the instructions he gave will help in unloading these trucks. Anyhow, you might also take some active interest in this matter and see that this jam is completely removed.

Yours sincerely,
[Jawaharlal Nehru]

485. Letter to the Home Minister.
486. See item 286.
487. Letter to the Minister for Railways.

468. To Mohanlal Sukhadia: Postpone NEFA Visit[488]

November 28, 1962

My dear Sukhadia,

Your letter of the 26th November. It will be a good thing for you to go to NEFA. But I think you might delay your visit for some little time. At the present moment, every person who goes there is a burden to the Army and other authorities there. Meanwhile, you might find out from our Defence authorities where the Rajasthan people are.

Yours sincerely,
[Jawaharlal Nehru]

469. To Prabhakar B. Mehta: Too Many Visitors to Assam[489]

November 29, 1962

Dear Shri Mehta,

Your letter of the 27th November. I entirely agree with you that it is not desirable for a large number of MPs to visit Assam. The story about forty MPs going there is due to some misunderstanding. Anyhow, that misunderstanding has been cleared, and I do not think they are going.[490]

We are not encouraging people to go to Assam because they are a burden in present circumstances there. Also, it is not easy to arrange transport. What we have said is that if some people are prepared to go there and spend some months there in the villages etc., looking after themselves, then they can go. At present, Shri U.N. Dhebar[491] has gone there and is going from village to village and is doing good work.

Yours sincerely,
[Jawaharlal Nehru]

---

488. Letter to the Chief Minister of Rajasthan.
489. Letter; address: Morarji Mansion, Nepean Sea Road, Bombay 26.
490. See item 321.
491. Lok Sabha Mp, Congress, from Rajkot, Gujarat. Former Chairman of Scheduled Areas and Scheduled Tribes Commission, 1960-1961.

470. For the Defence Forces: Armed Forces Flag Day[492]

My good wishes to our Defence Forces on the Armed Forces Flag Day. Our Defence Forces represent much that we cherish national unity, discipline, service of our country and people and protection of our far-flung frontiers. As our responsibilities grow, our Defence Forces have to carry greater burdens and responsibilities also. I send them my appreciation of their work, and I hope that all our people will also show their appreciation by contributing to the Flag Day Fund.

492. Message, 30 November 1962. PMO, File No. 9/2/61-PMP, Vol. 8, Sr. No. 99-A.

V. Miscellaneous

471. To Richard J. Margolis: Arnold Michaelis[1]

October 2, 1962

Dear Mr Margolis,
I have your letter of September 28, 1962. I have met Mr Arnold Michaelis[2] on some occasions. I do not pretend to know him very well. I rather doubt if he knows more about me than any man alive. That is a big statement to make about any one. Nor can I say anything about Mr Michaelis' special ability to explore man's feelings and convictions.

Yours sincerely,
[Jawaharlal Nehru]

472. To P. Subbarayan: Get Well[3]

3rd October, 1962

My dear Subbarayan,
When I arrived in Bombay two days ago on my return from abroad, I enquired about you. Last time I saw you in Bombay you were not quite well and I was anxious to find out how you were. I was told that you were in Madras and had not been well. I was sorry to learn this.

I have now learnt that you are very much better physically, but continue to be a little depressed and do not take your food properly. I hope you will get over this feeling and take adequate nourishment. I am sure that you will recover completely soon.

Why should you feel at all depressed? Anyone can fall ill and get well again. As you know, I was rather ill for a short period many months ago. After that I suffered from the reaction of anti-biotic medicines. (I gather you have had

---

1. Letter to Richard J. Margolis (1930-1991), author, freelance writer and columnist; address: Pageant, 26 West 47th Street, New York 36, New York, USA.
2. Arnold Michaelis (1915-1997), documentary film maker and TV interviewer. See also SWJN/SS/49/item 348. Interviews available at http://www.libs.uga.edu/media/ collections/audioradio/michaelis.htmlArnold Michaelis' interviews with Nehru, Audio, 1958 -- 1964. Date accessed 12 June 2018.
3. Letter to the Governor of Maharashtra; address: State Guest House, Mount Road, Madras. See item 7.

a similar experience). Now I am perfectly fit and have been declared so by a number of eminent doctors. I am sure you will be completely fit soon provided you set about it and take proper food, etc. I hope you will do so.[4]

Thank you for your letter which I have received on my return here.

Yours affectionately,
[Jawaharlal Nehru]

473. To Ali Yavar Jung: Leonardo da Vinci[5]

October 5, 1962

My dear Ali,

Thank you for your letter of the 27th September and for sending me a number of pictures of the house of Leonardo da Vinci. I am much interested to see these. I have always been a great admirer of Leonardo, and I think him one of the few very great men in history.

I enjoyed my brief stay in Paris. Thank you for it.

Yours sincerely,
[Jawaharlal Nehru]

474. To Vijaya Lakshmi Pandit: Stirling Castle in Simla[6]

October 6, 1962

[Nan dear,]

I have just received your letter of October 3rd with its enclosures. I know nothing about this matter and there is no question of my going to Simla for the purpose.

---

4. See also item 480.
5. Letter to the Ambassador in Paris.
6. A handwritten annotation by an unidentified person reads: "Re: opening of Stirling Castle in Simla." The Stirling Castle was purchased by "Save the Children Fund" for the children of Tibetan refugees in 1962 to function as an orphanage and school.

I suppose all you can do is to inform Saroj of Nabha[7] about the letter from Alexandra Metcalfe.[8] I do not think we should get entangled in this matter which has been carried on without consulting us or any reference to us.

I am returning the two letters you sent me.

[Jawahar]

475. To Christopher Mayhew: Acknowledging Book *Coexistence Plus*[9]

October 9, 1962

Dear Mr Mayhew,

Thank you for your letter of 28th September which I have just received together with a copy of your little book *Coexistence Plus*.[10] I shall gladly read this book.

It seems to me obvious that both communism and capitalism are toning down and, in a sense, approaching each other, although the gap is still wide. I have no doubt they will approach each other more rapidly but for the Cold War.

Yours sincerely,
[Jawaharlal Nehru]

476. To Ikram Aripov: Good Wishes on Birth of Daughter[11]

October 10, 1962

Dear Mr Aripov,

Thank for your letter of the 31st July which I have only just received. Perhaps the delay in receiving it is due to the fact that I have been abroad and have recently returned.

---

7. Sarojini Devi, wife of Ripudaman Singh, former Maharaja of Nabha.
8. Alexandra Metcalfe (1904-1995), joined Save the Children Fund in 1950 as a fund raiser and later became the Chairman of Overseas Relief Welfare Committee, the overseas wing of the Fund.
9. Letter to British Labour MP, (1915-1997), politician, author and broadcaster.
10. *Coexistence Plus: A Positive Approach to World Peace* (London: Bodley Head, 1962).
11. Letter to a Soviet citizen; address: House No. 36, 1ˢᵗ Street, Tangi-Arnk, Kirov District, Tashkent, Uzbek SSR, USSR.

I am glad to receive your letter and to learn of the birth of your daughter on the day I arrived in Tashkent. Also, that you have named her after my daughter Indira. I send all my good wishes to you and my love to your daughter Indira.

I agree with you that friendship between Soviet and Indian people is strong and unassailable. I wish you well.

Yours sincerely,
[Jawaharlal Nehru]

477. For Mohan Joshi's Biography[12]

मुझे खुशी है कि श्री मोहन जोशी का जीवन चरित्र लिखा गया है। श्री जोशी हमारी आज़ादी की लड़ाई में और असहयोग आन्दोलन में एक वीर सैनिक थे और उन्होंने सब कुछ उसके लिए त्याग किया। अलमोड़ा ज़िला में तो उनका बहुत असर था, और सब लोग उनके लिए श्रद्धा भक्ति रखते थे। लेकिन उनका असर ख़ाली अलमोड़ा ज़िला में नहीं, बल्कि उत्तर प्रदेश भर में था। मैं आशा करता हूं कि उनका जीवन-चरित्र पढ़कर आजकल के लोगों पर, विशेषकर नवजवानों पर, असर होगा, और उससे बहुत कुछ देश सेवा की बातें वह सीखेंगे।

[Translation begins:

I am pleased that the biography of Shri Mohan Joshi has been written. Shri Joshi was a brave warrior in our struggle for freedom and the non-cooperation movement and he had sacrificed everything for this struggle. He had great influence in Almora District and everybody had great reverence for him. But his influence was not limited to Almora District only, but was spread all over Uttar Pradesh. I hope that by reading his biography people, particularly the youth, will be inspired and that they will learn something about service to the nation.

Translation ends]

12. Message, 16 October 1962.

478. In New Delhi: To D.A. Low[13]

1. [Low[14] about Jawaharlal Nehru]: An elderly, quiet spoken, gentleman. Nothing dynamic about him. But a quiet persistence, although subdued. Very ready to listen, and give his mind to you, but – not surprisingly – had not given much thought to historical problems. A quick smile, and a ready response; but would occasionally dry up suddenly.

2. [It was] Clear from a phrase or two that [Nehru had] a profoundly deep-rooted, clear, if controlled passion against imperial domination. When I suggested that [it is] surprising that a man with Sapru's [Tej Bahadur Sapru] passion and temper should be a moderate; quickly and firmly, if gently, [Nehru] said that temper had really nothing to do with moderate or other politics.

3. [Low's question]: Regarding hopes that Sapru might lead them. Only a rambling answer [from Nehru] regarding a committee being formed (of which Sapru [was] probably [the] Chairman) to help recruiting in first world war for some additional volunteer corps, consisting of middle class people, who volunteered – including Nehru, Sapru sons[15] etc. But when Mrs Besant[16] [was] arrested, Jawaharlal Nehru withdrew, and [the] Committee collapse[d] -- Sapru [was] not very pleased – was what he [Nehru] seemed to say, but should check regarding this.

4. [Low's question]: Regarding end of Sapru's life. Close relationship. Imprecise answer here [by Nehru] but in [essential] terms; a) that personal relations [between them] had never been adversely affected[17]; b) they were both Kashmiris with a similar outlook, and, c) he [Nehru] now agreed with me [Low] that they shared a common secular outlook. This he said was typical of Kashmiris: in Kashmir, in old days, and even today – this [was] typical of India but more particularly pronounced in Kashmir – although Pandits [were] Hindus – he instanced their commensality rules – they were very "catholic" (his word) in their cultural universe. So that they

---

13. Notes on interview, 21 October 1962, New Delhi. The original of this document is with the Editor. Acronyms and abbreviations have been expanded.
14. Donald Anthony Low (1927--2015); historian.
15. The reference is most probably to T.B. Sapru and his eldest son Prakash Narain Sapru, who was an elected member (UP, Southern, non-Muslim) of the 2nd, 3rd, and 4th Council of States, since 1926.
16. Annie Besant was put under house arrest on 15 June 1917.
17. The reference here is probably to Sapru's support of the British war effort in 1939 and his being part of a Non- Party Committee to prepare a report (Sapru Committee Report 1945) on the "Communal Question", which the Indian National Congress, Muslim League and Communist Party of India boycotted.

were [illegible] good [illegible]. He [Nehru] agreed that this was very true of Sapru [too].

5. He [Nehru] characterised Sapru as a "constitutional moderate" who did not believe in what was implied by any revolutionary tendency. (By this he seemed clearly to separate as in paragraph 2 above, temperament from politics)

6. [Low's question]: Regarding Presidentship of [the] Constituent Assembly. They chose the oldest member – Sachidananda Sinha, who [was] of like politics with, and a close friend of Sapru's[18]. Sapru's name [never came up, since he was] too ill for question ever to be raised.

7. [Low's question regarding]: Indian National Army trials. Nehru went as [a defence] lawyer, because only he could be present. They wanted a good man to lead. He (J.N.) no doubt (nothing more definite than this) had something to do with getting him [Sapru] to appear. NB. There was something Nehru said to me, to be said for having someone whose politics were known to be moderate.

8. [Nehru]: Thinks Sapru drafted 2-3 chapters of Nehru Report.[19] Thinks it likely that he [Sapru] did more than just his fair share of it.

9. [Low's question]: Regarding Sapru's contribution to the whole process by 1947.[20] (nothing v. definite emerged). The 1935 Act was, of course one of the documents which they [the Constituent Assembly] had before them in 1947.

10. [Low's question]: Regarding Motilal and Round Table Conference [of] 1929. Did Motilal go to press Sapru regarding Round Table Conference? [Nehru Replied]: "may have mentioned it casually; or may have briefly expressed agreement with Sapru, who asked regarding this". [Nehru] did not think (N.B. here §1 of this note for the subdued nature of his conversation) that father [Motilal] would have made an issue of it? & experienced there after all they did not go to the 1[First] Round Table Conference (I would think that fairly clearly there was an elision of meaning here – not, of course, altogether surprising).

11. [Low's question]: Regarding National movement starting late in UP. But then Bengal [was] longest under British rule, & the partition: Maharashtra – Tilak, and the Maharatta belief that they were the last rulers of India

18. Sinha, a liberal and moderate politician, was chosen as the interim President of the Constituent Assembly on 9 December 1946.

19. An All Party Conference appointed committee's report headed by Motilal Nehru, 1928. Sapru was one of the signatories of the Report.

20. Here Low may be alluding to the impact of the recommendations of the Sapru Committee Report, 1945, on the Constituent Assembly proceedings.

(Muslims thought they were too); Punjab, a sturdy energetic peasantry, always prone to fight. [All Nehru's observations].

When Gandhi came, both Bengalis and Maharashtrians [were] surprised at [a] Gujarati Bania becoming a national leader. N.B. this one-man role: cf Joan of Arc on Gluckmann's terms![21]

[Low's question]: Did Taluqdars etc. have specific, dampening effect [on the belated rise of national movement in UP]. [Nehru] No, on the contrary, when Congress went to the peasantry [it] had an activating effect (but here, of course, he was referring to a late period).

UP however, he said, has had [a] reputation for providing great leaders: Malaviya, my father (pause – no mention of self) Dr Sapru...

[Nehru] Yes of course social distance [was] greater in UP than Punjab – zamindari settlement [in UP], whereas ryotwari in Punjab, Maharashtra & Madras.

12.   Here I [Low] finished by mentioning how many Sapru papers there were – [Nehru] the quiet smile and "Yes he was very careful."
13.   I [Low] had begun by asking whether he [Nehru] minded direct quotes – [Nehru] said it depended on the question – but no further mention of this.

[Low's notes on questions for the interview with Nehru]
To ask:

1.   What brought about change of attitude towards Sapru, from 30s to 40s (opposition to Pakistan[22] -- & nearness on constitutional issues).
2.   Was Sapru likely to have been 1) President Constituent Assembly 2) President of India?
3.   What was Motilal's view of Sapru in early twenties?
4.   Was it Motilal who urged Round Table Conference on Sapru [in] 1929-30?

---

21.   This seems to be a reference to Max Gluckman's thesis of outsiders as leaders, including the following observation: "we have only to recall Joan of Arc, not only a peasant but also a woman, managed to unite the squabbling noblemen of France against the English." See Max Gluckman, *Politics, Law and Rituals in Tribal Society* (London: Routledge, 2012), p. 102.
22.   See the Constituent Assembly Debates, Sapru Committee Report [SCR], paragraphs 12 and 34. https://cadindia.clpr.org.in/historical_constitutions/sapru_committee_report__sir_tej_bahadur_sapru__1945__1st%20December%201945 Accessed on 12 May 2018.

5. How much of drafting of Nehru Report 1928 did Sapru do?
6. How far would you distinguish Sapru from other non-Congressmen of 20s & 30s?

479. To Chas. Major: Quoting from Nehru's Books[23]

22nd October, 1962

Dear Mr Chas. Major,
I have your letter of the 14th October.

You can certainly use any extracts from my book for lectures and for other purposes in so far as I am concerned. I am not quite sure whether it will be necessary for you to ask for the permission of the publishers in case the extracts are long ones.

You can also translate any passages of my book into Afrikaans.

I do not know if there are any facilities for persons from other countries to come here and settle. Normally this does not take place. If you like, you can communicate with the Secretary of the Ministry of Home Affairs, Government of India, New Delhi.

Yours sincerely,
[Jawaharlal Nehru]

480. To P.P. Kumaramangalam: Pamphlet on P. Subbarayan[24]

October 26, 1962

Dear Kumaramangalam,
Thank you for sending me your little pamphlet about your father. I have read it with much interest. I have lasting and affectionate memories of your father which I shall treasure.

Yours sincerely,
[Jawaharlal Nehru]

---

23. Letter; address: "Karma", Klip Road, Grassy Park, Cape, South Africa.
24. Letter to P. Subbaryan's son. See also items 472 and 7.

481. To D.G. Tendulkar: Publishing the *Mahatma* Volumes[25]

November 15, 1962

My dear Tendulkar,

Your letter of November 12th. I do not know anything about the Belgian publishers whose letter you have sent me. We can, of course, enquire, if you so wish. But that will take some time. Anyhow, I am having an enquiry made.

I doubt very much if any publisher in Europe is likely to take up the publication of "*Mahatma*" in several volumes. They might accept a one volume book. In the French language especially, it is very rare to publish books in several volumes.

You may, if you like, send one or two volumes of your book to them and tell them what the total number of volumes will be, and ask them for their terms. It is only after you receive them that you need decide.

I now see from the letter you have sent that they have already been told that the book is in eight volumes of which six have been published. I think it would be worthwhile your sending a copy of the published volumes.

I am returning the papers you sent me.

Yours sincerely
Jawaharlal Nehru

482. To Lalitagauri Pant: Husband's Death[26]

November 15, 1962

My dear Lalitagauri,

Thank you for your letter of November 12th. I am sorry to learn that your husband died a little while ago. I had not heard of this before your letter reached me.

It seldom does good to think back and consider the various ifs and buts of life. We function as we think best at the time and naturally take the consequences.

I am glad you like the work you are doing in India House.

Yours sincerely,
[Jawaharlal Nehru]

---

25. Letter to biographer of Mahatma Gandhi. NMML, D.G. Tendulkar Papers.
26. Letter to the Rani of Aundh; address: India House, Aldwych, London WC2.

483. To Escott Reid: Welcome to Visit[27]

November 16, 1962

My dear Mr Reid,

It is good of you to have written to me and to have sent me your good wishes. We are going through a trying time and we are facing and will have to face much sorrow and distress. But I am certain that we shall win through whatever the difficulties might be.

I am glad to learn that you may be coming to India early next year. I hope your wife will also come and we shall have the pleasure of meeting you both again.

Yours sincerely,
[Jawaharlal Nehru]

484. To Ram Sewak[28]

नवम्बर 15, 1962

प्रिय राम सेवक जी,

आपका 13 नवम्बर का पत्र मिला। आकाशवाणी का जो आप लिखते हैं उसका कार्य-क्रम मैं नहीं बनाता। आम तौर से हमारी राय यह है कि बहुत भाषण न दिये जाये। उसके काम की शिकायतें कुछ आई हैं जो उनको भेज दी गई हैं। और अपनी कमेटी से सलाह कर के वह कार्य-क्रम बनाते हैं।

आपको मालूम होगा कि एक नागरिकों की केन्द्रीय कमेटी बनी हैं। असल में यह काम राज्य या प्रदेश का है। केन्द्रीय कमेटी तो ख़ाली कभी कभी सलाह उनको दे देती हैं। इन कमेटियों का विशेष काम है वस्तुओं के मूल्य स्थिर रहें।

आपका
जवाहरलाल नेहरु

27. Letter to the Director, South Asia and Middle East Department of the World Bank 1962-65; former Canadian High Commissioner to India, 1958-1962.
28. Letter to Congress MP from Jalaun, 15 November 1962; PMO, File No. 43 (192)/62-63-PMS Sr. No. 33-A.

[Translation begins:

Dear Ram Sewak Ji,
I received your letter of 13th November. What you write for the Akash Vani is not decided by us. My usual position is that there should not be too many speeches. Some complaints regarding this have come, and they have been sent to appropriate authorities. They have a committee which in consultation makes the programmes.

You may have come to know that there is a committee of Citizens at the centre. Actually, this is the work of the state governments. The central committee only gives suggestions at times. The main work of this committee is to keep the prices stable.

Yours,
Jawaharlal Nehru

Translation ends]

485. To Harshdeo Malaviya: Forgiven[29]

नवम्बर 17, 1962

प्रिय हर्षदेव,
तुम्हारा 16 तारीख़ का पत्र मिला। मेरे ख़्याल में तुम्हारे ख़िलाफ़ कोई विचार नहीं है। अगर तुम चाहते हो कि मैं कहूं कि मैंने तुम्हें माफ़ कर दिया तो यह मैं ख़ुशी से कह देता हूं।
तुम अच्छा काम कर सकते हो और इस समय कर भी रहे हो। मैं कोई नया काम तुम्हें क्या बताऊं।

तुम्हारा
जवाहरलाल नेहरु

29. Letter to Socialist journalist and economist; close aid of Narendra Dev, 17 November 1962; PMH, No.1999-62.

[Translation begins:

17 November 1962

My Dear Harshdeo,

I got your letter of 16th. I do not harbour any ill feelings towards you. If you wish that I should say that I have forgiven you, I am doing it gladly.

You can do a lot better and you are doing good work. What new work can I suggest to you?

Yours,
[J. Nehru]

Translation ends]

486. To Ralph Rogerson: Christmas Service for World Peace[30]

November 17, 1962

Dear Mr Rogerson,

Thank you for your letter of the 14th November. I am grateful for the sentiments you have expressed in it.

I send you my greetings and good wishes on the occasion of your having a special Christmas Service for World Peace. Indeed, that is the most important thing for the world today.

It is odd that just when I am sending you this little message, my country should be involved in a war with China. That was none of our seeking, and it has been thrust upon us by the aggression and invasion of China. We have to defend ourselves, and we shall do this to the best of our strength and ability. However long this may take, I am confident that we shall succeed.

Yours sincerely,
[Jawaharlal Nehru]

---

30. Letter to a Reverend in Isle of Man; address: "The Manse", 18 The Park, Onchan.

487. To Harriet Bunker: Acknowledging Birthday Greetings[31]

November 20, 1962

My dear Mrs Bunker,

Thank you for your letter of the 14th November. It was very good of you to remember my birthday and send me your good wishes. I appreciate them very much.

It is true that we are passing through very difficult times. I am confident, however, that we shall get over these difficulties and perhaps profit by passing through the fire which consumes many of us today.

Yours sincerely,
[Jawaharlal Nehru]

488. To Shiela Sokolov Grant: Good Wishes[32]

November 20, 1962

My dear Shiela,

Thank you for your letter of the 15th November. I was happy to receive it, and to have news of you. I hope you are well.

We are passing through very difficult days, and almost every day brings a fresh shock. I am confident, however, that we shall survive all these difficulties and perhaps, profiting by them, grow stronger in many ways.

With all good wishes,

Yours affectionately,
[Jawaharlal Nehru]

---

31. Letter to wife of Ellsworth Bunker, former US Ambassador to India; address: Dummerston Downs, Putney, Vermont, USA.
32. Letter to a British journalist, author and a longtime friend of Nehru. (1913-2004); address Bradley Green, Needham Market, Suffolk.

VI. APPENDICES

1. K.P.S. Menon to Indira Gandhi: Nehru's Message for Radhakrishnan Souvenir[1]
[Refer to item 3]

26th September, 1962

My dear Indu,

You may have heard of the Radhakrishnan Number, a souvenir proposed to be presented to Dr Radhakrishnan on his birthday this year. It has, however, been somewhat delayed.

V. Kalidas, the editor, had written to the PM for a contribution. PM has not been able to send one as he has been far too busy.

I enclose a list of the contributors to the Radhakrishnan Number. You will see that it includes world famous men like Albert Schweitzer, Bertrand Russell, Aldous Huxley, Horace Alexander and others, let alone prominent Indians. All of us including the editor and the sponsors—among whom I happen to be included, presumably because I had the honour of succeeding Dr Radhakrishnan in Moscow—feel that the absence of a contribution from PM will be a distinct omission, which will be noticed, regretted and even commented on. We would all be grateful if you could put this to PM and get him to write a few lines for the Souvenir. If he has no time to make a substantial contribution, a simple message to the Souvenir will do. That may kindly be sent to V. Kalidas, 12, Thambu Chetty Street, Madras-1.

Yours sincerely,
K.P.S. Menon

---

1. Letter from former Ambassador to the Soviet Union to Nehru's daughter. Sent from Palat House, Ottapalam, Kerala State. PMO, File No. 9/2/61-PMP, Vol. 7, Sr. No. 12-A.

711

2. Sri Prakasa on Kashmir[2]

[Refer to item 43 and 450]

Political Diary
Not to be published before October 2

Kashmir and Indo-Pakistan Relations: A Solution - I
by Sri Prakasa

(Radical and far-reaching proposals for improving Indo-Pakistan relations have been made by Mr Sri Prakasa in this thought-provoking article in two parts. What Mr Sri Prakasa has to suggest may or may not be acceptable to all. But, pleads the writer, "We cannot go on living in an atmosphere of fear forever. Whatever has to be done, must be done quickly. We cannot afford to drift any more. Time is passing fast and things can take an ugly turn any moment." Part two of the article will appear next Tuesday.)

As a citizen of Uttar Pradesh with its very large Hindu population and great centres of Hindu religious traditions and beliefs on the one hand and, on the other, the dominance of Muslim culture and thought in practically three-fourths of its urban regions; and, as one closely associated with its public life for over 45 years, I should not be unaware of the various forces that were working for the creation of Pakistan.

It will be remembered that on one occasion during his tour of the State—province as it then was—Mr Jinnah told his assembled friends that he had come to ask for the gift of Pakistan from the people of the then United Provinces, in view of the fact that they were likely to suffer as their proportion in the population was so small. Uttar Pradesh, therefore, can be regarded as having played a leading part in the then unfortunate situation that finally brought Pakistan into existence and must take its full share of responsibility for the unhappy results.

It was my misfortune to be the first High Commissioner for India (1947-49) of the newly established sovereign state of Pakistan when murder and violence were in the air and exoduses on an extensive scale were going on with their attendant sufferings and sorrows. Thus I was brought still nearer to the problem of Indo-Pakistan relationship. As a humble public worker, I

---

2. INFA Column, *India News and Feature Alliance*, Jeevan Deep, Parliament Street, New Delhi – 1. Edited, printed, and published by Durga Das. Available in MEA, File No. P.V 1022(B)/62, pp.1-6/Corr.

could see which way the wind was really blowing—though unable to change its direction—throughout the quarter of a century and more of the country's struggle both for the unity and for liberty under Mahatma Gandhi's guidance and leadership (1920-47).

As I have found no solution of the main problem in the partition of the land—cruel and tragic as it was—destroying at one stroke the work of integration that had taken quite two centuries of foreign rule and the people's earnest efforts to complete, I have in my own small way kept on thinking how best the same could be solved; and the endeavours of the Governments and the peoples of the two parts of what was one country and what should really have always been one, directed towards the welfare of all, and not against each other. As it is, a major portion of the resources on either side is being dissipated in mutual bickering and quarrellings and not in mutual co-operation and goodwill as the case should be.

I remember a talk with Mr Ghulam Mohammad who was a good friend of mine since we sat opposite to each other in the old Central Legislative Assembly at Delhi (1935-47). He became Pakistan's first Finance Minister when I went there as India's first High Commissioner (1947). He later became the Governor-General of Pakistan also, and was good enough to keep up contacts with me to the last. I recollect a visit of his to me when I was a Minister at Delhi (1950).

In the course of the very friendly conversation that we had, he said to me as so many have been saying all the time: "As soon as the Kashmir problem is solved, all troubles between Pakistan and India will end". That reminded me of Mr Jinnah's statement to me eight years earlier (1942); "As soon as Pakistan is conceded, all our problems will be solved". In deep sorrow, I replied: "Ghulam Mohammad, when Kashmir is solved, the question of river waters will come forward; and when that is cleared out of the way, evacuee property will raise its ugly head. When even that is finished, one of us will say to the other: 'Why is your nose bigger than mine?' So long as you and I are determined to quarrel, we shall go on quarrelling. Some reason will always be found for it. If we really and sincerely want peace, we can have it within five minutes". He agreed, but was as helpless as myself in getting anything really and effectively done. There are always too many forces at work in such matters, and the best intentioned individuals, even if apparently powerful, can do but little.

Mr Ghulam Mohammad asked me what my solution was, and I remember what I told him then. I cannot say I did so on the spur of the moment, for these thoughts had been with me since I went to Pakistan three years earlier in 1947, and I had not been able to shake them off. I said: "1) Common citizenship which will make all citizens of India also citizens of Pakistan and *vice versa*; 2) Freedom of movement for both the peoples all over the sub-continent

713

without the encumbrance of permit, passport and other formalities; and, 3) Neutrality of Kashmir guaranteed by all the surrounding powers—India, Pakistan, Afghanistan, Russia and China". "Will our Governments agree?" said Mr Ghulam Mohammad. The talk then ended with the usual expression of a pious wish, common on such occasions: "How nice it would be if they left the solution to you and me. All should then be well".

I will explain why I thought as I did at that time. To me it is quite clear that despite all the sad background of our history—of the rise and fall of kingdoms; of foreign invasions and internal conflicts—the people of India are really one and had become so politically also under British auspices when all parts thereof had begun to think in common terms as sons of a common motherland. Poems of Tagore and Iqbal describing and preaching the oneness of the country—apart from the work of social and political reformers—were coming to be known to all. India had at last assumed the boundaries and become the country as it had been in its racial consciousness through the ages. So far as I can see, all leaders whether of war or of peace, whether emperors or religious preachers—Asoka and Akbar, Buddha and Shankaracharya—had wanted this, and endeavoured to bring it about both physically and psychologically.

The people whether of India or Pakistan—all men and women living on either side of the border which was most indefinite at that time and continues still to be undefined—are basically and fundamentally one in every possible sense, and I felt they should continue to be one and helped to regard themselves as common citizens of the same country or sub-continent. It would not be difficult for them to continue to feel in the same way as common sons of the same soil. That is why I pleaded for common citizenship.

Then I found that the partition had not only divided the soil but also the homes of innumerable persons. Members of the self-same families—Hindu and Muslim alike—lived on either side. Their desire to meet each other was natural. Great difficulties were put in their way by governmental restrictions, whenever they wanted to do so. The situation appeared to me to be pathetic. It was the common people who suffered. They were the people who had never asked for any partition, and who still felt vividly the bond of common heritage and tradition.

The people who had wanted the partition and who were in authority, did not suffer in their own person from all the restrictions imposed by them on others in the matter of travel. They themselves had diplomatic passports and were free from even customs formalities. They did not know what others had to undergo. If the big-wigs as I know myself, wanted to visit their families across the borders, every facility was immediately afforded to them. The humble who had not taken any part in the agitation for partition—and never really wanted it—were the persons who suffered. I thought all this was wrong, and so pleaded for freedom of movement.

Then there was the problem of Kashmir. I was in Karachi when the United Nations Commission on India and Pakistan arrived (1948). Within two or three hours of their arrival, one of the most important members of the Commission holding the office of the Secretary, I believe, extended to me the courtesy of calling to see me, and we had a long and friendly chat. I joked at the name of "Lake Success", the then headquarters of the United Nations, as nothing seemed to succeed there, and wondered why the Secretary-General was named "Lie"[3] while the American President himself was "Truman".

We settled down to this talk on the basis of our common humanity. The talk turned on Gandhiji who had died only a few months earlier; and when my visitor saw tears in my eyes as I spoke of the great leader, he asked me if we all felt for him so very deeply. I told him that he could not understand how we mourned the tragic loss, and what great harm that had caused, to the mutual relations of India and Pakistan. Gandhiji, I told him, was working night and day towards the end of his life, to find ways and means of restoring peace and goodwill once again. He was so hurt, I told my visitor, that all the work of his life-time should have been so completely ruined as he had himself told me; for while he had striven for communal harmony, the partition had taken place on the basis of the supposed inability of the communities to live together.

After that, I had to be in touch, off and on, with the Commission while it was in Karachi, my own headquarters. I do not remember details, but I recollect that they were to send in some report to Delhi by a particular date. I had an urgent communication from the Prime Minister late one night to say that as the session of Parliament was ending, and as he had to make a statement before it on the basis of this report from the Commission, I should ask the President of the Commission to give it at once.

The report was sent to me late in the evening before the last day of Parliament. I immediately forwarded it by the night plane through one of my assistants, and the Prime Minister got it in time to make his report to Parliament that morning before it adjourned.

The Commission continues. Its presence has so far warded off a hot war between Pakistan and ourselves, but the situation remains as bad as ever, if not worse than before. The United Nations itself keeps discussing the problem from time to time. The cease fire line gets violated, and armed forces stand night and day, on either side to watch it. We want Pakistan to vacate the territory it has illegally occupied before we can have any further talk, and they want us

3. Trygve Lie, Secretary-General of the United Nations from 1946 to 1952.

715

to have a plebiscite straight off. The position is as foggy as ever, and no end is in sight. (Copyright *India News and Feature Alliance*)

New Delhi, September 28, 1962
Political Diary
Not to be published before October 9.

Kashmir and Indo-Pakistan Relations: A Solution – II
by Sri Prakasa

It will be recalled that when the wild men from across the border attacked Kashmir, Sir Mohammad Zafrullah in the United Nations, disclaimed any responsibility for this on behalf of Pakistan. The brigands who came, had thus no legal status, and we would have been fully justified to drive them away. Sardar Abdur Rab Nishtar, Pakistan's Minister, asked me rather irritably one evening at a cocktail party, as to how they could be held responsible for what bad men from across the borders did? It was we who insisted that Pakistan was implicated and responsible, and went to the United Nations instead of driving the marauders out as we were fully authorised to do.

My information is that we were deliberately wrongly advised by interested parties, and fell in their net, not directly knowing the facts ourselves. Later the stunt was invented that Mr Jinnah had given Kashmir to Pakistan by his political will and testament though he himself had, to my knowledge, never mentioned Kashmir even when he asked for the whole of the Punjab, the whole of Bengal and Assam. If my information is correct, then all that has happened, could have been easily and effectively avoided, anyway, all that is past beyond recall, and the chapter must be regarded as closed.

As matters now stand, it is quite clear to me that we ourselves on our own initiative, have given Kashmir a separate status. We are not prepared to resile from that position despite all that the public or members of Parliament may have to say on the subject. Kashmir is not like any other state of our Union. It had its own Constituent Assembly and has now its elected Sadar-i-Riyasat, and not Governor nominated by the President. It has its Prime Minister, and not a Chief Minister. It has its Parliament. In fact, it has more or less an independent status. Its administrative connection with the rest of the country is only tenuous. We are spending large sums of money for the protection and development of Kashmir without any expectation of or even desire for return. Our armed forces are on the borders, and we have given them roads, airfields, tunnels, cheap food—heavily subsidised—and if I am not mistaken, we have already spent quite five hundred crores of good money on Kashmir.

Our southern and western States are wondering why we are doing all that. Having been Governor both of Madras and Bombay, I should know those of us who belong to the north are immediately concerned and naturally and rightly feel anxious. I remember persons in Madras telling me that Kashmir did not concern them. It was no business of theirs, and we of the north must look after the matter. Taking all these circumstances into consideration, I have always had a feeling that Kashmir might just well get in Asia the status that Switzerland enjoys in Europe. Both are the most beautiful regions in their respective continents, and both attract tourists from all round, and mostly live on tourist traffic. The original suggestion of guaranteed neutrality that was in my mind, and that I had expressed to Mr Ghulam Mohammad, may now be out of date. Moreover, the fear could have haunted persons concerned from the very start that someone or other of the guaranteeing powers might not keep to his word.

It seems to me that time has come when we should reconsider the whole situation dispassionately and make up our minds. We cannot go on depending on armed forces and living in an atmosphere of fear forever. I personally see no harm in recognising the status of Kashmir de jure what it is de facto. It is also clear that no other power except India will help Kashmir to develop itself, and our age-old mutual associations give a right to Kashmir to ask for our help as it would be our duty to give it. Since, however, it is clear that the people of Kashmir itself are divided in their allegiance, it would be right and proper to think of a solution of the problem that it presents from other angles of vision.

The information of Pakistan itself is indeed strange. West Pakistan and East Pakistan have nothing to do with each other. They are moreover separated by about 1,000 miles of territory of so-called another country which they regard as hostile. I remember a talk with Nawabzada Liaquat Ali Khan, the first Prime Minister of Pakistan. He said that he was asking for Kashmir because it was contiguous to Pakistan, and had a majority Muslim population. He would never have thought of East Bengal at all if it had not been connected with Pakistan by sea.

According to him, the two parts of Pakistan were contiguous because of their connection with each other by a circuitous route across the open sea even if the distance was quite 2,500 miles. I remember an elderly, respected and retired member of the Madras Civil Service telling me in despair—and sick of endless squabbles—that it would be best to exchange East Bengal with Kashmir. That would show how even responsible persons in the South look at the problem that is exercising us, of the North, to such an extent.

All that naturally makes me anxious about the attitude of our people in general towards Kashmir. In any case, East Pakistan and West Pakistan have nothing to do with each other, and their contiguity with the help of the sea is an untenable proposition. Pakistan may regard itself as a Muslim or an Islamic State, and trace its existence to communal considerations; but we of India have not accepted that basis of governance at all, and have guaranteed equal rights and privileges to all our citizens of whatever creed or race they might be. We do not and cannot accept the right of any territory to belong to this sovereign State or to that, simply because of the religion of the majority of its people. I also think that after all that has happened, any attempt at fusion of any part of Pakistan with India or vice versa, would only cause further complications and embarrassments.

The next suggestion that I can think of would be preferably a confederation, a bundestaat; and failing that, a federation, a staatenbund of four entities—Ka shmir, West Pakistan, India as she is minus Kashmir Valley and East Pakistan which might just as well be celled East Bengal. To our ancients, Kashmir may have been as is described in the Sanskrit verse:

Sharada – math – marabhya,
Kunkumadri – tatantakah,
Tavet – Kashmir – desh – syat,
Pancha – shat – yojan – atmakah.

Starting from Sharada Math and going right up to the foot of the Kumkum-mountain, lies the country of Kashmir stretching across 500 yojans (roughly 4,000 miles).

But we live in different times, and must take into consideration facts as they are today. Kashmir in Sanskrit means saffron, and the poet rightly adds: Even the bitter things born in Kashmir are truly beautiful (Kashmira-jasyakatutapinitanta-ramya).

If the various parts of this sub-continent that used to be only one country India or Bharat before, could be combined together in some sort of a union—federation, confederation or by whatever name one might like to call it—whether loose or firm—provided all live in mutual sympathy and understanding, and work harmoniously for the common good, it would, indeed, be a great day for not only those who live in this territory, but for the world at large.

The whole sub-continent might be called India with its integral parts known as they are, the only exception being that what is "India that is Bharat" today may be called only Bharat, or even Hindustan. This should, to my mind, satisfy the susceptibilities of all, and enable us to make our contribution to the thought and activity of the world, instead of wasting all our talents end energies in mutual suspicion and hatred that sometimes take the form or even preparations for war and resulting ruination.

Whatever has to be done must be done quickly. We cannot afford to drift any more. Time is fleeting, and things can take an ugly turn any moment, I recall a talk with Sardar Vallabhbhai Patel. He was anxious to solve the problem, but felt for various reasons rather hesitant and embarrassed to do anything in the matter of Kashmir. He told me that he had been very greatly affected by what Nawabzada Liaquat Ali Khan had said to him.

Pakistan's Prime Minister had told our Home Minister: "Sardar Saheb, whatever can and should be done, must be done at once. Members of the present generation on either side have known each other and have worked with each other. We have mutual sympathy and affection. Our children and our children's children will not even know each other. It would be impossible to solve any problems when they are in charge of affairs. So let us be up and doing, and finish off all that we have to do quickly."

Sardar Vallabhbhai told me that this struck him as so true, so relevant and so correct that he readily yielded to the Pakistan Prime Minister on some of the issues, for the sake of peace and goodwill. As I see it, the safety and unity of our country at the present moment hangs by the slender thread of a single life; and whatever differences many people may have with our Prime Minister, it cannot be denied that it is he who is holding us together.

I do not like the situation; but facts are facts. No democracy or security of any country should be so entirely dependent on any individual, however great. I so fear that as soon as our Prime Minister's strong hands are withdrawn, there might be a terrible upsurge of communal passion which is just now kept in check. The solution of the Indo-Pakistan problem on which hangs the internal peace and security of the sub-continent brooks no delay. We dare not be complacent, feeling that now that Swaraj has been attained, no one can take it away and no harm can come to us. We can no more continue to bury our heads in the sand like the ostrich and imagine that all is well. I feel, therefore, even at the risk of being misunderstood, that I should speak out freely, fully and frankly all that I have in my mind.

My friends in the highest offices in Government have always known my views. It is time that the public might also know them for what they are worth; and I put them forward in all humility, so that if it should be regarded right and necessary, attention may be given to the position as it is, and solutions found and implemented before it is too late.

New Delhi.
October 5, 1962

3. From Mehr Chand Khanna: Decorating Public Buildings[4]

[Refer to item169]

29th September, 1962

My dear Panditji,

During your visit to the Rajghat Samadhi on the 31st August, 1962, you mentioned about the work of the Decoration Advisory Committee entrusted with the selection of artists and specific works of art for the decoration of public buildings. I myself had also not felt happy about the manner of functioning of the Committee and the pace of decoration under its supervision. We, therefore, invited a few selected artists of repute for an exchange of ideas on how best important public buildings could be decorated with really worthwhile works of art. To that end, we desired the fullest co-operation of the artists. Shrimati Devyani Krishna, and Sarvashri Satish Gujral, Manwal Krishna, K.S. Kulkarni, A.N. Sehgal, and Dhanraj Bhagat participated in the discussion.

In the course of a free and frank exchange of views, the artists stressed the following points:

I) The present composition of the Decoration Advisory committee is unsatisfactory since some of the members are not free from professional jealousy. It should be replaced by a smaller committee headed by the Secretary of this Ministry and with a few noted art critics as members.

II) The selected artist should not be required to submit any sketch or colour-scheme of the proposed work. He should be asked only to give a word picture of the work and then left completely free to execute it to the best of his ability.

III) The artist selected for the decoration of a particular building should have full freedom to choose the theme, medium, approach, and design.

The artists have since confirmed these points in writing and also suggested a few names for inclusion in the new committee. I largely agree with the artists that they should be given all the freedom necessary to execute their commissions. You are of the same view and so also is the Vice-President who has spoken to me on the subject.

I have now reconstituted the committee which will be known, as the Committee for Selection of Artists for the Decoration of Public Buildings. Its composition will be as follows:

---

4. Letter from Minister of Works, Housing and Supply. PMO, File No.2/129/56-71-PMS, Sr.No.20-A

1. The Secretary, Ministry of Works,   -Chairman
    Housing &Supply
2. Shri Bhagwan Sahay   -Member
3. Shri M. S. Randhawa   -Member
4. Dr. Mulkraj Anand   -Member
5. The Architect, designing the particular building   -Member

As far as possible, the committee will select an artist at an early stage of designing of a building so that he can be associated with the architect during the construction. After selection, the committee will leave the artist completely free to do the work. For the present, the scale of remuneration of artists will be left as it is, as suggested by the artists.

I now propose to give a trial to these new arrangements which, we hope, will prove to be more satisfactory and hasten the pace of decoration.

With kind regards,

Yours sincerely,
Mehr Chand Khanna

4. From Devika Rani: George Roerich Anniversary[5]

[Refer to item 242]

3rd October, 1962

My dearest Panditji,
On the 15th October 1962 the Institute of Oriental Studies of the USSR Academy of Science will celebrate the sixtieth Anniversary of my brother-in-law, the late Dr. George Roerich. There shall be a meeting of scholars and scientists dedicated to his work. This will be followed by the unveiling of a plaque in his memory on the 16th October.

This memorial meeting to George is of great significance and interest to the orientalists of the world, as he was the leading scholar in his field. He was a scholar in eighteen languages, besides his great and profound knowledge on Tibet, Mongolia and Central Asia.

---

5. Letter from Devika Rani, actor and film producer (1908-1994), wife of Svetoslav Roerich, sister-in-law of George Roerich (1902-1960). PMO, File No. 9/2/62-PMP, Vol. 7, Sr. No. 20-A.

A message from you would be greatly appreciated on this occasion, which may kindly be sent direct to:

Dr B.G. Gafurov,
Director,
Institute of Oriental Studies of the Academy of Science of USSR,
Armiansky-2,
Moscow.

I shall be grateful if the copy could be sent to me.
With our love and respects,

Ever yours affectionately,
Devika

5. From Moni Bagchee: Gandhism[6]
[Refer to item 8]

October 5, 1962

Dear Shri Nehru,

It is after an age that I am addressing this letter to you. We have left behind many long years since I first came into your contact. That was the time when you were still the General Secretary of the Congress and in that capacity you wrote me the first letter in reply to that of mine. I was then in the Indian Army, holding a non-commissioned post in the office of the Brigade Commander, Razmak Brigade in Waziristan District. It was then that at the risk of my life and service that I dispatched to you an important note in connection with the Bachhai Saqqo affairs that eventually resulted in the abdication of the King Amanullah. A few letters were then exchanged between us and in your last one you encouraged me to give up the Government Service which I did. Then I met you for the first time at the Lahore Congress. Many years later, when your *Autobiography* was published, I was then on the editorial staff of the *Ananda Bazar Patrika* and you will recollect that on reading your remarkable book I realised its importance and I could then divine the possibility of its being translated into Bengali. I then approached you with the suggestion to which you agreed. To make the long story short, the Bengali translation was subsequently

---

6. Letter from Moni Bagchee (1907-1983); writer and historian; address: 90, Baguiati Road, Dum Dum, Calcutta – 28. PMO, File No. 2(114)/56-66-PMS, Sr No. 86-A.

done by my esteemed colleague, the late Satyendra Nath Mazumdar and, as you know, it was well received.

With this short background let me now come to the actual purport of this lengthy letter. Enclosed please find a cutting from *The Statesman* which recently published a letter written by me. Since a long time it has been my feeling that within fifteen years of the passing away of Mahatma Gandhi, we are witnessing a phenomenon that his name has gone into the backwaters of the nation's memory. I do not know if you subscribe to the same view, but this remains a painful fact which I have attempted to give expression through the columns of the press. Mere chanting of Ramdhun in the daily programme of the AIR cannot go a long way to kindle in us the Gandhian ideals, in our everyday life. When I last visited Delhi, I went one evening to the Rajghat. While I was standing there in mute silence and over-awed with the magnitude of the surroundings, it struck me that this will not perpetuate the memory of Gandhiji in the manner we desire. Gandhi Jayanti celebrations have become no more than a formal affair. Something concrete should be done and done immediately for mass propagation of the Gandhian thoughts throughout India. I have a scheme and if you so desire, I can send it to you for your examination. Who lives if Gandhiji is forgotten, or Gandhism is eschewed?

With my regards,

Yours sincerely,
Moni Bagchee

6. From Naval H. Tata: Cotton Textile Industry[7]
[Refer to item 101]

October 5, 1962

My dear Jawaharlalji,

I am forwarding herewith, for your perusal, a copy of the Note I handed over to Shri M.G. Mane, Labour Minister with the Maharashtra Government, on the 3rd instant. I met him at his request and discussed in broad terms the pros and cons of my suggestion to utilise the present installed capacity of industries to the maximum extent possible. I have put down briefly in the annexed Note my ideas on the question.

---

7. Letter from Naval H. Tata; Chairman, Ahmedabad Advance Mills, Tata Group; Chairman, Tata Electric Company; Deputy Chairman, Tata Sons Ltd.; address: Bombay House, Fort, Bombay, 1. PMO, File No. 17(438)/60-64-PMS, (Vol I), Sr. No. 11-B.

2.   So far as the Cotton Textile Industry of India is concerned, I have prepared a statement showing the effect on production and employment if (a) all Sundays are added to the existing working days; and (b) the Industry is made to work round-the-clock throughout the year on three shift basis. The statement has been worked out purely on a hypothetical basis. I am aware of the fact that there are several difficulties in giving effect to the proposal, such as shortage of raw materials, power, etc. resistance from labour and the like. Nevertheless, I feel that even partially operated round-the-clock Textile Industry working on most Sundays can create substantial additional employment opportunities, apart from increased production of cloth for domestic market and export. Such decisions can go a great way in helping our national economy in which you are taking such keen and lively interest.

With kindest regards,

Yours sincerely,
Naval H. Tata

7.   From K. D. Malaviya: Administrative Reform[8]
[Refer to item 9]

6 October 1962

My dear Jawaharlal ji,
I spoke to you the other day regarding two matters:

  i)   Necessity of further changing our administrative system and the functioning of the administrators with a view to improving the working of our economic programmes; and

  ii)   to consider a change in the administrative set-up and control of "power" schemes with a view to speedy generation of greater quantum of power, and to evolve a new policy for "energy" in a more scientific and integrated way.

2.   I suggest for your consideration the appointment of two Committees for these purposes. The terms of reference can be laid down after due consideration of various aspects.

---

8.   Letter from K.D. Malviya, the Minister of Mines and Fuel. NMML, T.T. Krishnamachari Papers, File 1963, Auto.

3. I feel that there are still great hindrances in the smooth functioning of our public sector projects. Routine examination of issues by our administrators and counter-checks are more than any reasonable system of working can bear. Its justification itself seems to be outmoded because of the volume and dimensions of work-load weighing on individuals. There is acute shortage of top technicians and administrators. Those that are available in very many cases are not moved by a proper sense of idealism. Corruption and selfishness is very much in evidence. Naturally, therefore, we have to be careful yet we have to take risks. Greater responsibility for decisions have to be left on those individuals who have to undertake execution. That done, we can surely go ahead much more efficiently and promptly than the oldest of the private sector projects in the country. Examined from any angle, I come to the conclusion that the execution of our schemes get delayed because of the personal whims, interfering habits and lack of purposive enthusiasm of the individual senior officers of the various Ministries. They demand details without the capability of evaluating those details.

4. With regard to our "power" programme, I submit that a new policy for energy should be evolved now. Energy has to be generated from various types of fuel, low grade coal, natural and synthetic gas, petroleum products, atomic energy, hydro-electric energy etc. The demand for energy has increased tremendously and is further going to rise many times. All our railways and industries have ultimately to be run on electric power. All our kitchens even if they are centralised in a socialist society, have to be run on modern energy. The present system of control and ownership by the State Governments, by certain industrialists, municipal corporations and also somewhere by public sector projects, all need to be fused into a healthy national consortium-like organisation where though financial and administrative interests of the State Governments are safeguarded adequately, yet system of national control and creation of national grid may be clearly assured.

5. I submit that these two problems might be seriously considered by you and small committees be appointed to make recommendations in four to six months.

Yours affly,
Keshava Deva

8. Harishwar Dayal to M.J. Desai: Vinoba Bhave's Nepal Visit[9]

[Refer to item 219]

7th October 1962

My dear Desai,

Shri Tulsi Meher Shrestha, who spent some years with Mahatma Gandhi at Sabarmati and now runs the Gandhi Smarak Nidhi in Nepal and is the only genuine social worker in the country, is trying to arrange for Acharya Vinoba Bhave to come to Nepal. Apparently, he has been in touch with Vinobaji for some time. The other day he was called to the Palace at short notice for an audience for which he had applied several weeks previously, and the King asked him to go ahead with arrangements for the visit. It is not, however, yet known when, if at all, Vinobaji might be able to come.

2. So far as the King is concerned, this appears to be an attempt to gain the sympathy of our practising Gandhians, and at the same time to show that Nepal still wants to maintain the traditional links with India. As things are, I would doubt whether there is any genuine interest in Bhoodan in the Government or among those in Nepal who have something to give. On the other hand, there is a pressing need for land reform and of land for distribution among the landless, and it is just possible that the visit, if takes place, might set things moving. Be that as it may, I have no doubt that the King's motive in encouraging the visit is purely political.

With kind regards,

Harishwar Dayal

9. Jayaprakash Narayan on Nehru and Language[10]

[Refer to item 14]

I feel I must raise my voice, howsoever feeble, against the manner in which the Prime Minister is carrying on the language controversy since his return from abroad. It is a matter to be deeply regretted, as happened in the case of the States' Reorganisation issue, that it is the Prime Minister's manner of intervention that

---

9. Letter from the Ambassador to Nepal to the Foreign Secretary. MEA, File No. E II/122/5/Nepal/62, p. 1/corr.
10. Press statement by the Sarvodaya leader, issued in Patna, 7 October 1962.PMO, File No. 52(12)/57-63-PMS, Vol.I, Sr. No. 88-A.

often precipitates unnecessarily heated controversy. Controversy and debate are the food of democracy. But there are bounds beyond which these should not be carried on, if the democratic way of life is to grow in a healthy manner. No one, whatever his views, would like to be called stupid. Moreover, when the Prime Minister himself thinks it fit to use such language in a public debate, can it be wondered why marshals have to be called into allow our Legislatures to carry on their work with a modicum of decorum? The two things are not so unrelated as they might appear at first sight.

This, however, is the less serious aspect—though it is serious enough—of the Prime Minister's present role in this vital national debate. The more serious aspect is the deliberate manner in which the real issue has been confounded and clouded over. The Prime Minister seems to be hitting out against a shadow. For, barring a few extremists, no one is suggesting that English and other foreign languages should be banished from the schools. The vast majority of people in this country, including those who speak Hindi, would unhesitatingly agree with all that the Prime Minister has said about the importance of learning foreign languages in order to keep abreast with science and modern knowledge. They would even have no objection to compulsory teaching of English as a language at the appropriate stage.

But no matter how important learning foreign languages might be, no foreign language can become an effective and creative medium of education. There is general agreement that the medium of education must be the language of the child's environment. However desirable it might be for us to learn English, German or Russian, the medium of education in this country must be the regional language. Education through a foreign language can only result in mediocrity and stunting of originality and creativity.

All that, however, is not the real issue. The heart of the present controversy is the question whether any period of time should be defined within which English could be given up as an associate, or inter-state, language and Hindi alone could come to acquire that status. The Government of India proposes to fix no time-limit, which has aroused strong and widespread suspicion, not only among Hindi speaking people, but also among others who wish to see Hindi become the national language. The suspicion is that the absence of such a limit would release the centre from any pressing, and real, responsibility to take the necessary steps to make it possible for Hindi ever to assume the role of a national language. Already there is a deep and widespread feeling that the present unpreparedness of Hindi to take on that role is due not so much to obstruction from the South, as to the failure of the Central Government to fulfil its obligation in that behalf.

For instance, States that had already taken steps to make Hindi the medium of instruction at the university stage, had to reverse the gear just because competitive examinations for the Central Services continued to be held In English. It was not expected that those exams would be held only in Hindi. But if Hindi was to be enabled to become the national language, steps should have been taken to see that the Central examinations were held both in Hindi and English. This is only one example of the lapse of the Centre in this matter. Many more have been pointed out in the course of the present controversy.

For these reasons, the plea for some sort of time limit has been strongly, and to my mind, quite reasonably, put forward. There is no need to be dogmatic about the length of the period of time. Vinobaji's suggestion in this regard seems to be the wisest: namely that the non-Hindi speaking States themselves should be left free to determine the period of time required.

Cool consideration of this central question is likely to be far more useful in settling the present national debate than of general opinions on the wisdom of learning foreign languages.

Jayaprakash Narayan

10. From T. T. Krishnamachari: Naval Tata on Textile Policy[11]
[Refer to item 101]

October 10, 1962

My dear Jawaharlalji,

I have perused the letter and the note from Naval Tata, which I am returning herewith.

2. The basic proposition that he mentions, viz., full utilisation of existing equipment is unexceptionable. This matter has been raised in the Industries Advisory Council several times of which I had seen reports. Curiously enough, a *hokum* [direction] had gone from the Commerce and Industry Ministry to all industries to rate their installed capacity to approximate to their production. Perhaps this was to meet the criticism of there being unutilised capacity in the country. Nevertheless, the matter has to be investigated and our existing machinery utilised to the full.

---

11. Letter from Minister without Portfolio. PMO, File No. 17(438)/60-64-PMS, vol. I, Sr. No. 12-C.

3. Naval Tata's note deals specifically with cotton textile industry and he has himself stated the reasons that stand in the way of full utilisation of textile equipment. On page 2 of his note in paragraph 7, he has mentioned two of these reasons which at the moment are not easy to deal with. Expansion and production in the cotton textile industry is possible and in fact practicable, but what is in short supply now is cotton. We have not progressed in regard to the production of cotton during the last seven years. We were producing 27 lakhs of cotton bales at the time of the Partition. We stepped it up to over 50 lakh bales in 1955 and thereafter we have remained stagnant. Today with a significant expansion of spindles, we have to sustain the mills by importing cotton to the tune of 10 lakh bales a year from abroad, a part of which comes under PL 480. Therefore, the problem of supply and prices of cloth at the moment is merely a problem of shortage of cotton.

4. As you yourself know, the question of electric energy is one that is not easy to deal with. According to the latest estimates made by the Planning Commission, which in my view do not take into account the realities of demand, we shall still be short of power at the end of the Third Plan. In the overall power picture as it is today, even this is an understatement of the position. The composite problem he has mentioned in regard to industry could be dealt with. In fact, I think some attention is being paid to it at the moment. I would, therefore, suggest that you write to him and tell him that you agree to the basic proposition and would invite comprehensive suggestions from the industries to this end. But so far as cotton textile Industry is concerned on his own showing, there is nothing much to be done at the moment.

Yours affectionately,
T. T. Krishnamachari

11. From Sudhir Ghosh: Indonesian Politics[12]
[Refer to item 212]

10 October, 1962

My dear Panditji,
You will recollect that you approved of my participation in the Conference of about 60 young diplomats organised by the Quakers at Punjak Pas near Bandung, Indonesia. I was one of the ten older persons (consultants) who were asked to

12. Letter from Rajya Sabha MP, Congress; address: 95, South Avenue, New Delhi, NMML, Sudhir Ghosh Papers.

give the ten addresses which the diplomats discussed for 10 days. Russians and Americans, Communists and non-Communists, lived together for 10 days and talked from morning till midnight like undergraduates at Cambridge or Oxford; the results were very encouraging.

During the fortnight's stay in Indonesia I naturally kept my eyes and ears open. I spent a good deal of time with our Ambassador, Apa Pant, who arranged for me to have a series of talks with some of the prominent Indonesians viz.

1. Dr Roeslan Abdulgani, Cabinet Minister and the theoretician and political philosopher who tries to give sensible shape to the rather nebulous political conception of Dr Soekarno,

2. Dr Ali Sastroamidjojo, former Prime Minister and at present Cabinet Minister

3. Dr. Sudarshano, former Ambassador in New Delhi

4. The Russian Ambassador, Mr N.A. Mikhailov

5. The Yogoslav Ambassador, Dr. Ales Bebler and

6. The British Ambassador, Sir Leslie Fry.

I did not see the US Ambassador; he was out of the country. I checked all my impressions with Apa Pant and, for what it is worth, I venture to make a brief report to you on comments I heard on (1) the India-China border dispute, (2) strained relation between India and Indonesia, (3) the proposed Afro-Asian Conference, and (4) the formation of Malaysia.

One of the persons who addressed the young diplomats at the Quaker Conference was Dr Han Suyin, the author, who normally lives in Singapore but came to the Conference direct from Peking where, she said, she had been seeing Mr Mao Tse-tung, Mr Chou-En-lai, Mr Chen Yi and various other leaders. She promoted long conversations with me about the India-China border dispute and explained with great vehemence the Chinese point of view. Han Suyin was anxious to explain that Mr Chou-En-lai never said anything to Mr Nehru at any time to give the impression that he would respect the traditional frontier (McMahon Line) between India and China. I asked her if she could help me to understand why is it and how is it that China today is involved in a conflict with (a) Russia, and (b) India—the two countries that proved during the past years that they wanted the new regime in China to succeed. She explained that the quarrel between Russia and China was a "family quarrel" and the Indians did not understand the nature of it; it would be unwise of the Indians to bank on the differences between Russia and China. The conflict with India was a different matter. According to Han Suyin it was the Indian reaction to the flight of the Dalai Lama from Tibet and the treatment accorded to the Dalai Lama in India that was decisive; this "unfriendly act" made it plain to the leaders of the Chinese Government that India had no intention of maintaining friendly relations with Communist China. Han Suyin mentioned again and again the name of Mrs Lakshmi Menon; poor Mrs Menon, according to Peking, is supposed to have taken the lead in a signature campaign in Delhi in support of the Dalai Lama and is supposed to have done various other acts of unfriendliness to the Chinese Government. Han Suyin added that the Chinese know what they are doing and if what they are doing is a mistake they will pay for it, but they do not care.

Among the Indonesians the only man who talked frankly (and I felt a great deal of respect for him) was Dr Roeslan Abdulgani. He was obviously very eager to talk to an Indian MP and kept me for two hours. Dr Ali Sastroamidjojo also talked at great length but he really had nothing to say; he is evidently a spent force although he still holds the office of a Cabinet Minister. But I gathered from our own Ambassador and the British Ambassador, the Yugolsav Ambassador, the Italian Ambassador and various others that Dr Roeslan Abdulgani is still very much of a force in Indonesian politics and sure to come back to a more powerful position; since Belgrade he has been in some trouble with Dr Soekarno and is somewhat out of favour but I was told that he was about the only man in the Indonesian set up who can stand up to Dr Soekarno.

I told Dr Roeslan Abdulgani that Members of our Parliament were extremely unhappy about the unpleasant incident at the Asian games and the insult to the Indian National Anthem and the ransacking of the Indian Embassy and we wondered what was behind it all. "We have done many things together since the Asian Conference in Delhi in 1947" I said, "I thought India and Indonesia had a sense of affection for each other, Dr. Abdulgani, but you seem to have lost confidence in us. What has happened? Would you care to talk about it?" He first explained what had happened in the Asian games and confirmed that the insult to the Indian National Anthem and the ransacking of the Embassy were actually organised by the Communists (Dr Ali Sastroamidjojo also said the same thing). He also mentioned in the course of his explanation that the Taiwan participants in the games were not given visas because of persistent pressure from Peking. He said what had happened was very unfortunate but pointed out that wise men should not attach exaggerated importance to such a thing. He did, however, admit that these troubles were the symptoms of a disease and not the disease itself; he did think that relationship between India and Indonesia was seriously wrong and he enumerated three causes.

(1) Indonesian leaders feel that at the United Nations and elsewhere the representatives of India have for years treated the Indonesians and other Afro-Asian representatives as a bunch of school boys, as if

731

the Indians were the big brothers whose job it was to shepherd these immature children. Indonesians have for many years resented this superiority in Indian representatives at international gatherings.

(2) Dr Soekarno feels that India has drifted away from the path of true socialism. He is very bitter about the Western European Socialists, the Dutch Socialists, the British or French who all have, according to Dr Soekarno, let down Indonesia and other Asian and African countries in their struggle for freedom; India seems to be very close to those hated Western European Socialists. "Soekarno thinks", said Dr Abdulgani, "that Pandit Nehru and other Indian leaders are Mohamed Hatta type of people and Soekarno does not like Mohammed Hatta at all. He thinks that the mixture of private enterprises and public enterprises which India has accepted in her 5-Year Plans is no socialism at all. And what is more, India seems to be succeeding in a substantial way in her economic development; we have not had much success in our economic programmes and, human nature being what it is, many of us in Indonesia suffer from a sense of jealousy and a sense of inferiority although we do not like to admit it." I was impressed with Dr Abdulgani's frankness.

(3) At the Belgrade Conference (which Dr Roeslan Abdulgani also attended) Dr Soekarno resented the position taken by Pandit Nehru viz., that the Number one issue before the world was not colonialism but the issue of war and peace and the survival of mankind. Dr Soekarno who was then getting ready for the struggle to free West Irian felt that he had been badly let down. He still fosters a strong sense of grievance about it.

Dr Abdulgani then volunteered the comment that the proposed Afro-Asian Conference would be useless if there was no prior understanding between Pandit Nehru and Dr Soekarno at a personal level and if the existing damage in relationship was not repaired. "Do you think the damage can be repaired?" I asked. He was not prepared for the question and was taken unawares. He hesitated for some moments and said, "I think it can be repaired." And he added, "whatever lies in my power to repair it I certainly will do. My friend, I give you that assurance." He then expressed the view that even if Colonialism was on the way out the Afro-Asian Conference was still necessary and desirable and Panditji should be persuaded to come to it.

On the subject of the proposed Afro-Asian Conference the comments of Ambassador Mikhailov (who was a Minister of the Soviet Government and still holds the position of a member of the Central Committee of the Communist

Party) were interesting. He was very vocal and communicative on the subject and said that it was his Government's view that this time the Conference should be expanded to include Cuba and all the Latin American countries and thus a united front of all the underdeveloped countries should be presented to this neo- colonialism of the Western powers, the European Common Market, which is a new instrument of exploitation of the weak by the strong. He said again and again that it was very important that the Conference should be held and it was the earnest hope of his Government that India would decide to come. He also expressed the view that the formation of Malayasia was a bad thing; it was all being worked up by the British and the Americans and it was a threat to the democratic forces in that part of the world. About the India-China border conflict he was very cautious. I said that we in the Indian Parliament were very puzzled about it; we did not understand why the Chinese were doing what they have done and the way they have done it. The Ambassador observed that India and China were great countries and it should be possible for two such great countries to solve the problem by peaceful means and added "Nikita Sergeivich[13] is very proud of our friendship with India."

Indonesia today is a very depressing country. The people are very gentle and warm and hospitable. But the country's economics is in a mess; the price of a cup of hot milk in a Jakarta hotel is Rs 50 i.e. five Indian rupees; the minimum charge for a taxi for a 10 minute ride is Rs 250/- or twenty five Indian rupees; a hotel room is more expensive in Jakarta than in New York; they have nothing left in foreign exchange till 1965; all exports up to 1965 are virtually mortgaged. There is no sign of the country getting down to hard work and build itself up. The only activity which is on display everywhere is the army and its parades. On all accounts, there are two real forces in the country, the Army and the Communists and the present leadership survives by balancing one against the other. The leadership of the country seems to be living on one excitement after another. West Irian provided an excitement and there is now an anticlimax and almost a sense of disappointment because the UN has found a peaceful solution of the problem and the country could not go to war. A vast quantity of armaments was acquired from Russia (which have still to be paid for) and they do not know what to do with these armaments now. The proposed formation of Malaysia has provided another excitement. On the 4th October there was a great military parade in Jakarta at which Dr Soekarno made a big speech in the course of which he said that Indonesia was being encircled. The Malayans seem to fear that Dr Soekarno is preparing to use the proposed Afro-Asian Conference to wreck, if he can, the Malaysia plan which is to materialise by

13. Khrushchev.

the 31st August, 1963. One of the senior officials of the Malayan Government who was at the Quaker Conference, came up to me especially to explain that their Prime Minister, Tunku Abdul Rehman, was expecting trouble from Dr Soekarno and they earnestly hope that Mr Nehru would go to the Afro-Asian Conference and save the Malayans from Dr Soekarno and his friends. It appears that Indonesia is going to put all kinds of pressure on India to make India go to the Conference, so that it can be used as a platform for agitation against Malaysia, and the European Common Market. Where we stand with the ECM and whether it is really going to be an instrument of exploitation or not we can find out only by hard negotiations with them and not by making speeches at the Afro-Asian Conference. However, Apa Pant feels that, in spite of it all, India should go to the Conference, especially to the preparatory Committee in December, and take an active part in giving it a direction; otherwise the field will be left open for other forces. I told Apa that I did not agree with him.

With regards,

Yours sincerely,
Sudhir Ghosh

12. From Bertrand Russell, Bertrand Russell Peace Foundation[14]
[Refer to item 186]

During the past years of our struggle against nuclear war, my experience has forced upon me the conclusion that unless we are able to spread knowledge of the danger on a very large scale, our efforts to mobilise a sufficiently powerful, public opinion on behalf of sanity will be unsuccessful with dire consequences. I feel this is particularly true with regard to the peoples of belligerent countries who do not sufficiently grasp the irrelevance of previous means of treating disputes between great nations, if man is to survive. If we are unable to gain access to the public in this way in order to present continuous facts about the folly of current cold war policy, our efforts to promote conscientious protest and widespread consciousness cannot hope to rise above a certain threshold.

The propaganda which is being spread by those who are involved in the continuation of the Cold War is such as to overwhelm our efforts unless these efforts are conducted on a vastly larger scale.

---

14. Letter; sent from Plas Penrhyn, Penrhyndeudraeth, Merioneth. Salutation and signature not available.

I have become convinced of the need to have a great Peace Foundation which could receive very large sums and have those sums which are from private sources considered tax free. Such a foundation could reasonably promote the education of the public on a serious and continuing basis through the medium of the journals, press, films and radio it could finance for this purpose. I should wish it to have an entirely educative and informative purpose but on the very largest possible scale for us. I should hope such a foundation to be respectable enough in its purpose to appeal to those industrialists who quietly wish the Cold War to be resolved. Naturally, I should be anxious for it to be possible for neutral Governments to feel able to support the foundation as well so that the moderating influence they seek to bring to bear upon the Great Powers can be presented as well to the populations of their countries by media which are integrally part of the life of these countries.

I believe that if we can do this, the conditions from which a very large and militant public opinion can be brought to bear may be provided, I have been persuaded, with deeply felt reluctance, that the foundation be called the Bertrand Russell Peace Foundation. Although I am not altogether comfortable about this, it seems that it would be thereby assisted because of the prominence with which I have been mentioned publicly with such work in recent years.

I believe that these efforts could be immeasurably enhanced if you could agree to be a Sponsor of the Foundation. I am most anxious to have your support in this way for your support would create great confidence in the foundation around the world. As its purposes are explicitly educative and are intended to be formally charitable, I am hopeful that you will not feel that your public responsibility precludes your being a Sponsor of the foundation. I very eagerly await your decision and I should be pleased to know your thoughts on the undertaking.

13. From B. P. Chaliha: Mizo District[15]
[Refer to items 55,56, and 57]

12th October 1962

My dear Prime Minister,
I promised to submit an appreciation of the political situation in Mizo District after our officers have made a thorough study of it. Our officers, namely, the Commissioner for the Hill districts, the Deputy Commissioner of the Districts

15. Letter from the Chief Minister of Assam. MHA, File No. 15/1/62-SR(R)-A, vol. I, pp.95-97/c.

and the Sub-divisional Officers of the Lungleh subdivision have since made an extensive tour of the district and have submitted their reports. We have also held discussion with them and the Governor[16] was also pleased to grant them an interview. I enclose herewith copies of their reports in case you feel like going through the same. We have been assured both in their reports and in the discussions that there is nothing in the district to take an alarming view. They have however made some constructive suggestions for improvement of the situation in the district. I would endeavour to condense their recommendations in the following paragraphs for your information.

1. With a view to prevent the hostile Nagas, who had escaped to East Pakistan, from re-entering India through Mizo District there has been some military preparations in the district. These preparations although are meant against the hostile Nagas, the Mizo have got an impression that these preparations are against them and it has become a cause of irritation to them. Our officers therefore have advised that the Army and special police except the Assam Rifles should be withdrawn and if any preparation is necessary, such preparation should be strictly confined to the border of the Mizo District and East Pakistan. The rest of the district should be left out.

2. The percentage of literacy in the Mizo district is the highest in the whole of the State but unfortunately this district of 8000 square miles with a population of about 3 lakhs with steep hills is undeveloped in all respects and is therefore, poor. Partition of the country has deprived them of their market for fruits etc. in East Pakistan. They have therefore recommended taking up intensive development schemes for that district.

3. They have also recommended removal of misunderstandings created by the Assam Official Language Act.

We, as well as our Governor generally appreciate the approach of our officers and their recommendations. With regard to Army, I understand that our Governor had a discussion with Corps Commander Lieutenant General Umrao Singh and the Governor got an impression that there is no military necessity to keep the forces there but order for removal will have to come from the Government of India. I hope, you will advise the appropriate Ministry on this matter.

With regard to development plans and also about the other recommendations we are taking necessary steps.

16. Vishnu Sahay.

The APHLC members are going to meet on the 15th when they would decide about their visit to Delhi to meet you.

With regard to Chinese incursion in the NEFA area, the information given by the External Affairs Ministry and as it has come out in the Press are not adequate to satisfy the public. I wonder if some more information could be given to prevent speculations. We are also very much interested to know the developments and therefore, we shall be grateful if we are also informed of the developments. Till some days people of our State did not show much concern about the developments but since a few days with more movements of troops and more air activities people have become inquisitive to know more about the developments.

I am sending a copy of this letter to Shri Lal Bahadur Shastriji[17] for information.

With kind regards,

Yours sincerely,
B.P. Chaliha

14. From Mulraj Kersondas: Food Production[18]
[Refer to items 102 and 106]

October 12, 1962

My dear Panditji,

There are three major issues with which the country is faced at present. They are, high prices, shortage of foreign exchange and heavy gold smuggling.

I deeply feel that the primary price reduction in food grains is essential in restoring price equalism [equilibrium] of other things. The high prices of food grains results into higher cost of living which requires increase cost of dearness allowance and a higher cost of manufacture of other commodities which in turn brings again the prices increase cost of other commodities and these in turn will again increase in the cost of living.

It is essential therefore, that we should tackle the high prices of food grains by producing more rather than controls which create more evil and discontents than the good that it does.

---

17. Home Minister.
18. Letter from Gujarati entrepreneur and a long time acquaintance of Nehru. JNMF, 1.D-22/M Series.

737

In 1943, when the American technical mission came to India to investigate into the possibilities of making India as the main centre for producing war materials, that mission had recommended that Indian soil was deficient in nitrogen and therefore, they recommended immediately as a war measure to put in six plants [each of] 50000 tons capacity of Ammonium Sulphate in India in different provinces and save the country from threatened food shortage as those might interfere in the proposal of the manufacture of war [machinery] accepted by the Indian Government under the Viceroy[alty] of Lord Linlithgow.

The events that have followed have proved the correctness of this report and even today, we find that yield of food grain in India is about 900 lbs compare[d] to 2500 lbs [in] China, about 3000 lbs in Japan and over 4000 lbs in America.

With a view therefore to provide fertilisers to Indian farms, various steps have been contemplated and taken by the Government. Till now, however, there is very little increase in average production.

I had suggested to you for use of cow dung gas plants to supply these fertilisers. After your reply, I had written to the Planning Minister Mr Nanda and then to the Planning Secretary Mr Khera[19] with whom I had two to three meetings in Bombay and I was happy when on 5th July I got a D.O. letter from the Planning Commission that the scheme was approved by the Planning Commission. I am enclosing herewith a copy of the letter for your ready reference. I am however sorry to learn recently that in answer to Mr D.S. Patel[20] in Rajya Sabha the Government said that the matter was still under consideration.

I wish, therefore, to draw your attention to the fact that at a rough estimate the dung produced in India is about 80 crore tons of which about 30 crore tons is being used as fuel. If, instead, this portion is used in cow dung gas plant, it will produce 9 lakh tons of nitrogen besides, mythil [Methane] gas worth 210 crores to be used a[s] fuel [or] for power generation.

This 9 lakh tons of nitrogen thus produced is equivalent to 12 plants of the capacities of Sindri fertilisers [factory] and it will require 300 crore of rupees to put such 12 plants and it will take about five years to get them [to] produce fertilisers. While the cow-dung plants could be made and the results obtained in a year's time. It will also save foreign exchange of 150 crores which could be saved and diverted towards other essential needs of the country.

19. G.L. Nanda and S.S. Khera, respectively.
20. Probably D.V. Patel, leader of Swatantra Party or M.S. Patel, a Congress MP, Rajya Sabha, both from Gujarat.

For this purpose, it will not be necessary for Government to put all the plants [themselves]. If they only put up a few plants in every division of every state, its results would be known in a year and once its benefits are known to farmers, they would beg, borrow and steal and put up such plants, themselves. Though in initial cases a subsidy to the farmers is necessary for inducing them to have such plants at accelerated speed, I am sure if a person of your popularity thus propagates the use of this gas plant, the public will take up the work and our food production will be increased by about 50% in a couple of years. Such an increase in food production will bring down the prices of food grains without in the least affecting the profits of the farmers as that production will have increased and will have an exportable surplus of food grains. The decrease in food grain prices will reduce the cost of living, and be useful in checking or reducing your serious attention to this problem, i.e., universal use of cow dung plant by every farmer.

The other point [is] about gold smuggling. I feel that the correct remedy for stopping this evil is to bring down the prices of gold. This will be done if exploration is made in this country for finding out gold mines in the country. I know of one such place i.e. the Nilambur village, 30 miles from Ootacamand. This was the place where an Australian gold mining company had first discovered gold in India in 1875[21] but they had closed up because their working was uneconomical. The price of gold at that time was only about Rs 50/- per ounce which is equal to 1 1/7- 1 1/18 [sic] of the present price and there are large qualities [quantities] of gold ore at this place. I feel if your Ministry takes up mines in such places and sells the gold into the open market regularly, it will satisfy [the domestic need] and bring the gold prices down and if the gold prices are brought down to about Rs 80 to 90 per tola, the temptation in smuggling will greatly be reduced and this will save us a lot of foreign exchange which is disappearing in this racket.

I, therefore, suggest these two points for your careful consideration as they would also save the country a lot of foreign exchange.

With kind regards,

Yours sincerely,
Mulraj Kersondas

21. Probably Kolar Mines.

15. From K. B. Menon: A Confession[22]
[Refer to item 20]

October 12, 1962

My dear Punditji,

I am writing to you this letter after long long years as a salve to my conscience. It is the happy memories of the years that I spent working under you that encourage me to write.

Will you kindly recollect that Jaiprakash[23] introduced me to you in 1937 and that you took me in as Secretary of Indian Civil Liberties Union. I owe to you my public life ever since. When Jaiprakash sought my services years later, I thought that I should not forget the good turn he did to me. I did not realise at the moment that in trying to be fair to one I was being unfair to another. I joined him with your consent. He left me. I then tried to carry on, but past kept rebuking me by reminding me of my wrong. I came once or twice very near confessing to you. Fear held me back, fear that my motives might be misinterpreted, not by you but by others, and used against me. A crisis in the Party helped me to overcome that fear and hesitation. Acceptance of office by the PSP in Kerala had a corroding effect on the Party. The best in me revolted. Mental adjustment became difficult. I therefore quietly severed my connections with the Party.[24] It was not easy. I have been trying to serve the people almost from adolescence. I may continue to do that in my own limited way. That, however, is a small matter. What was worrying me was my behaviour towards you. I now feel relieved.

I am, as ever, at your service.
[K.B. Menon]

---

22. Letter from a former PSP leader from Kerala, (1897-1967); address: "Thripuram", Empress Hotel Road, Calicut-1, Kerala. NMML, K. B. Menon Papers, F.No.2, 1962.
23. Jayaprakash Narayan.
24. For Menon's differences with the PSP leadership, see NMML, K.B. Menon papers, F.No. 11/2, p.3. For Menon's resignation from PSP, see NMML, K.B. Menon papers, F.No.1/2, p.6.

16. From William Tubman: Settling India-China Dispute[25]
[Refer to item 386]

I have heard and read with great distress of the border difference between India and China and which now seems to be assuming dangerous proportions and I have therefore communicated with Members of the Bandung Conference Group and other African Asian States suggesting that we might intervene with a view of negotiating a settlement of this dispute between India and China and I am appealing to both sides to call a halt and cessation of further hostilities until we can get together and decide what action to take. With assurances of my highest esteem.

17. From C. P. Ramaswami Aiyar: Requesting Foreword for Book on Art[26]
[Refer to item 143]

October 18, 1962

My dear Prime Minister,

I have agreed to deliver a series of lectures at the Madras University on "India in the World of Art" dealing with the developments of Indian Architecture, Painting and Sculpture through the ages viewed in relation to similar evolutionary progress in China, Japan and Europe and America.

During over fifty years I have not only visited as a student of art most of the art galleries in Asia, Europe and North and South America but have been collecting specimens of painting and sculpture from all over the world and have specially been fortunate in securing some of the original paintings of the protagonists of the Bengal and Andhra Schools at a time when artists like Abanindranath Tagore, Gogonedranath Tagore, Chugtai, Nandlal Bose, Rama Rao and others were still struggling for recognition. I also possess reproductions of all the great pictures and sculptures of the West and in addition I have valuable specimens of Chinese painting and ceramic ware. Ultimately my ambition is to hand over these treasures to some public institution.

---

25. Cable, 17 October 1962, from the President of Liberia. MEA, File No. A/103/23/62, p.1/corr.
26. Letter from Chairman, Hindu Religious Endowment Commission. Sent from Ootacamund. PMO, File No. 9/2/62-PMP, Vol. 7, Sr.No.79-A.

In addition, I have made a special study of Indian architecture from early times up to the period of the great South Indian shrines.

With this background, I have completed my lectures and given them for printing. They will be produced in book form after delivery of the substance in the form of lectures.

I shall take it as a great personal favour if you will find time to go through the book when it is ready, (i.e. about the end of this year). If, after perusal, you think they deserve a foreword from you, I shall be specially obliged. My request is made not so much to the Prime Minister of India as to a person of ripe culture and wide historical perspective as well as a lover of beauty and the arts.

With my best regards,

Yours very sincerely
C. P. Ramaswami Aiyar

[P.S.] I shall be in New Delhi in my son's house from 24th October.

18. From T.T. Krishnamachari: Import Licences for Rayon[27]
[Refer to item 97]

October 19, 1962

My dear [Jawaharlal],

Please read the cutting enclosed.[28] It speaks of a Premium on import licences for rayon yarn issued as a result of export performance. Purchase of rayon yarn for export purposes at such high cost, both in regard to foreign exchange and also in respect of our moral well-being wants looking into. The so called exports under these schemes impose a fixed liability on the limited amount of foreign exchange that we have and the advantages we are supposed to get are in reality imaginary. I do not see why we should permit this type of illusory advantage to be gained by immoral methods to go on for all time.

[T.T. Krishnamachari]

27. Letter from the Minister without Portfolio. NMML, T.T. Krishnamachari Papers, File 1962, Copy.
28. Not reproduced; available in NMML, T.T. Krishnamachari Papers, File 1962.

19. From S. Radhakrishnan: Amending the Constitution[29]
[Refer to items 48 and 50]

October 20, 1962

My dear Prime Minister,

Your letter of the 17th October about the proposed amendments to the Constitution.

Article 84[a] may read "a citizen of India and pledges himself to preserve the Constitution and the integrity of the Union." In our Constitution there is no such thing as a 'citizen of a State.'

Before we modify article 19(1) and (4), we should take into account the impression that the Fundamental Rights are being slowly eroded and this may perhaps be looked upon as a further restriction. The expression 'preservation of the integrity of the State' should read 'preservation of the integrity of the Union'. Even then, it may be capable of varying interpretations.

Some way by which we can deprive a person of his citizenship rights, if he attempts to bring about disruption of the Union, may be considered. Any amendment should cover not only the DMK but also the secessionists in Mizo District (Assam) and Kashmir.

Yours affectionately,
S. Radhakrishnan

20. From Pyarelal: Gandhi on Africa[30]
[Refer to item 194]

20th October, 1962

My dear Panditji,

Some time back I wrote to Jomo Kenyatta in connection with an interview that he had with Bapu in London in 1931. While sending me Kenyatta's statement on that interview Shri Chanan Singh[31] has sent me the enclosed letter with some extracts from Bapu's writings.

---

29. Letter from the President. MHA, File No. 25/3/61-Poll (1), p.19.
30. Letter from Mahatma Gandhi's secretary, and biographer; sent from 2-4 Theatre Communication Building, Connaught Circus, New Delhi. PMO, File No. 2(114)/56-66-PMS, Sr. No. 88-A.
31. Parliamentary Secretary and a close aide of Jomo Kenyatta.

I am sending you with this the draft of my reply to Chanan Singh for your approval and advice. In view of the questions raised by Shri Chanan Singh I am also sending you for your perusal and return with your remarks the text of an article on "Gandhiji on the African Question" that I wrote for the Council for America at Balvantray Mehta's instance, and the script of a broadcast for the overseas services of the AIR which is to come on the 9th of November. As these writings have a bearing on our foreign relations, I seek your guidance.

I have to see you about a couple of matters relating to my work. I would feel obliged if you could spare a few minutes at your convenience.

I have to leave for Calcutta today. I shall be back here on the morning of Thursday, the 25th instant.

Yours sincerely,
Pyarelal

21. Pakistan-China Talks on Indo-US Arms Deal[32]
[Refer to item 228]

Chinese Embassy in Pakistan
20 October 1962

(Pakistan revealed that India and America had a secret agreement)

To the Ministry of Foreign Affairs:

On 21 October, the Parliament of Pakistan will hold an emergency meeting to discuss the Sino-Indian border clash and the weapons given to India by the United States and Britain. The President of Pakistan (Ayub Khan) will announce Pakistan's position toward the Sino-Indian border clash during a secret meeting and the Foreign Minister will address this during a public conference. The Secretary of Pakistan's Ministry of Foreign Affairs flew to Pindi [Rawalpindi] on the afternoon of 19 [October] to influence the decision of the President and Pakistan's Foreign Minister and prevent them from doing something unfavourable to China. Ambassador Ding [Guoyu] made an appointment with Pakistan's Foreign Affairs Secretary on the morning of 19 [October] and asked

32. Cable from Chinese Embassy, Pakistan, 20 October 1962; "Minutes of Conversation between Chinese Ambassador Ding Guoyu and Pakistan Foreign Secretary"; Wilson Centre Archives; http://digitalarchive.wilsoncenter.org/document/114763. Accessed on 6 September 2018.

him to arrange a meeting with Pakistan's President and Foreign Minister. The Secretary promised to reply after checking with them in Pindi. So Ambassador Ding may go to Pindi today. Even if he does not meet with Pakistan's President and Foreign Minister, he can exert his influence upon Pakistan's President and Foreign Minister through the Foreign Affairs Secretary, as foreign policy speeches are actually drafted by him.

Ambassador Ding and Pakistan's Foreign Affairs Secretary talked about the Sino-Indian border clash and Sino-Pakistani relations.

Pakistan's Foreign Affairs Secretary said that Pakistan was facing difficult circumstances in terms of the Sino-Indian border clash. If Pakistan had a good relationship with India, Pakistan could strive to contribute to the peaceful resolution of the Sino-Indian border issue through negotiations. Unfortunately, although Pakistan has always made efforts to solve issues with India, this has failed, Pakistan sympathizes with China, Pakistan's official position is that it hopes the issue can be resolved peacefully, that the clash will not escalate and that this does not turn into a kind of situation in which the Chinese government has to take further and stronger actions. On the other hand, Pakistan feels that India deserves [to be taught] a lesson and hopes that China will severely punish India and drag India down through a long-term struggle without making the issue too serious. Otherwise, the United States and Britain will do anything, even a world war, Pakistan could not say it in this way officially because if this had been spoken publicly, Pakistan would be seen as having a bias. In addition, Pakistan and China are negotiating border issues, thus, Pakistan has to be cautious when commenting on the Sino-Indian border issue. Otherwise, there will be misunderstandings.

The President of Pakistan has seen the letter from Premier Zhou En-lai and returned it to the Ministry of Foreign Affairs to be studied, Pakistan's Foreign Affairs Secretary said Pakistan paid close attention to the letter. The tone of the letter, which reveals India's attitude and method, was the same as Pakistan's, so Pakistan was familiar with the letter. The President of Pakistan will make an announcement during a secret meeting with the Parliament. He proposed clear written suggestions to the President not knowing to what degree he will take them or how (the President) will make use of them. However, the speech by Pakistan's Foreign Ministry at the public conference of the Parliament may be more frank or cite Premier Zhou's letter.

In regards of Sino-Pakistani relations, he said that the President of Pakistan completely knows the great significance of developing close relations with China and is paying close attention to [maintaining] friendly Sino-Pakistani relations.

The President of Pakistan is quite determined on this point. Although there are intense pressures from various areas, Pakistan will not allow anything to influence the Sino-Pakistan relationship, Pakistan will not do anything to hurt China and Pakistan will never offend China. Considering Pakistan's alignments and obligations, the way Pakistan talked is not a small matter.

[Pakistan] thus hopes that the Chinese government will appreciate this. Pakistan hopes Sino-Pakistan relations can produce more achievements. At the same time, he said that we could not underestimate the political and economic difficulties caused by past policies, Pakistan had to be good at using strategy to handle state affairs, and therefore hoped that Pakistan could gain China's support, sympathy and understanding. Even the strongest person also needs support, sympathy and assistance. He expressed that he sincerely hopes that China and Pakistan will soon conclude a border agreement. Border negotiations were suspended because the Pakistani ambassador needed to ask for instructions from his government and now that a reply has been written, we hope the negotiations can be conducted as soon as possible.

Concerning Pakistan's involvement in treaties, he said that Pakistan was still involved in treaties but he would not defend them. All of the notes and negotiations Pakistan has with other treaty nations have always put forth clauses for protest requirements against all forms of aggression, Pakistan has emphasised that this has always been [directed toward] India, and the reason Pakistan takes part in treaties is to defend itself against India, Pakistan never seriously considered a Russian attack and whether Pakistan could survive. As for China, the things which happened now show that China suffered an invasion, Pakistan has always appreciated China's understanding of Pakistan's difficulties and appreciates this very much.

On the issue of exposing the Nehru Government, he said that Nehru had always been telling big lies. Ostensibly, he was against imperialism and colonialism, executing "neutral" policies and actively opposing military treaties and agreements. But Pakistan has just received the "Agreement of Mutual Security" of 16 March 1951, signed by India and America based on Clause 408 in the American Mutual Security Act of 1949. He very mysteriously told Ambassador Ding about the agreement and the stipulation that the weapons supplied to India by the United States would be used for the following purposes: (1) Maintaining internal security; (2) Carrying out legal self-defense; (3) Taking part in the defense of territory belonging to India. This indicated that India was actually aligned with the United States and that Nehru was cheating the whole world, Pakistani newspapers have exposed this and hoped China would expose it to neutral nations in Asia and Africa without mentioning the point of "taking part in the defense of territory belonging to India"; otherwise, India would know that it was Pakistan who told China. Moreover, America sent a note to Pakistan which guaranteed that the weapons given to India would not be used to attack Pakistan on 17 October 1962. (He "secretly" showed me the note. But in fact, Pakistani newspapers already disclosed it on 19 (October).

Ambassador Ding expressed our appreciation to Pakistan's Foreign Affairs Secretary for his support in the Sino-Indian border clash and for the President of Pakistan's hope that the Sino-Indian border issue is resolved peacefully. Ding also hoped that he could exert influence on the President of Pakistan and introduce him to the truth: Who on earth invaded who? Who initiated peace negotiations? Who protested peace negotiations? Who refused peace negotiations? We believe that President of Pakistan will adopt a fair and impartial stance on the Sino-Indian border issue and that Pakistan will not succumb to pressures or adopt policies in line with national interests.

Ambassador Ding expressed the significance of the Sino-Pakistan border agreement and the visit to China by Pakistan's Foreign Minister. We hope that the border negotiations will continue to progress smoothly. As for the other issues mentioned, the Chinese government is considering these issues and believes that they will not be very difficult to resolve during the visit to China by Pakistan's Foreign Minister.

Concerning Pakistan's participation in treaties, Ambassador Ding said that there is an understanding between Pakistan and China. Foreign Minister Chen and La-di (sic), the former Ambassador of Pakistan in China, have discussed this issue. But we will never change our stance on the American imperialists' plots for these treaties, because military treaties obviously are in opposition to our nation.

Concerning the issue of exposing the Nehru Government, Ambassador Ding expressed that People's Daily had published two articles titled, "Re-discussing Nehru's Philosophies" and "The Appearance of Non-Alignment is being Taken Off."[33]

22. From B.K. Chandiwala: Night Shelters in Delhi[34]
[Refer to item 171]

श्री पंडित जी,
पिछले वर्ष दिल्ली में जब भयंकर सर्दी पड़ी थी तो कोर्पोरेशन ने चंद आर्ज़ी रैनबसेरे खोल दिये थे। गर्मी शुरू होने पर वह बंद हो गये थे उसके बाद हमने बहुत कोशिश की, कि

---

33. See the *Peking Review* the Vol.42, 19 October 1962, p.6.
34. From B.K. Chandiwala, 20/10 APP. NMML, B.K. Chandiwala Papers.

मकान बनाने के लिये कोई ज़मीन मिल जाए मगर कहीं नहीं मिली। अब जाड़ा फिर शुरू होने वाला है। और वही समस्या फिर उपस्थित होगी। कोर्पोरेशन ने यह तो मान लिया है कि गत वर्ष वाले स्थानों पर तीन बसेरे 15 नवम्बर को जारी कर देंगे। मैं तो इस बात पर ज़ोर दे रहा हूं कि दो तीन जगह मकान बना दिये जाएं। एक मकान बनाना कोर्पोरेशन ने मंज़ूर भी किया है। मेरी निगाह में दो जगहें ऐसी हैं जो रैन बसेरों के लिये बहुत ही उपयुक्त हैं। मकान बनाने के लिये रूपया भी मौजूद है। मगर एक स्थान है रेलवे मंत्रालय के अधीन और दूसरा है डिफ़ेंस के अधीन। रेलवे के अधीन तो है पीली कोठी, जो 1942 में जला दी गई थी। बीस वर्ष से वह जगह बेकार पड़ी है यदि वह हमें मिल जाए तो पांच सौ आदमियों के लिये रैन बसेरा बन सकता है। है भी वह खारी बाओली और चांदनी चौक के नज़दीक। दूसरी जगह है लाल क़िले के पास जहां कुछ महीने हुए आग लगी थी। यहां शरणार्थियों की एक बस्ती थी वह अब सीलमपूर भेज दी गई। जो जगह ख़ाली हुई है उसमें से यदि जगह मिल जाए तो वह चांदनी चौक के इलाक़े के लिये बहुत ही उपयुक्त है। मगर यह दोनों स्थान आप ही दिलवा सकते हैं। यदि आप कह दें तो हमारी एक बड़ी दिक़्क़त हल हो जाए। आप यदि राय साहब[35] से कह दें तो उनसे मिलकर मैं पूरी विगत उन्हें दे दूंगा।

आपका
ब्र.कृ

[Translation begins:

Shri Panditji,

Last year when Delhi faced severe winter, the Corporation had set up some temporary night shelters. They were shut down during the summer. After that we tried to get some land to build a permanent shelter, but could not get any suitable ones. Now the winter is about to set in and the same problem will recur. The Corporation has agreed to set up three shelters at the same place as last year, from 15th of November. I am trying to emphasise that houses should be set up in two or three places. The Corporation has agreed to build one such house. I have located a couple of spots which would be appropriate for night shelters. We have money for building too, but one is under the Ministry of Railway and the other is under Defence. The one under the Railways is the Pili Kothi, which was burnt down in 1942. That land has been lying unused for the last twenty years. If we can get that land, we can build a shelter for five

---

35. Most probably Mehr Chand Khanna.

hundred people. This is located near Khari Baoli and Chandni Chowk. The second one is near the Red Fort, where there was a major fire some months ago. There was a refugee camp, which has now been shifted to Seelam Puri. If we can get a piece of the vacated land, it would be most suitable for the Chandni Chowk area. Only you can make these plots available to us. If you put in a word, a major problem would be resolved. If you could speak to Rai Saheb,[36] I can meet him and apprise him of all the details.

Yours,
Brij Krishna

23. Soviet Position on Border Dispute[37]
[Refer to item 261 and appendix 27]

The government of the Soviet Union has carefully studied the current situation of the Sino-Indian border as introduced in the conversation between Comrade Zhou En-lai and the Soviet Ambassador on 8 October of this year and expressed its gratitude [for this introduction].

We understand the views of the Chinese comrades and recognize that the government of the People's Republic of China is making efforts to eliminate conflict and settle disputes peacefully. We are confident that this route is consistent with the interests of the entire socialist camp.

We all know that, although the Soviet Union has not issued any statement since 1959,[38] we consistently hold that such disputes should be resolved through peaceful means and take into account the interests of China and India. We are

---

36. See note 35 in this section.
37. Soviet Memorandum, 22 October 1962, handed over to Chinese Vice Minister Zhang Han-fu, Wilson Centre Archives; http://digitalarchive.wilsoncentre.org/document/1211895. Accessed on 6 September 2018.
38. On 9 September 1959 the Central Committee of the CPSU handed over to Chen Yi a letter and a TASS statement expressing "regret", "bewilderment" and "concern" over the border clash in Longju in August 1959. The statement claimed that the Chinese action "poisoned the international atmosphere" on the eve of Khrushchev's visit to the US. See "Report from the Chinese Foreign Ministry, 'The Soviet Union's Stance on Sino-Indian Boundary Question and Soviet-Indian Relations'," April, 1963. Wilson Centre Archives; http://digitalarchive.wilsoncentre.org/document/116949 Accessed on 6 September 2018.

closely watching how the situation develops and agree with your views, namely that the recent information regarding the Sino-Indian border is more worrisome.

It has become increasingly obvious that the tensions are continuing to build. This development is only beneficial to the imperialists and the reactionary clique of India. In the past and in the present, they are doing everything possible to sow the seeds of hostility between the People's Republic of China and India, to weaken the traditional friendship between the great Chinese and Indian people, and to provoke an armed conflict between them. We know very well that the imperialist clique has used every opportunity to take advantage of the Sino-Indian border issue in the dispute to speculate about relations between the Soviet Union and India and the Soviet Union and China in an attempt to divide us and sow dissension between the people of China and the Soviet Union.

Therefore, we are willing to clarify that the Soviet Union and China have an unbreakable fraternal friendship which is based on the Marxist-Leninist doctrine and the principles of Proletarian Internationalism. It is the fight against imperialism and for world peace that brings us together.

We fully support your desire to solve the border dispute with India through negotiations. Negotiations will prevent the further intensification of the conflict and create a good atmosphere for its peaceful settlement.

We understand your position that the McMahon Line is not an established boundary. It is a painful historical legacy.

When this line was delimited, Indian territory was still under the rule of a powerful colonial country—the United Kingdom. England drew and redrew the map of this area without considering the national interests of all ethnic groups, historical characteristics, and national characteristics. At that time, China was weak and could not resist the United Kingdom as it deserved. Nevertheless, China does not recognise the unilateral delimitation of the McMahon Line.

Of course, it is difficult to state the specific ways to resolve the border dispute between the People's Republic of China and India, but we believe that the recommendations put forward by the People's Republic of China to hold talks without preconditions and that the two forces should retreat 20 kilometers beyond the 1959 border are constructive suggestions. We believe that these recommendations are a good start for the peaceful solution to this problem which do not damage the prestige of either side and take into account the interests of both the People's Republic of China and India.

As for the comments made by Comrade Zhou En-lai on the sale of airplanes and helicopters to India by the Soviet Union, we are willing to tell you that, so far, the Soviet Union has sold India eight "AH-12" airplanes and twenty

"MU-4" helicopters. Obviously, these planes have no military significance and will not affect the balance of power.[39]

The government of the Soviet Union, in forming its policy towards India both in the past and at the present, begins from the desire of how to enable India to maintain a neutral position and prevent the reactionary forces in India from pulling India into the imperialist camp. When deciding to sell arms to India [we] considered how this measure can be used to serve our common interests and prevent India from becoming closer to the imperialist countries and, in particular, to prevent India's military clique from becoming closer to the militarists in the United States and other Western countries.

Finally, we hope that the border conflict will be cleared up and that the Sino-Indian border dispute will be solved in a reasonable manner.

24. From Amrit Kaur: Commonwealth Games[40]
[Refer to item 148]

October 23, 1962

My dear Jawaharlal,
A meeting of the All-India Council of Sports was held this morning and I presided over it in the absence of the Chairman.[41]

This meeting was called specially to look into the request of the Indian Olympic Association to send a team of athletes and players in other games to attend the Commonwealth Games which are being held in Perth, Australia, from November the 22nd onwards.

---

39. On 14 October 1962 the Central Committee of the CPSU took the following decisions (on the Indian-Chinese conflict). "1. Delay the shipment to India of MiG-21 aircraft. 2. On instructions to the Soviet ambassador in India, Cde. (Ivan) Benedictov. Say to (Indian Prime Minister Jawaharlal) Nehru: "We are disappointed." Are they thinking about how this conflict will end? ... The PRC's proposals for troop withdrawals spanning 20 km are reasonable. India's demands for troop withdrawals spanning an additional 20 km are humiliating for the PRC. We are in favour of eliminating the conflict, it will not bring any benefit. India is hardly going to gain anything from the conflict." "Central Committee of the Communist Party of the Soviet Union Presidium Protocol 59," October 14, 1962, Wilson Centre Archives; http://digitalarchive.wilsoncenter.org/document/114791. Accessed on 6 September 2018.
40. Letter from Rajya Sabha MP, Congress. address: 2 Willingdon Crescent, New Delhi. PMO, File No. 40(225)/61-72-PMS, Sr. No. 37-A.
41. Yadavindra Singh of Patiala.

We considered the personnel, etc, of the teams recommended by the IOA but, in the first instance, it was decided to write at once to you and seek your advice and guidance as to whether a team should go abroad under the present circumstances and whether any foreign exchange will be available to them. I may mention that eight out of the 12 athletes belong to the Army Services and 12 out of the entire contingent of 26 likewise. The Council would like to know whether it is possible for the Army, in the present circumstances, to spare these men.

If you and the Army authorities are of the opinion that no Army personnel shall go abroad for any purpose whatsoever at the present juncture the President of the Indian Olympic Association[42] informed us that, in that event, we would not send any athletes at all. Non-army personnel could go for wrestling, weight-lifting and swimming and perhaps one or two for boxing. But in the event of no Army personnel being available to our Olympic Team we would again like your advice as to whether a team should go at all.

Yours ever,
Amrit Kaur

25. US Analysis of Situation: R.W. Komer to Phillips Talbot[43]

[Refer to item 388 and 261 and appendices 23, 28 and 72]

Though we still see through a glass darkly, we may have a golden opportunity for a major gain in our relations with India. The sheer magnitude of India's reversal on the Chicom border may at long last awaken Delhi to the weakness of its position. Therefore, while I recognize the delicate tactical problems involved in handing this one, we ought to be prepared to move fast.

Now Delhi seems gripped (despite the brave words) by acute frustration, which may soon turn to despair. They don't know what to do next, and are clearly feeling out both us and the Russians for help.

---

42. Bhalinder Singh.
43. Internal memorandum, 24 October 2018, Deputy National Security Advisor to the US President to Assistant Secretary of State for Near East and South Asian Affairs https://www.jfklibrary.org/Asset-Viewer/Archives/JFKNSF-111-016.aspx Accessed on 21 August 2018.

We've had plenty of feelers (BK [Nehru] to [Carl] Kaysen, [M.J.] Desai to Galbraith,[44][G. Partha] Sarathy[45] to Bill Bundy[46], etc.). In this situation it's a close argument as to whether quiet receptiveness but no positive overtures on [our] part might not let an opportunity slip by. Indian pride, plus Menon's arguments, may lead Indians not to give us the clear signal we want. So, we ought urgently to canvas the possibilities (I gather Bill Bundy is working on this), and then perhaps at least tell Indians privately what's available.

Equally important is to do what we can to convince Delhi there's little hope in the Soviet track.

The Indians still seem to be relying largely on Soviets to help bail them out. Note Delhi's 1349 where Desai says that Soviet and Chinese have been "repairing differences" and "we cannot hasten a Sino-Soviet reconciliation." To our knowledge, he is inaccurate on both counts. Sino-Soviet relations have reached a nadir; we should document this to Indians and tell them we think Moscow has little if any leverage left with Peiping. It has already used up all its cards and would use more if possible. Indeed, Peiping must have already discounted the possibility of Soviet pressure on India's behalf. So this is a thin road in our view.

If we fear Indians would regard it as self-seeking if we were to advance this line of argument, why not get the British or other third parties to do so? Until the Indians are convinced that Moscow offers little hope (convincing them would also be a blow at Menon), the way for better US/Indian relationship will not be fully open.

The other direction from which India badly needs reassurance is Pakistan. It seems so desirable to press Ayub along these lines that I'd like to see us do more. In fact, I think we could argue honestly that Ayub will get better results on Kashmir, etc. in the long run by a forthcoming attitude now. While reviving the "joint defense" idea might be premature as yet, wouldn't it have an electric effect if Ayub broke off China border talks, saying no, wouldn't negotiate while Chicoms were invading India.

Even if Ayub turns us down, I see little risk in pressing him along these lines, because one of the things we want to do anyway is get across that we will not back Pakistan against India. So whether or not Ayub responds to our suggestions, he'll read their implications clearly enough.

An added reason for exploring the Pak angle is that the best and cheapest way to get Indian military resources freed for use against the Chicoms is from

44. J.K. Galbraith, Ambassador to India.
45. G. Parthasarathy, Indian Ambassador to Pakistan.
46. William Bundy, Foreign Affairs Advisor to Kennedy.

the Pak frontier. If the Indians go into a massive military buildup, it can only be at the expense of their current plan. This would be a tragedy from our standpoint. Therefore, the cheapest and most immediate way of freeing Indian military resources for next spring's campaign would be via rapprochement with the Paks. [See items 230 and 231].

We can't let our other current preoccupations, large as they loom, distract us unduly. The Sino-Indian conflict may have entered a stage whose long term implications are fully comparable to those arising from Cuba. If necessary, we should force these on the top echelon, once we've decided how we ought to move.

RWK

26. From Chou En-lai[47]
[Refer to items 247, 391, 395 and 419]

Your Excellency Respected Prime Minister,
It is most distressing that border clashes as serious as the present ones should have occurred between our two countries. Fierce fighting is still going on. At this critical moment, I do not propose to trace the origin of this conflict. I think we should look ahead, we should take measures to turn the tide. In order to seek a way to stop the border clashes, reopen peaceful negotiations and settle the Sino-Indian boundary question, the Chinese Government has already issued a statement, proposing the following:

1 Both parties affirm that the Sino-Indian boundary question must be settled peacefully through negotiations. Pending a peaceful settlement, the Chinese Government hopes that the Indian Government will agree that both parties respect the line of actual control between the two sides along the entire Sino-Indian border, and the armed forces of each side withdraw 20 kilometers from this line and disengage.

2 Provided that the Indian Government agrees to the above proposal, the Chinese Government is willing, through consultation between the two parties, to withdraw its frontier guards in the Eastern sector of the border to the north of the line of actual control; at the same time, both China and India undertake not to cross the line of actual control,

47. Letter from the Prime Minister of China 24 October 1962. Reproduced from *Chinese Aggression in War and Peace. Letters of the Prime Minister of India* (Ministry of Information and Broadcasting, Publications Division, 8 December 1962), pp. 35-36.

i.e., the traditional customary line, in the Middle and Western sectors of the border.

Matters relating to the disengagement of the armed forces of the two parties and the cessation of armed conflict shall be negotiated by officials designated by the Chinese and Indian Governments respectively.

3   In order to seek a friendly settlement of the Sino-Indian boundary question, talks should be held once again by the Prime Ministers of China and India. At a time considered to be appropriate by both parties, the Chinese Government would welcome the Indian Prime Minister to Peking; if this should be inconvenient to the Indian Government, the Chinese Premier would be ready to go to Delhi for talks.

For thousands of years, the peoples of China and India have been friendly to each other, and they should remain so from generation to generation. Our two countries jointly initiated the Five Principles of Peaceful Coexistence and took part in the Bandung Conference of historic significance. Our two peoples' common interests in their struggle against imperialism outweigh by far all the differences between our two countries. We have a major responsibility for Sino-Indian friendship, Asian-African solidarity and Asian peace. Driven by a deep sense of this responsibility, I sincerely appeal to you that you may respond positively to the above three proposals.

Please accept, Your Excellency, the assurances of my highest consideration.

Yours Sincerely,
Chou En-lai
Premier of the State Council of the People's Republic of China.

27. Sale of Aircraft to India[48]

[Refer to item 408 and appendices 23 and 26]

[To] All Chinese Embassies and Chargés d'Affaires

On 22 October, the Embassy of the Soviet Union submitted to Vice Minister Zhang [Han-fu] a memorandum from the Government of the Soviet Union in

---

48. Cable from Chinese Ministry of Foreign Affairs to all Chinese embassies and Chargés d'Affaires, 25 October 1962; Wilson Centre Archives; http://digitalarchive.wilsoncentre. org/document/114766. Accessed on 6 September 2018.

reply to Premier Zhou En-lai's talks with the Ambassador of the Soviet Union on the Sino-Indian border dispute. The key points of the memo are summarized as follows:

(1) It expresses serious worry about the situation in the Sino-Indian border and says that such a situation is only going to benefit the imperialists and the anti-revolutionary groups in India who always attempt to damage the Sino-Indian friendship, Soviet-Indian relations and Sino-Soviet relations.

(2) It emphasises the Soviet Union's perennial stance on the peaceful settlement of the dispute. It says that the Soviet Union fully supports our efforts to settle the dispute peacefully and our constructive proposal to hold unconditional negotiations and mutually withdraw by 20 kilometers. It expresses an understanding of our stance that the McMahon Line is not an established border.

(3) It pleads that the transport aircraft and helicopters that the Soviet Union sold to India "have no military significance" and "will not affect the balance of power." It also says that this "measure is for our common interest by preventing India from approaching the West."

Vice Minister Zhang says that what matters is India's encroachment on Chinese territory while China does not encroach on India's territory. It must be clearly understood that India is the invader and China has been forced to defend; that India has rejected peaceful negotiations on the Sino-Indian border dispute while China has always insisted on such a peaceful settlement; that India crossed the Chinese border, encroached on Chinese territory and launched full attacks against China's border defense units while China has been forced to fight back. It is also noteworthy that Nehru used to instigate riots in Tibet and met the Dalai Lama some days ago.[49] Indian governmental officials even claim to support and recognize the exile government of Tibet. It is necessary to clearly distinguish right from wrong.

Ministry of Foreign Affairs
25 October 1962

49. On 18 October 1962. See item 234.

28. From John F. Kennedy: Chinese Attack[50]
[Refer to item 388]

October 27, 1962

Dear Mr Prime Minister:

Your Ambassador handed me your letter last night. The occasion of it is a difficult and painful one for you and a sad one for the whole world. Yet there is a sense in which I welcome your letter, because it permits me to say to you what has been in my mind since the Chinese Communists have begun to press their aggressive attack into Indian territory. I know I can speak for my whole country when I say that our sympathy in this situation is wholeheartedly with you. You have displayed an impressive degree of forbearance and patience in dealing with the Chinese. You have put into practice what all great religious teachers have urged and so few of their followers have been able to do. Alas, this teaching seems to be effective only when it is shared by both sides in a dispute.

I want to give you support as well as sympathy. This is a practical matter and, if you wish, my Ambassador in New Delhi can discuss with you and the officials of your Government what we can do to translate our support into terms that are practically most useful to you as soon as possible.

With all sympathy for India and warmest personal good wishes,

Sincerely,
John. F. Kennedy

29. From Morarji Desai: Assam Oil Royalty[51]
[Refer to item 59]

28th October, 1962

My dear Jawaharlalji,

I am enclosing a Note containing my recommendations on the dispute regarding Oil Royalty which has arisen between the Assam Government and the Ministry of Mines and Fuel. I am enclosing also for your information a copy of the record of the discussion held on this subject with both the parties.

2.   As you would see from the Note, I have recommended that we should prescribe a specific rate of royalty of Rs 7.50 per metric ton as compared to the

---

50. Letter from the US President. MEA, File No. 1(China)/62, Vol. III, p.nil.
51. Letter from the Finance Minister. PMO, File No. 17(490)/62-70-PMS, Sr. No. 55-A.

rate calculated at more than Rs 10/- per ton which the Government of Assam had been getting hereto.

3. When communicating the Award to them, we should make it clear therefore that we cannot approve of any such measure to make up their revenues. We have given them an assurance that the Central Government will grant them additional financial assistance to compensate for such shortfall in their revenues during the remaining period of the Third Five Year Plan as would be caused by this reduction in the royalty, as compared to their original estimates of such revenues.

Yours sincerely,
Morarji Desai

30. From Karan Singh: Not Attending UNESCO Meeting[52]

[Refer to item 393]

29 October 1962

My dear Panditji,
There being no other nominee for the office, I was this morning declared duly elected by the Legislative Assembly for a third term as Sadar-i-Riyasat. The papers have now gone to the President for being placed to accord his recognition. It was, as you rightly guessed, a rather tame election, and I must see if I cannot come up with something more exciting next time. I would like to take this opportunity to express my deep gratitude for all your kindness and affection to me during the thirteen years that I have functioned as Head of this State. I venture to hope that in the future also I will continue to enjoy this privilege.

The Government of India have been good enough to include me as a member of the Indian delegation to the forthcoming General Conference of UNESCO beginning in Paris early next month. I feel, however, and I think you will agree, that in view of the National Emergency[53] and the serious military situation on our border including Ladakh, it would not be appropriate for me

---

52. Letter from the Sadar-i-Riyasat of Jammu and Kashmir, sent from Srinagar. Reproduced from J. Alam, ed., *Jammu and Kashmir (1949-64): Select Correspondence between Jawaharlal Nehru and Karan Singh*; (New Delhi: Penguin India ltd.2006); pp. 290-291.
53. The Government of India declared a state of national emergency on 26 October 1962.

to go abroad at this juncture. I would, therefore, request to be excused from attending this time. I need hardly add that in normal times I would have been honoured to avail of the opportunity to represent the country at this important Conference, and that in any case my services are always at the disposal of Government to be used in whatever capacity you think fit.

Asha and I look forward to seeing you and Indiraji in Delhi on the 3rd November when we will attend your kind invitation to lunch.

With respects and deep regards,

Yours as ever,
Tiger

31. From Ne Win: Offer of Help to end Conflict[54]
[Refer to item 425 and 388]

October 29, 1962

Your Excellency,

I thank you very much for your message of October 27, 1962 giving us a full and descriptive account of the crisis that has let to the present armed clashes over the Sino-Indian border dispute. I need hardly stress how grieved and concerned we are to find that the situation have developed to such serious and alarming proportions with armed clashes all along the frontier between our two most friendly neighbours.

I note also that your Excellency is not averse to a peaceful solution of the problem and is prepared to talk about a peaceful settlement provided an atmosphere conducive to such talks is created.

I on my part would naturally wish to see this unhappy dispute between our two most friendly neighbours brought to a speedy end and towards achieving this end I shall spare no efforts, in consultation with President Nasser and other likeminded Heads of States, to bring about an early reconciliation based on the five principles of peaceful co-existence between Asia's two foremost leaders.

Please accept, Your Excellency, the assurance of my highest consideration.

Ne Win

---

54. Letter from the Chairman of the Revolutionary Council of the Union of Burma. MEA, File No. 1 (China)/62, Vol. I, p. nil.

32. From John G. Diefenbaker: Offer of Help[55]
[Refer to item 429]

October 29, 1962

My dear Prime Minister,

I wish to thank you for the message which your High Commissioner transmitted to me on October 27. I much appreciated your courtesy in providing me with background information on the dispute with China concerning your northern border and the policy of your Government in the face of armed attack by the Chinese Peoples Republic.

2.   As I have already stated in the House of Commons, Canada deplores the unprovoked attack by China on India and I can assure you of the sympathy and support of the Canadian people for your determination to defend and protect your national territory and heritage. The Canadian Government stands ready to do what it can to be of help at this time.

3.   I have occasion yesterday in the House of Commons to refer to this matter and I spoke in the following terms:

4.   "I should now say a word with regard to another problem which faces the world. The Leader of the Opposition[56] (Mr Pearson) has referred to the Berlin situation and there is of course the problem which is being faced in India by the people of that nation".

5.   Last Monday I informed the House that if the Indian Government should approach Canada for assistance such a request would receive the fullest consideration. I now wish to report to the House that a request has been received from the Indian Government and that we are taking immediate steps to respond. On Friday we gave the Indian authorities a preliminary report on the kinds of military equipment available in Canada. These include Caribou transport planes. In a day or so I hope to be able to inform the House of the details of the supply equipment to India.

6.   Speaking for the Canadian Government, and I hope for all members of the House, we are deeply disturbed at the attacks which are being made at this time against India, a fellow member of the Commonwealth. India can rest assured that the Canadian Government will cooperate to the fullest in helping that nation acquire those items which it needs to defend itself in this critical hour.

With kind regards,

Yours sincerely,
John Diefenbaker

---

55. Letter from the Prime Minister of Canada. MEA, File No. 1 (China)/62, Vol. I, p. nil.
56. Lester B. Pearson.

33. From T. T. Krishnamachari: Despondent[57]
[Refer to item 266]

October 30, 1962

I have decided not to trouble you in person frequently hereafter. I am doubtful whether it is much use my writing to you either. If I could not do it, then I think the best place for me is my home in the village near Madras.

Every meeting that I attend deepens my disappointment with the existing state of affairs. At my age, I am incapable of getting angry, which I would like to if I can.

I will repeat what I said yesterday.

There is a tremendous amount of goodwill for us in most parts of the world. It would not stay long, as all sentiment is ultimately evanescent. We have to cash in on it quickly, and that is what we seem to be unable to do.

Whatever your views might be, and ultimately they count, your colleague, the Defence Minister,[58] has demonstrably showed his utter incapacity to act. I am told you think that he is the most intelligent man inside and outside the Cabinet. It might even be true. But intelligence in the abstract is of no use to anybody, least of all the possessor. It has also been indicated that the Defence organisation today, at any rate on the supply side, has been emasculated. I would not say the same thing of the operational side; it seems it is not consulted as often as it should be. But this is not the time to look into past misdeeds.

The Defence Minister's methods of going about things will not yield results. You cannot forget the fact that the Defence Minister is persona non-grata in most quarters, or at least in quarters that count for us at the moment. To go to Egypt and Indonesia for equipment is like searching for a needle in a haystock.

May I repeat again what I said to you yesterday. We have got to quickly approach people who can give us something. It may be that what they are going to give something. It may be that what they are going to give is what they are going to lay off and not of any use to them; but even this type of equipment would be adequate to fight our enemy.

Is it the time now to think of individual Ministers and individual officers as being the proper person or persons to do things? Do you want me to believe that the Defence Ministry is efficient when a senior officer of the Ministry when asked for a map for me says: "I open my mail only at 9 o'clock in the night;

---

57. Letter from the Minister without Portfolio. Salutation not available. NMML, T.T. Krishnamachari Papers, File 1962, Copy.
58. V. K. Krishna Menon.

then the request of your Minister will be considered?" Do you think that this type of man that is best to deal with public relations?

I mentioned to you yesterday about our methods of disseminating news. News has to be given in a form which the public will assimilate. And this cannot be done by people who do not know what the public mind is. If Krishna Menon and his minions have to put out the news, they can only do it from the angle which they know—that is that the public are fools, and do not realise the high value of Krishna Menon and his minions to the country.

We may not like the older journalists. They may have been against the Government. But today they will all play ball. A few of them can advise us on how public relations have to be tackled and how to put out the news. They will also advise us how to ask the papers to put out the news given. All this can be done only if there is a proper set-up in the Information Ministry, without Defence usurping its functions. If secrecy is a bar, I would like to say there is nothing secret anywhere.

We talked about our requirement of planes. In the context of the men that we have about us I see nobody who can take a decision in a big way about this matter. Why not send for J.R.D. Tata[59] and ask him to look after this kind of thing. He is individually an honest man and I am sure he is a patriot.

We talked about the creation of a supply organisation. Our officers may not know how to go about it. There is K.C. Mahindra[60] who ran the Supply Mission during the war time. He is not physically fit, but he is mentally alert. He can advise us how an organisation should be built up. He may be a tycoon, but he is a patriot.

What is needed is to rope in all elements which can help us now and will not hinder us. Meetings in Committees are of no use when these are composed of people who do not know what is wanted. What is wanted is action and we do not seem to be yet geared for it.

Please do something; something to prevent this atmosphere of a Greek tragedy deepening.

[T.T. Krishnamachari]

---

59. (1904-1993); Chairman Tata Group.
60. (1894-1963); Chairman of Mahindra and Mahindra group.

34. From Mahavir Tyagi: Israeli Offer of Weapons[61]
[Refer to item 448 and 453]

30th October 1962

My dear Jawaharlal ji,

The Trade Commissioner of Israel called on me this afternoon. He said that he came on a secret mission to inform me that the following weapons were available in his country and if the Indian Government were interested in them, he would make telegraphic (cipher) inquiries from his Government and let me know within a couple of days. He also mentioned to me that since their relations with Egypt were not very happy, our Government might feel some hesitation in dealing with Israel. As I had no time to consult you, I requested him to obtain all necessary details about the quantities, prices and period of availability of these weapons.

He gave the following details off hand:

1) 120 mm Mortar:
   Range 9 kilometre
   Bomb 36 lbs
   Accuracy precise
   Total weight of the mortar 250 kilograms
   Manhandled. Can be split into 4 parts
   Used in NATO countries.
2) 81 mm Mortar:
   Range 5½ kilometre
   Weight light.
   Weapons for Infantry:
3) "UZI" Sub machine guns: Very greatly admired all over the world and is in use with Dutch, Belgian and German armies.

I hope you will get this proposal examined.

Yours affectionately,
Mahavir Tyagi

---

61. Letter from Lok Sabha MP, Congress. Sent from 16, Dr. Rajendra Prasad Road, New Delhi. NMML, Mahavir Tyagi Papers.

35. From V. K. Krishna Menon: Change of Portfolio[62]
[Refer to items 336, 337 and appendix 33]

30th October 1962

In the situation that faces the country as the result of the unprovoked invasion of our territories by China, I submit that it is appropriate and necessary that the portfolio of Defence should be taken over by you.

I am conscious and concerned that this will impose a heavy burden on you. The determination of our people to eject the invader and to defend the honour and integrity of the motherland so overwhelmingly demonstrated by our people will, I feel sure, add to your strength and capacity. No one other than you can garner or help to maintain that resoluteness to the fullness of its purpose and without deterioration.

I conveyed these sentiments to you some days or weeks ago and much earlier in this crisis. I feel, however, that your assumption of the charge should not be delayed. I had offered to serve and assist you in the tasks that face us in any capacity you wished. I need hardly say that such abilities or energies I possess are unreservedly and entirely at your disposal now as always.

[V.K. Krishna Menon]

36. From Sirimavo Bandaranaike[63]
[Refer to item 417and 388]

I have read with very deep concern your message in regard to the present conflict on the borders between India and China, and I appreciate the gravity of the consequences that can ensue, not merely to India, but also to the rest of the world.

Your country and mine have always stood firmly against war and conflict as a means of the settlement of international issues, and you may rest assured that I shall do everything in my power to assist you towards a speedy and peaceful settlement by negotiation, with sympathy and understanding.

---

62. Letter from the Defence Minister. NMML, V.K. Krishna Menon Papers. Salutation not available.
63. Letter from the Prime Minster of Ceylon, 30 October 1962. MEA File No. 1 (China)/62, Vol I, p. nil. Salutation not available.

I have already addressed a personal letter to you on the 24th of October, in which I stated that it would be a calamity for Asia if the present conflict were to lead to war between India and China, and I offered such assistance as I am capable of giving to help to resolve and end the strife.

I have also sent a message to the Prime Minster of the People's Republic of China, and I shall keep you informed as to the progress that I am able to make.

I do appreciate very much that India would not want to do anything to prejudice her territorial integrity of self-respect by submitting to negotiations under pressure of armed force. Meanwhile, I should like to urge that every effort be made to bring the present fighting to an end, pending negotiations for a settlement of the larger border questions.

With kind regards,

[Sirimavo Bandaranaike]

37. From N.S. Khrushchev[64]
[Refer to items 388 and 395]

We have attentively studied your message of October 22 and 27, in which you gave the story of the Indo-Chinese border dispute and appraised the present state of relations existing now between India and China.

We had a talk on this question with your Minister Mr Malaviya.[65] I hope that he has informed you in detail about our point of view.

Now we should like to express once more our deep regret at the blood being shed by our friends and brothers—the Indians and the Chinese, at the military clashes taking place, which as it seems to us, could have been avoided.

A bloody conflict has arisen because of border questions which could have been solved by peaceful means. It is known that attempts to solve outstanding questions by means of war do not lead to good. When one seeks to settle disputes by military means new complications arise. We are extremely pained by the fact that the war which nobody needs is going on between India and China, the two great neighbouring countries. China is our neighbour and brother. We have very good friendly relations with India, we respect the Indian people. That is why we cannot remain indifferent when blood of the peoples friendly to us is being shed.

---

64. Letter from the Soviet Prime Minister, 31 October 1962. MEA, File No. 1(China)/62, Vol. I, p. nil. Salutation not available.
65. K. D. Malaviya, Minister of Mines and Fuel. He met Khrushchev on 26 October 1962.

I would like to say quite frankly and sincerely that nobody has authorised or asked us to assume the functions of a mediator in the Indo-Chinese border dispute. But, entertaining friendly feelings both to the Chinese and the Indian people, we would only like to express our opinion on this question. What sensible decision can be taken now? First of all, one should summon one's courage, rise above the heat of passion and hurt feelings which are naturally affecting both sides as a result of military clashes.

We think that one need not glance back at yesterday, one has to look into the future. In the interests of that future, in the interests of the people of India and China we would consider it the most reasonable to have an immediate cease fire. But to carry on shooting, while being governed by considerations of acquiring an advantageous position, means that the military conflict can continue indefinitely. Then a prolonged bloody struggle, a war of attrition will begin. If one side acquires an advantageous position, then the other side will also mobilise its manpower and material resources in order to achieve in its turn a position which it considers advantageous for itself. You can imagine where it could lead to. The war brings terrible disaster to both peoples. We consider proposals, which were put forward by the Chinese Government, reasonable because they contain the main basis for the settlement of the dispute—to cease fire immediately without any pre-conditions, to disengage opposing forces and to sit down at the table of negotiations. We consider it right that the Premier Chou En-lai in his appeal proposes that representatives of India go to Peking or representatives of China go to New Delhi, if it suited India better in order to put an end by mutual efforts to the conflict between the two friendly states, which to our great distress continues to deteriorate at present. As I know, there has never been a war between China and India. And now we do not see any reasons that could justify such a war. Both India and China are participants of the Bandung conference. The Indians and the Chinese showed a good example of peaceful co-existence of states with different social systems. They worked out the Panch Sheel principles. They signed the historic Bandung Declaration, which became an important contribution to the struggle of peoples for the cause of peace throughout the world.

So, is it possible that the necessary courage will not be found now and a sober understanding of the developments is not shown, in order to eliminate the conflict through negotiations? The fact cannot be really overlooked that the longer the conflict lasts the more sacrifices will be there and each country will accumulate the more obstacles to a peaceful solution of the conflict. Only one conclusion can be drawn from this: the faster a solution is found on a peaceful basis, the better it is for the people of India and China. We fervently wish that this decision is arrived at as soon as possible. We ask you to understand us correctly and to appreciate our anxiety correctly in regard to the still deteriorating conflict between China and India, to correctly understand the reasons, which impelled us to address this letter to you as answer to your messages.

As far as the explanations of the reasons of the emergence of the conflict and developments on the Indo-China border, contained in your messages are concerned, allow me, Mr Prime Minister, not to go into details of the conflict since each side has its own explanation and its own understanding of the existing situation.

I should like to express the belief that you, Mr Prime Minister, with your characteristic wise statesmanship will do everything within your power in order to cease fire on the Indo-Chinese border and to have the Indo-Chinese border conflict settled by peaceful means, through negotiations.

38. From T.T. Krishnamachari: Phone Tapping[66]
[Refer to items 88,89,91, and 92]

November 2, 1962

It was just like you to write so promptly in regard to my complaint about the tapping of my telephone. The DIB saw me in this connection today. The subsequent information that I got is that the tapping was done at the instance of the military authorities and the persons doing the tapping were withdrawn at 8 o'clock in the night of 31st October, presumably because of the change in the direction of the Defence Ministry—though it is asserted that no real change has taken place (by Krishna Menon)

[T.T. Krishnamachari]

39. From Chou En-lai[67]
[Refer to item 247 and appendix 26]

I thank you for your letter dated October 27. I have also received the enclosed copy of the Indian Government's statement dated October 24.

---

66. Letter from the Minister without Portfolio. NMML, T.T. Krishnamachari Papers, File: 1962, Copy. Salutations not available.
67. Letter from the Prime Minister of China, 4 November 1962. Reproduced from *Chinese Aggression in War and Peace. Letters of the Prime Minister of India* (Ministry of Information and Broadcasting, Publications Division, 8 December 1962), pp. 37-41.

It is indeed most painful to the Chinese Government and people that the current unfortunate border clashes should have eventually broken out and should have not yet ceased. The major enemy of China, as well as of the other Asian and African countries, is imperialism. The Chinese Government and people are by no means willing to see the two largest Asian countries crossing swords on account of differences between them, while they are confronted with the major enemy.

Though we interpret the cause of the current grave situation between China and India differently. I am glad that Your Excellency agrees that we should look ahead and should not merely turn the present tide but restore Sino-Indian relations to the warm and friendly pattern of earlier days and even improve on that pattern. I believe that if we really cherish such a common desire we shall certainly be able, through our joint efforts, to find a way to settle the Sino-Indian boundary question peacefully that is acceptable to both sides.

The three proposals of the Chinese Government of October 24 were advanced exactly in the spirit of resuming the friendly relations between the two countries prior to 1959. Your Excellency said that you and your colleagues were not clear about the precise meaning of the Chinese Government's proposals. Although the Chinese Government already pointed out in its statement the origin and meaning of its proposals, I am still willing here to make some further explanations.

As pointed out in the October 24 statement of the Chinese Government, the proposal for the armed forces of China and India to withdraw 20 kilometres each from the line of actual control and to disengage was first put forward by the Chinese Government back in 1959, to put it more specifically, in my letter to you dated November 7, 1959.[68] Now, the Chinese Government has reiterated these proposals. The "line of actual control" mentioned in the proposal is basically still the line of actual control as existed between the Chinese and Indian sides on November 7, 1959. To put it concretely, in the Eastern sector it coincides in the main with the so-called McMahon Line, and in the Western and Middle Sectors it coincides in the main with the traditional customary line which has consistently been pointed out by China. The reason why Chinese Government put forward this proposal again emphatically is that we have deeply realised from the bitter experience of the past three years that it is very hard to avoid clashes in border areas under dispute if the armed forces of the two sides are not disengaged. The fact that the Chinese Government's proposal has taken as its basis the 1959 line of actual control and not the present line of actual contact between the armed forces of the two sides is full proof that the Chinese side

68. SWJN/SS/54/p. 663.

has not tried to force any unilateral demand on the Indian side on account of the advances gained in the recent counter-attacks in self-defence. According to this proposal of the Chinese Government, the undertakings of both sides are equal. Moreover, as Your Excellency is surely aware, in concretely implementing this proposal the Chinese armed forces will have to withdraw much more than 20 kilometers from their present position in the eastern sector. The Chinese Government greatly regret that the Indian Government in its statement of 24th October should describe this fair proposal of the Chinese Government as a deceptive device to fool anybody. As Your Excellency is clearly aware, implementing of this proposal of the Chinese Government is not tantamount to the settlement of the boundary question, and so it will in no way prejudice the position of either side in maintaining its claims with regard to the boundary. No matter how differently our two sides view the Sino-Indian boundary question, the question has in fact been in existence for a long time. Yet this situation did not prevent our two countries from living together on friendly terms before 1959, then how is it that they can no longer do so after 1959? Of course, we both wish to see the boundary question settled speedily in a friendly way, yet why is it that our two countries must resort to arms before the boundary question is settled? The proposal of the Chinese Government relates to armed forces of the two sides to withdraw 20 kilometers each from the line of actual control along the entire boundary locations; disengaging is precisely designed to create an atmosphere for the peaceful settlement of the boundary question; and even if the boundary question cannot be settled for the time being, avoidance of clashes along the border can be ensured.

The Indian Government said in its statement that India can enter into talks "only on the basis of decency dignity and self-respect". I deem that the three proposals of the Chinese Government have precisely provided such a basis. Should the Indian Government agree to the Chinese Government's proposals, China and India can quickly designate officials to negotiate matters relating to the disengagement of the armed forces of the two sides and the cessation of their armed conflict. When these negotiations have yielded results and the results have been put into effect, the Prime Ministers of the two countries can then hold talks to proceed further to seek a friendly settlement of the Sino-Indian boundary question.

You have said in your letter that "a clear straight-forward way of reversing the deteriorating trend in India-China relations" is for the Chinese side to accept the suggestion made in point (v) of the Indian Government's statement, that is, to "revert to the position as it prevailed all along the India-China boundary prior to 8th September 1962". I cannot but state with regret, however, that this

Indian suggestion is contrary to the aim of turning the present tide and resume Sino-Indian friendly relations.

I do not wish to reopen the old argument. But since the state of the Sino-Indian boundary prior to 8th September 1962 has been referred, I cannot but point out that that state was unfair and pregnant with the danger of border conflict and hence should not be restored, so far as the Eastern sector is concerned, I believe the Indian Government must be in possession of the 1914 original map of the so-called McMahon Line. According to the original map, the Western end of the so-called McMahon line clearly starts from 27' 44.6' N. Yet the Indian Government arbitrarily said that it started from 27' 48' N and, on this pretext, it not only refused to withdraw the Indian troops from the Kechilang river area north of the line, but made active dispositions for a massive military attack, attempting to clear the area of Chinese frontier guards defending it. Such was the position in the Eastern sector of the Sino-Indian boundary prior to 8th September 1962. How can the Chinese Government agree to revert to such a position? As for the Western sector, the Aksai Chin area has always been under China's jurisdiction. It was through this area that back in 1950 the Chinese People's Liberation Army entered the Ari District of Tibet from Sinkiang. Again, it was through this area that, from 1956 to 1957, the Chinese Government constructed the Sinkiang-Tibet highway involving gigantic engineering work. Yet the Indian Government arbitrarily said that it was not until 1957 that the Chinese side came to this area and, on this pretext, unilaterally altered the state or the boundary in the Western sector by force from 1961 onwards, occupied large tracts of Chinese territory east of the 1959 line of actual control and set up over forty military points. Such was the position in the western sector of the Sino-Indian boundary prior to 8th September 1962. How can the Chinese Government agree to revert to such a position?

The Chinese Government hold that the present border clashes should not have occurred at all and that, in order quickly to stop the border clashes, re-open peaceful negotiations and settle the Sino-Indian boundary question, neither side should assume the attitude of a victor, no matter how the clashes may develop. It was precisely in this spirit that the Chinese Government put forward its three proposals of 24th October. The three proposals are reciprocal and not one-sided, they are equitable and not asking for submission of one side, they are based on mutual accommodation and not imposed on others, they are based on mutual respect and not bullying one side, and they are in the spirit of friendly negotiations and not arbitrary or dogmatic. However, the Indian Government has put to the Chinese Government humiliating conditions such as forced on a vanquished party. Your Excellency, Mr Prime Minister, both our countries are sovereign States and neither can force its unilateral demands on the other. India has its self-respect, so has China. It was for the upholding of the self-respect of both China and India that the Chinese Government put forward its three proposals of 24th October. I sincerely, appeal to Your Excellency once again to consider these three proposals and make a positive response.

Respected Mr Prime Minister, since the unfortunate Sino-Indian border clash began, many Asian and African countries have appealed to our two countries, expressing the hope that we may stop the clashes and resume negotiation. They say that imperialism and colonialism are the chief enemies of us newly-independent Asian and African countries, and that the Asian and African countries should settle the mutual dispute peacefully on the basis of mutual understanding and mutual accommodation. I am convinced that their intentions are good and the view point is correct, we should not disappoint their eager expectations.

Please accept, Your Excellency, the assurances of my highest consideration.

40. From Robert Frost: Support[69]
[Refer to item 438]

November 5, 1962

Dear Prime Minister,
May you find strength in yourself and friends to counter this wanton insult to your nation. And may you learn from this experience who your true friends are and what the English language does to find the speakers of it together in world politics.

Sincerely yours,
Robert Frost

41. From Sheikh Mohammed Abdullah: Chinese Invasion[70]
[Refer to item 274]

I am writing to you after a long spell of silence. It is neither opportune nor necessary to dilate on reasons for this silence. I am sure that you are not unaware

---

69. Letter from the poet. NMML, J.N. Papers – Robert Frost.
70. Letter from the former Prime Minister of Jammu and Kashmir, 5 November 1962, sent from Special Jail, Jammu. Salutation not available.

of what I and my colleagues have been going through during this period. Under compelling circumstances, I, however, feel that I must break this silence.

Due to the sudden flare up on our borders in the north, a grave situation has arisen which faces the country. Every son of the soil, therefore, has to address himself wholeheartedly to this question, and with single-mindedness think and act how to save the situation. Brushing aside all considerations of expediency, I, therefore, am sending this letter to you.

I am afraid that all of us have not yet fully realised the gravity of this situation. To my mind the danger is much more permanent and potential than it superficially seems to be. The causes of the clash lie much deeper and, as you have often pointed out, we shall have to prepare ourselves for a long struggle with unflinching determination. Now and then the situation may calm down on our borders. This should not lull us in a false sense of security. We have to prepare for sufferings and sacrifice in future in order to safeguard against inherent dangers in the situation. Any short sighted view, therefore, will be suicidal.

Emphasis to step up production, mobilise people, insistence on savings and austerity as also contributions to the National Defence Fund are unquestionably very important and no patriot can lose sight of them. But still more important is the factor which, I am afraid, has not and is not yet receiving adequate attention.

We have to realise fully that the present danger gravely jeopardises the hard-earned freedom of the whole sub-continent. It is, therefore, an onslaught on all the countries, big or small, of the sub-continent and our masses must view the situation in this perspective. It would be a sad commentary on our national and human outlook if anyone in any country in the sub-continent gloats over the misfortune facing the other. It should be our first duty to fight this mentality. At present unfortunately, I see no awareness of this aspect of the situation.

The question of questions is, how should we bring about this awareness so that everyone living in the sub-continent irrespective of caste, creed, colour or nationality faces the common danger with a will and determination without any consideration whether the target of the outside danger for the time being is India or any small country. My answer is: Freedom is indivisible and it has jointly to be preserved for the whole subcontinent. We must, therefore, take effective steps to root out the causes of dissension that strain our relations with our neighbours. The past history of the sub-continent tells us that her misfortunes always spring from her internal dissensions and distrust of the another. It was this misunderstanding and distrust which always encouraged an outsider to invade the sub-continent and become its master.

Partition, no doubt, divided our homeland into two parts and a geographical wall was artificially raised between the two. But is it at all necessary that we should allow such wall to separate our minds and hearts too? One should, however, sorrowfully admit that the most unfortunate legacy of the Partition has been raising such mental barriers in between the two big neighbours—India and Pakistan—who were one united country only a short while ago. It has left behind an aftermath of hate and distrust. Partition came about with the agreement of the Parties. Therefore, there should have been no room for mutual distrust. It is extremely sad that this mental attitude has persisted. There are, however, causes which accentuate this attitude and stand in the way of bringing nearer the two neighbours. It is, therefore, the foremost duty of those in authority to remove these causes. If the common peril has to be faced unitedly, all must stand unitedly.

India is a big and vast country with great international prestige. Therefore, its responsibility and obligations are equally great. It is for India to inspire confidence in her neighbours, and even to take initiative and give them full faith that she will spare no pains in protecting the common heritage of freedom and honour. I am sure that India can do it and the response from her neighbours will not be lacking.

In order to bring about this change in the situation the first and foremost step that needs to be taken is for those controlling the destiny of India at the moment, to take effective steps to amicably settle all outstanding disputes with her neighbours and remove all possible misunderstandings. India has done it in the past and, given the necessary will to do, can do it in future as well. Many ticklish and complicated disputes were settled with Pakistan. The only outstanding dispute which still remains unsettled is about Kashmir. This has resulted not only in the continued agony of Kashmiris but also in seriously embittering the relations of the two neighbours. Besides dissipating their vast resources by diverting them into unproductive channels, it has seriously disabled them to play their proper and complementary role in world affairs. In spite of the fact that both countries are committed to a peaceful and democratic solution, both are members of the United Nations Organisation and both are wedded to the principle of self-determination, this dispute lingers on confronting the whole sub-continent with grave potential dangers. How tragic it is that at the present juncture when both countries should have unitedly stood up to face the common danger, their armies are facing each other along the artificially drawn cease-fire line in Kashmir and elsewhere. This situation in itself is a grave danger fraught with serious disaster. It is impossible to create a sense of complete confidence, and security in the minds of the people, and remove their anxiety that nothing untoward is going to happen on the home front so long as this situation persists.

The present peril facing the country—which as I have said potentially faces the whole sub-continent—makes the settlement of the Kashmir dispute even more urgent. I, therefore, earnestly appeal to you to take effective steps for resolving it amicably.

It is not only now that I am advocating this approach to the problem. The experience gained during my stewardship of the State convinced me that in order to preserve the hard-earned freedom of the sub-continent it was absolutely essential that the two closest neighbours—India and Pakistan—should settle all their differences and come together and live as brothers. In my opinion, the main hurdle in the achievements of this happy result is the dispute over Kashmir. I doubt if posterity will forgive us in case we do not, even today, when the aggressor is on our territory, rise to the occasion and muster courage enough to tell the people boldly that in lasting brotherly relations between India and Pakistan lies the key to permanent peace and prosperity of the whole sub-continent. Gandhiji foresaw these disastrous consequences and therefore made moving appeals for resolving differences like brothers. Any sense of prestige never came in his way and he spoke the truth boldly. It was perhaps therefore that he achieved results which no ordinary mortal could. Are we not betraying him if we do not make an effort to emulate his example? Permit me to quote here his soul-stirring words:

> "If Pakistan was to become a worthy State, let the Pakistan and the Union Representatives sit down and thrash out the Kashmir affairs as they had already done in the case of many other things. If they could not do so, why could they not choose from among themselves two good and true persons who could direct their steps."

I strongly feel that the urgency to implement Gandhiji's advice was never greater than in the grave crisis facing the country at the present moment.

I and all my other colleagues including even those who later fell out in August 1953, unanimously shared the view that peaceful and democratic settlement of the dispute was essential, not only to end the agonies of the people of Kashmir but in order to permanently safeguard the freedom of the sub-continent, against any external danger. In spite of this unity of outlook, things, however, took unfortunately a sudden and unexpected turn in 1953 for reasons which is not necessary for me to detail out.

In regard to the present situation facing the country, you know full well where our sympathies are. Even in our present condition, I am sure, none will dispute the fact that I and my colleagues who are undergoing sufferings with me, have also made our humble contribution in the freedom struggle of the sub-continent. We have had the privilege of facing troubles and tribulations in that noble cause and sometimes shoulder to shoulder with you. Though we are not fortunate enough to enjoy the fruits of that struggle and are going through fresh suffering for the last decade, we can ill-afford to take an ostrich like attitude in regard to the dangerous situation facing the country. Fates have made us immobile. We can only convey our views to you in the hope that they will receive your due consideration. As I wrote to you in April, 1958, the key to the solution lies in your hands. I hope that you will take these suggestions in the spirit in which they are offered.

Your stature, vast experience in international affairs, and your deep sense of patriotism, give me hope and confidence that you will spare no pains to take steps to permanently preserve the hard-earned freedom of the sub-continent and thus earn the gratitude of the posterity.

[Sheikh Mohammed Abdullah]

42. From Ayub Khan[71]
[Refer to item 388]

Your Excellency,

I thank you for your letter of 27th October, 1962, in which you were good enough to give your Government's version of the dispute that has arisen between India and China on the question of border demarcation.

It is a matter of great regret to us that this dispute should have led to intensified military activities and induction of new war potential, thus endangering the peace and stability of the region in which Pakistan is vitally concerned.

I agree with you when you say that no efforts should be spared to eliminate deceit and force from relations. In this respect I am constrained to point out that various outstanding disputes between India and Pakistan can also be resolved amicably should the Government of India decide to apply these principles with sincerity and conviction.

We in Pakistan are wedded to a world of peace and friendly relations with all neighbouring countries, especially India. We have accepted this course for we believe this is the only method through which we can pursue the gigantic tasks of economic and industrial developments which must be carried forward in the interest of the prosperity and wellbeing of the people.

Mr Prime Minister we are fully conscious of the great responsibility that lies on your shoulders for the maintenance of peace, especially around this

71. Letter from the President of Pakistan, 6 November 1962, PIB.

775

subcontinent. We, therefore, hope that the conflict between India and China can be peacefully resolved.

With kind regards,

Yours sincerely,
Muhammad Ayub Khan

43. From Sudhir Ghosh: Publicity about US Arms Supplies[72]

[Refer to item 446 and appendix 44]

7 November, 1962

My dear Panditji,

I was in Calcutta for the last two days and I was somewhat shocked to hear from the Editor of *The Statesman*[73] and others about the kind of publicity that had been given by the US Government representatives to the details of arms delivered to our people by the US authorities at the Dum Dum airport. I wrote today a friendly letter to Ambassador Galbraith (whom I know well) drawing his attention to this unfortunate matter. I venture to send you a copy of it.

With regards,

Yours sincerely,
[Sudhir Ghosh]

44. Sudhir Ghosh to J.K. Galbraith: Publicity about US Arms Supplies[74]

[Refer to item 446 and appendix 43]

7 November, 1962

Dear Ken,

On the strength of your friendship, I venture to write this letter to draw your attention to the unfortunate publicity given by your people to the delivery of arms by the US authorities to our people at the Calcutta airport in this crisis.

---

72. Letter from Rajya Sabha MP, Congress; address: 95 South Avenue, New Delhi. NMML, Sudhir Ghosh Papers.
73. George Arthur Johnson.
74. Letter from Rajya Sabha MP, Congress, to the US Ambassador; sent from 95 South Avenue, New Delhi. NMML, Sudhir Ghosh Papers.

It was the editor of *The Statesman* (not an Indian)[75] who told me on Monday how shocked he was to find that your representatives at Calcutta had invited to the Dum Dum airport an extraordinary large number of journalists at the time of arrival of the first few jets carrying arms and all these journalists were given by your people handouts containing all manner of details of the types, sizes and varieties of arms delivered; it was like a big garlanding ceremony for the first lot of weapons.

I think you will agree with me that this was a very unwise thing to do. The Editor of *The Statesman* told me that the responsible ones amongst the journalists felt highly embarrassed because, if they were to print ever a part of the details given out by your people, they would land themselves in prison under the Defence of India Act. I am sure your officers are aware that this country is at war (even if undeclared) with a formidable opponent and a state of emergency has been proclaimed by the President; and it is very extraordinary in these circumstances, to give out to newspapermen details of the arrival of aircraft carrying arms to this country and even details about the weapons. Even in peace time this sort of thing is not permitted under normal security rules. Even this morning I saw an announcement in the newspapers by the USIS that the 14th jet plane carrying US arms had arrived at Calcutta yesterday. Is it really necessary to announce whether it was 10th or the 12th or the 14th plane? You may be sure that all the details given out by your people reached Peking very quickly.

If you will forgive my saying so, the big Press Conference you held in New Delhi on the 2nd November to announce the programme of delivery of US arms was perhaps not very appropriate either. Isn't it better that you leave it to our people to make whatever announcements they consider appropriate about the arrival of US arms? There is no lack of gratitude in the Indian for American help in this hour of need; but if your people create the impression that there is an excessive desire for publicity and kudos then people in this country will not like it. You must remember that we Indians are a proud people. This is personal letter and I hope you will take it in the spirit in which it is written.

With regards,

Yours sincerely,
[Sudhir Ghosh]

75. George Arthur Johnson.

45. From V. K. Krishna Menon: Resignation-I[76]

[Refer to items 269, 342 and 343]

November 7, 1962

My dear Prime Minister,

In the crisis that faces our country, the nation as well as our Party should be enabled in every possible way to face it in unity and zeal.

The people have responded energetically and in every way open to them. Not only have they spontaneously and in great dimensions come out in support of your and our national policies, they have done it with understanding and with the knowledge of the military reverses and the hard tasks ahead.

I am personally grateful in my heart to feel that in every place I have gone, even till last night, they have gathered to accord me their faith and support in considerable numbers with enthusiasm reminiscent of the election campaigns earlier this year. In some places they have broken previous records in both these respects.

Nevertheless, I am painfully aware of the fact that not only the opponents of our policy and Party but even perhaps an appreciable number of our Party Members, some leaders among them, have proclaimed or implied their lack of faith in me and in the Defence organisation under my stewardship.

These views may not, and in fact do not, represent the bulk of our Party or the people. Nevertheless, in my humble submission, the reservations amid the crisis that are theirs are a weak link in our national and Party unity. It can impede the vast efforts that we must make for the mobilisation, national and emotional, of our nation which must be effected both with speed and in great dimensions.

To a certain extent, rumours, misstatements of facts, and anti-morale sentiments emerge from such opposition. It is not purposeful to argue that such attitude or facts are unreasonable or indeed unfounded, or wrongly motivated.

It is, again, of little value, to argue that these hostilities are misdirected. It is wrong for me at the present time to seek to provide answers or to reveal the hollowness of charges and allegations.

The hard fact is that whatever the factors, domestic or foreign, and whoever are involved, the present situation must come to an end for the simple reason that we cannot afford to let our energies be dissipated.

---

76. Letter from the Minister of Defence Production. NMML, V.K. Krishna Menon Papers.

It is not possible now, and it will be increasingly impossible to isolate the present discontent from open and implied hostilities to our policies, national and international as they very well lead to the accentuation of the strength of anti-national, reactionary and democratic forces, even though many of the persons concerned may have no such notions or desires.

I am content to rest in the belief that facts are not altered by subsequent or non-factual representation of them. I have no adverse feelings towards those who have in their anxiety or concern about the country as a result of their reactions to the shock of invasion been led to misstatements or distortion of facts or of the character and role of persons.

Public statements by me even within the Party must be necessarily conditioned by, (a) considerations of security; (b) the view that I may not involve my colleagues or the Service except by way of factually relevant statements; (c) the knowledge that they may help the enemy; and (d) affect the morale of our troops.

The immediate concern and task of every Indian today is the defence and then the counter-offensives against the invaders for the redemption of the honour and integrity of our country. The retention of our anchorage in the basic principles and orientations of our international and domestic policies are essential for our survival to win the peace.

All this will be adversely affected by the present tensions and arguments and unwholesome propaganda within our Party. These have to come to an end in the interests of the Party and the nation, irrespective of the individuals.

The controversies centre round my person and my being in the Government. Furthermore, my defects or the shortcomings in the achievement of our tasks are sought to be attributed to these.

In the last several months and even more frequently in recent weeks and days I have repeatedly placed my office and personal services completely at your disposal to be used or dispensed with.

I request and hope that the length of this letter does not result in the deflection of your attention from its main purpose.

I once again submit my resignation from Government in the belief that it may be a small contribution to the war effort. Such experience or capacity I possess, if required, is at your disposal irrespective of the location and status in which I have to function.

I am grateful to you for all the affection and confidence that it has been my good fortune to enjoy at your hands. If events should prove when present excitements die out that this confidence was misplaced or betrayed, I would willingly accept all the consequences that must follow.

779

I tender to you once again my resignation and with it the reaffirmation of my respect and regards.

Yours affectionately,
V.K. Krishna Menon

46. From V. K. Krishna Menon: Resignation-II[77]
[Refer to items 269, 342 and 343]

7th November, 1962

My dear Prime Minister,
I have written to you at some length separately the reasons that prompt me to request you once again to accept my resignation from Government.

I have in the last few months, and even frequently in recent months and weeks, placed the office which you entrusted to me and myself at your disposal.

You have continued to place your confidence in me for which I am grateful.

I submit, however, that it may be in the interests of the Party that I should be relieved of office. Such experience or capacity as I may possess are always at your disposal, without considerations of office of status, if you should require them.

If my resignation serves even in a small measure to forge the strength and unity of the country, the party and Government, I am amply rewarded.

I need hardly say that this letter and the longer one I have sent are at your disposal for whatever use you wish to make of them. [See item 453].

I am grateful to you for the long years of your affection and confidence that it has been my privilege to enjoy.

I cannot be without regrets that I have not been able to serve the country with greater effect. I am grateful, however, in my heart and satisfied in my mind that is leaving you and the Government I shall be making a small contribution to the national effort.

Yours affectionately,
V.K. Krishna Menon

---

77. Letter from the Minister of Defence Production. NMML, V.K. Krishna Menon Papers.

47. From Ram Subhag Singh: Settlements in NEFA[78]
[Refer to items 297, 298 and 299]

November 8, 1962

Respected Panditji,

Kindly refer to your d.o. letter No. 1859-PMH/62 dated the 6th November, 1962. I shall keep in mind the views expressed by Shri Vishnu Sahay in regard to Nagaland.

What I propose to do at present is to induce some good cultivators to go to NEFA area. I respectfully submit that this scheme to get some good cultivators to go to NEFA and to undertake cultivation of vegetables etc., and later feel free to settle down there, if they so desire, should be undertaken and put into execution at an early date.

There are many areas in this border territory which could be brought into productive use if we arrange to introduce good cultivators from other parts of the country to go into this area and induce them to take to cultivation of those crops which have a good local demand. The entire territory is thinly populated. To my mind, for an effective defence also it should be desirable to have part of these areas taken up by good and sturdy farmers who are prepared to face the local hazards. Such an increase in local working population should incidentally be of help to the army itself. If necessary, the new settlers who go to these places could be given some kind of uniform and care could be taken to see that they do not displace any of the local hill population.

When I discussed these matters with you, I understood that you were agreeable to the scheme. Perhaps the matter has not been fully understood by Shri Vishnu Sahay whom I was unable to meet when I went to Assam and NEFA because at that time he was in Delhi. If the matters are fully explained to him and to the NEFA administration, I hope it will be possible to get their active support to the scheme and assistance to put it into execution.

If you agree, the NEFA administration may be asked to locate about 15 centres in that territory where some good cultivators could be taken to undertake cultivation of vegetables and other local products.

Yours sincerely,
Ram Subhag Singh

---

78. Letter from the Minister for Agriculture. MHA, File No. 16(7)-NI/62, p. 8/c.

48. From Lal Bahadur Shastri to B.P Chaliha[79]

[Refer to items 55, 56, and 57]

My dear Chaliha ji,

Please refer to your Top Secret letter of the 12th October1962 addressed to the Prime Minister, regarding the political situation in the Mizo District, of which you had sent me also a copy.

Since that letter was written, the situation has changed completely and you must now be busy with so many other pressing problems. However, I thought I might briefly indicate my reactions regarding the matters mentioned in those papers.

Regarding the troops, the U.P. Armed Police Battalion deputed to Mizo District has already been withdrawn and sent elsewhere and there is no army now in the area.

The most important needs of the District appear to be economic development and improvement of communications. No doubt you will be looking into this to the extent possible now-a-days, and in particular it seems desirable that there should be early improvement of communications.

Apart from these, perhaps some of the following measures might be considered:-

(i) Involvement of the Mizos in the Defence efforts to meet the present emergency. I am informed that the Mizo National Front which is the militant organisation, has already passed a resolution supporting the country's stand against China and has declared its intention not to embarrass the Government. Imaginative publicity with suitable enlistment opportunities to the Mizos should go a long way in improving their morale.

(ii) A scheme for giving greater autonomy to Hill Districts might be considered as and when other pressures permit. This is being proposed so that we may prepare ourselves to bring it into effect as early as possible after the emergency ends, and the militant organisations can be denied a ready cause for agitation.

(iii) I think something may have to be done regarding the Official Language Policy also. For the present, if you agree, it might be widely publicised that Assamese will not be imposed on the Hill people. This is what you have been saying all along, but it might be given greater publicity in these areas in order to remove any lurking doubts.

---

79. Letter to Chief Minister, Assam, 8 November 1962. NAI, MHA, File No.15/1/62-SR(R)-A.

In addition, the State Government must also build up its intelligence system. Perhaps you might also go ahead with the scheme for recruitment of an additional Assam Rifles Battalion for the Indo-Pak border in the Mizo District.

Last but not the least, I wonder whether you could consider associating some of the hill people's leaders with Government at the political level. In view of the present emergency it will help if they come together to play their full part in mobilising the people of the State and such a partnership will probably have beneficial results for the future also.

Yours sincerely,
Lal Bahadur

49. From Ram Subhag Singh to Vishnu Sahay: Settlements in NEFA[80]
[Refer to items 297, 298 and 299]

November 9, 1962

My dear [Vishnu Sahay,]

You are already aware of my suggestion that it would be desirable to select about 15 centres in NEFA where we could induce some good cultivators to go and take up cultivation on their own, or help the existing farmers in carrying on agricultural operations, and who may, at their option, eventually settle down on the land. This scheme would help in strengthening our defence. As you know, the territories are very thinly populated and if good and sturdy farmers can be induced to take up cultivation and eventually to settle there, the local working population would be strengthened and would help in effective defence of the area. Of course, in working out a scheme, care will have to be taken to select people who would be prepared to face the local difficulties and dangers. Further, it will be necessary to ensure that they do not displace any local population and arouse no resentment among the existing inhabitants. In this connection I am enclosing a copy of (1) the Prime Minister's letter to me dated November 6, 1962 (with which he forwarded your telegram referring to the news which appeared on page 6 of *The Statesman* of 3rd November, 1962), (2) my reply dated November 8, 1962. (3) Prime Minister's reply dated November 8, 1962. I shall be grateful if you would kindly examine this proposal and if you agree with it kindly let me know about the places where such centres can be established, the

80. Letter from Minister of Agriculture to the Governor of Assam. MHA, File No. 16 (7)-NI/62. P.15/c.

area of land that can be allotted for cultivation, the number of persons that can be brought in and the expenditure likely to be incurred with regard to reclamation of land, wherever necessary, provision for financial assistance to enable them to take up cultivation and provision for such amenities as may be necessary.

I shall be grateful for an early reply.

Yours sincerely
[Ram Subhag Singh]

50. From Mohanlal Sukhadia: Pak Movements on Border[81]

[Refer to items 226 and 228]

November 10, 1962

Respected Panditji,

I am writing this letter to inform you of the activities of the Pakistan Government on our Indo-Pak border. During last two to three months reports have received by us about the strengthening of the border defence. They have been equipping their posts particularly from northern edge of Rajasthan border commencing from Bikaner district and ending with Barmer.

2. They have started supplying arms and ammunition to the villagers along our border and have been linking their posts by telephone and other means of communication. Some reports have also been received that the Government of Pakistan have instructed the people of Pak territory to vacate the border by about 5 to 10 miles. Reports from Ganganagar district indicate that there has been intensive movement of the Pak Army. Civilians with fire arms have also been observed to have stationed along with Indo-Pak border, have also been constructed.

3. In Rajasthan there are military formations/units at the following places: Kota, Nasirabad, Jodhpur, Bikaner, Jaipur, Alwar and Mount Abu and the total strength is roughly fourteen battalions.

4. Under the present circumstances there has bean a movement of troops stationed in Rajasthan to our northern borders. I do not know whether there is a policy of replacing the troops who have gone out of Rajasthan. As a measure

---

81. Letter from the Chief Minister of Rajasthan. MHA, File No. 9/55/62-T, p.25/c. Enclosure with details of Rajasthan Armed Constabulary battalions omitted, but available in NMML.

of precaution, the State Government feel that it may be necessary to increase the strength of the military deployment in the areas adjacent to the borders. Of course, you are the best judge in this matter. I have only expressed my feeling resulting from the reports which I have received about the military activities being carried on by Pakistan all along the border adjacent to Rajasthan.

5. As regards the Rajasthan Armed Constabulary, in response to the request made by the Home Ministry some time back we have already placed one battalion at the disposal of the Army authorities and the same has been stationed at Jammu since the 1st October, 1962. We have raised another Battalion to replace the Battalion deputed to the Government of India and are taking steps to raise another two battalions and put them under command as soon as possible. Our difficulty is that the arms provided for Rajasthan Armed Constabulary are inadequate according to the scale recommended by the Army authorities and keeping in view the purpose for which the Battalions are being raised. It is necessary that the arms and ammunitions as required by the Army authorities should be supplied without any delay. I have already addressed the Minister for Home Affairs in this connection a few days back and the note on the scale of arms provided for the Rajasthan Armed Constabulary which was sent to them, is also enclosed for your information.

6. We also find that road communications in our border areas are poor from the security point of view. We need to construct more roads to facilitate movement in case of emergency. A statement of the proposed roads that need to be constructed along with estimates of the cost has already been forwarded to the Minister for Home Affairs.

Yours sincerely,
Mohanlal Sukhadia

51. From A. P. Jain: Visit to USA and Europe[82]
[Refer to item 446]

November 11, 1962

My dear Jawaharlalji,

Since my arrival in India on November 8, I have been trying to get time for meeting you, but it could not be done. I know how busy you are and, therefore,

---

82. Letter from the President of the UPPCC; address: 5 Rafi Marg, New Delhi. NMML, A.P. Jain Papers.

I am resorting to the device of writing to you. If you consider necessary you may call me.

At Washington I paid a visit to the State Department and among others I met Cameron[83] and Talbot.[84] It was just after Tawang had fallen to the Chinese. Talbot appeared to be greatly upset with the fall of Tawang and he expressed concern about the fighting on the Indo-Chinese border. He said that the US Government had refrained from making any statement supporting India because there was fear that it may embarrass the Indian Government. Americans had, however, full sympathy for India and were prepared to meet her request for arms and equipment. The offer would be unconditional and the terms of payment may be settled later. Talbot appreciated India's desire to buy arms on commercial basis. Among a fairly large number of non-officials whom I met was Ellsworth Bunker.[85] He was very sympathetic to India's cause. On the whole there was great sympathy for India and desire to help her.

There was by and large appreciation of India's non-alignment policy. It was recognised that India could, on account of its non-alignment, on many occasions play a useful role in settling disputes. But there was also a feeling that the policy of non-alignment had mostly been interpreted to the disadvantage of America and in favour of the Soviet Union. Those who wanted India to change its policy of non-alignment were very few.

It appears that the Indian Embassy at Washington is not kept promptly informed. The news of the fall of Tawang reached the State Department within half-an-hour while it reached the Indian Embassy quite a few hours afterwards.

In summing up, our policy of non-alignment is no more an issue in the United States and almost all sections including the administration are prepared to go far in helping India against the Chinese.

My stay in London was far too short to meet many people, but I could see Harold Wilson[86] and a few others. Harold Wilson has been taking great interest in our border's invasion. He had discussed the matter with the Government and there was full agreement about it between the Labour and the Conservatives. The Labour Party is totally in favour of India's policy of non-alignment and most of the Conservatives also share the same views. Wilson told me that there were

---

83. Turner C. Cameron, Director of the Office of South Asian Affairs.
84. William Philip Talbot, Assistant Secretary of State for Near East and South Asian Affairs.
85. Former US Ambassador to India.
86. Of the Labour Party.

large quantities of automatic weapons and other equipment in stock which could be given to India on request. In particular, he mentioned, saddles, Baily bridges, Walkie-Talkie, Loud-shouters, Electronic communication, tents, hospital tents, warm clothing, blankets, sten-gun, bren-gun, machine-gun, mortars, short range aircraft etc. etc. He had made a proposal to the Government that supplies to India may be made on "lend-lease" basis, articles consumed being paid for with small interest over a number of years and articles not used being returned. This proposal was acceptable to the Government and details would be worked out. There was general sympathy towards India and our policy of non-alignment had not many critics, though some would like to say, "I told you so".

I do not know what has actually been done on this side, but my feeling is that it would take us time before we could manufacture automatic weapons in sufficient numbers. A full and complete list of weapons and equipment which we require should be prepared and sent both to USA and UK for supply.

No matter on whatever scale we may get supplies from the USA and UK, we shall need plenty of money. Our own reserves are too meagre. With a proper approach I think it will be possible to get money from the United States. May I suggest that you may send your personal representatives to USA, U.K. and, if necessary, to West Germany with powers to negotiate about supplies and money.

I am left with little doubt that the climate both in USA and UK is extremely favourable. They are also careful not to do anything which may worsen our relations with USSR. We should cash [in] on the situation.

The attitude of Pakistan was full of uncertainty. Both the USA and UK are engaged in diplomatic activities to exert a moderating influence on Pakistan so that it may not take advantage of our involvement. Pakistan, however, has been complaining about India's attitude on Kashmir and the Americans see some justification in it. They ask a question "How far is India prepared to go". My impression is that they would like us to agree on a procedure which is also agreeable to Pakistan for settlement of the Kashmir dispute. It may be plebiscite or arbitration. I do not think that the Indo-Pakistan issue will in any event, whether there is an agreement or not, come in the way of the supply of arms and equipment to India.

With best of regards,

Sincerely yours,
Ajit Prasad Jain

52. From Josip Broz Tito[87]

[Refer to item 428]

[12 November 1962]

Dear Friend,

I am very thankful for your message of October 26, which reached me only on November 4, 1962. It was read carefully by me and, on the basis of your explanation, I have got a clear picture of serious happenings on the border of your country. I have already felt great concern from that very day when your border guards in Ladakh were attacked and when the attempt was made to solve this border problem between your country and China unilaterally, by the use of arms, instead of using peaceful methods, that is negotiations, in order to reach an agreement.

As you know, whenever in the past attempts were made to solve any disputed problem in the world by use of military force, we have nearly always, together with you and others who were inspired by the same aims and principles, expressed great anxiety. Together with you, we have always emphasised the necessity of solving the problems in a peaceful way through direct talks between the parties in dispute, because we were well aware of the fact that the use of force in such cases would again increase the tension and might even lead to the brink of war, which in the conditions of present bloc division and the possession of thermo-nuclear weapons, could not be easily localised. The principle that every international problem should be solved in peaceful way is the basis of the UN Charter and it was reaffirmed in the Declaration of the Conference of the Heads of State and Government of the non-aligned countries, held last year in Belgrade.

It is evident therefore, that in the present grave international situation all the efforts should made towards finding out such solution of the above-mentioned problem which would not only prevent the worsening of the present situation but would also help to bring about the normalisation of relations between the two countries on the basis of mutually accepted agreement.

Dear friend, it is well known to us and to the whole world that you and your country are devoted to the peace and to the principle of solving the problems among the peoples and nations in the peaceful way. We firmly believe that you personally will know best to assess the way which would lead to the honourable

---

87. Letter from the President of Yugoslavia. MEA, File No.1 China)/62, Vol.III, p. nil.

solution of this problem for your country. That will be of great importance in the present grave international situation.

I firmly believe that the well-intentioned initiative of some of our mutual friends from non-aligned countries could contribute in finding out the solution of this problem. In this regard our official representative of the Secretariat for Foreign Affairs gave the corresponding statement on behalf of the Government of the Federal People's Republic of Yugoslavia on November 2, 1962.

With kindest regards,

Yours sincerely,
Josip Broz Tito

53. From Phạm Văn Đồng and Consul-General Hanoi[88]
[Refer to item 418]

Foreign Minister[89] handed over to me following letter from Prime Minister Pham Van Dong to our Prime Minister.

[Message from Pham Van Dong begins]

Begins. "Your Excellency I have the honour to inform your Excellency that I have received your letter dated 27th October 1962 relating to the Sino-Indian border question.

Like the governments and peoples of all peace loving countries, the Government and people of the DRVN[90] are seriously concerned at the ever fiercer turn taken by the situation on the Sino-Indian border, which affects the age old ties of friendship between the two peoples and Asian-African Solidarity. As has been their consistent desire the imperialist forces are trying hard to make use of the dispute between India and China with a view to dividing and weakening the Asian and world peoples' general movement of struggle against colonialism and for peace.

China and India which have been till lately in the best of friendly relations, together laid down the five principles of peaceful coexistence which served

---

88. Telegram No. 82, 13 November 1982, from the Consul-General in Hanoi, S. Krishnamurthy.
89. Ung Văn Khiêm.
90. Democratic Republic of North Vietnam.

as standards for solidarity among Asian and African countries. At present the peoples of both countries still desire to live in peace and friendship with each other, proceeding from such a situation, it is our hope that the two parties shall, with goodwill and mutual effort, meet and discuss with a view to jointly finding out a mutual agreement. In the present dangerous situation peaceful negotiations are indeed the only way to a good settlement of border dispute between China and India.

In the superior interests of peace and friendship between the two great countries of Asia and of peace and friendship among nations of the world, we sincerely look forward to a satisfactory solution, through negotiations, of the Sino-Indian border question.

I take this opportunity to renew to your Excellency the assurances of my highest consideration." Ends.

[Message from Pham Van Dong ends]

[Note by Consul-General begins]

It is interesting that letter does not urge India specifically to negotiate on basis of China's 24th October proposals. Nor did the Foreign Minister give these proposals while explaining to me the content of the letter. Earlier DRVN, had officially supported the Chinese proposals. India having categorically rejected these they are probably just keeping diplomatic silence on this in their formal communication to us. However, I explained to Foreign Minister why the Chinese proposals are unacceptable to India and also protested that our own proposals for withdrawal to 8th September line offered a peaceful and honourable solution.

About damages being done to Afro-Asian solidarity I submitted to Foreign Minister that he should tell that to the Chinese who were responsible for present crisis. He said he was pointing out the fact to both parties. When I handed over to him a copy of the resolution by National Council of Indian Communist Party he put it aside saying it was a problem of the Indian Communists. I however emphasised that the resolution demonstrates how the entire Indian people were convinced that China is the aggressor and determined to resist it and that was a fact he should take into consideration."

[Note by Consul-General ends]

54. From Vishnu Sahay: Defence of Northeast[91]
[Refer to items 63, 277 and 468]

I have just returned from a short visit to Tezpur and Dirang, Tuting and Along in NEFA. Morale everywhere is high and I was flooded with donations from all kinds of people and with requests from the "tribals" that they should be given arms and cartridges to deal with the Chinese. We are handling this in concert with the Corps Commander.

I won't trouble you with details, but there are three matters, which I think I ought to mention. These are:

(a) Tezpur is being over-visited. Visits by national figures have done a lot of good but from now onwards visits by important people from Delhi might be spaced out a bit. As for visits by officials who have specific business, let everyone consider in each case where their business can really be best done, in Tezpur, or whether Shillong or Gauhati, though less thrilling, won't be better.

(b) Two months ago when I was in Kohima, my attention was drawn by the Chief Secretary of Nagaland to the danger of Chinese, directly or indirectly, coming in via Tirap, where they will get to the old Stilwell Road. The oil fields will then be exposed to easy attack and Nagaland will have a flank open to easy infiltration. East of Tirap, the Burmese Government's writ is apparently feeble and the Yunnan communists could organise something. I have just received a note from my Political Officer in Tirap, pointing out the same thing, namely, we have no forces to block this direction of attack or infiltration. I discussed this with Lt. General Kaul at Tezpur. He has no forces to deal with this loop-hole but he agreed with me that I should specifically mention this problem to you. I have no desire to set up as an amateur strategist, nor would I wish to burden you with shouts for special protection for any part of my area. I know very well that when one's forces are small, one can't attempt to guard all openings but this particular opening could be very serious. I dare say this matter is already being considered.

(c) A couple of weeks ago, I asked the External Affairs Ministry whether we could use our men and the tribals to organise resistance in that portion of Bhutan which is below Tawang and which according to some of their maps the Chinese apparently claim. For reasons which I fully

---

91. Letter from the Governor of Assam, 14 November 1962.

appreciate, the reply was that we had better not give the Chinese any pretext to enter Bhutan. But now the military position appears to be that we are strong at Sela and the Chinese are probing to the right and left of Sela to probe our strength. They may not attack us frontally at Sela and may try to turn the position by walking into the eastern part of Bhutan below Tawang. Then our forces in NEFA will be encircled and communications to Assam will be under direct threat.

I realise the dilemma. The last war's stories of Spain and Gibraltar and of Norway, with their different morals, readily come to mind. But I think I must bring this problem also to your notice. The army people whom I met in Dirang and General Kaul also think that we should immediately build up solid defence in this part of Bhutan to protect the left flank of our Sela position.

55. From T.T. Krishnamachari: Department of Supply[92]
[Refer to items 327, 328 and 329]

November 15, 1962

Now that the Presidential Order has been issued in regard to the creation of a Ministry of Economic and Defence Coordination and of a Minister of Defence Production in the Ministry of Defence, I venture to submit that the ancillary action has to be taken quickly. There appears to be a slight difference between what was contemplated in your letter to the President and what has ultimately emanated; and that is, it is emphasised that the Minister of Defence Production will be a Minister in the Ministry of Defence. In any event, it is not a matter which affects my work to any extent.

I had discussed with you the question of a creation of a Ministry of Supplies. Though personally, I would not like to assume the nomenclature, I am willing to assume the responsibilities for this Ministry. On second thoughts, I think it is better that the Ministry of Supply forms an integral part of the Ministry of Economic and Defence Coordination in the same way as the Technical Development Department will be part of it. Even if you are taking time to decide on the person who is to be the Minister of State for the Ministry of supply, I think it is better to get a Presidential Order issued:

92. Letter from the Minister of Economic & Defence Coordination. NMML, T.T. Krishnamachari Papers, File 1962, copy. Salutation not available.

(i)   Creating a Department of Supply, or a Ministry of Supply as you desire; and

(ii) Locating it in the Ministry of Economic and Defence Coordination.

It will be necessary simultaneously to create Department of Technical Development replacing the present Development Wing in the Ministry of Commerce and Industry, and locating it in the Ministry of Economic and Defence Coordination.

Please forgive me for troubling you in this matter. My only excuse is that I want to get going.

T.T. Krishnamachari

56. From Chou En-lai's to the Leaders of Asian and African Countries on the Sino-Indian Boundary Question[93]
[Refer to items 388 and 249]

Peking, November 15, 1962

Your Excellency,

The unfortunate border conflict between China and India has been going on for several weeks. There are indications that this conflict, far from being halted, will grow in scale. The Chinese Government feels deeply disturbed over this situation which has also evoked the profound concern of many Asian and African countries. I am taking the liberty of writing to you in the hope that my letter may be of help to Your Excellency in your endeavours to promote a peaceful settlement of the Sino-Indian boundary question.

(1) China has worked consistently for the peaceful settlement of questions related to its boundaries. China has a boundary question not only in relation to India, but also in relation to several of its other southwestern neighbours. Traced to their root, these boundary questions were largely created by the imperialists and colonialists before our countries attained independence. Since we won independence, the imperialists and colonialists have tried to make use of these boundary questions to create disputes among us, newly independent states. The Chinese

93. Published as a booklet; 15 November 1962. Original in English. (Foreign Language Press, Peking: 1973). Wilson Centre Archives, http://digitalarchive.wilsoncentre.org/document/175946 Accessed on 21 August 2018.

Government, therefore, considers that, in dealing with such boundary questions, we should clearly discern that these are issues between Asian and African countries which are not the same as issues between Asian-African countries and the imperialist powers; we should be on guard lest we be taken in by the imperialist attempt to sow discord among us.

Inasmuch as the boundary questions are a legacy of history, neither New China nor the other newly independent countries concerned should shoulder the blame. Hence the Chinese Government holds that, in dealing with the boundary questions, both the historical background and the actual situation that has come into being must be taken into account, and that, instead of trying to impose its claims on the other party, each of the parties concerned should seek a settlement that is reasonable and fair to both parties through friendly consultations and in a spirit of mutual understanding and mutual accommodation on the basis of the Five Principles of Peaceful Co-existence and the Ten Principles adopted at the Bandung Conference.

In this spirit China and Burma have settled in a friendly way their boundary question, which was in fact much more complicated than that between China and India. Similarly, a friendly settlement of the Sino-Nepalese boundary question was brought about not long ago. In regard to the Sino-Indian boundary question, the Chinese Government has, in the same spirit, striven for a friendly and peaceful settlement with India. Notwithstanding every conceivable effort on the part of China during the past three years or more, the question remains unsettled, and indeed has developed into the sanguinary border conflict of today. Why this is so is a question that deserves serious thought. For this reason, I deem it necessary here to review the background of Sino-Indian boundary question.

(2) Historically, the Chinese and Indian peoples have always lived together in peace and amity. Although the boundary between China and India has never been formally delimited, no border dispute had ever arisen between them before the British colonialists came to the East. This was so because a traditional customary boundary line had long taken shape on the basis of the extent of each side's administrative jurisdiction in the long course of time during which the two peoples lived together in peace. This line was respected by the Indian as well as the Chinese people. The Eastern sector of this traditional customary boundary runs along the southern foot of the Himalayas, the middle sector along the

Himalayas, and the western sector along the Karakoram range (see attached Map 1).[94]

In the eastern sector, the area disputed by the Indian Government north of the traditional customary line has always belonged to China. This area comprises Monyul, Loyul and Lower Tsayul, which are all part of the Tibet Region. It covers a total area of 90,000 square kilometres and is equivalent in size to three Belgiums or nine Lebanons. The inhabitants who have long lived in this area are either Tibetans or peoples closely akin to them. A case in point is the Monba people, who speak the Tibetan language and believe in Lamaism. Most of the geographical names here are in the Tibetan language. For instance, a river is called "chu" here, hence the Nyamjang River is called Nyamjang Chu; a mountain pass is called "la," hence the Se Pass is called "Sela"; a district is called "yul," hence the Mon district is called "Monyul." The administrative set-up here was the same as that in the other parts of Tibet; the basic administrative unit was called "dzong," as in the case of Senge Dzong and Dirang Dzong. Up to the time when the British colonialists and the Indians came to this area, the local authorities of China's Tibet region had always maintained administrative organs, appointed officials, collected taxes and exercised judicial authority here. This administrative jurisdiction was never called in question.

In the Middle sector, the places disputed by the Indian Government east of the traditional customary line have always belonged to China. They cover a total area of 2,000 square kilometres. The inhabitants are nearly all Tibetans. The Tibet local government had all along exercised jurisdiction over these places, and its archives to this day contain documents pertaining to this exercise of jurisdiction.

In the western sector, the area disputed by the Indian Government north and east of the traditional customary line has always belonged to China. This area consists mainly of Aksai Chin in China's Sinkiang and a part of the Ari district of Tibet. It covers a total area of 33,000 square kilometres and is equivalent in size to one Belgium or three Lebanons. Though sparsely inhabited, this area has always served as the traffic artery linking Sinkiang with Ari in Tibet. The Kirghiz and Uighur herdsmen of Sinkiang have the custom of grazing their cattle here. The name Aksai Chin is the Uighur term for "China's desert of white stones." To this day, this area remains under Chinese jurisdiction.

94. No attachments were found with this document.

The traditional customary boundary was not only respected by both China and India over a long period of time, but also reflected in early official British maps, before 1865, the delineation of the western sector of the Sino-Indian boundary on official British maps coincided roughly with the traditional customary line (see Reference Map 1), and before 1936 their delineation of the eastern sector similarly coincided roughly with the traditional customary line (see Reference Maps 2A and 2B).

(3) The Sino-Indian boundary dispute is a legacy of British imperialist aggression. After it had completely brought India under its domination, British imperialism, taking advantage of the powerless state of the Indian people, turned its spearhead of aggression and expansion towards China's southwestern and northwestern frontiers, using India as its base. From the second half of the nineteenth century to the beginning of the twentieth, British imperialism was actively engaged in conspiratorial activities of aggression against China's Tibet and Sinkiang. Its attempt to force open China's back door was designed to co-ordinate with its aggression along the coast and in the heartland of China. In 1911 there occurred the revolution which overthrew the absolute imperial rule in China. Seizing upon this as an opportune moment to detach Tibet from China, British imperialism sought to negate China's sovereignty in Tibet by recognizing merely China's so-called suzerainty there. It was against this historical background that the Simla Conference was convened in 1914. But even at that Conference the British representative dared not openly demand that China cede large tracts of its territory. It was outside the Conference and behind the back of the representative of the Chinese Central Government that the British representative drew the notorious "McMahon Line" through a secret exchange of letters with the representative of the Tibet local authorities, attempting thereby to annex 90,000 square kilometres of China's territory to British India. The then Chinese Government refused to recognize this illegal McMahon Line. So have all Chinese Governments since then. That is why even the British Government dared not publicly draw this Line on its maps before 1936.

The illegal McMahon Line was wholly imposed on the Chinese people by British imperialism. Although it contrived this Line, for quite a long time afterwards it dared not intrude into the area lying south of this illegal Line and north of the Sino-Indian traditional customary line. It was not until the last phase of the Second World War that British imperialism, utilizing the opportunity afforded by the then Chinese

Government's inability to look after its southwestern frontiers, seized a small part of this area.

In the western sector of the Sino-Indian border, British imperialism, seeking a short-cut for invading the heart of Sinkiang, laid covetous eyes on the relatively flat Aksai Chin in the eighteen sixties and dispatched military intelligence agents to infiltrate into the area for unlawful surveys. In compliance with the will of British imperialism, these agents worked out an assortment of boundary lines for truncating Sinkiang. The British Government did try at one time to alter according to its own wishes the traditional customary line in the western sector of the Sino-Indian border, but was promptly rebuffed by the Chinese Government.

Britain's attempt was to obliterate the traditional customary boundary line formed between China and India over a long period of time, and to attain its imperialist aims of aggression by carving up China's territory and expanding the territory of British India. Yet it dared not completely negate the traditional customary boundary line between China and India or bring out in their entirety the illegal boundary lines it had contrived. From 1865 to 1953 British and Indian maps either did not show any alignment of the boundary in the western sector at all, or showed it in an indistinct fashion and marked it as undefined. It was only from 1936 onwards that the illegal McMahon Line in the Eastern sector appeared on British and Indian maps, but up to the end of 1953 it was still designated as undemarcated {see Reference Map 3).

(4) India and China attained independence in 1947 and 1949 respectively. Friendly relations were developed by the two countries on a new basis. However, owing to causes from the Indian side, there has been a dark side to the Sino-Indian relations from the very beginning.

Thanks to their mutual efforts, China and India established diplomatic relations quite early, jointly initiated the famous Five Principles of Peaceful Co-existence, and signed the Agreement on Trade and Intercourse between the Tibet Region of China and India. This brought about a definite development in the friendly relations between the two countries. China and India ought to have cast away the entire legacy of imperialism and established and developed their relations of mutual friendship on a completely new basis. The Indian Government, however, inherited the British imperialists' covetous desires towards the Tibet region of China and persisted in regarding Tibet as India's sphere of influence, or sought at least to transform it into a buffer zone between China and India. For this reason, the Indian Government tried its best to obstruct the peaceful liberation of Tibet in 1950. When these attempts proved of no avail, India pressed forward in an all-out advance on the illegal McMahon Line in the eastern sector of the border and completely occupied China's territory south of that illegal Line and north of the traditional customary line. In the Middle sector of the Sino-Indian border, apart from long ago inheriting from British imperialism the encroachment on Sang and Tsungsha, India further encroached on Chuva, Chuje, Shipki Pass, Puling-Sumdo, Sangcha, and Lapthal after 1954. After 1954, India also encroached on Parigas in the Western sector of the border.

While it was occupying large tracts of Chinese territory, India suddenly made a unilateral alteration of the Sino-Indian traditional customary line on its official map published in 1954. It presented in its entirety the version of the Sino-Indian boundary insidiously contrived by British imperialism and tried to impose this version on China as the delimited boundary between China and India (see Reference Map 4).

The Chinese Government did not accept Indian encroachment on large tracts of Chinese territory, nonetheless it took the position that an amicable settlement of the Sino-Indian boundary question should be sought through peaceful negotiations, and that, pending a settlement, the status quo of the boundary should be maintained. China does not recognize the so-called McMahon Line, yet in the interest of settling the Sino-Indian boundary question through negotiations, it refrained from crossing this Line. As for maps of the two parties showing the boundary, they can be brought into conformity only after the boundary question has been settled through negotiations between the two parties. This was the procedure by which maps of China and Burma and maps of China and Nepal showing the boundary lines between them were brought into conformity. The delineation of the Sino-Indian boundary on maps published by China has its historical and factual basis. But in view of the fact that the Sino-Indian boundary has not been formally delimited, China has never imposed its maps on India; at the same time, China will under no circumstances accept the maps unilaterally altered by India.

From 1950 to 1958, tranquility generally prevailed along the Sino-Indian border because China adhered to the policy of seeking an amicable settlement of the boundary question through peaceful negotiations, although even in that period India was already sowing seeds for provoking future boundary disputes and border clashes.

(5) After the rebellion in Tibet, the Indian Government formally laid claim to large tracts of Chinese territory. In March 1959 a rebellion of serf-owners broke out in the Tibet region of China. The Indian Government not only aided and abetted this rebellion, but gave refuge to the remnant rebels after the rebellion had been put down, and connived at their anti-Chinese political activities in India. Soon after the rebellion broke out in Tibet, Prime Minister Nehru formally presented to the Chinese Government a claim to large tracts of Chinese territory. He asked the Chinese Government not only to recognize as legal Indian occupation of Chinese territory in the eastern sector of the Sino-Indian border, but also to recognize as part of India the Aksai Chin area in the Western sector of the Sino-Indian border which India had never occupied (see attached Map 2).

India's territorial claim to Aksai Chin was conjured up and is devoid of any basis whatever. China has always exercised its jurisdiction in this area. In 1950 it was through this area that units of the Chinese People's Liberation Army advanced from Sinkiang into Ari, Tibet. And it was through this area that between 1956 and 1957 the Chinese side constructed the Sinkiang-Tibet Highway, a gigantic task of engineering. As a matter of fact, up to 1958, India had never disputed the fact of China's exercise of jurisdiction over this area. But now the Indian Government asserted that this area had always belonged to India, and that it was not until 1957 that the Chinese had entered it clandestinely. If India had always exercised jurisdiction over this area, it is beyond comprehension how India could have been unaware of the passing of the Chinese People's Liberation Army units through this area to Tibet and of the construction of the gigantic highway. It was only from a pictorial magazine published in China that the Indian Government came to know that China had built the highway. In September 1958 the Indian side sent patrols to intrude into this area, but they were immediately detained by Chinese frontier guards. How could this have happened if India had really exercised jurisdiction over this area? In point of fact, Prime Minister Nehru himself said in the Indian Rajya Sabha on September 10, 1959 that this area "has not been under any kind of administration." On November 23 of the same year, he further stated in the Indian Rajya Sabha, "During British rule, as far as I know, this area was neither inhabited by any people nor were there any outposts." Though Prime Minister Nehru was in no position to assess correctly the situation on the Chinese side, his words nevertheless demonstrate authoritatively that India has never exercised jurisdiction over this area.

Having occupied 90,000 square kilometres of Chinese territory in the eastern sector and 2,000 square kilometres of Chinese territory in the Middle sector of the Sino-Indian border, India now wants to occupy another 33,000 square kilometres of Chinese territory in the Western sector. In other words, India views both the parts of Chinese territory it has occupied and the other parts of Chinese territory it has not yet occupied as belonging to India. This represents a demand which even the overbearing British imperialists dared not put to semi-colonial, old China. That a newly-independent India should have made such a demand came as a complete shock to China.

The gravity of the situation lies not only in India's extensive claims to Chinese territory, but also in its subsequent use of force to change unilaterally the state of the boundary that had emerged, so as to realize Indian territorial claims. Indian armed forces crossed the illegal McMahon Line in the Eastern sector, invaded and occupied Tamaden, Longju and Khinzemane north of the Line; and in August 1959, in the course of invading Longju, provoked the first sanguinary border clash.[95] In October 1959 Indian armed forces crossed the traditional customary boundary line in the western sector and provoked a san- guinary border clash of an even graver nature at Kongka Pass. These two border clashes were omens that India would further aggravate the situation on the Sino-Indian border.

(6) The Chinese Government held that, in order to avert conflict along the border, ways must be found to effect a disengagement of the armed forces of the two sides, and at the same time negotiations must be started quickly to seek a peaceful settlement of the boundary question. The Chinese Government was determined to take every possible measure within its power to prevent a deterioration of the situation.

On November 7, 1959, the Chinese Government proposed to the Indian Government that the armed forces of each side withdraw 20 kilometres from the line of actual control along the entire Sino- Indian border and halt patrols. The line of actual control referred to here coincided with the traditional customary line in the Western and Middle sectors except for the parts of Chinese territory which India had invaded and occupied as referred to in Section (4) above; in the

95. See SWJN/SS/51/ item 193 for India's position on the incident, statement on the Chinese claims in the Lok Sabha.

eastern sector, the line of actual control coincided with the illegal McMahon Line except for Khinzemane which was then still under Indian occupation (see attached Map 3). The Chinese Government also proposed that the Prime Ministers of the two countries hold talks to discuss the Sino-Indian boundary question. But these proposals were rejected by the Indian Government. On November 16, 1959 the Indian Government put forward a counter-proposal which would require all Chinese personnel in the Aksai Chin area of China's Sinkiang to withdraw to the east of the line which India claimed to be the international boundary, and all Indian personnel in this area to withdraw to the west of the line which China claimed to be the international boundary. Since Indian personnel had never actually come into this area, the Indian proposal was tantamount to demanding the unilateral withdrawal of Chinese personnel from vast tracts of their own territory. The Chinese government then put this question to the Indian Government: Since the Indian Government held that each side should withdraw behind the line claimed by the other side in the western sector of the Sino-Indian border, did this mean that the Indian Government agreed that in the Eastern sector as well, each side should withdraw behind the line claimed by the other side? –in other words, that India should withdraw to the south of the traditional customary line pointed out by China, while China should withdraw to the north of the so-called McMahon Line claimed by India? The Indian Government was at a loss to answer this question and merely kept insisting that its proposal was only applicable to the Western sector. Very clearly, the Indian Government had no interest in an amicable settlement of the Sino-Indian boundary question through peaceful negotiations on a fair and reasonable basis, nor had it any interest in separating the armed forces of the two sides on the basis of the line of actual control with a view to forestalling border clashes. What it was after was only to use armed forces to edge Chinese personnel out of Chinese territory in the Western sector of the Sino-Indian border.

Despite this, the Chinese Government still maintained that it was of paramount urgency to avert conflict along the border. Hence, after the Indian Government had rejected the Chinese Government's proposals that each side withdraw its armed forces 20 kilometres from the line of actual control and stop patrols, China unilaterally discontinued patrols on its side of the boundary. The Chinese Government hoped that, by so doing, at least a disengagement of the armed forces of the two sides could be effected which would be conducive to avoiding border clashes and maintaining tranquility in the border region.

(7) With a view to seeking a peaceful settlement of the Sino-Indian boundary question, the Chinese Premier visited New Delhi in April 1960 and held talks with Prime Minister Nehru. In the course of the talks, I repeatedly explained that the boundary question should be settled peacefully on a fair and reasonable basis; that if there could not be a settlement for the time being, the state of the boundary that had already emerged should be maintained; and that the armed forces of the two sides should be disengaged in order to forestall clashes. At the conclusion of the talks, I summed up the following six points as points of common ground or of close proximity emerging from the talks, namely:

(i) There exist disputes with regard to the boundary between the two sides.

(ii) There exists between the two countries a line of actual control up to which each side exercises administrative jurisdiction.

(iii) In determining the boundary between the two countries, certain geographical principles, such as watersheds, river valleys and mountain passes, should be equally applicable to all sectors of the boundary.

(iv) A settlement of the boundary question between the two countries should take into account the national feelings of the two peoples towards the Himalayas and the Karakoram Mountains.

(v) Pending a settlement of the boundary question between the two countries through discussions, both sides should keep to the line of actual control and should not put forward territorial claims as pre-conditions, but individual adjustments may be made.

(vi) In order to ensure tranquility on the border so as to facilitate the discussion, both sides should continue to refrain from patrolling along all sectors of the boundary.

I suggested that these points of common ground be affirmed so as to facilitate further discussions by the two governments. These six points are entirely equitable and involve no demands imposed by one side on the other. They include views expressed to me during the talks by Prime Minister Nehru himself. Yet Prime Minister Nehru refused to confirm these six points. His refusal in fact meant that the Indian Government was unwilling to recognize the existence of a line of actual control between the two countries, unwilling to agree to observe this line pending a settlement of the boundary question through negotiations and refrain from putting forward territorial claims as pre-conditions to negotiations, unwilling to disengage the armed forces of the two sides so as to forestall border clashes, and even unwilling to recognize the objective fact that there exist disputes between the two sides with regard to the boundary. In those talks, Prime Minister Nehru took the position that the Chinese Government must unconditionally accede to India's territorial claims and refused to leave any room for negotiation. These were claims which even British imperialism dared not put before the Chinese Government. Prime Minister Nehru was fully aware that the Chinese Government would in no circumstances agree to these claims. By pressing them he was clearly seeking, out of unrevealed motives, to keep the boundary question unsettled and the border situation tense indefinitely.

Subsequently, during the meetings between officials of the two countries held from June to December in 1960, the Chinese side proved with a large volume of conclusive data that the traditional customary boundary line as pointed out by China had a historical and factual basis. But the Indian side, mainly relying on obviously valueless material from British travellers and adventurers, insisted that the illegal McMahon Line was the traditional customary line in the Eastern sector of the Sino-Indian border, and that Aksai Chin over which China had always exercised jurisdiction belonged to India. Thus, the meetings between officials of the two countries also failed to yield results.

(8) The sincerity for conciliation demonstrated by the Chinese Government during the talks between the two Prime Ministers was taken by the Indian Government as an indication that China was weak and could be bullied, and China's unilateral halting of border patrols was taken as an opportunity to take advantage of. Therefore, after the meetings between the officials of the two countries had concluded, Indian troops crossed the line of actual control first in the western and then in the eastern sector of the border, occupied more and more Chinese territory and engaged in ever more serious armed provocations.

In the Western sector of the border, beginning from 1961, and particularly from last April on, Indian troops made repeated inroads into Chinese territory, and set up additional military strong points. Prior to the recent general outbreak of clashes on the border, India had established a total of 43 strong points encroaching on Chinese territory in the western sector of the border (see attached Map 4). Some were set up only a few metres away from Chinese posts, others even behind Chinese posts, cutting off their access to the rear. As

Prime Minister Nehru put it in addressing the Indian Lok Sabha on June 20, 1962, "India had opened some new patrol posts endangering the Chinese posts and it was largely due to movements on our side that the Chinese had also to make movements. It is well known in knowledgeable circles in the world that the position in this area had been changing to our advantage and the Chinese are concerned about it." The Indian weekly *Blitz* openly boasted at the time that India had occupied 2,500 square miles of territory there, which the weekly described as a "unique triumph for an audacious Napoleonic planning" worked out by Defence Minister Krishna Menon. Invading Indian troops again and again launched armed provocations against Chinese frontier guards. Indian aircraft again and again violated China's air space and recklessly carried out harassing raids. As a result of these increasingly frequent acts of provocation on the part of India, the situation in the Western sector of the Sino-Indian border grew sharply in tension and gravity.

Because China exercised great self-restraint and forbearance, India's encroachments in the western sector of the Sino-Indian border were not seriously resisted, whereupon India went further to extend its encroachments to the eastern sector of the border. From last June onwards, Indian troops crossed the illegal McMahon Line, intruded into the Che Dong area north of the Line, incessantly expanded their scope of occupation (see attached Map 4), and launched a series of armed attacks on Chinese frontier guards, inflicting forty-seven casualties on them. Thus, before the recent full-scale border conflict broke out, the Indian side had already created in both the eastern and western sectors of the Sino-Indian border a grave situation in which an explosion might be touched off at any moment.

(9) While the Indian encroachments and provocations increased in gravity and the border situation worsened day by day, the Chinese side maintained maximum self-restraint and forbearance throughout. Chinese frontier guards were ordered not to fire the first shot under any circumstances, nor to return fire except as a last resort. On the one hand, the Chinese Government sent protests and warnings to the Indian Government, declaring that it would never accept the Indian encroachments and firmly demanding that India evacuate Chinese territory. On the other hand, it did not relax in the least its efforts to seek an improvement in Sino-Indian relations and a peaceful settlement of the boundary issue through negotiations.

The Chinese side held that any steps conducive to improving Sino-Indian relations would without doubt also help promote a peaceful settlement of the boundary question. In view of the fact that the 1954 Agreement Between China and India on Trade and Intercourse Between the Tibet Region of China and India was due to expire in June 1962, the Chinese Government, from December 1961 to May 1962, proposed three times the conclusion of a new agreement to replace the old one. Although the conclusion of such a new agreement would have nothing to do with the boundary question, it would undoubtedly have helped to improve Sino-Indian relations. In advancing this proposal China had the best of intentions. But the Indian Government demanded China's acceptance of India's territorial claims as the pre-condition for the conclusion of such a new agreement, and unjustifiably rejected the proposal.

It was precisely because the Sino-Indian border situation was growing steadily more acute that the Chinese Government pointed more emphatically than ever to the necessity for a peaceful settlement of the boundary question through negotiations. But the Indian Government persisted in a negative attitude. It was not until July 26 this year that it expressed in vague terms a desire for further discussions on the boundary question on the basis of the report of the officials of the two sides. The Chinese Government responded promptly and positively in its note of August 4, and suggested that such discussions be held as soon as possible.

The Indian Government, however, suddenly adopted a different tone in a note dated August 22 and insisted that China must first evacuate large tracts of its own territory in the western sector of the border before any further boundary discussions on the basis of the officials' report could be held. This was a unilaterally posed pre-condition by which India sought to force its territorial claims on China. In its note of September 13, the Chinese Government pointed out that no pre-conditions should be set for further boundary discussions on the basis of the officials' report. It suggested, moreover, that representatives of the two sides begin discussions on the boundary question on October 15, first in Peking and then in Delhi alternately. At the same time, with a view to easing the border tension, the Chinese Government once again proposed that the armed forces of each side withdraw 20 kilometres along the entire border.

But the Indian Government, in its note of September, 19, rejected China's proposals for separation of the armed forces of the two sides and for holding discussions on the boundary question without pre-conditions. It merely agreed to the date and sites for the discussions proposed by China, while insisting that the discussions should be confined to China's withdrawal from large tracts of China's own territory in the western sector of the border. The Chinese Government, in its note dated October 3, repeated the proposal that the two sides should speedily enter into boundary discussions on the basis of the officials' report, and that in the course of the discussions neither side should refuse to discuss any question that might be raised by the other side concerning the boundary. This proposal was fair to both sides.

Nevertheless, the Indian Government in its reply note dated October 6 not only rejected the above-mentioned fair proposal of the Chinese Government, but added a new pre-condition to the old one, demanding that Chinese troops evacuate the Che Dong area, which is Chinese territory, north of the illegal McMahon Line. Thus, by going back on its own word and putting forward one precondition after another, the Indian Government finally blocked the door to negotiations on the boundary question.

(10) Making a series of miscalculations concerning China, India not only turned down China's peaceable proposals, but finally embarked on the road of military adventure. India thought that China's economic difficulties were so grave that it would not be able to overcome them, and that China's south western defences must have been weakened owing to the fact that its national defence forces were tied down by the attempt of the U.S.-supported Chiang Kai-shek clique to invade China's south eastern coastal areas. Therefore, India considered the opportunity ripe for launching massive armed attacks along the entire Sino-Indian border. On October 5 the Indian Ministry of Defence announced the establishment of a new corps under the "Eastern Command" for the sole purpose of dealing with China, and the appointment of Lt. General B. M. Kaul as its commander. On October 12 Prime Minister Nehru declared that he had issued orders to "free" what he termed invaded areas, in reality Chinese territory, of Chinese troops. On October 14 the then Indian Minister of Defence, Krishna Menon, called for fighting China to the last man and the last gun. On October 16, upon returning to New Delhi from abroad, Prime Minister Nehru immediately summoned a meeting of high-ranking military officers to accelerate combat preparations. On October 17 Indian troops in both the eastern and western sectors simultaneously began heavy "artillery attacks on the Chinese side. On October 18 officials

of the Indian Ministry of Defence declared that the Chinese had been "driven back two miles." Finally, in the early hours of October 20, Indian troops, on Prime Minister Nehru's orders, launched massive attacks all along the line. It was only when they had been repeatedly subjected to frenzied attacks by the Indian troops and had suffered heavy casualties that the Chinese frontier guards, pressed beyond the limits of forbearance and left with no room for retreat, struck back in resolute self-defence.

(11) All relevant facts show that the current grave Sino-Indian border conflict was wholly engineered by the Indian Government, deliberately and over a long period of time. At a mass meeting held in New Delhi on November 11 last, Prime Minister Nehru openly revealed that two years ago India had already drawn up a "plan of operations" against China, which had even worked out such details as the scale of the operations and how advance or falling back was to be made when the battle got under way. But the Indian Government, turning facts upside down, falsely accused Chinese frontier guards of crossing the western end of the illegal McMahon Line on September 8 and thereby touching off the current general border conflict. This accusation is an out-and-out lie. Actually, it was Indian troops that had crossed the western end of the illegal McMahon Line long before September 8. This is a fact that cannot be denied. The Chinese Government is in possession of the original 1914 map of the so-called McMahon Line. According to that map, the western extremity of the Line is clearly at latitude 27°44.6'N (see Reference Maps 5 and 6), The Indian Government, in order to justify its occupation of the Che Dong area north of the Line, insists that the western extremity of the Line is at 27°48'N and that the boundary between China and India in this area follows the so-called Thagla ridge, watershed. But the co-ordinates on the original map of the so-called McMahon Line are there and cannot be altered, and the name Thagla ridge does not even appear on the map. Moreover, the Indian military sketch maps captured by China during the current border clashes also clearly show the Che Dong area to be north of the illegal McMahon Line. The fact that India intentionally crossed the illegal McMahon Line, occupied the Che Dong area to its north, and publicly declared that India would "free" this area of Chinese frontier guards serves precisely to demonstrate that the current border clashes were solely and deliberately created by India.

The Chinese Government's stand on the illegal McMahon Line is a consistent one. China does not recognize the illegal McMahon

Line, yet it refrained from crossing it in the interest of a peaceful settlement of the Sino-Indian boundary question. The fact was that India first crossed to the north of the illegal McMahon Line and, using places south of the Line as its base, launched massive armed attacks on Chinese frontier guards. Thus, with its own hands the Indian Government finally destroyed the restrictive effect of this Line. In order to prevent the Indian troops from staging a come-back and launching fresh attacks, the Chinese frontier guards, fighting in self-defence, naturally need no longer be restricted by the illegal McMahon Line. China has consistently striven for the settlement of the Sino-Indian boundary question by peaceful means. The Chinese frontier guards have crossed the illegal McMahon Line because they had no alternative. But when China is compelled to strike back now in self-defence in the border conflict, it still aims at promoting a peaceful settlement of the Sino-Indian boundary question, just as it did in exercising forbearance and self-restraint over the past three years. The Chinese frontier guards have crossed the illegal McMahon Line and advanced to certain points, yet the Chinese side does not wish to rely on such a move to settle the question the Eastern sector of the Sino-Indian boundary. As in the past, the Chinese Government holds that only through peaceful negotiations can a settlement reasonable and fair to both sides be found not only for the eastern sector, but for the Sino-Indian boundary question as a whole.

(12) On October 24, that is, four days after the Sino-Indian border conflict broke out, the Chinese Government issued a statement putting forward the following three proposals with a view to stopping the border conflict, reopening peaceful negotiations and settling the Sino-Indian boundary question:

(i) Both parties affirm that the Sino-Indian boundary question must be settled peacefully through negotiations. Pending a peaceful settlement, the Chinese Government hopes that the Indian Government will agree that both parties respect the line of actual control between the two sides along the entire Sino-Indian border, and the armed forces of each side withdraw 20 kilometres from this line and disengage.

(ii) Provided that the Indian Government agrees to the above proposal, the Chinese Government is willing, through consultation between the two parties, to withdraw its frontier guards in the Eastern sector of the border to the north of the line of actual control; at the same time, both China and India undertake not to cross the line of actual control, i.e., the traditional customary line, in the Middle and Western sectors of the border.

(iii)   Matters relating to the disengagement of the armed forces of the two parties and the cessation of armed conflict shall be negotiated by officials designated by the Chinese and Indian Governments respectively.

(iv)   The Chinese Government considers that, in order to seek a friendly settlement of the Sino-Indian boundary question, talks should be held once again by the Prime Ministers of China and India. At a time considered to be appropriate by both parties, the Chinese Government would welcome the Indian Prime Minister to Peking; if this should be inconvenient to the Indian Government, the Chinese Premier would be ready to go to Delhi for talks.

The essence of the first of China's three proposals is to restore the state of the Sino-Indian boundary in 1959, that is, before complications arose in the border situation over the past three years, and to have the armed forces of each side withdraw 20 kilometres from the 1959 line of actual control. The obligations of both sides under this proposal would be equal. If the Indian Government agrees to this proposal, the Chinese frontier guards would have to withdraw from their present positions south of the so-called McMahon Line not only to the north of the line, but 20 kilometres further northward. The Indian troops, on the other hand, would only have to withdraw 20 kilometres southward from this line. If measured from Tawang and its vicinity south of the so-called McMahon Line, which Chinese frontier guards have now reached they would have to withdraw about 40 kilometres, while Indian troops would need to withdraw only one to two kilometres, or need not withdraw at all (see attached Map 5).

The reason why China has reiterated and emphasized its proposal for a 20-kilometre withdrawal by the armed forces of each side from the line of actual control is that, through its bitter experiences of the past three years, the Chinese Government has become acutely aware that it is very difficult to avoid clashes in border areas under dispute if the armed forces of the two sides are not disengaged. At the same time, it must be pointed out that the line of actual control is not equivalent to the boundary between the two countries. Acknowledging and

809

respecting the line of actual control would not prejudice each side's adherence to its claims on the boundary, but would create a favourable atmosphere for the reopening of peaceful negotiations to settle the boundary question.

(13) The Chinese Government had hoped that the Indian Government would give careful consideration to China's three proposals before making a response. But on the very day they were put forward by the Chinese Government, the Indian Government hastily rejected them and slanderously termed them deceptive. The Indian Government stated that no negotiations were possible unless the state of the entire boundary as it prevailed before September 8, 1962 was restored, and declared that the Indian Government was only prepared to hold negotiations "on the basis of decency, dignity and self-respect."

What is the implication of the Indian Government's proposed restoration of the state of the boundary as it prevailed before September 8? In the Eastern sector of the Sino-Indian border, it would mean that Indian troops again invade and occupy Chinese territory north of the illegal McMahon Line; in the western sector it would mean that they again invade and occupy the military strong points they set up on Chinese territory after 1959. And what kind of a state of affairs would this be? This would again be the state of affairs on October 20 when Indian troops, utilizing the advantageous military positions they had seized, launched large-scale armed attacks against Chinese frontier guards. It would be a state of affairs pregnant with so grave a danger as to make border clashes inevitable. It would not be fair, nor would it bring peace, to revert either to the state of the boundary as of September 8, or to that of October 20.

The fact that the Indian Government refuses to restore the state of the boundary of November 7, 1959 but wants to restore the state of the boundary of September 8, 1962 proves that since 1959 the Indian Government has seized by force large tracts of Chinese territory. What India proposes to restore is the situation that resulted from the Indian troops' crossing the line of actual control and encroaching on Chinese territory over the past three years; whereas the situation which China proposes to restore is one in which tranquility was basically maintained along the Sino-Indian border three years ago. According to the Indian proposal, only China would withdraw, while India would not withdraw, but advance and| again invade and occupy Chinese territory.

According to the Chinese proposals, both sides would withdraw, and in the eastern sector the distance the Chinese frontier guards would have to withdraw would far exceed the distance the Indian forces would have to withdraw. Looked at from any angle, India's proposal is a one-sided one by which it attempts to impose its will on China and make China submit; while China's proposals are equitable and in the spirit of mutual accommodation and mutual respect. Furthermore, the Chinese side proposed talks between the Prime Ministers of the two countries, expressed welcome for Prime Minister Nehru to come to Peking and stated that should the Indian Government find it inconvenient, the Chinese Premier was prepared to go to New Delhi once again. Clearly, full consideration had been given to India's prestige and sense of decency when China put forward these conciliatory proposals. The Indian Government has stressed that it is prepared to enter into negotiations only "on the basis of decency, dignity and self-respect." However, its proposal shows that it only considers its own decency, dignity and self-respect, but wants to deny decency, dignity and self-respect to the other party.

(14) After my first appeal was rejected by Prime Minister Nehru, I appealed to him a second time, hoping that he would return to the conference table. However, judging by present indications, the Indian Government, far from being ready to conduct peaceful negotiations, is resolved to continue the use of force. The Indian Government has publicly stated that India is in fact in a state of war with China. It presented in the Indian Parliament a resolution to "drive out the Chinese aggressors from the soil of India," and this resolution has been adopted. The President of India has proclaimed a "state of emergency" throughout the country. A wartime cabinet has been set up in India; military mobilization has been set in motion; war bonds have been issued; and India's economy has begun to go on "a war footing". War hysteria enshrouds the whole of India. Setting no store by the friendship of the Chinese and Indian peoples, Prime Minister Nehru has publicly spread seeds of hatred for the Chinese people and used every forum to call on the Indian people to wage a long drawn-out fight against the Chinese people.

The Indian Government has stepped up its persecution of Chinese nationals in India, arbitrarily ordered the closure of branch offices of the Bank of China in India, crudely restricted the movement of staff members of the Chinese Embassy and Consulates in India, and is even

811

considering severing diplomatic relations with China.[96] Casting off the cloak of "non-alignment," the Indian Government has openly begged for military aid from the United States of America and is receiving a continuous supply of U.S. arms. Large numbers of Indian troops and huge quantities of U.S. munitions are being rushed to the Sino-Indian border areas, Indian troops in both the Western and Eastern sectors of the Sino-Indian border have not ceased attacking the Chinese frontier guards. The Indian press has been trumpeting that India is about to launch a big counter-offensive. All this indicates that the threat of border conflicts on a bigger scale is growing perilously.

(15) There is no reason whatsoever for China and India to fight on account of the boundary question. In the past three years the Chinese Government has every possible effort to prevent the emergence of such an unfortunate situation. From the very beginning the Chinese Government has stood for an amicable settlement of the boundary question through peaceful negotiations. In the past three years, nearly all the proposals for negotiations were initiated by China. For the purpose of negotiation, the Chinese Premier went to New Delhi, and is prepared to go again. However, in the last three years the Indian Government usually refused to negotiate, or after reluctantly agreeing to negotiate, would not settle a single question capable of being settled. The Chinese Government stood for maintaining the state of the boundary which had taken shape, pending a peaceful settlement; concretely speaking, this means maintaining the line of actual control that existed between China and India in 1959. The Indian side, however, started off by crossing the line of actual control in the Western sector of the Sino-Indian border, and finally even violated the so-called McMahon Line which it claimed itself to be the boundary in the Eastern sector. China sought to disengage the armed forces of the two sides, while India persisted in keeping them in contact. To avoid border clashes, the Chinese Government proposed separating the armed forces of the two sides and halting patrols.

After these proposals were rejected by India, China unilaterally stopped patrolling on its side of the border. Taking advantage of China's unilateral cessation of patrols, however, India's armed forces

96. See "Cable from the Chinese Foreign Ministry, 'On India's Possible Severing Diplomatic Relations with China'," December 14, 1962, Wilson Centre Archives. http://digitalarchive.wilsoncenter.org/document/121794Accessed on 6 September 2018. See also item 248.

intruded into Chinese territory, set up military strong points and pressed steadily forward, thus eventually making border clashes between China and India unavoidable. Had the Indian Government entertained the slightest desire to settle the boundary question peacefully, the situation on the Sino-Indian border would never have deteriorated to the unfortunate degree it has.

The present unfortunate situation has been brought about solely by the Indian Government. The reasons for these actions of the Indian Government are to be found not so much in the boundary question per se as in its designs of utilizing this situation to whip up an anti-China campaign by which it seeks internally to divert the attention and increase the burden of the people and suppress the progressive forces, and externally to obtain more U.S. aid.

(16) Your Excellency, it is with a heavy heart that I have presented to you the history of the Sino-Indian boundary question in its entirety. But Your Excellency may rest assured that the Chinese Government is not discouraged, but will look ahead. However, complicated the situation may be now, the Chinese Government will never waver in its determination to seek a peaceful settlement of the Sino-Indian boundary question. So long as there remains a ray of hope, it will continue to seek a way to conciliation, and take the initiative to create conditions favouring the cessation of border clashes. There is no conflict of fundamental interests between China and India, and it is utterly unthinkable to the Chinese Government that the present border clashes should develop into a full-scale war between the two countries. The border clashes must and will eventually be settled peacefully.

Ever since the Sino-Indian border issue arose, leaders of many Asian and African countries have exerted great efforts to promote its peaceful settlement. Almost unanimously they hold that the arch enemy of us Asian and African countries is imperialism and colonialism, that our countries all face urgent tasks of reconstruction to transform the backward state of our economy, and that China and India, the two big Asian countries, should settle their boundary question peacefully, restore Sino-Indian friendship, enhance Asian-African solidarity and together cope with the main enemy before us. They appeal to China and India to halt the armed border clashes and immediately enter into negotiations, and they oppose foreign intervention.

Both China and India are big Asian countries. It is only through direct negotiations between China and India that a mutually satisfactory settlement of the boundary question can be secured. The

Chinese Government heartily, welcomes and sincerely thanks the leaders of friendly Asian and African countries for their fair-minded endeavours to promote direct negotiations between China and India, without themselves getting involved in the dispute. I sincerely hope that Your Excellency will uphold justice and continue to exercise your distinguished influence to promote a peaceful settlement of the Sino-Indian boundary question on a fair and reasonable basis.

Please accept, Your Excellency, the assurances of my highest consideration.

Chou En-lai
Premier of the State Council
of the People's Republic of China

57. Military Aid to India: US and UK consultations[97]
[Refer to items 420, 444, 445, 446 and 447]

Mr President:

You are having a meeting on the Indian military aid situation with State and Defense at 4:00 p.m., Monday.

The immediate subject for decision is the result of our discussion with the UK this past week. A team consisting of Jim Grant from State, Bill Bundy from Defence, and Bill Gaud from AID, has come to an agreed set of recommendations with a similar British group on what we should be prepared to do. In summary, this group recommends that we agree with the British and, to the extent that we can get them to contribute, other Commonwealth countries, to equip a force of about five divisions and their supporting formations. A preliminary guess is that the equipment involved might cost as much as $50 million. The associated supplies, especially ammunition, might be equally or more expensive depending on Indian production capabilities and present Indian stocks, neither of which are well known at the moment.

The rationale of the program is that, with such assistance, the Indians would be capable of holding the Chinese where they are now. If the Indians wish to

---

97. Briefing memorandum for J.F. Kennedy, drafted by Carl Kaysen, Deputy Special Assistant for National Security Affairs, 16 November 1962; Kennedy Papers, https://www.jfklibrary.org/Asset-Viewer/Archives/JFKNSF-111-016.aspx Accessed on 21 August 2018.

reconquer the Chinese-occupied area, they would have to use half to two-thirds of the forces they now have on their border with Pakistan. The idea is thus to combine a respectable amount of aid to the Indians with a continuation of pressure on them to improve their relations with Pakistan.

There is an indication of the dispositions of the Indian forces at two dates, 13 October and 16 November. The latter reflects information given to Galbraith by the Indians. One thing the map does not make clear is that the troops which are on the Kashmir border look to the Indians as back-up for the unit fighting at Ladakh, even though they look to the Paks the way they have always looked to the Paks.

The recent cables from New Delhi: Galbraith's latest on the opinions of Foreign Secretary Desai. It shows an increase in the realism of Indian assessments; Nehru's letter to Ayub; the present state of the discussion on non-alignment from New York—some indirect evidence on the effect of developments on Indian non-alignment. The effects have even reached Arthur Lall.[98]

This is the latest assessment from Karachi. McConaughy[99] obviously is somewhat frightened and thinks the situation is out of hand. Phil Talbot[100] and I do not agree with his suggestion that you reply to Ayub's letter immediately and cordially. We think a much better course of action would be for Secretary Rusk[101] to write to Muhammad Ali, Pak Foreign Minister. The occasion can be the transmission of a copy of our agreement with India on military aid. He can use the occasion to repeat our assurances to the Paks. We propose further, that at the same time we make the agreement public—late Saturday—we make a public statement of our commitment to go to Pakistan's aid if it is attacked, as well as our promise that the help we give to India will be used only against the Chinese Communists. The statement would come from State. It would put on the public record what you have already told Ayub privately in writing and orally several times.

There is a very interesting report from Malcolm MacDonald[102] on the Chinese position on the conflict. MacDonald talked with Chen Yi, the Foreign Secretary, on 29 October, and later with Chou En-lai.

The review will raise the deeper issues of our problems and possibilities on the Indian situation. The approach embodied in the US-UK memorandum is a

98. Member, Indian Delegation at the UN.
99. Walter P. McConaughy (1908-2000); US Ambassador to Pakistan, 1962-1966.
100. William Phillips Talbot (1915–2010); US Assistant Secretary of State for Near Eastern and South Asian affairs (1961–1965).
101. David Dean Rusk (1909-1994); Secretaryof State (1961-1969).
102. Former High Commissioner to India (1955-1960).

cautious one. It certainly makes sense as a first step, until events reveal more clearly what Chinese intentions are and how relations within the sub-continent will shift. Still, it is important to take a longer look ahead. Do we want to push the Indians hard enough and give them enough help to make sure that they do not seek a negotiated solution on Chinese terms and lapse back into neutralism? Continuance of the war may serve important U.S. policy objectives: the sharp decline of "positive neutralism" as a foreign policy stance in the unaligned countries, greatly improved relations between India and Pakistan, another setback to Chinese Communist prestige and power with consequences felt throughout Asia. On the other hand, continuance of the war may be increasingly at our expense. Can we and do we wish to bear the costs? Alternatively, it may well be beyond our power to promote a continuance of the war. The direct reaction of the Indians when confronted with the costs of reconquering what they have already lost may lead them to draw back no matter what we do. The effects on Pakistan of our aid to India may continue to be so unfavourable as to become a limiting factor in what we can do. It is neither necessary nor possible to answer these questions now. However, we must certainly begin to consider them and the policy decision we take on the narrower issue which will be before you on Monday is at best an interim one.

58. From A. P. Jain: Soviet Position Causing Anxiety[103]
[Refer to items 261, 395, 401 and 447]

November 16, 1962

My dear Jawaharlalji,

I am feeling greatly concerned to read the conflicting news about Russia. You had been trying to adopt a friendly attitude, I think correctly. You have recently said that Russia would fulfil its commitments both with regard to supplying MIG aircraft and putting up the manufacturing plant. I do not know if you have seen a reported denial of your statement published on page 9 of today's issue of the *Times of India*.[104] It says that a senior Soviet official in New Delhi said, "The position as far as we are concerned is that Russia will not supply India with MIGs while Mr Nehru's attitude continues to be what it is. He will not listen to our suggestion that he and the Chinese should hold talks." I have met with several who feel confused with this report.

---

103. Letter from the President of the UPCC; address: 5 Rafi Marg, New Delhi. NMML, A.P. Jain Papers.
104. See the *Times of India*, 16 November 1962, p.9, col.1.

At the top of it comes Chavan's speech from Poona that he firmly believed that "Russia would ultimately be on the side of China" etc. etc. I do not question the honesty or validity of Chavan's views, but there is no doubt that statements having contrary trends cause confusion among the people.

Please do not misunderstand me. I am a good friend of Chavan and I do not wish to create any prejudice when he is coming here to undertake a great responsibility.[105] I would wish that care should be taken to avoid expression of contradictory views by people in Government. We should better impose self-restraint and talk less.

Wishing you well,

Yours sincerely,
[Ajit Prasad Jain]

59. Galbraith on India's Requests[106]
[Refer to item 420]

(Eyes only for President, Secretary)

Following the message of 19 November from Nehru to you I have just learned under conditions of the greatest confidence that another is now (7:00 PM New Delhi time) in preparation. This is in reaction to new disasters and further large Chinese advance today. This will ask for some form of back up support to the Indian Air Force by the USAF amounting to joint Air Defence. This is to deter attacks on cities and lines of communications while Indians commit IAF to tactical operations and attacks on Chinese communications which they believe is now only chance of stopping Chinese and preventing cutoff of eastern India or more. There will also be indication of movement on sub-continental defence and preconditions in Kashmir or in any case this is much in mind. I have urged careful consideration of acceleration of conflict to air and believe, on reflection, that I should drive home this point further with Prime Minister. For the rest I have not reacted since Indian mood is desperate, the situation indeed grim and the request must obviously go to you. I will ascertain in morning if they have approached Russians for any assurances. I have learned of this move under conditions of greatest confidence even senior Ministers not being yet

---

105. As Defence Minister.
106. Telegram No. 1889 from New Delhi, 8 p.m., 19 November 1962. Kennedy Papers, https://www.jfklibrary.org/Asset-Viewer/Archives/JFKNSF-111-016.aspx Accessed on 21 August 2018.

informed. My staff is not informed. You must protect fact of my knowledge and this warning now and indefinitely.

60. From J.F. Kennedy: US Response to Request[107]
[Refer to items 419 and 420]

Dear Mr Prime Minister: I was on the point of responding to your two urgent letters, when we received news of the Chinese statements on a cease-fire. I, of course, wish your assessment of whether it makes any change in your situation. I had planned to write you that we are ready to be as responsive as possible to your needs, in association with the United Kingdom and the Commonwealth.[108] We remain prepared to do so. We had already organized a small group of top U.S. officials, who would arrive in New Delhi Friday, to help Ambassador Galbraith in concerting with your government how we can best help.[109] It seems useful to go ahead with this effort as planned and we will do so unless you think it inadvisable.

61. From Morarji Desai: Gold[110]
[Refer to item 100]

November 20, 1962

My dear Jawaharlalji,

This is in continuation of my brief talk with you the other day regarding gold. As you know, by tradition and custom most Indian families which can afford

---

107. Telegram from the Department of State to the Embassy in India, 20 November 1962, 22:31 p.m. Galbraith was instructed to personally deliver the telegram to the Prime Minister. Kennedy Papers, https://www.jfklibrary.org/Asset-Viewer/Archives/JFKNSF-111-016.aspx Accessed on 21 August 2018.
108. See briefing memo from Department of State, drafted by Carl Kaysen and Dean Rusk. Kennedy Papers, https://www.jfklibrary.org/Asset-Viewer/Archives/JFKNSF-111-016.aspx Accessed on 21 August 2018. The Embassy confirmed the request for the C-130s on November 20, and the Department of State responded the same day that the Department of Defense was dispatching 12 C-130 aircrafts to India. (Telegrams, 1914 from New Delhi and 2191 to New Delhi, both November 20, 1962). Ibid.
109. The group, headed by Averell Harriman, included Paul Nitze, Carl Kaysen, Roger Hilsman, and General Paul D. Adams, arrived on Thursday, November 22 1962.
110. Letter from the Finance Minister. PMO, File No. 37/114/63-66-PM, Vol. I, Sr. No. 1-D.

it, have in their possession gold in the form of ornaments, the quantity varying according to their means. While we should discourage this habit by encouraging people to put their savings to more useful and productive purposes, there can be no question of compelling the people to part with their gold ornaments.

2. Gold is, however, being used also for the purpose of concealing ill-gotten wealth. This, in turn, leads to smuggling, the scale of which far exceeds the quantum used for making ornaments.

3. To stop the smuggling of gold into the country we cannot go on adding to the Customs staff and intensifying the search of passengers and cargo coming into the country. What we need to do is to make it impossible for gold in the form of bars to be freely bought and sold. Towards this and, we propose to take the following steps:

(a) call for a declaration from all persons (including temples and religious places) of their holdings of gold in the form of bars, bullion and coins as well as in forms other than those which can be used for personal adornment, e.g. vessels and plates;

(b) to register all gold refiners as well as those dealers in gold who have been registered under the sales tax legislation of their respective States;

(c) to prescribe that after these declarations have been made, all sales and purchases of gold other than ornaments, should be only to and from the registered dealers who will have to maintain a careful account of such sales and purchases including the names of the people with whom the transactions have been completed; and

(d) to require registered dealers to handle only that gold in form of bars, etc. which is declared and held against a valid licence after making the necessary entries in the licence.

4. These will mean that the smuggler who brings in gold bars will not find it easy to dispose of these in the open market and what is more even if these bars are found later on with anyone in excess of what he has declared to Government, their possession would be held illegal and would invite the sanctions provided in the law. At the same time, ornaments as such will call neither for declaration nor anything else so that these measures would not involve the bulk of the people in any kind of form-filling. We even gave consideration to the question whether any special exemption should be given to temples, but there are so many of them, some private and some public, that it would be unsafe to exempt them from the simple act of making a declaration.

5. If you agree with the general approach, then we shall draft the necessary legal framework for operating this scheme in consultation with the Law Ministry.

Yours sincerely,
Morarji Desai

62. China Informs Fraternal Countries About Cease Fire[111]
[Refer to item 286]

Vice Minister Zhang Han-fu (hereafter Zhang): I am sorry for disturbing you today at such a late time,[112] but I have an important notification for you about the Sino-Indian boundary issue.

Comrades, as you all know, the Chinese government has consistently advocated settling the Sino-Indian boundary issue through peaceful means and friendly negotiations, but has not done so. I will not mention the events that occurred before the invasion and the provocation of the Indian army on 20 October of this year. On 20 October, the Indian army launched a massive assault on the Chinese army. On 15 November, the Indian Ministry of National Defense ordered another massive attack. Under such circumstances, China was forced to fight back.

Nevertheless, the Chinese government issued a statement on 24 October and proposed three recommendations to settle the military conflicts along the Sino-Indian border. We believed that these three recommendations are the most fair and reasonable, but India repeatedly refused such recommendations and asked the Chinese army without reason to retreat to the positions that were China's before 8 September [1962]; that is, to resume the situation in which the Indian army occupied a large portion of Chinese territory, set up forty-three strongholds, and was ready for a massive attack. The Chinese government steadfastly refused India's unreasonable and ridiculous claims.

India repeatedly refused China's recommendations, and it ordered another massive attack on 15 November, causing the Sino-Indian border to become tenser and more dangerous. Under such circumstances, the Chinese

---

111. Record of Minutes of meeting, 21 November 1962; Zhang Han-fu and ambassadors of fraternal countries. Wilson Centre Archives, http://digitalarchive.wilsoncenter.org/document/114775 Accessed on 6 September 2018.
112. The meeting was held at 1 p.m. Beijing time.

government proactively took measures to facilitate the realization of the three recommendations which could reverse the situation.

The Chinese government decided for a complete ceasefire along the Sino-Indian border on 22 November; that is, tomorrow. China also decided to withdraw the border defense forces from the Eastern, Middle, and Western sectors to more than 20 kilometres away from the 7 November 1959 Line of Actual Control. The Line of Actual Control mentioned here is the same as that referred to in the second recommendation of the three proposed by the Chinese government on 24 October. China is actively and unilaterally withdrawing.

China's active measures are enough to show China's great sincerity to stop the conflict along the border and peacefully settle the Sino-Indian boundary issue. We hope the Indian government will agree to take corresponding measures.

With respect to this issue, the Chinese government will make a statement today. We are all fraternal countries, so we are notifying you first. Please make it known to your government. After the statement is issued, the whole text will be sent to you and all of the embassies.

Ambassador of Mongolia: My understanding is that the contents of this statement are the same as that on 24 October and the issue is to withdraw to more than 20 kilometres from the Line of Actual Control.

Zhang: We are taking the initiative to withdraw. We are taking this measure in order to promote the realization of the three recommendations. In this regard, this statement is very different from that on 25 [24] October.

Ambassador of Czechoslovakia: What are the differences?

Zhang: The difference lies in that we are actively taking measures and initiating the withdrawal. I am sorry to disturb you at such a late time. We meant to notify you first because we are fraternal countries.

(The Vietnamese ambassador was late, so Zhang retold him the measures China would take after the other ambassadors left.)

Vietnamese Ambassador: You are welcome to take proactive measures, but some people believe that China is withdrawing because China lost.

Zhang: It is quite obvious which country won and which lost. At Parliament yesterday, Nehru was saying they lost Walong and how many people were killed or wounded. But we do not pose as a winner, nor are we doing so because it should be this way.

821

Vietnamese Ambassador: This is a good thing. I will report to the government after I return to the embassy.

63. From A. Sékou Touré: Welcoming Ceasefire[113]
[Refer to item 424]

Have learnt with satisfaction the decision of the Chinese Government to apply the cease fire unilaterally. This decision is an indication of the obvious desire of this Government to achieve a negotiated solution of the Sino-Indian frontier question and to ensure the reestablishment of friendly relations with your Government. (We) are convinced that your Government unmoved by the various pressures aimed at endangering the constructive solidarity of the third world group by encouraging localised conflicts and false antagonism among them knows how to remain faithful to the lofty ideals of peace which truly serve as a shining beacon in your great country. (We) are sure that your Government is only too well aware that the development of the Sino-Indian armed conflict affects the solidarity of the Afro-Asian world and might well encourage neo-colonialist aims. We would like to assure you of our wholehearted support for any decision which is consistent with the mutual interests of the developing countries founded on a reinforcement of the bases of peace in the world and an increased strengthening of the bonds of solidarity uniting the Peoples of Asia and Africa.

Highest consideration.

64. From Sudhir Ghosh: Galbraith's Message on Ceasefire[114]
[Refer to item 286]

November 21, 1962

My dear Panditji,

This morning I had gone to the airport to see off Senator Mansfield[115] and his colleagues whom I have known for a number of years. At the airport

---

113. Telegram, 21 November 1962, from the President of Guinea. MEA, File No. 1 (China)/62, Vol. II, p. nil.
114. Letter from Rajya Sabha MP, Congress. NMML, Sudhir Ghosh Papers.
115. Mike Mansfield (1903-2001), Senator from Montana from 1953-1977.

Ambassador Galbraith[116] took me to one side and asked me very earnestly to tell you something, if I got a chance, before you go to the Lok Sabha this morning.

Ambassador Galbraith says that even if Chinese statement about a cease fire and withdrawal beginning from December 1 is a mere trick, it would still be advisable for India to be silent and not to say anything definite on this peace offensive. His argument is that India needs precious time for further preparation and for securing effective British-American assistance and India does not lose anything if she waits to see what the Chinese actually do between today and December 1 and after December 1.

I venture to pass on to you in case it is any use to you.

With regards,

Yours sincerely
[Sudhir Ghosh]

65. From S.K. Patil: Not Enough Participation[117]
[Refer to item 332]

November 23, 1962

My dear Prime Minister,

During the last several weeks, since the Chinese invasion began, we have been receiving news of different kinds, often disturbing, sometimes quite alarming and at others disastrous. I have had the uncomfortable and uneasy feeling that as a Member of the Cabinet I was without such knowledge of events, policies and measures being taken to deal with the most emergent situation with which the country could be faced, as would be compatible with that position or as I would be expected to possess in that capacity. Often I and perhaps many of my colleagues have had to share that knowledge or information with the readers of newspapers or members of Parliament when it was given to them. In the absence of that knowledge or information, it was of course impossible for us to make any humble contribution to the solution of the difficulties with which we have been faced nor has it been easy for us to follow the course of events in the manner in which a Member of the Cabinet would be assumed to.

2. I do recognise that in a situation of this kind the Cabinet cannot meet every day and emergent actions have to be taken by appropriate committees of which we have quite a number. These committees however cover a fraction

---

116. J. K. Galbraith, US Ambassador.
117. Letter from the Minister of Food and Agriculture. NMML, S.K. Patil Papers.

of the members of the Cabinet as a whole and others have not the benefit or privilege of being participants in the deliberations. Since, generally the results of the deliberations of these committees are not communicated to the other members of the Cabinet, even this indirect knowledge of the situation and steps taken to deal with it is not available to us. I am sure that with your sympathetic insight into the minds of your colleagues, you will agree that such a position results in considerable sense of frustration and helplessness if not worse. Moreover, this is not conducive to the generation of that sense of responsibility which must permeate every member of the Cabinet particularly in such an emergency, nor does it promote that sense of participation which enables one to explain with authority and conviction the Government's approach to a particular situation or its implications or to assess and justify measures which are taken from time to time to deal with it.

3. I know how fully preoccupied you have been and what burden of anxiety you have carried in your own mind and of responsibility on your own shoulders during these weeks. It is for that reasons that I have hesitated to trouble you with these thoughts that were passing in my mind. I felt, however, that with the situation

putting on such a grave aspect, I would be failing in my duty to you as a humble member of your team, to extent what ever help and assistance I can, if I did not convey to you the position in which I find myself. I would, therefore, earnestly request you to give some thought to this aspect of our functioning and direct suitable steps to ensure that those of our colleagues who are not members of the various committees also acquire a sense of participation in the measures and policies that are being devised to deal with the situation and of sharing the knowledge and information of the situation as it develops day after day. In any case I feel that from time to time a meeting of the full Cabinet may be convened in which the situation could be discussed in such manner and to such an extent as would be advisable and thereby we may be enabled to render whatever help and assistance we can in dealing with this emergency.

4. I do hope this letter will not be an intrusion. I wrote to you only because I felt that I should bring these aspects to your notice, but certainly not in the nature of any grievance or complaint and I would earnestly request you to regard it as such. I leave the matter in your hands in full confidence that with your usual flair for understanding the minds of your colleagues and relieving them of what troubles their minds, you will take whatever action you deem appropriate.

Yours sincerely,
S.K. Patil

66. From S. Chellaswamy[118]
[Refer to item 319]

November 23, 1962

Dear Nehruji,

I am sending herewith the Prasadam of Lord Subrahmanya.

When you were suddenly taken ill I prayed to the Lord for restoration of your health and vowed that I would go and offer prayers to the Lord in Tiruchendur after you were restored to robust health. I have fulfilled the vow today and prayed to the Lord that you should be given spiritual strength and vigour to protect our country at this hour of grave crises. Just as Surapadman was destroyed by the "Vel" of Lord Subrahmanya the Asuric forces of the Chinese who have invaded the sacred soil of our motherland will also be destroyed by the Lord's grace under your leadership.

Believe me,

Sincerely yours,
S. Chellaswamy

67. J.F. Kennedy to Averrel Harriman[119]
[Refer to items 228, 230 and 408 and appendix 71]

While the ostensible purpose of your stopover in Pakistan is to inform Ayub generally on your Delhi talks, I also regard it as a major opportunity to show Ayub how radically the Sino-Indian confrontation has altered the situation in the subcontinent from our point of view. We have had to look at this situation in terms of Free World security and we regard it as a major test of our alliance ties as well as Ayub's statesmanship whether he does so too.

Up to this time we have been prepared to disregard as much as possible a basicdifference in viewpoint between us and the Pakistani as to what our alliance meant. They have always regarded it primarily as a basis for soliciting support of their aims vis-à-vis India. We have regarded it as part of the total

---

118. Letter from Convener, Union Language Convention, South India, and President, Madras Bar Association. Sent from Tiruchendur. Reproduced from *Letters from Late Prime Minister Mr Jawaharlal Nehru & Other Statesmen on National Issues. Selection of Letters To and From Mr S. Chellaswamy*, Printed in Madras, 1965, p. 32.
119. Telegram from Department of State, to Ambassador at Large, 25 November 1962. Kennedy Papers. https://www.jfklibrary.org/Asset-Viewer/Archives/JFKNSF-111-016. aspx Accessed on 21 August 2018.

free world defense against Bloc aggression, a contingency that Ayub seems to have regarded as remote. Now that it has actually occurred, however, it must take precedence in our thinking. It ought to do so in Pak and Indian thinking too. As and when this sinks in, our task of promoting Pak-Indian reconciliation will grow easier.

Regrettably, Ayub has elected instead to pursue at least initially a tough line toward India and, for obvious reasons, toward us. Though I recognise that he is under some domestic pressure, at a moment like this there are limits on how far we can live with this attitude. Whether the present Sino-Indian crisis ends in a negotiated settlement or continues to boil, the Indians will almost certainly wish to undertake a major modernization of their forces. We shall be pressed to become the chief underwriter and cannot sustain the additional costs implicit in continued Pak-Indian quarrels. These costs have already been great enough.

I also believe that the Sino-Indian confrontation has given us what may be a one-time opportunity to bring about a Pak-Indian reconciliation. Though this opportunity may be fleeting, we still ought to seize it if we can. Success will require movement in both the Pakistani and Indian positions. Yet unless both Pakistan and India look clearly at their fundamental interest in partnership this opportunity may be lost. We cannot expect quick results, but can hope to set in motion a trend which will bring about, with a lot of nursing along from us, a resolution of such issues as Kashmir.

I do not want to push Ayub so hard as to get his back up, yet I think it imperative that he be under no illusion as to where we stand. Frank talk carries risks, but these seem to me less than those entailed in failing to make our position clear. I count on you to do so. Therefore, while you and McConaughy[120] will of course choose the manner of your presentation, please tell Ayub that I have specifically asked you to make the following points to him:

(1) Whatever India's past follies, the Chicom attack and India's response to it create a basically new situation. We regard this as far more than a mere border squabble, even if it ends in a temporary settlement. By the Chinese action, the subcontinent has become a new area of major confrontation between the Free World and the Communists. We must take this fact into account in our global policy.

(2) The Indian themselves are at long last fully aware of the Chinese Communist thereat and appear to be determined to meet it. This creates a recognised community of interest between India and Pakistan, which India is beginning to acknowledge. It provides a basis for the resolution of Pak-Indian differences which did not previously exist.

120. Walter P. McConaughy (1908-2000); US Ambassador to Pakistan, 1962-1966.

(3) We for our part have made clear time and again that our alliance ties with Pakistan were for the express purpose meeting the Communist threat. Now that India too recognizes this threat and is seeking to cope with it, we intend to provide help to meet that threat.

(4) We regard such aid to India as fully consistent with our ties to Pakistan because there is no blinking the fact that the threat to the subcontinent is a threat to the security and independence of both.

(5) Were Pakistan to move closer to the Chinese at a time when we were assisting India to confront communist China, it would cut across the deep commitments of the entire free world. We know Ayub has no illusions about the Chicoms, but we would regard such gestures as wholly incompatible with Pakistan's own interests, traditions, and commitments. Pakistan must realise that there are certain limits which should not be overstepped if a fruitful Pak-US relationship can continue. The American people have a million men in uniform outside the United States defense of the freedom and independence of nations and are taking casualties every week. The esteem and friendship of the American people for Pakistan would melt away if Pakistan elects to draw close to those who are the sworn enemies of freedom.

(6) Indeed, we think the opposite course from that which Ayub pursuing publicly is far better calculated to lead to the resolution of Pak-Indian differences which we and Ayub seek. The more forthcoming Pakistan is toward India, the harder it will be for India to avoid movement in its direction. By the same token, the tougher the Pak attitude, the less likely India can risk the humiliation of appearing to knuckle under. Thus, the current Pak attitude risks diverting India from primary focus on the Chicom threat, a focus which can only benefit Pakistan in the long run.

(7) The US too will continue to do all it can to bring the two countries together. We have not been pressing Pakistan alone. But we cannot command we can only persuade. This means Ayub as well as Nehru. Nevertheless, we see the current situation as moving both parties toward the point where we can assist in a reasonable compromise involving some give by both parties. Indeed, should Ayub himself be prepared to be forthcoming, we are prepared to tell Nehru that if we give him major military aid he should agree to negotiate as a suitable point on Kashmir. Ayub cannot ask more of us, and we are unable to provide more.

(8) Meanwhile, though we recognize Ayub's public opinion problem, he should bear in mind: (a) that if he lets it get out of hand he may end up losing his room to manoeuvre; (b) current Pak outbursts make it that much more difficult for India to be forthcoming; (c) the US public and US Congress will be adversely affected by that they tend increasingly to regard as irrational Pak outbursts. In fact, you might cite the 23 Nov. *Washington Post* interview in which Eisenhower, whom the Paks regard as a friend, is reported as favouring all-out military aid to India, but warns that any US commitment must be carried through until the Chinese are decisively beaten, back.

(9) As to military aid, we are fulfilling our commitments to Pakistan and we intend to help India if it wants our help. Both steps are essential to the security the subcontinent. We have conveyed adequate security reassurances to both India and Pakistan. We've never committed ourselves to any particular military balance between the two, nor can we do so.

(10) In sum, we intend to stand by our commitments to Pakistan and to protect its integrity. I regard this as more than justifying Pakistan's reciprocal Alliance obligations to us. In return we ask Ayub to examine dispassionately the great opportunity he and Nehru have to resolve Pak-Indian difference in the cause of solidarity against the Chicom threat. We will press this case on both powers and be guided largely by their responses.

In requesting you to press Ayub along the above lines, I am proceeding on the assumption that in the last analysis he will go along with us. This is foreshadowed by Mohammed Ali's statement (Karachi 913) that Pakistan would not sacrifice its Alliance with us because it had no sound alternative course. So I am convinced that with the right combination of patience and firmness we can bring Ayub to take a reasonable course in his own interest.

Your mission will be an unqualified success if we can get the following from Ayub: (1) recognition that he must start re-educating his public before things drift too far; (2) indications of his willingness to respond to Indian overtures, so that we can encourage Nehru to make them; (3) minimising of attacks on the US, which only redound to Pak disadvantage; and (4) cutting off his flirtation with Peiping on matters other than their own border problem. In return we can assure Ayub that we will take full account of Pak interests in our dealings with India.

Both our sides are well aware of the difference between us on the boundary question. It is not necessary to repeat them at present. The Chinese Government holds that the present task before our two sides is to terminate the border conflict, separate the armed forces of the two parties and create a proper atmosphere so as to settle our boundary differences through negotiations; and we should be confident that these differences can be settled in a friendly way through peaceful negotiations. We should not get these differences entangled with the present task, lest the border conflict could not be terminated and negotiations could not be started at all. It was precisely out of these considerations that the Chinese Government decided to take the lead in ceasing fire and withdrawing the frontier guards.

In taking its decision, the Chinese Government had given full consideration to the decency, dignity and self respect of both sides. The initiative measures which the Chinese Government has decided to take are not conditional on simultaneous corresponding measures to be taken by the Indian side. According to the Chinese Government's decision, the Chinese frontier guards will withdraw 20 kilometres from the line of actual control of November 7, 1959. That is to say, they will not only evacuate the areas they reached in their recent fight in self- defence but will withdraw to positions far behind those they held on September 8 or October 20, 1962. The line of actual control of November 7, 1959 had taken shape on the basis of the extent of administration by each side at the time; it existed objectively and cannot be defined or interpreted according to the free will of either side. In withdrawing 20 kilometres from this line, the armed forces of each side would be evacuating areas under its own administration; hence the question of one side achieving gains and the other suffering losses does not arise. Moreover, this would not prevent either side from continuing to administer the area evacuated by its armed forces on its side of the line, nor will this prejudice either side's position in regard to the boundary alignment.

I would like to stress that withdrawal by China alone of its frontier guards beyond 20 kilometres on its side of the 1959 line of actual control cannot ensure the disengagement of the armed forces of the two sides, nor can it prevent the recurrence of border clashes. On the contrary, in case the Indian side should refuse to cooperate, even the cease fire which has been effected is liable to be upset. Therefore, the Chinese Government sincerely hopes that the Indian Government will take corresponding measures. If the Indian Government agrees to do so, I specifically [will] appoint officials to meet at places agreed upon by both parties in the various sectors of the Sino-Indian border to discuss matters relating to the 20 kilometres withdrawal of the armed forces of each party to form a demilitarised zone, the establishment of check-posts by each party on its own side of the line of actual control, and the return of captured personnel.

The meeting of the officials of the two countries will itself be of great positive significance because it will signify the return of our two sides from the battlefield to the conference table. If the meeting of the officials of the two countries achieves results and the results are put into effect, the Prime Ministers of our two countries can then hold talks and proceed further to seek a friendly settlement of the Sino-Indian boundary question.

The border conflict in the past month has greatly strained the relations between our two countries. China's Embassy, consulates, back establishments and nationals in India have been subjected to treatment which is rarely seen even when war has been formally declared between two states. In my view, such an abnormal state of affairs unnecessarily poisons the atmosphere between our two countries and obviously should not continue any longer.

Your Excellency, Mr Prime Minister, only a handful of ill-intentioned people in the world want our two countries to keep on fighting. The common friends of our two countries are all heartened by the realisation of cease fire between us. They ardently hope that we will make joint efforts to transform the cease fire which has been effected into the starting point of a peaceful settlement of the boundary question. The Chinese Government has taken the first step i.e., cease fire, and is going to take the second step i.e., withdrawal. I hope the Indian Government will give a positive response and made efforts in the same direction. I am awaiting your reply.

Please accept, Your Excellency, the assurances of my highest consideration.

71. Ayub Khan's Talk with Sandys and Harriman[131]
[Refer to items 230,231 and 408]

Rawalpindi, November 28, 1962.

Participants:

1. H.E. Mohammad Ayub Khan, President of Pakistan
2. H.E. Duncan Sandys, U.K. Minister for Commonwealth Relations
3. W. Averell Harriman, Assistant Secretary of State for Far Eastern Affairs

---

131. Record of conversation, drafted by Harriman; 29 November 1962.Wilson Centre Archives; http://digitalarchive.wilsoncenter.org/document/114791 Accessed on 6 September 2018.

On arrival in Rawalpindi (November 28, 5:00 p.m.) I was informed by Ambassador McConaughy that President Ayub wanted me to dine with him and Duncan Sandys alone and that Sandys wanted to see me half an hour before dinner in order to bring me up to date on what transpired. Ambassador McConaughy told me that Sandys had informed President Ayub of Nehru's willingness to start discussions regarding Kashmir without preconditions on any level; Sandys was proposing that first a preliminary meeting be held between Ayub and Nehru at New Delhi, since it was Ayub's turn to go to the Indian capital. President Ayub wanted to talk to me before making up his mind.

In my discussion with Sandys before dinner, he argued for a President-Prime Minister meeting, and I told him that I would think it wise to hold such a meeting only if the communiqué to be issued at the end of the meeting be agreed to in advance. Without such an agreement it would be dangerous since Ayub and Nehru found it difficult to negotiate due to the difference in the personalities of the two men. Sandys bought this idea. Sandys and I then drove to President Ayub's house and had a long talk with him before going into dinner.

Sandys produced a draft communiqué announcing a meeting between the President and the Prime Minister in New Delhi, including a sentence to the effect that the objective of the meeting would be to decide on methods and procedure to settle the differences between their two countries.

I then outlined my thought of an agreement in advance on the final communiqué to be issued at the close of the meeting. After some discussion, Ayub said if we are to agree upon a communiqué at the end of the discussions, why have a meeting at all—why not agree now on that communiqué by correspondence between himself and Nehru? I readily accepted this and so did Sandys. Taking the first sentence of Sandys' paper, Ayub dictated, with some discussion of each sentence, the following communiqué to be issued:

"The President of Pakistan and the Prime Minister of India have agreed that renewed effort should be made without delay to resolve the Kashmir problem so as to enable their two countries to live side by side free from anxiety. In consequence, they have decided to open negotiations at an early date with the object of reaching an honourable and equitable settlement. The negotiations will be conducted initially at the ministerial level. At the appropriate stage direct talks will be held between Mr Nehru and President Ayub."

Sandys agreed to take this draft to Nehru, attempt to get his approval and signature, and bring it back to Rawalpindi for President Ayub's signature. We all hoped that it might be possible to issue the communiqué on Friday morning.[132]

While the draft communiqué was being retyped, we had a discussion ranging over a wide area. In answer to Ayub's questions, Sandys and I expressed our views of the climate of opinion in India on the possibility of reaching a settlement on Kashmir. Sandys expressed himself somewhat more optimistically than I did. I explained that I had been struck by the unity of purpose which had developed in India in recognizing the long-range danger of Chinese Communist aggression. Domestic difficulties were being put aside by the people all over the country. In the villages people were enlisting, contributing funds, and asking what they could do to help in this national emergency. I explained I had found that everyone, with whom I had talked, unanimously spoke of the emergency in long-range terms. It was therefore natural that the minds of many were turned towards the importance of settling differences with Pakistan so that their entire energy could be directed towards the Communist menace. I told President Ayub that I thought some further time would be needed to get all the Ministers, as well as public opinion, in a mood to make a reasonable settlement but that I felt the time was running in the right direction and that it was essential to start negotiations which in themselves would focus public opinion on the issue.

Ayub insisted that Kashmir be named as the problem. He rejected the idea of a vaguer reference to "differences between the two countries." Both Sandys and I made it plain that it would be impossible to have a plebiscite, that the Vale as such could not be transferred to Pakistan, but that there was an understanding in India that they had to make certain concessions beyond the present cease-fire line. We both told him we had not discussed details and did not know how far the India Government was ready to go at the present time. Ayub accepted this situation and recognised that the negotiations on Kashmir might last a

---

132. Sandys returned to New Delhi on November 29 to discuss the text of the proposed joint statement with Nehru. Nehru amended the draft as follows: "to resolve the Kashmir problem" changed to read "to resolve the outstanding differences between their two countries on Kashmir and other matters." (Telegram 2158 from New Delhi, November 29; ibid.) Ayub further amended "other matters" to read "other related matters," The communiqué was issued on Friday, 30 November 1962 (Telegram 964 from Karachi, November 29; ibid.).

considerable time, but under the formula it was proposed in the communiqué there was considerable flexibility of continuing discussions even though the first talks might not reach a satisfactory conclusion.

We discussed Chinese intentions. Ayub said he believed that their intentions were only to insure control of the Sinkiang road and a certain part of Ladakh. I pointed out that this might be their immediate objective but that they did not have to attack in the NEFA area in order to achieve this objective. I underlined the opinion of all the Indians I had talked to that Red China was determined to destroy India's independence and way of life. Ayub did not contradict this and talked as if he recognized the long-range menace of Red China to the subcontinent. There was no suggestion of a non-aggression pact between Pakistan and Red China.

We discussed Khrushchev's motives in Cuba. President Ayub expressed great admiration for the manner in which President Kennedy handled the Cuban question.

President Ayub said he believed the differences between Moscow and Peiping were real but that if Red China got into military difficulties, the Soviet Union would come to her assistance. There seemed to be no intimation that President Ayub thought that Pakistan could make a special deal and thus avoid the dangers of either Soviet or Chinese Communist aggressive intentions.

We discussed at some length the relationship between Nehru and Krishna Menon with general agreement that Krishna Menon had spoken for Nehru. I believe that Sandys and I convinced Ayub that Krishna Menon was out for good, that Nehru did not have, any longer, the unchallenged authority to bring him back.

Sandys and I touched on the military situation in India but did not go into details as I explained that General Adams was here to brief President Ayub the next morning, although we did give some indication of the size of British and American assistance so far.

At dinner President Ayub reverted to the subject of our military assistance, turning to me and saying, "Now tell me about this assistance you are giving to India." I gave him the general order of dimensions emphasising that the loss of the equipment by the Fourth Division alone was far in excess in anything we had delivered or had agreed to deliver so far. I pointed out, however, that India had plans for long-range military build-up which the Government was now determined to undertake in order that they would not be helpless against Communist attack in the future. We left it that we would discuss this subject in more detail the next day. In answer to my question Ayub told me of the commencement of the de-salinisation program. He expressed hopes that it would be successful, although it would take a long time. He talked about his visit to the Hunza area and he expressed the hope that he could come to an agreement with Peiping over the boundary but would insist on retaining the Hunza grazing areas.

At one point, touching on Khrushchev's desire to avoid nuclear war, he said, "Yes, I know your views. I read your book which you had sent to me." He did not, however, take issue with this statement and agreed that at the present time Red China was more reckless. Cuba had been proof of Khrushchev's brinkmanship methods, leaving open always an opportunity to withdraw.

He spoke warmly of President Kennedy and with satisfaction of his visit to Washington. He pointed to a framed photograph on the wall.

Dehlavi was present throughout the evening but rarely injected himself in the discussion except at one point he mentioned that they had received an offer from Turkey to undertake mediation on Kashmir. Sandys pointed out that a Turkish offer would not go very well in New Delhi. President Ayub discussed at some length his difficulties with Nehru. He mentioned that when a subject came up which Nehru did not wish to discuss, he simply sat silent, which President Ayub said was most disconcerting. President Ayub asked about the Soviet MIGs. Sandys said that the Soviet Union had declined to furnish them. I said that my information maintained that they had postponed delivery, attempting to straddle the relationship (their "friend" India and their "ally" China).

President Ayub was cordial throughout the evening, relaxed, showed no strain or scars from the debate in the Assembly in the statements of the opposition.

I did not raise any of the other subjects I had in mind discussing, as I felt it was desirable to concentrate on the commencement of negotiations over Kashmir. He may well become more perturbed when we get into some of the questions about which he has been critical of US policy and actions.[133]

133. See also Memorandum by Harriman on his second conversation with Ayub Khan, 29 November 1962. Kennedy Papers, https://www.jfklibrary.org/Asset-Viewer/Archives/ JFKNSF-111-016.aspx Accessed on 21 August 2018.

72. Chester Bowles' Memorandum to J.F. Kennedy[134]
[Refer to items 444, 445, 447 and 448]

I. SOUTH ASIA

1. Initiate frank and comprehensive discussions with President Ayub of Pakistan, through a special designee of the President, to hammer out an understanding of the true purposes of the U.S.-Pakistan alliance and our respective responsibilities towards it, and clearly to redefine, in an exchange of Presidential letters, the aims, guarantees, and limitations of this alliance in regard to China, Russia, India and Afghanistan. (March 27, 1962)

2. In response to the confidential request made to me last February in New Delhi by General [B.M.] Kaul of the Indian Army, authorise covert exchanges of military information between U.S. and Indian military leaders with respect to the Chinese Communist threat, leading to firm assurances of US military support, and bringing the Pakistanis into these discussions if it should appear feasible (March 27, 1962)

3. Offer to sell modern aircraft and other sophisticated weapons to India on favourable terms and in quantities adequate to strengthen Indian capacity to resist the anticipated Chinese pressures. (March 27, 1962)

4. Simultaneously to press both Pakistan and India to consider fresh proposals for settling the Kashmir dispute. (March 27, 1962)

5. Make a carefully conditioned, long-range economic aid commitment to Afghanistan to bolster the independence of this strategically placed country which is under an increasingly effective pressure from the USSR. (March 27, 1962)

6. Politely reject Iranian requests for increased quantities of unnecessary and costly sophisticated military equipment; press the Shah of Iran vigorously to pursue essential economic and social reforms; make a generous commitment for future economic assistance programs firmly conditioned on a more effective mobilisation of Iranian economic resources and completion of a well-documented, long-range development plan. (March 27, 1962)

7. Assist Iran to build a new port on the Persian Gulf at Bandar Abbas and construct the connecting road system that will provide landlocked

---

134. "Summary of major policy recommendations during 1962", [only extracts available] 1 December 1962, by Chester Bowles, Ambassador at Large. Kennedy Papers, https://www.jfklibrary.org/Asset-Viewer/Archives/JFKNSF-111-016.aspx Accessed on 21 August 2018.

Afghanistan with an urgently needed alternative route to the sea through Iran (March 27, 1962)....

73. Averell Harriman's Note[135]
[Refer to items 408, 230, 231 and appendix 67]

Washington, December 8, 1962, 5:44 p.m.

1066. Following is summary of conclusions of Harriman Mission to India:

1. India now recognises Red China as its principal and long-term enemy, but is less clear about long-term threat of Soviet communism as imperialistic force.
2. Majority of Pakistanis consider India primary enemy of Pakistan. Notable exceptions are Ayub and some of immediate entourage who recognise communist north the long-term threat.
3. Dramatic reaction in Pakistan to US military assistance to India has at least in part been encouraged by Pakistan's leaders, including Ayub, as device for bringing pressure on US and in attempt achieve certain internal political objectives.
4. Only settlement Kashmir can change attitude of Pakistan towards India. There is some movement at least on Indian side towards easing tensions between two countries. Ayub appears believe there is unusual opportunity reach accommodation on Kashmir which, though unpopular with Pakistanis, will be acceptable. Ministerial talks must be encouraged by US and UK. We should continue press both governments persistently to move towards each other even if there some resentment this by both.
5. Indian leadership undergoing changes which should be encouraged. Malevolent influence Krishna Menon officially removed and Nehru's overpowering stature and freedom of action has been diminished to a point which permits rise of younger, more dynamic, generally more pragmatic leadership to top.
6. India is now determined to build and maintain larger military establishment. This determination, and degree of our association with it, are already producing increasing strains on subcontinent. Settlement with Pakistan could produce significant strengthening subcontinent against Communist China.

---

135. Circular telegram, 8 December 1962. Department of State, verbatim text, Kennedy Papers, https://www.jfklibrary.org/Asset-Viewer/Archives/JFKNSF-111-016.aspx Accessed on 21 August 2018.

7. Indian Armed Forces suffered severely under Krishna Menon. Indian Army has shaken up senior commands and is restoring leadership competence. Calibre of fighting men continues good and morale not seriously impaired. Army's plans for build-up appear soundly conceived and within its capacity execute with outside help. The Air Force effective at operational level, still has weaknesses at top. Effectiveness its plan for expansion requires considerable study by US and UK.

8. While India will not accept Chinese "cease-fire" plan, it will probably minimise provocation for resumption hostilities in near future. There is no guarantee Chinese will not initiate new fighting and we must be prepared for surprise Chinese attacks at times and places of their own choosing.

9. In case of further Chinese attacks, Indians should be in position use tactical air. This will require major political decision by GOI and may involve certain contingent arrangements for supplemental US and preferably Commonwealth air activity.

10. It doubtful India can rapidly expand defense production beyond simpler ordnance items. We will need more study before we can decide on degree to which India's intermediate requirements can be met from own resources. We should discourage India from attempting production of sophisticated military equipment and encourage concentration on feasible ordnance items.

11. India's diplomatic and propaganda efforts have been inept. Senior officials realise this and are correcting shortcomings. US and UK should discreetly assist.

12. India's "non-alignment" policy will undergo considerable substantive reinterpretation in manner favourable our interests. However, we should not seek formal association of India with US or West in general. Formal Western guaranty would tend diminish extent Indian effort and force a break with Soviet Union, bringing Soviet Union closer to Red China. However, there is great value in strengthening Commonwealth association both India and Pakistan.

GLOSSARY
(Including abbreviations and names of places)

AIIMS	All India Institute of Medical Sciences
AIR	All India Radio
AIR	All India Reporter
Akashvani	All India Radio
APHLC	All Party Hill Leaders Conference
BBC	British Broadcasting Corporation
Bewaqoof	Fool
Bundestaat	Federation
Calcutta	Kolkata
Cde	Comrade
CDU	Christian Democratic Union
CENTO	Central Treaty Organisation
Ceylon	Sri Lanka
Chicom	Chinese Communists
CONAKAT	Confédération des associations tribales du Katanga
CPP	Congress Parliamentary Party
CS	Commonwealth Secretary
CSU	Christian Socialist Union
DEFMIN	Defence Minister
DIB	Director, Intelligence Bureau, also Directorate of Intelligence Bureau
DMK	Dravida Munetra Kazhagam

FS	Foreign Secretary
GOC-in-C	General Officer Commanding--in--Chief
GOI	Government of India
Gur	Jaggery
IAF	Indian Air Force
INFA	Indian News and Features Alliance
Intekhab	Revenue receipt
INTUC	Indian National Trade Union Congress
IOA	Indian Olympic Association
IST	Indian Standard Time
Jawan	Soldier
Jehalat	Uninformed
JS	Joint Secretary
Lathi	Baton
Lekhpal	Village official
Manpatra	Welcome Address
Mashal	Fire light/torch
MEA	Ministry of External Affairs
NCC	National Cadet Corps
NEFA	North-East Frontier Agency
Ootacamand	Udhagamandalam
Panch sheel	Five Principles of peaceful co-existence
Peking/Peiping	Beijing
Poona	Pune
PPS	Personal Private Secretary
PS	Private Secretary
PSP	Praja Socialist Party
Ramdhun	A favourite devotional song of Gandhiji
Sampradayikta Virodhi	Anti-communal
Sattu	Mixture of ground pulses and cereals

SCR	Supreme Court Reporter
SEATO	Southeast Asia Treaty Organisation
SG	Secretary-General
Sifarishnama	Letter of appreciation
Staatenbund	Confederation
Tehsildar	Land Revenue Officer
Thana	Police station
UAR	United Arab Republic
UGC	University Grants Commission
UN	United Nations
UNESCO	United Nations Educational, Scientific and Cultural Organisation
Vel	Spear
YMCA	Young Men's Christian Association

INDEX

845

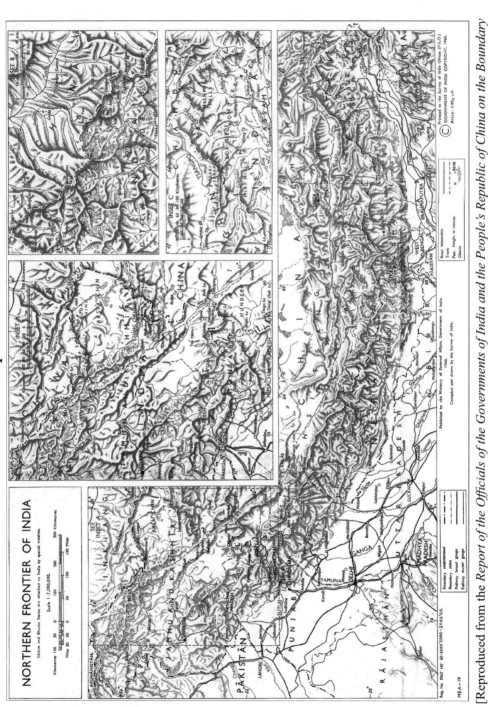

I

[Reproduced from the *Report of the Officials of the Governments of India and the People's Republic of China on the Boundary Question*, prepared by the Ministry of External Affairs and tabled in Parliament on 14 February 1961. Insets follow]

II

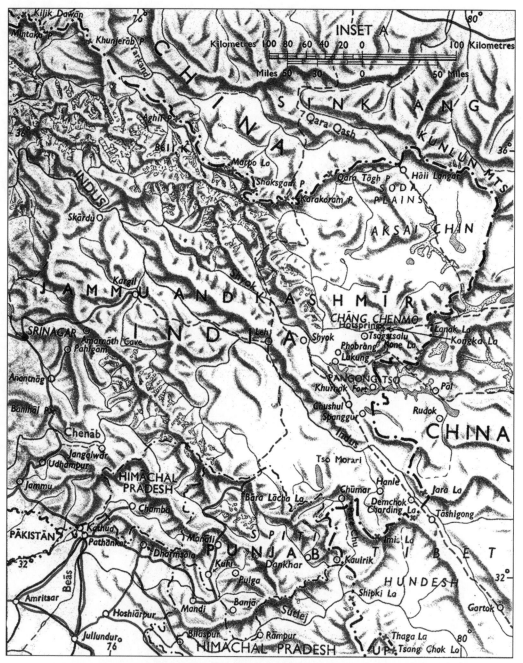

[Inset A, from map in *Report of the Officials of the Governments of India and the People's Republic of China on the Boundary Question*, prepared by the Ministry of External Affairs and tabled in Parliament on 14 February 1961]

III

[Inset B, from map in *Report of the Officials of the Governments of India and the People's Republic of China on the Boundary Question*, prepared by the Ministry of External Affairs and tabled in Parliament on 14 February 1961]